CONSTITUTIONAL STRUCTURE

EDITORIAL ADVISORS

ASPEN CASEBOOK SERIES

CONSTITUTIONAL STRUCTURE

Cases in Context

Second Edition

RANDY E. BARNETT

Carmack Waterhouse Professor of Legal Theory
Georgetown University Law Center

JOSH BLACKMAN

Associate Professor of Law
South Texas College of Law Houston

Wolters Kluwer

Published by Wolters Kluwer in New York.

Wolters Kluwer Legal & Regulatory U.S. serves customers worldwide with CCH, Aspen Publishers, and Kluwer Law International products. (www.WKLegaledu.com)

To contact Customer Service, e-mail customer.service@wolterskluwer.com, call 1-800-234-1660, fax 1-800-901-9075, or mail correspondence to:

Wolters Kluwer
Attn: Order Department
PO Box 990
Frederick, MD 21705

Printed in the United States of America.

2 3 4 5 6 7 8 9 0

ISBN 978-1-4548-9289-2

Library of Congress Cataloging-in-Publication Data

Names: Barnett, Randy E., author. | Blackman, Josh, author.
Title: Constitutional structure: cases in context / Randy E. Barnett, Carmack Waterhouse Professor of Legal Theory, Georgetown University Law Center; Josh Blackman Associate Professor of Law, South Texas College of Law, Houston.
Description: Second edition. | New York: Wolters Kluwer, [2018] | Series: Aspen casebook series | Includes bibliographical references and index.
Identifiers: LCCN 2017049901 | ISBN 9781454892892
Subjects: LCSH: Constitutional law — United States. | LCGFT: Casebooks
Classification: LCC KF4550 .B2762 2018 | DDC 342.73 — dc23
LC record available at https://lccn.loc.gov/2017049901

About Wolters Kluwer Legal & Regulatory U.S.

Wolters Kluwer Legal & Regulatory U.S. delivers expert content and solutions in the areas of law, corporate compliance, health compliance, reimbursement, and legal education. Its practical solutions help customers successfully navigate the demands of a changing environment to drive their daily activities, enhance decision quality and inspire confident outcomes.

Serving customers worldwide, its legal and regulatory portfolio includes products under the Aspen Publishers, CCH Incorporated, Kluwer Law International, ftwilliam.com and MediRegs names. They are regarded as exceptional and trusted resources for general legal and practice-specific knowledge, compliance and risk management, dynamic workflow solutions, and expert commentary.

To those whose vision of the Constitution is not limited to that of the Supreme Court

To my wife, Beth — Randy Barnett
To Militza — Josh Blackman

Summary of Contents

PART IV: THE JUDICIAL POWER

Contents

PART II: THE LEGISLATIVE POWER

PART III: THE EXECUTIVE POWER

Preface

Welcome to the Second Edition of *Constitutional Structure: Cases in Context*, which is based on the Third Edition of *Constitutional Law: Cases in Context*. We recognize that choosing a casebook is one of the most important decisions law professors make. For students, this selection is beyond their control, but often makes or breaks the foundation of their legal education.

In a crowded marketplace, our reinvigorated text stands out for professors and students alike because of its clarity, context, consideration, and the canon.

Clarity

In preparing the Second Edition, every page was reviewed and re-edited with a primary focus: clarity. Placing ourselves back in the shoes of a 1L who has never before studied this material, we rethought from the ground up what works, and what does not work. Specifically, we sought to provide students with a more accessible and engaging way to learn constitutional law than is now available in existing casebooks.

First, after extensive market research, we concluded that most textbooks — especially those that have evolved through many editions over a long period of time — are simply unrealistic about what students can actually learn in a three or four-credit course. Most books drown students with tedious notes, commentary, and "squibs" *after* the cases, which professors dread to prepare to field questions about, even as most students skip them. We chose a different path. *Before* each decision we include a clear, easy-to-understand study guide that consists of a series of precise questions. These learning objectives pinpoint what students should take away from the reading — we do not hide the ball.

Second, rather than assuming that students will grasp complicated postures, we provide them with the background information necessary to dive right into the cases. For example, if a decision involves a complicated regulatory scheme, or considers an obscure historical event, the study guide will offer a brief synopsis of extraneous facts so students can instead focus on the important analysis. Further, our casebook includes dozens of photographs of the people and places behind the cases. These additional pictures and tidbits of information will make the study of constitutional law come alive just a little more, and differentiate our text from all the others.

Third, we divided each chapter into a series of *Assignments*, which average thirty-pages in length. The readings are long enough to help students understand the arguments, but edited where necessary to prevent overwhelming them. Where feasible within each doctrinal category, the canonical cases are presented chronologically as they were decided. Learning how a line of cases developed conveys the story of constitutional law that every literate lawyer *ought* to know.

With our ready-made syllabi, professors can rearrange the materials to fit into three, four, and six-credit courses.

Finally, the Second Edition will allow professors to *flip* the classroom. Students will be able to access an online catalogue of short, focused, three-minute videos about each case in the book. The videos will discuss the facts, posture, analysis, and holding of the cases, centered around the study guide questions in the book. Building on modern learning techniques, students can better prepare themselves online *before* class. Professors will be empowered to spend more class time diving deeper into analysis and reasoning of the content, rather than consuming precious class time bringing every student up to speed on the facts.

Context

The theme of the book is reflected in its title: *Cases in Context*. Constitutional law has not developed in a vacuum. Rather, over the course of two centuries, all three branches of our government have interpreted the Constitution's seven articles and twenty-seven amendments in the context of complicated, real-world events. Professors take our knowledge of this story for granted, having picked it up along the way. But for most students it is entirely new and more than a little strange. This story is almost impossible to grasp when confronting disparate cases completely divorced from the context in which they were decided.

As with the previous edition, the Second Edition aims to place each of these developments, throughout the history of our republic, in the proper context. All students — even those unfamiliar with American history — will learn the essential background information to grasp how this body of law has come to be what it is today. To do that, we hew to discussions of first principles and method, rather than doctrinal details.

Consideration

By providing both cases and context, our book aims to nonjudgmentally convey the competing narratives that all lawyers ought to know. But it also provides consideration of different perspectives. We strive to always present competing points of view. Consideration of all sides of all issues will enrich the pedagogical experience, and more importantly, will better equip future attorneys with different modalities of argumentation. Regardless of how professors may view these issues, *Cases in Context* will provide students with a balanced perspective. With less opinionated supplementation by the casebook authors, each professor can put his or her own stamp on the story as it unfolds.

Before proceeding further, let us put our cards on the table. Though ascendant in recent years — "We are all originalists," Justice Kagan observed during her confirmation hearings — we concede that our views on originalism are not in the majority in faculty lounges across the country, or on the courts. But this is *not* an originalist casebook. Neither is it technically doctrinal. Rather, it is a book about the "canon" and the "anti-canon" that comprises constitutional law.

The Canon

The "canon" are the cases accepted by the vast majority of judges, lawyers, law professors as landmark cases to be followed and emulated. The "anti-canon" are the cases most everyone believes to have been wrongly decided in so egregious a manner as to be object lessons in how *not* to do constitutional law. Taken together, these decisions provide the basic vocabulary of constitutional law that every lawyer who practices constitutional law must somehow internalize.

It is not enough for students to memorize the good cases and the bad ones. To appreciate *why* some cases have become canonical and others have become reviled requires them to understand the *narrative* of constitutional law as it has developed since the Founding. No casebook presents the narrative of constitutional law as effectively or engagingly as this one.

The Second Edition includes all of the classic cases in the "canon," as well as those in "anti-canon" and the connective tissue that explains how and why they came be thought of in this way. At its heart, this is a story that dates back to the Founding. Our goal was to allow this story to emerge from the materials themselves rather than from us.

* * *

To the professors who have chosen to adopt this book, we thank you. To the students reading this preface before starting their course on constitutional law, brace yourselves: it's a wild ride.

Randy Barnett
Washington, D.C.
Josh Blackman
Houston, Texas

November 2017

Acknowledgments

The person most responsible for this book is Carol McGeehan who for many years persistently urged me to write it. No author could possibly ask for a more engaged, understanding, and constructive editor. Her faith in a junior contracts professor to write a solo-authored casebook led to *Contracts: Cases and Doctrine* (now in its fifth edition) and *Perspectives on Contracts* (now in its fourth). Her confidence that I could "double major" in writing a constitutional law casebook even before I had ever taught the course was truly inspirational.

For the Second Edition, I am delighted to welcome Josh Blackman to the casebook as my coauthor. Josh's teaching experience and enthusiasm has brought a new perspective on these materials. He has systematically edited the text for increased clarity and accessibility. And he is as committed as I am to illuminating the cases with photographs and other relevant graphics that help make the subjects come alive to professors and students alike.

At Wolters Kluwer, we are very grateful to grateful to John Devins, Maureen Kenealy, Joe Terry, and everyone else at Wolters Kluwer. At the Froebe Group, we are indebted to Darren Kelly, who allowed us to turn this edition out in less than six months, from start to finish.

As always, I am especially appreciative of the help and support I received from my dear friend and Georgetown colleague Larry Solum. Larry even taught from a tentative version of the casebook long before it was completed, and his suggestions for its improvement were invariably correct, as they always are. And it was Larry who first urged me years ago to pay close attention to *Chisholm v. Georgia*, a recommendation I failed to heed until I began writing the casebook and realized the enormous significance of this, the first great constitutional case.

I am grateful to my students in my Con Law I and II courses at the Georgetown Law Center for engaging with these materials so seriously over the years, and to my dean, William Treanor, for the research support that made writing this book possible. We also thank Betsy Kuhn at Georgetown, for her superlative proofreading talents.

Finally, I thank my wife, Beth, for her unfailing patience and support as I bury myself in all too many writing projects.

R.B.

In 2009, I invited Randy Barnett to speak at the George Mason University School of Law, where I was an inquisitive 3L. If you had told me that only seven years later, he would invite me to edit his constitutional law casebook, I would have never believed it. How it happened, only fate knows, but since then, Randy has served as a mentor, a co-author, and a friend. Collaborating with him on this casebook has been the highlight of my young career. I will forever be grateful for this amazing opportunity.

Every semester, I tell my students at the South Texas College of Law Houston that I learn more from them than they learn from me. Though they never believe me, my contributions to this book are proof. Thank you all for teaching me so much about teaching. Whatever insights I bring to this endeavor, I owe to my students. I am also in debt to my colleagues on the STCLH faculty. You have guided me throughout my career to become the best professor I can be; I promise, I am still not quite there yet.

I am very grateful to the followers of JoshBlackman.com and @JoshMBlackman. When I launched my blog and Twitter account in September 2009, I had no idea what I was doing. Eight years, ten thousand blog posts, and forty thousand tweets later, these forums have allowed me to exchange ideas, develop thoughts, and hone my writing. Without these online channels, I doubt I would have ever been invited to join this exciting casebook.

Finally, and most importantly, I owe a debt that I can never repay to my amazing family, Mom, Dad, and Alix. I am only where I am today because of what you have done for me. To Militza, thank you so much for your support, patience, and insights throughout this entire process. I love you all.

J.B.

The authors gratefully acknowledge the permissions granted to reproduce the following materials:

Cover images: Detail of Signing of the Constitution by Howard Chandler Christy, Architect of the Capitol (top); left: Courtesy Mary Lou Filbrun Spurgeon; center: Courtesy Ronald Reagan Library; right: National Portrait Gallery, Smithsonian Institution/Art Resource, NY.

p. i, Signing of the Constitution by Howard Chandler Christy, Architect of the Capitol; pp. 14, left: Library of Congress; p. 14, right: Photo © Philip Mould Ltd., London/The Bridgeman Art Library; p. 53: Collection of the Supreme Court of the United States; p. 65, left: Independence National Historic Park; p. 65, right: James Madison by Charles Wilson Peale, from the collection of Gilcrease Museum, Tulsa, Oklahoma; p. 91, left: By Larry Dodd Wheeler, Collection of the Supreme Court of the United States; p. 91, right: North Carolina Collection, University of North Carolina Library at Chapel Hill; p. 97, right: © Collection of the New-York Historical Society, USA/The Bridgeman Art Library; p. 132: Courtesy National Gallery of Art, Washington; p. 137: The Granger Collection, New York; p. 167: Historical & Special Collections, Harvard Law School Library; p. 185: Randy Barnett; p. 200: Library of Congress; p. 212: Library of Congress; p. 216: Library of Congress; p. 223: Library of Congress; p. 231: Courtesy Mary Lou Filbrun Spurgeon; p. 244: Special Collections and Archives, Georgia State University Library; p. 254: Josh Blackman; p. 288: Mannie Garcia/Getty Images; p. 306: Reuters/J. Scott Applewhite/Landov; p. 352: Courtesy Ronald Reagan Library; p. 371, top: Courtesy Ronald Reagan Library; p. 371, bottom: Randy Barnett; p. 372: Richard Ellis/Alamy Stock Photo; p. 421: AP Photo/LM Otero; p. 459: Photo Courtesy of Washington Apple Commission; p. 465: max blain/Shutterstock; p. 525: The Granger Collection, New York; p. 526: Historical & Special Collections, Harvard Law School Library; p. 535: Library of Congress; p. 567: Collection of the Supreme Court of the United States; p. 585, top left: National Archives; p. 585, bottom left: The Wing Luke Museum; p. 585, bottom right: National Portrait Gallery, Smithsonian Institution/Art Resource, NY; p. 595: Courtesy of National Archives; p. 676: © Roger Ressmeyer/CORBIS; p. 690: Nixon Presidential Library; p. 699, left: AP Photo/Ruth Fremson; p. 699, right: AP Photo/Danny Johnston; p. 711, top: Irwin Smith, Collection of the Supreme Court of the United States; p. 711, bottom: Antoine Taveneaux via Creative Commons; p. 725: Bruce Weaver/AFP/Newscom; p. 727: Kevork Djansezian/Getty Images; p. 768: University of Washington Libraries Special Collections, Negative no. UW35549.

The Constitution of the United States

Preamble

We the People of the United States, in Order to form a more perfect Union, establish Justice, insure domestic Tranquility, provide for the common defence, promote the general Welfare, and secure the Blessings of Liberty to ourselves and our Posterity, do ordain and establish this Constitution for the United States of America.

Article I

Section 1. All legislative Powers herein granted shall be vested in a Congress of the United States, which shall consist of a Senate and House of Representatives.

Section 2. The House of Representatives shall be composed of Members chosen every second Year by the People of the several States, and the Electors in each State shall have the Qualifications requisite for Electors of the most numerous Branch of the State Legislature.

No Person shall be a Representative who shall not have attained to the Age of twenty five Years, and been seven Years a Citizen of the United States, and who shall not, when elected, be an Inhabitant of that State in which he shall be chosen.

[Representatives and direct Taxes shall be apportioned among the several States which may be included within this Union, according to their respective Numbers, which shall be determined by adding to the whole Number of free Persons, including those bound to Service for a Term of Years, and excluding Indians not taxed, three fifths of all other Persons.]* The actual Enumeration shall be made within three Years after the first Meeting of the Congress of the United States, and within every subsequent Term of ten Years, in such Manner as they shall by Law direct. The number of Representatives shall not exceed one for every thirty Thousand, but each State shall have at Least one Representative; and until such enumeration shall be made, the State of New Hampshire shall be entitled to chuse three, Massachusetts eight, Rhode-Island and Providence Plantations one, Connecticut five, New-York six, New Jersey four, Pennsylvania eight, Delaware one, Maryland six, Virginia ten, North Carolina five, South Carolina five, and Georgia three.

When vacancies happen in the Representation from any State, the Executive Authority thereof shall issue Writs of Election to fill such Vacancies.

---

* Changed by Section 2 of the Fourteenth Amendment.

The House of Representatives shall chuse their Speaker and other Officers; and shall have the sole Power of Impeachment.

Section 3. The Senate of the United States shall be composed of two Senators from each State, [chosen by the Legislature thereof,]* for six Years; and each Senator shall have one Vote.

Immediately after they shall be assembled in Consequence of the first Election, they shall be divided as equally as may be into three Classes. The Seats of the Senators of the first Class shall be vacated at the Expiration of the second Year, of the second Class at the Expiration of the fourth Year, and of the third Class at the Expiration of the sixth Year, so that one third may be chosen every second Year; [and if Vacancies happen by Resignation, or otherwise, during the Recess of the Legislature of any State, the Executive thereof may make temporary Appointments until the next Meeting of the Legislature, which shall then fill such Vacancies.]*

No Person shall be a Senator who shall not have attained to the Age of thirty Years, and been nine Years a Citizen of the United States, and who shall not, when elected, be an Inhabitant of that State for which he shall be chosen.

The Vice President of the United States shall be President of the Senate, but shall have no Vote, unless they be equally divided.

The Senate shall chuse their other Officers, and also a President pro tempore, in the Absence of the Vice President, or when he shall exercise the Office of President of the United States.

The Senate shall have the sole Power to try all Impeachments. When sitting for that Purpose, they shall be on Oath or Affirmation. When the President of the United States is tried, the Chief Justice shall preside: And no Person shall be convicted without the Concurrence of two thirds of the Members present.

Judgment in Cases of Impeachment shall not extend further than to removal from Office, and disqualification to hold and enjoy any Office of honor, Trust or Profit under the United States: but the Party convicted shall nevertheless be liable and subject to Indictment, Trial, Judgment and Punishment, according to Law.

Section 4. The Times, Places and Manner of holding Elections for Senators and Representatives, shall be prescribed in each State by the Legislature thereof; but the Congress may at any time by Law make or alter such Regulations, except as to the Places of chusing Senators.

The Congress shall assemble at least once in every Year, and such Meeting shall be [on the first Monday in December,]** unless they shall by Law appoint a different Day.

Section 5. Each House shall be the Judge of the Elections, Returns and Qualifications of its own Members, and a Majority of each shall constitute a Quorum to do Business; but a smaller Number may adjourn from day to day, and may be authorized to compel the Attendance of absent Members, in such Manner, and under such Penalties as each House may provide.

Each House may determine the Rules of its Proceedings, punish its Members for disorderly Behaviour, and, with the Concurrence of two thirds, expel a Member.

Each House shall keep a Journal of its Proceedings, and from time to time publish the same, excepting such Parts as may in their Judgment require Secrecy; and the Yeas and Nays of the Members of either House on any question shall, at the Desire of one fifth of those Present, be entered on the Journal.

---

* Changed by the Seventeenth Amendment.

** Changed by Section 2 of the Twentieth Amendment.

Neither House, during the Session of Congress, shall, without the Consent of the other, adjourn for more than three days, nor to any other Place than that in which the two Houses shall be sitting.

Section 6. The Senators and Representatives shall receive a Compensation for their Services, to be ascertained by Law, and paid out of the Treasury of the United States. They shall in all Cases, except Treason, Felony and Breach of the Peace, be privileged from Arrest during their Attendance at the Session of their respective Houses, and in going to and returning from the same; and for any Speech or Debate in either House, they shall not be questioned in any other Place.

No Senator or Representative shall, during the Time for which he was elected, be appointed to any civil Office under the Authority of the United States, which shall have been created, or the Emoluments whereof shall have been encreased during such time; and no Person holding any Office under the United States, shall be a Member of either House during his Continuance in Office.

Section 7. All Bills for raising Revenue shall originate in the House of Representatives; but the Senate may propose or concur with Amendments as on other Bills.

Every Bill which shall have passed the House of Representatives and the Senate, shall, before it become a Law, be presented to the President of the United States; If he approve he shall sign it, but if not he shall return it, with his Objections to that House in which it shall have originated, who shall enter the Objections at large on their Journal, and proceed to reconsider it. If after such Reconsideration two thirds of that House shall agree to pass the Bill, it shall be sent, together with the Objections, to the other House, by which it shall likewise be reconsidered, and if approved by two thirds of that House, it shall become a Law. But in all such Cases the Votes of both Houses shall be determined by Yeas and Nays, and the Names of the Persons voting for and against the Bill shall be entered on the Journal of each House respectively. If any Bill shall not be returned by the President within ten Days (Sundays excepted) after it shall have been presented to him, the Same shall be a Law, in like Manner as if he had signed it, unless the Congress by their Adjournment prevent its Return, in which Case it shall not be a Law.

Every Order, Resolution, or Vote to which the Concurrence of the Senate and House of Representatives may be necessary (except on a question of Adjournment) shall be presented to the President of the United States; and before the Same shall take Effect, shall be approved by him, or being disapproved by him, shall be repassed by two thirds of the Senate and House of Representatives, according to the Rules and Limitations prescribed in the Case of a Bill.

Section 8. The Congress shall have Power To lay and collect Taxes, Duties, Imposts and Excises, to pay the Debts and provide for the common Defence and general Welfare of the United States; but all Duties, Imposts and Excises shall be uniform throughout the United States;

To borrow Money on the credit of the United States;

To regulate Commerce with foreign Nations, and among the several States, and with the Indian Tribes;

To establish an uniform Rule of Naturalization, and uniform Laws on the subject of Bankruptcies throughout the United States;

To coin Money, regulate the Value thereof, and of foreign Coin, and fix the Standard of Weights and Measures;

To provide for the Punishment of counterfeiting the Securities and current Coin of the United States;

To establish Post Offices and post Roads;

To promote the Progress of Science and useful Arts, by securing for limited Times to Authors and Inventors the exclusive Right to their respective Writings and Discoveries;

To constitute Tribunals inferior to the supreme Court;

To define and punish Piracies and Felonies committed on the high Seas, and Offenses against the Law of Nations;

To declare War, grant Letters of Marque and Reprisal, and make Rules concerning Captures on Land and Water;

To raise and support Armies, but no Appropriation of Money to that Use shall be for a longer Term than two Years;

To provide and maintain a Navy;

To make Rules for the Government and Regulation of the land and naval Forces;

To provide for calling forth the Militia to execute the Laws of the Union, suppress Insurrections and repel Invasions;

To provide for organizing, arming, and disciplining, the Militia, and for governing such Part of them as may be employed in the Service of the United States, reserving to the States respectively, the Appointment of the Officers, and the Authority of training the Militia according to the discipline prescribed by Congress;

To exercise exclusive Legislation in all Cases whatsoever, over such District (not exceeding ten Miles square) as may, by Cession of particular States, and the Acceptance of Congress, become the Seat of the Government of the United States, and to exercise like Authority over all Places purchased by the Consent of the Legislature of the State in which the Same shall be, for the Erection of Forts, Magazines, Arsenals, dock-Yards and other needful Buildings; — And

To make all Laws which shall be necessary and proper for carrying into Execution the foregoing Powers, and all other Powers vested by this Constitution in the Government of the United States, or in any Department or Officer thereof.

Section 9. The Migration or Importation of such Persons as any of the States now existing shall think proper to admit, shall not be prohibited by the Congress prior to the Year one thousand eight hundred and eight, but a Tax or duty may be imposed on such Importation, not exceeding ten dollars for each Person.

The Privilege of the Writ of Habeas Corpus shall not be suspended, unless when in Cases of Rebellion or Invasion the public Safety may require it.

No Bill of Attainder or ex post facto Law shall be passed.

[No Capitation, or other direct, Tax shall be laid, unless in Proportion to the Census or Enumeration herein before directed to be taken.]*

No Tax or Duty shall be laid on Articles exported from any State.

No Preference shall be given by any Regulation of Commerce or Revenue to the Ports of one State over those of another: nor shall Vessels bound to, or from, one State, be obliged to enter, clear, or pay Duties in another.

No Money shall be drawn from the Treasury, but in Consequence of Appropriations made by Law; and a regular Statement and Account of the Receipts and Expenditures of all public Money shall be published from time to time.

* See Sixth Amendment.

No Title of Nobility shall be granted by the United States: And no Person holding any Office of Profit or Trust under them, shall, without the Consent of the Congress, accept of any present, Emolument, Office, or Title, of any kind whatever, from any King, Prince, or foreign State.

Section 10. No State shall enter into any Treaty, Alliance, or Confederation; grant Letters of Marque and Reprisal; coin Money; emit Bills of Credit; make any Thing but gold and silver Coin a Tender in Payment of Debts; pass any Bill of Attainder, ex post facto Law, or Law impairing the Obligation of Contracts, or grant any Title of Nobility.

No State shall, without the Consent of the Congress, lay any Imposts or Duties on Imports or Exports, except what may be absolutely necessary for executing its inspection Laws: and the net Produce of all Duties and Imposts, laid by any State on Imports or Exports, shall be for the Use of the Treasury of the United States; and all such Laws shall be subject to the Revision and Controul of the Congress.

No State shall, without the Consent of Congress, lay any Duty of Tonnage, keep Troops, or Ships of War in time of Peace, enter into any Agreement or Compact with another State, or with a foreign Power, or engage in War, unless actually invaded, or in such imminent Danger as will not admit of delay.

Article II

Section 1. The executive Power shall be vested in a President of the United States of America. He shall hold his Office during the Term of four Years, and, together with the Vice President, chosen for the same Term, be elected, as follows:

Each State shall appoint, in such Manner as the Legislature thereof may direct, a Number of Electors, equal to the whole Number of Senators and Representatives to which the State may be entitled in the Congress: but no Senator or Representative, or Person holding an Office of Trust or Profit under the United States, shall be appointed an Elector.

[The Electors shall meet in their respective States, and vote by Ballot for two Persons, of whom one at least shall not be an Inhabitant of the same State with themselves. And they shall make a List of all the Persons voted for, and of the Number of Votes for each; which List they shall sign and certify, and transmit sealed to the Seat of the Government of the United States, directed to the President of the Senate. The President of the Senate shall, in the Presence of the Senate and House of Representatives, open all the Certificates, and the Votes shall then be counted. The Person having the greatest Number of Votes shall be the President, if such Number be a Majority of the whole Number of Electors appointed; and if there be more than one who have such Majority, and have an equal Number of Votes, then the House of Representatives shall immediately chuse by Ballot one of them for President; and if no Person have a Majority, then from the five highest on the List the said House shall in like Manner chuse the President. But in chusing the President, the Votes shall be taken by States, the Representation from each State having one Vote; A quorum for this Purpose shall consist of a Member or Members from two thirds of the States, and a Majority of all the States shall be necessary to a Choice. In every Case, after the Choice of the President, the Person having the greatest Number of Votes of the Electors shall be the Vice President. But if there should remain two or more who have equal Votes, the Senate shall chuse from them by Ballot the Vice President.]*

---

* Changed by the Twelfth Amendment.

The Congress may determine the Time of chusing the Electors, and the Day on which they shall give their Votes; which Day shall be the same throughout the United States.

No Person except a natural born Citizen, or a Citizen of the United States, at the time of the Adoption of this Constitution, shall be eligible to the Office of President; neither shall any person be eligible to that Office who shall not have attained to the Age of thirty five Years, and been fourteen Years a Resident within the United States.

[In Case of the Removal of the President from Office, or of his Death, Resignation, or Inability to discharge the Powers and Duties of the said Office, the Same shall devolve on the Vice President, and the Congress may by Law provide for the Case of Removal, Death, Resignation or Inability, both of the President and Vice President, declaring what Officer shall then act as President, and such Officer shall act accordingly, until the Disability be removed, or a President shall be elected.]*

The President shall, at stated Times, receive for his Services, a Compensation, which shall neither be increased nor diminished during the Period for which he shall have been elected, and he shall not receive within that Period any other Emolument from the United States, or any of them.

Before he enter on the Execution of his Office, he shall take the following Oath or Affirmation: "I do solemnly swear (or affirm) that I will faithfully execute the Office of President of the United States, and will to the best of my Ability, preserve, protect and defend the Constitution of the United States."

Section 2. The President shall be Commander in Chief of the Army and Navy of the United States, and of the Militia of the several States, when called into the actual Service of the United States; he may require the Opinion, in writing, of the principal Officer in each of the executive Departments, upon any Subject relating to the Duties of their respective Offices, and he shall have Power to grant Reprieves and Pardons for Offenses against the United States, except in Cases of Impeachment.

He shall have Power, by and with the Advice and Consent of the Senate, to make Treaties, provided two thirds of the Senators present concur; and he shall nominate, and by and with the Advice and Consent of the Senate, shall appoint Ambassadors, other public Ministers and Consuls, Judges of the supreme Court, and all other Officers of the United States, whose Appointments are not herein otherwise provided for, and which shall be established by Law: but the Congress may by Law vest the Appointment of such inferior Officers, as they think proper, in the President alone, in the Courts of Law, or in the Heads of Departments.

The President shall have Power to fill up all Vacancies that may happen during the Recess of the Senate, by granting Commissions which shall expire at the End of their next Session.

Section 3. He shall from time to time give to the Congress Information of the State of the Union, and recommend to their Consideration such Measures as he shall judge necessary and expedient; he may, on extraordinary Occasions, convene both Houses, or either of them, and in Case of Disagreement between them, with Respect to the Time of Adjournment, he may adjourn them to such Time as he shall think proper; he shall receive Ambassadors and other public Ministers; he shall take Care that the Laws be faithfully executed, and shall Commission all the Officers of the United States.

* Changed by the Twenty-Fifth Amendment.

Section 4. The President, Vice President and all civil Officers of the United States, shall be removed from Office on Impeachment for, and Conviction of, Treason, Bribery, or other high Crimes and Misdemeanors.

Article III

Section 1. The judicial Power of the United States, shall be vested in one supreme Court, and in such inferior Courts as the Congress may from time to time ordain and establish. The Judges, both of the supreme and inferior Courts, shall hold their Offices during good Behaviour, and shall, at stated Times, receive for their Services, a Compensation, which shall not be diminished during their Continuance in Office.

Section 2. The judicial Power shall extend to all Cases, in Law and Equity, arising under this Constitution, the Laws of the United States, and Treaties made, or which shall be made, under their Authority; — to all Cases affecting Ambassadors, other public Ministers and Consuls; — to all Cases of admiralty and maritime Jurisdiction; — to Controversies to which the United States shall be a Party; — to Controversies between two or more States; — [between a State and Citizens of another State; —]* between Citizens of different States; – between Citizens of the same State claiming Lands under Grants of different States [and between a State, or the Citizens thereof; – and foreign States, Citizens or Subjects.]**

In all Cases affecting Ambassadors, other public Ministers and Consuls, and those in which a State shall be Party, the supreme Court shall have original Jurisdiction. In all the other Cases before mentioned, the supreme Court shall have appellate Jurisdiction, both as to Law and Fact, with such Exceptions, and under such Regulations as the Congress shall make.

The Trial of all Crimes, except in Cases of Impeachment; shall be by Jury; and such Trial shall be held in the State where the said Crimes shall have been committed; but when not committed within any State, the Trial shall be at such Place or Places as the Congress may by Law have directed.

Section 3. Treason against the United States, shall consist only in levying War against them, or in adhering to their Enemies, giving them Aid and Comfort. No Person shall be convicted of Treason unless on the Testimony of two Witnesses to the same overt Act, or on Confession in open Court.

The Congress shall have Power to declare the Punishment of Treason, but no Attainder of Treason shall work Corruption of Blood, or Forfeiture except during the Life of the Person attainted.

Article IV

Section 1. Full Faith and Credit shall be given in each State to the public Acts, Records, and judicial Proceedings of every other State. And the Congress may by general Laws prescribe the Manner in which such Acts, Records and Proceedings shall be proved, and the Effect thereof.

Section 2. The Citizens of each State shall be entitled to all Privileges and Immunities of Citizens in the several States.

---

* Changed by the Eleventh Amendment.

** Changed by the Eleventh Amendment.

A Person charged in any State with Treason, Felony, or other Crime, who shall flee from Justice, and be found in another State, shall on Demand of the executive Authority of the State from which he fled, be delivered up, to be removed to the State having Jurisdiction of the Crime.

[No Person held to Service or Labour in one State, under the Laws thereof, escaping into another, shall, in Consequence of any Law or Regulation therein, be discharged from such Service or Labour, but shall be delivered up on Claim of the Party to whom such Service or Labour may be due.]*

Section 3. New States may be admitted by the Congress into this Union; but no new State shall be formed or erected within the Jurisdiction of any other State; nor any State be formed by the Junction of two or more States, or Parts of States, without the Consent of the Legislatures of the States concerned as well as of the Congress.

The Congress shall have Power to dispose of and make all needful Rules and Regulations respecting the Territory or other Property belonging to the United States; and nothing in this Constitution shall be so construed as to Prejudice any Claims of the United States, or of any particular State.

Section 4. The United States shall guarantee to every State in this Union a Republican Form of Government, and shall protect each of them against Invasion; and on Application of the Legislature, or of the Executive (when the Legislature cannot be convened) against domestic Violence.

Article V

The Congress, whenever two thirds of both Houses shall deem it necessary, shall propose Amendments to this Constitution, or, on the Application of the Legislatures of two thirds of the several States, shall call a Convention for proposing Amendments, which, in either Case, shall be valid to all Intents and Purposes, as Part of this Constitution, when ratified by the Legislatures of three fourths of the several States, or by Conventions in three fourths thereof, as the one or the other Mode of Ratification may be proposed by the Congress; Provided that no Amendment which may be made prior to the Year One thousand eight hundred and eight shall in any Manner affect the first and fourth Clauses in the Ninth Section of the first Article; and that no State, without its Consent, shall be deprived of its equal Suffrage in the Senate.

Article VI

All Debts contracted and Engagements entered into, before the Adoption of this Constitution, shall be as valid against the United States under this Constitution, as under the Confederation.

This Constitution, and the Laws of the United States which shall be made in Pursuance thereof; and all Treaties made, or which shall be made, under the Authority of the United States, shall be the supreme Law of the Land; and the Judges in every State shall be bound thereby, any Thing in the Constitution or Laws of any State to the Contrary notwithstanding.

The Senators and Representatives before mentioned, and the Members of the several State Legislatures, and all executive and judicial Officers, both of the United States and of the several States, shall be bound by Oath or Affirmation, to support this Constitution; but no religious Test shall ever be required as a Qualification to any Office or public Trust under the United States.

* Changed by the Thirteenth Amendment.

Article VII

The Ratification of the Conventions of nine States, shall be sufficient for the Establishment of this Constitution between the States so ratifying the Same.

Done in Convention by the Unanimous Consent of the States present the Seventeenth Day of September in the Year of our Lord one thousand seven hundred and Eighty seven and of the Independence of the United States of America the Twelfth.

In Witness whereof We have hereunto subscribed our Names,

Go. Washington — Presidt. and deputy from Virginia
New Hampshire: John Langdon, Nicholas Gilman
Massachusetts: Nathaniel Gorham, Rufus King
Connecticut: Wm. Saml. Johnson, Roger Sherman
New York: Alexander Hamilton
New Jersey: Wil. Livingston, David Brearley, Wm. Paterson, Jona: Dayton
Pennsylvania: B Franklin, Thomas Mifflin, Robt Morris, Geo. Clymer, Thos. FitzSimons, Jared Ingersoll, James Wilson, Gouv Morris
Delaware: Geo. Read, Gunning Bedford jun, John Dickinson, Richard Bassett, Jaco. Broom
Maryland: James McHenry, Dan of St. Thos. Jenifer, Danl. Carroll
Virginia: John Blair, James Madison Jr.
North Carolina: Wm. Blount, Richd. Dobbs Spaight, Hu Williamson
South Carolina: J. Rutledge, Charles Cotesworth Pinckney, Charles Pinckney, Pierce Butler
Georgia: William Few, Abr Baldwin
Attest William Jackson Secretary

In Convention Monday September 17th, 1787. Present The States of New Hampshire, Massachusetts, Connecticut, Mr. Hamilton from New York, New Jersey, Pennsylvania, Delaware, Maryland, Virginia, North Carolina, South Carolina and Georgia.

Resolved,

That the preceeding Constitution be laid before the United States in Congress assembled, and that it is the Opinion of this Convention, that it should afterwards be submitted to a Convention of Delegates, chosen in each State by the People thereof, under the Recommendation of its Legislature, for their Assent and Ratification; and that each Convention assenting to, and ratifying the Same, should give Notice thereof to the United States in Congress assembled. Resolved, That it is the Opinion of this Convention, that as soon as the Conventions of nine States shall have ratified this Constitution, the United States in Congress assembled should fix a Day on which Electors should be appointed by the States which shall have ratified the same, and a Day on which the Electors should assemble to vote for the President, and the Time and Place for commencing Proceedings under this Constitution.

That after such Publication the Electors should be appointed, and the Senators and Representatives elected: That the Electors should meet on the Day fixed for the Election of the President, and should transmit their Votes certified, signed, sealed and directed, as the Constitution requires, to the Secretary of the United States in Congress assembled, that the Senators and Representatives should convene at the Time and Place assigned; that the Senators should appoint a President of the Senate, for the sole Purpose of receiving, opening and counting the Votes for President; and, that after he shall be chosen, the Congress, together with the President, should, without Delay, proceed to execute this Constitution.

By the unanimous Order of the Convention
Go. Washington — Presidt.

W. JACKSON Secretary.

AMENDMENTS TO THE CONSTITUTION OF THE UNITED STATES

The Preamble to The Bill of Rights

Congress of the United States begun and held at the City of New-York, on Wednesday the fourth of March, one thousand seven hundred and eighty nine.

THE Conventions of a number of the States, having at the time of their adopting the Constitution, expressed a desire, in order to prevent misconstruction or abuse of its powers, that further declaratory and restrictive clauses should be added: And as extending the ground of public confidence in the Government, will best ensure the beneficent ends of its institution.

RESOLVED by the Senate and House of Representatives of the United States of America, in Congress assembled, two thirds of both Houses concurring, that the following Articles be proposed to the Legislatures of the several States, as amendments to the Constitution of the United States, all, or any of which Articles, when ratified by three fourths of the said Legislatures, to be valid to all intents and purposes, as part of the said Constitution; viz.

ARTICLES in addition to, and Amendment of the Constitution of the United States of America, proposed by Congress, and ratified by the Legislatures of the several States, pursuant to the fifth Article of the original Constitution.*

Amendment I

Congress shall make no law respecting an establishment of religion, or prohibiting the free exercise thereof; or abridging the freedom of speech, or of the press; or the right of the people peaceably to assemble, and to petition the Government for a redress of grievances.

Amendment II

A well regulated Militia, being necessary to the security of a free State, the right of the people to keep and bear Arms, shall not be infringed.

* The first ten amendments were ratified December 15, 1791, and form what is known as the "Bill of Rights."

Amendment III

No Soldier shall, in time of peace be quartered in any house, without the consent of the Owner, nor in time of war, but in a manner to be prescribed by law.

Amendment IV

The right of the people to be secure in their persons, houses, papers, and effects, against unreasonable searches and seizures, shall not be violated, and no Warrants shall issue, but upon probable cause, supported by Oath or affirmation, and particularly describing the place to be searched, and the persons or things to be seized.

Amendment V

No person shall be held to answer for a capital, or otherwise infamous crime, unless on a presentment or indictment of a Grand Jury, except in cases arising in the land or naval forces, or in the Militia, when in actual service in time of War or public danger; nor shall any person be subject for the same offence to be twice put in jeopardy of life or limb; nor shall be compelled in any criminal case to be a witness against himself, nor be deprived of life, liberty, or property, without due process of law; nor shall private property be taken for public use, without just compensation.

Amendment VI

In all criminal prosecutions, the accused shall enjoy the right to a speedy and public trial, by an impartial jury of the State and district wherein the crime shall have been committed, which district shall have been previously ascertained by law, and to be informed of the nature and cause of the accusation; to be confronted with the witnesses against him; to have compulsory process for obtaining witnesses in his favor, and to have the Assistance of Counsel for his defence.

Amendment VII

In suits at common law, where the value in controversy shall exceed twenty dollars, the right of trial by jury shall be preserved, and no fact tried by a jury, shall be otherwise reexamined in any Court of the United States, than according to the rules of the common law.

Amendment VIII

Excessive bail shall not be required, nor excessive fines imposed, nor cruel and unusual punishments inflicted.

Amendment IX

The enumeration in the Constitution, of certain rights, shall not be construed to deny or disparage others retained by the people.

Amendment X

The powers not delegated to the United States by the Constitution, nor prohibited by it to the States, are reserved to the States respectively, or to the people.

Amendment XI*

The Judicial power of the United States shall not be construed to extend to any suit in law or equity, commenced or prosecuted against one of the United States by Citizens of another State, or by Citizens or Subjects of any Foreign State.

Amendment XII**

The Electors shall meet in their respective states and vote by ballot for President and Vice-President, one of whom, at least, shall not be an inhabitant of the same state with themselves; they shall name in their ballots the person voted for as President, and in distinct ballots the person voted for as Vice-President, and they shall make distinct lists of all persons voted for as President, and of all persons voted for as Vice-President, and of the number of votes for each, which lists they shall sign and certify, and transmit sealed to the seat of the government of the United States, directed to the President of the Senate; — the President of the Senate shall, in the presence of the Senate and House of Representatives, open all the certificates and the votes shall then be counted; — The person having the greatest number of votes for President, shall be the President, if such number be a majority of the whole number of Electors appointed; and if no person have such majority, then from the persons having the highest numbers not exceeding three on the list of those voted for as President, the House of Representatives shall choose immediately, by ballot, the President. But in choosing the President, the votes shall be taken by states, the representation from each state having one vote; a quorum for this purpose shall consist of a member or members from two-thirds of the states, and a majority of all the states shall be necessary to a choice. [And if the House of Representatives shall not choose a President whenever the right of choice shall devolve upon them, before the fourth day of March next following, then the Vice-President shall act as President, as in case of the death or other constitutional disability of the President. —]*** The person having the greatest number of votes as Vice-President, shall be the Vice-President, if such number be a majority of the whole number of Electors appointed, and if no person have a majority, then from the two highest numbers on the list, the Senate shall choose the Vice-President; a quorum for the purpose shall consist of two-thirds of the whole number of Senators, and a majority of the whole number shall be necessary to a choice. But no person constitutionally ineligible to the office of President shall be eligible to that of Vice-President of the United States.

---

* Passed by Congress March 4, 1794. Ratified February 7, 1795. Article III, section 2, of the Constitution was modified by the Eleventh Amendment.

** Passed by Congress December 9, 1803. Ratified June 15, 1804. A portion of Article II, section 1 of the Constitution was superseded by the Twelfth Amendment.

*** Superseded by section 3 of the Twentieth Amendment.

Amendment XIII*

Section 1. Neither slavery nor involuntary servitude, except as a punishment for crime whereof the party shall have been duly convicted, shall exist within the United States, or any place subject to their jurisdiction.

Section 2. Congress shall have power to enforce this article by appropriate legislation.

Amendment XIV**

Section 1. All persons born or naturalized in the United States, and subject to the jurisdiction thereof, are citizens of the United States and of the State wherein they reside. No State shall make or enforce any law which shall abridge the privileges or immunities of citizens of the United States; nor shall any State deprive any person of life, liberty, or property, without due process of law; nor deny to any person within its jurisdiction the equal protection of the laws.

Section 2. Representatives shall be apportioned among the several States according to their respective numbers, counting the whole number of persons in each State, excluding Indians not taxed. But when the right to vote at any election for the choice of electors for President and Vice-President of the United States, Representatives in Congress, the Executive and Judicial officers of a State, or the members of the Legislature thereof, is denied to any of the male inhabitants of such State, being twenty-one years of age,*** and citizens of the United States, or in any way abridged, except for participation in rebellion, or other crime, the basis of representation therein shall be reduced in the proportion which the number of such male citizens shall bear to the whole number of male citizens twenty-one years of age in such State.

Section 3. No person shall be a Senator or Representative in Congress, or elector of President and Vice-President, or hold any office, civil or military, under the United States, or under any State, who, having previously taken an oath, as a member of Congress, or as an officer of the United States, or as a member of any State legislature, or as an executive or judicial officer of any State, to support the Constitution of the United States, shall have engaged in insurrection or rebellion against the same, or given aid or comfort to the enemies thereof. But Congress may by a vote of two-thirds of each House, remove such disability.

Section 4. The validity of the public debt of the United States, authorized by law, including debts incurred for payment of pensions and bounties for services in suppressing insurrection or rebellion, shall not be questioned. But neither the United States nor any State shall assume or pay any debt or obligation incurred in aid of insurrection or rebellion against the United States, or any claim for the loss or emancipation of any slave; but all such debts, obligations and claims shall be held illegal and void.

Section 5. The Congress shall have the power to enforce, by appropriate legislation, the provisions of this article.

---

* Passed by Congress January 31, 1865. Ratified December 6, 1865. A portion of Article IV, section 2, of the Constitution was superseded by the Thirteenth Amendment.

** Passed by Congress June 13, 1866. Ratified July 9, 1868. Article I, section 2, of the Constitution was modified by section 2 of the Fourteenth Amendment.

*** Changed by section 1 of the Twenty-Sixth Amendment.

Amendment XV*

Section 1. The right of citizens of the United States to vote shall not be denied or abridged by the United States or by any State on account of race, color, or previous condition of servitude.

Section 2. The Congress shall have the power to enforce this article by appropriate legislation.

Amendment XVI**

The Congress shall have power to lay and collect taxes on incomes, from whatever source derived, without apportionment among the several States, and without regard to any census or enumeration.

Amendment XVII***

The Senate of the United States shall be composed of two Senators from each State, elected by the people thereof, for six years; and each Senator shall have one vote. The electors in each State shall have the qualifications requisite for electors of the most numerous branch of the State legislatures.

When vacancies happen in the representation of any State in the Senate, the executive authority of such State shall issue writs of election to fill such vacancies: Provided, That the legislature of any State may empower the executive thereof to make temporary appointments until the people fill the vacancies by election as the legislature may direct.

This amendment shall not be so construed as to affect the election or term of any Senator chosen before it becomes valid as part of the Constitution.

Amendment XVIII****

Section 1. After one year from the ratification of this article the manufacture, sale, or transportation of intoxicating liquors within, the importation thereof into, or the exportation thereof from the United States and all territory subject to the jurisdiction thereof for beverage purposes is hereby prohibited.

Section 2. The Congress and the several States shall have concurrent power to enforce this article by appropriate legislation.

---

* Passed by Congress February 26, 1869. Ratified February 3, 1870.

** Passed by Congress July 2, 1909. Ratified February 3, 1913. Article I, section 9, of the Constitution was modified by the Sixteenth Amendment.

*** Passed by Congress May 13, 1912. Ratified April 8, 1913. Article I, section 3, of the Constitution was modified by the Seventeenth Amendment.

**** Passed by Congress December 18, 1917. Ratified January 16, 1919. Repealed by the Twenty-First Amendment, December 5, 1933.

Section 3. This article shall be inoperative unless it shall have been ratified as an amendment to the Constitution by the legislatures of the several States, as provided in the Constitution, within seven years from the date of the submission hereof to the States by the Congress.

Amendment XIX*

The right of citizens of the United States to vote shall not be denied or abridged by the United States or by any State on account of sex.

Congress shall have power to enforce this article by appropriate legislation.

Amendment XX**

Section 1. The terms of the President and the Vice President shall end at noon on the 20th day of January, and the terms of Senators and Representatives at noon on the 3d day of January, of the years in which such terms would have ended if this article had not been ratified; and the terms of their successors shall then begin.

Section 2. The Congress shall assemble at least once in every year, and such meeting shall begin at noon on the 3d day of January, unless they shall by law appoint a different day.

Section 3. If, at the time fixed for the beginning of the term of the President, the President elect shall have died, the Vice President elect shall become President. If a President shall not have been chosen before the time fixed for the beginning of his term, or if the President elect shall have failed to qualify, then the Vice President elect shall act as President until a President shall have qualified; and the Congress may by law provide for the case wherein neither a President elect nor a Vice President shall have qualified, declaring who shall then act as President, or the manner in which one who is to act shall be selected, and such person shall act accordingly until a President or Vice President shall have qualified.

Section 4. The Congress may by law provide for the case of the death of any of the persons from whom the House of Representatives may choose a President whenever the right of choice shall have devolved upon them, and for the case of the death of any of the persons from whom the Senate may choose a Vice President whenever the right of choice shall have devolved upon them.

Section 5. Sections 1 and 2 shall take effect on the 15th day of October following the ratification of this article.

Section 6. This article shall be inoperative unless it shall have been ratified as an amendment to the Constitution by the legislatures of three-fourths of the several States within seven years from the date of its submission.

---

* Passed by Congress June 4, 1919. Ratified August 18, 1920.

** Passed by Congress March 2, 1932. Ratified January 23, 1933. Article I, section 4, of the Constitution was modified by section 2 of this amendment. In addition, a portion of the Twelfth Amendment was superseded by section 3.

Amendment XXI*

Section 1. The eighteenth article of amendment to the Constitution of the United States is hereby repealed.

Section 2. The transportation or importation into any State, Territory, or Possession of the United States for delivery or use therein of intoxicating liquors, in violation of the laws thereof, is hereby prohibited.

Section 3. This article shall be inoperative unless it shall have been ratified as an amendment to the Constitution by conventions in the several States, as provided in the Constitution, within seven years from the date of the submission hereof to the States by the Congress.

Amendment XXII**

Section 1. No person shall be elected to the office of the President more than twice, and no person who has held the office of President, or acted as President, for more than two years of a term to which some other person was elected President shall be elected to the office of President more than once. But this Article shall not apply to any person holding the office of President when this Article was proposed by Congress, and shall not prevent any person who may be holding the office of President, or acting as President, during the term within which this Article becomes operative from holding the office of President or acting as President during the remainder of such term.

Section 2. This article shall be inoperative unless it shall have been ratified as an amendment to the Constitution by the legislatures of three-fourths of the several States within seven years from the date of its submission to the States by the Congress.

Amendment XXIII***

Section 1. The District constituting the seat of Government of the United States shall appoint in such manner as Congress may direct:

A number of electors of President and Vice President equal to the whole number of Senators and Representatives in Congress to which the District would be entitled if it were a State, but in no event more than the least populous State; they shall be in addition to those appointed by the States, but they shall be considered, for the purposes of the election of President and Vice President, to be electors appointed by a State; and they shall meet in the District and perform such duties as provided by the twelfth article of amendment.

Section 2. The Congress shall have power to enforce this article by appropriate legislation.

* Passed by Congress February 20, 1933. Ratified December 5, 1933.

** Passed by Congress March 21, 1947. Ratified February 27, 1951.

*** Passed by Congress June 16, 1960. Ratified March 29, 1961.

Amendment XXIV*

Section 1. The right of citizens of the United States to vote in any primary or other election for President or Vice President, for electors for President or Vice President, or for Senator or Representative in Congress, shall not be denied or abridged by the United States or any State by reason of failure to pay poll tax or other tax.

Section 2. The Congress shall have power to enforce this article by appropriate legislation.

Amendment XXV**

Section 1. In case of the removal of the President from office or of his death or resignation, the Vice President shall become President.

Section 2. Whenever there is a vacancy in the office of the Vice President, the President shall nominate a Vice President who shall take office upon confirmation by a majority vote of both Houses of Congress.

Section 3. Whenever the President transmits to the President pro tempore of the Senate and the Speaker of the House of Representatives his written declaration that he is unable to discharge the powers and duties of his office, and until he transmits to them a written declaration to the contrary, such powers and duties shall be discharged by the Vice President as Acting President.

Section 4. Whenever the Vice President and a majority of either the principal officers of the executive departments or of such other body as Congress may by law provide, transmit to the President pro tempore of the Senate and the Speaker of the House of Representatives their written declaration that the President is unable to discharge the powers and duties of his office, the Vice President shall immediately assume the powers and duties of the office as Acting President.

Thereafter, when the President transmits to the President pro tempore of the Senate and the Speaker of the House of Representatives his written declaration that no inability exists, he shall resume the powers and duties of his office unless the Vice President and a majority of either the principal officers of the executive department or of such other body as Congress may by law provide, transmit within four days to the President pro tempore of the Senate and the Speaker of the House of Representatives their written declaration that the President is unable to discharge the powers and duties of his office. Thereupon Congress shall decide the issue, assembling within forty-eight hours for that purpose if not in session. If the Congress, within twenty-one days after receipt of the latter written declaration, or, if Congress is not in session, within twenty-one days after Congress is required to assemble, determines by two-thirds vote of both Houses that the President is unable to discharge the powers and duties of his office, the Vice President shall continue to discharge the same as Acting President; otherwise, the President shall resume the powers and duties of his office.

---

* Passed by Congress August 27, 1962. Ratified January 23, 1964.

** Passed by Congress July 6, 1965. Ratified February 10, 1967. Article II, section 1, of the Constitution was affected by the Twenty-Fifth Amendment.

Amendment XXVI*

Section 1. The right of citizens of the United States, who are eighteen years of age or older, to vote shall not be denied or abridged by the United States or by any State on account of age.

Section 2. The Congress shall have power to enforce this article by appropriate legislation.

Amendment XXVII**

No law, varying the compensation for the services of the Senators and Representatives, shall take effect, until an election of representatives shall have intervened.

* Passed by Congress March 23, 1971. Ratified July 1, 1971. The Fourteenth Amendment, section 2, of the Constitution was modified by section 1 of the Twenty-Sixth Amendment.

** Originally proposed Sept. 25, 1789. Ratified May 7, 1992.

Articles of Confederation*

To all to whom these Presents shall come, we the undersigned Delegates of the States affixed to our Names send greeting.

Articles of Confederation and perpetual Union between the states of New Hampshire, Massachusetts-bay, Rhode Island and Providence Plantations, Connecticut, New York, New Jersey, Pennsylvania, Delaware, Maryland, Virginia, North Carolina, South Carolina and Georgia.

I.

The Stile of this Confederacy shall be "The United States of America."

II.

Each state retains its sovereignty, freedom, and independence, and every power, jurisdiction, and right, which is not by this Confederation expressly delegated to the United States, in Congress assembled.

III.

The said States hereby severally enter into a firm league of friendship with each other, for their common defense, the security of their liberties, and their mutual and general welfare, binding themselves to assist each other, against all force offered to, or attacks made upon them, or any of them, on account of religion, sovereignty, trade, or any other pretense whatever.

IV.

The better to secure and perpetuate mutual friendship and intercourse among the people of the different States in this Union, the free inhabitants of each of these States, paupers, vagabonds, and fugitives from justice excepted, shall be entitled to all privileges and immunities of free citizens in the several States; and the people of each State shall free ingress and regress to and from any other State, and shall enjoy therein all the privileges of trade and commerce, subject to the same duties, impositions, and restrictions as the inhabitants thereof respectively, provided that such restrictions shall not extend so far as to prevent the removal of property imported into

* Agreed to by Congress November 15, 1777. In force after ratification by Maryland, March 1, 1781.

any State, to any other State, of which the owner is an inhabitant; provided also that no imposition, duties or restriction shall be laid by any State, on the property of the United States, or either of them.

If any person guilty of, or charged with, treason, felony, or other high misdemeanor in any State, shall flee from justice, and be found in any of the United States, he shall, upon demand of the Governor or executive power of the State from which he fled, be delivered up and removed to the State having jurisdiction of his offense.

Full faith and credit shall be given in each of these States to the records, acts, and judicial proceedings of the courts and magistrates of every other State.

V.

For the most convenient management of the general interests of the United States, delegates shall be annually appointed in such manner as the legislatures of each State shall direct, to meet in Congress on the first Monday in November, in every year, with a power reserved to each State to recall its delegates, or any of them, at any time within the year, and to send others in their stead for the remainder of the year.

No State shall be represented in Congress by less than two, nor more than seven members; and no person shall be capable of being a delegate for more than three years in any term of six years; nor shall any person, being a delegate, be capable of holding any office under the United States, for which he, or another for his benefit, receives any salary, fees or emolument of any kind.

Each State shall maintain its own delegates in a meeting of the States, and while they act as members of the committee of the States.

In determining questions in the United States in Congress assembled, each State shall have one vote.

Freedom of speech and debate in Congress shall not be impeached or questioned in any court or place out of Congress, and the members of Congress shall be protected in their persons from arrests or imprisonments, during the time of their going to and from, and attendence on Congress, except for treason, felony, or breach of the peace.

VI.

No State, without the consent of the United States in Congress assembled, shall send any embassy to, or receive any embassy from, or enter into any conference, agreement, alliance or treaty with any King, Prince or State; nor shall any person holding any office of profit or trust under the United States, or any of them, accept any present, emolument, office or title of any kind whatever from any King, Prince or foreign State; nor shall the United States in Congress assembled, or any of them, grant any title of nobility.

No two or more States shall enter into any treaty, confederation or alliance whatever between them, without the consent of the United States in Congress assembled, specifying accurately the purposes for which the same is to be entered into, and how long it shall continue.

No State shall lay any imposts or duties, which may interfere with any stipulations in treaties, entered into by the United States in Congress assembled, with any King, Prince or State, in pursuance of any treaties already proposed by Congress, to the courts of France and Spain.

No vessel of war shall be kept up in time of peace by any State, except such number only, as shall be deemed necessary by the United States in Congress assembled, for the defense of such

State, or its trade; nor shall any body of forces be kept up by any State in time of peace, except such number only, as in the judgement of the United States in Congress assembled, shall be deemed requisite to garrison the forts necessary for the defense of such State; but every State shall always keep up a well-regulated and disciplined militia, sufficiently armed and accoutered, and shall provide and constantly have ready for use, in public stores, a due number of filed pieces and tents, and a proper quantity of arms, ammunition and camp equipage.

No State shall engage in any war without the consent of the United States in Congress assembled, unless such State be actually invaded by enemies, or shall have received certain advice of a resolution being formed by some nation of Indians to invade such State, and the danger is so imminent as not to admit of a delay till the United States in Congress assembled can be consulted; nor shall any State grant commissions to any ships or vessels of war, nor letters of marque or reprisal, except it be after a declaration of war by the United States in Congress assembled, and then only against the Kingdom or State and the subjects thereof, against which war has been so declared, and under such regulations as shall be established by the United States in Congress assembled, unless such State be infested by pirates, in which case vessels of war may be fitted out for that occasion, and kept so long as the danger shall continue, or until the United States in Congress assembled shall determine otherwise.

VII.

When land forces are raised by any State for the common defense, all officers of or under the rank of colonel, shall be appointed by the legislature of each State respectively, by whom such forces shall be raised, or in such manner as such State shall direct, and all vacancies shall be filled up by the State which first made the appointment.

VIII.

All charges of war, and all other expenses that shall be incurred for the common defense or general welfare, and allowed by the United States in Congress assembled, shall be defrayed out of a common treasury, which shall be supplied by the several States in proportion to the value of all land within each State, granted or surveyed for any person, as such land and the buildings and improvements thereon shall be estimated according to such mode as the United States in Congress assembled, shall from time to time direct and appoint.

The taxes for paying that proportion shall be laid and levied by the authority and direction of the legislatures of the several States within the time agreed upon by the United States in Congress assembled.

IX.

The United States in Congress assembled, shall have the sole and exclusive right and power of determining on peace and war, except in the cases mentioned in the sixth article — of sending and receiving ambassadors — entering into treaties and alliances, provided that no treaty of commerce shall be made whereby the legislative power of the respective States shall be restrained from imposing such imposts and duties on foreigners, as their own people are subjected to, or from prohibiting the exportation or importation of any species of goods or commodities whatsoever — of establishing rules for deciding in all cases, what captures on land or water shall be legal, and in what manner prizes taken by land or naval forces in the service of the United States shall be divided or appropriated — of granting letters of marque and reprisal in times of peace — appointing courts for the trial of piracies and felonies committed on the high seas and establishing courts for receiving and determining finally appeals in all cases of captures, provided that no member of Congress shall be appointed a judge of any of the said courts.

The United States in Congress assembled shall also be the last resort on appeal in all disputes and differences now subsisting or that hereafter may arise between two or more States concerning boundary, jurisdiction or any other causes whatever; which authority shall always be exercised in the manner following. Whenever the legislative or executive authority or lawful agent of any State in controversy with another shall present a petition to Congress stating the matter in question and praying for a hearing, notice thereof shall be given by order of Congress to the legislative or executive authority of the other State in controversy, and a day assigned for the appearance of the parties by their lawful agents, who shall then be directed to appoint by joint consent, commissioners or judges to constitute a court for hearing and determining the matter in question: but if they cannot agree, Congress shall name three persons out of each of the United States, and from the list of such persons each party shall alternately strike out one, the petitioners beginning, until the number shall be reduced to thirteen; and from that number not less than seven, nor more than nine names as Congress shall direct, shall in the presence of Congress be drawn out by lot, and the persons whose names shall be so drawn or any five of them, shall be commissioners or judges, to hear and finally determine the controversy, so always as a major part of the judges who shall hear the cause shall agree in the determination: and if either party shall neglect to attend at the day appointed, without showing reasons, which Congress shall judge sufficient, or being present shall refuse to strike, the Congress shall proceed to nominate three persons out of each State, and the secretary of Congress shall strike in behalf of such party absent or refusing; and the judgement and sentence of the court to be appointed, in the manner before prescribed, shall be final and conclusive; and if any of the parties shall refuse to submit to the authority of such court, or to appear or defend their claim or cause, the court shall nevertheless proceed to pronounce sentence, or judgement, which shall in like manner be final and decisive, the judgement or sentence and other proceedings being in either case transmitted to Congress, and lodged among the acts of Congress for the security of the parties concerned: provided that every commissioner, before he sits in judgement, shall take an oath to be administered by one of the judges of the supreme or superior court of the State, where the cause shall be tried, 'well and truly to hear and determine the matter in question, according to the best of his judgement, without favor, affection or hope of reward': provided also, that no State shall be deprived of territory for the benefit of the United States.

All controversies concerning the private right of soil claimed under different grants of two or more States, whose jurisdictions as they may respect such lands, and the States which passed such grants are adjusted, the said grants or either of them being at the same time claimed to have originated antecedent to such settlement of jurisdiction, shall on the petition of either party to the Congress of the United States, be finally determined as near as may be in the same manner as is before presecribed for deciding disputes respecting territorial jurisdiction between different States.

The United States in Congress assembled shall also have the sole and exclusive right and power of regulating the alloy and value of coin struck by their own authority, or by that of the respective States — fixing the standards of weights and measures throughout the United States — regulating the trade and managing all affairs with the Indians, not members of any of the States, provided that the legislative right of any State within its own limits be not infringed or violated—establishing or regulating post offices from one State to another, throughout all the United States, and exacting such postage on the papers passing through the same as may be requisite to defray the expenses of the said office—appointing all officers of the land forces, in the service of the United States, excepting regimental officers—appointing all the officers of the naval forces, and commissioning all officers whatever in the service of the United States—making rules for the government and regulation of the said land and naval forces, and directing their operations.

The United States in Congress assembled shall have authority to appoint a committee, to sit in the recess of Congress, to be denominated "A Committee of the States," and to consist of one delegate from each State; and to appoint such other committees and civil officers as may be necessary for managing the general affairs of the United States under their direction—to appoint one of their members to preside, provided that no person be allowed to serve in the office of president more than one year in any term of three years; to ascertain the necessary sums of money to be raised for the service of the United States, and to appropriate and apply the same for defraying the public expenses—to borrow money, or emit bills on the credit of the United States, transmitting every half-year to the respective States an account of the sums of money so borrowed or emitted—to build and equip a navy—to agree upon the number of land forces, and to make requisitions from each State for its quota, in proportion to the number of white inhabitants in such State; which requisition shall be binding, and thereupon the legislature of each State shall appoint the regimental officers, raise the men and cloath, arm and equip them in a solid-like manner, at the expense of the United States; and the officers and men so cloathed, armed and equipped shall march to the place appointed, and within the time agreed on by the United States in Congress assembled. But if the United States in Congress assembled shall, on consideration of circumstances judge proper that any State should not raise men, or should raise a smaller number of men than the quota thereof, such extra number shall be raised, officered, cloathed, armed and equipped in the same manner as the quota of each State, unless the legislature of such State shall judge that such extra number cannot be safely spread out in the same, in which case they shall raise, officer, cloath, arm and equip as many of such extra number as they judge can be safely spared. And the officers and men so cloathed, armed, and equipped, shall march to the place appointed, and within the time agreed on by the United States in Congress assembled.

The United States in Congress assembled shall never engage in a war, nor grant letters of marque or reprisal in time of peace, nor enter into any treaties or alliances, nor coin money, nor regulate the value thereof, nor ascertain the sums and expenses necessary for the defense and welfare of the United States, or any of them, nor emit bills, nor borrow money on the credit of the United States, nor appropriate money, nor agree upon the number of vessels of war, to be built or purchased, or the number of land or sea forces to be raised, nor appoint a commander in chief of the army or navy, unless nine States assent to the same: nor shall a question on any other point, except for adjourning from day to day be determined, unless by the votes of the majority of the United States in Congress assembled.

The Congress of the United States shall have power to adjourn to any time within the year, and to any place within the United States, so that no period of adjournment be for a longer duration than the space of six months, and shall publish the journal of their proceedings monthly, except such parts thereof relating to treaties, alliances or military operations, as in their judgement require secrecy; and the yeas and nays of the delegates of each State on any question shall be entered on the journal, when it is desired by any delegates of a State, or any of them, at his or their request shall be furnished with a transcript of the said journal, except such parts as are above excepted, to lay before the legislatures of the several States.

X.

The Committee of the States, or any nine of them, shall be authorized to execute, in the recess of Congress, such of the powers of Congress as the United States in Congress assembled, by the consent of the nine States, shall from time to time think expedient to vest them with; provided that no power be delegated to the said Committee, for the exercise of which, by the Articles of Confederation, the voice of nine States in the Congress of the United States assembled be requisite.

XI.

Canada acceding to this confederation, and adjoining in the measures of the United States, shall be admitted into, and entitled to all the advantages of this Union; but no other colony shall be admitted into the same, unless such admission be agreed to by nine States.

XII.

All bills of credit emitted, monies borrowed, and debts contracted by, or under the authority of Congress, before the assembling of the United States, in pursuance of the present confederation, shall be deemed and considered as a charge against the United States, for payment and satisfaction whereof the said United States, and the public faith are hereby solemnly pledged.

XIII.

Every State shall abide by the determination of the United States in Congress assembled, on all questions which by this confederation are submitted to them. And the Articles of this Confederation shall be inviolably observed by every State, and the Union shall be perpetual; nor shall any alteration at any time hereafter be made in any of them; unless such alteration be agreed to in a Congress of the United States, and be afterwards confirmed by the legislatures of every State.

And Whereas it hath pleased the Great Governor of the World to incline the hearts of the legislatures we respectively represent in Congress, to approve of, and to authorize us to ratify the said Articles of Confederation and perpetual Union. Know Ye that we the undersigned delegates, by virtue of the power and authority to us given for that purpose, do by these presents, in the name and in behalf of our respective constituents, fully and entirely ratify and confirm each and every of the said Articles of Confederation and perpetual Union, and all and singular the matters and things therein contained: And we do further solemnly plight and engage the faith of our respective constituents, that they shall abide by the determinations of the United States in Congress assembled, on all questions, which by the said Confederation are submitted to them. And that the Articles thereof shall be inviolably observed by the States we respectively represent, and that the Union shall be perpetual.

In Witness whereof we have hereunto set our hands in Congress. Done at Philadelphia in the State of Pennsylvania the ninth day of July in the Year of our Lord One Thousand Seven Hundred and Seventy-Eight, and in the Third Year of the independence of America.

Members of the Supreme Court of the United States

Name	State App't From	Appointed by President	Judicial Oath Taken	Date Service Terminated
Chief Justices				
Jay, John	New York	Washington	(a) October 19, 1789	June 29, 1795
Rutledge, John	South Carolina	Washington	August 12, 1795	December 15, 1795
Ellsworth, Oliver	Connecticut	Washington	March 8, 1796	December 15, 1800
Marshall, John	Virginia	Adams, John	February 4, 1801	July 6, 1835
Taney, Roger Brooke	Maryland	Jackson	March 28, 1836	October 12, 1864
Chase, Salmon Portland	Ohio	Lincoln	December 15, 1864	May 7, 1873
Waite, Morrison Remick	Ohio	Grant	March 4, 1874	March 23, 1888
Fuller, Melville Weston	Illinois	Cleveland	October 8, 1888	July 4, 1910
White, Edward Douglass	Louisiana	Taft	December 19, 1910	May 19, 1921
Taft, William Howard	Connecticut	Harding	July 11, 1921	February 3, 1930
Hughes, Charles Evans	New York	Hoover	February 24, 1930	June 30, 1941
Stone, Harlan Fiske	New York	Roosevelt, F.	July 3, 1941	April 22, 1946
Vinson, Fred Moore	Kentucky	Truman	June 24, 1946	September 8, 1953
Warren, Earl	California	Eisenhower	October 5, 1953	June 23, 1969
Burger, Warren Earl	Virginia	Nixon	June 23, 1969	September 26, 1986
Rehnquist, William H.	Virginia	Reagan	September 26, 1986	September 3, 2005
Roberts, John G., Jr.	Maryland	Bush, G. W.	September 29, 2005	
Associate Justices				
Rutledge, John	South Carolina	Washington	(a) February 15, 1790	March 5, 1791
Cushing, William	Massachusetts	Washington	(c) February 2, 1790	September 13, 1810
Wilson, James	Pennsylvania	Washington	(b) October 5, 1789	August 21, 1798
Blair, John	Virginia	Washington	(c) February 2, 1790	October 25, 1795
Iredell, James	North Carolina	Washington	(b) May 12, 1790	October 20, 1799
Johnson, Thomas	Maryland	Washington	(a) August 6, 1792	January 16, 1793
Paterson, William	New Jersey	Washington	(a) March 11, 1793	September 9, 1806
Chase, Samuel	Maryland	Washington	February 4, 1796	June 19, 1811
Washington, Bushrod	Virginia	Adams, John	(c) February 4, 1799	November 26, 1829

Name	State App't From	Appointed by President	Judicial Oath Taken	Date Service Terminated
Moore, Alfred	North Carolina	Adams, John	(a) April 21, 1800	January 26, 1804
Johnson, William	South Carolina	Jefferson	May 7, 1804	August 4, 1834
Livingston, Henry Brockholst	New York	Jefferson	January 20, 1807	March 18, 1823
Todd, Thomas	Kentucky	Jefferson	(a) May 4, 1807	February 7, 1826
Duvall, Gabriel	Maryland	Madison	(a) November 23, 1811	January 14, 1835
Story, Joseph	Massachusetts	Madison	(c) February 3, 1812	September 10, 1845
Thompson, Smith	New York	Monroe	(b) September 1, 1823	December 18, 1843
Trimble, Robert	Kentucky	Adams, J. Q.	(a) June 16, 1826	August 25, 1828
McLean, John	Ohio	Jackson	(c) January 11, 1830	April 4, 1861
Baldwin, Henry	Pennsylvania	Jackson	January 18, 1830	April 21, 1844
Wayne, James Moore	Georgia	Jackson	January 14, 1835	July 5, 1867
Barbour, Philip Pendleton	Virginia	Jackson	May 12, 1836	February 25, 1841
Catron, John	Tennessee	Jackson	May 1, 1837	May 30, 1865
McKinley, John	Alabama	Van Buren	(c) January 9, 1838	July 19, 1852
Daniel, Peter Vivian	Virginia	Van Buren	(c) January 10, 1842	May 31, 1860
Nelson, Samuel	New York	Tyler	February 27, 1845	November 28, 1872
Woodbury, Levi	New Hampshire	Polk	(b) September 23, 1845	September 4, 1851
Grier, Robert Cooper	Pennsylvania	Polk	August 10, 1846	January 31, 1870
Curtis, Benjamin Robbins	Massachusetts	Fillmore	(b) October 10, 1851	September 30, 1857
Campbell, John Archibald	Alabama	Pierce	(c) April 11, 1853	April 30, 1861
Clifford, Nathan	Maine	Buchanan	January 21, 1858	July 25, 1881
Swayne, Noah Haynes	Ohio	Lincoln	January 27, 1862	January 24, 1881
Miller, Samuel Freeman	Iowa	Lincoln	July 21, 1862	October 13, 1890
Davis, David	Illinois	Lincoln	December 10, 1862	March 4, 1877
Field, Stephen Johnson	California	Lincoln	May 20, 1863	December 1, 1897
Strong, William	Pennsylvania	Grant	March 14, 1870	December 14, 1880
Bradley, Joseph P.	New Jersey	Grant	March 23, 1870	January 22, 1892
Hunt, Ward	New York	Grant	January 9, 1873	January 27, 1882
Harlan, John Marshall	Kentucky	Hayes	December 10, 1877	October 14, 1911

Woods, William Burnham	Georgia	Hayes	January 5, 1881	May 14, 1887
Matthews, Stanley	Ohio	Garfield	May 17, 1881	March 22, 1889
Gray, Horace	Massachusetts	Arthur	January 9, 1882	September 15, 1902
Blatchford, Samuel	New York	Arthur	April 3, 1882	July 7, 1893
Lamar, Lucius Quintus C.	Mississippi	Cleveland	January 18, 1888	January 23, 1893
Brewer, David Josiah	Kansas	Harrison	January 6, 1890	March 28, 1910
Brown, Henry Billings	Michigan	Harrison	January 5, 1891	May 28, 1906
Shiras, George, Jr.	Pennsylvania	Harrison	October 10, 1892	February 23, 1903
Jackson, Howell Edmunds	Tennessee	Harrison	March 4, 1893	August 8, 1895
White, Edward Douglass	Louisiana	Cleveland	March 12, 1894	December 18, 1910*
Peckham, Rufus Wheeler	New York	Cleveland	January 6, 1896	October 24, 1909
McKenna, Joseph	California	McKinley	January 26, 1898	January 5, 1925
Holmes, Oliver Wendell	Massachusetts	Roosevelt, T.	December 8, 1902	January 12, 1932
Day, William Rufus	Ohio	Roosevelt, T.	March 2, 1903	November 13, 1922
Moody, William Henry	Massachusetts	Roosevelt, T.	December 17, 1906	November 20, 1910
Lurton, Horace Harmon	Tennessee	Taft	January 3, 1910	July 12, 1914
Hughes, Charles Evans	New York	Taft	October 10, 1910	June 10, 1916
Van Devanter, Willis	Wyoming	Taft	January 3, 1911	June 2, 1937
Lamar, Joseph Rucker	Georgia	Taft	January 3, 1911	January 2, 1916
Pitney, Mahlon	New Jersey	Taft	March 18, 1912	December 31, 1922
McReynolds, James Clark	Tennessee	Wilson	October 12, 1914	January 31, 1941
Brandeis, Louis Dembitz	Massachusetts	Wilson	June 5, 1916	February 13, 1939
Clarke, John Hessin	Ohio	Wilson	October 9, 1916	September 18, 1922
Sutherland, George	Utah	Harding	October 2, 1922	January 17, 1938
Butler, Pierce	Minnesota	Harding	January 2, 1923	November 16, 1939
Sanford, Edward Terry	Tennessee	Harding	February 19, 1923	March 8, 1930
Stone, Harlan Fiske	New York	Coolidge	March 2, 1925	July 2, 1941*
Roberts, Owen Josephus	Pennsylvania	Hoover	June 2, 1930	July 31, 1945
Cardozo, Benjamin Nathan	New York	Hoover	March 14, 1932	July 9, 1938
Black, Hugo Lafayette	Alabama	Roosevelt, F.	August 19, 1937	September 17, 1971

Name	State App't From	Appointed by President	Judicial Oath Taken	Date Service Terminated
Reed, Stanley Forman	Kentucky	Roosevelt, F.	January 31, 1938	February 25, 1957
Frankfurter, Felix	Massachusetts	Roosevelt, F.	January 30, 1939	August 28, 1962
Douglas, William Orville	Connecticut	Roosevelt, F.	April 17, 1939	November 12, 1975
Murphy, Frank	Michigan	Roosevelt, F.	February 5, 1940	July 19, 1949
Byrnes, James Francis	South Carolina	Roosevelt, F.	July 8, 1941	October 3, 1942
Jackson, Robert Houghwout	New York	Roosevelt, F.	July 11, 1941	October 9, 1954
Rutledge, Wiley Blount	Iowa	Roosevelt, F.	February 15, 1943	September 10, 1949
Burton, Harold Hitz	Ohio	Truman	October 1, 1945	October 13, 1958
Clark, Tom Campbell	Texas	Truman	August 24, 1949	June 12, 1967
Minton, Sherman	Indiana	Truman	October 12, 1949	October 15, 1956
Harlan, John Marshall	New York	Eisenhower	March 28, 1955	September 23, 1971
Brennan, William J., Jr.	New Jersey	Eisenhower	October 16, 1956	July 20, 1990
Whittaker, Charles Evans	Missouri	Eisenhower	March 25, 1957	March 31, 1962
Stewart, Potter	Ohio	Eisenhower	October 14, 1958	July 3, 1981
White, Byron Raymond	Colorado	Kennedy	April 16, 1962	June 28, 1993
Goldberg, Arthur Joseph	Illinois	Kennedy	October 1, 1962	July 25, 1965
Fortas, Abe	Tennessee	Johnson, L.	October 4, 1965	May 14, 1969
Marshall, Thurgood	New York	Johnson, L.	October 2, 1967	October 1, 1991
Blackmun, Harry A.	Minnesota	Nixon	June 9, 1970	August 3, 1994
Powell, Lewis F., Jr.	Virginia	Nixon	January 7, 1972	June 26, 1987
Rehnquist, William H.	Arizona	Nixon	January 7, 1972	September 26, 1986*
Stevens, John Paul	Illinois	Ford	December 19, 1975	June 29, 2010
O'Connor, Sandra Day	Arizona	Reagan	September 25, 1981	January 31, 2006
Scalia, Antonin	Virginia	Reagan	September 26, 1986	February 13, 2016
Kennedy, Anthony M.	California	Reagan	February 18, 1988	
Souter, David H.	New Hampshire	Bush, G. H. W.	October 9, 1990	June 29, 2009
Thomas, Clarence	Georgia	Bush, G. H. W.	October 23, 1991	
Ginsburg, Ruth Bader	New York	Clinton	August 10, 1993	
Breyer, Stephen G.	Massachusetts	Clinton	August 3, 1994	

Alito, Samuel A., Jr.	New Jersey	Bush, G. W.	January 31, 2006
Sotomayor, Sonia	New York	Obama	August 8, 2009
Kagan, Elena	Massachusetts	Obama	August 7, 2010
Neil M. Gorsuch	Colorado	Trump	April 9, 2017

Notes: The acceptance of the appointment and commission by the appointee, as evidenced by the taking of the prescribed oaths, is here implied; otherwise the individual is not carried on this list of the Members of the Court. Examples: Robert Hanson Harrison is not carried, as a letter from President Washington of February 9, 1790 states Harrison declined to serve. Neither is Edwin M. Stanton who died before he could take the necessary steps toward becoming a Member of the Court. Chief Justice Rutledge is included because he took his oaths, presided over the August Term of 1795, and his name appears on two opinions of the Court for that Term.

The date a Member of the Court took his/her Judicial oath (the Judiciary Act provided "That the Justices of the Supreme Court, and the district judges, before they proceed to execute the duties of their respective offices, shall take the following oath . . . ") is here used as the date of the beginning of his/her service, for until that oath is taken he/she is not vested with the prerogatives of the office. The dates given in this column are for the oaths taken following the receipt of the commissions. Dates without small-letter references are taken from the Minutes of the Court or from the original oath which are in the Curator's collection. The small letter (a) denotes the date is from the Minutes of some other court; (b) from some other unquestionable authority; (c) from authority that is questionable, and better authority would be appreciated.

[The foregoing was taken from a booklet prepared by the Supreme Court of the United States, and published with funding from the Supreme Court Historical Society.]

* Elevated.

CONSTITUTIONAL STRUCTURE

PART I

INTRODUCTION: THE FOUNDATION OF MODERN CONSTITUTIONAL LAW

CHAPTER 1

The Founding

A. THE ORIGINS OF THE CONSTITUTION

ASSIGNMENT 1

As you have already learned in contracts class — or soon will — no writing is or ever can be complete. This is because writings are based on background assumptions that can never be comprehensively articulated. In extreme cases, the failure of a basic assumption that is shared by both parties can result in the nonenforcement of a contract. And even when an assumption has not failed, it is sometimes necessary to examine the background assumptions of a writing to accurately assess its meaning.

In this regard, written constitutions are no different from written contracts. Therefore, we begin our studies by examining three of the most basic assumptions that underlie the original Constitution of the United States and its first ten amendments. The first of these is the idea that "first comes rights, then comes government" — that individuals have what were called "natural rights." This means very roughly that individuals have rights by virtue of being human that are not a grant from any government. The second of these assumptions, which follows from the first, is that government officials are servants, agents, or fiduciaries of the people, which is sometimes referred to as the *agency theory of government*. Third, by 1787, it was widely believed that the previous form of government as specified in the Articles of Confederation had failed miserably. While there was a widespread consensus among Americans on the first two of these assumptions, the third remained controversial even after the Constitution was adopted.

As with written contracts, to properly assess what the Constitution says, we must make ourselves aware of what it assumed. While the Constitution was enacted in 1789, the founding of the United States can be traced to the formal Declaration of Independence from Great Britain enacted by the Continental Congress in July of 1776. The assumption of natural rights was expressly recognized by the Continental Congress in the Declaration — though, as we will see, it abbreviated an equally canonical statement drafted by George Mason — and was offered as a legal justification for separation of the colonies from England.

1. The Declaration of Independence

When reading the Declaration, it is worth keeping in mind two very important facts. The Declaration constituted high treason against the Crown. Every person who signed it would be executed as traitors should they be caught by the British. Second, the Declaration was considered to be a legal document by which the revolutionaries justified their actions and explained why they were not truly traitors. It represented, as it were, a literal indictment of the Crown and Parliament, in the very same way that criminals are now publicly indicted for their alleged crimes by grand juries representing "the People."

But to justify a revolution, it was not thought to be enough that officials of the government of England, the Parliament, or even the sovereign himself had violated the rights of the people. No government is perfect; all governments violate rights. This was well known. So the Americans had to allege more than mere violations of rights. They had to allege nothing short of a criminal conspiracy to violate their rights systematically. Hence, the famous reference to "a long train of abuses and usurpations" and the list that follows. In some cases, these specific complaints account for provisions eventually included in the Constitution and Bill of Rights.

The Declaration of Independence used to be read aloud at public gatherings every Fourth of July. Today, while all Americans have heard of it, all too few have read more than its second sentence. Yet the Declaration shows the natural rights foundation of the American Revolution, and provides important information about what the founders believed makes a constitution or government legitimate. It also raises the question of how these fundamental rights are reconciled with the idea of "the consent of the governed," another idea for which the Declaration is famous.

THE DECLARATION OF INDEPENDENCE

In Congress, July 4, 1776.

The unanimous Declaration of the thirteen united States of America, When in the Course of human events, it becomes necessary for one people to dissolve the political bands which have connected them with another, and to assume among the powers of the earth, the separate and equal station to which the Laws of Nature and of Nature's God entitle them, a decent respect to the opinions of mankind requires that they should declare the causes which impel them to the separation.

We hold these truths to be self-evident, that all men are created equal, that they are endowed by their Creator with certain unalienable Rights, that among these are

Life, Liberty and the pursuit of Happiness. — That to secure these rights, Governments are instituted among Men, deriving their just powers from the consent of the governed, — That whenever any Form of Government becomes destructive of these ends, it is the Right of the People to alter or to abolish it, and to institute new Government, laying its foundation on such principles and organizing its powers in such form, as to them shall seem most likely to effect their Safety and Happiness. Prudence, indeed, will dictate that Governments long established should not be changed for light and transient causes; and accordingly all experience hath shewn, that mankind are more disposed to suffer, while evils are sufferable, than to right themselves by abolishing the forms to which they are accustomed. But when a long train of abuses and usurpations, pursuing invariably the same Object evinces a design to reduce them under absolute Despotism, it is their right, it is their duty, to throw off such Government, and to provide new Guards for their future security. — Such has been the patient sufferance of these Colonies; and such is now the necessity which constrains them to alter their former Systems of Government. The history of the present King of Great Britain is a history of repeated injuries and usurpations, all having in direct object the establishment of an absolute Tyranny over these States. To prove this, let Facts be submitted to a candid world.

He has refused his Assent to Laws, the most wholesome and necessary for the public good.

He has forbidden his Governors to pass Laws of immediate and pressing importance, unless suspended in their operation till his Assent should be obtained; and when so suspended, he has utterly neglected to attend to them.

He has refused to pass other Laws for the accommodation of large districts of people, unless those people would relinquish the right of Representation in the Legislature, a right inestimable to them and formidable to tyrants only.

He has called together legislative bodies at places unusual, uncomfortable, and distant from the depository of their public Records, for the sole purpose of fatiguing them into compliance with his measures.

He has dissolved Representative Houses repeatedly, for opposing with manly firmness his invasions on the rights of the people.

He has refused for a long time, after such dissolutions, to cause others to be elected; whereby the Legislative powers, incapable of Annihilation, have returned to the People at large for their exercise; the State remaining in the mean time exposed to all the dangers of invasion from without, and convulsions within.

He has endeavoured to prevent the population of these States; for that purpose obstructing the Laws for Naturalization of Foreigners; refusing to pass others to encourage their migrations hither, and raising the conditions of new Appropriations of Lands.

He has obstructed the Administration of Justice, by refusing his Assent to Laws for establishing Judiciary powers.

He has made Judges dependent on his Will alone, for the tenure of their offices, and the amount and payment of their salaries.

He has erected a multitude of New Offices, and sent hither swarms of Officers to harrass our people, and eat out their substance.

He has kept among us, in times of peace, Standing Armies without the Consent of our legislatures.

He has affected to render the Military independent of and superior to the Civil power.

He has combined with others to subject us to a jurisdiction foreign to our constitution, and unacknowledged by our laws; giving his Assent to their Acts of pretended Legislation:

For Quartering large bodies of armed troops among us:

For protecting them, by a mock Trial, from punishment for any Murders which they should commit on the Inhabitants of these States:

For cutting off our Trade with all parts of the world:

For imposing Taxes on us without our Consent:

For depriving us in many cases, of the benefits of Trial by Jury:

For transporting us beyond Seas to be tried for pretended offences:

For abolishing the free System of English Laws in a neighbouring Province, establishing therein an Arbitrary government, and enlarging its Boundaries so as to render it at once an example and fit instrument for introducing the same absolute rule into these Colonies:

For taking away our Charters, abolishing our most valuable Laws, and altering fundamentally the Forms of our Governments:

For suspending our own Legislatures, and declaring themselves invested with power to legislate for us in all cases whatsoever.

He has abdicated Government here, by declaring us out of his Protection and waging War against us.

He has plundered our seas, ravaged our Coasts, burnt our towns, and destroyed the lives of our people.

He is at this time transporting large Armies of foreign Mercenaries to compleat the works of death, desolation and tyranny, already begun with circumstances of Cruelty & perfidy scarcely paralleled in the most barbarous ages, and totally unworthy the Head of a civilized nation.

He has constrained our fellow Citizens taken Captive on the high Seas to bear Arms against their Country, to become the executioners of their friends and Brethren, or to fall themselves by their Hands.

He has excited domestic insurrections amongst us, and has endeavoured to bring on the inhabitants of our frontiers, the merciless Indian Savages, whose known rule of warfare, is an undistinguished destruction of all ages, sexes and conditions.

In every stage of these Oppressions We have Petitioned for Redress in the most humble terms: Our repeated Petitions have been answered only by repeated injury. A Prince whose character is thus marked by every act which may define a Tyrant, is unfit to be the ruler of a free people.

Nor have We been wanting in attentions to our Brittish brethren. We have warned them from time to time of attempts by their legislature to extend an unwarrantable jurisdiction over us. We have reminded them of the circumstances of our emigration and settlement here. We have appealed to their native justice and magnanimity, and we have conjured them by the ties of our common kindred to disavow these usurpations, which, would inevitably interrupt our connections and correspondence. They too have been deaf to the voice of justice and of consanguinity. We must, therefore, acquiesce in the necessity, which denounces our Separation, and hold them, as we hold the rest of mankind, Enemies in War, in Peace Friends.

We, therefore, the Representatives of the united States of America, in General Congress, Assembled, appealing to the Supreme Judge of the world for the rectitude of our intentions, do, in the Name, and by Authority of the good People of these Colonies, solemnly publish and declare, That these United Colonies are, and of Right ought to be Free and Independent States; that they are Absolved from all Allegiance to the British Crown, and that all political connection between them and the State of Great Britain, is and ought to be totally dissolved; and that as Free and Independent States, they have full Power to levy War, conclude Peace, contract Alliances, establish Commerce, and to do all other Acts and Things which Independent States may of right do. And for the support of this Declaration, with a firm reliance on the protection of divine Providence, we mutually pledge to each other our Lives, our Fortunes and our sacred Honor.

To appreciate all that is packed into this short document, it is useful to break down the Declaration into some of its key claims.

1. "*When in the Course of human events, it becomes necessary for one people to dissolve the political bands which have connected them with another, and to assume among the powers of the earth, the separate and equal station to which the Laws of Nature and of Nature's God entitle them, a decent respect to the opinions of mankind requires that they should declare the causes which impel them to the separation.*" This first sentence is often forgotten. It asserts that Americans as a whole (and not as members of their respective colonies) are a distinct "people." To "dissolve the political bands" revokes the "social compact" that existed between the Americans and the rest of "the People" of the British commonwealth, reinstates the "state of nature" between Americans and the government of Great Britain, and makes "the Laws of Nature" the standard by which this dissolution and whatever government is to follow are judged. "Declare the causes" amounts to a public statement of the reasons and justifications for their actions; the signatories were not acting as thieves in the night. The Declaration acts like the indictment in a criminal case that states the basis of charging someone who is normally presumed innocent with criminality. But the ultimate judge of the rightness of their cause will not be the opinions of mankind, but God, which is why the revolutionaries spoke of an "appeal to heaven" — an expression commonly found on revolutionary banners and flags. As British political theorist John Locke wrote: "The people have no other remedy in this, as in all other cases where they have no judge on earth, but to appeal to heaven." The reference to a "decent respect to the opinions of mankind" could be viewed as a test based on international public opinion. But perhaps the emphasis should be on the word "respect," recognizing the obligation to provide the rest of the world with an explanation they can evaluate for themselves, while reserving the ultimate judgment to God.

2. "*We hold these truths to be self-evident, that all men are created equal, that they are endowed by their Creator with* certain unalienable Rights, *that among these are Life, Liberty and the pursuit of Happiness.*" This is the most famous line of the Declaration. On the one hand, it will become a great embarrassment to a people who permitted slavery. On the other hand, making public claims like this has consequences — that's why people make them publicly: to be held to account. This promise will provide the heart of the abolitionist case in the nineteenth century, and it became a lynchpin of the moral and constitutional arguments of the nineteenth-century abolitionists. Leading up to the Civil War, the Declaration was much relied upon by Abraham Lincoln, and had to be explained away by the Supreme Court in *Dred Scott*. Eventually, the Declaration was repudiated by some defenders of slavery in the South because of its inconsistency with that institution. Ultimately, the Declaration formed the basis for Martin Luther King Jr.'s metaphor of the civil rights movement as a "promissory note" that a later generation has come to collect.

What are "unalienable," or more commonly, "inalienable rights"? Unlike other rights that you can agree to transfer or waive, inalienable rights cannot be given up, even if you want to and consent to do so. Why the claim that they are inalienable rights? The Founders wanted to counter England's claim that, by accepting the colonial governance, the colonists had waived or alienated their rights. The framers claimed that with inalienable rights, you always retain the ability to take back any right that has been given up.

A standard trilogy throughout this period was "life, liberty, and property." For example, the Declaration and Resolves of the First Continental Congress (1774) read: "That the inhabitants of the English colonies in North-America, by the immutable laws of nature, the principles of the English constitution, and the several charters or compacts, have the following RIGHTS: Resolved, 1. That they are entitled to life, liberty and property: and they have never ceded to any foreign power whatever, a right to dispose of either without their consent." Or, as John Locke wrote, "no one ought to harm another in his life, health, liberty, or possessions."

When drafting the Declaration in June of 1776, Jefferson based his formulation on a preliminary version of the Virginia Declaration of Rights that had been drafted by George Mason at the end of May for Virginia's provincial convention. Here is how Mason's draft read:

> THAT all men are born equally free and independent, and have certain inherent natural rights, of which they cannot, by any compact, deprive or divest their posterity; among which are, the enjoyment of life and liberty, with the means of acquiring and possessing property, and pursuing and obtaining happiness and safety.

Notice how George Mason's oft-repeated formulation combines the right of property with the pursuit of happiness. And, in his draft, not only do all persons have "certain . . . natural rights" of life, liberty, and property, but these rights cannot be taken away "by any compact." These inherent individual natural rights, of which the people cannot divest their posterity, are therefore retained by them, which is helpful in understanding the Ninth Amendment's reference to the "rights . . . retained by the people." (Some scholars speculate that Jefferson did not list "property" in the Declaration because it is in fact *alienable* — that is, it can be conveyed.)

Mason's draft was slightly altered by the Virginia convention in Williamsburg on June 11, 1776. After an extensive debate, the officially adopted version read (with the modifications in italics):

> That all men are *by nature* equally free and independent, and have certain *inherent rights*, of which, *when they enter into a state of society*, they cannot, by any compact, deprive or divest their posterity; namely, the enjoyment of life and liberty, with the means of acquiring and possessing property, and pursuing and obtaining happiness and safety.

This version is still in effect today.

According to historian Pauline Maier, by changing "are born equally free" to "are by nature equally free," and "inherent natural rights" to "inherent rights," and then by adding "when they enter into a state of society," defenders of slavery in the Virginia convention could contend that slaves were not covered because they "had never entered Virginia's society, which was confined to whites."[1] Yet it was the language of Mason's radical draft — rather than either Virginia's final wording or Jefferson's more succinct formulation — that became the canonical statement of first principles. Massachusetts, Pennsylvania, and Vermont adopted Mason's original references to "born equally free" and to "natural rights" into their declarations of rights while omitting the phrase "when they enter into a state of society." Indeed, it is remarkable that these states would have had Mason's draft language, rather than the version actually adopted by Virginia, from which to copy. Here is Massachusetts' version:

> All men are born free and equal, and have certain natural, essential, and unalienable rights; among which may be reckoned the right of enjoying and defending their lives and liberties; that of acquiring, possessing, and protecting property; in fine, that of seeking and obtaining their safety and happiness.

Virginia slaveholders' concerns about Mason's formulation proved to be warranted. In 1783, the Massachusetts Supreme Judicial Court relied upon this more radical language to invalidate slavery in that state. (What is today called "judicial review" was alive and well before *Marbury v. Madison.*) And its influence continued. In 1823, it was incorporated into an influential circuit court opinion by Justice Bushrod Washington (the nephew of the first President) defining the "privileges and immunities" of citizens in the several states as "protection by the Government, *the enjoyment of life and liberty, with the right to acquire and possess property of every kind, and to pursue and obtain happiness and safety.*"[2]

Justice Washington's opinion in *Corfield* (to which we will return in Chapter 5) embraced Mason's language at its core. This formulation was then repeatedly quoted by Republicans in the Thirty-Ninth Congress when they explained the meaning of the Privileges or Immunities Clause of the Fourteenth Amendment, which reads: "No state shall make or enforce any law which shall abridge the

---

[1] Pauline Maier, American Scripture: Making the Declaration of Independence 193 (1977). See also Randy E. Barnett, Our Republican Constitution: Securing the Liberty and Sovereignty of We the People 31-51 (2016) (discussing the political theory of the Declaration of Independence).

[2] Corfield v. Coryell, 6 F. Cas. 546, 551-552 (1823) (emphasis added).

privileges or immunities of citizens of the United States." It was this constitutional language that Republicans aimed at the discriminatory Black Codes by which Southerners were seeking to perpetuate the subordination of blacks, even after slavery had been abolished.

3. "*That* to secure these rights, *Governments are instituted among Men. . . .*" Another overlooked line, which is of greatest relevance to our discussion of the first underlying assumption of the Constitution: the assumption of natural rights. Here, even more clearly than in Mason's draft, the Declaration stipulates that the ultimate end or purpose of republican governments is "to secure these" preexisting natural rights that the previous sentence affirmed were the measure against which all government—whether of Great Britain or the United States—will be judged. This language identifies what is perhaps the central underlying "republican" assumption of the Constitution: that governments are instituted to secure the preexisting natural rights that are retained by the people. In short, that *first come rights and then comes government.*

4. ". . . *deriving their just powers from* the consent of the governed." Today, there is a tendency to focus entirely on the second half of this sentence, referencing "the consent of the governed," to the exclusion of the first part, which refers to securing our natural rights. Then, by reading "the consent of the governed" as equivalent to "the will of the people," the second part of the sentence seems to support majoritarian rule by the people's "representatives." In this way, "consent of the governed" is read to mean "consent to majoritarian rule." Put another way, the people can consent to *anything*, including rule by a majority in the legislature who will then decide the scope of their rights as individuals.

But read carefully, one sees that in this passage the Declaration speaks of "just powers," suggesting that only *some* powers are "justly" held by government, while others are beyond its proper authority. And notice also that "the consent *of the governed*" assumes that the people do not *themselves* rule or govern, but are "governed" by those individual persons who make up the "governments" that "are instituted among men."

The Declaration stipulates that those who govern the people are supposed "to secure" their preexisting rights, not impose the will of a majority of the people on the minority. And, as the Virginia Declaration of Rights made explicit, these inalienable rights cannot be surrendered "by any compact." Therefore, the "consent of the governed," to which the second half of this sentence refers, cannot be used to override the inalienable rights of the sovereign people that are reaffirmed by the first half.

In modern political discourse, people tend to favor one of these concepts over the other—either preexistent natural rights or popular consent—which leads them to stress one part of this sentence in the Declaration over the other. The fact that rights can be uncertain and disputed leads some to emphasize the consent part of this sentence and the legitimacy of popularly enacted legislation. But the fact that there is *never* unanimous consent to any particular law, or even to the government itself, leads others to emphasize the rights part of this sentence and the legitimacy of judges protecting the "fundamental" or "human" rights of individuals and minorities.

If we take both parts of this sentence seriously, however, this apparent tension can be reconciled by distinguishing between (a) the ultimate end or purpose of legitimate governance and (b) how any particular government gains jurisdiction to rule. So, while the protection of natural rights or justice is the ultimate end of governance, particular governments only gain jurisdiction to achieve this end by the consent of those who are governed. In other words, the "consent of the governed" tells us *which* government gets to undertake the mission of "securing" the natural rights that are retained by the people. After all, justifying the independence of Americans from the British government was the whole purpose of the Declaration of Independence.

5. "*That whenever any Form of Government becomes destructive of these ends, it is the Right of the People to alter or to abolish it, and to institute new Government, laying its foundation on such principles and organizing its powers in such form, as to them shall seem most likely to effect their Safety and Happiness.*" People have the right to take back power from the government. This provision restates the end—human safety and happiness—and connects the principles and forms of government as means to this end.

6. "*Prudence, indeed, will dictate that Governments long established should not be changed for light and transient causes; and accordingly all experience hath shewn, that mankind are more disposed to suffer, while evils are sufferable, than to right themselves by abolishing the forms to which they are accustomed.*" This clause affirms at least two propositions: on the one hand, long-established government should not be changed for just any reason. The mere fact that rights are violated is not enough to justify revolution. All governments on earth will sometimes violate rights. But things have to become very bad before anyone is going to organize a resistance. Therefore, the very existence of this Declaration is evidence that things are very bad indeed.

7. "*But when a long train of abuses and usurpations, pursuing invariably the same Object evinces a design to reduce them under absolute Despotism, it is their right, it is their duty, to throw off such Government, and to provide new Guards for their future security.*" Revolution is justified only if there "is a long train of abuses and usurpations, pursuing invariably the same Object"—evidence of what amounts to an actual criminal conspiracy by the government against the rights of the people. Such charges are the opposite of "light and transient causes," that is, the more ordinary, acceptable violations of rights by government.

8. "*Such has been the patient sufferance of these Colonies; and such is now the necessity which constrains them to alter their former Systems of Government. The history of the present King of Great Britain* [George III—Eds.] *is a history of repeated injuries and usurpations, all having in direct object the establishment of an absolute Tyranny over these States. To prove this, let Facts be submitted to a candid world.*" What follows is a bill of indictment. Several of these items end up in the

Bill of Rights. Others are addressed by the form of the government established—first by the Articles of Confederation, and ultimately by the Constitution.

The assumption of natural rights expressed in the Declaration of Independence can be summed up by the following proposition: "First comes rights, then comes government." According to this view: (1) the rights of individuals do not originate with any government, but preexist its formation; (2) the protection of these rights is the first duty of government; (3) even after government is formed, these rights provide a standard by which its performance is measured and, in extreme cases, its systemic failure to protect rights—or its systematic violation of rights—can justify its alteration or abolition; and (4) at least some of these rights are so fundamental that they are "inalienable," meaning they are so intimately connected to one's nature as a human being that they cannot be transferred to another even if one consents to do so. This is powerful stuff.

At the Founding, these ideas were considered so true as to be "self-evident." However, today the idea of natural rights is obscure and controversial. Oftentimes, when the idea comes up, it is deemed to be archaic. Moreover, the discussion by many of natural rights, as reflected in the Declaration's claim that such rights "are endowed by their Creator," leads many to characterize natural rights as religiously based rather than secular. So it is useful to attempt to understand natural rights the way the founding generation that wrote and ratified the Bill of Rights understood them.

a. Popular Sovereignty, the Social Compact, and the State of Nature

As we previously discussed, the Declaration employs a form of reasoning that hypothesizes a "social compact" or "social contract" that a declaration of independence then "dissolved." "We the people" then agree to form a new political arrangement—the exact form of which is expressed in a written constitution. In those days, political theory instructed that, in every society, there must be a "sovereign" with the ultimate authority to rule. Because they viewed "the People" as the ultimate authority deciding when governments are formed and dissolved, the American revolutionaries replaced the concept of monarchical sovereignty with that of "popular sovereignty." This justified their withdrawing consent to be ruled by the English king so that they might adopt their own political order.

Social compact theory postulates a preexisting and natural social situation prior to the adoption of the social compact that then creates a political order to explain *why* the compact is adopted. In other words, it is this preexisting situation that gives rise to the *need* to adopt a social compact, which in turn then *justifies* the resulting social order. This preexisting situation was called the "state of nature." How the state of nature is imagined shapes why a social compact is needed and also the terms of that agreement.

Prior to the American Revolution, two powerful but inconsistent conceptions of the state of nature were formulated in the seventeenth century by English political theorists Thomas Hobbes and John Locke. In his book *Leviathan* (1651),

Hobbes described the state of nature and the resultant need for a sovereign as follows:

> [D]uring the time men live without a common power to keep them all in awe, they are in that condition which is called war; and such a war as is of every man against every man. . . . In such condition there is no place for industry, because the fruit thereof is uncertain: and consequently no culture of the earth; no navigation, nor use of the commodities that may be imported by sea; no commodious building; no instruments of moving and removing such things as require much force; no knowledge of the face of the earth; no account of time; no arts; no letters; no society; and which is worst of all, continual fear, and danger of violent death; and the life of man, solitary, poor, nasty, brutish, and short. . . .
>
> To this war of every man against every man, this also is consequent; that nothing can be unjust. The notions of right and wrong, justice and injustice, have there no place. Where there is no common power, there is no law; where no law, no injustice. Force and fraud are in war the two cardinal virtues. Justice and injustice are none of the faculties neither of the body nor mind. If they were, they might be in a man that were alone in the world, as well as his senses and passions. They are qualities that relate to men in society, not in solitude. It is consequent also to the same condition that there be no propriety, no dominion, no mine and thine distinct; but only that to be every man's that he can get, and for so long as he can keep it. . . .
>
> By liberty is understood, according to the proper signification of the word, the absence of external impediments; which impediments may oft take away part of a man's power to do what he would, but cannot hinder him from using the power left him according as his judgement and reason shall dictate to him. . . . And because the condition of man . . . is a condition of war of every one against every one, in which case every one is governed by his own reason, and there is nothing he can make use of that may not be a help unto him in preserving his life against his enemies; it followeth that in such a condition every man has a right to every thing, even to one another's body. And therefore, as long as this natural right of every man to every thing endureth, there can be no security to any man, how strong or wise soever he be, of living out the time which nature ordinarily alloweth men to live. . . .
>
> The only way to erect such a common power, as may be able to defend them from the invasion of foreigners, and the injuries of one another, and thereby to secure them in such sort as that by their own industry and by the fruits of the earth they may nourish themselves and live contentedly, is to confer all their power and strength upon one man, or upon one assembly of men, that may reduce all their wills, by plurality of voices, unto one will: which is as much as to say, to appoint one man, or assembly of men, to bear their person . . . and therein to submit their wills, every one to his will, and their judgements to his judgement. This is more than consent, or concord; it is a real unity of them all in one and the same person, made by covenant of every man with every man, in such manner as if every man should say to every man: I authorise and give up my right of governing myself to this man, or to this assembly of men, on this condition; that thou give up, thy right to him, and authorise all his actions in like manner. This done, the multitude so united in one person is called a COMMONWEALTH; in Latin, CIVITAS. This is the generation of that great LEVIATHAN, or rather, to speak more reverently, of that mortal god to which we owe, under the immortal God, our peace and defence. . . .
>
> And in him consisteth the essence of the Commonwealth; which, to define it, is: one person, of whose acts a great multitude, by mutual covenants one with another, have made themselves every one the author, to the end he may use the strength and means of them all as he shall think expedient for their peace and common defence. And

> he that carryeth this person is called sovereign, and said to have sovereign power; and every one besides, his subject.

For Hobbes, therefore, there are no rights in the state of nature — or, more accurately, in the state of nature, everyone's rights or "liberty" are unlimited, including even the right to use other persons as each sees fit. A sovereign ruler or government is therefore needed precisely to *limit* this liberty and these natural rights, and to establish in their place enforceable or "legal" rights. Otherwise there will be chaos.

A quite difference conception of the state of nature was described by John Locke in his *Second Treatise of Government* (1690), which was subtitled "An Essay Concerning the True Original, Extent and End of Civil Government." A physician by training, Locke was heavily immersed in English revolutionary politics in the late seventeenth century. He had to flee the country due to his close association with opponents of King Charles II who had hatched the Rye House Plot to assassinate the king and his brother James II, the heir to the throne. Locke returned to England only after the Glorious Revolution of 1688 deposed Charles's successor James and put William and Mary on the throne. Locke's Treatise was considered so inflammatory and potentially treasonous when it appeared that he published it anonymously and acknowledged his authorship in a codicil to his will.

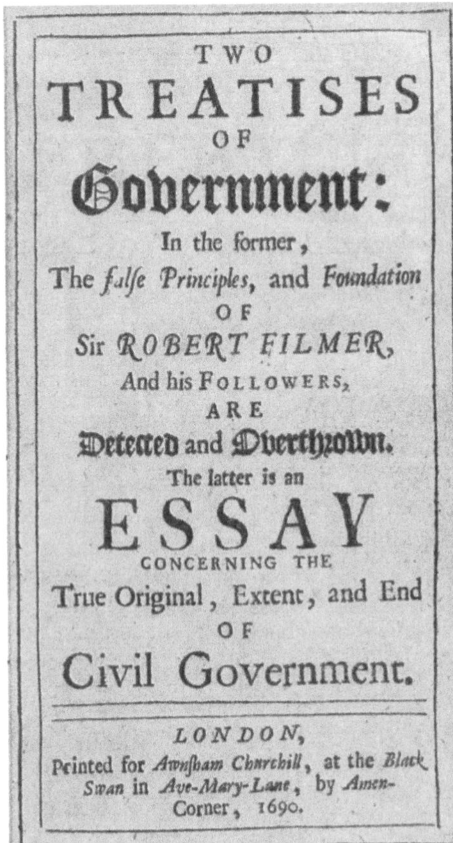

TWO
TREATISES
OF
Government:
In the former,
The *falſe Principles*, and *Foundation*
OF
Sir ROBERT FILMER,
And his FOLLOWERS,
ARE
Detected and Overthrown.
The latter is an
ESSAY
CONCERNING THE
True Original, Extent, and End
OF
Civil Government.

LONDON,
Printed for *Awnſham Churchill*, at the *Black Swan* in *Ave-Mary-Lane*, by *Amen-Corner*, 1690.

Frontispiece of the Second Treatise of Government *and author John Locke*

You will see a very close affinity between Locke's "state of nature" and that described in the Declaration:

> To understand political power right, and derive it from its original, we must consider, what state all men are naturally in, and that is, a state of perfect freedom to order their actions, and dispose of their possessions and persons, as they think fit, within the bounds of the law of nature, without asking leave, or depending upon the will of any other man.
>
> A state also of equality, wherein all the power and jurisdiction is reciprocal, no one having more than another; there being nothing more evident, than that creatures of the same species and rank, promiscuously born to all the same advantages of nature, and the use of the same faculties, should also be equal one amongst another without subordination or subjection, unless the lord and master of them all should, by any manifest declaration of his will, set one above another, and confer on him, by an evident and clear appointment, an undoubted right to dominion and sovereignty. . . .
>
> But though this be a state of liberty, yet it is not a state of licence. . . . The state of nature has a law of nature to govern it, which obliges every one: and reason, which is that law, teaches all mankind, who will but consult it, that being all equal and independent, no one ought to harm another in his life, health, liberty, or possessions: for men being all the workmanship of one omnipotent, and infinitely wise maker; all the servants of one sovereign master, sent into the world by his order, and about his business; they are his property, whose workmanship they are, made to last during his, not one another's pleasure: and being furnished with like faculties, sharing all in one community of nature, there cannot be supposed any such subordination among us, that may authorize us to destroy one another, as if we were made for one another's uses, as the inferior ranks of creatures are for ours. . . .
>
> And that all men may be restrained from invading others' rights, and from doing hurt to one another, and the law of nature be observed, which willeth the peace and preservation of all mankind, the execution of the law of nature is, in that state, put into every man's hands, whereby every one has a right to punish the transgressors of that law to such a degree, as may hinder its violation. . . .
>
> To this strange doctrine, viz. That in the state of nature every one has the executive power of the law of nature, I doubt not but it will be objected, that it is unreasonable for men to be judges in their own cases, that self-love will make men partial to themselves and their friends: and on the other side, that ill nature, passion and revenge will carry them too far in punishing others; and hence nothing but confusion and disorder will follow, and that therefore God hath certainly appointed government to restrain the partiality and violence of men.

There is some dispute about whether the "state of nature" was viewed by these theorists as a real historical event or as a thought experiment. On the one hand, while these writers may not have believed there was ever a time in which government emerged from a state of nature in so pristine a way, it seems plain that many writers — and the founders themselves — believed that a real state of nature could exist between persons, including the rulers of nations, who were not governed by a common authority. Locke addresses this point:

> It is often asked as a mighty objection, where are, or ever were there any men in such a state of nature? To which it may suffice as an answer at present, that since all princes and rulers of independent governments all through the world, are in a state of nature, it

is plain the world never was, nor ever will be, without numbers of men in that state. I have named all governors of independent communities, whether they are, or are not, in league with others: for it is not every compact that puts an end to the state of nature between men, but only this one of agreeing together mutually to enter into one community, and make one body politic; other promises, and compacts, men may make one with another, and yet still be in the state of nature. The promises and bargains for truck, &c. between the two men in the desert island, mentioned by Garcilasso de la Vega, in his history of Peru; or between a Swiss and an Indian, in the woods of America, are binding to them, though they are perfectly in a state of nature, in reference to one another: for truth and keeping of faith belongs to men, as men, and not as members of society. . . .

Locke was far from being the only prominent natural rights advocate of his day. Nor was he the only natural rights theorist with whom the founding generation was intimately familiar (though they largely ignored Hobbes). But Locke was a careful and systematic writer of enormous influence. Whatever else can be said about the respective merits of each work, there is little question that the founding generation is more accurately described as Lockean than Hobbesian in its views.

b. The Separation of Powers

According to Locke, the social compact establishes a government that addresses the inconveniences in the state of nature, primarily the inconvenience of executing or enforcing the laws of nature to protect one's natural rights.

If man in the state of nature be so free, as has been said; if he be absolute lord of his own person and possessions, equal to the greatest, and subject to no body, why will he part with his freedom? Why will he give up this empire, and subject himself to the dominion and controul of any other power? To which it is obvious to answer, that though in the state of nature he hath such a right, yet the enjoyment of it is very uncertain, and constantly exposed to the invasion of others: for all being kings as much as he, every man his equal, and the greater part no strict observers of equity and justice, the enjoyment of the property he has in this state is very unsafe, very unsecure. This makes him willing to quit a condition, which, however free, is full of fears and continual dangers: and it is not without reason, that he seeks out, and is willing to join in society with others, who are already united, or have a mind to unite, for the mutual preservation of their lives, liberties and estates, which I call by the general name, property.

The great and chief end, therefore, of men's uniting into commonwealths, and putting themselves under government, is the preservation of their property. To which in the state of nature there are many things wanting.

But Locke then goes on to identify three distinct problems in the state of nature that lead to three distinct powers of a government, which is established to protect the natural rights of the people.

First, There wants an established, settled, known law, received and allowed by common consent to be the standard of right and wrong, and the common measure to decide all

> controversies between them: for though the law of nature be plain and intelligible to all rational creatures; yet men being biassed by their interest, as well as ignorant for want of study of it, are not apt to allow of it as a law binding to them in the application of it to their particular cases.

The first problem is addressed by the legislative power to enact statutes.

> Secondly, In the state of nature there wants a known and indifferent judge, with authority to determine all differences according to the established law: for every one in that state being both judge and executioner of the law of nature, men being partial to themselves, passion and revenge is very apt to carry them too far, and with too much heat, in their own cases; as well as negligence, and unconcernedness, to make them too remiss in other men's.

The second problem is addressed by the judicial power to decide cases impartially.

> Thirdly, In the state of nature there often wants power to back and support the sentence when right, and to give it due execution, They who by any injustice offended, will seldom fail, where they are able, by force to make good their injustice; such resistance many times makes the punishment dangerous, and frequently destructive, to those who attempt it.

The third problem is addressed by the executive power to enforce the laws.

Although Locke clearly distinguished the legislative, judicial, and executive powers, he did not emphasize that these powers ought to be separated and placed in different hands. This is understandable given that they were merged under the British political system. The idea of a separation of these powers is identified with the French political thinker Charles Louis de Secondat, who was known as the Baron de Montesquieu. Although he did not originate the notion, in his book *De l'Esprit des Loix* (1748) — or "The Spirit of the Law" — Montesquieu advocated a division of political power among different persons comprising an executive, a legislature, and a judiciary, which greatly influenced the founding generation.

> When the legislative and executive powers are united in the same person, or in the same body of magistrates, there can be no liberty. . . . Again, there is no liberty, if the judiciary power be not separated from the legislative and executive. Were it joined with the legislative, the life and liberty of the subject would be exposed to arbitrary control; for the judge would then be the legislator. Were it joined to the executive power, the judge might behave with violence and oppression. There would be an end to everything, were the same man, or the same body, whether of the nobles or of the people, to exercise those three powers, that of enacting laws, that of executing the public resolutions, and of trying the causes of individuals.

We will see that, unlike the Articles of Confederation, the U.S. Constitution reflects this idea by explicitly separating and placing legislative powers in Congress (Article I), executive powers in the President (Article II), and judicial power in the judiciary (Article III).

c. Natural Rights as a Constraint on Government

After a people have consented to form a government to protect their natural rights, Locke maintained that these rights provide a standard or criterion by which the actions of governments are to be judged:

> I easily grant, that civil government is the proper remedy for the inconveniencies of the state of nature, which must certainly be great, where men may be judges in their own case, since it is easy to be imagined, that he who was so unjust as to do his brother an injury, will scarce be so just as to condemn himself for it: but I shall desire those who make this objection, to remember, that absolute monarchs are but men; and if government is to be the remedy of those evils, which necessarily follow from men's being judges in their own cases, and the state of nature is therefore not to be endured, I desire to know what kind of government that is, and how much better it is than the state of nature, where one man, commanding a multitude, has the liberty to be judge in his own case, and may do to all his subjects whatever he pleases, without the least liberty to any one to question or controul those who execute his pleasure and in whatsoever he doth, whether led by reason, mistake or passion, must be submitted to. Much better it is in the state of nature, wherein men are not bound to submit to the unjust will of another. And if he that judges, judges amiss in his own, or any other case, he is answerable for it to the rest of mankind.

Locke elaborates on this idea by invoking the idea of presumed or "supposed" consent.

> But though men, when they enter into society, give up the equality, liberty, and executive power they had in the state of nature, into the hands of the society, to be so far disposed of by the legislative, as the good of the society shall require; yet it being only with an intention in every one the better to preserve himself, his liberty and property; (for no rational creature *can be supposed* to change his condition with an intention to be worse) the power of the society, or legislative constituted by them, can never be supposed to extend farther, than the common good; but is obliged to secure every one's property, by providing against those three defects above mentioned, that made the state of nature so unsafe and uneasy. And so whoever has the legislative or supreme power of any commonwealth, is bound to govern by established standing laws, promulgated and known to the people, and not by extemporary decrees; by indifferent and upright judges, who are to decide controversies by those laws; and to employ the force of the community at home, only in the execution of such laws, or abroad to prevent or redress foreign injuries, and secure the community from inroads and invasion. And all this to be directed to no other end, but the peace, safety, and public good of the people (emphasis added).

Later in this chapter, we will see appeals to this idea of "supposed" or presumed consent by Justice Samuel Chase in the case of *Calder v. Bull.*

For students who often do not learn much about natural rights before coming to law school, this widespread background assumption by the Founders can seem a bit mysterious. To illuminate their thinking, consider this portion of an "election sermon" delivered in Hartford to the governor and Connecticut General Assembly by Elizur Goodrich, the pastor of the Church of Christ in Durham, Connecticut. Both before and after the Founding, it was commonplace for members of the clergy to give a formal lecture or sermon to the newly elected representatives and members of the government to guide them in the performance of their duties. Goodrich's sermon, entitled "The Principles of Civil Union and Happiness Considered and Recommended," was delivered on May 10, 1787, on the eve of the convening of the Constitutional Convention in Philadelphia (which was scheduled to begin on May 14). It is worth examining, not because Goodrich was prominent, but because his relative obscurity demonstrates how commonplace such thinking was. Here is a portion of Goodrich's sermon (with certain key passages highlighted):

> [T]he great occasion, on which we are assembled in the house of God, justify a discourse on the great principles and maxims, of civil union — the importance of a good, public administration, to answer the ends of government — and the necessity of the joint exertions of subjects, and their rulers, in promoting the public peace and happiness. I am then, in the first place, to point out some of the great principles and maxims, which are the foundation and cement of civil society. *The principles of society are the laws, which Almighty God has established in the moral world, and made necessary to be observed by mankind; in order to promote their true happiness,* in their transactions and intercourse. These laws may be considered as principles, in respect of their fixedness and operation, and as maxims, since *by the knowledge of them, we discover the rules of conduct, which direct mankind to the highest perfection, and supreme happiness of their nature.* They are as fixed and unchangeable as the laws which operate in the natural world. Human art in order to produce certain effects, must conform to the principles and laws, which the Almighty Creator has established in the natural world. *He who neglects the cultivation of his field, and the proper time of sowing, may not expect a harvest. He, who would assist mankind in raising weights, and overcoming obstacles, depends on certain rules, derived from the knowledge of mechanical principles applied to the construction of machines, in order to give the most useful effect to the smallest force: And every builder should well understand the best position of firmness and strength, when he is about to erect an edifice.* For he, who attempts these things, on other principles, than those of nature, *attempts to make a new world*; and his aim will prove absurd and his labour lost. No more can mankind be conducted to happiness; or civil societies united, and enjoy peace and prosperity, without observing the moral principles and connections, which the Almighty Creator has established for the government of the moral world.
>
> *Moral connections and causes in different circumstances produce harmony or discord, peace or war, happiness or woe among mankind, with the same certainty, as physical causes produce their effect.* To institute these causes and connexions belongs not to men, to nations or to human laws, but to build upon them. It is no more in the power of the greatest earthly potentate to hinder their operation, than it is to govern the flowing and ebbing of the ocean.

In this excerpt, Goodrich explains how natural rights, or what he calls the "principles of society," were viewed as on a par with principles in other fields — in particular, agriculture and engineering. Unlike such *descriptive* bodies of knowledge like mathematics, biology, or physics, fields like agriculture, engineering, architecture and medicine, are *normative* disciplines that developed to guide human conduct. In other words, normative disciplines purport to answer the question of *how* men should act when faced with practical problems. When Goodrich says "he, who attempts these things, on other principles, than those of nature, *attempts to make a new world*; and his aim will prove absurd and his labour lost," he is merely claiming that our world has certain characteristics — like gravity — that cannot be wished away — by, for example, jumping off a building thinking one can fly. Attempting "to make a new world" in our world will be self-defeating.

Notice that, while these "principles of society" are traced by Goodrich to God, so too are agriculture and engineering. All were based on the order in the world (for which God is responsible). This means that they could be just as valid even if the natural order on which they are based was not of divine origin. As the renowned Dutch natural rights theorist Hugo Grotius famously (and bravely) affirmed: "What we have been saying [about the existence of a natural law of justice] would have a degree of validity even if we were to concede what cannot be conceded without the utmost wickedness, that there is no God, or that the affairs of men are of no concern to Him."[3]

2. The Origin of American Federalism

We see in the excerpt from John Locke a horizontal structural division of powers between the legislative, executive, and judiciary, or what has come to be called in American constitutional law "the separation of powers." Another primary structural division of power is between the national or federal government and the governments of the several states. This vertical division of authority is commonly referred to as "federalism." The origin of American federalism is much studied and debated.[4] But one source of the idea of separate governments divided hierarchically by subject matter stemmed from the fierce debate in the colonies over the power of Parliament over the colonies. While the colonists pledged their allegiance to the King, they denied the authority of Parliament over them, because they lacked representation in that body. Instead, they claimed the legislative authority in America rested with their own colonial legislators, subject to the higher authority of the Crown.

A memorable public written debate on this idea of divided sovereignty occurred in 1773 between the governor of Massachusetts, Thomas Hutchinson, and the Massachusetts General Court, its legislature comprising the Council and

---

[3] Hugo Grotius, 2 De Jure Belli ac Pacis Libri Tres 12 (Francis W. Kelsey trans., Clarendon Press 1925) (1690) (citation omitted). The passage continues:

> To this sphere of law belong the abstaining from that which is another's, the restoration to another of anything of his which we may have, together with any gain which we may have received from it; the obligation to fulfil promises, the making good of a loss incurred through our fault, and the inflicting of penalties upon men according to their deserts.

Id. at 12-13 (citation omitted).

[4] See Alison L. LaCroix, The Ideological Origins of American Federalism 1-10 (2010) (describing the academic debate over the origins of American federalism). For a critical commentary on Professor LaCroix's approach, see Gordon S. Wood, Federalism from the Bottom Up, 78 U. Chi. L. Rev. 705 (2011). For Professor LaCroix's reply, see Alison L. LaCroix, Rhetoric and Reality in Early American Legal History: A Reply to Gordon Wood, 78 U. Chi. L. Rev. 733 (2011).

House of Representatives. In response to growing unrest, on January 6, 1773, Governor Hutchison convened an emergency session of the General Court to consider the question of whether Parliament possessed exclusive legislative authority over the colonies.[5] What follows is a short excerpt focusing on the different conceptions of sovereignty or authority expressed by each side.

STUDY GUIDE

- Notice the colonists' insistence on the difference between "supreme" and "unlimited" legislative power. Notice how their arguments culminate in a division of power according to the "constitutional objects" or purposes of the legislation. Notice how they respond to the governor's claim that all of government was an infringement of natural rights, and the primacy they accorded to the rights of property.
- You can see in Hutchinson's contention that even injustice does not justify disobedience; the revolutionaries agreed, which was the reason why the Declaration of Independence alleged "a long train of abuses," not merely injustice.
- Finally, notice how the colonists derive a "natural right" of representation from the natural right of property. Unlike the universal consensus on behalf of property rights, the status of suffrage (the right to vote) was a matter of considerable controversy among early Americans.

SPEECH BY GOVERNOR THOMAS HUTCHINSON TO THE MASSACHUSETTS GENERAL COURT, January 6, 1773. Gentlemen of the Council, and Gentlemen of the House of Representatives, . . . That the government is at present in a disturbed and disordered state, is a truth too evident to be denied. The cause of this disorder, appears to me equally evident. I wish I may be able to make it appear so to you, for then, I may not doubt that you will agree with me in the proper measures for the removal of it. I have pleased myself, for several years past, with hopes, that the cause would cease of itself, and the effect with it, but I am disappointed; and I may not any longer, consistent with my duty to the King, and my regard to the interest of the province, delay communicating my sentiments to you upon a matter of so great importance. I shall be explicit, and treat the subject without reserve. I hope you will receive what I have to say upon it, with candor, and, if you shall not agree in sentiments with me, I promise you, with candor, likewise, to receive and consider what you may offer in answer.

When our predecessors first took possession of this plantation, or colony, under a grant and charter from the Crown of England, it was their sense, and it

[5] See LaCroix, The Ideological Origins of American Federalism 74-104 (describing this debate).

was the sense of the kingdom, that they were to remain subject to the supreme authority of Parliament. This appears from the charter itself, and from other irresistible evidence. This supreme authority has, from time to time, been exercised by Parliament, and submitted to by the colony, and hath been, in the most express terms, acknowledged by the Legislature. . . .

So much, however, of the spirit of liberty breathes through all parts of the English constitution, that, although from the nature of government, there must be one supreme authority over the whole, yet this constitution will adroit of subordinate powers with Legislative and Executive authority, greater or less, according to local and other circumstances. Thus we see a variety of corporations formed within the kingdom, with powers to make and execute such by-laws as are for their immediate use and benefit, the members of such corporations still remaining subject to the general laws of the kingdom. We see also governments established in the plantations, which, from their separate and remote situation, require more general and extensive powers of legislation within themselves, than those formed within the kingdom, but subject, nevertheless, to all such laws of the kingdom as immediately respect them, or are designed to extend to them; and, accordingly, we, in this province have, from the first settlement of it, been left to the exercise of our Legislative and Executive powers, Parliament occasionally, though rarely, interposing, as in its wisdom has been judged necessary. . . .

They who claim exemption, as part of their rights by nature, should consider that every restraint which men are laid under by a state of government, is a privation of part of their natural rights; and of all the different forms of government which exist, there can be no two of them in which the departure from natural rights is exactly the same. Even in case of representation by election, do they not give up part of their natural rights when they consent to be represented by such person as shall be chosen by the majority of the electors, although their own voices may be for some other person? And is it not contrary to their natural rights to be obliged to submit to a representative for seven years, or even one year, after they are dissatisfied with his conduct, although they gave their voices for him when he was elected? This must, therefore, be considered as an objection against a state of government; rather than against any particular form.

If what I have said shall not be sufficient to satisfy such as object to the supreme authority of Parliament over the plantations, there may something further be added to induce them to an acknowledgment of it, which, I think, will well deserve their consideration. I know of no line that can be drawn between the supreme authority of Parliament and the total independence of the colonies: it is impossible there should be two independent Legislatures in one and the same state; for, although there may be but one head, the King, yet the two Legislative bodies will make two governments as distinct as the kingdoms of England and Scotland before the union. If we might be suffered to be altogether independent of Great Britain, could we have any claim to the protection of that government, of which we are no longer a part? Without this protection, should we not become the prey of one or the other powers of Europe, such as should first seize upon us? Is there any thing which we have more reason to dread than independence? I hope it never will be our misfortune to know, by experience, the difference between the liberties of an English colonist, and those of the Spanish, French, or Dutch.

If then, the supremacy of Parliament over the whole British dominions shall no longer be denied, it will follow that the mere exercise of its authority can be no matter of grievance. If it has been, or shall be exercised in such way and manner as shall appear to be grievous, still this cannot be sufficient ground for immediately denying or renouncing the authority, or refusing to submit to it. The acts and doings of authority, in the most perfect form of government, will not always be thought just and equitable by all the parts of which it consists; but it is the greatest absurdity, to admit the several parts to be at liberty to obey, or disobey, according as the acts of such authority may be approved, or disapproved of by them, for this necessarily works a dissolution of the government. . . .

I have disclosed my sentiments to you without reserve. Let me entreat you to consider them calmly, and not be too sudden in your determination. . . . With the same principles, our ancestors were easy and happy for a long course of years together. The people, influenced by you, will desist from their unconstitutional principles, and desist from their irregularities, which are the consequence of them; they will be convinced that every thing which is valuable to them, depend upon their connexion with their parent state; that this connexion cannot be carried in any other way, than such as will also continue their dependence upon the supreme authority of the British dominions; and that, notwithstanding this dependence, they will enjoy as great a proportion of those, to which they have a claim by nature, or as Englishmen) as can be enjoyed by a plantation or colony.

ANSWER OF THE COUNCIL TO THE SPEECH OF GOVERNOR HUTCHINSON, OF JANUARY 6, January 25, 1773. *May it please your Excellency* . . . . You are pleased to observe, that when our predecessors first took possession of this colony, under a grant and charter from the Crown of England, it was their sense, and the sense of the whole kingdom, that they were to remain subject to the supreme authority of Parliament; and to prove that subjection, the greater part of your speech is employed.

In order to a right conception of this matter, it is necessary to guard against any improper idea of the term *supreme* authority. In your idea of it, your Excellency seems to include *unlimited* authority; for, you are pleased to say, that you know of no line which can be drawn between the supreme authority of Parliament, and the real independence of the colonies. But if no such line can be drawn, a denial of that authority, in any instance whatever, implies and amounts to a declaration of total independence. But if supreme authority, includes unlimited authority, the subjects of it are emphatically slaves; and equally so, whether residing in the colonies, or Great Britain. And, indeed, in this respect, all the nations on earth, among whom government exists in any of its forms, would be alike conditioned, excepting so far as the mere grace and favor of their Governors might make a difference, for from, the nature of government there must be, as your Excellency has observed, one supreme authority over the whole.

We cannot think, that when our predecessors took possession of this colony, it was their sense, or the sense of the kingdom, that they were to remain subject to the supreme authority of Parliament in this idea of it. Nor can we find, that this appears from the charter; or, that such authority has ever been exercised by Parliament, submitted to by the colony, or acknowledged by the Legislature.

Supreme, or unlimited authority, can with fitness, belong only to the Sovereign of the universe; and that fitness is derived from the perfection of his nature. To such authority, directed by infinite wisdom and infinite goodness, is due both active and passive obedience; which, as it constitutes the happiness of rational creatures, should, with cheerfulness, and from choice, be unlimitedly paid by them. But, this can be said with truth, of no other authority whatever. If, then, from the nature and end of government, the supreme authority of every government is limited, the supreme authority of Parliament must be limited; and the inquiry will be, what are the limits of that authority, with regard to this colony? . . .

But your Excellency is pleased to say, "that they who claim exemption as part of their rights by nature, should consider that every restraint which men are laid under by a state of government, is a privation of part of their natural rights. Even in case of representation by election, do they not give up part of their natural rights, when they consent to be represented by such persons as shall be chosen by the majority of the electors, although their own voices may be for some other person. And is it not contrary to their natural rights, to be obliged to submit to a representation for seven years, or even one year, after they are dissatisfied with his conduct, although they gave their voices for him when he was elected. This must, therefore, be considered as an objection against a state of government, rather than against any particular form."

Your Excellency's premises are true, but we do not think your conclusion follows from them. It is true, that every restraint of government is a privation of natural right; and the two cases you have been pleased to mention, may be instances of that privation. But, as they arise from the nature of society and government; and as government is necessary to secure other natural rights, infinitely more valuable, they cannot, therefore, be considered as an objection, either against a state government, or against any particular form of it.

Life, liberty, property, and the disposal of that property, with our own consent, are natural rights. Will any one put the other in competition with these; or infer, that, because those others must be given up in a state of government, these must be given up also? The preservation of these rights, is the great end of government. But is it probable, they will be effectually secured by a government, which the proprietors of them, have no part in the direction of, and over which, they have no power or influence, whatever? Hence, is deducible representation, which being necessary to preserve these invaluable rights of nature, is itself, for that reason, a natural right, coinciding with, and running into that great law of nature, self preservation.

Thus have we considered the most material parts of your Excellency's speech, and, agreeable to your desire, disclosed to you our sentiments on the subject of it. "Independence," as you have rightly judged, "we have not in contemplation." We cannot, however, adopt your principles of government, or acquiesce in all the inferences you have drawn from them.

We have the highest respect for that august body, the Parliament, and do not presume to prescribe the exact limits of its authority; yet, with the deference which is due to it, we are humbly of opinion, that, as all human authority is, in the nature of it, and ought to be, limited, it cannot, constitutionally, extend, for the reasons we have suggested, to the levying of taxes, in any form, on his Majesty's subjects in this province. . . .

ANSWER OF THE COUNCIL TO THE SPEECH OF GOVERNOR HUTCHINSON, OF FEBRUARY SIXTEENTH, February 25, 1773. *May it please your Excellency*, . . . [there is] another matter, on which we would make a few further observations. What we refer to, is the general nature of supreme authority. We have already offered reasons, in which your Excellency seems to acquiesce, to shew that, though the term *supreme*, sometimes carries with it the idea of *unlimited* authority, it cannot, in that sense, be applied to that which is human. What is usually denominated the supreme authority of a nation, must nevertheless be limited in its acts to the objects that are properly or constitutionally cognizable by it. To illustrate our meaning, we beg leave to quote a passage from your speech, at the opening of the session, where your Excellency says, "so much of the spirit of liberty breathes through all parts of the English constitution, that, although from the nature of government, there must be one supreme authority over the whole, yet, this constitution will admit of subordinate powers, with legislative and executive authority, greater or less, according to local and other circumstances." This is very true, and implies that the legislative and executive authority granted to the subordinate powers, should extend and operate, as far as the grant allows; and that, if it does not exceed the limits prescribed to it, and no forfeiture be incurred, the supreme power has no rightful authority to take away or diminish it, or to substitute its own acts, in cases wherein the acts of the subordinate power can, according to its constitution, operate. To suppose the contrary, is to suppose, that it has no property in the privileges granted to it; for, if it holds them at the will of the supreme power, which it must do, by the above supposition, it can have no property in them. Upon which principle, which involves the contradiction, that what is granted, is, in reality, not granted, no subordinate power can exist. But, as in fact, the two powers are not incompatible, and do subsist together, each restraining its acts to their constitutional objects, can we not from hence, see how the supreme power may supervise, regulate, and make general laws for the kingdom, without interfering with the privileges of the subordinate powers within it? And also, see how it may extend its care and protection to its colonies, without injuring their constitutional rights? What has been here said, concerning supreme authority, has no reference to the manner in which it has been, in fact, exercised; but is wholly confined to its general nature. And, if it conveys any just idea of it, the inferences that have been, at any time, deduced from it, injurious to the rights of the colonists, are not well founded; and have, probably, arisen from a misconception of the nature of that authority. . . .

3. The Agency Theory of Government

What does the assumption that "first come rights and then comes government" entail for the relationship between the sovereign people and what the Declaration refers to as "governments [that are] instituted among Men" "to secure" their inalienable rights? A second widely held basic assumption was that the subset of the people who work for the government are "fiduciaries" who hold their powers "in trust" for the benefit of the people. Or, to use the legal concepts of agency law that you have studied or will study in Contracts or Business Associations, those persons who "serve" in government are the "agents" or "servants" of the sovereign people, who are their "principals" or "masters." This is sometimes referred to as the agency theory of government.

Consider the argument made by James Iredell — a representative to the Philadelphia convention and one of the original members of the Supreme Court — during the North Carolina ratification debates. To defend the Constitution from the objection that it lacked a bill of rights (akin to that which George Mason had drafted for Virginia), Iredell characterized the Constitution as "a great power of attorney":

> Of what use, therefore, can a bill of rights be in this Constitution, where the people expressly declare how much power they do give, and consequently retain all they do not? It is a declaration of particular powers by the people to their representatives, for particular purposes. It may be considered as *a great power of attorney*, under which no power can be exercised but what is expressly given. Did any man ever hear, before, that at the end of a power of attorney it was said that the attorney should not exercise more power than was there given him? Suppose, for instance, a man had lands in the counties of Anson and Caswell, and he should give another a power of attorney to sell his lands in Anson, would the other have any authority to sell the lands in Caswell? — or could he, without absurdity, say, "Tis true you have not expressly authorized me to sell the lands in Caswell; but as you had lands there, and did not say I should not, I thought I might as well sell those lands as the other." A bill of rights, as I conceive, would not only be incongruous, but dangerous.[6]

At the Founding, the term "attorney" did not necessarily refer to a "lawyer" as it does today. It was a term for an agent who was authorized to act in the name of the principal, say, to receive money owed. For example, one dictionary defined attorneys as "those Persons who take it upon them the Business of other Men, by whom they are retained."[7] As such, lawyers very often served as "attorneys" of their clients. But "attorneys" need not have been lawyers then (or now).

Building on the work of Robert G. Natelson,[8] Gary Lawson and Guy Seidman have identified the intellectual roots and pervasiveness of the agency theory of government at the time that the Constitution was drafted, which provided a background assumption of the document. They trace the concept from the classical

6 The Debates in the Several State Conventions on the Adoption of the Federal Constitution 148-149 (Jonathan Elliot ed., 2d ed. 1907) (emphasis added).

7 Gile Jacob, A New Law Dictionary (6th ed. 1750).

8 See Robert G. Natelson, The Agency Law Origins of the Necessary and Proper Clause, 55 Case W. Res. L. Rev. 243 (2004); and Judicial Review of Special Interest Spending: The General Welfare Clauses and the Fiduciary Law of the Founders, 11 Tex. Rev. L. & Pol. 239 (2007).

writers like Plato, Aristotle, and Cicero, through English political writers like Milton, Locke, and the pamphleteers Trenchard and Gordon.[9]

STUDY GUIDE

- Consider the implications of interpreting the Constitution as "a great power of attorney" for the idea that Congress has only enumerated and delegated powers. How should these powers be construed in light of the fact that the people are sovereign and retain their natural rights?
- Consider also the implications of a "fiduciary" or agency theory of government for the proper role of the judiciary in a scheme of separated powers. If judges too are considered agents or servants of the people, what is their proper role when a member of the sovereign public contests whether his or her servants in the legislature have exceeded their proper or delegated powers?

GARY LAWSON & GUY SEIDMAN, THE FIDUCIARY GOVERNMENT BACKGROUND OF THE FOUNDING ERA (2017). One of the classical authors most highly regarded in the founding era was Cicero. To the founding generation, Cicero was more than just a vehicle for the study of Latin. He was a symbol of civic virtue and practical wisdom. . . . There is good reason to think that Cicero's views had an especially potent influence on founding-era thinking.

Cicero had much to say about fiduciary government. . . . According to Cicero, a political leader must "bear in mind that he represents the state and that it is his duty to uphold its honour and its dignity, to enforce the law, to dispense to all their constitutional rights, and to remember that all this has been committed to him as a sacred trust."[10] He wrote that "the chief thing in all public administration and public service is to avoid even the slightest suspicion of self-seeking."[11] . . . For Cicero "[t]here is . . . no vice more offensive than avarice, especially in men who stand foremost and hold the helm of state. For to exploit the state for selfish profit is not only immoral; it is criminal, infamous."[12] In sum, "[t]he use of *fides*, 'trust' or 'faith,' by Cicero to describe the relationship between magistrate and citizen . . . recalls in particular the common Roman fiduciary nexus between patron and client. . . . The patron holds a trust for his clients just as the magistrate does for citizens under his jurisdiction."[13]

---

[9] Gary Lawson & Guy Seidman, "A Great Power of Attorney": Understanding the Fiduciary Constitution 33-43 (2017) (some footnotes omitted).

[10] [M. Tullius Cicero, De Officiis, Bk. 1, §124 (Walter Miller ed., 1913). — EDS.]

[11] *Id.* bk. 2, §75.

[12] *Id.* bk. 2, §77.

[13] [Neal Wood, Cicero's Social and Political Thought 136 (1988). — EDS.]

Cicero, of course, was not writing on a blank slate. He expressly took Plato as the jumping-off point for his discussion, folding Plato's rules for governance into the fiduciary law of Rome. Plato, along with his student Aristotle, were also familiar companions to the founding generation; recall that education in that time included a study of Greek as well as Latin. The rulers of Plato's ideal state . . . were expected to rule on behalf of the community rather than themselves[14] — and indeed were expected to live a most, for lack of a better term, Spartan life.[15] Aristotle similarly proposed fiduciary-like standards for rulers.[16] Cicero may have expressed the classical tradition more precisely than did his predecessors, but he was expressing a tradition. This was the tradition in which the founding generation was raised and schooled.

Fast-forwarding more than fifteen centuries to someone closer in time to the founding, John Milton also emphasized the fiduciary character of government in his mid-seventeenth-century anti-monarchical tract, *The Tenure of Kings and Magistrates*.[17] Milton, who was one of the sources for the American tradition of natural law,[18] located the origins of government in natural law theory, in which people designate other persons to provide protection. . . . In another essay, Milton described the oaths sworn by Charles I and his subjects: "He swore fidelity to his trust (not as a deluding ceremony, but as a real condition of their admitting him for a king) . . . [and] [t]hey swore homage and fealty to his person in that trust."[19] Milton was laying out the foundation of a fiduciary or agency theory of government.

Even the advocates of absolute monarchy to whom Milton was responding agreed, in their own way, with Milton's fiduciary model of government. In 1598, James VI of Scotland, soon to become James I of England, wrote that it is the King's duty "to procure the weale and flourishing of his people . . . as a loving Father, and careful watchman, caring for them more then for himselfe, knowing himselfe to be ordained for them, and they not for him; and therefore countable to that great God, who place him as his lieutenant over them, upon the peril of his soule to procure the weale of both soules and bodies, as farre as in him lieth, of all them that are committed to his charge."[20] In essence, according to James, the King is an agent of God, charged with administering his (and His) responsibilities in a fiduciary manner. The kingship is really a divinely constituted and ordained trust. . . . And Charles I of England emphasized the idea of a divine trusteeship right up to his execution in

---

[14] Plato, The Republic 178-80 (Desmond Lee, 2d ed. 1984).

[15] *See id.* at 184-85.

[16] *See* [Robert G. Natelson, The Constitution and the Public Trust, 52 Buff. L. Rev. 1077, 1097-1099 (2004) — Eds.].

[17] John Milton, The Tenure of Kings and Magistrates, in John Milton: Complete Poems and Major Prose 750 (Merritt Y. Hughes ed., 1957).

[18] *See* [Meyer Reinhold, The Classics and the Quest for Virtue in Eighteenth-Century America, in The Usefulness of Classical Learning in the Eighteenth Century 37 (Susan Ford Wiltshire ed., 1977) — Eds.].

[19] [John Milton, The Tenure of Kings and Magistrates, *in* John Milton: Complete Poems and Major Prose 811 (Merritt Y. Hughes ed., 1957) — Eds.]

[20] James Stuart, The Trew Law of Free Monarchies: Or, the Reciprock and Mutual Duetie Betwixt a Free King, and His Naturall Subjects 53, 55, in The Political Works of James I (Charles Howard McIlwain ed., 1918).

1649. He and his executioners debated to the last whether the King was a trustee for God or for the people, but they all agreed that he was a trustee.

Similar themes played throughout the seventeenth and early eighteenth centuries in English political thought, especially in so-called "country party," or anti-royalist, thought. Perhaps the most important expressions of an agency theory of government in this era came from John Locke. . . . Locke observed that "the legislative [power] being only a Fiduciary Power to act for certain ends, there remains still in the people a Supream Power to remove or alter the Legislative, when they find the Legislative act contrary to the trust reposed in them. For all Power given with trust for the attaining an end, being limited by that end, whenever that end is manifestly neglected or opposed, the trust must necessarily be forfeited. . . ."[21] The executive, for its part, was also a fiduciary power, at least with regard to the power to summon or adjourn the legislature: "The power of assembling and dismissing the legislative, placed in the executive, gives not the executive a superiority over it, but is a fiduciary trust placed in him for the safety of the people. . . ."[22] . . . Locke made clear that these concepts of agency applied to government as much as — and perhaps even more than — they do to private law arrangements. . . . Locke applied the agency or trustee theory of government not merely to the King but to the legislature as well. That application was well established by the seventeenth century, and references to legislators as trustees in Locke's time were commonplace.[23] Hence, "whether applied to executive or to legislature, the trust concept reached Locke in a well-developed form, and . . . he did no more than receive and apply it."[24]

The idea of government as a trust continued with vigor in the early eighteenth century through, inter alia, *Cato's Letters*, a series of Whig-inspired essays on a wide range of topics written between 1720 and 1723 by John Trenchard and Thomas Gordon. In the founding era, those writings "ranked with the treatises of Locke as the most authoritative statement of the nature of political liberty and above Locke as an exposition of the social sources of the threats it faced,"[25] and they were "widely circulated in America before the Revolution."[26] They also set forth an agency theory of government. . . .[27] And, in words that might have been the progenitors of some of James Madison's most famous observations about the nature of government, Trenchard and Gordon highlighted "[t]he great Point of Nicety and Care in forming the Constitution that the Persons entrusted and representing, shall neither never have any interest detached from the Persons entrusting and

---

[21] John Locke, The Second Treatise of Civil Government §149 (J.W. Gough ed., 1946) (1690).

[22] *Id.* §129.

[23] *See* [J.W. Gough, John Locke's Political Philosophy 156-161 (1950) — Eds.].

[24] *See id.* at 163.

[25] Bernard Bailyn, The Ideological Origins of the American Revolution 36 (1967).

[26] Michael Kent Curtis, The Fraying Fabric of Freedom: Crisis and Criminal Law in Struggles for Democracy and Freedom of Expression, 44 Texas Tech L. Rev. 89, 94 (2011).

[27] 3 John Trenchard & Thomas Gordon, Cato's Letters, Or Essays on Liberty, Civil and Religious, and Other Important Subjects 557 (Ronald Hamowy ed., 1995). Trenchard and Gordon were also great admirers of Cicero. *See id.*

represented, or never the Means to pursue it."[28] Many of their other essays exhibit similar themes in a fashion too elaborate to quote here.

Trenchard and Gordon's linkage between entrustment and representation surfaced in one of the most intriguing illustrations of the power of the idea of fiduciary government in America in the pre-constitutional era. Gordon Wood has trenchantly documented the changing conceptions of representation in revolutionary America, as old English ideals of virtual representation gave way to new theories of actual representation.[29] The latter, in turn, led in some quarters to strong movements in favor of an obligation on the part of representatives to follow specific instructions of the electorate, grounded in a strict agency theory of government. As Professor Wood explains, "[i]nstructing . . . implied that the delegate represented no one but the people who elected him, and that he was simply a mistrusted agent of the electors, bound to follow their directions."[30] . . .

[In 1776, Mecklenburg County, North Carolina inhabitants instructed] their provincial representatives to approve the Declaration of Independence and to "endeavor to establish a free government under the authority of the people of the State of North Carolina."[31] They specifically insisted upon a bill of rights that would recognize, among other maxims of governance:

> 1st. Political power is of two kinds, one principal and superior, the other derived and inferior.
>
> 2d. The principal supreme power is possessed by the people at large, the derived and inferior power by the servants which they employ.
>
> 3d. Whatever persons are delegated, chosen, employed and intrusted by the people are their servants and can possess only derived inferior power.
>
> 4th. Whatever is constituted and ordained by the principal supreme power can not be altered, suspended or abrogated by any other power, but the same power that ordained may alter, suspend and abrogate its own ordinances. . . .

Not only do these instructions reflect a strong agency or fiduciary theory of government, but they do so using language — "constituted and ordained" — that is redolent both of the later Preamble to the United States Constitution and of powers of attorney in North Carolina at that time. . . .

Our point is not that an agency theory of government leads inexorably to, or even logically tends toward, a right of instruction. Our point is only that an agency theory of government was prominent enough in the founding era to give rise to those kinds of thoughts among a large and respectable group of people. . . . Thus, at the time of the founding, "[v]irtually all contemporary English writers agreed that

---

28 2 John Trenchard, Cato's Letters, June 24, 1721 to March 3, 1722, No. 60 (LF ed. 1721).

29 *See* Gordon S. Wood, Representation in the American Revolution (rev. ed. 2008).

30 *Id.* at 33.

31 Instructions from inhabitants of Mecklenburg County to their delegates to the Provincial Congress of North Carolina, in 10 Colonial and State Records of North Carolina 870a (William Saunders ed., 1890).

public officials should adhere to standards comparable to those imposed on private sector fiduciaries."[32]

Nor was the background assumption about the agency theory of government solely expressed in political writings and local resolutions. Several constitutions officially adopted by the states made this assumption explicit (emphases added): Virginia (1776): "All power is vested in, and consequently derived from, the people; that magistrates are their *trustees and servants*, and at all times amenable to them." Pennsylvania (1776): "All power being originally inherent in, and consequently derived from, the people; therefore all officers of government, whether legislative or executive, are their *trustees and servants*, and at all times accountable to them." Maryland (1776): "All persons invested with the legislative or executive powers of government are the *trustees* of the public, and, as such, accountable for their conduct." Massachusetts (1780): "All power residing originally in the people, and being derived from them, the several magistrates and officers of government, vested with authority, whether legislative, executive or judicial, are their substitutes and *agents*, and are at all times accountable to them."

ASSIGNMENT 2

4. The Articles of Confederation

The third important background assumption behind the Constitution of 1787 was the widespread — though far from unanimous — view that the existing governmental structure was highly deficient. Following the Revolutionary War, the United States was governed by the Articles of Confederation, which functioned much like a treaty organization among the thirteen separate states. Under the Articles, there was a single house of Congress composed of delegates from the states, and no executive or judicial branches. This Congress operated mainly by consensus, and lacked the power to raise revenue by imposing taxes. Instead, Congress could only "requisition," or request revenue from the states; the states were then supposed to tax their own citizens to pay their share.

During the post-Revolutionary period, many Americans became unhappy with the general state of the economy and with the behavior of state governments. In an essay prepared in advance of the Philadelphia convention, in April 1787, James Madison of Virginia summarized what he and others perceived as the deficiencies or "vices" in the form of government defined by the Articles. Bear in mind that not everyone at the time shared these complaints, or thought they justified a wholesale replacement of the Articles. Still, the list provides a useful summary of the defects the drafters of the Constitution had in mind as they set about to improve upon the form of government.

- Failure of the States to comply with the Constitutional requisitions.
- Encroachments by the States on the federal authority.

---

[32] Natelson, *supra* note [16], at 1122.

- Violations of the law of nations and of treaties.
- Trespasses of the States on the rights of each other.
- Want of concert in matters where common interest requires it.
- Want of guaranty to the States of their Constitutions & laws against internal violence.
- Want of sanction to the laws, and of coercion in the Government of the Confederation.
- Want of ratification by the people of the Articles of Confederation.
- Multiplicity (over regulation) of laws in the several States.
- Mutability (rapidly changing) of the laws of the States.
- Injustice of the laws of the States.

The last of these vices, Madison wrote, raised a fundamental challenge to the prevailing theory of "republicanism" or popular rule:

> If the multiplicity and mutability of laws prove a want of wisdom, their injustice betrays a defect still more alarming: more alarming not merely because it is a greater evil in itself, but because it brings more into question the fundamental principle of republican Government, that the majority who rule in such Governments, are the safest Guardians both of public Good and of private rights. To what causes is this evil to be ascribed?[33]

Madison attributed part of this evil to deficiencies in the elected representatives. But the other part he boldly attributed to "the people themselves." At the time, state governments were largely run by a single popularly elected assembly, to which the executive and judiciary were subservient. Such governments were widely thought to be the proper alternative to rule by an aristocracy, as a means of protecting the retained rights of the people. Yet those who favored a new constitutional structure believed these republican governments to be pervasively violating the peoples' rights. Under prevailing "republican" political theory, this was simply not supposed to happen. In his essay Madison attempts to answer why this was happening, with an early version of the argument he later presents in *Federalist No. 10* (which appears below). His theory of "faction" explains how majoritarian rule can come to unjustly violate the rights of the people.

5. Drafting and Ratifying the Constitution

The Constitutional Convention took place in Philadelphia from May 25 to September 17, 1787. Every state except for Rhode Island sent delegates. Originally charged with proposing revisions to the Articles of Confederation (which would have required the unanimous consent of all the states in Congress), the members of the Convention soon decided to devise an entirely new replacement for the Articles. While convening the Convention was a highly public act, its deliberations were carefully kept secret. The Convention considered a number of plans before reaching what is sometimes called the *Great Compromise*.

---

[33] James Madison, Vices of the Political System of the United States, Papers 9:348-57 (April 1787).

The Virginia Plan. The Virginia Plan was the unofficial agenda for the Convention. The Virginia delegation arrived before the other delegations to Philadelphia and began meeting daily to discuss plans for the new government. Most of the plan was written by James Madison, but was reported to the Convention by the more senior Edmund Randolph (who later became attorney general in the Washington administration). It included:

- A very powerful bicameral legislature.
- Both houses' membership determined proportionately.
- A lower house elected by the people of the several states.
- An upper house elected by the lower house based on nominations from the state legislatures.
- An executive chosen by the legislature to ensure that its will was carried out.
- Formation of a judiciary, with life terms of service.
- A council of revision, consisting of the executive and some of the national judiciary, with the power to veto and revise national legislation, subject to override by the legislature.
- The national legislature would be able to veto state laws.

The New Jersey Plan. Some, including William Paterson, feared that if too much power were given to larger states, they could swallow up the smaller states and take over the House, leaving the smaller states with little influence. The New Jersey Plan was largely a response to the Virginia Plan. Paterson reported the plan to the Convention on June 15, 1787. It included:

- The retention of the Confederation Congress, but vested with new powers. For example, the Congress could set taxes and force their collection.
- An executive, elected by Congress. The plan permitted a multiperson executive.
- A single-term limit for the executives, who were subject to recall based on the request of state governors.
- A judiciary appointed by the executives, with life terms of service.
- The supremacy of laws enacted by Congress over state laws.
- One vote per state in the unicameral legislature.

Hamilton's Plan. On June 18, Alexander Hamilton of New York reported his own plan for the U.S. government. In a marathon speech, Hamilton outlined a plan calling for a President and Senators, who when elected, would serve for life on "good behavior." Members of the House of Representatives would be directly elected for three-year terms. Hamilton's model was largely based on the British form of government: the Monarch served for life, as did members of the House of Lords; members of the House of Commons stood for election. This plan was never seriously considered by the Convention. Although the delegates had agreed that the debates of the Convention were to be kept confidential, in later years Hamilton's political foes leaked elements of his plan in an effort to cast him as a monarchist.

The Great Compromise. The issue of representation in Congress stymied the Convention more than any other. Ultimately, the delegates accepted the so-called *Great Compromise*, originally proposed by Roger Sherman of Connecticut: members of the House of Representatives would be allocated based on population, while each state would receive two senators, regardless of population. The decision to give small states equal representation in the Senate immediately caused delegates from larger states, who had previously supported the Virginia Plan's broad statement of congressional powers, to reverse themselves; now, since they were no longer assured of control, they insisted upon an enumeration or list of the limited powers of Congress.

Another issue that jeopardized the prospect of a new constitution was that of slavery. Once again, representation was the principal issue. To bolster their legislative power, Southern slave-holding states wanted their slaves to count as full persons for purposes of calculating representation in Congress. Contrary to what you may have learned, Northern states in fact opposed the inclusion of *any* slaves in calculating representation, so as to deprive the Southern states of that additional representation. Eventually, the Convention compromised in counting slaves as three-fifths of a person for purposes of representation. One price slaveholders would have to pay for this concession is that their slaves were also counted as three-fifths of a person for purpose of calculating any "direct" taxes that were supposed to be apportioned based on the population of a state. (As it turned out — and perhaps not coincidentally — few such taxes were ever levied, with the national government relying on excise taxes and duties instead.) The increase in the representation of the Southern states in Congress and in the Electoral College due to counting three-fifths of their slave population greatly strengthened the South's political power in the early years of the Republic. Although the abolition of slavery within the states was never seriously considered, several states did want to prohibit the further importation of slaves. Others threatened to leave the Convention if the slave trade was banned. Eventually another compromise was reached by which Congress would have the power to ban the slave trade after January 1, 1808.

A Committee of Detail — comprised of Oliver Ellsworth, Nathaniel Gorham, Edmund Randolph, John Rutledge, and James Wilson — was formed to reduce the Convention's many resolutions to specific text. After further debate, a Committee of Style — headed by Gouverneur Morris, and including Alexander Hamilton, William Samuel Johnson, Rufus King, and James Madison — refined the draft into its final form. The Constitution was signed by fifty-five delegates on September 17, 1787. Of those still in Philadelphia, three delegates refused to sign: Edmund Randolph and George Mason of Virginia, and Elbridge Gerry of Massachusetts. Among the complaints voiced by George Mason, in Philadelphia and afterward, was the absence in the Constitution of a bill of rights.

After receiving the proposal of the Convention, Congress in turn referred the charter to the states for their ratification (expressing neither its approval nor disapproval). By its terms (in Article VII), the Constitution was to go into effect when nine of the original thirteen states adopted it, though it would bind only those states that had ratified. The states deliberated on ratification in "conventions" consisting of delegates elected by eligible voters in local communities. Unlike a standing legislature that was part of the existing government, a convention was considered at the time to be the means by which the people themselves could directly express their consent. This method of ratification would figure importantly in later discussions of popular sovereignty.

The first five ratifications occurred quickly:

- Delaware, December 7, 1787 (unanimous)
- Pennsylvania, December 12, 1787 (46-23)
- New Jersey, December 18, 1787 (unanimous)
- Georgia, January 2, 1788 (unanimous)
- Connecticut, January 9, 1788 (128-40)

Anti-Federalists became better organized in later conventions and approval was much harder fought and in many instances closer. Notice in particular the close vote in Virginia, despite the fact that it was widely assumed that George Washington would be the first President:

- Massachusetts, February 6, 1788 (187-168)
- Maryland, April 28, 1788 (63-11)
- South Carolina, May 23, 1788 (149-73)
- New Hampshire, June 21, 1788 (57-47)
- Virginia, June 25, 1788 (89-79)
- New York, July 26, 1788 (30-27)

North Carolina and Rhode Island did not ratify and join the Union until after the new government was formed.[34]

Those who opposed the Constitution were dubbed "Anti-Federalists" by supporters of the Constitution, who called themselves "Federalists" — though the objectors considered themselves to be *true* federalists. The opponents considered those who supported the Constitution to be nationalists who favored "consolidation" rather than a confederation. Nevertheless, the label "Anti-Federalists" stuck, and it is by that name we refer to them today.

6. *The Federalist* Papers

While the state conventions were considering the ratification of the Constitution, Federalist and Anti-Federalists published a flurry of pamphlets and newspaper essays. Among the most popular were a coordinated series of essays by Alexander Hamilton of New York, James Madison of Virginia, and (briefly) John Jay of New York, who joined forces to defend the Constitution. These papers were eventually compiled into a single volume called *The Federalist*, and have become highly influential. When reading these papers, one must remember that they were partisan polemics on behalf of the political cause of ratification. But the cogency of their

[34] For a recent, comprehensive, and engaging account of the ratification process, see Pauline Maier, Ratification: Americans Debate the Constitution, 1787-1788 (2010).

reasoning has stood the test of time, and they rank among the most important works in political theory.

Possibly the most famous of these essays is *Federalist No. 10*, in which Madison expanded upon his defense of a large republic he previously presented in his *Vices* essay. In particular, Madison sought to explain why popular rule in the states had unexpectedly led to laws not based on "the rules of justice and the rights of the minor party," and why the "extended republic" governed by the proposed Constitution would be better able to deal with this most serious problem. Because the conventional political wisdom at the time was that a republican form of government could *only* work with small populations, Madison's novel argument was a singular contribution to political theory and has, as a result, become famous.

a. Federalist No. 10: *The Problem of Faction*

STUDY GUIDE

- How does Madison define "faction"? Does this concept differ from what we now call "interest groups"?
- How does he distinguish between the causes and effects of the problem of faction? Why does he reject going after its causes? Does majority rule solve the problem of faction, or does it instead contribute to it?
- How does he distinguish between a "pure" democracy and a republic? How does an extended republic ameliorate the effects of faction without restricting the liberty that gives rise to it?
- Has today's communication technology rendered his analysis of this approach impractical? Do we still live in an "extended republic" as Madison conceived of it?

JAMES MADISON, *FEDERALIST No. 10*, Friday, November 23, 1787

To the People of the State of New York:

AMONG the numerous advantages promised by a well constructed Union, none deserves to be more accurately developed than its tendency to break and control the violence of faction. . . . Complaints are everywhere heard from our most considerate and virtuous citizens, equally the friends of public and private faith, and of public and personal liberty, that our governments are too unstable, that the public good is disregarded in the conflicts of rival parties, and that measures are too often decided, not according to the rules of justice and the rights of the minor party, but by the superior force of an interested and overbearing majority. However anxiously we may wish that these complaints had no foundation, the evidence, of known facts will not permit us to deny that they are in some degree true. It will be found, indeed, on a candid review of our situation, that some of the distresses under which we labor have been erroneously charged on the operation of our governments; but it will be found, at the same time, that other causes will not alone account for many of our heaviest misfortunes; and, particularly, for that prevailing and increasing distrust of public engagements, and alarm for private rights, which are echoed from one end of the continent to the other. These must be chiefly, if not wholly, effects of the unsteadiness and injustice with which a factious spirit has tainted our public administrations.

By a faction, I understand a number of citizens, whether amounting to a majority or a minority of the whole, who are united and actuated by some common impulse of passion, or of interest, adversed to the rights of other citizens, or to the permanent and aggregate interests of the community.

There are two methods of curing the mischiefs of faction: the one, by removing its causes; the other, by controlling its effects.

There are again two methods of removing the causes of faction: the one, by destroying the liberty which is essential to its existence; the other, by giving to every citizen the same opinions, the same passions, and the same interests.

It could never be more truly said than of the first remedy, that it was worse than the disease. Liberty is to faction what air is to fire, an aliment without which it instantly expires. But it could not be less folly to abolish liberty, which is essential to political life, because it nourishes faction, than it would be to wish the annihilation of air, which is essential to animal life, because it imparts to fire its destructive agency.

The second expedient is as impracticable as the first would be unwise. As long as the reason of man continues fallible, and he is at liberty to exercise it, different opinions will be formed. As long as the connection subsists between his reason and his self-love, his opinions and his passions will have a reciprocal influence on each other; and the former will be objects to which the latter will attach themselves. The diversity in the faculties of men, from which the rights of property originate, is not less an insuperable obstacle to a uniformity of interests. The protection of these faculties is the first object of government. From the protection of different and unequal faculties of acquiring property, the possession of different degrees and kinds of property immediately results; and from the influence of these on the sentiments and views of the respective proprietors, ensues a division of the society into different interests and parties.

The latent causes of faction are thus sown in the nature of man; and we see them everywhere brought into different degrees of activity, according to the different circumstances of civil society. A zeal for different opinions concerning religion, concerning government, and many other points, as well of speculation as of practice; an attachment to different leaders ambitiously contending for preeminence and power; or to persons of other descriptions whose fortunes have been interesting to the human passions, have, in turn, divided mankind into parties, inflamed them with mutual animosity, and rendered them much more disposed to vex and oppress each other than to co-operate for their common good. So strong is this propensity of mankind to fall into mutual animosities, that where no substantial occasion presents itself, the most frivolous and fanciful distinctions have been sufficient to kindle their unfriendly passions and excite their most violent conflicts. But the most common and durable source of factions has been the various and unequal distribution of property. Those who hold and those who are without property have ever formed distinct interests in society. Those who are creditors, and those who are debtors, fall under a like discrimination. A landed interest, a manufacturing interest, a mercantile interest, a moneyed interest, with many lesser interests, grow up of necessity in civilized nations, and divide them into different classes, actuated by different sentiments and views. The regulation of these various and interfering interests forms the principal task of modern legislation, and involves the spirit of party and faction in the necessary and ordinary operations of the government.

No man is allowed to be a judge in his own cause, because his interest would certainly bias his judgment, and, not improbably, corrupt his integrity. With equal, nay with greater reason, a body of men are unfit to be both judges and parties at the same time; yet what are many of the most important acts of legislation, but so many judicial determinations, not indeed concerning the rights of single persons, but concerning the rights of large bodies of citizens? And what are the different classes of legislators but advocates and parties to the causes which they determine? Is a law proposed concerning private debts? It is a question to which the creditors are parties on one side and the debtors on the other. Justice ought to hold the balance between them. Yet the parties are, and must be, themselves the judges; and the most numerous party, or, in other words, the most powerful faction must be expected to prevail. Shall domestic manufactures be encouraged, and in what degree, by restrictions on foreign manufactures? are questions which would be differently decided by the landed and the manufacturing classes, and probably by neither with a sole regard to justice and the public good. The apportionment of taxes on the various descriptions of property is an act which seems to require the most exact impartiality; yet there is, perhaps, no legislative act in which greater opportunity and temptation are given to a predominant party to trample on the rules of justice. Every shilling with which they overburden the inferior number, is a shilling saved to their own pockets.

It is in vain to say that enlightened statesmen will be able to adjust these clashing interests, and render them all subservient to the public good. Enlightened statesmen will not always be at the helm. Nor, in many cases, can such an adjustment be made at all without taking into view indirect and remote considerations, which will rarely prevail over the immediate interest which one party may find in disregarding the rights of another or the good of the whole.

The inference to which we are brought is, that the CAUSES of faction cannot be removed, and that relief is only to be sought in the means of controlling its EFFECTS.

If a faction consists of less than a majority, relief is supplied by the republican principle, which enables the majority to defeat its sinister views by regular vote. It may clog the administration, it may convulse the society; but it will be unable to execute and mask its violence under the forms of the Constitution. When a majority is included in a faction, the form of popular government, on the other hand, enables it to sacrifice to its ruling passion or interest both the public good and the rights of other citizens. To secure the public good and private rights against the danger of such a faction, and at the same time to preserve the spirit and the form of popular government, is then the great object to which our inquiries are directed. . . .

By what means is this object attainable? Evidently by one of two only. Either the existence of the same passion or interest in a majority at the same time must be prevented, or the majority, having such coexistent passion or interest, must be rendered, by their number and local situation, unable to concert and carry into effect schemes of oppression. If the impulse and the opportunity be suffered to coincide, we well know that neither moral nor religious motives can be relied on as an adequate control. They are not found to be such on the injustice and violence of individuals, and lose their efficacy in proportion to the number combined together, that is, in proportion as their efficacy becomes needful.

From this view of the subject it may be concluded that a pure democracy, by which I mean a society consisting of a small number of citizens, who assemble and administer the government in person, can admit of no cure for the mischiefs of faction. A common passion or interest will, in almost every case, be felt by a majority of the whole; a communication and concert result from the form of government itself; and there is nothing to check the inducements to sacrifice the weaker party or an obnoxious individual. Hence it is that such democracies have ever been spectacles of turbulence and contention; have ever been found incompatible with personal security or the rights of property; and have in general been as short in their lives as they have been violent in their deaths. Theoretic politicians, who have patronized this species of government, have erroneously supposed that by reducing mankind to a perfect equality in their political rights, they would, at the same time, be perfectly equalized and assimilated in their possessions, their opinions, and their passions.

A republic, by which I mean a government in which the scheme of representation takes place, opens a different prospect, and promises the cure for which we are seeking. Let us examine the points in which it varies from pure democracy, and we shall comprehend both the nature of the cure and the efficacy which it must derive from the Union.

The two great points of difference between a democracy and a republic are: first, the delegation of the government, in the latter, to a small number of citizens elected by the rest; secondly, the greater number of citizens, and greater sphere of country, over which the latter may be extended.

The effect of the first difference is, on the one hand, to refine and enlarge the public views, by passing them through the medium of a chosen body of citizens, whose wisdom may best discern the true interest of their country, and whose patriotism and love of justice will be least likely to sacrifice it to temporary or partial considerations. Under such a regulation, it may well happen that the public voice, pronounced by the representatives of the people, will be more consonant to the public good than if pronounced by the people themselves, convened for the purpose. On the other hand, the effect may be inverted. Men of factious tempers, of local prejudices, or of sinister designs, may, by intrigue, by corruption, or by other means, first obtain the suffrages, and then betray the interests, of the people. The question resulting is, whether small or extensive republics are more favorable to the election of proper guardians of the public weal; and it is clearly decided in favor of the latter by two obvious considerations:

In the first place, it is to be remarked that, however small the republic may be, the representatives must be raised to a certain number, in order to guard against the cabals of a few; and that, however large it may be, they must be limited to a certain number, in order to guard against the confusion of a multitude. Hence, the number of representatives in the two cases not being in proportion to that of the two constituents, and being proportionally greater in the small republic, it follows that, if the proportion of fit characters be not less in the large than in the small republic, the former will present a greater option, and consequently a greater probability of a fit choice.

In the next place, as each representative will be chosen by a greater number of citizens in the large than in the small republic, it will be more difficult for unworthy candidates to practice with success the vicious arts by which elections are too often carried; and the suffrages of the people being more free, will be more likely to centre in men who possess the most attractive merit and the most diffusive and established characters.

It must be confessed that in this, as in most other cases, there is a mean, on both sides of which inconveniences will be found to lie. By enlarging too much the number of electors, you render the representatives too little acquainted with all their local circumstances and lesser interests; as by reducing it too much, you render him unduly attached to these, and too little fit to comprehend and pursue great and national objects. The federal Constitution forms a happy combination in this respect; the great and aggregate interests being referred to the national, the local and particular to the State legislatures.

The other point of difference is, the greater number of citizens and extent of territory which may be brought within the compass of republican than of democratic government; and it is this circumstance principally which renders factious combinations less to be dreaded in the former than in the latter. The smaller the society, the fewer probably will be the distinct parties and interests composing it; the fewer the distinct parties and interests, the more frequently will a majority be found of the same party; and the smaller the number of individuals composing a majority, and the smaller the compass within which they are placed, the more easily will they concert and execute their plans of oppression. Extend the sphere, and you take in a greater variety of parties and interests; you make it less probable that a majority of the whole will have a common motive to invade the rights of other citizens; or if such a common motive exists, it will be more difficult for all who feel it to discover their own strength, and to act in unison with each other. Besides other impediments, it may be remarked that, where there is a consciousness of unjust or dishonorable purposes, communication is always checked by distrust in proportion to the number whose concurrence is necessary.

Hence, it clearly appears, that the same advantage which a republic has over a democracy, in controlling the effects of faction, is enjoyed by a large over a small republic, — is enjoyed by the Union over the States composing it. Does the advantage consist in the substitution of representatives whose enlightened views and virtuous sentiments render them superior to local prejudices and schemes of injustice? It will not be denied that the representation of the Union will be most likely to possess these requisite endowments. Does it consist in the greater security afforded by a greater variety of parties, against the event of any one party being able to outnumber and oppress the rest? In an equal degree does the increased variety of parties comprised within the Union, increase this security. Does it, in fine, consist in the greater obstacles opposed to the concert and accomplishment of the secret wishes of an unjust and interested majority? Here, again, the extent of the Union gives it the most palpable advantage.

The influence of factious leaders may kindle a flame within their particular States, but will be unable to spread a general conflagration through the other States. A religious sect may degenerate into a political faction in a part of the Confederacy; but the variety of sects dispersed over the entire face of it must secure the national councils against any danger from that source. A rage for paper money, for an abolition of debts, for an equal division of property, or for any other improper or wicked project, will be less apt to pervade the whole body of the Union than a particular member of it; in the same proportion as such a malady is more likely to taint a particular county or district, than an entire State.

In the extent and proper structure of the Union, therefore, we behold a republican remedy for the diseases most incident to republican government. And according to the degree of pleasure and pride we feel in being republicans, ought to be our zeal in cherishing the spirit and supporting the character of Federalists.

PUBLIUS.

b. Federalist No. 78: *The Judicial Duty to Declare Unconstitutional Laws to Be Void*

A close second to Madison's *Federalist No. 10* in fame and influence is Alexander Hamilton's *Federalist No. 78*, which explains and defends what is now commonly called the "power of judicial review." The term "judicial review" is a modern one, however. Hamilton speaks, not of power, but of the judicial *duty* to follow the law and, where two laws may conflict, to follow the law of the superior rather than of the subordinate authority. Since the authority of the People is superior to that of their representatives in Congress, judges are bound to follow the law of the former as embodied in the Constitution when in conflict with laws made by the latter. Together, *Federalist No. 10* and *Federalist No. 78* provide two distinct structural ways to mitigate the problem of faction: first, the check provided by representative government over a large and diverse population and, second, the check provided by a sufficiently independent judiciary.

STUDY GUIDE

- This essay is famous for a number of reasons, including its designation of the judiciary as the "least dangerous" branch of the federal government.
- Notice the connection Hamilton makes between the role of the judiciary and the fact that the national government is "limited" in its powers.
- How does he respond to the complaint that judicial nullification makes the judges superior over the other branches? Notice that, like Madison, Hamilton also relies on the maxim that no one should be a judge in his own case, which leads him to deny the proposition that the "legislative body are themselves the constitutional judges of their own powers, and that the construction they put upon them is conclusive upon the other departments."
- One of Hamilton's crucial moves is his claim that the Constitution is law, but a law higher than that of a statute. How does he use this to bolster the judicial power to nullify unconstitutional laws? How does he use this to describe the relationship of judicial review to the popular will?
- Notice that, like Madison, Hamilton emphasizes the rights of the minority against the will of the majority.

ALEXANDER HAMILTON, *FEDERALIST No. 78*, Saturday, June 14, 1788

To the People of the State of New York:

WE PROCEED now to an examination of the judiciary department of the proposed government. . . .

According to the plan of the convention, all judges who may be appointed by the United States are to hold their offices DURING GOOD BEHAVIOR; which is conformable to the most approved of the State constitutions and among the rest, to that of this State. . . .

Whoever attentively considers the different departments of power must perceive, that, in a government in which they are separated from each other, the judiciary, from the nature of its functions, will always be the least dangerous to the political rights of the Constitution; because it will be least in a capacity to annoy or injure them. The Executive not only dispenses the honors, but holds the sword of the community. The legislature not only commands the purse, but prescribes the rules by which the duties and rights of every citizen are to be regulated. The judiciary, on the contrary, has no influence over either the sword or the purse; no direction either of the strength or of the wealth of the society; and can take no active resolution whatever. It may truly be said to have neither FORCE nor WILL, but merely judgment; and must ultimately depend upon the aid of the executive arm even for the efficacy of its judgments.

This simple view of the matter suggests several important consequences. It proves incontestably, that the judiciary is beyond comparison the weakest of the three departments of power[35]; that it can never attack with success either of the other two; and that all possible care is requisite to enable it to defend itself against their attacks. It equally proves, that though individual oppression may now and then proceed from the courts of justice, the general liberty of the people can never be endangered from that quarter; I mean so long as the judiciary remains truly distinct from both the legislature and the Executive. For I agree, that "there is no liberty, if the power of judging be not separated from the legislative and executive powers."[36] And it proves, in the last place, that as liberty can have nothing to fear from the judiciary alone, but would have every thing to fear from its union with either of the other departments; that as all the effects of such a union must ensue from a dependence of the former on the latter, notwithstanding a nominal and apparent separation; that as, from the natural feebleness of the judiciary, it is in continual jeopardy of being overpowered, awed, or influenced by its co-ordinate branches; and that as nothing can contribute so much to its firmness and independence as permanency in office, this quality may therefore be justly regarded as an indispensable ingredient in its constitution, and, in a great measure, as the citadel of the public justice and the public security.

The complete independence of the courts of justice is peculiarly essential in a limited Constitution. By a limited Constitution, I understand one which contains certain specified exceptions to the legislative authority; such, for instance, as that it shall pass no bills of attainder, no ex-post-facto laws, and the like. Limitations of this kind can be preserved in practice no other way than through the medium of courts of justice, whose duty it must be to declare all acts contrary to the manifest tenor of the Constitution void. Without this, all the reservations of particular rights or privileges would amount to nothing.

Some perplexity respecting the rights of the courts to pronounce legislative acts void, because contrary to the Constitution, has arisen from an imagination that the doctrine would imply a superiority of the judiciary to the legislative power. It is urged that the authority which can declare the acts of another void, must necessarily be superior to the one whose acts may be declared void. As this doctrine is of great importance in all the American constitutions, a brief discussion of the ground on which it rests cannot be unacceptable.

There is no position which depends on clearer principles, than that every act of a delegated authority, contrary to the tenor of the commission under which it is exercised, is void. No legislative act, therefore, contrary to the Constitution, can be valid. To deny this, would be to affirm, that the deputy is greater than his principal; that the servant is above his master; that the representatives of the people are superior to the people themselves; that men acting by virtue of powers, may do not only what their powers do not authorize, but what they forbid.

If it be said that the legislative body are themselves the constitutional judges of their own powers, and that the construction they put upon them is conclusive upon

---

[35] The celebrated Montesquieu, speaking of them, says: "Of the three powers above mentioned, the judiciary is next to nothing." Spirit of Laws.

[36] Id.

the other departments, it may be answered, that this cannot be the natural presumption, where it is not to be collected from any particular provisions in the Constitution. It is not otherwise to be supposed, that the Constitution could intend to enable the representatives of the people to substitute their WILL to that of their constituents. It is far more rational to suppose, that the courts were designed to be an intermediate body between the people and the legislature, in order, among other things, to keep the latter within the limits assigned to their authority. The interpretation of the laws is the proper and peculiar province of the courts. A constitution is, in fact, and must be regarded by the judges, as a fundamental law. It therefore belongs to them to ascertain its meaning, as well as the meaning of any particular act proceeding from the legislative body. If there should happen to be an irreconcilable variance between the two, that which has the superior obligation and validity ought, of course, to be preferred; or, in other words, the Constitution ought to be preferred to the statute, the intention of the people to the intention of their agents.

Nor does this conclusion by any means suppose a superiority of the judicial to the legislative power. It only supposes that the power of the people is superior to both; and that where the will of the legislature, declared in its statutes, stands in opposition to that of the people, declared in the Constitution, the judges ought to be governed by the latter rather than the former. They ought to regulate their decisions by the fundamental laws, rather than by those which are not fundamental.

This exercise of judicial discretion, in determining between two contradictory laws, is exemplified in a familiar instance. It not uncommonly happens, that there are two statutes existing at one time, clashing in whole or in part with each other, and neither of them containing any repealing clause or expression. In such a case, it is the province of the courts to liquidate and fix their meaning and operation. So far as they can, by any fair construction, be reconciled to each other, reason and law conspire to dictate that this should be done; where this is impracticable, it becomes a matter of necessity to give effect to one, in exclusion of the other. The rule which has obtained in the courts for determining their relative validity is, that the last in order of time shall be preferred to the first. But this is a mere rule of construction, not derived from any positive law, but from the nature and reason of the thing. It is a rule not enjoined upon the courts by legislative provision, but adopted by themselves, as consonant to truth and propriety, for the direction of their conduct as interpreters of the law. They thought it reasonable, that between the interfering acts of an EQUAL authority, that which was the last indication of its will should have the preference.

But in regard to the interfering acts of a superior and subordinate authority, of an original and derivative power, the nature and reason of the thing indicate the converse of that rule as proper to be followed. They teach us that the prior act of a superior ought to be preferred to the subsequent act of an inferior and subordinate authority; and that accordingly, whenever a particular statute contravenes the Constitution, it will be the duty of the judicial tribunals to adhere to the latter and disregard the former.

It can be of no weight to say that the courts, on the pretense of a repugnancy, may substitute their own pleasure to the constitutional intentions of the legislature.

This might as well happen in the case of two contradictory statutes; or it might as well happen in every adjudication upon any single statute. The courts must declare the sense of the law; and if they should be disposed to exercise WILL instead of JUDGMENT, the consequence would equally be the substitution of their pleasure to that of the legislative body. The observation, if it prove any thing, would prove that there ought to be no judges distinct from that body.

If, then, the courts of justice are to be considered as the bulwarks of a limited Constitution against legislative encroachments, this consideration will afford a strong argument for the permanent tenure of judicial offices, since nothing will contribute so much as this to that independent spirit in the judges which must be essential to the faithful performance of so arduous a duty.

This independence of the judges is equally requisite to guard the Constitution and the rights of individuals from the effects of those ill humors, which the arts of designing men, or the influence of particular conjunctures, sometimes disseminate among the people themselves, and which, though they speedily give place to better information, and more deliberate reflection, have a tendency, in the meantime, to occasion dangerous innovations in the government, and serious oppressions of the minor party in the community. Though I trust the friends of the proposed Constitution will never concur with its enemies, in questioning that fundamental principle of republican government, which admits the right of the people to alter or abolish the established Constitution, whenever they find it inconsistent with their happiness, yet it is not to be inferred from this principle, that the representatives of the people, whenever a momentary inclination happens to lay hold of a majority of their constituents, incompatible with the provisions in the existing Constitution, would, on that account, be justifiable in a violation of those provisions; or that the courts would be under a greater obligation to connive at infractions in this shape, than when they had proceeded wholly from the cabals of the representative body. Until the people have, by some solemn and authoritative act, annulled or changed the established form, it is binding upon themselves collectively, as well as individually; and no presumption, or even knowledge, of their sentiments, can warrant their representatives in a departure from it, prior to such an act. But it is easy to see, that it would require an uncommon portion of fortitude in the judges to do their duty as faithful guardians of the Constitution, where legislative invasions of it had been instigated by the major voice of the community.

But it is not with a view to infractions of the Constitution only, that the independence of the judges may be an essential safeguard against the effects of occasional ill humors in the society. These sometimes extend no farther than to the injury of the private rights of particular classes of citizens, by unjust and partial laws. Here also the firmness of the judicial magistracy is of vast importance in mitigating the severity and confining the operation of such laws. It not only serves to moderate the immediate mischiefs of those which may have been passed, but it operates as a check upon the legislative body in passing them; who, perceiving that obstacles to the success of iniquitous intention are to be expected from the scruples of the courts, are in a manner compelled, by the very motives of the injustice they meditate, to qualify their attempts. . . .

That inflexible and uniform adherence to the rights of the Constitution, and of individuals, which we perceive to be indispensable in the courts of justice, can certainly not be expected from judges who hold their offices by a temporary commission. Periodical appointments, however regulated, or by whomsoever made, would, in some way or other, be fatal to their necessary independence. If the power of making them was committed either to the Executive or legislature, there would be danger of an improper complaisance to the branch which possessed it; if to both, there would be an unwillingness to hazard the displeasure of either; if to the people, or to persons chosen by them for the special purpose, there would be too great a disposition to consult popularity, to justify a reliance that nothing would be consulted but the Constitution and the laws. . . .

Upon the whole, there can be no room to doubt that the convention acted wisely in copying from the models of those constitutions which have established GOOD BEHAVIOR as the tenure of their judicial offices, in point of duration; and that so far from being blamable on this account, their plan would have been inexcusably defective, if it had wanted this important feature of good government. The experience of Great Britain affords an illustrious comment on the excellence of the institution.

PUBLIUS.

c. Federalist No. 51: *The Structure of the Government Must Furnish the Proper Checks and Balances Between the Different Departments*

After *Federalist No. 10*, Madison's most famous essay was No. 51, which discusses how the separation of powers can preserve government structures, and ultimately individual liberty. Indeed, Madison's essay is as much a reflection on government as it is on human nature itself. "If men were angels," he writes, then "no government would be necessary." But because we are not angels, the "great difficulty lies in this: you must first enable the government to control the governed; and in the next place oblige it to control itself."

STUDY GUIDE

- Madison views the separation of powers as a method of allowing each branch to counteract the other branches. He writes, "Ambition must be made to counteract ambition." What does this mean?
- How does Madison see the interaction between the federal and state governments as creating a "double security" for freedom?
- How will a "multiplicity of interests" protect "civil rights"?

JAMES MADISON, *FEDERALIST No. 51*, Friday, February 8, 1788

To the People of the State of New York:

TO WHAT expedient, then, shall we finally resort, for maintaining in practice the necessary partition of power among the several departments, as laid down in the Constitution? The only answer that can be given is, that as all these exterior provisions are found to be inadequate, the defect must be supplied, by so contriving the interior structure of the government as that its several constituent parts may, by their mutual relations, be the means of keeping each other in their proper places. Without presuming to undertake a full development of this important idea, I will hazard a few general observations, which may perhaps place it in a clearer light, and enable us to form a more correct judgment of the principles and structure of the government planned by the convention.

In order to lay a due foundation for that separate and distinct exercise of the different powers of government, which to a certain extent is admitted on all hands to be essential to the preservation of liberty, it is evident that each department should have a will of its own; and consequently should be so constituted that the members of each should have as little agency as possible in the appointment of the members of the others. Were this principle rigorously adhered to, it would require that all the appointments for the supreme executive, legislative, and judiciary magistracies should be drawn from the same fountain of authority, the people, through channels having no communication whatever with one another. Perhaps such a plan of constructing the several departments would be less difficult in practice than it may in contemplation appear. Some difficulties, however, and some additional expense would attend the execution of it. Some deviations, therefore, from the principle must be admitted. In the constitution of the judiciary department in particular, it might be inexpedient to insist rigorously on the principle: first, because peculiar qualifications being essential in the members, the primary consideration ought to be to select that mode of choice which best secures these qualifications; secondly, because the permanent tenure by which the appointments are held in that department, must soon destroy all sense of dependence on the authority conferring them.

It is equally evident, that the members of each department should be as little dependent as possible on those of the others, for the emoluments annexed to their offices. Were the executive magistrate, or the judges, not independent of the legislature in this particular, their independence in every other would be merely nominal. But the great security against a gradual concentration of the several powers in the same department, consists in giving to those who administer each department the necessary constitutional means and personal motives to resist encroachments of the others. The provision for defense must in this, as in all other cases, be made commensurate to the danger of attack. Ambition must be made to counteract ambition. The interest of the man must be connected with the constitutional rights of the place. It may be a reflection on human nature, that such devices should be necessary to control the abuses of government. But what is government itself, but the greatest of all reflections on human nature? If men were angels, no government would be necessary. If angels were to govern men, neither external nor internal controls on government would be necessary. In framing a government which is to be administered by men over men, the great difficulty lies in this: you must first enable the government to control the governed; and in the next place oblige it to control itself.

A dependence on the people is, no doubt, the primary control on the government; but experience has taught mankind the necessity of auxiliary precautions. This policy of supplying, by opposite and rival interests, the defect of better motives, might be traced through the whole system of human affairs, private as well as public. We see it particularly displayed in all the subordinate distributions of power, where the constant aim is to divide and arrange the several offices in such a manner as that each may be a check on the other that the private interest of every individual may be a sentinel over the public rights. These inventions of prudence cannot be less requisite in the distribution of the supreme powers of the State. But it is not possible to give to each department an equal power of self-defense. In republican government, the legislative authority necessarily predominates. The remedy for this inconveniency is to divide the legislature into different branches; and to render them, by different modes of election and different principles of action, as little connected with each other as the nature of their common functions and their common dependence on the society will admit. It may even be necessary to guard against dangerous encroachments by still further precautions. As the weight of the legislative authority requires that it should be thus divided, the weakness of the executive may require, on the other hand, that it should be fortified.

An absolute negative on the legislature appears, at first view, to be the natural defense with which the executive magistrate should be armed. But perhaps it would be neither altogether safe nor alone sufficient. On ordinary occasions it might not be exerted with the requisite firmness, and on extraordinary occasions it might be perfidiously abused. May not this defect of an absolute negative be supplied by some qualified connection between this weaker department and the weaker branch of the stronger department, by which the latter may be led to support the constitutional rights of the former, without being too much detached from the rights of its own department? If the principles on which these observations are founded be just, as I persuade myself they are, and they be applied as a criterion to the several State constitutions, and to the federal Constitution it will be found that if the latter does not perfectly correspond with them, the former are infinitely less able to bear such a test.

There are, moreover, two considerations particularly applicable to the federal system of America, which place that system in a very interesting point of view. First. In a single republic, all the power surrendered by the people is submitted to the administration of a single government; and the usurpations are guarded against by a division of the government into distinct and separate departments. In the compound republic of America, the power surrendered by the people is first divided between two distinct governments, and then the portion allotted to each subdivided among distinct and separate departments. Hence a double security arises to the rights of the people. The different governments will control each other, at the same time that each will be controlled by itself. Second. It is of great importance in a republic not only to guard the society against the oppression of its rulers, but to guard one part of the society against the injustice of the other part. Different interests necessarily exist in different classes of citizens. If a majority be united by a common interest, the rights of the minority will be insecure.

There are but two methods of providing against this evil: the one by creating a will in the community independent of the majority that is, of the society itself; the other, by comprehending in the society so many separate descriptions of citizens as will render an unjust combination of a majority of the whole very improbable, if not impracticable. The first method prevails in all governments possessing an hereditary or self-appointed authority. This, at best, is but a precarious security; because a power independent of the society may as well espouse the unjust views of the major, as the rightful interests of the minor party, and may possibly be turned against both parties. The second method will be exemplified in the federal republic of the United States. Whilst all authority in it will be derived from and dependent on the society, the society itself will be broken into so many parts, interests, and classes of citizens, that the rights of individuals, or of the minority, will be in little danger from interested combinations of the majority.

In a free government the security for civil rights must be the same as that for religious rights. It consists in the one case in the multiplicity of interests, and in the other in the multiplicity of sects. The degree of security in both cases will depend on the number of interests and sects; and this may be presumed to depend on the extent of country and number of people comprehended under the same government. This view of the subject must particularly recommend a proper federal system to all the sincere and considerate friends of republican government, since it shows that in exact proportion as the territory of the Union may be formed into more circumscribed Confederacies, or States oppressive combinations of a majority will be facilitated: the best security, under the republican forms, for the rights of every class of citizens, will be diminished: and consequently the stability and independence of some member of the government, the only other security, must be proportionately increased. Justice is the end of government. It is the end of civil society. It ever has been and ever will be pursued until it be obtained, or until liberty be lost in the pursuit. In a society under the forms of which the stronger faction can readily unite and oppress the weaker, anarchy may as truly be said to reign as in a state of nature, where the weaker individual is not secured against the violence of the stronger; and as, in the latter state, even the stronger individuals are prompted, by the uncertainty of their condition, to submit to a government which may protect the weak as well as themselves; so, in the former state, will the more powerful factions or parties be gradually induced, by a like motive, to wish for a government which will protect all parties, the weaker as well as the more powerful.

It can be little doubted that if the State of Rhode Island was separated from the Confederacy and left to itself, the insecurity of rights under the popular form of government within such narrow limits would be displayed by such reiterated oppressions of factious majorities that some power altogether independent of the people would soon be called for by the voice of the very factions whose misrule had proved the necessity of it. In the extended republic of the United States, and among the great variety of interests, parties, and sects which it embraces, a coalition of a majority of the whole society could seldom take place on any other principles than those of justice and the general good; whilst there being thus less danger to a minor from the will of a major party, there must be less pretext, also, to provide for the security of the former, by introducing into the government a will not dependent on the latter, or, in other words, a will independent of the society itself. It is no less certain than it is important, notwithstanding the contrary opinions which have been entertained, that the larger the society, provided it lie within a practical sphere, the more duly capable it will be of self-government. And happily for the REPUBLICAN CAUSE, the practicable sphere may be carried to a very great extent, by a judicious modification and mixture of the FEDERAL PRINCIPLE.

PUBLIUS.

ASSIGNMENT 3

B. THE ORIGINS OF THE BILL OF RIGHTS

It is often forgotten that, for a period of two years, there was a Constitution but no bill of rights. (During this time, could Congress have enacted a law restricting the freedom of the press? Under which enumerated power could Congress enact such a law?) What we have come to know as the Bill of Rights was added by amendment after the Constitution was adopted, a process of drafting and ratification that took two years to unfold. The absence of a bill of rights in the Constitution became a potent objection to its ratification.

1. Anti-Federalist Complaints About the Lack of a Bill of Rights

Perhaps the most telling objection to the Constitution was the fact it lacked a "bill of rights," something that even the English had (though England's written Bill of Rights applied only to the Crown). However, it is not at all clear that Anti-Federalists were concerned about actually getting a bill of rights adopted. Rather, many opponents stressed this argument because it resonated with the general public. Their true aim was either to defeat the Constitution outright or to get the proposal recommitted to a new convention where it would die. On the other side, Federalist supporters of the Constitution were obliged to defend the absence of a bill of rights. In what follows we read one version of the Anti-Federalist objection, and responses to it by two prominent Federalist framers — James Wilson of Pennsylvania and James Iredell of North Carolina. Both Wilson and Iredell later became Justices on the first Supreme Court, where they found themselves on opposite sides of some important disputes.

STUDY GUIDE

When reading Centinel, keep in mind that the lack of a bill of rights was just one of a long list of objections made to the Constitution. We are focusing on this particular one because it explains the origins of the Bill of Rights and helps us to understand its meaning.

CENTINEL I, *INDEPENDENT GAZETTEER,* October 5, 1787 [Attributed to Samuel Bryan]. *Friends, Countrymen and Fellow Citizens,* . . . [t]he late convention have submitted to your consideration a plan of a new federal government — The subject is highly interesting to your future welfare — Whether it be calculated to promote the great ends of civil society, *viz.* the happiness and prosperity of the community; it behooves you well to consider, uninfluenced by the authority of names. . . . From this investigation into the organization of this government, it appears that it is devoid of all responsibility or accountability to the great body of the people, and that so far from being a regular balanced government, it would be in practice a *permanent* ARISTOCRACY.

The framers of it, actuated by the true spirit of such a government, which ever abominates and suppresses all free enquiry and discussion, have made no provision for the *liberty of the press*, that grand *palladium of freedom*, and *scourge of tyrants*, but observed a total silence on that head. It is the opinion of some great writers, that if the liberty of the press, by an institution of religion, or otherwise, could be rendered sacred, even in *Turkey*, that despotism would fly before it. And it is worthy of remark, that there is no declaration of personal rights, premised in most free constitutions; and that trial by *jury* in *civil* cases is taken away. . . .

But our situation is represented to be so *critically* dreadful that, however reprehensible and exceptionable the proposed plan of government may be, there is no alternative, between the adoption of it and absolute ruin. — My fellow citizens, things are not at that crisis, it is the argument of tyrants; the present distracted state of Europe secures us from injury on that quarter, and as to domestic dissensions, we have not so much to fear from them, as to precipitate us into this form of government, without it is a safe and a proper one. For remember, of all *possible* evils that of *despotism* is the *worst* and the most to be *dreaded*. . . .

2. Federalist Objections to a Bill of Rights

STUDY GUIDE

These two Federalist arguments are important to understanding whether the Bill of Rights lists all of the rights that the people have, or whether "other" unenumerated rights "retained by the people" may also be protected. Compare Iredell's position here to the views he expresses as a Justice of the Supreme Court in the case of *Calder v. Bull*, which appears later in this chapter.

JAMES WILSON, SPEECH IN THE STATEHOUSE YARD, PHILADELPHIA, October 6, 1787. When the people established the powers of legislation under their separate governments, they invested their representatives with every right and authority which they did not in explicit terms reserve; and therefore upon every question, respecting the jurisdiction of the house of assembly, if the frame of government is silent, the jurisdiction is efficient and complete. But in delegating federal powers, another criterion was necessarily introduced, and the congressional authority is to be collected, not from tacit implication, but from the positive grant expressed in the instrument of union. Hence it is evident, that in the former case everything which is not reserved is given, but in the latter the reverse of the proposition prevails, and everything which is not given, is reserved. This distinction being recognized, will furnish an answer to those who think the omission of a bill of rights, a defect in the proposed Constitution; for it would have been superfluous and absurd to have stipulated with a federal body of our own creation, that we should enjoy those privileges, of which we are not divested wither by the intention or the act, that has brought that body into existence. For instance, the liberty of the press, which has been a copious source of declamation and opposition, what control can proceed from the federal government to shackle or destroy that sacred palladium of national freedom? If indeed, a power similar to that which has been granted for the regulation of commerce, had been granted to regulate literary publications, it would have been as necessary to stipulate that the liberty of the press should be preserved inviolate, as that the impost should be general in its operation.... In truth then, the proposed system possesses no influence whatever upon the press, and it would have been merely nugatory to have introduced a formal declaration upon the subject — nay, that very declaration might have been construed to imply that some degree of power was given, since we undertook to define its extent....

James Wilson was a member of the Philadelphia Convention that drafted the Constitution, where he served as a member of the Committee of Detail that selected the actual language of the text. He was the first professor of law at the College of Philadelphia, which became the University of Pennsylvania.

JAMES WILSON, SPEECH TO THE PENNSYLVANIA RATIFICATION CONVENTION. WEDNESDAY, October 28, 1787, A.M. . . . [I]n a government consisting of enumerated powers, such as is proposed for the United States, a bill of rights would not only be unnecessary, but, in my humble judgment, highly imprudent. . . . If we attempt an enumeration, every thing that is not enumerated is presumed to be given. The consequence is, that an imperfect enumeration would throw all implied power into the scale of the government, and the rights of the people would be rendered incomplete. On the other hand, an imperfect enumeration of the powers of government reserves all implied power to the people; and by that means the constitution becomes incomplete. But of the two, it is much safer to run the risk on the side of the constitution; for an omission in the enumeration of the powers of government is neither so dangerous nor important as an omission in the enumeration of the rights of the people.

TUESDAY, December 4, 1787, A.M. . . . I apprehend that the powers given and reserved form the whole rights of the people, as men and as citizens. I consider that there are very few who understand the whole of these rights. All the political writers, from Grotius and Puffendorf down to Vattel, have treated on this subject; but in no one of those books, nor in the aggregate of them all, can you find a complete enumeration of rights appertaining to the people as men and as citizens. . . . Enumerate all the rights of men! I am sure, sir, that no gentleman in the late Convention would have attempted such a thing.

JAMES IREDELL, SPEECH TO THE NORTH CAROLINA RATIFICATION CONVENTION, July 29, 1788. I thought the objection against the want of a bill of rights had been obviated unanswerably. It appears to me most extraordinary. Shall we give up any thing but what is positively granted by that instrument? It would be the greatest absurdity for any man to pretend that, when a legislature is formed for a particular purpose, it can have any authority but what is so expressly given to it, any more than a man acting under a power of attorney could depart from the authority it conveyed to him. . . . Negative words, in my opinion, could make the matter no plainer than it was before. The gentleman says that unalienable rights ought not to be given up. Those rights which are unalienable are not alienated. They still remain with the great body of the people. . . . [I]t would be not only useless, but dangerous, to enumerate a number of rights which are not intended to be given up; because it would be implying, in the strongest manner, that every right not included in the exception might be impaired by the government without usurpation; and it would be impossible to enumerate every one. Let any one make what collection or enumeration of rights he pleases, I will immediately mention twenty or thirty more rights not contained in it.

3. The Anti-Federalist Reply

STUDY GUIDE

- What does Brutus identify as the purpose of written constitutions?
- Notice the extent to which he relies on the natural rights reasoning of the sort presented by John Locke.
- Compare the sophistication of these appeals by both sides in this debate to those made today. What does this tell us about the sophistication of the audience to whom these speeches and essays were aimed? Could the sophistication of both advocates and audience help account for the Constitution's longevity?

BRUTUS II, *THE NEW YORK JOURNAL*, November 1, 1787 [Attributed to Robert Yates]. The common good . . . is the end of civil government, and common consent, the foundation on which it is established. To effect this end, it was necessary that a certain portion of natural liberty should be surrendered, in order that what remained should be preserved. . . . But it is not necessary, for this purpose, that individuals should relinquish all their natural rights. Some are of such a nature that they cannot be surrendered. Of this kind are the rights of conscience, the right of enjoying and defending life, etc. Others are not necessary to be resigned in order to attain the end for which government is instituted; these therefore ought not to be given up. To surrender them, would counteract the very end of government, to wit, the common good. From these observations it appears, that in forming a government on its true principles, the foundation should be laid . . . by expressly reserving to the people such of their essential rights as are not necessary to be parted with. . . . [R]ulers have the same propensities as other men; they are as likely to use the power with which they are vested, for private purposes, and to the injury and oppression of those over whom they are placed, as individuals in a state of nature are to injure and oppress one another. It is therefore as proper that bounds should be set to their authority, as that government should have at first been instituted to restrain private injuries. . . .

It has been said . . . that such declarations of rights, however requisite they might be in the Constitutions of the States, are not necessary in the general Constitution, because, "in the former case, every thing which is not reserved is given; but in the latter, the reverse of the proposition prevails, and every thing which is not given is reserved." It requires but little attention to discover, that this mode of reasoning is rather specious than solid. The powers, rights and authority, granted to the general government by this Constitution, are as complete, with respect to every object to which they extend, as that of any State government — it reaches to every thing which concerns human happiness — life, liberty, and property are under its control. There is the same reason, therefore, that the exercise of power, in this case, should be restrained within proper limits, as in that of the State governments. . . .

Besides, it is evident that the reason here assigned was not the true one, why the framers of this Constitution omitted a bill of rights; if it had been, they would not have made certain reservations, while they totally omitted others of more importance. We find they have . . . declared, that the writ of habeas corpus shall not be suspended, unless in cases of rebellion, — that no bill of attainder, or ex post facto law, shall be passed, — that no title of nobility shall be granted by the United States, etc. If every thing which is not given is reserved, what propriety is there in these exceptions? Does this Constitution any where grant the power of suspending the habeas corpus, to make ex post facto laws, pass bills of attainder, or grant titles of nobility? It certainly does not in express terms. The only answer that can be given is, that these are implied in the general powers granted. With equal truth it may be said, that all the powers which the bills of rights guard against the abuse of, are contained or implied in the general ones granted by this Constitution. . . .

4. James Madison Delivers on the Promise of a Bill of Rights

There is general consensus among historians that the Constitution was headed for defeat until the Federalists solemnly promised to adopt, after ratification, a bill of rights in the form of amendments. This promise turned the tide in key state ratification conventions. After it was made, state conventions began to accompany their approvals with sometimes long lists of proposed amendments. Some of these amendments were designated "rights"; others were simply desired alterations in the Constitution.

When it came time for the first Congress to formulate and propose amendments, however, the Federalists who now dominated both houses had little interest in the subject. Then-Representative James Madison of Virginia repeatedly urged the House to take up the matter, only to be opposed by other congressmen who were more concerned with enacting taxes than with proposing a bill of rights. Eventually, Madison prevailed in getting the matter assigned to a select committee to which he was named a member. Congress eventually proposed twelve amendments to the states. The first two initially failed of ratification, leaving the ten amendments we call the Bill of Rights. (One of those first two amendments proposed by Congress was ratified in 1992, becoming the Twenty-Seventh Amendment.)

STUDY GUIDE

- Notice how Madison begins his speech with arguments about why the House should take up the matter. At this point, only eleven states had ratified the Constitution. Note how tenuous Madison considers the new federal government to be.
- Notice also that Madison does not consider all his proposed amendments to be literally a "bill of rights" but only some. Indeed, until around the time of the Civil War, these amendments were rarely referred to as "the Bill of Rights" but were more typically called "the amendments." This could suggest that, while all of the first ten amendments are meant to limit federal power, not all are to be considered individual rights, privileges, or immunities of citizenship.
- What is Madison's response to the Federalist objections to adding a bill of rights? How is it related to the Necessary and Proper Clause?
- Finally, notice that Madison's proposal includes restrictions on the powers of states, which were not adopted. This omission is relevant to understanding the scope of the Bill of Rights, as addressed by the Supreme Court in *Barron v. Baltimore*, which appears in Chapter 2.

MADISON'S SPEECH TO THE HOUSE INTRODUCING AMENDMENTS, June 8, 1789[37]

[*Why the Congress should propose amendments*]

I will state my reasons why I think it proper to propose amendments; and state the amendments themselves, so far as I think they ought to be proposed. . . . It appears to me that this house is bound by every motive of prudence, not to let the first session pass over without proposing to the state legislatures some things to be incorporated into the constitution, as will render it as acceptable to the whole people of the United States, as it has been found acceptable to a majority of them. I wish, among other reasons why something should be done, that those who have been friendly to the adoption of this constitution, may have the opportunity of proving to those who were opposed to it, that they were as sincerely devoted to liberty and a republican government, as those who charged them with wishing the adoption of this constitution in order to lay the foundation of an aristocracy or despotism. It will be a desirable thing to extinguish from the bosom of every member of the community any apprehensions, that there are those among his countrymen who wish to deprive them of the liberty for which they valiantly fought and honorably bled. And if there are amendments desired, of such a nature as will not injure the constitution, and they can be engrafted so as to give satisfaction to the doubting part of our fellow citizens; the friends of the federal government will evince that spirit of deference and concession for which they have hitherto been distinguished.

It cannot be a secret to the gentlemen in this house, that, notwithstanding the ratification of this system of government by eleven of the thirteen United States, in some cases unanimously, in others by large majorities; yet still there is a great number of our constituents who are dissatisfied with it; among whom are many respectable for their talents, their patriotism, and respectable for the jealousy they have for their liberty, which, though mistaken in its object, is laudable in its motive.

There is a great body of the people falling under this description, who as present feel much inclined to join their support to the cause of federalism, if they were satisfied in this one point: We ought not to disregard their inclination, but, on principles of amity and moderation, conform to their wishes, and expressly declare the great rights of mankind secured under this constitution. The acquiescence which our fellow citizens show under the government, calls upon us for a like return of moderation.

But perhaps there is a stronger motive than this for our going into a consideration of the subject; it is to provide those securities for liberty which are required by a part of the community. I allude in a particular manner to those two states[38] who have not thought fit to throw themselves into the bosom of the confederacy: it is a desirable thing, on our part as well as theirs, that a re-union should take place as

---

[37] [The formatting of this speech has been modified for easier comprehension. Topic headings have been inserted and some paragraphs have been broken up. —Eds.]

[38] [North Carolina and Rhode Island. —Eds.]

soon as possible. I have no doubt, if we proceed to take those steps which would be prudent and requisite at this juncture, that in a short time we should see that disposition prevailing in those states that are not come in, that we have seen prevailing [in] those states which are.

But I will candidly acknowledge, that, over and above all these considerations, . . . if all power is subject to abuse, that then it is possible the abuse of the powers of the general government may be guarded against in a more secure manner than is now done, while no one advantage, arising from the exercise of that power, shall be damaged or endangered by it. We have in this way something to gain, and, if we proceed with caution, nothing to lose; and in this case it is necessary to proceed with caution; for while we feel all these inducements to go into a revisal of the constitution, we must feel for the constitution itself, and make that revisal a moderate one.

I should be unwilling to see a door opened for a re-consideration of the whole structure of the government, for a re-consideration of the principles and the substance of the powers given; because I doubt, if such a door was opened, if we should be very likely to stop at that point which would be safe to the government itself: But I do wish to see a door opened to consider, so far as to incorporate those provisions for the security of rights, against which I believe no serious objection has been made by any class of our constituents, such as would be likely to meet with the concurrence of two-thirds of both houses, and the approbation of three-fourths of the state legislatures.

I will not propose a single alteration which I do not wish to see take place, as intrinsically proper in itself, or proper because it is wished for by a respectable number of my fellow citizens; and therefore I shall not propose a single alteration but is likely to meet the concurrence required by the constitution.

[*Why some Americans have opposed the Constitution*]

There have been objections of various kinds made against the constitution: Some were levelled against its structure, because the president was without a council; because the senate, which is a legislative body, had judicial powers in trials on impeachments; and because the powers of that body were compounded in other respects, in a manner that did not correspond with a particular theory; because it grants more power than is supposed to be necessary for every good purpose; and controls the ordinary powers of the state governments.

I know some respectable characters who opposed this government on these grounds; but I believe that the great mass of the people who opposed it, disliked it because it did not contain effectual provision against encroachments on particular rights, and those safeguards which they have been long accustomed to have interposed between them and the magistrate who exercised the sovereign power: nor ought we to consider them safe, while a great number of our fellow citizens think these securities necessary.

It has been a fortunate thing that the objection to the government has been made on the ground I stated; because it will be practicable on that ground to obviate the objection, so far as to satisfy the public mind that their liberties will be perpetual, and this without endangering any part of the constitution, which is considered as essential to the existence of the government by those who promoted its adoption.

[*Madison's "first" amendment, or what he called a "bill of rights"*]

The amendments which have occurred to me, proper to be recommended by congress to the state legislatures are these:

First. That there be prefixed to the constitution a declaration

> That all power is originally vested in, and consequently derived from the people.
>
> That government is instituted, and ought to be exercised for the benefit of the people; which consists in the enjoyment of life and liberty, with the right of acquiring and using property, and generally of pursuing and obtaining happiness and safety.
>
> That the people have an indubitable, unalienable, and indefeasible right to reform or change their government, whenever it be found adverse or inadequate to the purposes of its institution. . . .

The first of these amendments, relates to what may be called a bill of rights; I will own that I never considered this provision so essential to the federal constitution, as to make it improper to ratify it, until such an amendment was added; at the same time, I always conceived, that in a certain form and to a certain extent, such a provision was neither improper nor altogether useless.

I am aware, that a great number of the most respectable friends to the government and champions for republican liberty, have thought such a provision, not only unnecessary, but even improper, nay, I believe some have gone so far as to think it even dangerous. . . .

I acknowledge the ingenuity of those arguments which were drawn against the constitution, by a comparison with the policy of Great-Britain, in establishing a declaration of rights; but there is too great a difference in the case to warrant the comparison: therefore the arguments drawn from that source, were in a great measure inapplicable. In the declaration of rights which that country has established, the truth is, they have gone no farther, than to raise a barrier against the power of the crown; the power of the legislature is left altogether indefinite. Although I know whenever the great rights, the trial by jury, freedom of the press, or liberty of conscience, came in question in that body, the invasion of them is resisted by able advocates, yet their Magna Charta does not contain any one provision for the security of those rights, respecting which, the people of America are most alarmed. The freedom of the press and rights of conscience, those choicest privileges of the people, are unguarded in the British constitution.

But although the case may be widely different, and it may not be thought necessary to provide limits for the legislative power in that country, yet a different opinion prevails in the United States. The people of many states, have thought it necessary to raise barriers against power in all forms and departments of government, and I am inclined to believe, if once bills of rights are established in all the states as well as the federal constitution, we shall find that although some of them are rather unimportant, yet, upon the whole, they will have a salutary tendency.

[*The different kinds of rights included in state bills of rights (and in Madison's proposed amendments)*]

It may be said, in some instances they do no more than state the perfect equality of mankind; this to be sure is an absolute truth, yet it is not absolutely necessary to be inserted at the head of a constitution.

In some instances they assert those rights which are exercised by the people in forming and establishing a plan of government. In other instances, they specify those rights which are retained when particular powers are given up to be exercised by the legislature.[39]

In other instances, they specify positive rights, which may seem to result from the nature of the compact. Trial by jury cannot be considered as a natural right, but a right resulting from the social compact which regulates the action of the community, but is as essential to secure the liberty of the people as any one of the pre-existent rights of nature. In other instances they lay down dogmatic maxims with respect to the construction of the government; declaring, that the legislative, executive, and judicial branches shall be kept separate and distinct: Perhaps the best way of securing this in practice is to provide such checks, as will prevent the encroachment of the one upon the other.

But whatever may be the form which the several states have adopted in making declarations in favor of particular rights, the great object in view is to limit and qualify the powers of government, by excepting out of the grant of power those cases in which the government ought not to act, or to act only in a particular mode. They point these exceptions sometimes against the abuse of the executive power, sometimes against the legislative, and, in some cases, against the community itself; or, in other words, against the majority in favor of the minority.

[*Why the Congress is the most dangerous branch, but the greater danger in a Republican government lies in the abuse of the minority by a majority of the community*]

In our government it is, perhaps, less necessary to guard against the abuse in the executive department than any other; because it is not the stronger branch of the system, but the weaker: It therefore must be levelled against the legislative, for it is the most powerful, and most likely to be abused, because it is under the least control; hence, so far as a declaration of rights can tend to prevent the exercise of undue power, it cannot be doubted but such declaration is proper.

---

[39] [Madison's notes for this speech support the conclusion that by "retained" rights he meant natural rights, and that he viewed the freedom of speech as a retained natural right:

> Contents of Bill of Rhts.
> 1. assertion of primitive equality &c.
> 2. do. of rights exerted in formg. of Govts.
> 3. natural rights retained as speach [illegible].
> 4. positive rights resultg. as trial by jury.
> 5. Doctrinl. artics vs. Depts. distinct electn.
> 6. moral precepts for the administrn. & natl. character — as justice — economy — &c. — Eds.]

But . . . in a government modified like this of the United States, the great danger lies rather in the abuse of the community than in the legislative body. The prescriptions in favor of liberty, ought to be levelled against that quarter where the greatest danger lies, namely, that which possesses the highest prerogative of power: But this [is] not found in either the executive or legislative departments of government, but in the body of the people, operating by the majority against the minority.

It may be thought all paper barriers against the power of the community are too weak to be worthy of attention. I am sensible they are not so strong as to satisfy gentlemen of every description who have seen and examined thoroughly the texture of such a defence; yet, as they have a tendency to impress some degree of respect for them, to establish the public opinion in their favor, and rouse the attention of the whole community, it may be one means to control the majority from those acts to which they might be otherwise inclined.

[*Why a bill of rights is necessary: the danger of the Necessary and Proper Clause*]

It has been said by way of objection to a bill of rights, by many respectable gentlemen out of doors, and I find opposition on the same principles likely to be made by gentlemen on this floor, that they are unnecessary articles of a republican government, upon the presumption that the people have those rights in their own hands, and that is the proper place for them to rest. It would be a sufficient answer to say that this objection lies against such provisions under the state governments as well as under the general government; and there are, I believe, but few gentlemen who are inclined to push their theory so far as to say that a declaration of rights in those cases is either ineffectual or improper.

It has been said that in the federal government they are unnecessary, because the powers are enumerated, and it follows that all that are not granted by the constitution are retained: that the constitution is a bill of powers, the great residuum being the rights of the people; and therefore a bill of rights cannot be so necessary as if the residuum was thrown into the hands of the government. I admit that these arguments are not entirely without foundation; but they are not conclusive to the extent which has been supposed.

It is true the powers of the general government are circumscribed; they are directed to particular objects; but even if government keeps within those limits, it has certain discretionary powers with respect to the means, which may admit of abuse to a certain extent, in the same manner as the powers of the state governments under their constitutions may to an indefinite extent; because in the constitution of the United States there is a clause granting to Congress the power to make all laws which shall be necessary and proper for carrying into execution all the powers vested in the government of the United States, or in any department or officer thereof; this enables them to fulfil every purpose for which the government was established.

Now, may not laws be considered necessary and proper by Congress, for it is them who are to judge of the necessity and propriety to accomplish those special purposes which they may have in contemplation, which laws in themselves are neither necessary or proper; as well as improper laws could be enacted by the state legislatures, for fulfilling the more extended objects of those governments.

I will state an instance which I think in point, and proves that this might be the case. The general government has a right to pass all laws which shall be necessary to collect its revenue; the means for enforcing the collection are within the direction of the legislature: may not general warrants be considered necessary for this purpose, as well as for some purposes which it was supposed at the framing of their constitutions the state governments had in view. If there was reason for restraining the state governments from exercising this power, there is like reason for restraining the federal government. . . .

[*How the alleged danger of enumerating certain rights can be addressed with what came to be the Ninth Amendment; and the importance of judicial nullification*]

It has been objected also against a bill of rights, that, by enumerating particular exceptions to the grant of power, it would disparage those rights which were not placed in that enumeration, and it might follow by implication, that those rights which were not singled out, were intended to be assigned into the hands of the general government, and were consequently insecure. This is one of the most plausible arguments I have ever heard urged against the admission of a bill of rights into this system; but, I conceive, that may be guarded against. I have attempted it, as gentlemen may see by turning to the last clause of the 4th resolution.

[The exceptions here or elsewhere in the constitution, made in favor of particular rights, shall not be so construed as to diminish the just importance of other rights retained by the people; or as to enlarge the powers delegated by the constitution; but either as actual limitations of such powers, or as inserted merely for greater caution.]

It has been said, that it is unnecessary to load the constitution with this provision, because it was not found effectual in the constitution of the particular states. It is true, there are a few particular states in which some of the most valuable articles have not, at one time or other, been violated; but does it not follow but they may have, to a certain degree, a salutary effect against the abuse of power.

If they are incorporated into the constitution, independent tribunals of justice will consider themselves in a peculiar manner the guardians of those rights; they will be an impenetrable bulwark against every assumption of power in the legislative or executive; they will be naturally led to resist every encroachment upon rights expressly stipulated for in the constitution by the declaration of rights.

Beside this security, there is a great probability that such a declaration in the federal system would be enforced; because the state legislatures will jealously and closely watch the operation of this government, and be able to resist with more effect every assumption of power than any other power on earth can do; and the greatest opponents to a federal government admit the state legislatures to be sure guardians of the people's liberty. I conclude from this view of the subject, that it will be proper in itself, and highly politic, for the tranquility of the public mind, and the stability of the government, that we should offer something, in the form I have proposed, to be incorporated in the system of government, as a declaration of the rights of the people. . . .

[*Why and how the powers of states should also be further restricted*]

I wish also, in revising the constitution, we may throw into that section, which interdicts the abuse of certain powers in the state legislatures, some other provisions of equal if not greater importance than those already made. The words, "No state shall pass any bill of attainder, ex post facto law, &c." were wise and proper restrictions in the constitution. I think there is more danger of those powers being abused by the state governments than by the government of the United States. The same may be said of other powers which they possess, if not controlled by the general principle, that laws are unconstitutional which infringe the rights of the community. I should therefore wish to extend this interdiction, and add, as I have stated in the 5th resolution. . . .

> [No state shall violate the equal rights of conscience, or the freedom of the press, or the trial by jury in criminal cases.]

[B]ecause it is proper that every government should be disarmed of powers which trench upon those particular rights. I know in some of the state constitutions the power of the government is controlled by such a declaration, but others are not. I cannot see any reason against obtaining even a double security on those points; and nothing can give a more sincere proof of the attachment of those who opposed this constitution to these great and important rights, than to see them join in obtaining the security I have now proposed; because it must be admitted, on all hands, that the state governments are as liable to attack these invaluable privileges as the general government is, and therefore ought to be as cautiously guarded against. . . .

[*Madison's comment on what came to be the Tenth Amendment*]

I find, from looking into the amendments proposed by the state conventions, that several are particularly anxious that it should be declared in the constitution, that the powers not therein delegated, should be reserved to the several states. Perhaps words which may define this more precisely, than the whole of the instrument now does, may be considered as superfluous. I admit they may be deemed unnecessary; but there can be no harm in making such a declaration, if gentlemen will allow that the fact is as stated. I am sure I understand it so, and do therefore propose it.

[* * *]

These are the points on which I wish to see a revision of the constitution take place. . . . I have proposed nothing that does not appear to me as proper in itself, or eligible as patronized by a respectable number of our fellow citizens; and if we can make the constitution better in the opinion of those who are opposed to it, without weakening its frame, or abridging its usefulness, in the judgment of those who are attached to it, we act the part of wise and liberal men to make such alterations as shall produce that effect.

Having done what I conceived was my duty, in bringing before this house the subject of amendments, and also stated such as wish for and approve, and offered the reasons which occurred to me in their support; I shall content myself for the present with moving, that a committee be appointed to consider of and report such amendments as ought to be proposed by congress to the legislatures of the states, to become, if ratified by three-fourths thereof, part of the constitution of the United States. . . .

C. THE SCOPE OF CONGRESSIONAL POWER: THE DEBATE OVER THE FIRST NATIONAL BANK

While today we expect major constitutional controversies to be decided by the Supreme Court, two of the earliest constitutional disputes — the constitutionality of a national bank and of the Alien and Sedition Acts — were fought out in other arenas. And, although a third early controversy — the ability of a state to be sued by a citizen of another state in federal court — was initially dealt with by the Supreme Court, its decision was rapidly reversed by Congress and the states through the enactment of the Eleventh Amendment.

The creation of a national bank was proposed to Congress by Secretary of the Treasury Alexander Hamilton, who lobbied hard for its adoption. It was opposed in President Washington's cabinet by Secretary of State Thomas Jefferson,[40] and in Congress by James Madison. Madison and Hamilton were allies in the fight to ratify the Constitution and were coauthors of *The Federalist* papers. But their views on the proper scope of federal power diverged early on, as reflected by their disagreement over the bank. Eventually, Madison and Jefferson joined forces to organize a political opposition to the Federalists in Congress. This happened at a time when the idea of a political "party" was anathema to the founding generation. Parties were seen as a form of factionalism in conflict with the ideal of governance by "disinterested" statesmen acting purely in the public interest. Members of Madison's and Jefferson's opposition alliance called themselves "Republicans." Having successfully labeled those who opposed the Constitution with the pejorative "Anti-Federalists," the Federalists dubbed their new opponents "democrats" — a highly pejorative term connoting pure majoritarian or direct popular rule. For a time, those affiliated with the Jeffersonian group were variously known as "Republicans," "Democratic societies," "democratic-republicans," or "The Democracy," before eventually adopting the current name: the Democratic Party. "The Democracy" connoted that, rather than being a faction or "party," they purported to speak

[40] For a comprehensive overview of all the disagreements between Hamilton and Jefferson when they were in Washington's cabinet, see Carson Holloway, Hamilton versus Jefferson in the Washington Administration: Completing the Founding or Betraying the Founding? (2016).

for "the people" as a whole. One of the early hallmarks of the Democratic Party was its contention that the constitutional powers of the national government ought to be "strictly" construed, a stance that can be traced to Madison's and Jefferson's position concerning the bank. In contrast, Federalists such as Hamilton favored a more "liberal" construction of national powers.

STUDY GUIDE

- How does Madison interpret the Necessary and Proper Clause? What does he mean by an "incidental" power, as distinct from an "important" one?
- Consider his proposed "rules" of constitutional interpretation.
- When Madison refers to the 11th and 12th articles, this is a reference to what eventually became the Ninth and Tenth Amendments. The numbering changed when it was finally determined that the first two proposed amendments had failed of ratification (though one of them became the Twenty-Seventh Amendment in 1992). How does Madison distinguish between the Ninth and Tenth Amendments?
- Finally, it should be noted that this is just one reported version of Madison's speech, which is why it is written in the third person and why its complete accuracy cannot be assumed.

"Alexander Hamilton" by Charles Willson Peale, from life, c. 1790-1795

"James Madison" by Charles Willson Peale

JAMES MADISON, SPEECH IN CONGRESS OPPOSING THE NATIONAL BANK, February 2, 1791. . . . Is the power of establishing an incorporated bank among the powers vested by the constitution in the legislature of the United States? This is the question to be examined. . . . The only clauses under which such a power could be pretended, are either—

1. The power to lay and collect taxes to pay the debts, and provide for the common defence and general welfare: Or,
2. The power to borrow money on the credit of the United States: Or,
3. The power to pass all laws necessary and proper to carry into execution those powers.

The bill did not come within the first power. It laid no tax to pay the debts, or provide for the general welfare. It laid no tax whatever. It was altogether foreign to the subject.

No argument could be drawn from the terms "common defence, and general welfare." The power as to these general purposes, was limited to acts laying taxes for them; and the general purposes themselves were limited and explained by the particular enumeration subjoined. To understand these terms in any sense, that would justify the power in question, would give to Congress an unlimited power; would render nugatory the enumeration of particular powers; would supercede all the powers reserved to the state governments. These terms are copied from the articles of confederation; had it ever been pretended, that they were to be understood otherwise than as here explained? . . .

The second clause to be examined is that, which empowers Congress to borrow money.

Is this a bill to borrow money? It does not borrow a shilling. Is there any fair construction by which the bill can be deemed an exercise of the power to borrow money? The obvious meaning of the power to borrow money, is that of accepting it from, and stipulating payment to those who are able and willing to lend.

To say that the power to borrow involves a power of creating the ability, where there may be the will, to lend, is not only establishing a dangerous principle, as will be immediately shewn, but is as forced a construction, as to say that it involves the power of compelling the will, where there may be the ability, to lend.

The third clause is that which gives the power to pass all laws necessary and proper to execute the specified powers.

Whatever meaning this clause may have, none can be admitted, that would give an unlimited discretion to Congress.

Its meaning must, according to the natural and obvious force of the terms and the context, be limited to means necessary to the end, and incident to the nature of the specified powers.

The clause is in fact merely declaratory of what would have resulted by unavoidable implication, as the appropriate, and as it were, technical means of executing those powers. In this sense it had been explained by the friends of the constitution, and ratified by the state conventions.

The essential characteristic of the government, as composed of limited and enumerated powers, would be destroyed: If instead of direct and incidental means, any means could be used, which in the language of the preamble to the bill, "might be conceived to be conducive to the successful conducting of the finances; or might be conceived to tend to give facility to the obtaining of loans." . . . If . . . Congress, by virtue of the power to borrow, can create the means of lending, and in pursuance of these means, can incorporate a Bank, they may do any thing whatever creative of like means. . . .

The doctrine of implication is always a tender one. The danger of it has been felt in other governments. The delicacy was felt in the adoption of our own, the danger may also be felt, if we do not keep close to our chartered authorities.

Mark the reasoning on which the validity of the bill depends. To borrow money is made the end and the accumulation of capitals, implied as the means. The accumulation of capitals is then the end, and a bank implied as the means. The bank is then the end, and a charter of incorporation, a monopoly, capital punishments, &c. implied as the means.

If implications, thus remote and thus multiplied, can be linked together, a chain may be formed that will reach every object of legislation, every object within the whole compass of political economy.

The latitude of interpretation required by the bill is condemned by the rule furnished by the constitution itself.

Congress have power "to regulate the value of money," yet it is expressly added not left to be implied, that counterfeiters may be punished.

They have the power "to declare war," to which armies are more incident, than incorporated Banks, to borrowing, yet is expressly added, the power "to raise and support armies," and to this again, the express power "to make rules and regulations for the government of armies," a like remark is applicable to the powers as to a navy.

The regulation and calling out of the militia are more appurtenant to war, than the proposed bank, to borrowing, yet the former is not left to construction.

The very power to borrow money is a less remote implication from the power of war, than an incorporated monopoly bank, from the power of borrowing — yet the power to borrow is not left to implication.

It is not pretended that every insertion or omission in the constitution is the effect of systematic attention. This is not the character of any human work, particularly the work of a body of men. The examples cited, with others that might be added, sufficiently inculcate nevertheless a rule of interpretation, very different from that on which the bill rests. They condemn the exercise of any power, particularly a great and important power, which is not evidently and necessarily involved in an express power. . . .

It cannot be denied that the power proposed to be exercised is an important power. . . . [I]t could never be deemed an accessary or subaltern power, to be deduced by implication, as a means of executing another power; it was in its nature a distinct, an independent and substantive prerogative, which not being enumerated in the constitution could never have been meant to be included in it, and not being included could never be rightfully exercised.

He here adverted to a distinction, which he said had not been sufficiently kept in view, between a power necessary and proper for the government or union, and a power necessary and proper for executing the enumerated powers. In the latter case, the powers included in each of the enumerated powers were not expressed, but to be drawn from the nature of each. In the former, the powers composing the government were expressly enumerated. This constituted the peculiar nature of the government, no power therefore not enumerated, could be inferred from the general nature of government. Had the power of making treaties, for example, been omitted, however necessary it might have been, the defect could only have been lamented, or supplied by an amendment of the constitution.

But the proposed bank could not even be called necessary to the government; at most it could be but convenient. Its uses to the government could be supplied by keeping the taxes a little in advance — by loans from individuals — by the other banks, over which the government would have equal command; nay greater, as it may grant or refuse to these the privilege, made a free and irrevocable gift to the proposed bank, of using their notes in the federal revenue.

He proceeded next to the contemporary expositions given to the constitution.

The defence against the charge founded on the want of a bill of rights, presupposed, he said, that the powers not given were retained; and that those given were not to be extended by remote implications. On any other supposition, the power of Congress to abridge the freedom of the press, or the rights of conscience, &c. could not have been disproved.

The explanations in the state conventions all turned on the same fundamental principle, and on the principle that the terms necessary and proper gave no additional powers to those enumerated. . . .

The explanatory amendments proposed by Congress themselves, at least, would be good authority with them; all these renunciations of power proceeded on a rule of construction, excluding the latitude now contended for. These explanations were the more to be respected, as they had not only been proposed by Congress, but ratified by nearly three-fourths of the states. He read several of the articles proposed, remarking particularly on the 11th. and 12th. the former, as guarding against a latitude of interpretation — the latter, as excluding every source of power not within the constitution itself. . . .

[W]ill it not be said, if the bill should pass, that its adoption was brought about by one set of arguments, and that it is now administered under the influence of another set. . . . In fine, if the power were in the constitution, the immediate exercise of it cannot be essential — if not there, the exercise of it involves the guilt of usurpation, and establishes a precedent of interpretation, levelling all the barriers which limit the powers of the general government, and protect those of the state governments. . . .

It appeared on the whole, he concluded, that the power exercised by the bill was condemned by the silence of the constitution; was condemned by the rule of interpretation arising out of the constitution; was condemned by its tendency to destroy the main characteristic of the constitution; was condemned by the expositions of the friends of the constitution, whilst depending before the public; was condemned by the apparent intention of the parties which ratified the constitution; was condemned by the explanatory amendments proposed by Congress themselves to the Constitution; and he hoped it would receive its final condemnation, by the vote of this house.

Despite Madison's impassioned opposition, the bank was approved by the House and then by the Senate. In deciding whether to sign the bill, President Washington sought opinions on the bill's constitutionality from members of his cabinet, Attorney General Edmund Randolph, Secretary of State Thomas Jefferson, and Secretary of the Treasury Alexander Hamilton. Hamilton's proposal ultimately prevailed when the President signed the bill.

Edmund Randolph was not only a delegate from Virginia to the Constitutional Convention in Philadelphia, he also was a member of the five-person Committee of Detail that converted the resolutions of the Convention to precise text — including the text of the Necessary and Proper Clause. Four of the five members of the Committee (including Randolph) were highly respected practicing attorneys. Although he refused to sign the Constitution in Philadelphia, citing as one of its objectionable features the "general clause concerning necessary and proper laws," in the end Randolph supported ratification by the Virginia convention.

STUDY GUIDE

- What significance does Attorney General Edmund Randolph attach to the fact that the Constitution is written?
- How does his definition of "necessary" differ from that of Madison, Jefferson, and Hamilton? On what does he base his "rule of interpretation"?
- What relationship does he see between the consent of the governed and the "paramount rights" of a free people? (We will see this argument again in Justice Chase's opinion in *Calder v. Bull.*) How does he rely on the Tenth Amendment?

OPINION OF ATTORNEY GENERAL EDMUND RANDOLPH, February 12, 1791. It must be acknowledged, that, if any part of the bill does either encounter the constitution, or is not warranted by it, the clause of incorporation is the only one. . . . If it can be exercised by them, it must be,

1st. Because the nature of the Federal Government implies it; or,

2d. Because it is involved in some of the specified powers of legislation; or,

3d. Because it is necessary and proper to carry into execution some of the specified powers:

1st. To be implied in the nature of the Federal Government, would beget a doctrine so indefinite as to grasp every power.

Governments having no written constitution may, perhaps, claim a latitude of power not always easy to be determined. Those which have written constitutions are circumscribed by a just interpretation of the words contained in them. Nay, farther; a legislature, instituted even by a written constitution but without a special demarcation of powers, may perhaps, be presumed to be left at large, as to all authority which is communicable by the people, and does not affect any of those paramount rights, which a free people cannot be supposed to confide even to their representatives. Essentially otherwise is the condition of a legislature whose powers are described. An example of the former, is in the State Legislatures; of the latter in the Legislature of the Federal Government, the characteristic of which has been confessed by Congress, in the twelfth amendment, to be, that it claims no powers which are not delegated to it. . . .

2d. We ask, then, in the second place, whether, upon any principle of fair construction, the specified powers of legislation involve the power of granting charters of incorporation? We say charters of incorporation, without confining the question to the bank; because the admission of it in that instance, is an admission of it in every other, in which Congress may think the use of it equally expedient. . . .

If the laying and collecting of taxes brings with it every thing which, in the opinion of Congress, may facilitate the payment of taxes; if to borrow money sets political speculation loose, to conceive which may create an ability to lend; if to regulate commerce is to range in the boundless mazes of projects for the apparently best scheme to invite from abroad, or to diffuse at home, the precious metals; if to dispose of, or to regulate, property of the United States, is to incorporate a bank, that stock may be subscribed to it by them, it may, without exaggeration, be affirmed, that a similar construction on every specified federal power, will stretch the arm of Congress into the whole circle of State legislation.

[3d.] The general qualities of the Federal Government, independent of the constitution and the specified powers, being thus insufficient to uphold the incorporation of a bank, we come to the last inquiry, which has been already anticipated, whether it be sanctified by the power to make all laws, which shall be necessary and proper for carrying into execution the powers vested by the constitution. To be necessary is to be incidental, or, in other words, may be denominated the natural means of executing a power.

The phrase "and Proper," if it has any meaning, does not enlarge the powers of Congress, but rather restricts them. For no power is to be assumed under the general clause, but such as is not only necessary, but proper, or perhaps expedient also. But as the friends to the bill ought not to claim any advantage from this clause, so ought not the enemies to it, to quote the clause as having a restrictive effect. Both ought to consider it as among the surplusage which as often proceeds from inattention as caution.

However, let it be propounded as an eternal question to those who build new powers on this clause, whether the latitude of construction, which they arrogate will not terminate in an unlimited power in Congress.

In every respect, therefore, under which the Attorney General can view the act, so far as it incorporates the bank, he is bound to declare his opinion to be against its constitutionality.

Thomas Jefferson, a Virginia lawyer who gained early fame as the author of the Declaration of Independence, was ambassador to France at the time of the Constitutional Convention. Therefore, unlike Madison, Randolph, and Hamilton, Jefferson did not participate in the deliberations, though he did carry on an active correspondence with Madison.

STUDY GUIDE

- Does the fact that Jefferson was not a member of the Constitutional Convention undermine the authoritativeness of his constitutional interpretation?
- How does Jefferson's interpretation of "necessary" compare to that of Madison and Randolph? If adopting one of three different means was essential to accomplishing an enumerated power or end, would any of them be deemed "necessary" under his conception? Would this entail that Congress could employ none of these means?
- Notice also his urging the President to afford acts of Congress some degree of deference. Would this deference depend on whether Congress itself had carefully considered the constitutional scope of its powers (as it did in fact do with respect to the bank)?

OPINION OF SECRETARY OF STATE THOMAS JEFFERSON, February 15, 1791. . . . I consider the foundation of the Constitution as laid on this ground: That "all powers not delegated to the United States, by the Constitution, nor prohibited by it to the States, are reserved to the States or to the people." To take a single step beyond the boundaries thus specially drawn around the powers of Congress, is to take possession of a boundless field of power, no longer susceptible of any definition.

The incorporation of a bank, and the powers assumed by this bill, have not, in my opinion, been delegated to the United States, by the Constitution. They are not among the powers specially enumerated. . . . Nor are they within either of the general phrases, which are the two following:

1. To lay taxes to provide for the general welfare of the United States, that is to say, "to lay taxes for the purpose of providing for the general welfare." For the laying of taxes is the power, and the general welfare the purpose for which the power is to be exercised. They are not to lay taxes ad libitum for any purpose they please; but only to pay the debts or provide for the welfare of the Union. In like manner, they are not to do anything they please to provide for the general welfare, but only to lay taxes for that purpose. To consider the latter phrase, not as describing the purpose

of the first, but as giving a distinct and independent power to do any act they please, which might be for the good of the Union, would render all the preceding and subsequent enumerations of power completely useless.

It would reduce the whole instrument to a single phrase, that of instituting a Congress with power to do whatever would be for the good of the United States; and, as they would be the sole judges of the good or evil, it would be also a power to do whatever evil they please.

It is an established rule of construction where a phrase will bear either of two meanings, to give it that which will allow some meaning to the other parts of the instrument, and not that which would render all the others useless. Certainly no such universal power was meant to be given them. It was intended to lace them up straitly within the enumerated powers, and those without which, as means, these powers could not be carried into effect. It is known that the very power now proposed as a means was rejected as an end by the Convention which formed the Constitution. A proposition was made to them to authorize Congress to open canals, and an amendatory one to empower them to incorporate. But the whole was rejected, and one of the reasons for rejection urged in debate was, that then they would have a power to erect a bank, which would render the great cities, where there were prejudices and jealousies on the subject, adverse to the reception of the Constitution.

2. The second general phrase is, "to make all laws necessary and proper for carrying into execution the enumerated powers." But they can all be carried into execution without a bank. A bank therefore is not necessary, and consequently not authorized by this phrase.

It has been urged that a bank will give great facility or convenience in the collection of taxes. Suppose this were true: yet the Constitution allows only the means which are "necessary," not those which are merely "convenient" for effecting the enumerated powers. If such a latitude of construction be allowed to this phrase as to give any non-enumerated power, it will go to everyone, for there is not one which ingenuity may not torture into a convenience in some instance or other, to some one of so long a list of enumerated powers. It would swallow up all the delegated powers, and reduce the whole to one power, as before observed. Therefore it was that the Constitution restrained them to the necessary means, that is to say, to those means without which the grant of power would be nugatory. . . .

The negative of the President is the shield provided by the Constitution to protect against the invasions of the legislature: 1. The right of the Executive. 2. Of the Judiciary. 3. Of the States and State legislatures. The present is the case of a right remaining exclusively with the States, and consequently one of those intended by the Constitution to be placed under its protection,

It must be added, however, that unless the President's mind on a view of everything which is urged for and against this bill, is tolerably clear that it is unauthorized by the Constitution; if the pro and the con hang so even as to balance his judgment, a just respect for the wisdom of the legislature would naturally decide the balance in favor of their opinion. It is chiefly for cases where they are clearly misled by error, ambition, or interest, that the Constitution has placed a check in the negative of the President.

As we saw earlier, Hamilton had proposed to the Constitutional Convention a more British-style government in which there would be no enumerated limits on congressional power. Nevertheless, in his contributions to *The Federalist* papers, he insisted that the powers of Congress were limited.

STUDY GUIDE

- How does Hamilton's interpretation of the Necessary and Proper Clause differ from Madison's? Does Hamilton see any enforceable limits on this power?
- Notice the degree to which Hamilton's argument depends on a particular background assumption about "sovereignty." The debate over this assumption, which continues to the present day, was taken up in 1793 by the Supreme Court in its first major constitutional case: *Chisholm v. Georgia*. The decision in *Chisholm* was then reversed by the adoption of the Eleventh Amendment.
- In his opinion, Hamilton also makes some interesting observations about the scope of the Commerce Clause.

OPINION OF SECRETARY OF THE TREASURY ALEXANDER HAMILTON, February 23, 1791. Now it appears to the Secretary of the Treasury, that this *general principle* is *inherent* in the very *definition* of *Government* and *essential* to every step of progress to be made by that of the United States, namely— that every power vested in a Government is in its nature *sovereign*, and includes, by *force* of the *term,* a right to employ all the *means* requisite and fairly *applicable* to the attainment of the *ends* of such power; and which are not precluded by restrictions & exceptions specified in the constitution; or not immoral, or not contrary to the essential ends of political society.

This principle in its application to Government in general would be admitted as an axiom. And it will be incumbent upon those who may incline to deny it, to *prove* a distinction; and to shew that a rule which in the general system of things is essential to the preservation of the social order is inapplicable to the United States.

The circumstance that the powers of sovereignty are in this country divided between the National and State governments, does not afford the distinction required. It does not follow from this, that each of the *portion* of powers delegated to the one or to the other is not sovereign *with regard to its proper objects*. It will only *follow* from it, that each has sovereign power as to certain *things*, and not as to *other things*. To deny that the government of the United States has sovereign power, as to its declared purposes & trusts, because its power does not extend to all cases, would be equally to deny, that the State Governments have sovereign power in any case, because their power does not extend to every case. The tenth section of the first article of the constitution exhibits a long list of very important things which they may not do. And thus the United States would furnish the singular spectacle of a *political society* without *sovereignty*, or of a people *governed* without *government*.

If it would be necessary to bring proof to a proposition so clear, as that which affirms that the powers of the federal government, *as to its objects*, are sovereign, there is a clause of its constitution which would be decisive. It is that which declares, that the constitution and the laws of the United States made in pursuance of it, and all treaties made or which shall be made under their authority shall be the supreme law of the land. The power which can create the *Supreme law* of the land, in any case, is doubtless sovereign *as to such case*.

This general & indisputable principle puts at once an end to the *abstract* question — Whether the United States have power to *erect a corporation*? that is to say, to give a *legal* or *artificial capacity* to one or more persons, distinct from the natural. For it is unquestionably incident to *sovereign* power to erect corporations, and consequently to *that* of the United States, in *relation to the objects* intrusted to the management of the government. The difference is this — where the authority of the government is general, it can create corporations in *all cases*; where it is confined to certain branches of legislation, it can create corporations only in those cases. . . .

To return — It is conceded that implied powers are to be considered as delegated equally with express ones.

Then it follows, that as a power of erecting a corporation may as well be *implied* as any other thing; it may as well be employed as an *instrument* or *mean* of carrying into execution any of the specified powers, as any other instrument or mean whatever. The only question must be, in this as in every other case, whether the mean to be employed, or in this instance the corporation to be erected, has a natural relation to any of the acknowledged objects or lawful ends of the government. Thus a corporation may not be erected by congress for superintending the police of the city of Philadelphia because they are not authorized to *regulate* the *police* of that city; but one may be erected in relation to the collection of taxes, or to the trade with foreign countries, or to the trade between the States, or with the Indian tribes; because it is the province of the federal government to regulate those objects & because it is incident to a general *sovereign* or *legislative power* to *regulate* a thing, to employ all the means which relate to its regulation to the *best & greatest advantage*. . . .

To this mode of reasoning respecting the right of employing all the means requisite to the execution of the specified powers of the Government, it is objected that none but *necessary* & proper means are to be employed; & the Secretary of State maintains, that no means are to be considered as *necessary*, but those without which the grant of the power would be *nugatory*. Nay so far does he go in his restrictive interpretation of the word, as even to make the case of *necessity* which shall warrant the constitutional exercise of the power to depend on *casual* & *temporary* circumstances, an idea which alone refutes the construction. The *expediency* of exercising a particular power, at a particular time, must indeed depend on *circumstances*; but the constitutional right of exercising it must be uniform & invariable, the same today as tomorrow.

All the arguments, therefore, against the constitutionality of the bill derived from the accidental existence of certain State banks: institutions which *happen* to exist today, & for ought that concerns the government of the United States, may disappear tomorrow, must not only be rejected as fallacious, but must be viewed as demonstrative, that there is a *radical* source of error in the reasoning.

It is essential to the being of the National government, that so erroneous a conception of the meaning of the word *necessary* should be exploded.

It is certain, that neither the grammatical, nor popular sense of the term requires that construction. According to both, *necessary* often means no more than *needful, requisite, incidental, useful,* or *conducive to.* It is a common mode of expression to say, that it is *necessary* for a government or a person to do this or that thing, when nothing more is intended or understood, than that the interests of the government or person require, or will be promoted by, the doing of this or that thing. The imagination can be at no loss for exemplifications of the use of the word in this sense.

And it is the true one in which it is to be understood as used in the constitution. The whole turn of the clause containing it, indicates, that it was the intent of the convention, by that clause to give a liberal latitude to the exercise of the specified powers.... To understand the word as the Secretary of State does, would be to depart from its obvious & popular sense, and to give it a *restrictive* operation; an idea never before entertained. It would be to give it the same force as if the word *absolutely* or *indispensably* had been prefixed to it.

Such a construction would beget endless uncertainty & embarrassment. The cases must be palpable & extreme in which it could be pronounced with certainty, that a measure was absolutely necessary, or one without which the exercise of a given power would be nugatory. There are few measures of any government, which would stand so severe a test. To insist upon it, would be to make the criterion of the exercise of any implied power a *case of extreme necessity*; which is rather a rule to justify the overleaping of the bounds of constitutional authority, than to govern the ordinary exercise of it....

The degree in which a measure is necessary, can never be a test of the *legal* right to adopt it — That must be a matter of opinion; and can only be a test of expediency. The *relation* between the *measure* and the *end*, between the *nature* of *the mean* employed toward the execution of a power and the object of that power, must be the criterion of constitutionality, not the more or less of *necessity* or *utility*....

This restrictive interpretation of the word *necessary* is also contrary to this sound maxim of construction namely, that the powers contained in a constitution of government, especially those which concern the general administration of the affairs of a country, its finances, trade, defense &c. ought to be construed liberally, in advancement of the public good. This rule does not depend on the particular form of a government or on the particular demarcation of the boundaries of its powers, but on the nature and object of government itself. The means by which national exigencies are to be provided for, national inconveniences obviated, national prosperity promoted, are of such infinite variety, extent & complexity, that there must, of necessity, be great latitude of discretion in the selection & application of those means. Hence consequently, the necessity & propriety of exercising the authorities intrusted to a government on principles of liberal construction....

But while, on the one hand, the construction of the Secretary of State is deemed inadmissible, it will not be contended on the other, that the clause in question gives any *new* or *independent* power. . . .

It is no valid objection to the doctrine to say, that it is calculated to extend the power of the government throughout the entire sphere of State legislation. The same thing has been said, and may be said, with regard to every exercise of power by *implication* or *construction.* The moment the literal meaning is departed from, there is a chance of error and abuse. And yet an adherence to the letter of its powers would at once arrest the motions of government. . . .

The truth is, that difficulties on this point are inherent in the nature of the federal constitution. They result inevitably from a division of the legislative power. The consequence of this division is, that there will be cases clearly within the power of the National Government; others clearly without its powers; and a third class, which will leave room for controversy & difference of opinion, & concerning which a reasonable latitude of judgment must be allowed.

But the doctrine which is contended for . . . does not affirm that the National government is sovereign in all respects, but that it is sovereign to a certain extent: that is, to the extent of the objects of its specified powers. It leaves therefore a criterion of what is constitutional, and of what is not so. This criterion is the *end* to which the measure relates as a *mean.* If the end be clearly comprehended within any of the specified powers, & if the measure have an obvious relation to that end, and is not forbidden by any particular provision of the constitution it may safely be deemed to come within the compass of the national authority. . . .

To establish such a right, it remains to shew the relation of such an institution to one or more of the specified powers of the government. Accordingly it is affirmed, that it has a relation more or less direct to the power of *collecting taxes*; to that of borrowing money, to that of regulating trade between the states, and to those of raising, and maintaining fleets & armies. . . .

The institution of a bank has also a natural relation to the regulation of trade between the States: insofar as it is conducive to the creation of a convenient medium of *exchange* between them, and to the keeping up a full circulation by preventing the frequent displacement of the metals in reciprocal remittances. Money is the very hinge on which commerce turns. And this does not merely mean gold & silver; many other things have served the purpose with different degrees of utility. Paper has been extensively employed. . . .

[T]he Secretary of the Treasury, with all deference conceives . . . that all the special powers of government are sovereign as to the proper objects; that the incorporation of a bank is a constitutional measure, and that the objections taken to the bill, in this respect, are ill founded. . . .

Ultimately, the view of the Secretary of the Treasury prevailed in the courts. In 1819, Chief Justice Marshall largely echoed Hamilton's reasoning in upholding the constitutionality of the second national bank in the case of *McCulloch v. Maryland*, which we will read in Chapter 2.

ASSIGNMENT 4

D. POPULAR SOVEREIGNTY VS. STATE SOVEREIGNTY

The constitutional controversy over the national bank concerned the proper scope of *federal* power. But the first major constitutional controversy to be decided by the Supreme Court was over the constitutional limits on *state* power — in particular, whether the Constitution permitted a state to be sued by a citizen of another state in federal court. Here is the relevant text of the Constitution, from Article III, Section 2 (emphasis added):

> Section 2. *The judicial power shall extend* to all cases, in law and equity, arising under this Constitution, the laws of the United States, and treaties made, or which shall be made, under their authority; — to all cases affecting ambassadors, other public ministers and consuls; — to all cases of admiralty and maritime jurisdiction; — *to controversies* to which the United States shall be a party; — to controversies between two or more states; — *between a state and citizens of another state*; — between citizens of different states; — between citizens of the same state claiming lands under grants of different states, and between a state, or the citizens thereof, and foreign states, citizens or subjects.

Because Georgia objected to being a defendant in such a lawsuit on grounds of its "sovereignty," this case involved "first principles" that have been debated ever since. We will return repeatedly to these principles in the chapters that follow, especially in Chapter 4 where the modern Eleventh Amendment cases are discussed.

STUDY GUIDE

- Notice the sharp disagreement on the issue of "sovereignty" between Justice Iredell and rest of the Court, particularly Justice Wilson. We are so accustomed to thinking of sovereignty residing in the states or in the national government that it is hard to grasp why someone of Wilson's stature and intellectual sophistication would resist this idea. Pay close attention to his reasons for doing so and where he thinks sovereignty resides. Do you see a different conception of "popular sovereignty" in Wilson's opinion than we are accustomed to today?
- Observe Wilson's repeated reliance on "general principles of right" and his only secondary reliance on the text of the Constitution. Contrast his approach with that of Justice Blair. Notice also his reliance on the agency theory of government.
- Notice Justice Iredell's assumption of the Court's duty to "void" unconstitutional legislation well before the decision in *Marbury v. Madison*. Also notice his reliance on a "clear statement" rule.
- Of what relevance is foreign law, according to Justice Blair?
- Chief Justice John Jay (speaking last) was the third coauthor of *The Federalist* papers (though his role in that project was minor). What difference does he see between sovereignty in Europe and in the United States?

Chisholm v. Georgia

2 U.S. (2 Dall.) 419 (1793)

[In 1777, during the Revolutionary War, the Executive Council of Georgia authorized the purchase of clothing from a South Carolina businessman. After receiving the supplies, Georgia did not deliver payments as promised. After the merchant's death, the executor of his estate, Alexander Chisholm, represented by Attorney General Edmund Randolph, took the case to the Supreme Court in an attempt to collect from the state. Georgia refused to appear, claiming immunity from the suit as a sovereign and independent state. Before the practice was later discouraged by Chief Justice John Marshall, opinions of the Supreme Court were delivered separately or "seriatim" from the bench. So the first opinion that follows, delivered by Justice Iredell, was actually the lone dissent in a 4-1 decision of the Court on behalf of Chisholm and against Georgia. — Eds.]

Mr. Justice Iredell.

A general question of great importance here occurs. What controversy of a civil nature can be maintained against a State by an individual? . . . This appears to me to be one of those cases, with many others, in which an article of the Constitution cannot be effectuated without the intervention of the Legislative authority. . . . Upon this authority, there is, that I know, but one limit; that is, "that they shall not exceed their authority." If they do, I have no hesitation to say, that any act to that effect would be utterly void, because it would be inconsistent with the Constitution, which is a fundamental law paramount to all others, which we are not only bound to consult, but sworn to observe; and, therefore, where there is an interference, being superior in obligation to the other, we must unquestionably obey that in preference.

Subject to this restriction, the whole business of organizing the Courts, and directing the methods of their proceeding where necessary, I conceive to be in the discretion of Congress. . . . There is no part of the Constitution that I know of, that authorises this Court to take up any business where they left it, and, in order that the powers given in the Constitution may be in full activity, supply their omission by making new laws for new cases; or, which I take to be the same thing, applying old principles to new cases materially different from those to which they were applied before. . . .

If therefore, . . . we must receive our directions from the Legislature in this particular, and have no right to . . . take any other short method of doing what the Constitution has chosen (and, in my opinion, with the most perfect propriety) should be done in another manner. . . .

I believe there is no doubt that neither in the State now in question, nor in any other in the Union, any particular Legislative mode, authorizing a compulsory suit for the recovery of money against a State, was in being either when the Constitution was adopted, or at the time the judicial act was passed. . . .

Every State in the Union in every instance where its sovereignty has not been delegated to the United States, I consider to be as completely sovereign, as the United States are in respect to the powers surrendered. The United States are sovereign as to all the powers of Government actually surrendered: Each State in the Union is sovereign as to all the powers reserved. It must necessarily be so, because the United States have no claim to any authority but such as the States have surrendered to them: Of course the part not surrendered must remain as it did before. . . .

Now let us consider the case of a debt due from a State. . . . Every man must know that no suit can lie against a Legislative body. His only dependence therefore can be, that the Legislature on principles of public duty, will make a provision for the execution of their own contracts, and if that fails, whatever reproach the Legislature may incur, the case is certainly without remedy in any of the Courts of the State. It never was pretended, even in the case of the crown in England, that if any contract was made with Parliament, or with the crown by virtue of an authority from Parliament, that a Petition to the crown would in such case lie. . . .

I have now, I think, established the following particulars. 1st. That the Constitution, so far as it respects the judicial authority, can only be carried into effect by acts of the Legislature appointing Courts, and prescribing their methods of proceeding. 2nd. That Congress has provided no new law in regard to this case, but expressly referred us to the old. 3rd. That there are no principles of the old law, to which, we must have recourse, that in any manner authorise the present suit, either by precedent or by analogy. The consequence of which, in my opinion, clearly is, that the suit in question cannot be maintained, nor, of course, the motion made upon it be complied with. . . .

Mr. Justice Blair.

In considering this important case, I have thought it best to pass over all the strictures which have been made on the various European confederations; because, as, on the one hand, their likeness to our own is not sufficiently close to justify any analogical application; so, on the other, they are utterly destitute of any binding authority here. The Constitution of the United States is the only fountain from which I shall draw; the only authority to which I shall appeal. Whatever be the true language of that, it is obligatory upon every member of the Union; for, no State could have become a member, but by an adoption of it by the people of that State. What then do we find there requiring the submission of individual States to the judicial authority of the United States? This is expressly extended, among other things, to controversies between a State and citizens of another State. Is then the case before us one of that description? Undoubtedly it is. . . . It seems to me, that if this Court should refuse to hold jurisdiction of a case where a State is Defendant, it would renounce part of the authority conferred, and, consequently, part of the duty imposed on it by the Constitution; because it would be a refusal to take cognizance of a case where a State is a party. Nor does the jurisdiction of this Court, in relation to a State, seem to me to be questionable, on the ground that Congress has not provided any form of execution, or pointed out any mode of making the judgment against a State effectual. . . .

MR. JUSTICE WILSON.

This is a case of uncommon magnitude. One of the parties to it is a State; certainly respectable, claiming to be sovereign. The question to be determined is, whether this State, so respectable, and whose claim soars so high, is amenable to the jurisdiction of the Supreme Court of the United States? This question, important in itself, will depend on others, more important still; and, may, perhaps, be ultimately resolved into one, no less radical than this "do the people of the United States form a Nation?" . . .

To the Constitution of the United States the term SOVEREIGN, is totally unknown. There is but one place where it could have been used with propriety. But, even in that place it would not, perhaps, have comported with the delicacy of those, who ordained and established that Constitution. They might have announced themselves "SOVEREIGN" people of the United States: But serenely conscious of the fact, they avoided the ostentatious declaration.

Having thus avowed my disapprobation of the purposes, for which the terms, State and sovereign, are frequently used, and of the object, to which the application of the last of them is almost universally made; it is now proper that I should disclose the meaning, which I assign to both, and the application, which I make of the latter. In doing this, I shall have occasion incidently to evince, how true it is, that States and Governments were made for man; and, at the same time, how true it is, that his creatures and servants have first deceived, next vilified, and, at last, oppressed their master and maker. . . .

As the State has claimed precedence of the people; so, in the same inverted course of things, the Government has often claimed precedence of the State; and to this perversion in the second degree, many of the volumes of confusion concerning sovereignty owe their existence. The ministers, dignified very properly by the appellation of the magistrates, have wished, and have succeeded in their wish, to be considered as the sovereigns of the State. This second degree of perversion is confined to the old world, and begins to diminish, even there: but the first degree is still too prevalent, even in the several States, of which our union is composed.

By a State I mean, a complete body of free persons united together for their common benefit, to enjoy peaceably what is their own, and to do justice to others. It is an artificial person. It has its affairs and its interests: It has its rules: It has its rights: And it has its obligations. It may acquire property distinct from that of its members: It may incur debts to be discharged out of the public stock, not out of the private fortunes of individuals. It may be bound by contracts; and for damages arising from the breach of those contracts. In all our contemplations, however, concerning this feigned and artificial person, we should never forget, that, in truth and nature, those, who think and speak, and act, are men. . . .

Is there any part of this description, which intimates, in the remotest manner, that a State, any more than the men who compose it, ought not to do justice and fulfil engagements? It will not be pretended that there is. If justice is not done; if engagements are not fulfilled; is it upon general principles of right, less proper, in the case of a great number, than in the case of an individual, to secure, by compulsion, that, which will not be voluntarily performed? Less proper it surely cannot be.

The only reason, I believe, why a free man is bound by human laws, is, that he binds himself. Upon the same principles, upon which he becomes bound by the laws, he becomes amenable to the Courts of Justice, which are formed and authorised by those laws. If one free man, an original sovereign, may do all this; why may not an aggregate of free men, a collection of original sovereigns, do this likewise? If the dignity of each singly is undiminished; the dignity of all jointly must be unimpaired. A State, like a merchant, makes a contract. A dishonest State, like a dishonest merchant, wilfully refuses to discharge it: The latter is amenable to a Court of Justice: Upon general principles of right, shall the former when summoned to answer the fair demands of its creditor, be permitted, proteus-like, to assume a new appearance, and to insult him and justice, by declaring I am a Sovereign State? Surely not. Before a claim, so contrary, in its first appearance, to the general principles of right and equality, be sustained by a just and impartial tribunal, the person, natural or artificial, entitled to make such claim, should certainly be well known and authenticated.

Who, or what, is a sovereignty? What is his or its sovereignty? . . . In one sense, the term sovereign has for its correlative, subject. In this sense, the term can receive no application; for it has no object in the Constitution of the United States. Under that Constitution there are citizens, but no subjects. "Citizen of the United States." "Citizens of another State." "Citizens of different States." "A State or citizen thereof." The term, subject, occurs, indeed, once in the instrument; but to mark the contrast strongly, the epithet "foreign"[41] is prefixed. In this sense, I presume the State of Georgia has no claim upon her own citizens: In this sense, I am certain, she can have no claim upon the citizens of another State.

In another sense, according to some writers,[42] every State, which governs itself without any dependence on another power, is a sovereign State. Whether, with regard to her own citizens, this is the case of the State of Georgia; whether those citizens have done, as the individuals of England are said, by their late instructors, to have done, surrendered the Supreme Power to the State or Government, and reserved nothing to themselves; or whether, like the people of other States, and of the United States, the citizens of Georgia have reserved the Supreme Power in their own hands; and on that Supreme Power have made the State dependent, instead of being sovereign; these are questions, to which, as a Judge in this cause, I can neither know nor suggest the proper answers; though, as a citizen of the Union, I know, and am interested to know, that the most satisfactory answers can be given.

As a citizen, I know the Government of that State to be republican; and my short definition of such a Government is, one constructed on this principle, that the Supreme Power resides in the body of the people. As a Judge of this Court, I know, and can decide upon the knowledge, that the citizens of Georgia, when they acted upon the large scale of the Union, as a part of the "People of the United States," did

---

[41] Art. 3. §3.

[42] [Vattel] B. 1. c. s. 4.

not surrender the Supreme or Sovereign Power to that State; but, as to the purposes of the Union, retained it to themselves. As to the purposes of the Union, therefore, Georgia is NOT a sovereign State. . . .

There is a third sense, in which the term sovereign is frequently used, and which . . . furnishes a basis for what I presume to be one of the principal objections against the jurisdiction of this Court over the State of Georgia. In this sense, sovereignty is derived from a feudal source; and like many other parts of that system so degrading to man, still retains its influence over our sentiments and conduct, though the cause, by which that influence was produced, never extended to the American States. . . .

Into England this system was introduced by the conqueror: and to this era we may, probably, refer the English maxim, that the King or sovereign is the fountain of Justice. But, in the case of the King, the sovereignty had a double operation. While it vested him with jurisdiction over others, it excluded all others from jurisdiction over him. With regard to him, there was no superior power; and, consequently, on feudal principles, no right of jurisdiction. "The law," says Sir William Blackstone, "ascribes to the King the attribute of sovereignty: he is sovereign and independent within his own dominions; and owes no kind of objection to any other potentate upon earth. Hence it is, that no suit or action can be brought against the King, even in civil matters; because no Court can have jurisdiction over him: for all jurisdiction implies superiority of power."

This last position is only a branch of a much more extensive principle, on which a plan of systematic despotism has been lately formed in England, and prosecuted with unwearied assiduity and care. Of this plan the author of the Commentaries was, if not the introducer, at least the great supporter. He has been followed in it by writers later and less known; and his doctrines have, both on the other and this side of the Atlantic, been implicitly and generally received by those, who neither examined their principles nor their consequences, The principle is, that all human law must be prescribed by a superior. This principle I mean not now to examine. Suffice it, at present to say, that another principle, very different in its nature and operations, forms, in my judgment, the basis of sound and genuine jurisprudence; laws derived from the pure source of equality and justice must be founded on the CONSENT of those, whose obedience they require. The sovereign, when traced to his source, must be found in the man. . . .

With the strictest propriety, therefore, classical and political, our national scene opens with the most magnificent object, which the nation could present. "The PEOPLE of the United States" are the first personages introduced. Who were those people? They were the citizens of thirteen States, each of which had a separate Constitution and Government, and all of which were connected together by articles of confederation. To the purposes of public strength and felicity, that confederacy was totally inadequate. A requisition on the several States terminated its Legislative authority: Executive or Judicial authority it had none. In order, therefore, to form a more perfect union, to establish justice, to ensure domestic tranquillity, to provide for common defence, and to secure the blessings of liberty, those people, among whom were the people of Georgia, ordained and established the present Constitution. By that Constitution Legislative power is vested, Executive power is vested, Judicial power is vested.

The question now opens fairly to our view, could the people of those States, among whom were those of Georgia, bind those States, and Georgia among the others, by the Legislative, Executive, and Judicial power so vested? If the principles, on which I have founded myself, are just and true; this question must unavoidably receive an affirmative answer. If those States were the work of those people; those people . . . could alter, as they pleased, their former work: To any given degree, they could diminish as well as enlarge it. Any or all of the former State-powers, they could extinguish or transfer. The inference, which necessarily results, is, that the Constitution ordained and established by those people; and, . . . in particular by the people of Georgia, could vest jurisdiction or judicial power over those States and over the State of Georgia in particular.

The next question under this head, is, Has the Constitution done so? . . . Did those people intend to bind those states by the Legislative power vested by that Constitution? . . . Whoever considers, in a combined and comprehensive view, the general texture of the Constitution, will be satisfied, that the people of the United States intended to form themselves into a nation for national purposes. They instituted, for such purposes, a national Government, complete in all its parts, with powers Legislative, Executive and Judiciary; and, in all those powers, extending over the whole nation.

Is it congruous, that, with regard to such purposes, any man or body of men, any person natural or artificial, should be permitted to claim successfully an entire exemption from the jurisdiction of the national Government? Would not such claims, crowned with success, be repugnant to our very existence as a nation? When so many trains of deduction, coming from different quarters, converge and unite, at last, in the same point; we may safely conclude, as the legitimate result of this Constitution, that the State of Georgia is amenable to the jurisdiction of this Court.

But, in my opinion, this doctrine rests not upon the legitimate result of fair and conclusive deduction from the Constitution: It is confirmed, beyond all doubt, by the direct and explicit declaration of the Constitution itself. . . . "The judicial power of the United States shall extend to controversies, between a state and citizens of another State." Could . . . this strict and appropriate language, describe, with more precise accuracy, the cause now depending before the tribunal? . . .

I have now tried this question by all the touchstones, to which I proposed to apply it. I have examined it by the principles of general jurisprudence; by the laws and practice of States and Kingdoms; and by the Constitution of the United States. From all, the combined inference is; that the action lies.

Mr. Justice Cushing.

The grand and principal question in this case is, whether a State can, by the Federal Constitution, be sued by an individual citizen of another State? The point turns not upon the law or practice of England, although perhaps it may be in some measure elucidated thereby, nor upon the law of any other country whatever; but upon the Constitution established by the people of the United States; and particularly upon the extent of powers given to the Federal Judicial in the second section of the third article of the Constitution. . . . The judicial power . . . is expressly extended to "controversies between a State and citizens of another State." When a citizen makes a demand against a State, of which he is not a citizen, it is as really a controversy between a State and a citizen of another State, as if such State made a demand against such citizen. The case, then, seems clearly to fall within the letter of the Constitution. It may be suggested that it could not be intended to subject a State to be a Defendant, because it would effect the sovereignty of States. If that be the case, what shall we do with the immediate preceding clause; "controversies between two or more States," where a State must of necessity be Defendant? If it was not the intent, in the very next clause also, that a State might be made Defendant, why was it so expressed as naturally to lead to and comprehend that idea? Why was not an exception made if one was intended?

Again what are we to do with the last clause of the section of judicial powers, viz. "Controversies between a state, or the citizens thereof, and foreign states or citizens?" Here again, States must be suable or liable to be made Defendants by this clause, which has a similar mode of language with the two other clauses I have remarked upon. For if the judicial power extends to a controversy between one of the United States and a foreign State, as the clause expresses, one of them must be Defendant. And then, what becomes of the sovereignty of States as far as suing affects it? . . . Further; if a State is entitled to Justice in the Federal Court, against a citizen of another State, why not such citizen against the State, when the same language equally comprehends both? The rights of individuals and the justice due to them, are as dear and precious as those of States. Indeed the latter are founded upon the former; and the great end and object of them must be to secure and support the rights of individuals, or else vain is Government. . . .

As to individual States and the United States, the Constitution marks the boundary of powers. Whatever power is deposited with the Union by the people for their own necessary security, is so far a curtailing of the power and prerogatives of States. This is, as it were, a self-evident proposition; at least it cannot be contested. . . . So that, I think, no argument of force can be taken from the sovereignty of States. Where it has been abridged, it was thought necessary for the greater indispensable good of the whole. If the Constitution is found inconvenient in practice in this or any other particular, it is well that a regular mode is pointed out for amendment. But, while it remains, all offices Legislative, Executive, and Judicial, both of the States and of the Union, are bound by oath to support it. . . .

Mr. Chief Justice Jay.

The question we are now to decide has been accurately stated, viz. Is a State suable by individual citizens of another State?

It is said, that Georgia refuses to appear and answer to the Plaintiff in this action, because she is a sovereign State, and therefore not liable to such actions. In order to ascertain the merits of this objection, let us enquire, 1st. In what sense Georgia is a sovereign State. 2nd. Whether suability is incompatable with such sovereignty. 3rd. Whether the Constitution (to which Georgia is a party) authorises such an action against her. Suability and suable are words not in common use, but they concisely and correctly convey the idea annexed to them.

1st. In determining the sense in which Georgia is a sovereign State, it may be useful to turn our attention to the political situation we were in, prior to the

Revolution, and to the political rights which emerged from the Revolution. All the country now possessed by the United States was then a part of the dominions appertaining to the crown of Great Britain. Every acre of land in this country was then held mediately or immediately by grants from that crown. All the people of this country were then, subjects of the King of Great Britain, and owed allegiance to him; and all the civil authority then existing or exercised here, flowed from the head of the British Empire. They were in strict sense fellow subjects, and in a variety of respects one people. . . .

The Revolution, or rather the Declaration of Independence, found the people already united for general purposes, and at the same time providing for their more domestic concerns by State conventions, and other temporary arrangements. . . . [T]hirteen sovereignties were considered as emerged from the principles of the Revolution, combined with local convenience and considerations; the people nevertheless continued to consider themselves, in a national point of view, as one people; and they continued without interruption to manage their national concerns accordingly; afterwards, in the hurry of the war, and in the warmth of mutual confidence, they made a confederation of the States, the basis of a general Government.

Experience disappointed the expectations they had formed from it; and then the people, in their collective and national capacity, established the present Constitution. It is remarkable that in establishing it, the people exercised their own rights, and their own proper sovereignty, and conscious of the plenitude of it, they declared with becoming dignity, "We the people of the United States, do ordain and establish this Constitution." Here we see the people acting as sovereigns of the whole country; and in the language of sovereignty, establishing a Constitution by which it was their will, that the State Governments should be bound, and to which the State Constitutions should be made to conform. Every State Constitution is a compact made by and between the citizens of a State to govern themselves in a certain manner; and the Constitution of the United States is likewise a compact made by the people of the United States to govern themselves as to general objects, in a certain manner. By this great compact however, many prerogatives were transferred to the national Government, such as those of making war and peace, contracting alliances, coining money, etc. etc.

If then it be true, that the sovereignty of the nation is in the people of the nation, and the residuary sovereignty of each State in the people of each State, it may be useful to compare these sovereignties with those in Europe, that we may thence be enabled to judge, whether all the prerogatives which are allowed to the latter, are so essential to the former. There is reason to suspect that some of the difficulties which embarrass the present question, arise from inattention to differences which subsist between them.

It will be sufficient to observe briefly, that the sovereignties in Europe, and particularly in England, exist on feudal principles. That system considers the Prince as the sovereign, and the people as his subjects; it regards his person as the object of allegiance, and excludes the idea of his being on an equal footing with a subject, either in a Court of Justice or elsewhere. That system contemplates him as being the fountain of honor and authority; and from his grace and grant derives all franchises, immunities and privileges; it is easy to perceive that such a sovereign could not be amenable to a Court of Justice, or subjected to judicial controul and actual constraint. It was of necessity, therefore, that suability became incompatible with such sovereignty. Besides, the Prince having all the Executive powers, the judgment of the Courts would, in fact, be only monitory, not mandatory to him, and a capacity to be advised, is a distinct thing from a capacity to be sued.

The same feudal ideas run through all their jurisprudence, and constantly remind us of the distinction between the Prince and the subject. No such ideas obtain here; at the Revolution, the sovereignty devolved on the people; and they are truly the sovereigns of the country, but they are sovereigns without subjects (unless the African slaves among us may be so called) and have none to govern but themselves; the citizens of America are equal as fellow citizens, and as joint tenants in the sovereignty.

From the differences existing between feudal sovereignties and Governments founded on compacts, it necessarily follows that their respective prerogatives must differ. Sovereignty is the right to govern; a nation or State-sovereign is the person or persons in whom that resides. In Europe the sovereignty is generally ascribed to the Prince; here it rests with the people; there, the sovereign actually administers the Government; here, never in a single instance; our Governors are the agents of the people, and at most stand in the same relation to their sovereign, in which regents in Europe stand to their sovereigns. Their Princes have personal powers, dignities, and pre-eminences, our rulers have none but official; nor do they partake in the sovereignty otherwise, or in any other capacity, than as private citizens.

2nd. The second object of enquiry [is] whether suability is compatible with State sovereignty.

Suability, by whom? Not a subject, for in this country there are none; not an inferior, for all the citizens being as to civil rights perfectly equal, there is not, in that respect, one citizen inferior to another. It is agreed, that one free citizen may sue another; the obvious dictates of justice, and the purposes of society demanding it. It is agreed, that one free citizen may sue any number on whom process can be conveniently executed; nay, in certain cases one citizen may sue forty thousand; for where a corporation is sued, all the members of it are actually sued, though not personally, sued. In this city there are forty odd thousand free citizens, all of whom may be collectively sued by any individual citizen. In the State of Delaware, there are fifty odd thousand free citizens, and what reason can be assigned why a free citizen who has demands against them should not prosecute them?

Can the difference between forty odd thousand, and fifty odd thousand make any distinction as to right? Is it not as easy, and as convenient to the public and parties, to serve a summons on the Governor and Attorney General of Delaware, as on the Mayor or other Officers of the Corporation of Philadelphia? Will it be said, that the fifty odd thousand citizens in Delaware being associated under a State Government, stand in a rank so superior to the forty odd thousand of Philadelphia, associated under their charter, that although it may become the latter to meet an individual on an equal footing in a Court of Justice, yet that such a procedure would not comport with the dignity of the former? In this land of equal liberty, shall forty odd thousand in one place be compellable to do justice, and yet fifty odd thousand in another place be privileged to do justice only as they may think proper? Such objections would not correspond with the equal rights we claim; with the equality we profess to admire and maintain, and with that popular sovereignty in which every citizen partakes. Grant that the Governor of Delaware holds an office of superior rank to the Mayor of Philadelphia, they are both nevertheless the officers of the people; and however more exalted the one may be than the other, yet in the opinion of those who dislike aristocracy, that circumstance cannot be a good reason for impeding the course of justice. . . .

As one State may sue another State in this Court, it is plain that no degradation to a State is thought to accompany her appearance in this Court. It is not therefore to an appearance in this Court that the objection points. To what does it point? It points to an appearance at the suit of one or more citizens. But why it should be more incompatible, that all the people of a State should be sued by one citizen, than by one hundred thousand, I cannot perceive, the process in both cases being alike; and the consequences of a judgment alike. Nor can I observe any greater inconveniencies in the one case than in the other, except what may arise from the feelings of those who may regard a lesser number in an inferior light. But if any reliance be made on this inferiority as an objection, at least one half of its force is done away by this fact, viz. that it is conceded that a State may appear in this Court as Plaintiff against a single citizen as Defendant; and the truth is, that the State of Georgia is at this moment prosecuting an action in this Court against two citizens of South Carolina.[43]

The only remnant of objection therefore that remains is, that the State is not bound to appear and answer as a Defendant at the suit of an individual: but why it is unreasonable that she should be so bound, is hard to conjecture: That rule is said to be a bad one, which does not work both ways; the citizens of Georgia are content with a right of suing citizens of other States; but are not content that citizens of other States should have a right to sue them. . . .

Let us now turn to the Constitution. . . . If the Constitution really meant to extend these powers only to those controversies in which a State might be Plaintiff, to the exclusion of those in which citizens had demands against a State, it is inconceivable that it should have attempted to convey that meaning in words, not only so incompetent, but also repugnant to it; if it meant to exclude a certain class of these controversies, why were they not expressly excepted; on the contrary, not even an intimation of such intention appears in any part of the Constitution.

It cannot be pretended that where citizens urge and insist upon demands against a State, which the State refuses to admit and comply with, that there is no controversy between them. If it is a controversy between them, then it clearly falls not only within the spirit, but the very words of the Constitution. What is it to the cause of justice, and how can it effect the definition of the word controversy,

[43] Georgia v. Brailsford, et al. Ant. 1.

whether the demands which cause the dispute, are made by a State against citizens of another State, or by the latter against the former? When power is thus extended to a controversy, it necessarily, as to all judicial purposes, is also extended to those, between whom it subsists.

The exception contended for, would contradict and do violence to the great and leading principles of a free and equal national government, one of the great objects of which is, to ensure justice to all: To the few against the many, as well as to the many against the few. It would be strange, indeed, that the joint and equal sovereigns of this country, should, in the very Constitution by which they professed to establish justice, so far deviate from the plain path of equality and impartiality, as to give to the collective citizens of one State, a right of suing individual citizens of another State, and yet deny to those citizens a right of suing them. . . .

I am convinced that the sense in which I understand and have explained the words "controversies between States and citizens of another State," is the true sense. The extension of the judiciary power of the United States to such controversies, appears to me to be wise, because it is honest, and because it is useful. It is honest, because it provides for doing justice without respect of persons, and by securing individual citizens as well as States, in their respective rights, performs the promise which every free Government makes to every free citizen, of equal justice and protection. It is useful, because it is honest, because it leaves not even the most obscure and friendless citizen without means of obtaining justice from a neighbouring State; because it obviates occasions of quarrels between States on account of the claims of their respective citizens; because it recognizes and strongly rests on this great moral truth, that justice is the same whether due from one man or a million, or from a million to one man; because it teaches and greatly appreciates the value of our free republican national Government, which places all our citizens on an equal footing, and enables each and every of them to obtain justice without any danger of being overborne by the weight and number of their opponents; and, because it brings into action, and enforces this great and glorious principle, that the people are the sovereign of this country, and consequently that fellow citizens and joint sovereigns cannot be degraded by appearing with each other in their own Courts to have their controversies determined. . . .

THE ELEVENTH AMENDMENT (1795). *Chisholm v. Georgia* was argued on February 5, 1793, and decided on February 18, 1793. Soon thereafter, on March 4, 1794, Congress proposed the following amendment. It became part of the Constitution on February 7, 1795, when it was ratified by the twelfth of what were then fifteen states:

> Amendment XI: The Judicial power of the United States shall not be construed to extend to any suit in law or equity, commenced or prosecuted against one of the United States by Citizens of another State, or by Citizens or Subjects of any Foreign State.

As a result, the writ issued against the State of Georgia was never executed.

STUDY GUIDE

- What is the legal significance of this Amendment? Does it stand for the proposition that the Court in *Chisholm* was wrong in its interpretation of the Constitution and that Congress later corrected it? Or does it signify that, while the Court's interpretation may have been correct, this interpretation of the Constitution was politically unacceptable? Or is there no right or wrong in the matter; the Court simply thought one way about state sovereignty, while the Congress and the states thought another?
- Does it matter which of these descriptions of the relation between the ruling in *Chisholm* and the Eleventh Amendment is right? Put another way, how would the interpretation of the Eleventh Amendment by the Court today be affected by which of these descriptions of its relationship to *Chisholm* is correct?
- What does passage of the Eleventh Amendment say about the use of amendments either to correct judicial mistakes (assuming the Court erred) or to correct mistakes in the Constitution itself (assuming the Court was correct)? Should the amendment process be used more often? How would such a practice affect the Supreme Court and the Constitution itself? To fully appreciate the significance of these issues, you should know that there is now a modern "Eleventh Amendment" line of cases concerning the immunities of states from lawsuits in federal court (discussed in Chapter 4 of this casebook).

E. FUNDAMENTAL PRINCIPLES VS. EXPRESSED CONSTRAINTS

One of the striking aspects of the opinions in *Chisholm* is the degree to which the justices based their decision primarily on fundamental principles, and only secondarily on the text of the Constitution. This practice, commonplace at the time, was the subject of a famous disagreement between Justices Samuel Chase (not to be confused with Chief Justice Salmon P. Chase) and James Iredell in the next case. Justice Chase's position is often characterized as favoring the judicial use of unwritten fundamental or natural rights as a constraint on the exercise of legislative power, perhaps because of how Justice Iredell framed the debate. But Chase's reasoning is similar to the "presumed consent" approach we earlier saw employed by John Locke. This approach is consistent with what is called the *doctrine of equitable interpretation*, by which a document — be it a constitution or a statute — is construed in a light most favorable to its justice. The difference is that this doctrine concedes that a written constitution *could* expressly violate natural rights deemed to be fundamental and, if it did, these unenumerated rights would not authorize a court to override the meaning of the text. In this sense, natural rights provide a baseline or "default rule" that governs unless a text clearly conflicts with and thereby displaces them.

STUDY GUIDE

- Does Justice Chase say that natural rights trump the constitutional allocation of legislative power? If not, what does he say? How does "consent" fit into Chase's analysis? Compare Chase's statement that "it cannot be presumed that" a people have entrusted "a legislature with such powers," with Attorney General Randolph's opinion on the constitutionality of a bank, in which he refers to "those paramount rights, which a free people cannot be supposed to confide even to their representatives," and with John Locke's statement that "the power of the society, or legislative constituted by them, can never be supposed to extend farther, than the common good." Do these statements referring to the "presumed" or "supposed" consent of the people help resolve any of the tension in the Declaration of Independence between the purpose of government to secure the preexisting rights of the People and the authority of the government resting on the People's consent?
- Remember that Iredell, at the North Carolina ratification convention (quoted in Section B), said that "it would be not only useless, but dangerous, to enumerate a number of rights which are not intended to be given up; because it would be implying, in the strongest manner, that every right not included in the exception might be impaired by the government without usurpation; and it would be impossible to enumerate every one. Let any one make what collection or enumeration of rights he pleases, I will immediately mention twenty or thirty more rights not contained in it." Does Justice Iredell's opinion here contradict that position? If not, was his previous affirmation misleading in any respect?
- What is the significance to Chase and to Iredell of the fact that we have a written Constitution?

***CALDER v. BULL*, 3 U.S. (3 DALL.) 386 (1798).** The Court of Probate for Hartford disapproved a will naming Caleb Bull and his wife beneficiaries of the estate of Norman Morrison. As a result Calder and his wife were to inherit the estate. When the Bulls were prevented from contesting the probate court's decision because of a statute barring appeals initiated eighteen months after a ruling, they successfully prevailed upon the Connecticut legislature to enact a statute that permitted the appeal. They prevailed in their suit, thereby disinheriting the Calders who then brought this lawsuit. The Calders "contend, that the said resolution or law of the Legislature of Connecticut, granting a new hearing, in the above case, is an ex post facto law, prohibited by the Constitution of the United States; that any

Justice Samuel Chase

Justice James Iredell

In 1804, Federalist Samuel Chase became the only Supreme Court Justice ever impeached when Jeffersonian Democratic-Republicans in the House brought charges based on his allegedly intemperate conduct as a trial judge in the circuit court. He was acquitted by the Senate.

law of the Federal government, or of any of the State governments, contrary to the Constitution of the United States, is void; and that this court possesses the power to declare such law void." The Court held that the statute was not an ex post facto law, but a disagreement arose between Justices Chase and Iredell on the source of the prohibition on ex post facto laws.

In a famous passage, Justice Chase maintained that the prohibition rested, in important part, on what he called "certain vital principles in our free Republican governments":

> I cannot subscribe to the omnipotence of a State Legislature, or that it is absolute and without control; although its authority should not be expressly restrained by the Constitution, or fundamental law, of the State. The people of the United States erected their Constitutions, or forms of government, to establish justice, to promote the general welfare, to secure the blessings of liberty; and to protect their persons and property from violence. The purposes for which men enter into society will determine the nature and terms of the social compact; and as they are the foundation of the legislative power, they will decide what are the proper objects of it: The nature, and ends of legislative

> power will limit the exercise of it. This fundamental principle flows from the very nature of our free Republican governments, that no man should be compelled to do what the laws do not require; nor to refrain from acts which the laws permit. There are acts which the Federal, or State, Legislature cannot do, without exceeding their authority. There are certain vital principles in our free Republican governments, which will determine and over-rule an apparent and flagrant abuse of legislative power; as to authorize manifest injustice by positive law; or to take away that security for personal liberty, or private property, for the protection whereof of the government was established. An ACT of the Legislature (for I cannot call it a law) contrary to the great first principles of the social compact, cannot be considered a rightful exercise of legislative authority. The obligation of a law in governments established on express compact, and on republican principles, must be determined by the nature of the power, on which it is founded. A few instances will suffice to explain what I mean. A law that punished a citizen for an innocent action, or, in other words, for an act, which, when done, was in violation of no existing law; a law that destroys, or impairs, the lawful private contracts of citizens; a law that makes a man a Judge in his own cause; or a law that takes property from A and gives it to B: It is against all reason and justice, for a people to entrust a Legislature with SUCH powers; and, therefore, it cannot be presumed that they have done it. The genius, the nature, and the spirit, of our State Governments, amount to a prohibition of such acts of legislation; and the general principles of law and reason forbid them. The Legislature may enjoin, permit, forbid, and punish; they may declare new crimes; and establish rules of conduct for all its citizens in future cases; they may command what is right, and prohibit what is wrong; but they cannot change innocence into guilt; or punish innocence as a crime; or violate the right of an antecedent lawful private contract; or the right of private property. To maintain that our Federal, or State, Legislature possesses such powers, if they had not been expressly restrained; would, in my opinion, be a political heresy, altogether inadmissible in our free republican governments.

In stark contrast, Justice Iredell adopted the opposite "default rule" or baseline: state legislatures have all powers not expressly prohibited by the federal and state constitutions

> Though I concur in the general result of the opinions, which have been delivered, I cannot entirely adopt the reasons that are assigned upon the occasion. . . . If . . . a government, composed of Legislative, Executive and Judicial departments, were established, by a Constitution, which imposed no limits on the legislative power, the consequence would inevitably be, that whatever the legislative power chose to enact, would be lawfully enacted, and the judicial power could never interpose to pronounce it void. It is true, that some speculative jurists have held, that a legislative act against natural justice must, in itself, be void; but I cannot think that, under such a government, any Court of Justice would possess a power to declare it so. Sir William Blackstone, having put the strong case of an act of Parliament, which should authorise a man to try his own cause, explicitly adds, that even in that case, "there is no court that has power to defeat the intent of the Legislature, when couched in such evident and express words, as leave no doubt whether it was the intent of the Legislature, or no."
>
> In order, therefore, to guard against so great an evil, it has been the policy of all the American states, which have, individually, framed their state constitutions since the revolution, and of the people of the United States, when they framed the Federal Constitution, to define with precision the objects of the legislative power, and to restrain its

exercise within marked and settled boundaries. If any act of Congress, or of the Legislature of a state, violates those constitutional provisions, it is unquestionably void; though, I admit, that as the authority to declare it void is of a delicate and awful nature, the Court will never resort to that authority, but in a clear and urgent case. If, on the other hand, the Legislature of the Union, or the Legislature of any member of the Union, shall pass a law, within the general scope of their constitutional power, the Court cannot pronounce it to be void, merely because it is, in their judgment, contrary to the principles of natural justice. The ideas of natural justice are regulated by no fixed standard: the ablest and the purest men have differed upon the subject; and all that the Court could properly say, in such an event, would be, that the Legislature (possessed of an equal right of opinion) had passed an act which, in the opinion of the judges, was inconsistent with the abstract principles of natural justice. There are then but two lights, in which the subject can be viewed: 1st. If the Legislature pursue the authority delegated to them, their acts are valid. 2nd. If they transgress the boundaries of that authority, their acts are invalid. In the former case, they exercise the discretion vested in them by the people, to whom alone they are responsible for the faithful discharge of their trust: but in the latter case, they violate a fundamental law, which must be our guide, whenever we are called upon as judges to determine the validity of a legislative act.

CHAPTER 2

Foundational Cases on Constitutional Structure: The Marshall Court

Only weeks before Democratic-Republican Thomas Jefferson took office as President in the "Revolution of 1800," Federalist John Marshall became Chief Justice of the United States. The stage was set for a showdown between the President (and his new party) and the judiciary — the last branch of government controlled by the Federalists. While the political nature of the dispute was very real, it should not be overestimated. Ironically, it turned out that the Court continued to rule in ways displeasing to Democratic-Republicans even after Jefferson had appointed a majority of Justices.

The first three cases in this chapter concern what is today called the power of judicial review, whereby the Justices nullify laws that they deem unconstitutional. The next four cases concern the scope of federal versus state power. All seven cases illustrate a clash between two distinct approaches to the scope of national power in a federal system. Both approaches have been advocated from the time of the Founding to the present. More importantly, all of the cases discussed in this chapter are considered fountainheads of contemporary constitutional law and are repeatedly cited by the Supreme Court. All literate lawyers must know what they are about.

A. THE JUDICIAL POWER

ASSIGNMENT 1

Article III of the Constitution begins:

> The judicial power of the United States, shall be vested in one Supreme Court, and in such inferior courts as the Congress may from time to time ordain and establish. . . . The judicial power shall extend to all cases, in law and equity, arising under this Constitution, the laws of the United States, and treaties made, or which shall be made, under their authority.

We start our study with *Marbury v. Madison* and the issue of whether the "judicial power" in Article III includes the power to nullify unconstitutional laws. Chief Justice John Marshall's opinion in *Marbury* was the start of the 200-year tradition of "grand" constitutional opinions. Through his concerted efforts, the Justices abandoned the practice of each Justice issuing his own separate opinion *seriatim* — or "one after the other" — as was done in *Chisholm v. Georgia*, and instead they joined a single "opinion of the court" (often written by the Chief Justice).

Marshall's opinion only hints at the bitter conflict that led to Jefferson's defeat of President John Adams. Prior to the adoption of the Twelfth Amendment in 1804, members of the Electoral College could vote only for President. The candidate with the most electoral votes became President, and the one with the next highest number became Vice President. This explains how Thomas Jefferson could be Vice President in the administration of his arch-foe John Adams from 1796-1800. This irregularity also illustrates that the framers of the Constitution were far from perfect in their constitutional design and their foresight.

> Four years later, in 1804, Burr shot and killed Hamilton in a duel on the shore of Weehawken, New Jersey. Both men boated there from New York, where dueling was illegal.

In the election of 1800, Jefferson's party made the mistake of assigning the same number of electoral votes to Jefferson as it did to Aaron Burr of New York, the candidate for Vice President. This tie threw the election into the House of Representatives, which was still controlled by the outgoing "lame-duck" Federalists. In the House, each state received a single vote for President, irrespective of the size of the state. Greatly fearing a Jefferson presidency for many reasons, Federalists in the House supported Burr. There followed a deadlock that lasted from February 11th to 17th. In the end, Alexander Hamilton, who disliked Jefferson but despised his fellow New Yorker Burr — in part for reasons of Burr's personal character — shifted his support to Jefferson. Jefferson was elected President on the thirty-sixth ballot, a mere two weeks before Inauguration Day.

Marbury v. Madison arose from the passage of the Judiciary Act of 1801 by the lame-duck Federalist Congress after Jefferson's election, but before his inauguration in March. The Act created a number of new judgeships to which outgoing President Adams nominated and Congress confirmed forty-two Federalist supporters, who came to be known as the "midnight judges." One of the midnight judges was William Marbury, appointed as a Justice of the Peace. The Act also reduced the number of Supreme Court Justices from six to five. John Marshall had himself been appointed Chief Justice on February 4th but continued to serve as Adams's secretary of state. It was in this capacity that Marshall, who was being assisted by his brother, inadvertently failed to deliver Marbury's commission that had been signed by Adams.

Marshall became Chief Justice and administered the oath of office to Jefferson on March 4th. Jefferson instructed James Madison, his new secretary of state, not to deliver the commissions that had been left behind by Marshall and his brother, including Marbury's commission. In March 1802, the Congress, now controlled by the Democratic-Republicans, repealed the Judiciary Act of 1801 and also eliminated the Court's 1802 term (to prevent it from hearing Marbury's challenge, and other challenges to the Repeal Act, until February 1803). This put the Court on notice that it confronted Congress at its peril.

Chief Justice John Marshall

Thomas Jefferson

STUDY GUIDE

- In one of the most famous "jiu jitsu" maneuvers in legal history, Marshall is able both to assert the power of the Court to nullify unconstitutional legislation AND to avoid the possibility that President Jefferson would ignore an adverse ruling by the Court. How does he accomplish this?

- The *Marbury* case has become associated with the "power of judicial review," yet the opinion never uses that term. Like Hamilton in *Federalist No. 78*, Marshall employs the concept of judicial *duty* to follow the law of the superior as opposed to the subordinate authority. What difference does this difference in terminology make? (*Hints:* Could judges properly refrain from doing their "duty" in the same way they could refrain from exercising their "power"? Would such a duty likely have been specified in the constitutional text?)
- On what does Marshall ground this judicial duty of nullification? Text? History? First principles? Structure?
- What is Marshall's distinction between "political" questions and those involving "individual rights"? What presumption does he adopt when construing the meaning of express clauses in the Constitution?
- Should Marshall have even been sitting on a case in which he was so intimately involved? (He personally failed to deliver Marbury's commission on time.) What conception of law might explain why this would not have been a completely unacceptable conflict of interest?

Marbury v. Madison

5 U.S. (1 Cranch) 137 (1803)

[In 1789, Congress enacted the first Judiciary Act establishing inferior courts and defining the scope of federal courts. The constitutionality of the italicized portion of the following provision became the subject of the next case:

> SEC. 13. . . . *The Supreme Court* shall also have *appellate jurisdiction* from the circuit courts and courts of the several states, in the cases herein after specially provided for; and *shall have power to issue* writs of prohibition to the district courts, when proceeding as courts of admiralty and maritime jurisdiction, and *writs of mandamus, in cases warranted by the principles and usages of law, to any courts appointed, or persons holding office, under the authority of the United States.*

In *Marbury*, the Court would decide whether this statute was consistent with Article III, Section 2 of the Constitution, which provides:

> The judicial Power shall extend to all Cases, in Law and Equity, arising under this Constitution. . . . In all Cases affecting Ambassadors, other public Ministers and Consuls, and those in which a State shall be Party, the supreme Court shall have *original Jurisdiction*. In all the other Cases before mentioned, the supreme Court shall have *appellate Jurisdiction*, both as to Law and Fact, with such Exceptions, and under such Regulations as the Congress shall make. — EDS.]

At the December term 1801, William Marbury [and others] . . . moved the court for a rule to James Madison, secretary of state of the United States, to show cause why a mandamus should not issue commanding him to cause to be delivered to them respectively their several commissions as justices of the peace in the district of Columbia. This motion was supported by affidavits of the following facts: that notice of this motion had been given to Mr. Madison; that Mr. Adams, the late president of the United States, nominated the applicants to the senate for their advice and consent to be appointed justices of the peace of the district of Columbia; that the senate advised and consented to the appointments; that commissions in due form were signed by the said president appointing them justices, &c. and that the seal of the United States was in due form affixed to the said commissions by the secretary of state [At the time, Marshall was simultaneously serving as Secretary of State and Chief Justice. — EDS.]; that the applicants have requested Mr. Madison to deliver them their said commissions, who has not complied with that request; and that their said commissions are withheld from them; that the applicants have made application to Mr. Madison as secretary of state of the United States at his office, for information whether the commissions were signed and sealed as aforesaid; that explicit and satisfactory information has not been given in answer to that inquiry, either by the secretary of state, or any officer in the department of state; that application has been made to the secretary of the senate for a certificate of the nomination of the applicants, and of the advice and consent of the senate, who has declined giving such a certificate; whereupon a rule was made to show cause on the fourth day of this term. . . .

MR. CHIEF JUSTICE MARSHALL delivered the opinion of the court. . . .

In the order in which the court has viewed this subject, the following questions have been considered and decided:

> 1st. Has the applicant a right to the commission he demands?
> 2d. If he has a right, and that right has been violated, do the laws of his country afford him a remedy?
> 3d. If they do afford him a remedy, is it a *mandamus* issuing from this court?

The first object of inquiry is — 1st. Has the applicant a right to the commission he demands?

His right originates in an act of congress passed in February 1801, concerning the district of Columbia . . . [which] enacts, "that there shall be appointed in and for each of the said counties, such number of discreet persons to be justices of the peace as the president of the United States shall, from time to time, think expedient, to continue in office for five years." It appears from the affidavits, that in compliance with this law, a commission for William Marbury as a justice of peace for the county of Washington was signed by John Adams, then president of the United States; after which the seal of the United States was affixed to it; but the commission has never reached the person for whom it was made out. . . .

It [is] decidedly the opinion of the court, that when a commission has been signed by the president, the appointment is made; and that the commission is complete, when the seal of the United States has been affixed to it by the secretary of state. . . . To withhold his commission, therefore, is an act deemed by the court not warranted by law, but violative of a vested legal right.

This brings us to the second inquiry; which is, 2dly. If he has a right, and that right has been violated, do the laws of his country afford him a remedy?

The very essence of civil liberty certainly consists in the right of every individual to claim the protection of the laws, whenever he receives an injury. One of the first duties of government is to afford that protection. . . . The government of the United States has been emphatically termed a government of laws, and not of men.[1] It will certainly cease to deserve this high appellation, if the laws furnish no remedy for the violation of a vested legal right. . . .

By the constitution of the United States, the President is invested with certain important political powers, in the exercise of which he is to use his own discretion, and is accountable only to his country in his political character, and to his own conscience. To aid him in the performance of these duties, he is authorized to appoint certain officers, who act by his authority and in conformity with his orders.

In such cases, their acts are his acts; and whatever opinion may be entertained of the manner in which executive discretion may be used, still there exists, and can exist, no power to control that discretion. The subjects are political. They respect the nation, not individual rights, and being entrusted to the executive, the decision of the executive is conclusive. . . .

But when the legislature proceeds to impose on that officer other duties; when he is directed peremptorily to perform certain acts; when the rights of individuals are dependent on the performance of those acts; he is so far the officer of the law; is amenable to the laws for his conduct; and cannot at his discretion sport away the vested rights of others.

The conclusion from this reasoning is, that where the heads of departments are the political or confidential agents of the executive, merely to execute the will of the President, or rather to act in cases in which the executive possesses a constitutional or legal discretion, nothing can be more perfectly clear than that their acts are only politically examinable. But where a specific duty is assigned by law, and individual rights depend upon the performance of that duty, it seems equally clear, that the individual who considers himself injured, has a right to resort to the laws of his country for a remedy. . . .

It is, then, the opinion of the Court, 1st. That by signing the commission of Mr. Marbury, the president of the United States appointed him a justice of peace for the county of Washington in the district of Columbia; and that the seal of the United States, affixed thereto by the secretary of state, is conclusive testimony of the verity of the signature, and of the completion of the appointment; and that the appointment conferred on him a legal right to the office for the space of five years.

2dly. That, having this legal title to the office, he has a consequent right to the commission; a refusal to deliver which is a plain violation of that right, for which the laws of his country afford him a remedy.

---

[1] [The concept of *a government of laws, not of men*, was famously invoked by John Adams, who authored the Massachusetts Constitution of 1780. Section 30 ("The executive shall never exercise the legislative and judicial powers, or either of them: The judicial shall never exercise the legislative and executive powers, or either of them: to the end it may be a government of laws and not of men."). — EDS.]

It remains to be enquired whether, 3dly. He is entitled to the remedy for which he applies. This depends on

1st. The nature of the writ applied for, and,
2dly. The power of this court.

1st. The nature of the writ. . . .

This writ, if awarded, would be directed to an officer of government, and its mandate to him would be, to use the words of Blackstone, "to do a particular thing therein specified, which appertains to his office and duty, and which the court has previously determined or at least supposes to be consonant to right and justice." . . .

These circumstances certainly concur in this case.

This, then, is a plain case for a mandamus, either to deliver the commission, or a copy of it from the record; and it only remains to be enquired, Whether it can issue from this court.

The act to establish the judicial courts of the United States authorizes the Supreme Court "to issue writs of mandamus in cases warranted by the principles and usages of law, to any courts appointed, or persons holding office, under the authority of the United States."

The Secretary of State, being a person holding an office under the authority of the United States, is precisely within the letter of the description; and if this court is not authorized to issue a writ of mandamus to such an officer, it must be because the law is unconstitutional, and therefore incapable of conferring the authority, and assigning the duties which its words purport to confer and assign.

The constitution vests the whole judicial power of the United States in one Supreme Court, and such inferior courts as congress shall, from time to time, ordain and establish. This power is expressly extended to all cases arising under the laws of the United States; and, consequently, in some form, may be exercised over the present case; because the right claimed is given by a law of the United States.

In the distribution of this power it is declared that "the Supreme Court shall have original jurisdiction in all cases affecting ambassadors, other public ministers and consuls, and those in which a state shall be a party. In all other cases, the Supreme Court shall have appellate jurisdiction."

It has been insisted, at the bar, that as the original grant of jurisdiction, to the supreme and inferior courts, is general, and the clause, assigning original jurisdiction to the Supreme Court, contains no negative or restrictive words, the power remains to the legislature, to assign original jurisdiction to that court in other cases than those specified in the article which has been recited; provided those cases belong to the judicial power of the United States.

If it had been intended to leave it in the discretion of the legislature to apportion the judicial power between the supreme and inferior courts according to the will of that body, it would certainly have been useless to have proceeded further than to have defined the judicial power, and the tribunals in which it should be vested. The subsequent part of the section is mere surplusage, is entirely without meaning, if such is to be the construction. If congress remains at liberty to give this court appellate jurisdiction, where the constitution has declared their jurisdiction shall be original; and original jurisdiction where the constitution has declared it shall be appellate; the distribution of jurisdiction, made in the constitution, is form without substance.

Affirmative words are often, in their operation, negative of other objects than those affirmed; and in this case, a negative or exclusive sense must be given to them or they have no operation at all.

It cannot be presumed that any clause in the constitution is intended to be without effect; and, therefore, such a construction is inadmissible, unless the words require it.

If the solicitude of the convention, respecting our peace with foreign powers, induced a provision that the supreme court should take original jurisdiction in cases which might be supposed to affect them; yet the clause would have proceeded no further than to provide for such cases, if no further restriction on the powers of congress had been intended. That they should have appellate jurisdiction in all other cases, with such exceptions as congress might make, is no restriction; unless the words be deemed exclusive of original jurisdiction.

When an instrument organizing fundamentally a judicial system, divides it into one supreme, and so many inferior courts as the legislature may ordain and establish; then enumerates its powers, and proceeds so far to distribute them, as to define the jurisdiction of the supreme court by declaring the cases in which it shall take original jurisdiction, and that in others it shall take appellate jurisdiction; the plain import of the words seems to be, that in one class of cases its jurisdiction is original, and not appellate; in the other it is appellate, and not original. If any other construction would render the clause inoperative, that is an additional reason for rejecting such other construction, and for adhering to their obvious meaning.

To enable this court, then, to issue a mandamus, it must be shown to be an exercise of appellate jurisdiction, or to be necessary to enable them to exercise appellate jurisdiction.

It has been stated at the bar that the appellate jurisdiction may be exercised in a variety of forms, and that if it be the will of the legislature that a mandamus should be used for that purpose, that will must be obeyed. This is true, yet the jurisdiction must be appellate, not original.

It is the essential criterion of appellate jurisdiction, that it revises and corrects the proceedings in a cause already instituted, and does not create that cause. Although, therefore, a mandamus may be directed to courts, yet to issue such a writ to an officer for the delivery of a paper, is in effect the same as to sustain an original action for that paper, and, therefore, seems not to belong to appellate, but to original jurisdiction. Neither is it necessary in such a case as this, to enable the court to exercise its appellate jurisdiction.

The authority, therefore, given to the Supreme Court, by the act establishing the judicial courts of the United States, to issue writs of mandamus to public officers, appears not to be warranted by the constitution; and it becomes necessary to enquire whether a jurisdiction, so conferred, can be exercised.

The question, whether an act, repugnant to the constitution, can become the law of the land, is a question deeply interesting to the United States; but happily, not of an intricacy proportioned to its interest. It seems only necessary to recognize certain principles, supposed to have been long and well established, to decide it.

That the people have an original right to establish, for their future government, such principles as, in their opinion, shall most conduce to their own happiness, is the basis on which the whole American fabric has been erected. The exercise of this original right is a very great exertion; nor can it, nor ought it, to be frequently repeated. The principles, therefore, so established, are deemed fundamental. And as the authority from which they proceed is supreme, and can seldom act, they are designed to be permanent.

This original and supreme will organizes the government, and assigns to different departments their respective powers. It may either stop here, or establish certain limits not to be transcended by those departments.

The government of the United States is of the latter description. The powers of the legislature are defined and limited; and that those limits may not be mistaken, or forgotten, the constitution is written. To what purpose are powers limited, and to what purpose is that limitation committed to writing, if these limits may, at any time, be passed by those intended to be restrained? The distinction between a government with limited and unlimited powers is abolished, if those limits do not confine the persons on whom they are imposed, and if acts prohibited and acts allowed, are of equal obligation. It is a proposition too plain to be contested, that the constitution controls any legislative act repugnant to it; or, that the legislature may alter the constitution by an ordinary act.

Between these alternatives there is no middle ground. The constitution is either a superior, paramount law, unchangeable by ordinary means, or it is on a level with ordinary legislative acts, and, like other acts, is alterable when the legislature shall please to alter it.

If the former part of the alternative be true, then a legislative act contrary to the constitution is not law: if the latter part be true, then written constitutions are absurd attempts, on the part of the people, to limit a power in its own nature illimitable.

Certainly all those who have framed written constitutions contemplate them as forming the fundamental and paramount law of the nation, and consequently, the theory of every such government must be, that an act of the legislature, repugnant to the constitution, is void.

This theory is essentially attached to a written constitution, and is, consequently, to be considered, by this court, as one of the fundamental principles of our society. It is not therefore to be lost sight of in the further consideration of this subject.

If an act of the legislature, repugnant to the constitution, is void, does it, notwithstanding its invalidity, bind the courts, and oblige them to give it effect? Or, in other words, though it be not law, does it constitute a rule as operative as if it was a law? This would be to overthrow in fact what was established in theory; and would seem, at first view, an absurdity too gross to be insisted on. It shall, however, receive a more attentive consideration.

It is emphatically the province and duty of the judicial department to say what the law is. Those who apply the rule to particular cases, must of necessity expound and interpret that rule. If two laws conflict with each other, the courts must decide on the operation of each.

So if a law be in opposition to the constitution; if both the law and the constitution apply to a particular case, so that the court must either decide that case conformably to the law, disregarding the constitution; or conformably to the constitution, disregarding the law; the court must determine which of these conflicting rules governs the case. This is of the very essence of judicial duty.

If, then, the courts are to regard the constitution, and the constitution is superior to any ordinary act of the legislature, the constitution, and not such ordinary act, must govern the case to which they both apply.

Those then who controvert the principle that the constitution is to be considered, in court, as a paramount law, are reduced to the necessity of maintaining that the courts must close their eyes on the constitution, and see only the law.

This doctrine would subvert the very foundation of all written constitutions. It would declare that an act which, according to the principles and theory of our government, is entirely void, is yet, in practice, completely obligatory. It would declare that if the legislature shall do what is expressly forbidden, such act, notwithstanding the express prohibition, is in reality effectual. It would be giving to the legislature a practical and real omnipotence, with the same breath which professes to restrict their powers within narrow limits. It is prescribing limits, and declaring that those limits may be passed at pleasure.

That it thus reduces to nothing what we have deemed the greatest improvement on political institutions — a written constitution — would of itself be sufficient, in America, where written constitutions have been viewed with so much reverence, for rejecting the construction. But the peculiar expressions of the constitution of the United States furnish additional arguments in favour of its rejection.

The judicial power of the United States is extended to all cases arising under the constitution.

Could it be the intention of those who gave this power, to say that in using it the constitution should not be looked into? That a case arising under the constitution should be decided without examining the instrument under which it arises?

This is too extravagant to be maintained.

In some cases, then, the constitution must be looked into by the judges. And if they can open it at all, what part of it are they forbidden to read or to obey?

There are many other parts of the constitution which serve to illustrate this subject.

It is declared that "no tax or duty shall be laid on articles exported from any state." Suppose a duty on the export of cotton, of tobacco, or of flour; and a suit instituted to recover it. Ought judgment to be rendered in such a case? Ought the judges to close their eyes on the constitution, and only see the law?

The constitution declares that "no bill of attainder or *ex post facto* law shall be passed." If, however, such a bill should be passed, and a person should be prosecuted under it; must the court condemn to death those victims whom the constitution endeavors to preserve?

"No person," says the constitution, "shall be convicted of treason unless on the testimony of two witnesses to the same overt act, or on confession in open court."

Here the language of the constitution is addressed especially to the courts. It prescribes, directly for them, a rule of evidence not to be departed from. If the legislature should change that rule, and declare *one* witness, or a confession *out* of court, sufficient for conviction, must the constitutional principle yield to the legislative act?

From these, and many other selections which might be made, it is apparent, that the framers of the constitution contemplated that instrument as a rule for the government of *courts,* as well as of the legislature. Why otherwise does it direct the judges to take an oath to support it? This oath certainly applies, in an especial manner, to their conduct in their official character. How immoral to impose it on them, if they were to be used as the instruments, and the knowing instruments, for violating what they swear to support!

The oath of office, too, imposed by the legislature, is completely demonstrative of the legislative opinion on this subject. It is in these words: "I do solemnly swear that I will administer justice without respect to persons, and do equal right to the poor and to the rich; and that I will faithfully and impartially discharge all the duties incumbent on me as ________________, according to the best of my abilities and understanding, agreeably to the *constitution*, and laws of the United States." Why does a Judge swear to discharge his duties agreeably to the constitution of the United States, if that constitution forms no rule for his government? If it is closed upon him, and cannot be inspected by him?

If such be the real state of things, this is worse than solemn mockery. To prescribe, or to take this oath, becomes equally a crime.

It is also not entirely unworthy of observation that in declaring what shall be the *supreme* law of the land, the *constitution* itself is first mentioned; and not the laws of the United States generally, but those only which shall be made in *pursuance* of the constitution, have that rank.

Thus, the particular phraseology of the constitution of the United States confirms and strengthens the principle, supposed to be essential to all written constitutions, that a law repugnant to the constitution is void; and that *courts*, as well as other departments, are bound by that instrument.

The rule must be discharged.

1. Evidence of the Meaning of the "Judicial Power"

We begin by noting that the term "power of judicial review" is of recent vintage, arising sometime in the twentieth century. Founding era sources referred instead to the judicial "duty" to "nullify," "negative," or "declare to be null and void" unconstitutional "laws" or "acts" of legislatures.[2] But, with this caveat, in what follows, we will nevertheless refer to the power of judicial review. Some scholars (including the late Alexander Bickel, a law professor at Yale) credit John Marshall's opinion in *Marbury* with inventing and establishing judicial review. Others (such as Stanford

[2] See Philip Hamburger, Law and Judicial Duty (2008).

historian Jack Rakove) have argued that the founding generation assumed that the Court would have this power, and thus the decision to establish judicial review was in some sense inevitable. There is quite a bit of evidence that, at the time of the Constitution's adoption, the public meaning of the term "judicial power" included the duty to nullify legislation that conflicted with the Constitution.[3]

The Constitutional Convention. Several members of the Constitutional Convention explicitly assumed the power of judicial review to reside in the judiciary — even before they settled on the particular wording of the various clauses. Roger Sherman of Connecticut argued that a congressional power to negative (i.e., veto) state laws was "unnecessary, as the Courts of the States would not consider as valid any law contravening the Authority of the Union. . . ." James Madison of Virginia favored such a legislative veto because states "will accomplish their injurious objects before they can be . . . set aside by the National Tribunals." He then cited the example of Rhode Island, where "the Judges who refused to execute an unconstitutional law were displaced, and others substituted, by the Legislature. . . ." Gouverneur Morris of Pennsylvania argued that the legislative negative was unnecessary because "a law that ought to be negatived will be set aside in the Judiciary department." (*Gouverneur* was his first name, not an elected office.) There is no evidence that anyone at the Convention disputed the power of the judiciary to set aside unconstitutional laws passed by a state.

Nor was it disputed that federal judges would have the power to set aside unconstitutional legislation enacted by Congress. During a debate concerning whether judges should be included with the executive in a council empowered to revise laws — what is sometimes referred to as a "council of revision" — the comments of several delegates revealed their assumption that federal judges had the inherent power to hold federal laws unconstitutional. Luther Martin of Maryland stated that "as to the Constitutionality of laws, that point will come before the Judges in their proper official character. In this character they have a negative on the laws." George Mason of Virginia observed that "in their expository capacity of Judges they would have one negative. . . . They could declare an unconstitutional law void." While he favored the idea of the council, James Wilson of Pennsylvania conceded that there "was weight in this observation" that "the Judges, as expositors of the Laws would have an opportunity of defending their constitutional rights." Some infer from the Convention's rejection of the proposed council of revision an intention that the judiciary defer to legislative will. But the most discussed and influential reason for rejecting the council of revision proposal was the presumed existence of a judicial negative on unconstitutional legislation, which gave rise to the argument that such a council would involve judges in review of the legislation for a second time.

The assumption that judges possess the inherent power to nullify unconstitutional laws crops up in a variety of other contexts during the Convention. For example, Gouverneur Morris favored ratification of the Constitution by the people in convention because legislative ratification of the new Constitution was

[3] For additional authority, see John C. Yoo & Saikrishna Prakash, The Origins of Judicial Review, 70 U. Chi. L. Rev. 887 (2003).

prohibited by the terms of the Articles of Confederation. "Legislative alterations not conformable to the federal compact, would clearly not be valid. The Judges would consider them as null & void." James Madison argued that a difference between a league or confederation among states and a Constitution was precisely its status as binding law on judges. "A law violating a treaty ratified by a pre-existing law, might be respected by the Judges as a law, though an unwise or perfidious one. A law violating a constitution established by the people themselves, would be considered by the Judges as null & void." Hugh Williamson of North Carolina stated that an express prohibition on ex post facto laws by states "may do good here, because the Judges can take hold of it."

The fact that judicial nullification was taken as given by virtually all members of the Constitutional Convention does not mean everyone liked this power. John Mercer of Maryland "disapproved of the Doctrine that the Judges as expositors of the Constitution should have authority to declare a law void." Instead he "thought laws ought to be well and cautiously made, and then to be uncontroulable." But Mercer's was a lone voice. Even John Dickinson of Delaware who "was strongly impressed with the remark of Mr. Mercer as to the power of the Judges to set aside the law," said he "was at the same time at a loss to know what expedient to substitute." Gouverneur Morris took issue with Mercer more sharply, stating that he could not agree that the judiciary "should be bound to say that a direct violation of the Constitution was law. A control over the legislature might have its inconveniences. But view the danger on the other side."

The principal criticism of judicial nullification was not its existence but its weakness. Some framers were less than sanguine about the ability of courts to stand up for constitutional principle when necessary. James Wilson thought that Congress should have the power to nullify state laws because "[t]he firmness of Judges is not itself sufficient." Moreover, he argued — in words that assume a judicial power to declare "improper" laws unconstitutional — that it "would be better to prevent the passage of an improper law, than to declare it void when passed." Despite this concern, a congressional negative on state laws and proposals for the council of revision were rejected by the Convention, leaving the other structural constraints, including the doctrine of judicial nullification, to keep state and national governments from exceeding their proper powers.

The Federalist. Perhaps the most well-known endorsement of the power of judicial nullification came in *Federalist No. 78*, authored by Alexander Hamilton. Here is an excerpt of the essay, which is reproduced in full in Chapter 1:

> The complete independence of the courts of justice is peculiarly essential in a limited Constitution. By a limited Constitution, I understand one which contains certain specified exceptions to the legislative authority; such, for instance, as that it shall pass no bills of attainder, no ex post facto laws, and the like. Limitations of this kind can be preserved in practice no other way than through the medium of courts of justice, whose duty it must be to declare all acts contrary to the manifest tenor of the Constitution void. Without this, all the reservations of particular rights or privileges would amount to nothing.

> Some perplexity respecting the rights of the courts to pronounce legislative acts void, because contrary to the Constitution, has arisen from an imagination that the doctrine would imply a superiority of the judiciary to the legislative power. It is urged that the authority which can declare the acts of another void, must necessarily be superior to the one whose acts may be declared void. As this doctrine is of great importance in all the American constitutions, a brief discussion of the ground on which it rests cannot be unacceptable.
>
> There is no position which depends on clearer principles, than that every act of a delegated authority, contrary to the tenor of the commission under which it is exercised, is void. No legislative act, therefore, contrary to the Constitution, can be valid. To deny this, would be to affirm, that the deputy is greater than his principal; that the servant is above his master; that the representatives of the people are superior to the people themselves; that men acting by virtue of powers, may do not only what their powers do not authorize, but what they forbid.

Ratification Conventions. The state ratification debates are replete with assertions of the power of judicial nullification. Supporters of the Constitution offered it as a means of limiting the powers of government. Speaking to the Pennsylvania convention, James Wilson stated: "If a law should be made inconsistent with those powers vested by this instrument in Congress, the judges, as a consequence of their independence, and the particular powers of government being defined, will declare such law to be null and void; for the power of the Constitution predominates. Any thing, therefore, that shall be enacted by Congress contrary thereto, will not have the force of law." To the objection that judges would "be impeached, because they decide an act null and void, that was made in defiance of the Constitution," Wilson replied: "What House of Representatives would dare to impeach, or Senate to commit, judges for the performance of their duty?" In the Virginia convention, future-Chief Justice John Marshall openly stated the principle of nullification he would later enunciate in *Marbury*. If the government of the United States "were to make a law not warranted by any of the powers enumerated," said Marshall, "it would be considered by the judges as an infringement of the Constitution which they are to guard. They would not consider such a law as coming under their jurisdiction. They would declare it void."

Perhaps the clearest equating of the "judicial power" with judicial nullification was future–Chief Justice Oliver Ellsworth's ringing endorsement in the Connecticut convention of the judicial power to nullify unconstitutional acts of both Congress and state legislatures:

> This Constitution defines the extent of the powers of the general government. If the general legislature should at any time overleap their limits, the judicial department is a constitutional check. If the United States go beyond their powers, if they make a law which the Constitution does not authorize, it is void; and *the judicial power*, the national judges, who, to secure their impartiality, are to be made independent, will declare it to be void. On the other hand, if the states go beyond their limits, if they make a law which is a usurpation upon the general government, the law is void; and upright, independent judges will declare it to be so.

The power of the federal judiciary to strike down unconstitutional state laws was also asserted in the North Carolina convention by William Davie, who stated that "every member will agree that the positive regulations ought to be carried into execution, and that the negative restrictions ought not to [be] disregarded or violated. Without a judiciary, the injunctions of the Constitution may be disobeyed, and the positive regulations neglected or contravened." He then argued that should states impose duties on imported goods, "the Constitution might be violated with impunity, if there were no power in the general government to correct and counteract such laws. This great object can only be safely and completely obtained by the instrumentality of the federal judiciary."

Even opponents of the Constitution conceded the existence of judicial nullification, though again some questioned its efficacy. In his statement to the legislature of Maryland, Luther Martin said: "Whether, therefore, any laws *or regulations* of the Congress, any acts of *its President or other officers*, are contrary to, or not warranted by, the Constitution, rests only with the judges, who are appointed by Congress, to determine; by whose determinations every state must *be bound*." In the Virginia ratification convention, Patrick Henry made a similar charge in a manner that suggests he included judicial nullification within the meaning of the word "judiciary":

> The honorable gentleman did our judiciary honor in saying that they had firmness to counteract the legislature in some cases. Yes, sir, our judges opposed the acts of the legislature. We have this landmark to guide us. They had fortitude to declare that *they were the judiciary*, and would oppose unconstitutional acts. Are you sure that your federal judiciary will act thus? Is that judiciary as well constructed, and as independent of the other branches, as our state judiciary? Where are your landmarks in this government? I will be bold to say you cannot find any in it. I take it as the highest encomium on this country, that the acts of the legislature, if unconstitutional, are liable to be opposed by the judiciary. (Emphasis added.)

Also in Virginia, William Grayson, another opponent of the Constitution, observed that "[i]f the Congress cannot make a law against the Constitution, I apprehend they cannot make a law to abridge it. The judges are to defend it."

2. Judicial Nullification of State Statutes and State Supreme Court Decisions

In the years following *Marbury*, the Marshall Court went on to employ the doctrine of judicial review to invalidate state statutes and to assert the power to review and reverse decisions of state supreme courts.

In Fletcher v. Peck, 10 U.S. (6 Cranch) 87 (1810), the Court struck down a state statute that repealed a previous sale of Indian property by a corrupt legislature to private speculators in return for bribes. In so doing, Chief Justice Marshall defended the "security of property" and "human rights" and denied that state legislatures can rightly be the judges in their own case when evaluating their claim of powers, and he relied on "certain great principles of justice" to reach the outcome in the case.

> If the Legislature of Georgia was not bound to submit its pretensions to those tribunals which are established for the security of property, and to decide on human rights, if it might claim to itself the power of judging in its own case, yet there are certain great principles of justice, whose authority is universally acknowledged, that ought not to be entirely disregarded. . . .
>
> The principle asserted is that one Legislature is competent to repeal any act which a former legislature was competent to pass, and that one legislature cannot abridge the powers of a succeeding legislature.
>
> The correctness of this principle, so far as respects general legislation, can never be controverted. But if an act be done under a law, a succeeding legislature cannot undo it. The past cannot be recalled by the most absolute power. Conveyances have been made, those conveyances have vested legal estate, and, if those estates may be seized by the sovereign authority, still that they originally vested is a fact, and cannot cease to be a fact.
>
> When, then, a law is in its nature a contract, when absolute rights have vested under that contract, a repeal of the law cannot devest those rights; and the act of annulling them, if legitimate, is rendered so by a power applicable to the case of every individual in the community.
>
> It may well be doubted whether the nature of society and of government does not prescribe some limits to the legislative power; and, if any be prescribed, where are they to be found if the property of an individual, fairly and honestly acquired, may be seized without compensation?
>
> To the Legislature all legislative power is granted, but the question whether the act of transferring the property of an individual to the public be in the nature of the legislative power is well worthy of serious reflection.

As an aside, later in this opinion, Chief Justice Marshall obliquely offers his opinion that *Chisholm v. Georgia* was correctly decided (despite the fact that it had been reversed by the Eleventh Amendment). Because he mentions neither the case nor amendment by name, this passage is sometimes overlooked.

> The Constitution, *as passed*, gave the courts of the United States jurisdiction in suits brought against individual States. A State, then, which violated its own contract was suable in the courts of the United States for that violation. Would it have been a defence in such a suit to say that the State had passed a law absolving itself from the contract? It is scarcely to be conceived that such a defence could be set up. And yet, if a State is neither restrained by the general principles of our political institutions nor by the words of the Constitution from impairing the obligation of its own contracts, such a defence would be a valid one. *This feature is no longer found in the Constitution*, but it aids in the construction of those clauses with which it was originally associated. (Emphases added.)

In Martin v. Hunter's Lessee, 14 U.S. (1 Wheat.) 304 (1816), the Supreme Court asserted the power to review and reverse state supreme court decisions. Before this decision, it was unclear whether the Supreme Court of the United States even had jurisdiction over state court judgments. As in the previous cases we have read so far, the opinion (in this instance written by Justice Story) began by relying on first principles and, in particular, first principles of sovereignty.

> The Constitution of the United States was ordained and established not by the States in their sovereign capacities, but emphatically, as the preamble of the Constitution declares, by "the people of the United States." There can be no doubt that it was competent to the people to invest the general government with all the powers which they might deem proper and necessary, to extend or restrain these powers according to their own good pleasure, and to give them a paramount and supreme authority. As little doubt can there be that the people had a right to prohibit to the States the exercise of any powers which were, in their judgment, incompatible with the objects of the general compact, to make the powers of the State governments, in given cases, subordinate to those of the nation, or to reserve to themselves those sovereign authorities which they might not choose to delegate to either. The Constitution was not, therefore, necessarily carved out of existing State sovereignties, nor a surrender of powers already existing in State institutions, for the powers of the States depend upon their own Constitutions, and the people of every State had the right to modify and restrain them according to their own views of the policy or principle. On the other hand, it is perfectly clear that the sovereign powers vested in the State governments by their respective Constitutions remained unaltered and unimpaired except so far as they were granted to the Government of the United States. . . . The government, then, of the United States can claim no powers which are not granted to it by the Constitution, and the powers actually granted, must be such as are expressly given, or given by necessary implication.

But these express delegations of powers

> are to be taken in their natural and obvious sense, and not in a sense unreasonably restricted or enlarged. The Constitution unavoidably deals in general language. It did not suit the purposes of the people, in framing this great charter of our liberties, to provide for minute specifications of its powers or to declare the means by which those powers should be carried into execution. It was foreseen that this would be a perilous and difficult, if not an impracticable, task. The instrument was not intended to provide merely for the exigencies of a few years, but was to endure through a long lapse of ages, the events of which were locked up in the inscrutable purposes of Providence. . . . Hence its powers are expressed in general terms, leaving to the legislature from time to time to adopt its own means to effectuate legitimate objects and to mould and model the exercise of its powers as its own wisdom and the public interests, should require.

(In Chapter 3, we will see Justice Story employing the same method — a broad construction of implied powers — to uphold the constitutionality of the Fugitive Slave Act of 1793 over the objection that the Constitution gave Congress no express power to enforce the Fugitive Slave Clause of Article IV.)

Justice Story then used this conception of sovereignty to deny that the federal government operates only on individuals and never on the states.

> It is a mistake to contend that the Constitution was not designed to operate upon States in their corporate capacities. It is crowded with provisions which restrain or annul the sovereignty of the States in some of the highest branches of their prerogatives. The tenth section of the first article contains a long list of disabilities and prohibitions imposed upon the States. Surely, when such essential portions of State sovereignty are taken away or prohibited to be exercised, it cannot be correctly asserted that the Constitution does not act upon the States. The language of the Constitution is also

> imperative upon the States as to the performance of many duties. It is imperative upon the State legislatures to make laws prescribing the time, places, and manner of holding elections for senators and representatives, and for electors of President and Vice-President. And in these as well as some other cases, Congress have a right to revise, amend, or supersede the laws which may be passed by State legislatures. When therefore the States are stripped of some of the highest attributes of sovereignty, and the same are given to the United States; when the legislatures of the States are, in some respects, under the control of Congress, and in every case are, under the Constitution, bound by the paramount authority of the United States, it is certainly difficult to support the argument that the appellate power over the decisions of State courts is contrary to the genius of our institutions. The courts of the United States can, without question, revise the proceedings of the executive and legislative authorities of the States, and if they are found to be contrary to the Constitution, may declare them to be of no legal validity. Surely the exercise of the same right over judicial tribunals is not a higher or more dangerous act of sovereign power. . . .

One passage of Justice Story's opinion seems to contradict Chief Justice Marshall's contention that Congress has the power to strip federal courts of jurisdiction in certain cases.

> The judicial power of the United States shall be vested (not may be vested) in one Supreme Court, and in such inferior Courts as Congress may, from time to time, ordain and establish. Could Congress have lawfully refused to create a Supreme Court, or to vest in it the constitutional jurisdiction? . . .
>
> The judicial power must, therefore, be vested in some court by Congress; and to suppose that it was not an obligation binding on them, but might, at their pleasure, be omitted or declined, is to suppose that, under the sanction of the Constitution, they might defeat the Constitution itself, a construction which would lead to such a result cannot be sound. . . .
>
> If, then, it is a duty of Congress to vest the judicial power of the United States, it is a duty to vest the whole judicial power. The language, if imperative as to one part, is imperative as to all. If it were otherwise, this anomaly would exist, that Congress might successively refuse to vest the jurisdiction in any one class of cases enumerated in the Constitution, and thereby defeat the jurisdiction as to all, for the Constitution has not singled out any class on which Congress are bound to act in preference to others. . . .
>
> The judicial power shall extend to all the cases enumerated in the Constitution. As the mode is not limited, it may extend to all such cases, in any form, in which judicial power may be exercised. It may therefore extend to them in the shape of original or appellate jurisdiction, or both, for there is nothing in the nature of the cases which binds to the exercise of the one in preference to the other. . . .

If Story was correct about this, then John Marshall's so-called jiu jitsu maneuver to assert the power of judicial review while denying President Jefferson a ruling he could then defy was too clever by half. It has led to the general acceptance of the principle that Congress may "strip" the jurisdiction of the federal courts over certain subject matters that they would otherwise have the judicial power to hear. Most scholars, however, believe there may be structural limits on how far Congress can go in doing this.

B. THE NECESSARY AND PROPER CLAUSE

ASSIGNMENT 2

As discussed in Chapter 1, the constitutionality of a national bank was hotly disputed as early as the first Congress. Ultimately, President Washington agreed with Secretary of the Treasury Alexander Hamilton that Congress had the power to establish a bank. The first bank's charter expired in 1811. Five years later, Congress chartered the second bank, which gave rise to the constitutional challenge in *McCulloch v. Maryland.* Chief Justice Marshall's decision for the Court became the authoritative interpretation of the Necessary and Proper Clause, which grants Congress the power: "To make all laws which shall be necessary and proper for carrying into execution the foregoing powers, and all other powers vested by this Constitution in the government of the United States, or in any department or officer thereof." *McCulloch* contains perhaps the most quoted sentence of any Supreme Court opinion: "[W]e must never forget that it is *a constitution* we are expounding." (As you learn more throughout the course, you might want to think about exactly what that means.)

McCulloch was not the first time that Marshall interpreted the meaning of the Necessary and Proper Clause. In the case of United States v. Fisher, 6 U.S. (2 Cranch) 358 (1805), he wrote:

> In construing this clause it would be incorrect and would produce endless difficulties, if the opinion should be maintained that no law was authorized which was not indispensably necessary to give effect to a specified power. Where various systems might be adopted for that purpose, it might be said with respect to each, that it was not necessary because the end might be obtained by other means. Congress must possess the choice of means, and must be empowered to use any means which are in fact conducive to the exercise of a power granted by the constitution.

STUDY GUIDE

- As always, you should pay attention to the basis of Marshall's opinion. How much does he rely on "first principles"? On text? On history? On structure? On the consequences of adopting the alternative interpretation?
- What exactly is Marshall's interpretation of the Necessary and Proper Clause? Is it unmodified from his earlier formulation in *Fisher*? How does it differ from that of James Madison? Is it identical to that of Alexander Hamilton? Is there any difference between Madison's interpretation (as reflected in his speech to Congress about the first bank in Chapter 1) and that of the State of Maryland?

- Notice Marshall's analysis of whether a power of incorporation is "a great substantive and independent power which cannot be implied as incidental to other powers or used as a means of executing them" before he gets to the question of whether the bank may be "necessary" to execute another power. The distinction between "principal" and "incidental" powers was a staple of founding era agency law. After being moribund for nearly 200 years, it will again be invoked by Chief Justice Roberts in *NFIB v. Sebelius* (Chapter 3) when considering the constitutionality of an individual purchase mandate.
- Are you surprised that Marshall does not rely more on textual interpretation, especially in a case that has become the authoritative interpretation of a specific clause?
- Does Marshall's interpretation amount to a blank check to Congress? If not, what are the limits of Congress's powers under the clause?
- Marshall discusses "the former proceedings of the nation" to support his conclusion. Given that the Supreme Court had never previously adjudicated this issue, of what relevance are past practices to the issue of constitutionality?
- You might want to compare the list of implied powers offered by Marshall with the list of powers that Madison said in his bank speech could not be implied without undermining the scheme of enumerated powers.

McCulloch v. Maryland[4]

17 U.S. (4 Wheat.) 316 (1819)

[The charter of the first Bank of the United States, which was the object of the debate described in Chapter 1, was allowed by Congress to lapse in 1811. In April 1816, Congress incorporated the second Bank of the United States. In 1818, the General Assembly of Maryland imposed a tax on all Maryland banks that the legislature did not charter. The Bank of the United States was organized in Pennsylvania, but operated a branch in Baltimore without any authorization by Maryland. John James, the original plaintiff, sued on behalf of himself and the State of Maryland to recover the taxes due on the Bank of the United States from the original defendant, the Bank's cashier, James William McCulloch. The Court of Appeals of the State of Maryland issued a judgment for the plaintiff, and McCulloch appealed, as the plaintiff in error (appellant), arguing that the Maryland law taxing the Bank was unconstitutional. The defendant, now the State of Maryland, contested the validity of the Bank. — Eds.]

[4] [In Henry Wheaton's official report, the case is styled *M'Culloch v. The State of Maryland et al.* "[T]he upside down and backwards apostrophe ['] turns out to have been a routine way for eighteenth and early nineteenth century printers to recreate a lower case, superscript 'c' after the letter 'M.'" See Michael G. Collins, M'Culloch and the Turned Comma, 12 Green Bag 2d 265 (2009). — Eds.]

Mr. Chief Justice Marshall delivered the opinion of the Court.

In the case now to be determined, the defendant, a sovereign State, denies the obligation of a law enacted by the legislature of the Union, and the plaintiff, on his part, contests the validity of an act which has been passed by the legislature of that State. The constitution of our country, in its most interesting and vital parts, is to be considered; the conflicting powers of the government of the Union and of its members, as marked in that constitution, are to be discussed; and an opinion given, which may essentially influence the great operations of the government. No tribunal can approach such a question without a deep sense of its importance, and of the awful responsibility involved in its decision. But it must be decided peacefully, or remain a source of hostile legislation, perhaps of hostility of a still more serious nature; and if it is to be so decided, by this tribunal alone can the decision be made. On the Supreme Court of the United States has the constitution of our country devolved this important duty.

The first question made in the cause is, has Congress power to incorporate a bank?

It has been truly said that this can scarcely be considered as an open question, entirely unprejudiced by the former proceedings of the nation respecting it. The principle now contested was introduced at a very early period of our history, has been recognized by many successive legislatures, and has been acted upon by the judicial department, in cases of peculiar delicacy, as a law of undoubted obligation.

It will not be denied, that a bold and daring usurpation might be resisted, after an acquiescence still longer and more complete than this. But it is conceived, that a doubtful question, one on which human reason may pause, and the human judgment be suspended, in the decision of which the great principles of liberty are not concerned, but the respective powers of those who are equally the representatives of the people, are to be adjusted; if not put at rest by the practice of the government, ought to receive a considerable impression from that practice. An exposition of the constitution, deliberately established by legislative acts, on the faith of which an immense property has been advanced, ought not to be lightly disregarded.

The power now contested was exercised by the first Congress elected under the present constitution. The bill for incorporating the bank of the United States did not steal upon an unsuspecting legislature, and pass unobserved. Its principle was completely understood, and was opposed with equal zeal and ability. After being resisted, first in the fair and open field of debate, and afterwards in the executive cabinet, with as much persevering talent as any measure has ever experienced, and being supported by arguments which convinced minds as pure and as intelligent as this country can boast, it became a law. The original act was permitted to expire; but a short experience of the embarrassments to which the refusal to revive it exposed the government, convinced those who were most prejudiced against the measure of its necessity, and induced the passage of the present law. It would require no ordinary share of intrepidity to assert that a measure adopted under these circumstances was a bold and plain usurpation, to which the constitution gave no countenance.

These observations belong to the cause; but they are not made under the impression that, were the question entirely new, the law would be found irreconcilable with the constitution.

In discussing this question, the counsel for the State of Maryland have deemed it of some importance, in the construction of the constitution, to consider that instrument not as emanating from the people, but as the act of sovereign and independent States. The powers of the general government, it has been said, are delegated by the States, who alone are truly sovereign; and must be exercised in subordination to the States, who alone possess supreme dominion.

It would be difficult to sustain this proposition. The Convention which framed the constitution was indeed elected by the State legislatures. But the instrument, when it came from their hands, was a mere proposal, without obligation, or pretensions to it. It was reported to the then existing Congress of the United States, with a request that it might "be submitted to a convention of delegates, chosen in each State by the people thereof, under the recommendation of its legislature, for their assent and ratification." This mode of proceeding was adopted; and by the convention, by Congress, and by the State legislatures, the instrument was submitted to the *people*. They acted upon it in the only manner in which they can act safely, effectively, and wisely, on such a subject, by assembling in convention. It is true, they assembled in their several States — and where else should they have assembled? No political dreamer was ever wild enough to think of breaking down the lines which separate the States, and of compounding the American people into one common mass. Of consequence, when they act, they act in their States. But the measures they adopt do not, on that account, cease to be the measures of the people themselves, or become the measures of the State governments.

From these conventions the constitution derives its whole authority. The government proceeds directly from the people; is "ordained and established" in the name of the people; and is declared to be ordained, "in order to form a more perfect union, establish justice, ensure domestic tranquility, and secure the blessings of liberty to themselves and to their posterity." The assent of the States, in their sovereign capacity, is implied in calling a convention, and thus submitting that instrument to the people. But the people were at perfect liberty to accept or reject it; and their act was final. It required not the affirmance, and could not be negatived, by the State governments. The constitution, when thus adopted, was of complete obligation, and bound the State sovereignties.

It has been said, that the people had already surrendered all their powers to the state sovereignties, and had nothing more to give. But, surely, the question whether they may resume and modify the powers granted to government, does not remain to be settled in this country. Much more might the legitimacy of the general government be doubted, had it been created by the states. The powers delegated to the state sovereignties were to be exercised by themselves, not by a distinct and independent sovereignty, created by themselves. To the formation of a league, such as was the confederation, the state sovereignties were certainly competent. But when, "in order to form a more perfect union," it was deemed necessary to change this alliance into an effective government, possessing great and sovereign powers, and acting directly on the people, the necessity of referring it to the people, and of deriving its powers directly from them, was felt and acknowledged by all. The government of the Union, then (whatever may be the influence of this fact on the case), is emphatically, and truly, a government of the people. In form and in substance it emanates from them. Its powers are granted by them, and are to be exercised directly on them, and for their benefit.

This government is acknowledged by all, to be one of enumerated powers. The principle, that it can exercise only the powers granted to it, would seem too apparent, to have required to be enforced by all those arguments, which its enlightened friends, while it was depending before the people, found it necessary to urge; that principle is now universally admitted. But the question respecting the extent of the powers actually granted, is perpetually arising, and will probably continue to arise, so long as our system shall exist.

In discussing these questions, the conflicting powers of the general and state governments must be brought into view, and the supremacy of their respective laws, when they are in opposition, must be settled.

If any one proposition could command the universal assent of mankind, we might expect it would be this — that the government of the Union, though limited in its powers, is supreme within its sphere of action. This would seem to result, necessarily, from its nature. It is the government of all; its powers are delegated by all; it represents all, and acts for all. Though any one state may be willing to control its operations, no state is willing to allow others to control them. The nation, on those subjects on which it can act, must necessarily bind its component parts. But this question is not left to mere reason: the people have, in express terms, decided it, by saying, "this constitution, and the laws of the United States, which shall be made in pursuance thereof," "shall be the supreme law of the land," and by requiring that the members of the state legislatures, and the officers of the executive and judicial departments of the states, shall take the oath of fidelity to it. The government of the United States, then, though limited in its powers, is supreme; and its laws, when made in pursuance of the constitution, form the supreme law of the land, "anything in the constitution or laws of any state to the contrary notwithstanding."

Among the enumerated powers, we do not find that of establishing a bank or creating a corporation. But there is no phrase in the instrument which, like the articles of confederation, excludes incidental or implied powers; and which requires that everything granted shall be expressly and minutely described. Even the 10th amendment, which was framed for the purpose of quieting the excessive jealousies which had been excited, omits the word "expressly," and declares only that the powers "not delegated to the United States, nor prohibited to the States, are reserved to the States or to the people"; thus leaving the question, whether the particular power which may become the subject of contest has been delegated to the one government, or prohibited to the other, to depend on a fair construction of the whole instrument. The men who drew and adopted this amendment had experienced the embarrassments resulting from the insertion of this word in the articles of confederation, and probably omitted it to avoid those embarrassments. A constitution, to contain an accurate detail of all the subdivisions of which its great powers will admit, and of all the means by which they may be carried into execution, would partake of the prolixity of a legal code, and could scarcely be embraced by the human mind. It would probably never be understood by the public. Its nature, therefore, requires, that only its great outlines should be marked, its important objects designated, and the minor ingredients which compose those objects be deduced from the nature of the objects themselves. That this idea was entertained by the framers of the American constitution, is not only to be inferred from the nature of the instrument, but from the language. Why else were some of the limitations, found in the ninth section of the 1st article, introduced? It is also, in some degree, warranted by their having omitted to use any restrictive term which might prevent its receiving a fair and just interpretation. In considering this question, then, we must never forget that it is a *constitution* we are expounding.

Although, among the enumerated powers of government, we do not find the word "bank," or "incorporation," we find the great powers to lay and collect taxes; to borrow money; to regulate commerce; to declare and conduct a war; and to raise and support armies and navies. The sword and the purse, all the external relations, and no inconsiderable portion of the industry of the nation, are entrusted to its government. It can never be pretended that these vast powers draw after them others of inferior importance, merely because they are inferior. Such an idea can never be advanced. But it may with great reason be contended, that a government, entrusted with such ample powers, on the due execution of which the happiness and prosperity of the nation so vitally depends, must also be entrusted with ample means for their execution. The power being given, it is the interest of the nation to facilitate its execution. It can never be their interest, and cannot be presumed to have been their intention, to clog and embarrass its execution by withholding the most appropriate means. Throughout this vast republic, from the St. Croix to the Gulf of Mexico, from the Atlantic to the Pacific, revenue is to be collected and expended, armies are to be marched and supported. The exigencies of the nation may require, that the treasure raised in the north should be transported to the south, that raised in the east, conveyed to the west, or that this order should be reversed. Is that construction of the constitution to be preferred, which would render these operations difficult, hazardous and expensive? Can we adopt that construction (unless the words imperiously require it) which would impute to the framers of that instrument, when granting these powers for the public good, the intention of impeding their exercise by withholding a choice of means? If, indeed, such be the mandate of the constitution, we have only to obey; but that instrument does not profess to enumerate the means by which the powers it confers may be executed; nor does it prohibit the creation of a corporation, if the existence of such a being be essential to the beneficial exercise of those powers. It is, then, the subject of fair inquiry, how far such means may be employed.

It is not denied, that the powers given to the government imply the ordinary means of execution. That, for example, of raising revenue, and applying it to national purposes, is admitted to imply the power of conveying money from place to place, as the exigencies of the nation may require, and of employing the usual means of conveyance. But it is denied that the government has its choice of means; or, that it may employ the most convenient means, if, to employ them, it be necessary to erect a corporation.

On what foundation does this argument rest? On this alone: the power of creating a corporation, is one appertaining to sovereignty, and is not expressly conferred on congress. This is true. But all legislative powers appertain to sovereignty. The original power of giving the law on any subject whatever, is a sovereign power;

and if the government of the Union is restrained from creating a corporation, as a means for performing its functions, on the single reason that the creation of a corporation is an act of sovereignty; if the sufficiency of this reason be acknowledged, there would be some difficulty in sustaining the authority of congress to pass other laws for the accomplishment of the same objects.

The government which has a right to do an act, and has imposed on it, the duty of performing that act, must, according to the dictates of reason, be allowed to select the means; and those who contend that it may not select any appropriate means, that one particular mode of effecting the object is excepted, take upon themselves the burden of establishing that exception.

The creation of a corporation, it is said, appertains to sovereignty. This is admitted. But to what portion of sovereignty does it appertain? Does it belong to one more than to another? In America, the powers of sovereignty are divided between the government of the Union, and those of the states. They are each sovereign, with respect to the objects committed to it, and neither sovereign, with respect to the objects committed to the other. We cannot comprehend that train of reasoning, which would maintain, that the extent of power granted by the people is to be ascertained, not by the nature and terms of the grant, but by its date. Some state constitutions were formed before, some since that of the United States. We cannot believe, that their relation to each other is in any degree dependent upon this circumstance. Their respective powers must, we think, be precisely the same, as if they had been formed at the same time. Had they been formed at the same time, and had the people conferred on the general government the power contained in the constitution, and on the states the whole residuum of power, would it have been asserted, that the government of the Union was not sovereign, with respect to those objects which were intrusted to it, in relation to which its laws were declared to be supreme? If this could not have been asserted, we cannot well comprehend the process of reasoning which maintains, that a power appertaining to sovereignty cannot be connected with that vast portion of it which is granted to the general government, so far as it is calculated to subserve the legitimate objects of that government. The power of creating a corporation, though appertaining to sovereignty, is not, like the power of making war, or levying taxes, or of regulating commerce, a great substantive and independent power, which cannot be implied as incidental to other powers, or used as a means of executing them. It is never the end for which other powers are exercised, but a means by which other objects are accomplished. No contributions are made to charity, for the sake of an incorporation, but a corporation is created to administer the charity; no seminary of learning is instituted, in order to be incorporated, but the corporate character is conferred to subserve the purposes of education. No city was ever built, with the sole object of being incorporated, but is incorporated as affording the best means of being well governed. The power of creating a corporation is never used for its own sake, but for the purpose of effecting something else. No sufficient reason is, therefore, perceived, why it may not pass as incidental to those powers which are expressly given, if it be a direct mode of executing them.

But the constitution of the United States has not left the right of Congress to employ the necessary means, for the execution of the powers conferred on the government, to general reasoning. To its enumeration of powers is added that of making "all laws which shall be necessary and proper for carrying into execution the foregoing powers, and all other powers vested by this constitution, in the government of the United States, or in any department thereof."

The counsel for the State of Maryland have urged various arguments, to prove that this clause, though in terms a grant of power, is not so in effect; but is really restrictive of the general right, which might otherwise be implied, of selecting means for executing the enumerated powers. In support of this proposition, they have found it necessary to contend, that this clause was inserted for the purpose of conferring on congress the power of making laws. That, without it, doubts might be entertained, whether congress could exercise its powers in the form of legislation.

But could this be the object for which it was inserted? A government is created by the people, having legislative, executive and judicial powers. Its legislative powers are vested in a congress, which is to consist of a senate and house of representatives. Each house may determine the rule of its proceedings; and it is declared, that every bill which shall have passed both houses, shall, before it becomes a law, be presented to the president of the United States. The 7th section describes the course of proceedings, by which a bill shall become a law; and, then, the 8th section enumerates the powers of congress. Could it be necessary to say, that a legislature should exercise legislative powers, in the shape of legislation? After allowing each house to prescribe its own course of proceeding, after describing the manner in which a bill should become a law, would it have entered into the mind of a single member of the convention, that an express power to make laws was necessary, to enable the legislature to make them? That a legislature, endowed with legislative powers, can legislate, is a proposition too self-evident to have been questioned.

But the argument on which most reliance is placed, is drawn from that peculiar language of this clause. Congress is not empowered by it to make all laws, which may have relation to the powers conferred on the government, but such only as may be *"necessary and proper"* for carrying them into execution. The word *"necessary"* is considered as controlling the whole sentence, and as limiting the right to pass laws for the execution of the granted powers, to such as are indispensable, and without which the power would be nugatory. That it excludes the choice of means, and leaves to congress, in each case, that only which is most direct and simple.

Is it true, that this is the sense in which the word "necessary" is always used? Does it always import an absolute physical necessity, so strong, that one thing to which another may be termed necessary, cannot exist without that other? We think it does not. If reference be had to its use, in the common affairs of the world, or in approved authors, we find that it frequently imports no more than that one thing is convenient, or useful, or essential to another. To employ the means necessary to an end, is generally understood as employing any means calculated to produce the end, and not as being confined to those single means, without which the end would be entirely unattainable. Such is the character of human language, that no word conveys to the mind, in all situations, one single definite idea; and nothing is more common than to use words in a figurative sense.

Almost all compositions contain words, which, taken in their rigorous sense, would convey a meaning different from that which is obviously intended. It is essential to just construction, that many words which import something excessive should be understood in a more mitigated sense — in that sense which common usage justifies. The word "necessary" is of this description. It has not a fixed character peculiar to itself. It admits of all degrees of comparison; and is often connected with other words, which increase or diminish the impression the mind receives of the urgency it imports. A thing may be necessary, very necessary, absolutely or indispensably necessary. To no mind would the same idea be conveyed by these several phrases. This comment on the word is well illustrated by the passage cited at the bar, from the 20th section of the 1st article of the constitution. It is, we think, impossible to compare the sentence which prohibits a State from laying "imposts, or duties on imports or exports, except what may be *absolutely* necessary for executing its inspection laws," with that which authorizes Congress "to make all laws which shall be necessary and proper for carrying into execution" the powers of the general government, without feeling a conviction that the convention understood itself to change materially the meaning of the word "necessary," by prefixing the word "absolutely." This word, then, like others, is used in various senses; and, in its construction, the subject, the context, the intention of the person using them, are all to be taken into view.

Let this be done in the case under consideration. The subject is the execution of those great powers on which the welfare of a nation essentially depends. It must have been the intention of those who gave these powers, to insure, as far as human prudence could insure, their beneficial execution. This could not be done by confiding the choice of means to such narrow limits as not to leave it in the power of Congress to adopt any which might be appropriate, and which were conducive to the end. This provision is made in a constitution intended to endure for ages to come, and, consequently, to be adapted to the various *crises* of human affairs. To have prescribed the means by which government should, in all future time, execute its powers, would have been to change, entirely, the character of the instrument, and give it the properties of a legal code. It would have been an unwise attempt to provide, by immutable rules, for exigencies which, if foreseen at all, must have been seen dimly, and which can be best provided for as they occur. To have declared that the best means shall not be used, but those alone without which the power given would be nugatory, would have been to deprive the legislature of the capacity to avail itself of experience, to exercise its reason, and to accommodate its legislation to circumstances. If we apply this principle of construction to any of the powers of the government, we shall find it so pernicious in its operation that we shall be compelled to discard it.

The powers vested in congress may certainly be carried into execution, without prescribing an oath of office. The power to exact this security for the faithful performance of duty, is not given, nor is it indispensably necessary. The different departments may be established; taxes may be imposed and collected; armies and navies may be raised and maintained; and money may be borrowed, without requiring an oath of office. It might be argued, with as much plausibility as other incidental powers have been assailed, that the convention was not unmindful of this subject. The oath which might be exacted — that of fidelity to the constitution — is prescribed, and no other can be required. Yet, he would be charged with insanity, who should contend, that the legislature might not superadd, to the oath directed by the constitution, such other oath of office as its wisdom might suggest.[5]

So, with respect to the whole penal code of the United States: whence arises the power to punish, in cases not prescribed by the constitution? All admit, that the government may, legitimately, punish any violation of its laws; and yet, this is not among the enumerated powers of congress. The right to enforce the observance of law, by punishing its infraction, might be denied, with the more plausibility, because it is expressly given in some cases.

Congress is empowered "to provide for the punishment of counterfeiting the securities and current coin of the United States," and "to define and punish piracies and felonies committed on the high seas, and offences against the law of nations." The several powers of congress may exist, in a very imperfect state, to be sure, but they may exist and be carried into execution, although no punishment should be inflicted, in cases where the right to punish is not expressly given.

Take, for example, the power "to establish post-offices and post-roads." This power is executed, by the single act of making the establishment. But, from this has been inferred the power and duty of carrying the mail along the post-road, from one post-office to another. And from this implied power, has again been inferred the right to punish those who steal letters from the post-office, or rob the mail. It may be said, with some plausibility, that the right to carry the mail, and to punish those who rob it, is not indispensably necessary to the establishment of a post-office and post-road. This right is indeed essential to the beneficial exercise of the power, but not indispensably necessary to its existence. So, of the punishment of the crimes of stealing or falsifying a record or process of a court of the United States, or of perjury in such court. To punish these offences, is certainly conducive to the due administration of justice. But courts may exist, and may decide the causes brought before them, though such crimes escape punishment.

The baneful influence of this narrow construction on all the operations of the government, and the absolute impracticability of maintaining it, without rendering the government incompetent to its great objects, might be illustrated by numerous examples drawn from the constitution, and from our laws. The good sense of the public has pronounced, without hesitation, that the power of punishment appertains to sovereignty, and may be exercised, whenever the sovereign has a right to act, as incidental to his constitutional powers. It is a means for carrying into execution all sovereign powers, and may be used, although not indispensably necessary. It is a right incidental to the power, and conducive to its beneficial exercise.

If this limited construction of the word "necessary" must be abandoned, in order to punish, whence is derived the rule which would reinstate it, when the government would carry its powers into execution, by means not vindictive in their nature? If the word "necessary" means "needful," "requisite," "essential,"

[5] [Article VI reads, in part: "The Senators and Representatives before mentioned, and the members of the several state legislatures, and all executive and judicial officers, both of the United States and of the several states, shall be bound by oath or affirmation, to support this Constitution." Marshall appears to be referring to terms of a congressional oath extending beyond simply supporting the Constitution. — EDS.]

"conducive to," in order to let in the power of punishment for the infraction of law; why is it not equally comprehensive, when required to authorize the use of means which facilitate the execution of the powers of government, without the infliction of punishment?

In ascertaining the sense in which the word "necessary" is used in this clause of the constitution, we may derive some aid from that with which it is associated. Congress shall have power "to make all laws which shall be necessary and proper to carry into execution" the powers of the government. If the word "necessary" was used in that strict and rigorous sense for which the counsel for the State of Maryland contend, it would be an extraordinary departure from the usual course of the human mind, as exhibited in composition, to add a word, the only possible effect of which is, to qualify that strict and rigorous meaning; to present to the mind the idea of some choice of means of legislation, not strained and compressed within the narrow limits for which gentlemen contend.

But the argument which most conclusively demonstrates the error of the construction contended for by the counsel for the State of Maryland, is founded on the intention of the convention, as manifested in the whole clause. To waste time and argument in proving that, without it, congress might carry its powers into execution, would be not much less idle, than to hold a lighted taper to the sun. As little can it be required to prove, that in the absence of this clause, congress would have some choice of means. That it might employ those which, in its judgment, would most advantageously effect the object to be accomplished. That any means adapted to the end, any means which tended directly to the execution of the constitutional powers of the government, were in themselves constitutional. This clause, as construed by the State of Maryland, would abridge, and almost annihilate, this useful and necessary right of the legislature to select its means. That this could not be intended, is, we should think, had it not been already controverted, too apparent for controversy.

We think so for the following reasons: 1st. The clause is placed among the powers of congress, not among the limitations on those powers. 2d. Its terms purport to enlarge, not to diminish the powers vested in the government. It purports to be an additional power, not a restriction on those already granted. No reason has been, or can be assigned, for thus concealing an intention to narrow the discretion of the national legislature, under words which purport to enlarge it. The framers of the constitution wished its adoption, and well knew that it would be endangered by its strength, not by its weakness. Had they been capable of using language which would convey to the eye one idea, and, after deep reflection, impress on the mind, another, they would rather have disguised the grant of power, than its limitation. If, then, their intention had been, by this clause, to restrain the free use of means which might otherwise have been implied, that intention would have been inserted in another place, and would have been expressed in terms resembling these. "In carrying into execution the foregoing powers, and all others," &c., "no laws shall be passed but such as are necessary and proper." Had the intention been to make this clause restrictive, it would unquestionably have been so in form as well as in effect.

The result of the most careful and attentive consideration bestowed upon this clause is, that if it does not enlarge, it cannot be construed to restrain the powers of Congress, or to impair the rights of the legislature to exercise its best judgment in the selection of measures to carry into execution the constitutional powers of the government. If no other motive for its insertion can be suggested, a sufficient one is found in the desire to remove all doubts respecting the right to legislate on that vast mass of incidental powers which must be involved in the constitution, if that instrument be not a splendid bauble.

We admit, as all must admit, that the powers of the government are limited, and that its limits are not to be transcended. But we think the sound construction of the constitution must allow to the national legislature that discretion, with respect to the means by which the powers it confers are to be carried into execution, which will enable that body to perform the high duties assigned to it, in the manner most beneficial to the people. Let the end be legitimate, let it be within the scope of the constitution, and all means which are appropriate, which are plainly adapted to that end, which are not prohibited, but consist with the letter and spirit of the constitution, are constitutional.

That a corporation must be considered as a means not less usual, not of higher dignity, not more requiring a particular specification than other means, has been sufficiently proved. If we look to the origin of corporations, to the manner in which they have been framed in that government from which we have derived most of our legal principles and ideas, or to the uses to which they have been applied, we find no reason to suppose, that a constitution, omitting, and wisely omitting, to enumerate all the means for carrying into execution the great powers vested in government, ought to have specified this. Had it been intended to grant this power, as one which should be distinct and independent, to be exercised in any case whatever, it would have found a place among the enumerated powers of the government. But being considered merely as a means, to be employed only for the purpose of carrying into execution the given powers, there could be no motive for particularly mentioning it. . . .

If a corporation may be employed, indiscriminately with other means, to carry into execution the powers of the government, no particular reason can be assigned for excluding the use of a bank, if required for its fiscal operations. To use one, must be within the discretion of congress, if it be an appropriate mode of executing the powers of government. That it is a convenient, a useful, and essential instrument in the prosecution of its fiscal operations, is not now a subject of controversy. All those who have been concerned in the administration of our finances, have concurred in representing its importance and necessity; and so strongly have they been felt, that statesmen of the first class, whose previous opinions against it had been confirmed by every circumstance which can fix the human judgment, have yielded those opinions to the exigencies of the nation. Under the confederation, Congress, justifying the measure by its necessity, transcended, perhaps, its powers, to obtain the advantage of a bank; and our own legislation attests the universal conviction of the utility of this measure. The time has passed away, when it can be necessary to enter into any discussion, in order to prove the importance of this instrument, as a means to effect the legitimate objects of the government.

But were its necessity less apparent, none can deny its being an appropriate measure; and if it is, the degree of its necessity, as has been very justly observed, is to be discussed in another place. Should Congress, in the execution of its powers, adopt measures which are prohibited by the constitution; or should Congress, under the pretext of executing its powers, pass laws for the accomplishment of objects not entrusted to the government; it would become the painful duty of this tribunal, should a case requiring such a decision come before it, to say that such an act was not the law of the land. But where the law is not prohibited, and is really calculated to effect any of the objects entrusted to the government, to undertake here to inquire into the degree of its necessity, would be to pass the line which circumscribes the judicial department, and to tread on legislative ground. This court disclaims all pretensions to such a power.

After this declaration, it can scarcely be necessary to say that the existence of State banks can have no possible influence on the question. No trace is to be found in the constitution of an intention to create a dependence of the government of the Union on those of the States, for the execution of the great powers assigned to it. Its means are adequate to its ends; and on those means alone was it expected to rely for the accomplishment of its ends. To impose on it the necessity of resorting to means which it cannot control, which another government may furnish or withhold, would render its course precarious, the result of its measures uncertain, and create a dependence on other governments, which might disappoint its most important designs, and is incompatible with the language of the constitution. But were it otherwise, the choice of means implies a right to choose a national bank in preference to State banks, and Congress alone can make the election.

After the most deliberate consideration, it is the unanimous and decided opinion of this Court, that the act to incorporate the Bank of the United States is a law made in pursuance of the constitution, and is a part of the supreme law of the land. . . .

STUDY GUIDE *(to Part Two of the opinion)*

- Assuming Marshall's basic premise is correct — that the power to tax is the power to destroy — does that automatically lead to the conclusion that the state cannot impose a nondiscriminatory tax on the bank? Would such a nondiscrimination principle address Marshall's concern? If the Court adopted such a rule, would there be any clear standard as to what is or is not discriminatory? Does the absence of such a standard in the Constitution argue against adopting such a rule?
- Does Marshall determine that the state has an impermissible purpose — destroying the bank? Or just that the tax could lead to that result? Although it would have been widely understood that destroying the bank was Maryland's purpose, how would the Court know that? Should the purpose matter?

2. Whether the State of Maryland may, without violating the constitution, tax that branch? . . .

That the power to tax involves the power to destroy; that the power to destroy may defeat and render useless the power to create; that there is a plain repugnance, in conferring on one government a power to control the constitutional measures of another, which other, with respect to those very measures, is declared to be supreme over that which exerts the control, are propositions not to be denied. . . .

If we apply the principle for which the State of Maryland contends, to the constitution generally, we shall find it capable of changing totally the character of that instrument. We shall find it capable of arresting all the measures of the government, and of prostrating it at the foot of the States. The American people have declared their constitution, and the laws made in pursuance thereof, to be supreme; but this principle would transfer the supremacy, in fact, to the States.

If the States may tax one instrument, employed by the government in the execution of its powers, they may tax any and every other instrument. They may tax the mail; they may tax the mint; they may tax patent rights; they may tax the papers of the custom-house; they may tax judicial process; they may tax all the means employed by the government, to an excess which would defeat all the ends of government. This was not intended by the American people. They did not design to make their government dependent on the States. . . .

The Court has bestowed on this subject its most deliberate consideration. The result is a conviction that the States have no power, by taxation or otherwise, to retard, impede, burden, or in any manner control, the operations of the constitutional laws enacted by Congress to carry into execution the powers vested in the general government. This is, we think, the unavoidable consequence of that supremacy which the constitution has declared.

We are unanimously of opinion, that the law passed by the legislature of Maryland, imposing a tax on the Bank of the United States, is unconstitutional and void. . . .

Using the pseudonyms "A Friend to the Union" and "A Friend of the Constitution," John Marshall published two essays in the *Philadelphia Union* and nine essays in the *Alexandria Gazette* responding to harsh attacks on *McCulloch*.[6] (Imagine if today Chief Justice Roberts wrote an anonymous op-ed in the *New York Times* defending his opinion in a landmark case!)

Given the emphasis placed on Marshall's defining "necessary" as "convenient" in *McCulloch*, it is noteworthy that in the *Philadelphia Union* he insisted that "[t]he court does not say that the word 'necessary' means whatever may be 'convenient' or 'useful.'"[7] Earlier in this essay he refers to the synonyms for "necessary" in this often overlooked passage of *McCulloch*: "If the word *'necessary' means 'needful,' 'requisite,' 'essential,' 'conducive to,'* in order to let in the power of punishment for the infraction of law; why is it not equally comprehensive, when required to authorize the use of means which facilitate the execution of the powers of government, without the infliction of punishment?"[8]

---

[6] See John Marshall's Defense of McCulloch v. Maryland (Gerald Gunther ed., 1969).

[7] *Id.* at 100.

[8] *Id.* at 99 (emphasis added).

Marshall's "Friend of the Constitution" essays were responding to a particularly vituperative criticism authored by Virginia Supreme Court Justice Spencer Roane, who used the pseudonym "Hampden." What follows is a brief excerpt from the nine essays.

STUDY GUIDE

Does Marshall's defense of his own opinion in *McCulloch* add anything to our understanding of the case? Keep this in mind when we consider modern claims about the meaning of the Necessary and Proper Clause as established in *McCulloch*.

JOHN MARSHALL, "A FRIEND OF THE CONSTITUTION," ***ALEXANDRIA GAZETTE,*** **June 30-July 15, 1819.** . . . The zealous and persevering hostility with which the constitution was originally opposed, cannot be forgotten. The deep rooted and vindictive hate, which grew of unfounded jealousies, and was aggravated by defeat, though suspended for a time, seems never to have been appeased. The desire to strip the government of those effective powers, which enable it to accomplish the objects for which it was created; and, by construction, essentially to reintroduce that miserable confederation, whose incompetency to the preservation of our union . . . seems to have recovered all its activity. . . .

[The Constitution] is the act of a people, creating a government, without which they cannot exist as a people. The powers of this government are conferred for their own benefit, are essential to their own prosperity, and are to be exercised for their own good, by persons chosen for that purpose by themselves. The object of the instrument is not a single one which can be minutely described, with all its circumstances. The attempt to do so, would totally change its nature, and defeat its purpose. It is intended to be a general system for all future times, to be adapted by those who administer it, to all future occasions that may come within its own view. From its nature, such an instrument can describe only the great objects it is intended to accomplish, and state in general terms, the specific powers which are deemed necessary for those objects. To direct the manner in which these powers are to be exercised, the means by which the objects of government are to be effected, a legislature is granted. This would be totally useless, if its office and duty were performed in the constitution. This legislature is an emanation from the people themselves. It is a part chosen to represent the whole, and to mark, according to the judgment of the nation, its course, within those great outlines which are given in the constitution. . . .

[N]ot a syllable uttered by the court, applies to an enlargement of the powers of congress. The reasoning of the judges is opposed to that restricted construction which would embarrass congress, in the execution of its acknowledged powers; and maintains that such construction, if not required by the words of the instrument, ought not to be adopted of choice; but makes no allusion to a construction enlarging the grant beyond the meaning of its ends. . . .

The whole opinion of the court proceeds upon this basis, as a truth not to be controverted. The principal it labors to establish is, not that congress may select means beyond the limits of the constitution, but means within those limits. . . .

I say, without fear of contradiction, that the general principles maintained by the supreme court are, that the constitution may be construed as if the clause which has been so much discussed, had been entirely omitted. That the powers of congress are expressed in terms which, without its aid, enable and require the legislature to execute them, and of course, to take means for their execution. That the choice of these means devolve on the legislature, whose right, and whose duty it is, to adopt those which are most advantageous to the people, provided they be within the limits of the constitution. Their constitutionality depends on their being the natural, direct, and appropriate means, or the known and usual means, for the execution of a given power.

In no single instance does the court admit the unlimited power of congress to adopt any means whatever, and thus to pass the limits prescribed by the Constitution. Not only is the discretion claimed for the legislature in the selection of its means, always limited in terms, to such as are appropriate, but the court expressly says, "should congress under the pretext of executing its powers, pass laws for the accomplishment of objects, not entrusted to the government, it would become the painful duty of this tribunal . . . to say that such an act was not the law of the land."

The bank bill upheld in *McCulloch* was signed into law by President James Madison, who, you will recall, strongly objected to the constitutionality of the first national bank. In the following letter to Justice Roane, Madison nevertheless criticizes the constitutional reasoning by which Marshall upholds the bill.

STUDY GUIDE

How do the views expressed by Madison in this letter compare with those he offered when a congressman thirty years earlier? How do they compare with the views he expressed in his Report of 1799 on the Alien and Sedition Act (Chapter 1)?

Madison begins by criticizing the "general and abstract" form of Marshall's opinion, as well as the new practice of having a single opinion of the Court, rather than a series of opinions by each Justice explaining his vote. How do you think these two practices have affected the exercise of the judicial power by the Supreme Court? Notice Madison's assumption that the judicial power includes "controul on the Legislative exercise of unconstitutional powers." Once again, see how the theory of sovereignty affects the analysis.

Notice also Madison's invocation of the "legitimate" and "regular mode" of amending the Constitution, rather than relying on innovative "constructive assumption of powers never meant to be granted."

JAMES MADISON, LETTER TO JUDGE SPENCER ROANE, September 2, 1819

Dear Sir

I have recd. your favor of the 22d Ult inclosing a copy of your observations on the Judgment of the Supreme Court of the U.S. in the case of M'Culloch agst. the State of Maryland. . . . It appears to me as it does to you that the occasion did not call for the general and abstract doctrine interwoven with the decision of the particular case. I have always supposed that the meaning of a law, and for a like reason, of a Constitution, so far as it depends on Judicial interpretation, was to result from a course of particular decisions, and not these from a previous and abstract comment on the subject. . . .

I could have wished also that the Judges had delivered their opinions seriatim. The case was of such magnitude, in the scope given to it, as to call, if any case could do so, for the views of the subject separately taken by them. This might either by the harmony of their reasoning have produced a greater conviction in the Public mind; or by its discordance have impaired the force of the precedent now ostensibly supported by a unanimous & perfect concurrence in every argument & dictum in the judgment pronounced.

But what is of most importance is the high sanction given to a latitude in expounding the Constitution which seems to break down the landmarks intended by a specification of the Powers of Congress, and to substitute for a definite connection between means and ends, a Legislative discretion as to the former to which no practical limit can be assigned. In the great system of Political Economy having for its general object the national welfare, everything is related immediately or remotely to every other thing; and consequently a Power over any one thing, if not limited by some obvious and precise affinity, may amount to a Power over every other. Ends & means may shift their character at the will & according to the ingenuity of the Legislative Body. What is an end in one case may be a means in another; nay in the same case, may be either an end or a means at the Legislative option. The British Parliament in collecting a revenue from the commerce of America found no difficulty in calling it either a tax for the regulation of trade, or a regulation of trade with a view to the tax, as it suited the argument or the policy of the moment.

Is there a Legislative power in fact, not expressly prohibited by the Constitution, which might not, according to the doctrine of the Court, be exercised as a means of carrying into effect some specified Power?

Does not the Court also relinquish by their doctrine, all controul on the Legislative exercise of unconstitutional powers? According to that doctrine, the expediency & constitutionality of means for carrying into effect a specified Power are convertible terms; and Congress are admitted to be Judges of the expediency. The Court certainly cannot be so; a question, the moment it assumes the character of mere expediency or policy, being evidently beyond the reach of Judicial cognizance.

It is true, the Court are disposed to retain a guardianship of the Constitution against legislative encroachments. "Should Congress," say they, "under the pretext of executing its Powers, pass laws for the accomplishment of objects not entrusted to the Government, it would become the painful duty of this Tribunal to say that such an act was not the law of the land." But suppose Congress should, as would doubtless happen, pass unconstitutional laws not to accomplish objects not specified in the Constitution, but the same laws as means expedient, convenient or conducive to the accomplishment of objects entrusted to the Government; by what handle could the Court take hold of the case? . . .

It could not but happen, and was foreseen at the birth of the Constitution, that difficulties and differences of opinion might occasionally arise in expounding terms & phrases necessarily used in such a charter; more especially those which divide legislation between the General & local Governments; and that it might require a regular course of practice to liquidate & settle the meaning of some of them. But it was anticipated I believe by few if any of the friends of the Constitution, that a rule of construction would be introduced as broad & as pliant as what has occurred. And those who recollect, and still more those who shared in what passed in the State Conventions, thro' which the people ratified the Constitution, with respect to the extent of the powers vested in Congress, cannot easily be persuaded that the avowal of such a rule would not have prevented its ratification. It has been the misfortune, if not the reproach, of other nations, that their Govts. have not been freely and deliberately established by themselves. It is the boast of ours that such has been its source and that it can be altered by the same authority only which established it. It is a further boast that a regular mode of making proper alterations has been providently inserted in the Constitution itself. It is anxiously to be wished therefore, that no innovations may take place in other modes, one of which would be a constructive assumption of powers never meant to be granted. If the powers be deficient, the legitimate source of additional ones is always open, and ought to be resorted to.

Much of the error in expounding the Constitution has its origin in the use made of the species of sovereignty implied in the nature of Govt. The specified powers vested in Congress, it is said, are sovereign powers, and that as such they carry with them an unlimited discretion as to the means of executing them. It may surely be remarked that a limited Govt. may be limited in its sovereignty as well with respect to the means as to the objects of his powers; and that to give an extent to the former, superseding the limits to the latter, is in effect to convert a limited into an unlimited Govt. There is certainly a reasonable medium between expounding the Constitution with the strictness of a penal law, or other ordinary statute, and expounding it with a laxity which may vary its essential character, and encroach on the local sovereignties with wch. it was meant to be reconcilable. . . .

In establishing [the General] Govt. the people retained other Govts. capable of exercising such necessary and useful powers as were not to be exercised by the General Govt. No necessary presumption therefore arises from the importance of any particular power in itself, that it has been vested in that Govt. because tho' not vested there, it may exist elsewhere, and the exercise of it elsewhere might be preferred by those who alone had a right to make the distribution. . . .

Here, Madison reconciled his previous constitutional objections as a congressman to a national bank decision with his decision as President to sign the bill authorizing the second bank by relying on the idea of following precedent. Years later, when he was in retirement, he elaborated on this idea. Understanding the relationship between the original meaning of the text and the doctrine of precedent remains a vexatious issue of constitutional law and theory.

STUDY GUIDE

Are you persuaded by Madison's reconciliation of his two different stances? What exactly does he see as the role of precedent and practice in establishing constitutional meaning? On his view, can precedent trump or supersede the text? If the Constitution is the "law to the legislature," why does the legislature get to decide its meaning? Doesn't that make it the judge in its own case?

JAMES MADISON, LETTER TO CHARLES J. INGERSOLL, February 2, 1831. . . . The charge of inconsistency between my objection to the constitutionality of such a bank in 1791, and my assent in 1817, turns on the question, how far legislative precedents, expounding the Constitution, ought to guide succeeding legislatures, and to overrule individual opinions. . . . The case in question has its true analogy in the obligation arising from judicial expositions of the law on succeeding judges; the constitution being a law to the legislator, as the law is a rule of decision to the judge.

And why are judicial precedents, when formed on due discussion and consideration, and deliberately sanctioned by reviews and repetitions, regarded as of binding influence, or rather of authoritative force, in settling the meaning of a law? It must be answered: 1st. Because it is a reasonable and established axiom, that the good of society requires that the rules of conduct of its members should be certain and known, which would not be the case, if any judge, disregarding the decisions of his predecessors, should vary the rule of law according to his individual interpretation of it. . . . 2d. Because an exposition of the law publicly made, and repeatedly confirmed by the constituted authority, carries with it, by fair inference, the sanction of those who, having made the law through their legislative organ, appear under such circumstances to have determined its meaning through their judiciary organ.

Can it be of less consequence that the meaning of a constitution should be fixed and known, than that the meaning of a law should be so? Can indeed a law be fixed in its meaning and operation, unless the constitution be so? On the contrary, if a particular legislature, differing in the construction of the constitution, from a series of preceding constructions, proceed to act on that difference, they not only introduce uncertainty and instability in the constitution, but in the laws themselves; inasmuch as all laws preceding the new construction and inconsistent with it, are not only annulled for the future, but virtually pronounced nullities from the beginning.

But it is said that the legislator, having sworn to support the constitution, must support it in his own construction of it, however different from that put on it by his predecessors, or whatever be the consequences of the construction. And is not the judge under the same oath to support the law? Yet has it ever been supposed that he was required, or at liberty to disregard all precedents, however solemnly repeated and regularly observed; and, by giving effect to his own abstract and individual opinions, to disturb the established course of practice in the business of the community? Has the wisest and most conscientious judge ever scrupled to acquiesce in decisions in which he has been overruled by the mature opinions of the majority of his colleagues, and subsequently to conform himself thereto, as to authoritative expositions of the law? And is it not reasonable that the same view of the official oath should be taken by a legislator, acting under the constitution, which is his guide, as is taken by a judge, acting under the law, which is his?

There is in fact and in common understanding, a necessity of regarding a course of practice, as above characterized, in the light of a legal rule of interpreting a law; and there is a like necessity of considering it a constitutional rule of interpreting a constitution. . . .

It was in conformity with the view here taken of the respect due to deliberate and reiterated precedents, that the Bank of the United States, though on the original question held to be unconstitutional, received the executive signature in the year 1817. The act originally establishing a bank had undergone ample discussions in its passage through the several branches of the government. It had been carried into execution throughout a period of twenty years with annual legislative recognitions; in one instance indeed, with a positive ramification of it into a new state; and with the entire acquiescence of all the local authorities, as well as of the nation at large, to all of which may be added, a decreasing prospect of any change in the public opinion adverse to the constitutionality of such an institution. A veto from the executive under these circumstances, with an admission of the expediency, and almost necessity of the measure, would have been a defiance of all the obligations derived from a course of precedents amounting to the requisite evidence of the national judgment and intention. . . .

President Andrew Jackson

In July 1832, President Andrew Jackson vetoed a bill reauthorizing the charter of the second bank. As was then and is still the practice, he sent a message to Congress explaining the reasons for his veto, in this case because he believed the bank to be unconstitutional. Jackson's veto message has also become famous because of his reference to "the rich and powerful."

STUDY GUIDE

- How does Jackson respond to the argument, endorsed by Madison, that precedent established the constitutionality of the bank? Does he dispute Marshall's interpretation of the Necessary and Proper Clause in *McCulloch*? Can his stance be reconciled with that decision?
- What is Jackson's view on the supremacy of Supreme Court interpretations of the Constitution? Is he arguing that he as President would not be bound by a decision of the Court, or that he as President could make an independent judgment on the necessity of a law when the issue at hand is whether to veto a bill?
- What does Jackson see as the problem of "the rich and powerful," and what is his solution to it?

ANDREW JACKSON, VETO MESSAGE, July 10, 1832

To the Senate:

The bill "to modify and continue" the act entitled "An act to incorporate the subscribers to the Bank of the United States" was presented to me on the 4th July instant. Having considered it with that solemn regard to the principles of the Constitution which the day was calculated to inspire, and come to the conclusion that it ought not to become a law, I herewith return it to the Senate, in which it originated, with my objections. . . .

It is maintained by the advocates of the bank that its constitutionality in all its features ought to be considered as settled by precedent and by the decision of the Supreme Court. To this conclusion I can not assent. Mere precedent is a dangerous source of authority, and should not be regarded as deciding questions of constitutional power except where the acquiescence of the people and the States can be considered as well settled. So far from this being the case on this subject, an argument against the bank might be based on precedent. One Congress, in 1791, decided in favor of a bank; another, in 1811, decided against it. One Congress, in 1815, decided against a bank; another, in 1816, decided in its favor. Prior to the present Congress, therefore, the precedents drawn from that source were equal. If we resort to the States, the expressions of legislative, judicial, and executive opinions against the bank have been probably to those in its favor as 4 to 1. There is nothing in precedent, therefore, which, if its authority were admitted, ought to weigh in favor of the act before me.

If the opinion of the Supreme Court covered the whole ground of this act, it ought not to control the coordinate authorities of this Government. The Congress, the Executive, and the Court must each for itself be guided by its own opinion of the Constitution. Each public officer who takes an oath to support the Constitution swears that he will support it as he understands it, and not as it is understood by others. It is as much the duty of the House of Representatives, of the Senate, and of the President to decide upon the constitutionality of any bill or resolution which may be presented to them for passage or approval as it is of the supreme judges when it may be brought before them for judicial decision. The opinion of the judges has no more authority over Congress than the opinion of Congress has over the judges, and on that point the President is independent of both. The authority of the Supreme Court must not, therefore, be permitted to control the Congress or the Executive when acting in their legislative capacities, but to have only such influence as the force of their reasoning may deserve.

Historians doubt that President Jackson wrote his famous veto message himself. Although many attribute the drafting of the message to Jackson's attorney general (and future Chief Justice) Roger Taney, who claimed credit for its authorship, evidence suggests it was initially drafted by Amos Kendall, a Kentucky newspaperman whom Jackson had rewarded with a position in the Treasury Department.[9]

But in the case relied upon the Supreme Court have not decided that all the features of this corporation are compatible with the Constitution. It is true that the court have said that the law incorporating the bank is a constitutional exercise of power by Congress; but taking into view the whole opinion of the court and the reasoning by which they have come to that conclusion, I understand them to have decided that inasmuch as a bank is an appropriate means for carrying into effect the enumerated powers of the General Government, therefore the law incorporating it is in accordance with that provision of the Constitution which declares that Congress shall have power "to make all laws which shall be necessary and proper for carrying those powers into execution." Having satisfied themselves that the word *"necessary"* in the Constitution means *"needful," "requisite," "essential," "conducive to,"* and that "a bank" is a convenient, a useful, and essential instrument in the prosecution of the Government's "fiscal operations," they conclude that to "use one must be within the discretion of Congress" and that "the act to incorporate the Bank of the United States is a law made in pursuance of the Constitution;" "but," say they, *"where the law is not prohibited and is really calculated to effect any of the objects intrusted to the Government, to undertake here to inquire into the degree of its necessity would be to pass the line which circumscribes the judicial department and to tread on legislative ground."*

[9] See Lynn L. Marshall, The Authorship of Jackson's Bank Veto Message, 50 Miss. Valley Historical Rev. 466 (1963).

The principle here affirmed is that the "degree of its necessity," involving all the details of a banking institution, is a question exclusively for legislative consideration. A bank is constitutional, but it is the province of the Legislature to determine whether this or that particular power, privilege, or exemption is "necessary and proper" to enable the bank to discharge its duties to the Government, and from their decision there is no appeal to the courts of justice. Under the decision of the Supreme Court, therefore, it is the exclusive province of Congress and the President to decide whether the particular features of this act are *necessary* and *proper* in order to enable the bank to perform conveniently and efficiently the public duties assigned to it as a fiscal agent, and therefore constitutional, or *unnecessary* and *improper*, and therefore unconstitutional.

Without commenting on the general principle affirmed by the Supreme Court, let us examine the details of this act in accordance with the rule of legislative action which they have laid down. It will be found that many of the powers and privileges conferred on it can not be supposed necessary for the purpose for which it is proposed to be created, and are not, therefore, means necessary to attain the end in view, and consequently not justified by the Constitution. . . .

It can not be *necessary* to the character of the bank as a fiscal agent of the Government that its private business should be exempted from that taxation to which all the State banks are liable, nor can I conceive it *"proper"* that the substantive and most essential powers reserved by the States shall be thus attacked and annihilated as a means of executing the powers delegated to the General Government. It may be safely assumed that none of those sages who had an agency in forming or adopting our Constitution ever imagined that any portion of the taxing power of the States not prohibited to them nor delegated to Congress was to be swept away and annihilated as a means of executing certain powers delegated to Congress.

If our power over means is so absolute that the Supreme Court will not call in question the constitutionality of an act of Congress the subject of which "is not prohibited, and is really calculated to effect any of the objects intrusted to the Government," although, as in the case before me, it takes away powers expressly granted to Congress and rights scrupulously reserved to the States, it becomes us to proceed in our legislation with the utmost caution. . . . We may not pass an act prohibiting the States to tax the banking business carried on within their limits, but we may, as a means of executing our powers over other objects, place that business in the hands of our agents and then declare it exempt from State taxation in their hands. Thus may our own powers and the rights of the States, which we can not directly curtail or invade, be frittered away and extinguished in the use of means employed by us to execute other powers. That a bank of the United States, competent to all the duties which may be required by the Government, might be so organized as not to infringe on our own delegated powers or the reserved rights of the States I do not entertain a doubt. Had the Executive been called upon to furnish the project of such an institution, the duty would have been cheerfully performed. In the absence of such a call it was obviously proper that he should confine himself to pointing out those prominent features in the act presented which in his opinion make it incompatible with the Constitution and sound policy. . . .

It is to be regretted that the rich and powerful too often bend the acts of government to their selfish purposes. Distinctions in society will always exist under every just government. Equality of talents, of education, or of wealth can not be produced by human institutions. In the full enjoyment of the gifts of Heaven and the fruits of superior industry, economy, and virtue, every man is equally entitled to protection by law; but when the laws undertake to add to these natural and just advantages artificial distinctions, to grant titles, gratuities, and exclusive privileges, to make the rich richer and the potent more powerful, the humble members of society — the farmers, mechanics, and laborers — who have neither the time nor the means of securing like favors to themselves, have a right to complain of the injustice of their Government. There are no necessary evils in government. Its evils exist only in its abuses. If it would confine itself to equal protection, and, as Heaven does its rains, shower its favors alike on the high and the low, the rich and the poor, it would be an unqualified blessing. In the act before me there seems to be a wide and unnecessary departure from these just principles. . . .

Experience should teach us wisdom. Most of the difficulties our Government now encounters and most of the dangers which impend over our Union have sprung from an abandonment of the legitimate objects of Government by our national legislation, and the adoption of such principles as are embodied in this act. Many of our rich men have not been content with equal protection and equal benefits, but have besought us to make them richer by act of Congress. By attempting to gratify their desires we have in the results of our legislation arrayed section against section, interest against interest, and man against man, in a fearful commotion which threatens to shake the foundations of our Union. It is time to pause in our career to review our principles, and if possible revive that devoted patriotism and spirit of compromise which distinguished the sages of the Revolution and the fathers of our Union. If we can not at once, in justice to interests vested under improvident legislation, make our Government what it ought to be, we can at least take a stand against all new grants of monopolies and exclusive privileges, against any prostitution of our Government to the advancement of the few at the expense of the many, and in favor of compromise and gradual reform in our code of laws and system of political economy.

I have now done my duty to my country. If sustained by my fellow citizens, I shall be grateful and happy; if not, I shall find in the motives which impel me ample grounds for contentment and peace. In the difficulties which surround us and the dangers which threaten our institutions there is cause for neither dismay nor alarm. For relief and deliverance let us firmly rely on that kind Providence which I am sure watches with peculiar care over the destinies of our Republic, and on the intelligence and wisdom of our countrymen. Through *His* abundant goodness and *their* patriotic devotion our liberty and Union will be preserved.

C. THE COMMERCE CLAUSE

ASSIGNMENT 3

The Necessary and Proper Clause refers to executing the "foregoing" powers that are "enumerated" in Article I, Section 8. The enumerated power most commonly combined with the Necessary and Proper Clause to justify national regulations is often the power of Congress "[t]o regulate commerce . . . among the several States." The fountainhead of Commerce Clause interpretation remains Chief Justice Marshall's opinion in *Gibbons v. Ogden*. *Gibbons* is another grand statement of the Federalists' theory of federalism and what it means to be a government of limited and enumerated powers.

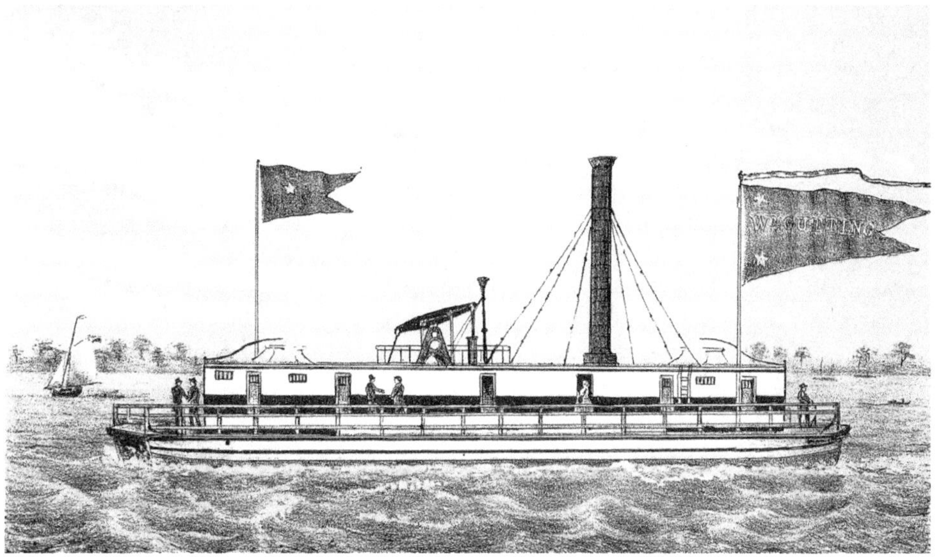

Steamboat, circa 1824

STUDY GUIDE

- How does Marshall go about defining the terms of the Commerce Clause? Does his interpretation affirm or undermine the idea of limited and enumerated powers? Under his interpretation what, if anything, is outside the power of Congress to reach? What does he see as the relationship between the powers of Congress and those of the states?
- Is this sentence referring to the text of the Necessary and Proper Clause in conflict with what he said about the clause in *McCulloch*: "But this limitation on the means which may be used, is not extended to the powers which are conferred"? Can his "pretext" language in *McCulloch* be reconciled with his statement in *Gibbons* that "the sovereignty of Congress, though limited to specified objects, is plenary as to those objects, [and] the power over commerce . . . is vested in Congress as absolutely as it would be in a single government"?
- What does Marshall's discussion of inspection laws, and Justice Johnson's discussion of health laws, imply about the limits of Congress's power under the Commerce Clause?
- Notice Justice Johnson's emphasis on the "objects" or purposes for which a measure is enacted as the way of assessing whether it is within or without the power of Congress or the states.

Gibbons v. Ogden

22 U.S. (9 Wheat.) 1 (1824)

[The Legislature of the State of New York granted Robert R. Livingston and Robert Fulton exclusive rights to operate steamboats within the state for 30 years, beginning in 1808. The rights were assigned to Aaron Ogden, the original plaintiff. In violation of this monopoly, Thomas Gibbons, the original defendant, had operated two steamboats within New York, and Ogden sued to enjoin his operation. Gibbons argued that he was authorized to do so by a 1793 act of Congress licensing his ships. The New York Court of Chancery and the Court for the Trial of Impeachments and Correction of Errors of the State of New York upheld the state law and enjoined Gibbons's operation. Gibbons appealed, arguing that the New York law granting the monopoly violated the federal Constitution. — EDS.]

MR. CHIEF JUSTICE MARSHALL delivered the opinion of the Court, and, after stating the case, proceeded as follows. . . .

As preliminary to the very able discussions of the constitution, which we have heard from the bar, and as having some influence on its construction, reference has been made to the political situation of these States, anterior to its formation. It has been said, that they were sovereign, were completely independent, and were connected with each other only by a league. This is true. But, when these allied sovereigns converted their league into a government, when they converted their Congress of Ambassadors, deputed to deliberate on their common concerns, and to recommend measures of general utility, into a Legislature, empowered to enact laws on the most interesting subjects, the whole character in which the States appear, underwent a change, the extent of which must be determined by a fair consideration of the instrument by which that change was effected.

This instrument contains an enumeration of powers expressly granted by the people to their government. It has been said, that these powers ought to be construed strictly. But why ought they to be so construed? Is there one sentence in the constitution which gives countenance to this rule? In the last of the enumerated powers, that which grants, expressly, the means for carrying all others into execution, Congress is authorized "to make all laws which shall be necessary and proper" for the purpose. But this limitation on the means which may be used, is not extended to the powers which are conferred; nor is there one sentence in the constitution, which has been pointed out by the gentlemen of the bar, or which we have been able to discern, that prescribes this rule. We do not, therefore, think ourselves justified in adopting it. What do gentlemen mean, by a strict construction? If they contend only against that enlarged construction, which would extend words beyond their natural and obvious import, we might question the application of the term, but should not controvert the principle. If they contend for that narrow construction which, in support of some theory not to be found in the constitution, would deny to the government those powers which the words of the grant, as usually understood, import, and which are consistent with the general views and objects of the instrument; for that narrow construction, which would cripple the government, and render it unequal to the object for which it is declared to be instituted, and to which the powers given, as fairly understood, render it competent; then we cannot perceive the propriety of this strict construction, nor adopt it as the rule by which the constitution is to be expounded. As men, whose intentions require no concealment, generally employ the words which most directly and aptly express the ideas they intend to convey, the enlightened patriots who framed our constitution, and the people who adopted it, must be understood to have employed words in their natural sense, and to have intended what they have said. If, from the imperfection of human language, there should be serious doubts respecting the extent of any given power, it is a well settled rule, that the objects for which it was given, especially when those objects are expressed in the instrument itself, should have great influence in the construction. We know of no reason for excluding this rule from the present case. The grant does not convey power which might be beneficial to the grantor, if retained by himself, or which can enure solely to the benefit of the grantee; but is an investment of power for the general advantage, in the hands of agents selected for that purpose; which power can never be exercised by the people themselves, but must be placed in the hands of agents, or lie dormant. We know of no rule for construing the extent of such powers, other than is given by the language of the instrument which confers them, taken in connexion with the purposes for which they were conferred.

The words are, "Congress shall have power to regulate commerce with foreign nations, and among the several States, and with the Indian tribes."

The subject to be regulated is commerce; and our constitution being, as was aptly said at the bar, one of enumeration, and not of definition, to ascertain the extent of the power, it becomes necessary to settle the meaning of the word. The counsel for the appellee would limit it to traffic, to buying and selling, or the interchange of commodities, and do not admit that it comprehends navigation. This would restrict a general term, applicable to many objects, to one of its significations. Commerce, undoubtedly, is traffic, but it is something more — it is intercourse. It describes the commercial intercourse between nations, and parts of nations, in all its branches, and is regulated by prescribing rules for carrying on that intercourse. . . .

If commerce does not include navigation, the government of the Union has no direct power over that subject, and can make no law prescribing what shall constitute American vessels, or requiring that they shall be navigated by American seamen. Yet this power has been exercised from the commencement of the government, has been exercised with the consent of all, and has been understood by all to be a commercial regulation. All America understands, and has uniformly understood, the word "commerce," to comprehend navigation. It was so understood, and must have been so understood, when the constitution was framed. The power over commerce, including navigation, was one of the primary objects for which the people of America adopted their government, and must have been contemplated in forming it. The convention must have used the word in that sense, because all have understood it in that sense; and the attempt to restrict it comes too late.

If the opinion that "commerce," as the word is used in the constitution, comprehends navigation also, requires any additional confirmation, that additional confirmation is, we think, furnished by the words of the instrument itself.

It is a rule of construction, acknowledged by all, that the exceptions from a power mark its extent; for it would be absurd, as well as useless, to except from a granted power, that which was not granted — that which the words of the grant could not comprehend. If, then, there are in the constitution plain exceptions from the power over navigation, plain inhibitions to the exercise of that power in a particular way, it is a proof that those who made these exceptions, and prescribed these inhibitions, understood the power to which they applied as being granted.

The 9th section of the 1st article declares, that "no preference shall be given, by any regulation of commerce or revenue, to the ports of one State over those of another." This clause cannot be understood as applicable to those laws only which are passed for the purposes of revenue, because it is expressly applied to commercial regulations; and the most obvious preference which can be given to one port over another, in regulating commerce, relates to navigation. But the subsequent part of the sentence is still more explicit. It is, "nor shall vessels bound to or from one State, be obliged to enter, clear, or pay duties, in another." These words have a direct reference to navigation. . . .

The universally acknowledged power of the government to impose embargoes, must also be considered as showing, that all America is united in that construction which comprehends navigation in the word commerce. . . . When Congress imposed that embargo which, for a time, engaged the attention of every man in the United States, the avowed object of the law was, the protection of commerce, and the avoiding of war. By its friends and its enemies it was treated as a commercial, not as a war measure. . . . They did, indeed, contest the constitutionality of the act, but, on a principle which admits the construction for which the appellant contends. They denied that the particular law in question was made in pursuance of the constitution, not because the power could not act directly on vessels, but because a perpetual embargo was the annihilation, and not the regulation of commerce. . . .

The word used in the constitution, then, comprehends, and has been always understood to comprehend, navigation within its meaning; and a power to regulate navigation, is as expressly granted, as if that term had been added to the word "commerce."

To what commerce does this power extend? The constitution informs us, to commerce "with foreign nations, and among the several States, and with the Indian tribes."

It has, we believe, been universally admitted, that these words comprehend every species of commercial intercourse between the United States and foreign nations. No sort of trade can be carried on between this country and any other, to which this power does not extend. It has been truly said, that commerce, as the word is used in the constitution, is a unit, every part of which is indicated by the term.

If this be the admitted meaning of the word, in its application to foreign nations, it must carry the same meaning throughout the sentence, and remain a unit, unless there be some plain intelligible cause which alters it.

The subject to which the power is next applied, is to commerce "among the several States." The word "among" means intermingled with. A thing which is among others, is intermingled with them. Commerce among the States, cannot stop at the external boundary line of each State, but may be introduced into the interior.

It is not intended to say that these words comprehend that commerce, which is completely internal, which is carried on between man and man in a State, or between different parts of the same State, and which does not extend to or affect other States. Such a power would be inconvenient, and is certainly unnecessary.

Comprehensive as the word "among" is, it may very properly be restricted to that commerce which concerns more States than one. The phrase is not one which would probably have been selected to indicate the completely interior traffic of a State, because it is not an apt phrase for that purpose; and the enumeration of the particular classes of commerce, to which the power was to be extended, would not have been made, had the intention been to extend the power to every description. The enumeration presupposes something not enumerated; and that something, if we regard the language or the subject of the sentence, must be the exclusively internal commerce of a State. The genius and character of the whole government seem to be, that its action is to be applied to all the external concerns of the nation, and to those internal concerns which affect the States generally; but not to those which are completely within a particular State, which do not affect other States, and with which it is not necessary to interfere, for the purpose of executing some of the general powers of the government. The completely internal commerce of a State, then, may be considered as reserved for the State itself.

But, in regulating commerce with foreign nations, the power of Congress does not stop at the jurisdictional lines of the several States. It would be a very useless power, if it could not pass those lines. The commerce of the United States with foreign nations, is that of the whole United States. Every district has a right to participate in it. The deep streams which penetrate our country in every direction, pass through the interior of almost every State in the Union, and furnish the means of exercising this right. If Congress has the power to regulate it, that power must be exercised whenever the subject exists. If it exists within the States, if a foreign voyage may commence or terminate at a port within a State, then the power of Congress may be exercised within a State.

This principle is, if possible, still more clear, when applied to commerce "among the several States." They either join each other, in which case they are separated by a mathematical line, or they are remote from each other, in which case other States lie between them. What is commerce "among" them; and how is it to be conducted? Can a trading expedition between two adjoining States, commence and terminate outside of each? And if the trading intercourse be between two States remote from each other, must it not commence in one, terminate in the other, and probably pass through a third? Commerce among the States must, of necessity, be commerce with the States. In the regulation of trade with the Indian tribes, the action of the law, especially when the constitution was made, was chiefly within a State. The power of Congress, then, whatever it may be, must be exercised within the territorial jurisdiction of the several States. . . .

We are now arrived at the inquiry — What is this power?

It is the power to regulate; that is, to prescribe the rule by which commerce is to be governed. This power, like all others vested in Congress, is complete in itself, may be exercised to its utmost extent, and acknowledges no limitations, other than are prescribed in the constitution. These are expressed in plain terms, and do not affect the questions which arise in this case, or which have been discussed at the bar. If, as has always been understood, the sovereignty of Congress, though limited to specified objects, is plenary as to those objects, the power over commerce with foreign nations, and among the several States, is vested in Congress as absolutely as it would be in a single government, having in its constitution the same restrictions on the exercise of the power as are found in the constitution of the United States. The wisdom and the discretion of Congress, their identity with the people, and the influence which their constituents possess at elections, are, in this, as in many other instances, as that, for example, of declaring war, the sole restraints on which they have relied, to secure them from its abuse. They are the restraints on which the people must often rely solely, in all representative governments.

The power of Congress, then, comprehends navigation, within the limits of every State in the Union; so far as that navigation may be, in any manner, connected with "commerce with foreign nations, or among the several States, or with the Indian tribes." It may, of consequence, pass the jurisdictional line of New York, and act upon the very waters to which the prohibition now under consideration applies.

But it has been urged with great earnestness, that . . . the States may severally exercise the same power, within their respective jurisdictions. In support of this argument, it is said, that they possessed it as an inseparable attribute of sovereignty, before the formation of the constitution, and still retain it, except so far as they have surrendered it by that instrument; that this principle results from the nature of the government, and is secured by the tenth amendment; that an affirmative grant of power is not exclusive, unless in its own nature it be such that the continued exercise of it by the former possessor is inconsistent with the grant, and that this is not of that description. . . .

The grant of the power to lay and collect taxes is, like the power to regulate commerce, made in general terms, and has never been understood to interfere with the exercise of the same power by the State. . . . But the two grants are not, it is conceived, similar in their terms or their nature. Although many of the powers formerly exercised by the States, are transferred to the government of the Union, yet the State governments remain, and constitute a most important part of our system. The power of taxation is indispensable to their existence, and is a power which, in its own nature, is capable of residing in, and being exercised by, different authorities at the same time. We are accustomed to see it placed, for different purposes, in different hands. Taxation is the simple operation of taking small portions from a perpetually accumulating mass, susceptible of almost infinite division; and a power in one to take what is necessary for certain purposes, is not, in its nature, incompatible with a power in another to take what is necessary for other purposes. Congress is authorized to lay and collect taxes, &c. to pay the debts, and provide for the common defence and general welfare of the United States. This does not interfere with the power of the States to tax for the support of their own governments; nor is the exercise of that power by the States, an exercise of any portion of the power that is granted to the United States. In imposing taxes for State purposes, they are not doing what Congress is empowered to do. Congress is not empowered to tax for those purposes which are within the exclusive province of the States. When, then, each government exercises the power of taxation, neither is exercising the power of the other. But, when a State proceeds to regulate commerce with foreign nations, or among the several States, it is exercising the very power that is granted to Congress, and is doing the very thing which Congress is authorized to do. There is no analogy, then, between the power of taxation and the power of regulating commerce.

In discussing the question, whether this power is still in the States, in the case under consideration, we may dismiss from it the inquiry, whether it is surrendered by the mere grant to Congress, or is retained until Congress shall exercise the power. We may dismiss that inquiry, because it has been exercised, and the regulations which Congress deemed it proper to make, are now in full operation. The sole question is, can a State regulate commerce with foreign nations and among the States, while Congress is regulating it?

The counsel for the respondent answer this question in the affirmative, and rely very much on the restrictions in the 10th section, as supporting their opinion. They say, very truly, that limitations of a power, furnish a strong argument in favour of the existence of that power, and that the section which prohibits the States from laying duties on imports or exports, proves that this power might have been exercised, had it not been expressly forbidden; and, consequently, that any other commercial regulation, not expressly forbidden, to which the original power of the State was competent, may still be made.

That this restriction shows the opinion of the Convention, that a State might impose duties on exports and imports, if not expressly forbidden, will be conceded; but that it follows as a consequence, from this concession, that a State may regulate commerce with foreign nations and among the States, cannot be admitted.

We must first determine whether the act of laying "duties or imposts on imports or exports," is considered in the constitution as a branch of the taxing power, or of the power to regulate commerce. We think it very clear, that it is considered as a branch of the taxing power. It is so treated in the first clause of the 8th section: "Congress shall have power to lay and collect taxes, duties, imposts, and excises"; and, before commerce is mentioned, the rule by which the exercise of this power must be governed, is declared. It is, that all duties, imposts, and excises, shall be uniform. In a separate clause of the enumeration, the power to regulate commerce is given, as being entirely distinct from the right to levy taxes and imposts, and as being a new power, not before conferred. The constitution, then, considers these powers as substantive, and distinct from each other; and so places them in the enumeration it contains. The power of imposing duties on imports is classed with the power to levy taxes, and that seems to be its natural place. But the power to levy taxes could never be considered as abridging the right of the States on that subject; and they might, consequently, have exercised it by levying duties on imports or exports, had the constitution contained no prohibition on this subject. This prohibition, then, is an exception from the acknowledged power of the States to levy taxes, not from the questionable power to regulate commerce. . . .

These restrictions, then, are on the taxing power, not on that to regulate commerce; and presuppose the existence of that which they restrain, not of that which they do not purport to restrain.

But, the inspection laws are said to be regulations of commerce, and are certainly recognised in the constitution, as being passed in the exercise of a power remaining with the States.

That inspection laws may have a remote and considerable influence on commerce, will not be denied; but that a power to regulate commerce is the source from which the right to pass them is derived, cannot be admitted. The object of inspection laws, is to improve the quality of articles produced by the labour of a country; to fit them for exportation; or, it may be, for domestic use. They act upon the subject before it becomes an article of foreign commerce, or of commerce among the States, and prepare it for that purpose. They form a portion of that immense mass of legislation, which embraces every thing within the territory of a State, not surrendered to the general government: all which can be most advantageously exercised by the States themselves. Inspection laws, quarantine laws, health laws of every description, as well as laws for regulating the internal commerce of a State, and those which respect turnpike roads, ferries, &c., are component parts of this mass.

No direct general power over these objects is granted to Congress; and, consequently, they remain subject to State legislation. If the legislative power of the Union can reach them, it must be for national purposes; it must be where the power is expressly given for a special purpose, or is clearly incidental to some power which is expressly given. It is obvious, that the government of the Union, in the exercise of its express powers, that, for example, of regulating commerce with foreign nations and among the States, may use means that may also be employed by a State, in the exercise of its acknowledged powers; that, for example, of regulating commerce within the State. If Congress license vessels to sail from one port to another, in the same State, the act is supposed to be, necessarily, incidental to the power expressly granted to Congress, and implies no claim of a direct power to regulate the purely internal commerce of a State, or to act directly on its system of police. So, if a State, in passing laws on subjects acknowledged to be within its control, and with a view to those subjects, shall adopt a measure of the same character with one which Congress may adopt, it does not derive its authority from the particular power which has been granted, but from some other, which remains with the State, and may be executed by the same means. All experience shows, that the same measures, or measures scarcely distinguishable from each other, may flow from distinct powers; but this does not prove that the powers themselves are identical. Although the means used in their execution may sometimes approach each other so nearly as to be confounded, there are other situations in which they are sufficiently distinct to establish their individuality.

In our complex system, presenting the rare and difficult scheme of one general government, whose action extends over the whole, but which possesses only certain enumerated powers; and of numerous State governments, which retain and exercise all powers not delegated to the Union, contests respecting power must arise. Were it even otherwise, the measures taken by the respective governments to execute their acknowledged powers, would often be of the same description, and might, sometimes, interfere. This, however, does not prove that the one is exercising, or has a right to exercise, the powers of the other. . . .

The act passed in 1803, prohibiting the importation of slaves into any State which shall itself prohibit their importation, implies, it is said, an admission that the States possessed the power to exclude or admit them; from which it is inferred, that they possess the same power with respect to other articles. . . . But it is obvious, that the power of the States over this subject, previous to the year 1808, constitutes an exception to the power of Congress to regulate commerce, and the exception is expressed in such words, as to manifest clearly the intention to continue the pre-existing right of the States to admit or exclude, for a limited period. . . .

It has been contended by the counsel for the appellant, that, as the word "to regulate" implies in its nature, full power over the thing to be regulated, it excludes, necessarily, the action of all others that would perform the same operation on the same thing. That regulation is designed for the entire result, applying to those parts which remain as they were, as well as to those which are altered. It produces a uniform whole, which is as much disturbed and deranged by changing what the regulating power designs to leave untouched, as that on which it has operated.

There is great force in this argument, and the Court is not satisfied that it has been refuted. . . .

In argument . . . it has been contended that, if a law passed by a State, in the exercise of its acknowledged sovereignty, comes into conflict with a law passed by Congress in pursuance of the Constitution, they affect the subject and each other like equal opposing powers.

But the framers of our Constitution foresaw this state of things, and provided for it by declaring the supremacy not only of itself, but of the laws made in pursuance of it. The nullity of any act inconsistent with the Constitution is produced by the declaration that the Constitution is the supreme law. The appropriate application of that part of the clause which confers the same supremacy on laws and treaties is to such acts of the State Legislatures as do not transcend their powers, but, though enacted in the execution of acknowledged State powers, interfere with, or are contrary to, the laws of Congress made in pursuance of the Constitution or some treaty made under the authority of the United States. In every such case, the act of Congress or the treaty is supreme, and the law of the State, though enacted in the exercise of powers not controverted, must yield to it. . . .

Powerful and ingenious minds, taking, as postulates, that the powers expressly granted to the government of the Union, are to be contracted by construction, into the narrowest possible compass, and that the original powers of the States are retained, if any possible construction will retain them, may, by a course of well digested, but refined and metaphysical reasoning, founded on these premises, explain away the constitution of our country, and leave it, a magnificent structure, indeed, to look at, but totally unfit for use. They may so entangle and perplex the understanding, as to obscure principles, which were before thought quite plain, and induce doubts where, if the mind were to pursue its own course, none would be perceived. In such a case, it is peculiarly necessary to recur to safe and fundamental principles to sustain those principles, and when sustained, to make them the tests of the arguments to be examined.

MR. JUSTICE JOHNSON . . .

The "power to regulate commerce," here meant to be granted, was that power to regulate commerce which previously existed in the States. But what was that power? . . . When speaking of the power of Congress over navigation, I do not regard it as a power incidental to that of regulating commerce; I consider it as the thing itself; inseparable from it as vital motion is from vital existence.

Commerce, in its simplest signification, means an exchange of goods; but in the advancement of society, labour, transportation, intelligence, care, and various mediums of exchange, become commodities, and enter into commerce; the subject, the vehicle, the agent, and their various operations, become the objects of commercial regulation. Ship building, the carrying trade, and propagation of seamen, are such vital agents of commercial prosperity, that the nation which could not legislate over these subjects, would not possess power to regulate commerce. . . .

It is no objection to the existence of distinct, substantive powers, that, in their application, they bear upon the same subject. The same bale of goods, the same cask of provisions, or the same ship, that may be the subject of commercial regulation, may also be the vehicle of disease. And the health laws that require them to be stopped and ventilated, are no more intended as regulations on commerce, than the laws which permit their importation, are intended to innoculate the community with disease. Their different purposes mark the distinction between the powers brought into action; and while frankly exercised, they can produce no serious collision. . . .

Wherever the powers of the respective governments are frankly exercised, with a distinct view to the ends of such powers, they may act upon the same object, or use the same means, and yet the powers be kept perfectly distinct. A resort to the same means, therefore, is no argument to prove the identity of their respective powers. . . .

Evidence of the Meaning of the Word "Commerce"

One of the questions raised by *Gibbons* concerns the meaning of the word "commerce" as used in the Commerce Clause. "Commerce" might be limited to trade or exchange of goods, which would exclude, for example, agriculture, manufacturing, and other methods of production, or it might be interpreted expansively to refer to any gainful activity.[10] The use of the term "commerce" in the drafting and ratification process was remarkably uniform, however. Indeed, there appears to be not a single example from the reports of these proceedings that unambiguously used a broad meaning of "commerce" and many instances where the context makes clear that the speaker intended a narrow meaning. As we shall see in Chapter 3, when the Supreme Court expanded its construction of federal power in cases involving economic regulations, it did so by stressing the Necessary and Proper Clause rather than by expanding the meaning of the term "commerce" itself.

---

[10] See Robert J. Pushaw, Jr. & Grant S. Nelson, A Critique of the Narrow Interpretation of the Commerce Clause, 96 Nw. U. L. Rev. 695 (2002) (contending that the term "commerce" in the Commerce Clause meant gainful activity). Jack Balkin has proposed that "commerce" in the Commerce Clause be read even more broadly to mean "interaction" between persons. See Jack M. Balkin, Commerce, 109 Mich. L. Rev. 1 (2010). For a reply, see Randy E. Barnett, Jack Balkin's Interaction Theory of "Commerce," 2012 U. Ill. L. Rev. 623.

STUDY GUIDE

Even if the original meaning of the term "commerce" was limited to trade and excluded productive activities such as agriculture and manufacturing, would this necessarily limit the scope of the powers of Congress under Marshall's interpretation of the Necessary and Proper Clause in *McCulloch*? What is the relationship between the Necessary and Proper Clause and the enumerated powers that precede it in Article I, Section 8? We will return to these questions repeatedly as we consider the materials that concern the structure of government established by the Constitution.

Contemporary Dictionaries. The Oxford English Dictionary gives the etymology of "commerce" as "with merchandise": "com 'with'; merci 'merchandise.'"[11] The 1785 edition of Samuel Johnson's Dictionary of the English Language defines "commerce" as "1. Intercourse; exchange of one thing for another; interchange of any thing; trade; traffick." In contrast, "manufacture" is defined as "1. The practice of making any piece of workmanship. 2. Any thing made by art." "Agriculture" is defined as "[t]he art of cultivating the ground; tillage; husbandry, as distinct from pasturage." If Johnson is accurate, commerce referred predominantly to exchange or trade as distinct from the agricultural or manufacturing production of those things that are subsequently traded. Johnson's definition of "commerce" is borne out by other dictionaries of the time.[12] It is also the usage most closely associated with the drafting and adoption of the Constitution.

The Constitutional Convention. In Madison's notes on the Constitutional Convention, the term "commerce" appears thirty-four times in the speeches of the delegates. Eight of these entries are unambiguous references to commerce with foreign nations, which can consist only of trade. In every other instance, the terms "trade" or "exchange" could be substituted for the term "commerce" with the apparent meaning of the statement preserved. In no instance is the term "commerce" clearly used to refer to "any gainful activity" or anything broader than trade. One congressional power proposed by Madison, but not ultimately adopted, suggests that the delegates shared the limited meaning of "commerce" described in Johnson's dictionary. Madison proposed to grant Congress the power "[t]o establish public institutions, rewards, and immunities for the promotion of agriculture,

---

[11] Oxford English Dictionary 552 (2d ed. 1989).

[12] See, e.g., Nathan Bailey, An Universal Etymological English Dictionary, 26th ed. (Edinburgh: Neill & Co., 1789) ("trade or traffic"); T. Sheridan, A Complete Dictionary of the English Language 585-586, 6th ed. (Philadelphia: W. Young, Mills & Son, 1796) ("Exchange of one thing for another; trade, traffick").

commerce, trades and manufactures,"[13] strongly indicating that the members understood the term "commerce" to mean trade or exchange, as distinct from the productive processes that made the things to be traded.

The Federalist. In several of his contributions to *The Federalist*, Alexander Hamilton repeatedly recognized the commonplace distinction between commerce, or trade, and production. In *Federalist No. 11*, he also explained the purpose of the Commerce Clause, a purpose entirely consistent with the prevailing "core" meaning of the term "commerce":

> An unrestrained intercourse between the States themselves will advance the trade of each by an interchange of their respective productions, not only for the supply of reciprocal wants at home, but for exportation to foreign markets. The veins of commerce in every part will be replenished and will acquire additional motion and vigor from a free circulation of the commodities of every part. Commercial enterprise will have much greater scope from the diversity in the productions of different States.

In *Federalist No. 12*, he referred to the "rivalship," now silenced, "between agriculture and commerce," while in *Federalist No. 17*, he distinguished between the power to regulate such national matters as commerce and "the supervision of agriculture and of other concerns of a similar nature, all those things, in short, which are proper to be provided for by local legislation." In *Federalist No. 21*, Hamilton maintained that causes of the wealth of nations were of "an infinite variety," including "[s]ituation, soil, climate, the nature of the productions, the nature of the government, the genius of the citizens, the degree of information they possess, the state of commerce, of arts, of industry." In *Federalist No. 35*, he asked, "Will not the merchant understand and be disposed to cultivate, as far as may be proper, the interests of the mechanic and manufacturing arts to which his commerce is so nearly allied?"

In none of the sixty-three appearances of the term "commerce" in *The Federalist* is it ever used to refer unambiguously to any activity beyond trade or exchange. Later, Hamilton's usage did not change. As secretary of the treasury, his official opinion to President Washington advocating a broad congressional power to incorporate a national bank (that appears in Chapter 1) repeatedly referred to Congress's power under the Commerce Clause as the power to regulate the "trade between the States."

Ratification Conventions. In the state ratification conventions, speakers uniformly used the term "commerce" as a synonym for trade or exchange, including shipping — and did not include agriculture, manufacturing, or other business (apart from shipping or navigation).

In the records of the Massachusetts convention, the word "commerce" is used nineteen times — every use consistent with it meaning trade — mostly foreign trade — and no use clearly indicating a broader meaning. The most explicit distinction was made by Thomas Dawes, a prominent revolutionary and legislator, who began his discussion on the importance of the national taxation powers, "We have

---

[13] The term "trades" connotes crafts and other types of trades, not trade or exchange.

suffered for want of such authority in the federal head. This will be evident if we take a short view of our agriculture, commerce, and manufactures." He then expounded at some length, giving separate attention to each of these activities and the beneficial effect the Constitution would have on them. Under the heading of "commerce," he referred to "our own domestic traffic that passes from state to state."

In the New York convention, the delegate who repeatedly made the clearest distinction between commerce and other economic activity was Alexander Hamilton. As part of a lengthy speech, he observed: "The Southern States possess certain staples, — tobacco, rice, indigo, &c., — which must be capital objects in treaties of commerce with foreign nations." The same distinction is implicit in his denial that the regulation of commerce was outside the competency of a central government: "What are the objects of the government? Commerce, taxation, &c. In order to comprehend the interests of commerce, is it necessary to know how wheat is raised, and in what proportion it is produced in one district and in another? By no means." Later, in defending the power of direct taxation, Hamilton predicted that in its absence, the "general government . . . will push imposts [on our commerce] to an extreme." As a result, "[o]ur neighbors, not possessed of our advantages for commerce and agriculture, will become manufacturers: their property will, in a great measure, be vested in the commodities of their own productions; but a small proportion will be in trade or in lands. Thus, on the gentleman's scheme, they will be almost free from burdens, while we shall be loaded with them."

In the report of the Pennsylvania ratification convention, all eight uses of the term are consistent with the narrow meaning of "commerce"; none clearly uses a broader meaning. The most revealing comment is made by James Wilson, a member of the Constitutional Convention:

> Suppose we reject this system of government; what will be the consequence? Let the farmer say, he whose produce remains unasked for; nor can he find a single market for its consumption, though his fields are blessed with luxuriant abundance. Let the manufacturer, and let the mechanic, say; they can feel, and tell their feelings. Go along the wharves of Philadelphia, and observe the melancholy silence that reigns. . . . Let the merchants tell you what is our commerce.

In the North Carolina debates, "commerce" is mentioned eighteen times. As elsewhere, there are no clear uses of it in any sense broader than "trade" or "exchange" and a few clear examples of its use in the narrow sense in speeches by William Davie. Davie defined the "general objects of the union" to be "1st, to protect us against foreign invasion; 2nd, to defend us against internal commotions and insurrections; 3rd, to promote the commerce, agriculture, and manufactures, of America." Later, he explained why the regulation of commerce, though distinct from agriculture and manufacturing, promoted them: "Commerce, sir, is the nurse of both. The merchant furnishes the planter with such articles as he cannot manufacture himself, and finds him a market for his produce. Agriculture cannot flourish if commerce languishes; they are mutually dependent on each other."

In the reports of the South Carolina convention, the word "commerce" is used twenty-six times. Charles Pinckney — a delegate to the Constitutional Convention — equated "the regulation of commerce" and mere "privileges with regard to shipping," when he asked, "If our government is to be founded on equal compact, what inducement can [the Eastern states] possibly have to be united with us, if we do not grant them some privileges with regard to their shipping?"

Virginia wins the prize, with seventy-four mentions of "commerce." Here, as elsewhere, there is not a single instance of "commerce" being used unambiguously in the broader sense. To the contrary, the most striking evidence is the dominance of a conception of commerce that is even narrower than "trade" or "exchange" — also manifested by Pinckney's reference in the South Carolina debates to "privileges with regard to shipping." In Virginia, at least seventeen references link "commerce" in some way to ports, shipping, navigation, or the "carrying trades." In other words, on these occasions, the term "commerce" is limited to conveying or transporting the articles of trade, rather than to the entire act of trading. Common as was such usage, "commerce" was not used solely to refer to shipping in Virginia. Others of the sort seen elsewhere appear here as well. Edmund Pendleton, for instance, viewed "commerce" as the means by which "the people may have an opportunity of disposing of their crops at market, and of procuring such supplies as they may be in want of." So synonymous was "commerce" with "trade" that William Grayson worried that "the whole commerce of the United States may be exclusively carried on by merchants residing within the seat of government," referring to what became the District of Columbia.

These findings confirm Madison's observation, made late in his life, that "[i]f, in citing the Constitution, the word trade was put in the place of commerce, the word foreign made it synonymous with commerce. Trade and commerce are, in fact, used indiscriminately, both in books and in conversation."

D. THE "BILL OF RIGHTS"

ASSIGNMENT 4

Today most people take for granted that state governments must respect the rights contained in the Bill of Rights. But this is a relatively modern development that took place only after the adoption of the Fourteenth Amendment. Indeed, it was not until sometime in the twentieth century that the first ten amendments came commonly to be called "the Bill of Rights." Prior to then, they were generally referred to merely as "amendments." In *Barron v. Baltimore*, Chief Justice Marshall described what came to be the settled view (pre–Fourteenth Amendment) of how and why the rights in the first ten amendments did *not* apply to the states. Reading *Barron* in its entirety is essential to understanding the objectives of the Republicans in the Thirty-ninth Congress who drafted the Fourteenth Amendment, portions of which were meant to reverse *Barron*. In this respect, *Barron* is to the Fourteenth Amendment what *Chisholm v. Georgia* is to the Eleventh. The reasoning of *Barron* is also crucial to appreciating both the need for, and the controversy surrounding, the so-called incorporation doctrine — developed in the twentieth century — by which selected *portions* of these rights were "incorporated" into the Fourteenth Amendment and applied to the states.

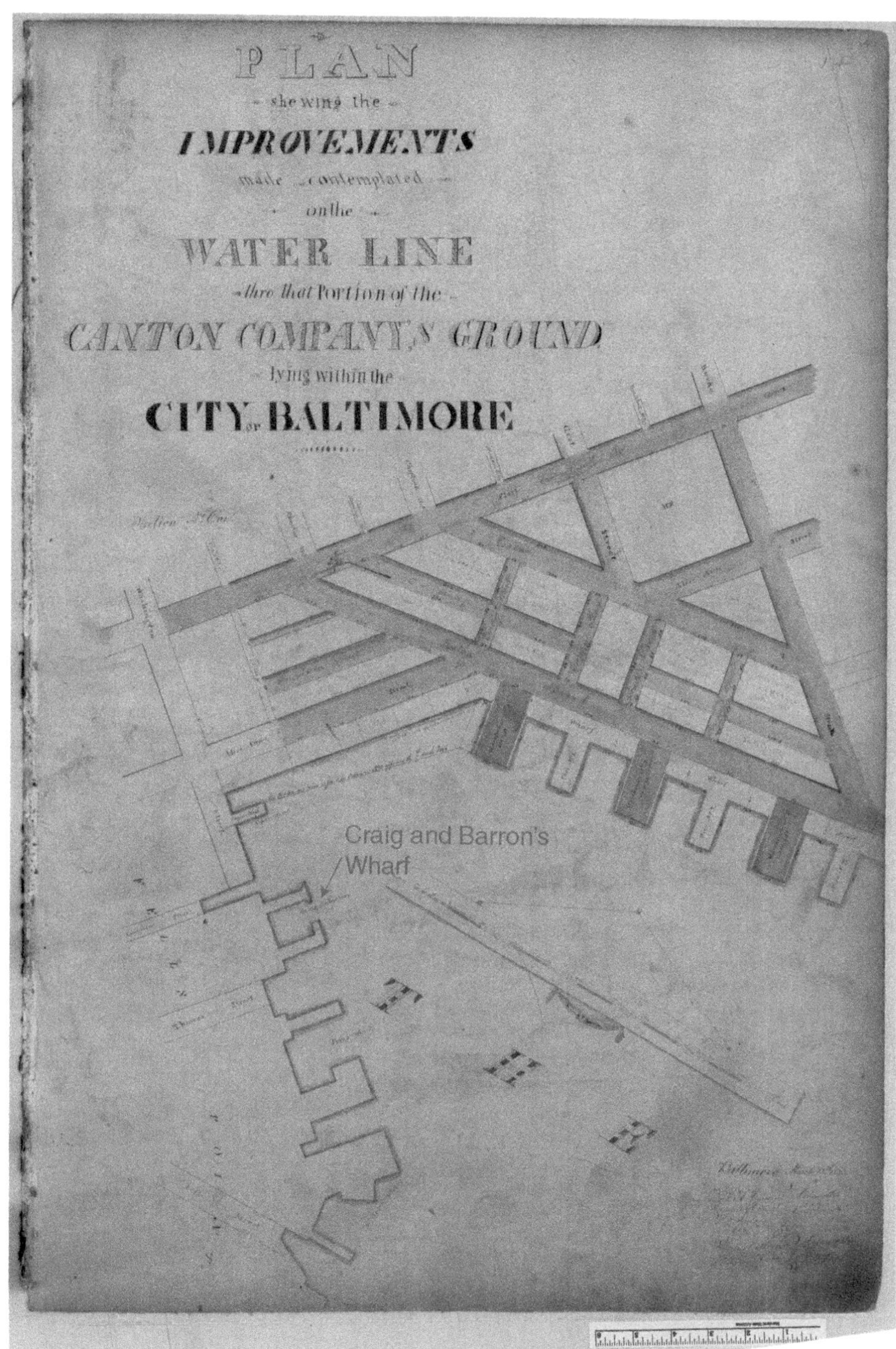

John Barron's Wharf in Baltimore from Bouldin Atlas (1833)

STUDY GUIDE

- Is Marshall's limitation of the Bill of Rights grounded in its text? In its historical origins? In the problems that were supposed to be addressed by a Bill of Rights?
- Look at the first ten amendments to see if they specify against which level of government they are supposed to apply.
- Is Marshall's opinion supported by Madison's initial proposal to Congress for a bill of rights (Chapter 1)?
- Can you see how Marshall's theory of the Bill of Rights derives from his views of sovereignty, and will undercut the later claim of a right of states to secede from the Union?

Barron v. City of Baltimore

32 U.S. (7 Pet.) 243 (1833)

[John Barron owned a profitable wharf in the Baltimore harbor. He sued the mayor of Baltimore for damages, claiming that (1) when the city had diverted the flow of streams while engaging in street construction, it had created mounds of sand and earth near his wharf, making the water too shallow for most vessels; and (2) that this constituted a "taking" of private property for public use without just compensation under the Fifth Amendment. — EDS.]

MR. CHIEF JUSTICE MARSHALL, delivered the opinion of the court.

The judgment brought up by this writ of error having been rendered by the court of a state, this tribunal can exercise no jurisdiction over it, unless it be shown to come within the provisions of the 25th section of the judiciary act. The plaintiff in error contends, that it comes within that clause in the fifth amendment to the constitution, which inhibits the taking of private property for public use, without just compensation. He insists, that this amendment being in favor of the liberty of the citizen, ought to be so construed as to restrain the legislative power of a state, as well as that of the United States. If this proposition be untrue, the court can take no jurisdiction of the cause.

> One of the lawyers for the City of Baltimore was future Chief Justice Roger Taney.

The question thus presented is, we think, of great importance, but not of much difficulty. The constitution was ordained and established by the people of the United States for themselves, for their own government, and not for the government of the individual states. Each state established a constitution for itself, and in that constitution, provided such limitations and restrictions on the powers of its particular government, as its judgment dictated. The people of the United States framed such a government for the United States as they supposed best adapted to their situation and best calculated to promote their interests. The powers they conferred on this government were to be exercised by itself; and the limitations on power, if expressed in general terms, are naturally, and, we think, necessarily, applicable to the government created by the instrument. They are limitations of power granted in the instrument itself; not of distinct governments, framed by different persons and for different purposes.

If these propositions be correct, the fifth amendment must be understood as restraining the power of the general government, not as applicable to the states. In their several constitutions, they have imposed such restrictions on their respective governments, as their own wisdom suggested; such as they deemed most proper for themselves. It is a subject on which they judge exclusively, and with which others interfere no further than they are supposed to have a common interest.

The counsel for the plaintiff in error insists, that the constitution was intended to secure the people of the several states against the undue exercise of power by their respective state governments; as well as against that which might be attempted by their general government. In support of this argument he relies on the inhibitions contained in the tenth section of the first article. We think, that section affords a strong, if not a conclusive, argument in support of the opinion already indicated by the court. The preceding section contains restrictions which are obviously intended for the exclusive purpose of restraining the exercise of power by the departments of the general government. Some of them use language applicable only to congress; others are expressed in general terms. The third clause, for example, declares, that "no bill of attainder or ex post facto law shall be passed." No language can be more general; yet the demonstration is complete, that it applies solely to the government of the United States. In addition to the general arguments furnished by the instrument itself, some of which have been already suggested, the succeeding section, the avowed purpose of which is to restrain state legislation, contains in terms the very prohibition. It declares, that "no state shall pass any bill of attainder or ex post facto law." This provision, then, of the ninth section, however comprehensive its language, contains no restriction on state legislation.

The ninth section having enumerated, in the nature of a bill of rights, the limitations intended to be imposed on the powers of the general government, the tenth proceeds to enumerate those which were to operate on the state legislatures. These restrictions are brought together in the same section, and are by express words applied to the states. "No state shall enter into any treaty," &c. Perceiving, that in a constitution framed by the people of the United States, for the government of all, no limitation of the action of government on the people would apply to the state government, unless expressed in terms, the restrictions contained in the tenth section are in direct words so applied to the states.

It is worthy of remark, too, that these inhibitions generally restrain state legislation on subjects intrusted to the general government, or in which the people of all the states feel an interest. A state is forbidden to enter into any treaty, alliance or confederation. If these compacts are with foreign nations, they interfere with the treaty-making power, which is conferred entirely on the general government; if with each other, for political purposes, they can scarcely fail to interfere with the general purpose and intent of the constitution. To grant letters of marque and reprisal, would lead directly to war; the power of declaring which is expressly given to congress. To coin money is also the exercise of a power conferred on congress. It would be tedious to recapitulate the several limitations on the powers of the states which are contained in this section. They will be found, generally, to restrain state legislation on subjects intrusted to the government of the Union, in which the citizens of all the states are interested. In these alone, were the whole people concerned. The question of their application to states is not left to construction. It is averred in positive words.

If the original constitution, in the ninth and tenth sections of the first article, draws this plain and marked line of discrimination between the limitations it imposes on the powers of the general government, and on those of the state; if, in every inhibition intended to act on state power, words are employed, which directly express that intent; some strong reason must be assigned for departing from this safe and judicious course, in framing the amendments, before that departure can be assumed. We search in vain for that reason.

Had the people of the several states, or any of them, required changes in their constitutions; had they required additional safe-guards to liberty from the apprehended encroachments of their particular governments; the remedy was in their own hands, and could have been applied by themselves. A convention could have been assembled by the discontented state, and the required improvements could have been made by itself. The unwieldy and cumbrous machinery of procuring a recommendation from two-thirds of congress, and the assent of three-fourths of their sister states, could never have occurred to any human being, as a mode of doing that which might be effected by the state itself. Had the framers of these amendments intended them to be limitations on the powers of the state governments, they would have imitated the framers of the original constitution, and have expressed that intention. Had congress engaged in the extraordinary occupation of improving the constitutions of the several states, by affording the people additional protection from the exercise of power by their own governments, in matters which concerned themselves alone, they would have declared this purpose in plain and intelligible language.

But it is universally understood, it is a part of the history of the day, that the great revolution which established the constitution of the United States, was not effected without immense opposition. Serious fears were extensively entertained, that those powers which the patriot statesmen, who then watched over the interests of our country, deemed essential to union, and to the attainment of those invaluable objects for which union was sought, might be exercised in a manner dangerous to liberty. In almost every convention by which the constitution was adopted, amendments to guard against the abuse of power were recommended. These amendments demanded security against the apprehended encroachments of the general government — not against those of the local governments. In compliance with a sentiment thus generally expressed, to quiet fears thus extensively entertained, amendments were proposed by the required majority in congress, and adopted by the states. These amendments contain no expression indicating an intention to apply them to the state governments. This court cannot so apply them.

We are of opinion, that the provision in the fifth amendment to the constitution, declaring that private property shall not be taken for public use, without just compensation, is intended solely as a limitation on the exercise of power by the government of the United States, and is not applicable to the legislation of the states. We are, therefore, of opinion, that there is no repugnancy between the several acts of the general assembly of Maryland, given in evidence by the defendants at the trial of this cause, in the court of that state, and the constitution of the United States. This court, therefore, has no jurisdiction of the cause, and it is dismissed.

PART II

THE LEGISLATIVE POWER

CHAPTER 3

Enumerated Powers

ASSIGNMENT 1

Article I, Section 1 of the Constitution reads, "All legislative powers herein granted shall be vested in a Congress of the United States, which shall consist of a Senate and House of Representatives." Note that "herein granted" qualifies the legislative power of Congress; no such comparable qualification exists with respect to "the executive power" in Article II, Section 1 or "the judicial power" in Article III, Section 1. Thus it should not be surprising that in *Marbury v. Madison* (Chapter 2) Chief Justice John Marshall pronounced the federal government to be one of "defined and limited" powers:

> This original and supreme will organizes the government, and assigns to different departments their respective powers. It may either stop here, or establish certain limits not to be transcended by those departments.
>
> The government of the United States is of the latter description. The powers of the legislature are defined and limited; and that those limits may not be mistaken, or forgotten, the constitution is written. To what purpose are powers limited, and to what purpose is that limitation committed to writing, if these limits may, at any time, be passed by those intended to be restrained? The distinction between a government with limited and unlimited powers is abolished, if those limits do not confine the persons on whom they are imposed, and if acts prohibited and acts allowed, are of equal obligation. It is a proposition too plain to be contested, that the constitution controls any legislative act repugnant to it; or, that the legislature may alter the constitution by an ordinary act.

When trying to ascertain the limits of legislative power, courts have employed both "internal" and "external" limitations. An *internal* approach examines whether a federal power itself contains some inherent limitations. For example, action Y cannot be within Congress's power to do X, when X is properly defined. The three powers most often used today to justify federal legislation are the powers of Congress to tax and spend, to regulate commerce among the several states, and to enforce the Fourteenth Amendment. In this chapter, we will consider judicial efforts to ascertain if these congressional powers are limited by their own terms.

In contrast, an *external* approach looks at outside constraints on the exercise of delegated powers. The most obvious example would be constraints imposed by the Bill of Rights, such as the First Amendment's protection of speech. With this sort of analysis, Congress is free to do X, provided that doing so does not violate constraint Y. That is, it can regulate any activity affecting the national economy (as some maintain), so long as it does not abridge the freedom of speech protected by the First Amendment. In Chapter 4, we consider the argument that there is an "external" constraint on federal legislative power arising from the Court's concern for preserving "federalism" or dual sovereignty. The logic, accepted in some eras and rejected in others, is that Congress may not exercise its enumerated powers in such a way as to violate the principle of federalism.

A. THE TANEY COURT

In 1836, Roger Brooke Taney[1] was appointed by President Andrew Jackson to succeed John Marshall as Chief Justice of the United States. Taney was descended from a wealthy and influential tobacco-growing Maryland family. Originally a Federalist, he became a staunch Democrat, and served as Jackson's attorney general. His tenure as Chief Justice is remembered most for the treatment of the slavery issue.

Taney married the sister of Francis Scott Key (composer of "The Star Spangled Banner," written during the bombardment of Baltimore in 1814).

It is difficult to understand the structure of the original Constitution without considering it against the backdrop of slavery. For example, sectional disagreement about the justice of slavery led the framers to adopt a federalist system where states retain powers over this central question. A divided approach to law-making obviated the need to address this issue on a national basis. In fact, any effort to create a one-size-fits-all solution would have doomed the new Constitution. Further, to understand the meaning of the Thirteenth and Fourteenth Amendments, students should understand the constitutional treatment of slavery leading up to the Civil War.

The institution of slavery was imported into North America by European settlers. The first African slaves in North America landed at Jamestown, Virginia in 1619.

---

[1] Chief Justice Taney's name is pronounced "Taw-nee."

Initially, few slaves were imported, and their status was unofficial. It was not until 1641 that slavery was first recognized by statutes concerning fugitive slaves in Massachusetts, then in Connecticut (1650) and Virginia (1661). The growth of the plantation system in the Southern colonies in the latter half of the seventeenth century led to greatly increased importation of African slave laborers. In the Northern colonies, slaves were used mainly as domestics and in trade. In the Middle Atlantic colonies, they were used more in agriculture. In the Southern colonies, where most slaves were used to work the plantations, the principal economic institution in the South, slavery became the mainstay of the Southern economy. The legal apparatus surrounding slavery grew gradually and fitfully. By the time of the American Revolution, the Africans in the South were slaves in the fullest sense of the term, with specific laws defining their legal, political, and social status with respect to their owners.

In the North, slaves were emancipated, or freed, at varying rates and by various means. By 1800, just 36,505 of the nation's 893,602 slaves resided in the Northern states. By 1804, Vermont, Pennsylvania, Massachusetts, Rhode Island, Connecticut, New York, and New Jersey had emancipated all their slaves. Even in the South, by the time of the Constitution's ratification, slavery was considered by many prominent Americans to be an unjust and inefficient economic institution fated to eventual extinction, though many greatly feared what would happen if and when slaves were freed.

However, with the invention in 1793 of the cotton gin — a simple device that quickly and easily separates cotton fibers from sticky seeds — plantation agriculture using slaves became enormously profitable. The rising profitability of cotton gave rise to a growing Southern ideology that, with increasing boldness, defended slavery as inevitable and just. By the census of 1860, the number of slaves in the United States had risen to 3,953,760, all of whom were in the Southern states.

In 1836, opponents of slavery inundated Congress with petitions to abolish slavery in the District of Columbia and the territories. A select committee of the House of Representatives concluded that eliminating slavery in the federal district would deprive slaveholders of their property without due process of law, and thereby violate the Fifth Amendment. "We lay it down as a rule," the committee observed, "that no Government can do anything directly repugnant to the principles of natural justice and of the social compact." Consequently, the members wrote, "[n]o republican could approve of any system of legislation by which the property of an individual, lawfully acquired, should be arbitrarily wrested from him by the high hand of power."[2] The report then relied on a lengthy passage from Justice Chase's opinion in *Calder v. Bull.* Some twenty years later, in 1857, Chief Justice Taney adopted this same reasoning, when he concluded in *Dred Scott v. Sandford* that restricting the rights of slaveholders to take their slaves into the territories violated the Due Process Clause.

In 1837, Theodore Dwight Weld published an article in the *New York Evening Post* contending that it was slavery itself that violated the Fifth Amendment, because it deprived slaves of their liberty without any process of law whatsoever.

---

[2] H.R. Rep. No. 691, 24th Cong. 1st Sess. (May 18, 1836), p. 14.

This argument became a staple among abolitionists, who argued that the Bill of Rights prohibited slavery and discrimination against free blacks. Weld's argument fueled the growth of a subset of the abolitionist movement that could be called "constitutional abolitionism."[3]

These constitutional abolitionists also contended that the Constitution's scheme of limited and enumerated powers imposed limitations on the federal government's power to protect slavery. For example, Salmon P. Chase, who would serve as the Chief Justice of the United States from 1864-1873, argued forcefully that Congress lacked the delegated powers to implement the Fugitive Slave Act. As a result, judges were under no obligation to assist slave owners who were attempting to return runaway slaves.

Chase first developed this argument as a 29-year-old lawyer in 1837 with his representation of a runaway slave named Matilda. At the time, Matilda was employed as a maid in Cincinnati by the abolitionist newspaper editor and attorney James Birney. Birney recounted that Matilda was fathered by her slave owner, who had brought her into free territory by passing her off as his white daughter. Having breathed free air, she pleaded with her father for a certificate of emancipation, but he refused. She then fled to the small neighborhood of free blacks in Cincinnati, where she found refuge before coming into Birney's employ.[4] Alas, Matilda was soon seized by slave catchers. Chase brought a writ of habeas corpus for her freedom and argued the case before the local judge. Based on ideas developed by Birney in his paper, *The Philanthropist*, Chase's hastily prepared argument was multifaceted, but his principal claim was that Congress lacked the authority to enact the Fugitive Slave Act of 1793. This law authorized a slave owner to seize a fugitive (that is, runaway) slave in a free state and return him or her to bondage after obtaining a certificate of removal from a federal judge or state magistrate.

In 1846, Chase would present a more developed version of this argument before the Supreme Court in the case of *Jones v. Van Zandt*. The structural arguments advanced by Chase and others against the congressional power over fugitive slaves, and in favor of a congressional power to abolish slavery in the District of Columbia and the territories, undercut the commonly held view that federalism and "states' rights" arguments were used exclusively to defend slavery. In fact, Southerners were more than willing to use *federal* power to bolster the slave system whenever they could muster the votes to do so.

---

[3] See Randy E. Barnett, Whence Comes Section One? The Abolitionist Origins of the Fourteenth Amendment, 3 J. Leg. Anal. 165 (2011) (describing the evolution of the arguments made by constitutional abolitionists); *id.* at 166 (quoting Benjamin F. Shaw: "[T]he fight for liberty in this land was begun by the Radical Abolitionists long before the final battle. They were followed, however, by a class known as Constitutional Abolitionists; equally bold and brave, but more practical."). At the same time, most of these constitutional abolitionists were a part of what has been called "political abolitionism," which strove to work within the political system to end slavery. See Richard H. Sewell, Ballots for Freedom: Antislavery Politics in the United States, 1837-1860 (1976).

[4] The events surrounding the *Matilda* case and Chase's involvement are discussed in John Niven, Salmon P. Chase 50-54 (1995).

Consider this excerpt of Chase's argument on behalf of Matilda, which was published in a widely distributed pamphlet.

STUDY GUIDE

- Article IV, Section 2 of the Constitution provides, "No person held to service or labor in one state, under the laws thereof, escaping into another, shall, in consequence of any law or regulation therein, be discharged from such service or labor, but shall be delivered up on claim of the party to whom such service or labor may be due." Chase makes much of the fact that the Fugitive Slave Clause is located in Article IV. What is the significance of the fact that the Fugitive Slave Clause is in Article IV?
- Given the existence of this clause, what is Chase's argument that the Fugitive Slave Act of 1793 was outside the power of Congress to enact? How does he distinguish the provisions of Article IV from the first three articles?
- How does Chase interpret the Necessary and Proper Clause? How does he use the Tenth Amendment? How does he reconcile his legal and constitutional analysis with natural rights?

SPEECH OF SALMON P. CHASE, IN THE CASE OF THE COLORED WOMAN, MATILDA. WHO WAS BROUGHT BEFORE THE COURT OF COMMON PLEAS OF HAMILTON COUNTY, OHIO, BY WRIT OF HABEAS CORPUS, March 11, 1837. . . . Slavery is admitted, on all hands, to be contrary to natural right. Wherever it exists at all, it exists only in virtue of positive law. The right to hold a man as a slave is a naked legal right. It is a right which, in its own nature, can have no existence beyond the territorial limits of the state which sanctions it, except in other states whose positive law recognises and protects it. It vanishes when the master and the slave meet together in a state where positive law interdicts slavery. The moment the slave comes within such a state, he acquires a legal right to freedom. The petitioner, Matilda, is now within the limits of Ohio, by whose fundamental law slavery is positively and forever interdicted. Admitting then, that she was once a slave, and is now claimed as such: admitting that if she is a slave, the present detention is lawful, still, it by no means follows that she is now a slave, or now legally restrained. On the contrary, she is now legally free: legally restored to her natural right; unless some exception to the great interdict can be clearly shown. And is there a man of all who hear me, who would rejoice that this poor woman, if legally free, should nevertheless be given up because once a slave? Is there a citizen of Ohio within these walls, who regards this woman as a mere article of property, the title to which is founded in natural right, and is recognised by the law of nations, and is protected by the positive laws of all states, and as bound to her owner by the same permanent ties which connect him with his horse or his ox? — If there be, let me tell that individual, that the constitution of Ohio frowns upon him, and that the soil of Ohio is dishonored by his tread. . . .

I maintain . . . that the act of congress which authorizes justices of the peace, without a jury, to try and decide the most important questions of personal liberty, which makes the certificate of a justice a sufficient warrant for the transportation out of the state, of any person, whom he may adjudge to be an escaping servant,— is not . . . warranted by the constitution of the United States. The leading object of the framers of our federal constitution was to create a national government, and confer upon it adequate powers. A secondary object was to adjust and settle certain matters of right and duty, between the states and between the citizens of different states, by permanent stipulations having the force and effect of a treaty. Both objects were happily accomplished.

The constitution establishes a form of government, declares its principles, defines its sphere, and confers its powers. It creates the artificial being, denominated "the government," and breathes into it the breath of life, and imparts to each branch and member, the necessary energies and faculties. It also establishes certain articles of compact or agreement between the states. It prescribes certain duties to be performed by each state and its citizens, towards every other state and its citizens: and it confers certain rights upon each state and its citizens, and binds all the states to the recognition and enforcement of these rights.

These different ends of the constitution — the creation of a government and the establishment of a compact, are entirely distinct in their nature. Either might be attained independently of the other. If all the clauses of compact in the constitution were stricken out, the government created by it would still exist. If the articles and sections, establishing a form of government, were blotted from the constitution, the clauses of compact might still remain in full force, as articles of agreement among the states.

The clauses of compact confer no powers on the government: and the powers of government cannot be exerted, except in virtue of express provisions, to enforce the matters of compact. . . . Now what is the clause in the constitution in regard to fugitives from labor, but an article of agreement between the states? It is expressed in these words, "No person held to service or labor in one state, under the laws thereof, escaping into another, shall, in consequence of any law or regulation thereof, be discharged from such service or labor; but shall be delivered up on claim of the party to whom such service or labor may be due." Does this clause confer any power on government, or on any officer or department of government? — Clearly not. It says nothing about the government, or its officers, or its departments. It declares that the citizens of no state in the Union, legally entitled to the service of any person, shall be deprived of that right to service, by the operation of the laws of any state into which the servant may escape; and it requires such state to deliver him up, on the claim of the lawful master.

The clause, then, restrains the operation of state constitutions and state laws in a particular class of cases; and it obliges, so far as a compact can oblige, each state to the performance of certain duties towards the citizens of other states. The clause has nothing to do with the creation of a form of government. It is, in the strictest sense, a clause of compact. The parties to the agreement are the states. The general government is not a party to it, nor affected by it. If the clause stood alone in the constitution, it would mean precisely what it does now, and would be just as obligatory as it is now. Nothing can be plainer, then, than that this clause cannot be construed as vesting any power in the government, or in any of its departments, or in any of its officers; and this is the only provision in the constitution which at all relates to fugitives from labor.

Now the whole legislative power of congress is derived, either from the general grant of power, "to make all laws, necessary and proper for carrying into execution all the powers vested by the constitution in the government of the United States, or in any department or officer thereof"; or from special provisions in relation to particular subjects. If congress has any power to legislate upon the subject of fugitives from labor, it must be derived from one of these sources, — from the general grant, or from some special provision.

It cannot be derived from the general grant, because the clause in regard to fugitives from labor, vests no power in the national government, or in any of its departments or officers; and the general grant of legislative power is expressly confined to the enactment of laws, necessary and proper to carry into execution the powers so vested. Nor can it be derived from any special provision: for none is attached to the clause relating to fugitives from service. The conclusion seems inevitable, that the constitution confers on congress no power to legislate in regard to escaping servants.

Where then is this power? Undoubtedly it is reserved to the states; for "all powers not delegated to the United States, nor prohibited to the states, are reserved to the states or to the people." The constitution restrains the operation of the state constitutions and the state laws, which would enfranchise the fugitive. It also binds the states to deliver him up on the claim of the master, and by necessary inference, it obliges them to provide a tribunal before which such claim may be asserted and tried, and by which such claims may be decided upon, and, if valid, enforced: but it confers no jot of legislative power on congress.

This construction of this clause in the constitution, is strengthened by reference to another provision. The first clause of the first section of the same article, in which the provision in regard to escaping servants is found, is in these words: "full faith and credit shall be given, in each state, to the public acts, records, and judicial proceedings of every other state." This clause, so far, is of the same nature with the clause in regard to fugitives from labor. It is a clause of compact, and it pledges the faith of each state to the faithful observance of it. But it confers no power on government, or any of its departments or officers. Congress, therefore, could not legislate in reference to the subject of it in virtue of the general grant of legislative power.

Aware of this, the framers of the constitution annexed to this first clause, a second, specially providing that congress might "prescribe, by general laws, the manner in which such acts, records, and proceedings shall be proved, and the effect thereof." Am I not right in saying that the framers of the constitution were aware, that without this special provision, congress would have no power to legislate upon the subject of the section? If the first clause, *propria vigore*, confers on Congress legislative power, why add the second? Why add it, if legislative power is conferred by the general grant, or by any other provision in the constitution? . . .

The framers of the constitution were men of large experience, comprehensive knowledge, sound judgment, and great ability. Among them were Hamilton, and Madison, and Washington. Such men, in framing such an instrument would avoid all needless repetition. They would not incorporate into the constitution a special provision upon any subject unnecessarily. To them, therefore, the second clause of the section under consideration, must have appeared not only fit, but necessary. But if a special provision was necessary to enable congress to legislate in regard to the authentication and effect of records, why is not a special provision necessary to enable congress to legislate in regard to fugitive servants? Can the counsel explain?

Both clauses of the constitution are of the same nature. Neither has any thing to do with creating, organizing, or energizing a form of the government. Both are articles of compact. If then, the framers of the constitution had intended that congress might legislate in reference to the subjects of both, would not special provisions, conferring such legislative power, have been annexed to both? Is not the annexation of such a special provision to one clause, and not to the other, decisive evidence that the convention intended to confer legislative power in regard to the subject of one clause, and to withhold legislative power in reference to the subject of the other? This conclusion seems to me inevitable. I see not how the counsel for the claimant, with all their ability and ingenuity, can frame an argument which will conduct to any other.

Nor is it difficult to assign valid and substantial reasons why the convention should not entrust to congress any legislative power upon this subject. Let us suppose that, when this clause about escaping servants was under discussion, a member had proposed to annex another clause in these words, "And congress shall have power to appoint officers in each state to try and determine the validity of such claims; and to provide by law for the apprehension and re-delivery of persons so escaping." Would not the answer have been, "What! give congress power to appoint officers to try questions of personal liberty, and to provide for the arrest and redelivery of all persons who may be claimed as escaping servants? Who would be safe under such a constitution? What personal right, conferred by God and guarantied by the state constitutions, might not be prostrated under it? Who might not be claimed as a fugitive from labor? Who would be secure against condemnation to servitude? To little purpose has liberty been achieved, if only to be placed in jeopardy like this." And if this answer had failed to satisfy the convention, and the clause had been incorporated into the constitution, can any one believe that it would have received the assent of the states?

Let it be remembered that the states existed before the federal constitution, and that the fundamental law of each asserted and guarantied the absolute, inherent, and unalienable rights of every citizen. Among these were reckoned "life, liberty, and the pursuit of happiness": and can it be supposed that any state, especially any nonslaveholding state, would have assented to a constitution which would withdraw from either of these rights, the ample shield of the fundamental law, and leave it exposed to the almost unlimited discretion of congress, and of officers appointed by congress? I think not. . . .

I have now done with this case. I have presented, feebly perhaps and unsuccessfully, but honestly and fearlessly, the great principles, legal and constitutional, which, in my judgment, ought to govern it. I have not asked — I do not now ask, in behalf of my humble client, deliverance from imprisonment, because that imprisonment is against natural right, but because it is against the constitution and against the law. I claim, however in her behalf, that it be borne in mind that there is such a thing as natural right, derived, not from any civil constitution or civil code, but from the constitution of human nature and the code of heaven.

This court, I am sure, need not to be reminded of the original, paramount truth, written upon the hearts of all men by the finger of God, the same in all ages and in all climes, and destined to no change, proclaimed by our fathers, in the declaration of independence, to be selfevident, and reiterated in our state constitution as its fundamental axiom, that all men are born "equally free." And if the petitioner at the bar cannot expect, here, the full benefit of this fundamental truth; if her right to freedom must, here, be vindicated upon narrower grounds, let her have, at least this advantage from it.

Let her be regarded as free, until it be shown by the fullest and clearest evidence, that her case falls within some exception to the universal law of human liberty. Let the proceedings by which she is now, without the accusation of crime, and without the suspicion of guilt, deprived of freedom and driven a suppli[c]ant to this bar, be narrowly scrutinized. Let every provision, unfavorable to liberty, whether legal or constitutional, receive a strict and rigorous interpretation. And if, when thus scrutinized, these proceedings shall be found insufficient, and especially if they shall be found to be warranted by no law and repugnant to the most vital principles of our social system; if, when thus interpreted, those provisions, which exclude a certain class of persons from the benefit of these vital principles, shall be found not broad enough to reach the case of this petitioner; I demand her discharge in the name of justice, of liberty, and of our common humanity.

The local judge in Cincinnati rejected Chase's arguments, and Matilda was taken "down the river" by boat the next day, to be sold in New Orleans and never to be heard of again. Eventually, the Supreme Court considered the constitutionality of the Fugitive Slave Act in *Prigg v. Pennsylvania* (1842).

Justice Joseph Story

STUDY GUIDE

- How does Justice Story address the argument made by Chase that Article IV, Section 2, does not empower Congress to enact any laws? (*Hint:* How exactly does he use the Necessary and Proper Clause?) Can you think of any answer to Story's claim that this clause was essential to the ratification of the Constitution? (*Hint:* Did it exist in the Articles of Confederation?)
- Doesn't Story's analysis assume what must be shown: that a particular individual is a fugitive slave that must be surrendered up? Does the assertion by Congress of the power to enact the Fugitive Slave Act, and the outcome of this case, cloud that picture?

Prigg v. Pennsylvania

41 U.S. (16 Pet.) 539 (1842)

[With the apparent acquiescence of her owner, John Ashmore, Margaret Morgan left Maryland to marry a free black man in Pennsylvania, where at least one of their children were born. Five years later, after John Ashmore's death, his daughter, Margaret Ashmore sent Edward Prigg and others to recapture Morgan. They captured Morgan, her husband, and their children in York County, Pennsylvania. After the York County justice of the peace refused to consider the case, Prigg took Morgan and her children (but not her husband) to Maryland, in violation of Pennsylvania's "personal liberty law," which required that certificates of removal be obtained from a state judge, justice of the peace, or alderman. The York County prosecutor obtained indictments against Prigg and his helpers for kidnapping and violating the Pennsylvania statute. After a public outcry and extensive negotiations between state officials, Maryland sent Prigg to Pennsylvania, where he was convicted of kidnapping. Morgan and her children were "sold down the river" and shipped south, where they remained in bondage. After the Pennsylvania Supreme Court affirmed his conviction, Prigg challenged its constitutionality in the U.S. Supreme Court. — Eds.]

Mr. Justice Story delivered the opinion of the court....

Few questions which have ever come before this Court involve more delicate and important considerations; and few upon which the public at large may be presumed to feel a more profound and pervading interest....

Before, however, we proceed to the points more immediately before us, it may be well — in order to clear the case of difficulty — to say, that in the exposition of this part of the Constitution, we shall limit ourselves to those considerations which appropriately and exclusively belong to it, without laying down any rules of interpretation of a more general nature. It will, indeed, probably, be found, when we look to the character of the Constitution itself, the objects which it seeks to attain, the powers which it confers, the duties which it enjoins, and the rights which it secures, as well as the known historical fact that many of its provisions were matters of compromise of opposing interests and opinions; that no uniform rule of interpretation can be applied to it which may not allow, even if it does not positively demand, many modifications in its actual application to particular clauses. And, perhaps, the safest rule of interpretation after all will be found to be to look to the nature and objects of the particular powers, duties, and rights, with all the lights and aids of contemporary history; and to give to the words of each just such operation and force, consistent with their legitimate meaning, as may fairly secure and attain the ends proposed.

There are two clauses in the Constitution upon the subject of fugitives, which stand in juxtaposition with each other, and have been thought mutually to illustrate each other. They are both contained in the second section of the fourth article, and are in the following words:

> A person charged in any state with treason, felony or other crime, who shall flee from justice, and be found in another state, shall, on demand of the executive authority of the state from which he fled, be delivered up, to be removed to the state having jurisdiction of the crime.
>
> No person held to service or labor in one state under the laws thereof, escaping into another, shall in consequence of any law or regulation therein, be discharged from such service or labor; but shall be delivered up, on claim of the party to whom such service or labor may be due.

The . . . true interpretation [of the last clause] is directly in judgment before us. Historically, it is well known, that the object of this clause was to secure to the citizens of the slaveholding states the complete right and title of ownership in their slaves, as property, in every state in the Union into which they might escape from the state where they were held in servitude. The full recognition of this right and title was indispensable to the security of this species of property in all the slaveholding states; and, indeed, was so vital to the preservation of their domestic interests and institutions, that it cannot be doubted that it constituted a fundamental article, without the adoption of which the Union could not have been formed. Its true design was, to guard against the doctrines and principles prevalent in the non-slaveholding states, by preventing them from intermeddling with, or obstructing, or abolishing the rights of the owners of slaves.

By the general law of nations, no nation is bound to recognise the state of slavery, as to foreign slaves found within its territorial dominions, when it is in opposition to its own policy and institutions, in favour of the subjects of other nations where slavery is recognised. If it does it, it is as a matter of comity, and not as a matter of international right. . . . It is manifest from this consideration, that if the Constitution had not contained this clause, every non-slaveholding state in the Union would have been at liberty to have declared free all runaway slaves coming within its limits, and to have given them entire immunity and protection against the claims of their masters; a course which would have created the most bitter animosities, and engendered perpetual strife between the different states. The clause was, therefore, of the last importance to the safety and security of the southern states; and could not have been surrendered by them without endangering their whole property in slaves. The clause was accordingly adopted into the

Constitution, by the unanimous consent of the framers of it; a proof at once of its intrinsic and practical necessity.

How, then, are we to interpret the language of the clause? The true answer is, in such a manner, as, consistently with the words, shall fully and completely effectuate the whole objects of it. If by one mode of interpretation, the right must become shadowy and unsubstantial, and without any remedial power adequate to the end; and by another mode it will attain its just end and secure its manifest purpose; it would seem, upon principles of reasoning, absolutely irresistible, that the latter ought to prevail. No Court of justice can be authorized so to construe any clause of the Constitution as to defeat its obvious ends, when another construction, equally accordant with the words and sense thereof, will enforce and protect them.

The clause manifestly contemplates the existence of a positive, unqualified right on the part of the owner of the slave, which no state law or regulation can in any way qualify, regulate, control, or restrain. The slave is not to be discharged from service or labor, in consequence of any state law or regulation. Now, certainly, without indulging in any nicety of criticism upon words, it may fairly and reasonably be said, that any state law or state regulation, which interrupts, limits, delays, or postpones the right of the owner to the immediate possession of the slave, and the immediate command of his service and labour, operates, pro tanto, a discharge of the slave therefrom. . . .

[T]he clause contains a positive and unqualified recognition of the right of the owner in the slave, unaffected by any state law or legislation whatsoever, because there is no qualification or restriction of it to be found therein; and we have no right to insert any which is not expressed, and cannot be fairly implied. . . . If this be so, then . . . the owner must, therefore, have the right to seize and repossess the slave, which the local laws of his own state confer upon him as property; and we all know that this right of seizure and recaption is universally acknowledged in all the slaveholding states. . . . Upon this ground we have not the slightest hesitation in holding, that, under and in virtue of the Constitution, the owner of a slave is clothed with entire authority, in every state in the Union, to seize and recapture his slave, whenever he can do it, without any breach of the peace, or any illegal violence. In this sense, and to this extent this clause of the Constitution may properly be said to execute itself; and to require no aid from legislation, state or national.

But the clause of the Constitution does not stop here; nor indeed, consistently with its professed objects, could it do so. Many cases must arise in which, if the remedy of the owner were confined to the mere right of seizure and recaption, he would be utterly without any adequate redress. He may not be able to lay his hands upon the slave. He may not be able to enforce his rights against persons who either secrete or conceal, or withhold the slave. He may be restricted by local legislation, as to the mode of proofs of his ownership; as to the Courts in which he shall sue, and as to the actions which he may bring; or the process he may use to compel the delivery of the slave. Nay, the local legislation may be utterly inadequate to furnish the appropriate redress . . . ; and this may be innocently as well as designedly done, since every state is perfectly competent, and has the exclusive right, to prescribe the remedies in its own judicial tribunals, to limit the time as well as the mode of redress, and to deny jurisdiction over cases, which its own policy and its own institutions either prohibit or discountenance.

If, therefore, the clause of the Constitution had stopped at the mere recognition of the right, without providing or contemplating any means by which it might be established and enforced, in cases where it did not execute itself, it is plain, that it would have been, in a great variety of cases, a delusive and empty annunciation. . . .

And this leads us to the consideration of the other part of the clause, which implies at once a guarantee and duty. It says, "But he (the slave) shall be delivered up, on claim of the party to whom such service or labor may be due." Now, we think it exceedingly difficult, if not impracticable, to read this language and not to feel that it contemplated some further remedial redress than that which might be administered at the hands of the owner himself. . . . If, indeed, the Constitution guaranties the right, and if it requires the delivery upon the claim of the owner, (as cannot well be doubted), the natural inference certainly is, that the national government is clothed with the appropriate authority and functions to enforce it. The fundamental principle applicable to all cases of this sort, would seem to be, that where the end is required, the means are given; and where the duty is enjoined, the ability to perform it is contemplated to exist on the part of the functionaries to whom it is intrusted. The clause is found in the national Constitution, and not in that of any state. It does not point out any state functionaries, or any state action to carry its provisions into effect. The states cannot, therefore, be compelled to enforce them; and it might well be deemed an unconstitutional exercise of the power of interpretation, to insist that the states are bound to provide means to carry into effect the duties of the national government, nowhere delegated or intrusted to them by the Constitution. On the contrary, the natural, if not the necessary conclusion is, that the national government, in the absence of all positive provisions to the contrary, is bound, through its own proper departments, legislative, judicial, or executive, as the case may require, to carry into effect all the rights and duties imposed upon it by the Constitution. . . .

Congress has taken this very view of the power and duty of the national government. . . . The result of their deliberations was the passage of the act of the 12th of February 1793. . . . [This] legislation of Congress, if constitutional, must supersede all state legislation upon the same subject; and by necessary implication prohibit it. . . . [W]here Congress have exercised a power over a particular subject given them by the Constitution, it is not competent for state legislation to add to the provisions of Congress upon that subject; for that the will of Congress upon the whole subject is as clearly established by what it has not declared, as by what it has expressed.

But it has been argued, that the act of Congress is unconstitutional, because it does not fall within the scope of any of the enumerated powers of legislation confided to that body; and therefore it is void. Stripped of its artificial and technical structure, the argument comes to this, that although rights are exclusively secured by, or duties are exclusively imposed upon the national government, yet, unless the power to enforce these rights, or to execute these duties can be found among the express powers of legislation enumerated in the Constitution, they remain without any means of giving them effect by any act of Congress; and they must operate solely *proprio vigore* ["by its own force" — EDS.], however defective may be their operation; nay, even although, in a practical sense, they may become a nullity from the want of a proper remedy to enforce them, or to provide against their violation. If this be the true interpretation of the Constitution, it must, in a great measure, fail to attain many of its avowed and positive objects as a security of rights, and a recognition of duties. Such a limited construction of the Constitution has never yet been adopted as correct, either in theory or practice. No one has ever supposed that Congress could, constitutionally, by its legislation, exercise powers, or enact laws beyond the powers delegated to it by the Constitution; but it has, on various occasions, exercised powers which were necessary and proper as means to carry into effect rights expressly given, and duties expressly enjoined thereby. The end being required, it has been deemed a just and necessary implication, that the means to accomplish it are given also; or, in other words, that the power flows as a necessary means to accomplish the ends. . . .

The provisions of the act of 12th February, 1793, relative to fugitive slaves is clearly constitutional in all its leading provisions. . . . Upon these grounds, we are of the opinion that the act of Pennsylvania upon which this indictment is founded, is unconstitutional and void. It purports to punish as a public offence against that state, the very act of seizing and removing a slave, by his master, which the Constitution of the United States was designed to justify and uphold. . . .

The Supreme Court's decision in *Prigg* led many in the North to believe that the South would eventually seek to impose slavery on the whole country. This sentiment was instrumental to the formation of the Republican party in 1854. In his 1858 address to the Republican state convention of Illinois that nominated him as its candidate for the Senate, Abraham Lincoln espoused this view:

> "A house divided against itself cannot stand." I believe this government cannot endure, permanently half slave and half free. I do not expect the Union to be dissolved — I do not expect the house to fall — but I do expect it will cease to be divided. It will become all one thing or all the other. Either the opponents of slavery, will arrest the further spread of it, and place it where the public mind shall rest in the belief that it is in the course of ultimate extinction; or its advocates will push it forward, till it shall become alike lawful in all the States, old as well as new — North as well as South.

Lincoln's claim may appear farfetched to us today. But it came in the wake of the Supreme Court's decision in *Dred Scott v. Sandford* in which Chief Justice Taney held that the deprivation of a slaveholder's rights to his slave in a territory deprived him of "property" without due process of law in violation of the Fifth Amendment (just as the House Select Committee on Slavery in the District of Columbia had contended in 1836). Other cases working their way through the courts involved slaveholders taking their slaves in transit through free states. If the Fifth Amendment protected their "property" right to their slaves in federal territory, rather than in a state in which slavery existed as a matter of positive (i.e., statutory) law, it seemed only a matter of time before the Supreme Court would uphold the "property" right of slaveholders to take their slaves into a free state.

The abolitionist movement was sharply divided on the issue of whether the Constitution sanctioned slavery. On one side was the group associated with William Lloyd Garrison and his close associate, attorney Wendell Phillips. They maintained that the Constitution recognized slavery. For this reason, they characterized "the compact which exists between the North and the South" as "a covenant with death and an agreement with hell" and advocated "no union with the slave power." In other words, they favored secession from the Union, in part to deny the slave system the legal reinforcement provided by the federal Fugitive Slave Act as interpreted in *Prigg*. They believed that if the North seceded from the Union, the border states would either be drained of slaves by those fleeing to freedom in the North, or the South would bankrupt itself trying to keep slaves from escaping. Either way, eventually the slave system would collapse. It is far from clear that this strategy would have failed.

On the other side of the dispute were abolitionists such as Lysander Spooner, William Goodell, and Gerrit Smith. They contended that, because the Constitution did not explicitly sanction slavery by name, such an unjust meaning could not be attributed to it under sound approaches to interpretation. The most comprehensive version of the argument was presented in Spooner's 280-page book *The Unconstitutionality of Slavery*, the first version of which appeared in 1845. Spooner's book was a reply to an earlier pamphlet by Phillips entitled *The Constitution: A Pro-Slavery Compact*, in which Phillips relied upon extensive excerpts from Madison's notes of the Constitutional Convention that had only recently been released to the public. Phillips, a former law student of Justice Story at Harvard, then replied to Spooner in a ninety-page essay published at his own expense.

One important feature of their exchange was the difference in their approaches to constitutional interpretation. Phillips relied on evidence of the *original intentions of the framers* of the Constitution. Spooner denied that this evidence was relevant, basing his claims instead on the *original public meaning* of the text. Their debate is the earliest and clearest account of these two distinct forms of originalism. In the next excerpt, Spooner summarizes some of the arguments he made in *The Unconstitutionality of Slavery* and chastises Justice Story for the method of constitutional interpretation employed in *Prigg*.

STUDY GUIDE

- Spooner, and later Frederick Douglass, placed great stress on the principle of statutory interpretation advanced by Chief Justice Marshall in *United States v. Fisher* (1805): "Where rights are infringed, where fundamental principles are overthrown, where the general system of the laws is departed from, the legislative intention must be expressed with irresistible clearness, to induce a court of justice to suppose a design to effect such objects." (The entire passage appears in Chapter 2 before *McCulloch*. Does the rest of the passage add anything of relevance?)
- Notice how this rule of construction allows a function for natural rights without calling for their direct protection by the courts. Is there anything wrong with adopting such a rule of construction? Does this qualify the "originalist" nature of Spooner's interpretive method?

LYSANDER SPOONER, A DEFENCE FOR FUGITIVE SLAVES AGAINST THE ACTS OF CONGRESS OF FEBRUARY 12, 1793, AND SEPTEMBER 18, 1850. Neither the constitutional provision, nor either of said acts of Congress, uses the word slave, nor slavery, nor any language that can *legally* be made to apply to slaves. The only "person" required by the constitution to be delivered up, is described in the constitution as a "person held to service or labor in one state, under the laws thereof." This language is no legal description of a slave, and can be made to apply to a slave only by a violation of all the most imperative rules of interpretation, by which the meaning of all legal instruments is to be ascertained. . . .

The word "*held*" being, in law, synonymous with the word "*bound*," the description, "person held to service or labor," is synonymous with the description in another Section, (Art. 1, Sec. 2), to wit, "those *bound* to service for a term of years." . . . In fact, every body, courts and people, admit that "persons *bound* to service for a term of years," as apprentices and other indented servants, are to be delivered up under the provision relative to "persons *held* to service or labor." The word "*held*," then, is regarded as synonymous with "*bound*," whenever it is wished to deliver up "persons *bound* to service." If, then, it be synonymous with the word "*bound*," it applies only to persons who are "*bound*," in a *legal* sense,—that is, by some legal contract, obligation, or duty, which the law will enforce. The words cannot be stretched beyond their *necessary* and proper *legal* meaning; because all legal provisions in derogation of liberty must be construed strictly. The same words that are used to describe a "person held to service or labor," by a *legal* contract, or obligation, certainly cannot be legally construed to apply also to one who is "held" only by private violence, and brute force. . . .

The Supreme Court of the United States, in the *Prigg* case, . . . made no pretence that the *language itself* of the constitution afforded any justification for a claim to a fugitive slave. On the contrary, they made the audacious and atrocious avowal, that for the sole purpose of making the clause apply to slaves, they would disregard,—as they acknowledged themselves obliged to disregard,—all the primary, established, and imperative rules of legal interpretation, *and be governed solely by the history of men's intentions, outside of the constitution*. . . .

Thus it will be seen, that on the strength of *history alone*, they assume that "*many of the provisions of the constitution were matters of compromise*," (that is, in regard to slavery); but they admit that the words of those provisions cannot be made to express any such compromise, if they are interpreted according to any "*uniform rule of interpretation*," or "*any rules of interpretation of a more general nature*," than the mere history of those particular clauses. Hence, "*in order to clear the case of [that] difficulty*," they conclude that "*perhaps the safest rule of interpretation after all will be found to be to look to the nature and objects of the particular powers, duties, and rights, with all the lights and aids of contemporary history; and to give to the words of each just such operation and force*, consistent with their legitimate meaning, *as may fairly secure and attain the ends proposed*." . . .

Stripped, then, of the covering, which that falsehood was intended to throw over their conduct, the plain English of the language of the Court is this,—that history tells us that certain clauses of the constitution were intended to recognize and support slavery; but inasmuch as such is not the legal meaning of the words of those clauses, if interpreted by the established rules of interpretation, we will, "*in order to clear the case of [that] difficulty,*" just discard those rules, and pervert the words so as to *make* them accomplish whatever ends *history* tells us were intended to be accomplished by them.

It was only by such a naked and daring fraud as this, that the court could make the constitution authorize the recovery of fugitive slaves.

And what were the rules of interpretation, which they thus discarded, "in order to clear the case of difficulty," and make the constitution subserve the purposes of slavery? One of them is this, laid down by the Supreme Court of the United States: "The intention of the instrument must prevail; *this intention must be collected from its words.*" 12 Wheaton, 332. Without an adherence to this rule, it is plain we could never know what is, and what was not, the constitution.

Another rule is that universal one, acknowledged by all courts to be imperative, that language used must be construed strictly in favor of liberty and justice. The Supreme Court of the United States have laid down this rule in these strong terms.

> Where rights are infringed, where fundamental principles are overthrown, where the general system of the laws is departed from, the legislative intention must be expressed with *irresistible clearness,* to induce a court of justice to suppose a design to effect such objects. United States vs. Fisher, 2 Cranch, 390.

Story delivered this opinion of the court (in the *Prigg* case), discarding all other rules of interpretation, and resorting to history to make the clause apply to slaves. And yet no judge has ever scouted more contemptuously than Story, the idea of going out of the words of the law, or the constitution, and being governed by what history may say were the intentions of the authors. He says,

> . . . Nothing but the text itself was adopted by the people. . . . Is the sense of the constitution to be ascertained, not by its own text, but by the "probable meaning," to be gathered by conjectures from scattered documents, from private papers, from the table-talk of some statesman, or the jealous exaggerations of others? Is the constitution of the United States to be the only instrument, which is not to be interpreted by what is written, but by probable guesses, aside from the text? What would be said of interpreting a statute of a state legislature, by endeavoring to find out, from private sources, the objects and opinions of every member; how every one thought; what he wished; how he interpreted it? Suppose different persons had different opinions, what is to be done? Suppose different persons are not agreed as to the "probable meaning" of the framers, or of the people, what interpretation is to be followed? These, and many questions of the same sort, might be asked. It is obvious, that there can be no security to the people in any constitution of government, if they are not to judge of it by the fair meaning of the words of the text, but the words are to be bent and broken by the "probable meaning" of persons, whom they never knew, and whose opinions, and means of information, may be no better than their own. The people adopted the constitution, according to the words of the text in their reasonable interpretation, and not according to the private interpretation of any particular men. 1 Story's Comm. on Const., 387 to 392.

And Story has said much more of the same sort as to the absurdity of relying upon "history" for the meaning of the constitution.

It is manifest that if the meaning of the constitution is to be warped in the least, it may be warped to any extent, on the authority of history; and thus it would follow that the constitution would in reality be made by the historians, and not by the people. It would be impossible for the people to make a constitution, which the historians might not change at pleasure, by simply asserting that the people intended thus or so. . . .

But it will be said that the constitution of the United States itself recognizes slavery, to wit, in the provision requiring "the whole number of *free* persons" and "three-fifths of all other persons" to be counted in making up the basis of representation and taxation. But this interpretation of the word "free" is only another of the fraudulent interpretations, which the slaveholders and their northern accomplices have succeeded in placing upon the constitution.

The legal and technical meaning of the word "free," as used in England for centuries, has been to designate a native or naturalized member of the state, as distinguished from an alien, or foreigner not naturalized. Thus the term "free British subject" means, not a person who is not a slave, but a native born, or naturalized subject, who is a member of the state, and entitled to all the rights of a member of the state, in contradistinction to aliens, and persons not thus entitled. . . .

But we are told again that the constitution recognizes the legality of the slave trade, and by consequence the legality of slavery, in the clause respecting the "importation of persons." But the word "importation," when applied to "persons," no more implies that the persons are slaves, than does the word "transportation." It was perfectly understood, in the convention that framed the constitution — and the language was chosen with special care to that end — that there was nothing in the language itself, that legally recognized the slavery of the persons to be imported; although some of the members, (how many we do not know), while choosing language with an avowed caution against "admitting, *in the constitution*, the idea that there could be property in man," intended, if they could induce the people to adopt the constitution, and could then get the control of the government, to pervert this language into a license to the slave trade.

This fraudulent perversion of the legal meaning of the language of the constitution, is all the license the constitution ever gave to the slave trade.

Chief Justice Marshall, in the case of the Brig Wilson . . . held that the words "import" and "imported," in an act of Congress, applied to free persons as well as to slaves. If, then, the word "Importation," in the constitution, applies properly to free persons, it certainly cannot imply that any of the persons imported are slaves.

If the constitution, truly interpreted, contain no sanction of slavery, the slaves of this country are as much entitled to the writ of habeas corpus at the hands of the United States government, as are the whites.

Salmon P. Chase's position lay somewhere between the Garrisonians, who thought that the Constitution positively sanctioned slavery, and that of Spooner, Goodell, and Douglass, who maintained that slavery was unconstitutional even in those states that recognized it. Chase insisted that slavery was constitutional within any of the original states that still retained it. But with a moral and constitutional fervor equal to that of Spooner, Chase also contended that Congress had the power to abolish slavery in the District of Columbia and the territories.

Chase favored an antislavery program of (1) "repealing all legislation, and discontinuing all action, in favor of slavery, at home and abroad"; (2) "prohibiting the practice of slaveholding in all places of exclusive national jurisdiction, in the District of Columbia, in American vessels upon the seas, in forts, arsenals, navy yards"; (3) "forbidding the employment of slaves upon any public work"; (4) "adopting resolutions in Congress, declaring that slaveholding, in all States created out of national territories, is unconstitutional, and recommending to the others the immediate adoption of measures for its extinction within their respective limits"; and (5) electing and appointing to public office only those who "openly avow our principles, and will honestly carry out our measures." Chase maintained that the "constitutionality of this line of action cannot be successfully impeached."[5]

Chase was active in the formation of the Liberty, Free Soil, and Republican parties, becoming a United States senator from Ohio in 1849 on the Free Soil ticket. As historian Eric Foner has noted, "Chase's interpretation of the Constitution . . . formed the legal basis for the political programs which were created by the Liberty party and inherited in large part by the Free Soilers and Republicans."[6] The Republican party's national platforms for the elections of 1856 and 1860 largely adopted Chase's constitutional views on slavery. With this in mind, it becomes clearer exactly why the Republican victory of 1860 provoked the Southern states to secede from the Union. Despite Lincoln's insistence that he would not interfere with the practice of slavery in the existing states, Southerners apparently shared Chase's judgment that the Republican program would hasten the extinction of slavery throughout the United States.

In 1855, Chase was elected governor of Ohio, the first Republican governor in the nation. At the 1860 Republican National Convention in Chicago, Chase was a serious candidate for the Republican presidential nomination, but Abraham Lincoln was chosen instead. Chase was again elected to the United States Senate by the Ohio legislature. He resigned his seat after three days when Lincoln appointed him Secretary of the Treasury, where he was faced with the enormous challenge of financing the Civil War without raising taxes.

Chase served as the Secretary of Treasury from 1861 to 1864. "[He] alone among cabinet heads hired thousands of blacks and females as civil servants and even placed an impressive number of black males in supervisory positions over white females."[7]

[5] Salmon P. Chase, The Address of the Southern and Western Liberty Convention, held at Cincinnati, June 11 and 12, 1845, in Salmon P. Chase & Charles D. Cleveland, Anti-Slavery Addresses of 1844 and 1855 (1867), p. 100.

[6] Eric Foner, Free Soil, Free Labor, Free Men 87 (1995). For a description of Chase's constitutional ideas and their reception by the Liberty, Free Soil, and Republican parties, see *id.* at 73-102.

[7] Harold M. Hyman, The Reconstruction Justice of Salmon P. Chase 81 (1997).

B. THE CHASE COURT

ASSIGNMENT 2

When Chief Justice Taney died in October of 1864, President Lincoln nominated Salmon P. Chase to be the sixth Chief Justice of the United States. The former political rival administered the oath of office to Lincoln during his second inaugural. As Chief Justice, Chase agreed to the admission of the first black lawyer to be a member of the Supreme Court bar. Massachusetts attorney John Rock had been denied admission the previous year by the Taney Court on the basis of his race. Now, upon the motion of Massachusetts Senator Charles Sumner, Rock was admitted with Chase's approval. *Harper's Weekly* observed that this event represented an "extraordinary reversal" of *Dred Scott*, and would "be regarded by the future historian as a remarkable indication of the revolution which is going on in the sentiment of a great people."[8]

When Lincoln was murdered by the Maryland-born actor and Southern sympathizer John Wilkes Booth on April 14, 1865, Chief Justice Chase administered the oath of office to Vice President Andrew Johnson, a Democrat from Tennessee. When Johnson was later impeached by the House of Representatives for resisting the efforts of the Republican Congress to "reconstruct" the South,[9] Chase presided over his trial in the Senate. In part because Chase established a judicial-style proceeding, Johnson escaped conviction and removal from office by a single vote.[10]

In 1873, the gravely ill Chase joined three other Justices in dissenting from the Court's decision in the *Slaughter-House Cases*, which effectively gutted the Privileges or Immunities Clause of the Fourteenth Amendment. The very next day, the Chief Justice was the only dissenting vote in *Bradwell v. Illinois*, a case in which the other *Slaughter-House* dissenters joined with the *Slaughter-House* majority to uphold Illinois's power to deny to women the right to practice law. Chase was too weak and ill to write opinions in either case, and one may wonder if their outcomes might have been changed had he retained his previous vitality. Three weeks later, a second stroke took his life. The Chase National Bank, originally founded in 1877, was named in his honor.

---

[8] See Doris Kearns Goodwin, Team of Rivals 681 (2006).

[9] President Johnson's specific offence concerned the alleged violation of the Tenure in Office Act, which provided that certain federal officials whose appointment required Senate confirmation could not be removed without the consent of the Senate. The bill had been enacted over Johnson's veto, which was based on his objections to its constitutionality.

[10] "Impeaching" an official is like indicting a criminal. Only if convicted is the official removed from office. Under the Constitution, the House impeaches and the Senate, presided over by the Chief Justice, convicts or acquits.

In *United States v. Dewitt*, Chief Justice Chase addressed the scope of Congress's enumerated powers.

STUDY GUIDE

How exactly does the Court limit Congress's power to regulate commerce that takes place solely within a single state? If Congress can ban the local sale of lamp oil, even if a state has permitted it, could it also ban the local slave trade where a state has permitted it?

United States v. Dewitt

76 U.S. (9 Wall.) 41 (1869)

[In 1867, Congress enacted a law providing:

> That no person shall mix for sale naphtha and illuminating oils, or shall knowingly sell or keep for sale, or offer for sale such mixture, or shall sell or offer for sale oil made from petroleum for illuminating purposes, inflammable at less temperature or fire-test than 110 degrees Fahrenheit; and any person so doing, shall be held to be guilty of a misdemeanor, and on conviction thereof by indictment or presentment in any court of the United States having competent jurisdiction, shall be punished by fine, &c., and imprisonment, . . .

"Under this section one Dewitt was indicted, the offence charged being the offering for sale, at Detroit, in Michigan, oil made of petroleum of the description specified." — Eds.]

Mr. Chief Justice Chase delivered the opinion of the court.

The questions certified resolve themselves into this: Has Congress power, under the Constitution, to prohibit trade within the limits of a State?

That Congress has power to regulate commerce with foreign nations and among the several States, and with the Indian tribes, the Constitution expressly declares. But this express grant of power to regulate commerce among the States has always been understood as limited by its terms; and as a virtual denial of any power to interfere with the internal trade and business of the separate States; except, indeed, as a necessary and proper means for carrying into execution some other power expressly granted or vested.

It has been urged in argument that the provision under which this indictment was framed is within this exception; that the prohibition of the sale of the illuminating oil described in the indictment was in aid and support of the internal revenue tax imposed on other illuminating oils. And we have been referred to provisions, supposed to be analogous, regulating the business of distilling liquors, and the mode of packing various manufactured articles; but the analogy appears to fail at the essential point, for the regulations referred to are restricted to the very articles which are the subject of taxation, and are plainly adapted to secure the collection of the tax imposed; while, in the case before us, no tax is imposed on the oils the sale of which is prohibited. If the prohibition, therefore, has any relation to taxation at all, it is merely that of increasing the production and sale of other oils, and, consequently, the revenue derived from them, by excluding from the market the particular kind described.

This consequence is too remote and too uncertain to warrant us in saying that the prohibition is an appropriate and plainly adapted means for carrying into execution the power of laying and collecting taxes.

There is, indeed, no reason for saying that it was regarded by Congress as such a means, except that it is found in an act imposing internal duties. Standing by itself, it is plainly a regulation of police; and that it was so considered, if not by the Congress which enacted, it, certainly by the succeeding Congress, may be inferred from the circumstance, that while all special taxes on illuminating oils were repealed by the act of July 20th, 1868, which subjected distillers and refiners to the tax on sales as manufacturers, this prohibition was left unrepealed.

As a police regulation, relating exclusively to the internal trade of the State, it can only have effect where the legislative authority of Congress excludes, territorially, all State legislation, as for example, in the District of Columbia. Within State limits, it can have no constitutional operation. This has been so frequently declared by this court, results so obviously from the terms of the Constitution, and has been so fully explained and supported on former occasions, that we think it unnecessary to enter again upon the discussion. . . .

The *Legal Tender Cases* were a series of Supreme Court decisions concerning the constitutionality of paper money, as opposed to money made from valuable metals like gold or silver. To understand the dispute, one needs to know that "legal tender" refers to a medium of payment that, by law, *must* be accepted as payment for a money debt. So the issue in these cases was not whether Congress could issue paper promissory notes — everyone agreed it could — but whether it could make these paper notes a "legal tender" so that private creditors would *have* to accept them in payment of debts even if their contracts stipulated that repayment be in gold or silver. The *Legal Tender Cases* are worth studying as a surprisingly early harbinger of the twentieth-century debates over the scope of implied federal powers and the relationship between the enumerated powers in Article I, Section 8 and the Necessary and Proper Clause, as well as the meaning of Chief Justice Marshall's opinion in *McCulloch v. Maryland.*

STUDY GUIDE

- Notice Chief Justice Chase's use of Chief Justice Marshall's test for constitutionality articulated in *McCulloch v. Maryland* (Chapter 2). This should tell you something important about the close connection between the Commerce Clause and the Necessary and Proper Clause.
- In the next case, how does Chase approach finding an implied power under the Necessary and Proper Clause? How does he distinguish between the power to issue paper notes as currency, and the power to make those notes a "legal tender" in satisfaction of debts? Where does he locate the power to define legal tender?

Hepburn v. Griswold

The Legal Tender Cases, 75 U.S. 603 (1870)

[The Legal Tender Act of 1862 was enacted to issue paper money to finance the Civil War without raising taxes. The paper money or "greenbacks" depreciated in terms of gold and became the subject of controversy, particularly because debts contracted earlier could be paid in this cheaper currency. This lawsuit originated when Mrs. Hepburn attempted to pay a debt due to Mr. Griswold on a promissory note using paper notes issued by the United States. Griswold sued Hepburn in the Louisville Chancery Court (i.e., a court of equity) on the note and refused Hepburn's tender of U.S. notes to satisfy his claim. She then tendered the notes to the chancery court, which declared her debt satisfied. When the Court of Errors of Kentucky reversed the chancery court's judgment, Mrs. Griswold appealed to the U.S. Supreme Court, where Chief Justice Salmon P. Chase was called to pass upon the constitutionality of the legal tender laws he had supported as treasury secretary. This support was reluctant, however, as he had long been an advocate of "hard money." — EDS.]

Mr. CHIEF JUSTICE CHASE delivered the opinion of the court.

The question presented for our determination by the record in this case is, whether or not the payee or assignee of a note . . . is obliged by law to accept in payment United States notes, equal in nominal amount to the sum due according to its terms, when tendered by the maker or other party bound to pay it? . . . We are thus brought to the question, whether Congress has power to make notes issued under its authority a legal tender in payment of debts, which, when contracted, were payable by law in gold and silver coin. . . .

It is generally, if not universally, conceded, that the government of the United States is one of limited powers, and that no department possesses any authority not granted by the Constitution.

It is not necessary, however, in order to prove the existence of a particular authority to show a particular and express grant. The design of the Constitution was to establish a government competent to the direction and administration of the affairs of a great nation, and, at the same time, to mark, by sufficiently definite lines, the sphere of its operations. To this end it was needful only to make express grants of general powers, coupled with a further grant of such incidental and auxiliary powers as might be required for the exercise of the powers expressly granted. These powers are necessarily extensive. It has been found, indeed, in the practical administration of the government, that a very large part, if not the largest part, of its functions have been performed in the exercise of powers thus implied.

But the extension of power by implication was regarded with some apprehension by the wise men who framed, and by the intelligent citizens who adopted, the Constitution. This apprehension is manifest in the terms by which the grant of incidental and auxiliary powers is made. All powers of this nature are included under the description of "power to make all laws necessary and proper for carrying into execution the powers expressly granted to Congress or vested by the Constitution in the government or in any of its departments or officers."

The same apprehension is equally apparent in the tenth article of the amendments, which declares that "the powers not delegated to the United States by the Constitution, nor prohibited by it to the States, are reserved to the States or the people."

We do not mean to say that either of these constitutional provisions is to be taken as restricting any exercise of power fairly warranted by legitimate derivation from one of the enumerated or express powers. The first was undoubtedly introduced to exclude all doubt in respect to the existence of implied powers; while the words "necessary and proper" were intended to have a "sense," to use the words of Mr. Justice Story, "at once admonitory and directory," and to require that the means used in the execution of an express power "should be bona fide, appropriate to the end." [2 Story on the Constitution p. 142 §1253.] The second provision was intended to have a like admonitory and directory sense, and to restrain the limited government established under the Constitution from the exercise of powers not clearly delegated or derived by just inference from powers so delegated.

It has not been maintained in argument, nor, indeed, would any one, however slightly conversant with constitutional law, think of maintaining that there is in the Constitution any express grant of legislative power to make any description of credit currency a legal tender in payment of debts. We must inquire then whether this can be done in the exercise of an implied power.

The rule for determining whether a legislative enactment can be supported as an exercise of an implied power was stated by Chief Justice Marshall, speaking for the whole court, in the case of *McCullough v. The State of Maryland*; and the statement then made has ever since been accepted as a correct exposition of the Constitution. . . . It must be taken then as finally settled, so far as judicial decisions can settle anything, that the words "all laws necessary and proper for carrying into execution" powers expressly granted or vested, have, in the Constitution, a sense equivalent to that of the words, laws, not absolutely necessary indeed, but appropriate, plainly adapted to constitutional and legitimate ends; laws not prohibited, but consistent with the letter and spirit of the Constitution; laws really calculated to effect objects intrusted to the government.

The question before us, then, resolves itself into this: "Is the clause which makes United States notes a legal tender for debts contracted prior to its enactment, a law of the description stated in the rule?"

It is not doubted that the power to establish a standard of value by which all other values may be measured, or, in other words, to determine what shall be lawful money and a legal tender, is in its nature, and of necessity, a governmental power. It is in all countries exercised by the government. In the United States, so far as it relates to the precious metals, it is vested in Congress by the grant of the power to coin money. But can a power to impart these qualities to notes, or promises to pay money, when offered in discharge of pre-existing debts, be derived from the coinage power, or from any other power expressly given?

It is certainly not the same power as the power to coin money. Nor is it in any reasonable or satisfactory sense an appropriate or plainly adapted means to the exercise of that power. Nor is there more reason for saying that it is implied in, or incidental to, the power to regulate the value of coined money of the United States, or of foreign coins. This power of regulation is a power to determine the weight, purity, form, impression, and denomination of the several coins, and their relation to each other, and the relations of foreign coins to the monetary unit of the United States.

Nor is the power to make notes a legal tender the same as the power to issue notes to be used as currency. The old Congress, under the Articles of Confederation, was clothed by express grant with the power to emit bills of credit, which are in fact notes for circulation as currency; and yet that Congress was not clothed with the power to make these bills a legal tender in payment. . . . Indeed, we are not aware that it has ever been claimed that the power to issue bills or notes has any identity with the power to make them a legal tender. On the contrary, the whole history of the country refutes that notion. The States have always been held to possess the power to authorize and regulate the issue of bills for circulation by banks or individuals, subject, as has been lately determined, to the control of Congress, for the purpose of establishing and securing a National currency; and yet the States are expressly prohibited by the Constitution from making anything but gold and silver coin a legal tender. This seems decisive on the point that the power to issue notes and the power to make them a legal tender are not the same power, and that they have no necessary connection with each other. . . .

[T]here is abundant evidence, that whatever benefit is possible from that compulsion to some individuals or to the government, is far more than outweighed by the losses of property, the derangement of business, the fluctuations of currency and values, and the increase of prices to the people and the government, and the long train of evils which flow from the use of irredeemable paper money. It is true that these evils are not to be attributed altogether to making it a legal tender. But this increases these evils. It certainly widens their extent and protracts their continuance.

We are unable to persuade ourselves that an expedient of this sort is an appropriate and plainly adapted means for the execution of the power to declare and carry on war. If it adds nothing to the utility of the notes, it cannot be upheld as a means to the end in furtherance of which the notes are issued. Nor can it, in our judgment, be upheld as such, if, while facilitating in some degree the circulation of the notes, it debases and injures the currency in its proper use to a much greater degree. And these considerations seem to us equally applicable to the powers to regulate commerce and to borrow money. Both powers necessarily involve the use of money by the people and by the government, but neither, as we think, carries with it as an appropriate and plainly adapted means to its exercise, the power of making circulating notes a legal tender in payment of pre-existing debts. . . .

But there is another view, which seems to us decisive, to whatever express power the supposed implied power in question may be referred. In the rule stated by Chief Justice Marshall, the words appropriate, plainly adapted, really calculated, are qualified by the limitation that the means must be not prohibited, but consistent with the letter and spirit of the Constitution. Nothing so prohibited or inconsistent can be regarded as appropriate, or plainly adapted, or really calculated means to any end. Let us inquire, then, first, whether making bills of credit a legal tender, to the extent indicated, is consistent with the spirit of the Constitution. [Discussion of the "cardinal principles" embodied in the Contracts, Takings, and Due Process Clauses omitted. — EDS.] . . .

We confess ourselves unable to perceive any solid distinction between such an act and an act compelling all citizens to accept, in satisfaction of all contracts for money, half or three-quarters or any other proportion less than the whole of the value actually due, according to their terms. It is difficult to conceive what act would take private property without process of law if such an act would not.

We are obliged to conclude that an act making mere promises to pay dollars a legal tender in payment of debts previously contracted, is not a means appropriate, plainly adapted, really calculated to carry into effect any express power vested in Congress; that such an act is inconsistent with the spirit of the Constitution; and that it is prohibited by the Constitution.

It is not surprising that amid the tumult of the late civil war, and under the influence of apprehensions for the safety of the Republic almost universal, different views, never before entertained by American statesmen or jurists, were adopted by many. The time was not favorable to considerate reflection upon the constitutional limits of legislative or executive authority. If power was assumed from patriotic motives, the assumption found ready justification in patriotic hearts. Many who doubted yielded their doubts; many who did not doubt were silent. Some who were strongly averse to making government notes a legal tender felt themselves constrained to acquiesce in the views of the advocates of the measure. Not a few who then insisted upon its necessity, or acquiesced in that view, have, since the return of peace, and under the influence of the calmer time, reconsidered their conclusions, and now concur in those which we have just announced. These conclusions seem to us to be fully sanctioned by the letter and spirit of the Constitution. . . .

Mr. Justice MILLER (with whom concurred SWAYNE and DAVIS, JJ.), dissenting.

Altering the Size of the Supreme Court

In 1871, barely a year after deciding *Hepburn*, the Supreme Court reversed itself in *Knox v. Lee*. This highly unusual reversal resulted from a complicated series of events concerning the composition of the Supreme Court. You may be surprised to learn that the Constitution does not specify the number of Supreme Court Justices. Instead, it lets Congress organize the federal courts by passing what are called "judiciary acts." The Judiciary Act of 1789 set the number of Justices at six, which was increased to seven in 1807, to nine in 1837, and to ten in 1863. This last change allowed President Lincoln to appoint Stephen Field to the Court. (The power of Congress to set the number of Justices figured in a so-called court-packing scheme by President Franklin Roosevelt, which we will discuss later in this chapter.)

Courtroom in Philadelphia's Old City Hall where the Supreme Court sat from 1791 to 1800 [Photo: Randy Barnett]

After the death of Justice John Catron in 1865, Congress passed a judiciary act providing that the next three Justices to leave the bench by retirement or death would not be replaced, which would lower the number from ten to seven through attrition. When Justice James Moore died in 1867, the number of Justices was reduced to eight. *Hepburn v. Griswold* was then decided in November 1869 by a conference vote of 5-3. (The Justices meet in "conference" to vote on each case, after which opinions are written. When that process is completed, the Court's decision is officially announced and the opinions are issued.) Around the same time, Congress passed a judiciary act restoring the number of justices to nine.

In January of 1870, Justice Grier — who had voted with the majority in *Hepburn* — resigned due to poor health. Because the *Hepburn* decision was publicly announced after his retirement, this made the official vote 4-3. The same day the decision was announced, newly elected Republican President Grant — a strong supporter of paper money — nominated William Strong and Joseph Bradley to fill the two vacancies on the Court. Strong had previously been on record as supporting the constitutionality of the Legal Tender Acts. Two days after joining the Court, Strong and Bradley joined with Justices Swayne, Miller, and Davis to attempt to rehear the *Hepburn* case. After a long and very bitter internal struggle, that motion was denied. But the new five-Justice majority quickly agreed to hear the case of *Knox v. Lee* as a vehicle to reverse *Hepburn*. "It is I think a sad day for the [country]," Chase wrote in his diary after the reversal, "& for the cause of constitutional government. The consequences of the sanction this day given to irredeemable paper currency may not soon manifest themselves but are sure to come."

STUDY GUIDE

- How does the *Knox* majority justify its reversal of a two-year-old precedent?
- How does its method of evaluating a claim of implied power differ from that of Chase in *Hepburn*?
- Notice the Court's reliance on a presumption of constitutionality. Notice also its heavy reliance on the "purpose" for granting enumerated powers to the federal government as well as for recognizing implied powers.
- Does the Court's invocation of the Constitution's amendments vindicate James Wilson's warning about the dangerousness of a bill of rights?
- What enumerated power was the legal tender laws a necessary and proper means of implementing?
- What role does the concept of an "emergency" play? Does the Court say what happens to unenumerated powers after the emergency passes? Is there anything about the Civil War that is likely to have distorted the views people might have about limited congressional power in a federalist constitutional system? Does the end of the emergency caused by the Civil War entail the end of the power to enact legal tender laws under nonemergency situations? Or is something less than a true emergency needed to justify such powers?
- Justice Strong makes reference to the opinion of the then-Secretary of the Treasury that the legal tender law was necessary. That person was Salmon P. Chase. Chief Justice Chase then replies to this point in his dissent.

Chase on a greenback

As treasury secretary, Salmon Chase had his picture placed on the one-dollar greenback. As a result of this case, Chase's picture now appears on the $10,000 bill.

Chase on a $10,000 bill

Knox v. Lee

The Legal Tender Cases, 79 U.S. 457 (1871)

Mr. Justice Strong delivered the opinion of the court. . . .

If it be held by this court that Congress has no constitutional power, under any circumstances, or in any emergency, to make treasury notes a legal tender for the payment of all debts (a power confessedly possessed by every independent sovereignty other than the United States), the government is without those means of self-preservation which, all must admit, may, in certain contingencies, become indispensable, even if they were not when the acts of Congress now called in question were enacted. It is also clear that if we hold the acts invalid as applicable to debts incurred, or transactions which have taken place since their enactment, our decision must cause, throughout the country, great business derangement, widespread distress, and the rankest injustice. . . .

A decent respect for a co-ordinate branch of the government demands that the judiciary should presume, until the contrary is clearly shown, that there has been no transgression of power by Congress — all the members of which act under the obligation of an oath of fidelity to the Constitution. Such has always been the rule. . . . It is incumbent, therefore, upon those who affirm the unconstitutionality of an act of Congress to show clearly that it is in violation of the provisions of the Constitution. It is not sufficient for them that they succeed in raising a doubt.

Nor can it be questioned that, when investigating the nature and extent of the powers conferred by the Constitution upon Congress, it is indispensable to keep in view the objects for which those powers were granted. This is a universal rule of construction applied alike to statutes, wills, contracts, and constitutions. If the general purpose of the instrument is ascertained, the language of its provisions must be construed with reference to that purpose and so as to subserve it. In no other way can the intent of the framers of the instrument be discovered. And there are more urgent reasons for looking to the ultimate purpose in examining the powers conferred by a constitution than there are in construing a statute, a will, or a contract. We do not expect to find in a constitution minute details. It is necessarily brief and comprehensive. It prescribes outlines, leaving the filling up to be deduced from the outlines. . . .

If these are correct principles, if they are proper views of the manner in which the Constitution is to be understood, the powers conferred upon Congress must be regarded as related to each other, and all means for a common end. Each is but part of a system, a constituent of one whole. No single power is the ultimate end for which the Constitution was adopted. It may, in a very proper sense, be treated as a means for the accomplishment of a subordinate object, but that object is itself a means designed for an ulterior purpose. Thus the power to levy and collect taxes, to coin money and regulate its value, to raise and support armies, or to provide for and maintain a navy, are instruments for the paramount object, which was to establish a government, sovereign within its sphere, with capability of self-preservation, thereby forming a union more perfect than that which existed under the old Confederacy.

The same may be asserted also of all the non-enumerated powers included in the authority expressly given "to make all laws which shall be necessary and proper for carrying into execution the specified powers vested in Congress, and all other powers vested by the Constitution in the government of the United States, or in any department or officer thereof." It is impossible to know what those non-enumerated powers are, and what is their nature and extent, without considering the purposes they were intended to subserve. Those purposes, it must be noted, reach beyond the mere execution of all powers definitely intrusted to Congress and mentioned in detail. They embrace the execution of all other powers vested by the Constitution in the government of the United States, or in any department or officer thereof. It certainly was intended to confer upon the government the power of self-preservation. . . .

That would appear, then, to be a most unreasonable construction of the Constitution which denies to the government created by it, the right to employ freely every means, not prohibited, necessary for its preservation, and for the fulfilment of its acknowledged duties. Such a right, we hold, was given by the last clause of the eighth section of its first article. The means or instrumentalities referred to in that clause, and authorized, are not enumerated or defined. In the nature of things enumeration and specification were impossible. But they were left to the discretion of Congress, subject only to the restrictions that they be not prohibited, and be necessary and proper for carrying into execution the enumerated powers given to Congress, and all other powers vested in the government of the United States, or in any department or officer thereof.

And here it is to be observed it is not indispensable to the existence of any power claimed for the Federal government that it can be found specified in the words of the Constitution, or clearly and directly traceable to some one of the specified powers. Its existence may be deduced fairly from more than one of the substantive powers expressly defined, or from them all combined. It is allowable to group together any number of them and infer from them all that the power claimed has been conferred. Such a treatment of the Constitution is recognized by its own provisions. This is well illustrated in its language respecting the writ of habeas corpus. The power to suspend the privilege of that writ is not expressly given, nor can it be deduced from any one of the particularized grants of power. Yet it is provided that the privileges of the writ shall not be suspended except in certain defined contingencies. This is no express grant of power. It is a restriction. But it shows irresistibly that somewhere in the Constitution power to suspend the privilege of the writ was granted, either by some one or more of the specifications of power, or by them all combined. And, that important powers were understood by the people who adopted the Constitution to have been created by it, powers not enumerated, and not included incidentally in any one of those enumerated, is shown by the amendments. The first ten of these were suggested in the conventions of the States, and proposed at the first session of the first Congress, before any complaint was made of a disposition to assume doubtful powers. The preamble to the resolution submitting them for adoption recited that the "conventions of a number of the States had, at the time of their adopting the Constitution, expressed a desire, in order to prevent misconstruction or abuse of its powers, that further declaratory and restrictive clauses should be added." This was the origin of the amendments, and they are significant. They tend plainly to show that, in the judgment of those who adopted the Constitution, there were powers created by it, neither expressly specified nor deducible from any one specified power, or ancillary to it alone, but which grew out of the aggregate of powers conferred upon the government, or out of the sovereignty instituted. Most of these amendments are denials of power which had not been expressly granted, and which cannot be said to have been necessary and proper for carrying into execution any other powers. Such, for example, is the prohibition of any laws respecting the establishment of religion, prohibiting the free exercise thereof, or abridging the freedom of speech or of the press.

And it is of importance to observe that Congress has often exercised, without question, powers that are not expressly given nor ancillary to any single enumerated power. . . . Under the power to establish post-offices and post-roads Congress has provided for carrying the mails, punishing theft of letters and mail robberies, and even for transporting the mails to foreign countries. Under the power to regulate commerce, provision has been made by law for the improvement of harbors, the establishment of observatories, the erection of lighthouses, breakwaters, and buoys, the registry, enrolment, and construction of ships, and a code has been enacted for the government of seamen. Under the same power and other powers over the revenue and the currency of the country, for the convenience of the treasury and internal commerce, a corporation known as the United States Bank was early created. . . . Its incorporation was a constitutional exercise of congressional power for no other reason than that it was deemed to be a convenient instrument or means for accomplishing one or more of the ends for which the government was established, or, in the language of the first article, already quoted, "necessary and proper" for carrying into execution some or all the powers vested in the government. Clearly this necessity, if any existed, was not a direct and obvious one. . . .

Happily the true meaning of the clause authorizing the enactment of all laws necessary and proper for carrying into execution the express powers conferred upon Congress, and all other powers vested in the government of the United States, or in any of its departments or officers, has long since been settled. . . . It was . . . in *McCulloch v. Maryland* that the fullest consideration was given to this clause of the Constitution granting auxiliary powers, and a construction adopted that has ever since been accepted as determining its true meaning. . . . Suffice it to say, in that case it was finally settled that in the gift by the Constitution to Congress of authority to enact laws "necessary and proper" for the execution of all the powers created by it, the necessity spoken of is not to be understood as an absolute one. On the contrary, this court then held that the sound construction of the Constitution must allow to the national legislature that discretion with respect to the means by which the powers it confers are to be carried into execution, which will enable that body to perform the high duties assigned to it in the manner most beneficial to the people. . . .

With these rules of constitutional construction before us, settled at an early period in the history of the government, hitherto universally accepted, and not even now doubted, we have a safe guide to a right decision of the questions before us. Before we can hold the legal tender acts unconstitutional, we must be convinced they were not appropriate means, or means conducive to the execution of any or all of the powers of Congress, or of the government, not appropriate in any degree (for we are not judges of the degree of appropriateness), or we must hold that they were prohibited.

This brings us to the inquiry whether they were, when enacted, appropriate instrumentalities for carrying into effect, or executing any of the known powers of Congress, or of any department of the government. Plainly to this inquiry, a consideration of the time when they were enacted, and of the circumstances in which the government then stood, is important. It is not to be denied that acts may be adapted to the exercise of lawful power, and appropriate to it, in seasons of exigency, which would be inappropriate at other times.

We do not propose to dilate at length upon the circumstances in which the country was placed, when Congress attempted to make treasury notes a legal tender. They are of too recent occurrence to justify enlarged description. Suffice it to say that a civil war was then raging which seriously threatened the overthrow of the government and the destruction of the Constitution itself. It demanded the equipment and support of large armies and navies, and the employment of money to an extent beyond the capacity of all ordinary sources of supply. Meanwhile the public treasury was nearly empty, and the credit of the government, if not stretched to its utmost tension, had become nearly exhausted. Moneyed institutions had advanced largely of their means, and more could not be expected of them. They had been compelled to suspend specie payments. Taxation was inadequate to pay even the interest on the debt already incurred, and it was impossible to await the income of additional taxes. The necessity was immediate and pressing. The army was unpaid. There was then due to the soldiers in the field nearly a score of millions of dollars. The requisitions from the War and Navy Departments for supplies exceeded fifty millions, and the current expenditure was over one million per day. The entire amount of coin in the country, including that in private hands, as well as that in banking institutions, was insufficient to supply the need of the government three months, had it all been poured into the treasury. Foreign credit we had none. We say nothing of the overhanging paralysis of trade, and of business generally, which threatened loss of confidence in the ability of the government to maintain its continued existence, and therewith the complete destruction of all remaining national credit.

It was at such a time and in such circumstances that Congress was called upon to devise means for maintaining the army and navy, for securing the large supplies of money needed, and, indeed, for the preservation of the government created by the Constitution. It was at such a time and in such an emergency that the legal tender acts were passed. Now, if it were certain that nothing else would have supplied the absolute necessities of the treasury, that nothing else would have enabled the government to maintain its armies and navy, that nothing else would have saved the government and the Constitution from destruction, while the legal tender acts would, could any one be bold enough to assert that Congress transgressed its powers? Or if these enactments did work these results, can it be maintained now that they were not for a legitimate end, or "appropriate and adapted to that end," in the language of Chief Justice Marshall? That they did work such results is not to be doubted. Something revived the drooping faith of the people; something brought immediately to the government's aid the resources of the nation, and something enabled the successful prosecution of the war, and the preservation of the national life. What was it, if not the legal tender enactments?

But if it be conceded that some other means might have been chosen for the accomplishment of these legitimate and necessary ends, the concession does not weaken the argument. It is urged now, after the lapse of nine years, and when the emergency has passed, that treasury notes without the legal tender clause might have been issued, and that the necessities of the government might thus have been supplied. Hence it is inferred there was no necessity for giving to the notes issued the capability of paying private debts. At best this is mere conjecture. But admitting it to be true, what does it prove? Nothing more than that Congress had the choice of means for a legitimate end, each appropriate, and adapted to that end, though, perhaps, in different degrees. What then? Can this court say that it ought to have adopted one rather than the other? Is it our province to decide that the means selected were beyond the constitutional power of Congress, because we may think that other means to the same ends would have been more appropriate and equally efficient? That would be to assume legislative power, and to disregard the accepted rules for construing the Constitution. The degree of the necessity for any congressional enactment, or the relative degree of its appropriateness, if it have any appropriateness, is for consideration in Congress, not here. . . .

It is plain to our view, however, that none of those measures which it is now conjectured might have been substituted for the legal tender acts, could have met the exigencies of the case, at the time when those acts were passed. We have said that the credit of the government had been tried to its utmost endurance. Every new issue of notes which had nothing more to rest upon than government credit, must have paralyzed it more and more, and rendered it increasingly difficult to keep the army in the field, or the navy afloat. It is an historical fact that many persons and institutions refused to receive and pay those notes that had been issued, and even the head of the Treasury represented to Congress the necessity of making the new issues legal tenders, or rather, declared it impossible to avoid the necessity. . . .

It may be conceded that Congress is not authorized to enact laws in furtherance even of a legitimate end, merely because they are useful, or because they make the government stronger. There must be some relation between the means and the end; some adaptedness or appropriateness of the laws to carry into execution the powers created by the Constitution. But when a statute has proved effective in the execution of powers confessedly existing, it is not too much to say that it must have had some appropriateness to the execution of those powers. The rules of construction heretofore adopted, do not demand that the relationship between the means and the end shall be direct and immediate. . . .

We are accustomed to speak for mere convenience of the express and implied powers conferred upon Congress. But in fact the auxiliary powers, those necessary and appropriate to the execution of other powers singly described, are as expressly given as is the power to declare war, or to establish uniform laws on the subject of bankruptcy. They are not catalogued, no list of them is made, but they are grouped in the last clause of section eight of the first article, and granted in the same words in which all other powers are granted to Congress. . . .

[In holding] the acts of Congress constitutional as applied to contracts made either before or after their passage . . . , we overrule so much of what was decided in Hepburn v. Griswold, as ruled the acts unwarranted by the Constitution so far as they apply to contracts made before their enactment. That case was decided by a divided court, and by a court having a less number of judges than the law then in existence provided this court shall have. These cases have been heard before a full court, and they have received our most careful consideration. The questions involved are constitutional questions of the most vital importance to the government and to the public at large. We have been in the habit of treating cases involving a consideration of constitutional power differently from those which concern merely private right. We are not accustomed to hear them in the absence of a full court, if it can be avoided. Even in cases involving only private rights, if convinced we had made a mistake, we would hear another argument and correct our error. And it is no unprecedented thing in courts of last resort, both in this country and in England, to overrule decisions previously made. We agree this should not be done inconsiderately, but in a case of such far-reaching consequences as the present, thoroughly convinced as we are that Congress has not transgressed its powers, we regard it as our duty so to decide and to affirm both these judgments.

THE CHIEF JUSTICE, dissenting:

We dissent from the argument and conclusion in the opinion just announced. . . .

The rule by which the constitutionality of an act of Congress passed in the alleged exercise of an implied power is to be tried is no longer, in this Court, open to question. It was laid down in the case of *McCulloch v. Maryland*, by Chief Justice Marshall, in these words:

> Let the end be legitimate, let it be within the scope of the Constitution, and all means which are appropriate, which are plainly adapted to that end, which are not prohibited but consistent with the letter and spirit of the Constitution, are constitutional.

And it is the plain duty of the Court to pronounce acts of Congress not made in the exercise of an express power nor coming within the reasonable scope of this rule, if made in virtue of an implied power, unwarranted by the Constitution. Acts of Congress not made in pursuance of the Constitution are not laws.

Neither of these propositions was questioned in the case of *Hepburn v. Griswold*. The judges who dissented in that case maintained that the clause in the Act of February 25, 1862, making the United States notes a legal tender in payment of debts, was an appropriate, plainly adapted means to a constitutional end, not prohibited but consistent with the letter and spirit of the Constitution. The majority of the court as then constituted, five judges out of eight, felt obliged to conclude that an act making mere promises to pay dollars a legal tender in payments of debts previously contracted is not a means appropriate, plainly adapted, really calculated to carry into effect any express power vested in Congress, is inconsistent with the spirit of the Constitution, and is prohibited by the Constitution.

In the case of the *United States v. De Witt*, we held unanimously that a provision of the internal revenue law prohibiting the sale of certain illuminating oil in the states was unconstitutional, though it might increase the production and sale of other oils, and consequently the revenue derived from them, because this consequence was too remote and uncertain to warrant the court in saying that the prohibition was an appropriate and plainly adapted means for carrying into execution the power to lay and collect taxes.

We agree, then, that the question whether a law is a necessary and proper means to execution of an express power, within the meaning of these words as defined by the rule — that is to say, a means appropriate, plainly adapted, not prohibited but consistent with the latter and spirit of the Constitution — is a judicial question. Congress may not adopt any means for the execution of an express power that Congress may see fit to adopt. It must be a necessary and proper means within the fair meaning of the rule. If not such it cannot be employed consistently with the Constitution. Whether the means actually employed in a given case are such or not, the court must decide. The court must judge of the fact, Congress of the degree of necessity.

A majority of the Court, five of four, in the opinion which has just been read, reverses the judgment rendered by the former majority of five to three, in pursuance of an opinion formed after repeated arguments, at successive terms, and careful consideration, and declares the legal tender clause to be constitutional. . . . And this reversal, unprecedented in the history of the Court, has been produced by no change in the opinions of those who concurred in the former judgment. One closed an honorable judicial career by resignation after the case had been decided, after the opinion had been read and agreed to in conference, and after the day when it would have been delivered in court had not the delivery been postponed for a week to give time for the preparation of the dissenting opinion. The Court was then full, but the vacancy caused by the resignation of Mr. Justice Grier having been subsequently filled and an additional justice having been appointed under the act increasing the number of judges to nine, which took effect on the first Monday of December, 1869, the then majority find themselves in a minority of the Court, as now constituted, upon the question.

Their convictions, however, remain unchanged. We adhere to the opinion pronounced in *Hepburn v. Griswold*. Reflection has only wrought a firmer belief in the soundness of the constitutional doctrines maintained, and in the importance of them to the country. . . .

We perceive no connection between the express power to coin money and the inference that the government may, in any contingency, make its securities perform the functions of coined money, as a legal tender in payment of debts. We have supposed that the power to exclude from circulation notes not authorized by the national government might perhaps be deduced from the power to regulate the value of coin, but that the power of the government to emit bills of credit was an exercise of the power to borrow money, and that its power over the currency was incidental to that power and to the power to regulate commerce. . . .

The opinion of the then minority affirmed the power on the ground that it was a necessary and proper means, within the definition of the Court in the case of *McCulloch v. Maryland*, to carry on war, and that it was not prohibited by the spirit or letter of the Constitution, though it was admitted to be a law impairing the obligation of contracts and notwithstanding the objection that it deprived many persons of their property without compensation and without due process of law.

We shall not add much to what was said in the opinion of the then majority on these points.

The reference made in the opinion just read, as well as in the argument at the bar to the opinions of the Chief Justice when Secretary of the Treasury, seems to warrant, if it does not require, some observations before proceeding further in the discussion.

It was his fortune at the time the legal tender clause was inserted in the bill to authorize the issue of United States notes and received the sanction of Congress, to be charged with the anxious and responsible duty of providing funds for the prosecution of the war. In no report made by him to Congress was the expedient of making the notes of the United States a legal tender suggested. . . . In his report of December, 1862, he said that . . . "The Secretary recommends, therefore, no mere paper money scheme, but on the contrary a series of measures looking to a safe and gradual return to gold and silver as the only permanent basis, standard, and measure of value recognized by the Constitution."

At the session of Congress before this report was made, the bill containing the legal tender clause had become a law. He was extremely and avowedly averse to this clause, but was very solicitous for the passage of the bill to authorize the issue of United States notes then pending. He thought it indispensably necessary that the authority to issue these notes should be granted by Congress. The passage of the bill was delayed, if not jeoparded, by the difference of opinion which prevailed on the question of making them a legal tender. It was under these circumstances that he expressed the opinion, when called upon by the Committee of Ways and Means, that it was necessary, and he was not sorry to find it sustained by the decisions of respected courts, not unanimous indeed, nor without contrary decisions of state courts equally respectable. Examination and reflection under more propitious circumstances have satisfied him that this opinion was erroneous, and he does not hesitate to declare it. . . .

It is unnecessary to say that we reject wholly the doctrine, advanced for the first time, we believe, in this Court by the present majority that the legislature has any "powers under the Constitution which grow out of the aggregate of powers conferred upon the government or out of the sovereignty instituted by it." If this proposition be admitted, and it be also admitted that the legislature is the sole judge of the necessity for the exercise of such powers, the government becomes practically absolute and unlimited. . . .

Until recently, no one in Congress ever suggested that that body possessed power to make anything else a standard of value.

Statesmen who have disagreed widely on other points have agreed in the opinion that the only constitutional measures of value are metallic coins, struck as regulated by the authority of Congress. . . .

The present majority of the Court say that legal tender notes "have become the universal measure of values," and they hold that the legislation of Congress substituting such measures for coin by making the notes a legal tender in payment is warranted by the Constitution.

But if the plain sense of words, if the contemporaneous exposition of parties, if common consent in understanding, if the opinions of courts avail anything in determining the meaning of the Constitution, it seems impossible to doubt that the power to coin money is a power to establish a uniform standard of value, and that no other power to establish such a standard, by making notes a legal tender, is conferred upon Congress by the Constitution.

My brothers Clifford and Field concur in these views, but in consideration of the importance of the principles involved, will deliver their separate opinions. My brother Nelson also dissents.

STUDY GUIDE

- In the next case, how does the Court move beyond emergencies as a justification for implied powers under the Necessary and Proper Clause?
- Is "implying" a power pursuant to the Necessary and Proper Clause the same as finding a power to be "inherent" in sovereignty?

Juilliard v. Greenman

110 U.S. 421 (1884)

JUSTICE GRAY. . . .

The constitutional authority of congress to provide a currency for the whole country is now firmly established. . . . The power, as incident to the power of borrowing money, and issuing bills or notes of the government for money borrowed, of impressing upon those bills or notes the quality of being a legal tender for the payment of private debts, was a power universally understood to belong to sovereignty, in Europe and America, at the time of the framing and adopting of the constitution of the United States. The governments of Europe, acting through the monarch or the legislature, according to the distribution of powers under their respective constitutions, had and have as sovereign a power of issuing paper money as of stamping coin. . . .

The power of issuing bills of credit, and making them, at the discretion of the legislature, a tender in payment of private debts, had long been exercised in this country by the several colonies and states; and during the revolutionary war the states, upon the recommendation of the congress of the confederation, had made the bills issued by congress a legal tender. The exercise of this power not being prohibited to congress by the constitution, it is included in the power expressly granted to borrow money on the credit of the United States. . . .

Such being our conclusion in matter of law, the question whether at any particular time, in war or in peace, the exigency is such, by reason of unusual and pressing demands on the resources of the government, or of the inadequacy of the supply of gold and silver coin to furnish the currency needed for the uses of the government and of the people, that it is, as matter of fact, wise and expedient to resort to this means, is a political question, to be determined by congress when the question of exigency arises, and not a judicial question, to be afterwards passed upon by the courts. To quote once more from the judgment in *McCulloch v. Maryland*: "Where the law is not prohibited, and is really calculated to effect any of the objects intrusted to the government, to undertake here to inquire into the degree of its necessity would be to pass the line which circumscribes the judicial department, and to tread on legislative ground."

C. PROGRESSIVE ERA CASES

ASSIGNMENT 3

At the end of the nineteenth century, two social and political movements arose advocating increased government intervention in both economic and personal affairs: the progressive and populist movements. As a result, the constitutionality of various regulatory measures enacted, first by states and then by Congress, came to be challenged. The progressive movement is difficult to define without distorting its complexity. Some understanding of its ideology is needed, however, to grasp the political climate that produced many of the laws that the Supreme Court reviewed during this period. Here is one sympathetic description of progressivism:

> Progressivism [was] a broadly based reform movement that reached its height early in the 20th century. In the decades following the Civil War rapid industrialization transformed the United States. A national rail system was completed; agriculture was mechanized; the factory system spread; and cities grew rapidly in size and number. The progressive movement arose as a response to the vast changes brought by industrialization.
>
> *Urban Reform.* Progressivism began in the cities, where the problems were most acute. Dedicated men and women of middle-class background moved into the slums and established settlement houses. Led by women such as Jane Addams in Chicago and Lillian Wald in New York City, they hoped to improve slum life through programs of self-help. Other reformers attacked corruption in municipal government; they formed nonpartisan leagues to defeat the entrenched bosses and their political machines. During the 1890s, reform mayors such as Hazen Pingree in Detroit, Samuel Jones in Toledo, and James Phelan in San Francisco were elected on platforms promising municipal ownership of public utilities, improved city services, and tenement housing codes. Urban reformers were often frustrated, however, because state legislatures, controlled by railroads and large corporations, obstructed the municipal struggle for home rule.
>
> *Reform on the State Level.* Reformers turned to state politics, where progressivism reached its fullest expression. Robert La Follette's term as governor of Wisconsin (1901-6) was a model of progressive reform. He won from the legislature an antilobbying law directed at large corporations, a state banking control measure, and a direct primary law. Taxes on corporations were raised, a railroad commission was created to set rates, and a conservation commission was set up.
>
> In state after state, progressives advocated a wide range of political, economic, and social reforms. They urged adoption of the secret ballot, direct primaries, the initiative, the referendum, and direct election of senators. They struck at the excessive power of corporate wealth by regulating railroads and utilities, restricting lobbying, limiting monopoly, and raising corporate taxes. To correct the worst features of industrialization, progressives advocated workers' compensation, child labor laws, minimum wage and maximum hours legislation (especially for women workers), and widows' pensions.

Reform on the National Level. As progressives gained strength on the state level, they turned to national politics. Little headway was made, however, since conservatives controlled the Senate. Some progress was made against the trusts during [Republican] Theodore Roosevelt's administration, and Congress passed two bills regulating railroads, the Elkins Act (1903) and the Hepburn Act (1906). The exposés of business practices by the muckrakers aroused public opinion. The Pure Food and Drug Act and the Meat Inspection Act were passed (1906) to eliminate the worst practices of the food industry. Although Roosevelt supported the progressive drive for regulation of corporations and for social-welfare legislation, Congress remained adamant.

Roosevelt's [Republican] successor, William Howard Taft, was a determined opponent of progressive reform; in 1911 progressives, whose ranks had been swelled by middle-class professionals, small businessmen, and farmers, formed the National Progressive Republican League to prevent Taft's renomination. When this failed, progressives united in a third party and nominated (1912) Roosevelt for President. Although Roosevelt was defeated, the new President, [Democrat] Woodrow Wilson, sponsored many progressive measures. The Federal Reserve Act of 1913 reformed the currency system; the Clayton Antitrust Act and the Federal Trade Commission Act (1914) extended government regulation of big business; and the Keating-Owen Act (1916) restricted child labor.

Progressivism's Legacy. America's entry into World War I diverted the energy of reformers, and after the war progressivism virtually died. Its legacy endured, however, in the political reforms that it achieved and the acceptance that it won for the principle of government regulation of business. Most of the social-welfare measures advocated by progressives had to await the New Deal years for passage.[11]

Whereas progressives sometimes tended to support reforms based on the wisdom of scientifically enlightened experts, populism was based on the "belief that greater popular participation in government and business is necessary to protect individuals from exploitation by inflexible bureaucracy and financial conglomerates."[12] Or, more colorfully, populism is defined as "an ideology which pits a virtuous and homogeneous people against a set of elites and dangerous 'others' who are together depicted as depriving (or attempting to deprive) the sovereign people of their rights, values, prosperity, identity and voice."[13] The Seventeenth Amendment, which required the direct election of senators, could therefore be viewed as populist as well as progressive.

In evaluating whether the progressive political program was consistent with the constraints of the Constitution, one must bear in mind that the text of the Constitution was amended in important ways to reflect the progressive agenda. These are:

[11] The Columbia Encyclopedia (6th ed. 2001-2005).

[12] The New Dictionary of Cultural Literacy (3d ed. 2002).

[13] Daniele Albertazzi & Duncan McDonnell, Twenty-First Century Populism: The Spectre of Western European Democracy (2007).

1. the Sixteenth Amendment (1913) authorizing a national income tax, which reversed a Supreme Court decision holding such a tax to be unconstitutional;
2. the Seventeenth Amendment (1913) requiring the direct popular election of senators, who previously were selected by state legislatures;
3. the Eighteenth Amendment (1919) empowering Congress to prohibit the manufacture, sale, and transportation (but not the possession) of alcohol; and
4. the Nineteenth Amendment (1920) giving women the right to vote.

A strong argument can be made that the first two of these amendments fundamentally altered the American form of government more than any judicial decision.

While most "progressive" legislation originated at the state level, enactment of the Sherman Antitrust Act of 1890 tested the limits of congressional power and marked the beginning of judicial resistance to Progressive Era legislation.

STUDY GUIDE

- Notice how Justice Harlan's dissent in *United States v. E.C. Knight* relies on the Necessary and Proper Clause. Can you see how, in light of the Marshall Court precedents (and the *Legal Tender Cases* that are not cited in these opinions), emphasizing the Commerce Clause leads in one direction while emphasizing the Necessary and Proper Clause leads in another?
- What authority does Chief Justice Fuller give for his interpretation of the word "commerce"? If there was evidence from the founding era as to intent or understanding, why didn't he cite it?
- In 1790, 90 percent of the labor force worked in agriculture. Most manufacturing was local in nature. The first private corporation capitalized at one million dollars (the Delaware and Hudson Canal Company) was not formed until 1825. The first billion-dollar corporation was U.S. Steel in 1901. Should the tremendous changes in the economy since the Founding affect how the Court interprets the Commerce Clause?
- Notice how the Court uses a narrowing construction of the statute to avoid finding it to be unconstitutional. This is sometimes called a "saving construction." We will see Chief Justice Roberts utilize this device in *NFIB v. Sebelius* later in this chapter.

The Sherman Antitrust Act was authored by John Sherman (above), who succeeded Salmon Chase as senator from Ohio. Sherman wrote the Act after leaving the Senate for a time to serve as secretary of the treasury. Sherman's older brother was Union General William Tecumseh Sherman.

United States v. E.C. Knight Co.

156 U.S. 1 (1895)

[Defendants were charged with violating the provision of the Sherman Antitrust Act of 1890, "providing that every contract, combination in the form of trust, or otherwise, or conspiracy in restraint of trade and commerce among the several states is illegal, and that persons who shall monopolize or shall attempt to monopolize, or combine or conspire with other persons to monopolize trade and commerce among the several states, shall be guilty of a misdemeanor." The bill alleged that the E.C. Knight Company, the Franklin Sugar Company, the Spreckels Sugar Refining Company, and the Delaware Sugar House "were independently engaged in the manufacture and sale of sugar" and "the product of their refineries amounted to 33 percent of the sugar refined in the United States." These four companies were competitors with the American Sugar Refining Company, which had "obtained the control of all the sugar refineries of the United States with the exception of the Revere of Boston and the refineries of the four defendants above mentioned."

"The bill then alleged that, in order that the American Sugar Refining Company might obtain complete control of the price of sugar in the United States, that company . . . entered into an unlawful and fraudulent scheme to purchase the stock, machinery, and real estate of the other four corporations defendant, by which they attempted to control all the sugar refineries for the purpose of restraining the trade thereof with other states as theretofore carried on independently by said defendants. . . . It was further averred that the American Sugar Refining Company monopolized the manufacture and sale of refined sugar in the United States, and controlled the price of sugar; that in making the contracts, . . . the American Sugar Refining Company combined and conspired with the other defendants to restrain trade and commerce in refined sugar among the several states and foreign nations. . . ." — EDS.]

MR. CHIEF JUSTICE FULLER, after stating the cases, delivered the opinion of the court. . . .

The fundamental question is, whether conceding that the existence of a monopoly in manufacture is established by the evidence, that monopoly can be directly suppressed under the act of Congress in the mode attempted by this bill.

It cannot be denied that the power of a State to protect the lives, health, and property of its citizens, and to preserve good order and the public morals, "the power to govern men and things within the limits of its dominion," is a power originally and always belonging to the States, not surrendered by them to the general government, nor directly restrained by the Constitution of the United States, and essentially exclusive. The relief of the citizens of each State from the burden of monopoly and the evils resulting from the restraint of trade among such citizens was left with the States to deal with, and this court has recognized their possession of that power even to the extent of holding that an employment or business carried on by private individuals, when it becomes a matter of such public interest and importance as to create a common charge or burden upon the citizen; in other words, when it becomes a practical monopoly, to which the citizen is compelled to resort, and by means of which a tribute can be exacted from the community, is subject to regulation by state legislative power. On the other hand, the power of Congress to regulate commerce among the several states is also exclusive. . . . That which belongs to commerce is within the jurisdiction of the United States, but that which does not belong to commerce is within the jurisdiction of the police power of the State. *Gibbons v. Ogden* (1824). . . .

The argument is that the power to control the manufacture of refined sugar is a monopoly over a necessary of life, to the enjoyment of which by a large part of the population of the United States interstate commerce is indispensable, and that, therefore, the general government in the exercise of the power to regulate commerce may repress such monopoly directly and set aside the instruments which have created it. But this argument cannot be confined to necessaries of life merely, and must include all articles of general consumption. Doubtless the power to control the manufacture of a given thing involves in a certain sense the control of its disposition but this is a secondary and not the primary sense; and although the exercise of that power may result in bringing the operation of commerce into play, it does not control it, and affects it only incidentally and indirectly. Commerce succeeds to manufacture, and is not a part of it. The power to regulate commerce is the power to prescribe the rule by which commerce shall be governed, and is a power independent of the power to suppress monopoly. But it may operate in repression of monopoly whenever that comes within the rules by which commerce is governed, or whenever the transaction is itself a monopoly of commerce.

It is vital that the independence of the commercial power and of the police power, and the delimitation between them, however sometimes perplexing, should always be recognized and observed, for while the one furnishes the strongest bond of union, the other is essential to the preservation of the autonomy of the States as required by our dual form of government; and acknowledged evils, however grave and urgent they may appear to be, had better be borne, than the risk be run, in the effort to suppress them, of more serious consequences by resort to expedients of even doubtful constitutionality.

It will be perceived how far-reaching the proposition is that the power of dealing with a monopoly directly may be exercised by the general government whenever interstate or international commerce may be ultimately affected. The regulation of commerce applies to the subjects of commerce, and not to matters of internal police. Contracts to buy, sell, or exchange goods to be transported among the several states, the transportation and its instrumentalities, and articles bought, sold, or exchanged for the purposes of such transit among the states, or put in the way of transit, may be regulated, but this is because they form part of interstate trade or commerce. The fact that an article is manufactured for export to another state does not of itself make it an article of interstate commerce, and the intent of the manufacturer does not determine the time when the article or product passes from the control of the state and belongs to commerce. . . .

[As] Mr. Justice Lamar remarked [in *Kidd v. Pearson* (1888)]:

> No distinction is more popular to the common mind, or more clearly expressed in economic and political literature, than that between manufacture and commerce. Manufacture is transformation — the fashioning of raw materials into a change of form for use. The functions of commerce are different. The buying and selling, and the transportation incidental thereto, constitute commerce; and the regulation of commerce in the constitutional sense embraces the regulation at least of such transportation. . . . If it be held that the term includes the regulation of all such manufactures as are intended to be the subject of commercial transactions in the future, it is impossible to deny that it would also include all productive industries that contemplate the same thing. The result would be that Congress would be invested, to the exclusion of the States, with the power to regulate, not only manufactures, but also agriculture, horticulture, stock-raising, domestic fisheries, mining — in short, every branch of human industry. For is there one of them that does not contemplate, more or less clearly, an interstate or foreign market? Does not the wheat grower of the Northwest, and the cotton planter of the South, plant, cultivate, and harvest his crop with an eye on the prices at Liverpool, New York, and Chicago? The power being vested in Congress and denied to the states, it would follow as an inevitable result that the duty would devolve on Congress to regulate all of these delicate, multiform, and vital interests — interests which in their nature are, and must be, local in all the details of their successful management. . . . The demands of such supervision would require, not uniform legislation generally applicable throughout the United States, but a swarm of statutes only locally applicable, and utterly inconsistent. Any movement towards the establishment of rules of production in this vast country, with its many different climates and opportunities, would only be at the

> sacrifice of the peculiar advantages of a large part of the localities in it, if not of every one of them. On the other hand, any movement towards the local, detailed, and incongruous legislation required by such interpretation would be about the widest possible departure from the declared object of the clause in question. [. . .] A situation more paralyzing to the state governments, and more provocative of conflicts between the general government and the states, and less likely to have been what the framers of the constitution intended, it would be difficult to imagine.

In *Gibbons v. Ogden* (1824), *Brown v. Maryland* (1827), and other cases often cited, the state laws, which were held inoperative, were instances of direct interference with, or regulations of, interstate or international commerce; yet in *Kidd v. Pearson* the refusal of a State to allow articles to be manufactured within her borders, even for export, was held not to directly affect external commerce; and state legislation which, in a great variety of ways, affected interstate commerce and persons engaged in it, has been frequently sustained because the interference was not direct. . . .

It was in the light of well-settled principles that the [Sherman Act] was framed. Congress did not attempt thereby to assert the power to deal with monopoly directly as such; or to limit and restrict the rights of corporations created by the States or the citizens of the States in the acquisition, control, or disposition of property; or to regulate or prescribe the price or prices at which such property or the products thereof should be sold; or to make criminal the acts of persons in the acquisition and control of property which the States of their residence or creation sanctioned or permitted. Aside from the provisions applicable where Congress might exercise municipal power, what the law struck at was combinations, contracts, and conspiracies to monopolize trade and commerce among the several states or with foreign nations; but the contracts and acts of the defendants related exclusively to the acquisition of the Philadelphia refineries and the business of sugar refining in Pennsylvania, and bore no direct relation to commerce between the states or with foreign nations. . . .

Decree [dismissing the bill filed by the United States against E.C. Knight Company] *affirmed.*

MR. JUSTICE HARLAN, dissenting. . . .

It is the Constitution, the supreme law of the land, which invests Congress with power to protect commerce among the States against burdens and exactions arising from unlawful restraints by whatever authority imposed. Surely, a right secured or granted by that instrument is under the protection of the government which that instrument creates. Any combination, therefore, that disturbs or unreasonably obstructs freedom in buying and selling articles manufactured to be sold to persons in other States, or to be carried to other States — a freedom that cannot exist if the right to buy and sell is fettered by unlawful restraints that crush out competition — affects, not incidentally, but directly, the people of all the States; and the remedy for such an evil is found only in the exercise of powers confided to a government which, this court has said, was the government of all, exercising powers delegated by all, representing all, acting for all. *McCulloch v. Maryland* (1819). . . .

In my judgment, the citizens of the several States composing the Union are entitled of right to buy goods in the State where they are manufactured, or in any other State, without being confronted by an illegal combination whose business extends throughout the whole country, which, by the law everywhere, is an enemy to the public interests, and which prevents such buying, except at prices arbitrarily fixed by it. I insist that the free course of trade among the States cannot coexist with such combinations. When I speak of trade I mean the buying and selling of articles of every kind that are recognized articles of interstate commerce. Whatever improperly obstructs the free course of interstate intercourse and trade, as involved in the buying and selling of articles to be carried from one State to another, may be reached by Congress under its authority to regulate commerce among the States. The exercise of that authority so as to make trade among the States in all recognized articles of commerce absolutely free from unreasonable or illegal restrictions imposed by combinations is justified by an express grant of power to Congress, and would redound to the welfare of the whole country. I am unable to perceive that any such result would imperil the autonomy of the States, especially as that result cannot be attained through the action of any one State. . . .

In committing to Congress the control of commerce with foreign nations and among the several States, the Constitution did not define the means that may be employed to protect the freedom of commercial intercourse and traffic established for the benefit of all the people of the Union. It wisely forbore to impose any limitations upon the exercise of that power except those arising from the general nature of the government, or such as are embodied in the fundamental guaranties of liberty and property. It gives to Congress, in express words, authority to enact all laws necessary and proper for carrying into execution the power to regulate commerce; and whether an act of Congress, passed to accomplish an object to which the general government is competent, is within the power granted, must be determined by the rule announced through Chief Justice Marshall three-quarters of a century ago, and which has been repeatedly affirmed by this court. That rule is: "The sound construction of the Constitution must allow to the national legislature the discretion with respect to the means by which the powers it confers are to be carried into execution, which will enable that body to perform the high duties assigned to it in the manner most beneficial to the people. Let the end be legitimate, let it be within the scope of the Constitution, and all means which are appropriate, which are plainly adapted to that end, which are not prohibited, but consistent with the letter and spirit of the Constitution, are constitutional." *McCulloch v. Maryland.* The end proposed to be accomplished by the Act of 1890 is the protection of trade and commerce among the States against unlawful restraints. Who can say that that end is not legitimate or is not within the scope of the Constitution? The means employed are the suppression, by legal proceedings, of combinations, conspiracies, and monopolies which, by their inevitable and admitted tendency, improperly restrain trade and commerce among the States. Who can say that such means are not appropriate to attain the end of freeing commercial intercourse among the States from burdens and exactions imposed upon it by combinations which, under principles long recognized in this country, as well as at the common law, are illegal and dangerous to the public welfare? What clause of the Constitution can be referred to which prohibits the means thus prescribed in the act of Congress? . . .

To the general government has been committed the control of commercial intercourse among the States, to the end that it may be free at all times from any restraints except such as Congress may impose or permit for the benefit of the whole country. The common government of all the people is the only one that can adequately deal with a matter which directly and injuriously affects the entire commerce of the country, which concerns equally all the people of the Union, and which, it must be confessed, cannot be adequately controlled by any one State. Its authority should not be so weakened by construction that it cannot reach and eradicate evils that, beyond all question, tend to defeat an object which that government is entitled, by the Constitution, to accomplish. . . .

For the reasons stated, I dissent from the opinion and judgment of the court.

Legislation from as early as the 1820s at the state level attempted to control the sale and use of alcohol and lottery tickets. The Progressive movement endorsed these and other forms of social legislation, in part as "public health" measures.[14] The movement for temperance culminated in the passage of the Eighteenth Amendment in 1919 prohibiting the manufacture, sale, and transportation of alcohol. The belief that a federal prohibition of alcohol required the adoption of the Prohibition amendment reveals much about the then-reigning interpretation of the Commerce Clause. The anti-lottery sentiment led to the law that is the subject of *Champion v. Ames.* In its opinion, which is still relied upon today, the Supreme Court confronts the intersection of morals or social legislation and the commerce power.

STUDY GUIDE

- *Champion v. Ames* is still cited as the principal authority for the proposition that the power to "regulate" commerce includes the power to prohibit it as well. Today, the use of "regulate" to mean prohibit or ban is so widespread that it is hard to conceive of any distinction between the two phrases. Can you think of any other meaning of "regulate" that would exclude complete prohibition?
- How does Justice Harlan circumscribe the power upheld by the Court? These limitations are generally ignored today when the case is cited. Does this tell us something about the wisdom of making "exceptions" to prohibitions on governmental powers? Do you agree with Harlan's statement that "the possible abuse of a power is not an argument against its existence"? Notice his reference to "public health or morality."

---

[14] See Ronald Hamowy, Preventive Medicine and the Criminalization of Sexual Immorality in Nineteenth Century America, in Assessing the Criminal: Restitution, Retribution, and the Legal Process 33-95 (Randy E. Barnett & John Hagel, III eds., 1977) (describing Progressive Era laws against masturbation and providing state-by-state data on the origins of age of consent, sodomy, and prostitution laws).

Champion v. Ames

The Lottery Case, 188 U.S. 321 (1903)

[Appellants were indicted for conspiring to transport tickets of the Pan-American Lottery Company (based in Paraguay) from Texas to California in violation of an 1895 congressional act prohibiting the sending of lottery tickets from one state to another by any means. Appellants shipped them by railroad with the Wells Fargo Express Company. — EDS.]

MR. JUSTICE HARLAN delivered the opinion of the court.

The appellant insists that the carrying of lottery tickets from one State to another State by an express company engaged in carrying freight and packages from State to State, although such tickets may be contained in a box or package, does not constitute, and cannot by any act of Congress be legally made to constitute, *commerce* among the States within the meaning of the clause of the Constitution of the United States. . . .

The Government insists that express companies when engaged, for hire, in the business of transportation from one State to another, are instrumentalities of commerce among the States; that the carrying of lottery tickets from one State to another is commerce which Congress may regulate; and that as a means of executing the power to regulate interstate commerce Congress may make it an offense against the United States to cause lottery tickets to be carried from one State to another.

The questions presented by these opposing contentions are of great moment, and are entitled to receive, as they have received, the most careful consideration.

What is the import of the word "commerce" as used in the Constitution? It is not defined by that instrument. Undoubtedly, the carrying from one State to another by independent carriers of things or commodities that are ordinary subjects of traffic, and which have in themselves a recognized value in money, constitutes interstate commerce. But does not commerce among the several States include something more? Does not the carrying from one State to another, by independent carriers, of lottery tickets that entitle the holder to the payment of a certain amount of money therein specified, also constitute commerce among the States? . . . We are of opinion that lottery tickets are subjects of traffic and therefore are subjects of commerce, and the regulation of the carriage of such tickets from State to State, at least by independent carriers, is a regulation of commerce among the several States.

But it is said that the statute in question does not regulate the carrying of lottery tickets from State to State, but by punishing those who cause them to be so carried Congress in effect prohibits such carrying; that in respect of the carrying from one state to another of articles or things that are, in fact, or according to usage in business, the subjects of commerce, the authority given Congress was not to *prohibit*, but only to *regulate*. This view was earnestly pressed at the bar by learned counsel, and must be examined. . . .

In determining whether regulation may not under some circumstances properly take the form or have the effect of prohibition, the nature of the interstate traffic which it was sought by the act of May 2, 1895, to suppress cannot be overlooked. When enacting that statute Congress no doubt shared the views upon the subject of lotteries heretofore expressed by this court.

In *Phalen v. Virginia* (1850), after observing that the suppression of nuisances injurious to public health or morality is among the most important duties of Government, this court said: "Experience has shown that the common forms of gambling are comparatively innocuous when placed in contrast with the widespread pestilence of lotteries. The former are confined to a few persons and places, but the latter infests the whole community; it enters every dwelling; it reaches every class; it preys upon the hard earnings of the poor; it plunders the ignorant and simple." In other cases we have adjudged that authority given by legislative enactment to carry on a lottery, although based upon a consideration in money, was not protected by the contract clause of the Constitution; this, for the reason that no state may bargain away its power to protect the public morals, nor excuse its failure to perform a public duty by saying that it had agreed, by legislative enactment, not to do so.

If a State, when considering legislation for the suppression of lotteries within its own limits, may properly take into view the evils that inhere in the raising of money, in that mode, why may not Congress, invested with the power to regulate commerce among the several States, provide that such commerce shall not be polluted by the carrying of lottery tickets from one State to another? In this connection it must not be forgotten that the power of Congress to regulate commerce among the States is plenary, is complete in itself, and is subject to no limitations except such as may be found in the Constitution. What provision in that instrument can be regarded as limiting the exercise of the power granted? What clause can be cited which, in any degree, countenances the suggestion that one may, of right, carry or cause to be carried from one State to another that which will harm the public morals? We cannot think of any clause of that instrument that could possibly be invoked by those who assert their right to send lottery tickets from State to State except the one providing that no person shall be deprived of his liberty without due process of law. We have said that the liberty protected by the Constitution embraces the right to be free in the enjoyment of one's faculties; "to be free to use them in all lawful ways; to live and work where he will; to earn his livelihood by any lawful calling; to pursue any livelihood or avocation, and for that purpose to enter into all contracts which may be proper." *Allgeyer v. Louisiana* (1897). But surely it will not be said to be a part of anyone's liberty, as recognized by the supreme law of the land, that he shall be allowed to introduce into commerce among the States an element that will be confessedly injurious to the public morals.

If it be said that the act of 1895 is inconsistent with the Tenth Amendment, reserving to the States respectively or to the people the powers not delegated to the United States, the answer is that the power to regulate commerce among the States has been expressly delegated to Congress.

Besides, Congress, by that act, does not assume to interfere with traffic or commerce in lottery tickets carried on exclusively within the limits of any State, but has in view only commerce of that kind among the several States. It has not assumed to interfere with the completely internal affairs of any State, and has only legislated in respect of a matter which concerns the people of the United States. As a State may, for the purpose of guarding the morals of its own people, forbid all sales of lottery tickets within its limits, so Congress, for the purpose of guarding the people of the United States against the "widespread pestilence of lotteries" and to protect the commerce which concerns all the States, may prohibit the carrying of lottery tickets from one State to another. In legislating upon the subject of the traffic in lottery tickets, as carried on through interstate commerce, Congress only supplemented the action of those States — perhaps all of them — which, for the protection of the public morals, prohibit the drawing of lotteries, as well as the sale or circulation of lottery tickets, within their respective limits. It said, in effect, that it would not permit the declared policy of the States, which sought to protect their people against the mischiefs of the lottery business, to be overthrown or disregarded by the agency of interstate commerce. We should hesitate long before adjudging that an evil of such appalling character, carried on through interstate commerce, cannot be met and crushed by the only power competent to that end. We say competent to that end, because Congress alone has the power to occupy, by legislation, the whole field of interstate commerce. . . .

It is said, however, that if, in order to suppress lotteries carried on through interstate commerce, Congress may exclude lottery tickets from such commerce, that principle leads necessarily to the conclusion that Congress may arbitrarily exclude from commerce among the States any article, commodity, or thing, of whatever kind or nature, or however useful or valuable, which it may choose, no matter with what motive, to declare shall not be carried from one State to another. It will be time enough to consider the constitutionality of such legislation when we must do so. The present case does not require the court to declare the full extent of the power that Congress may exercise in the regulation of commerce among the States. We may, however, repeat, in this connection, what the court has heretofore said, that the power of Congress to regulate commerce among the States, although plenary, cannot be deemed arbitrary, since it is subject to such limitations or restrictions as are prescribed by the Constitution. This power, therefore, may not be exercised so as to infringe rights secured or protected by that instrument. It would not be difficult to imagine legislation that would be justly liable to such an objection as that stated, and be hostile to the objects for the accomplishment of which Congress was invested with the general power to regulate commerce among the several States. But, as often said, the possible abuse of a power is not an argument against its existence. There is probably no governmental power that may not be exerted to the injury of the public. If what is done by Congress is manifestly in excess of the powers granted to it, then upon the courts will rest the duty of adjudging that its action is neither legal nor binding upon the people. . . .

The whole subject is too important, and the questions suggested by its consideration are too difficult of solution, to justify any attempt to lay down a rule for determining in advance the validity of every statute that may be enacted under the commerce clause. We decide nothing more in the present case than that lottery tickets are subjects of traffic among those who choose to sell or buy them; that the carriage of such tickets by independent carriers from one State to another is therefore interstate commerce; that under its power to regulate commerce among the several States Congress — subject to the limitations imposed by the Constitution upon the exercise of the powers granted — has plenary authority over such commerce, and may prohibit the carriage of such tickets from State to State; and that legislation to that end, and of that character, is not inconsistent with any limitation or restriction imposed upon the exercise of the powers granted to Congress.

The judgment is *Affirmed.*

MR. CHIEF JUSTICE FULLER, with whom concur MR. JUSTICE BREWER, MR. JUSTICE SHIRAS, and MR. JUSTICE PECKHAM, dissenting. . . .

The power of the State to impose restraints and burdens on persons and property in conservation and promotion of the public health, good order, and prosperity is a power originally and always belonging to the States, not surrendered by them to the general government, nor directly restrained by the Constitution of the United States, and essentially exclusive, and the suppression of lotteries as a harmful business falls within this power, commonly called, of police.

It is urged, however, that because Congress is empowered to regulate commerce between the several States, it, therefore, may suppress lotteries by prohibiting the carriage of lottery matter. Congress may indeed make all laws necessary and proper for carrying the powers granted to it into execution, and doubtless an act prohibiting the carriage of lottery matter would be necessary and proper to the execution of a power to suppress lotteries; but that power belongs to the States and not to Congress. To hold that Congress has general police power would be to hold that it may accomplish objects not intrusted to the general government, and to defeat the operation of the Tenth Amendment. . . .

[T]his act cannot be brought within the power to regulate commerce among the several States, unless lottery tickets are articles of commerce, and, therefore, when carried across State lines, of interstate commerce; or unless the power to regulate interstate commerce includes the absolute and exclusive power to prohibit the transportation of anything or anybody from one State to another. . . . It cannot be successfully contended that either Congress or the States can, by their own legislation, enlarge their powers, and the question of the extent and limit of the powers of either is a judicial question under the fundamental law. If a particular article is not the subject of commerce, the determination of Congress that it is, cannot be so conclusive as to exclude judicial inquiry.

When Chief Justice Marshall said that commerce embraced intercourse, he added, commercial intercourse, and this was necessarily so since, as Chief Justice Taney pointed out, if intercourse were a word of larger meaning than the word commerce, it could not be substituted for the word of more limited meaning contained in the Constitution.

Is the carriage of lottery tickets from one State to another commercial intercourse?

The lottery ticket purports to create contractual relations, and to furnish the means of enforcing a contract right.

This is true of insurance policies, and both are contingent in their nature. Yet this court has held that the issuing of fire, marine, and life insurance policies, in one state, and sending them to another, to be there delivered to the insured on payment of premium, is not interstate commerce. . . . In *Paul v. Virginia*, Mr. Justice Field, in delivering the unanimous opinion of the court, said:

> Issuing a policy of insurance is not a transaction of commerce. The policies are simple contracts of indemnity against loss by fire, entered into between the corporations and the assured, for a consideration paid by the latter. These contracts are not articles of commerce in any proper meaning of the word. They are not subjects of trade and barter offered in the market as something having an existence and value independent of the parties to them. They are not commodities to be shipped or forwarded from one State to another, and then put up for sale. They are like other personal contracts between parties which are completed by their signature and the transfer of the consideration. Such contracts are not interstate transactions, though the parties may be domiciled in different States. The policies do not take effect — are not executed contracts — until delivered by the agent in Virginia. They are, then, local transactions, and are governed by the local law. They do not constitute a part of the commerce between the States any more than a contract for the purchase and sale of goods in Virginia by a citizen of New York whilst in Virginia would constitute a portion of such commerce.

. . .

If a lottery ticket is not an article of commerce, how can it become so when placed in an envelope or box or other covering, and transported by an express company? To say that the mere carrying of an article which is not an article of commerce in and of itself nevertheless becomes such the moment it is to be transported from one State to another, is to transform a non-commercial article into a commercial one simply because it is transported. I cannot conceive that any such result can properly follow.

It would be to say that everything is an article of commerce the moment it is taken to be transported from place to place, and of interstate commerce if from State to State.

An invitation to dine, or to take a drive, or a note of introduction, all become articles of commerce under the ruling in this case, by being deposited with an express company for transportation. This in effect breaks down all the differences between that which is, and that which is not, an article of commerce, and the necessary consequence is to take from the States all jurisdiction over the subject so far as interstate communication is concerned. It is a long step in the direction of wiping out all traces of State lines, and the creation of a centralized Government.

Does the grant to Congress of the power to regulate interstate commerce import the absolute power to prohibit it? . . .

It will not do to say . . . that State laws have been found to be ineffective for the suppression of lotteries, and therefore Congress should interfere. The scope of the commerce clause of the Constitution cannot be enlarged because of present views of public interest. In countries whose fundamental law is flexible it may be that the homely maxim, "to ease the shoe where it pinches" may be applied, but under the Constitution of the United States it cannot be availed of to justify action by Congress or by the courts. The Constitution gives no countenance to the theory that Congress is vested with the full powers of the British Parliament, and that, although subject to constitutional limitations, it is the sole judge of their extent and application; and the decisions of this court from the beginning have been to the contrary.

"To what purpose are powers limited, and to what purpose is that limitation committed to writing, if these limits may, at any time, be passed by those intended to be restrained?" asked Marshall, in *Marbury v. Madison*. "Should Congress," said the same great magistrate in *McCulloch v. Maryland*, "under the pretext of executing its powers, pass laws for the accomplishment of objects not intrusted to the Government; it would become the painful duty of this tribunal, should a case requiring such a decision come before it, to say that such an act was not the law of the land." . . .

It is argued that the power to regulate commerce among the several States is the same as the power to regulate commerce with foreign nations, and with the Indian tribes. But is its scope the same? . . . [T]he power to regulate interstate commerce . . . was intended to secure equality and freedom in commercial intercourse as between the States, not to permit the creation of impediments to such intercourse; while the [power to regulate commerce with foreign nations] clothed Congress with that power over international commerce, pertaining to a sovereign nation in its intercourse with foreign nations, and subject, generally speaking, to no implied or reserved power in the States. The laws which would be necessary and proper in the one case would not be necessary or proper in the other. . . .

The power to prohibit the transportation of diseased animals and infected goods over railroads or on steamboats is an entirely different thing, for they would be in themselves injurious to the transaction of interstate commerce, and, moreover, are essentially commercial in their nature. And the exclusion of diseased persons rests on different ground, for nobody would pretend that persons could be kept off the trains because they were going from one State to another to engage in the lottery business. However enticing that business may be, we do not understand these pieces of paper themselves can communicate bad principles by contact.

The same view must be taken as to commerce with Indian tribes. There is no reservation of police powers or any other to a foreign nation or to an Indian tribe, and the scope of the power is not the same as that over interstate commerce. . . .

I regard this decision as inconsistent with the views of the framers of the Constitution, and of Marshall, its great expounder. Our form of government may remain notwithstanding legislation or decision, but, as long ago observed, it is with governments, as with religions, the form may survive the substance of the faith. . . .

Children working in Cherryville Mfg. Co. cotton mill, Cherryville, North Carolina

STUDY GUIDE

- Is the holding of *Hammer v. Dagenhart* consistent with that of *Champion v. Ames*?
- Are you persuaded by the majority's effort to distinguish the *Lottery* case? The limitations adopted by the majority in *Hammer* were later rejected by the Supreme Court in *United States v. Darby* (1941).

Hammer v. Dagenhart

247 U.S. 251 (1918)

Mr. Justice Day delivered the opinion of the court.

A bill was filed in the United States District Court for the Western District of North Carolina by a father in his own behalf and as next friend of his two minor sons, one under the age of fourteen years and the other between the ages of fourteen and sixteen years, employees in a cotton mill at Charlotte, North Carolina, to enjoin the enforcement of the act of Congress intended to prevent interstate commerce in the products of child labor. . . . The District Court held the act unconstitutional and entered a decree enjoining its enforcement. This appeal brings the case here. The first section of the act is in the margin.[15]

The controlling question for decision is: Is it within the authority of Congress in regulating commerce among the states to prohibit the transportation in interstate commerce of manufactured goods, the product of a factory in which, within thirty days prior to their removal therefrom, children under the age of fourteen have been employed or permitted to work, or children between the ages of fourteen and sixteen years have been employed or permitted to work more than eight hours in any day, or more than six days in any week, or after the hour of seven o'clock P.M. or before the hour of six o'clock A.M.?

The power essential to the passage of this act, the Government contends, is found in the commerce clause of the Constitution which authorizes Congress to regulate commerce with foreign nations and among the States. . . . [I]t is insisted that adjudged cases in this court establish the doctrine that the power to regulate given to Congress incidentally includes the authority to prohibit the movement of ordinary commodities and therefore that the subject is not open for discussion. The cases demonstrate the contrary. They rest upon the character of the particular subjects dealt with and the fact that the scope of governmental authority, state or national, possessed over them is such that the authority to prohibit is as to them but the exertion of the power to regulate.

The first of these cases is *Champion v. Ames* (1903), the so-called *Lottery Case*, in which it was held that Congress might pass a law having the effect to keep the channels of commerce free from use in the transportation of tickets used in the promotion of lottery schemes. In *Hipolite Egg Co. v. United States* (1911), this court sustained the power of Congress to pass the Pure Food and Drug Act, which prohibited the introduction into the States by means of interstate commerce of impure foods and drugs. In *Hoke v. United States* (1913), this court sustained the constitutionality of the so-called "White Slave Traffic Act," whereby the transportation of a woman in interstate commerce for the purpose of prostitution was forbidden. . . . In *Caminetti v. United* States (1917), we held that Congress might prohibit the transportation of women in interstate commerce for the purposes of debauchery and kindred purposes. In *Clark Distilling Co. v. Western Maryland Railway Co.* (1917), the power of Congress over the transportation of intoxicating liquors was sustained. . . .

In each of these instances the use of interstate transportation was necessary to the accomplishment of harmful results. In other words, although the power over

[15] That no producer, manufacturer, or dealer shall ship or deliver for shipment in interstate or foreign commerce any article or commodity the product of any mine or quarry, situated in the United States, in which within thirty days prior to the time of the removal of such product therefrom children under the age of sixteen years have been employed or permitted to work, or any article or commodity the product of any mill, cannery, workshop, factory, or manufacturing establishment, situated in the United States, in which within thirty days prior to the removal of such product therefrom children under the age of fourteen years have been employed or permitted to work, or children between the ages of fourteen years and sixteen years have been employed or permitted to work more than eight hours in any day, or more than six days in any week, or after the hour of seven o'clock postmeridian, or before the hour of six o'clock antemeridian. . . .

interstate transportation was to regulate, that could only be accomplished by prohibiting the use of the facilities of interstate commerce to effect the evil intended.

This element is wanting in the present case. The thing intended to be accomplished by this statute is the denial of the facilities of interstate commerce to those manufacturers in the States who employ children within the prohibited ages. The act in its effect does not regulate transportation among the States, but aims to standardize the ages at which children may be employed in mining and manufacturing within the States. The goods shipped are of themselves harmless. The act permits them to be freely shipped after thirty days from the time of their removal from the factory. When offered for shipment, and before transportation begins, the labor of their production is over, and the mere fact that they were intended for interstate commerce transportation does not make their production subject to federal control under the commerce power. . . .

It is further contended that the authority of Congress may be exerted to control interstate commerce in the shipment of child-made goods because of the effect of the circulation of such goods in other States where the evil of this class of labor has been recognized by local legislation, and the right to thus employ child labor has been more rigorously restrained than in the state of production. In other words, that the unfair competition, thus engendered, may be controlled by closing the channels of interstate commerce to manufacturers in those states where the local laws do not meet what Congress deems to be the more just standard of other States.

There is no power vested in Congress to require the states to exercise their police power so as to prevent possible unfair competition. Many causes may cooperate to give one state, by reason of local laws or conditions, an economic advantage over others. The Commerce Clause was not intended to give to Congress a general authority to equalize such conditions. In some of the states laws have been passed fixing minimum wages for women, in others the local law regulates the hours of labor of women in various employments. Business done in such States may be at an economic disadvantage when compared with States which have no such regulations; surely, this fact does not give Congress the power to deny transportation in interstate commerce to those who carry on business where the hours of labor and the rate of compensation for women have not been fixed by a standard in use in other States and approved by Congress.

The grant of power of Congress over the subject of interstate commerce was to enable it to regulate such commerce, and not to give it authority to control the States in their exercise of the police power over local trade and manufacture.

The grant of authority over a purely federal matter was not intended to destroy the local power always existing and carefully reserved to the states in the Tenth Amendment to the Constitution. . . . Police regulations relating to the internal trade and affairs of the states have been uniformly recognized as within such control. "This," said this court in *United States v. Dewitt* (1869), "has been so frequently declared by this court, results so obviously from the terms of the Constitution, and has been so fully explained and supported on former occasions, that we think it unnecessary to enter again upon the discussion." See . . . Cooley's Constitutional Limitations (7th Ed.) p. 11. . . .

That there should be limitations upon the right to employ children in mines and factories in the interest of their own and the public welfare, all will admit. That such employment is generally deemed to require regulation is shown by the fact that the brief of counsel states that every state in the Union has a law upon the subject, limiting the right to thus employ children. In North Carolina, the State wherein is located the factory in which the employment was had in the present case, no child under twelve years of age is permitted to work.

It may be desirable that such laws be uniform, but our Federal Government is one of enumerated powers; "this principle," declared Chief Justice Marshall in *McCulloch v. Maryland*, "is universally admitted." . . . In interpreting the Constitution it must never be forgotten that the nation is made up of States to which are entrusted the powers of local government. And to them and to the people the powers not expressly delegated to the National Government are reserved. The power of the States to regulate their purely internal affairs by such laws as seem wise to the local authority is inherent and has never been surrendered to the general government. *New York v. Miln*, *Slaughter-House Cases*. To sustain this statute would not be in our judgment a recognition of the lawful exertion of congressional authority over interstate commerce, but would sanction an invasion by the federal power of the control of a matter purely local in its character, and over which no authority has been delegated to Congress in conferring the power to regulate commerce among the States. . . .

In our view the necessary effect of this act is, by means of a prohibition against the movement in interstate commerce of ordinary commercial commodities to regulate the hours of labor of children in factories and mines within the States, a purely state authority. Thus the act in a two-fold sense is repugnant to the Constitution. It not only transcends the authority delegated to Congress over commerce but also exerts a power as to a purely local matter to which the federal authority does not extend. The far-reaching result of upholding the act cannot be more plainly indicated than by pointing out that if Congress can thus regulate matters entrusted to local authority by prohibition of the movement of commodities in interstate commerce, all freedom of commerce will be at an end, and the power of the states over local matters may be eliminated, and thus our system of government be practically destroyed.

Affirmed.

Mr. Justice Holmes, with whom Mr. Justice McKenna, Mr. Justice Brandeis, and Mr. Justice Clarke concur, dissenting. . . .

The act does not meddle with anything belonging to the States. They may regulate their internal affairs and their domestic commerce as they like. But when they seek to send their products across the state line they are no longer within their rights. If there were no Constitution and no Congress their power to cross the line would depend upon their neighbors. Under the Constitution such commerce belongs not to the States but to Congress to regulate. It may carry out its views of public policy whatever indirect effect they may have upon the activities of the States. Instead of being encountered by a prohibitive tariff at her boundaries the State encounters the public policy of the United States which it is for Congress to express. The public policy of the United States is shaped with a view to the benefit of the nation as a whole. If, as has been the case within the memory of men still living, a State should take a different view of the propriety of sustaining a lottery from that which generally prevails, I cannot believe that the fact would require a different decision from that reached in *Champion v. Ames*. Yet in that case it would be said with quite as much force as in this that

Congress was attempting to intermeddle with the State's domestic affairs. The national welfare as understood by Congress may require a different attitude within its sphere from that of some self-seeking State. It seems to me entirely constitutional for Congress to enforce its understanding by all the means at its command.

STUDY GUIDE

In the next case, Justices Brandeis and Cardozo (who almost always voted to uphold New Deal legislation) and Chief Justice Hughes (who sometimes did) all voted to strike down the law.

Chief Justice Charles Evans Hughes

The Schechter brothers were immigrants who ran two kosher butcher shops in Brooklyn. Fittingly, in Hebrew, the word *schecht* means "to slaughter meat." Under Kashrut (Kosher) religious dietary laws, which also served as an informal health code in the Jewish community, the lungs of chickens were examined by rabbinical inspectors to ensure that they were free of illnesses or other blemishes. Under Jewish law, buyers — both retailers and individual customers — had the right to refuse a specific animal. However, the federal regulations in place prohibited customers from rejecting the animal offered. After repeated inspections by federal authorities, the Schechters told their clientele that they could not reject individual birds, causing their deeply religious customer base to dwindle.

Schechter Poultry Corp. v. United States

295 U.S. 495 (1935)

MR. CHIEF JUSTICE HUGHES delivered the opinion of the Court. . . .

New York City is the largest live poultry market in the United States. Ninety-six percent of the live poultry there marketed comes from other States. . . . A.L.A. Schechter Poultry Corporation and Schechter Live Poultry Market are corporations conducting wholesale poultry slaughterhouse markets in Brooklyn, New York City. . . . Defendants ordinarily purchase their live poultry from commission men at the West Washington Market in New York City or at the railroad terminals serving the City, but occasionally they purchase from commission men in Philadelphia. They buy the poultry for slaughter and resale. After the poultry is trucked to their slaughterhouse markets in Brooklyn, it is there sold, usually within twenty-four hours, to retail poultry dealers and butchers who sell directly to consumers. The poultry purchased from defendants is immediately slaughtered, prior to delivery, by *schochtim* [Kosher butchers in Hebrew — EDS.] in defendants' employ. Defendants do not sell poultry in interstate commerce.

The "Live Poultry Code" was promulgated under §3 of the National Industrial Recovery Act. That section . . . authorizes the President to approve "codes of fair competition."[16]

. . . The "Live Poultry Code" was approved by the President on April 13, 1934. . . . The Code is established as "a code of fair competition for the live poultry industry of the metropolitan area in and about the City of New York." . . . The Code fixes the number of hours for workdays. It provides that no employee, with certain exceptions, shall be permitted to work in excess of forty (40) hours in any one week, and that no employee, save as stated, "shall be paid in any pay period less than at the rate of fifty (50) cents per hour." The article containing "general labor provisions" prohibits the employment of any person under sixteen years of age, and declares that employees shall have the right of "collective bargaining," and freedom of choice with respect to labor organizations, in the terms of §7(a) of the Act. The minimum number of employees who shall be employed by slaughterhouse operators is fixed, the number being graduated according to the average volume of weekly sales. . . . The seventh article, containing "trade practice provisions," prohibits various practices which are said to constitute "unfair methods of competition." . . .

Of the eighteen counts of the indictment upon which the defendants were indicted, aside from the count for conspiracy, two counts charged violation of the minimum wage and maximum hour provisions of the Code, and ten counts

---

[16] CODES OF FAIR COMPETITION

> Sec. 3. (a) Upon the application to the President by one or more trade or industrial associations or groups, the President may approve a code or codes of fair competition for the trade or industry or subdivision thereof, represented by the applicant or applicants. . . .
>
> (f) When a code of fair competition has been approved or prescribed by the President under this title, any violation of any provision thereof in any transaction in or affecting interstate or foreign commerce shall be a misdemeanor and upon conviction thereof an offender shall be fined not more than $500 for each offense, and each day such violation continues shall be deemed a separate offense.

were for violation of the requirement (found in the "trade practice provisions") of "straight killing." This requirement was really one of "straight" selling. The term "straight killing" was defined in the Code as "the practice of requiring persons purchasing poultry for resale to accept the run of any half coop, coop, or coops, as purchased by slaughterhouse operators, except for culls." The charges in the ten counts, respectively, were that the defendants, in selling to retail dealers and butchers, had permitted "selections of individual chickens taken from particular coops and half-coops." . . . We are told that the provision of the statute authorizing the adoption of codes must be viewed in the light of the grave national crisis with which Congress was confronted. Undoubtedly, the conditions to which power is addressed are always to be considered when the exercise of power is challenged. Extraordinary conditions may call for extraordinary remedies. But the argument necessarily stops short of an attempt to justify action which lies outside the sphere of constitutional authority. Extraordinary conditions do not create or enlarge constitutional power.[17] The Constitution established a national government with powers deemed to be adequate, as they have proved to be both in war and peace, but these powers of the national government are limited by the constitutional grants. Those who act under these grants are not at liberty to transcend the imposed limits because they believe that more or different power is necessary. Such assertions of extraconstitutional authority were anticipated and precluded by the explicit terms of the Tenth Amendment — "The powers not delegated to the United States by the Constitution, nor prohibited by it to the States, are reserved to the States respectively, or to the people." . . .

Although the validity of the codes . . . rests upon the commerce clause of the Constitution, §3(a) is not, in terms, limited to interstate and foreign commerce. From the generality of its terms, and from the argument of the Government at the bar, it would appear that §3(a) was designed to authorize codes without that limitation. But, under §3(f), penalties are confined to violations of a code provision "in any transaction in or affecting interstate or foreign commerce." This aspect of the case presents the question whether the particular provisions of the Live Poultry Code, which the defendants were convicted for violating and for having conspired to violate, were within the regulating power of Congress.

These provisions relate to the hours and wages of those employed by defendants in their slaughterhouses in Brooklyn, and to the sales there made to retail dealers and butchers.

(1) Were these transactions "*in*" interstate commerce? Much is made of the fact that almost all the poultry coming to New York is sent there from other States. But the code provisions, as here applied, do not concern the transportation of the poultry from other States to New York, or the transactions of the commission men or others to whom it is consigned, or the sales made by such consignees to defendants. When defendants had made their purchases, whether at the West Washington Market in New York City or at the railroad terminals serving the City, or elsewhere, the poultry was trucked to their slaughterhouses in Brooklyn for local disposition.

---

[17] See *Ex parte Milligan* (1866); *Home Building & Loan Assn. v. Blaisdell* (1934).

The interstate transactions in relation to that poultry then ended. Defendants held the poultry at their slaughterhouse markets for slaughter and local sale to retail dealers and butchers who, in turn, sold directly to consumers. Neither the slaughtering nor the sales by defendants were transactions in interstate commerce.

The undisputed facts thus afford no warrant for the argument that the poultry handled by defendants at their slaughterhouse markets was in a "*current*" or "*flow*" of interstate commerce, and was thus subject to congressional regulation. The mere fact that there may be a constant flow of commodities into a State does not mean that the flow continues after the property has arrived, and has become commingled with the mass of property within the State, and is there held solely for local disposition and use. So far as the poultry here in question is concerned, the flow in interstate commerce had ceased. The poultry had come to a permanent rest within the State. It was not held, used, or sold by defendants in relation to any further transactions in interstate commerce, and was not destined for transportation to other States. Hence, decisions which deal with a stream of interstate commerce — where goods come to rest within a State temporarily and are later to go forward in interstate commerce — and with the regulations of transactions involved in that practical continuity of movement, are not applicable here.

(2) Did the defendants' transactions directly "*affect*" interstate commerce, so as to be subject to federal regulation? The power of Congress extends not only to the regulation of transactions which are part of interstate commerce, but to the protection of that commerce from injury. It matters not that the injury may be due to the conduct of those engaged in intrastate operations. Thus, Congress may protect the safety of those employed in interstate transportation "no matter what may be the source of the dangers which threaten it." *Southern Ry. Co. v. United States* (1911). We said in *Second Employers' Liability Cases* (1912), that it is the "effect upon interstate commerce," not "the source of the injury," which is "the criterion of congressional power." We have held that, in dealing with common carriers engaged in both interstate and intrastate commerce, the dominant authority of Congress necessarily embraces the right to control their intrastate operations in all matters having such a close and substantial relation to interstate traffic that the control is essential or appropriate to secure the freedom of that traffic from interference or unjust discrimination and to promote the efficiency of the interstate service. And combinations and conspiracies to restrain interstate commerce, or to monopolize any part of it, are nonetheless within the reach of the Anti-Trust Act because the conspirators seek to attain their end by means of intrastate activities. . . .

The instant case is not of that sort. This is not a prosecution for a conspiracy to restrain or monopolize interstate commerce in violation of the Anti-Trust Act. Defendants have been convicted not upon direct charges of injury to interstate commerce or of interference with persons engaged in that commerce, but of violations of certain provisions of the Live Poultry Code and of conspiracy to commit these violations. Interstate commerce is brought in only upon the charge that violations of these provisions — as to hours and wages of employees and local sales — "*affected*" interstate commerce.

In determining how far the federal government may go in controlling intrastate transactions upon the ground that they "affect" interstate commerce, there is a necessary and well established distinction between direct and indirect effects. The precise line can be drawn only as individual cases arise, but the distinction is clear in principle. Direct effects are illustrated by the railroad cases . . . as, *e.g.*, the effect of failure to use prescribed safety appliances on railroads which are the highways of both interstate and intrastate commerce, injury to an employee engaged in interstate transportation by the negligence of an employee engaged in an intrastate movement, the fixing of rates for intrastate transportation which unjustly discriminate against interstate commerce. But where the effect of intrastate transactions upon interstate commerce is merely indirect, such transactions remain within the domain of state power. If the commerce clause were construed to reach all enterprise and transactions which could be said to have an indirect effect upon interstate commerce, the federal authority would embrace practically all the activities of the people, and the authority of the State over its domestic concerns would exist only by sufferance of the federal government. Indeed, on such a theory, even the development of the State's commercial facilities would be subject to federal control. . . .

[T]he distinction between direct and indirect effects of intrastate transactions upon interstate commerce must be recognized as a fundamental one, essential to the maintenance of our constitutional system. Otherwise, as we have said, there would be virtually no limit to the federal power, and, for all practical purposes, we should have a completely centralized government. We must consider the provisions here in question in the light of this distinction.

The question of chief importance relates to the provisions of the Code as to the hours and wages of those employed in defendants' slaughterhouse markets. It is plain that these requirements are imposed in order to govern the details of defendants' management of their local business. The persons employed in slaughtering and selling in local trade are not employed in interstate commerce. Their hours and wages have no direct relation to interstate commerce. The question of how many hours these employees should work and what they should be paid differs in no essential respect from similar questions in other local businesses which handle commodities brought into a State and there dealt in as a part of its internal commerce. This appears from an examination of the considerations urged by the Government with respect to conditions in the poultry trade. Thus, the Government argues that hours and wages affect prices; that slaughterhouse men sell at a small margin above operating costs; that labor represents 50 to 60 percent of these costs; that a slaughterhouse operator paying lower wages or reducing his cost by exacting long hours of work translates his saving into lower prices; that this results in demands for a cheaper grade of goods, and that the cutting of prices brings about a demoralization of the price structure. Similar conditions may be adduced in relation to other businesses. The argument of the Government proves too much. If the federal government may determine the wages and hours of employees in the internal commerce of a State, because of their relation to cost and prices and their indirect effect upon interstate commerce, it would seem that a similar control might be exerted over other elements of cost also affecting prices, such as the number of employees, rents, advertising, methods of doing business, etc. All the processes of production and distribution that enter into cost could likewise be controlled. If the cost of doing an intrastate business is, in itself, the permitted object of federal control, the extent of the regulation of cost would be a question of discretion, and not of power.

The Government also makes the point that efforts to enact state legislation establishing high labor standards have been impeded by the belief that, unless similar action is taken generally, commerce will be diverted from the States adopting such standards, and that this fear of diversion has led to demands for federal legislation on the subject of wages and hours. The apparent implication is that the federal authority under the commerce clause should be deemed to extend to the establishment of rules to govern wages and hours in intrastate trade and industry generally throughout the country, thus overriding the authority of the States to deal with domestic problems arising from labor conditions in their internal commerce.

It is not the province of the Court to consider the economic advantages or disadvantage of such a centralized system. It is sufficient to say that the Federal Constitution does not provide for it. Our growth and development have called for wide use of the commerce power of the federal government in its control over the expanded activities of interstate commerce, and in protecting that commerce from burdens, interferences, and conspiracies to restrain and monopolize it. But the authority of the federal government may not be pushed to such an extreme as to destroy the distinction, which the commerce clause itself establishes, between commerce "among the several States" and the internal concerns of a State. . . .

We are of the opinion that the attempt, through the provisions of the Code, to fix the hours and wages of employees of defendants in their intrastate business was not a valid exercise of federal power. . . .

D. THE NEW DEAL COURT

ASSIGNMENT 4

In 1932, President Franklin D. Roosevelt was elected in a landslide on the promise that he would bring the United States out of the Great Depression. Through his New Deal agenda, President Roosevelt sought to promote economic recovery by vastly expanding the powers of the federal government. During this time, the executive branch often clashed with the judiciary, though not in the way you may have learned.

Until recently, the conventional account of the transition between the Progressive Era and the New Deal Era went as follows. During the Progressive Era, the "*Lochner* Court" — named after the 1905 decision in *Lochner v. New York* — used the Commerce Clause and Due Process Clause to engage in conservative "judicial activism." These decisions impeded progress and thwarted the popular will by declaring progressive legislation unconstitutional. During the early years of the Roosevelt administration, the Democratic Congress enacted the first planks of the New Deal agenda. The Supreme Court, however, found portions of the legislation unconstitutional.

In response, the President proposed the so-called court-packing scheme, which would have had the effect of increasing the number of Supreme Court Justices, thus creating new vacancies that could be filled with Justices sympathetic to the New

Deal. (Recall from earlier in the chapter that Congress has the power to set the number of Supreme Court Justices. As we saw, it has varied that number from as low as six to as many as ten.) Roosevelt's 1937 plan was presented under the guise that the oldest members of the Court could not handle the workload, but everyone knew this was not the true reason.

After the court-packing scheme was made public, the story goes, the Justices announced their decision in *West Coast Hotel Co. v. Parrish*. In that case, a five-Justice majority upheld the constitutionality of a law that imposed a minimum wage for women. This decision reversed the Court's prior 1923 decision in *Adkins v. Children's Hospital*, which invalidated a nearly identical law. Justice Owen Roberts (no relation to Chief Justice John Roberts) had previously joined the four conservative Justices in striking down a similar minimum wage law in New York just the year before in *Morehead v. New York ex rel. Tipaldo*, 298 U.S. 587 (1936). His decision to uphold the minimum wage law in *West Coast Hotel* was thus dubbed "the switch in time that saved nine," a take-off on the adage "a stitch in time saves nine."

Although no one denies that a seismic change in constitutional law occurred in 1936 and 1937, the conventional account of how and when it occurred has been contested.[18] Here are some countervailing facts:

1. The changes did not occur abruptly after the court-packing plan was announced. In fact, the transition began gradually, as early as 1931 after President Hoover appointed to the Court Charles Evans Hughes and Owen Roberts in 1930, followed by Benjamin Cardozo in 1932. Though elected as a Republican, Hoover was a political progressive.
2. The constitutional sea change took until at least 1942 to be fully effected. By that point, President Franklin D. Roosevelt, a Democrat, had appointed seven out of the nine Justices.
3. The conference vote in *West Coast Hotel* took place *before* the court-packing scheme was publicly announced.
4. Because key Democrats in Congress were vocal in their opposition to the plan, it was not perceived as a realistic threat to the Court.
5. The shift in constitutional law initially concerned only the Due Process Clauses. In contrast, the Court's shift with respect to the Commerce Clause only happened later and with considerable hesitance.
6. Many doctrines limiting federal and state power that were developed during the Progressive Era — including important features of the Court's approach to due process — were never repudiated by the New Deal or Warren Courts and are still good law today.

Another question in dispute is whether this change in constitutional law by the New Deal Court represented a *restoration* of the original Constitution or, instead, a genuine constitutional *revolution*. At the time, some claimed that the change restored the original meaning of the Constitution as reflected in early Marshall

[18] The pathbreaking revisionist work can be studied in Barry Cushman, Rethinking the New Deal Court (1998).

Jones & Laughlin Steel Factory

Court decisions such as *Gibbons v. Ogden* and *McCulloch v. Maryland.*[19] However, many prominent contemporary scholars who favor the wisdom and legitimacy of the change now freely accept that it was indeed a revolutionary departure from a 150-year-old constitutional tradition.[20] Indeed, Rexford Tugwell, a member of President Roosevelt's so-called *Brain Trust*, admitted that New Deal programs could only be reconciled with the Constitution through "tortured interpretations of a document intended to prevent them." Finally, some advocates, who sought *even greater change* than the New Deal Court was willing to accept, may have exaggerated the scope of the Court's revolution. The doctrines actually enunciated by the Court may not have been quite so radical.

When considering the development of constitutional law as it unfolded during the New Deal, keep the different doctrinal areas distinct and pay careful attention to the actual reasoning of the New Deal cases. In this chapter we confine our study to cases involving the Commerce and Necessary and Proper Clauses, which reversed much — but not all — of the doctrine developed during the Progressive Era.

---

[19] See, e.g., Walton H. Hamilton & Douglass Adair, The Power to Govern: The Constitution — Then and Now 184-194 (1937).

[20] See Bruce Ackerman, We the People: Foundations (1991); Howard Gillman, The Constitution Besieged: The Rise and Demise of *Lochner* Era Police Powers Jurisprudence (1993).

STUDY GUIDE

- What limits, if any, did the Court place on the commerce power of Congress?
- How does the Court alter the approach previously taken in *Schechter Poultry*?

1. The Substantial Effects Doctrine

NLRB v. Jones & Laughlin Steel Corp.

301 U.S. 1 (1937)

MR. CHIEF JUSTICE HUGHES delivered the opinion of the Court.

In a proceeding under the National Labor Relations Act of 1935 the National Labor Relations Board found that the respondent, Jones & Laughlin Steel Corporation, had violated the act by engaging in unfair labor practices affecting commerce. . . . The unfair labor practices charged were that the corporation was discriminating against members of the union with regard to hire and tenure of employment, and was coercing and intimidating its employees in order to interfere with their self-organization. . . .

The scheme of the National Labor Relations Act — which is too long to be quoted in full — may be briefly stated. The first section sets forth findings with respect to the injury to commerce resulting from the denial by employers of the right of employees to organize and from the refusal of employers to accept the procedure of collective bargaining. There follows a declaration that it is the policy of the United States to eliminate these causes of obstruction to the free flow of commerce. . . . It creates the National Labor Relations Board and prescribes its organization. . . . The Board is empowered to prevent the described unfair labor practices affecting commerce and the act prescribes the procedure to that end. . . .

The facts as to the nature and scope of the business of the Jones & Laughlin Steel Corporation have been found by the Labor Board and, so far as they are essential to the determination of this controversy, they are not in dispute. The Labor Board has found: The corporation is organized under the laws of Pennsylvania and has its principal office at Pittsburgh. It is engaged in the business of manufacturing iron and steel in plants situated in Pittsburgh and nearby Aliquippa, Pennsylvania. It manufactures and distributes a widely diversified line of steel and pig iron, being the fourth largest producer of steel in the United States. With its subsidiaries — nineteen in number — it is a completely integrated enterprise, owning and operating ore, coal and limestone properties, lake and river transportation facilities and terminal railroads located at its manufacturing plants. It owns or controls mines in Michigan and Minnesota. It operates four ore steamships on the Great Lakes, used in the transportation of ore to its factories. It owns coal mines in Pennsylvania. It operates towboats and steam barges used in carrying coal to its factories. It owns limestone properties in various places in Pennsylvania and West Virginia. It owns the Monongahela connecting railroad which connects the plants of the Pittsburgh works and forms an interconnection with the Pennsylvania, New York Central and Baltimore & Ohio Railroad systems. It owns the Aliquippa & Southern Railroad Company, which connects the Aliquippa works with the Pittsburgh & Lake Erie, part of the New York Central system. Much of its product is shipped to its warehouses in Chicago, Detroit, Cincinnati and Memphis — to the last two places by means of its own barges and transportation equipment. In Long Island City, New York, and in New Orleans it operates structural steel fabricating shops in connection with the warehousing of semifinished materials sent from its works. Through one of its wholly owned subsidiaries it owns, leases, and operates stores, warehouses, and yards for the distribution of equipment and supplies for drilling and operating oil and gas wells and for pipe lines, refineries and pumping stations. It has sales offices in twenty cities in the United States and a wholly owned subsidiary which is devoted exclusively to distributing its product in Canada. Approximately 75 per cent of its product is shipped out of Pennsylvania. . . .

The Act is challenged in its entirety as an attempt to regulate all industry, thus invading the reserved powers of the States over their local concerns. It is asserted that the references in the Act to interstate and foreign commerce are colorable at best; that the act is not a true regulation of such commerce or of matters which directly affect it, but on the contrary has the fundamental object of placing under the compulsory supervision of the federal government all industrial labor relations within the nation. The argument seeks support in the broad words of the preamble and in the sweep of the provisions of the Act, and it is further insisted that its legislative history shows an essential universal purpose in the light of which its scope cannot be limited by either construction or by the application of the separability clause.

If this conception of terms, intent and consequent inseparability were sound, the Act would necessarily fall by reason of the limitation upon the federal power which inheres in the constitutional grant, as well as because of the explicit reservation of the Tenth Amendment. The authority of the federal government may not be pushed to such an extreme as to destroy the distinction, which the commerce clause itself establishes, between commerce "among the several States" and the internal concerns of a State. That distinction between what is national and what is local in the activities of commerce is vital to the maintenance of our federal system.

But we are not at liberty to deny effect to specific provisions, which Congress has constitutional power to enact, by superimposing upon them inferences from general legislative declarations of an ambiguous character, even if found in the same statute. The cardinal principle of statutory construction is to save and not to destroy. . . .

We think it clear that the National Labor Relations Act may be construed so as to operate within the sphere of constitutional authority. The jurisdiction conferred upon the Board, and invoked in this instance, is found in section 10(a), which provides:

> SEC. 10(a). The Board is empowered, as hereinafter provided, to prevent any person from engaging in any unfair labor practice [. . .] affecting commerce.

The critical words of this provision, prescribing the limits of the Board's authority in dealing with the labor practices, are "affecting commerce." The act specifically defines the "commerce" to which it refers:

> The term "commerce" means trade, traffic, commerce, transportation, or communication among the several States, or between the District of Columbia or any Territory of the United States and any State or other Territory, or between any foreign country and any State, Territory, or the District of Columbia, or within the District of Columbia or any Territory, or between points in the same State but through any other State or any Territory or the District of Columbia or any foreign country.

There can be no question that the commerce thus contemplated by the act (aside from that within a Territory or the District of Columbia) is interstate and foreign commerce in the constitutional sense. The act also defines the term "affecting commerce":

> The term "affecting commerce" means in commerce, or burdening or obstructing commerce or the free flow of commerce, or having led or tending to lead to a labor dispute burdening or obstructing commerce or the free flow of commerce.

This definition is one of exclusion as well as inclusion. The grant of authority to the Board does not purport to extend to the relationship between all industrial employees and employers. Its terms do not impose collective bargaining upon all industry regardless of effects upon interstate or foreign commerce. It purports to reach only what may be deemed to burden or obstruct that commerce and, thus qualified, it must be construed as contemplating the exercise of control within constitutional bounds. It is a familiar principle that acts which directly burden or obstruct interstate or foreign commerce, or its free flow, are within the reach of the congressional power. Acts having that effect are not rendered immune because they grow out of labor disputes. It is the effect upon commerce, not the source of the injury, which is the criterion. . . .

The congressional authority to protect interstate commerce from burdens and obstructions is not limited to transactions which can be deemed to be an essential part of a "flow" of interstate or foreign commerce. Burdens and obstructions may be due to injurious action springing from other sources. The fundamental principle is that the power to regulate commerce is the power to enact "all appropriate legislation" for "its protection and advancement" to adopt measures "to promote its growth and insure its safety" "to foster, protect, control and restrain." That power is plenary, and may be exerted to protect interstate commerce "no matter what the source of the dangers which threaten it." Although activities may be intrastate in character when separately considered, if they have such a close and substantial relation to interstate commerce that their control is essential or appropriate to protect that commerce from burdens and obstructions, Congress cannot be denied the power to exercise that control. Undoubtedly the scope of this power must be considered in the light of our dual system of government, and may not be extended so as to embrace effects upon interstate commerce so indirect and remote that to embrace them, in view of our complex society, would effectually obliterate the distinction between what is national and what is local and create a completely centralized government. The question is necessarily one of degree. . . .

Our conclusion is that the order of the Board was within its competency and that the Act is valid as here applied. The judgment of the Circuit Court of Appeals is reversed and the cause is remanded for further proceedings in conformity with this opinion.

Reversed.

STUDY GUIDE

- Does *Darby* add anything to the interpretation of the scope of the Commerce Clause in *Jones & Laughlin*? Notice that the Court considers separately two different portions of the statute, and applies a different test to each. Is there any indication that the Court is relying on the Necessary and Proper Clause, rather than solely on the Commerce Clause, in evaluating the scope of Congress's power?
- What role does the Court see for "motive and purpose"? Can this inquiry be reconciled with Chief Justice Marshall's discussion of pretextual legislation in *McCulloch* (Chapter 2) and his later defense of his opinion?
- Given how Madison described the Tenth Amendment in his Bill of Rights speech, isn't the Court correct in describing it as merely a "truism"? Is there any response you think Madison would make to such a characterization in the context of this case?

United States v. Darby

312 U.S. 100 (1941)

Mr. Justice Stone delivered the opinion of the Court.

The two principal questions raised by the record in this case are, *first*, whether Congress has constitutional power to prohibit the shipment in interstate commerce of lumber manufactured by employees whose wages are less than a prescribed minimum or whose weekly hours of labor at that wage are greater than a prescribed maximum, and, *second*, whether it has power to prohibit the employment of workmen in the production of goods "for interstate commerce" at other than prescribed wages and hours. . . .

The Fair Labor Standards Act set up a comprehensive legislative scheme for preventing the shipment in interstate commerce of certain products and commodities produced in the United States under labor conditions as respects wages and hours which fail to conform to standards set up by the Act. Its purpose, as we judicially know from the declaration of policy in §2(a) of the Act, and the reports of Congressional committees proposing the legislation, is to exclude from interstate commerce goods produced for the commerce and to prevent their production for interstate commerce, under conditions detrimental to the maintenance of the minimum standards of living necessary for health and general well-being; and to prevent the use of interstate commerce as the means of competition in the distribution of goods so produced, and as the means of spreading and perpetuating such substandard labor conditions among the workers of the several states. . . .

While manufacture is not of itself interstate commerce, the shipment of manufactured goods interstate is such commerce and the prohibition of such shipment by Congress is indubitably a regulation of the commerce. The power to regulate commerce is the power "to prescribe the rule by which commerce is to be governed." *Gibbons v. Ogden* (1824). It extends not only to those regulations which aid, foster and protect the commerce, but embraces those which prohibit it. It is conceded that the power of Congress to prohibit transportation in interstate commerce includes noxious articles; stolen articles; kidnapped persons, and articles such as intoxicating liquor or convict made goods, traffic in which is forbidden or restricted by the laws of the state of destination.

But it is said that the present prohibition falls within the scope of none of these categories; that while the prohibition is nominally a regulation of the commerce its motive or purpose is regulation of wages and hours of persons engaged in manufacture, the control of which has been reserved to the states and upon which Georgia and some of the states of destination have placed no restriction; that the effect of the present statute is not to exclude the prescribed articles from interstate commerce in aid of state regulation . . . , but instead, under the guise of a regulation of interstate commerce, it undertakes to regulate wages and hours within the state contrary to the policy of the state which has elected to leave them unregulated.

The power of Congress over interstate commerce "is complete in itself, may be exercised to its utmost extent, and acknowledges no limitations, other than are prescribed by the Constitution." *Gibbons v. Ogden*. That power can neither be enlarged nor diminished by the exercise or non-exercise of state power. Congress, following its own conception of public policy concerning the restrictions which may appropriately be imposed on interstate commerce, is free to exclude from the commerce articles whose use in the states for which they are destined it may conceive to be injurious to the public health, morals or welfare, even though the state has not sought to regulate their use.

Such regulation is not a forbidden invasion of state power merely because either its motive or its consequence is to restrict the use of articles of commerce within the states of destination and is not prohibited unless by other Constitutional provisions. It is no objection to the assertion of the power to regulate interstate commerce that its exercise is attended by the same incidents which attend the exercise of the police power of the states.

The motive and purpose of the present regulation are plainly to make effective the Congressional conception of public policy that interstate commerce should not be made the instrument of competition in the distribution of goods produced under substandard labor conditions, which competition is injurious to the commerce and to the states from and to which the commerce flows. The motive and purpose of a regulation of interstate commerce are matters for the legislative judgment upon the exercise of which the Constitution places no restriction and over which the courts are given no control. . . . Whatever their motive and purpose, regulations of commerce which do not infringe some constitutional prohibition are within the plenary power conferred on Congress by the Commerce Clause. Subject only to that limitation, presently to be considered, we conclude that the prohibition of the shipment interstate of goods produced under the forbidden substandard labor conditions is within the constitutional authority of Congress.

In the more than a century which has elapsed since the decision of *Gibbons v. Ogden*, these principles of constitutional interpretation have been so long and repeatedly recognized by this Court as applicable to the Commerce Clause, that there would be little occasion for repeating them now were it not for the decision of this Court twenty-two years ago in *Hammer v. Dagenhart* (1918). In that case it was held by a bare majority of the Court over the powerful and now classic dissent of Mr. Justice Holmes setting forth the fundamental issues involved, that Congress was without power to exclude the products of child labor from interstate commerce. The reasoning and conclusion of the Court's opinion there cannot be reconciled with the conclusion which we have reached, that the power of Congress under the Commerce Clause is plenary to exclude any article from interstate commerce subject only to the specific prohibitions of the Constitution.

Hammer v. Dagenhart has not been followed. The distinction on which the decision was rested that Congressional power to prohibit interstate commerce is limited to articles which in themselves have some harmful or deleterious property — a distinction which was novel when made and unsupported by any provision of the Constitution — has long since been abandoned. The thesis of the opinion that the motive of the prohibition or its effect to control in some measure the use or production within the states of the article thus excluded from the commerce can operate to deprive the regulation of its constitutional authority has long since ceased to have force. . . .

The conclusion is inescapable that *Hammer v. Dagenhart* was a departure from the principles which have prevailed in the interpretation of the Commerce Clause both before and since the decision and that such vitality, as a precedent, as it then had has long since been exhausted. It should be and now is overruled. . . .

There remains the question whether such restriction on the production of goods for commerce is a permissible exercise of the commerce power. The power of Congress over interstate commerce is not confined to the regulation of commerce among the states. It extends to those activities intrastate which so affect interstate commerce or the exercise of the power of Congress over it as to make regulation of them appropriate means to the attainment of a legitimate end, the exercise of the granted power of Congress to regulate interstate commerce. See *McCulloch v. Maryland* (1819).

In the absence of Congressional legislation on the subject, state laws which are not regulations of the commerce itself or its instrumentalities are not forbidden even though they affect interstate commerce. But it does not follow that Congress may not by appropriate legislation regulate intrastate activities where they have a substantial effect on interstate commerce. . . .

The means adopted by [the Act] for the protection of interstate commerce by the suppression of the production of the condemned goods for interstate commerce is so related to the commerce and so affects it as to be within the reach of the commerce power. Congress, to attain its objective in the suppression of nationwide competition in interstate commerce by goods produced under substandard labor conditions, has made no distinction as to the volume or amount of shipments in the commerce or of production for commerce by any particular shipper or producer. It recognized that in present day industry, competition by a small part may affect the whole and that the total effect of the competition of many small producers may be great. The legislation aimed at a whole embraces all its parts. . . .

Our conclusion is unaffected by the Tenth Amendment which provides: "The powers not delegated to the United States by the Constitution, nor prohibited by it to the States, are reserved to the States respectively, or to the people." The amendment states but a truism that all is retained which has not been surrendered. There is nothing in the history of its adoption to suggest that it was more than declaratory of the relationship between the national and state governments as it had been established by the Constitution before the amendment or that its purpose was other than to allay fears that the new national government might seek to exercise powers not granted, and that the states might not be able to exercise fully their reserved powers.

From the beginning and for many years the amendment has been construed as not depriving the national government of authority to resort to all means for the exercise of a granted power which are appropriate and plainly adapted to the permitted end. *Martin v. Hunter's Lessee* (1816); *McCulloch v. Maryland* (1819); . . . *Lottery Case* (1903). . . . Whatever doubts may have arisen of the soundness of that conclusion they have been put at rest by the decisions under the Sherman Act and the National Labor Relations Act which we have cited. . . .

2. The Aggregation Principle

STUDY GUIDE

- Even after *Jones & Laughlin* and *Darby*, and the near-complete control of the Court by Roosevelt appointees, *Wickard v. Filburn* was considered to be so controversial it was held over for re-argument in a subsequent term. Why do you think this might have been?
- Does the Court in *Wickard* retain any role in constraining Congress's powers under the Necessary and Proper Clause?

After the ruling against him, Ohio farmer Roscoe Filburn (above) changed his name to Fibrun, which was how his father spelled the family name.

Wickard v. Filburn

317 U.S. 111 (1942)

MR. JUSTICE JACKSON delivered the opinion of the Court.

The appellee . . . sought to enjoin enforcement against himself of the marketing penalty imposed by the . . . Agricultural Adjustment Act of 1938, upon that part of his 1941 wheat crop which was available for marketing in excess of the marketing quota established [pursuant to the Act] for his farm. He also sought a declaratory judgment that the wheat marketing quota provisions of the Act as amended and applicable to him were unconstitutional because not sustainable under the Commerce Clause. . . .

The appellee for many years past has owned and operated a small farm in Montgomery County, Ohio, maintaining a herd of dairy cattle, selling milk, raising poultry, and selling poultry and eggs. It has been his practice to raise a small acreage of winter wheat, sown in the Fall and harvested in the following July; to sell a portion of the crop; to feed part to poultry and livestock on the farm, some of which is sold; to use some in making flour for home consumption; and to keep the rest for the following seeding. . . .

In July of 1940, pursuant to the [Act,] there were established for the appellee's 1941 crop a wheat acreage allotment of 11.1 acres and a normal yield of 20.1 bushels of wheat an acre. He was given notice of such allotment in July of 1940 before the Fall planting of his 1941 crop of wheat, and again in July of 1941, before it was harvested. He sowed, however, 23 acres, and harvested from his 11.9 acres of excess acreage 239 bushels, which under the terms of the Act, constituted farm marketing excess, subject to a penalty of 49 cents a bushel, or $117.11 in all. The appellee has not paid the penalty. . . .

The general scheme of the Agricultural Adjustment Act of 1938 as related to wheat is to control the volume moving in interstate and foreign commerce in order to avoid surpluses and shortages and the consequent abnormally low or high wheat prices and obstructions to commerce. Within prescribed limits and by prescribed standards the Secretary of Agriculture is directed to ascertain and proclaim each year a national acreage allotment for the next crop of wheat, which is then apportioned to the states and their counties, and is eventually broken up into allotments for individual farms. . . .

The Act provides further that whenever it appears that the total supply of wheat as of the beginning of any marketing year, beginning July 1, will exceed a normal year's domestic consumption and export by more than 35 per cent, the Secretary shall so proclaim not later than May 15 prior to the beginning of such marketing year; and that during the marketing year a compulsory national marketing quota shall be in effect with respect to the marketing of wheat. Between the issuance of the proclamation and June 10, the Secretary must, however, conduct a referendum of farmers who will be subject to the quota to determine whether they favor or oppose it; and if more than one-third of the farmers voting in the referendum do oppose, the Secretary must prior to the effective date of the quota by proclamation suspend its operation.

On May 19, 1941, the Secretary of Agriculture made a radio address to the wheat farmers of the United States in which he advocated approval of the quotas. . . .

Pursuant to the Act, the referendum of wheat growers was held on May 31, 1941. According to the required published statement of the Secretary of Agriculture, 81 per cent of those voting favored the marketing quota, with 19 per cent opposed. . . .

It is urged that under the Commerce Clause of the Constitution, Article I, §8, Clause 3, Congress does not possess the power it has in this instance sought to exercise. The question would merit little consideration since our decision in *United States v. Darby* (1941), sustaining the federal power to regulate production of goods for commerce except for the fact that this Act extends federal regulation to production not intended in any part for commerce but wholly for consumption on the farm. The Act includes a definition of "market" and its derivatives so that as related to wheat in addition to its conventional meaning it also means to dispose of "by feeding (in any form) to poultry or livestock which, or the products of which, are sold, bartered, or exchanged, or to be so disposed of." Hence, marketing quotas not only embrace all that may be sold without penalty but also what may be consumed on the premises. . . .

But even if appellee's activity be local and though it may not be regarded as commerce, it may still, whatever its nature, be reached by Congress if it exerts a substantial economic effect on interstate commerce and this irrespective of whether such effect is what might at some earlier time have been defined as "direct" or "indirect."

The parties have stipulated a summary of the economics of the wheat industry. Commerce among the states in wheat is large and important. Although wheat is raised in every state but one, production in most states is not equal to consumption. Sixteen states on average have had a surplus of wheat above their own requirements for feed, seed, and food. Thirty-two states and the District of Columbia, where production has been below consumption, have looked to these surplus-producing states for their supply as well as for wheat for export and carryover.

The wheat industry has been a problem industry for some years. Largely as a result of increased foreign production and import restrictions, annual exports of wheat and flour from the United States during the ten-year period ending in 1940 averaged less than 10 per cent of total production, while during the 1920's they averaged more than 25 per cent. The decline in the export trade has left a large surplus in production which in connection with an abnormally large supply of wheat and other grains in recent years caused congestion in a number of markets; tied up railroad cars; and caused elevators in some instances to turn away grains, and railroads to institute embargoes to prevent further congestion.

Many countries, both importing and exporting, have sought to modify the impact of the world market conditions on their own economy. Importing countries have taken measures to stimulate production and self-sufficiency. The four large exporting countries of Argentina, Australia, Canada, and the United States have all undertaken various programs for the relief of growers. Such measures have been designed in part at least to protect the domestic price received by producers. Such plans have generally evolved towards control by the central government.

In the absence of regulation the price of wheat in the United States would be much affected by world conditions. During 1941 producers who cooperated with the Agricultural Adjustment program received an average price on the farm of about $1.16 a bushel as compared with the world market price of 40 cents a bushel.

Differences in farming conditions, however, make these benefits mean different things to different wheat growers. There are several large areas of specialization in wheat, and the concentration on this crop reaches 27 per cent of the crop land, and the average harvest runs as high as 155 acres. Except for some use of wheat as stock feed and for seed, the practice is to sell the crop for cash. Wheat from such areas constitutes the bulk of the interstate commerce therein.

On the other hand, in some New England states less than one percent of the crop land is devoted to wheat, and the average harvest is less than five acres per farm. In 1940 the average percentage of the total wheat production that was sold in each state as measured by value ranged from 29 per cent thereof in Wisconsin to 90 per cent in Washington. Except in regions of large-scale production, wheat is usually grown in rotation with other crops; for a nurse crop for grass seeding; and as a cover crop to prevent soil erosion and leaching. Some is sold, some kept for seed, and a percentage of the total production much larger than in areas of specialization is consumed on the farm and grown for such purpose. Such farmers, while growing some wheat, may even find the balance of their interest on the consumer's side.

The effect of consumption of homegrown wheat on interstate commerce is due to the fact that it constitutes the most variable factor in the disappearance of the wheat crop. Consumption on the farm where grown appears to vary in an amount greater than 20 per cent of average production. The total amount of wheat consumed as food varies but relatively little, and use as seed is relatively constant.

The maintenance by government regulation of a price for wheat undoubtedly can be accomplished as effectively by sustaining or increasing the demand as by limiting the supply. The effect of the statute before us is to restrict the amount which may be produced for market and the extent as well to which one may forestall resort to the market by producing to meet his own needs. That appellee's own contribution to the demand for wheat may be trivial by itself is not enough to remove him from the scope of federal regulation where, as here, his contribution, taken together with that of many others similarly situated, is far from trivial.

It is well established by decisions of this Court that the power to regulate commerce includes the power to regulate the prices at which commodities in that commerce are dealt in and practices affecting such prices. One of the primary purposes of the Act in question was to increase the market price of wheat and to that end to limit the volume thereof that could affect the market. It can hardly be denied that a factor of such volume and variability as home-consumed wheat would have a substantial influence on price and market conditions. This may arise because being in marketable condition such wheat overhangs the market and if induced by rising prices tends to flow into the market and check price increases. But if we assume that it is never marketed, it supplies a need of the man who grew it which would otherwise be reflected by purchases in the open market. Home-grown wheat in this sense competes with wheat in commerce. The stimulation of commerce is a use of the regulatory function quite as definitely as prohibitions or restrictions thereon. This record leaves us in no doubt that Congress may properly have considered that wheat consumed on the farm where grown if wholly outside the scheme of regulation would have a substantial effect in defeating and obstructing its purpose to stimulate trade therein at increased prices.

It is said, however, that this Act, forcing some farmers into the market to buy what they could provide for themselves, is an unfair promotion of the markets and prices of specializing wheat growers. It is of the essence of regulation that it lays a restraining hand on the self-interest of the regulated and that advantages from the regulation commonly fall to others. The conflicts of economic interest between the regulated and those who advantage by it are wisely left under our system to resolution by the Congress under its more flexible and responsible legislative process. Such conflicts rarely lend themselves to judicial determination. And with the wisdom, workability, or fairness, of the plan of regulation we have nothing to do. . . .

Reversed.

STUDY GUIDE

- In the following excerpt, Professor Barry Cushman describes the judicial anguish surrounding the decision in *Wickard.* Do you see any potential implication for constitutional law of his concluding observation that "while the published opinion repudiated the first of Jackson's proposed alternative holdings, and refrained from a clear embrace of the second, it similarly avoided the frank recognition that he had called for in his memorandum"?
- Is *Wickard* a precedent for something more than what even the ardently pro–New Deal Justices were willing to say in print?

BARRY CUSHMAN, RETHINKING THE NEW DEAL COURT: THE STRUCTURE OF A CONSTITUTIONAL REVOLUTION, pp. 212-219, 1998.* The case was initially docketed for the 1941 term and was argued May 4, 1942. At the initial conference, every participating justice except Roberts agreed with Stone's view that "this is a regulation of commerce." Justice Roberts passed, however, saying he was "in doubt" over whether the commerce clause authorized such a far-reaching regulation. Yet eventually a majority of the court came to share Roberts's reservations with respect to the commerce power issues the case presented. The growth of wheat for home consumption was not itself interstate commerce, nor was it intended for interstate commerce. Only if the activity produced a substantial effect on interstate commerce, therefore, was it properly subject to federal regulation. In spring of 1942, the Court was not prepared to find such an effect. Justice Jackson produced two drafts of an opinion, in each of which the Court refused to reach the commerce clause issue. In each he remanded the case to the district court for additional factual findings that might better enable the Court to determine whether such an effect on commerce existed. . . .

The legislative history and the facts on the record did not demonstrate to Jackson's satisfaction that the growth of wheat for home consumption exerted a substantial effect on interstate commerce, and he and his colleagues were unprepared to assume without proof that it did. The legislative findings had merely declared the necessity of the Act's provisions for effective regulation of interstate commerce in wheat. This, Jackson wrote, was clearly an inadequate constitutional foundation. "A mere finding of convenience will not sustain federal invasion of the intrastate field. Undivided power is usually exercised more conveniently than divided power, but our federal system is not to be disposed of for the convenience of federal administrators."

The absence of factual findings bearing on the effect of Filburn's activity on interstate commerce, Jackson concluded, "have left us without adequate materials for confident judgment that an affirmative answer to the question of power would not 'effectively obliterate the distinction between what is national [and what is

---

local] and create a completely centralized government.'" The source of this quotation was, of course, Hughes's opinion in *Jones & Laughlin.*

Justices Roberts, Frankfurter, Murphy, and Byrnes each agreed to this draft. This opinion, however, never saw the light of day. At a subsequent conference the justices reached a tentative agreement that the case be set for reargument rather than remanded. . . . The order directed counsel "to discuss the question whether the Act in question in so far as it deals with wheat consumed on the farm of the producer is within the power of Congress to regulate interstate commerce."

The shift from a decision to remand to a decision to order reargument was substantial. . . . The decision to remand in Jackson's draft opinion had been based on the proposition that a factually detailed analysis of the effects on interstate commerce of production of wheat for home consumption was required in order to decide the case. Now no such analysis was requested or even mentioned. By the end of the term it was apparent that what the justices wanted was more time to think, not more facts to think about. The earlier decision to remand may have been in reality a device to buy the time the justices thought they needed. In any event, the decision to order reargument testifies to the uncertainty that a majority of the justices felt in the spring of 1942 concerning the scope of the commerce power. . . .

During the summer of '42 Jackson wrote two memoranda to his law clerk in which he attempted to think his way through the commerce clause issue. Jackson confessed at the outset that the question in *Filburn* "presents a good deal of a problem to me. It seems idle to disguise it, for it appears to be a regulation of production and of production not for commerce either actually or in contemplation." Such a regulation penetrated "the domain ordinarily reserved to the states to an extent not sustained by any prior precedent of this Court." Under these circumstances, wrote Jackson, there were three possible holdings. First, the Court might hold that "production and consumption not for commerce is exclusively within the control of the state." Such a holding would be consistent with the line of cases descending from [*E.C.*] *Knight*, which held that local activities of production were presumptively subject solely to state control. Second, the Court might hold that such production "is normally within the control of the state but is transferred to federal control upon judicial findings that it is necessary to protect exercises of the commerce power." This holding would have been consistent with the line of cases descending from *Swift* and *Shreveport*, which stood for the proposition that particular facts could transform what was otherwise a local activity into a national one subject to federal control. But Jackson's third alternative was without precedent: "That it is normally within the control of the state but that it is transferred to federal control upon a mere Congressional assumption of control." . . .

Jackson recognized that it was this case that had brought the Court to a jurisprudential Rubicon. "If we sustain the present Act, I don't see how we can ever sustain states' rights again as against a Congressional exercise of the commerce power." "If we sustain the present case, the judicial shibboleths as to limitation of the commerce power are without practical meaning, and that is within the commerce power which Congress desires to regulate."

That summer, Jackson was ready to cross that Rubicon at high noon. "It is perhaps time that we recognize that the introduction of economic determinism into constitutional law of interstate commerce marked the end of judicial control of the scope of federal activity," he wrote.

> A frank holding that the interstate commerce power has no limits except those which Congress sees fit to observe might serve a wholesome purpose. In order to be unconstitutional by the judicial process if this Act is sustained, the relation between interstate commerce and the regulated activity would have to be so absurd that it would be laughed out of Congress.
>
> . . .

Adopting the third alternative made the case simple rather than troubling. No additional factual information was necessary.

> Congress has seen fit to regulate small and casual wheat growers in the interest of large and specialized ones. It has seen fit to extend its regulation to the grower of wheat for home consumption. Whether this is necessary, whether it is just, whether it is wise, is not for us to say. We cannot say that there is no economic relationship between the growth of wheat for home consumption and interstate commerce in wheat. As to the weight to be given the effects, we have no legal standards by which to set our own judgment against the policy judgment of Congress.

Paraphrasing Hughes's oft-quoted remark about the judges and the Constitution, Jackson concluded that the growth of wheat for home consumption "is within the federal power to regulate interstate commerce, if for no better reason than the commerce clause is what the Congress says it is."

In Jackson's view, "[a] candid recognition that the extent of the commerce power depends upon the facts of each case and that Congress is the primary and final judge of the meaning of those facts can be objectionable only because of its candor, and not because of its result." Jackson's colleagues were apparently prepared for the result, but not for the candor. For while the published opinion repudiated the first of Jackson's proposed alternative holdings and refrained from a clear embrace of the second, it similarly avoided the frank recognition he had called for in his memoranda. Nevertheless, it appears that the justices in fact selected the third alternative. . . .

STUDY GUIDE

- *United States v. South-Eastern Underwriters* provides important background information to assess the constitutionality of the Patient Protection and Affordable Care Act of 2010. In *Jones & Laughlin*, *Darby*, and *Wickard*, the Court did not expand the meaning of "commerce," but used the Necessary and Proper Clause to allow Congress to regulate intrastate activity — whether it be commerce or not — if that activity in the aggregate has a substantial effect on interstate commerce. In *South-Eastern Underwriters*, does the Court actually reject the original meaning of "commerce" in favor of an updated meaning to accommodate changing times?

- Does its analysis of the meaning of "commerce" comport with the evidence considered in Chapter 2? How did the previous decisions of the Court comport with that evidence?
- How did the Court in *Paul v. Virginia* reach its contrary conclusion about the meaning of "commerce"? How does the Court distinguish these previous cases?
- Does the Court consider itself bound by *stare decisis* or "precedent"? How does the Court treat the previous line of cases?
- Notice the reference at the end to the power "to govern intercourse among the states." Does this have exactly the same meaning as the power "to regulate commerce among the several states"? Why substitute one set of words for the other?

United States v. South-Eastern Underwriters

322 U.S. 533 (1944)

MR. JUSTICE BLACK delivered the opinion of the Court.

For seventy-five years, this Court has held, whenever the question has been presented, that the Commerce Clause of the Constitution does not deprive the individual states of power to regulate and tax specific activities of foreign insurance companies which sell policies within their territories. Each state has been held to have this power, even though negotiation and execution of the companies' policy contracts involved communications of information and movements of persons, moneys, and papers across state lines. Not one of all these cases, however, has involved an Act of Congress which required the Court to decide the issue of whether the Commerce Clause grants to Congress the power to regulate insurance transactions stretching across state lines. Today, for the first time in the history of the Court, that issue is squarely presented, and must be decided.

Appellees — the South-Eastern Underwriters Association (SEUA), and its membership of nearly 200 private stock fire insurance companies, and 27 individuals — were indicted in the District Court for alleged violations of the Sherman Anti-Trust Act. . . . [D]o fire insurance transactions which stretch across state lines constitute "Commerce among the several States" so as to make them subject to regulation by Congress under the Commerce Clause? . . .

Ordinarily courts do not construe words used in the Constitution so as to give them a meaning more narrow than one which they had in the common parlance of the times in which the Constitution was written. To hold that the word "commerce," as used in the Commerce Clause, does not include a business such as insurance would do just that. Whatever other meanings "commerce" may have included in 1787, the dictionaries, encyclopedias, and other books of the period show that it included trade: business in which persons bought and sold, bargained and contracted.[21] And this meaning has persisted to modern times. Surely, therefore, a heavy burden is on him who asserts that the plenary power which the Commerce Clause grants to Congress to regulate "Commerce among the several States" does not include the power to regulate trading in insurance to the same extent that it includes power to regulate other trades or businesses conducted across state lines.[22]

The modern insurance business holds a commanding position in the trade and commerce of our Nation. Built upon the sale of contracts of indemnity, it has become one of the largest and most important branches of commerce. . . . Perhaps no modern commercial enterprise directly affects so many persons in all walks of life as does the insurance business. Insurance touches the home, the family, and the occupation or the business of almost every person in the United States.

This business is not separated into 48 distinct territorial compartments which function in isolation from each other. Interrelationship, interdependence, and integration of activities in all the states in which they operate are practical aspects of the insurance companies' methods of doing business. A large share of the insurance business is concentrated in a comparatively few companies located, for the most part, in the financial centers of the East. Premiums collected from policyholders in every part of the United States flow into these companies for investment. As policies become payable, checks and drafts flow back to the many states where the policyholders reside. The result is a continuous and indivisible stream of intercourse among the states composed of collections of premiums, payments of policy obligations, and the countless documents and communications which are essential to the negotiation and execution of policy contracts. Individual policyholders living in many different states who own policies in a single company have their separate interests blended in one assembled fund of assets upon which all are equally dependent for payment of their policies. The decisions which that company makes at its home office — the risks it insures, the premiums it charges, the investments it makes, the losses it pays — concern not just the people of the state where the home office happens to be located. They concern people living far beyond the boundaries of that state. . . .

Despite all of this, despite the fact that most persons, speaking from common knowledge, would instantly say that, of course, such a business is engaged in trade and commerce, the District Court felt compelled by decisions of this Court to conclude that the insurance business can never be trade or commerce within the meaning of the Commerce Clause. We must therefore consider these decisions.

---

[21] See Gibbons v. Ogden, 9 Wheat. 1; also, Hamilton and Adair, The Power to Govern (1937), pp. 53-63.

[22] Alexander Hamilton, in 1791, stating his opinion on the constitutionality of the Bank of the United States, declared that it would "admit of little if any question" that the federal power to regulate foreign commerce included "the regulation of policies of insurance." Speaking of the need of a federal power to regulate "commerce," Hamilton had earlier said,

> It is, indeed, evident on the most superficial view that there is no object, either as it respects the interests of trade or finance, that more strongly demands a federal superintendence.

Federalist No. XXII.

In 1869, this Court held, in sustaining a statute of Virginia which regulated foreign insurance companies, that the statute did not offend the Commerce Clause because "issuing a policy of insurance is not a transaction of commerce." [*Paul v. Virginia* (1868).][23] Since then, in similar cases, this statement has been repeated, and has been broadened. In *Hooper v. California*, decided in 1895, the *Paul* statement was reaffirmed, and the Court added that, "The business of insurance is not commerce." In 1913, the New York Life Insurance Company, protesting against a Montana tax, challenged these broad statements, strongly urging that its business, at least, was so conducted as to be engaged in interstate commerce. But the Court again approved the *Paul* statement and held against the company, saying that "contracts of insurance are not commerce at all, neither state nor interstate." *New York Life Ins. Co. v. Deer Lodge County* (1913).

In all cases in which the Court has relied upon the proposition that "the business of insurance is not commerce," its attention was focused on the validity of state statutes the extent to which the Commerce Clause automatically deprived states of the power to regulate the insurance business. Since Congress had at no time attempted to control the insurance business, invalidation of the state statutes would practically have been equivalent to granting insurance companies engaged in interstate activities a blanket license to operate without legal restraint. As early as 1866, the insurance trade, though still in its infancy, was subject to widespread abuses. To meet the imperative need for correction of these abuses, the various state legislatures, including that of Virginia, passed regulatory legislation. *Paul v. Virginia* upheld one of Virginia's statutes. To uphold insurance laws of other states, including tax laws, *Paul v. Virginia*'s generalization and reasoning have been consistently adhered to.

Today, however, we are asked to apply this reasoning not to uphold another state law, but to strike down an Act of Congress which was intended to regulate certain aspects of the methods by which interstate insurance companies do business, and, in so doing, to narrow the scope of the federal power to regulate the activities of a great business carried on back and forth across state lines. But past decisions of this Court emphasize that legal formulae devised to uphold state power cannot uncritically be accepted as trustworthy guides to determine Congressional power under the Commerce Clause.[24] Furthermore, the reasons given in support of the generalization that "the business of insurance is not commerce" and can never

[23] "The defect of the argument lies in the character of their business. Issuing a policy of insurance is not a transaction of commerce. The policies are simple contracts of indemnity against loss by fire, entered into between the corporations and the assured, for a consideration paid by the latter. These contracts are not articles of commerce in any proper meaning of the word. They are not subjects of trade and barter offered in the market as something having an existence and value independent of the parties to them. They are not commodities to be shipped or forwarded from one State to another, and then put up for sale. They are like other personal contracts between parties which are completed by their signature and the transfer of the consideration. Such contracts are not interstate transactions, though the parties may be domiciled in different States. The policies do not take effect — are not executed contracts — until delivered by the agent in Virginia. They are, then, local transactions, and are governed by the local law." [*Paul v. Virginia*.]

[24] See, e.g., *Wickard v. Filburn*. . . .

be conducted so as to constitute "Commerce among the States" are inconsistent with many decisions of this Court which have upheld federal statutes regulating interstate commerce under the Commerce Clause.

One reason advanced for the rule in the *Paul* case has been that insurance policies "are not commodities to be shipped or forwarded from one State to another." But both before and since *Paul v. Virginia*, this Court has held that Congress can regulate traffic though it consist of intangibles.[25] Another reason much stressed has been that insurance policies are mere personal contracts subject to the laws of the state where executed. But this reason rests upon a distinction between what has been called "local" and what "interstate," a type of mechanical criterion which this Court has not deemed controlling in the measurement of federal power. Cf. *Wickard v. Filburn* (1942)....

We may grant that a contract of insurance, considered as a thing apart from negotiation and execution, does not itself constitute interstate commerce. But it does not follow from this that the Court is powerless to examine the entire transaction, of which that contract is but a part, in order to determine whether there may be a chain of events which becomes interstate commerce. Only by treating the Congressional power over commerce among the states as a "technical legal conception," rather than as a "practical one, drawn from the course of business" could such a conclusion be reached. *Swift & Co. v. United States* (1905). In short, a nationwide business is not deprived of its interstate character merely because it is built upon sales contracts which are local in nature. Were the rule otherwise, few businesses could be said to be engaged in interstate commerce....

The real answer to the question before us is to be found in the Commerce Clause itself, and in some of the great cases which interpret it. Many decisions make vivid the broad and true meaning of that clause. It is interstate commerce subject to regulation by Congress to carry lottery tickets from state to state. So also is it interstate commerce to transport a woman from Louisiana to Texas in a common carrier; to carry across a state line in a private automobile five quarts of whiskey intended for personal consumption; to drive a stolen automobile from Iowa to South Dakota. Diseased cattle ranging between Georgia and Florida are in commerce, and the transmission of an electrical impulse over a telegraph line between Alabama and Florida is intercourse, and subject to paramount federal regulation. Not only, then, may transactions be commerce though noncommercial; they may be commerce though illegal and sporadic, and though they do not utilize common carriers or concern the flow of anything more tangible than electrons and information. These activities having already been held to constitute interstate commerce, and persons engaged in them therefore having been held subject to federal regulation, it would indeed be difficult now to hold that no activities of any insurance company can ever constitute interstate commerce so as to make it subject to such regulation; — activities which, as part of the conduct of a legitimate and useful commercial enterprise, may embrace integrated operations in many states

---

[25] See, for illustration, . . . *Lottery Case*. . . .

and involve the transmission of great quantities of money, documents, and communications across dozens of state lines.

The precise boundary between national and state power over commerce has never yet been, and doubtless never can be, delineated by a single abstract definition. The most widely accepted general description of that part of commerce which is subject to the federal power is that given in 1824 by Chief Justice Marshall: "Commerce, undoubtedly, is traffic, but it is something more: it is intercourse. It describes the commercial intercourse between nations, and parts of nations, in all its branches. . . ." *Gibbons v. Ogden* (1824). Commerce is interstate, he said, when it "concerns more States than one." No decision of this Court has ever questioned this as too comprehensive a description of the subject matter of the Commerce Clause. To accept a description less comprehensive, the Court has recognized, would deprive the Congress of that full power necessary to enable it to discharge its Constitutional duty to govern commerce among the states.[26]

The power confined to Congress by the Commerce Clause is declared in *The Federalist* to be for the purpose of securing the "maintenance of harmony and proper intercourse among the States." But its purpose is not confined to empowering Congress with the negative authority to legislate against state regulations of commerce deemed inimical to the national interest. The power granted Congress is a positive power. It is the power to legislate concerning transactions which, reaching across State boundaries, affect the people of more states than one; — to govern affairs which the individual states, with their limited territorial jurisdictions, are not fully capable of governing. This federal power to determine the rules of intercourse across state lines was essential to weld a loose confederacy into a single, indivisible Nation; its continued existence is equally essential to the welfare of that Nation.

Our basic responsibility in interpreting the Commerce Clause is to make certain that the power to govern intercourse among the states remains where the Constitution placed it. That power, as held by this Court from the beginning, is vested in the Congress, available to be exercised for the national welfare as Congress shall deem necessary. No commercial enterprise of any kind which conducts its activities across state lines has been held to be wholly beyond the regulatory power of Congress under the Commerce Clause. We cannot make an exception of the business of insurance. . . . Having power to enact the Sherman Act, Congress did so; if exceptions are to be written into the Act, they must come from the Congress, not this Court. . . .

Reversed.

Mr. Justice Roberts and Mr. Justice Reed took no part in the consideration or decision of this case.

Mr. Chief Justice Stone, dissenting. . . .

---

[26] ". . . A government ought to contain, in itself, every power requisite to the full accomplishment of the objects committed to its care, and to the complete execution of the trusts for which it is responsible, free from every other control, but a regard to the public good and to the sense of the people." *Federalist No. 31.*

If an insurance company in New York executes and delivers, either in that state or another, a policy insuring the owner of a building in New Jersey against loss by fire, no act of interstate commerce has occurred. True, if the owner comes to New York to procure the insurance or, after delivery in New York, carries the policy to New Jersey, or the company sends it there by mail or messenger, such would be acts of interstate commerce. Similarly, if the owner pays the premiums by mail to the company in New York, or the company's New Jersey agent sends the premiums to New York, or the company in New York sends money to New Jersey on the occurrence of the loss insured against, acts of interstate commerce would occur. But the power of the Congress to regulate them is derived not from its authority to regulate the business of insurance, but from its power to regulate interstate communication and transportation. And such incidental use of the facilities of interstate commerce does not render the insurance business itself interstate commerce. Nor is the nature of a single insurance transaction or a few such transactions not involving interstate commerce altered in that regard merely because their number is multiplied. The power of Congress to regulate interstate communication and transportation incidental to the insurance business is not any more or any less because the number of insurance transactions is great or small.... The contract of insurance makes no stipulation for the sale or delivery of commodities in interstate commerce or for any other interstate transaction. It provides only for the payment of a sum of money in the event of the loss insured against....

The conclusion seems inescapable that the formation of insurance contracts, like many others, and the business of so doing, is not, without more, commerce within the protection of the commerce clause of the Constitution and thereby, in large measure, excluded from state control and regulation. This conclusion seems, upon analysis, not only correct on principle and in complete harmony with the uniform rulings by which this Court has held that the formation of all types of contract which do not stipulate for the performance of acts of interstate commerce, are likewise not interstate commerce, but it has the support of an unbroken line of decisions of this Court beginning with *Paul v. Virginia*, seventy-five years ago, and extending down to the present time.... [T]he immediate and only practical effect of the decision now rendered is to withdraw from the states, in large measure, the regulation of insurance, and to confer it on the national government, which has adopted no legislative policy and evolved no scheme of regulation with respect to the business of insurance....

The judgment should be *Affirmed*.

In response to this case, in 1945, Congress enacted the McCarran-Ferguson Act, 15 U.S.C. §§1011-1015, exempting the business of insurance from most federal regulation, including, to a limited extent, federal antitrust laws. It did so by providing that Acts of Congress that do not expressly purport to regulate the "business of insurance" will not preempt state laws or regulations that regulate the "business of insurance." As a result of this Act, until the Affordable Care Act of 2010, the business of insurance was largely regulated by state insurance commissions.

The Heart of Atlanta Motel was torn down in 1976 to be replaced by the Atlanta Hilton. The owner of the motel, Moreton Rolleston, Jr., argued the case on his own behalf before the Supreme Court. The United States was represented by Solicitor General Archibald Cox, on leave from the faculty of Harvard Law School. Cox later served as the first Watergate special prosecutor.

E. THE WARREN COURT

Although the New Deal Court could be considered the start of the modern era of constitutional law, the Warren Court made important changes to the doctrines discussed in the previous chapter.

ASSIGNMENT 5

1. The Commerce Clause

The Civil Rights Revolution of the 1950s and 1960s — sometimes referred to as the Second Reconstruction — ushered in monumental improvements for the rights and equality of African Americans in the United States. When this story is told, however, the importance of the role played by the courts is often exaggerated.[27] Although *Brown v. Board of Education* was decided in 1954, even ten years later schools and other public institutions remained segregated. Beyond the courts, the primary drivers in this revolution were the elected branches. For example, the enactment of the Civil Rights Act of 1964, and its ensuing enforcement by the executive branch, was of inestimable importance in addressing segregation. The Act was the direct product of the powerful political forces unleashed by African Americans in what came to be called the Civil Rights Movement, under the inspirational, courageous, and charismatic leadership of Martin Luther King Jr. In many respects, the Civil Rights Act of 1964 closely resembled the largely forgotten Civil Rights Act of 1875. However, the Supreme Court invalidated this foundational law in the *Civil Rights Cases* (1883), finding that Congress lacked the authority under Section 5 of the Fourteenth Amendment to prohibit racial discrimination in private business transactions. In part because of this precedent, Congress chose to enact the Civil Rights Act of 1964 on the basis of its newly expanded powers under the Commerce Clause, rather than under Section 5 of the Fourteenth Amendment.

STUDY GUIDE

- In *Heart of Atlanta Motel v. United States*, does the Court expand the meaning of "commerce" to uphold Title II of the Civil Rights Act of 1964?
- If the *Civil Rights Cases* (1883) were wrongly decided, would there be any advantage to implementing the protections of the Civil Rights Act of 1964 under Section 5 of the Fourteenth Amendment rather than using the Commerce Clause? If the *Civil Rights Cases* were correctly decided, does this ruling justify an expansive nonoriginalist interpretation of the Commerce Clause to compensate?
- Does the Court expand the scope of the Commerce Clause here by defining what "affects commerce" more broadly than before the New Deal, or can this case be understood as regulating what the Court later comes to call the channels and instrumentalities of commerce?

Heart of Atlanta Motel v. United States

379 U.S. 241 (1964)

MR. JUSTICE CLARK delivered the opinion of the Court.

This is a declaratory judgment action, attacking the constitutionality of Title II of the Civil Rights Act of 1964. . . .

[27] This argument was most prominently advanced in Gerald N. Rosenberg, The Hollow Hope: Can Courts Bring About Social Change? (1991). A second edition of the book was published in 2008.

1. The Factual Background and Contentions of the Parties

The case comes here on admissions and stipulated facts. Appellant owns and operates the Heart of Atlanta Motel which has 216 rooms available to transient guests. The motel is located on Courtland Street, two blocks from downtown Peachtree Street. It is readily accessible to interstate highways 75 and 85 and state highways 23 and 41. Appellant solicits patronage from outside the State of Georgia through various national advertising media, including magazines of national circulation; it maintains over 50 billboards and highway signs within the State, soliciting patronage for the motel; it accepts convention trade from outside Georgia and approximately 75% of its registered guests are from out of State. Prior to passage of the Act the motel had followed a practice of refusing to rent rooms to Negroes, and it alleged that it intended to continue to do so. In an effort to perpetuate that policy this suit was filed.

The appellant contends that Congress in passing this Act exceeded its power to regulate commerce under Art. I, §8, cl. 3, of the Constitution of the United States; [and] that the Act violates the Fifth Amendment because appellant is deprived of the right to choose its customers and operate its business as it wishes, resulting in a taking of its liberty and property without due process of law. . . .

The appellees counter that the unavailability to Negroes of adequate accommodations interferes significantly with interstate travel, and that Congress, under the Commerce Clause, has power to remove such obstructions and restraints; [and] that the Fifth Amendment does not forbid reasonable regulation. . . . At the trial the appellant offered no evidence, submitting the case on the pleadings, admissions and stipulation of facts; however, appellees proved the refusal of the motel to accept Negro transients after the passage of the Act. . . .

2. The History of the Act

Congress first evidenced its interest in civil rights legislation in the Civil Rights or Enforcement Act of April 9, 1866. There followed four Acts, with a fifth, the Civil Rights Act of March 1, 1875, culminating the series. In 1883 this Court struck down the public accommodations sections of the 1875 Act in the Civil Rights Cases. No major legislation in this field had been enacted by Congress for 82 years when the Civil Rights Act of 1957 became law. It was followed by the Civil Rights Act of 1960. Three years later, on June 19, 1963, the late President Kennedy called for civil rights legislation in a message to Congress to which he attached a proposed bill. Its stated purpose was

> to promote the general welfare by eliminating discrimination based on race, color, religion, or national origin in . . . public accommodations through the exercise by Congress of the powers conferred upon it . . . to enforce the provisions of the fourteenth and fifteenth amendments, to regulate commerce among the several States, and to make laws necessary and proper to execute the powers conferred upon it by the Constitution.

. . .

Bills were introduced in each House of the Congress, embodying the President's suggestion. . . . However, it was not until July 2, 1964, upon the recommendation of President Johnson, that the Civil Rights Act of 1964, here under attack, was finally passed. . . .

3. Title II of the Act

This Title is divided into seven sections beginning with §201(a) which provides that:

> All persons shall be entitled to the full and equal enjoyment of the goods, services, facilities, privileges, advantages, and accommodations of any place of public accommodation, as defined in this section, without discrimination or segregation on the ground of race, color, religion, or national origin.

There are listed in §201(b) four classes of business establishments, each of which "serves the public" and "is a place of public accommodation" within the meaning of §201(a) "if its operations affect commerce, or if discrimination or segregation by it is supported by State action." The covered establishments are:

> (1) any inn, hotel, motel, or other establishment which provides lodging to transient guests, other than an establishment located within a building which contains not more than five rooms for rent or hire and which is actually occupied by the proprietor of such establishment as his residence;
>
> (2) any restaurant, cafeteria . . . [not here involved];
>
> (3) any motion picture house . . . [not here involved];
>
> (4) any establishment . . . which is physically located within the premises of any establishment otherwise covered by this subsection, or . . . within the premises of which is physically located any such covered establishment . . . [not here involved].

Section 201(c) defines the phrase "affect commerce" as applied to the above establishments. It first declares that "any inn, hotel, motel, or other establishment which provides lodging to transient guests" affects commerce *per se*. Restaurants, cafeterias, etc., in class two affect commerce only if they serve or offer to serve interstate travelers or if a substantial portion of the food which they serve or products which they sell have "moved in commerce." Motion picture houses and other places listed in class three affect commerce if they customarily present films, performances, etc., "which move in commerce." And the establishments listed in class four affect commerce if they are within, or include within their own premises, an establishment "the operations of which affect commerce." Private clubs are excepted under certain conditions. See §201(e).

Section §201(d) declares that "discrimination or segregation" is supported by state action when carried on under color of any law, statute, ordinance, regulation or any custom or usage required or enforced by officials of the State or any of its subdivisions.

In addition, §202 affirmatively declares that all persons "shall be entitled to be free, at any establishment or place, from discrimination or segregation of any kind on the ground of race, color, religion, or national origin, if such discrimination or segregation is or purports to be required by any law, statute, ordinance, regulation, rule, or order of a State or any agency or political subdivision thereof."

Finally, §203 prohibits the withholding or denial, etc., of any right or privilege secured by §201 and §202 or the intimidation, threatening or coercion of any person with the purpose of interfering with any such right or the punishing, etc., of any person for exercising or attempting to exercise any such right. . . .

4. Application of Title II to Heart of Atlanta Motel

It is admitted that the operation of the motel brings it within the provisions of §201(a) of the Act and that appellant refused to provide lodging for transient Negroes because of their race or color and that it intends to continue that policy unless restrained.

The sole question posed is, therefore, the constitutionality of the Civil Rights Act of 1964 as applied to these facts. The legislative history of the Act indicates that Congress based the Act on §5 and the Equal Protection Clause of the Fourteenth Amendment as well as its power to regulate interstate commerce under Art. I, §8, cl. 3, of the Constitution.

The Senate Commerce Committee made it quite clear that the fundamental object of Title II was to vindicate "the deprivation of personal dignity that surely accompanies denials of equal access to public establishments." At the same time, however, it noted that such an objective has been and could be readily achieved "by congressional action based on the commerce power of the Constitution." Our study of the legislative record, made in the light of prior cases, has brought us to the conclusion that Congress possessed ample power in this regard, and we have therefore not considered the other grounds relied upon. This is not to say that the remaining authority upon which it acted was not adequate, a question upon which we do not pass, but merely that since the commerce power is sufficient for our decision here we have considered it alone. . . .

5. The *Civil Rights Cases* (1883), and Their Application

In light of our ground for decision, it might be well at the outset to discuss the *Civil Rights Cases*, which declared provisions of the Civil Rights Act of 1875 unconstitutional. We think that decision inapposite, and without precedential value in determining the constitutionality of the present Act. Unlike Title II of the present legislation, the 1875 Act broadly proscribed discrimination in "inns, public conveyances on land or water, theaters, and other places of public amusement," without limiting the categories of affected businesses to those impinging upon interstate commerce. In contrast, the applicability of Title II is carefully limited to enterprises having a direct and substantial relation to the interstate flow of goods and people, except where state action is involved. Further, the fact that certain kinds of businesses may not in 1875 have been sufficiently involved in interstate commerce to warrant bringing them within the ambit of the commerce power is not necessarily dispositive of the same question today. Our populace had not reached its present mobility, nor were facilities, goods and services circulating as readily in interstate commerce as they are today. Although the principles which we apply today are those first formulated by Chief Justice Marshall in *Gibbons v. Ogden* (1824), the conditions of transportation and commerce have changed dramatically, and we must apply those principles to the present state of commerce. The sheer increase in volume of interstate traffic alone would give discriminatory practices which inhibit travel a far larger impact upon the Nation's commerce than such practices had on the economy of another day. Finally, there is language in the *Civil*

Rights Cases which indicates that the Court did not fully consider whether the 1875 Act could be sustained as an exercise of the commerce power. Though the Court observed that "no one will contend that the power to pass it was contained in the Constitution before the adoption of the last three amendments [Thirteenth, Fourteenth, and Fifteenth]," the Court went on specifically to note that the Act was not "conceived" in terms of the commerce power and expressly pointed out:

> Of course, these remarks [as to lack of congressional power] do not apply to those cases in which Congress is clothed with direct and plenary powers of legislation over the whole subject, accompanied with an express or implied denial of such power to the States, as in the regulation of commerce with foreign nations, among the several States, and with the Indian tribes. . . . In these cases Congress has power to pass laws for regulating the subjects specified in every detail, and the conduct and transactions of individuals in respect thereof.

. . . [S]uch a limitation renders the opinion devoid of authority for the proposition that the Commerce Clause gives no power to Congress to regulate discriminatory practices now found substantially to affect interstate commerce. We, therefore, conclude that the *Civil Rights Cases* have no relevance to the basis of decision here where the Act explicitly relies upon the commerce power, and where the record is filled with testimony of obstructions and restraints resulting from the discriminations found to be existing. We now pass to that phase of the case.

6. The Basis of Congressional Action

While the Act as adopted carried no congressional findings the record of its passage through each house is replete with evidence of the burdens that discrimination by race or color places upon interstate commerce. This testimony included the fact that our people have become increasingly mobile with millions of people of all races traveling from State to State; that Negroes in particular have been the subject of discrimination in transient accommodations, having to travel great distances to secure the same; that often they have been unable to obtain accommodations and have had to call upon friends to put them up overnight; and that these conditions had become so acute as to require the listing of available lodging for Negroes in a special guidebook which was itself "dramatic testimony to the difficulties" Negroes encounter in travel. These exclusionary practices were found to be nationwide, the Under Secretary of Commerce testifying that there is "no question that this discrimination in the North still exists to a large degree" and in the West and Midwest as well. This testimony indicated a qualitative as well as quantitative effect on interstate travel by Negroes. The former was the obvious impairment of the Negro traveler's pleasure and convenience that resulted when he continually was uncertain of finding lodging. As for the latter, there was evidence that this uncertainty stemming from racial discrimination had the effect of discouraging travel on the part of a substantial portion of the Negro community. This was the conclusion not only of the Under Secretary of Commerce but also of the Administrator of the Federal Aviation Agency who wrote the Chairman of the Senate Commerce Committee that it was his "belief that air commerce is adversely affected by the denial to a substantial segment of the traveling public of adequate and desegregated public accommodations." We shall not burden this opinion with further details since the voluminous testimony presents overwhelming evidence that discrimination by hotels and motels impedes interstate travel.

7. The Power of Congress over Interstate Travel

The power of Congress to deal with these obstructions depends on the meaning of the Commerce Clause. Its meaning was first enunciated 140 years ago by the great Chief Justice John Marshall in *Gibbons v. Ogden* (1824). . . . In short, the determinative test of the exercise of power by the Congress under the Commerce Clause is simply whether the activity sought to be regulated is "commerce which concerns more States than one" and has a real and substantial relation to the national interest. Let us now turn to this facet of the problem.

That the "intercourse" of which the Chief Justice spoke included the movement of persons through more States than one was settled as early as 1849, in the *Passenger Cases*, where Mr. Justice McLean stated: "That the transportation of passengers is a part of commerce is not now an open question." Again in 1913 Mr. Justice McKenna, speaking for the Court, said: "Commerce among the States, we have said, consists of intercourse and traffic between their citizens, and includes the transportation of persons and property." *Hoke v. United States* (1913). And only four years later in 1917 in *Caminetti v. United States*, Mr. Justice Day held for the Court:

> The transportation of passengers in interstate commerce, it has long been settled, is within the regulatory power of Congress, under the commerce clause of the Constitution, and the authority of Congress to keep the channels of interstate commerce free from immoral and injurious uses has been frequently sustained, and is no longer open to question.

Nor does it make any difference whether the transportation is commercial in character. . . .

The same interest in protecting interstate commerce which led Congress to deal with segregation in interstate carriers and the white-slave traffic has prompted it to extend the exercise of its power to gambling, *Lottery Case* (1903); to criminal enterprises; to deceptive practices in the sale of products; to fraudulent security transactions; to misbranding of drugs; to wages and hours, *United States, v. Darby* (1941); to members of labor unions, *National Labor Relations Board v. Jones & Laughlin Steel Corp.* (1937); to crop control, *Wickard v. Filburn* (1942); to discrimination against shippers; to the protection of small business from injurious price cutting; to resale price maintenance; to professional football; and to racial discrimination by owners and managers of terminal restaurants.

That Congress was legislating against moral wrongs in many of these areas rendered its enactments no less valid. In framing Title II of this Act Congress was also dealing with what it considered a moral problem. But that fact does not detract from the overwhelming evidence of the disruptive effect that racial discrimination has had on commercial intercourse. It was this burden which empowered Congress to enact appropriate legislation, and, given this basis for the exercise of its power, Congress was not restricted by the fact that the particular obstruction to interstate commerce with which it was dealing was also deemed a moral and social wrong.

It is said that the operation of the motel here is of a purely local character. But, assuming this to be true, "[i]f it is interstate commerce that feels the pinch, it does not matter how local the operation which applies the squeeze." *United States v. Women's Sportswear Mfrs. Assn.* (1949). See *NLRB v. Jones & Laughlin Steel Corp., supra.* As Chief Justice Stone put it in *United States v. Darby* (1941), *supra*:

> The power of Congress over interstate commerce is not confined to the regulation of commerce among the states. It extends to those activities intrastate which so affect interstate commerce or the exercise of the power of Congress over it as to make regulation of them appropriate means to the attainment of a legitimate end, the exercise of the granted power of Congress to regulate interstate commerce. See McCulloch v. Maryland, 4 Wheat. 316, 421.

Thus the power of Congress to promote interstate commerce also includes the power to regulate the local incidents thereof, including local activities in both the States of origin and destination, which might have a substantial and harmful effect upon that commerce. One need only examine the evidence which we have discussed above to see that Congress may — as it has — prohibit racial discrimination by motels serving travelers, however "local" their operations may appear.

Nor does the Act deprive appellant of liberty or property under the Fifth Amendment. The commerce power invoked here by the Congress is a specific and plenary one authorized by the Constitution itself. The only questions are: (1) whether Congress had a rational basis for finding that racial discrimination by motels affected commerce, and (2) if it had such a basis, whether the means it selected to eliminate that evil are reasonable and appropriate. If they are, appellant has no "right" to select its guests as it sees fit, free from governmental regulation. . . .

We, therefore, conclude that the action of the Congress in the adoption of the Act as applied here to a motel which concededly serves interstate travelers is within the power granted it by the Commerce Clause of the Constitution, as interpreted by this Court for 140 years. It may be argued that Congress could have pursued other methods to eliminate the obstructions it found in interstate commerce caused by racial discrimination. But this is a matter of policy that rests entirely with the Congress not with the courts. How obstructions in commerce may be removed — what means are to be employed — is within the sound and exclusive discretion of the Congress. It is subject only to one caveat — that the means chosen by it must be reasonably adapted to the end permitted by the Constitution. We cannot say that its choice here was not so adapted. The Constitution requires no more.

Affirmed.

MR. JUSTICE DOUGLAS, concurring.[28]

Though I join the Court's opinions, I am somewhat reluctant here . . . to rest solely on the Commerce Clause. My reluctance is not due to any conviction that

---

[28] This opinion applies also to *Katzenbach v. McClung.*

Congress lacks power to regulate commerce in the interests of human rights. It is rather my belief that the right of people to be free of state action that discriminates against them because of race, like the "right of persons to move freely from State to State," *Edwards v. California* (1941), "occupies a more protected position in our constitutional system than does the movement of cattle, fruit, steel and coal across state lines." Moreover, . . . the result reached by the Court is for me much more obvious as a protective measure under the Fourteenth Amendment than under the Commerce Clause. For the former deals with the constitutional status of the individual not with the impact on commerce of local activities or vice versa.

Hence I would prefer to rest on the assertion of legislative power contained in §5 of the Fourteenth Amendment which states: "The Congress shall have power to enforce, by appropriate legislation, the provisions of this article" — a power which the Court concedes was exercised at least in part in this Act.

A decision based on the Fourteenth Amendment would have a more settling effect, making unnecessary litigation over whether a particular restaurant or inn is within the commerce definitions of the Act or whether a particular customer is an interstate traveler. Under my construction, the Act would apply to all customers in all the enumerated places of public accommodation. And that construction would put an end to all obstructionist strategies and finally close one door on a bitter chapter in American history. . . .

I think the Court is correct in concluding that the Act is not founded on the Commerce Clause to the exclusion of the Enforcement Clause of the Fourteenth Amendment.

In determining the reach of an exertion of legislative power, it is customary to read various granted powers together. As stated in *McCulloch v. Maryland* (1819):

> We admit, as all must admit, that the powers of the government are limited, and that its limits are not to be transcended. But we think the sound construction of the constitution must allow to the national legislature that discretion, with respect to the means by which the powers it confers are to be carried into execution, which will enable that body to perform the high duties assigned to it, in the manner most beneficial to the people. Let the end be legitimate, let it be within the scope of the constitution, and all means which are appropriate, which are plainly adapted to that end, which are not prohibited, but consist with the letter and spirit of the constitution, are constitutional.

The "means" used in the present Act are in my view "appropriate" and "plainly adapted" to the end of enforcing Fourteenth Amendment rights as well as protecting interstate commerce. . . .

Thus while I agree with the Court that Congress in fashioning the present Act used the Commerce Clause to regulate racial segregation, it also used (and properly so) some of its power under §5 of the Fourteenth Amendment.

I repeat what I said earlier, that our decision should be based on the Fourteenth Amendment, thereby putting an end to all obstructionist strategies and allowing every person — whatever his race, creed, or color — to patronize all places of public accommodation without discrimination whether he travels interstate or intrastate.

Mr. Justice Goldberg, concurring.[29]

I join in the opinions and judgments of the Court, since I agree "that the action of the Congress in the adoption of the Act as applied here . . . is within the power granted it by the Commerce Clause of the Constitution, as interpreted by this Court for 140 years." . . .

In my concurring opinion in *Bell v. Maryland* (1964), however, I expressed my conviction that §1 of the Fourteenth Amendment guarantees to all Americans the constitutional right "to be treated as equal members of the community with respect to public accommodations," and that "Congress [has] authority under §5 of the Fourteenth Amendment, or under the Commerce Clause, Art. I, §8, to implement the rights protected by §1 of the Fourteenth Amendment. In the give-and-take of the legislative process, Congress can fashion a law drawing the guidelines necessary and appropriate to facilitate practical administration and to distinguish between genuinely public and private accommodations." The challenged Act is just such a law and, in my view, Congress clearly had authority under both §5 of the Fourteenth Amendment and the Commerce Clause to enact the Civil Rights Act of 1964.

STUDY GUIDE

- Is *Katzenbach v. McClung* best understood as being about interstate commerce or about fundamental rights of citizenship?
- Was Congress truly addressing "a national commercial problem of the first magnitude"? Is there a price to be paid for using this type of rationale? What if there is simply no other viable option?

Katzenbach v. McClung

379 U.S. 294 (1964)

Mr. Justice Clark delivered the opinion of the Court.

This case was argued with *Heart of Atlanta Motel v. United States*, decided this date, in which we upheld the constitutional validity of Title II of the Civil Rights Act of 1964 against an attack by hotels, motels, and like establishments. This complaint for injunctive relief against appellants attacks the constitutionality of the Act as applied to a restaurant. . . .

---

[29] This opinion applies also to *Katzenbach v. McClung*.

Ollie's Barbecue closed in 2001.

Professor Blackman purchased a matchbook from Ollie's Barbecue that was manufactured in Atlanta. Is this proof that the restaurant engaged in interstate commerce?

Ollie's Barbecue is a family-owned restaurant in Birmingham, Alabama, specializing in barbecued meats and homemade pies, with a seating capacity of 220 customers. It is located on a state highway 11 blocks from an interstate one and a somewhat greater distance from railroad and bus stations. The restaurant caters to a family and white-collar trade with a take-out service for Negroes. It employs 36 persons, two-thirds of whom are Negroes.

In the 12 months preceding the passage of the Act, the restaurant purchased locally approximately $150,000 worth of food, $69,683 or 46% of which was meat that it bought from a local supplier who had procured it from outside the State. The District Court expressly found that a substantial portion of the food served in the restaurant had moved in interstate commerce. The restaurant has refused to serve Negroes in its dining accommodations since its original opening in 1927, and since July 2, 1964, it has been operating in violation of the Act. The court below concluded that if it were required to serve Negroes it would lose a substantial amount of business.

On the merits, the District Court held that the Act could not be applied under the Fourteenth Amendment because it was conceded that the State of Alabama was not involved in the refusal of the restaurant to serve Negroes. It was also admitted that the Thirteenth Amendment was authority neither for validating nor for invalidating the Act. As to the Commerce Clause, the court found that it was "an express grant of power to Congress to regulate interstate commerce, which consists of the movement of persons, goods or information from one state to another"; and it found that the clause was also a grant of power "to regulate intrastate activities, but only to the extent that action on its part is necessary or appropriate to the effective execution of its expressly granted power to regulate interstate commerce." There must be, it said, a close and substantial relation between local activities and interstate commerce which requires control of the former in the protection of the latter. The court concluded, however, that the Congress, rather than finding facts sufficient to meet this rule, had legislated a conclusive presumption that a restaurant affects interstate commerce if it serves or offers to serve interstate travelers or if a substantial portion of the food which it serves has moved in commerce. This, the court held, it could not do because there was no demonstrable connection between food purchased in interstate commerce and sold in a restaurant and the conclusion of Congress that discrimination in the restaurant would affect that commerce.

The basic holding in *Heart of Atlanta Motel*, answers many of the contentions made by the appellees. There we outlined the overall purpose and operational plan of Title II and found it a valid exercise of the power to regulate interstate commerce insofar as it requires hotels and motels to serve transients without regard to their race or color. In this case we consider its application to restaurants which serve food a substantial portion of which has moved in commerce. . . .

As we noted in *Heart of Atlanta Motel* both Houses of Congress conducted prolonged hearings on the Act. And, as we said there, while no formal findings were made, which of course are not necessary, it is well that we make mention of the testimony at these hearings the better to understand the problem before Congress and determine whether the Act is a reasonable and appropriate means toward its solution. The record is replete with testimony of the burdens placed on interstate commerce by racial discrimination in restaurants. A comparison of per capita spending by Negroes in restaurants, theaters, and like establishments indicated less spending, after discounting income differences, in areas where discrimination is widely practiced. This condition, which was especially aggravated in the South, was attributed in the testimony of the Under Secretary of Commerce to racial segregation. This diminutive spending springing from a refusal to serve Negroes and their total loss as customers has, regardless of the absence of direct evidence, a close connection to interstate commerce. The fewer customers a restaurant enjoys the less food it sells and consequently the less it buys. In addition, the Attorney General testified that this type of discrimination imposed "an artificial restriction on the market" and interfered with the flow of merchandise. In addition, there were many references to discriminatory situations causing wide unrest and having a depressant effect on general business conditions in the respective communities.

Moreover there was an impressive array of testimony that discrimination in restaurants had a direct and highly restrictive effect upon interstate travel by Negroes. This resulted, it was said, because discriminatory practices prevent Negroes from buying prepared food served on the premises while on a trip, except in isolated and unkempt restaurants and under most unsatisfactory and often unpleasant conditions. This obviously discourages travel and obstructs interstate commerce for one can hardly travel without eating. Likewise, it was said, that discrimination deterred professional, as well as skilled, people from moving into areas where such practices occurred and thereby caused industry to be reluctant to establish there.

We believe that this testimony afforded ample basis for the conclusion that established restaurants in such areas sold less interstate goods because of the discrimination, that interstate travel was obstructed directly by it, that business in general suffered and that many new businesses refrained from establishing there as a result of it. Hence the District Court was in error in concluding that there was no connection between discrimination and the movement of interstate commerce. The court's conclusion that such a connection is outside "common experience" flies in the face of stubborn fact.

It goes without saying that, viewed in isolation, the volume of food purchased by Ollie's Barbecue from sources supplied from out of state was insignificant when compared with the total foodstuffs moving in commerce. But, as our late Brother Jackson said for the Court in *Wickard v. Filburn* (1942):

> That appellee's own contribution to the demand for wheat may be trivial by itself is not enough to remove him from the scope of federal regulation where, as here, his contribution, taken together with that of many others similarly situated, is far from trivial.

... Article I, §8, cl. 3, confers upon Congress the power "[t]o regulate Commerce ... among the several States" and Clause 18 of the same Article grants it the power "[t]o make all Laws which shall be necessary and proper for carrying into Execution the foregoing Powers. ..." This grant, as we have pointed out in *Heart of Atlanta Motel* "extends to those activities intrastate which so affect interstate commerce, or the exertion of the power of Congress over it, as to make regulation of them appropriate means to the attainment of a legitimate end, the effective execution of the granted power to regulate interstate commerce." *United States v. Wrightwood Dairy Co.* (1942). Much is said about a restaurant business being local but "even if appellee's activity be local and though it may not be regarded as commerce, it may still, whatever its nature, be reached by Congress if it exerts a substantial economic effect on interstate commerce. . . ." *Wickard v. Filburn*. The activities that are beyond the reach of Congress are "those which are completely within a particular State, which do not affect other States, and with which it is not necessary to interfere, for the purpose of executing some of the general powers of the government." *Gibbons v. Ogden* (1824). This rule is as good today as it was when Chief Justice Marshall laid it down almost a century and a half ago.

This Court has held time and again that this power extends to activities of retail establishments, including restaurants, which directly or indirectly burden or obstruct interstate commerce. We have detailed the cases in *Heart of Atlanta Motel*, and will not repeat them here. . . .

The appellees contend that Congress has arbitrarily created a conclusive presumption that all restaurants meeting the criteria set out in the Act "affect commerce." Stated another way, they object to the omission of a provision for a case-by-case determination — judicial or administrative — that racial discrimination in a particular restaurant affects commerce.

But Congress' action in framing this Act was not unprecedented. In *United States v. Darby* (1941), this Court held constitutional the Fair Labor Standards Act of 1938. There Congress determined that the payment of substandard wages to employees engaged in the production of goods for commerce, while not itself commerce, so inhibited it as to be subject to federal regulation. The appellees in that case argued, as do the appellees here, that the Act was invalid because it included no provision for an independent inquiry regarding the effect on commerce of substandard wages in a particular business. But the Court rejected the argument, observing that:

> [S]ometimes Congress itself has said that a particular activity affects the commerce, as it did in the present Act, the Safety Appliance Act and the Railway Labor Act. In passing on the validity of legislation of the class last mentioned the only function of courts is to determine whether the particular activity regulated or prohibited is within the reach of the federal power.

Here, as there, Congress has determined for itself that refusals of service to Negroes have imposed burdens both upon the interstate flow of food and upon the movement of products generally. Of course, the mere fact that Congress has said when particular activity shall be deemed to affect commerce does not preclude further examination by this Court. But where we find that the legislators, in light of the facts and testimony before them, have a rational basis for finding a chosen regulatory scheme necessary to the protection of commerce, our investigation is at an end. The only remaining question — one answered in the affirmative by the court below — is whether the particular restaurant either serves or offers to serve interstate travelers or serves food a substantial portion of which has moved in interstate commerce. . . .

Confronted as we are with the facts laid before Congress, we must conclude that it had a rational basis for finding that racial discrimination in restaurants had a direct and adverse effect on the free flow of interstate commerce. Insofar as the sections of the Act here relevant are concerned, §§201(b)(2) and (c), Congress prohibited discrimination only in those establishments having a close tie to interstate commerce, *i.e.*, those, like the McClungs', serving food that has come from out of the State. We think in so doing that Congress acted well within its power to protect and foster commerce in extending the coverage of Title II only to those restaurants offering to serve interstate travelers or serving food, a substantial portion of which has moved in interstate commerce.

The absence of direct evidence connecting discriminatory restaurant service with the flow of interstate food, a factor on which the appellees place much reliance, is not, given the evidence as to the effect of such practices on other aspects of commerce, a crucial matter.

The power of Congress in this field is broad and sweeping; where it keeps within its sphere and violates no express constitutional limitation it has been the rule of this Court, going back almost to the founding days of the Republic, not to interfere. The Civil Rights Act of 1964, as here applied, we find to be plainly appropriate in the resolution of what the Congress found to be a national commercial problem of the first magnitude. We find it in no violation of any express limitations of the Constitution and we therefore declare it valid.

The judgment is therefore *Reversed.*

2. The Due Process Clause

The bane of the progressives and the New Deal Court was the reliance on the Due Process Clause by the Supreme Court during the Progressive Era, which they felt was used to thwart the will of the majority as manifest in popularly enacted legislation. In cases such as *Lochner v. New York* (1905), the court struck down economic regulations because they interfered with liberty without adequate justification. (The court in that era also protected personal liberties using the same type of approach. But these cases have not been questioned in the way *Lochner* has been, and they remain good law today.) In the 1930s, the Court began restricting its use of the Due Process Clause by adopting a presumption in favor of the constitutionality of legislation. But in principle this presumption was rebuttable in two ways.

The first was articulated in the most famous footnote in all of constitutional law and one that provides the foundation of modern constitutional doctrine: Footnote Four in *United States v. Carolene Products*, which reads (with case citations omitted):

> There may be narrower scope for operation of the presumption of constitutionality when legislation appears on its face to be within a specific prohibition of the Constitution, such as those of the first ten Amendments, which are deemed equally specific when held to be embraced within the Fourteenth.
>
> It is unnecessary to consider now whether legislation which restricts those political processes which can ordinarily be expected to bring about repeal of undesirable legislation, is to be subjected to more exacting judicial scrutiny under the general prohibitions of the Fourteenth Amendment than are most other types of legislation.

> Nor need we enquire whether similar considerations enter into the review of statutes directed at particular religious, or national, or racial minorities, [or] whether prejudice against discrete and insular minorities may be a special condition, which tends seriously to curtail the operation of those political processes ordinarily to be relied upon to protect minorities, and which may call for a correspondingly more searching judicial inquiry.

This short passage provided the basis for a powerful theory of judicial review, most prominently articulated by John Hart Ely in his 1980 book *Democracy and Distrust*. In it, Ely elaborates a "representation reinforcing" theory that judges should usually defer to the democratic, representative legislature because such institutions ordinarily reflect majority will that normally should prevail. One can then interpret each paragraph of Footnote Four as identifying a different situation that raises an exception to the general principle:

1. when a majority of representatives violate the enumerated restrictions on its powers that a previous super-majority of the people themselves had included in the Constitution;
2. when a majority of representatives manipulates the electoral process by which they are selected; and
3. when a majority of representatives oppresses identifiable minorities who may lack adequate representation in the legislative process by which they may protect themselves.

Consequently, when any of these circumstances are shown to exist, there should be a "narrower scope for the operation of the presumption of constitutionality."

But in *Carolene Products*, the New Deal justices also recognized another way to rebut the presumption of constitutionality (emphasis added):

> We may assume for present purposes that no pronouncement of a legislature can forestall attack upon the constitutionality of the prohibition which it enacts by applying opprobrious epithets to the prohibited act, and that *a statute would deny due process which precluded the disproof in judicial proceedings of all facts which would show or tend to show that a statute depriving the suitor of life, liberty, or property had a rational basis*. . . .
>
> Where the existence of a rational basis for legislation whose constitutionality is attacked depends upon facts beyond the sphere of judicial notice, such facts may properly be made the subject of judicial inquiry, and the constitutionality of a statute predicated upon the existence of *a particular state of facts may be challenged by showing to the court* that those facts have ceased to exist. Similarly we recognize that the constitutionality of a statute, valid on its face, *may be assailed by proof of facts* tending to show that the statute as applied to a particular article is without support in reason because the article, although within the prohibited class, is so different from others of the class as to be without the reason for the prohibition, though the effect of such proof depends on the relevant circumstances of each case, as for example the administrative difficulty of excluding the article from the regulated class.

In other words, the factual presumption on behalf of the rationality of legislation could be rebutted by presenting evidence of conflicting facts, with the courts to decide whether the case against the legislation had been proved. Often these facts indicate that representatives were seeking to aid favored "special interest" groups, rather than the public in general.

In the next case, the Warren Court changed the rules, virtually eliminating this second road to "Scrutiny Land." The Due Process Clause is ordinarily studied in a course on constitutional rights. But we need to know this case because whether or not the form of "rational basis" scrutiny it adopts now applies in Commerce and Necessary and Proper Clause cases is currently a matter of some dispute.[30]

STUDY GUIDE

- Does Justice Douglas's method of interpretation more closely resemble that of Justice Harlan or of Justice Holmes in *Lochner*?
- Which approach is more "realist"? Which is more "formalist"?

Williamson v. Lee Optical of Oklahoma

348 U.S. 483 (1955)

MR. JUSTICE DOUGLAS delivered the opinion of the Court.

This suit was instituted in the District Court to have an Oklahoma law declared unconstitutional and to enjoin state officials from enforcing it for the reason that it allegedly violated various provisions of the Federal Constitution. . . . That court held certain provisions of the law unconstitutional. . . .

The Oklahoma law may exact a needless, wasteful requirement in many cases. But it is for the legislature, not the courts, to balance the advantages and disadvantages of the new requirement. It appears that in many cases the optician can easily supply the new frames or new lenses without reference to the old written prescription. It also appears that many written prescriptions contain no directive data in regard to fitting spectacles to the face. But in some cases the directions contained in the prescription are essential, if the glasses are to be fitted so as to correct the particular defects of vision or alleviate the eye condition. The legislature might have concluded that the frequency of occasions when a prescription is necessary was sufficient to justify this regulation of the fitting of eyeglasses. Likewise, when it is necessary to duplicate a lens, a written prescription may or may not be necessary. But the legislature might have concluded that one was needed often enough to require one in every case. Or the legislature may have concluded that eye examinations were so critical, not only for correction of vision but also for detection of latent

[30] For an elaboration of the rise and fall of these two types of judicial scrutiny, see Randy E. Barnett, Scrutiny Land, 106 Mich. L. Rev. 1479 (2008).

ailments or diseases, that every change in frames and every duplication of a lens should be accompanied by a prescription from a medical expert. To be sure, the present law does not require a new examination of the eyes every time the frames are changed or the lenses duplicated. For if the old prescription is on file with the optician, he can go ahead and make the new fitting or duplicate the lenses. But the law need not be in every respect logically consistent with its aims to be constitutional. It is enough that there is an evil at hand for correction, and that it might be thought that the particular legislative measure was a rational way to correct it.

The day is gone when this Court uses the Due Process Clause of the Fourteenth Amendment to strike down state laws, regulatory of business and industrial conditions, because they may be unwise, improvident, or out of harmony with a particular school of thought. See *Nebbia v. New York* (1934); *West Coast Hotel Co. v. Parrish* (1937). . . . We emphasize again what Chief Justice Waite said in *Munn v. Illinois* (1877), "For protection against abuses by legislatures the people must resort to the polls, not to the courts."

Secondly, the District Court held that it violated the Equal Protection Clause of the Fourteenth Amendment to subject opticians to this regulatory system and to exempt, as §3 of the Act does, all sellers of ready-to-wear glasses.

The problem of legislative classification is a perennial one, admitting of no doctrinaire definition. Evils in the same field may be of different dimensions and proportions, requiring different remedies. Or so the legislature may think. Or the reform may take one step at a time, addressing itself to the phase of the problem which seems most acute to the legislative mind. The legislature may select one phase of one field and apply a remedy there, neglecting the others. The prohibition of the Equal Protection Clause goes no further than the invidious discrimination. We cannot say that that point has been reached here. For all this record shows, the ready-to-wear branch of this business may not loom large in Oklahoma or may present problems of regulation distinct from the other branch.

Third, the District Court held unconstitutional, as violative of the Due Process Clause of the Fourteenth Amendment, that portion of §3 which makes it unlawful "to solicit the sale of . . . frames, mountings . . . or any other optical appliances." . . .

An eyeglass frame, considered in isolation, is only a piece of merchandise. But an eyeglass frame is not used in isolation . . . ; it is used with lenses; and lenses, pertaining as they do to the human eye, enter the field of health. Therefore, the legislature might conclude that to regulate one effectively it would have to regulate the other. Or it might conclude that both the sellers of frames and the sellers of lenses were in a business where advertising should be limited or even abolished in the public interest. The advertiser of frames may be using his ads to bring in customers who will buy lenses. If the advertisement of lenses is to be abolished or controlled, the advertising of frames must come under the same restraints; or so the legislature might think. We see no constitutional reason why a State may not treat all who deal with the human eye as members of a profession who should use no merchandising methods for obtaining customers.

Fourth, the District Court held unconstitutional, as violative of the Due Process Clause of the Fourteenth Amendment, the provision of §4 of the Oklahoma Act which reads as follows: "No person, firm, or corporation engaged in the business of retailing merchandise to the general public shall rent space, sublease departments, or otherwise permit any person purporting to do eye examination or visual care to occupy space in such retail store."

It seems to us that this regulation is on the same constitutional footing as the denial to corporations of the right to practice dentistry. It is an attempt to free the profession, to as great an extent as possible, from all taints of commercialism. It certainly might be easy for an optometrist with space in a retail store to be merely a front for the retail establishment. In any case, the opportunity for that nexus may be too great for safety, if the eye doctor is allowed inside the retail store. Moreover, it may be deemed important to effective regulation that the eye doctor be restricted to geographical locations that reduce the temptations of commercialism. Geographical location may be an important consideration in a legislative program which aims to raise the treatment of the human eye to a strictly professional level. We cannot say that the regulation has no rational relation to that objective and therefore is beyond constitutional bounds. . . .

F. THE REHNQUIST COURT

ASSIGNMENT 6

1. The Spending Power

Article I, Section 8, Clause 1 of the Constitution provides, "The Congress shall have power to lay and collect taxes, duties, imposts and excises, to pay the debts and provide for the common defense and general welfare of the United States; but all duties, imposts and excises shall be uniform throughout the United States." Though there is no explicit authority that allows Congress to spend money, this provision is often referred to as the *Spending Clause*. Because this power is not expressly enumerated, a constitutional question arose in the early days of our republic: does the power to tax in order "to pay the debts and provide for the common defense and general welfare of the United States" provide Congress with the power to spend *for any purpose* whatsoever? Or, does this power limit Congress to spending money *pursuant to the other enumerated powers* that follow in Article I, Section 8? *South Dakota v. Dole* illustrates the Court's current approach to an additional question: whether Congress can put strings, or conditions, on money it gives to the states in order to accomplish objectives that are not independently supported by an enumerated power. *Dole* is followed by President James Madison's 1817 veto statement, in which he describes what he believed to be the proper relationship between the enumerated powers scheme and Congress's power to tax and spend.

STUDY GUIDE

- According to *South Dakota v. Dole*, are there any limits to Congress's power to place conditions on spending?
- What test does the Court announce? Why does Justice O'Connor dissent?

South Dakota v. Dole

483 U.S. 203 (1987)

CHIEF JUSTICE REHNQUIST delivered the opinion of the Court.

Petitioner South Dakota permits persons 19 years of age or older to purchase beer containing up to 3.2% alcohol. In 1984 Congress enacted 23 U.S.C. §158 which directs the Secretary of Transportation to withhold a percentage of federal highway funds otherwise allocable from States "in which the purchase or public possession . . . of any alcoholic beverage by a person who is less than twenty-one years of age is lawful." The State sued in United States District Court seeking a declaratory judgment that §158 violates the constitutional limitations on congressional exercise of the spending power. . . . The District Court rejected the State's claims, and the Court of Appeals for the Eighth Circuit affirmed. . . .

The Constitution empowers Congress to "lay and collect Taxes, Duties, Imposts, and Excises, to pay the Debts and provide for the common Defence and general Welfare of the United States." Art. I, §8, cl. 1. Incident to this power, Congress may attach conditions on the receipt of federal funds, and has repeatedly employed the power "to further broad policy objectives by conditioning receipt of federal moneys upon compliance by the recipient with federal statutory and administrative directives." *Fullilove v. Klutznick* (1980) (opinion of Burger, C.J.). The breadth of this power was made clear in *United States v. Butler* (1936), where the Court, resolving a longstanding debate over the scope of the Spending Clause, determined that "the power of Congress to authorize expenditure of public moneys for public purposes is not limited by the direct grants of legislative power found in the Constitution." Thus, objectives not thought to be within Article I's "enumerated legislative fields," may nevertheless be attained through the use of the spending power and the conditional grant of federal funds.

The spending power is of course not unlimited, but is instead subject to several general restrictions articulated in our cases. The first of these limitations is derived from the language of the Constitution itself: the exercise of the spending power must be in pursuit of "the general welfare." In considering whether a particular expenditure is intended to serve general public purposes, courts should defer substantially to the judgment of Congress. Second, we have required that if Congress desires to condition the States' receipt of federal funds, it "must do so unambiguously . . . enabl[ing] the States to exercise their choice knowingly, cognizant of the consequences of their participation." *Pennhurst State School and Hospital v. Halderman* (1981). Third, our cases have suggested (without significant elaboration) that conditions on federal grants might be illegitimate if they are unrelated "to the federal interest in particular national projects or programs." *Massachusetts v. United States* (1978) (plurality opinion). Finally, we have noted that other constitutional provisions may provide an independent bar to the conditional grant of federal funds.

South Dakota does not seriously claim that §158 is inconsistent with any of the first three restrictions mentioned above. We can readily conclude that the provision is designed to serve the general welfare, especially in light of the fact that "the concept of welfare or the opposite is shaped by Congress. . . ." *Helvering v. Davis* (1937). Congress found that the differing drinking ages in the States created particular incentives for young persons to combine their desire to drink with their ability to drive, and that this interstate problem required a national solution. The means it chose to address this dangerous situation were reasonably calculated to advance the general welfare. The conditions upon which States receive the funds, moreover, could not be more clearly stated by Congress. And the State itself, rather than challenging the germaneness of the condition to federal purposes, admits that it "has never contended that the congressional action was . . . unrelated to a national concern in the absence of the Twenty-first Amendment." Brief for Petitioner. Indeed, the condition imposed by Congress is directly related to one of the main purposes for which highway funds are expended — safe interstate travel.

This goal of the interstate highway system had been frustrated by varying drinking ages among the States. A Presidential commission appointed to study alcohol-related accidents and fatalities on the Nation's highways concluded that the lack of uniformity in the States' drinking ages created "an incentive to drink and drive" because "young persons commut[e] to border States where the drinking age is lower." Presidential Commission on Drunk Driving, Final Report 11 (1983). By enacting §158, Congress conditioned the receipt of federal funds in a way reasonably calculated to address this particular impediment to a purpose for which the funds are expended. . . .

Our decisions have recognized that in some circumstances the financial inducement offered by Congress might be so coercive as to pass the point at which "pressure turns into compulsion." *Steward Machine Co. v. Davis* (1937). Here, however, Congress has directed only that a State desiring to establish a minimum drinking age lower than 21 lose a relatively small percentage of certain federal highway funds. Petitioner contends that the coercive nature of this program is evident from the degree of success it has achieved. We cannot conclude, however, that a conditional grant of federal money of this sort is unconstitutional simply by reason of its success in achieving the congressional objective.

When we consider, for a moment, that all South Dakota would lose if she adheres to her chosen course as to a suitable minimum drinking age is 5% of the funds otherwise obtainable under specified highway grant programs, the argument as to coercion is shown to be more rhetoric than fact. . . .

Here Congress has offered relatively mild encouragement to the States to enact higher minimum drinking ages than they would otherwise choose. But the enactment of such laws remains the prerogative of the States not merely in theory but in fact. Even if Congress might lack the power to impose a national minimum drinking age directly, we conclude that encouragement to state action found in §158 is a valid use of the spending power. Accordingly, the judgment of the Court of Appeals is

Affirmed.

JUSTICE O'CONNOR, dissenting. . . .

My disagreement with the Court is relatively narrow on the spending power issue: it is a disagreement about the application of a principle rather than a disagreement on the principle itself. I agree with the Court that Congress may attach conditions on the receipt of federal funds to further "the federal interest in particular national projects or programs." *Massachusetts v. United States* (1978). I also subscribe to the established proposition that the reach of the spending power "is not limited by the direct grants of legislative power found in the Constitution." *United States v. Butler* (1936). Finally, I agree that there are four separate types of limitations on the spending power: the expenditure must be for the general welfare, the conditions imposed must be unambiguous, they must be reasonably related to the purpose of the expenditure, and the legislation may not violate any independent constitutional prohibition. Insofar as two of those limitations are concerned, the Court is clearly correct that §158 is wholly unobjectionable. Establishment of a national minimum drinking age certainly fits within the broad concept of the general welfare and the statute is entirely unambiguous. . . .

But the Court's application of the requirement that the condition imposed be reasonably related to the purpose for which the funds are expended is cursory and unconvincing. We have repeatedly said that Congress may condition grants under the spending power only in ways reasonably related to the purpose of the federal program. In my view, establishment of a minimum drinking age of 21 is not sufficiently related to interstate highway construction to justify so conditioning funds appropriated for that purpose.

In support of its contrary conclusion . . . the Court asserts the reasonableness of the relationship between the supposed purpose of the expenditure — "safe interstate travel" — and the drinking age condition. The Court reasons that Congress wishes that the roads it builds may be used safely, that drunken drivers threaten highway safety, and that young people are more likely to drive while under the influence of alcohol under existing law than would be the case if there were a uniform national drinking age of 21. It hardly needs saying, however, that if the purpose of §158 is to deter drunken driving, it is far too over- and under-inclusive. It is over-inclusive because it stops teenagers from drinking even when they are not about to drive on interstate highways. It is under-inclusive because teenagers pose only a small part of the drunken driving problem in this Nation.

When Congress appropriates money to build a highway, it is entitled to insist that the highway be a safe one. But it is not entitled to insist as a condition of the use of highway funds that the State impose or change regulations in other areas of the State's social and economic life because of an attenuated or tangential relationship to highway use or safety. Indeed, if the rule were otherwise, the Congress could effectively regulate almost any area of a State's social, political, or economic life on the theory that use of the interstate transportation system is somehow enhanced. If, for example, the United States were to condition highway moneys upon moving the state capital, I suppose it might argue that interstate transportation is facilitated by locating local governments in places easily accessible to interstate highways — or, conversely, that highways might become overburdened if they had to carry traffic to and from the state capital. In my mind, such a relationship is hardly more attenuated than the one which the Court finds supports §158.

There is a clear place at which the Court can draw the line between permissible and impermissible conditions on federal grants. It is the line identified in the Brief for the National Conference of State Legislatures et al. as *Amici Curiae*:

> Congress has the power to *spend* for the general welfare, it has the power to *legislate* only for delegated purposes. . . .
>
> The appropriate inquiry, then, is whether the spending requirement or prohibition is a condition on a grant or whether it is regulation. The difference turns on whether the requirement specifies in some way how the money should be spent, so that Congress' intent in making the grant will be effectuated. Congress has no power under the Spending Clause to impose requirements on a grant that go beyond specifying how the money should be spent. A requirement that is not such a specification is not a condition, but a regulation, which is valid only if it falls within one of Congress' delegated regulatory powers.

This approach harks back to *United States v. Butler* (1936), the last case in which this Court struck down an Act of Congress as beyond the authority granted by the Spending Clause. There the Court wrote that "[t]here is an obvious difference between a statute stating the conditions upon which moneys shall be expended and one effective only upon assumption of a contractual obligation to submit to a regulation which otherwise could not be enforced." The *Butler* Court saw the Agricultural Adjustment Act for what it was — an exercise of regulatory, not spending, power. The error in *Butler* was not the Court's conclusion that the Act was essentially regulatory, but rather its crabbed view of the extent of Congress' regulatory power under the Commerce Clause. The Agricultural Adjustment Act was regulatory but it was regulation that today would likely be considered within Congress' commerce power. See, e.g., *Katzenbach v. McClung* (1964); *Wickard v. Filburn* (1942).

While *Butler*'s authority is questionable insofar as it assumes that Congress has no regulatory power over farm production, its discussion of the spending power and its description of both the power's breadth and its limitations remain sound. The Court's decision in *Butler* also properly recognizes the gravity of the task of appropriately limiting the spending power. If the spending power is to be limited only by Congress' notion of the general welfare, the reality, given the vast financial resources of the Federal Government, is that the Spending Clause gives "power to the Congress to tear down the barriers, to invade the states' jurisdiction, and to become a parliament of the whole people, subject to no restrictions save such as are self-imposed." *United States v. Butler*. This, of course, as *Butler* held, was not the Framers' plan and it is not the meaning of the Spending Clause.

Our later cases are consistent with the notion that, under the spending power, the Congress may only condition grants in ways that can fairly be said to be related to the expenditure of federal funds. For example, in *Oklahoma v. CSC* (1947), the

Court upheld application of the Hatch Act to a member of the Oklahoma State Highway Commission who was employed in connection with an activity financed in part by loans and grants from a federal agency. This condition is appropriately viewed as a condition relating to how federal moneys were to be expended. Other conditions that have been upheld by the Court may be viewed as independently justified under some regulatory power of the Congress. Thus, in *Fullilove v. Klutznick* (1980), the Court upheld a condition on federal grants that 10% of the money be "set aside" for contracts with minority business enterprises. But the Court found that the condition could be justified as a valid regulation under the commerce power and §5 of the Fourteenth Amendment.

This case, however, falls into neither class. As discussed above, a condition that a State will raise its drinking age to 21 cannot fairly be said to be reasonably related to the expenditure of funds for highway construction. The only possible connection, highway safety, has nothing to do with how the funds Congress has appropriated are expended. Rather than a condition determining how federal highway money shall be expended, it is a regulation determining who shall be able to drink liquor. As such it is not justified by the spending power. . . .

The immense size and power of the Government of the United States ought not obscure its fundamental character. It remains a Government of enumerated powers. *McCulloch v. Maryland* (1819). Because 23 U.S.C. 158 cannot be justified as an exercise of any power delegated to the Congress, it is not authorized by the Constitution. The Court errs in holding it to be the law of the land, and I respectfully dissent.

STUDY GUIDE

- Is there any difference between Madison's view of the spending power and that of the Court in *Dole*?
- When reading Madison's opinion, bear in mind that others — including his former *Federalist* coauthor Alexander Hamilton — understood the spending power to be much broader.

PRESIDENT JAMES MADISON, VETO OF FEDERAL PUBLIC WORKS BILL, March 3, 1817. To the House of Representatives of the United States: Having considered the bill this day presented to me entitled "An act to set apart and pledge certain funds for internal improvements," and which sets apart and pledges funds "for constructing roads and canals, and improving the navigation of water courses, in order to facilitate, promote, and give security to internal commerce among the several States, and to render more easy and less expensive the means and provisions for the common defense," I am constrained by the insuperable difficulty I feel in reconciling the bill with the Constitution of the United States to return it with that objection to the House of Representatives, in which it originated.

The legislative powers vested in Congress are specified and enumerated in the eighth section of the first article of the Constitution, and it does not appear that the power proposed to be exercised by the bill is among the enumerated powers, or that it falls by any just interpretation with the power to make laws necessary and proper for carrying into execution those or other powers vested by the Constitution in the Government of the United States.

"The power to regulate commerce among the several States" can not include a power to construct roads and canals, and to improve the navigation of water courses in order to facilitate, promote, and secure such commerce without a latitude of construction departing from the ordinary import of the terms, strengthened by the known inconveniences which doubtless led to the grant of this remedial power to Congress.

To refer the power in question to the clause "to provide for common defense and general welfare" would be contrary to the established and consistent rules of interpretation, as rendering the special and careful enumeration of powers which follow the clause nugatory and improper. Such a view of the Constitution would have the effect of giving to Congress a general power of legislation instead of the defined and limited one hitherto understood to belong to them, the terms "common defense and general welfare" embracing every object and act within the purview of a legislative trust. It would have the effect of subjecting both the Constitution and laws of the several States in all cases not specifically exempted to be superseded by laws of Congress, it being expressly declared "that the Constitution of the United States and laws made in pursuance thereof shall be the supreme law of the land, and the judges of every state shall be bound thereby, anything in the constitution or laws of any State to the contrary notwithstanding." Such a view of the Constitution, finally, would have the effect of excluding the judicial authority of the United States from its participation in guarding the boundary between the legislative powers of the General and the State Governments, inasmuch as questions relating to the general welfare, being questions of policy and expediency, are unsusceptible of judicial cognizance and decision.

A restriction of the power "to provide for the common defense and general welfare" to cases which are to be provided for by the expenditure of money would still leave within the legislative power of Congress all the great and most important measures of Government, money being the ordinary and necessary means of carrying them into execution.

If a general power to construct roads and canals, and to improve the navigation of water courses, with the train of powers incident thereto, be not possessed by Congress, the assent of the States in the mode provided in the bill can not confer the power. The only cases in which the consent and cession of particular States can extend the power of Congress are those specified and provided for in the Constitution.

I am not unaware of the great importance of roads and canals and the improved navigation of water courses, and that a power in the National Legislature to provide for them might be exercised with signal advantage to the general prosperity. But seeing that such a power is not expressly given by the Constitution, and believing that it can not be deduced from any part of it without an inadmissible latitude of construction and reliance on insufficient precedents; believing also that the permanent success of the Constitution depends on a definite partition of powers between the General and the State Governments, and that no adequate landmarks would be left by the constructive extension of the powers of Congress as proposed in the bill, I have no option but to withhold my signature from it, and to cherishing the hope that its beneficial objects may be attained by a resort for the necessary powers to the same wisdom and virtue in the nation which established the Constitution in its actual form and providently marked out in the instrument itself a safe and practicable mode of improving it as experience might suggest.

2. The Commerce Clause and Necessary and Proper Clause

ASSIGNMENT 7

As we saw earlier in this chapter, the first time the Court struck down a federal statute for exceeding the power to regulate commerce among the several states was in the 1869 case of *United States v. Dewitt*. There, Chief Justice Chase wrote:

> But this express grant of power to regulate commerce among the States has always been understood as limited by its terms; and as a virtual denial of any power to interfere with the internal trade and business of the separate States; except, indeed, as a necessary and proper means for carrying into execution some other power expressly granted or vested.

During the Progressive Era, the Court attempted to police the line between what was national and what was local by paying close attention to the definitions of "commerce" and "among the several states." However, the New Deal Court effectively withdrew from this endeavor.

Beginning in the 1970s, members of the Court, led by Justice William H. Rehnquist, began to reinvigorate the idea of federalism in a variety of doctrinal areas. Some of these developments led to decisions striking down federal laws or upholding state laws; others achieved less long-lasting success (at least to date). These cases included:

1. Defining judicially enforceable limits on the scope of congressional power pursuant to the Commerce Clause and Necessary and Proper Clause (*United States v. Lopez*, *United States v. Morrison*, and most recently in *NFIB v. Sebelius*);
2. Limiting congressional power under the spending clause, particularly as it relates to conditions on grants given to states (*South Dakota v. Dole* and *NFIB v. Sebelius*);
3. Limiting the ability of Congress to regulate state and local governments by applying laws of general applicability (*National League of Cities v. Usery*, a case later overturned by *Garcia v. San Antonio Metropolitan Transit Authority*, which was then qualified by *Gregory v. Ashcroft*);

4. Developing the "anti-commandeering" principle, which was used to invalidate laws that direct state legislative- and executive-branch officials to take certain actions (*New York v. United States* and *Printz v. United States*);
5. Expanding the idea of sovereign immunity, which has been explained by the Court as deriving from the underlying "principles" of the Eleventh Amendment rather than its text (*Seminole Tribe of Florida v. Florida* and *Alden v. Maine*);
6. Showing deference to state laws when applying the dormant Commerce Clause (Chief Justice Rehnquist's dissent in *Kassel v. Consolidated Freightways Corp.*, which will be discussed in Chapter 5);
7. Emphasizing the federalism aspects of standing (*Allen v. Wright*).

In *United States v. Lopez*, for the first time in sixty years, the Supreme Court struck down a law Congress had enacted because it exceeded the legislature's powers under the Commerce Clause.

STUDY GUIDE

- What approach to enumerated powers does the Court take in *Lopez*? Why does the Court think that the Gun-Free School Zones Act exceeded Congress's enumerated powers? How does Chief Justice Rehnquist reconcile this stance with the cases decided since the New Deal? What does the Court require Congress to demonstrate in order for its laws to pass constitutional scrutiny?
- Chief Justice Rehnquist observes that "even *Wickard* . . . involved economic activity. . . ." Did *Wickard* limit its approach to economic activity?
- How does Justice Kennedy's approach in his concurring opinion compare to that of the majority? Does the distinction between "external" and "internal" limitations on federal power help distinguish one approach from the other?
- Does Justice Thomas offer a different methodology than the majority?
- Under the dissenters' interpretation, are there any limits to Congress's powers?
- Assume for argument's sake that Justice Thomas is right about the original meaning of the Commerce Clause. Also assume that there has been a long period of time (and many precedents) during which the Court has reached a different conclusion as to how to interpret the Commerce Clause. If Justice Thomas (or any Justice) feels his interpretation is "more correct," what should that Justice do? Vote and write the way Thomas did in the case? Is there any argument to be made that a Justice should defer to those precedents, under the doctrine of *stare decisis*, even if the Justice feels they are "incorrect"? If so, what factors should the Justice take into account in deviating from his or her own convictions?

United States v. Lopez

514 U.S. 549 (1995)

CHIEF JUSTICE REHNQUIST delivered the opinion of the Court.

In the Gun-Free School Zones Act of 1990, Congress made it a federal offense "for any individual knowingly to possess a firearm at a place that the individual knows, or has reasonable cause to believe, is a school zone." The Act neither regulates a commercial activity nor contains a requirement that the possession be connected in any way to interstate commerce. We hold that the Act exceeds the authority of Congress "[t]o regulate Commerce . . . among the several States. . . ."

On March 10, 1992, respondent, who was then a 12th-grade student, arrived at Edison High School in San Antonio, Texas, carrying a concealed .38 caliber handgun and five bullets. Acting upon an anonymous tip, school authorities confronted respondent, who admitted that he was carrying the weapon. He was arrested and charged under Texas law with firearm possession on school premises. The next day, the state charges were dismissed after federal agents charged respondent by complaint with violating the Gun-Free School Zones Act of 1990.[31] . . . On appeal, respondent challenged his conviction based on his claim that §922(q) exceeded Congress' power to legislate under the Commerce Clause. . . .

We start with first principles. The Constitution creates a Federal Government of enumerated powers. See U.S. Const., Art. I, §8. As James Madison wrote, "[t]he powers delegated by the proposed Constitution to the federal government are few and defined. Those which are to remain in the State governments are numerous and indefinite." *Federalist No. 45*. This constitutionally mandated division of authority "was adopted by the Framers to ensure protection of our fundamental liberties." *Gregory v. Ashcroft* (1991). "Just as the separation and independence of the coordinate branches of the Federal Government serves to prevent the accumulation of excessive power in any one branch, a healthy balance of power between the States and the Federal Government will reduce the risk of tyranny and abuse from either front." . . .

For nearly a century [after *Gibbons v. Ogden* (1824),] the Court's Commerce Clause decisions dealt but rarely with the extent of Congress' power, and [instead] almost entirely with the Commerce Clause as a limit on state legislation that discriminated against interstate commerce. Under this line of precedent, the Court held that certain categories of activity such as "production," "manufacturing," and "mining" were within the province of state governments, and thus were beyond the power of Congress under the Commerce Clause.

In 1887, Congress enacted the Interstate Commerce Act, and in 1890, Congress enacted the Sherman Antitrust Act, 26 Stat. 209, as amended, 15 U.S.C. §1 *et seq.* These laws ushered in a new era of federal regulation under the commerce power. When cases involving these laws first reached this Court, we imported from our negative Commerce Clause cases the approach that Congress could not regulate

---

[31] The term "school zone" is defined as "in, or on the grounds of, a public, parochial or private school" or "within a distance of 1,000 feet from the grounds of a public, parochial or private school."

activities such as "production," "manufacturing," and "mining." See, e.g., *United States v. E.C. Knight Co.* (1895). Simultaneously, however, the Court held that, where the interstate and intrastate aspects of commerce were so mingled together that full regulation of interstate commerce required incidental regulation of intrastate commerce, the Commerce Clause authorized such regulation. . . .

Jones & Laughlin Steel, Darby, and *Wickard* ushered in an era of Commerce Clause jurisprudence that greatly expanded the previously defined authority of Congress under that Clause. In part, this was a recognition of the great changes that had occurred in the way business was carried on in this country. Enterprises that had once been local or at most regional in nature had become national in scope. But the doctrinal change also reflected a view that earlier Commerce Clause cases artificially had constrained the authority of Congress to regulate interstate commerce.

But even these modern-era precedents which have expanded congressional power under the Commerce Clause confirm that this power is subject to outer limits. . . . [W]e have identified three broad categories of activity that Congress may regulate under its commerce power. First, Congress may regulate the use of the channels of interstate commerce. See, e.g., *Darby, Heart of Atlanta Motel.* Second, Congress is empowered to regulate and protect the instrumentalities of interstate commerce, or persons or things in interstate commerce, even though the threat may come only from intrastate activities. Finally, Congress' commerce authority includes the power to regulate those activities having a substantial relation to interstate commerce, *Jones & Laughlin Steel,* those activities that substantially affect interstate commerce.

Within this final category, admittedly, our case law has not been clear whether an activity must "affect" or "substantially affect" interstate commerce in order to be within Congress' power to regulate it under the Commerce Clause. We conclude, consistent with the great weight of our case law, that the proper test requires an analysis of whether the regulated activity "substantially affects" interstate commerce.

We now turn to consider the power of Congress, in the light of this framework, to enact §922(q). The first two categories of authority may be quickly disposed of: §922(q) is not a regulation of the use of the channels of interstate commerce, nor is it an attempt to prohibit the interstate transportation of a commodity through the channels of commerce; nor can §922(q) be justified as a regulation by which Congress has sought to protect an instrumentality of interstate commerce or a thing in interstate commerce. Thus, if §922(q) is to be sustained, it must be under the third category as a regulation of an activity that substantially affects interstate commerce.

First, we have upheld a wide variety of congressional Acts regulating intrastate economic activity where we have concluded that the activity substantially affected interstate commerce. Examples include the regulation of intrastate coal mining, intrastate extortionate credit transactions, restaurants utilizing substantial interstate supplies, *McClung,* inns and hotels catering to interstate guests, *Heart of Atlanta Motel,* and production and consumption of home-grown wheat, *Wickard v. Filburn* (1942). These examples are by no means exhaustive, but the pattern is clear. Where economic activity substantially affects interstate commerce, legislation regulating that activity will be sustained.

Even *Wickard*, which is perhaps the most far reaching example of Commerce Clause authority over intrastate activity, involved economic activity in a way that the possession of a gun in a school zone does not. . . . Section 922(q) is a criminal statute that by its terms has nothing to do with "commerce" or any sort of economic enterprise, however broadly one might define those terms.[32] Section 922(q) is not an essential part of a larger regulation of economic activity, in which the regulatory scheme could be undercut unless the intrastate activity were regulated. It cannot, therefore, be sustained under our cases upholding regulations of activities that arise out of or are connected with a commercial transaction, which viewed in the aggregate, substantially affects interstate commerce.

Second, §922(q) contains no jurisdictional element which would ensure, through case-by-case inquiry, that the firearm possession in question affects interstate commerce. For example, in United States v. Bass (1971), the Court interpreted former 18 U.S.C. §1202(a), which made it a crime for a felon to "receiv[e], posses[s], or transpor[t] in commerce or affecting commerce . . . any firearm." . . . Unlike the statute in *Bass*, §922(q) has no express jurisdictional element which might limit its reach to a discrete set of firearm possessions that additionally have an explicit connection with or effect on interstate commerce.

Although as part of our independent evaluation of constitutionality under the Commerce Clause we of course consider legislative findings, and indeed even congressional committee findings, regarding effect on interstate commerce, the Government concedes that "[n]either the statute nor its legislative history contain[s] express congressional findings regarding the effects upon interstate commerce of gun possession in a school zone." We agree with the Government that Congress normally is not required to make formal findings as to the substantial burdens that an activity has on interstate commerce. But to the extent that congressional findings would enable us to evaluate the legislative judgment that the activity in question substantially affected interstate commerce, even though no such substantial effect was visible to the naked eye, they are lacking here. . . .

The Government's essential contention, *in fine*, is that we may determine here that §922(q) is valid because possession of a firearm in a local school zone does indeed substantially affect interstate commerce. The Government argues that possession of a firearm in a school zone may result in violent crime and that violent crime can be expected to affect the functioning of the national economy in two ways. First, the costs of violent crime are substantial, and, through the mechanism of insurance, those costs are spread throughout the population. Second, violent crime reduces the willingness of individuals to travel to areas within the country that are perceived to be unsafe. Cf. *Heart of Atlanta Motel*. The Government also

---

[32] Under our federal system, the "States possess primary authority for defining and enforcing the criminal law." When Congress criminalizes conduct already denounced as criminal by the States, it effects a "change in the sensitive relation between federal and state criminal jurisdiction." *United States v. Enmons* (1973).

argues that the presence of guns in schools poses a substantial threat to the educational process by threatening the learning environment. A handicapped educational process, in turn, will result in a less productive citizenry. That, in turn, would have an adverse effect on the Nation's economic well-being. As a result, the Government argues that Congress could rationally have concluded that §922(q) substantially affects interstate commerce.

We pause to consider the implications of the Government's arguments. The Government admits, under its "costs of crime" reasoning, that Congress could regulate not only all violent crime, but all activities that might lead to violent crime, regardless of how tenuously they relate to interstate commerce. Similarly, under the Government's "national productivity" reasoning, Congress could regulate any activity that it found was related to the economic productivity of individual citizens: family law (including marriage, divorce, and child custody), for example. Under the theories that the Government presents in support of §922(q), it is difficult to perceive any limitation on federal power, even in areas such as criminal law enforcement or education where States historically have been sovereign. Thus, if we were to accept the Government's arguments, we are hard-pressed to posit any activity by an individual that Congress is without power to regulate.

Although Justice Breyer argues that acceptance of the Government's rationales would not authorize a general federal police power, he is unable to identify any activity that the States may regulate but Congress may not. . . . Justice Breyer focuses, for the most part, on the threat that firearm possession in and near schools poses to the educational process and the potential economic consequences flowing from that threat. Specifically, the dissent reasons that (1) gun-related violence is a serious problem; (2) that problem, in turn, has an adverse effect on classroom learning; and (3) that adverse effect on classroom learning, in turn, represents a substantial threat to trade and commerce. This analysis would be equally applicable, if not more so, to subjects such as family law and direct regulation of education.

For instance, if Congress can, pursuant to its Commerce Clause power, regulate activities that adversely affect the learning environment, then, *a fortiori*, it also can regulate the educational process directly. Congress could determine that a school's curriculum has a "significant" effect on the extent of classroom learning. As a result, Congress could mandate a federal curriculum for local elementary and secondary schools because what is taught in local schools has a significant "effect on classroom learning," and that, in turn, has a substantial effect on interstate commerce.

Justice Breyer rejects our reading of precedent and argues that "Congress . . . could rationally conclude that schools fall on the commercial side of the line." Again, Justice Breyer's rationale lacks any real limits because, depending on the level of generality, any activity can be looked upon as commercial. Under the dissent's rationale, Congress could just as easily look at child rearing as "fall[ing] on the commercial side of the line" because it provides a "valuable service — namely, to equip [children] with the skills they need to survive in life and, more specifically, in the workplace." We do not doubt that Congress has authority under the Commerce Clause to regulate numerous commercial activities that substantially affect interstate commerce and also affect the educational process. That authority, though broad, does not include the authority to regulate each and every aspect of local schools.

Admittedly, a determination whether an intrastate activity is commercial or noncommercial may in some cases result in legal uncertainty. But, so long as Congress' authority is limited to those powers enumerated in the Constitution, and so long as those enumerated powers are interpreted as having judicially enforceable outer limits, congressional legislation under the Commerce Clause always will engender "legal uncertainty." As Chief Justice Marshall stated in *McCulloch v. Maryland* (1819): "Th[e] [federal] government is acknowledged by all to be one of enumerated powers. The principle, that it can exercise only the powers granted to it . . . is now universally admitted. But the question respecting the extent of the powers actually granted, is perpetually arising, and will probably continue to arise, as long as our system shall exist." See also *Gibbons v. Ogden* ("The enumeration presupposes something not enumerated"). The Constitution mandates this uncertainty by withholding from Congress a plenary police power that would authorize enactment of every type of legislation. See U.S. Const., Art. I, §8. Congress has operated within this framework of legal uncertainty ever since this Court determined that it was the judiciary's duty "to say what the law is." *Marbury v. Madison* (1803) (Marshall, C.J.). Any possible benefit from eliminating this "legal uncertainty" would be at the expense of the Constitution's system of enumerated powers. . . .

To uphold the Government's contentions here, we would have to pile inference upon inference in a manner that would bid fair to convert congressional authority under the Commerce Clause to a general police power of the sort retained by the States. Admittedly, some of our prior cases have taken long steps down that road, giving great deference to congressional action. The broad language in these opinions has suggested the possibility of additional expansion, but we decline here to proceed any further. To do so would require us to conclude that the Constitution's enumeration of powers does not presuppose something not enumerated, and that there never will be a distinction between what is truly national and what is truly local, cf. *Jones & Laughlin Steel.* This we are unwilling to do.

For the foregoing reasons the judgment of the Court of Appeals is

Affirmed.

Justice Kennedy, with whom Justice O'Connor joins, concurring.

The history of the judicial struggle to interpret the Commerce Clause during the transition from the economic system the Founders knew to the single, national market still emergent in our own era counsels great restraint before the Court determines that the Clause is insufficient to support an exercise of the national power. That history gives me some pause about today's decision, but I join the Court's opinion with these observations on what I conceive to be its necessary though limited holding. . . .

This case requires us to consider our place in the design of the Government and to appreciate the significance of federalism in the whole structure of the Constitution. Of the various structural elements in the Constitution, separation of powers, checks and balances, judicial review, and federalism, only concerning the last does there seem to be much uncertainty respecting the existence, and the content, of standards that allow the judiciary to play a significant role in maintaining the design contemplated by the Framers. . . . There is irony in this, because of the four structural elements in the Constitution just mentioned, federalism was the unique contribution of the Framers to political science and political theory. Though on the surface the idea may seem counterintuitive, it was the insight of the Framers that freedom was enhanced by the creation of two governments, not one. . . .

The theory that two governments accord more liberty than one requires for its realization two distinct and discernable lines of political accountability: one between the citizens and the Federal Government; the second between the citizens and the States. If, as Madison expected, the federal and state governments are to control each other, see *Federalist No. 51*, and hold each other in check by competing for the affections of the people, see *Federalist No. 46*, those citizens must have some means of knowing which of the two governments to hold accountable for the failure to perform a given function. . . . Were the Federal Government to take over the regulation of entire areas of traditional state concern, areas having nothing to do with the regulation of commercial activities, the boundaries between the spheres of federal and state authority would blur and political responsibility would become illusory. The resultant inability to hold either branch of the government answerable to the citizens is more dangerous even than devolving too much authority to the remote central power. . . .

For these reasons, it would be mistaken and mischievous for the political branches to forget that the sworn obligation to preserve and protect the Constitution in maintaining the federal balance is their own in the first and primary instance. . . . At the same time, the absence of structural mechanisms to require those officials to undertake this principled task, and the momentary political convenience often attendant upon their failure to do so, argue against a complete renunciation of the judicial role. Although it is the obligation of all officers of the Government to respect the constitutional design, the federal balance is too essential a part of our constitutional structure and plays too vital a role in securing freedom for us to admit inability to intervene when one or the other level of Government has tipped the scales too far. . . .

The substantial element of political judgment in Commerce Clause matters leaves our institutional capacity to intervene more in doubt than when we decide cases, for instance, under the Bill of Rights even though clear and bright lines are often absent in the latter class of disputes. But our cases do not teach that we have no role at all in determining the meaning of the Commerce Clause. . . .

The statute now before us forecloses the States from experimenting and exercising their own judgment in an area to which States lay claim by right of history and expertise, and it does so by regulating an activity beyond the realm of commerce in the ordinary and usual sense of that term. . . . This is not a case where the etiquette of federalism has been violated by a formal command from the National Government directing the State to enact a certain policy, or to organize its governmental functions in a certain way. While the intrusion on state sovereignty may not be as severe in this instance as in some of our recent Tenth Amendment cases, the intrusion is nonetheless significant. Absent a stronger connection or identification with commercial concerns that are central to the Commerce Clause, that interference contradicts the federal balance the Framers designed and that this Court is obliged to enforce.

For these reasons, I join in the opinion and judgment of the Court.

JUSTICE THOMAS, concurring.

. . . Although I join the majority, I write separately to observe that our case law has drifted far from the original understanding of the Commerce Clause. In a future case, we ought to temper our Commerce Clause jurisprudence in a manner that both makes sense of our more recent case law and is more faithful to the original understanding of that Clause.

We have said that Congress may regulate not only "Commerce . . . among the several states," but also anything that has a "substantial effect" on such commerce. This test, if taken to its logical extreme, would give Congress a "police power" over all aspects of American life. Unfortunately, we have never come to grips with this implication of our substantial effects formula. Although we have supposedly applied the substantial effects test for the past 60 years, we *always* have rejected readings of the Commerce Clause and the scope of federal power that would permit Congress to exercise a police power; our cases are quite clear that there are real limits to federal power. . . .

In an appropriate case, I believe that we must further reconsider our "substantial effects" test with an eye toward constructing a standard that reflects the text and history of the Commerce Clause without totally rejecting our more recent Commerce Clause jurisprudence.

Today, however, I merely support the Court's conclusion with a discussion of the text, structure, and history of the Commerce Clause and an analysis of our early case law. My goal is simply to show how far we have departed from the original understanding and to demonstrate that the result we reach today is by no means "radical." I also want to point out the necessity of refashioning a coherent test that does not tend to "obliterate the distinction between what is national and what is local and create a completely centralized government." *Jones & Laughlin Steel Corp.*

At the time the original Constitution was ratified, "commerce" consisted of selling, buying, and bartering, as well as transporting for these purposes. See 1 S. Johnson, *A Dictionary of the English Language* 361 (4th ed. 1773) (defining commerce as "Intercour[s]e; exchange of one thing for another; interchange of any thing; trade; traffick"); N. Bailey, *An Universal Etymological English Dictionary* (26th ed. 1789) ("trade or traffic"); T. Sheridan, *A Complete Dictionary of the English Language* (6th ed. 1796) ("Exchange of one thing for another; trade, traffick"). This understanding finds support in the etymology of the word, which literally means "with merchandise." See 3 *Oxford English Dictionary* 552 (2d ed. 1989) (com — "with"; merci — "merchandise"). In fact, when Federalists and Anti-Federalists discussed the Commerce Clause during the ratification period, they often used trade (in its selling/bartering sense) and commerce interchangeably. See *Federalist No. 4* (J. Jay) (asserting that countries will cultivate our friendship when our "trade" is prudently regulated by Federal Government); *id., No. 7* (A. Hamilton) (discussing "competitions of commerce" between States resulting from state "regulations of trade"); *id., No. 40* (J. Madison) (asserting that it was an "acknowledged object of the Convention ... that the regulation of trade should be submitted to the general government"). . . .

As one would expect, the term "commerce" was used in contradistinction to productive activities such as manufacturing and agriculture. Alexander Hamilton, for example, repeatedly treated commerce, agriculture, and manufacturing as three separate endeavors. See, e.g., *Federalist No. 36* (referring to "agriculture, commerce, manufactures"); *id., No. 21* (distinguishing commerce, arts, and industry); *id., No. 12* (asserting that commerce and agriculture have shared interests). The same distinctions were made in the state ratification conventions. . . .

Moreover, interjecting a modern sense of commerce into the Constitution generates significant textual and structural problems. For example, one cannot replace "commerce" with a different type of enterprise, such as manufacturing. When a manufacturer produces a car, assembly cannot take place "with a foreign nation" or "with the Indian Tribes." Parts may come from different States or other nations and hence may have been in the flow of commerce at one time, but manufacturing takes place at a discrete site. Agriculture and manufacturing involve the production of goods; commerce encompasses traffic in such articles.

The Port Preference Clause also suggests that the term "commerce" denoted sale and/or transport rather than business generally. According to that Clause, "[n]o Preference shall be given by any Regulation of Commerce or Revenue to the Ports of one State over those of another." U.S. Const., Art. I, §9, cl. 6. Although it is possible to conceive of regulations of manufacturing or farming that prefer one port over another, the more natural reading is that the Clause prohibits Congress from using its commerce power to channel commerce through certain favored ports.

The Constitution not only uses the word "commerce" in a narrower sense than our case law might suggest, it also does not support the proposition that Congress has authority over all activities that "substantially affect" interstate commerce. The Commerce Clause does not state that Congress may "regulate matters that substantially affect commerce with foreign Nations, and among the several States, and with the Indian Tribes." In contrast, the Constitution itself temporarily prohibited amendments that would "affect" Congress' lack of authority to prohibit or restrict the slave trade or to enact unproportioned direct taxation. [U.S. Const.,] Art. V. Clearly, the Framers could have drafted a Constitution that contained a "substantially affects interstate commerce" clause had that been their objective.

In addition to its powers under the Commerce Clause, Congress has the authority to enact such laws as are "necessary and proper" to carry into execution its power to regulate commerce among the several States. U.S. Const., Art. I, §8, cl. 18. But on this Court's understanding of congressional power under these two Clauses, many of Congress' other enumerated powers under Art. I, §8 are wholly superfluous. After all, if Congress may regulate all matters that substantially affect commerce, there is no need for the Constitution to specify that Congress may enact bankruptcy laws, or coin money and fix the standard of weights and measures, or punish counterfeiters of United States coin and securities. Likewise, Congress would not need the separate authority to establish post-offices and post-roads, cl. 7, or to grant patents and copyrights, or to "punish Piracies and Felonies committed on the high Seas." It might not even need the power to raise and support an Army and Navy, for fewer people would engage in commercial shipping if they thought that a foreign power could expropriate their property with ease. Indeed, if Congress could regulate matters that substantially affect interstate commerce, there would have been no need to specify that Congress can regulate international trade and commerce with the Indians. As the Framers surely understood, these other branches of trade substantially affect interstate commerce.

Put simply, much if not all of Art. I, §8 (including portions of the Commerce Clause itself) would be surplusage if Congress had been given authority over matters that substantially affect interstate commerce. An interpretation of cl. 3 that makes the rest of §8 superfluous simply cannot be correct. Yet this Court's Commerce Clause jurisprudence has endorsed just such an interpretation: the power we have accorded Congress has swallowed Art. I, §8.

Indeed, if a "substantial effects" test can be appended to the Commerce Clause, why not to every other power of the Federal Government? There is no reason for singling out the Commerce Clause for special treatment. Accordingly, Congress could regulate all matters that "substantially affect" the Army and Navy, bankruptcies, tax collection, expenditures, and so on. In that case, the clauses of §8 all mutually overlap, something we can assume the Founding Fathers never intended.

Our construction of the scope of congressional authority has the additional problem of coming close to turning the Tenth Amendment on its head. Our case law could be read to reserve to the United States all powers not expressly *prohibited* by the Constitution. Taken together, these fundamental textual problems should, at the very least, convince us that the "substantial effects" test should be reexamined. . . .

Early Americans understood that commerce, manufacturing, and agriculture, while distinct activities, were intimately related and dependent on each other — that each "substantially affected" the others. After all, items produced by farmers and manufacturers were the primary articles of commerce at the time. If commerce was more robust as a result of federal superintendence, farmers and manufacturers could benefit. Thus, Oliver Ellsworth of Connecticut attempted to convince farmers of the benefits of regulating commerce. "Your property and riches depend on a ready demand and generous price for the produce you can annually spare," he wrote, and these conditions exist "where trade flourishes and when the merchant can freely export the produce of the country" to nations that will pay the highest price. William Davie, a delegate to the North Carolina Convention, illustrated the close link best: "Commerce, sir, is the nurse of [agriculture and manufacturing]. The merchant furnishes the planter with such articles as he cannot manufacture himself, and finds him a market for his produce. Agriculture cannot flourish if commerce languishes; they are mutually dependent on each other."

Yet, despite being well aware that agriculture, manufacturing, and other matters substantially affected commerce, the founding generation did not cede authority over all these activities to Congress. Hamilton, for instance, acknowledged that the Federal Government could not regulate agriculture and like concerns: "The administration of private justice between the citizens of the same State, the supervision of agriculture and of other concerns of a similar nature, all those things in short which are proper to be provided for by local legislation, can never be desirable cares of a general jurisdiction." *Federalist No. 17*. . . .

In short, the Founding Fathers were well aware of what the principal dissent [by Justice Breyer] calls "economic . . . realities." Even though the boundary between commerce and other matters may ignore "economic reality" and thus seem arbitrary or artificial to some, we must nevertheless respect a constitutional line that does not grant Congress power over all that substantially affects interstate commerce. . . .

I am aware of no cases prior to the New Deal that characterized the power flowing from the Commerce Clause as sweepingly as does our substantial effects test. My review of the case law indicates that the substantial effects test is but an innovation of the 20th century. . . . As recently as 1936, the Court continued to insist that the Commerce Clause did not reach the wholly internal business of the States. . . . [F]rom the time of the ratification of the Constitution to the mid 1930's, it was widely understood that the Constitution granted Congress only limited powers, notwithstanding the Commerce Clause. Moreover, there was no question that activities wholly separated from business, such as gun possession, were beyond the reach of the commerce power. If anything, the "wrong turn" was the Court's dramatic departure in the 1930's from a century and a half of precedent.

Apart from its recent vintage and its corresponding lack of any grounding in the original understanding of the Constitution, the substantial effects test suffers from the further flaw that it appears to grant Congress a police power over the Nation. When asked at oral argument if there were any limits to the Commerce Clause, the Government was at a loss for words. Tr. of Oral Arg. 5. Likewise, the principal dissent insists that there are limits, but it cannot muster even one example. Indeed, the dissent implicitly concedes that its reading has no limits when it criticizes the Court for "threaten[ing] legal uncertainty in an area of law that . . . seemed reasonably well settled." The one advantage of the dissent's standard is certainty: it is certain that under its analysis everything may be regulated under the guise of the Commerce Clause.

The substantial effects test suffers from this flaw, in part, because of its "aggregation principle." Under so-called "class of activities" statutes, Congress can regulate whole categories of activities that are not themselves either "interstate" or "commerce." In applying the effects test, we ask whether the class of activities *as a whole* substantially affects interstate commerce, not whether any specific activity within the class has such effects when considered in isolation.

The aggregation principle is clever, but has no stopping point. Suppose all would agree that gun possession within 1,000 feet of a school does not substantially affect commerce, but that possession of weapons generally (knives, brass knuckles, nunchakus, etc.) does. Under our substantial effects doctrine, even though Congress cannot single out gun possession, it can prohibit weapon possession generally. But one *always* can draw the circle broadly enough to cover an activity that, when taken in isolation, would not have substantial effects on commerce. Under our jurisprudence, if Congress passed an omnibus "substantially affects interstate commerce" statute, purporting to regulate every aspect of human existence, the Act apparently would be constitutional. Even though particular sections may govern only trivial activities, the statute in the aggregate regulates matters that substantially affect commerce.

This extended discussion of the original understanding and our first century and a half of case law does not necessarily require a wholesale abandonment of our more recent opinions.[33] It simply reveals that our substantial effects test is far removed from both the Constitution and from our early case law and that the Court's opinion should not be viewed as "radical" or another "wrong turn" that must be corrected in the future. . . .

At an appropriate juncture, I think we must modify our Commerce Clause jurisprudence. Today, it is easy enough to say that the Clause certainly does not empower Congress to ban gun possession within 1,000 feet of a school.

JUSTICE BREYER, with whom JUSTICE STEVENS, JUSTICE SOUTER, and JUSTICE GINSBURG join, dissenting. . . .

In my view, the statute falls well within the scope of the commerce power as this Court has understood that power over the last half century. . . . [T]he Constitution requires us to judge the connection between a regulated activity and interstate commerce, not directly, but at one remove. Courts must give Congress a degree of leeway in determining the existence of a significant factual connection between the regulated activity and interstate commerce — both because the Constitution delegates the commerce power directly to Congress and because the determination requires an empirical judgment of a kind that a legislature is more likely than a court to make with accuracy. The traditional words "rational basis" capture this leeway. Thus, the specific question before us, as the Court recognizes, is not whether the "regulated activity sufficiently affected interstate commerce," but, rather, whether Congress could have had "a *rational basis*" for so concluding. . . . [W]e must ask whether Congress could have had a *rational basis* for finding a significant (or substantial) connection between gun-related school violence and interstate commerce. . . . Or, to put the question in the language of the *explicit* finding that Congress made when it amended this law in 1994: Could Congress rationally have found that "violent crime in school zones," through its effect on the "quality of education," significantly (or substantially) affects "interstate" or "foreign commerce"? As long as one views the commerce connection, not as a "technical legal conception," but as "a practical one," *Swift & Co. v. United States* (1905) (Holmes, J.), the answer to this question must be yes. Numerous reports and studies — generated both inside and outside government — make clear that Congress could reasonably have found the empirical connection that its law, implicitly or explicitly, asserts. . . .

Specifically, Congress could have found that gun-related violence near the classroom poses a serious economic threat (1) to consequently inadequately educated workers who must endure low-paying jobs, and (2) to communities and businesses that might (in today's "information society") otherwise gain, from a well-educated work force, an important commercial advantage of a kind that

---

33 Although I might be willing to return to the original understanding, I recognize that many believe that it is too late in the day to undertake a fundamental reexamination of the past 60 years. Consideration of stare decisis and reliance interests may convince us that we cannot wipe the slate clean.

location near a railhead or harbor provided in the past. Congress might also have found these threats to be no different in kind from other threats that this Court has found within the commerce power, such as the threat that loan sharking poses to the "funds" of "numerous localities," and that unfair labor practices pose to instrumentalities of commerce. . . . The violence related facts, the educational facts, and the economic facts, taken together, make this conclusion rational. And, because under our case law, the sufficiency of the constitutionally necessary Commerce Clause link between a crime of violence and interstate commerce turns simply upon size or degree, those same facts make the statute constitutional. . . .

The majority's holding — that §922 falls outside the scope of the Commerce Clause — creates three serious legal problems. First, the majority's holding runs contrary to modern Supreme Court cases that have upheld congressional actions despite connections to interstate or foreign commerce that are less significant than the effect of school violence. . . .

The second legal problem the Court creates comes from its apparent belief that it can reconcile its holding with earlier cases by making a critical distinction between "commercial" and noncommercial "transaction[s]." That is to say, the Court believes the Constitution would distinguish between two local activities, each of which has an identical effect upon interstate commerce, if one, but not the other, is "commercial" in nature. As a general matter, this approach fails to heed this Court's earlier warning not to turn "questions of the power of Congress" upon "formula[s]" that would give "controlling force to nomenclature such as 'production' and 'indirect' and foreclose consideration of the actual effects of the activity in question upon interstate commerce." *Wickard.*

Moreover, the majority's test is not consistent with what the Court saw as the point of the cases that the majority now characterizes. Although the majority today attempts to categorize *Perez, McClung,* and *Wickard* as involving intrastate "economic activity," the Courts that decided each of those cases did not focus upon the economic nature of the activity regulated. Rather, they focused upon whether that activity affected interstate or foreign commerce. In fact, the *Wickard* Court expressly held that Wickard's consumption of homegrown wheat, "*though it may not be regarded as commerce,*" could nevertheless be regulated — "*whatever its nature*" — so long as "it exerts a substantial economic effect on interstate commerce." (emphasis added).

More importantly, if a distinction between commercial and noncommercial activities is to be made, this is not the case in which to make it. . . . Schools that teach reading, writing, mathematics, and related basic skills serve both social and commercial purposes, and one cannot easily separate the one from the other. . . . In 1990, the year Congress enacted the statute before us, primary and secondary schools spent $230 billion — that is, nearly a quarter of a trillion dollars — which accounts for a significant portion of our $5.5 trillion Gross Domestic Product for that year. . . . Why could Congress, for Commerce Clause purposes, not consider schools as roughly analogous to commercial investments from which the Nation derives the benefit of an educated work force?

The third legal problem created by the Court's holding is that it threatens legal uncertainty in an area of law that, until this case, seemed reasonably well settled. . . .

Upholding this legislation would do no more than simply recognize that Congress had a "rational basis" for finding a significant connection between guns in or near schools and (through their effect on education) the interstate and foreign commerce they threaten. For these reasons, I would reverse the judgment of the Court of Appeals. Respectfully, I dissent.

STUDY GUIDE

- Does *United States v. Morrison* address any issues left open by *Lopez*?
- Why does the *Morrison* Court base its Commerce Clause doctrine on the distinction between "economic" and "noneconomic" activity?

United States v. Morrison

529 U.S. 598 (2000)

CHIEF JUSTICE REHNQUIST delivered the opinion of the Court.

In these cases we consider the constitutionality of 42 U.S.C. §13981, which provides a federal civil remedy for the victims of gender-motivated violence. . . . Section 13981 was part of the Violence Against Women Act of 1994. It states that "[a]ll persons within the United States shall have the right to be free from crimes of violence motivated by gender." To enforce that right, subsection (c) declares:

> A person (including a person who acts under color of any statute, ordinance, regulation, custom, or usage of any State) who commits a crime of violence motivated by gender and thus deprives another of the right declared in subsection (b) of this section shall be liable to the party injured, in an action for the recovery of compensatory and punitive damages, injunctive and declaratory relief, and such other relief as a court may deem appropriate.

. . .

Every law enacted by Congress must be based on one or more of its powers enumerated in the Constitution. "The powers of the legislature are defined and limited; and that those limits may not be mistaken or forgotten, the constitution is written." *Marbury v. Madison* (1803). Congress explicitly identified the sources of federal authority on which it relied in enacting §13981. It said that a "federal civil rights cause of action" is established "[p]ursuant to the affirmative power of Congress . . . under section 5 of the Fourteenth Amendment to the Constitution, as well as under section 8 of Article I of the Constitution." We address Congress' authority to enact this remedy under each of these constitutional provisions in turn. [The Court's discussion of Section 5 appears in Chapter 4. — EDS.]

Due respect for the decisions of a coordinate branch of Government demands that we invalidate a congressional enactment only upon a plain showing that

Congress has exceeded its constitutional bounds. With this presumption of constitutionality in mind, we turn to the question whether §13981 falls within . . . the third clause of the Article, which gives Congress power "[t]o regulate Commerce with foreign Nations, and among the several States, and with the Indian Tribes."

As we discussed at length in *Lopez*, . . . even under our modern, expansive interpretation of the Commerce Clause, Congress' regulatory authority is not without effective bounds. . . . Reviewing our case law, we noted that "we have upheld a wide variety of congressional Acts regulating intrastate economic activity where we have concluded that the activity substantially affected interstate commerce." . . . [A] fair reading of *Lopez* shows that the noneconomic, criminal nature of the conduct at issue was central to our decision in that case. . . .

Gender-motivated crimes of violence are not, in any sense of the phrase, economic activity. While we need not adopt a categorical rule against aggregating the effects of any noneconomic activity in order to decide these cases, thus far in our Nation's history our cases have upheld Commerce Clause regulation of intrastate activity only where that activity is economic in nature.

Like the Gun-Free School Zones Act at issue in *Lopez*, §13981 contains no jurisdictional element establishing that the federal cause of action is in pursuance of Congress' power to regulate interstate commerce. Although *Lopez* makes clear that such a jurisdictional element would lend support to the argument that §13981 is sufficiently tied to interstate commerce, Congress elected to cast §13981's remedy over a wider, and more purely intrastate, body of violent crime.

In contrast with the lack of congressional findings that we faced in *Lopez*, §13981 *is* supported by numerous findings regarding the serious impact that gender-motivated violence has on victims and their families. But the existence of congressional findings is not sufficient, by itself, to sustain the constitutionality of Commerce Clause legislation. As we stated in *Lopez*, "[S]imply because Congress may conclude that a particular activity substantially affects interstate commerce does not necessarily make it so." Rather, "[w]hether particular operations affect interstate commerce sufficiently to come under the constitutional power of Congress to regulate them is ultimately a judicial rather than a legislative question, and can be settled finally only by this Court."

In these cases, Congress' findings are substantially weakened by the fact that they rely so heavily on a method of reasoning that we have already rejected as unworkable if we are to maintain the Constitution's enumeration of powers. Congress found that gender-motivated violence affects interstate commerce "by deterring potential victims from traveling interstate, from engaging in employment in interstate business, and from transacting with business, and in places involved in interstate commerce; . . . by diminishing national productivity, increasing medical and other costs, and decreasing the supply of and the demand for interstate products." Given these findings and petitioners' arguments, the concern that we expressed in *Lopez* that Congress might use the Commerce Clause to completely obliterate the Constitution's distinction between national and local authority seems well founded. The reasoning that petitioners advance seeks to follow the but-for causal chain from the initial occurrence of violent crime (the suppression of which has always been the prime object of the States' police power) to every attenuated effect upon interstate commerce. If accepted, petitioners' reasoning would allow Congress to regulate any crime as long as the nationwide, aggregated impact of that crime has substantial effects on employment, production, transit, or consumption. Indeed, if Congress may regulate gender-motivated violence, it would be able to regulate murder or any other type of violence since gender-motivated violence, as a subset of all violent crime, is certain to have lesser economic impacts than the larger class of which it is a part. . . .

We accordingly reject the argument that Congress may regulate noneconomic, violent criminal conduct based solely on that conduct's aggregate effect on interstate commerce. The Constitution requires a distinction between what is truly national and what is truly local. In recognizing this fact we preserve one of the few principles that has been consistent since the Clause was adopted. The regulation and punishment of intrastate violence that is not directed at the instrumentalities, channels, or goods involved in interstate commerce has always been the province of the States. Indeed, we can think of no better example of the police power, which the Founders denied the National Government and reposed in the States, than the suppression of violent crime and vindication of its victims. . . .

Justice Thomas, concurring.

The majority opinion correctly applies our decision in *United States v. Lopez* (1995), and I join it in full. I write separately only to express my view that the very notion of a "substantial effects" test under the Commerce Clause is inconsistent with the original understanding of Congress' powers and with this Court's early Commerce Clause cases. By continuing to apply this rootless and malleable standard, however circumscribed, the Court has encouraged the Federal Government to persist in its view that the Commerce Clause has virtually no limits. Until this Court replaces its existing Commerce Clause jurisprudence with a standard more consistent with the original understanding, we will continue to see Congress appropriating state police powers under the guise of regulating commerce.

Justice Souter, with whom Justice Stevens, Justice Ginsburg, and Justice Breyer join, dissenting. . . .

[This] Act would have passed muster at any time between *Wickard* in 1942 and *Lopez* in 1995, a period in which the law enjoyed a stable understanding that congressional power under the Commerce Clause, complemented by the authority of the Necessary and Proper Clause, Art. I., §8, cl. 18, extended to all activity that, when aggregated, has a substantial effect on interstate commerce. The fact that the Act does not pass muster before the Court today is therefore proof, to a degree that *Lopez* was not, that the Court's nominal adherence to the substantial effects test is merely that. Although a new jurisprudence has not emerged with any distinctness, it is clear that some congressional conclusions about obviously substantial, cumulative effects on commerce are being assigned lesser values than the once-stable doctrine would assign them. These devaluations are accomplished not by any express repudiation of the substantial effects test or its application through the aggregation of individual conduct, but by supplanting rational basis scrutiny with a new criterion of review.

Thus the elusive heart of the majority's analysis in these cases is its statement that Congress' findings of fact are "weakened" by the presence of a disfavored "method of reasoning." This seems to suggest that the "substantial effects" analysis is not a factual enquiry, for Congress in the first instance with subsequent judicial review looking only to the rationality of the congressional conclusion, but one of a rather different sort, dependent upon a uniquely judicial competence. . . .

[W]ickard applied an aggregate effects test to ostensibly domestic, noncommercial farming. . . . If we now ask why the formalistic economic/noneconomic distinction might matter today, after its rejection in *Wickard*, the answer is not that the majority fails to see causal connections in an integrated economic world. The answer is that in the minds of the majority there is a new animating theory that makes categorical formalism seem useful again. Just as the old formalism had value in the service of an economic conception, the new one is useful in serving a conception of federalism. It is the instrument by which assertions of national power are to be limited in favor of preserving a supposedly discernible, proper sphere of state autonomy to legislate or refrain from legislating as the individual States see fit. The legitimacy of the Court's current emphasis on the noncommercial nature of regulated activity, then, does not turn on any logic serving the text of the Commerce Clause or on the realism of the majority's view of the national economy. The essential issue is rather the strength of the majority's claim to have a constitutional warrant for its current conception of a federal relationship enforceable by this Court through limits on otherwise plenary commerce power. . . .

All of this convinces me that today's ebb of the commerce power rests on error, and at the same time leads me to doubt that the majority's view will prove to be enduring law. . . . As our predecessors learned then, the practice of such ad hoc review cannot preserve the distinction between the judicial and the legislative, and this Court, in any event, lacks the institutional capacity to maintain such a regime for very long. This one will end when the majority realizes that the conception of the commerce power for which it entertains hopes would inevitably fail the test expressed in Justice Holmes's statement that "[t]he first call of a theory of law is that it should fit the facts." The facts that cannot be ignored today are the facts of integrated national commerce and a political relationship between States and Nation much affected by their respective treasuries and constitutional modifications adopted by the people. The federalism of some earlier time is no more adequate to account for those facts today than the theory of laissez-faire was able to govern the national economy 70 years ago.

JUSTICE BREYER, with whom JUSTICE STEVENS joins, and with whom JUSTICE SOUTER and JUSTICE GINSBURG join as to Part I-A, dissenting. . . .

The majority holds that the federal commerce power does not extend to such "noneconomic" activities as "noneconomic, violent criminal conduct" that significantly affects interstate commerce only if we "aggregate" the interstate "effect[s]" of individual instances. . . . [T]he majority's holding illustrates the difficulty of finding a workable judicial Commerce Clause touchstone — a set of comprehensible interpretive rules that courts might use to impose some meaningful limit, but not too great a limit, upon the scope of the legislative authority that the Commerce Clause delegates to Congress.

Consider the problems. The "economic/noneconomic" distinction is not easy to apply. Does the local street corner mugger engage in "economic" activity or "noneconomic" activity when he mugs for money? Would evidence that desire for economic domination underlies many brutal crimes against women save the present statute?

The line becomes yet harder to draw given the need for exceptions. The Court itself would permit Congress to aggregate, hence regulate, "noneconomic" activity taking place at economic establishments. See *Heart of Atlanta Motel, Inc. v. United States* (1964) (upholding civil rights laws forbidding discrimination at local motels); *Katzenbach v. McClung* (1964) (same for restaurants). And it would permit Congress to regulate where that regulation is "an essential part of a larger regulation of economic activity, in which the regulatory scheme could be undercut unless the intrastate activity were regulated." *Lopez*; cf. Controlled Substances Act, 21 U.S.C. §801 *et seq.* (regulating drugs produced for home consumption). Given the former exception, can Congress simply rewrite the present law and limit its application to restaurants, hotels, perhaps universities, and other places of public accommodation? Given the latter exception, can Congress save the present law by including it, or much of it, in a broader "Safe Transport" or "Workplace Safety" act?

More important, why should we give critical constitutional importance to the economic, or noneconomic, nature of an interstate-commerce-affecting *cause*? If chemical emanations through indirect environmental change cause identical, severe commercial harm outside a State, why should it matter whether local factories or home fireplaces release them? The Constitution itself refers only to Congress' power to "regulate Commerce . . . among the several States," and to make laws "necessary and proper" to implement that power. Art. I, §8, cls. 3, 18. The language says nothing about either the local nature, or the economic nature, of an interstate-commerce-affecting cause. . . .

STUDY GUIDE

- Do you see how the majority in *Gonzales v. Raich* used *Webster's* 3rd Edition dictionary to keep its holding within the doctrine of *Lopez* and *Morrison*?
- Are you persuaded by Justice Scalia's concurring opinion that offers a "more nuanced" analysis of the case under the Necessary and Proper Clause? Wasn't the Necessary and Proper Clause in effect when *Lopez* and *Morrison* were decided? How did that clause figure into the decisions in those cases, which Justice Scalia joined?
- Notice Justice Scalia's reference in his final paragraph to "Congress could reasonably conclude. . . ." This echoes the extremely deferential standard of scrutiny known as "rational basis review." Can you see how adopting this standard was crucial to his conclusion that the statute was constitutional under the Necessary and Proper Clause?
- Can you explain Justice Kennedy's shift from *Lopez* and *Morrison*, where he voted twice to invalidate the federal law?
- What part of Justice O'Connor's dissent did the Chief Justice and Justice Thomas not join?

Angel Raich after oral argument, with Diane Monson and Randy Barnett

Angel Raich (pronounced "raytch") was represented in the Supreme Court by Professor Randy Barnett, while Paul Clement defended the law as acting solicitor general. Chief Justice Rehnquist was seriously ill with cancer during the term in which *Raich* was decided and was not present for oral argument in December 2004. He most likely participated in the conference vote by telephone. He died during the summer of 2005, thereby marking the end of the "Rehnquist Court."

Gonzales v. Raich

545 U.S. 1 (2005)

Justice Stevens delivered the opinion of the Court.

California is one of at least nine States that authorize the use of marijuana for medicinal purposes. The question presented in this case is whether the power vested in Congress by Article I, §8, of the Constitution "[t]o make all Laws which shall be necessary and proper for carrying into Execution" its authority to "regulate Commerce with foreign Nations, and among the several States" includes the power to prohibit the local cultivation and use of marijuana in compliance with California law.

I

. . . In 1996, California voters passed Proposition 215, now codified as the Compassionate Use Act of 1996. The proposition was designed to ensure that "seriously ill" residents of the State have access to marijuana for medical purposes, and to encourage Federal and State Governments to take steps towards ensuring the safe and affordable distribution of the drug to patients in need. The Act creates an exemption from criminal prosecution for physicians, as well as for patients and primary caregivers who possess or cultivate marijuana for medicinal purposes with the recommendation or approval of a physician. A "primary caregiver" is a person who has consistently assumed responsibility for the housing, health, or safety of the patient.

Respondents Angel Raich and Diane Monson are California residents who suffer from a variety of serious medical conditions and have sought to avail themselves of medical marijuana pursuant to the terms of the Compassionate Use Act. They are being treated by licensed, board-certified family practitioners, who have concluded, after prescribing a host of conventional medicines to treat respondents' conditions and to alleviate their associated symptoms, that marijuana is the only drug available that provides effective treatment. Both women have been using marijuana as a medication for several years pursuant to their doctors' recommendation, and both rely heavily on cannabis to function on a daily basis. Indeed, Raich's physician believes that forgoing cannabis treatments would certainly cause Raich excruciating pain and could very well prove fatal.

Respondent Monson cultivates her own marijuana, and ingests the drug in a variety of ways including smoking and using a vaporizer. Respondent Raich, by contrast, is unable to cultivate her own, and thus relies on two caregivers, litigating as "John Does," to provide her with locally grown marijuana at no charge. These caregivers also process the cannabis into hashish or keif, and Raich herself processes some of the marijuana into oils, balms, and foods for consumption.

On August 15, 2002, county deputy sheriffs and agents from the federal Drug Enforcement Administration (DEA) came to Monson's home. After a thorough investigation, the county officials concluded that her use of marijuana was entirely lawful as a matter of California law. Nevertheless, after a 3-hour standoff, the federal agents seized and destroyed all six of her cannabis plants. . . .

II

[I]n 1970, after declaration of the national "war on drugs," . . . Congress enacted the Comprehensive Drug Abuse Prevention and Control Act. . . . Title II of that Act, the CSA [Controlled Substances Act — Eds.], repealed most of the earlier antidrug laws in favor of a comprehensive regime to combat the international and interstate traffic in illicit drugs. The main objectives of the CSA were to conquer drug abuse and to control the legitimate and illegitimate traffic in controlled substances. Congress was particularly concerned with the need to prevent the diversion of drugs from legitimate to illicit channels.

To effectuate these goals, Congress devised a closed regulatory system making it unlawful to manufacture, distribute, dispense, or possess any controlled substance except in a manner authorized by the CSA. The CSA categorizes all controlled substances into five schedules. The drugs are grouped together based on their accepted medical uses, the potential for abuse, and their psychological and physical effects on the body. Each schedule is associated with a distinct set of controls regarding the manufacture, distribution, and use of the substances listed therein. The CSA and its implementing regulations set forth strict requirements regarding registration, labeling and packaging, production quotas, drug security, and recordkeeping.

In enacting the CSA, Congress classified marijuana as a Schedule I drug. This preliminary classification was based, in part, on the recommendation of the Assistant Secretary of HEW "that marihuana be retained within schedule I at least until the completion of certain studies now underway." Schedule I drugs are categorized as such because of their high potential for abuse, lack of any accepted medical use, and absence of any accepted safety for use in medically supervised treatment. These three factors, in varying gradations, are also used to categorize drugs in the other four schedules. For example, Schedule II substances also have a high potential for abuse which may lead to severe psychological or physical dependence, but unlike Schedule I drugs, they have a currently accepted medical use. By classifying marijuana as a Schedule I drug, as opposed to listing it on a lesser schedule, the manufacture, distribution, or possession of marijuana became a criminal offense, with the sole exception being use of the drug as part of a Food and Drug Administration pre-approved research study. . . .

III

Respondents in this case do not dispute that passage of the CSA, as part of the Comprehensive Drug Abuse Prevention and Control Act, was well within Congress' commerce power. Nor do they contend that any provision or section of the CSA amounts to an unconstitutional exercise of congressional authority. Rather, respondents' challenge is actually quite limited; they argue that the CSA's categorical prohibition of the manufacture and possession of marijuana as applied to the intrastate manufacture and possession of marijuana for medical purposes pursuant to California law exceeds Congress' authority under the Commerce Clause. . . .

Our case law firmly establishes Congress' power to regulate purely local activities that are part of an economic "class of activities" that have a substantial effect on interstate commerce. As we stated in *Wickard*, "even if appellee's activity be local and though it may not be regarded as commerce, it may still, whatever its nature, be reached by Congress if it exerts a substantial economic effect on interstate commerce." We have never required Congress to legislate with scientific exactitude. When Congress decides that the "'total incidence'" of a practice poses a threat to a national market, it may regulate the entire class. . . . In this vein, we have reiterated that when "'a general regulatory statute bears a substantial relation to commerce, the *de minimis* character of individual instances arising under that statute is of no consequence.'" *Lopez*.

Our decision in *Wickard*, is of particular relevance. In *Wickard*, we upheld the application of regulations promulgated under the Agricultural Adjustment Act of 1938 which were designed to control the volume of wheat moving in interstate and foreign commerce in order to avoid surpluses and consequent abnormally low prices.... *Wickard*... establishes that Congress can regulate purely intrastate activity that is not itself "commercial," in that it is not produced for sale, if it concludes that failure to regulate that class of activity would undercut the regulation of the interstate market in that commodity.

The similarities between this case and *Wickard* are striking. Like the farmer in *Wickard*, respondents are cultivating, for home consumption, a fungible commodity for which there is an established, albeit illegal, interstate market. Just as the Agricultural Adjustment Act was designed "to control the volume [of wheat] moving in interstate and foreign commerce in order to avoid surpluses..." and consequently control the market price, a primary purpose of the CSA is to control the supply and demand of controlled substances in both lawful and unlawful drug markets. In *Wickard*, we had no difficulty concluding that Congress had a rational basis for believing that, when viewed in the aggregate, leaving home-consumed wheat outside the regulatory scheme would have a substantial influence on price and market conditions. Here too, Congress had a rational basis for concluding that leaving home-consumed marijuana outside federal control would similarly affect price and market conditions.

More concretely, one concern prompting inclusion of wheat grown for home consumption in the 1938 Act was that rising market prices could draw such wheat into the interstate market, resulting in lower market prices. The parallel concern making it appropriate to include marijuana grown for home consumption in the CSA is the likelihood that the high demand in the interstate market will draw such marijuana into that market. While the diversion of homegrown wheat tended to frustrate the federal interest in stabilizing prices by regulating the volume of commercial transactions in the interstate market, the diversion of homegrown marijuana tends to frustrate the federal interest in eliminating commercial transactions in the interstate market in their entirety. In both cases, the regulation is squarely within Congress' commerce power because production of the commodity meant for home consumption, be it wheat or marijuana, has a substantial effect on supply and demand in the national market for that commodity.

Nonetheless, respondents suggest that *Wickard* differs from this case in three respects: (1) the Agricultural Adjustment Act, unlike the CSA, exempted small farming operations; (2) *Wickard* involved a "quintessential economic activity" — a commercial farm — whereas respondents do not sell marijuana; and (3) the *Wickard* record made it clear that the aggregate production of wheat for use on farms had a significant impact on market prices. Those differences, though factually accurate, do not diminish the precedential force of this Court's reasoning.

The fact that Filburn's own impact on the market was "trivial by itself" was not a sufficient reason for removing him from the scope of federal regulation. That the Secretary of Agriculture elected to exempt even smaller farms from regulation does not speak to his power to regulate all those whose aggregated production was significant, nor did that fact play any role in the Court's analysis. Moreover, even though Filburn was indeed a commercial farmer, the activity he was engaged in — the cultivation of wheat for home consumption — was not treated by the Court as part of his commercial farming operation.[34] And while it is true that the record in the *Wickard* case itself established the causal connection between the production for local use and the national market, we have before us findings by Congress to the same effect.

Findings in the introductory sections of the CSA explain why Congress deemed it appropriate to encompass local activities within the scope of the CSA. The submissions of the parties and the numerous *amici* all seem to agree that the national, and international, market for marijuana has dimensions that are fully comparable to those defining the class of activities regulated by the Secretary pursuant to the 1938 statute. Respondents nonetheless insist that the CSA cannot be constitutionally applied to their activities because Congress did not make a specific finding that the intrastate cultivation and possession of marijuana for medical purposes based on the recommendation of a physician would substantially affect the larger interstate marijuana market. Be that as it may, we have never required Congress to make particularized findings in order to legislate absent a special concern such as the protection of free speech. While congressional findings are certainly helpful in reviewing the substance of a congressional statutory scheme, particularly when the connection to commerce is not self-evident, and while we will consider congressional findings in our analysis when they are available, the absence of particularized findings does not call into question Congress' authority to legislate.

In assessing the scope of Congress' authority under the Commerce Clause, we stress that the task before us is a modest one. We need not determine whether respondents' activities, taken in the aggregate, substantially affect interstate commerce in fact, but only whether a "rational basis" exists for so concluding. Given the enforcement difficulties that attend distinguishing between marijuana cultivated locally and marijuana grown elsewhere, and concerns about diversion into illicit channels, we have no difficulty concluding that Congress had a rational basis for believing that failure to regulate the intrastate manufacture and possession of marijuana would leave a gaping hole in the CSA. Thus, as in *Wickard*, when it enacted comprehensive legislation to regulate the interstate market in a fungible commodity, Congress was acting well within its authority to "make all Laws which shall be necessary and proper" to "regulate Commerce . . . among the several States." U.S. Const., Art. I, §8. That the regulation ensnares some purely intrastate activity is of no moment. As we have done many times before, we refuse to excise individual components of that larger scheme.

IV

To support their contrary submission, respondents rely heavily on two of our more recent Commerce Clause cases. . . . Those two cases, of course, are *Lopez*, and *U.S. v. Morrison* (2005). As an initial matter, the statutory challenges at issue in

---

[34] See *Wickard* (recognizing that Filburn's activity "may not be regarded as commerce").

those cases were markedly different from the challenge respondents pursue in the case at hand. Here, respondents ask us to excise individual applications of a concededly valid statutory scheme. In contrast, in both *Lopez* and *Morrison*, the parties asserted that a particular statute or provision fell outside Congress' commerce power in its entirety. This distinction is pivotal for we have often reiterated that "[w]here the class of activities is regulated and that class is within the reach of federal power, the courts have no power 'to excise, as trivial, individual instances' of the class." . . .

Unlike those at issue in *Lopez* and *Morrison*, the activities regulated by the CSA are quintessentially economic. "Economics" refers to "the production, distribution, and consumption of commodities." Webster's Third New International Dictionary (1966). The CSA is a statute that regulates the production, distribution, and consumption of commodities for which there is an established, and lucrative, interstate market. Prohibiting the intrastate possession or manufacture of an article of commerce is a rational (and commonly utilized) means of regulating commerce in that product.[35] Such prohibitions include specific decisions requiring that a drug be withdrawn from the market as a result of the failure to comply with regulatory requirements as well as decisions excluding Schedule I drugs entirely from the market. Because the CSA is a statute that directly regulates economic, commercial activity, our opinion in *Morrison* casts no doubt on its constitutionality. . . .

Respondents . . . contend that their activities were not "an essential part of a larger regulatory scheme" because they had been "isolated by the State of California, and [are] policed by the State of California," and thus remain "entirely separated from the market." Tr. of Oral Arg. 27. The dissenters fall prey to similar reasoning. The notion that California law has surgically excised a discrete activity that is hermetically sealed off from the larger interstate marijuana market is a dubious proposition, and, more importantly, one that Congress could have rationally rejected. . . .

The exemption for cultivation by patients and caregivers can only increase the supply of marijuana in the California market. The likelihood that all such production will promptly terminate when patients recover or will precisely match the patients' medical needs during their convalescence seems remote; whereas the danger that excesses will satisfy some of the admittedly enormous demand for recreational use seems obvious. Moreover, that the national and international narcotics trade has thrived in the face of vigorous criminal enforcement efforts suggests that no small number of unscrupulous people will make use of the California exemptions to serve their commercial ends whenever it is feasible to do so. Taking into account the fact that California is only one of at least nine States to have authorized the medical use of marijuana, a fact Justice O'Connor's dissent conveniently disregards in arguing that the demonstrated effect on commerce while admittedly "plausible" is ultimately "unsubstantiated," Congress could have rationally concluded that the aggregate impact on the national market of all the transactions exempted from federal supervision is unquestionably substantial. . . .

[35] See 16 U.S.C. §668(a) (bald and golden eagles); 18 U.S.C. §175(a) (biological weapons); §831(a) (nuclear material); §842(n)(1) (certain plastic explosives); §2342(a) (contraband cigarettes).

JUSTICE SCALIA, concurring in the judgment.

I agree with the Court's holding that the Controlled Substances Act (CSA) may validly be applied to respondents' cultivation, distribution, and possession of marijuana for personal, medicinal use. I write separately because my understanding of the doctrinal foundation on which that holding rests is, if not inconsistent with that of the Court, at least more nuanced. . . .

NCP

I

Our cases show that the regulation of intrastate activities may be necessary to and proper for the regulation of interstate commerce in two general circumstances. Most directly, the commerce power permits Congress not only to devise rules for the governance of commerce between States but also to facilitate interstate commerce by eliminating potential obstructions, and to restrict it by eliminating potential stimulants. See *NLRB v. Jones & Laughlin Steel Corp.* (1937). That is why the Court has repeatedly sustained congressional legislation on the ground that the regulated activities had a substantial effect on interstate commerce. *Lopez* and *Morrison* recognized the expansive scope of Congress' authority in this regard: "[T]he pattern is clear. Where economic activity substantially affects interstate commerce, legislation regulating that activity will be sustained."

This principle is not without limitation. In *Lopez* and *Morrison*, the Court — conscious of the potential of the "substantially affects" test to '"obliterate the distinction between what is national and what is local'" — rejected the argument that Congress may regulate *noneconomic* activity based solely on the effect that it may have on interstate commerce through a remote chain of inferences. "[I]f we were to accept [such] arguments," the Court reasoned in *Lopez*, "we are hard pressed to posit any activity by an individual that Congress is without power to regulate." Thus, although Congress' authority to regulate intrastate activity that substantially affects interstate commerce is broad, it does not permit the Court to "pile inference upon inference," in order to establish that noneconomic activity has a substantial effect on interstate commerce.

As we implicitly acknowledged in *Lopez*, however, Congress' authority to enact laws necessary and proper for the regulation of interstate commerce is not limited to laws directed against economic activities that have a substantial effect on interstate commerce. Though the conduct in *Lopez* was not economic, the Court nevertheless recognized that it could be regulated as "an essential part of a larger regulation of economic activity, in which the regulatory scheme could be undercut unless the intrastate activity were regulated." This statement referred to those cases permitting the regulation of intrastate activities "which in a substantial way interfere with or obstruct the exercise of the granted power." . . .[36]

---

[36] *Wickard v. Filburn* presented such a case. Because the unregulated production of wheat for personal consumption diminished demand in the regulated wheat market, the Court said, it carried with it the potential to disrupt Congress' price regulation by driving down prices in the market. This potential disruption of Congress' interstate regulation, and not only the effect that personal consumption of wheat had on interstate commerce, justified Congress' regulation of that conduct.

... The regulation of an intrastate activity may be essential to a comprehensive regulation of interstate commerce even though the intrastate activity does not itself "substantially affect" interstate commerce. Moreover, as the passage from *Lopez* quoted above suggests, Congress may regulate even noneconomic local activity if that regulation is a necessary part of a more general regulation of interstate commerce. The relevant question is simply whether the means chosen are "reasonably adapted" to the attainment of a legitimate end under the commerce power. ...

II

Today's principal dissent objects that, by permitting Congress to regulate activities necessary to effective interstate regulation, the Court reduces *Lopez* and *Morrison* to "little more than a drafting guide." I think that criticism unjustified. Unlike the power to regulate activities that have a substantial effect on interstate commerce, the power to enact laws enabling effective regulation of interstate commerce can only be exercised in conjunction with congressional regulation of an interstate market, and it extends only to those measures necessary to make the interstate regulation effective. As *Lopez* itself states, and the Court affirms today, Congress may regulate noneconomic intrastate activities only where the failure to do so "could ... undercut" its regulation of interstate commerce. This is not a power that threatens to obliterate the line between "what is truly national and what is truly local."

Lopez and *Morrison* affirm that Congress may not regulate certain "purely local" activity within the States based solely on the attenuated effect that such activity may have in the interstate market. But those decisions do not declare noneconomic intrastate activities to be categorically beyond the reach of the Federal Government. Neither case involved the power of Congress to exert control over intrastate activities in connection with a more comprehensive scheme of regulation; *Lopez* expressly disclaimed that it was such a case, and *Morrison* did not even discuss the possibility that it was. The Court of Appeals in *Morrison* made clear that it was not. To dismiss this distinction as "superficial and formalistic," is to misunderstand the nature of the Necessary and Proper Clause, which empowers Congress to enact laws in effectuation of its enumerated powers that are not within its authority to enact in isolation. See *McCulloch v. Maryland* (1819).

And there are other restraints upon the Necessary and Proper Clause authority. As Chief Justice Marshall wrote in *McCulloch v. Maryland* even when the end is constitutional and legitimate, the means must be "appropriate" and "plainly adapted" to that end. Moreover, they may not be otherwise "prohibited" and must be "consistent with the letter and spirit of the constitution." These phrases are not merely hortatory. For example, cases such as *Printz v. United States* (1997), and *New York v. United States* (1992), affirm that a law is not "'*proper* for carrying into Execution the Commerce Clause'" "[w]hen [it] violates [a constitutional] principle of state sovereignty."

III

The application of these principles to the case before us is straightforward. In the CSA, Congress has undertaken to extinguish the interstate market in Schedule I controlled substances, including marijuana. The Commerce Clause unquestionably permits this. The power to regulate interstate commerce "extends not only to those regulations which aid, foster and protect the commerce, but embraces those which prohibit it." *Darby*. See also *Lottery Case* (1903). To effectuate its objective, Congress has prohibited almost all intrastate activities related to Schedule I substances — both economic activities (manufacture, distribution, possession with the intent to distribute) and noneconomic activities (simple possession). That simple possession is a noneconomic activity is immaterial to whether it can be prohibited as a necessary part of a larger regulation. Rather, Congress' authority to enact all of these prohibitions of intrastate controlled-substance activities depends only upon whether they are appropriate means of achieving the legitimate end of eradicating Schedule I substances from interstate commerce.

By this measure, I think the regulation must be sustained. Not only is it impossible to distinguish "controlled substances manufactured and distributed intrastate" from "controlled substances manufactured and distributed interstate," but it hardly makes sense to speak in such terms. Drugs like marijuana are fungible commodities. As the Court explains, marijuana that is grown at home and possessed for personal use is never more than an instant from the interstate market — and this is so whether or not the possession is for medicinal use or lawful use under the laws of a particular State.[37] . . .

Finally, neither respondents nor the dissenters suggest any violation of state sovereignty of the sort that would render this regulation "inappropriate," — except to argue that the CSA regulates an area typically left to state regulation. That is not enough to render federal regulation an inappropriate means. The Court has repeatedly recognized that, if authorized by the commerce power, Congress may regulate private endeavors "even when [that regulation] may pre-empt express state-law determinations contrary to the result which has commended itself to the collective wisdom of Congress." *National League of Cities v. Usery* (1976). At bottom, respondents' state-sovereignty argument reduces to the contention that federal regulation of the activities permitted by California's Compassionate Use Act is not sufficiently necessary to be "necessary and proper" to Congress's regulation of the interstate market. For the reasons given above and in the Court's opinion, I cannot agree.

* * *

I thus agree with the Court that, however the class of regulated activities is subdivided, Congress could reasonably conclude that its objective of prohibiting marijuana from the interstate market "could be undercut" if those activities were

---

[37] The principal dissent claims that, if this is sufficient to sustain the regulation at issue in this case, then it should also have been sufficient to sustain the regulation at issue in *United States v. Lopez*. This claim founders upon the shoals of *Lopez* itself, which made clear that the statute there at issue was "*not* an essential part of a larger regulation of economic activity." On the dissent's view of things, that statement is inexplicable. . . .

excepted from its general scheme of regulation. That is sufficient to authorize the application of the CSA to respondents.

JUSTICE O'CONNOR, with whom THE CHIEF JUSTICE and JUSTICE THOMAS join as to all but Part III, dissenting.

We enforce the "outer limits" of Congress' Commerce Clause authority not for their own sake, but to protect historic spheres of state sovereignty from excessive federal encroachment and thereby to maintain the distribution of power fundamental to our federalist system of government. One of federalism's chief virtues, of course, is that it promotes innovation by allowing for the possibility that "a single courageous State may, if its citizens choose, serve as a laboratory; and try novel social and economic experiments without risk to the rest of the country." *New State Ice Co. v. Liebmann* (1932) (Brandeis, J., dissenting).

This case exemplifies the role of States as laboratories. The States' core police powers have always included authority to define criminal law and to protect the health, safety, and welfare of their citizens. Exercising those powers, California (by ballot initiative and then by legislative codification) has come to its own conclusion about the difficult and sensitive question of whether marijuana should be available to relieve severe pain and suffering. Today the Court sanctions an application of the federal Controlled Substances Act that extinguishes that experiment, without any proof that the personal cultivation, possession, and use of marijuana for medicinal purposes, if economic activity in the first place, has a substantial effect on interstate commerce and is therefore an appropriate subject of federal regulation. In so doing, the Court announces a rule that gives Congress a perverse incentive to legislate broadly pursuant to the Commerce Clause — nestling questionable assertions of its authority into comprehensive regulatory schemes — rather than with precision. That rule and the result it produces in this case are irreconcilable with our decisions in [*United States v. Lopez*] and *United States v. Morrison*. Accordingly I dissent. . . .

II

A

. . . Today's decision allows Congress to regulate intrastate activity without check, so long as there is some implication by legislative design that regulating intrastate activity is essential (and the Court appears to equate "essential" with "necessary") to the interstate regulatory scheme. Seizing upon our language in *Lopez* that the statute prohibiting gun possession in school zones was "not an essential part of a larger regulation of economic activity, in which the regulatory scheme could be undercut unless the intrastate activity were regulated," the Court appears to reason that the placement of local activity in a comprehensive scheme confirms that it is essential to that scheme. If the Court is right, then *Lopez* stands for nothing more than a drafting guide: Congress should have described the relevant crime as "transfer or possession of a firearm anywhere in the nation" — thus including commercial and noncommercial activity, and clearly encompassing some activity with assuredly substantial effect on interstate commerce. Had it done so, the majority hints, we would have sustained its authority to regulate possession of firearms in school zones. Furthermore, today's decision suggests we would readily sustain a congressional decision to attach the regulation of intrastate activity to a pre-existing comprehensive (or even not-so-comprehensive) scheme. If so, the Court invites increased federal regulation of local activity even if, as it suggests, Congress would not enact a *new* interstate scheme exclusively for the sake of reaching intrastate activity. . . .

B

. . . The Court's definition of economic activity is breathtaking. It defines as economic any activity involving the production, distribution, and consumption of commodities. And it appears to reason that when an interstate market for a commodity exists, regulating the intrastate manufacture or possession of that commodity is constitutional either because that intrastate activity is itself economic, or because regulating it is a rational part of regulating its market. Putting to one side the problem endemic to the Court's opinion — the shift in focus from the activity at issue in this case to the entirety of what the CSA regulates, see *Lopez* ("depending on the level of generality, any activity can be looked upon as commercial") — the Court's definition of economic activity for purposes of Commerce Clause jurisprudence threatens to sweep all of productive human activity into federal regulatory reach.

The Court uses a dictionary definition of economics to skirt the real problem of drawing a meaningful line between "what is national and what is local," *Jones & Laughlin Steel.* It will not do to say that Congress may regulate noncommercial activity simply because it may have an effect on the demand for commercial goods, or because the noncommercial endeavor can, in some sense, substitute for commercial activity. Most commercial goods or services have some sort of privately producible analogue. Home care substitutes for daycare. Charades games substitute for movie tickets. Backyard or windowsill gardening substitutes for going to the supermarket. To draw the line wherever private activity affects the demand for market goods is to draw no line at all, and to declare everything economic. We have already rejected the result that would follow — a federal police power. *Lopez.*

In *Lopez* and *Morrison*, we suggested that economic activity usually relates directly to commercial activity. The homegrown cultivation and personal possession and use of marijuana for medicinal purposes has no apparent commercial character. Everyone agrees that the marijuana at issue in this case was never in the stream of commerce, and neither were the supplies for growing it. (Marijuana is highly unusual among the substances subject to the CSA in that it can be cultivated without any materials that have traveled in interstate commerce.) *Lopez* makes clear that possession is not itself commercial activity. And respondents have not come into possession by means of any commercial transaction; they have simply grown, in their own homes, marijuana for their own use, without acquiring, buying, selling, or bartering a thing of value.

The Court suggests that *Wickard*, which we have identified as "perhaps the most far-reaching example of Commerce Clause authority over intrastate activity," *Lopez*, established federal regulatory power over any home consumption of a commodity for which a national market exists. I disagree. *Wickard* involved a challenge to the Agricultural Adjustment Act of 1938 (AAA), which directed the Secretary of Agriculture to set national quotas on wheat production, and penalties for excess production. The AAA itself confirmed that Congress made an explicit choice not to reach — and thus the Court could not possibly have approved of federal control over — small-scale, noncommercial wheat farming. In contrast to the CSA's limitless assertion of power, Congress provided an exemption within the AAA for small producers. When Filburn planted the wheat at issue in *Wickard*, the statute exempted plantings less than 200 bushels (about six tons), and when he harvested his wheat it exempted plantings less than six acres. *Wickard*, then, did not extend Commerce Clause authority to something as modest as the home cook's herb garden. This is not to say that Congress may never regulate small quantities of commodities possessed or produced for personal use, or to deny that it sometimes needs to enact a zero tolerance regime for such commodities. It is merely to say that *Wickard* did not hold or imply that small-scale production of commodities is always economic, and automatically within Congress' reach.

Even assuming that economic activity is at issue in this case, the Government has made no showing in fact that the possession and use of homegrown marijuana for medical purposes, in California or elsewhere, has a substantial effect on interstate commerce. Similarly, the Government has not shown that regulating such activity is necessary to an interstate regulatory scheme. Whatever the specific theory of "substantial effects" at issue (i.e., whether the activity substantially affects interstate commerce, whether its regulation is necessary to an interstate regulatory scheme, or both), a concern for dual sovereignty requires that Congress' excursion into the traditional domain of States be justified.

That is why characterizing this as a case about the Necessary and Proper Clause does not change the analysis significantly. Congress must exercise its authority under the Necessary and Proper Clause in a manner consistent with basic constitutional principles. As Justice Scalia recognizes, Congress cannot use its authority under the Clause to contravene the principle of state sovereignty embodied in the Tenth Amendment. Likewise, that authority must be used in a manner consistent with the notion of enumerated powers — a structural principle that is as much part of the Constitution as the Tenth Amendment's explicit textual command. Accordingly, something more than mere assertion is required when Congress purports to have power over local activity whose connection to an intrastate market is not self-evident. Otherwise, the Necessary and Proper Clause will always be a back door for unconstitutional federal regulation. Cf. *Printz v. United States* (1997) (the Necessary and Proper Clause is "the last, best hope of those who defend ultra vires congressional action"). Indeed, if it were enough in "substantial effects" cases for the Court to supply conceivable justifications for intrastate regulation related to an interstate market, then we could have surmised in *Lopez* that guns in school zones are "never more than an instant from the interstate market" in guns already subject to extensive federal regulation, recast *Lopez* as a Necessary and Proper Clause case, and thereby upheld the Gun-Free School Zones Act of 1990. . . .

There is simply no evidence that homegrown medicinal marijuana users constitute, in the aggregate, a sizable enough class to have a discernable, let alone substantial, impact on the national illicit drug market — or otherwise to threaten the CSA regime. Explicit evidence is helpful when substantial effect is not "visible to the naked eye." See *Lopez*. And here, in part because common sense suggests that medical marijuana users may be limited in number and that California's Compassionate Use Act and similar state legislation may well isolate activities relating to medicinal marijuana from the illicit market, the effect of those activities on interstate drug traffic is not self-evidently substantial.

In this regard, again, this case is readily distinguishable from *Wickard*. To decide whether the Secretary could regulate local wheat farming, the Court looked to "the actual effects of the activity in question upon interstate commerce." Critically, the Court was able to consider "actual effects" because the parties had "stipulated a summary of the economics of the wheat industry." After reviewing in detail the picture of the industry provided in that summary, the Court explained that consumption of homegrown wheat was the most variable factor in the size of the national wheat crop, and that on-site consumption could have the effect of varying the amount of wheat sent to market by as much as 20 percent. With real numbers at hand, the *Wickard* Court could easily conclude that "a factor of such volume and variability as home-consumed wheat would have a substantial influence on price and market conditions" nationwide. . . .

The Court refers to a series of declarations in the introduction to the CSA. . . . [But] the CSA's introductory declarations are too vague and unspecific to demonstrate that the federal statutory scheme will be undermined if Congress cannot exert power over individuals like respondents. The declarations are not even specific to marijuana. . . . Because here California, like other States, has carved out a limited class of activity for distinct regulation, the inadequacy of the CSA's findings is especially glaring. The California Compassionate Use Act exempts from other state drug laws patients and their caregivers "who posses[s] or cultivat[e] marijuana for the *personal* medical purposes of the patient upon the written or oral recommendation of a physician" to treat a list of serious medical conditions. The Act specifies that it should not be construed to supersede legislation prohibiting persons from engaging in acts dangerous to others, or to condone the diversion of marijuana for nonmedical purposes. To promote the Act's operation and to facilitate law enforcement, California recently enacted an identification card system for qualified patients. We generally assume States enforce their laws and have no reason to think otherwise here. . . .

The Court . . . offers some arguments about the effect of the Compassionate Use Act on the national market. It says that the California statute might be vulnerable to exploitation by unscrupulous physicians, that Compassionate Use Act patients may overproduce, and that the history of the narcotics trade shows the difficulty of cordoning off any drug use from the rest of the market. These arguments are plausible; if borne out in fact they could justify prosecuting Compassionate Use Act patients under the federal CSA. But, without substantiation, they add little to the CSA's conclusory statements about diversion, essentiality, and market effect. Piling assertion upon assertion does not, in my view, satisfy the substantiality test of *Lopez* and *Morrison.*

III

We would do well to recall how James Madison, the father of the Constitution, described our system of joint sovereignty to the people of New York: "The powers delegated by the proposed constitution to the federal government are few and defined. Those which are to remain in the State governments are numerous and indefinite. . . . The powers reserved to the several States will extend to all the objects which, in the ordinary course of affairs, concern the lives, liberties, and properties of the people, and the internal order, improvement, and prosperity of the State." *Federalist No. 45.* . . .

If I were a California citizen, I would not have voted for the medical marijuana ballot initiative; if I were a California legislator I would not have supported the Compassionate Use Act. But whatever the wisdom of California's experiment with medical marijuana, the federalism principles that have driven our Commerce Clause cases require that room for experiment be protected in this case. For these reasons I dissent.

JUSTICE THOMAS, dissenting.

Respondents Diane Monson and Angel Raich use marijuana that has never been bought or sold, that has never crossed state lines, and that has had no demonstrable effect on the national market for marijuana. If Congress can regulate this under the Commerce Clause, then it can regulate virtually anything—and the Federal Government is no longer one of limited and enumerated powers. . . .

I

. . . [N]either the Commerce Clause nor the Necessary and Proper Clause grants Congress the power to regulate respondents' conduct.

A

As I explained at length in *United States v. Lopez* (1995), the Commerce Clause empowers Congress to regulate the buying and selling of goods and services trafficked across state lines. . . . Certainly no evidence from the founding suggests that "commerce" included the mere possession of a good or some purely personal activity that did not involve trade or exchange for value. In the early days of the Republic, it would have been unthinkable that Congress could prohibit the local cultivation, possession, and consumption of marijuana.

On this traditional understanding of "commerce," the Controlled Substances Act regulates a great deal of marijuana trafficking that is interstate and commercial in character. The CSA does not, however, criminalize only the interstate buying and selling of marijuana. Instead, it bans the entire market—intrastate or interstate, noncommercial or commercial—for marijuana. Respondents are correct that the

CSA exceeds Congress' commerce power as applied to their conduct, which is purely intrastate and noncommercial.

B

More difficult, however, is whether the CSA is a valid exercise of Congress' power to enact laws that are "necessary and proper for carrying into Execution" its power to regulate interstate commerce. The Necessary and Proper Clause is not a warrant to Congress to enact any law that bears some conceivable connection to the exercise of an enumerated power. Nor is it, however, a command to Congress to enact only laws that are absolutely indispensable to the exercise of an enumerated power.

In *McCulloch v. Maryland* (1819), this Court, speaking through Chief Justice Marshall, set forth a test for determining when an Act of Congress is permissible under the Necessary and Proper Clause: "Let the end be legitimate, let it be within the scope of the constitution, and all means which are appropriate, which are plainly adapted to that end, which are not prohibited, but consist with the letter and spirit of the constitution, are constitutional." To act under the Necessary and Proper Clause, then, Congress must select a means that is "appropriate" and "plainly adapted" to executing an enumerated power; the means cannot be otherwise "prohibited" by the Constitution; and the means cannot be inconsistent with "the letter and spirit of the [C]onstitution." The CSA, as applied to respondents' conduct, is not a valid exercise of Congress' power under the Necessary and Proper Clause.

1

... On its face, a ban on the intrastate cultivation, possession and distribution of marijuana may be plainly adapted to stopping the interstate flow of marijuana. Unregulated local growers and users could swell both the supply and the demand sides of the interstate marijuana market, making the market more difficult to regulate. But respondents do not challenge the CSA on its face. Instead, they challenge it as applied to their conduct. The question is thus whether the intrastate ban is "necessary and proper" as applied to medical marijuana users like respondents.[38] ... [E]ven assuming Congress has "obvious" and "plain" reasons why regulating intrastate cultivation and possession is necessary to regulating the interstate drug trade, none of those reasons applies to medical marijuana patients like Monson and Raich.

California's Compassionate Use Act sets respondents' conduct apart from other intrastate producers and users of marijuana. The Act channels marijuana use to "seriously ill Californians," and prohibits "the diversion of marijuana for

---

[38] Because respondents do not challenge on its face the CSA's ban on marijuana, our adjudication of their as-applied challenge casts no doubt on this Court's practice in *Lopez* and *Morrison*. In those cases, we held that Congress, in enacting the statutes at issue, had exceeded its Article I powers.

nonmedical purposes." California strictly controls the cultivation and possession of marijuana for medical purposes. To be eligible for its program, California requires that a patient have an illness that cannabis can relieve, such as cancer, AIDS, or arthritis, and that he obtain a physician's recommendation or approval. Qualified patients must provide personal and medical information to obtain medical identification cards, and there is a statewide registry of cardholders. Moreover, the Medical Board of California has issued guidelines for physicians' cannabis recommendations, and it sanctions physicians who do not comply with the guidelines. . . .

These controls belie the Government's assertion that placing medical marijuana outside the CSA's reach "would prevent effective enforcement of the interstate ban on drug trafficking." Enforcement of the CSA can continue as it did prior to the Compassionate Use Act. Only now, a qualified patient could avoid arrest or prosecution by presenting his identification card to law enforcement officers. In the event that a qualified patient is arrested for possession or his cannabis is seized, he could seek to prove as an affirmative defense that, in conformity with state law, he possessed or cultivated small quantities of marijuana intrastate solely for personal medical use. Moreover, under the CSA, certain drugs that present a high risk of abuse and addiction but that nevertheless have an accepted medical use — drugs like morphine and amphetamines — are available by prescription. No one argues that permitting use of these drugs under medical supervision has undermined the CSA's restrictions. . . .

In sum, neither in enacting the CSA nor in defending its application to respondents has the Government offered any obvious reason why banning medical marijuana use is necessary to stem the tide of interstate drug trafficking. Congress' goal of curtailing the interstate drug trade would not plainly be thwarted if it could not apply the CSA to patients like Monson and Raich. That is, unless Congress' aim is really to exercise police power of the sort reserved to the States in order to eliminate even the intrastate possession and use of marijuana.

2

Even assuming the CSA's ban on locally cultivated and consumed marijuana is "necessary," that does not mean it is also "proper." The means selected by Congress to regulate interstate commerce cannot be "prohibited" by, or inconsistent with the "letter and spirit" of, the Constitution. *McCulloch.*

In *Lopez,* I argued that allowing Congress to regulate intrastate, noncommercial activity under the Commerce Clause would confer on Congress a general "police power" over the Nation. This is no less the case if Congress ties its power to the Necessary and Proper Clause rather than the Commerce Clause. When agents from the Drug Enforcement Administration raided Monson's home, they seized six cannabis plants. If the Federal Government can regulate growing a half-dozen cannabis plants for personal consumption (not because it is interstate commerce, but because it is inextricably bound up with interstate commerce), then Congress' Article I powers — as expanded by the Necessary and Proper Clause — have no meaningful limits. . . .

Even if Congress may regulate purely intrastate activity when essential to exercising some enumerated power, see *United States v. Dewitt* (1870); but see Barnett, The Original Meaning of the Necessary and Proper Clause, 6 U. Pa. J. Const. L. 183, 186 (2003) (detailing statements by Founders that the Necessary and Proper Clause was not intended to expand the scope of Congress' enumerated powers), Congress may not use its incidental authority to subvert basic principles of federalism and dual sovereignty.

Here, Congress has encroached on States' traditional police powers to define the criminal law and to protect the health, safety, and welfare of their citizens. Further, the Government's rationale — that it may regulate the production or possession of any commodity for which there is an interstate market — threatens to remove the remaining vestiges of States' traditional police powers. This would convert the Necessary and Proper Clause into precisely what Chief Justice Marshall did not envision, a "pretext . . . for the accomplishment of objects not intrusted to the government."

II

. . . The majority holds that Congress may regulate intrastate cultivation and possession of medical marijuana under the Commerce Clause, because such conduct arguably has a substantial effect on interstate commerce. The majority's decision is further proof that the "substantial effects" test is a "rootless and malleable standard" at odds with the constitutional design. *Morrison* (Thomas, J., concurring).

The majority's treatment of the substantial effects test is rootless, because it is not tethered to either the Commerce Clause or the Necessary and Proper Clause. Under the Commerce Clause, Congress may regulate interstate commerce, not activities that substantially affect interstate commerce — any more than Congress may regulate activities that do not fall within, but that affect, the subjects of its other Article I powers. Whatever additional latitude the Necessary and Proper Clause affords, the question is whether Congress' legislation is essential to the regulation of interstate commerce itself — not whether the legislation extends only to economic activities that substantially affect interstate commerce.

The majority's treatment of the substantial effects test is malleable, because the majority expands the relevant conduct. By defining the class at a high level of generality (as the intrastate manufacture and possession of marijuana), the majority overlooks that individuals authorized by state law to manufacture and possess medical marijuana exert no demonstrable effect on the interstate drug market. The majority ignores that whether a particular activity substantially affects interstate commerce — and thus comes within Congress' reach on the majority's approach — can turn on a number of objective factors, like state action or features of the regulated activity itself. For instance, here, if California and other States are effectively regulating medical marijuana users, then these users have little effect on the interstate drug trade. . . .

This Court has never held that Congress can regulate noneconomic activity that substantially affects interstate commerce. To evade even that modest restriction on federal power, the majority defines economic activity in the broadest possible terms as "the production, distribution, and consumption of commodities."[39] This carves out a vast swath of activities that are subject to federal regulation. If the majority is to be taken seriously, the Federal Government may now regulate quilting bees, clothes drives, and potluck suppers throughout the 50 States. This makes a mockery of Madison's assurance to the people of New York that the "powers delegated" to the Federal Government are "few and defined," while those of the States are "numerous and indefinite." *Federalist No. 45.*

Moreover, even a Court interested more in the modern than the original understanding of the Constitution ought to resolve cases based on the meaning of words that are actually in the document. Congress is authorized to regulate "Commerce," and respondents' conduct does not qualify under any definition of that term.[40] The majority's opinion only illustrates the steady drift away from the text of the Commerce Clause. There is an inexorable expansion from "commerce," to "commercial" and "economic" activity, and finally to all "production, distribution, and consumption" of goods or services for which there is an "established . . . interstate market." Federal power expands, but never contracts, with each new locution. The majority is not interpreting the Commerce Clause, but rewriting it.

The majority's rewriting of the Commerce Clause seems to be rooted in the belief that, unless the Commerce Clause covers the entire web of human activity, Congress will be left powerless to regulate the national economy effectively. The interconnectedness of economic activity is not a modern phenomenon unfamiliar to the Framers. Moreover, the Framers understood what the majority does not appear to fully appreciate: There is a danger to concentrating too much, as well as too little, power in the Federal Government. This Court has carefully avoided stripping Congress of its ability to regulate *inter*state commerce, but it has casually allowed the Federal Government to strip States of their ability to regulate *intra*state commerce — not to mention a host of local activities, like mere drug possession, that are not commercial. . . .

[T]oday's decision will add no measure of stability to our Commerce Clause jurisprudence: This Court is willing neither to enforce limits on federal power, nor to declare the Tenth Amendment a dead letter. If stability is possible, it is only by discarding the stand-alone substantial effects test and revisiting our definition of "Commerce among the several States." Congress may regulate interstate

---

[39] Other dictionaries do not define the term "economic" as broadly as the majority does. See, e.g., The American Heritage Dictionary of the English Language 583 (3d ed. 1992) (defining "economic" as "[o]f or relating to the production, development, and management of *material wealth*, as of a country, household, or business enterprise" (emphasis added)). The majority does not explain why it selects a remarkably expansive 40-year-old definition.

[40] See, e.g., *id.*, at 380 ("[t]he buying and selling of goods, especially on a large scale, as between cities or nations"); The Random House Dictionary of the English Language 411 (2d ed. 1987) ("an interchange of goods or commodities, esp. on a large scale between different countries . . . or between different parts of the same country"); Webster's 3d 456 ("the exchange or buying and selling of commodities esp. on a large scale and involving transportation from place to place").

commerce — not things that affect it, even when summed together, unless truly "necessary and proper" to regulating interstate commerce. . . .

The majority prevents States like California from devising drug policies that they have concluded provide much-needed respite to the seriously ill. It does so without any serious inquiry into the necessity for federal regulation or the propriety of "displac[ing] state regulation in areas of traditional state concern," *Lopez* (Kennedy, J., concurring). The majority's rush to embrace federal power "is especially unfortunate given the importance of showing respect for the sovereign States that comprise our Federal Union." *United States v. Oakland Cannabis Buyers' Cooperative* (2001) (Stevens, J., concurring in judgment). Our federalist system, properly understood, allows California and a growing number of other States to decide for themselves how to safeguard the health and welfare of their citizens. I would affirm the judgment of the Court of Appeals.

I respectfully dissent.

G. THE ROBERTS COURT

1. The Commerce and Necessary and Proper Clauses

Chief Justice John G. Roberts, Jr.

ASSIGNMENT 8

In March 2010, Congress passed the Patient Protection and Affordable Care Act (ACA).[41] Moments after it was signed into law, a group of state attorneys general challenged its constitutionality in the Northern District of Florida. The parties eventually grew to include twenty-six states and the National Federation of Independent Business (NFIB). They challenged the constitutionality of the ACA's so-called individual mandate, which required nearly all Americans to purchase qualifying health insurance policies or pay a monetary penalty. They also challenged the provisions of the ACA that required states to expand the number of low-income individuals who would be eligible to enroll in Medicaid. Others challenged the constitutionality of the individual mandate in other circuits, which reached different conclusions.

In March 2012, the Supreme Court heard more than six hours of oral argument spread over three days. This schedule was exceptional. Since the late twentieth century, oral arguments have been strictly limited to one hour. The Court granted four hours of oral argument on the constitutionality of the McCain-Feingold campaign finance law. But it had been forty-seven years since the Court had granted as many as six hours.

At issue was the scope of three of Congress's enumerated powers in Article I, Section 8: the Commerce Clause, the Necessary and Proper Clause, and the taxing power from which the spending power is inferred. In short, at issue was the scope of the principal powers that Congress has used since the New Deal as the basis for much of its legislation.

In the two years leading up to the argument, it became clear that the case posed a choice between two competing visions of the expansion of federal power since the New Deal. Did it mean that Article I gives Congress the power to regulate, in its discretion, any aspect of the "national economy." That is, could Congress address any problem that can be deemed "national" in scope, subject only to the express (or "external") limits in other parts of the Constitution? Or did the New Deal cases represent the "high water mark" of congressional power? Does any new claim of more expansive power require serious justification based on reasons that do not then establish a limitless national police power? Is there any "internal" limit imposed by the enumeration of powers?

We begin by considering the Court's treatment of the Commerce and Necessary and Proper Clauses, and the tax power.

Paul Clement, who defended the government in *Gonzales v. Raich* as solicitor general, argued *NFIB v. Sebelius* in the Supreme Court on behalf of 26 states. Randy Barnett, who represented Angel Raich, was one of the lawyers representing the NFIB.

[41] For a history of the enactment of the law, and the ensuing litigation, see Josh Blackman, Unprecedented: The Constitutional Challenge to Obamacare (2013).

STUDY GUIDE

- Which vision of the New Deal is adopted by a majority of the Justices in *NFIB v. Sebelius*?
- How does Chief Justice Roberts's analysis of the Commerce and Necessary and Proper Clauses fit with *Lopez, Morrison*, and *Raich*?
- Pay particular attention to his distinction between "incidental powers" and "great substantive and independent power[s]," a distinction also relied upon by Chief Justice Marshall in *McCulloch v. Maryland* (Chapter 2), but generally neglected in the interim. How does this distinction operate when utilizing the Necessary and Proper Clause? How does this distinction relate to the difference between "regulating" commerce and requiring that people engage in economic activity with a private company?
- Did the parties contest whether the individual mandate was "necessary"? If not, what exactly did Chief Justice Roberts think was "improper" about it? Did the parties in *Raich* contest the necessity or the propriety of applying the Controlled Substances Act to the activity permitted by California law?
- Can you imagine why two cable news networks announced that the ACA had been invalidated when they quickly read the slip opinion? How and where did the Chief Justice pivot to reach a different result?
- What does the Chief Justice mean by a "saving construction," and what work did it do in his analysis? In the end, did he uphold or invalidate the individual insurance mandate?
- What was the holding or holdings of the case? (*Hint:* Notice which portions of the Chief Justice's opinion were joined by four (or more) other Justices and what is said about the holding there. Consider also whether Justice Ginsburg and those who joined her would feel bound by the limits set out in *Lopez* in a future case.)
- In particular, did Chief Justice Roberts rule that, although the individual insurance mandate was unconstitutional under the Commerce and Necessary and Proper Clauses, Congress could have enacted it under its taxing power?

NFIB v. Sebelius

567 U.S. 519 (2012)

CHIEF JUSTICE ROBERTS announced the judgment of the Court and delivered the opinion of the Court with respect to Parts I, II, and III-C . . . and an opinion with respect to Parts III-A, III-B, and III-D.

Today we resolve constitutional challenges to two provisions of the Patient Protection and Affordable Care Act of 2010: the individual mandate, which requires individuals to purchase a health insurance policy providing a minimum level of coverage; and the Medicaid expansion, which gives funds to the States on the condition that they provide specified health care to all citizens whose income falls below a certain threshold. We do not consider whether the Act embodies sound policies. That judgment is entrusted to the Nation's elected leaders. We ask only whether Congress has the power under the Constitution to enact the challenged provisions.

In our federal system, the National Government possesses only limited powers; the States and the people retain the remainder. Nearly two centuries ago, Chief Justice Marshall observed that "the question respecting the extent of the powers actually granted" to the Federal Government "is perpetually arising, and will probably continue to arise, as long as our system shall exist." *McCulloch v. Maryland* (1819). In this case we must again determine whether the Constitution grants Congress powers it now asserts, but which many States and individuals believe it does not possess. Resolving this controversy requires us to examine both the limits of the Government's power, and our own limited role in policing those boundaries.

The Federal Government "is acknowledged by all to be one of enumerated powers." *Ibid.* That is, rather than granting general authority to perform all the conceivable functions of government, the Constitution lists, or enumerates, the Federal Government's powers. Congress may, for example, "coin Money," "establish Post Offices," and "raise and support Armies." Art. I, §8, cls. 5, 7, 12. The enumeration of powers is also a limitation of powers, because "[t]he enumeration presupposes something not enumerated." *Gibbons v. Ogden* (1824). The Constitution's express conferral of some powers makes clear that it does not grant others. And the Federal Government "can exercise only the powers granted to it." *McCulloch*.

Today, the restrictions on government power foremost in many Americans' minds are likely to be affirmative prohibitions, such as contained in the Bill of Rights. These affirmative prohibitions come into play, however, only where the Government possesses authority to act in the first place. If no enumerated power authorizes Congress to pass a certain law, that law may not be enacted, even if it would not violate any of the express prohibitions in the Bill of Rights or elsewhere in the Constitution.

Indeed, the Constitution did not initially include a Bill of Rights at least partly because the Framers felt the enumeration of powers sufficed to restrain the Government. As Alexander Hamilton put it, "the Constitution is itself, in every rational sense, and to every useful purpose, A BILL OF RIGHTS." *Federalist No. 84*. And when the Bill of Rights was ratified, it made express what the enumeration of powers necessarily implied: "The powers not delegated to the United States by the Constitution . . . are reserved to the States respectively, or to the people." U.S. Const., Amdt. 10. The Federal Government has expanded dramatically over the past two centuries, but it still must show that a constitutional grant of power authorizes each of its actions. See, e.g., *United States v. Comstock* (2010).

The same does not apply to the States, because the Constitution is not the source of their power. The Constitution may restrict state governments — as it does, for example, by forbidding them to deny any person the equal protection of the laws. But where such prohibitions do not apply, state governments do not need constitutional authorization to act. The States thus can and do perform many of the vital functions of modern government — punishing street crime, running public schools, and zoning property for development, to name but a few — even though the Constitution's text does not authorize any government to do so. Our cases refer to this general power of governing, possessed by the States but not by the Federal Government, as the "police power." See, e.g., *United States v. Morrison* (2000).

"State sovereignty is not just an end in itself: Rather, federalism secures to citizens the liberties that derive from the diffusion of sovereign power." *New York v. United States* (1992). Because the police power is controlled by 50 different States instead of one national sovereign, the facets of governing that touch on citizens' daily lives are normally administered by smaller governments closer to the governed. The Framers thus ensured that powers which "in the ordinary course of affairs, concern the lives, liberties, and properties of the people" were held by governments more local and more accountable than a distant federal bureaucracy. *Federalist No. 45* (J. Madison). The independent power of the States also serves as a check on the power of the Federal Government: "By denying any one government complete jurisdiction over all the concerns of public life, federalism protects the liberty of the individual from arbitrary power." *Bond v. United States* (2011).

This case concerns two powers that the Constitution does grant the Federal Government, but which must be read carefully to avoid creating a general federal authority akin to the police power. The Constitution authorizes Congress to "regulate Commerce with foreign Nations, and among the several States, and with the Indian Tribes." Art. I, §8, cl. 3. Our precedents read that to mean that Congress may regulate "the channels of interstate commerce," "persons or things in interstate commerce," and "those activities that substantially affect interstate commerce." *Morrison*. The power over activities that substantially affect interstate commerce can be expansive. That power has been held to authorize federal regulation of such seemingly local matters as a farmer's decision to grow wheat for himself and his livestock, and a loan shark's extortionate collections from a neighborhood butcher shop. See *Wickard v. Filburn* (1942); *Perez v. United States* (1971).

Congress may also "lay and collect Taxes, Duties, Imposts and Excises, to pay the Debts and provide for the common Defence and general Welfare of the United States." U.S. Const., Art. I, §8, cl. 1. Put simply, Congress may tax and spend. This grant gives the Federal Government considerable influence even in areas where it cannot directly regulate. The Federal Government may enact a tax on an activity that it cannot authorize, forbid, or otherwise control. See, e.g., *License Tax Cases* (1867). And in exercising its spending power, Congress may offer funds to the States, and may condition those offers on compliance with specified conditions. See, e.g., *College Savings Bank v. Florida Prepaid Postsecondary Ed. Expense Bd.* (1999). These offers may well induce the States to adopt policies that the Federal Government itself could not impose. See, e.g., *South Dakota v. Dole* (1987) (conditioning federal highway funds on States raising their drinking age to 21).

The reach of the Federal Government's enumerated powers is broader still because the Constitution authorizes Congress to "make all Laws which shall be necessary and proper for carrying into Execution the foregoing Powers." Art. I, §8, cl. 18. We have long read this provision to give Congress great latitude in exercising its powers: "Let the end be legitimate, let it be within the scope of the constitution, and all means which are appropriate, which are plainly adapted to that end, which are not prohibited, but consist with the letter and spirit of the constitution, are constitutional." *McCulloch.*

Our permissive reading of these powers is explained in part by a general reticence to invalidate the acts of the Nation's elected leaders. "Proper respect for a co-ordinate branch of the government" requires that we strike down an Act of Congress only if "the lack of constitutional authority to pass [the] act in question is clearly demonstrated." *United States v. Harris* (1883). Members of this Court are vested with the authority to interpret the law; we possess neither the expertise nor the prerogative to make policy judgments. Those decisions are entrusted to our Nation's elected leaders, who can be thrown out of office if the people disagree with them. It is not our job to protect the people from the consequences of their political choices.

Our deference in matters of policy cannot, however, become abdication in matters of law. "The powers of the legislature are defined and limited; and that those limits may not be mistaken, or forgotten, the constitution is written." *Marbury v. Madison* (1803). Our respect for Congress's policy judgments thus can never extend so far as to disavow restraints on federal power that the Constitution carefully constructed. "The peculiar circumstances of the moment may render a measure more or less wise, but cannot render it more or less constitutional." Chief Justice John Marshall, A Friend of the Constitution No. V, *Alexandria Gazette*, July 5, 1819. And there can be no question that it is the responsibility of this Court to enforce the limits on federal power by striking down acts of Congress that transgress those limits. *Marbury.*

The questions before us must be considered against the background of these basic principles.

I

In 2010, Congress enacted the Patient Protection and Affordable Care Act. The Act aims to increase the number of Americans covered by health insurance and decrease the cost of health care. The Act's 10 titles stretch over 900 pages and contain hundreds of provisions. This case concerns constitutional challenges to two key provisions, commonly referred to as the individual mandate and the Medicaid expansion. The individual mandate requires most Americans to maintain "minimum essential" health insurance coverage. 26 U.S.C. §5000A. The mandate does not apply to some individuals, such as prisoners and undocumented aliens. Many individuals will receive the required coverage through their employer, or from a government program such as Medicaid or Medicare. But for individuals who are not exempt and do not receive health insurance through a third party, the means of satisfying the requirement is to purchase insurance from a private company. Beginning in 2014, those who do not comply with the mandate must make a "[s]hared responsibility payment" to the Federal Government. That payment, which the Act describes as a "penalty," is calculated as a percentage of household income, subject to a floor based on a specified dollar amount and a ceiling based on the average annual premium the individual would have to pay for qualifying private health insurance. In 2016, for example, the penalty will be 2.5 percent of an individual's household income, but no less than $695 and no more than the average yearly premium for insurance that covers 60 percent of the cost of 10 specified services (e.g., prescription drugs and hospitalization). The Act provides that the penalty will be paid to the Internal Revenue Service with an individual's taxes, and "shall be assessed and collected in the same manner" as tax penalties, such as the penalty for claiming too large an income tax refund. The Act, however, bars the IRS from using several of its normal enforcement tools, such as criminal prosecutions and levies. And some individuals who are subject to the mandate are nonetheless exempt from the penalty — for example, those with income below a certain threshold and members of Indian tribes.

On the day the President signed the Act into law, Florida and 12 other States filed a complaint in the Federal District Court for the Northern District of Florida. Those plaintiffs — who are both respondents and petitioners here, depending on the issue — were subsequently joined by 13 more States, several individuals, and the National Federation of Independent Business. The plaintiffs alleged, among other things, that the individual mandate provisions of the Act exceeded Congress's powers under Article I of the Constitution. . . .

The second provision of the Affordable Care Act directly challenged here is the Medicaid expansion. Enacted in 1965, Medicaid offers federal funding to States to assist pregnant women, children, needy families, the blind, the elderly, and the disabled in obtaining medical care. In order to receive that funding, States must comply with federal criteria governing matters such as who receives care and what services are provided at what cost. By 1982 every State had chosen to participate in Medicaid. Federal funds received through the Medicaid program have become a substantial part of state budgets, now constituting over 10 percent of most States' total revenue.

The Affordable Care Act expands the scope of the Medicaid program and increases the number of individuals the States must cover. For example, the Act requires state programs to provide Medicaid coverage to adults with incomes up to 133 percent of the federal poverty level, whereas many States now cover adults with children only if their income is considerably lower, and do not cover childless adults at all. The Act increases federal funding to cover the States' costs in expanding Medicaid coverage, although States will bear a portion of the costs on their own. If a State does not comply with the Act's new coverage requirements, it may lose not only the federal funding for those requirements, but all of its federal Medicaid funds. . . .

III

The Government advances two theories for the proposition that Congress had constitutional authority to enact the individual mandate. First, the Government argues that Congress had the power to enact the mandate under the Commerce

Clause. Under that theory, Congress may order individuals to buy health insurance because the failure to do so affects interstate commerce, and could undercut the Affordable Care Act's other reforms. Second, the Government argues that if the commerce power does not support the mandate, we should nonetheless uphold it as an exercise of Congress's power to tax. According to the Government, even if Congress lacks the power to direct individuals to buy insurance, the only effect of the individual mandate is to raise taxes on those who do not do so, and thus the law may be upheld as a tax.

A

The Government's first argument is that the individual mandate is a valid exercise of Congress's power under the Commerce Clause and the Necessary and Proper Clause. According to the Government, the health care market is characterized by a significant cost-shifting problem. Everyone will eventually need health care at a time and to an extent they cannot predict, but if they do not have insurance, they often will not be able to pay for it. Because state and federal laws nonetheless require hospitals to provide a certain degree of care to individuals without regard to their ability to pay, hospitals end up receiving compensation for only a portion of the services they provide. To recoup the losses, hospitals pass on the cost to insurers through higher rates, and insurers, in turn, pass on the cost to policy holders in the form of higher premiums. Congress estimated that the cost of uncompensated care raises family health insurance premiums, on average, by over $1,000 per year. In the Affordable Care Act, Congress addressed the problem of those who cannot obtain insurance coverage because of preexisting conditions or other health issues. It did so through the Act's "guaranteed-issue" and "community-rating" provisions. These provisions together prohibit insurance companies from denying coverage to those with such conditions or charging unhealthy individuals higher premiums than healthy individuals. The guaranteed-issue and community-rating reforms do not, however, address the issue of healthy individuals who choose not to purchase insurance to cover potential health care needs. In fact, the reforms sharply exacerbate that problem, by providing an incentive for individuals to delay purchasing health insurance until they become sick, relying on the promise of guaranteed and affordable coverage.

The reforms also threaten to impose massive new costs on insurers, who are required to accept unhealthy individuals but prohibited from charging them rates necessary to pay for their coverage. This will lead insurers to significantly increase premiums on everyone.

The individual mandate was Congress's solution to these problems. By requiring that individuals purchase health insurance, the mandate prevents cost-shifting by those who would otherwise go without it. In addition, the mandate forces into the insurance risk pool more healthy individuals, whose premiums on average will be higher than their health care expenses. This allows insurers to subsidize the costs of covering the unhealthy individuals the reforms require them to accept. The Government claims that Congress has power under the Commerce and Necessary and Proper Clauses to enact this solution.

1

The Government contends that the individual mandate is within Congress's power because the failure to purchase insurance "has a substantial and deleterious effect on interstate commerce" by creating the cost-shifting problem. The path of our Commerce Clause decisions has not always run smooth, see *United States v. Lopez* (1995), but it is now well established that Congress has broad authority under the Clause. We have recognized, for example, that "[t]he power of Congress over interstate commerce is not confined to the regulation of commerce among the states," but extends to activities that "have a substantial effect on interstate commerce." *United States v. Darby* (1941). Congress's power, moreover, is not limited to regulation of an activity that by itself substantially affects interstate commerce, but also extends to activities that do so only when aggregated with similar activities of others. See *Wickard.*

Given its expansive scope, it is no surprise that Congress has employed the commerce power in a wide variety of ways to address the pressing needs of the time. But Congress has never attempted to rely on that power to compel individuals not engaged in commerce to purchase an unwanted product. Legislative novelty is not necessarily fatal; there is a first time for everything. But sometimes "the most telling indication of [a] severe constitutional problem . . . is the lack of historical precedent" for Congress's action. *Free Enterprise Fund v. Public Company Accounting Oversight Bd.* (2010). At the very least, we should "pause to consider the implications of the Government's arguments" when confronted with such new conceptions of federal power. *Lopez.*

The Constitution grants Congress the power to "*regulate* Commerce." Art. I, §8, cl. 3 (emphasis added). The power to *regulate* commerce presupposes the existence of commercial activity to be regulated. If the power to "regulate" something included the power to create it, many of the provisions in the Constitution would be superfluous. For example, the Constitution gives Congress the power to "coin Money," in addition to the power to "regulate the Value thereof." And it gives Congress the power to "raise and support Armies" and to "provide and maintain a Navy," in addition to the power to "make Rules for the Government and Regulation of the land and naval Forces." If the power to regulate the armed forces or the value of money included the power to bring the subject of the regulation into existence, the specific grant of such powers would have been unnecessary. The language of the Constitution reflects the natural understanding that the power to regulate assumes there is already something to be regulated. See *Gibbons* ("[T]he enlightened patriots who framed our constitution, and the people who adopted it, must be understood to have employed words in their natural sense, and to have intended what they have said").

Our precedent also reflects this understanding. As expansive as our cases construing the scope of the commerce power have been, they all have one thing in common: They uniformly describe the power as reaching "activity." It is nearly impossible to avoid the word when quoting them. See, e.g., *Lopez* ("Where economic activity substantially affects interstate commerce, legislation regulating that activity will be sustained"); *Perez* ("Where the *class of activities* is regulated and that *class* is within the reach of federal power, the courts have no power to excise, as trivial, individual instances of the class" (emphasis in original)); *Wickard* ("[E]ven if appellee's activity be local and though it may not be regarded as commerce, it may still, whatever its nature, be reached by Congress if it exerts a substantial economic effect on interstate commerce"); NLRB v. Jones & Laughlin Steel Corp., 301 U.S. 1, 37 (1937) ("Although activities may be intrastate in character when separately considered, if they have such a close and substantial relation to interstate commerce that their control is essential or appropriate to protect that commerce from burdens and obstructions, Congress cannot be denied the power to exercise that control").

The individual mandate, however, does not regulate existing commercial activity. It instead compels individuals to become active in commerce by purchasing a product, on the ground that their failure to do so affects interstate commerce. Construing the Commerce Clause to permit Congress to regulate individuals precisely *because* they are doing nothing would open a new and potentially vast domain to congressional authority. Every day individuals do not do an infinite number of things. In some cases they decide not to do something; in others they simply fail to do it. Allowing Congress to justify federal regulation by pointing to the effect of inaction on commerce would bring countless decisions an individual could potentially make within the scope of federal regulation, and — under the Government's theory — empower Congress to make those decisions for him.

Applying the Government's logic to the familiar case of *Wickard v. Filburn* shows how far that logic would carry us from the notion of a government of limited powers. In *Wickard*, the Court famously upheld a federal penalty imposed on a farmer for growing wheat for consumption on his own farm. That amount of wheat caused the farmer to exceed his quota under a program designed to support the price of wheat by limiting supply. The Court rejected the farmer's argument that growing wheat for home consumption was beyond the reach of the commerce power. It did so on the ground that the farmer's decision to grow wheat for his own use allowed him to avoid purchasing wheat in the market. That decision, when considered in the aggregate along with similar decisions of others, would have had a substantial effect on the interstate market for wheat.

Wickard has long been regarded as "perhaps the most far reaching example of Commerce Clause authority over intrastate activity," *Lopez*, but the Government's theory in this case would go much further. Under *Wickard* it is within Congress's power to regulate the market for wheat by supporting its price. But price can be supported by increasing demand as well as by decreasing supply. The aggregated decisions of some consumers not to purchase wheat have a substantial effect on the price of wheat, just as decisions not to purchase health insurance have on the price of insurance. Congress can therefore command that those not buying wheat do so, just as it argues here that it may command that those not buying health insurance do so. The farmer in *Wickard* was at least actively engaged in the production of wheat, and the Government could regulate that activity because of its effect on commerce. The Government's theory here would effectively override that limitation, by establishing that individuals may be regulated under the Commerce Clause whenever enough of them are not doing something the Government would have them do.

Indeed, the Government's logic would justify a mandatory purchase to solve almost any problem. To consider a different example in the health care market, many Americans do not eat a balanced diet. That group makes up a larger percentage of the total population than those without health insurance. The failure of that group to have a healthy diet increases health care costs, to a greater extent than the failure of the uninsured to purchase insurance. Those increased costs are borne in part by other Americans who must pay more, just as the uninsured shift costs to the insured. Congress addressed the insurance problem by ordering everyone to buy insurance. Under the Government's theory, Congress could address the diet problem by ordering everyone to buy vegetables.

People, for reasons of their own, often fail to do things that would be good for them or good for society. Those failures — joined with the similar failures of others — can readily have a substantial effect on interstate commerce. Under the Government's logic, that authorizes Congress to use its commerce power to compel citizens to act as the Government would have them act.

That is not the country the Framers of our Constitution envisioned. James Madison explained that the Commerce Clause was "an addition which few oppose and from which no apprehensions are entertained." *Federalist No. 45*. While Congress's authority under the Commerce Clause has of course expanded with the growth of the national economy, our cases have "always recognized that the power to regulate commerce, though broad indeed, has limits." *Maryland v. Wirtz* (1968). The Government's theory would erode those limits, permitting Congress to reach beyond the natural extent of its authority, "everywhere extending the sphere of its activity and drawing all power into its impetuous vortex." *Federalist No. 48*, at 309 (J. Madison). Congress already enjoys vast power to regulate much of what we do. Accepting the Government's theory would give Congress the same license to regulate what we do not do, fundamentally changing the relation between the citizen and the Federal Government.

To an economist, perhaps, there is no difference between activity and inactivity; both have measurable economic effects on commerce. But the distinction between doing something and doing nothing would not have been lost on the Framers, who were "practical statesmen," not metaphysical philosophers. Industrial Union Dept., AFL-CIO v. American Petroleum Institute (1980) (Rehnquist, J., concurring in judgment). . . . The Framers gave Congress the power to *regulate* commerce, not to *compel* it, and for over 200 years both our decisions and Congress's actions have reflected this understanding. There is no reason to depart from that understanding now. . . . The individual mandate forces individuals into commerce precisely because they elected to refrain from commercial activity. Such a law cannot be sustained under a clause authorizing Congress to "regulate Commerce."

2

The Government next contends that Congress has the power under the Necessary and Proper Clause to enact the individual mandate because the mandate is an "integral part of a comprehensive scheme of economic regulation" — the guaranteed-issue and community-rating insurance reforms. Under this argument, it is not necessary to consider the effect that an individual's inactivity may have on interstate commerce; It is enough that Congress regulate commercial activity in a way that requires regulation of inactivity to be effective.

The power to "make all Laws which shall be necessary and proper for carrying into Execution" the powers enumerated in the Constitution, vests Congress with authority to enact provisions "incidental to the [enumerated] power, and conducive to its beneficial exercise," *McCulloch*. Although the Clause gives Congress authority to "legislate on that vast mass of incidental powers which must be involved in the constitution," it does not license the exercise of any "great substantive and independent power[s]" beyond those specifically enumerated. *Id.* Instead, the Clause is "'merely a declaration, for the removal of all uncertainty, that the means of carrying into execution those [powers] otherwise granted are included in the grant.'" *Kinsella v. United States ex rel. Singleton* (1960) (quoting James Madison).

As our jurisprudence under the Necessary and Proper Clause has developed, we have been very deferential to Congress's determination that a regulation is "necessary." We have thus upheld laws that are "'convenient, or useful' or 'conducive' to the authority's 'beneficial exercise.'" *Comstock*. But we have also carried out our responsibility to declare unconstitutional those laws that undermine the structure of government established by the Constitution. Such laws, which are not "consist[ent] with the letter and spirit of the constitution," *McCulloch*, are not "*proper* [means] for carrying into Execution" Congress's enumerated powers. Rather, they are, "in the words of The Federalist, 'merely acts of usurpation' which 'deserve to be treated as such.'" *Printz v. United States* (1997) (quoting *Federalist No. 33* (A. Hamilton)); see also *New York*; *Comstock* (Kennedy, J., concurring in judgment) ("It is of fundamental importance to consider whether essential attributes of state sovereignty are compromised by the assertion of federal power under the Necessary and Proper Clause . . .").

Applying these principles, the individual mandate cannot be sustained under the Necessary and Proper Clause as an essential component of the insurance reforms. Each of our prior cases upholding laws under that Clause involved exercises of authority derivative of, and in service to, a granted power. For example, we have upheld provisions permitting continued confinement of those *already in federal custody* when they could not be safely released, *Comstock*; criminalizing bribes involving organizations *receiving federal funds*, *Sabri v. United States* (2004); and tolling state statutes of limitations while cases are *pending in federal court*, *Jinks v. Richland County* (2003). The individual mandate, by contrast, vests Congress with the extraordinary ability to create the necessary predicate to the exercise of an enumerated power.

This is in no way an authority that is "narrow in scope," *Comstock*, or "incidental" to the exercise of the commerce power, *McCulloch*. Rather, such a conception of the Necessary and Proper Clause would work a substantial expansion of federal authority. No longer would Congress be limited to regulating under the Commerce Clause those who by some preexisting activity bring themselves within the sphere of federal regulation. Instead, Congress could reach beyond the natural limit of its authority and draw within its regulatory scope those who otherwise would be outside of it. Even if the individual mandate is "necessary" to the Act's insurance reforms, such an expansion of federal power is not a "proper" means for making those reforms effective.

The Government relies primarily on our decision in *Gonzales v. Raich*. In *Raich*, we considered "comprehensive legislation to regulate the interstate market" in marijuana. Certain individuals sought an exemption from that regulation on the ground that they engaged in only intrastate possession and consumption. We denied any exemption, on the ground that marijuana is a fungible commodity, so that any marijuana could be readily diverted into the interstate market. Congress's attempt to regulate the interstate market for marijuana would therefore have been substantially undercut if it could not also regulate intrastate possession and consumption. Accordingly, we recognized that "Congress was acting well within its authority" under the Necessary and Proper Clause even though its "regulation ensnare[d] some purely intrastate activity." *Raich* thus did not involve the exercise of any "great substantive and independent power," *McCulloch*, of the sort at issue here. Instead, it concerned only the constitutionality of "individual *applications* of a concededly valid statutory scheme." *Raich* (emphasis added).

Just as the individual mandate cannot be sustained as a law regulating the substantial effects of the failure to purchase health insurance, neither can it be upheld as a "necessary and proper" component of the insurance reforms. The commerce power thus does not authorize the mandate.

B

That is not the end of the matter. Because the Commerce Clause does not support the individual mandate, it is necessary to turn to the Government's second argument: that the mandate may be upheld as within Congress's enumerated power to "lay and collect Taxes." Art. I, §8, cl. 1.

The Government's tax power argument asks us to view the statute differently than we did in considering its commerce power theory. In making its Commerce Clause argument, the Government defended the mandate as a regulation requiring individuals to purchase health insurance. The Government does not claim that the taxing power allows Congress to issue such a command. Instead, the Government asks us to read the mandate not as ordering individuals to buy insurance, but rather as imposing a tax on those who do not buy that product.

The text of a statute can sometimes have more than one possible meaning. To take a familiar example, a law that reads "no vehicles in the park" might, or might not, ban bicycles in the park. And it is well established that if a statute has two possible meanings, one of which violates the Constitution, courts should adopt the meaning that does not do so. Justice Story said that 180 years ago: "No court ought, unless the terms of an act rendered it unavoidable, to give a construction to it which should involve a violation, however unintentional, of the constitution." *Parsons v. Bedford* (1830). Justice Holmes made the same point a century later: "[T]he rule is settled that as between two possible interpretations of a statute, by one of which it would be unconstitutional and by the other valid, our plain duty is to adopt that which will save the Act." *Blodgett v. Holden* (1927) (concurring opinion).

The most straightforward reading of the mandate is that it commands individuals to purchase insurance. After all, it states that individuals "shall" maintain health insurance. Congress thought it could enact such a command under the Commerce Clause, and the Government primarily defended the law on that basis. But, for the reasons explained above, the Commerce Clause does not give Congress that power. Under our precedent, it is therefore necessary to ask whether the Government's alternative reading of the statute — that it only imposes a tax on those without insurance — is a reasonable one.

Under the mandate, if an individual does not maintain health insurance, the only consequence is that he must make an additional payment to the IRS when he pays his taxes. That, according to the Government, means the mandate can be regarded as establishing a condition — not owning health insurance — that triggers a tax — the required payment to the IRS. Under that theory, the mandate is not a legal command to buy insurance. Rather, it makes going without insurance just another thing the Government taxes, like buying gasoline or earning income. And if the mandate is in effect just a tax hike on certain taxpayers who do not have health insurance, it may be within Congress's constitutional power to tax.

The question is not whether that is the most natural interpretation of the mandate, but only whether it is a "fairly possible" one. *Crowell v. Benson* (1932). As we have explained, "every reasonable construction must be resorted to, in order to save a statute from unconstitutionality." *Hooper v. California* (1895). The Government asks us to interpret the mandate as imposing a tax, if it would otherwise violate the Constitution. Granting the Act the full measure of deference owed to federal statutes, it can be so read, for the reasons set forth below.

C

The exaction the Affordable Care Act imposes on those without health insurance looks like a tax in many respects. The "[s]hared responsibility payment," as the statute entitles it, is paid into the Treasury by "taxpayer[s]" when they file their tax returns. It does not apply to individuals who do not pay federal income taxes because their household income is less than the filing threshold in the Internal Revenue Code. For taxpayers who do owe the payment, its amount is determined by such familiar factors as taxable income, number of dependents, and joint filing status. The requirement to pay is found in the Internal Revenue Code and enforced by the IRS, which — as we previously explained — must assess and collect it "in the same manner as taxes." This process yields the essential feature of any tax: it produces at least some revenue for the Government. Indeed, the payment is expected to raise about $4 billion per year by 2017. It is of course true that the Act describes the payment as a "penalty," not a "tax." But . . . that label . . . does not determine whether the payment may be viewed as an exercise of Congress's taxing power. . . .

We have . . . held that exactions not labeled taxes nonetheless were authorized by Congress's power to tax. In the *License Tax Cases*, for example, we held that federal licenses to sell liquor and lottery tickets — for which the licensee had to pay a fee — could be sustained as exercises of the taxing power. And in *New York v. United States* we upheld as a tax a "surcharge" on out-of-state nuclear waste shipments, a portion of which was paid to the Federal Treasury. We thus ask whether the shared responsibility payment falls within Congress's taxing power, "[d]isregarding the designation of the exaction, and viewing its substance and application." *United States v. Constantine* (1935)

Our cases confirm this functional approach. For example, in *Bailey v. Drexel Furniture* (1922), we focused on three practical characteristics of the so-called tax on employing child laborers that convinced us the "tax" was actually a penalty. First, the tax imposed an exceedingly heavy burden — 10 percent of a company's net income — on those who employed children, no matter how small their infraction. Second, it imposed that exaction only on those who knowingly employed underage laborers. Such scienter requirements are typical of punitive statutes, because Congress often wishes to punish only those who intentionally break the law. Third, this "tax" was enforced in part by the Department of Labor, an agency responsible for punishing violations of labor laws, not collecting revenue.

The same analysis here suggests that the shared responsibility payment may for constitutional purposes be considered a tax, not a penalty: First, for most Americans the amount due will be far less than the price of insurance, and, by statute, it can never be more. It may often be a reasonable financial decision to make the payment rather than purchase insurance, unlike the "prohibitory" financial punishment in *Drexel Furniture*. Second, the individual mandate contains no scienter requirement. Third, the payment is collected solely by the IRS through the normal means of taxation — except that the Service is *not* allowed to use those means most suggestive of a punitive sanction, such as criminal prosecution. The reasons the Court in *Drexel Furniture* held that what was called a "tax" there was a penalty support the conclusion that what is called a "penalty" here may be viewed as a tax.[42]

None of this is to say that the payment is not intended to affect individual conduct. Although the payment will raise considerable revenue, it is plainly designed to expand health insurance coverage. But taxes that seek to influence conduct are nothing new. Some of our earliest federal taxes sought to deter the purchase of imported manufactured goods in order to foster the growth of domestic industry. Today, federal and state taxes can compose more than half the retail price of cigarettes, not just to raise more money, but to encourage people to quit smoking. And we have upheld such obviously regulatory measures as taxes on selling marijuana and sawed-off shotguns. See *United States v. Sanchez* (1950); *Sonzinsky v. United States* (1937). Indeed, "[e]very tax is in some measure regulatory. To some extent it interposes an economic impediment to the activity taxed as compared with others not taxed." *Sonzinsky*. That §5000A seeks to shape decisions about whether

[42] We do not suggest that any exaction lacking a scienter requirement and enforced by the IRS is within the taxing power. See (joint opinion of Scalia, Kennedy, Thomas, and Alito, JJ., dissenting). Congress could not, for example, expand its authority to impose criminal fines by creating strict liability offenses enforced by the IRS rather than the FBI. But the fact the exaction here is paid like a tax, to the agency that collects taxes — rather than, for example, exacted by Department of Labor inspectors after ferreting out willful malfeasance — suggests that this exaction may be viewed as a tax.

to buy health insurance does not mean that it cannot be a valid exercise of the taxing power.

In distinguishing penalties from taxes, this Court has explained that "if the concept of penalty means anything, it means punishment for an unlawful act or omission." *United States v. Reorganized CF&I Fabricators of Utah, Inc.* (1996); see also *United States v. La Franca* (1931) ("[A] penalty, as the word is here used, is an exaction imposed by statute as punishment for an unlawful act"). While the individual mandate clearly aims to induce the purchase of health insurance, it need not be read to declare that failing to do so is unlawful. Neither the Act nor any other law attaches negative legal consequences to not buying health insurance, beyond requiring a payment to the IRS. The Government agrees with that reading, confirming that if someone chooses to pay rather than obtain health insurance, they have fully complied with the law.

Indeed, it is estimated that four million people each year will choose to pay the IRS rather than buy insurance. We would expect Congress to be troubled by that prospect if such conduct were unlawful. That Congress apparently regards such extensive failure to comply with the mandate as tolerable suggests that Congress did not think it was creating four million outlaws. It suggests instead that the shared responsibility payment merely imposes a tax citizens may lawfully choose to pay in lieu of buying health insurance. . . .

The joint dissenters argue that we cannot uphold §5000A as a tax because Congress did not "frame" it as such. In effect, they contend that even if the Constitution permits Congress to do exactly what we interpret this statute to do, the law must be struck down because Congress used the wrong labels. An example may help illustrate why labels should not control here. Suppose Congress enacted a statute providing that every taxpayer who owns a house without energy efficient windows must pay $50 to the IRS. The amount due is adjusted based on factors such as taxable income and joint filing status, and is paid along with the taxpayer's income tax return. Those whose income is below the filing threshold need not pay. The required payment is not called a "tax," a "penalty," or anything else. No one would doubt that this law imposed a tax, and was within Congress's power to tax. That conclusion should not change simply because Congress used the word "penalty" to describe the payment. Interpreting such a law to be a tax would hardly "[i]mpos[e] a tax through judicial legislation." Rather, it would give practical effect to the Legislature's enactment.

Our precedent demonstrates that Congress had the power to impose the exaction in §5000A under the taxing power, and that §5000A need not be read to do more than impose a tax. That is sufficient to sustain it. The "question of the constitutionality of action taken by Congress does not depend on recitals of the power which it undertakes to exercise." *Woods v. Cloyd W. Miller Co.* (1948).

Even if the taxing power enables Congress to impose a tax on not obtaining health insurance, any tax must still comply with other requirements in the Constitution. Plaintiffs argue that the shared responsibility payment does not do so, citing Article I, §9, clause 4. That clause provides: "No Capitation, or other direct, Tax shall be laid, unless in Proportion to the Census or Enumeration herein before directed to be taken." This requirement means that any "direct Tax" must be apportioned so that each State pays in proportion to its population. According to the plaintiffs, if the individual mandate imposes a tax, it is a direct tax, and it is unconstitutional because Congress made no effort to apportion it among the States.

Even when the Direct Tax Clause was written it was unclear what else, other than a capitation (also known as a "head tax" or a "poll tax"), might be a direct tax. Soon after the framing, Congress passed a tax on ownership of carriages, over James Madison's objection that it was an unapportioned direct tax. This Court upheld the tax, in part reasoning that apportioning such a tax would make little sense, because it would have required taxing carriage owners at dramatically different rates depending on how many carriages were in their home State. See *Hylton v. United States* (1796) (opinion of Chase, J.). The Court was unanimous, and those Justices who wrote opinions either directly asserted or strongly suggested that only two forms of taxation were direct: capitations and land taxes.

That narrow view of what a direct tax might be persisted for a century. . . .

There may, however, be a more fundamental objection to a tax on those who lack health insurance. Even if only a tax, the payment under §5000A(b) remains a burden that the Federal Government imposes for an omission, not an act. If it is troubling to interpret the Commerce Clause as authorizing Congress to regulate those who abstain from commerce, perhaps it should be similarly troubling to permit Congress to impose a tax for not doing something.

Three considerations allay this concern. First, and most importantly, it is abundantly clear the Constitution does not guarantee that individuals may avoid taxation through inactivity. A capitation, after all, is a tax that everyone must pay simply for existing, and capitations are expressly contemplated by the Constitution. The Court today holds that our Constitution protects us from federal regulation under the Commerce Clause so long as we abstain from the regulated activity. But from its creation, the Constitution has made no such promise with respect to taxes. See Letter from Benjamin Franklin to M. Le Roy (Nov. 13, 1789) ("Our new Constitution is now established . . . but in this world nothing can be said to be certain, except death and taxes").

Whether the mandate can be upheld under the Commerce Clause is a question about the scope of federal authority. Its answer depends on whether Congress can exercise what all acknowledge to be the novel course of directing individuals to purchase insurance. Congress's use of the Taxing Clause to encourage buying something is, by contrast, not new. Tax incentives already promote, for example, purchasing homes and professional educations. Sustaining the mandate as a tax depends only on whether Congress has properly exercised its taxing power to encourage purchasing health insurance, not whether it can. Upholding the individual mandate under the Taxing Clause thus does not recognize any new federal power. It determines that Congress has used an existing one.

Second, Congress's ability to use its taxing power to influence conduct is not without limits. A few of our cases policed these limits aggressively, invalidating punitive exactions obviously designed to regulate behavior otherwise regarded at the time as beyond federal authority. See, e.g., *United States v. Butler* (1936); *Drexel Furniture*. More often and more recently we have declined to closely examine the regulatory motive or effect of revenue-raising measures. We have nonetheless maintained that "'there comes a time in the extension of the penalizing features of the so-called tax when it loses its character as such and becomes a mere penalty with the characteristics of regulation and punishment.'" *Kurth Ranch* (quoting *Drexel Furniture*).

We have already explained that the shared responsibility payment's practical characteristics pass muster as a tax under our narrowest interpretations of the taxing power. Because the tax at hand is within even those strict limits, we need not here decide the precise point at which an exaction becomes so punitive that the taxing power does not authorize it. It remains true, however, that the "'power to tax is not the power to destroy while this Court sits.'" *Oklahoma Tax Comm'n v. Texas Co.* (1949) (quoting *Panhandle Oil Co. v. Mississippi ex rel. Knox* (1928) (Holmes, J., dissenting)).

Third, although the breadth of Congress's power to tax is greater than its power to regulate commerce, the taxing power does not give Congress the same degree of control over individual behavior. Once we recognize that Congress may regulate a particular decision under the Commerce Clause, the Federal Government can bring its full weight to bear. Congress may simply command individuals to do as it directs. An individual who disobeys may be subjected to criminal sanctions. Those sanctions can include not only fines and imprisonment, but all the attendant consequences of being branded a criminal: deprivation of otherwise protected civil rights, such as the right to bear arms or vote in elections; loss of employment opportunities; social stigma; and severe disabilities in other controversies, such as custody or immigration disputes.

By contrast, Congress's authority under the taxing power is limited to requiring an individual to pay money into the Federal Treasury, no more. If a tax is properly paid, the Government has no power to compel or punish individuals subject to it. We do not make light of the severe burden that taxation — especially taxation motivated by a regulatory purpose — can impose. But imposition of a tax nonetheless leaves an individual with a lawful choice to do or not do a certain act, so long as he is willing to pay a tax levied on that choice.

The Affordable Care Act's requirement that certain individuals pay a financial penalty for not obtaining health insurance may reasonably be characterized as a tax. Because the Constitution permits such a tax, it is not our role to forbid it, or to pass upon its wisdom or fairness. . . .

D

Justice Ginsburg questions the necessity of rejecting the Government's commerce power argument, given that §5000A can be upheld under the taxing power. But the statute reads more naturally as a command to buy insurance than as a tax, and I would uphold it as a command if the Constitution allowed it. It is only because the Commerce Clause does not authorize such a command that it is necessary to reach the taxing power question. And it is only because we have a duty to construe a statute to save it, if fairly possible, that §5000A can be interpreted as a tax. Without deciding the Commerce Clause question, I would find no basis to adopt such a saving construction. The Federal Government does not have the power to order people to buy health insurance. Section 5000A would therefore be unconstitutional if read as a command. The Federal Government does have the power to impose a tax on those without health insurance. Section 5000A is therefore constitutional, because it can reasonably be read as a tax. . . .

* * *

The Affordable Care Act is constitutional in part and unconstitutional in part. The individual mandate cannot be upheld as an exercise of Congress's power under the Commerce Clause. That Clause authorizes Congress to regulate interstate commerce, not to order individuals to engage in it. In this case, however, it is reasonable to construe what Congress has done as increasing taxes on those who have a certain amount of income, but choose to go without health insurance. Such legislation is within Congress's power to tax. [The Court's treatment of the Medicaid expansion appears below. — EDS.]

The Framers created a Federal Government of limited powers, and assigned to this Court the duty of enforcing those limits. The Court does so today. But the Court does not express any opinion on the wisdom of the Affordable Care Act. Under the Constitution, that judgment is reserved to the people.

The judgment of the Court of Appeals for the Eleventh Circuit is affirmed in part and reversed in part.

It is so ordered.

JUSTICE GINSBURG, with whom JUSTICE SOTOMAYOR joins, and with whom JUSTICE BREYER and JUSTICE KAGAN join as to Parts I, II, III, and IV, concurring in part, concurring in the judgment in part, and dissenting in part. . . .

Unlike The Chief Justice, . . . I would hold, alternatively, that the Commerce Clause authorizes Congress to enact the minimum coverage provision. I would also hold that the Spending Clause permits the Medicaid expansion exactly as Congress enacted it.

I

The provision of health care is today a concern of national dimension, just as the provision of old-age and survivors' benefits was in the 1930's. In the Social Security Act, Congress installed a federal system to provide monthly benefits to retired wage earners and, eventually, to their survivors. Beyond question, Congress could have adopted a similar scheme for health care. Congress chose, instead, to preserve a central role for private insurers and state governments. According to The Chief Justice, the Commerce Clause does not permit that preservation. This rigid reading of the Clause makes scant sense and is stunningly retrogressive. Since 1937, our precedent has recognized Congress' large authority to set the Nation's course in the economic and social welfare realm. See *United States v. Darby* (1941) (overruling *Hammer v. Dagenhart* (1918), and recognizing that "regulations of commerce which do not infringe some constitutional prohibition are within the plenary power conferred on Congress by the Commerce Clause"); *NLRB v. Jones & Laughlin Steel Corp.* (1937) ("[The commerce] power is plenary and may be exerted to protect interstate commerce no matter what the source of the dangers which threaten it."). The Chief Justice's crabbed reading of the Commerce Clause harks back to the era in which the Court routinely thwarted Congress' efforts to regulate the national economy in the interest of those who labor to sustain it. It is a reading that should not have staying power. . . .

II

A

The Commerce Clause, it is widely acknowledged, "was the Framers' response to the central problem that gave rise to the Constitution itself." *EEOC v. Wyoming* (1983) (Stevens, J., concurring). Under the Articles of Confederation, the Constitution's precursor, the regulation of commerce was left to the States. This scheme proved unworkable, because the individual States, understandably focused on their own economic interests, often failed to take actions critical to the success of the Nation as a whole. See Vices of the Political System of the United States, in James Madison: Writings (As a result of the "want of concert in matters where common interest requires it," the "national dignity, interest, and revenue [have] suffered.").

What was needed was a "national Government . . . armed with a positive & compleat authority in all cases where uniform measures are necessary." See Letter from James Madison to Edmund Randolph (Apr. 8, 1787). See also Letter from George Washington to James Madison (Nov. 30, 1785) ("We are either a United people, or we are not. If the former, let us, in all matters of general concern act as a nation, which ha[s] national objects to promote, and a national character to support."). The Framers' solution was the Commerce Clause, which, as they perceived it, granted Congress the authority to enact economic legislation "in all Cases for the general Interests of the Union, and also in those Cases to which the States are separately incompetent." Records of the Federal Convention of 1787.

The Framers understood that the "general Interests of the Union" would change over time, in ways they could not anticipate. Accordingly, they recognized that the Constitution was of necessity a "great outlin[e]," not a detailed blueprint, see *McCulloch v. Maryland* (1819), and that its provisions included broad concepts, to be "explained by the context or by the facts of the case," Letter from James Madison to N. P. Trist (Dec. 1831). "Nothing . . . can be more fallacious," Alexander Hamilton emphasized, "than to infer the extent of any power, proper to be lodged in the national government, from . . . its immediate necessities. There ought to be a CAPACITY to provide for future contingencies[,] as they may happen; and as these are illimitable in their nature, it is impossible safely to limit that capacity." *Federalist No. 34*. See also *McCulloch* (The Necessary and Proper Clause is lodged "in a constitution[,] intended to endure for ages to come, and consequently, to be adapted to the various crises of human affairs.").

B

Consistent with the Framers' intent, we have repeatedly emphasized that Congress' authority under the Commerce Clause is dependent upon "practical" considerations, including "actual experience." *Jones & Laughlin Steel Corp.* We afford Congress the leeway "to undertake to solve national problems directly and realistically." *American Power & Light Co. v. SEC* (1946).

Until today, this Court's pragmatic approach to judging whether Congress validly exercised its commerce power was guided by two familiar principles. First, Congress has the power to regulate economic activities "that substantially affect interstate commerce." *Gonzales v. Raich* (2005). This capacious power extends even to local activities that, viewed in the aggregate, have a substantial impact on interstate commerce. See also *Wickard* ("[E]ven if appellee's activity be local and though it may not be regarded as commerce, it may still, *whatever its nature*, be reached by Congress if it exerts a substantial economic effect on interstate commerce." (emphasis added)).

Second, we owe a large measure of respect to Congress when it frames and enacts economic and social legislation. See *Raich*. When appraising such legislation, we ask only (1) whether Congress had a "rational basis" for concluding that the regulated activity substantially affects interstate commerce, and (2) whether there is a "reasonable connection between the regulatory means selected and the asserted ends." [*Hodel v. Indiana* (1981).] See also *Raich*; *Lopez*; *Hodel v. Virginia Surface Mining & Reclamation Assn., Inc.* (1981); *Katzenbach v. McClung* (1964); *Heart of Atlanta Motel, Inc. v. United States* (1964); *United States v. Carolene Products Co.* (1938). In answering these questions, we presume the statute under review is constitutional and may strike it down only on a "plain showing" that Congress acted irrationally. *United States v. Morrison* (2000).

C

Straightforward application of these principles would require the Court to hold that the minimum coverage provision is proper Commerce Clause legislation. Beyond dispute, Congress had a rational basis for concluding that the uninsured, as a class, substantially affect interstate commerce. Those without insurance consume billions of dollars of health-care products and services each year. Those goods are produced, sold, and delivered largely by national and regional companies who routinely transact business across state lines. The uninsured also cross state lines to receive care. Some have medical emergencies while away from home. Others, when sick, go to a neighboring State that provides better care for those who have not prepaid for care.

Not only do those without insurance consume a large amount of health care each year; critically, . . . their inability to pay for a significant portion of that consumption drives up market prices, foists costs on other consumers, and reduces market efficiency and stability. Given these far-reaching effects on interstate commerce, the decision to forgo insurance is hardly inconsequential or equivalent to "doing nothing," *ante*; it is, instead, an economic decision Congress has the authority to address under the Commerce Clause. See *Wickard* ("It is well established by decisions of this Court that the power to regulate commerce includes the power to regulate the prices at which commodities in that commerce are dealt in and *practices affecting such prices*." (emphasis added)).

The minimum coverage provision, furthermore, bears a "reasonable connection" to Congress' goal of protecting the health-care market from the disruption caused by individuals who fail to obtain insurance. By requiring those who do not carry insurance to pay a toll, the minimum coverage provision gives individuals a strong incentive to insure. This incentive, Congress had good reason to believe, would reduce the number of uninsured and, correspondingly, mitigate the adverse impact the uninsured have on the national health-care market.

Congress also acted reasonably in requiring uninsured individuals, whether sick or healthy, either to obtain insurance or to pay the specified penalty. As earlier observed, because every person is at risk of needing care at any moment, all those who lack insurance, regardless of their current health status, adversely affect the price of health care and health insurance. Moreover, an insurance-purchase requirement limited to those in need of immediate care simply could not work. Insurance companies would either charge these individuals prohibitively expensive premiums, or, if community rating regulations were in place, close up shop.

"[W]here we find that the legislators . . . have a rational basis for finding a chosen regulatory scheme necessary to the protection of commerce, our investigation is at an end." *Katzenbach*. Congress' enactment of the minimum coverage provision, which addresses a specific interstate problem in a practical, experience informed manner, easily meets this criterion.

D

Rather than evaluating the constitutionality of the minimum coverage provision in the manner established by our precedents, The Chief Justice relies on a newly minted constitutional doctrine. The commerce power does not, The Chief Justice announces, permit Congress to "compe[l] individuals to become active in commerce by purchasing a product." (emphasis deleted).

1

a

The Chief Justice's novel constraint on Congress' commerce power gains no force from our precedent and for that reason alone warrants disapprobation. But even assuming, for the moment, that Congress lacks authority under the Commerce Clause to "compel individuals not engaged in commerce to purchase an unwanted product," such a limitation would be inapplicable here. Everyone will, at some point, consume health-care products and services. Thus, if The Chief Justice is correct that an insurance purchase requirement can be applied only to those who "actively" consume health care, the minimum coverage provision fits the bill. . . .

Maintaining that the uninsured are not active in the health-care market, The Chief Justice draws an analogy to the car market. An individual "is not 'active in the car market,'" The Chief Justice observes, simply because he or she may someday buy a car. The analogy is inapt. The inevitable yet unpredictable need for medical care and the guarantee that emergency care will be provided when required are conditions nonexistent in other markets. That is so of the market for cars, and of the market for broccoli as well. Although an individual might buy a car or a crown of broccoli one day, there is no certainty she will ever do so. And if she eventually wants a car or has a craving for broccoli, she will be obliged to pay at the counter before receiving the vehicle or nourishment. She will get no free ride or food, at the expense of another consumer forced to pay an inflated price. Upholding the minimum coverage provision on the ground that all are participants or will be participants in the health-care market would therefore carry no implication that Congress may justify under the Commerce Clause a mandate to buy other products and services. . . .

b

In any event, The Chief Justice's limitation of the commerce power to the regulation of those actively engaged in commerce finds no home in the text of the Constitution or our decisions. Article I, §8, of the Constitution grants Congress the power "[t]o regulate Commerce . . . among the several States." Nothing in this language implies that Congress' commerce power is limited to regulating those actively engaged in commercial transactions. . . . Arguing to the contrary, The Chief Justice notes that "the Constitution gives Congress the power to 'coin Money,' in addition to the power to 'regulate the Value thereof,'" and similarly "gives Congress the power to 'raise and support Armies' and to 'provide and maintain a Navy,' in addition to the power to 'make Rules for the Government and Regulation of the land and naval Forces.'" In separating the power to regulate from the power to bring the subject of the regulation into existence, The Chief Justice asserts, "[t]he language of the Constitution reflects the natural understanding that the power to regulate assumes there is already something to be regulated."

This argument is difficult to fathom. Requiring individuals to obtain insurance unquestionably regulates the interstate health-insurance and health-care markets, both of them in existence well before the enactment of the ACA. See *Wickard* ("The stimulation of commerce is a use of the regulatory function quite as definitely as prohibitions or restrictions thereon."). Thus, the "something to be regulated" was surely there when Congress created the minimum coverage provision.

Nor does our case law toe the activity versus inactivity line. In *Wickard*, for example, we upheld the penalty imposed on a farmer who grew too much wheat, even though the regulation had the effect of compelling farmers to purchase wheat in the open market. "[F]orcing some farmers into the market to buy what they could provide for themselves" was, the Court held, a valid means of regulating commerce. . . .

In concluding that the Commerce Clause does not permit Congress to regulate commercial "inactivity," and therefore does not allow Congress to adopt the practical solution it devised for the health-care problem, The Chief Justice views the Clause as a "technical legal conception," precisely what our case law tells us not to do. *Wickard*. This Court's former endeavors to impose categorical limits on the commerce power have not fared well. In several pre-New Deal cases, the Court attempted to cabin Congress' Commerce Clause authority by distinguishing "commerce" from activity once conceived to be noncommercial, notably, "production," "mining," and "manufacturing." See, e.g., *United States v. E. C. Knight Co.* (1895) ("Commerce succeeds to manufacture, and is not a part of it."); *Carter v. Carter Coal Co.* (1936) ("Mining brings the subject matter of commerce into existence. Commerce disposes of it."). The Court also sought to distinguish activities having a "direct" effect on interstate commerce, and for that reason, subject to federal regulation, from those having only an "indirect" effect, and therefore not amenable to federal control. See, e.g., *A. L. A. Schechter Poultry Corp. v. United States* (1935) ("[T]he distinction between direct and indirect effects of intrastate transactions upon interstate commerce must be recognized as a fundamental one.").

These line-drawing exercises were untenable, and the Court long ago abandoned them. "[Q]uestions of the power of Congress [under the Commerce Clause]," we held in *Wickard*, "are not to be decided by reference to any formula which would give controlling force to nomenclature such as 'production' and 'indirect' and foreclose consideration of the actual effects of the activity in question upon interstate commerce." Failing to learn from this history, The Chief Justice plows ahead with his formalistic distinction between those who are "active in commerce," and those who are not.

It is not hard to show the difficulty courts (and Congress) would encounter in distinguishing statutes that regulate "activity" from those that regulate "inactivity." . . . Take this case as an example. An individual who opts not to purchase insurance from a private insurer can be seen as actively selecting another form of insurance: self-insurance. The minimum coverage provision could therefore be described as regulating activists in the self-insurance market. *Wickard* is another example. Did the statute there at issue target activity (the growing of too much wheat) or inactivity (the farmer's failure to purchase wheat in the marketplace)? If anything, the Court's analysis suggested the latter. At bottom, The Chief Justice's and the joint dissenters' "view that an individual cannot be subject to Commerce Clause regulation absent voluntary, affirmative acts that enter him or her into, or affect, the interstate market expresses a concern for individual liberty that [is] more redolent of Due Process Clause arguments." *Seven-Sky v. Holder* (D.C. Cir. 2011). Plaintiffs have abandoned any argument pinned to substantive due process, however, and now concede that the provisions here at issue do not offend the Due Process Clause. . . .

Underlying The Chief Justice's view that the Commerce Clause must be confined to the regulation of active participants in a commercial market is a fear that the commerce power would otherwise know no limits. This concern is unfounded. . . . [A]bsent The Chief Justice's "activity" limitation[,] Congress would remain unable to regulate noneconomic conduct that has only an attenuated effect on interstate commerce and is traditionally left to state law. See *Lopez*. . . .

As an example of the type of regulation he fears, The Chief Justice cites a Government mandate to purchase green vegetables. One could call this concern "the broccoli horrible." Congress, The Chief Justice posits, might adopt such a mandate, reasoning that an individual's failure to eat a healthy diet, like the failure to purchase health insurance, imposes costs on others.

Consider the chain of inferences the Court would have to accept to conclude that a vegetable-purchase mandate was likely to have a substantial effect on the health-care costs borne by lithe Americans. The Court would have to believe that individuals forced to buy vegetables would then eat them (instead of throwing or giving them away), would prepare the vegetables in a healthy way (steamed or raw, not deep-fried), would cut back on unhealthy foods, and would not allow other factors (such as lack of exercise or little sleep) to trump the improved diet.[43] Such "pil[ing of] inference upon inference" is just what the Court refused to do in *Lopez* and *Morrison.*

Other provisions of the Constitution also check congressional overreaching. A mandate to purchase a particular product would be unconstitutional if, for example, the edict impermissibly abridged the freedom of speech, interfered with the free exercise of religion, or infringed on a liberty interest protected by the Due Process Clause. . . .

Supplementing these legal restraints is a formidable check on congressional power: the democratic process. As the controversy surrounding the passage of the Affordable Care Act attests, purchase mandates are likely to engender political resistance. This prospect is borne out by the behavior of state legislators. Despite their possession of unquestioned authority to impose mandates, state governments have rarely done so.

When contemplated in its extreme, almost any power looks dangerous. The commerce power, hypothetically, would enable Congress to prohibit the purchase and home production of all meat, fish, and dairy goods, effectively compelling Americans to eat only vegetables. Yet no one would offer the "hypothetical and unreal possibilit[y]," *Pullman Co. v. Knott* (1914), of a vegetarian state as a credible reason to deny Congress the authority ever to ban the possession and sale of goods. The Chief Justice accepts just such specious logic when he cites the broccoli horrible as a reason to deny Congress the power to pass the individual mandate. . . .

To bolster his argument that the minimum coverage provision is not valid Commerce Clause legislation, The Chief Justice emphasizes the provision's novelty. . . . For decades, [however,] the Court has declined to override legislation because of its novelty, and for good reason. As our national economy grows and changes, we have recognized, Congress must adapt to the changing "economic and financial realities." Hindering Congress' ability to do so is shortsighted; if history is any guide, today's constriction of the Commerce Clause will not endure.

---

[43] The failure to purchase vegetables in The Chief Justice's hypothetical, then, is *not* what leads to higher health-care costs for others; rather, it is the failure of individuals to maintain a healthy diet, and the resulting obesity, that creates the cost-shifting problem. Requiring individuals to purchase vegetables is thus several steps removed from solving the problem. The failure to obtain health insurance, by contrast, is the *immediate cause* of the cost-shifting Congress sought to address through the ACA. Requiring individuals to obtain insurance attacks the source of the problem directly, in a single step.

III

A

For the reasons explained above, the minimum coverage provision is valid Commerce Clause legislation. When viewed as a component of the entire ACA, the provision's constitutionality becomes even plainer.

The Necessary and Proper Clause "empowers Congress to enact laws in effectuation of its [commerce] powe[r] that are not within its authority to enact in isolation." *Raich* (Scalia, J., concurring in judgment). Hence, "[a] complex regulatory program . . . can survive a Commerce Clause challenge without a showing that every single facet of the program is independently and directly related to a valid congressional goal." *Indiana*, 452 U.S., at 329, n. 17. "It is enough that the challenged provisions are an integral part of the regulatory program and that the regulatory scheme when considered as a whole satisfies this test." Ibid. (collecting cases). See also *Raich*, 545 U.S., at 24-25 (A challenged statutory provision fits within Congress' commerce authority if it is an "essential par[t] of a larger regulation of economic activity," such that, in the absence of the provision, "the regulatory scheme could be undercut." (quoting *Lopez*)); *Raich* (Scalia, J., concurring in judgment) ("Congress may regulate even noneconomic local activity if that regulation is a necessary part of a more general regulation of interstate commerce. The relevant question is simply whether the means chosen are 'reasonably adapted' to the attainment of a legitimate end under the commerce power."). . . .

Recall that one of Congress' goals in enacting the Affordable Care Act was to eliminate the insurance industry's practice of charging higher prices or denying coverage to individuals with preexisting medical conditions. The commerce power allows Congress to ban this practice, a point no one disputes. See *United States v. South-Eastern Underwriters Assn.* (1944) (Congress may regulate "the methods by which interstate insurance companies do business.").

Congress knew, however, that simply barring insurance companies from relying on an applicant's medical history would not work in practice. Without the individual mandate, Congress learned, guaranteed-issue and community rating requirements would trigger an adverse-selection death-spiral in the health-insurance market: Insurance premiums would skyrocket, the number of uninsured would increase, and insurance companies would exit the market. When complemented by an insurance mandate, on the other hand, guaranteed issue and community rating would work as intended, increasing access to insurance and reducing uncompensated care. The minimum coverage provision is thus an "essential par[t] of a larger regulation of economic activity"; without the provision, "the regulatory scheme [w]ould be undercut." *Raich*. Put differently, the minimum coverage provision, together with the guaranteed issue and community-rating requirements, is "'reasonably adapted' to the attainment of a legitimate end under the commerce power": the elimination of pricing and sales practices that take an applicant's medical history into account. See *id.* (Scalia, J., concurring in judgment).

B

Asserting that the Necessary and Proper Clause does not authorize the minimum coverage provision, The Chief Justice focuses on the word "proper." A mandate to purchase health insurance is not "proper" legislation, The Chief Justice urges, because the command "undermine[s] the structure of government established by the Constitution." If long on rhetoric, The Chief Justice's argument is short on substance. The Chief Justice cites only two cases in which this Court concluded that a federal statute impermissibly transgressed the Constitution's boundary between state and federal authority: *Printz v. United States* (1997), and *New York v. United States* (1992). The statutes at issue in both cases, however, compelled state officials to act on the Federal Government's behalf.

The minimum coverage provision, in contrast, acts "directly upon individuals, without employing the States as intermediaries." *New York*. The provision is thus entirely consistent with the Constitution's design. See *Printz* ("[T]he Framers explicitly chose a Constitution that confers upon Congress the power to regulate individuals, not States." (internal quotation marks omitted)).

Lacking case law support for his holding, The Chief Justice nevertheless declares the minimum coverage provision not "proper" because it is less "narrow in scope" than other laws this Court has upheld under the Necessary and Proper Clause (citing *United States v. Comstock* (2010)). . . . The Chief Justice's reliance on cases in which this Court has affirmed Congress' "broad authority to enact federal legislation" under the Necessary and Proper Clause, *Comstock*, is underwhelming.

Nor does The Chief Justice pause to explain why the power to direct either the purchase of health insurance or, alternatively, the payment of a penalty collectible as a tax is more far-reaching than other implied powers this Court has found meet under the Necessary and Proper Clause. These powers include the power to enact criminal laws, the power to imprison, including civil imprisonment, and the power to create a national bank.

In failing to explain why the individual mandate threatens our constitutional order, The Chief Justice disserves future courts. How is a judge to decide, when ruling on the constitutionality of a federal statute, whether Congress employed an "independent power," or merely a "derivative." Whether the power used is "substantive," or just "incidental." The instruction The Chief Justice, in effect, provides lower courts: You will know it when you see it. . . .[44]

[44] In a separate argument, the joint dissenters contend that the minimum coverage provision is not necessary and proper because it was not the "only . . . way" Congress could have made the guaranteed-issue and community-rating reforms work. . . . But even assuming there were "practicable" alternatives to the minimum coverage provision, "we long ago rejected the view that the Necessary and Proper Clause demands that an Act of Congress be 'absolutely necessary' to the exercise of an enumerated power." *Jinks v. Richland County* 462 (2003) (quoting *McCulloch*). Rather, the statutory provision at issue need only be "conducive" and "[reasonably] adapted" to the goal Congress seeks to achieve. *Jinks*. The minimum coverage provision meets this requirement.

IV

In the early 20th century, this Court regularly struck down economic regulation enacted by the peoples' representatives in both the States and the Federal Government. See, e.g., *Carter Coal Co*; *Dagenhart*; *Lochner v. New York* (1905). The Chief Justice's Commerce Clause opinion . . . bear[s] a disquieting resemblance to those long-overruled decisions.

Ultimately, the Court upholds the individual mandate as a proper exercise of Congress' power to tax and spend "for the . . . general Welfare of the United States." I concur in that determination, which makes The Chief Justice's Commerce Clause essay all the more puzzling. Why should The Chief Justice strive so mightily to hem in Congress' capacity to meet the new problems arising constantly in our ever developing modern economy? I find no satisfying response to that question in his opinion.[45]

JUSTICE SCALIA, JUSTICE KENNEDY, JUSTICE THOMAS, and JUSTICE ALITO, dissenting.

Congress has set out to remedy the problem that the best health care is beyond the reach of many Americans who cannot afford it. It can assuredly do that, by exercising the powers accorded to it under the Constitution. The question in this case, however, is whether the complex structures and provisions of the Patient Protection and Affordable Care Act (Affordable Care Act or ACA) go beyond those powers. We conclude that they do.

This case is in one respect difficult: it presents two questions of first impression. The first of those is whether failure to engage in economic activity (the purchase of health insurance) is subject to regulation under the Commerce Clause. Failure to act does result in an effect on commerce, and hence might be said to come under this Court's "affecting commerce" criterion of Commerce Clause jurisprudence. But in none of its decisions has this Court extended the Clause that far. The second question is whether the congressional power to tax and spend permits the conditioning of a State's continued receipt of all funds under a massive state-administered federal welfare program upon its acceptance of an expansion to that program. Several of our opinions have suggested that the power to tax and spend cannot be used to coerce state administration of a federal program, but we have never found a law enacted under the spending power to be coercive. Those questions are difficult.

The case is easy and straightforward, however, in another respect. What is absolutely clear, affirmed by the text of the 1789 Constitution, by the Tenth Amendment ratified in 1791, and by innumerable cases of ours in the 220 years since, is that there are structural limits upon federal power — upon what it can prescribe with respect to private conduct, and upon what it can impose upon the sovereign States. Whatever may be the conceptual limits upon the Commerce

---

[45] The Chief Justice states that he must evaluate the constitutionality of the minimum coverage provision under the Commerce Clause because the provision "reads more naturally as a command to buy insurance than as a tax." The Chief Justice ultimately concludes, however, that interpreting the provision as a tax is a "fairly possible" construction. That being so, I see no reason to undertake a Commerce Clause analysis that is not outcome determinative.

Clause and upon the power to tax and spend, they cannot be such as will enable the Federal Government to regulate all private conduct and to compel the States to function as administrators of federal programs.

That clear principle carries the day here. The striking case of *Wickard v. Filburn* (1942), which held that the economic activity of growing wheat, even for one's own consumption, affected commerce sufficiently that it could be regulated, always has been regarded as the *ne plus ultra* ["the most extreme example" — Eds.] of expansive Commerce Clause jurisprudence. To go beyond that, and to say the failure to grow wheat (which is not an economic activity, or any activity at all) nonetheless affects commerce and therefore can be federally regulated, is to make mere breathing in and out the basis for federal prescription and to extend federal power to virtually all human activity. . . .

The Act before us here exceeds federal power both in mandating the purchase of health insurance and in denying nonconsenting States all Medicaid funding. These parts of the Act are central to its design and operation, and all the Act's other provisions would not have been enacted without them. In our view it must follow that the entire statute is inoperative. . . .

I. The Individual Mandate

A

. . . [T]he scope of the Necessary and Proper Clause is exceeded not only when the congressional action directly violates the sovereignty of the States but also when it violates the background principle of enumerated (and hence limited) federal power.

The case upon which the Government principally relies to sustain the Individual Mandate under the Necessary and Proper Clause is *Gonzales v. Raich* (2005). That case held that Congress could, in an effort to restrain the interstate market in marijuana, ban the local cultivation and possession of that drug. *Raich* is no precedent for what Congress has done here. That case's prohibition of growing (cf. *Wickard*), and of possession (cf. innumerable federal statutes) did not represent the expansion of the federal power to direct into a broad new field. The mandating of economic activity does, and since it is a field so limitless that it converts the Commerce Clause into a general authority to direct the economy, that mandating is not "consist[ent] with the letter and spirit of the constitution." *McCulloch*.

Moreover, *Raich* is far different from the Individual Mandate in another respect. The Court's opinion in *Raich* pointed out that the growing and possession prohibitions were the only practicable way of enabling the prohibition of interstate traffic in marijuana to be effectively enforced. See also *Shreveport Rate Cases* (1914) (Necessary and Proper Clause allows regulations of intrastate transactions if necessary to the regulation of an interstate market). Intrastate marijuana could no more be distinguished from interstate marijuana than, for example, endangered-species trophies obtained before the species was federally protected can be distinguished from trophies obtained afterwards — which made it necessary and proper to prohibit the sale of all such trophies, see *Andrus v. Allard* (1979).

With the present statute, by contrast, there are many ways other than this unprecedented Individual Mandate by which the regulatory scheme's goals of reducing insurance premiums and ensuring the profitability of insurers could be achieved. For instance, those who did not purchase insurance could be subjected to a surcharge when they do enter the health insurance system. Or they could be denied a full income tax credit given to those who do purchase the insurance.

The Government was invited, at oral argument, to suggest what federal controls over private conduct (other than those explicitly prohibited by the Bill of Rights or other constitutional controls) could not be justified as necessary and proper for the carrying out of a general regulatory scheme. See Tr. of Oral Arg. 27-30, 43-45 (Mar. 27, 2012). It was unable to name any. . . . [W]hereas the precise scope of the Commerce Clause and the Necessary and Proper Clause is uncertain, the proposition that the Federal Government cannot do everything is a fundamental precept. See *Lopez*, 514 U.S., at 564 ("[I]f we were to accept the Government's arguments, we are hard pressed to posit any activity by an individual that Congress is without power to regulate"). Section 5000A is defeated by that proposition. . . .

C

. . . A few respectful responses to Justice Ginsburg's dissent on the issue of the Mandate are in order. That dissent duly recites the test of Commerce Clause power that our opinions have applied, but disregards the premise the test contains. It is true enough that Congress needs only a "'rational basis' for concluding that the *regulated activity* substantially affects interstate commerce" (emphasis added). But it must be *activity* affecting commerce that is regulated, and not merely the failure to engage in commerce. And one is not now purchasing the health care covered by the insurance mandate simply because one is likely to be purchasing it in the future. Our test's premise of regulated activity is not invented out of whole cloth, but rests upon the Constitution's requirement that it be commerce which is regulated. If all inactivity affecting commerce is commerce, commerce is everything. Ultimately the dissent is driven to saying that there is really no difference between action and inaction, a proposition that has never recommended itself, neither to the law nor to common sense. To say, for example, that the inaction here consists of activity in "the self insurance market," seems to us wordplay. By parity of reasoning the failure to buy a car can be called participation in the non-private-car-transportation market. Commerce becomes everything.

The dissent claims that we "fai[l] to explain why the individual mandate threatens our constitutional order." But we have done so. It threatens that order because it gives such an expansive meaning to the Commerce Clause that all private conduct (including failure to act) becomes subject to federal control, effectively destroying the Constitution's division of governmental powers. Thus the dissent, on the theories proposed for the validity of the Mandate, would alter the accepted constitutional relation between the individual and the National Government. The dissent protests that the Necessary and Proper Clause has been held to include "the power to enact criminal laws, . . . the power to imprison, . . . and the power to create a national bank." Is not the power to compel purchase of health insurance much lesser? No, not if (unlike those other dispositions) its application rests upon a theory that everything is within federal control simply because it exists.

The dissent's exposition of the wonderful things the Federal Government has achieved through exercise of its assigned powers, such as "the provision of old-age and survivors' benefits" in the Social Security Act, is quite beside the point. The issue here is whether the federal government can impose the Individual Mandate through the Commerce Clause. And the relevant history is not that Congress has achieved wide and wonderful results through the proper exercise of its assigned powers in the past, but that it has never before used the Commerce Clause to compel entry into commerce. The dissent treats the Constitution as though it is an enumeration of those problems that the Federal Government can address — among which, it finds, is "the Nation's course in the economic and social welfare realm," and more specifically "the problem of the uninsured." The Constitution is not that. It enumerates not federally soluble problems, but federally available powers. The Federal Government can address whatever problems it wants but can bring to their solution only those powers that the Constitution confers, among which is the power to regulate commerce. None of our cases say anything else. Article I contains no whatever-it-takes-to-solve-a-national problem power.

The dissent dismisses the conclusion that the power to compel entry into the health-insurance market would include the power to compel entry into the new-car or broccoli markets. The latter purchasers, it says, "will be obliged to pay at the counter before receiving the vehicle or nourishment," whereas those refusing to purchase health-insurance will ultimately get treated anyway, at others' expense. "[T]he unique attributes of the health-care market . . . give rise to a significant free riding problem that does not occur in other markets." And "a vegetable-purchase mandate" (or a car-purchase mandate) is not "likely to have a substantial effect on the health-care costs" borne by other Americans. Those differences make a very good argument by the dissent's own lights, since they show that the failure to purchase health insurance, unlike the failure to purchase cars or broccoli, creates a national, social-welfare problem that is (in the dissent's view) included among the unenumerated "problems" that the Constitution authorizes the Federal Government to solve. But those differences do not show that the failure to enter the health-insurance market, unlike the failure to buy cars and broccoli, is an *activity* that Congress can "regulate." (Of course one day the failure of some of the public to purchase American cars may endanger the existence of domestic automobile manufacturers; or the failure of some to eat broccoli may be found to deprive them of a newly discovered cancer fighting chemical which only that food contains, producing health-care costs that are a burden on the rest of us — in which case, under the theory of Justice Ginsburg's dissent, moving against those inactivities will also come within the Federal Government's unenumerated problem solving powers.)

II. The Taxing Power

As far as §5000A is concerned, we would stop there. Congress has attempted to regulate beyond the scope of its Commerce Clause authority, and §5000A is therefore invalid. The Government contends, however, as expressed in the caption to Part II of its brief, that "THE MINIMUM COVERAGE PROVISION IS INDEPENDENTLY AUTHORIZED BY CONGRESS'S TAXING POWER." The phrase "independently authorized" suggests the existence of a creature never hitherto seen in the United States Reports: A penalty for constitutional purposes that is also a tax for constitutional purposes. In all our cases the two are mutually exclusive. The provision challenged under the Constitution is either a penalty or else a tax. Of course in many cases what was a regulatory mandate enforced by a penalty could have been imposed as a tax upon permissible action; or what was imposed as a tax upon permissible action could have been a regulatory mandate enforced by a penalty. But we know of no case, and the Government cites none, in which the imposition was, for constitutional purposes, both. The two are mutually exclusive. Thus, what the Government's caption should have read was "ALTERNATIVELY, THE MINIMUM COVERAGE PROVISION IS NOT A MANDATE-WITH-PENALTY BUT A TAX." It is important to bear this in mind in evaluating the tax argument of the Government and of those who support it: The issue is not whether Congress had the *power* to frame the minimum-coverage provision as a tax, but whether it *did so*.

In answering that question we must, if "fairly possible," *Crowell v. Benson* (1932), construe the provision to be a tax rather than a mandate-with-penalty, since that would render it constitutional rather than unconstitutional (*ut res magis valeat quam pereat* ["the law should be given effect rather than be destroyed" — EDS.]). But we cannot rewrite the statute to be what it is not. "'[A]lthough this Court will often strain to construe legislation so as to save it against constitutional attack, it must not and will not carry this to the point of perverting the purpose of a statute . . . ' or judicially rewriting it." *Commodity Futures Trading Comm'n v. Schor* (1986). In this case, there is simply no way, "without doing violence to the fair meaning of the words used," *Grenada County Supervisors v. Brogden* (1884), to escape what Congress enacted: a mandate that individuals maintain minimum essential coverage, enforced by a penalty.

Our cases establish a clear line between a tax and a penalty: "'[A] tax is an enforced contribution to provide for the support of government; a penalty . . . is an exaction imposed by statute as punishment for an unlawful act.'" *United States v. Reorganized CF&I Fabricators of Utah, Inc.* (1996) (quoting *United States v. La Franca* (1931)). In a few cases, this Court has held that a "tax" imposed upon private conduct was so onerous as to be in effect a penalty. But we have never held — *never* — that a penalty imposed for violation of the law was so trivial as to be in effect a tax. We have never held that *any* exaction imposed for violation of the law is an exercise of Congress' taxing power — even when the statute *calls* it a tax, much less when (as here) the statute repeatedly calls it a penalty. When an act "adopt[s] the criteria of wrongdoing" and then imposes a monetary penalty as the "principal consequence on those who transgress its standard," it creates a regulatory penalty, not a tax. *Child Labor Tax Case* (1922).

So the question is, quite simply, whether the exaction here is imposed for violation of the law. It unquestionably is. The minimum-coverage provision is found in 26 U.S.C. §5000A, entitled "*Requirement* to maintain minimum essential coverage." (Emphasis added.) It commands that every "applicable individual *shall* . . . ensure that the individual . . . is covered under minimum essential coverage." Ibid. (emphasis added). And the immediately following provision states that, "[i]f . . . an applicable individual . . . fails to meet the *requirement* of subsection (a) . . . there is hereby imposed . . . a *penalty*." §5000A(b) (emphasis added). And several of Congress' legislative "findings" with regard to §5000A confirm that it sets forth a legal requirement and constitutes the assertion of regulatory power, not mere taxing power. See 42 U.S.C. §18091(2)(A) ("The requirement regulates activity . . ."); §18091(2)(C) ("The requirement . . . will add millions of new consumers to the health insurance market . . ."); §18091(2)(D) ("The requirement achieves near-universal coverage"); §18091(2)(H) ("The requirement is an essential part of this larger regulation of economic activity, and the absence of the requirement would undercut Federal regulation of the health insurance market"); §18091(3) ("[T]he Supreme Court of the United States ruled that insurance is interstate commerce subject to Federal regulation"). . . .

Quite separately, the fact that Congress (in its own words) "imposed . . . a penalty," 26 U.S.C. §5000A(b)(1), for failure to buy insurance is alone sufficient to render that failure unlawful. It is one of the canons of interpretation that a statute that penalizes an act makes it unlawful: "[W]here the statute inflicts a penalty for doing an act, although the act itself is not expressly prohibited, yet to do the act is unlawful, because it cannot be supposed that the Legislature intended that a penalty should be inflicted for a lawful act." *Powhatan Steamboat Co. v. Appomattox R. Co.* (1861). Or in the words of Chancellor Kent: "If a statute inflicts a penalty for doing an act, the penalty implies a prohibition, and the thing is unlawful, though there be no prohibitory words in the statute." J. Kent, Commentaries on American Law (1826).

We never have classified as a tax an exaction imposed for violation of the law, and so too, we never have classified as a tax an exaction described in the legislation itself as a penalty. To be sure, we have sometimes treated as a tax a statutory exaction (imposed for something other than a violation of law) which bore an agnostic label that does not entail the significant constitutional consequences of a penalty — such as "license" (*License Tax Cases* (1867)) or "surcharge" (*New York v. United States*). But we have never — *never* — treated as a tax an exaction which faces up to the critical difference between a tax and a penalty, and explicitly denominates the exaction a "penalty." Eighteen times in §5000A itself and elsewhere throughout the Act, Congress called the exaction in §5000A(b) a "penalty."

That §5000A imposes not a simple tax but a mandate to which a penalty is attached is demonstrated by the fact that some are exempt from the tax who are not exempt from the mandate — a distinction that would make no sense if the mandate were not a mandate. Section 5000A(d) exempts three classes of people from the definition of "applicable individual" subject to the minimum coverage requirement: Those with religious objections or who participate in a "health care sharing ministry"; those who are "not lawfully present" in the United States; and those who are incarcerated. Section 5000A(e) then creates a separate set of exemptions, excusing from liability for the penalty certain individuals who are subject to the minimum coverage requirement: Those who cannot afford coverage; who earn too little income to require filing a tax return; who are members of an Indian tribe; who experience only short gaps in coverage; and who, in the judgment of the Secretary of Health and Human Services, "have suffered a hardship with respect to the capability to obtain coverage." If §5000A were a tax, these two classes of exemption would make no sense; there being no requirement, all the exemptions would attach to the penalty (renamed tax) alone. . . .

Against the mountain of evidence that the minimum coverage requirement is what the statute calls it — a requirement — and that the penalty for its violation is what the statute calls it — a penalty — the Government brings forward the flimsiest of indications to the contrary. It notes that "[t]he minimum coverage provision amends the Internal Revenue Code to provide that a non-exempted individual . . . will owe a monetary penalty, in addition to the income tax itself," and that "[t]he [Internal Revenue Service (IRS)] will assess and collect the penalty in the same manner as assessable penalties under the Internal Revenue Code." The manner of collection could perhaps suggest a tax if IRS penalty-collection were unheard-of or rare. It is not. See, e.g., 26 U.S.C. §527(j) (2006 ed.) (IRS-collectible penalty for failure to make campaign-finance disclosures); §5761(c) (IRS-collectible penalty for domestic sales of tobacco products labeled for export); §9707 (IRS-collectible penalty for failure to make required health-insurance premium payments on behalf of mining employees). In *Reorganized CF&I Fabricators of Utah, Inc.* (1996), we held that an exaction not only enforced by the Commissioner of Internal Revenue but even called a "tax" was in fact a penalty. "[I]f the concept of penalty means anything," we said, "it means punishment for an unlawful act or omission." Moreover, while the penalty is assessed and collected by the IRS, §5000A is administered both by that agency and by the Department of Health and Human Services (and also the Secretary of Veteran Affairs), which is responsible for defining its substantive scope — a feature that would be quite extraordinary for taxes.

The Government points out that "[t]he amount of the penalty will be calculated as a percentage of household income for federal income tax purposes, subject to a floor and [a] ca[p]," and that individuals who earn so little money that they "are not required to file income tax returns for the taxable year are not subject to the penalty" (though they are, as we discussed earlier, subject to the mandate). But varying a penalty according to ability to pay is an utterly familiar practice. See, e.g., 33 U.S.C. §1319(d) ("In determining the amount of a civil penalty the court shall consider . . . the economic impact of the penalty on the violator").

The last of the feeble arguments in favor of petitioners that we will address is the contention that what this statute repeatedly calls a penalty is in fact a tax because it contains no scienter requirement. The presence of such a requirement suggests a penalty — though one can imagine a tax imposed only on willful action; but the absence of such a requirement does not suggest a tax. Penalties for absolute-liability offenses are commonplace. And where a statute is silent as to scienter, we traditionally presume a mens rea requirement if the statute imposes a "severe penalty." *Staples v. United States* (1994). Since we have an entire jurisprudence addressing when it is that a scienter requirement should be inferred from a penalty, it is quite illogical to suggest that a penalty is not a penalty for want of an express scienter requirement.

And the nail in the coffin is that the mandate and penalty are located in Title I of the Act, its operative core, rather than where a tax would be found — in Title IX, containing the Act's "Revenue Provisions." In sum, "the terms of [the] act rende[r] it unavoidable," *Parsons v. Bedford* (1830), that Congress imposed a regulatory penalty, not a tax.

For all these reasons, to say that the Individual Mandate merely imposes a tax is not to interpret the statute but to rewrite it. Judicial tax-writing is particularly troubling. Taxes have never been popular, see, e.g., Stamp Act of 1765, and in part for that reason, the Constitution requires tax increases to originate in the House of Representatives. See Art. I, §7, cl. 1. That is to say, they must originate in the legislative body most accountable to the people, where legislators must weigh the need for the tax against the terrible price they might pay at their next election, which is never more than two years off. *Federalist No. 58* "defend[ed] the decision to give the origination power to the House on the ground that the Chamber that is more accountable to the people should have the primary role in raising revenue." *United States v. Munoz-Flores* (1990). We have no doubt that Congress knew precisely what it was doing when it rejected an earlier version of this legislation that imposed a tax instead of a requirement-with-penalty. See Affordable Health Care for America Act, H.R. 3962 (2009); America's Healthy Future Act of 2009, S. 1796. Imposing a tax through judicial legislation inverts the constitutional scheme, and places the power to tax in the branch of government least accountable to the citizenry.

Finally, we must observe that rewriting §5000A as a tax in order to sustain its constitutionality would force us to confront a difficult constitutional question: whether this is a direct tax that must be apportioned among the States according to their population. Art. I, §9, cl. 4. Perhaps it is not (we have no need to address the point); but the meaning of the Direct Tax Clause is famously unclear, and its application here is a question of first impression that deserves more thoughtful consideration than the lick-and-a-promise accorded by the Government and its supporters. The Government's opening brief did not even address the question — perhaps because, until today, no federal court has accepted the implausible argument that §5000A is an exercise of the tax power. And once respondents raised the issue, the Government devoted a mere 21 lines of its reply brief to the issue. At oral argument, the most prolonged statement about the issue was just over 50 words. One would expect this Court to demand more than fly-by-night briefing and argument before deciding a difficult constitutional question of first impression. . . .

The Constitution, though it dates from the founding of the Republic, has powerful meaning and vital relevance to our own times. The constitutional protections that this case involves are protections of structure. Structural protections — notably, the restraints imposed by federalism and separation of powers — are less romantic and have less obvious a connection to personal freedom than the provisions of the Bill of Rights or the Civil War Amendments. Hence they tend to be undervalued or even forgotten by our citizens. It should be the responsibility of the Court to teach otherwise, to remind our people that the Framers considered structural protections of freedom the most important ones, for which reason they alone were embodied in the original Constitution and not left to later amendment. The fragmentation of power produced by the structure of our Government is central to liberty, and when we destroy it, we place liberty at peril. Today's decision should have vindicated, should have taught, this truth; instead, our judgment today has disregarded it.

For the reasons here stated, we would find the Act invalid in its entirety. We respectfully dissent.

JUSTICE THOMAS, dissenting.

I dissent for the reasons stated in our joint opinion, but I write separately to say a word about the Commerce Clause. The joint dissent and The Chief Justice correctly apply our precedents to conclude that the Individual Mandate is beyond the power granted to Congress under the Commerce Clause and the Necessary and Proper Clause. Under those precedents, Congress may regulate "economic activity [that] substantially affects interstate commerce." *United States v. Lopez* (1995). I adhere to my view that "the very notion of a 'substantial effects' test under the Commerce Clause is inconsistent with the original understanding of Congress' powers and with this Court's early Commerce Clause cases." *United States v. Morrison* (2000) (Thomas, J., concurring); see also *Gonzales v. Raich* (2005) (Thomas, J., dissenting). As I have explained, the Court's continued use of that test "has encouraged the Federal Government to persist in its view that the Commerce Clause has virtually no limits." *Morrison*. The Government's unprecedented claim in this suit that it may regulate not only economic activity but also inactivity that substantially affects interstate commerce is a case in point.

ASSIGNMENT 9

2. The Spending Power

NFIB v. Sebelius

567 U.S. 519 (2012)

CHIEF JUSTICE ROBERTS announced the judgment of the Court and delivered . . . an opinion with respect to Part IV, in which JUSTICE BREYER and JUSTICE KAGAN join.

IV

A

The States also contend that the Medicaid expansion exceeds Congress's authority under the Spending Clause. They claim that Congress is coercing the

States to adopt the changes it wants by threatening to withhold all of a State's Medicaid grants, unless the State accepts the new expanded funding and complies with the conditions that come with it. This, they argue, violates the basic principle that the "Federal Government may not compel the States to enact or administer a federal regulatory program." *New York v. United States* (1992).

There is no doubt that the Act dramatically increases state obligations under Medicaid. The current Medicaid program requires States to cover only certain discrete categories of needy individuals — pregnant women, children, needy families, the blind, the elderly, and the disabled. There is no mandatory coverage for most childless adults, and the States typically do not offer any such coverage. The States also enjoy considerable flexibility with respect to the coverage levels for parents of needy families. On average States cover only those unemployed parents who make less than 37 percent of the federal poverty level, and only those employed parents who make less than 63 percent of the poverty line.

The Medicaid provisions of the Affordable Care Act, in contrast, require States to expand their Medicaid programs by 2014 to cover *all* individuals under the age of 65 with incomes below 133 percent of the federal poverty line. The Act also establishes a new "[e]ssential health benefits" package, which States must provide to all new Medicaid recipients — a level sufficient to satisfy a recipient's obligations under the individual mandate. The Affordable Care Act provides that the Federal Government will pay 100 percent of the costs of covering these newly eligible individuals through 2016. In the following years, the federal payment level gradually decreases, to a minimum of 90 percent. In light of the expansion in coverage mandated by the Act, the Federal Government estimates that its Medicaid spending will increase by approximately $100 billion per year, nearly 40 percent above current levels.

The Spending Clause grants Congress the power "to pay the Debts and provide for the . . . general Welfare of the United States." We have long recognized that Congress may use this power to grant federal funds to the States, and may condition such a grant upon the States' "taking certain actions that Congress could not require them to take." *College Savings Bank*. Such measures "encourage a State to regulate in a particular way, [and] influenc[e] a State's policy choices." *New York*. The conditions imposed by Congress ensure that the funds are used by the States to "provide for the . . . general Welfare" in the manner Congress intended.

At the same time, our cases have recognized limits on Congress's power under the Spending Clause to secure state compliance with federal objectives. "We have repeatedly characterized . . . Spending Clause legislation as 'much in the nature of a contract.'" *Barnes v. Gorman* (2002) (quoting *Pennhurst State School and Hospital v. Halderman* (1981)). The legitimacy of Congress's exercise of the spending power "thus rests on whether the State voluntarily and knowingly accepts the terms of the 'contract.'" *Pennhurst*. Respecting this limitation is critical to ensuring that Spending Clause legislation does not undermine the status of the States as independent sovereigns in our federal system. That system "rests on what might at first seem a counterintuitive insight, that 'freedom is enhanced by the creation of two governments, not one.'" *Bond* (quoting *Alden v. Maine* (1999).) For this reason, "the Constitution has never been understood to confer upon Congress the ability to require the States to govern according to Congress' instructions." *New York*.

Otherwise the two-government system established by the Framers would give way to a system that vests power in one central government, and individual liberty would suffer.

That insight has led this Court to strike down federal legislation that commandeers a State's legislative or administrative apparatus for federal purposes. *Printz* (striking down federal legislation compelling state law enforcement officers to perform federally mandated background checks on handgun purchasers); *New York* (invalidating provisions of an Act that would compel a State to either take title to nuclear waste or enact particular state waste regulations). It has also led us to scrutinize Spending Clause legislation to ensure that Congress is not using financial inducements to exert a "power akin to undue influence." *Steward Machine Co. v. Davis* (1937). Congress may use its spending power to create incentives for States to act in accordance with federal policies. But when "pressure turns into compulsion," *ibid.*, the legislation runs contrary to our system of federalism. "[T]he Constitution simply does not give Congress the authority to require the States to regulate." *New York*. That is true whether Congress directly commands a State to regulate or indirectly coerces a State to adopt a federal regulatory system as its own.

Permitting the Federal Government to force the States to implement a federal program would threaten the political accountability key to our federal system. "[W]here the Federal Government directs the States to regulate, it may be state officials who will bear the brunt of public disapproval, while the federal officials who devised the regulatory program may remain insulated from the electoral ramifications of their decision." *Id.* Spending Clause programs do not pose this danger when a State has a legitimate choice whether to accept the federal conditions in exchange for federal funds. In such a situation, state officials can fairly be held politically accountable for choosing to accept or refuse the federal offer. But when the State has no choice, the Federal Government can achieve its objectives without accountability, just as in *New York* and *Printz*. Indeed, this danger is heightened when Congress acts under the Spending Clause, because Congress can use that power to implement federal policy it could not impose directly under its enumerated powers. . . .

The States . . . object that Congress has "crossed the line distinguishing encouragement from coercion," *New York*, in the way it has structured the funding: Instead of simply refusing to grant the new funds to States that will not accept the new conditions, Congress has also threatened to withhold those States' existing Medicaid funds. The States claim that this threat serves no purpose other than to force unwilling States to sign up for the dramatic expansion in health care coverage effected by the Act.

Given the nature of the threat and the programs at issue here, we must agree. We have upheld Congress's authority to condition the receipt of funds on the States' complying with restrictions on the use of those funds, because that is the means by which Congress ensures that the funds are spent according to its view of the "general Welfare." Conditions that do not here govern the use of the funds, however, cannot be justified on that basis. When, for example, such conditions take the form of threats to terminate other significant independent grants, the conditions are properly viewed as a means of pressuring the States to accept policy changes.

In *South Dakota v. Dole*, we considered a challenge to a federal law that threatened to withhold five percent of a State's federal highway funds if the State did not raise its drinking age to 21. The Court found that the condition was "directly related to one of the main purposes for which highway funds are expended — safe interstate travel." At the same time, the condition was not a restriction on how the highway funds — set aside for specific highway improvement and maintenance efforts — were to be used.

We accordingly asked whether "the financial inducement offered by Congress" was "so coercive as to pass the point at which 'pressure turns into compulsion.'" (quoting *Steward Machine*). By "financial inducement" the Court meant the threat of losing five percent of highway funds; no new money was offered to the States to raise their drinking ages. We found that the inducement was not impermissibly coercive, because Congress was offering only "relatively mild encouragement to the States." *Dole*. We observed that "all South Dakota would lose if she adheres to her chosen course as to a suitable minimum drinking age is 5%" of her highway funds. In fact, the federal funds at stake constituted less than half of one percent of South Dakota's budget at the time. In consequence, "we conclude[d] that [the] encouragement to state action [was] a valid use of the spending power." Whether to accept the drinking age change "remain[ed] the prerogative of the States not merely in theory but in fact."

In this case, the financial "inducement" Congress has chosen is much more than "relatively mild encouragement" — it is a gun to the head. Section 1396c of the Medicaid Act provides that if a State's Medicaid plan does not comply with the Act's requirements, the Secretary of Health and Human Services may declare that "further payments will not be made to the State." A State that opts out of the Affordable Care Act's expansion in health care coverage thus stands to lose not merely "a relatively small percentage" of its existing Medicaid funding, but all of it. *Dole*. Medicaid spending accounts for over 20 percent of the average State's total budget, with federal funds covering 50 to 83 percent of those costs. The Federal Government estimates that it will pay out approximately $3.3 trillion between 2010 and 2019 in order to cover the costs of pre-expansion Medicaid. In addition, the States have developed intricate statutory and administrative regimes over the course of many decades to implement their objectives under existing Medicaid. It is easy to see how the *Dole* Court could conclude that the threatened loss of less than half of one percent of South Dakota's budget left that State with a "prerogative" to reject Congress's desired policy, "not merely in theory but in fact." 483 U.S., at 211-212. The threatened loss of over 10 percent of a State's overall budget, in contrast, is economic dragooning that leaves the States with no real option but to acquiesce in the Medicaid expansion. . . .

B

Nothing in our opinion precludes Congress from offering funds under the Affordable Care Act to expand the availability of health care, and requiring that

States accepting such funds comply with the conditions on their use. What Congress is not free to do is to penalize States that choose not to participate in that new program by taking away their existing Medicaid funding. . . . In light of the Court's holding, the Secretary cannot apply §1396c to withdraw existing Medicaid funds for failure to comply with the requirements set out in the expansion.

That fully remedies the constitutional violation we have identified. . . . Congress has no authority to order the States to regulate according to its instructions. Congress may offer the States grants and require the States to comply with accompanying conditions, but the States must have a genuine choice whether to accept the offer. The States are given no such choice in this case: They must either accept a basic change in the nature of Medicaid, or risk losing all Medicaid funding. The remedy for that constitutional violation is to preclude the Federal Government from imposing such a sanction. That remedy does not require striking down other portions of the Affordable Care Act. . . .

Justice Ginsburg, with whom Justice Sotomayor joins [dissenting from this part of the judgment of the Court]. . . .

V

. . . The Spending Clause authorizes Congress "to pay the Debts and provide for the . . . general Welfare of the United States." To ensure that federal funds granted to the States are spent "to 'provide for the . . . general Welfare' in the manner Congress intended." Congress must of course have authority to impose limitations on the States' use of the federal dollars. This Court, time and again, has respected Congress' prescription of spending conditions, and has required States to abide by them. In particular, we have recognized Congress' prerogative to condition a State's receipt of Medicaid funding on compliance with the terms Congress set for participation in the program.

Congress' authority to condition the use of federal funds is not confined to spending programs as first launched. The legislature may, and often does, amend the law, imposing new conditions grant recipients henceforth must meet in order to continue receiving funds.

Yes, there are federalism-based limits on the use of Congress' conditional spending power. In the leading decision in this area, *South Dakota v. Dole* (1987), the Court identified four criteria. The conditions placed on federal grants to States must (a) promote the "general welfare," (b) "unambiguously" inform States what is demanded of them, (c) be germane "to the federal interest in particular national projects or programs," and (d) not "induce the States to engage in activities that would themselves be unconstitutional."

The Court in *Dole* mentioned, but did not adopt, a further limitation, one hypothetically raised a half-century earlier: In "some circumstances," Congress might be prohibited from offering a "financial inducement . . . so coercive as to pass the point at which 'pressure turns into compulsion'" (quoting *Steward Machine Co. v. Davis* (1937)). Prior to today's decision, however, the Court has never ruled that the terms of any grant crossed the indistinct line between temptation and coercion. . . .

This case does not present the concerns that led the Court in *Dole* even to consider the prospect of coercion. In *Dole*, the condition — set 21 as the minimum drinking age — did not tell the States how to use funds Congress provided for highway construction. Further, in view of the Twenty-First Amendment, it was an open question whether Congress could directly impose a national minimum drinking age.

The ACA, in contrast, relates solely to the federally funded Medicaid program; if States choose not to comply, Congress has not threatened to withhold funds earmarked for any other program. Nor does the ACA use Medicaid funding to induce States to take action Congress itself could not undertake. The Federal Government undoubtedly could operate its own health-care program for poor persons, just as it operates Medicare for seniors' health care.

That is what makes this such a simple case, and the Court's decision so unsettling. Congress, aiming to assist the needy, has appropriated federal money to subsidize state health-insurance programs that meet federal standards. The principal standard the ACA sets is that the state program cover adults earning no more than 133% of the federal poverty line. Enforcing that prescription ensures that federal funds will be spent on health care for the poor in furtherance of Congress' present perception of the general welfare. . . .

The Chief Justice ultimately asks whether "the financial inducement offered by Congress . . . pass[ed] the point at which pressure turns into compulsion." The financial inducement Congress employed here, he concludes, crosses that threshold: The threatened withholding of "existing Medicaid funds" is "a gun to the head" that forces States to acquiesce.

The Chief Justice sees no need to "fix the outermost line," *Steward Machine* "where persuasion gives way to coercion." . . . When future Spending Clause challenges arrive, as they likely will in the wake of today's decision, how will litigants and judges assess whether "a State has a legitimate choice whether to accept the federal conditions in exchange for federal funds"? Are courts to measure the number of dollars the Federal Government might withhold for noncompliance? The portion of the State's budget at stake? And which State's — or States' — budget is determinative: the lead plaintiff, all challenging States (26 in this case, many with quite different fiscal situations), or some national median? Does it matter that Florida, unlike most States, imposes no state income tax, and therefore might be able to replace foregone federal funds with new state revenue? Or that the coercion state officials in fact fear is punishment at the ballot box for turning down a politically popular federal grant?

The coercion inquiry, therefore, appears to involve political judgments that defy judicial calculation. . . . At bottom, my colleagues' position is that the States' reliance on federal funds limits Congress' authority to alter its spending programs. This gets things backwards: Congress, not the States, is tasked with spending federal money in service of the general welfare. And each successive Congress is empowered to appropriate funds as it sees fit. When the 110th Congress reached a conclusion about Medicaid funds that differed from its predecessors' view, it abridged no State's right to "existing," or "pre-existing," funds. For, in fact, there are no such funds. There is only money States anticipate receiving from future Congresses. . . .

For the foregoing reasons, I disagree that any such withholding would violate the Spending Clause. . . . But in view of The Chief Justice's disposition, I agree with him that the Medicaid Act's severability clause determines the appropriate remedy. . . . The Chief Justice is undoubtedly right to conclude that Congress may offer States funds "to expand the availability of health care, and requir[e] that States accepting such funds comply with the conditions on their use." I therefore concur in the judgment with respect to Part IV-B of The Chief Justice's opinion.

Justice Scalia, Justice Kennedy, Justice Thomas, and Justice Alito, dissenting. . . .

Seven Members of the Court agree that the Medicaid Expansion, as enacted by Congress, is unconstitutional. Because the Medicaid Expansion is unconstitutional, the question of remedy arises. The most natural remedy would be to invalidate the Medicaid Expansion. However, the Government proposes — in two cursory sentences at the very end of its brief — preserving the Expansion. Under its proposal, States would receive the additional Medicaid funds if they expand eligibility, but States would keep their pre-existing Medicaid funds if they do not expand eligibility. We cannot accept the Government's suggestion.

The reality that States were given no real choice but to expand Medicaid was not an accident. Congress assumed States would have no choice, and the ACA depends on States' having no choice, because its Mandate requires low-income individuals to obtain insurance many of them can afford only through the Medicaid Expansion. Furthermore, a State's withdrawal might subject everyone in the State to much higher insurance premiums. That is because the Medicaid Expansion will no longer offset the cost to the insurance industry imposed by the ACA's insurance regulations and taxes, a point that is explained in more detail in the severability section below. To make the Medicaid Expansion optional despite the ACA's structure and design "'would be to make a new law, not to enforce an old one. This is no part of our duty.'" *Trade-Mark Cases* (1879).

Worse, the Government's proposed remedy introduces a new dynamic: States must choose between expanding Medicaid or paying huge tax sums to the federal fisc for the sole benefit of expanding Medicaid in other States. If this divisive dynamic between and among States can be introduced at all, it should be by conscious congressional choice, not by Court-invented interpretation. We do not doubt that States are capable of making decisions when put in a tight spot. We do doubt the authority of this Court to put them there.

The Government cites a severability clause codified with Medicaid in Chapter 7 of the United States Code stating that if "any provision of this chapter, or the application thereof to any person or circumstance, is held invalid, the remainder of the chapter, and the application of such provision to other persons or circumstances shall not be affected thereby." 42 U.S.C. §1303 (2006 ed.). But that clause tells us only that other provisions in Chapter 7 should not be invalidated if §1396c, the authorization for the cut-off of all Medicaid funds, is unconstitutional. It does not tell us that §1396c can be judicially revised, to say what it does not say. Such a judicial power would not be called the doctrine of severability but perhaps the doctrine of amendatory invalidation — similar to the amendatory veto that permits the Governors of some States to reduce the amounts appropriated in legislation. The proof that such a power does not exist is the fact that it would not preserve other congressional dispositions, but would leave it up to the Court what the "validated" legislation will contain. The Court today opts for permitting the cut-off of only incremental Medicaid funding, but it might just as well have permitted, say, the cut-off of funds that represent no more than *x* percent of the State's budget. The Court severs nothing, but simply revises §1396c to read as the Court would desire.

We should not accept the Government's invitation to attempt to solve a constitutional problem by rewriting the Medicaid Expansion so as to allow States that reject it to retain their pre-existing Medicaid funds. Worse, the Government's remedy, now adopted by the Court, takes the ACA and this Nation in a new direction and charts a course for federalism that the Court, not the Congress, has chosen; but under the Constitution, that power and authority do not rest with this Court. . . .

The Court today decides to save a statute Congress did not write. It rules that what the statute declares to be a requirement with a penalty is instead an option subject to a tax. And it changes the intentionally coercive sanction of a total cut-off of Medicaid funds to a supposedly noncoercive cut-off of only the incremental funds that the Act makes available.

The Court regards its strained statutory interpretation as judicial modesty. It is not. It amounts instead to a vast judicial overreaching. It creates a debilitated, inoperable version of health-care regulation that Congress did not enact and the public does not expect. It makes enactment of sensible health-care regulation more difficult, since Congress cannot start afresh but must take as its point of departure a jumble of now senseless provisions, provisions that certain interests favored under the Court's new design will struggle to retain. And it leaves the public and the States to expend vast sums of money on requirements that may or may not survive the necessary congressional revision.

The Court's disposition, invented and atextual as it is, does not even have the merit of avoiding constitutional difficulties. It creates them. The holding that the Individual Mandate is a tax raises a difficult constitutional question (what is a direct tax?) that the Court resolves with inadequate deliberation. And the judgment on the Medicaid Expansion issue ushers in new federalism concerns and places an unaccustomed strain upon the Union. Those States that decline the Medicaid Expansion must subsidize, by the federal tax dollars taken from their citizens, vast grants to the States that accept the Medicaid Expansion. If that destabilizing political dynamic, so antagonistic to a harmonious Union, is to be introduced at all, it should be by Congress, not by the Judiciary.

The values that should have determined our course today are caution, minimalism, and the understanding that the Federal Government is one of limited powers. But the Court's ruling undermines those values at every turn. In the name of restraint, it overreaches. In the name of constitutional avoidance, it creates new constitutional questions. In the name of cooperative federalism, it undermines state sovereignty. . . .

CHAPTER 4

Federalism Limits on Congressional Power

ASSIGNMENT 1

The rights enumerated in the Bill of Rights are commonly thought to provide constraints on the exercise of legislative power. These constraints are "external" to the definition of that power. For example, the rights protected by the First Amendment are "external" to the definition of Congress's enumerated powers. So, however narrowly or broadly "commerce" is defined, and whatever may be the scope of the commerce power considered on its own, this power may not be exercised in a way that violates "the freedom of speech" or "the free exercise of religion" protected by the First Amendment. Does federalism operate in a similar fashion? That is, regardless of how broadly congressional power is defined, does the allocation of powers between the federal and state governments impose an external constraint on congressional power? In other words, is the permissible scope of Congress's authority — however it is defined in Article I — further narrowed by federalism concerns? This question has arisen when the Court invokes the Tenth and Eleventh Amendments.

A. THE TENTH AMENDMENT

In 1976, for the first time since the New Deal, the Court struck down a federal law because it violated the principles of federalism. The question presented in *National League of Cities v. Usery* was whether Congress could constitutionally regulate the wages paid by states to their employees. At that time, federal law already imposed a minimum wage law for employees in the private sector. In his opinion for the Court, then-Associate Justice Rehnquist explained that federalism imposes certain "external" constraints on federal power, which he termed "affirmative limitations":

> Appellants in no way challenge these decisions establishing the breadth of authority granted Congress under the commerce power. Their contention, on the contrary, is that when Congress seeks to regulate directly the activities of States as public employers, it transgresses an affirmative limitation on the exercise of its power akin to other commerce power affirmative limitations contained in the Constitution. Congressional enactments which may be fully within the grant of legislative authority contained in the Commerce Clause may nonetheless be invalid because found to offend against the right to trial by jury contained in the Sixth Amendment, or the Due Process Clause of the Fifth Amendment. Appellants' essential contention is that the 1974 amendments to the Act, while undoubtedly within the scope of the Commerce Clause, encounter a similar constitutional barrier because they are to be applied directly to the States and subdivisions of States as employers.

He based the existence of such an affirmative limitation on the Tenth Amendment:

> This Court has never doubted that there are limits upon the power of Congress to override state sovereignty, even when exercising its otherwise plenary powers to tax or to regulate commerce which are conferred by Art. I of the Constitution. . . . In *Fry v. United States* (1975), the Court recognized that an express declaration of this limitation is found in the Tenth Amendment:
>
> > While the Tenth Amendment has been characterized as a "truism," stating merely that "all is retained which has not been surrendered," *United States v. Darby*, it is not without significance. The Amendment expressly declares the constitutional policy that Congress may not exercise power in a fashion that impairs the States' integrity or their ability to function effectively in a federal system.
>
> . . .
>
> It is one thing to recognize the authority of Congress to enact laws regulating individual businesses necessarily subject to the dual sovereignty of the government of the Nation and of the State in which they reside. It is quite another to uphold a similar exercise of congressional authority directed, not to private citizens, but to the States as States. We have repeatedly recognized that there are attributes of sovereignty attaching to every state government which may not be impaired by Congress, not because Congress may lack an affirmative grant of legislative authority to reach the matter, but because the Constitution prohibits it from exercising the authority in that manner.

In the end, the Court concluded that the statute unconstitutionally interfered with the State's power to determine the wages and hours of its employees, a function that is "essential to separate and independent existence" of a state. This decision, however, did not last long.

Just nine years later, the Court reversed course in *Garcia v. San Antonio Metropolitan Transit Authority* (1985). Justice Blackmun changed his position, concluding that the identification of "traditional state functions" had proven to be unworkable in practice and contrary to a correct understanding of federalism:

> What has proved problematic is not the perception that the Constitution's federal structure imposes limitations on the Commerce Clause, but rather the nature and content of those limitations. . . . We doubt that courts ultimately can identify principled constitutional limitations on the scope of Congress' Commerce Clause powers over the States merely by relying on a priori definitions of state sovereignty. In part, this is because of the elusiveness of objective criteria for "fundamental" elements of state sovereignty, a problem we have witnessed in the search for "traditional governmental functions." There is, however, a more fundamental reason: the sovereignty of the States is limited by the Constitution itself. . . . The power of the Federal Government is a "power to be respected" as well, and the fact that the States remain sovereign as to all powers not vested in Congress or denied them by the Constitution offers no guidance about where the frontier between state and federal power lies. In short, we have no license to employ freestanding conceptions of state sovereignty when measuring congressional authority under the Commerce Clause.

In other words, so long as a law is within the scope of a granted power under the post–New Deal interpretation of federal powers, the Tenth Amendment imposes no external or "affirmative limitation" on federal laws that apply to a state. The role of states in our federal system was not to be protected by affirmative limitations enforced by courts. Instead, Justice Blackmun observed, the "political process" imposes all appropriate constraints:

> [T]he principal and basic limit on the federal commerce power is that inherent in all congressional action — the built-in restraints that our system provides through state participation in federal governmental action. The political process ensures that laws that unduly burden the States will not be promulgated. In the factual setting of these cases the internal safeguards of the political process have performed as intended.

Justice Rehnquist's dissent in *Garcia* was terse and ended with the following: "I do not think it incumbent on those of us in dissent to spell out further the fine points of a principle that will, I am confident, in time again command the support of a majority of this Court."

After Justice Rehnquist became Chief Justice, the Court somewhat vindicated his prediction that federalism limits would one day be imposed on the powers of Congress. The early crucial decisions in this area were authored by his fellow Arizonan, Justice Sandra Day O'Connor. These cases each raise fundamental questions about federalism's constraints on Congress's powers: Are the constraints justified on the basis of the Tenth Amendment? Is the adoption of these "external" constraints a reaction to the lack of serious "internal" constraints on the power of Congress rather than an accurate interpretation of the Constitution itself? In other words, if the scope of Congress's enumerated powers were defined in a more limited fashion, would there be any need for the Court to create this affirmative protection of states?

STUDY GUIDE

- According to Justice O'Connor, what is the purpose of federalism? Could the majority's approach be reconciled with the dissent's contention that the protection of federalism is best left to the political sphere?
- Why do the concerns expressed by Justice O'Connor for the hardships imposed on state governments by the statutory scheme not also apply to private entities? If they do, where do these interests fit into modern constitutional analysis of the Court?
- How does the constitutional limitation found in *Gregory v. Ashcroft* differ from those the Court adopted in *National League of Cities* and later rejected in *Garcia*?
- Consider whether Justice O'Connor's approach is reminiscent of Chief Justice Marshall's analysis in *United States v. Fisher* (Chapter 2): "Where rights are infringed, where fundamental principles are overthrown, where the general system of the laws is departed from, the legislative intention must be expressed with irresistible clearness to induce a court of justice to suppose a design to effect such objects."

President Ronald Reagan and Justice Sandra Day O'Connor

O'Connor was a member of the Arizona State Senate, where she became the first woman to serve as its majority leader. In 1975, she was elected to the Maricopa County Superior Court, in 1979 she was elevated to the Arizona State Court of Appeals, and in 1981 she was appointed to the Supreme Court. She stepped down in 2006, the last Justice to have served in a legislature and the last Justice to have served in any elected public office.

Gregory v. Ashcroft

501 U.S. 452 (1991)

JUSTICE O'CONNOR delivered the opinion of the Court in which CHIEF JUSTICE REHNQUIST, and JUSTICES SCALIA, KENNEDY, and SOUTER, joined, and in Parts I and III of which JUSTICES WHITE and STEVENS joined.

Article V, §26 of the Missouri Constitution provides that "[a]ll judges other than municipal judges shall retire at the age of seventy years." We consider whether this mandatory retirement provision . . . violates the federal Age Discrimination in Employment Act of 1967 (ADEA). . . .

The ADEA makes it unlawful for an "employer" "to discharge any individual" who is at least 40 years old "because of such individual's age." The term "employer" is defined to include "a State or political subdivision of a State." Petitioners work for the State of Missouri. They contend that the Missouri mandatory retirement requirement for judges violates the ADEA. . . .

As every schoolchild learns, our Constitution establishes a system of dual sovereignty between the States and the Federal Government. . . . The Constitution created a Federal Government of limited powers. "The powers not delegated to the United States by the Constitution, nor prohibited by it to the States, are reserved to the States respectively, or to the people." U.S. Const., Amdt. 10. The States thus retain substantial sovereign authority under our constitutional system. As James Madison put it:

> The powers delegated by the proposed Constitution to the federal government are few and defined. Those which are to remain in the State governments are numerous and indefinite. . . . The powers reserved to the several States will extend to all the objects which, in the ordinary course of affairs, concern the lives, liberties, and properties of the people, and the internal order, improvement, and prosperity of the State. *The Federalist, No. 45.*

This federalist structure of joint sovereigns preserves to the people numerous advantages. It assures a decentralized government that will be more sensitive to the diverse needs of a heterogeneous society; it increases opportunity for citizen involvement in democratic processes; it allows for more innovation and experimentation in government; and it makes government more responsive by putting the States in competition for a mobile citizenry.

Perhaps the principal benefit of the federalist system is a check on abuses of government power. "The 'constitutionally mandated balance of power' between the States and the Federal Government was adopted by the Framers to ensure the protection of 'our fundamental liberties.'" *Atascadero State Hospital v. Scanlon* (1985), quoting *Garcia v. San Antonio Metropolitan Transit Authority* (Powell, J., dissenting). Just as the separation and independence of the coordinate Branches of the Federal Government serve to prevent the accumulation of excessive power in any one Branch, a healthy balance of power between the States and the Federal Government will reduce the risk of tyranny and abuse from either front. Alexander Hamilton explained to the people of New York, perhaps optimistically, that the new federalist system would suppress completely "the attempts of the government to establish a tyranny":

> [I]n a confederacy the people, without exaggeration, may be said to be entirely the masters of their own fate. Power being almost always the rival of power, the general government will at all times stand ready to check usurpations of the state governments, and these will have the same disposition towards the general government. The people, by throwing themselves into either scale, will infallibly make it preponderate. If their rights are invaded by either, they can make use of the other as the instrument of redress. *The Federalist, No. 28.*

James Madison made much the same point:

> In a single republic, all the power surrendered by the people is submitted to the administration of a single government; and the usurpations are guarded against by a division of the government into distinct and separate departments. In the compound republic of America, the power surrendered by the people is first divided between two distinct governments, and then the portion allotted to each subdivided among distinct and separate departments. Hence a double security arises to the rights of the people. The different governments will control each other, at the same time that each will be controlled by itself. [*The Federalist*], *No. 51.*

One fairly can dispute whether our federalist system has been quite as successful in checking government abuse as Hamilton promised, but there is no doubt about the design. If this "double security" is to be effective, there must be a proper balance between the States and the Federal Government. These twin powers will act as mutual restraints only if both are credible. In the tension between federal and state power lies the promise of liberty.

The Federal Government holds a decided advantage in this delicate balance: the Supremacy Clause. U.S. Const., Art. VI. As long as it is acting within the powers granted it under the Constitution, Congress may impose its will on the States. Congress may legislate in areas traditionally regulated by the States. This is an extraordinary power in a federalist system. It is a power that we must assume Congress does not exercise lightly.

The present case concerns a state constitutional provision through which the people of Missouri establish a qualification for those who sit as their judges. This provision goes beyond an area traditionally regulated by the States; it is a decision of the most fundamental sort for a sovereign entity. Through the structure of its government, and the character of those who exercise government authority, a State defines itself as a sovereign. "It is obviously essential to the independence of the States, and to their peace and tranquility, that their power to prescribe the qualifications of their own officers . . . should be exclusive, and free from external interference, except so far as plainly provided by the Constitution of the United States." *Taylor v. Beckham* (1900).

Congressional interference with this decision of the people of Missouri, defining their constitutional officers, would upset the usual constitutional balance of federal and state powers. For this reason, "it is incumbent upon the federal courts to be certain of Congress' intent before finding that federal law overrides" this balance. We explained recently: "[I]f Congress intends to alter the 'usual constitutional balance between the States and the Federal Government,' it must make its intention to do so 'unmistakably clear in the language of the statute.'" *Atascadero State Hospital v. Scanlon* (1985). *Atascadero* was an Eleventh Amendment case, but a similar approach is applied in other contexts. . . . This plain statement rule is nothing more than an acknowledgment that the States retain substantial sovereign powers under our constitutional scheme, powers with which Congress does not readily interfere. . . .

The authority of the people of the States to determine the qualifications of their government officials is, of course, not without limit. Other constitutional provisions, most notably the Fourteenth Amendment, proscribe certain qualifications; our review of citizenship requirements under the political function exception is less exacting, but it is not absent.

Here, we must decide what Congress did in extending the ADEA to the States, pursuant to its powers under the Commerce Clause. As against Congress' powers "[t]o regulate Commerce . . . among the several States," the authority of the people of the States to determine the qualifications of their government officials may be inviolate.

We are constrained in our ability to consider the limits that the state-federal balance places on Congress' powers under the Commerce Clause. See *Garcia* (declining to review limitations placed on Congress' Commerce Clause powers by our federal system). But there is no need to do so if we hold that the ADEA does not apply to state judges. Application of the plain statement rule thus may avoid a potential constitutional problem. Indeed, inasmuch as this Court, in *Garcia*, has left primarily to the political process the protection of the States against intrusive exercises of Congress' Commerce Clause powers, we must be absolutely certain that Congress intended such an exercise. . . .

In 1974, Congress extended the substantive provisions of the ADEA to include the States as employers. At the same time, Congress amended the definition of "employee" to exclude all elected and most high-ranking government officials. Under the Act, as amended:

> The term "employee" means an individual employed by any employer except that the term "employee" shall not include any person elected to public office in any State or political subdivision of any State by the qualified voters thereof, or any person chosen by such officer to be on such officer's personal staff, or an appointee on the policy-making level or an immediate adviser with respect to the exercise of the constitutional or legal powers of the office.

Governor Ashcroft contends that the 630(f) exclusion of certain public officials also excludes judges, like petitioners, who are appointed to office by the Governor and are then subject to retention election. The Governor points to two passages in 630(f). First, he argues, these judges are selected by an elected official and, because they make policy, are "appointee[s] on the 'policymaking level.'" Petitioners counter that judges merely resolve factual disputes and decide questions of law; they do not make policy. . . .

The Governor argues that state judges, in fashioning and applying the common law, make policy. Missouri is a common law state. The common law, unlike a constitution or statute, provides no definitive text; it is to be derived from the interstices of prior opinions and a well-considered judgment of what is best for the community. . . .

Governor Ashcroft contends that Missouri judges make policy in other ways as well. The Missouri Supreme Court and Courts of Appeals have supervisory authority over inferior courts. The Missouri Supreme Court has the constitutional duty to establish rules of practice and procedure for the Missouri court system, and inferior courts exercise policy judgment in establishing local rules of practice. The state courts have supervisory powers over the state bar, with the Missouri Supreme Court given the authority to develop disciplinary rules.

The Governor stresses judges' policymaking responsibilities, but it is far from plain that the statutory exception requires that judges actually make policy. The statute refers to appointees "on the policymaking level," not to appointees "who make policy." It may be sufficient that the appointee is in a position requiring the exercise of discretion concerning issues of public importance. This certainly describes the bench, regardless of whether judges might be considered policymakers in the same sense as the executive or legislature.

Nonetheless, "appointee at the policymaking level," particularly in the context of the other exceptions that surround it, is an odd way for Congress to exclude judges; a plain statement that judges are not "employees" would seem the most efficient phrasing. But in this case, we are not looking for a plain statement that judges are excluded. We will not read the ADEA to cover state judges unless Congress has made it clear that judges are included. This does not mean that the Act must mention judges explicitly, though it does not. Rather, it must be plain to anyone reading the Act that it covers judges. In the context of a statute that plainly excludes most important state public officials, "appointee on the policymaking level" is sufficiently broad that we cannot conclude that the statute plainly covers appointed state judges. Therefore, it does not. . . .

The people of Missouri have a legitimate, indeed compelling, interest in maintaining a judiciary fully capable of performing the demanding tasks that judges must perform. It is an unfortunate fact of life that physical and mental capacity sometimes diminish with age. The people may therefore wish to replace some older judges. Voluntary retirement will not always be sufficient. Nor may impeachment — with its public humiliation and elaborate procedural machinery — serve acceptably the goal of a fully functioning judiciary. . . .

The people of Missouri have established a qualification for those who would be their judges. It is their prerogative as citizens of a sovereign State to do so. . . .

Justice White, with whom Justice Stevens joins, concurring in part, dissenting in part, and concurring in the judgment.

I agree with the majority that . . . the ADEA [does not] prohibit[] Missouri's mandatory retirement provision as applied to petitioners, and I therefore concur in the judgment and in Parts I and III of the majority's opinion. I cannot agree, however, with the majority's reasoning in Part II of its opinion, which ignores several areas of well-established precedent and announces a rule that is likely to prove both unwise and infeasible. That the majority's analysis in Part II is completely unnecessary to the proper resolution of this case makes it all the more remarkable. . . .

While acknowledging [the] principle of federal legislative supremacy, the majority nevertheless imposes upon Congress a "plain statement" requirement. The majority claims to derive this requirement from the plain statement approach developed in our Eleventh Amendment cases. The issue in those cases, however, was whether Congress intended a particular statute to extend to the States at all. . . . In the present case, by contrast, Congress has expressly extended the coverage of the ADEA to the States and their employees. Its intention to regulate age discrimination by States is thus "unmistakably clear in the language of the statute." *Atascadero*. The only dispute is over the precise details of the statute's application. We have never extended the plain statement approach that far, and the majority offers no compelling reason for doing so.

The majority's plain statement rule is not only unprecedented, it contravenes our decisions in *Garcia v. San Antonio Metropolitan Transit Authority* (1985), and *South Carolina v. Baker* (1988). In those cases, we made it clear "that States must find their protection from congressional regulation through the national political process, not through judicially defined spheres of unregulable state activity." We also rejected as "unsound in principle and unworkable in practice" any test for state immunity that requires a judicial determination of which state activities are "traditional," "integral," or "necessary." The majority disregards those decisions in its attempt to carve out areas of state activity that will receive special protection from federal legislation. . . .

As long as "the national political process did not operate in a defective manner, the Tenth Amendment is not implicated." *Baker*. There is no claim in this case that the political process by which the ADEA was extended to state employees was inadequate to protect the States from being "unduly burden[ed]" by the Federal Government. In any event, . . . a straightforward analysis of the ADEA's definition of "employee" reveals that the ADEA does not apply here. Thus, even if there were potential constitutional problems in extending the ADEA to state judges, the majority's proposed plain statement rule would not be necessary to avoid them in this case. . . .

STUDY GUIDE

- Is there any textual support for the anti-commandeering principle standing on its own? Or does Congress lack the authority to enact laws that commandeer the states? That is, is the power to commandeer states "incidental" to the enumerated powers and therefore within the scope of the Necessary and Proper Clause? Or is the power to commandeer states instead a "great substantive and independent power," which both Chief Justices Marshall and Roberts said needed to be enumerated? If commandeering is not expressly barred by the Constitution, why can't Congress command a state to enact laws as a "necessary" means of "carrying into execution," say, its power to regulate interstate commerce? Are such laws perhaps "necessary" but not "proper"?

- Does *New York v. United States* represent a different approach from that of *Gregory*? Does it differ from the inquiry into "traditional state function" employed by Justice Rehnquist in *National League*? According to Justice O'Connor, what are the "two ways" in which the question of the scope of federal powers can be viewed?
- Does the majority concede the irrelevance of the Tenth Amendment to this line of cases?
- In *New York v. United States*, and the follow-up case, *Printz v. United States*, do the majority and dissenting opinions treat the presence or absence of specific text the way they normally do? Or has each side seemingly adopted the interpretive method normally associated with the other? If so, can you imagine why?
- One of the weaknesses of the Articles of Confederation was the absence of any executive structure (Chapter 1), and there were fears by some of a strong centralized national government under the new Constitution. If those who drafted the Constitution intended that the national government should not be able to "commandeer" state officials, would you expect them to have explicitly forbidden the practice? Or would they have been able to make the assumption that the change in the nature and location of sovereignty under the new Constitution would preclude such a practice?

New York v. United States

505 U.S. 144 (1992)

JUSTICE O'CONNOR delivered the opinion of the Court.

This case implicates one of our Nation's newest problems of public policy, and perhaps our oldest question of constitutional law. The public policy issue involves the disposal of radioactive waste. . . . The constitutional question is as old as the Constitution: it consists of discerning the proper division of authority between the Federal Government and the States. We conclude that, while Congress has substantial power under the Constitution to encourage the States to provide for the disposal of the radioactive waste generated within their borders, the Constitution does not confer upon Congress the ability simply to compel the States to do so. . . .

I

We live in a world full of low-level radioactive waste. Radioactive material is present in luminous watch dials, smoke alarms, measurement devices, medical fluids, research materials, and the protective gear and construction materials used by workers at nuclear power plants. . . . Millions of cubic feet of low-level radioactive waste must be disposed of each year. . . . [S]ince 1979, only three disposal sites — those in Nevada, Washington, and South Carolina — have been in operation. Waste generated in the rest of the country must be shipped to one of these three sites for disposal. . . .

Faced with the possibility that the Nation would be left with no disposal sites for low-level radioactive waste, Congress responded by enacting the Low-Level Radioactive Waste Policy Act[, which] declared a federal policy of holding each State "responsible for providing for the availability of capacity either within or outside the State for the disposal of low-level radioactive waste generated within its borders," and found that such waste could be disposed of "most safely and efficiently . . . on a regional basis." The 1980 Act authorized States to enter into regional compacts that, once ratified by Congress, would have the authority, beginning in 1986, to restrict the use of their disposal facilities to waste generated within member States. The 1980 Act included no penalties for States that failed to participate in this plan.

By 1985, only three approved regional compacts had operational disposal facilities; not surprisingly, these were the compacts formed around South Carolina, Nevada, and Washington, the three sited States. The following year, the 1980 Act would have given these three compacts the ability to exclude waste from nonmembers, and the remaining 31 States would have had no assured outlet for their low-level radioactive waste. With this prospect looming, Congress once again took up the issue of waste disposal. The result was the legislation challenged here, the Low-Level Radioactive Waste Policy Amendments Act of 1985.

The 1985 Act was again based largely on a proposal submitted by the National Governors' Association. In broad outline, the Act embodies a compromise among the sited and unsited States. The sited States agreed to extend for seven years the period in which they would accept low-level radioactive waste from other States. In exchange, the unsited States agreed to end their reliance on the sited States by 1992.

The mechanics of this compromise are intricate. The Act directs: "Each State shall be responsible for providing, either by itself or in cooperation with other States, for the disposal of . . . low-level radioactive waste generated within the State," with the exception of certain waste generated by the Federal Government. The Act authorizes States to "enter into such [interstate] compacts as may be necessary to provide for the establishment and operation of regional disposal facilities for low-level radioactive waste." For an additional seven years beyond the period contemplated by the 1980 Act, from the beginning of 1986 through the end of 1992, the three existing disposal sites "shall make disposal capacity available for low-level radioactive waste generated by any source," with certain exceptions not relevant here. But the three States in which the disposal sites are located are permitted to exact a graduated surcharge for waste arriving from outside the regional compact. . . . After the 7-year transition period expires, approved regional compacts may exclude radioactive waste generated outside the region.

The Act provides three types of incentives to encourage the States to comply with their statutory obligation to provide for the disposal of waste generated within their borders.

1. Monetary incentives. . . .
2. Access incentives. The second type of incentive involves the denial of access to disposal sites. . . .
3. The take-title provision. The third type of incentive is the most severe. The Act provides:

> If a State (or, where applicable, a compact region) in which low-level radioactive waste is generated is unable to provide for the disposal of all such waste generated within such State or compact region by January 1, 1996, each State in which such waste is generated, upon the request of the generator or owner of the waste, shall take title to the waste, be obligated to take possession of the waste, and shall be liable for all damages directly or indirectly incurred by such generator or owner as a consequence of the failure of the State to take possession of the waste as soon after January 1, 1996, as the generator or owner notifies the State that the waste is available for shipment. [. . .]

In the seven years since the Act took effect, Congress has approved nine regional compacts, encompassing 42 of the States. . . .

New York, a State whose residents generate a relatively large share of the Nation's low-level radioactive waste, did not join a regional compact. Instead, the State complied with the Act's requirements by enacting legislation providing for the siting and financing of a disposal facility in New York. The State has identified five potential sites, three in Allegany County and two in Cortland County. Residents of the two counties oppose the State's choice of location.

Petitioners — the State of New York and the two counties — filed this suit against the United States in 1990. They sought a declaratory judgment that the Act is inconsistent with the Tenth . . . Amendment[]. . . . The States of Washington, Nevada, and South Carolina intervened as defendants. . . .

II

A

. . . While no one disputes the proposition that "[t]he Constitution created a Federal Government of limited powers," *Gregory v. Ashcroft* (1991); and while the Tenth Amendment makes explicit that "[t]he powers not delegated to the United States by the Constitution, nor prohibited by it to the States, are reserved to the States respectively, or to the people," the task of ascertaining the constitutional line between federal and state power has given rise to many of the Court's most difficult and celebrated cases. . . .

These questions can be viewed in either of two ways. In some cases, the Court has inquired whether an Act of Congress is authorized by one of the powers delegated to Congress in Article I of the Constitution. . . . *McCulloch v. Maryland* (1819). In other cases, the Court has sought to determine whether an Act of Congress invades the province of state sovereignty reserved by the Tenth Amendment. See, e.g., *Garcia v. San Antonio Metropolitan Transit Authority* (1985). In a case like this one, involving the division of authority between federal and state governments, the two inquiries are mirror images of each other. If a power is delegated to Congress in the Constitution, the Tenth Amendment expressly disclaims any reservation of that power to the States; if a power is an attribute of state sovereignty reserved by the Tenth Amendment, it is necessarily a power the Constitution has not conferred on Congress.

It is in this sense that the Tenth Amendment "states but a truism that all is retained which has not been surrendered." *United States v. Darby* (1941). As Justice

Story put it, "This amendment is a mere affirmation of what, upon any just reasoning, is a necessary rule of interpreting the constitution. Being an instrument of limited and enumerated powers, it follows irresistibly that what is not conferred is withheld, and belongs to the state authorities." 3 J. Story, Commentaries on the Constitution of the United States 752 (1833). This has been the Court's consistent understanding: "The States unquestionably do retai[n] a significant measure of sovereign authority . . . to the extent that the Constitution has not divested them of their original powers and transferred those powers to the Federal Government." *Garcia.*

Congress exercises its conferred powers subject to the limitations contained in the Constitution. Thus, for example, under the Commerce Clause, Congress may regulate publishers engaged in interstate commerce, but Congress is constrained in the exercise of that power by the First Amendment. The Tenth Amendment likewise restrains the power of Congress, but this limit is not derived from the text of the Tenth Amendment itself, which, as we have discussed, is essentially a tautology. Instead, the Tenth Amendment confirms that the power of the Federal Government is subject to limits that may, in a given instance, reserve power to the States. The Tenth Amendment thus directs us to determine, as in this case, whether an incident of state sovereignty is protected by a limitation on an Article I power.

The benefits of this federal structure have been extensively catalogued elsewhere, see, e.g., *Gregory v. Ashcroft*, but they need not concern us here. Our task would be the same even if one could prove that federalism secured no advantages to anyone. It consists not of devising our preferred system of government, but of understanding and applying the framework set forth in the Constitution. "The question is not what power the Federal Government ought to have, but what powers in fact have been given by the people." *United States v. Butler* (1936).

This framework has been sufficiently flexible over the past two centuries to allow for enormous changes in the nature of government. The Federal Government undertakes activities today that would have been unimaginable to the Framers in two senses; first, because the Framers would not have conceived that any government would conduct such activities; and second, because the Framers would not have believed that the Federal Government, rather than the States, would assume such responsibilities. Yet the powers conferred upon the Federal Government by the Constitution were phrased in language broad enough to allow for the expansion of the Federal Government's role. . . .

The volume of interstate commerce and the range of commonly accepted objects of government regulation have, however, expanded considerably in the last 200 years, and the regulatory authority of Congress has expanded along with them. As interstate commerce has become ubiquitous, activities once considered purely local have come to have effects on the national economy, and have accordingly come within the scope of Congress' commerce power. See, e.g., *Katzenbach v. McClung* (1964); *Wickard v. Filburn* (1942). . . . The Court's broad construction of Congress' power under the Commerce [Clause] has of course been guided, as it has with respect to Congress' power generally, by the Constitution's Necessary and Proper Clause. . . . *McCulloch v. Maryland* (1819). . . .

The actual scope of the Federal Government's authority with respect to the States has changed over the years, therefore, but the constitutional structure underlying and limiting that authority has not. In the end, just as a cup may be half empty or half full, it makes no difference whether one views the question at issue in this case as one of ascertaining the limits of the power delegated to the Federal Government under the affirmative provisions of the Constitution or one of discerning the core of sovereignty retained by the States under the Tenth Amendment. Either way, we must determine whether any of the three challenged provisions of the Low-Level Radioactive Waste Policy Amendments Act of 1985 oversteps the boundary between federal and state authority.

B

[Unlike *National League* and *Garcia*], this is not a case in which Congress has subjected a State to the same legislation applicable to private parties. This case instead concerns the circumstances under which Congress may use the States as implements of regulation; that is, whether Congress may direct or otherwise motivate the States to regulate in a particular field or a particular way. Our cases have established a few principles that guide our resolution of the issue.

As an initial matter, Congress may not simply "commandee[r] the legislative processes of the States by directly compelling them to enact and enforce a federal regulatory program." *Hodel v. Virginia Surface Mining & Reclamation Assn., Inc.* (1981). . . . The Court reached the same conclusion the following year in *FERC v. Mississippi* (1982), . . . [where we] observed that "this Court never has sanctioned explicitly a federal command to the States to promulgate and enforce laws and regulations." . . .

These statements in *FERC* and *Hodel* were not innovations. While Congress has substantial powers to govern the Nation directly, including in areas of intimate concern to the States, the Constitution has never been understood to confer upon Congress the ability to require the States to govern according to Congress' instructions. . . . Indeed, the question whether the Constitution should permit Congress to employ state governments as regulatory agencies was a topic of lively debate among the Framers. Under the Articles of Confederation, Congress lacked the authority in most respects to govern the people directly. . . .

The inadequacy of this governmental structure was responsible in part for the Constitutional Convention. Alexander Hamilton observed: "The great and radical vice in the construction of the existing Confederation is in the principle of LEGISLATION for STATES or GOVERNMENTS, in their CORPORATE or COLLECTIVE CAPACITIES, and as contra-distinguished from the INDIVIDUALS of whom they consist." *The Federalist, No. 16.* As Hamilton saw it, "we must resolve to incorporate into our plan those ingredients which may be considered as forming the characteristic difference between a league and a government; we must extend the authority of the Union to the persons of the citizens — the only proper objects of government." The new National Government "must carry its agency to the persons of the citizens. It must stand in need of no intermediate legislations. . . . The government of the Union, like that of each State, must be able to address itself immediately to the hopes and fears of individuals."

The Convention generated a great number of proposals for the structure of the new Government, but two quickly took center stage. Under the Virginia Plan, as first introduced by Edmund Randolph, Congress would exercise legislative authority directly upon individuals, without employing the States as intermediaries. Under the New Jersey Plan, as first introduced by William Paterson, Congress would continue to require the approval of the States before legislating, as it had under the Articles of Confederation. These two plans underwent various revisions as the Convention progressed, but they remained the two primary options discussed by the delegates. One frequently expressed objection to the New Jersey Plan was that it might require the Federal Government to coerce the States into implementing legislation. As Randolph explained the distinction, "[t]he true question is whether we shall adhere to the federal plan [i.e., the New Jersey Plan], or introduce the national plan. The insufficiency of the former has been fully displayed. . . . There are but two modes by which the end of a Gen[eral] Gov[ernment] can be attained: the 1st is by coercion as proposed by Mr. P[aterson's] plan[, the 2nd] by real legislation as prop[osed] by the other plan. Coercion [is] impracticable, *expensive, cruel to individuals. . . .* We must resort therefore to a national *Legislation over individuals.*" (emphasis in original). Madison echoed this view: "The practicability of making laws, with coercive sanctions, for the States as political bodies, had been exploded on all hands." . . .

In the end, the Convention opted for a Constitution in which Congress would exercise its legislative authority directly over individuals, rather than over States; for a variety of reasons, it rejected the New Jersey Plan in favor of the Virginia Plan. This choice was made clear to the subsequent state ratifying conventions. Oliver Ellsworth, a member of the Connecticut delegation in Philadelphia, explained the distinction to his State's convention: "This Constitution does not attempt to coerce sovereign bodies, states, in their political capacity. . . . But this legal coercion singles out the . . . individual." Charles Pinckney, another delegate at the Constitutional Convention, emphasized to the South Carolina House of Representatives that, in Philadelphia, "the necessity of having a government which should at once operate upon the people, and not upon the states, was conceived to be indispensable by every delegation present." Rufus King, one of Massachusetts' delegates, returned home to support ratification by recalling the Commonwealth's unhappy experience under the Articles of Confederation and arguing: "Laws, to be effective, therefore, must not be laid on states, but upon individuals." At New York's convention, Hamilton (another delegate in Philadelphia) exclaimed: "But can we believe that one state will ever suffer itself to be used as an instrument of coercion? The thing is a dream; it is impossible. Then we are brought to this dilemma — either a federal standing army is to enforce the requisitions, or the federal treasury is left without supplies, and the government without support. What, sir, is the cure for this great evil? Nothing but to enable the national laws to operate on individuals, in the same manner as those of the states do." At North Carolina's convention, Samuel Spencer recognized that "all the laws of the Confederation were binding on the states in their political capacities, . . . but now the thing is entirely different. The laws of Congress will be binding on individuals." In providing for a stronger central government, therefore, the Framers explicitly chose a Constitution that confers upon Congress the power to regulate individuals, not States. . . .

This is not to say that Congress lacks the ability to encourage a State to regulate in a particular way, or that Congress may not hold out incentives to the States as a method of influencing a State's policy choices. Our cases have identified a variety of methods, short of outright coercion, by which Congress may urge a State to adopt a legislative program consistent with federal interests. Two of these methods are of particular relevance here.

First, under Congress' spending power, "Congress may attach conditions on the receipt of federal funds." *South Dakota v. Dole* (1987). Such conditions must (among other requirements) bear some relationship to the purpose of the federal spending; otherwise, of course, the spending power could render academic the Constitution's other grants and limits of federal authority. Where the recipient of federal funds is a State, as is not unusual today, the conditions attached to the funds by Congress may influence a State's legislative choices. . . .

Second, where Congress has the authority to regulate private activity under the Commerce Clause, we have recognized Congress' power to offer States the choice of regulating that activity according to federal standards or having state law pre-empted by federal regulation. This arrangement, which has been termed "a program of cooperative federalism," is replicated in numerous federal statutory schemes. These include the Clean Water Act; the Occupational Safety and Health Act of 1970; the Resource Conservation and Recovery Act of 1976; and the Alaska National Interest Lands Conservation Act.

By either of these two methods, as by any other permissible method of encouraging a State to conform to federal policy choices, the residents of the State retain the ultimate decision as to whether or not the State will comply. If a State's citizens view federal policy as sufficiently contrary to local interests, they may elect to decline a federal grant. If state residents would prefer their government to devote its attention and resources to problems other than those deemed important by Congress, they may choose to have the Federal Government, rather than the State, bear the expense of a federally mandated regulatory program, and they may continue to supplement that program to the extent state law is not pre-empted. Where Congress encourages state regulation, rather than compelling it, state governments remain responsive to the local electorate's preferences; state officials remain accountable to the people.

By contrast, where the Federal Government compels States to regulate, the accountability of both state and federal officials is diminished. If the citizens of New York, for example, do not consider that making provision for the disposal of radioactive waste is in their best interest, they may elect state officials who share their view. That view can always be pre-empted under the Supremacy Clause if it is contrary to the national view, but, in such a case, it is the Federal Government that makes the decision in full view of the public, and it will be federal officials that suffer the consequences if the decision turns out to be detrimental or unpopular. But where the Federal Government directs the States to regulate, it may be state officials who will bear the brunt of public disapproval, while the federal officials who devised the regulatory program may remain insulated from the electoral ramifications of their decision. Accountability is thus diminished when, due to federal coercion, elected state officials cannot regulate in accordance with the views of the local electorate in matters not preempted by federal regulation.

With these principles in mind, we turn to the three challenged provisions of the Low-Level Radioactive Waste Policy Amendments Act of 1985.

III

. . . The first set of incentives works in three steps. First, Congress has authorized States with disposal sites to impose a surcharge on radioactive waste received from other States. Second, the Secretary of Energy collects a portion of this surcharge and places the money in an escrow account. Third, States achieving a series of milestones receive portions of this fund.

The first of these steps is an unexceptionable exercise of Congress' power to authorize the States to burden interstate commerce. . . . The second step, the Secretary's collection of a percentage of the surcharge, is no more than a federal tax on interstate commerce, which petitioners do not claim to be an invalid exercise of either Congress' commerce or taxing power. The third step is a conditional exercise of Congress' authority under the Spending Clause: Congress has placed conditions — the achievement of the milestones — on the receipt of federal funds. . . . Because the first set of incentives is supported by affirmative constitutional grants of power to Congress, it is not inconsistent with the Tenth Amendment.

In the second set of incentives, Congress has authorized States and regional compacts with disposal sites gradually to increase the cost of access to the sites, and then to deny access altogether, to radioactive waste generated in States that do not meet federal deadlines. As a simple regulation, this provision would be within the power of Congress to authorize the States to discriminate against interstate commerce. Where federal regulation of private activity is within the scope of the Commerce Clause, we have recognized the ability of Congress to offer states the choice of regulating that activity according to federal standards or having state law preempted by federal regulation. . . . As a result, the second set of incentives does not intrude on the sovereignty reserved to the States by the Tenth Amendment.

The take-title provision is of a different character. This third so-called "incentive" offers States, as an alternative to regulating pursuant to Congress' direction, the option of taking title to and possession of the low-level radioactive waste generated within their borders and becoming liable for all damages waste generators suffer as a result of the States' failure to do so promptly. In this provision, Congress has crossed the line distinguishing encouragement from coercion. . . .

Because an instruction to state governments to take title to waste, standing alone, would be beyond the authority of Congress, and because a direct order to regulate, standing alone, would also be beyond the authority of Congress, it follows that Congress lacks the power to offer the States a choice between the two. . . . Either way, "the Act commandeers the legislative processes of the States by directly compelling them to enact and enforce a federal regulatory program," *Hodel*, an outcome that has never been understood to lie within the authority conferred upon Congress by the Constitution. . . .

The take-title provision appears to be unique. No other federal statute has been cited which offers a state government no option other than that of implementing legislation enacted by Congress. Whether one views the take-title provision as lying outside Congress' enumerated powers or as infringing upon the core of state sovereignty reserved by the Tenth Amendment, the provision is inconsistent with the federal structure of our Government established by the Constitution.

IV

Respondents raise a number of objections to this understanding of the limits of Congress' power. . . . [T]he United States argues that the Constitution does, in some circumstances, permit federal directives to state governments. . . . Federal statutes enforceable in state courts do, in a sense, direct state judges to enforce them, but this sort of federal "direction" of state judges is mandated by the text of the Supremacy Clause. No comparable constitutional provision authorizes Congress to command state legislatures to legislate. . . .

The sited state respondents focus their attention on the process by which the Act was formulated. They correctly observe that public officials representing the State of New York lent their support to the Act's enactment. . . . Respondents note that the Act embodies a bargain among the sited and unsited States, a compromise to which New York was a willing participant, and from which New York has reaped much benefit. Respondents then pose what appears at first to be a troubling question: how can a federal statute be found an unconstitutional infringement of state sovereignty when state officials consented to the statute's enactment?

The answer follows from an understanding of the fundamental purpose served by our Government's federal structure. The Constitution does not protect the sovereignty of States for the benefit of the States or state governments as abstract political entities, or even for the benefit of the public officials governing the States. To the contrary, the Constitution divides authority between federal and state governments for the protection of individuals. State sovereignty is not just an end in itself: "Rather, federalism secures to citizens the liberties that derive from the diffusion of sovereign power." "Just as the separation and independence of the coordinate branches of the Federal Government serve to prevent the accumulation of excessive power in any one branch, a healthy balance of power between the States and the Federal Government will reduce the risk of tyranny and abuse from either front." *Gregory v. Ashcroft.*

Where Congress exceeds its authority relative to the States, therefore, the departure from the constitutional plan cannot be ratified by the "consent" of state officials. An analogy to the separation of powers among the branches of the Federal Government clarifies this point. The Constitution's division of power among the three branches is violated where one branch invades the territory of another, whether or not the encroached-upon branch approves the encroachment. . . . The constitutional authority of Congress cannot be expanded by the "consent" of the governmental unit whose domain is thereby narrowed, whether that unit is the Executive Branch or the States.

State officials thus cannot consent to the enlargement of the powers of Congress beyond those enumerated in the Constitution. Indeed, the facts of this case raise the possibility that powerful incentives might lead both federal and state officials to view departures from the federal structure to be in their personal interests. Most citizens recognize the need for radioactive waste disposal sites, but few want sites near their homes. As a result, while it would be well within the authority of either federal or state officials to choose where the disposal sites will be, it is likely to be in the political interest of each individual official to avoid being held accountable to the voters for the choice of location. If a federal official is faced with the alternatives of choosing a location or directing the States to do it, the official may well prefer the latter, as a means of shifting responsibility for the eventual decision. If a state official is faced with the same set of alternatives — choosing a location or having Congress direct the choice of a location — the state official may also prefer the latter, as it may permit the avoidance of personal responsibility. The interests of public officials thus may not coincide with the Constitution's intergovernmental allocation of authority. Where state officials purport to submit to the direction of Congress in this manner, federalism is hardly being advanced.

Nor does the State's prior support for the Act estop it from asserting the Act's unconstitutionality. While New York has received the benefit of the Act in the form of a few more years of access to disposal sites in other States, New York has never joined a regional radioactive waste compact. Any estoppel implications that might flow from membership in a compact, thus do not concern us here. The fact that the Act, like much federal legislation, embodies a compromise among the States does not elevate the Act (or the antecedent discussions among representatives of the States) to the status of an interstate agreement requiring Congress' approval under the Compact Clause. That a party collaborated with others in seeking legislation has never been understood to estop the party from challenging that legislation in subsequent litigation. . . .

VII

Some truths are so basic that, like the air around us, they are easily overlooked. Much of the Constitution is concerned with setting forth the form of our government, and the courts have traditionally invalidated measures deviating from that form. The result may appear "formalistic" in a given case to partisans of the measure at issue, because such measures are typically the product of the era's perceived necessity. But the Constitution protects us from our own best intentions: it divides power among sovereigns and among branches of government precisely so that we may resist the temptation to concentrate power in one location as an expedient solution to the crisis of the day. The shortage of disposal sites for radioactive waste is a pressing national problem, but a judiciary that licensed extraconstitutional government with each issue of comparable gravity would, in the long run, be far worse.

States are not mere political subdivisions of the United States. State governments are neither regional offices nor administrative agencies of the Federal Government. The positions occupied by state officials appear nowhere on the Federal Government's most detailed organizational chart. The Constitution instead "leaves to the several States a residuary and inviolable sovereignty," *The Federalist, No. 39*, reserved explicitly to the States by the Tenth Amendment.

Whatever the outer limits of that sovereignty may be, one thing is clear: the Federal Government may not compel the States to enact or administer a federal regulatory program. The Constitution permits both the Federal Government and the States to enact legislation regarding the disposal of low-level radioactive waste. The Constitution enables the Federal Government to pre-empt state regulation contrary to federal interests, and it permits the Federal Government to hold out incentives to the States as a means of encouraging them to adopt suggested regulatory schemes. It does not, however, authorize Congress simply to direct the States to provide for the disposal of the radioactive waste generated within their borders. . . .

JUSTICE WHITE, with whom JUSTICE BLACKMUN and JUSTICE STEVENS join, concurring in part and dissenting in part. . . .

In my view, New York's actions subsequent to enactment of the 1980 and 1986 Acts fairly indicate its approval of the interstate agreement process embodied in those laws within the meaning of Art. I, §10, cl. 3, of the Constitution, which provides that "no State shall, without the Consent of Congress, . . . enter into any Agreement or Compact with another State." . . . The State should be estopped from asserting the unconstitutionality of a provision that seeks merely to ensure that, after deriving substantial advantages from the 1985 Act, New York in fact must live up to its bargain by establishing an in-state low-level radioactive waste facility or assuming liability for its failure to act. . . .

The Court's distinction between a federal statute's regulation of States and private parties for general purposes, as opposed to a regulation solely on the activities of States, is unsupported by our recent Tenth Amendment cases. . . . Moreover, the Court makes no effort to explain why this purported distinction should affect the analysis of Congress' power under general principles of federalism and the Tenth Amendment. . . . The alleged diminution in state authority over its own affairs is not any less because the federal mandate restricts the activities of private parties. . . .

In *Garcia*, we stated the proper inquiry: "[W]e are convinced that the fundamental limitation that the constitutional scheme imposes on the Commerce Clause to protect the 'States as States' is one of process, rather than one of result. Any substantive restraint on the exercise of Commerce Clause powers must find its justification in the procedural nature of this basic limitation, and it must be tailored to compensate for possible failings in the national political process, rather than to dictate a 'sacred province of state autonomy.'" [T]he Court tacitly concedes that a failing of the political process cannot be shown in this case, because it refuses to rebut the unassailable arguments that the States were well able to look after themselves in the legislative process that culminated in the 1985 Act's passage. . . . The Court rejects this process-based argument by resorting to generalities and platitudes about the purpose of federalism being to protect individual rights.

Ultimately, I suppose, the entire structure of our federal constitutional government can be traced to an interest in establishing checks and balances to prevent the exercise of tyranny against individuals. But these fears seem extremely far distant to me in a situation such as this. We face a crisis of national proportions in the disposal of low-level radioactive waste, and Congress has acceded to the wishes of the States by permitting local decisionmaking, rather than imposing a solution from Washington. New York itself participated and supported passage of this legislation at both the gubernatorial and federal representative levels, and then enacted state laws specifically to comply with the deadlines and timetables agreed upon by the

States in the 1985 Act. For me, the Court's civics lecture has a decidedly hollow ring at a time when action, rather than rhetoric, is needed to solve a national problem.[1]

The ultimate irony of the decision today is that, in its formalistically rigid obeisance to "federalism," the Court gives Congress fewer incentives to defer to the wishes of state officials in achieving local solutions to local problems. This legislation was a classic example of Congress acting as arbiter among the States in their attempts to accept responsibility for managing a problem of grave import. The States urged the National Legislature not to impose from Washington a solution to the country's low-level radioactive waste management problems. Instead, they sought a reasonable level of local and regional autonomy consistent with Art. I, §10, cl. 3, of the Constitution. By invalidating the measure designed to ensure compliance for recalcitrant States, such as New York, the Court upsets the delicate compromise achieved among the States, and forces Congress to erect several additional formalistic hurdles to clear before achieving exactly the same objective. Because the Court's justifications for undertaking this step are unpersuasive to me, I respectfully dissent.

JUSTICE STEVENS, concurring in part and dissenting in part.

Under the Articles of Confederation, the Federal Government had the power to issue commands to the States. See Arts. VIII, IX. Because that indirect exercise of federal power proved ineffective, the Framers of the Constitution empowered the Federal Government to exercise legislative authority directly over individuals within the States, even though that direct authority constituted a greater intrusion on state sovereignty. Nothing in that history suggests that the Federal Government may not also impose its will upon the several States as it did under the Articles. The Constitution enhanced, rather than diminished, the power of the Federal Government.

---

[1] With selective quotations from the era in which the Constitution was adopted, the majority attempts to bolster its holding that the take-title provision is tantamount to federal "commandeering" of the States. In view of the many Tenth Amendment cases decided over the past two decades in which resort to the kind of historical analysis generated in the majority opinion was not deemed necessary, I do not read the majority's many invocations of history to be anything other than elaborate window dressing. Certainly nowhere does the majority announce that its rule is compelled by an understanding of what the Framers may have thought about statutes of the type at issue here. Moreover, I would observe that, while its quotations add a certain flavor to the opinion, the majority's historical analysis has a distinctly wooden quality. One would not know from reading the majority's account, for instance, that the nature of federal-state relations changed fundamentally after the Civil War. That conflict produced in its wake a tremendous expansion in the scope of the Federal Government's lawmaking authority, so much so that the persons who helped to found the Republic would scarcely have recognized the many added roles the National Government assumed for itself. Moreover, the majority fails to mention the New Deal era, in which the Court recognized the enormous growth in Congress' power under the Commerce Clause. While I believe we should not be blind to history, neither should we read it so selectively as to restrict the proper scope of Congress' powers under Article 1, especially when the history not mentioned by the majority fully supports a more expansive understanding of the legislature's authority than may have existed in the late 18th century. Given the scanty textual support for the majority's position, it would be far more sensible to defer to a coordinate branch of government in its decision to devise a solution to a national problem of this kind. . . .

The notion that Congress does not have the power to issue "a simple command to state governments to implement legislation enacted by Congress," is incorrect and unsound. There is no such limitation in the Constitution. The Tenth Amendment surely does not impose any limit on Congress' exercise of the powers delegated to it by Article I. Nor does the structure of the constitutional order or the values of federalism mandate such a formal rule. To the contrary, the Federal Government directs state governments in many realms. The Government regulates state-operated railroads, state school systems, state prisons, state elections, and a host of other state functions. Similarly, there can be no doubt that, in time of war, Congress could either draft soldiers itself or command the States to supply their quotas of troops. I see no reason why Congress may not also command the States to enforce federal water and air quality standards or federal standards for the disposition of low-level radioactive wastes. . . .

With respect to the problem presented by the case at hand, if litigation should develop between States that have joined a compact, we would surely have the power to grant relief in the form of specific enforcement of the take-title provision. Indeed, even if the statute had never been passed, if one State's radioactive waste created a nuisance that harmed its neighbors, it seems clear that we would have had the power to command the offending State to take remedial action. If this Court has such authority, surely Congress has similar authority.

For these reasons, as well as those set forth by Justice White, I respectfully dissent.

STUDY GUIDE

- Is there any principled distinction to be made between federal "commandeering" of state legislatures and state executive branch officials?
- How does Justice Scalia justify this extension of the anti-commandeering doctrine? Recall that his treatment of the Necessary and Proper Clause was relied upon by Chief Justice Roberts and the four dissenting Justices in *NFIB v. Sebelius* (Chapter 3), who found that the individual mandate may be "necessary" but not "proper."
- How does Justice Thomas's self-described "revisionist view" compare with that of Justice Scalia?
- What do you think of Justice Stevens's use of historical and textualist arguments?
- Why does the majority reject the dissenters' "natural reading" of *Federalist No. 27*, which seems to assume there would be what the Court now calls "commandeering"?
- Is there a functional or structural argument for protecting the states based on changed circumstances in the political system? Is it fair for an originalist to also make a functional argument, or does that undermine the cogency of an originalist approach?
- Are state judges commandeered when they are required to apply federal law? Look carefully at Article VI, Section 3 of the Constitution. If so, how is that different from commandeering the legislative or executive branches?

Shooting of James Brady during assassination attempt on President Reagan

Washington, D.C., Hilton Hotel

The Brady Act was named for James Brady, the White House press secretary who was shot by John Hinckley, Jr., during an assassination attempt in March 1981 on President Reagan outside of the Washington, D.C., Hilton Hotel. After the shooting, the Hilton built a new drive-through structure allowing the President to exit safely from his limo within its shelter.

Printz v. United States

521 U.S. 898 (1997)

[Provisions of the Brady Handgun Violence Prevention Act require the attorney general to establish a national system for instantly checking the background of prospective handgun purchasers. While that electronic system was being developed, the law commanded the "chief law enforcement officer" (CLEO) of each local jurisdiction to conduct such checks and perform related tasks on an interim basis. Petitioners, the CLEOs for counties in Montana and Arizona, filed separate actions challenging the interim provisions' constitutionality. — Eds.]

Justice Scalia delivered the opinion of the Court. . . .

Sheriffs Richard Mack (left) and Jay Printz (right) with their attorney, Stephen P. Halbrook (center), at the Supreme Court

II

Petitioners here object to being pressed into federal service, and contend that congressional action compelling state officers to execute federal laws is unconstitutional. Because there is no constitutional text speaking to this precise question, the answer to the CLEOs' challenge must be sought in historical understanding and practice, in the structure of the Constitution, and in the jurisprudence of this Court. . . .

Petitioners contend that compelled enlistment of state executive officers for the administration of federal programs is, until very recent years at least, unprecedented. The Government contends, to the contrary, that "the earliest Congresses enacted statutes that required the participation of state officials in the implementation of federal laws." . . . Conversely if, as petitioners contend, earlier Congresses avoided use of this highly attractive power, we would have reason to believe that the power was thought not to exist. . . .

The Government observes that statutes enacted by the first Congresses required state courts to record applications for citizenship, to transmit abstracts of citizenship applications and other naturalization records to the Secretary of State, and to register aliens seeking naturalization and issue certificates of registry. . . . Other statutes of that era apparently or at least arguably required state courts to perform functions unrelated to naturalization, such as resolving controversies between a captain and the crew of his ship concerning the seaworthiness of the vessel, hearing the claims of slave owners who had apprehended fugitive slaves and issuing certificates authorizing the slave's forced removal to the State from which he had fled, taking proof of the claims of Canadian refugees who had assisted the United States during the Revolutionary War, and ordering the deportation of alien enemies in times of war.

These early laws establish, at most, that the Constitution was originally understood to permit imposition of an obligation on state *judges* to enforce federal prescriptions, insofar as those prescriptions related to matters appropriate for the judicial power. That assumption was perhaps implicit in one of the provisions of the Constitution, and was explicit in another. In accord with the so-called Madisonian Compromise, Article III, §1, established only a Supreme Court, and made the creation of lower federal courts optional with the Congress — even though it was obvious that the Supreme Court alone could not hear all federal cases throughout the United States. And the Supremacy Clause, Art. VI, cl. 2, announced that "the Laws of the United States . . . shall be the supreme Law of the Land; and the Judges in every State shall be bound thereby." It is understandable why courts should have been viewed distinctively in this regard; unlike legislatures and executives, they applied the law of other sovereigns all the time. The principle underlying so-called "transitory" causes of action was that laws which operated elsewhere created obligations in justice that courts of the forum State would enforce. The Constitution itself, in the Full Faith and Credit Clause, Art. IV, §1, generally required such enforcement with respect to obligations arising in other States.

For these reasons, we do not think the early statutes imposing obligations on state courts imply a power of Congress to impress the state executive into its service. Indeed, it can be argued that the numerousness of these statutes, contrasted with the utter lack of statutes imposing obligations on the States' executive (notwithstanding the attractiveness of that course to Congress), suggests an assumed absence of such power.[2] The only early federal law the Government has brought to our attention that imposed duties on state executive officers is the Extradition Act of 1793, which required the "executive authority" of a State to cause the arrest and delivery of a fugitive from justice upon the request of the executive authority of the State from which the fugitive had fled. That was in direct

---

[2] Bereft of even a single early, or indeed even pre-20th-century, statute compelling state executive officers to administer federal laws, the dissent is driven to claim that early federal statutes compelled state judges to perform executive functions, which implies a power to compel state executive officers to do so as well. Assuming that this implication would follow (which is doubtful), the premise of the argument is in any case wrong. None of the early statutes directed to state judges or court clerks required the performance of functions more appropriately characterized as executive than judicial. . . . Given that state courts were entrusted with the quintessentially adjudicative task of determining whether applicants for citizenship met the requisite qualifications, it is unreasonable to maintain that the ancillary functions of recording, registering, and certifying the citizenship applications were unalterably executive rather than judicial in nature. . . .

implementation, however, of the Extradition Clause of the Constitution itself, see Art. IV, §2. . . .

[T]he Government also appeals to other sources we have usually regarded as indicative of the original understanding of the Constitution. It points to portions of *The Federalist* which reply to criticisms that Congress's power to tax will produce two sets of revenue officers. . . . "Publius" responded that Congress will probably "make use of the State officers and State regulations, for collecting" federal taxes, *The Federalist, No. 36*, and predicted that "the eventual collection [of internal revenue] under the immediate authority of the Union, will generally be made by the officers, and according to the rules, appointed by the several States," *No. 45* (J. Madison). The Government also invokes *The Federalist*'s more general observations that the Constitution would "enable the [national] government to employ the ordinary magistracy of each [State] in the execution of its laws," *No. 27* (A. Hamilton), and that it was "extremely probable that in other instances, particularly in the organization of the judicial power, the officers of the States will be clothed with the correspondent authority of the Union," *No. 45* (J. Madison). But none of these statements necessarily implies — what is the critical point here — that Congress could impose these responsibilities without the consent of the States. They appear to rest on the natural assumption that the States would consent to allowing their officials to assist the Federal Government. . . . Another passage of *The Federalist* reads as follows:

> It merits particular attention . . . that the laws of the Confederacy as to the *enumerated* and *legitimate* objects of its jurisdiction will become the SUPREME LAW of the land; to the observance of which all officers, legislative, executive, and judicial in each State will be bound by the sanctity of an oath. Thus, the legislatures, courts, and magistrates, of the respective members will be incorporated into the operations of the national government *as far as its just and constitutional authority extends*; and will be rendered auxiliary to the enforcement of its laws.

The Federalist, No. 27 (A. Hamilton) (emphasis in original). . . .

Justice Souter finds "[t]he natural reading" of the phrases "will be incorporated into the operations of the national government" and "will be rendered auxiliary to the enforcement of its laws" to be that the National Government will have "authority . . . , when exercising an otherwise legitimate power (the commerce power, say), to require state 'auxiliaries' to take appropriate action." There are several obstacles to such an interpretation. First, the consequences in question ("incorporated into the operations of the national government" and "rendered auxiliary to the enforcement of its laws") are said in the quoted passage to flow automatically from the officers' oath to observe "the laws of the Confederacy as to the *enumerated* and *legitimate* objects of its jurisdiction." Thus, if the passage means that state officers must take an active role in the implementation of federal law, it means that they must do so without the necessity for a congressional directive that they implement it. But no one has ever thought, and no one asserts in the present litigation, that that is the law. The second problem with Justice Souter's reading is that it makes state *legislatures* subject to federal direction. (The passage in question, after all, does not include legislatures merely incidentally, as by referring to "all state officers"; it refers to legislatures *specifically* and *first of all.*) We have held, however, that state legislatures are *not* subject to federal direction. *New York v. United States* (1992).

These problems are avoided, of course, if the calculatedly vague consequences the passage recites — "incorporated into the operations of the national government" and "rendered auxiliary to the enforcement of its laws" — are taken to refer to nothing more (or less) than the duty owed to the National Government, on the part of all state officials, to enact, enforce, and interpret state law in such fashion as not to obstruct the operation of federal law, and the attendant reality that all state actions constituting such obstruction, even legislative Acts, are *ipso facto* invalid. This meaning accords well with the context of the passage, which seeks to explain why the new system of federal law directed to individual citizens, unlike the old one of federal law directed to the States, will "bid much fairer to avoid the necessity of using force" against the States, *The Federalist, No. 27.* It also reconciles the passage with Hamilton's statement in *Federalist, No. 36* that the Federal Government would in some circumstances do well "to employ the state officers as much as possible, and to attach them to the Union by an accumulation of their emoluments" — which surely suggests inducing state officers to come aboard by paying them, rather than merely commandeering their official services.[3] . . .

III

. . . We turn next to consideration of the structure of the Constitution, to see if we can discern among its "essential postulate[s]," a principle that controls the present cases.

It is incontestible that the Constitution established a system of "dual sovereignty." *Gregory v. Ashcroft* (1991). Although the States surrendered many of their powers to the new Federal Government, they retained "a residuary and inviolable sovereignty," *The Federalist, No. 39* (J. Madison). This is reflected throughout the Constitution's text, including (to mention only a few examples) the prohibition on any involuntary reduction or combination of a State's territory, Art. IV, §3; the Judicial Power Clause, Art. III, §2, and the Privileges and Immunities Clause, Art. IV, §2, which speak of the "Citizens" of the States; the amendment provision, Article V, which requires the votes of three-fourths of the States to amend the Constitution; and the Guarantee Clause, Art. IV, §4, which "presupposes the continued existence of the states and . . . those means and instrumentalities which are the creation of their sovereign and reserved rights." Residual state sovereignty was also implicit, of course, in the Constitution's conferral upon Congress of not all governmental powers, but only discrete, enumerated ones, Art. I, §8, which implication was rendered express by the Tenth Amendment's assertion that

[3] Justice Souter deduces from this passage in *No. 36* that although the Federal Government may commandeer state officers, it must compensate them for their services. This is a mighty leap, which would create a constitutional jurisprudence (for determining when the compensation was adequate) that would make takings cases appear clear and simple.

"[t]he powers not delegated to the United States by the Constitution, nor prohibited by it to the States, are reserved to the States respectively, or to the people." . . .

[T]he Framers rejected the concept of a central government that would act upon and through the States, and instead designed a system in which the state and federal governments would exercise concurrent authority over the people. . . . We have set forth the historical record in more detail elsewhere, see *New York v. United States*, and need not repeat it here. It suffices to repeat the conclusion: "The Framers explicitly chose a Constitution that confers upon Congress the power to regulate individuals, not States."[4] The great innovation of this design was that "our citizens would have two political capacities, one state and one federal, each protected from incursion by the other."[5]

. . . This separation of the two spheres is one of the Constitution's structural protections of liberty. . . . To quote Madison once again:

> In the compound republic of America, the power surrendered by the people is first divided between two distinct governments, and then the portion allotted to each subdivided among distinct and separate departments. Hence a double security arises to the rights of the people. The different governments will control each other, at the same time that each will be controlled by itself.

The Federalist, No. 51.

[4] The dissent, reiterating Justice Stevens' dissent in *New York*, maintains that the Constitution merely *augmented* the pre-existing power under the Articles to issue commands to the States with the additional power to make demands directly on individuals. That argument, however, was squarely rejected by the Court in *New York*, and with good reason. Many of Congress' powers under Art. I, §8, were copied almost verbatim from the Articles of Confederation, indicating quite clearly that "[w]here the Constitution intends that our Congress enjoy a power once vested in the Continental Congress, it specifically grants it." Prakash, Field Office Federalism, 79 Va. L. Rev. 1957, 1972 (1993).

[5] Justice Breyer's dissent would have us consider the benefits that other countries, and the European Union, believe they have derived from federal systems that are different from ours. We think such comparative analysis inappropriate to the task of interpreting a constitution, though it was of course quite relevant to the task of writing one. The Framers were familiar with many federal systems, from classical antiquity down to their own time; they are discussed in *Nos. 18-20* of *The Federalist.* Some were (for the purpose here under discussion) quite similar to the modern "federal" systems that Justice Breyer favors. Madison's and Hamilton's opinion of such systems could not be clearer. *Federalist, No. 20,* after an extended critique of the system of government established by the Union of Utrecht for the United Netherlands, concludes:

> I make no apology for having dwelt so long on the contemplation of these federal precedents. Experience is the oracle of truth; and where its responses are unequivocal, they ought to be conclusive and sacred. The important truth, which it unequivocally pronounces in the present case, is that a sovereignty over sovereigns, a government over governments, a legislation for communities, as contradistinguished from individuals, as it is a solecism in theory, so in practice it is subversive of the order and ends of civil polity. . . .

Antifederalists, on the other hand, pointed specifically to Switzerland — and its then 400 years of success as a "confederate republic" — as proof that the proposed Constitution and its federal structure was unnecessary. The fact is that our federalism is not Europe's. . . .

The power of the Federal Government would be augmented immeasurably if it were able to impress into its service — and at no cost to itself — the police officers of the 50 States.

We have thus far discussed the effect that federal control of state officers would have upon the first element of the "double security" alluded to by Madison: the division of power between State and Federal Governments. It would also have an effect upon the second element: the separation and equilibration of powers between the three branches of the Federal Government itself. The Constitution does not leave to speculation who is to administer the laws enacted by Congress; the President, it says, "shall take Care that the Laws be faithfully executed." . . . The Brady Act effectively transfers this responsibility to thousands of CLEOs in the 50 States, who are left to implement the program without meaningful Presidential control (if indeed meaningful Presidential control is possible without the power to appoint and remove). The insistence of the Framers upon unity in the Federal Executive — to insure both vigor and accountability — is well known. See *The Federalist, No. 70* (A. Hamilton); see also Calabresi & Prakash, The President's Power to Execute the Laws, 104 Yale L.J. 541 (1994). That unity would be shattered, and the power of the President would be subject to reduction, if Congress could act as effectively without the President as with him, by simply requiring state officers to execute its laws.[6]

The dissent of course resorts to the last, best hope of those who defend ultra vires congressional action, the Necessary and Proper Clause. It reasons that the power to regulate the sale of handguns under the Commerce Clause, coupled with the power to "make all Laws which shall be necessary and proper for carrying into Execution the foregoing Powers," conclusively establishes the Brady Act's constitutional validity, because the Tenth Amendment imposes no limitations on the *exercise* of *delegated* powers but merely prohibits the exercise of powers "not delegated to the United States." What destroys the dissent's Necessary and Proper Clause argument, however, is not the Tenth Amendment but the Necessary and Proper Clause itself.[7] When a "La[w] . . . for carrying into Execution" the Commerce Clause violates the principle of state sovereignty reflected in the various constitutional provisions we mentioned earlier, it is not a "La[w] . . . proper for carrying into Execution the Commerce Clause," and is thus, in the words of *The Federalist*, "merely [an] ac[t] of usurpation" which "deserve[s] to be treated as such." *The Federalist, No. 33*, at 204 (A. Hamilton). See Lawson & Granger, The "Proper" Scope of Federal Power: A Jurisdictional Interpretation of the Sweeping Clause, 43 Duke L.J. 267 (1993). . . .

---

[6] [C]ontrol by the unitary Federal Executive is also sacrificed when States voluntarily administer federal programs, but the condition of voluntary state participation significantly reduces the ability of Congress to use this device as a means of reducing the power of the Presidency.

[7] This argument also falsely presumes that the Tenth Amendment is the exclusive textual source of protection for principles of federalism. Our system of dual sovereignty is reflected in numerous constitutional provisions and not only those, like the Tenth Amendment, that speak to the point explicitly. It is not at all unusual for our resolution of a significant constitutional question to rest upon reasonable implications.

The dissent perceives a simple answer in that portion of Article VI which requires that "all executive and judicial Officers, both of the United States and of the several States, shall be bound by Oath or Affirmation, to support this Constitution," arguing that by virtue of the Supremacy Clause this makes "not only the Constitution, but every law enacted by Congress as well," binding on state officers, including laws requiring state officer enforcement. The Supremacy Clause, however, makes "Law of the Land" only "Laws of the United States which shall be made in Pursuance [of the Constitution]"; so the Supremacy Clause merely brings us back to the question discussed earlier, whether laws conscripting state officers violate state sovereignty and are thus not in accord with the Constitution. . . .

IV

Finally, and most conclusively in the present litigation, we turn to the prior jurisprudence of this Court. Federal commandeering of state governments is such a novel phenomenon that this Court's first experience with it did not occur until the 1970s. . . . We held in *New York* that Congress cannot compel the States to enact or enforce a federal regulatory program. Today we hold that Congress cannot circumvent that prohibition by conscripting the State's officers directly. The Federal Government may neither issue directives requiring the States to address particular problems, nor command the States' officers, or those of their political subdivisions, to administer or enforce a federal regulatory program. It matters not whether policymaking is involved, and no case by case weighing of the burdens or benefits is necessary; such commands are fundamentally incompatible with our constitutional system of dual sovereignty.

Accordingly, the judgment of the Court of Appeals for the Ninth Circuit is reversed.

JUSTICE O'CONNOR, concurring. . . .

Our holding, of course, does not spell the end of the objectives of the Brady Act. States and chief law enforcement officers may voluntarily continue to participate in the federal program. Moreover, the directives to the States are merely interim provisions scheduled to terminate November 30, 1998. Congress is also free to amend the interim program to provide for its continuance on a contractual basis with the States if it wishes, as it does with a number of other federal programs.

In addition, the Court appropriately refrains from deciding whether other purely ministerial reporting requirements imposed by Congress on state and local authorities pursuant to its Commerce Clause powers are similarly invalid. See, e.g., 42 U.S.C. §5779(a) (requiring state and local law enforcement agencies to report cases of missing children to the Department of Justice). The provisions invalidated here, however, which directly compel state officials to administer a federal regulatory program, utterly fail to adhere to the design and structure of our constitutional scheme.

JUSTICE THOMAS, concurring. . . .

In my "revisionist" view, the Federal Government's authority under the Commerce Clause, which merely allocates to Congress the power "to regulate Commerce . . . among the several states," does not extend to the regulation of wholly intrastate, point of sale transactions. Absent the underlying authority to regulate the intrastate transfer of firearms, Congress surely lacks the corollary power to impress state law enforcement officers into administering and enforcing such regulations. Although this Court has long interpreted the Constitution as ceding Congress extensive authority to regulate commerce (interstate or otherwise), I continue to believe that we must "temper our Commerce Clause jurisprudence" and return to an interpretation better rooted in the Clause's original understanding.

Even if we construe Congress' authority to regulate interstate commerce to encompass those intrastate transactions that "substantially affect" interstate commerce, I question whether Congress can regulate the particular transactions at issue here. The Constitution, in addition to delegating certain enumerated powers to Congress, places whole areas outside the reach of Congress' regulatory authority. The First Amendment, for example, is fittingly celebrated for preventing Congress from "prohibiting the free exercise" of religion or "abridging the freedom of speech." The Second Amendment similarly appears to contain an express limitation on the government's authority. That Amendment provides: "A well regulated Militia, being necessary to the security of a free State, the right of the people to keep and bear arms, shall not be infringed." This Court has not had recent occasion to consider the nature of the substantive right safeguarded by the Second Amendment. If, however, the Second Amendment is read to confer a personal right to "keep and bear arms," a colorable argument exists that the Federal Government's regulatory scheme, at least as it pertains to the purely intrastate sale or possession of firearms, runs afoul of that Amendment's protections.[8] As the parties did not raise this argument, however, we need not consider it here. Perhaps, at some future date, this Court will have the opportunity to determine whether Justice Story was correct when he wrote that the right to bear arms "has justly been considered, as the palladium of the liberties of a republic." 3 J. Story, Commentaries §1890, p. 746 (1833). In the meantime, I join the Court's opinion striking down the challenged provisions of the Brady Act as inconsistent with the Tenth Amendment.

JUSTICE STEVENS, with whom JUSTICE SOUTER, JUSTICE GINSBURG, and JUSTICE BREYER join, dissenting.

When Congress exercises the powers delegated to it by the Constitution, it may impose affirmative obligations on executive and judicial officers of state and local governments as well as ordinary citizens. . . .

[8] Marshaling an impressive array of historical evidence, a growing body of scholarly commentary indicates that the "right to keep and bear arms" is, as the Amendment's text suggests, a personal right.

I

The text of the Constitution provides a sufficient basis for a correct disposition of this case.

Article I, §8, grants the Congress the power to regulate commerce among the States. . . . [T]here can be no question that that provision adequately supports the regulation of commerce in handguns effected by the Brady Act. . . .

Unlike the First Amendment, which prohibits the enactment of a category of laws that would otherwise be authorized by Article I, the Tenth Amendment imposes no restriction on the exercise of delegated powers. . . . The Amendment confirms the principle that the powers of the Federal Government are limited to those affirmatively granted by the Constitution, but it does not purport to limit the scope or the effectiveness of the exercise of powers that are delegated to Congress. Thus, the Amendment provides no support for a rule that immunizes local officials from obligations that might be imposed on ordinary citizens.[9] Indeed, it would be more reasonable to infer that federal law may impose greater duties on state officials than on private citizens because another provision of the Constitution requires that "all executive and judicial Officers, both of the United States and of the several States, shall be bound by Oath or Affirmation, to support this Constitution." U.S. Const., Art. VI, cl. 3.

It is appropriate for state officials to make an oath or affirmation to support the Federal Constitution because, as explained in *The Federalist*, they "have an essential agency in giving effect to the federal Constitution." *The Federalist, No. 44* (J. Madison). There can be no conflict between their duties to the State and those owed to the Federal Government because Article VI unambiguously provides that federal law "shall be the supreme Law of the Land," binding in every State. Thus, not only the Constitution, but every law enacted by Congress as well, establishes policy for the States just as firmly as do laws enacted by state legislatures. . . .

There is not a clause, sentence, or paragraph in the entire text of the Constitution of the United States that supports the proposition that a local police officer can ignore a command contained in a statute enacted by Congress pursuant to an express delegation of power enumerated in Article I.

II

Under the Articles of Confederation the National Government had the power to issue commands to the several sovereign states, but it had no authority to govern individuals directly. Thus, it raised an army and financed its operations by issuing requisitions to the constituent members of the Confederacy, rather than by creating federal agencies to draft soldiers or to impose taxes.

That method of governing proved to be unacceptable, not because it demeaned the sovereign character of the several States, but rather because it was cumbersome

[9] Recognizing the force of the argument, the Court suggests that this reasoning is in error because — even if it is responsive to the submission that the Tenth Amendment roots the principle set forth by the majority today — it does not answer the possibility that the Court's holding can be rooted in a "principle of state sovereignty" mentioned nowhere in the constitutional text. As a ground for invalidating important federal legislation, this argument is remarkably weak. . . .

and inefficient. Indeed, a confederation that allows each of its members to determine the ways and means of complying with an overriding requisition is obviously more deferential to state sovereignty concerns than a national government that uses its own agents to impose its will directly on the citizenry. The basic change in the character of the government that the Framers conceived was designed to enhance the power of the national government, not to provide some new, unmentioned immunity for state officers. . . .

Indeed, the historical materials strongly suggest that the Founders intended to enhance the capacity of the federal government by empowering it — as a part of the new authority to make demands directly on individual citizens — to act through local officials. Hamilton made clear that the new Constitution, "by extending the authority of the federal head to the individual citizens of the several States, will enable the government to employ the ordinary magistracy of each, in the execution of its laws." *The Federalist, No. 27.* Hamilton's meaning was unambiguous; the federal government was to have the power to demand that local officials implement national policy programs. As he went on to explain: "It is easy to perceive that this will tend to destroy, in the common apprehension, all distinction between the sources from which [the state and federal governments] might proceed; and will give the federal government the same advantage for securing a due obedience to its authority which is enjoyed by the government of each State."

More specifically, during the debates concerning the ratification of the Constitution, it was assumed that state agents would act as tax collectors for the federal government. Opponents of the Constitution had repeatedly expressed fears that the new federal government's ability to impose taxes directly on the citizenry would result in an overbearing presence of federal tax collectors in the States. Federalists rejoined that this problem would not arise because, as Hamilton explained, "the United States . . . will make use of the State officers and State regulations for collecting" certain taxes. *Id., No. 36.* Similarly, Madison made clear that the new central government's power to raise taxes directly from the citizenry would "not be resorted to, except for supplemental purposes of revenue . . . and that the eventual collection, under the immediate authority of the Union, will generally be made by the officers . . . appointed by the several States." *Id., No. 45.*

The Court's response to this powerful historical evidence is weak. The majority suggests that "none of these statements necessarily implies . . . Congress could impose these responsibilities without the consent of the States." (emphasis omitted). No fair reading of these materials can justify such an interpretation. . . . This point is made especially clear in Hamilton's statement that "the legislatures, courts, and magistrates, of the respective members, will be incorporated into the operations of the national government *as far as its just and constitutional authority extends;* and *will be rendered auxiliary to the enforcement of its laws.*" (second emphasis added). It is hard to imagine a more unequivocal statement that state judicial and executive branch officials may be required to implement federal law where the National Government acts within the scope of its affirmative powers.

[A]ccording to the majority, because Hamilton mentioned the Supremacy Clause without specifically referring to any "congressional directive," the statement does not mean what it plainly says. But the mere fact that the Supremacy Clause is the source of the obligation of state officials to implement congressional directives does not remotely suggest that they might be "incorporat[ed] into the operations of the national government" before their obligations have been defined by Congress. Federal law establishes policy for the States just as firmly as laws enacted by state legislatures, but that does not mean that state or federal officials must implement directives that have not been specified in any law. . . .

Bereft of support in the history of the founding, the Court rests its conclusion on the claim that there is little evidence the National Government actually exercised such a power in the early years of the Republic. This reasoning is misguided in principle and in fact. While we have indicated that the express consideration and resolution of difficult constitutional issues by the First Congress in particular "provides 'contemporaneous and weighty evidence' of the Constitution's meaning since many of [its] Members . . . 'had taken part in framing that instrument,'" *Bowsher v. Synar* (1986) (quoting *Marsh v. Chambers* (1983)), we have never suggested that the failure of the early Congresses to address the scope of federal power in a particular area or to exercise a particular authority was an argument against its existence. That position, if correct, would undermine most of our post–New Deal Commerce Clause jurisprudence. . . .

More importantly, the fact that Congress did elect to rely on state judges and the clerks of state courts to perform a variety of executive functions, is surely evidence of a contemporary understanding that their status as state officials did not immunize them from federal service. The majority's description of these early statutes is both incomplete and at times misleading.

For example, statutes of the early Congresses required in mandatory terms that state judges and their clerks perform various executive duties with respect to applications for citizenship. The First Congress enacted a statute requiring that the state courts consider such applications, specifying that the state courts "*shall* administer" an oath of loyalty to the United States, and that "the clerk of such court shall record such application." (emphasis added). Early legislation passed by the Fifth Congress also imposed reporting requirements relating to naturalization on court clerks, specifying that failure to perform those duties would result in a fine. Not long thereafter, the Seventh Congress mandated that state courts maintain a registry of aliens seeking naturalization. Court clerks were required to receive certain information from aliens, record that data, and provide certificates to the aliens; the statute specified fees to be received by local officials in compensation.

Similarly, the First Congress enacted legislation requiring state courts to serve, functionally, like contemporary regulatory agencies in certifying the seaworthiness of vessels. The majority casts this as an adjudicative duty, but that characterization is misleading. The law provided that upon a complaint raised by a ship's crew members, the state courts were (if no federal court was proximately located) to appoint an investigative committee of three persons "most skilful in maritime affairs" to report back. On this basis, the judge was to determine whether the ship was fit for its intended voyage. The statute sets forth, in essence, procedures for an expert inquisitorial proceeding, supervised by a judge but otherwise more characteristic of executive activity. . . .

We are far truer to the historical record by applying a functional approach in assessing the role played by these early state officials. The use of state judges and their clerks to perform executive functions was, in historical context, hardly unusual. As one scholar has noted, "two centuries ago, state and local judges and associated judicial personnel performed many of the functions today performed by executive officers, including such varied tasks as laying city streets and ensuring the seaworthiness of vessels." Caminker, State Sovereignty and Subordinacy: May Congress Commandeer State Officers to Implement Federal Law?, 95 Colum. L. Rev. 1001, 1045, n.176 (1995). . . . The majority's insistence that this evidence of federal enlistment of state officials to serve executive functions is irrelevant simply because the assistance of "judges" was at issue rests on empty formalistic reasoning of the highest order.[10]

The Court's evaluation of the historical evidence, furthermore, fails to acknowledge the important difference between policy decisions that may have been influenced by respect for state sovereignty concerns, and decisions that are compelled by the Constitution.[11] . . . [T]he majority's opinion consists almost entirely of arguments against the substantial evidence weighing in opposition to its view; the Court's ruling is strikingly lacking in affirmative support. Absent even a modicum of textual foundation for its judicially crafted constitutional rule, there should be a presumption that if the Framers had actually intended such a rule, at least one of them would have mentioned it.

III

The Court's "structural" arguments are not sufficient to rebut that presumption. The fact that the Framers intended to preserve the sovereignty of the several States simply does not speak to the question whether individual state employees may be required to perform federal obligations, such as registering young adults for the draft, creating state emergency response commissions designed to manage the release of hazardous substances, collecting and reporting data on underground storage tanks that may pose an environmental hazard, and reporting traffic fatalities and missing children to a federal agency.

As we explained in *Garcia*: "[T]he principal means chosen by the Framers to ensure the role of the States in the federal system lies in the structure of the Federal Government itself. It is no novelty to observe that the composition of the Federal Government was designed in large part to protect the States from overreaching by Congress." Given the fact that the Members of Congress are elected by the people of the several States, with each State receiving an equivalent number of Senators in order to ensure that even the smallest States have a powerful voice in the legislature,

---

[10] The majority's view that none of the statutes referred to in the text required judges to perform anything other than "quintessentially adjudicative tasks[s]," is quite wrong. The evaluation of applications for citizenship and the acceptance of Revolutionary War claims for example, . . . are hard to characterize as the sort of adversarial proceedings to which common law courts are accustomed. . . .

[11] Indeed, an entirely appropriate concern for the prerogatives of state government readily explains Congress' sparing use of this otherwise "highly attractive" power. Congress' discretion, contrary to the majority's suggestion, indicates not that the power does not exist, but rather that the interests of the States are more than sufficiently protected by their participation in the National Government.

it is quite unrealistic to assume that they will ignore the sovereignty concerns of their constituents. It is far more reasonable to presume that their decisions to impose modest burdens on state officials from time to time reflect a considered judgment that the people in each of the States will benefit therefrom.

Indeed, the presumption of validity that supports all congressional enactments has added force with respect to policy judgments concerning the impact of a federal statute upon the respective States. The majority points to nothing suggesting that the political safeguards of federalism identified in *Garcia* need be supplemented by a rule, grounded in neither constitutional history nor text, flatly prohibiting the National Government from enlisting state and local officials in the implementation of federal law.[12] . . . [U]nelected judges are better off leaving the protection of federalism to the political process in all but the most extraordinary circumstances.

Perversely, the majority's rule seems more likely to damage than to preserve the safeguards against tyranny provided by the existence of vital state governments. By limiting the ability of the Federal Government to enlist state officials in the implementation of its programs, the Court creates incentives for the National Government to aggrandize itself. In the name of States' rights, the majority would have the Federal Government create vast national bureaucracies to implement its policies. This is exactly the sort of thing that the early Federalists promised would not occur, in part as a result of the National Government's ability to rely on the magistracy of the states. . . .

The provision of the Brady Act that crosses the Court's newly defined constitutional threshold is more comparable to a statute requiring local police officers to report the identity of missing children to the Crime Control Center of the Department of Justice than to an offensive federal command to a sovereign state. If Congress believes that such a statute will benefit the people of the Nation, and serve the interests of cooperative federalism better than an enlarged federal bureaucracy, we should respect both its policy judgment and its appraisal of its constitutional power.

Accordingly, I respectfully dissent.

JUSTICE SOUTER, dissenting. . . .

In deciding these cases, which I have found closer than I had anticipated, it is *The Federalist* that finally determines my position. I believe that the most straightforward reading of *No. 27* is authority for the Government's position here, and that this reading is both supported by *No. 44* and consistent with *Nos.*

---

[12] The majority also makes the more general claim that requiring state officials to carry out federal policy causes states to "tak[e] the blame" for failed programs. The Court cites no empirical authority to support the proposition, relying entirely on the speculations of a law review article. This concern is vastly overstated. Unlike state legislators, local government executive officials routinely take action in response to a variety of sources of authority: local ordinance, state law, and federal law. It doubtless may therefore require some sophistication to discern under which authority an executive official is acting, just as it may not always be immediately obvious what legal source of authority underlies a judicial decision. . . . Moreover, we can be sure that CLEOs will inform disgruntled constituents who have been denied permission to purchase a handgun about the origins of the Brady Act requirements. The Court's suggestion that voters will be confused over who is to "blame" for the statute reflects a gross lack of confidence in the electorate that is at war with the basic assumptions underlying any democratic government.

36 and *45*. . . . I do not read any of *The Federalist* material as requiring the conclusion that Congress could require administrative support without an obligation to pay fair value for it. . . . If, therefore, my views were prevailing in these cases, I would remand for development and consideration of petitioners' points, that they have no budget provision for work required under the Act and are liable for unauthorized expenditures.

JUSTICE BREYER, with whom JUSTICE STEVENS joins, dissenting.

I would add to the reasons Justice Stevens sets forth the fact that the United States is not the only nation that seeks to reconcile the practical need for a central authority with the democratic virtues of more local control. At least some other countries, facing the same basic problem, have found that local control is better maintained through application of a principle that is the direct opposite of the principle the majority derives from the silence of our Constitution. The federal systems of Switzerland, Germany, and the European Union, for example, all provide that constituent states, not federal bureaucracies, will themselves implement many of the laws, rules, regulations, or decrees enacted by the central "federal" body. They do so in part because they believe that such a system interferes less, not more, with the independent authority of the "state," member nation, or other subsidiary government, and helps to safeguard individual liberty as well.

Of course, we are interpreting our own Constitution, not those of other nations, and there may be relevant political and structural differences between their systems and our own. Cf. *The Federalist, No. 20* (J. Madison and A. Hamilton) (rejecting certain aspects of European federalism). But their experience may nonetheless cast an empirical light on the consequences of different solutions to a common legal problem — in this case the problem of reconciling central authority with the need to preserve the liberty-enhancing autonomy of a smaller constituent governmental entity. Cf. *id., No. 42* (J. Madison) (looking to experiences of European countries); *id., No. 43* (J. Madison) (same). . . .

As comparative experience suggests, there is no need to interpret the Constitution as containing an absolute principle — forbidding the assignment of virtually any federal duty to any state official. . . .

B. THE ELEVENTH AMENDMENT

ASSIGNMENT 2

The Supreme Court's 1793 decision in *Chisholm v. Georgia*, which allowed a South Carolina citizen to sue the State of Georgia, was met with widespread opposition. Two years later, the Eleventh Amendment was ratified. It provides:

> The Judicial power of the United States shall not be construed to extend to any suit in law or equity, commenced or prosecuted against one of the United States by Citizens of another State, or by Citizens or Subjects of any Foreign State.

From this amendment, the Supreme Court has developed the doctrine known as sovereign immunity. Notwithstanding the text of the Amendment referring only to "citizens of another state," under the Court's case law, citizens are also barred from suing their own state, without the state's consent. But beyond who can sue which states, the Court ruled in *Hans v. Louisiana* that the Eleventh Amendment reaffirmed the doctrine of state sovereign immunity that had been repudiated in *Chisholm v. Georgia.*

Without question, the Eleventh Amendment reversed the outcome in *Chisholm.* Citizens were barred from bringing suit against *another* state in federal court. But whether it did more than this remains a matter of dispute. Consider this comment by Chief Justice Marshall in *Fletcher v. Peck* (1810):

> The Constitution, *as passed*, gave the courts of the United States jurisdiction in suits brought against individual States. A State, then, which violated its own contract was suable in the courts of the United States for that violation. Would it have been a defence in such a suit to say that the State had passed a law absolving itself from the contract? It is scarcely to be conceived that such a defence could be set up. And yet, if a State is neither restrained by the general principles of our political institutions nor by the words of the Constitution from impairing the obligation of its own contracts, such a defence would be a valid one. *This feature is no longer found in the Constitution*, but it aids in the construction of those clauses with which it was originally associated. (Emphases added.)

This passage suggests that Marshall did not consider the principles affirmed in *Chisholm* to have been completely repudiated. Because he mentions neither the case nor amendment by name, this passage is sometimes overlooked.

STUDY GUIDE

- The next case was decided after the Reconstruction Era ended. Does anything about its timing help account for the decision?
- Is there any textual objection to applying the Eleventh Amendment in this situation? How does the Court deal with this issue? Does the Court's argument depend on whether *Chisholm v. Georgia* (Chapter 1) was correctly decided?

Hans v. State of Louisiana

134 U.S. 1 (1890)

[A citizen of Louisiana sued that state in federal circuit court in Louisiana, to recover interest due on state bonds. The state answered with the defense of sovereign immunity. — EDS.]

MR. JUSTICE BRADLEY delivered the opinion of the court. . . .

The ground taken is, that under the Constitution, as well as under the act of Congress passed to carry it into effect, a case is within the jurisdiction of the federal courts, without regard to the character of the parties, if it arises under the Constitution or laws of the United States. . . . The language relied on is that clause of the 3rd article of the Constitution, which declares that "the judicial power of the United States shall extend to all cases in law and equity arising under this constitution, the laws of the United States, and treaties made, or which shall be made, under their authority"; and the corresponding clause of the act conferring jurisdiction upon the circuit court, which, as found in the act of March 3, 1875, is as follows, to wit: "That the circuit courts of the United States shall have original cognizance, concurrent with the courts of the several states, of all suits of a civil nature, at common law or in equity, . . . arising under the Constitution or laws of the United States, or treaties made, or which shall be made, under their authority." It is said that these jurisdictional clauses make no exception arising from the character of the parties, and therefore that a State can claim no exemption from suit, if the case is really one arising under the Constitution, laws or treaties of the United States. . . . The question now to be decided is, whether it is true where one of the parties is a State, and is sued as a defendant by one of its own citizens.

That a State cannot be sued by a citizen of another State, or of a foreign State, on the mere ground that the case is one arising under the Constitution or laws of the United States, is clearly established by the decisions of this court in several recent cases. Those were cases arising under the Constitution of the United States, upon laws complained of as impairing the obligation of contracts, one of which was the constitutional amendment of Louisiana, complained of in the present case. . . . This court held that the suits were . . . against the states . . . and were consequently violative of the Eleventh Amendment of the Constitution, and could not be maintained. It was not denied that they presented cases arising under the Constitution; but, notwithstanding that, they were held to be prohibited by the amendment referred to.

In the present case the plaintiff in error contends that he, being a citizen of Louisiana, is not embarrassed by the obstacle of the Eleventh Amendment, inasmuch as that amendment only prohibits suits against a State which are brought by the citizens of another State, or by citizens or subjects of a foreign State. It is true, the amendment does so read: and if there were no other reason or ground for abating his suit, it might be maintainable; and then we should have this anomalous result, that in cases arising under the Constitution or laws of the United States, a State may be sued in the federal courts by its own citizens, though it cannot be sued for a like cause of action by the citizens of other States, or of a foreign State; and may be thus sued in the federal courts, although not allowing itself to be sued in its own courts. If this is the necessary consequence of the language of the Constitution and the law, the result is no less startling and unexpected than was the original decision of this court, that, under the language of the Constitution and of the Judiciary Act of 1789, a State was liable to be sued by a citizen of another State, or of a foreign country. That decision was made in the case of *Chisholm v. Georgia* (1793), and created such a shock of surprise throughout the country that, at the first meeting of Congress thereafter, the Eleventh Amendment to the Constitution was almost unanimously proposed, and was in due course adopted by the legislatures of the states. This amendment, expressing the will of the ultimate sovereignty of the whole country, superior to all legislatures and all courts, actually reversed the decision of the Supreme Court. It did not in terms prohibit suits by individuals against the States, but declared that the Constitution should not be construed to import any power to authorize the bringing of such suits. The language of the amendment is that "the judicial power of the United States shall *not be construed to extend* to any suit in law or equity, commenced or prosecuted against one of the United States by citizens of another State or by citizens or subjects of any foreign State." The Supreme Court had construed the judicial power as extending to such a suit, and its decision was thus overruled. . . . Looking back from our present standpoint at the decision in Chisholm v. Georgia, we do not greatly wonder at the effect which it had upon the country. Any such power as that of authorizing the federal judiciary to entertain suits by individuals against the States, had been expressly disclaimed, and even resented, by the great defenders of the Constitution while it was on its trial before the American people. As some of their utterances are directly pertinent to the question now under consideration, we deem it proper to quote them.

The eighty-first number of the *Federalist*, written by Hamilton, has the following profound remarks:

> It has been suggested that an assignment of the public securities of one state to the citizens of another would enable them to prosecute that state in the federal courts for the amount of those securities; a suggestion which the following considerations prove to be without foundation: It is inherent in the nature of sovereignty not to be amenable to the suit of an individual *without its consent*. This is the general sense and the general practice of mankind; and the exemption, as one of the attributes of sovereignty, is now enjoyed by the government of every state in the Union. Unless, therefore, there is a surrender of this immunity in the plan of the convention, it will remain with the states, and the danger intimated must be merely ideal. The circumstances which are necessary to produce an alienation of state sovereignty were discussed in considering the article of taxation, and need not be repeated here. A recurrence to the principles there established will satisfy us that there is no color to pretend that the state governments would, by the adoption of that plan, be divested of the privilege of paying their own debts in their own way, free from every constraint but that which flows from the obligations of good faith. The contracts between a nation and individuals are only binding on the conscience of the sovereign, and have no pretension to a compulsive force. They confer no right of action independent of the sovereign will. To what purpose would it be to authorize suits against states for the debts they owe? How could recoveries be enforced? It is evident that it could not be done without waging war against the contracting state; and to ascribe to the federal courts by mere implication, and in destruction of a pre-existing right of the state governments, a power which would involve such a consequence, would be altogether forced and unwarrantable.

The obnoxious clause to which Hamilton's argument was directed, and which was the ground of the objections which he so forcibly met, was that which declared that "the judicial power shall extend to all . . . controversies between a State and citizens of another State, . . . and between a State and foreign States, citizens, or subjects." It was argued by the opponents of the Constitution that this clause would authorize jurisdiction to be given to the federal courts to entertain suits against a State brought by the citizens of another State or of a foreign State. Adhering to the mere letter, it might be so; and so, in fact, the Supreme Court held in *Chisholm v. Georgia*; but looking at the subject as Hamilton did, and as Mr. Justice Iredell did, in the light of history and experience and the established order of things, the views of the latter were clearly right — as the people of the United States in their sovereign capacity subsequently decided.

But Hamilton was not alone in protesting against the construction put upon the Constitution by its opponents. In the Virginia convention the same objections were raised by George Mason and Patrick Henry, and were met by Madison and Marshall as follows. Madison said: "Its jurisdiction [the federal jurisdiction] in controversies between a State and citizens of another State is much objected to, and perhaps without reason. It is not in the power of individuals to call any State into court. The only operation it can have is that, if a State should wish to bring a suit against a citizen, it must be brought before the federal court. This will give satisfaction to individuals, as it will prevent citizens on whom a State may have a claim being dissatisfied with the State courts. . . . It appears to me that this [clause] can have no operation but this — to give a citizen a right to be heard in the federal courts; and if a State should condescend to be a party, this court may take cognizance of it." . . . Marshall, in answer to the same objection, said: "With respect to disputes between a State and the citizens of another State, its jurisdiction has been decried with unusual vehemence. I hope that no gentleman will think that a state will be called at the bar of the federal court. . . . It is not rational to suppose that the sovereign power should be dragged before a court. The intent is to enable States to recover claims of individuals residing in other States. . . . But, say they, there will be partiality in it if a State cannot be a defendant — if an individual cannot proceed to obtain judgment against a State, though he may be sued by a State. It is necessary to be so, and cannot be avoided. I see a difficulty in making a State defendant which does not prevent its being plaintiff."

It seems to us that these views of those great advocates and defenders of the Constitution were most sensible and just, and they apply equally to the present case as to that then under discussion. The letter is appealed to now, as it was then, as a ground for sustaining a suit brought by an individual against a State. The reason against it is as strong in this case as it was in that. It is an attempt to strain the Constitution and the law to a construction never imagined or dreamed of. Can we suppose that, when the Eleventh Amendment was adopted, it was understood to be left open for citizens of a State to sue their own State in the federal courts, while the idea of suits by citizens of other States, or of foreign States, was indignantly repelled? Suppose that Congress, when proposing the Eleventh Amendment, had appended to it a proviso that nothing therein contained should prevent a state from being sued by its own citizens in cases arising under the Constitution or laws of the United States: can we imagine that it would have been adopted by the States? The supposition that it would is almost an absurdity on its face. . . .

It is not necessary that we should enter upon an examination of the reason or expediency of the rule which exempts a sovereign State from prosecution in a court of justice at the suit of individuals. This is fully discussed by writers on public law. It is enough for us to declare its existence. The legislative department of a State represents its polity and its will, and is called upon by the highest demands of natural and political law to preserve justice and judgment, and to hold inviolate the public obligations. Any departure from this rule, except for reasons most cogent, (of which the legislature, and not the courts, is the judge), never fails in the end to incur the odium of the world, and to bring lasting injury upon the State itself. But to deprive the legislature of the power of judging what the honor and safety of the state may require, even at the expense of a temporary failure to discharge the public debts, would be attended with greater evils than such failure can cause. The judgment of the Circuit Court is *Affirmed.*

MR. JUSTICE HARLAN, concurring . . .

I concur with the court in holding that a suit directly against a State by one of its own citizens is not one to which the judicial power of the United States extends, unless the State itself consents to be sued. Upon this ground alone I assent to the judgment. But I cannot give my assent to many things said in the opinion. The comments made upon the decision in *Chisholm v. Georgia* do not meet my approval. They are not necessary to the determination of the present case. Besides, I am of opinion that the decision in that case was based upon a sound interpretation of the Constitution as that instrument then was.

STUDY GUIDE

- Is the next opinion based on the text of the Eleventh Amendment? If not, what is its basis?
- What does Justice Souter think was wrong with the reasoning of *Hans v. Louisiana*? What does he identify as the "two plausible readings" of the Eleventh Amendment's text? To understand his argument, you need to remember that there are two separate sources of federal jurisdiction under Article III: (a) diversity jurisdiction, which arises when parties are from different states, and (b) federal question jurisdiction, which arises when the Constitution or a federal statute is alleged to be violated.
- Did the enactment of the Eleventh Amendment necessarily "decredit" (in the words of Chief Justice Rehnquist) *Chisholm v. Georgia*?

Seminole Tribe of Florida v. Florida

517 U.S. 44 (1996)

CHIEF JUSTICE REHNQUIST delivered the opinion of the Court.

The Indian Gaming Regulatory Act [IGRA] provides that an Indian tribe may conduct certain gaming activities only in conformance with a valid compact between the tribe and the State in which the gaming activities are located. The Act, passed by Congress under the Indian Commerce Clause, U.S. Const., Art. I, §8, cl. 3, imposes upon the States a duty to negotiate in good faith with an Indian tribe toward the formation of a compact, and authorizes a tribe to bring suit in federal court against a State in order to compel performance of that duty. We hold that notwithstanding Congress' clear intent to abrogate the States' sovereign immunity, the Indian Commerce Clause does not grant Congress that power, and therefore [IGRA] cannot grant jurisdiction over a State that does not consent to be sued. We further hold that the doctrine of *Ex parte Young* (1908), may not be used to enforce [the IGRA] against a state official. . . .

The Eleventh Amendment provides:

> The Judicial power of the United States shall not be construed to extend to any suit in law or equity, commenced or prosecuted against one of the United States by Citizens of another State, or by Citizens or Subjects of any Foreign State.

Although the text of the Amendment would appear to restrict only the Article III diversity jurisdiction of the federal courts, "we have understood the Eleventh Amendment to stand not so much for what it says, but for the presupposition . . . which it confirms." That presupposition, first observed over a century ago in *Hans v. Louisiana* (1890), has two parts: first, that each State is a sovereign entity in our federal system; and second, that "[i]t is inherent in the nature of sovereignty not to be amenable to the suit of an individual without its consent." For over a century we have reaffirmed that federal jurisdiction over suits against unconsenting States "was not contemplated by the Constitution when establishing the judicial power of the United States." *Hans.*

Here, petitioner has sued the State of Florida and it is undisputed that Florida has not consented to the suit. Petitioner nevertheless contends that its suit is not barred by state sovereign immunity. . . . [I]t argues that Congress, through the Act, abrogated the States' sovereign immunity. . . . In order to determine whether Congress has abrogated the States' sovereign immunity, we ask two questions: first, whether Congress has "unequivocally expresse[d] its intent to abrogate the immunity," and second, whether Congress has acted "pursuant to a valid exercise of power."

Congress' intent to abrogate the States' immunity from suit must be obvious from "a clear legislative statement." This rule arises from a recognition of the important role played by the Eleventh Amendment and the broader principles that it reflects. . . . Here, we agree with the parties, with the Eleventh Circuit in the decision below, and with virtually every other court that has confronted the question that Congress has in [the IGRA] provided an "unmistakably clear" statement of its intent to abrogate. . . .

. . . [W]e turn now to consider whether the Act was passed "pursuant to a valid exercise of power." . . . [O]ur inquiry into whether Congress has the power to abrogate unilaterally the States' immunity from suit is narrowly focused on one question: Was the Act in question passed pursuant to a constitutional provision granting Congress the power to abrogate? . . . Previously, in conducting that inquiry, we have found authority to abrogate under only two provisions of the

Constitution. In *Fitzpatrick v. Bitzer* (1976), we recognized that the Fourteenth Amendment, by expanding federal power at the expense of state autonomy, had fundamentally altered the balance of state and federal power struck by the Constitution. We noted that §1 of the Fourteenth Amendment contained prohibitions expressly directed at the States and that §5 of the Amendment expressly provided that "The Congress shall have power to enforce, by appropriate legislation, the provisions of this article." We held that through the Fourteenth Amendment, federal power extended to intrude upon the province of the Eleventh Amendment and therefore that §5 of the Fourteenth Amendment allowed Congress to abrogate the immunity from suit guaranteed by that Amendment.

In only one other case has congressional abrogation of the States' Eleventh Amendment immunity been upheld. In *Pennsylvania v. Union Gas Co.* (1989), a plurality of the Court found that the Interstate Commerce Clause, Art. I, §8, cl. 3, granted Congress the power to abrogate state sovereign immunity, stating that the power to regulate interstate commerce would be "incomplete without the authority to render States liable in damages." . . .

Never before the decision in *Union Gas* had we suggested that the bounds of Article III could be expanded by Congress operating pursuant to any constitutional provision other than the Fourteenth Amendment. Indeed, it had seemed fundamental that Congress could not expand the jurisdiction of the federal courts beyond the bounds of Article III. *Marbury v. Madison* (1803). . . .

In the five years since it was decided, *Union Gas* has proven to be a solitary departure from established law. Reconsidering the decision in *Union Gas*, we conclude that none of the policies underlying stare decisis require our continuing adherence to its holding. The decision has, since its issuance, been of questionable precedential value, largely because a majority of the Court expressly disagreed with the rationale of the plurality. The case involved the interpretation of the Constitution and therefore may be altered only by constitutional amendment or revision by this Court. Finally, both the result in *Union Gas* and the plurality's rationale depart from our established understanding of the Eleventh Amendment and undermine the accepted function of Article III. We feel bound to conclude that *Union Gas* was wrongly decided, and that it should be, and now is, overruled. . . .

For over a century, we have grounded our decisions in the oft-repeated understanding of state sovereign immunity as an essential part of the Eleventh Amendment. . . . The dissent, to the contrary, disregards our case law in favor of a theory cobbled together from law review articles and its own version of historical events. The dissent cites not a single decision since *Hans* (other than *Union Gas*) that supports its view of state sovereign immunity, instead relying upon the now-discredited decision in *Chisholm v. Georgia* (1793). Its undocumented and highly speculative extralegal explanation of the decision in *Hans* is a disservice to the Court's traditional method of adjudication.

The dissent mischaracterizes the *Hans* opinion. That decision found its roots not solely in the common law of England, but in the much more fundamental "jurisprudence in all civilized nations." *Hans*. The dissent's proposition that the common law of England, where adopted by the States, was open to change by the Legislature is wholly unexceptionable and largely beside the point: that common law provided the substantive rules of law rather than jurisdiction. . . . It also is noteworthy that the principle of state sovereign immunity stands distinct from other principles of the common law in that only the former prompted a specific constitutional amendment.

Hans — with a much closer vantage point than the dissent — recognized that the decision in *Chisholm* was contrary to the well-understood meaning of the Constitution. The dissent's conclusion that the decision in *Chisholm* was "reasonable," certainly would have struck the Framers of the Eleventh Amendment as quite odd: That decision created "such a shock of surprise that the Eleventh Amendment was at once proposed and adopted." The dissent's lengthy analysis of the text of the Eleventh Amendment is directed at a straw man — we long have recognized that blind reliance upon the text of the Eleventh Amendment is "to strain the Constitution and the law to a construction never imagined or dreamed of." *Hans*. The text dealt in terms only with the problem presented by the decision in *Chisholm*; in light of the fact that the federal courts did not have federal question jurisdiction at the time the Amendment was passed (and would not have it until 1875), it seems unlikely that much thought was given to the prospect of federal-question jurisdiction over the States. . . .

In putting forward a new theory of state sovereign immunity, the dissent develops its own vision of the political system created by the Framers, concluding with the statement that "[t]he Framers' principal objectives in rejecting English theories of unitary sovereignty . . . would have been impeded if a new concept of sovereign immunity had taken its place in federal-question cases, and would have been substantially thwarted if that new immunity had been held untouchable by any congressional effort to abrogate it." This sweeping statement ignores the fact that the Nation survived for nearly two centuries without the question of the existence of such power ever being presented to this Court. And Congress itself waited nearly a century before even conferring federal-question jurisdiction on the lower federal courts.

In overruling *Union Gas* today, we reconfirm that the background principle of state sovereign immunity embodied in the Eleventh Amendment is not so ephemeral as to dissipate when the subject of the suit is an area, like the regulation of Indian commerce, that is under the exclusive control of the Federal Government. Even when the Constitution vests in Congress complete law-making authority over a particular area, the Eleventh Amendment prevents congressional authorization of suits by private parties against unconsenting States. The Eleventh Amendment restricts the judicial power under Article III, and Article I cannot be used to circumvent the constitutional limitations placed upon federal jurisdiction. Petitioner's suit against the State of Florida must be dismissed for a lack of jurisdiction. . . .

JUSTICE STEVENS, dissenting. . . .

The importance of the majority's decision to overrule the Court's holding in *Pennsylvania v. Union Gas Co.* cannot be overstated. The majority's opinion does not simply preclude Congress from establishing the rather curious statutory scheme under which Indian tribes may seek the aid of a federal court to secure a State's good faith negotiations over gaming regulations. Rather, it prevents

Congress from providing a federal forum for a broad range of actions against States, from those sounding in copyright and patent law, to those concerning bankruptcy, environmental law, and the regulation of our vast national economy.

There may be room for debate over whether, in light of the Eleventh Amendment, Congress has the power to ensure that such a cause of action may be enforced in federal court by a citizen of another State or a foreign citizen. There can be no serious debate, however, over whether Congress has the power to ensure that such a cause of action may be brought by a citizen of the State being sued. Congress' authority in that regard is clear. . . .

JUSTICE SOUTER, with whom JUSTICE GINSBURG and JUSTICE BREYER join, dissenting.

In holding the State of Florida immune to suit under the Indian Gaming Regulatory Act, the Court today holds for the first time since the founding of the Republic that Congress has no authority to subject a State to the jurisdiction of a federal court at the behest of an individual asserting a federal right. Although the Court invokes the Eleventh Amendment as authority for this proposition, the only sense in which that amendment might be claimed as pertinent here was tolerantly phrased by Justice Stevens in his concurring opinion in *Union Gas*. There, he explained how it has come about that we have two Eleventh Amendments, the one ratified in 1795, the other (so-called) invented by the Court nearly a century later in *Hans v. Louisiana* (1890). Justice Stevens saw in that second Eleventh Amendment no bar to the exercise of congressional authority under the Commerce Clause in providing for suits on a federal question by individuals against a State, and I can only say that after my own canvass of the matter I believe he was entirely correct in that view, for reasons given below. . . .

I

It is useful to separate three questions: (1) whether the States enjoyed sovereign immunity if sued in their own courts in the period prior to ratification of the National Constitution; (2) if so, whether after ratification the States were entitled to claim some such immunity when sued in a federal court exercising jurisdiction either because the suit was between a State and a nonstate litigant who was not its citizen, or because the issue in the case raised a federal question; and (3) whether any state sovereign immunity recognized in federal court may be abrogated by Congress.

The answer to the first question is not clear, although some of the Framers assumed that States did enjoy immunity in their own courts. The second question was not debated at the time of ratification, . . . but in due course the Court in Chisholm v. Georgia, answered that a state defendant enjoyed no such immunity. As to federal-question jurisdiction, state sovereign immunity seems not to have been debated prior to ratification, the silence probably showing a general understanding at the time that the States would have no immunity in such cases.

The adoption of the Eleventh Amendment soon changed the result in *Chisholm*, not by mentioning sovereign immunity, but by eliminating citizen-state diversity jurisdiction over cases with state defendants. I will explain why the Eleventh Amendment did not affect federal-question jurisdiction, a notion that needs to be understood for the light it casts on the soundness of *Hans*'s holding that States did enjoy sovereign immunity in federal-question suits. The *Hans* Court erroneously assumed that a State could plead sovereign immunity against a non-citizen suing under federal-question jurisdiction, and for that reason held that a State must enjoy the same protection in a suit by one of its citizens. . . .

Whatever the scope of sovereign immunity might have been in the Colonies, . . . or during the period of Confederation, the proposal to establish a National Government under the Constitution drafted in 1787 presented a prospect unknown to the common law prior to the American experience: the States would become parts of a system in which sovereignty over even domestic matters would be divided or parcelled out between the States and the Nation, the latter to be invested with its own judicial power and the right to prevail against the States whenever their respective substantive laws might be in conflict. With this prospect in mind, the 1787 Constitution . . . in fact said nothing on the subject, and it was this very silence that occasioned some, though apparently not widespread, dispute among the Framers and others over whether ratification of the Constitution would preclude a State sued in federal court from asserting sovereign immunity as it could have done on any matter of nonfederal law litigated in its own courts. As it has come down to us, the discussion gave no attention to congressional power under the proposed Article I but focused entirely on the limits of the judicial power provided in Article III. And although the jurisdictional bases together constituting the judicial power of the national courts under §2 of Article III included questions arising under federal law and cases between States and individuals who are not citizens, it was only upon the latter citizen-state diversity provisions that preratification questions about state immunity from suit or liability centered. . . .

The argument among the Framers and their friends about sovereign immunity in federal citizen-state diversity cases, in any event, was short lived and ended when this Court, in *Chisholm*, chose between the constitutional alternatives of abrogation and recognition of the immunity enjoyed at common law. The 4-to-1 majority adopted the reasonable (although not compelled) interpretation that the first of the two Citizen-State Diversity Clauses abrogated for purposes of federal jurisdiction any immunity the States might have enjoyed in their own courts, and Georgia was accordingly held subject to the judicial power in a common-law assumpsit action by a South Carolina citizen suing to collect a debt. The case also settled, by implication, any question there could possibly have been about recognizing state sovereign immunity in actions depending on the federal question (or "arising under") head of jurisdiction as well. The constitutional text on federal-question jurisdiction, after all, was just as devoid of immunity language as it was on citizen-state diversity. . . .

Justice Iredell's dissent in *Chisholm* . . . is largely devoted to stating the position taken by several federalists that state sovereign immunity was cognizable under the Citizen-State Diversity Clauses, not that state immunity was somehow invisibly codified as an independent constitutional defense. . . . Justice Iredell's dissent focused on the construction of the Judiciary Act of 1789, not Article III. . . . [O]n Justice Iredell's view, States sued in diversity retained the common-law sovereignty "where no special act of Legislation controuls it, to be in force in each State, as it existed in England, (unaltered by any statute) at the time of the first settlement of the country." While in at least some circumstances States might be held liable to "the authority of the United States," any such liability would depend upon "laws passed under the Constitution and in conformity to it." Finding no congressional action abrogating Georgia's common-law immunity, Justice Iredell concluded that the State should not be liable to suit.

The Eleventh Amendment, of course, repudiated *Chisholm* and clearly divested federal courts of some jurisdiction as to cases against state parties. . . . There are two plausible readings of this provision's text. Under the first, it simply repeals the Citizen-State Diversity Clauses of Article III for all cases in which the State appears as a defendant. Under the second, it strips the federal courts of jurisdiction in any case in which a state defendant is sued by a citizen not its own, even if jurisdiction might otherwise rest on the existence of a federal question in the suit. . . . [W]e need to choose between the competing readings for the light that will be shed on the *Hans* doctrine and the legitimacy of inflating that doctrine to the point of constitutional immutability as the Court has chosen to do.

The history and structure of the Eleventh Amendment convincingly show that it reaches only to suits subject to federal jurisdiction exclusively under the Citizen-State Diversity Clauses. In precisely tracking the language in Article III providing for citizen-state diversity jurisdiction, the text of the Amendment does, after all, suggest to common sense that only the Diversity Clauses are being addressed. If the Framers had meant the Amendment to bar federal question suits as well, they could not only have made their intentions clearer very easily, but could simply have adopted the first post-*Chisholm* proposal, introduced in the House of Representatives by Theodore Sedgwick of Massachusetts on instructions from the Legislature of that Commonwealth. Its provisions would have had exactly that expansive effect:

> [N]o state shall be liable to be made a party defendant, in any of the judicial courts, established, or which shall be established under the authority of the United States at the suit of any person or persons, whether a citizen or citizens, or a foreigner or foreigners, or of any body politic or corporate, whether within or without the United States.

With its references to suits by citizens as well as non-citizens, the Sedgwick amendment would necessarily have been applied beyond the Diversity Clauses, and for a reason that would have been wholly obvious to the people of the time. Sedgwick sought such a broad amendment because many of the States, including his own, owed debts subject to collection under the Treaty of Paris. Suits to collect such debts would "arise under" that Treaty, and thus be subject to federal question jurisdiction under Article III. . . . Congress took no action on Sedgwick's proposal, however, and the Amendment as ultimately adopted two years later could hardly have been meant to limit federal question jurisdiction, or it would never have left the states open to federal question suits by their own citizens. . . .

In sum, reading the Eleventh Amendment solely as a limit on citizen-state diversity jurisdiction has the virtue of coherence with this Court's practice, with the views of John Marshall, with the history of the Amendment's drafting, and with its allusive language. Today's majority does not appear to disagree at least insofar as the constitutional text is concerned; the Court concedes, after all, that "the text of the Amendment would appear to restrict only the Article III diversity jurisdiction of the federal courts."

Thus, regardless of which of the two plausible readings one adopts, the further point to note here is that there is no possible argument that the Eleventh Amendment, by its terms, deprives federal courts of jurisdiction over all citizen lawsuits against the States. Not even the Court advances that proposition, and there would be no textual basis for doing so. Because the plaintiffs in today's case are citizens of the State that they are suing, the Eleventh Amendment simply does not apply to them. We must therefore look elsewhere for the source of that immunity by which the Court says their suit is barred from a federal court.

II

The obvious place to look elsewhere, of course, is *Hans v. Louisiana* (1890), and *Hans* was indeed a leap in the direction of today's holding, even though it does not take the Court all the way. The parties in *Hans* raised, and the Court in that case answered, only what I have called the second question, that is, whether the Constitution, without more, permits a State to plead sovereign immunity to bar the exercise of federal-question jurisdiction.... A critical examination of that case will show that it was wrongly decided, as virtually every recent commentator has concluded. It follows that the Court's further step today of constitutionalizing *Hans*'s rule against abrogation by Congress compounds and immensely magnifies the century-old mistake of *Hans* itself and takes its place with other historic examples of textually untethered elevations of judicially derived rules to the status of inviolable constitutional law.

Hans ... addressed the issue implicated (though not directly raised) in the preratification debate about the Citizen-State Diversity Clauses and implicitly settled by *Chisholm*: whether state sovereign immunity was cognizable by federal courts on the exercise of federal-question jurisdiction. According to *Hans*, and contrary to *Chisholm*, it was.... Taking *Hans* only as far as its holding, its vulnerability is apparent. The Court rested its opinion on avoiding the supposed anomaly of recognizing jurisdiction to entertain a citizen's federal-question suit, but not one brought by a noncitizen. There was, however, no such anomaly at all. As already explained, federal-question cases are not touched by the Eleventh Amendment, which leaves a State open to federal-question suits by citizens and noncitizens alike. If *Hans* had been from Massachusetts the Eleventh Amendment would not have barred his action against Louisiana.

Although there was thus no anomaly to be cured by *Hans*, the case certainly created its own anomaly in leaving federal courts entirely without jurisdiction to enforce paramount federal law at the behest of a citizen against a State that broke it. It destroyed the congruence of the judicial power under Article III with the substantive guarantees of the Constitution, and with the provisions of statutes passed by Congress in the exercise of its power under Article I: when a State injured an individual in violation of federal law no federal forum could provide direct relief....

How such a result could have been threatened on the basis of a principle not so much as mentioned in the Constitution is difficult to understand. But history provides the explanation. . . . *Hans* was one episode in a long story of debt repudiation by the States of the former Confederacy after the end of Reconstruction. The turning point in the States' favor came with the Compromise of 1877, when the Republican Party agreed effectively to end Reconstruction and to withdraw federal troops from the South in return for Southern acquiescence in the decision of the Electoral Commission that awarded the disputed 1876 presidential election to Rutherford B. Hayes. The troop withdrawal, of course, left the federal judiciary "effectively without power to resist the rapidly coalescing repudiation movement." Contract Clause suits like the one brought by *Hans* thus presented this Court with "a draconian choice between repudiation of some of its most inviolable constitutional doctrines and the humiliation of seeing its political authority compromised as its judgments met the resistance of hostile state governments." . . . Given the likelihood that a judgment against the State could not be enforced, it is not wholly surprising that the *Hans* Court found a way to avoid the certainty of the State's contempt.

So it is that history explains, but does not honor, *Hans*. The ultimate demerit of the case centers, however, not on its politics but on the legal errors on which it rested. . . .

III

Three critical errors in *Hans* weigh against constitutionalizing its holding as the majority does today. The first we have already seen: the *Hans* Court misread the Eleventh Amendment. It also misunderstood the conditions under which common-law doctrines were received or rejected at the time of the founding, and it fundamentally mistook the very nature of sovereignty in the young Republic that was supposed to entail a State's immunity to federal-question jurisdiction in a federal court. . . .

[T]he Framers and their contemporaries did not agree about the place of common-law state sovereign immunity even as to federal jurisdiction resting on the Citizen-State Diversity Clauses. Edmund Randolph argued in favor of ratification on the ground that the immunity would not be recognized, leaving the States subject to jurisdiction. Patrick Henry opposed ratification on the basis of exactly the same reading. On the other hand, James Madison, John Marshall, and Alexander Hamilton all appear to have believed that the common-law immunity from suit would survive the ratification of Article III, so as to be at a State's disposal when jurisdiction would depend on diversity. This would have left the States free to enjoy a traditional immunity as defendants without barring the exercise of judicial power over them if they chose to enter the federal courts as diversity plaintiffs or to waive their immunity as diversity defendants. . . . The majority sees in these statements, and chiefly in Hamilton's discussion of sovereign immunity in *The Federalist, No. 81*, an unequivocal mandate "which would preclude all federal jurisdiction over an unconsenting State." But there is no such mandate to be found. . . .

[T]he immediate context of Hamilton's discussion in *Federalist, No. 81* has nothing to do with federal question cases. It addresses a suggestion "that an assignment of the public securities of one state to the citizens of another, would enable them to prosecute that state in the federal courts for the amount of those securities." Hamilton is plainly talking about a suit subject to a federal court's jurisdiction under the Citizen-State Diversity Clauses of Article III.

The general statement on sovereign immunity emphasized by the majority then follows, along with a reference back to *Federalist, No. 32.* What Hamilton draws from that prior paper, however, is not a general conclusion about state sovereignty but a particular point about state contracts:

> A recurrence to the principles there established will satisfy us, that there is no colour to pretend that the state governments, would by the adoption of that plan, be divested of the privilege of paying their own debts in their own way, free from every constraint but that which flows from the obligations of good faith. The contracts between a nation and individuals are only binding on the conscience of the sovereign, and have no pretensions to a compulsive force. They confer no right of action independent of the sovereign will.

The most that can be inferred from this is . . . that, in diversity cases applying state contract law, the immunity that a State would have enjoyed in its own courts is carried into the federal court. When, therefore, the *Hans* Court relied in part upon Hamilton's statement, its reliance was misplaced; Hamilton was addressing diversity jurisdiction, whereas *Hans* involved federal question jurisdiction under the Contracts Clause. No general theory of federal question immunity can be inferred from Hamilton's discussion of immunity in contract suits. But that is only the beginning of the difficulties that accrue to the majority from reliance on *Federalist, No. 81.*

Hamilton says that a State is "not . . . amenable to the suit of an individual without its consent . . . [u]nless . . . there is a surrender of this immunity in the plan of the convention." *The Federalist, No. 81* (emphasis omitted). He immediately adds, however, that "[t]he circumstances which are necessary to produce an alienation of state sovereignty, were discussed in considering the article of taxation, and need not be repeated here." The reference is to *Federalist, No. 32*, also by Hamilton, which has this to say about the alienation of state sovereignty:

> [A]s the plan of the Convention aims only at a partial Union or consolidation, the State Governments would clearly retain all the rights of sovereignty which they before had and which were not by that act exclusively delegated to the United States. This exclusive delegation or rather this alienation of State sovereignty would only exist in three cases; where the Constitution in express terms granted an exclusive authority to the Union; where it granted in one instance an authority to the Union and in another prohibited the States from exercising the like authority; and where it granted an authority to the Union, to which a similar authority in the States would be absolutely and totally *contradictory* and *repugnant*. I use these terms to distinguish this last case from another which might appear to resemble it; but which would in fact be essentially different; I mean where the exercise of a concurrent jurisdiction might be productive of occasional interferences in the *policy* of any branch of administration, but would not imply any direct contradiction or repugnancy in point of constitutional authority. (emphasis in original).

As an instance of the last case, in which exercising concurrent jurisdiction may produce interferences in "policy," Hamilton gives the example of concurrent power to tax the same subjects. . . . The first embarrassment Hamilton's discussion creates for the majority turns on the fact that the power to regulate commerce with Indian Tribes has been interpreted as making "Indian relations . . . the exclusive province of federal law." . . . In sum, since the States have no sovereignty in the regulation of commerce with the tribes, on Hamilton's view, there is no source of sovereign immunity to assert in a suit based on congressional regulation of that commerce. If Hamilton is good authority, the majority of the Court today is wrong. . . .

In sum, either the majority reads Hamilton as I do, to say nothing about sovereignty or immunity in such a case, or it will have to read him to say something about it that bars any state immunity claim. . . . The Court's difficulty is far more fundamental however, than inconsistency with a particular quotation, for the Court's position runs afoul of the general theory of sovereignty that gave shape to the Framers' enterprise. An enquiry into the development of that concept demonstrates that American political thought had so revolutionized the concept of sovereignty itself that calling for the immunity of a State as against the jurisdiction of the national courts would have been sheer illogic. . . .

While there is no need here to calculate exactly how close the American States came to sovereignty in the classic sense prior to ratification of the Constitution, it is clear that the act of ratification affected their sovereignty in a way different from any previous political event in America or anywhere else. For the adoption of the Constitution made them members of a novel federal system that sought to balance the States' exercise of some sovereign prerogatives delegated from their own people with the principle of a limited but centralizing federal supremacy. . . .

Before the new federal scheme appeared, 18th-century political theorists had assumed that "there must reside somewhere in every political unit a single, undivided, final power, higher in legal authority than any other power, subject to no law, a law unto itself." B. Bailyn, The Ideological Origins of the American Revolution 198 (1967). . . . The American development of divided sovereign powers . . . was made possible only by a recognition that the ultimate sovereignty rests in the people themselves. The People possessing this plenary bundle of specific powers were free to parcel them out to different governments and different branches of the same government as they saw fit. . . .

Under such a scheme, Alexander Hamilton explained, "[i]t does not follow . . . that each of the portions of powers delegated to [the national or state government] is not sovereign *with regard to its proper objects*." Hamilton, Opinion on the Constitutionality of an Act to Establish a Bank (emphasis in original). A necessary consequence of this view was that "the Government of the United States has sovereign power as to its declared purposes & trusts." Justice Iredell was to make the same observation in his *Chisholm* dissent, commenting that "[t]he United States are sovereign as to all the powers of Government actually surrendered: Each State in the Union is sovereign as to all the powers reserved." And to the same point was Chief Justice Marshall's description of the National and State Governments as "each sovereign, with respect to the objects committed to it, and neither sovereign with respect to the objects committed to the other." *McCulloch*.

Given this metamorphosis of the idea of sovereignty in the years leading up to 1789, the question whether the old immunity doctrine might have been received as something suitable for the new world of federal-question jurisdiction is a crucial one. The answer is that sovereign immunity as it would have been known to the Framers before ratification thereafter became inapplicable as a matter of logic in a federal suit raising a federal question. The old doctrine, after all, barred the involuntary subjection of a sovereign to the system of justice and law of which it was itself the font, since to do otherwise would have struck the common-law mind from the Middle Ages onward as both impractical and absurd. But the ratification demonstrated that state governments were subject to a superior regime of law in a judicial system established, not by the State, but by the people through a specific delegation of their sovereign power to a National Government that was paramount within its delegated sphere. When individuals sued States to enforce federal rights, the Government that corresponded to the "sovereign" in the traditional common-law sense was not the State but the National Government, and any state immunity from the jurisdiction of the Nation's courts would have required a grant from the true sovereign, the people, in their Constitution, or from the Congress that the Constitution had empowered. . . .

Without citing a single source to the contrary, the Court dismisses the historical evidence regarding the Framers' vision of the relationship between national and state sovereignty, and reassures us that "the Nation survived for nearly two centuries without the question of the existence of [the abrogation] power ever being presented to this Court." But we are concerned here not with the survival of the Nation but the opportunity of its citizens to enforce federal rights in a way that Congress provides. The absence of any general federal-question statute for nearly a century following ratification of Article III (with a brief exception in 1800) hardly counts against the importance of that jurisdiction either in the Framers' conception or in current reality; likewise, the fact that Congress has not often seen fit to use its power of abrogation (outside the Fourteenth Amendment context, at least) does not compel a conclusion that the power is not important to the federal scheme. In the end, is it plausible to contend that the plan of the convention was meant to leave the National Government without any way to render individuals capable of enforcing their federal rights directly against an intransigent State? . . .

Because neither text, precedent, nor history supports the majority's abdication of our responsibility to exercise the jurisdiction entrusted to us in Article III, I would reverse the judgment of the Court of Appeals.

STUDY GUIDE

- What does Justice Kennedy mean by "ahistoric literalism"? Does his opinion represent a shift in the underlying theory of state immunities? (*Hint:* How does his opinion in *Alden* compare with his concurring opinion in *Lopez*?)

- Notice Justice Kennedy's reliance on the statements of Constitution supporters Hamilton, Madison, and Marshall in ratification conventions. These reassurances are often cited as providing a "gloss" on the original meaning of the text. What is the proper relationship of these explanations to the text of the Constitution itself?
- Who has the better of the historical argument — Kennedy or Souter? How does this history bear on the original meaning of the text? Why should we care?

Alden v. Maine

527 U.S. 706 (1999)

JUSTICE KENNEDY delivered the opinion of the Court.

In 1992, petitioners, a group of probation officers . . . alleged the State had violated the overtime provisions of the Fair Labor Standards Act of 1938 (FLSA), and sought compensation and liquidated damages. . . . [After] this Court decided *Seminole Tribe of Fla. v. Florida* (1996), which made it clear that Congress lacks power under Article I to abrogate the States' sovereign immunity from suits commenced or prosecuted in the federal courts[, the officers filed this] action in state court. The state trial court dismissed the suit on the basis of sovereign immunity, and the Maine Supreme Judicial Court affirmed. . . .

We hold that the powers delegated to Congress under Article I of the United States Constitution do not include the power to subject nonconsenting States to private suits for damages in state courts. . . .

I

The Eleventh Amendment makes explicit reference to the States' immunity from suits "commenced or prosecuted against one of the United States by Citizens of another State, or by Citizens or Subjects of any Foreign State." U.S. Const., Amdt. 11. We have, as a result, sometimes referred to the States' immunity from suit as "Eleventh Amendment immunity." The phrase is convenient shorthand but something of a misnomer, for the sovereign immunity of the States neither derives from, nor is limited by, the terms of the Eleventh Amendment. Rather, as the Constitution's structure, its history, and the authoritative interpretations by this Court make clear, the States' immunity from suit is a fundamental aspect of the sovereignty which the States enjoyed before the ratification of the Constitution, and which they retain today (either literally or by virtue of their admission into the Union upon an equal footing with the other States) except as altered by the plan of the Convention or certain constitutional Amendments.

A

Although the Constitution establishes a National Government with broad, often plenary authority over matters within its recognized competence, the founding document "specifically recognizes the States as sovereign entities." *Seminole Tribe of Fla. v. Florida*. Various textual provisions of the Constitution assume the States' continued existence and active participation in the fundamental processes of governance. See *Printz v. United States* (citing Art. III, §2; Art. IV, §§2-4; Art. V). The limited and enumerated powers granted to the Legislative, Executive, and Judicial Branches of the National Government, moreover, underscore the vital role reserved to the States by the constitutional design, see, e.g., Art. I, §8; Art. II, §§2-3; Art. III, §2. Any doubt regarding the constitutional role of the States as sovereign entities is removed by the Tenth Amendment, which, like the other provisions of the Bill of Rights, was enacted to allay lingering concerns about the extent of the national power. The Amendment confirms the promise implicit in the original document: "The powers not delegated to the United States by the Constitution, nor prohibited by it to the States, are reserved to the States respectively, or to the people." U.S. Const., Amdt. 10.

The federal system established by our Constitution preserves the sovereign status of the States in two ways. First, it reserves to them a substantial portion of the Nation's primary sovereignty, together with the dignity and essential attributes inhering in that status. The States "form distinct and independent portions of the supremacy, no more subject, within their respective spheres, to the general authority than the general authority is subject to them, within its own sphere." The Federalist No. 39 (J. Madison).

Second, even as to matters within the competence of the National Government, the constitutional design secures the founding generation's rejection of "the concept of a central government that would act upon and through the States" in favor of "a system in which the State and Federal Governments would exercise concurrent authority over the people who were, in Hamilton's words, 'the only proper objects of government.'" *Printz* (quoting The Federalist No. 15); accord, *New York* ("The Framers explicitly chose a Constitution that confers upon Congress the power to regulate individuals, not States"). In this the Founders achieved a deliberate departure from the Articles of Confederation: Experience under the Articles had "exploded on all hands" the "practicality of making laws, with coercive sanctions, for the States as political bodies." 2 Records of the Federal Convention of 1787 (J. Madison).

The States thus retain "a residuary and inviolable sovereignty." The Federalist No. 39, at 245. They are not relegated to the role of mere provinces or political corporations, but retain the dignity, though not the full authority, of sovereignty.

B

The generation that designed and adopted our federal system considered immunity from private suits central to sovereign dignity. When the Constitution was ratified, it was well established in English law that the Crown could not be sued without consent in its own courts. See *Chisholm v. Georgia* (1793) (Iredell, J., dissenting) (surveying English practice). . . . In reciting the prerogatives of the Crown, Blackstone — whose works constituted the preeminent authority on English law for the founding generation — underscored the close and necessary relationship understood to exist between sovereignty and immunity from suit:

"And, first, the law ascribes to the king the attribute of sovereignty, or pre-eminence.... Hence it is, that no suit or action can be brought against the king, even in civil matters, because no court can have jurisdiction over him. For all jurisdiction implies superiority of power...." 1 W. Blackstone, Commentaries on the Laws of England (1765).

Although the American people had rejected other aspects of English political theory, the doctrine that a sovereign could not be sued without its consent was universal in the States when the Constitution was drafted and ratified. See *Chisholm* (Iredell, J., dissenting) ("I believe there is no doubt that neither in the State now in question, nor in any other in the Union, any particular Legislative mode, authorizing a compulsory suit for the recovery of money against a State, was in being either when the Constitution was adopted, or at the time the judicial act was passed"); *Hans v. Louisiana* (1890) ("The suability of a State, without its consent, was a thing unknown to the law. This has been so often laid down and acknowledged by courts and jurists that it is hardly necessary to be formally asserted").

The ratification debates, furthermore, underscored the importance of the States' sovereign immunity to the American people. Grave concerns were raised by the provisions of Article III, which extended the federal judicial power to controversies between States and citizens of other States or foreign nations....

The leading advocates of the Constitution assured the people in no uncertain terms that the Constitution would not strip the States of sovereign immunity. One assurance was contained in The Federalist No. 81, written by Alexander Hamilton:

> It is inherent in the nature of sovereignty not to be amenable to the suit of an individual *without its consent*. This is the general sense and the general practice of mankind; and the exemption, as one of the attributes of sovereignty, is now enjoyed by the government of every State in the Union. Unless, therefore, there is a surrender of this immunity in the plan of the convention, it will remain with the States and the danger intimated must be merely ideal.... [T]here is no color to pretend that the State governments would, by the adoption of that plan, be divested of the privilege of paying their own debts in their own way, free from every constraint but that which flows from the obligations of good faith. The contracts between a nation and individuals are only binding on the conscience of the sovereign, and have no pretensions to a compulsive force. They confer no right of action independent of the sovereign will. To what purpose would it be to authorize suits against States for the debts they owe? How could recoveries be enforced? It is evident that it could not be done without waging war against the contracting State; and to ascribe to the federal courts, by mere implication, and in destruction of a preexisting right of the State governments, a power which would involve such a consequence, would be altogether forced and unwarrantable. (emphasis in original).

At the Virginia ratifying convention, James Madison echoed this theme:

> Its jurisdiction in controversies between a state and citizens of another state is much objected to, and perhaps without reason. It is not in the power of individuals to call any state into court.... It appears to me that this [clause] can have no operation but this — to give a citizen a right to be heard in the federal courts; and if a state should

> condescend to be a party, this court may take cognizance of it. 3 Debates on the Federal Constitution (1854).

When Madison's explanation was questioned, John Marshall provided immediate support:

> With respect to disputes between *a state and the citizens of another state*, its jurisdiction has been decried with unusual vehemence. I hope no gentleman will think that a state will be called at the bar of the federal court. Is there no such case at present? Are there not many cases in which the legislature of Virginia is a party, and yet the state is not sued? It is not rational to suppose that the sovereign power should be dragged before a court. The intent is, to enable states to recover claims of individuals residing in other states. I contend this construction is warranted by the words. But, say they, there will be partiality in it if a state cannot be defendant. . . . It is necessary to be so, and cannot be avoided. I see a difficulty in making a state defendant, which does not prevent its being plaintiff. (emphasis in original).

Although the state conventions which addressed the issue of sovereign immunity in their formal ratification documents sought to clarify the point by constitutional amendment, they made clear that they, like Hamilton, Madison, and Marshall, understood the Constitution as drafted to preserve the States' immunity from private suits. The Rhode Island Convention thus proclaimed that "[i]t is declared by the Convention, that the judicial power of the United States, in cases in which a state may be a party, does not extend to criminal prosecutions, or to authorize any suit by any person against a state." The convention sought, in addition, an express amendment "to remove all doubts or controversies respecting the same." In a similar fashion, the New York Convention "declare[d] and ma[d]e known," its understanding "[t]hat the judicial power of the United States, in cases in which a state may be a party, does not extend to criminal prosecutions, or to authorize any suit by any person against a state." The convention proceeded to ratify the Constitution "[u]nder these impressions, and declaring that the rights aforesaid cannot be abridged or violated, and that the explanations aforesaid are consistent with the said Constitution, and in confidence that the amendments which shall have been proposed to the said Constitution will receive an early and mature consideration."

Despite the persuasive assurances of the Constitution's leading advocates and the expressed understanding of the only state conventions to address the issue in explicit terms, this Court held, just five years after the Constitution was adopted, that Article III authorized a private citizen of another State to sue the State of Georgia without its consent. *Chisholm v. Georgia* (1793). Each of the four Justices who concurred in the judgment issued a separate opinion. The common theme of the opinions was that the case fell within the literal text of Article III, which by its terms granted jurisdiction over controversies "between a State and Citizens of another State," and "between a State, or the Citizens thereof, and foreign States, Citizens, or Subjects." U.S. Const., Art. III, §2. The argument that this provision granted jurisdiction only over cases in which the State was a plaintiff was dismissed as inconsistent with the ordinary meaning of "between," and with the provision extending jurisdiction to "Controversies between two or more States," which by necessity contemplated jurisdiction over suits to which States were defendants. Two

Justices also argued that sovereign immunity was inconsistent with the principle of popular sovereignty established by the Constitution. . . .

Justice Iredell dissented, relying on American history, English history, and the principles of enumerated powers and separate sovereignty. . . . The Court's decision "fell upon the country with a profound shock." 1 C. Warren, The Supreme Court in United States History (rev. ed. 1926). "Newspapers representing a rainbow of opinion protested what they viewed as an unexpected blow to state sovereignty. Others spoke more concretely of prospective raids on state treasuries." D. Currie, The Constitution in Congress: The Federalist Period 1789-1801 (1997).

The States, in particular, responded with outrage to the decision. . . . An initial proposal to amend the Constitution was introduced in the House of Representatives the day after *Chisholm* was announced; the proposal adopted as the Eleventh Amendment was introduced in the Senate promptly following an intervening recess. Congress turned to the latter proposal with great dispatch; little more than two months after its introduction it had been endorsed by both Houses and forwarded to the States.

Each House spent but a single day discussing the Amendment, and the vote in each House was close to unanimous. All attempts to weaken the Amendment were defeated. Congress in succession rejected proposals to limit the Amendment to suits in which "the cause of action shall have arisen before the ratification of the amendment," or even to cases "where such State shall have previously made provision in their own Courts, whereby such suit may be prosecuted to effect"; it refused as well to make an exception for "cases arising under treaties made under the authority of the United States."

It might be argued that the *Chisholm* decision was a correct interpretation of the constitutional design and that the Eleventh Amendment represented a deviation from the original understanding. This, however, seems unsupportable. First, despite the opinion of Justice Iredell, the majority failed to address either the practice or the understanding that prevailed in the States at the time the Constitution was adopted. Second, even a casual reading of the opinions suggests the majority suspected the decision would be unpopular and surprising. Finally, two Members of the majority acknowledged that the United States might well remain immune from suit despite Article III's grant of jurisdiction over "Controversies to which the United States shall be a Party" (Cushing, J.), (Jay, C.J.); and, invoking the example of actions to collect debts incurred before the Constitution was adopted, one raised the possibility of "exceptions," suggesting the rule of the case might not "extend to all the demands, and to every kind of action," (Jay, C.J.). These concessions undercut the crucial premise that either the Constitution's literal text or the principle of popular sovereignty necessarily overrode widespread practice and opinion.

The text and history of the Eleventh Amendment also suggest that Congress acted not to change but to restore the original constitutional design. Although earlier drafts of the Amendment had been phrased as express limits on the judicial power granted in Article III ("The Judicial Power of the United States shall not extend to any suits in law or equity, commenced or prosecuted against one of the United States . . ."), the adopted text addressed the proper interpretation of that provision of the original Constitution, see U.S. Const., Amdt. 11 ("The Judicial power of the United States shall not be construed to extend to any suit in law or equity, commenced or prosecuted against one of the United States . . ."). By its terms, then, the Eleventh Amendment did not redefine the federal judicial power but instead overruled the Court. . . .

The text reflects the historical context and the congressional objective in endorsing the Amendment for ratification. Congress chose not to enact language codifying the traditional understanding of sovereign immunity but rather to address the specific provisions of the Constitution that had raised concerns during the ratification debates and formed the basis of the *Chisholm* decision. Given the outraged reaction to *Chisholm*, as well as Congress' repeated refusal to otherwise qualify the text of the Amendment, it is doubtful that if Congress meant to write a new immunity into the Constitution it would have limited that immunity to the narrow text of the Eleventh Amendment. . . .

The more natural inference is that the Constitution was understood, in light of its history and structure, to preserve the States' traditional immunity from private suits. As the Amendment clarified the only provisions of the Constitution that anyone had suggested might support a contrary understanding, there was no reason to draft with a broader brush.

Finally, the swiftness and near unanimity with which the Eleventh Amendment was adopted suggest "either that the Court had not captured the original understanding, or that the country had changed its collective mind most rapidly." D. Currie, The Constitution in the Supreme Court: The First Hundred Years: 1789-1888 (1985). The more reasonable interpretation, of course, is that regardless of the views of four Justices in *Chisholm*, the country as a whole which had adopted the Constitution just five years earlier had not understood the document to strip the States of their immunity from private suits. Cf. Currie, The Constitution in Congress ("It is plain that just about everybody in Congress agreed the Supreme Court had misread the Constitution").

Although the dissent attempts to rewrite history to reflect a different original understanding, its evidence is unpersuasive. The handful of state statutory and constitutional provisions authorizing suits or petitions of right against States only confirms the prevalence of the traditional understanding that a State could not be sued in the absence of an express waiver, for if the understanding were otherwise, the provisions would have been unnecessary. The constitutional amendments proposed by the New York and Rhode Island Conventions undercut rather than support the dissent's view of history, and the amendments proposed by the Virginia and North Carolina Conventions do not cast light upon the original understanding of the States' immunity to suit. It is true that, in the course of all but eliminating federal-question and diversity jurisdiction, the amendments would have removed the language in the Constitution relied upon by the *Chisholm* Court. While the amendments do reflect dissatisfaction with the scope of federal jurisdiction as a general matter, there is no evidence that they were directed toward the question of sovereign immunity or that they reflect an understanding that the States would be subject to private suits without consent under Article III as drafted.

The dissent's remaining evidence cannot bear the weight the dissent seeks to place on it. The views voiced during the ratification debates by Edmund Randolph and James Wilson, when reiterated by the same individuals in their respective capacities as advocate and Justice in *Chisholm*, were decisively rejected by the Eleventh Amendment, and General Pinkney did not speak to the issue of sovereign immunity at all. Furthermore, Randolph appears to have recognized that his views were in tension with the traditional understanding of sovereign immunity ("I think, whatever the law of nations may say, that any doubt respecting the construction that a state may be plaintiff, and not defendant, is taken away by the words where a state shall be a party"), and Wilson and Pinkney expressed a radical nationalist vision of the constitutional design that not only deviated from the views that prevailed at the time but, despite the dissent's apparent embrace of the position, remains startling even today, see post (quoting with approval Wilson's statement that "the government of each state ought to be subordinate to the government of the United States"). . . .

In short, the scanty and equivocal evidence offered by the dissent establishes no more than what is evident from the decision in *Chisholm* — that some members of the founding generation disagreed with Hamilton, Madison, Marshall, Iredell, and the only state conventions formally to address the matter. The events leading to the adoption of the Eleventh Amendment, however, make clear that the individuals who believed the Constitution stripped the States of their immunity from suit were at most a small minority.

Not only do the ratification debates and the events leading to the adoption of the Eleventh Amendment reveal the original understanding of the States' constitutional immunity from suit; they also underscore the importance of sovereign immunity to the founding generation. Simply put, "The Constitution never would have been ratified if the States and their courts were to be stripped of their sovereign authority except as expressly provided by the Constitution itself." *Atascadero State Hospital v. Scanlon* (1985). . . .

II

In this case we must determine whether Congress has the power, under Article I, to subject nonconsenting States to private suits in their own courts. . . . [T]he fact that the Eleventh Amendment by its terms limits only "[t]he Judicial power of the United States" does not resolve the question. To rest on the words of the Amendment alone would be to engage in the type of ahistorical literalism we have rejected in interpreting the scope of the States' sovereign immunity since the discredited decision in *Chisholm*. . . . Whether Congress has authority under Article I to abrogate a State's immunity from suit in its own courts is . . . a question of first impression. In determining whether there is "compelling evidence" that this derogation of the States' sovereignty is "inherent in the constitutional compact," we continue our discussion of history, practice, precedent, and the structure of the Constitution.

We look first to evidence of the original understanding of the Constitution. Petitioners contend that because the ratification debates and the events surrounding the adoption of the Eleventh Amendment focused on the States' immunity from suit in federal courts, the historical record gives no instruction as to the founding generation's intent to preserve the States' immunity from suit in their own courts.

We believe, however, that the founders' silence is best explained by the simple fact that no one, not even the Constitution's most ardent opponents, suggested the document might strip the States of the immunity. In light of the overriding concern regarding the States' war-time debts, together with the well known creativity, foresight, and vivid imagination of the Constitution's opponents, the silence is most instructive. It suggests the sovereign's right to assert immunity from suit in its own courts was a principle so well established that no one conceived it would be altered by the new Constitution.

The arguments raised against the Constitution confirm this strong inference. In England, the rule was well established that "no lord could be sued by a vassal in his own court, but each petty lord was subject to suit in the courts of a higher lord." It was argued that, by analogy, the States could be sued without consent in federal court. The point of the argument was that federal jurisdiction under Article III would circumvent the States' immunity from suit in their own courts. The argument would have made little sense if the States were understood to have relinquished the immunity in all events.

The response the Constitution's advocates gave to the argument is also telling. Relying on custom and practice — and, in particular, on the States' immunity from suit in their own courts — they contended that no individual could sue a sovereign without its consent. It is true the point was directed toward the power of the Federal Judiciary, for that was the only question at issue. The logic of the argument, however, applies with even greater force in the context of a suit prosecuted against a sovereign in its own courts, for in this setting, more than any other, sovereign immunity was long established and unquestioned.

Similarly, while the Eleventh Amendment by its terms addresses only "the Judicial power of the United States," nothing in *Chisholm*, the catalyst for the Amendment, suggested the States were not immune from suits in their own courts. The only Justice to address the issue, in fact, was explicit in distinguishing between sovereign immunity in federal court and in a State's own courts. See 2 Dall., at 452 (opinion of Blair, J.) ("When sovereigns are sued in their own Courts, such a method [a petition of right] may have been established as the most respectful form of demand; but we are not now in a State-Court; and if sovereignty be an exemption from suit in any other than the sovereign's own Courts, it follows that when a State, by adopting the Constitution, has agreed to be amenable to the judicial power of the United States, she has, in that respect, given up her right of sovereignty").

The language of the Eleventh Amendment, furthermore, was directed toward the only provisions of the constitutional text believed to call the States' immunity from private suits into question. Although Article III expressly contemplated jurisdiction over suits between States and individuals, nothing in the Article or in any other part of the Constitution suggested the States could not assert immunity from private suit in their own courts or that Congress had the power to abrogate sovereign immunity there.

Finally, the Congress which endorsed the Eleventh Amendment rejected language limiting the Amendment's scope to cases where the States had made available a remedy in their own courts. Implicit in the proposal, it is evident, was the premise that the States retained their immunity and the concomitant authority to decide whether to allow private suits against the sovereign in their own courts.

In light of the language of the Constitution and the historical context, it is quite apparent why neither the ratification debates nor the language of the Eleventh Amendment addressed the States' immunity from suit in their own courts. The concerns voiced at the ratifying conventions, the furor raised by *Chisholm*, and the speed and unanimity with which the Amendment was adopted, moreover, underscore the jealous care with which the founding generation sought to preserve the sovereign immunity of the States. To read this history as permitting the inference that the Constitution stripped the States of immunity in their own courts and allowed Congress to subject them to suit there would turn on its head the concern of the founding generation — that Article III might be used to circumvent state-court immunity. In light of the historical record it is difficult to conceive that the Constitution would have been adopted if it had been understood to strip the States of immunity from suit in their own courts and cede to the Federal Government a power to subject nonconsenting States to private suits in these fora. . . .

Our final consideration is whether a congressional power to subject nonconsenting States to private suits in their own courts is consistent with the structure of the Constitution. We look both to the essential principles of federalism and to the special role of the state courts in the constitutional design.

Although the Constitution grants broad powers to Congress, our federalism requires that Congress treat the States in a manner consistent with their status as residuary sovereigns and joint participants in the governance of the Nation. See, e.g., *United States v. Lopez* (concurring opinion); *Printz*; *New York*. . . . Petitioners contend that immunity from suit in federal court suffices to preserve the dignity of the States. Private suits against nonconsenting States, however, present "the indignity of subjecting a State to the coercive process of judicial tribunals at the instance of private parties," regardless of the forum. Not only must a State defend or default but also it must face the prospect of being thrust, by federal fiat and against its will, into the disfavored status of a debtor, subject to the power of private citizens to levy on its treasury or perhaps even government buildings or property which the State administers on the public's behalf.

In some ways, of course, a congressional power to authorize private suits against nonconsenting States in their own courts would be even more offensive to state sovereignty than a power to authorize the suits in a federal forum. Although the immunity of one sovereign in the courts of another has often depended in part on comity or agreement, the immunity of a sovereign in its own courts has always been understood to be within the sole control of the sovereign itself. A power to press a State's own courts into federal service to coerce the other branches of the State, furthermore, is the power first to turn the State against itself and ultimately to commandeer the entire political machinery of the State against its will and at the behest of individuals. Such plenary federal control of state governmental processes denigrates the separate sovereignty of the States.

It is unquestioned that the Federal Government retains its own immunity from suit not only in state tribunals but also in its own courts. In light of our constitutional system recognizing the essential sovereignty of the States, we are reluctant to conclude that the States are not entitled to a reciprocal privilege.

Underlying constitutional form are considerations of great substance. Private suits against nonconsenting States — especially suits for money damages — may threaten the financial integrity of the States. It is indisputable that, at the time of the founding, many of the States could have been forced into insolvency but for their immunity from private suits for money damages. Even today, an unlimited congressional power to authorize suits in state court to levy upon the treasuries of the States for compensatory damages, attorney's fees, and even punitive damages could create staggering burdens, giving Congress a power and a leverage over the States that is not contemplated by our constitutional design. The potential national power would pose a severe and notorious danger to the States and their resources. . . .

A general federal power to authorize private suits for money damages would place unwarranted strain on the States' ability to govern in accordance with the will of their citizens. Today, as at the time of the founding, the allocation of scarce resources among competing needs and interests lies at the heart of the political process. While the judgment creditor of the State may have a legitimate claim for compensation, other important needs and worthwhile ends compete for access to the public fisc. Since all cannot be satisfied in full, it is inevitable that difficult decisions involving the most sensitive and political of judgments must be made. If the principle of representative government is to be preserved to the States, the balance between competing interests must be reached after deliberation by the political process established by the citizens of the State, not by judicial decree mandated by the Federal Government and invoked by the private citizen. . . .

Congress cannot abrogate the States' sovereign immunity in federal court; were the rule to be different here, the National Government would wield greater power in the state courts than in its own judicial instrumentalities. . . . We are aware of no constitutional precept that would admit of a congressional power to require state courts to entertain federal suits which are not within the judicial power of the United States and could not be heard in federal courts. . . .

In light of history, practice, precedent, and the structure of the Constitution, we hold that the States retain immunity from private suit in their own courts, an immunity beyond the congressional power to abrogate by Article I legislation. . . .

JUSTICE SOUTER, with whom JUSTICE STEVENS, JUSTICE GINSBURG, and JUSTICE BREYER join, dissenting.

In *Seminole Tribe of Fla. v. Florida* (1996), a majority of this Court invoked the Eleventh Amendment to declare that the federal judicial power under Article III of the Constitution does not reach a private action against a State, even on a federal question. In the Court's conception, however, the Eleventh Amendment was understood as having been enhanced by a "background principle" of state sovereign immunity (understood as immunity to suit) that operated beyond its limited codification in the Amendment, dealing solely with federal citizen-state diversity jurisdiction. . . .

Today's issue arises naturally in the aftermath of the decision in *Seminole Tribe*. In . . . complementing its earlier decision, the Court of course confronts the fact that the state forum renders the Eleventh Amendment beside the point, and it has responded by discerning a simpler and more straightforward theory of state sovereign immunity than it found in *Seminole Tribe*: a State's sovereign immunity from all individual suits is a "fundamental aspect" of state sovereignty "confirm[ed]" by the Tenth Amendment. As a consequence, *Seminole Tribe*'s contorted reliance on the Eleventh Amendment and its background was presumably unnecessary; the Tenth would have done the work with an economy that the majority in *Seminole Tribe* would have welcomed. Indeed, if the Court's current reasoning is correct, the Eleventh Amendment itself was unnecessary. Whatever Article III may originally have said about the federal judicial power, the embarrassment to the State of Georgia occasioned by attempts in federal court to enforce the State's war debt could easily have been avoided if only the Court that decided Chisholm v. Georgia had understood a State's inherent, Tenth Amendment right to be free of any judicial power, whether the court be state or federal, and whether the cause of action arise under state or federal law. . . .

There is no evidence that the Tenth Amendment constitutionalized a concept of sovereign immunity as inherent in the notion of statehood, and no evidence that any concept of inherent sovereign immunity was understood historically to apply when the sovereign sued was not the font of the law. Nor does the Court fare any better with its subsidiary lines of reasoning, that the state-court action is barred by the scheme of American federalism, a result supposedly confirmed by a history largely devoid of precursors to the action considered here. . . .

On each point the Court has raised it is mistaken, and I respectfully dissent from its judgment.

I

The Court rests its decision principally on the claim that immunity from suit was "a fundamental aspect of the sovereignty which the States enjoyed before the ratification of the Constitution," an aspect which the Court understands to have survived the ratification of the Constitution in 1788 and to have been "confirm[ed]" and given constitutional status by the adoption of the Tenth Amendment in 1791. If the Court truly means by "sovereign immunity" what that term meant at common law, its argument would be insupportable. While sovereign immunity entered many new state legal systems as a part of the common law selectively received from England, it was not understood to be indefeasible or to have been given any such status by the new National Constitution, which did not mention it. Had the question been posed, state sovereign immunity could not have been thought to shield a State from suit under federal law on a subject committed to national jurisdiction by Article I of the Constitution. Congress exercising its conceded Article I power may unquestionably abrogate such immunity. I set out this position at length in my dissent in *Seminole Tribe* and will not repeat it here.

The Court does not, however, offer today's holding as a mere corollary to its reasoning in *Seminole Tribe*, substituting the Tenth Amendment for the Eleventh as the occasion demands, and it is fair to read its references to a "fundamental aspect" of state sovereignty as referring not to a prerogative inherited from the Crown, but to a conception necessarily implied by statehood itself. The conception is thus not one of common law so much as of natural law, a universally applicable proposition discoverable by reason. . . .

The Court's principal rationale for today's result, then, turns on history: was the natural law conception of sovereign immunity as inherent in any notion of an independent State widely held in the United States in the period preceding the ratification of 1788 (or the adoption of the Tenth Amendment in 1791)? The answer is certainly no. There is almost no evidence that the generation of the Framers thought sovereign immunity was fundamental in the sense of being unalterable. Whether one looks at the period before the framing, to the ratification controversies, or to the early republican era, the evidence is the same. Some Framers thought sovereign immunity was an obsolete royal prerogative inapplicable in a republic; some thought sovereign immunity was a common-law power defeasible, like other common-law rights, by statute; and perhaps a few thought, in keeping with a natural law view distinct from the common-law conception, that immunity was inherent in a sovereign because the body that made a law could not logically be bound by it. Natural law thinking on the part of a doubtful few will not, however, support the Court's position.

The American Colonies did not enjoy sovereign immunity, that being a privilege understood in English law to be reserved for the Crown alone; "antecedent to the Declaration of Independence, none of the colonies were, or pretended to be, sovereign states," J. Story, Commentaries on the Constitution. Several colonial charters, including those of Massachusetts, Connecticut, Rhode Island, and Georgia, expressly specified that the corporate body established thereunder could sue and be sued. . . .

Starting in the mid-1760s, ideas about sovereignty in colonial America began to shift as Americans argued that, lacking a voice in Parliament, they had not in any express way consented to being taxed. The story of the subsequent development of conceptions of sovereignty is complex and uneven; here, it is enough to say that by the time independence was declared in 1776, the locus of sovereignty was still an open question, except that almost by definition, advocates of independence denied that sovereignty with respect to the American Colonies remained with the King in Parliament.

As the concept of sovereignty was unsettled, so was that of sovereign immunity. Some States appear to have understood themselves to be without immunity from suit in their own courts upon independence. Connecticut and Rhode Island adopted their pre-existing charters as constitutions, without altering the provisions specifying their suability. Other new States understood themselves to be inheritors of the Crown's common-law sovereign immunity and so enacted statutes authorizing legal remedies against the State parallel to those available in England. There, although the Crown was immune from suit, the contemporary practice allowed private litigants to seek legal remedies against the Crown through the petition of right or the monstrans de droit in the Chancery or Exchequer. . . .

Around the time of the Constitutional Convention, then, there existed among the States some diversity of practice with respect to sovereign immunity; but despite a tendency among the state constitutions to announce and declare certain inalienable and natural rights of men and even of the collective people of a State, no State declared that sovereign immunity was one of those rights. To the extent that States were thought to possess immunity, it was perceived as a prerogative of the sovereign under common law. And where sovereign immunity was recognized as barring suit, provisions for recovery from the State were in order, just as they had been at common law in England.

At the Constitutional Convention, the notion of sovereign immunity, whether as natural law or as common law, was not an immediate subject of debate, and the sovereignty of a State in its own courts seems not to have been mentioned. This comes as no surprise, for although the Constitution required state courts to apply federal law, the Framers did not consider the possibility that federal law might bind States, say, in their relations with their employees. In the subsequent ratification debates, however, the issue of jurisdiction over a State did emerge in the question whether States might be sued on their debts in federal court, and on this point, too, a variety of views emerged and the diversity of sovereign immunity conceptions displayed itself.

The only arguable support for the Court's absolutist view that I have found among the leading participants in the debate surrounding ratification was . . . that of Alexander Hamilton in *The Federalist, No. 81*, where he described the sovereign immunity of the States in language suggesting principles associated with natural law. . . . Hamilton chose his words carefully, and he acknowledged the possibility that at the Convention the States might have surrendered sovereign immunity in some circumstances, but the thrust of his argument was that sovereign immunity was "inherent in the nature of sovereignty." . . . The apparent novelty and uniqueness of Hamilton's employment of natural law terminology to explain the sovereign immunity of the States is worth remarking, because it stands in contrast to formulations indicating no particular position on the natural-law-versus-common-law origin, to the more widespread view that sovereign immunity derived from common law, and to the more radical stance that the sovereignty of the people made sovereign immunity out of place in the United States. . . .

At the farthest extreme from Hamilton, James Wilson made several comments in the Pennsylvania Convention that suggested his hostility to any idea of state sovereign immunity. First, he responded to the argument that "the sovereignty of the states is destroyed" if they are sued by the United States. . . . For Wilson, "[t]he answer [was] plain and easy: the government of each state ought to be subordinate to the government of the United States." Wilson was also pointed in commenting on federal jurisdiction over cases between a State and citizens of another State: "When this power is attended to, it will be found to be a necessary one. Impartiality is the leading feature in this Constitution; it pervades the whole. When a citizen has a controversy with another state, there ought to be a tribunal where both parties may stand on a just and equal footing." Finally, Wilson laid out his view that sovereignty was in fact not located in the States at all: "Upon what principle is it contended that the sovereign power resides in the state governments? The honorable gentleman has said truly, that there can be no subordinate sovereignty. Now, if there cannot, my position is, that the sovereignty resides in the people; they have not parted with it; they have only dispensed such portions of the power as were conceived necessary for the public welfare." While this statement did not specifically address sovereign immunity, it expressed the major premise of what would later become Justice Wilson's position in *Chisholm*: that because the people, and not the States, are sovereign, sovereign immunity has no applicability to the States.

From a canvass of this spectrum of opinion expressed at the ratifying conventions, one thing is certain. No one was espousing an indefeasible, natural law view of sovereign immunity. The controversy over the enforceability of state debts subject to state law produced emphatic support for sovereign immunity from eminences as great as Madison and Marshall, but neither of them indicated adherence to any immunity conception outside the common law....

If the natural law conception of sovereign immunity as an inherent characteristic of sovereignty enjoyed by the States had been broadly accepted at the time of the founding, one would expect to find it reflected somewhere in the five opinions delivered by the Court in *Chisholm*. Yet that view did not appear in any of them. And since a bare two years before *Chisholm*, the Bill of Rights had been added to the original Constitution, if the Tenth Amendment had been understood to give federal constitutional status to state sovereign immunity so as to endue it with the equivalent of the natural law conception, one would be certain to find such a development mentioned somewhere in the *Chisholm* writings. In fact, however, not one of the opinions espoused the natural law view, and not one of them so much as mentioned the Tenth Amendment. Not even Justice Iredell, who alone among the Justices thought that a State could not be sued in federal court, echoed Hamilton or hinted at a constitutionally immutable immunity doctrine....

In ... *Chisholm* two Justices (Jay and Wilson), both of whom had been present at the Constitutional Convention, took a position suggesting that States should not enjoy sovereign immunity (however conceived) even in their own courts; one (Cushing) was essentially silent on the issue of sovereign immunity in state court; one (Blair) took a cautious position affirming the pragmatic view that sovereign immunity was a continuing common-law doctrine and that States would permit suit against themselves as of right; and one (Iredell) expressly thought that state sovereign immunity at common law rightly belonged to the sovereign States. Not a single Justice suggested that sovereign immunity was an inherent and indefeasible right of statehood, and neither counsel for Georgia before the Circuit Court, nor Justice Iredell seems even to have conceived the possibility that the new Tenth Amendment produced the equivalent of such a doctrine. This dearth of support makes it very implausible for today's Court to argue that a substantial (let alone a dominant) body of thought at the time of the framing understood sovereign immunity to be an inherent right of statehood, adopted or confirmed by the Tenth Amendment.

The Court's discomfort is evident in its obvious recognition that its natural law or Tenth Amendment conception of state sovereign immunity is insupportable if *Chisholm* stands. Hence the Court's attempt to discount the *Chisholm* opinions, an enterprise in which I believe it fails.

The Court, citing *Hans*, says that the Eleventh Amendment "overruled" *Chisholm*, but the animadversion is beside the point. The significance of *Chisholm* is its indication that in 1788 and 1791 it was not generally assumed (indeed, hardly assumed at all) that a State's sovereign immunity from suit in its own courts was an inherent, and not merely a common-law, advantage. On the contrary, the testimony of five eminent legal minds of the day confirmed that virtually everyone who understood immunity to be legitimate saw it as a common-law prerogative (from which it follows that it was subject to abrogation by Congress as to a matter within Congress's Article I authority). . . .

Nor can the Court make good on its claim that the enactment of the Eleventh Amendment retrospectively reestablished the view that had already been established at the time of the framing (though eluding the perception of all but one Member of the Supreme Court), and hence "acted . . . to restore the original constitutional design." There was nothing "established" about the position espoused by Georgia in the effort to repudiate its debts. . . . There was no received view either of the role this sovereign immunity would play in the circumstances of the case or of a conceptual foundation for immunity doctrine at odds with *Chisholm*'s reading of Article III. As an author on whom the Court relies has it, "there was no unanimity among the Framers that immunity would exist," D. Currie, *The Constitution in the Supreme Court: The First Century* 19 (1985).

It should not be surprising, then, to realize that although much post-*Chisholm* discussion was disapproving (as the States saw their escape from debt cut off), the decision had champions "every bit as vigorous in defending their interpretation of the Constitution as were those partisans on the other side of the issue." The federal citizen-state diversity jurisdiction was settled by the Eleventh Amendment; Article III was not "restored." . . .

II

. . . The State of Maine is not sovereign with respect to the national objective of the FLSA. It is not the authority that promulgated the FLSA, on which the right of action in this case depends. That authority is the United States acting through the Congress, whose legislative power under Article I of the Constitution to extend FLSA coverage to state employees has already been decided, see *Garcia v. San Antonio Metropolitan Transit Authority* (1985), and is not contested here.

Nor can it be argued that because the State of Maine creates its own court system, it has authority to decide what sorts of claims may be entertained there, and thus in effect to control the right of action in this case. Maine has created state courts of general jurisdiction; once it has done so, the Supremacy Clause of the Constitution, which requires state courts to enforce federal law and state-court judges to be bound by it, requires the Maine courts to entertain this federal cause of action. Maine has advanced no "valid excuse" for its courts' refusal to hear federal-law claims in which Maine is a defendant, and sovereign immunity cannot be that excuse, simply because the State is not sovereign with respect to the subject of the claim against it. The Court's insistence that the federal structure bars Congress from making States susceptible to suit in their own courts is, then, plain mistake. . . .

C. THE ENFORCEMENT CLAUSE OF THE FOURTEENTH AMENDMENT

ASSIGNMENT 3

The enactment of the Fourteenth Amendment expressly expanded the legislative power of Congress. Section 5 of the Fourteenth Amendment reads: "The Congress shall have power to enforce, by appropriate legislation, the provisions of this article" (i.e., Sections 1-4 of the Amendment). Although the Supreme Court shied away from relying on Section 5 of the Fourteenth Amendment to uphold the Civil Rights Act of 1964, it did use the Enforcement Clause to uphold a provision of the Voting Rights Act of 1965. (Lawyers often use "Section 5" as a shorthand to refer to Section 5 of the Fourteenth Amendment.)

STUDY GUIDE

- Why might the Court have been comfortable using Section 5 to uphold the Voting Rights Act, but not the Civil Rights Act of 1964? What is the difference between the judicial enforcement of the Equal Protection Clause and allowing Congress to enforce the very same clause using Section 5?
- Notice the Court's reliance on the reasoning in *McCulloch v. Maryland* (Chapter 2). What is the relation between Section 5 and the Necessary and Proper Clause?

Katzenbach v. Morgan

384 U.S. 641 (1966)

MR. JUSTICE BRENNAN delivered the opinion of the Court.

These cases concern the constitutionality of §4(e) of the Voting Rights Act of 1965. That law, in the respects pertinent in these cases, provides that no person who has successfully completed the sixth primary grade in a public school in, or a private school accredited by, the Commonwealth of Puerto Rico in which the language of instruction was other than English shall be denied the right to vote in any election because of his inability to read or write English. Appellees, registered voters in New York City, brought this suit to challenge the constitutionality of §4(e) insofar as it pro tanto prohibits the enforcement of the election laws of New York requiring an ability to read and write English as a condition of voting. Under these laws many of the several hundred thousand New York City residents who have migrated there from the Commonwealth of Puerto Rico had previously been denied the right to vote, and appellees attack §4(e) insofar as it would enable many of these citizens to vote. . . .

Under the distribution of powers effected by the Constitution, the States establish qualifications for voting for state officers, and the qualifications established by the States for voting for members of the most numerous branch of the state legislature also determine who may vote for United States Representatives and Senators, Art. I, §2. But, of course, the States have no power to grant or withhold the franchise on conditions that are forbidden by the Fourteenth Amendment, or any other provision of the Constitution. Such exercises of state power are no more immune to the limitations of the Fourteenth Amendment than any other state action. The Equal Protection Clause itself has been held to forbid some state laws that restrict the right to vote.

The Attorney General of the State of New York argues that an exercise of congressional power under §5 of the Fourteenth Amendment that prohibits the enforcement of a state law can only be sustained if the judicial branch determines that the state law is prohibited by the provisions of the Amendment that Congress sought to enforce. More specifically, he urges that §4(e) cannot be sustained as appropriate legislation to enforce the Equal Protection Clause unless the judiciary decides — even with the guidance of a congressional judgment — that the application of the English literacy requirement prohibited by §4(e) is forbidden by the Equal Protection Clause itself. We disagree. Neither the language nor history of §5 supports such a construction. As was said with regard to §5 in *Ex parte Virginia* (1879), "It is the power of Congress which has been enlarged. Congress is authorized to enforce the prohibitions by appropriate legislation. Some legislation is contemplated to make the amendments fully effective." A construction of §5 that would require a judicial determination that the enforcement of the state law precluded by Congress violated the Amendment, as a condition of sustaining the congressional enactment, would depreciate both congressional resourcefulness and congressional responsibility for implementing the Amendment. . . .

Thus our task in this case is not to determine whether the New York English literacy requirement as applied to deny the right to vote to a person who successfully completed the sixth grade in a Puerto Rican school violates the Equal Protection Clause. . . . [T]he question before us here [is] could Congress prohibit the enforcement of the state law by legislating under §5 of the Fourteenth Amendment? In answering this question, our task is limited to determining whether such legislation is, as required by §5, appropriate legislation to enforce the Equal Protection Clause.

By including §5 the draftsmen sought to grant to Congress, by a specific provision applicable to the Fourteenth Amendment, the same broad powers expressed in the Necessary and Proper Clause, Art. I, §8, cl. 18. The classic formulation of the reach of those powers was established by Chief Justice Marshall in *McCulloch v. Maryland* (1819): "Let the end be legitimate, let it be within the scope of the constitution, and all means which are appropriate, which are plainly adapted to that end, which are not prohibited, but consist with the letter and spirit of the constitution, are constitutional." . . .

The *McCulloch v. Maryland* standard is the measure of what constitutes "appropriate legislation" under §5 of the Fourteenth Amendment. Correctly viewed, §5 is a positive grant of legislative power authorizing Congress to exercise its discretion in determining whether and what legislation is needed to secure the guarantees of the Fourteenth Amendment.

We therefore proceed to the consideration whether §4(e) is "appropriate legislation" to enforce the Equal Protection Clause, that is, under the *McCulloch v. Maryland* standard, whether §4(e) may be regarded as an enactment to enforce the Equal Protection Clause, whether it is "plainly adapted to that end" and whether it is not prohibited by but is consistent with "the letter and spirit of the constitution."[13]

There can be no doubt that §4(e) may be regarded as an enactment to enforce the Equal Protection Clause. Congress explicitly declared that it enacted §4(e) "to secure the rights under the fourteenth amendment of persons educated in American-flag schools in which the predominant classroom language was other than English." The persons referred to include those who have migrated from the Commonwealth of Puerto Rico to New York and who have been denied the right to vote because of their inability to read and write English, and the Fourteenth Amendment rights referred to include those emanating from the Equal Protection Clause. More specifically, §4(e) may be viewed as a measure to secure for the Puerto Rican community residing in New York nondiscriminatory treatment by government — both in the imposition of voting qualifications and the provision or administration of governmental services, such as public schools, public housing and law enforcement.

Section 4(e) may be readily seen as "plainly adapted" to furthering these aims of the Equal Protection Clause. The practical effect of §4(e) is to prohibit New York from denying the right to vote to large segments of its Puerto Rican community. Congress has thus prohibited the State from denying to that community the right that is "preservative of all rights." This enhanced political power will be helpful in gaining nondiscriminatory treatment in public services for the entire Puerto Rican community. §4(e) thereby enables the Puerto Rican minority better to obtain "perfect equality of civil rights and the equal protection of the laws." It was well within

[13] Contrary to the suggestion of the dissent, §5 does not grant Congress power to exercise discretion in the other direction and to enact "statutes so as in effect to dilute equal protection and due process decisions of this Court." We emphasize that Congress' power under §5 is limited to adopting measures to enforce the guarantees of the Amendment; §5 grants Congress no power to restrict, abrogate, or dilute these guarantees. Thus, for example, an enactment authorizing the States to establish racially segregated systems of education would not be — as required by §5 — a measure "to enforce" the Equal Protection Clause, since that clause, of its own force, prohibits such state laws.

congressional authority to say that this need of the Puerto Rican minority for the vote warranted federal intrusion upon any state interests served by the English literacy requirement. It was for Congress, as the branch that made this judgment, to assess and weigh the various conflicting considerations — the risk or pervasiveness of the discrimination in governmental services, the effectiveness of eliminating the state restriction on the right to vote as a means of dealing with the evil, the adequacy or availability of alternative remedies, and the nature and significance of the state interests that would be affected by the nullification of the English literacy requirement as applied to residents who have successfully completed the sixth grade in a Puerto Rican school. It is not for us to review the congressional resolution of these factors. It is enough that we be able to perceive a basis upon which the Congress might resolve the conflict as it did. There plainly was such a basis to support §4(e) in the application in question in this case. Any contrary conclusion would require us to be blind to the realities familiar to the legislators.

The result is no different if we confine our inquiry to the question whether §4(e) was merely legislation aimed at the elimination of an invidious discrimination in establishing voter qualifications. We are told that New York's English literacy requirement originated in the desire to provide an incentive for non-English speaking immigrants to learn the English language, and in order to assure the intelligent exercise of the franchise. Yet Congress might well have questioned, in light of the many exemptions provided, and some evidence suggesting that prejudice played a prominent role in the enactment of the requirement, whether these were actually the interests being served. Congress might have also questioned whether denial of a right deemed so precious and fundamental in our society was a necessary or appropriate means of encouraging persons to learn English, or of furthering the goal of an intelligent exercise of the franchise. Finally, Congress might well have concluded that, as a means of furthering the intelligent exercise of the franchise, an ability to read or understand Spanish is as effective as ability to read English for those to whom Spanish language newspapers and Spanish language radio and television programs are available to inform them of election issues and governmental affairs. Since Congress undertook to legislate so as to preclude the enforcement of the state law, and did so in the context of a general appraisal of literacy requirements for voting, to which it brought a specially informed legislative competence, it was Congress' prerogative to weigh these competing considerations. Here again, it is enough that we perceive a basis upon which Congress might predicate a judgment that the application of New York's English literacy requirement to deny the right to vote to a person with a sixth grade education in Puerto Rican schools in which the language of instruction was other than English constituted an invidious discrimination in violation of the Equal Protection Clause. . . .

We therefore conclude that §4(e), in the application challenged in this case, is appropriate legislation to enforce the Equal Protection Clause and that the judgment of the District Court must be and hereby is reversed.

Although Section 5 of the Fourteenth Amendment is an additional enumerated power of Congress, it is included in this chapter, rather than in Chapter 3, because of how the Court's federalism case law constrains Congress's exercise of this authority. These limitations resemble the constraints imposed under the rubric of the Tenth and Eleventh Amendments.

STUDY GUIDE

- Do you see any parallel between Section 5 of the Fourteenth Amendment and the Necessary and Proper Clause of Article I? Does the Court approach the two clauses in a similar manner? What is the difference between a "remedial" and a "substantive" provision?
- Are you persuaded by Justice Kennedy's interpretation of *Katzenbach v. Morgan*?
- The excerpt below includes the Court's only reference to *McCulloch v. Maryland* in this opinion. Contrast this with the Warren Court's treatment of *McCulloch* in *Morgan*.

St. Peter Catholic Church in Boerne, Texas

City of Boerne v. Flores

521 U.S. 507 (1997)

Justice Kennedy delivered the opinion of the Court, in which Chief Justice Rehnquist and Justices Stevens, Thomas, and Ginsburg, joined, and in which Justice Scalia joined as to all but Part III-A-1.

A decision by local zoning authorities to deny a church a building permit was challenged under the Religious Freedom Restoration Act of 1993 (RFRA or Act). The case calls into question the authority of Congress to enact RFRA. We conclude the statute exceeds Congress' power.

I

Situated on a hill in the city of Boerne, Texas, some 28 miles northwest of San Antonio, is St. Peter Catholic Church. Built in 1923, the church's structure replicates the mission style of the region's earlier history. The church seats about 230 worshippers, a number too small for its growing parish. . . . In order to meet the needs of the congregation the Archbishop of San Antonio gave permission to the parish to plan alterations to enlarge the building.

A few months later, the Boerne City Council passed an ordinance authorizing the city's Historic Landmark Commission to prepare a preservation plan with proposed historic landmarks and districts. Under the ordinance, the commission must preapprove construction affecting historic landmarks or buildings in a historic district.

Soon afterwards, the Archbishop applied for a building permit so construction to enlarge the church could proceed. City authorities, relying on the ordinance and the designation of a historic district . . . denied the application. . . .

II

Congress enacted RFRA in direct response to the Court's decision in *Employment Div., Dept. of Human Resources of Oregon v. Smith* (1990). There we considered a Free Exercise Clause claim brought by members of the Native American Church who were denied unemployment benefits when they lost their jobs because they had used peyote. Their practice was to ingest peyote for sacramental purposes, and they challenged an Oregon statute of general applicability which made use of the drug criminal. . . . *Smith* held that neutral, generally applicable laws may be applied to religious practices even when not supported by a compelling governmental interest.

Four Members of the Court disagreed. They argued the law placed a substantial burden on the Native American Church members so that it could be upheld only if the law served a compelling state interest and was narrowly tailored to achieve that end. . . .

These points of constitutional interpretation were debated by Members of Congress in hearings and floor debates. Many criticized the Court's reasoning, and this disagreement resulted in the passage of RFRA. Congress announced:

(1) [T]he framers of the Constitution, recognizing free exercise of religion as an unalienable right, secured its protection in the First Amendment to the Constitution;
(2) laws 'neutral' toward religion may burden religious exercise as surely as laws intended to interfere with religious exercise;
(3) governments should not substantially burden religious exercise without compelling justification;
(4) in Employment Division v. Smith, the Supreme Court virtually eliminated the requirement that the government justify burdens on religious exercise imposed by laws neutral toward religion; and
(5) the compelling interest test as set forth in prior Federal court rulings is a workable test for striking sensible balances between religious liberty and competing prior governmental interests.

The Act's stated purposes are:

(1) to restore the compelling interest test as set forth in *Sherbert v. Verner* (1963) and *Wisconsin v. Yoder* (1972) and to guarantee its application in all cases where free exercise of religion is substantially burdened; and
(2) to provide a claim or defense to persons whose religious exercise is substantially burdened by government.

RFRA prohibits "[g]overnment" from "substantially burden[ing]" a person's exercise of religion even if the burden results from a rule of general applicability unless the government can demonstrate the burden "(1) is in furtherance of a compelling governmental interest; and (2) is the least restrictive means of furthering that compelling governmental interest." The Act's mandate applies to any "branch, department, agency, instrumentality, and official (or other person acting under color of law) of the United States," as well as to any "State, or . . . subdivision of a State." . . . RFRA "applies to all Federal and State law, and the implementation of that law, whether statutory or otherwise, and whether adopted before or after [RFRA's enactment]." In accordance with RFRA's usage of the term, we shall use "state law" to include local and municipal ordinances.

III

A

Under our Constitution, the Federal Government is one of enumerated powers. *McCulloch v. Maryland* (1819); see also *The Federalist No. 45* (J. Madison). The judicial authority to determine the constitutionality of laws, in cases and controversies, is based on the premise that the "powers of the legislature are defined and limited; and that those limits may not be mistaken, or forgotten, the constitution is written." *Marbury v. Madison* (1803).

Congress relied on its Fourteenth Amendment enforcement power in enacting the most far-reaching and substantial of RFRA's provisions, those which impose its requirements on the States. The Fourteenth Amendment provides, in relevant part:

> Section 1. . . . No State shall make or enforce any law which shall abridge the privileges or immunities of citizens of the United States; nor shall any State deprive any person of life, liberty, or property, without due process of law, nor deny to any person within its jurisdiction the equal protection of the laws. . . .
>
> Section 5. The Congress shall have power to enforce, by appropriate legislation, the provisions of this article.

The parties disagree over whether RFRA is a proper exercise of Congress' §5 power "to enforce" by "appropriate legislation" the constitutional guarantee that no State shall deprive any person of "life, liberty, or property, without due process of law" nor deny any person "equal protection of the laws."

In defense of the Act, respondent the Archbishop contends, with support from the United States, that RFRA is permissible enforcement legislation. Congress, it is said, is only protecting by legislation one of the liberties guaranteed by the Fourteenth Amendment's Due Process Clause, the free exercise of religion, beyond what is necessary under *Smith*. It is said the congressional decision to dispense with proof of deliberate or overt discrimination and instead concentrate on a law's effects accords with the settled understanding that §5 includes the power to enact legislation designed to prevent, as well as remedy, constitutional violations. It is further contended that Congress' §5 power is not limited to remedial or preventive legislation.

All must acknowledge that §5 is "a positive grant of legislative power" to Congress, *Katzenbach v. Morgan* (1966). . . . Legislation which deters or remedies constitutional violations can fall within the sweep of Congress' enforcement power even if in the process it prohibits conduct which is not itself unconstitutional and intrudes into "legislative spheres of autonomy previously reserved to the States." *Fitzpatrick v. Bitzer* (1976). For example, the Court upheld a suspension of literacy tests and similar voting requirements under Congress' parallel power to enforce the provisions of the Fifteenth Amendment as a measure to combat racial discrimination in voting, *South Carolina v. Katzenbach* (1966), despite the facial constitutionality of the tests. . . . We have also concluded that other measures protecting voting rights are within Congress' power to enforce the Fourteenth and Fifteenth Amendments, despite the burdens those measures placed on the States.

It is also true, however, that "[a]s broad as the congressional enforcement power is, it is not unlimited." *Oregon v. Mitchell* (1970). In assessing the breadth of §5's enforcement power, we begin with its text. Congress has been given the power "to enforce" the "provisions of this article." We agree with respondent, of course, that Congress can enact legislation under §5 enforcing the constitutional right to the free exercise of religion. The "provisions of this article," to which §5 refers, include the Due Process Clause of the Fourteenth Amendment. Congress' power to enforce the Free Exercise Clause follows from our holding in *Cantwell v. Connecticut* (1940), that the "fundamental concept of liberty embodied in [the Fourteenth Amendment's Due Process Clause] embraces the liberties guaranteed by the First Amendment."

Congress' power under §5, however, extends only to "enforc[ing]" the provisions of the Fourteenth Amendment. The Court has described this power as "remedial," *Katzenbach*. The design of the Amendment and the text of §5 are inconsistent with the suggestion that Congress has the power to decree the substance of the Fourteenth Amendment's restrictions on the States. Legislation which alters the meaning of the Free Exercise Clause cannot be said to be enforcing the Clause. Congress does not enforce a constitutional right by changing what the right is. It has been given the power "to enforce," not the power to determine what constitutes a constitutional violation. Were it not so, what Congress would be enforcing would no longer be, in any meaningful sense, the "provisions of [the Fourteenth Amendment]."

While the line between measures that remedy or prevent unconstitutional actions and measures that make a substantive change in the governing law is not easy to discern, and Congress must have wide latitude in determining where it lies, the distinction exists and must be observed. There must be a congruence and proportionality between the injury to be prevented or remedied and the means adopted to that end. Lacking such a connection, legislation may become substantive in operation and effect. History and our case law support drawing the distinction, one apparent from the text of the Amendment.

1[14]

The Fourteenth Amendment's history confirms the remedial, rather than substantive, nature of the Enforcement Clause. The Joint Committee on Reconstruction of the 39th Congress began drafting what would become the Fourteenth Amendment in January 1866. The objections to the Committee's first draft of the Amendment, and the rejection of the draft, have a direct bearing on the central issue of defining Congress' enforcement power. In February, Republican Representative John Bingham of Ohio reported the following draft Amendment to the House of Representatives on behalf of the Joint Committee:

> The Congress shall have power to make all laws which shall be necessary and proper to secure to the citizens of each State all privileges and immunities of citizens in the several States, and to all persons in the several States equal protection in the rights of life, liberty, and property.

The proposal encountered immediate opposition, which continued through three days of debate. Members of Congress from across the political spectrum criticized the Amendment, and the criticisms had a common theme: The proposed Amendment gave Congress too much legislative power at the expense of the existing constitutional structure. Democrats and conservative Republicans argued that the proposed Amendment would give Congress a power to intrude into traditional areas of state responsibility, a power inconsistent with the federal design central to the Constitution. Typifying these views, Republican Representative Robert Hale of

---

[14] [This is the portion of the opinion of the Court in which Justice Scalia did not join. — EDS.]

New York labeled the Amendment "an utter departure from every principle ever dreamed of by the men who framed our Constitution," and warned that under it "all State legislation, in its codes of civil and criminal jurisprudence and procedure . . . may be overridden, may be repealed or abolished, and the law of Congress established instead." Senator William Stewart of Nevada likewise stated the Amendment would permit "Congress to legislate fully upon all subjects affecting life, liberty, and property," such that "there would not be much left for the State Legislatures," and would thereby "work an entire change in our form of government." Some radicals . . . also objected that giving Congress primary responsibility for enforcing legal equality would place power in the hands of changing congressional majorities.

As a result of these objections having been expressed from so many different quarters, the House voted to table the proposal until April . . . [when] the Joint Committee began drafting a new article of Amendment, which it reported to Congress on April 30, 1866.

Section 1 of the new draft Amendment imposed self-executing limits on the States. Section 5 prescribed that "[t]he Congress shall have power to enforce, by appropriate legislation, the provisions of this article." Under the revised Amendment, Congress' power was no longer plenary but remedial. Congress was granted the power to make the substantive constitutional prohibitions against the States effective. Representative Bingham said the new draft would give Congress "the power . . . to protect by national law the privileges and immunities of all the citizens of the Republic . . . whenever the same shall be abridged or denied by the unconstitutional acts of any State." Representative Stevens described the new draft Amendment as "allow[ing] Congress to correct the unjust legislation of the States." See also statement of Sen. Howard (§5 "enables Congress, in case the States shall enact laws in conflict with the principles of the amendment, to correct that legislation by a formal congressional enactment"). See generally T. Cooley, *Constitutional Limitations* (2d ed. 1871) ("This amendment of the Constitution does not concentrate power in the general government for any purpose of police government within the States; its object is to preclude legislation by any State which shall 'abridge the privileges or immunities of citizens of the United States'"). The revised Amendment proposal did not raise the concerns expressed earlier regarding broad congressional power to prescribe uniform national laws with respect to life, liberty, and property. After revisions not relevant here, the new measure passed both Houses and was ratified in July 1868 as the Fourteenth Amendment. . . .

The design of the Fourteenth Amendment has proved significant also in maintaining the traditional separation of powers between Congress and the Judiciary. The first eight Amendments to the Constitution set forth self-executing prohibitions on governmental action, and this Court has had primary authority to interpret those prohibitions. The Bingham draft, some thought, departed from that tradition by vesting in Congress primary power to interpret and elaborate on the meaning of the new Amendment through legislation. Under it, "Congress, and not the courts, was to judge whether or not any of the privileges or immunities were not secured to citizens in the several States." While this separation-of-powers aspect did not occasion the widespread resistance which was caused by the proposal's threat to the federal balance, it nonetheless attracted the attention of various Members. As enacted, the Fourteenth Amendment confers substantive rights against the States which, like the provisions of the Bill of Rights, are self-executing. The power to interpret the Constitution in a case or controversy remains in the Judiciary.

2

The remedial and preventive nature of Congress' enforcement power, and the limitation inherent in the power, were confirmed in our earliest cases on the Fourteenth Amendment. In the *Civil Rights Cases* (1883), the Court invalidated sections of the Civil Rights Act of 1875 which prescribed criminal penalties for denying to any person "the full enjoyment of" public accommodations and conveyances, on the grounds that it exceeded Congress' power by seeking to regulate private conduct. The Enforcement Clause, the Court said, did not authorize Congress to pass "general legislation upon the rights of the citizen, but corrective legislation, that is, such as may be necessary and proper for counteracting such laws as the States may adopt or enforce, and which, by the amendment, they are prohibited from making or enforcing. . . ." The power to "legislate generally upon" life, liberty, and property, as opposed to the "power to provide modes of redress" against offensive state action, was "repugnant" to the Constitution. Although the specific holdings of these early cases might have been superseded or modified, see, e.g., *Heart of Atlanta Motel, Inc. v. United States* (1964), their treatment of Congress' §5 power as corrective or preventive, not definitional, has not been questioned. . . .

3

. . . There is language in our opinion in *Katzenbach v. Morgan* (1966), which could be interpreted as acknowledging a power in Congress to enact legislation that expands the rights contained in §1 of the Fourteenth Amendment. This is not a necessary interpretation, however, or even the best one. In *Morgan*, the Court considered the constitutionality of §4(e) of the Voting Rights Act of 1965, which provided that no person who had successfully completed the sixth primary grade in a public school in, or a private school accredited by, the Commonwealth of Puerto Rico in which the language of instruction was other than English could be denied the right to vote because of an inability to read or write English. New York's Constitution, on the other hand, required voters to be able to read and write English. The Court provided two related rationales for its conclusion that §4(e) could "be viewed as a measure to secure for the Puerto Rican community residing in New York nondiscriminatory treatment by government." Under the first rationale, Congress could prohibit New York from denying the right to vote to large segments of its Puerto Rican community, in order to give Puerto Ricans "enhanced political power" that would be "helpful in gaining nondiscriminatory treatment in public services for the entire Puerto Rican community." Section 4(e) thus could be justified as a remedial measure to deal with "discrimination in governmental services." The second rationale, an alternative holding, did not address discrimination in the provision of public services but "discrimination in establishing voter qualifications." The Court perceived a factual basis on which Congress could have concluded that New York's literacy requirement "constituted an invidious discrimination in violation of the Equal Protection Clause." Both rationales for upholding §4(e) rested on unconstitutional discrimination by New York and Congress' reasonable attempt to combat it. . . .

If Congress could define its own powers by altering the Fourteenth Amendment's meaning, no longer would the Constitution be "superior paramount law, unchangeable by ordinary means." It would be "on a level with ordinary legislative acts, and, like other acts, . . . alterable when the legislature shall please to alter it." *Marbury v. Madison*. Under this approach, it is difficult to conceive of a principle that would limit congressional power. Shifting legislative majorities could change the Constitution and effectively circumvent the difficult and detailed amendment process contained in Article V.

We now turn to consider whether RFRA can be considered enforcement legislation under §5 of the Fourteenth Amendment.

B

Respondent contends that RFRA is a proper exercise of Congress' remedial or preventive power. The Act, it is said, is a reasonable means of protecting the free exercise of religion as defined by *Smith*. It prevents and remedies laws which are enacted with the unconstitutional object of targeting religious beliefs and practices. To avoid the difficulty of proving such violations, it is said, Congress can simply invalidate any law which imposes a substantial burden on a religious practice unless it is justified by a compelling interest and is the least restrictive means of accomplishing that interest. If Congress can prohibit laws with discriminatory effects in order to prevent racial discrimination in violation of the Equal Protection Clause, then it can do the same, respondent argues, to promote religious liberty.

While preventive rules are sometimes appropriate remedial measures, there must be a congruence between the means used and the ends to be achieved. The appropriateness of remedial measures must be considered in light of the evil presented. Strong measures appropriate to address one harm may be an unwarranted response to another, lesser one.

A comparison between RFRA and the Voting Rights Act is instructive. In contrast to the record which confronted Congress and the Judiciary in the voting rights cases, RFRA's legislative record lacks examples of modern instances of generally applicable laws passed because of religious bigotry. The history of persecution in this country detailed in the hearings mentions no episodes occurring in the past 40 years. Rather, the emphasis of the hearings was on laws of general applicability which place incidental burdens on religion. Much of the discussion centered upon anecdotal evidence of autopsies performed on Jewish individuals and Hmong immigrants in violation of their religious beliefs, and on zoning regulations and historic preservation laws (like the one at issue here), which, as an incident of their normal operation, have adverse effects on churches and synagogues. It is difficult to maintain that they are examples of legislation enacted or enforced due to animus or hostility to the burdened religious practices or that they indicate some widespread pattern of religious discrimination in this country. Congress' concern was with the incidental burdens imposed, not the object or purpose of the legislation. This lack of support in the legislative record, however, is not RFRA's most serious shortcoming. . . .

Regardless of the state of the legislative record, RFRA cannot be considered remedial, preventive legislation, if those terms are to have any meaning. RFRA is so out of proportion to a supposed remedial or preventive object that it cannot be understood as responsive to, or designed to prevent, unconstitutional behavior. It appears, instead, to attempt a substantive change in constitutional protections. Preventive measures prohibiting certain types of laws may be appropriate when there is reason to believe that many of the laws affected by the congressional enactment have a significant likelihood of being unconstitutional. . . .

RFRA is not so confined. Sweeping coverage ensures its intrusion at every level of government, displacing laws and prohibiting official actions of almost every description and regardless of subject matter. RFRA's restrictions apply to every agency and official of the Federal, State, and local Governments. RFRA applies to all federal and state law, statutory or otherwise, whether adopted before or after its enactment. RFRA has no termination date or termination mechanism. Any law is subject to challenge at any time by any individual who alleges a substantial burden on his or her free exercise of religion.

The reach and scope of RFRA distinguish it from other measures passed under Congress' enforcement power, even in the area of voting rights. [T]he challenged provisions [of the Voting Rights Act] were confined to those regions of the country where voting discrimination had been most flagrant, and affected a discrete class of state laws, i.e., state voting laws. Furthermore, to ensure that the reach of the Voting Rights Act was limited to those cases in which constitutional violations were most likely (in order to reduce the possibility of overbreadth), the coverage under the Act would terminate "at the behest of States and political subdivisions in which the danger of substantial voting discrimination has not materialized during the preceding five years." The provisions restricting and banning literacy tests attacked a particular type of voting qualification, one with a long history as a "notorious means to deny and abridge voting rights on racial grounds." . . . This is not to say, of course, that §5 legislation requires termination dates, geographic restrictions, or egregious predicates. Where, however, a congressional enactment pervasively prohibits constitutional state action in an effort to remedy or to prevent unconstitutional state action, limitations of this kind tend to ensure Congress' means are proportionate to ends legitimate under §5.

The stringent test RFRA demands of state laws reflects a lack of proportionality or congruence between the means adopted and the legitimate end to be achieved. If an objector can show a substantial burden on his free exercise, the State must demonstrate a compelling governmental interest and show that the law is the least restrictive means of furthering its interest. Claims that a law substantially burdens someone's exercise of religion will often be difficult to contest. Requiring a State to demonstrate a compelling interest and show that it has adopted the least restrictive means of achieving that interest is the most demanding test known to constitutional law. . . . Laws valid under *Smith* would fail under RFRA without regard to whether they had the object of stifling or punishing free exercise. We make these observations not to reargue the position of the majority in *Smith* but to illustrate the substantive alteration of its holding attempted by RFRA. Even assuming RFRA would be interpreted in effect to mandate some lesser test, say, one equivalent to intermediate scrutiny, the statute nevertheless would require searching judicial scrutiny of state law with the attendant likelihood of invalidation. This is a considerable congressional intrusion into the States' traditional prerogatives and general authority to regulate for the health and welfare of their citizens.

The substantial costs RFRA exacts, both in practical terms of imposing a heavy litigation burden on the States and in terms of curtailing their traditional general regulatory power, far exceed any pattern or practice of unconstitutional conduct under the Free Exercise Clause as interpreted in *Smith*. Simply put, RFRA is not designed to identify and counteract state laws likely to be unconstitutional because of their treatment of religion. In most cases, the state laws to which RFRA applies are not ones which will have been motivated by religious bigotry. If a state law disproportionately burdened a particular class of religious observers, this circumstance might be evidence of an impermissible legislative motive. RFRA's substantial-burden test, however, is not even a discriminatory effects or disparate-impact test. It is a reality of the modern regulatory state that numerous state laws, such as the zoning regulations at issue here, impose a substantial burden on a large class of individuals. When the exercise of religion has been burdened in an incidental way by a law of general application, it does not follow that the persons affected have been burdened any more than other citizens, let alone burdened because of their religious beliefs. . . .

Our national experience teaches that the Constitution is preserved best when each part of the Government respects both the Constitution and the proper actions and determinations of the other branches. When the Court has interpreted the Constitution, it has acted within the province of the Judicial Branch, which embraces the duty to say what the law is. *Marbury*. When the political branches of the Government act against the background of a judicial interpretation of the Constitution already issued, it must be understood that in later cases and controversies the Court will treat its precedents with the respect due them under settled principles, including stare decisis, and contrary expectations must be disappointed. RFRA was designed to control cases and controversies, such as the one before us; but as the provisions of the federal statute here invoked are beyond congressional authority, it is this Court's precedent, not RFRA, which must control. . . . Broad as the power of Congress is under the Enforcement Clause of the Fourteenth Amendment, RFRA contradicts vital principles necessary to maintain separation of powers and the federal balance.

JUSTICE SOUTER, dissenting.

To decide whether the Fourteenth Amendment gives Congress sufficient power to enact the Religious Freedom Restoration Act of 1993, the Court measures the legislation against the free-exercise standard of *Smith*. . . . I have serious doubts about the precedential value of the *Smith* rule and its entitlement to adherence. . . . [T]his case should be set down for reargument permitting plenary reexamination of the issue. Since the Court declines to follow that course, our free-exercise law remains marked by an "intolerable tension," and the constitutionality of the Act of Congress to enforce the free-exercise right cannot now be soundly decided. I would therefore dismiss the writ of certiorari as improvidently granted, and I accordingly dissent from the Court's disposition of this case.

STUDY GUIDE

- In *United States v. Morrison*, the Court claims to adhere to its Reconstruction Era decision in the *Civil Rights Cases* (1883). (A reminder: The facts of the case and other portions of the opinion appear in Chapter 3.) Is there any way to distinguish *Morrison* from the *Civil Rights Cases*?
- Can you spot language in Chief Justice Rehnquist's opinion that identifies a literal lack of the "equal protection of the laws" being afforded the freedmen by the states, which the Civil Rights Acts of 1871 and 1875 were attempting to remedy?
- Would the adoption of Justice Harlan's dissent from the *Civil Rights Cases* have changed the outcome in this case?

United States v. Morrison

529 U.S. 598 (2000)

Chief Justice Rehnquist delivered the opinion of the Court. . . .

Because we conclude that the Commerce Clause does not provide Congress with authority to enact §13981, we address petitioners' alternative argument that the section's civil remedy should be upheld as an exercise of Congress' remedial power under §5 of the Fourteenth Amendment. As noted above, Congress expressly invoked the Fourteenth Amendment as a source of authority to enact §13981.

The principles governing an analysis of congressional legislation under §5 are well settled. Section 5 states that Congress may "'enforce,' by 'appropriate legislation' the constitutional guarantee that no State shall deprive any person of 'life, liberty or property, without due process of law,' nor deny any person 'equal protection of the laws.'" *City of Boerne v. Flores* (1997). Section 5 is "a positive grant of legislative power," *Katzenbach v. Morgan* (1966), that includes authority to "prohibit conduct which is not itself unconstitutional and [to] intrud[e] into 'legislative spheres of autonomy previously reserved to the States.'" *Flores*. However, "[a]s broad as the congressional enforcement power is, it is not unlimited." *Oregon v. Mitchell* (1970). In fact, as we discuss in detail below, several limitations inherent in §5's text and constitutional context have been recognized since the Fourteenth Amendment was adopted.

Petitioners' §5 argument is founded on an assertion that there is pervasive bias in various state justice systems against victims of gender-motivated violence. This assertion is supported by a voluminous congressional record. Specifically, Congress received evidence that many participants in state justice systems are perpetuating an array of erroneous stereotypes and assumptions. Congress concluded that these discriminatory stereotypes often result in insufficient investigation and prosecution of gender-motivated crime, inappropriate focus on the behavior and credibility of the victims of that crime, and unacceptably lenient punishments for those who are actually convicted of gender-motivated violence. Petitioners contend that this bias denies victims of gender-motivated violence the equal protection of the laws and that Congress therefore acted appropriately in enacting a private civil remedy against the perpetrators of gender-motivated violence to both remedy the States' bias and deter future instances of discrimination in the state courts. . . .

However, the language and purpose of the Fourteenth Amendment place certain limitations on the manner in which Congress may attack discriminatory conduct. These limitations are necessary to prevent the Fourteenth Amendment from obliterating the Framers' carefully crafted balance of power between the States and the National Government. Foremost among these limitations is the time-honored principle that the Fourteenth Amendment, by its very terms, prohibits only state action. "[T]he principle has become firmly embedded in our constitutional law that the action inhibited by the first section of the Fourteenth Amendment is only such action as may fairly be said to be that of the States. That Amendment erects no shield against merely private conduct, however discriminatory or wrongful." *Shelley v. Kraemer* (1948).

Shortly after the Fourteenth Amendment was adopted, we decided two cases interpreting the Amendment's provisions, *United States v. Harris* (1883), and the *Civil Rights Cases* (1883). In *Harris*, the Court considered a challenge to §2 of the Civil Rights Act of 1871. That section sought to punish "private persons" for "conspiring to deprive any one of the equal protection of the laws enacted by the State." We concluded that this law exceeded Congress' §5 power because the law was "directed exclusively against the action of private persons, without reference to the laws of the State, or their administration by her officers." . . . We reached a similar conclusion in the *Civil Rights Cases*. In those consolidated cases, we held that the public accommodation provisions of the Civil Rights Act of 1875, which applied to purely private conduct, were beyond the scope of the §5 enforcement power.

The force of the doctrine of stare decisis behind these decisions stems not only from the length of time they have been on the books, but also from the insight attributable to the Members of the Court at that time. Every Member had been appointed by President Lincoln, Grant, Hayes, Garfield, or Arthur — and each of their judicial appointees obviously had intimate knowledge and familiarity with the events surrounding the adoption of the Fourteenth Amendment. . . .

Petitioners . . . argue that, unlike the situation in the *Civil Rights Cases*, here there has been gender-based disparate treatment by state authorities, whereas in those cases there was no indication of such state action. There is abundant evidence, however, to show that the Congresses that enacted the Civil Rights Acts of 1871 and

1875 had a purpose similar to that of Congress in enacting §13981: There were state laws on the books bespeaking equality of treatment, but in the administration of these laws there was discrimination against newly freed slaves. The statement of Representative Garfield in the House and that of Senator Sumner in the Senate are representative:

> [T]he chief complaint is not that the laws of the State are unequal, but that even where the laws are just and equal on their face, yet, by a systematic maladministration of them, or a neglect or refusal to enforce their provisions, a portion of the people are denied equal protection under them. (Statement of Rep. Garfield).
>
> The Legislature of South Carolina has passed a law giving precisely the rights contained in your "supplementary civil rights bill." But such a law remains a dead letter on her statute-books, because the State courts, comprised largely of those whom the Senator wishes to obtain amnesty for, refuse to enforce it. (Statement of Sen. Sumner).

But even if that distinction were valid, we do not believe it would save §13981's civil remedy. For the remedy is simply not "corrective in its character, adapted to counteract and redress the operation of such prohibited [s]tate laws or proceedings of [s]tate officers." *Civil Rights Cases.* Or, as we have phrased it in more recent cases, prophylactic legislation under §5 must have a "congruence and proportionality between the injury to be prevented or remedied and the means adopted to that end." *Florida Prepaid Postsecondary Ed. Expense Bd. v. College Savings Bank* (1999); *Flores.* Section 13981 is not aimed at proscribing discrimination by officials which the Fourteenth Amendment might not itself proscribe; it is directed not at any State or state actor, but at individuals who have committed criminal acts motivated by gender bias.

In the present cases, for example, §13981 visits no consequence whatever on any Virginia public official involved in investigating or prosecuting Brzonkala's assault. The section is, therefore, unlike any of the §5 remedies that we have previously upheld. For example, in *Katzenbach v. Morgan*, Congress prohibited New York from imposing literacy tests as a prerequisite for voting because it found that such a requirement disenfranchised thousands of Puerto Rican immigrants who had been educated in the Spanish language of their home territory. That law, which we upheld, was directed at New York officials who administered the State's election law and prohibited them from using a provision of that law. In *South Carolina v. Katzenbach* (1966), Congress imposed voting rights requirements on States that, Congress found, had a history of discriminating against blacks in voting. The remedy was also directed at state officials in those States. Similarly, in *Ex parte Virginia* (1880), Congress criminally punished state officials who intentionally discriminated in jury selection; again, the remedy was directed to the culpable state official.

Section 13981 is also different from these previously upheld remedies in that it applies uniformly throughout the Nation. Congress' findings indicate that the problem of discrimination against the victims of gender-motivated crimes does not exist in all States, or even most States. By contrast, the §5 remedy upheld in *Katzenbach v. Morgan*, was directed only to the State where the evil found by

Congress existed, and in *South Carolina v. Katzenbach*, the remedy was directed only to those States in which Congress found that there had been discrimination.

For these reasons, we conclude that Congress' power under §5 does not extend to the enactment of §13981.

STUDY GUIDE

- The next case exemplifies how the approach adopted in *City of Boerne* can be used to limit Congress's enforcement powers under Section 5 of the Fourteenth Amendment.
- How does the Court distinguish the Americans with Disabilities Act from the Voting Rights Act of 1965?

Board of Trustees of University of Alabama v. Garrett

531 U.S. 356 (2001)

Chief Justice Rehnquist delivered the opinion of the Court.

We decide here whether employees of the State of Alabama may recover money damages by reason of the State's failure to comply with the provisions of Title I of the Americans with Disabilities Act of 1990 (ADA or Act). . . . The ADA prohibits certain employers, including the States, from "discriminat[ing] against a qualified individual with a disability because of the disability of such individual in regard to job application procedures, the hiring, advancement, or discharge of employees, employee compensation, job training, and other terms, conditions, and privileges of employment." To this end, the Act requires employers to "mak[e] reasonable accommodations to the known physical or mental limitations of an otherwise qualified individual with a disability who is an applicant or employee, unless [the employer] can demonstrate that the accommodation would impose an undue hardship on the operation of the [employer's] business." . . .

Respondent Patricia Garrett, a registered nurse, was employed as the Director of Nursing, OB/Gyn/Neonatal Services, for the University of Alabama in Birmingham Hospital. In 1994, Garrett was diagnosed with breast cancer and subsequently underwent a lumpectomy, radiation treatment, and chemotherapy. Garrett's treatments required her to take substantial leave from work. Upon returning to work in July 1995, Garrett's supervisor informed Garrett that she would have to give up her Director position. Garrett then applied for and received a transfer to another, lower paying position as a nurse manager. . . . [Garrett's lawsuit for money damages under the ADA was rejected by the District Court and the Court of Appeals. — Eds.] We granted certiorari to resolve a split among the Courts of Appeals on the question whether an individual may sue a State for money damages in federal court under the ADA. . . .

Section 5 of the Fourteenth Amendment grants Congress the power to enforce the substantive guarantees contained in §1 by enacting "appropriate legislation." See *City of Boerne v. Flores* (1997). Congress is not limited to mere legislative repetition of this Court's constitutional jurisprudence. "Rather, Congress' power 'to enforce' the Amendment includes the authority both to remedy and to deter violation of rights guaranteed thereunder by prohibiting a somewhat broader swath of conduct, including that which is not itself forbidden by the Amendment's text." *Kimel v. Florida Bd. of Regents* (2000); *City of Boerne*. *City of Boerne* also confirmed, however, the long-settled principle that it is the responsibility of this Court, not Congress, to define the substance of constitutional guarantees. Accordingly, §5 legislation reaching beyond the scope of §1's actual guarantees must exhibit "congruence and proportionality between the injury to be prevented or remedied and the means adopted to that end."

The first step in applying these now familiar principles is to identify with some precision the scope of the constitutional right at issue. . . . Once we have determined the metes and bounds of the constitutional right in question, we examine whether Congress identified a history and pattern of unconstitutional employment discrimination by the States against the disabled. Just as §1 of the Fourteenth Amendment applies only to actions committed "under color of state law," Congress' §5 authority is appropriately exercised only in response to state transgressions.

The legislative record of the ADA, however, simply fails to show that Congress did in fact identify a pattern of irrational state discrimination in employment against the disabled. . . . Congress made a general finding in the ADA that "historically, society has tended to isolate and segregate individuals with disabilities, and, despite some improvements, such forms of discrimination against individuals with disabilities continue to be a serious and pervasive social problem." The record assembled by Congress includes many instances to support such a finding. But the great majority of these incidents do not deal with the activities of States. . . .

Even were it possible to squeeze out of these examples a pattern of unconstitutional discrimination by the States, the rights and remedies created by the ADA against the States would raise the same sort of concerns as to congruence and proportionality as were found in *City of Boerne*. For example, whereas it would be entirely rational (and therefore constitutional) for a state employer to conserve scarce financial resources by hiring employees who are able to use existing facilities, the ADA requires employers to "mak[e] existing facilities used by employees readily accessible to and usable by individuals with disabilities"[except] where the employer "can demonstrate that the accommodation would impose an undue hardship on the operation of the business of such covered entity." However, even with this exception, the accommodation duty far exceeds what is constitutionally required in that it makes unlawful a range of alternate responses that would be reasonable but would fall short of imposing an "undue burden" upon the employer. . . .

The ADA's constitutional shortcomings are apparent when the Act is compared to Congress' efforts in the Voting Rights Act of 1965 to respond to a serious pattern of constitutional violations. . . . In that Act, Congress documented a marked pattern of unconstitutional action by the States. State officials, Congress found, routinely applied voting tests in order to exclude African-American citizens from registering to vote. Congress also determined that litigation had proved ineffective and that there persisted an otherwise inexplicable 50-percentage-point gap in the registration of white and African-American voters in some States. Congress' response was to promulgate in the Voting Rights Act a detailed but limited remedial scheme designed to guarantee meaningful enforcement of the Fifteenth Amendment in those areas of the Nation where abundant evidence of States' systematic denial of those rights was identified.

The contrast between this kind of evidence, and the evidence that Congress considered in the present case, is stark. . . . Congress is the final authority as to desirable public policy, but in order to authorize private individuals to recover money damages against the States, there must be a pattern of discrimination by the States which violates the Fourteenth Amendment, and the remedy imposed by Congress must be congruent and proportional to the targeted violation. Those requirements are not met here, and to uphold the Act's application to the States would allow Congress to rewrite the Fourteenth Amendment law laid down by this Court. . . . Section 5 does not so broadly enlarge congressional authority. The judgment of the Court of Appeals is therefore

Reversed.

Justice Kennedy, with whom Justice O'Connor joins, concurring. . . .

If the States had been transgressing the Fourteenth Amendment by their mistreatment or lack of concern for those with impairments, one would have expected to find in decisions of the courts of the States and also the courts of the United States extensive litigation and discussion of the constitutional violations. This confirming judicial documentation does not exist. . . .

Justice Breyer, with whom Justice Stevens, Justice Souter and Justice Ginsburg join, dissenting. . . .

[T]he Court fails to find in the legislative record sufficient indication that Congress has "negative[d]" the presumption that state action is rationally related to a legitimate objective. The problem with the Court's approach is that neither the "burden of proof" that favors States nor any other rule of restraint applicable to *judges* applies to *Congress* when it exercises its §5 power. . . . Rational-basis review — with its presumptions favoring constitutionality — is "a paradigm of *judicial* restraint." *FCC v. Beach Communications, Inc.* (1993) (emphasis added). And the Congress of the United States is not a lower court. . . .

There is simply no reason to require Congress, seeking to determine facts relevant to the exercise of its §5 authority, to adopt rules or presumptions that reflect a court's institutional limitations. Unlike courts, Congress can readily gather facts from across the Nation, assess the magnitude of a problem, and more easily find an appropriate remedy. Unlike courts, Congress directly reflects public attitudes and beliefs, enabling Congress better to understand where, and to what extent, refusals to accommodate a disability amount to behavior that is callous or unreasonable to the point of lacking constitutional justification. Unlike judges, Members of Congress can directly obtain information from constituents who have firsthand experience with discrimination and related issues. . . . To apply a rule designed to restrict courts as if it restricted Congress' legislative power is to stand the underlying principle — a principle of judicial restraint — on its head.

STUDY GUIDE

- Can *Nevada Department of Human Resources v. Hibbs* be reconciled with *Garrett*? Justice Ginsburg has hinted that Chief Justice Rehnquist joined the majority in *Hibbs* due to "life experience." His daughter was a recently divorced single mother with a demanding career.
- Did the Court alter its approach to congruence and proportionality? Or did it apply the same standard in a different way?

Nevada Department of Human Resources v. Hibbs

538 U.S. 721 (2003)

Chief Justice Rehnquist delivered the opinion of the Court.

The Family and Medical Leave Act of 1993 (FMLA or Act) entitles eligible employees to take up to 12 work weeks of unpaid leave annually for any of several reasons, including the onset of a "serious health condition" in an employee's spouse, child, or parent. The Act creates a private right of action to seek both equitable relief and money damages "against any employer (including a public agency) in any Federal or State court of competent jurisdiction," should that employer "interfere with, restrain, or deny the exercise of" FMLA rights. We hold that employees of the State of Nevada may recover money damages in the event of the State's failure to comply with the family-care provision of the Act. . . .

This case turns . . . on whether Congress acted within its constitutional authority when it sought to abrogate the States' immunity for purposes of the FMLA's family-leave provision. . . . Two provisions of the Fourteenth Amendment are relevant here: Section 5 grants Congress the power "to enforce" the substantive guarantees of §1 — among them, equal protection of the laws — by enacting "appropriate legislation." Congress may, in the exercise of its §5 power, do more than simply proscribe conduct that we have held unconstitutional. "Congress' power 'to enforce' the Amendment includes the authority both to remedy and to deter violation of rights guaranteed thereunder by prohibiting a somewhat broader swath of conduct, including that which is not itself forbidden by the Amendment's text." *Board of Trustees of Univ. of Ala. v. Garrett* (2001); *City of Boerne v. Flores* (1997); *Katzenbach v. Morgan* (1966). In other words, Congress may enact so-called prophylactic legislation that proscribes facially constitutional conduct, in order to prevent and deter unconstitutional conduct.

City of Boerne also confirmed, however, that it falls to this Court, not Congress, to define the substance of constitutional guarantees. . . . Section 5 legislation reaching beyond the scope of §1's actual guarantees must be an appropriate remedy for identified constitutional violations, not "an attempt to substantively redefine the States' legal obligations." We distinguish appropriate prophylactic legislation from "substantive redefinition of the Fourteenth Amendment right at issue," *id.*, at 81, by applying the test set forth in *City of Boerne*: Valid §5 legislation must exhibit "congruence and proportionality between the injury to be prevented or remedied and the means adopted to that end."

The FMLA aims to protect the right to be free from gender-based discrimination in the workplace. We have held that statutory classifications that distinguish between males and females are subject to heightened scrutiny. For a gender-based classification to withstand such scrutiny, it must "serv[e] important governmental objectives," and "the discriminatory means employed [must be] substantially related to the achievement of those objectives." *United States v. Virginia* (1996). The State's justification for such a classification "must not rely on overbroad generalizations about the different talents, capacities, or preferences of males and females." *Ibid.* We now inquire whether Congress had evidence of a pattern of constitutional violations on the part of the States in this area. . . .

According to evidence that was before Congress when it enacted the FMLA, States continue to rely on invalid gender stereotypes in the employment context, specifically in the administration of leave benefits. Reliance on such stereotypes cannot justify the States' gender discrimination in this area. The . . . persistence of such unconstitutional discrimination by the States justifies Congress' passage of prophylactic §5 legislation.

As the FMLA's legislative record reflects, a 1990 Bureau of Labor Statistics (BLS) survey stated that 37 percent of surveyed private-sector employees were covered by maternity leave policies, while only 18 percent were covered by paternity leave policies. The corresponding numbers from a similar BLS survey the previous year were 33 percent and 16 percent, respectively. While these data show an increase in the percentage of employees eligible for such leave, they also show a widening of the gender gap during the same period. Thus, stereotype-based beliefs about the allocation of family duties remained firmly rooted, and employers' reliance on them in establishing discriminatory leave policies remained widespread.

Congress also heard testimony that "[p]arental leave for fathers . . . is rare. Even . . . [w]here child-care leave policies do exist, men, both in the public and private sectors, receive notoriously discriminatory treatment in their requests for such leave." Many States offered women extended "maternity" leave that far exceeded the typical 4- to 8-week period of physical disability due to pregnancy and childbirth, but very few States granted men a parallel benefit: Fifteen States provided women up to one year of extended maternity leave, while only four provided men with the same. M. Lord & M. King, The State Reference Guide to Work-Family Programs for State Employees 30 (1991). This and other differential leave policies were not attributable to any differential physical needs of men and women, but rather to the pervasive sex-role stereotype that caring for family members is women's work.

Finally, Congress had evidence that, even where state laws and policies were not facially discriminatory, they were applied in discriminatory ways. It was aware of the "serious problems with the discretionary nature of family leave," because when "the authority to grant leave and to arrange the length of that leave rests with individual supervisors," it leaves "employees open to discretionary and possibly unequal treatment." Testimony supported that conclusion, explaining that "[t]he lack of uniform parental and medical leave policies in the work place has created an environment where [sex] discrimination is rampant." . . . In sum, the States' record of unconstitutional participation in, and fostering of, gender-based discrimination in the administration of leave benefits is weighty enough to justify the enactment of prophylactic §5 legislation.

The impact of the discrimination targeted by the FMLA is significant. . . . Stereotypes about women's domestic roles are reinforced by parallel stereotypes presuming a lack of domestic responsibilities for men. Because employers continued to regard the family as the woman's domain, they often denied men similar accommodations or discouraged them from taking leave. These mutually reinforcing stereotypes created a self-fulfilling cycle of discrimination that forced women to continue to assume the role of primary family caregiver, and fostered employers' stereotypical views about women's commitment to work and their value as employees. Those perceptions, in turn, Congress reasoned, lead to subtle discrimination that may be difficult to detect on a case-by-case basis.

We believe that Congress' chosen remedy, the family-care leave provision of the FMLA, is "congruent and proportional to the targeted violation," *Garrett*. Congress had already tried unsuccessfully to address this problem through Title VII and the amendment of Title VII by the Pregnancy Discrimination Act. Here, as in *Katzenbach*, Congress again confronted a "difficult and intractable proble[m]," where previous legislative attempts had failed. Such problems may justify added prophylactic measures in response.

By creating an across-the-board, routine employment benefit for all eligible employees, Congress sought to ensure that family-care leave would no longer be stigmatized as an inordinate drain on the workplace caused by female employees, and that employers could not evade leave obligations simply by hiring men. By setting a minimum standard of family leave for all eligible employees, irrespective of gender, the FMLA attacks the formerly state-sanctioned stereotype that only women are responsible for family caregiving, thereby reducing employers' incentives to engage in discrimination by basing hiring and promotion decisions on stereotypes. . . .

The dissent characterizes the FMLA as a "substantive entitlement program" rather than a remedial statute because it establishes a floor of 12 weeks' leave. In the dissent's view, in the face of evidence of gender-based discrimination by the States in the provision of leave benefits, Congress could do no more in exercising its §5 power than simply proscribe such discrimination. But this position cannot be squared with our recognition that Congress "is not confined to the enactment of legislation that merely parrots the precise wording of the Fourteenth Amendment," but may prohibit "a somewhat broader swath of conduct, including that which is not itself forbidden by the Amendment's text." *Kimel v. Florida Bd. of Regents* (2000). For example, this Court has upheld certain prophylactic provisions of the Voting Rights Act as valid exercises of Congress' §5 power, including the literacy test ban and preclearance requirements for changes in States' voting procedures. . . .

Unlike the statutes at issue in *City of Boerne*, *Kimel*, and *Garrett*, which applied broadly to every aspect of state employers' operations, the FMLA is narrowly targeted at the fault line between work and family — precisely where sex-based overgeneralization has been and remains strongest — and affects only one aspect of the employment relationship.

For the above reasons, we conclude that §2612(a)(1)(C) is congruent and proportional to its remedial object, and can "be understood as responsive to, or designed to prevent, unconstitutional behavior." *City of Boerne*.

The judgment of the Court of Appeals is therefore

Affirmed.

JUSTICE KENNEDY, with whom JUSTICE SCALIA and JUSTICE THOMAS join, dissenting. . . .

Congress does not have authority to define the substantive content of the Equal Protection Clause; it may only shape the remedies warranted by the violations of that guarantee. *City of Boerne*. . . . The Court is unable to show that States have engaged in a pattern of unlawful conduct which warrants the remedy of opening state treasuries to private suits. The inability to adduce evidence of alleged discrimination, coupled with the inescapable fact that the federal scheme is not a remedy but a benefit program, demonstrate the lack of the requisite link between any problem Congress has identified and the program it mandated.

In examining whether Congress was addressing a demonstrated "pattern of unconstitutional employment discrimination by the States," the Court gives superficial treatment to the requirement that we "identify with some precision the scope of the constitutional right at issue." *Garrett*. . . . The relevant question . . . is whether, notwithstanding the passage of Title VII and similar state legislation, the States continued to engage in widespread discrimination on the basis of gender in the provision of family leave benefits. . . . The evidence to substantiate this charge must be far more specific, however, than a simple recitation of a general history of employment discrimination against women. . . .

Respondents fail to make the requisite showing. . . . [T]he evidence considered by Congress concerned discriminatory practices of the private sector, not those of state employers. The statistical information compiled by the Bureau of Labor Statistics (BLS), which are the only factual findings the Court cites, surveyed only private employers. While the evidence of discrimination by private entities may be relevant, it does not, by itself, justify the abrogation of States' sovereign immunity. *Garrett* ("Congress' §5 authority is appropriately exercised only in response to state transgressions"). . . .

The question is not whether the family leave provision is a congruent and proportional response to general gender-based stereotypes in employment which "ha[ve] historically produced discrimination in the hiring and promotion of women"; the question is whether it is a proper remedy to an alleged pattern of unconstitutional discrimination by States in the grant of family leave. The evidence of gender-based stereotypes is too remote to support the required showing. . . . [Nor] does the Constitution require States to provide their employees with any family leave at all. A State's failure to devise a family leave program is not, then, evidence of unconstitutional behavior. Considered in its entirety, the evidence fails to document a pattern of unconstitutional conduct sufficient to justify the abrogation of States' sovereign immunity. . . .

Our concern with gender discrimination, which is subjected to heightened scrutiny . . . does not alter this conclusion. . . . This consideration does not divest respondents of their burden to show that "Congress identified a history and pattern of unconstitutional employment discrimination by the States." *Garrett*. . . . Congress was not responding with a congruent and proportional remedy to a perceived course of unconstitutional conduct. Instead, it enacted a substantive entitlement program of its own. If Congress had been concerned about different treatment of men and women with respect to family leave, a congruent remedy would have sought to ensure the benefits of any leave program enacted by a State are available to men and women on an equal basis. Instead, the Act imposes, across the board, a requirement that States grant a minimum of 12 weeks of leave per year. 29 U.S.C. §2612(a)(1)(C). This requirement may represent Congress' considered judgment as to the optimal balance between the family obligations of workers and the interests of employers. . . . It does not follow, however, that if the States choose to enact a different benefit scheme, they should be deemed to engage in unconstitutional conduct and forced to open their treasuries to private suits for damages. . . .

Were more proof needed to show that this is an entitlement program, not a remedial statute, it should suffice to note that the Act does not even purport to bar discrimination in some leave programs the States do enact and administer. Under the Act, a State is allowed to provide women with, say, 24 weeks of family leave per year but provide only 12 weeks of leave to men. A law of this kind might run afoul of the Equal Protection Clause or Title VII, but it would not constitute a violation of the Act. The Act on its face is not drawn as a remedy to gender-based discrimination in family leave. . . .

JUSTICE SCALIA, dissenting.

I join Justice Kennedy's dissent, and add one further observation: The constitutional violation that is a prerequisite to "prophylactic" congressional action to "enforce" the Fourteenth Amendment is a violation *by the State against which the enforcement action is taken*. There is no guilt by association, enabling the sovereignty of one State to be abridged under §5 of the Fourteenth Amendment because of violations by another State, or by most other States, or even by 49 other States. Congress has sometimes displayed awareness of this self-evident limitation. That is presumably why the most sweeping provisions of the Voting Rights Act of 1965 — which we upheld in City of Rome v. United States (1980), as a valid exercise of congressional power under §2 of the Fifteenth Amendment — were restricted to States "with a demonstrable history of intentional racial discrimination in voting."

Today's opinion for the Court does not even attempt to demonstrate that each one of the 50 States covered by [the Act] was in violation of the Fourteenth Amendment. It treats "the States" as some sort of collective entity which is guilty or innocent as a body. "[T]he States' record of unconstitutional participation in, and fostering of, gender-based discrimination," it concludes, "is weighty enough to justify the enactment of prophylactic §5 legislation." This will not do. Prophylaxis in the sense of extending the remedy beyond the violation is one thing; prophylaxis in the sense of extending the remedy beyond the violator is something else. . . .

CHAPTER 5

Federalism Limits on State Power

Chapter 4 considered the constraints on congressional power derived from principles of federalism. This chapter analyzes how federalism limits the powers of the states — topics that will be more likely to show up in legal practice. Students who go on in their professional careers to represent corporate clients are more likely to litigate a Dormant Commerce Clause or Privileges and Immunities Clause claim than any other type of constitutional case. However, because these areas are enormously complicated, the coverage in this chapter is limited to exposing you to the basic doctrines so you can better spot the issues in practice. These cases also raise the issue of whether the Court should "second-guess" the political branches when economic legislation is involved. Some of the cases touch on when the Court should look behind laws to the motives of those who passed them (an issue we came across in earlier chapters on the powers of Congress, and that we will see again). This sort of analysis is central to the debate on how the Court deals with cases under the Equal Protection Clause.

A. THE DORMANT COMMERCE CLAUSE

ASSIGNMENT 1

Article I, Section 8, Clause 3 gives Congress the power "[t]o regulate Commerce with foreign Nations . . . among the several States." Historically, the Commerce

Clause functioned first as a limitation on state power and only later (when the national government began to legislate more broadly) as a grant of power for the federal regulation of commerce. When Congress chooses to regulate interstate commerce, any state laws that conflict with the federal law are "preempted." But what happens if states attempt to legislate aspects of interstate commerce that Congress has not regulated? The Court has developed the so-called *Dormant Commerce Clause* doctrine to address these latter situations. (Note that the text of the Constitution does not include such a "negative" provision.) The most prominent early Supreme Court case to suggest the doctrine was *Gibbons v. Ogden* (1824), which we discussed in Chapter 2. Four years later, Chief Justice Marshall issued a follow-up decision in *Willson v. Black Bird Creek Marsh* (1829). After reading how Chief Justice John Marshall handled this issue, and then seeing how it was dealt with in the nineteenth century, we will look at a small part of the complex modern Dormant Commerce Clause doctrine.

In this chapter, you will continually want to ask yourself this question: Should the Court be involved at all in reviewing state laws that arguably burden interstate commerce? On the one hand, it is widely recognized that, under the Articles of Confederation, some states struggled with the existence of trade barriers to commerce imposed by other states, and the economy of the United States suffered as a result. Thus, one traditional core justification of the Dormant Commerce Clause has been the desire to remove those barriers and to create a single national market. On the other hand, decisions in this area inevitably involve economic policy judgments for which courts are arguably ill-suited.

STUDY GUIDE

Note that the passage where Marshall refers to "the power to regulate commerce in its dormant state" is confusingly written. Marshall is referring here to a situation where Congress's "*power* to regulate commerce" is "in its dormant state"—meaning that Congress has not used its power. Marshall is not referring to a congressional power to regulate "*commerce* in its dormant state" (whatever that might mean). In short, it is the power that is dormant, not commerce.

Willson v. Black Bird Creek Marsh Co.

27 U.S. (2 Pet.) 245 (1829)

[The General Assembly of Delaware incorporated the Black Bird Creek Marsh Company in 1822 and authorized it to build a dam across Black Bird Creek. The company sued Willson, whose boat broke the dam that previously stood at the creek. Willson argued that he did not commit a trespass because the creek was a navigable highway available to all citizens of Delaware and the United States. Therefore, he contended, the Delaware act authorizing construction of the dam violated Congress's power to regulate interstate commerce. The Delaware courts disagreed, and ruled for the company. Willson then appealed to the U.S. Supreme Court — EDS.]

MR. CHIEF JUSTICE MARSHALL delivered the opinion of the Court. . . .

The jurisdiction of the Court being established, the more doubtful question is to be considered, whether the act incorporating the Black Bird Creek Marsh Company is repugnant to the constitution, so far as it authorizes a dam across the creek. The plea states the creek to be navigable, in the nature of a highway, through which the tide ebbs and flows.

The act of assembly by which the plaintiffs were authorized to construct their dam, shows plainly that this is one of those many creeks, passing through a deep level marsh adjoining the Delaware, up which the tide flows for some distance. The value of the property on its banks must be enhanced by excluding the water from the marsh, and the health of the inhabitants probably improved. Measures calculated to produce these objects, provided they do not come into collision with the powers of the general government, are undoubtedly within those which are reserved to the states. But the measure authorised by this act stops a navigable creek, and must be supposed to abridge the rights of those who have been accustomed to use it. But this abridgement, unless it comes in conflict with the constitution or a law of the United States, is an affair between the government of Delaware and its citizens, of which this Court can take no cognizance.

The counsel for the plaintiffs in error insist that it comes in conflict with the power of the United States "to regulate commerce with foreign nations and among the several states." If congress had passed any act which bore upon the case; any act in execution of the power to regulate commerce, the object of which was to control state legislation over those small navigable creeks into which the tide flows, and which abound throughout the lower country of the middle and southern states; we should feel not much difficulty in saying that a state law coming in conflict with such act would be void. But congress has passed no such act. The repugnancy of the law of Delaware to the constitution is placed entirely on its repugnancy to the power to regulate commerce with foreign nations and among the several states; a power which has not been so exercised as to affect the question. We do not think that the act empowering the Black Bird Creek Marsh Company to place a dam across the creek, can, under all the circumstances of the case, be considered as repugnant to the power to regulate commerce in its dormant state, or as being in conflict with any law passed on the subject. There is no error, and the judgment is affirmed.

STUDY GUIDE

- Notice the Court's use of categories — subjects of national concern and subjects of local concern. Does this categorical approach remind you of any cases from the Commerce Clause material?

Justice McLean was a mentor to fellow Ohioan and future Chief Justice Salmon P. Chase. Like Chase, McLean had presidential ambitions. Known as "The Politician on the Supreme Court," McLean, originally a Jackson Democrat, joined the Anti-Jackson Democrats, then the Anti-Masonic Party, the Whigs, the Free Soilers, and finally the Republicans.

Cooley v. Board of Wardens

53 U.S. (12 How.) 299 (1851)

[In 1803, Pennsylvania's legislature passed a statute requiring ships that did not take a pilot to pay a fee to the master warden. The Board of Wardens sued defendant Cooley for failing to pay the fee for his ship that sailed from Pennsylvania without a pilot. The Supreme Court of Pennsylvania rejected Cooley's argument that the statute was unconstitutional — EDS.]

MR. JUSTICE CURTIS delivered the opinion of the court. . . .

We think this particular regulation concerning half-pilotage fees, is an appropriate part of a general system of regulations of this subject. . . . [T]hey rest upon the propriety of securing lives and property exposed to the perils of a dangerous navigation, by taking on board a person peculiarly skilled to encounter or avoid them; upon the policy of discouraging the commanders of vessels from refusing to receive such persons on board at the proper times and places; and upon the expediency, and even intrinsic justice, of not suffering those who have incurred labor, and expense, and danger, to place themselves in a position to render important service generally necessary, to go unrewarded, because the master of a particular vessel either rashly refuses their proffered assistance, or, contrary to the general experience, does not need it. . . .

It remains to consider the objection, that it is repugnant to the [Commerce Clause]. That the power to regulate commerce includes the regulation of navigation, we consider settled. And when we look to the nature of the service performed by pilots, to the relations which that service and its compensations bear to navigation between the several states, and between the ports of the United States and foreign countries, we are brought to the conclusion, that the regulation of the qualifications of pilots, of the modes and times of offering and rendering their services, of the responsibilities which shall rest upon them, of the powers they shall possess, of the compensation they may demand, and of the penalties by which their rights and duties may be enforced, do constitute regulations of navigation, and consequently of commerce, within the just meaning of this clause of the Constitution. . . .

[W]e are brought directly and unavoidably to the consideration of the question, whether the grant of the commercial power to Congress, did *per se* deprive the States of all power to regulate pilots. . . . Now the power to regulate commerce, embraces a vast field, containing not only many, but exceedingly various subjects, quite unlike in their nature; some imperatively demanding a single uniform rule, operating equally on the commerce of the United States in every port; and some, like the subject now in question, as imperatively demanding that diversity, which alone can meet the local necessities of navigation.

Either absolutely to affirm, or deny that the nature of this power requires exclusive legislation by Congress, is to lose sight of the nature of the subjects of this power, and to assert concerning all of them, what is really applicable but to a part. Whatever subjects of this power are in their nature national, or admit only of one uniform system, or plan of regulation, may justly be said to be of such a nature as to require exclusive legislation by Congress. That this cannot be affirmed of laws for the regulation of pilots and pilotage is plain. The . . . nature of this subject is such, that until Congress should find it necessary to exert its power, it should be left to the legislation of the states; that it is local and not national; that it is likely to be the best provided for, not by one system, or plan of regulations, but by as many as the legislative discretion of the several states should deem applicable to the local peculiarities of the ports within their limits. . . .

It is the opinion of a majority of the court that the mere grant to Congress of the power to regulate commerce, did not deprive the States of power to regulate pilots. . . . [This opinion] does not extend to the question what other subjects, under the commercial power, are within the exclusive control of Congress, or may be regulated by the states in the absence of all congressional legislation; nor to the general question how far any regulation of a subject by Congress, may be deemed to operate as an exclusion of all legislation by the States upon the same subject. We decide the precise questions before us, upon what we deem sound principles, applicable to this particular subject in the state in which the legislation of Congress has left it. We go no further. . . .

We are of opinion that this State law was enacted by virtue of a power, residing in the State to legislate; that it is not in conflict with any law of Congress; that it does not interfere with any system which Congress has established by making regulations, or by intentionally leaving individuals to their own unrestricted action; that this law is therefore valid, and the judgment of the Supreme Court of Pennsylvania in each case must be affirmed.

Mr. Justice McLean [dissenting].

It is with regret that I feel myself obliged to dissent from the opinion of a majority of my brethren in this case. . . . That a State may regulate foreign commerce, or commerce among the States, is a doctrine which has been advanced by individual judges of this court; but never before, I believe, has such a power been sanctioned by the decision of this court. In this case, the power to regulate pilots is admitted to belong to the commercial power of Congress; and yet it is held, that a State, by virtue of its inherent power, may regulate the subject, until such regulation shall be annulled by Congress. This is the principle established by this decision. Its language is guarded, in order to apply the decision only to the case before the court. But such restriction can never operate, so as to render the principle inapplicable to other cases. And it is in this light that the decision is chiefly to be regretted. The power is recognised in the State, because the subject is more appropriate for State than Federal action; and consequently, it must be presumed the Constitution cannot have intended to inhibit State action. This is not a rule by which the Constitution is to be construed. It can receive but little support from the discussions which took place on the adoption of the Constitution, and none at all from the earlier decisions of this court.

It will be found that the principle in this case, if carried out, will deeply affect the commercial prosperity of the country. If a State has power to regulate foreign commerce, such regulation must be held valid, until Congress shall repeal or annul it. . . . I speak of the principle of the opinion, and not of the restricted application given to it by the learned judge who delivered it. The noted *Blackbird Creek* case shows what little influence the facts and circumstances of a case can have in restraining the principle it is supposed to embody. . . .

The decision in *Cooley* introduced what came to be known as the *doctrine of selective exclusiveness*. The national government would have exclusive power to regulate those matters that were national in scope or which, by their nature, required uniform regulation. As to such matters, if Congress chose to legislate, it would preempt state law. If Congress chose not to legislate, the subject was beyond the reach of state legislation. Purely intrastate commerce was exclusively within the power of the states to regulate (because the Commerce Clause did not give Congress the power to regulate such activity). Interstate commerce not considered to be national in scope or requiring uniform regulation could be regulated concurrently by the states and by Congress. Of course, the application of these categories was subject to interpretation. And it should be noted that, broadly speaking, until the Progressive Era the national government did very little regulating. So if a particular matter fell into the first category — being national in scope or requiring uniform regulation — the practical effect was to have no regulation of the activity at all.

South Carolina State Highway Department v. Barnwell Bros.

303 U.S. 177 (1938)

Mr. Justice Stone delivered the opinion of the Court.

Act No. 259 of the General Assembly of South Carolina, of April 28, 1933 prohibits use on the state highways of motor trucks and "semi-trailer motor trucks" whose width exceeds 90 inches, and whose weight including load exceeds 20,000 pounds. For purposes of the weight limitation, section 2 of the statute provides that a semitrailer motortruck, which is a motor propelled truck with a trailer whose front end is designed to be attached to and supported by the truck, shall be considered a single unit. The principal question for decision is whether these prohibitions impose an unconstitutional burden upon interstate commerce.

The District Court of three judges, after hearing evidence, ruled that the challenged provisions of the statute have not been superseded by the Federal Motor Carrier Act and adopted as its own the ruling of the state Supreme Court . . . that the challenged provisions, being an exercise of the state's power to

When Associate Justice Harlan Fiske Stone became Chief Justice in 1941, he was the first Chief Justice never to have held an elected office.

regulate the use of its highways so as to protect them from injury and to insure their safe and economical use, do not violate the Fourteenth Amendment. But it held that the weight and width prohibitions place an unlawful burden on interstate motor traffic passing over specified highways of the state, which for the most part are of concrete or a concrete base surfaced with asphalt. It accordingly enjoined the enforcement of the weight provision against interstate motor carriers on the specified highway, and also the width limitation of 90 inches, except in the case of vehicles exceeding 96 inches in width. It exempted from the operation of the decree, bridges on those highways "not constructed with sufficient strength to support the heavy trucks of modern traffic or too narrow to accommodate such traffic safely," provided the state highway department should place at each end of the bridge proper notices warning that the use of the bridge is forbidden by trucks exceeding the weight or width limits and provided the proper authorities take the necessary steps to enforce the law against such use of the bridges. . . .

The trial court rested its decision that the statute unreasonably burdens interstate commerce, upon findings, not assailed here, that there is a large amount of motortruck traffic passing interstate in the southeastern part of the United States, which would normally pass over the highways of South Carolina, but which will be barred from the state by the challenged restrictions if enforced, and upon its conclusion that, when viewed in the light of their effect upon interstate commerce, these restrictions are unreasonable.

To reach [its] conclusion [enjoining the enforcement of the state law based on the Commerce Clause] the [trial] court weighed conflicting evidence and made its own determinations as to the weight and width of motortrucks commonly used in interstate traffic and the capacity of the specified highways of the state to accommodate such traffic without injury to them or danger to their users. It found that interstate carriage by motortrucks has become a national industry; that from 85 to 90 per cent of the motor trucks used in interstate transportation are 96 inches wide and of a gross weight, when loaded, of more than 10 tons; that only four other states prescribe a gross load weight as low as 20,000 pounds; and that the American Association of State Highway Officials and the National Conference on Street and Highway Safety in the Department of Commerce have recommended for adoption weight and width limitations in which weight is limited to axle loads of 16,000 to 18,000 pounds and width is limited to 96 inches.

It found in detail that compliance with the weight and width limitations demanded by the South Carolina act would seriously impede motortruck traffic passing to and through the state and increase its cost; that 2,417 miles of state highways, including most of those affected by the injunction, are of the standard construction of concrete or concrete base with asphalt surface; that they are capable of sustaining without injury a wheel load of 8,000 to 9,000 pounds or an axle load of double those amounts; that all but 100 miles of the specified highways are from 18 to 20 feet in width; that they constitute a connected system of highways which have been improved with the aid of federal money grants, as a part of a national system of highways; and that they constitute one of the best highway systems in the southeastern part of the United States.

It also found that the gross weight of vehicles is not a factor to be considered in the preservation of concrete highways, but that the appropriate factor to be considered is wheel or axle weight; that vehicles engaged in interstate commerce are so designed and the pressure of their weight is so distributed by their wheels and axles that gross loads of more than 20,000 pounds can be carried over concrete roads without damage to the surface; that a gross weight limitation of that amount, especially as applied to semitrailer motortrucks, is unreasonable as a means of preserving the highways; that it has no reasonable relation to safety of the public using the highways; and that the width limitation of 90 inches is unreasonable when applied to standard concrete highways of the state, in view of the fact that all other states permit a width of 96 inches, which is the standard width of trucks engaged in interstate commerce.

South Carolina has built its highways and owns and maintains them. It has received from the federal government, in aid of its highway improvements, money grants which have been expended upon the highways to which the injunction applies. . . . Congress has not undertaken to regulate the weight and size of motor vehicles in interstate motor traffic. . . .

While the constitutional grant to Congress of power to regulate interstate commerce has been held to operate of its own force to curtail state power in some measure, it did not forestall all state action affecting interstate commerce. Ever since *Willson v. Black Bird Creek Marsh Co.* (1829) and *Cooley v. Board of Port Wardens* (1851) it has been recognized that there are matters of local concern, the regulation of which unavoidably involves some regulation of interstate commerce but which, because of their local character and their number and diversity, may never be fully dealt with by Congress. . . .

The commerce clause by its own force, prohibits discrimination against interstate commerce, whatever its form or method, and the decisions of this Court have recognized that there is scope for its like operation when state legislation nominally of local concern is in point of fact aimed at interstate commerce, or by its necessary operation is a means of gaining a local benefit by throwing the attendant burdens on those without the state. It was to end these practices that the commerce clause was adopted. See *Gibbons v. Ogden* (1824); II Farrand, Records of the Federal Convention, 308; III Farrand, Records of the Federal Convention, 478, 547, 548; The Federalist, No. XLII; 1 Curtis, History of the Constitution, 502; Story on the Constitution, §259. . . .

Few subjects of state regulation are so peculiarly of local concern as is the use of state highways. There are few, local regulation of which is so inseparable from a substantial effect on interstate commerce. Unlike the railroads, local highways are built, owned, and maintained by the state or its municipal subdivisions. The present regulations, or any others of like purpose, if they are to accomplish their end, must be applied alike to interstate and intrastate traffic both moving in large volume over the highways. The fact that they affect alike shippers in interstate and intrastate commerce in large number within as well as without the state is a safeguard against their abuse. . . .

But so long as the state action does not discriminate, the burden is one which the Constitution permits because it is an inseparable incident of the exercise of a legislative authority, which, under the Constitution, has been left to the states.

Congress, in the exercise of its plenary power to regulate interstate commerce, may determine whether the burdens imposed on it by state regulation, otherwise permissible, are too great, and may, by legislation designed to secure uniformity or in other respects to protect the national interest in the commerce, curtail to some extent the state's regulatory power. But that is a legislative, not a judicial, function, to be performed in the light of the congressional judgment of what is appropriate regulation of interstate commerce, and the extent to which, in that field, state power and local interests should be required to yield to the national authority and interest. In the absence of such legislation the judicial function, under the commerce clause, as well as the Fourteenth Amendment, stops with the inquiry whether the state Legislature in adopting regulations such as the present has acted within its province, and whether the means of regulation chosen are reasonably adapted to the end sought.

Here the first inquiry has already been resolved by our decisions that a state may impose nondiscriminatory restrictions with respect to the character of motor vehicles moving in interstate commerce as a safety measure and as a means of securing the economical use of its highways. In resolving the second, courts do not sit as Legislatures, either state or national. . . .

[I]n reviewing a state highway regulation where Congress has not acted, a court is not called upon, as are state Legislatures, to determine what, in its judgment, is the most suitable restriction to be applied of those that are possible, or to choose that one which in its opinion is best adapted to all the diverse interests affected. . . . When the action of a Legislature is within the scope of its power, fairly debatable questions as to its reasonableness, wisdom, and propriety are not for the determination of courts, but for the legislative body, on which rests the duty and responsibility of decision. This is equally the case when the legislative power is one which may legitimately place an incidental burden on interstate commerce. It is not any the less a legislative power committed to the states because it affects interstate commerce, and courts are not any the more entitled, because interstate commerce is affected, to substitute their own for the legislative judgment. . . .

Hence, in reviewing the present determination, we examine the record, not to see whether the findings of the court below are supported by evidence, but to ascertain upon the whole record whether it is possible to say that the legislative choice is without rational basis. . . .

While there is evidence that weight stresses on concrete roads are determined by wheel rather than gross load weights, other elements enter into choice of the type of weight limitation. . . .

The choice is not to be condemned because the Legislature prefers a workable standard, less likely to be violated than another under which the violations will probably be increased but more easily detected. It is for the Legislature to say whether the one test or the other will in practical operation better protect the highways from the risk of excessive loads. . . .

Much of this testimony appears to have been based on theoretical strength of concrete highways laid under ideal conditions, and none of it was based on an actual study of the highways of South Carolina or of the subgrade and other road building conditions which prevail there and which have a material bearing on the strength and durability of such highways. . . .

These considerations, with the presumption of constitutionality, afford adequate support for the weight limitation without reference to other items of the testimony tending to support it. Furthermore, South Carolina's own experience is not to be ignored. Before adoption of the limitation South Carolina had had experience with higher weight limits. In 1924 it had adopted a combined gross weight limit of 20,000 pounds for vehicles of four wheels or less, and an axle weight limit of 15,000 pounds. In 1930 it had adopted a combined gross weight limit of 12 1/2 tons with a five-ton axle weight limit for vehicles having more than two axles. In 1931 it appointed a commission to investigate motor transportation in the state, to recommend legislation, and to report in 1932. The present weight limitation was recommended by the commission after a full consideration of relevant data, including a report by the state engineer who had constructed the concrete highways of the state and who advised a somewhat lower limitation as necessary for their preservation. The fact that many states have adopted a different standard is not persuasive. The conditions under which highways must be built in the several states, their construction, and the demands made upon them, are not uniform. The road building art, as the record shows, is far from having attained a scientific certainty and precision, and scientific precision is not the criterion for the exercise of the constitutional regulatory power of the states. The Legislature, being free to exercise its own judgment, is not bound by that of other legislatures. It would hardly be contended that if all the states had adopted a single standard, none, in the light of its own experience and in the exercise of its judgment upon all the complex elements which enter into the problem, could change it.

Only a word need be said as to the width limitation. . . . The 90-inch limitation has been in force in South Carolina since 1920, and the concrete highways which it has built appear to be adopted to vehicles of that width. The record shows without contradiction that the use of heavy loaded trucks on the highways tends to force other traffic off the concrete surface onto the shoulders of the road adjoining its edges, and to increase repair costs materially. It appears also that as the width of trucks is increased it obstructs the view of the highway, causing much inconvenience and increased hazard in its use. It plainly cannot be said that the width of trucks used on the highways in South Carolina is unrelated to their safety and cost of maintenance, or that a 90-inch width limitation, adopted to safeguard the highways of the state, is not within the range of the permissible legislative choice.

The regulatory measures taken by South Carolina are within its legislative power. They do not infringe the Fourteenth Amendment, and the resulting burden on interstate commerce is not forbidden.

Reversed.

Mr. Justice Cardozo and Mr. Justice Reed took no part in the consideration or decision of this case.

STUDY GUIDE

- In *City of Philadelphia v. New Jersey*, is there agreement between the majority opinion and the dissent as to whether solid waste can be an article of commerce?
- Would Justice Rehnquist's dissenting statement that "solid waste is an article of commerce" be consistent with the original meaning of "commerce"? Compare that passage of his dissent with the constitutional objections rejected in the *Lottery Case* (*Champion v. Ames*) and in *Hammer v. Dagenhart*.
- Can you see why businesses would be likely to bring constitutional claims under this clause?
- Is this law about keeping something from coming into the state (which raises the question of whether solid waste is or is not an article of commerce)? Or can it be better understood as preserving a natural resource — here, landfill capacity — which makes the case akin to others where a state tried to keep something from leaving the state for the benefit of the state's residents (e.g., wildlife or resources)?
- Is there a disagreement between the majority and the dissent as to whether the state has a valid purpose in enacting this law?
- Does the law discriminate against out-of-state commerce? How can the Court tell? Is there agreement between the majority and the dissent on this point?
- If there is discrimination, is that discrimination purposeful (with intent) or only based on the effects of the law in the real world? Does that matter, or should it matter, in a case based on the Dormant Commerce Clause? Keep this issue in mind as you read *Hunt v. Washington State Apple Advertising Commission* and *Kassel v. Consolidated Freightways Corporation of Delaware.*

City of Philadelphia v. New Jersey

437 U.S. 617 (1978)

MR. JUSTICE STEWART delivered the opinion of the Court.

A New Jersey law prohibits the importation of most "solid or liquid waste which originated or was collected outside the territorial limits of the State. . . ." In this case we are required to decide whether this statutory prohibition violates the Commerce Clause of the United States Constitution.

I

The statutory provision in question is ch. 363 of 1973 N.J. Laws, which took effect in early 1974. In pertinent part it provides:

> No person shall bring into this State any solid or liquid waste which originated or was collected outside the territorial limits of the State, except garbage to be fed to swine in

> the State of New Jersey, until the commissioner [of the State Department of Environmental Protection] shall determine that such action can be permitted without endangering the public health, safety and welfare and has promulgated regulations permitting and regulating the treatment and disposal of such waste in this State.
>
> . . .

Immediately affected by these developments were the operators of private landfills in New Jersey, and several cities in other States that had agreements with these operators for waste disposal. They brought suit against New Jersey and its Department of Environmental Protection in state court, attacking the statute and regulations on a number of state and federal grounds. In an oral opinion granting the plaintiffs' motion for summary judgment, the trial court declared the law unconstitutional because it discriminated against interstate commerce. The New Jersey Supreme Court consolidated this case with another reaching the same conclusion. It found that ch. 363 advanced vital health and environmental objectives with no economic discrimination against, and with little burden upon, interstate commerce, and that the law was therefore permissible under the Commerce Clause of the Constitution.

The plaintiffs then appealed to this Court. . . . We agree with the New Jersey court that the state law has not been pre-empted by federal legislation. The dispositive question, therefore, is whether the law is constitutionally permissible in light of the Commerce Clause of the Constitution. . . .

The state court expressed the view that there may be two definitions of "commerce" for constitutional purposes. When relied on "to support some exertion of federal control or regulation," the Commerce Clause permits "a very sweeping concept" of commerce. But when relied on "to strike down or restrict state legislation," that Clause and the term "commerce" have a "much more confined . . . reach."

The state court reached this conclusion in an attempt to reconcile modern Commerce Clause concepts with several old cases of this Court holding that States can prohibit the importation of some objects because they "are not legitimate subjects of trade and commerce." These articles include items "which, on account of their existing condition, would bring in and spread disease, pestilence, and death, such as rags or other substances infected with the germs of yellow fever or the virus of small-pox, or cattle or meat or other provisions that are diseased or decayed, or otherwise, from their condition and quality, unfit for human use or consumption." . . .

We think the state court misread our cases, and thus erred in assuming that they require a two-tiered definition of commerce. In saying that innately harmful articles "are not legitimate subjects of trade and commerce," the *Bowman* Court was stating its conclusion, not the starting point of its reasoning. All objects of interstate trade merit Commerce Clause protection; none is excluded by definition at the outset. . . .

III

A

The bounds of these restraints appear nowhere in the words of the Commerce Clause, but have emerged gradually in the decisions of this Court giving effect to its basic purpose. That broad purpose was well expressed by Mr. Justice Jackson in his opinion for the Court in *H. P. Hood & Sons, Inc. v. Du Mond* (1949):

"This principle that our economic unit is the Nation, which alone has the gamut of powers necessary to control of the economy, including the vital power of erecting customs barriers against foreign competition, has as its corollary that the states are not separable economic units." ...

The opinions of the Court through the years have reflected an alertness to the evils of "economic isolation" and protectionism, while at the same time recognizing that incidental burdens on interstate commerce may be unavoidable when a State legislates to safeguard the health and safety of its people. Thus, where simple economic protectionism is effected by state legislation, a virtually *per se* rule of invalidity has been erected. The clearest example of such legislation is a law that overtly blocks the flow of interstate commerce at a State's borders. But where other legislative objectives are credibly advanced and there is no patent discrimination against interstate trade, the Court has adopted a much more flexible approach, the general contours of which were outlined in *Pike v. Bruce Church, Inc.* (1970):

> Where the statute regulates evenhandedly to effectuate a legitimate local public interest, and its effects on interstate commerce are only incidental, it will be upheld unless the burden imposed on such commerce is clearly excessive in relation to the putative local benefits. ... If a legitimate local purpose is found, then the question becomes one of degree. And the extent of the burden that will be tolerated will of course depend on the nature of the local interest involved, and on whether it could be promoted as well with a lesser impact on interstate activities.

...

The crucial inquiry, therefore, must be directed to determining whether ch. 363 is basically a protectionist measure, or whether it can fairly be viewed as a law directed to legitimate local concerns, with effects upon interstate commerce that are only incidental.

B

The purpose of ch. 363 is set out in the statute itself as follows:

> The Legislature finds and determines that ... the volume of solid and liquid waste continues to rapidly increase, that the treatment and disposal of these wastes continues to pose an even greater threat to the quality of the environment of New Jersey, that the available and appropriate land fill sites within the State are being diminished, that the environment continues to be threatened by the treatment and disposal of waste which originated or was collected outside the State, and that the public health, safety and welfare require that the treatment and disposal within this State of all wastes generated outside of the State be prohibited.

The New Jersey Supreme Court accepted this statement of the state legislature's purpose. The state court additionally found that New Jersey's existing landfill sites will be exhausted within a few years; that to go on using these sites or to develop new ones will take a heavy environmental toll, both from pollution and from loss of scarce open lands; that new techniques to divert waste from landfills to other methods of disposal and resource recovery processes are under development, but that these changes will require time; and finally, that "the extension of the lifespan of existing landfills, resulting from the exclusion of out-of-state waste, may be of crucial importance in preventing further virgin wetlands or other undeveloped lands from being devoted to landfill purposes." Based on these findings, the court concluded that ch. 363 was designed to protect, not the State's economy, but its environment, and that its substantial benefits outweigh its "slight" burden on interstate commerce. . . .

[The appellants] cite passages of legislative history suggesting that the problem addressed by ch. 363 is primarily financial: Stemming the flow of out-of-state waste into certain landfill sites will extend their lives, thus delaying the day when New Jersey cities must transport their waste to more distant and expensive sites.

The appellees, on the other hand, deny that ch. 363 was motivated by financial concerns or economic protectionism. In the words of their brief, "[n]o New Jersey commercial interests stand to gain advantage over competitors from outside the state as a result of the ban on dumping out-of-state waste." Noting that New Jersey landfill operators are among the plaintiffs, the appellee's brief argues that "[t]he complaint is not that New Jersey has forged an economic preference for its own commercial interests, but rather that it has denied a small group of its entrepreneurs an economic opportunity to traffic in waste in order to protect the health, safety and welfare of the citizenry at large."

This dispute about ultimate legislative purpose need not be resolved. Contrary to the evident assumption of the state court and the parties, the evil of protectionism can reside in legislative means as well as legislative ends. Thus, it does not matter whether the ultimate aim of ch. 363 is to reduce the waste disposal costs of New Jersey residents or to save remaining open lands from pollution, for we assume New Jersey has every right to protect its residents' pocketbooks as well as their environment. And it may be assumed as well that New Jersey may pursue those ends by slowing the flow of *all* waste into the State's remaining landfills, even though interstate commerce may incidentally be affected. But whatever New Jersey's ultimate purpose, it may not be accomplished by discriminating against articles of commerce coming from outside the State unless there is some reason, apart from their origin, to treat them differently. Both on its face and in its plain effect, ch. 363 violates this principle of nondiscrimination. . . .

Also relevant here are the Court's decisions holding that a State may not accord its own inhabitants a preferred right of access over consumers in other States to natural resources located within its borders. These cases stand for the basic principle that a "State is without power to prevent privately owned articles of trade from being shipped and sold in interstate commerce on the ground that they are required to satisfy local demands or because they are needed by the people of the State." . . .

On its face, it imposes on out-of-state commercial interests the full burden of conserving the State's remaining landfill space. It is true that in our previous cases the scarce natural resource was itself the article of commerce, whereas here the scarce resource and the article of commerce are distinct. But that difference is without consequence. It does not matter that the State has shut the article of commerce inside the State in one case and outside the State in the other. What is crucial is the attempt by one State to isolate itself from a problem common to many by erecting a barrier against the movement of interstate trade. . . .

[The appellees] point to quarantine laws, which this Court has repeatedly upheld even though they appear to single out interstate commerce for special treatment. . . . But those quarantine laws banned the importation of articles such as diseased livestock that required destruction as soon as possible because their very movement risked contagion and other evils. Those laws thus did not discriminate against interstate commerce as such, but simply prevented traffic in noxious articles, whatever their origin.

The New Jersey statute is not such a quarantine law. There has been no claim here that the very movement of waste into or through New Jersey endangers health, or that waste must be disposed of as soon and as close to its point of generation as possible. The harms caused by waste are said to arise after its disposal in landfill sites, and at that point, as New Jersey concedes, there is no basis to distinguish out-of-state waste from domestic waste. If one is inherently harmful, so is the other. . . .

Today, cities in Pennsylvania and New York find it expedient or necessary to send their waste into New Jersey for disposal, and New Jersey claims the right to close its borders to such traffic. Tomorrow, cities in New Jersey may find it expedient or necessary to send their waste into Pennsylvania or New York for disposal, and those States might then claim the right to close their borders. The Commerce Clause will protect New Jersey in the future, just as it protects her neighbors now, from efforts by one State to isolate itself in the stream of interstate commerce from a problem shared by all. The judgment is

Reversed.

Mr. Justice Rehnquist, with whom The Chief Justice joins, dissenting.

A growing problem in our Nation is the sanitary treatment and disposal of solid waste. For many years, solid waste was incinerated. Because of the significant environmental problems attendant on incineration, however, this method of solid waste disposal has declined in use in many localities, including New Jersey. In ch. 363 of the 1973 N.J. Laws, the State of New Jersey legislatively recognized the unfortunate fact that landfills also present extremely serious health and safety problems. First, in New Jersey, "virtually all sanitary landfills can be expected to produce leachate, a noxious and highly polluted liquid which is seldom visible and frequently pollutes . . . ground and surface waters." The natural decomposition process which occurs in landfills also produces large quantities of methane and thereby presents a significant explosion hazard. Landfills can also generate "health hazards caused by rodents, fires and scavenger birds" and, "needless to say, do not help New Jersey's aesthetic appearance nor New Jersey's noise or water or air pollution problems." . . .

Other, hopefully safer, methods of disposing of solid wastes are still in the development stage and cannot presently be used. But appellees obviously cannot completely stop the tide of solid waste that its citizens will produce in the interim. For the moment, therefore, appellees must continue to use sanitary landfills to dispose of New Jersey's own solid waste despite the critical environmental problems thereby created.

The question presented in this case is whether New Jersey must also continue to receive and dispose of solid waste from neighboring States, even though these will inexorably increase the health problems discussed above. The Court answers this question in the affirmative. New Jersey must either prohibit *all* landfill operations, leaving itself to cast about for a presently nonexistent solution to the serious problem of disposing of the waste generated within its own borders, or it must accept waste from every portion of the United States, thereby multiplying the health and safety problems which would result if it dealt only with such wastes generated within the State. Because past precedents establish that the Commerce Clause does not present appellees with such a Hobson's choice, I dissent. . . .

As the Court points out, . . . "quarantine laws have not been considered forbidden protectionist measures, *even though they were directed against out-of-state commerce.*" (emphasis added).

In my opinion, these cases are dispositive of the present one. . . . The physical fact of life that New Jersey must somehow dispose of its own noxious items does not mean that it must serve as a depository for those of every other State. Similarly, New Jersey should be free under our past precedents to prohibit the importation of solid waste because of the health and safety problems that such waste poses to its citizens. . . .

The Court's effort to distinguish these prior cases is unconvincing. . . . According to the Court, the New Jersey law is distinguishable from these other laws, and invalid, because the concern of New Jersey is not with the *movement* of solid waste but with the present inability to safely *dispose* of it once it reaches its destination. But I think it far from clear that the State's law has as limited a focus as the Court imputes to it: Solid waste which is a health hazard when it reaches its destination may in all likelihood be an equally great health hazard in transit.

Even if the Court is correct in its characterization of New Jersey's concerns, I do not see why a State may ban the importation of items whose movement risks contagion, but cannot ban the importation of items which, although they may be transported into the State without undue hazard, will then simply pile up in an ever increasing danger to the public's health and safety. The Commerce Clause was not drawn with a view to having the validity of state laws turn on such pointless distinctions.

Second, the Court implies that the challenged laws must be invalidated because New Jersey has left its landfills open to domestic waste. New Jersey must out of sheer necessity treat and dispose of its solid waste in some fashion, just as it must treat New Jersey cattle suffering from hoof-and-mouth disease. It does not follow that New Jersey must, under the Commerce Clause, accept solid waste or diseased cattle from outside its borders and thereby exacerbate its problems.

The Supreme Court of New Jersey expressly found that ch. 363 was passed "to preserve the health of New Jersey residents by keeping their exposure to solid waste and landfill areas to a minimum." The Court points to absolutely no evidence that would contradict this finding by the New Jersey Supreme Court. Because I find no basis for distinguishing the laws under challenge here from our past cases upholding state laws that prohibit the importation of items that could endanger the population of the State, I dissent.

STUDY GUIDE

- Does the North Carolina law discriminate between in-state and out-of-state commerce on its face? If not, does that mean there is no discrimination? If there is discrimination, is it intentional?
- Is the law unconstitutional because of an invalid purpose, because of discrimination, or because of the undue burden the law places on interstate commerce? What does the Court say is its reason?
- What is the burden the law imposes — the cost of sorting and relabeling crates of apples, or something else?

Washington State Apple Advertising Commission logo

Hunt v. Washington State Apple Advertising Commission

432 U.S. 333 (1977)

MR. CHIEF JUSTICE BURGER delivered the opinion of the Court.

In 1973, North Carolina enacted a statute which required, inter alia, all closed containers of apples sold, offered for sale, or shipped into the State to bear "no grade other than the applicable U.S. grade or standard." N.C. Gen. Stat. §106-189.1 (1973). In an action brought by the Washington State Apple Advertising Commission, a three-judge Federal District Court invalidated the statute insofar as it prohibited the display of Washington State apple grades on the ground that it unconstitutionally discriminated against interstate commerce.

The specific questions presented on appeal are (a) whether the Commission had standing to bring this action; (b) if so, whether it satisfied the jurisdictional-amount requirement . . . and (c) whether the challenged North Carolina statute constitutes an unconstitutional burden on interstate commerce. [The lower court and the Supreme Court answered the first two questions in the affirmative — EDS.]

1

Washington State is the Nation's largest producer of apples, its crops accounting for approximately 30% of all apples grown domestically and nearly half of all apples shipped in closed containers in interstate commerce. Because of the importance of the apple industry to the State, its legislature has undertaken to protect and enhance the reputation of Washington apples by establishing a stringent, mandatory inspection program, administered by the State's Department of Agriculture, which requires all apples shipped in interstate commerce to be tested under strict quality standards and graded accordingly. In all cases, the Washington State grades, which have gained substantial acceptance in the trade, are the equivalent of, or superior to, the comparable grades and standards adopted by the United States Department of Agriculture (USDA). Compliance with the Washington inspection scheme costs the State's growers approximately $1 million each year.

In addition to the inspection program, the state legislature has sought to enhance the market for Washington apples through the creation of a state agency, the Washington State Apple Advertising Commission, charged with the statutory duty of promoting and protecting the State's apple industry. . . .

In 1972, the North Carolina Board of Agriculture adopted an administrative regulation, unique in the 50 States, which in effect required all closed containers of apples shipped into or sold in the State to display either the applicable USDA grade or none at all. State grades were expressly prohibited. In addition to its obvious consequence prohibiting the display of Washington State apple grades on containers of apples shipped into North Carolina, the regulation presented the Washington apple industry with a marketing problem of potentially nationwide significance. Washington apple growers annually ship in commerce approximately 40 million closed containers of apples, nearly 500,000 of which eventually find their way into

North Carolina, stamped with the applicable Washington State variety and grade. It is the industry's practice to purchase these containers preprinted with the various apple varieties and grades, prior to harvest. Since the ultimate destination of these apples is unknown at the time they are placed in storage, compliance with North Carolina's unique regulation would have required Washington growers to obliterate the printed labels on containers shipped to North Carolina, thus giving their product a damaged appearance. Alternatively, they could have changed their marketing practices to accommodate the needs of the North Carolina market, *i.e.*, repack apples to be shipped to North Carolina in containers bearing only the USDA grade, and/or store the estimated portion of the harvest destined for that market in such special containers. As a last resort, they could discontinue the use of the preprinted containers entirely. None of these costly and less efficient options was very attractive to the industry. Moreover, in the event a number of other States followed North Carolina's lead, the resultant inability to display the Washington grades could force the Washington growers to abandon the State's expensive inspection and grading system which their customers had come to know and rely on over the 60-odd years of its existence.

With these problems confronting the industry, the Washington State Apple Advertising Commission petitioned the North Carolina Board of Agriculture to amend its regulation to permit the display of state grades. An administrative hearing was held on the question but no relief was granted. Indeed, North Carolina hardened its position shortly thereafter by enacting the regulation into law:

> All apples sold offered for sale, or shipped into this State in closed containers shall bear on the container, bag or other receptacle, no grade other than the applicable U.S. grade or standard or the marking "unclassified," "not graded" or "grade not determined."

Nonetheless, the Commission once again requested an exemption which would have permitted the Washington apple growers to display both the United States and the Washington State grades on their shipments to North Carolina. This request, too, was denied.

Unsuccessful in its attempts to secure administrative relief, the Commission instituted this action. . . . A three-judge Federal District Court was convened. . . .

After a hearing, the District Court granted the requested relief. . . . Proceeding to the merits, the District Court found that the North Carolina statute, while neutral on its face, actually discriminated against Washington State growers and dealers in favor of their local counterparts. This discrimination resulted from the fact that North Carolina, unlike Washington, had never established a grading and inspection system. Hence, the statute had no effect on the existing practices of North Carolina producers; they were still free to use the USDA grade or none at all. Washington growers and dealers, on the other hand, were forced to alter their long-established procedures, at substantial cost, or abandon the North Carolina market. The District Court then concluded that this discrimination against out-of-state competitors was not justified by the asserted local interest — the elimination of deception and confusion from the marketplace — arguably furthered by the statute. Indeed, it noted that the statute was "irrationally" drawn to accomplish that alleged goal since it permitted the marketing of closed containers of apples without any grade at all. . . .

Appellants do not really contest the District Court's determination that the challenged statute burdened the Washington apple industry by increasing its costs of doing business in the North Carolina market and causing it to lose accounts there. Rather, they maintain that any such burdens on the interstate sale of Washington apples were far outweighed by the local benefits flowing from what they contend was a valid exercise of North Carolina's inherent police powers designed to protect its citizenry from fraud and deception in the marketing of apples.

Prior to the statute's enactment, appellants point out, apples from 13 different States were shipped into North Carolina for sale. Seven of those States, including the State of Washington, had their own grading systems which, while differing in their standards, used similar descriptive labels (e. g., fancy, extra fancy, etc.). This multiplicity of inconsistent state grades, as the District Court itself found, posed dangers of deception and confusion not only in the North Carolina market, but in the Nation as a whole. Moreover, it is contended that North Carolina sought to accomplish this goal of uniformity in an evenhanded manner as evidenced by the fact that its statute applies to all apples sold in closed containers in the State without regard to their point of origin.

... [O]ur opinions have long recognized that, "in the absence of conflicting legislation by Congress, there is a residuum of power in the state to make laws governing matters of local concern which nevertheless in some measure affect interstate commerce or even, to some extent, regulate it."

Moreover, as appellants correctly note, that "residuum" is particularly strong when the State acts to protect its citizenry in matters pertaining to the sale of foodstuffs. By the same token, however, a finding that state legislation furthers matters of legitimate local concern, even in the health and consumer protection areas, does not end the inquiry. Such a view, we have noted, "would mean that the Commerce Clause of itself imposes no limitations on state action ... save for the rare instance where a state artlessly discloses an avowed purpose to discriminate against interstate goods." ...

As the District Court correctly found, the challenged statute has the practical effect of not only burdening interstate sales of Washington apples, but also discriminating against them. This discrimination takes various forms. The first, and most obvious, is the statute's consequence of raising the costs of doing business in the North Carolina market for Washington apple growers and dealers, while leaving those of their North Carolina counterparts unaffected. As previously noted, this disparate effect results from the fact that North Carolina apple producers, unlike their Washington competitors, were not forced to alter their marketing practices in order to comply with the statute. They were still free to market their wares under the USDA grade or none at all as they had done prior to the statute's enactment. Obviously, the increased costs imposed by the statute would tend to shield the local apple industry from the competition of Washington apple growers and dealers who are already at a competitive disadvantage because of their great distance from the North Carolina market.

Second, the statute has the effect of stripping away from the Washington apple industry the competitive and economic advantages it has earned for itself through its expensive inspection and grading system. The record demonstrates that the

Washington apple-grading system has gained nationwide acceptance in the apple trade. Indeed, it contains numerous affidavits from apple brokers and dealers located both inside and outside of North Carolina who state their preference, and that of their customers, for apples graded under the Washington, as opposed to the USDA, system because of the former's greater consistency, its emphasis on color, and its supporting mandatory inspections. Once again, the statute had no similar impact on the North Carolina apple industry and thus operated to its benefit.

Third, by prohibiting Washington growers and dealers from marketing apples under their State's grades, the statute has a leveling effect which insidiously operates to the advantage of local apple producers. As noted earlier, the Washington State grades are equal or superior to the USDA grades in all corresponding categories. Hence, with free market forces at work, Washington sellers would normally enjoy a distinct market advantage vis-à-vis local producers in those categories where the Washington grade is superior. However, because of the statute's operation, Washington apples which would otherwise qualify for and be sold under the superior Washington grades will now have to be marketed under their inferior USDA counterparts. Such "downgrading" offers the North Carolina apple industry the very sort of protection against competing out-of-state products that the Commerce Clause was designed to prohibit. At worst, it will have the effect of an embargo against those Washington apples in the superior grades as Washington dealers withhold them from the North Carolina market. At best, it will deprive Washington sellers of the market premium that such apples would otherwise command.

Despite the statute's facial neutrality, the Commission suggests that its discriminatory impact on interstate commerce was not an unintended byproduct and there are some indications in the record to that effect. The most glaring is the response of the North Carolina Agriculture Commissioner to the Commission's request for an exemption following the statute's passage in which he indicated that before he could support such an exemption, he would "want to have the sentiment from our apple producers, *since they were mainly responsible for this legislation being passed*. . . ." (emphasis added). Moreover, we find it somewhat suspect that North Carolina singled out only closed containers of apples, the very means by which apples are transported in commerce, to effectuate the statute's ostensible consumer protection purpose when apples are not generally sold at retail in their shipping containers. However, we need not ascribe an economic protection motive to the North Carolina Legislature to resolve this case; we conclude that the challenged statute cannot stand insofar as it prohibits the display of Washington State grades even if enacted for the declared purpose of protecting consumers from deception and fraud in the marketplace.

When discrimination against commerce of the type we have found is demonstrated, the burden falls on the State to justify it both in terms of the local benefits flowing from the statute and the unavailability of nondiscriminatory alternatives adequate to preserve the local interests at stake. North Carolina has failed to sustain that burden on both scores. . . .

[T]he challenged statute does remarkably little to further that laudable goal at least with respect to Washington apples and grades. The statute, as already noted, permits the marketing of closed containers of apples under no grades at all. Such a result can hardly be thought to eliminate the problems of deception and confusion created by the multiplicity of differing state grades; indeed, it magnifies them by depriving purchasers of all information concerning the quality of the contents of closed apple containers. Moreover, although the statute is ostensibly a consumer protection measure, it directs its primary efforts, not at the consuming public at large, but at apple wholesalers and brokers who are the principal purchasers of closed containers of apples. And those individuals are presumably the most knowledgeable individuals in this area. Finally, we note that any potential for confusion and deception created by the Washington grades[1] was not of the type that led to the statute's enactment. Since Washington grades are in all cases equal or superior to their USDA counterparts, they could only "deceive" or "confuse" a consumer to his benefit, hardly a harmful result.

In addition, it appears that nondiscriminatory alternatives to the outright ban of Washington State grades are readily available. For example, North Carolina could effectuate its goal by permitting out-of-state growers to utilize state grades only if they also marked their shipments with the applicable USDA label. North Carolina might consider banning those state grades which, unlike Washington's could not be demonstrated to be equal or superior to the corresponding USDA categories. Concededly, even in this latter instance, some potential for "confusion" might persist. However, it is the type of "confusion" that the national interest in the free flow of goods between the States demands be tolerated.

The judgment of the District Court is

Affirmed.

MR. JUSTICE REHNQUIST took no part in the consideration or decision of the case.

ASSIGNMENT 2

STUDY GUIDE

- In *Kassel v. Consolidated Freightways Corporation of Delaware*, does Justice Powell find discrimination by the State of Iowa? Does Brennan? Does Rehnquist?
- If there is discrimination, what kind is it? *Hint:* Is it that the measure *itself* was discriminatory, or that its passage was motivated by a discriminatory *intent*?

[1] Indeed, the District Court specifically indicated in its findings of fact that there had been no showing that the Washington State grades had caused any confusion in the North Carolina market.

- How do the Justices who suggest or find there is discrimination determine that? If it is not based on the *language* of the Iowa statute, but on the "purposes" or *motives* of those who enacted it, how do the Justices disagree about the way courts should inquire into such motives, if at all? *Hint:* Must it be the *actual* purposes, or can it be a "rationally conceivable" purpose?
- Does it matter if discrimination is established? In other words, if no discrimination is found against out-of-state commerce, does that mean the law is valid? How do Justices Powell and Rehnquist deal with this question? Do they differ as to how the balancing test should be applied?
- Notice Justice Rehnquist's deference to the state government here, consistent with his belief in the importance of federalism (which we have seen earlier).

Kassel v. Consolidated Freightways Corporation of Delaware

450 U.S. 662 (1981)

JUSTICE POWELL announced the judgment of the Court and delivered an opinion, in which JUSTICE WHITE, JUSTICE BLACKMUN, and JUSTICE STEVENS joined.

The question is whether an Iowa statute that prohibits the use of certain large trucks within the State unconstitutionally burdens interstate commerce.

Double truck

I

Appellee Consolidated Freightways Corporation of Delaware (Consolidated) is one of the largest common carriers in the country. . . . Among other routes, Consolidated carries commodities through Iowa on Interstate 80, the principal east-west route linking New York, Chicago, and the west coast, and on Interstate 35, a major north-south route.

Consolidated mainly uses two kinds of trucks. One consists of a three-axle tractor pulling a 40-foot two-axle trailer. This unit, commonly called a single, or "semi," is 55 feet in length overall. Such trucks have long been used on the Nation's highways. Consolidated also uses a two-axle tractor pulling a single-axle trailer which, in turn, pulls a single-axle dolly and a second single-axle trailer. This combination, known as a double, or twin, is 65 feet long overall. Many trucking companies, including Consolidated, increasingly prefer to use doubles to ship certain kinds of commodities. Doubles have larger capacities, and the trailers can be detached and routed separately if necessary. Consolidated would like to use 65-foot doubles on many of its trips through Iowa.

The State of Iowa, however, by statute restricts the length of vehicles that may use its highways. Unlike all other States in the West and Midwest Iowa generally prohibits the use of 65-foot doubles within its borders. Instead, most truck combinations are restricted to 55 feet in length. Doubles, mobile homes, trucks carrying vehicles such as tractors and other farm equipment, and singles hauling livestock, are permitted to be as long as 60 feet. Notwithstanding these restrictions, Iowa's statute permits cities abutting the state line by local ordinance to adopt the length limitations of the adjoining State. . . .

Iowa also provides for two other relevant exemptions. An Iowa truck manufacturer may obtain a permit to ship trucks that are as large as 70 feet. Permits also are available to move oversized mobile homes, provided that the unit is to be moved from a point within Iowa or delivered for an Iowa resident.[2]

Because of Iowa's statutory scheme, Consolidated cannot use its 65-foot doubles to move commodities through the State. Instead, the company must do one of four things: (i) use 55-foot singles; (ii) use 60-foot doubles; (iii) detach the trailers of a 65-foot double and shuttle each through the State separately; or (iv) divert 65-foot doubles around Iowa. . . .

The State assert[s] that 65-foot doubles are more dangerous than 55-foot singles and, in any event, that the law promotes safety and reduces road wear within the State by diverting much truck traffic to other States.[3]

---

[2] The parochial restrictions in the mobile home provision were enacted after Governor Ray vetoed a bill that would have permitted the interstate shipment of all mobile homes through Iowa. Governor Ray commented, in his veto message:

> This bill . . . would make Iowa a bridge state as these oversized units are moved into Iowa after being manufactured in another state and sold in a third. None of this activity would be of particular economic benefit to Iowa.

[3] In this Court, Iowa places little or no emphasis on the constitutional validity of this second argument.

In a 14-day trial, both sides adduced evidence on safety, and on the burden on interstate commerce imposed by Iowa's law. On the question of safety, the District Court found that the "evidence clearly establishes that the twin is as safe as the semi." For that reason,

> there is no valid safety reason for barring twins from Iowa's highways because of their configuration. The evidence convincingly, if not overwhelmingly, establishes that the 65 foot twin is as safe as, if not safer than, the 60 foot twin and the 55 foot semi. . . .
>
> Twins and semis have different characteristics. Twins are more maneuverable, are less sensitive to wind, and create less splash and spray. However, they are more likely than semis to jackknife or upset. They can be backed only for a short distance. The negative characteristics are not such that they render the twin less safe than semis overall. Semis are more stable but are more likely to "rear end" another vehicle.

In light of these findings, the District Court applied the standard we enunciated in *Raymond Motor Transportation, Inc. v. Rice* (1978) and concluded that the state law impermissibly burdened interstate commerce:

> [T]he balance here must be struck in favor of the federal interests. The *total effect* of the law as a safety measure in reducing accidents and casualties is so slight and problematical that it does not outweigh the national interest in keeping interstate commerce free from interferences that seriously impede it. (emphasis in original).

The Court of Appeals accepted the District Court's finding that 65-foot doubles were as safe as 55-foot singles. . . . Thus, the only apparent safety benefit to Iowa was that resulting from forcing large trucks to detour around the State, thereby reducing overall truck traffic on Iowa's highways. The Court of Appeals noted that this was not a constitutionally permissible interest. It also commented that the several statutory exemptions identified above, such as those applicable to border cities and the shipment of livestock, suggested that the law in effect benefited Iowa residents at the expense of interstate traffic. The combination of these exemptions weakened the presumption of validity normally accorded a state safety regulation. For these reasons, the Court of Appeals agreed with the District Court that the Iowa statute unconstitutionally burdened interstate commerce.

Iowa appealed, We now affirm.

II

It is unnecessary to review in detail the evolution of the principles of Commerce Clause adjudication. The Clause is both a "prolific sourc[e] of national power and an equally prolific source of conflict with legislation of the state[s]." . . . The Clause requires that some aspects of trade generally must remain free from interference by the States. When a State ventures excessively into the regulation of these aspects of commerce, it "trespasses upon national interests," and the courts will hold the state regulation invalid under the Clause alone.

The Commerce Clause does not, of course, invalidate all state restrictions on commerce. . . . The extent of permissible state regulation is not always easy to measure. It may be said with confidence, however, that a State's power to regulate commerce is never greater than in matters traditionally of local concern. For example, regulations that touch upon safety — especially highway safety — are those that "the Court has been most reluctant to invalidate." Indeed, "if safety justifications are not illusory, the Court will not second-guess legislative judgment about their importance in comparison with related burdens on interstate commerce." Those who would challenge such bona fide safety regulations must overcome a "strong presumption of validity."

But the incantation of a purpose to promote the public health or safety does not insulate a state law from Commerce Clause attack. Regulations designed for that salutary purpose nevertheless may further the purpose so marginally, and interfere with commerce so substantially, as to be invalid under the Commerce Clause. . . . Th[e] "weighing" by a court requires — and indeed the constitutionality of the state regulation depends on — "a sensitive consideration of the weight and nature of the state regulatory concern in light of the extent of the burden imposed on the course of interstate commerce." . . .

Here, as in *Raymond*, the State failed to present any persuasive evidence that 65-foot doubles are less safe than 55-foot singles. Moreover, Iowa's law is now out of step with the laws of all other Midwestern and Western States. Iowa thus substantially burdens the interstate flow of goods by truck. In the absence of congressional action to set uniform standards, some burdens associated with state safety regulations must be tolerated. But where, as here, the State's safety interest has been found to be illusory, and its regulations impair significantly the federal interest in efficient and safe interstate transportation, the state law cannot be harmonized with the Commerce Clause.

A

. . . [T]he State points to only three ways in which the 55-foot single is even arguably superior: singles take less time to be passed and to clear intersections; they may back up for longer distances; and they are somewhat less likely to jackknife.

The first two of these characteristics are of limited relevance on modern interstate highways. . . . Similarly, although doubles tend to jackknife somewhat more than singles, 65-foot doubles actually are less likely to jackknife than 60-foot doubles. [The Court then discussed various statistical studies and testimony from insurance executives and federal transportation officials. — Eds.]

In sum, although Iowa introduced more evidence on the question of safety than did Wisconsin in *Raymond*, the record as a whole was not more favorable to the State.

B

Consolidated, meanwhile, demonstrated that Iowa's law substantially burdens interstate commerce. Trucking companies that wish to continue to use 65-foot doubles must route them around Iowa or detach the trailers of the doubles and ship them through separately. Alternatively, trucking companies must use the smaller 55-foot singles or 60-foot doubles permitted under Iowa law. Each of these options engenders inefficiency and added expense. The record shows that Iowa's law added about $12.6 million each year to the costs of trucking companies. Consolidated alone incurred about $2 million per year in increased costs.

In addition to increasing the costs of the trucking companies (and, indirectly, of the service to consumers), Iowa's law may aggravate, rather than ameliorate, the problem of highway accidents. Fifty-five foot singles carry less freight than 65-foot doubles. . . . [T]he restriction requires more highway miles to be driven to transport the same quantity of goods. Other things being equal, accidents are proportional to distance traveled. Thus, if 65-foot doubles are as safe as 55-foot singles, Iowa's law tends to *increase* the number of accidents, and to shift the incidence of them from Iowa to other States.

IV

. . . The Court normally does accord "special deference" to state highway safety regulations. This traditional deference "derives in part from the assumption that where such regulations do not discriminate on their face against interstate commerce, their burden usually falls on local economic interests as well as other States' economic interests, thus insuring that a State's own political processes will serve as a check against unduly burdensome regulations." *Raymond.* Less deference to the legislative judgment is due, however, where the local regulation bears disproportionately on out-of-state residents and businesses. Such a disproportionate burden is apparent here. . . .

At the time of trial there were two particularly significant exemptions. First, singles hauling livestock or farm vehicles were permitted to be as long as 60 feet. . . . Second cities abutting other States were permitted to enact local ordinances adopting the larger length limitation of the neighboring State. This exemption offered the benefits of longer trucks to individuals and businesses in important border cities[4] without burdening Iowa's highways with interstate through traffic.

The origin of the "border cities exemption" also suggests that Iowa's statute may not have been designed to ban dangerous trucks, but rather to discourage interstate truck traffic. In 1974, the legislature passed a bill that would have permitted 65-foot doubles in the State. Governor Ray vetoed the bill. He said:

> I find sympathy with those who are doing business in our state and whose enterprises could gain from increased cargo carrying ability by trucks. However, with this bill, the Legislature has pursued a course that would benefit only a few Iowa-based companies while providing a great advantage for out-of-state trucking firms and competitors at the expense of our Iowa citizens.[5]

After the veto, the "border cities exemption" was immediately enacted and signed by the Governor.

---

[4] Five of Iowa's ten largest cities — Davenport, Sioux City, Dubuque, Council Bluffs, and Clinton — are by their location entitled to use the "border cities exemption."

[5] Governor Ray further commented that "if we have thousands more trucks crossing our state, there will be millions of additional miles driven in Iowa and that does create a genuine concern for safety."

It is thus far from clear that Iowa was motivated primarily by a judgment that 65-foot doubles are less safe than 55-foot singles. Rather, Iowa seems to have hoped to limit the use of its highways by deflecting some through traffic.[6] . . .

V

In sum, the statutory exemptions, their history, and the arguments Iowa has advanced in support of its law in this litigation, all suggest that the deference traditionally accorded a State's safety judgment is not warranted. . . .

Because Iowa has imposed this burden without any significant countervailing safety interest,[7] its statute violates the Commerce Clause. The judgment of the Court of Appeals is affirmed.

Justice Brennan, with whom Justice Marshall joins, concurring in the judgment.

Iowa's truck-length regulation challenged in this case is nearly identical to the Wisconsin regulation struck down in *Raymond*, as in violation of the Commerce Clause. In my view the same Commerce Clause restrictions that dictated that holding also require invalidation of Iowa's regulation insofar as it prohibits 65-foot doubles.

The reasoning bringing me to that conclusion does not require, however, that I engage in the debate between my Brothers Powell and Rehnquist over what the District Court record shows on the question whether 65-foot doubles are more dangerous than shorter trucks. With all respect, my Brothers ask and answer the wrong question.

For me, analysis of Commerce Clause challenges to state regulations must take into account three principles: (1) The courts are not empowered to second-guess the empirical judgments of lawmakers concerning the utility of legislation. (2) The burdens imposed on commerce must be balanced against the local benefits actually sought to be achieved by the State's lawmakers, and not against those suggested after the fact by counsel. (3) Protectionist legislation is unconstitutional under the Commerce Clause, even if the burdens and benefits are related to safety rather than economics.

---

[6] The dissenting opinion insists that we defer to Iowa's truck-length limitations because they represent the collective judgment of the Iowa Legislature. This position is curious because, as noted above, the Iowa Legislature approved a bill legalizing 65-foot doubles. The bill was vetoed by the Governor, primarily for parochial rather than legitimate safety reasons. The dissenting opinion is at a loss to explain the Governor's interest in deflecting interstate truck traffic around Iowa.

[7] . . . [T]he District Court and the Court of Appeals held that the Iowa statutory scheme unconstitutionally burdened interstate commerce. The District Court, however, found that the statute did not discriminate against such commerce. Because the record fully supports the decision below with respect to the burden on interstate commerce, we need not consider whether the statute also operated to discriminate against that commerce. The latter theory was neither briefed nor argued in this Court.

I

Both the opinion of my Brother Powell and the opinion of my Brother Rehnquist are predicated upon the supposition that the constitutionality of a state regulation is determined by the factual record created by the State's lawyers in trial court. But that supposition cannot be correct, for it would make the constitutionality of state laws and regulations depend on the vagaries of litigation rather than on the judgments made by the State's lawmakers.

In considering a Commerce Clause challenge to a state regulation, the judicial task is to balance the burden imposed on commerce against the local benefits sought to be achieved by the State's *lawmakers.* See *Pike v. Bruce Church, Inc.* (1970). In determining those benefits, a court should focus ultimately on the regulatory purposes identified by the lawmakers and on the evidence before or available to them that might have supported their judgment. Since the court must confine its analysis to the purposes the lawmakers had for maintaining the regulation, the only relevant evidence concerns whether the lawmakers could rationally have believed that the challenged regulation would foster those purposes. It is not the function of the court to decide whether *in fact* the regulation promotes its intended purpose, so long as an examination of the evidence before or available to the lawmaker indicates that the regulation is not wholly irrational in light of its purposes.[8]

My Brothers Powell and Rehnquist make the mistake of disregarding the intention of Iowa's lawmakers and assuming that resolution of the case must hinge upon the argument offered by Iowa's attorneys: that 65-foot doubles are more dangerous than shorter trucks. They then canvass the factual record and findings of the courts below and reach opposite conclusions as to whether the evidence adequately supports that empirical judgment. I repeat: my Brothers Powell and Rehnquist have asked and answered the wrong question. . . . Iowa's actual rationale for maintaining the regulation had nothing to do with these purported differences. Rather, Iowa sought to discourage interstate truck traffic on Iowa's highways. Thus, the safety advantages and disadvantages of the types and lengths of trucks involved in this case are irrelevant to the decision.[9]

---

[8] In the field of safety, once the court has established that the intended safety benefit is not illusory, insubstantial, or nonexistent, it must defer to the State's lawmakers on the appropriate balance to be struck against other interests. I therefore disagree with my Brother Powell when he asserts that the degree of interference with interstate commerce may in the first instance be "weighed" against the State's safety interests.

[9] My Brother Rehnquist claims that the "argument" that a court should defer to the actual purposes of the lawmakers rather than to the *post hoc* justifications of counsel "has been consistently rejected by the Court in other contexts." Apparently, he has overlooked such cases as *Allied Stores of Ohio, Inc. v. Bowers* (1959), where we described the rationale for our earlier decision in *Wheeling Steel Corp. v. Glander* (1949):

> The statutes, on their face admittedly discriminatory against nonresidents, themselves declared their purpose. . . . Having themselves specifically declared their purpose, the Ohio statute left no room to conceive of any other purpose for their existence. And the declared purpose having been found arbitrarily discriminatory against nonresidents, the Court could hardly escape the conclusion. . . .

. . .

Although the Court has stated that "[i]n no field has . . . deference to state regulation been greater than that of highway safety," it has declined to go so far as to presume that size restrictions are inherently tied to public safety. The Court has emphasized that the "strong presumption of validity" of size restrictions "cannot justify a court in closing its eyes to uncontroverted evidence of record," — here the obvious fact that the safety characteristics of 65-foot doubles did not provide the motivation for either legislators or Governor in maintaining the regulation.

III

Though my Brother Powell recognizes that the State's actual purpose in maintaining the truck-length regulation was "to limit the use of its highways by deflecting some through traffic," he fails to recognize that this purpose, being *protectionist* in nature, is *impermissible* under the Commerce Clause. The Governor admitted that he blocked legislative efforts to raise the length of trucks because the change "would benefit only a few Iowa-based companies while providing a great advantage for out-of-state trucking firms and competitors at the expense of our Iowa citizens." Appellant Raymond Kassel, Director of the Iowa Department of Transportation, while admitting that the greater 65-foot length standard would be *safer* overall, defended the more restrictive regulations because of their benefits *within Iowa*. . . .

Iowa may not shunt off its fair share of the burden of maintaining interstate truck routes, nor may it create increased hazards on the highways of neighboring States in order to decrease the hazards on Iowa highways. Such an attempt has all

---

And in *Weinberger v. Wiesenfeld* (1975) we said:

> This Court need not . . . accept at face value assertions of legislative purposes, when an examination of the legislative scheme and its history demonstrates that the asserted purpose could not have been a goal of the legislation. (Citing cases.)

And in *Massachusetts Board of Retirement v. Murgia* (1976), we stated that a classification challenged as being discriminatory will be upheld only if it "rationally furthers the purpose identified by the State." [*Weinberger* and *Murgia* were both equal protection cases (involving gender discrimination), not Dormant Commerce Clause cases. — Eds.]

The extent to which we may rely upon *post hoc* justifications of counsel depends on the circumstances surrounding passage of the legislation. Where there is no evidence bearing on the actual purpose for a legislative classification, our analysis necessarily focuses on the suggestions of counsel. . . . But where the lawmakers' purposes in enacting a statute are explicitly set forth or are clearly discernible from the legislative history this Court should not take — and, with the possible exception of *United States Railroad Retirement Board v. Fritz* (1980) (Brennan, J., dissenting), has not taken — the extraordinary step of disregarding the *actual* purpose in favor of some "imaginary basis or purpose." The principle of separation of powers requires, after all, that we defer to the elected lawmakers' judgment as to the appropriate means to accomplish an end, not that we defer to the arguments of lawyers.

If, as here, the only purpose ever articulated by the State's lawmakers for maintaining a regulation is illegitimate, I consider it contrary to precedent as well as to sound principles of constitutional adjudication for the courts to base their analysis on purposes never conceived by the lawmakers. This is especially true where, as the dissent's strained analysis of the relative safety of 65-foot doubles to shorter trucks amply demonstrates, the *post hoc* justifications are implausible as well as imaginary.

the hallmarks of the "simple . . . protectionism" this Court has condemned in the economic area. *Philadelphia v. New Jersey*. . . . Just as a State's attempt to avoid interstate competition in economic goods may damage the prosperity of the Nation as a whole, so Iowa's attempt to deflect interstate truck traffic has been found to make the Nation's highways as a whole more hazardous. That attempt should therefore be subject to "a virtually *per se* rule of invalidity."

This Court's heightened deference to the judgments of state lawmakers in the field of safety, is largely attributable to a judicial disinclination to weigh the interests of safety against other societal interests, such as the economic interest in the free flow of commerce. Here, the decision of Iowa's lawmakers to promote *Iowa's* safety and other interests at the direct expense of the safety and other interests of neighboring States merits no such deference. No special judicial acuity is demanded to perceive that this sort of parochial legislation violates the Commerce Clause. As Justice Cardozo has written, the Commerce Clause "was framed upon the theory that the peoples of the several states must sink or swim together, and that in the long run prosperity and salvation are in union and not division." *Baldwin v. G. A. F. Seelig, Inc.* (1935).

I therefore concur in the judgment.

JUSTICE REHNQUIST, with whom THE CHIEF JUSTICE and JUSTICE STEWART join, dissenting.

The result in this case suggests, to paraphrase Justice Jackson, that the only state truck-length limit "that is valid is one which this Court has not been able to get its hands on." Although the plurality opinion and the opinion concurring in the judgment strike down Iowa's law by different routes, I believe the analysis in both opinions oversteps our "limited authority to review state legislation under the commerce clause," and seriously intrudes upon the fundamental right of the States to pass laws to secure the safety of their citizens. Accordingly, I dissent.

I

It is necessary to elaborate somewhat on the facts as presented in the plurality opinion to appreciate fully what the Court does today. Iowa's action in limiting the length of trucks which may travel on its highways is in no sense unusual. Every State in the Union regulates the length of vehicles permitted to use the public roads. Nor is Iowa a renegade in having length limits which operate to exclude the 65-foot doubles favored by Consolidated. These trucks are prohibited in other areas of the country as well, some 17 States and the District of Columbia, including all of New England and most of the Southeast. While pointing out that Consolidated carries commodities through Iowa on Interstate 80, "the principal east-west route linking New York, Chicago, and the west coast," the plurality neglects to note that both Pennsylvania and New Jersey, through which Interstate 80 runs before reaching New York, also ban 65-foot doubles. In short, the persistent effort in the plurality opinion to paint Iowa as an oddity standing alone to block commerce carried in 65-foot doubles is simply not supported by the facts. . . .

II

... Although it is phrased in terms of an affirmative grant of power to the National Legislature, we have read the Commerce Clause as imposing some limitations on the States as well, even in the absence of any action by Congress. See Philadelphia v. New Jersey. The Court has hastened to emphasize, however, that the negative implication it has discerned in the Commerce Clause does not invalidate state legislation simply because the legislation burdens interstate commerce....

The Commerce Clause is, after all, a grant of authority to Congress, not to the courts. Although the Court when it interprets the "dormant" aspect of the Commerce Clause will invalidate unwarranted state intrusion, such action is a far cry from simply undertaking to regulate when Congress has not because we believe such regulation would facilitate interstate commerce....

The propriety of state regulation of the use of public highways was explicitly recognized in *Morris v. Duby* (1927), where Chief Justice Taft wrote that "[i]n the absence of national legislation especially covering the subject of interstate commerce, the State may rightfully prescribe uniform regulations adapted to promote safety upon its highways and the conservation of their use, applicable alike to vehicles moving in interstate commerce and those of its own citizens." ...

A determination that a state law is a rational safety measure does not end the Commerce Clause inquiry. A "sensitive consideration" of the safety purpose in relation to the burden on commerce is required. *Raymond.* When engaging in such a consideration the Court does not directly compare safety benefits to commerce costs and strike down the legislation if the latter can be said in some vague sense to "outweigh" the former. Such an approach would make an empty gesture of the strong presumption of validity accorded state safety measures, particularly those governing highways. It would also arrogate to this Court functions of forming public policy, functions which, in the absence of congressional action, were left by the Framers of the Constitution to state legislatures....

The purpose of the "sensitive consideration" referred to above is rather to determine if the asserted safety justification, although rational, is merely a pretext for discrimination against interstate commerce. We will conclude that it is if the safety benefits from the regulation are demonstrably trivial while the burden on commerce is great.... The nature of the inquiry is perhaps best illustrated by examining those cases in which state safety laws have been struck down on Commerce Clause grounds. In *Southern Pacific v. Arizona* (1945) a law regulating train lengths was viewed by the Court as having "at most slight and dubious advantage, if any, over unregulated train lengths," the lower courts concluded the law actually tended to *increase* the number of accidents by increasing the number of trains, In *Bibb v. Navajo Freight Lines, Inc.* (1959) the contoured mudguards required by Illinois, alone among the States, had *no* safety advantages over conventional mudguards and, as in *Southern Pacific*, actually *increased* hazards. (Harlan, J., concurring). In *Great A&P Tea Co. v. Cottrell* (1976), the Court struck down a Mississippi "reciprocity clause" concerning milk inspection because it "disserve[d] rather than promote[d] any higher Mississippi milk quality standards." ...

III

. . . Iowa adduced evidence supporting the relation between vehicle length and highway safety. The evidence indicated that longer vehicles take greater time to be passed, thereby increasing the risks of accidents, particularly during the inclement weather not uncommon in Iowa. The 65-foot vehicle exposes a passing driver to visibility-impairing splash and spray during bad weather for a longer period than do the shorter trucks permitted in Iowa. Longer trucks are more likely to clog intersections, and although there are no intersections on the Interstate Highways, the order below went beyond the highways themselves and the concerns about greater length at intersections would arise "[a]t every trip origin, every trip destination, every intermediate stop for picking up trailers, reconfiguring loads, change of drivers, eating, refueling — every intermediate stop would generate this type of situation." The Chief of the Division of Patrol in the Iowa Department of Public Safety testified that longer vehicles pose greater problems at the scene of an accident. For example, trucks involved in accidents often must be unloaded at the scene which would take longer the bigger the load.

In rebuttal of Consolidated's evidence on the relative safety of 65-foot doubles to trucks permitted on Iowa's highways, Iowa introduced evidence that doubles are more likely than singles to jackknife or upset. The District Court concluded that this was so and that singles are more stable than doubles.[10] Iowa also introduced evidence from Consolidated's own records showing that Consolidated's overall accident rate for doubles exceeded that of semis for three of the last four years, and that some of Consolidated's own drivers expressed a preference for the handling characteristics of singles over doubles. . . .

[T]here was sufficient evidence presented at trial to support the legislative determination that length is related to safety, and nothing in Consolidated's evidence undermines this conclusion. . . . The question . . . is whether the Iowa Legislature has acted rationally in regulating vehicle lengths and whether the safety benefits from this regulation are more than slight or problematical. . . .

Any direct balancing of marginal safety benefits against burdens on commerce would make the burdens on commerce the sole significant factor, and make likely the odd result that similar state laws enacted for identical safety reasons might violate the Commerce Clause in one part of the country but not another. For example, Mississippi and Georgia prohibit trucks over 55 feet. Since doubles are not operated in the Southeast, the demonstrable burden on commerce may not be sufficient to strike down these laws. . . .

Forcing Iowa to yield to the policy choices of neighboring States perverts the primary purpose of the Commerce Clause, that of vesting power to regulate interstate commerce in Congress, where all the States are represented. In *Barnwell Brothers*, the Court upheld a South Carolina width limit of 90 inches even though "all other states permit a width of 96 inches which is the standard width of trucks

---

[10] Although the District Court noted that doubles are more maneuverable, it certainly is reasonable for a legislature to conclude that stability is a more critical factor than maneuverability on the straight expanses of the Interstates.

engaged in interstate commerce." Then Justice Stone, writing for the Court, stressed:

> The fact that many states have adopted a different standard is not persuasive. . . . The legislature, being free to exercise its own judgment, is not bound by that of other legislatures. It would hardly be contended that if all the states had adopted a single standard none, in the light of its own experience and in the exercise of its judgment upon all the complex elements which enter into the problem, could change it. . . .

The border-cities exception to the Iowa length limit does not [discriminate on its face]. Iowa shippers in cities with border-city ordinances may use longer vehicles in interstate commerce, but interstate shippers coming into such cities may do so as well. Cities without border-city ordinances may neither export nor import on oversized vehicles. . . . The population of the eight cities with border-city ordinances is only 13 percent of the population of the State.

My Brother Brennan argues that the Court should consider only *the* purpose the Iowa legislators *actually* sought to achieve by the length limit, and not the purposes advanced by Iowa's lawyers in defense of the statute. . . . The argument has been consistently rejected by the Court in other contexts. . . . The problems with a view such as that advanced in the opinion concurring in the judgment are apparent. To name just a few, it assumes that individual legislators are motivated by one discernible "actual" purpose, and ignores the fact that different legislators may vote for a single piece of legislation for widely different reasons. How, for example, would a court adhering to the views expressed in the opinion concurring in the judgment approach a statute, the legislative history of which indicated that 10 votes were based on safety considerations, 10 votes were based on protectionism, and the statute passed by a vote of 40-20? What would the *actual* purpose of the *legislature* have been in that case? This Court has wisely "never insisted that a legislative body articulate its reasons for enacting a statute." *Fritz.*[11]

---

[11] It is not a particularly pleasant task for the author of a dissent joined by two other Members of the Court to take issue with a statement made by the author of a concurrence in that same case which is joined by only one Member of the Court. Such fragmentation, particularly between two opinions neither of which command the adherence of a majority of the Court, cannot help but further unsettle what certainty there may be in the legal principles which govern our decision of Commerce Clause cases such as this and lay a foundation for similar uncertainty in other sorts of constitutional adjudication. Nonetheless, I feel obliged to take up the cudgels, however unwillingly, because Justice Brennan's concurrence, joined by Justice Marshall, is mistaken not only in its analysis but also in its efforts to interpret the meaning of today's decision.

Although both my Brother Brennan and I have cited cases from the equal protection area, it is not clear that the analysis of legislative purpose in that area is the same as in the present context. It may be more reasonable to suppose that proffered purposes of a statute, whether advanced by a legislature or *post hoc* by lawyers, cloak impermissible aims in Commerce Clause cases than in equal protection cases. Statutes generally favor one group at the expense of another, and the Equal Protection Clause was not designed to proscribe this in the way that the Commerce Clause was designed to prevent local barriers to interstate commerce. Thus even if my Brother Brennan's arguments were supportable in Commerce Clause cases, that analysis would not carry over of its own force into the realm of equal protection generally.

But even in the Commerce Clause area, his arguments are unpersuasive. . . .

Both the plurality and the concurrence attach great significance to the Governor's veto of a bill passed by the Iowa Legislature permitting 65-foot doubles. Whatever views one may have about the significance of legislative motives, it must be emphasized that the law which the Court strikes down today was not passed to achieve the protectionist goals the plurality and the concurrence ascribe to the Governor. Iowa's 60-foot length limit was established in 1963, at a time when very few States permitted 65-foot doubles. Striking down legislation on the basis of asserted legislative motives is dubious enough, but the plurality and concurrence strike down the legislation involved in this case because of asserted impermissible motives for *not* enacting *other* legislation, motives which could not possibly have been present when the legislation under challenge here was considered and passed. Such action is, so far as I am aware, unprecedented in this Court's history.

Furthermore, the effort in both the plurality and the concurrence to portray the legislation involved here as protectionist is in error. Whenever a State enacts more stringent safety measures than its neighbors, in an area which affects commerce, the safety law will have the incidental effect of deflecting interstate commerce to the neighboring States. Indeed, the safety and protectionist motives cannot be separated: The whole purpose of safety regulation of vehicles is to *protect* the State from unsafe vehicles. If a neighboring State chooses *not* to protect its citizens from the danger discerned by the enacting State, that is its business, but the enacting State should not be penalized when the vehicles it considers unsafe travel through the neighboring State.

The other States with truck-length limits that exclude Consolidated's 65-foot doubles would not at all be paranoid in assuming that they might be next on Consolidated's "hit list." [Consolidated was a plaintiff in the *Raymond* case as well as this one. — EDS.] The true problem with today's decision is that it gives no guidance whatsoever to these States as to whether their laws are valid or how to defend them. For that matter, the decision gives no guidance to Consolidated or other trucking firms either. Perhaps, after all is said and done, the Court today neither says nor does very much at all. We know only that Iowa's law is invalid and that the

---

Nor do the more recent decisions cited by my Brother Brennan support his argument. For example, the fact that we "*need not* . . . accept at face value assertions of legislative purposes, when an examination of the legislative scheme and its history demonstrates that the asserted purpose *could not* have been a goal of the legislation," *Weinberger v. Wiesenfeld* (1975) (emphasis supplied), hardly supports the proposition that we *cannot* consider assertions of legislative purpose which *could* have been a goal of the legislation, even though such purposes may not have been identified as goals by the legislature. To take another example, the upholding of the law in *Massachusetts Board of Retirement v. Murgia* (1976), because it "rationally furthers the purpose identified by the State," certainly does not suggest that by "State" this Court meant only "legislature," and not the State's attorneys, or that *only* those purposes identified by the State could be considered in reviewing legislation.

Although Justice Brennan "would emphasize" the significance the plurality opinion attaches to the Governor's articulation of what is viewed as an impermissible purpose, this hardly supports the proposition that permissible purposes cannot be considered by a court unless they were somehow identified by the legislature as goals of the statute. The plurality opinion in fact examines the asserted safety purpose of the Iowa statute at some length. Indeed, Justice Brennan criticizes the plurality for examining the safety purpose and "disregarding the intention of Iowa's lawmakers." . . .

jurisprudence of the "negative side" of the Commerce Clause remains hopelessly confused.

In recent years, two Justices have expressed reservations about having courts enforce the Dormant Commerce Clause. The following excerpts are from concurring opinions of Justices Scalia and Thomas, in which they explain their disagreement with the Court's current treatment of the Dormant Commerce Clause.

STUDY GUIDE

- Given the difficulties of interpreting text in this area, and also given the consensus understanding of at least one purpose of the Dormant Commerce Clause — to break down trade barriers — what, then, should be the position of an originalist in this debate? What should be the position of someone who believes in interpreting the Constitution in light of modern circumstances?
- Does the current balance between federal and state governments make the idea of courts withdrawing from enforcement a better or worse idea than it might have been in earlier times?
- If the Court withdrew from its policing of state laws that interfere with interstate commerce, would out-of-state interests be sufficiently protected? Or is it possible that state interests would be "overprotected," with Congress reluctant to preempt laws even if they clearly discriminated against or burdened out-of-state commerce?

Tyler Pipe v. Washington Department of Revenue

483 U.S. 232 (1987)

JUSTICE SCALIA . . . concurring in part and dissenting in part. . . .

The fact is that, in the 114 years since the doctrine of the negative Commerce Clause was formally adopted as holding of this Court, and in the 50 years prior to that in which it was alluded to in various dicta of the Court, our applications of the doctrine have, not to put too fine a point on the matter, made no sense.

That uncertainty in application has been attributable in no small part to the lack of any clear theoretical underpinning for judicial "enforcement" of the Commerce Clause. The text of the Clause states that "Congress shall have Power . . . To regulate Commerce with foreign Nations, and among the several States, and with the Indian Tribes." Art. I, §8, cl. 3. On its face, this is a charter for Congress, not the courts, to ensure "an area of trade free from interference by the States." *Boston Stock Exchange v. State Tax Comm'n* (1977). The preemption of state legislation would automatically follow, of course, if the grant of power to Congress to regulate interstate commerce were exclusive, as Charles Pinckney's draft constitution would have provided, and as John Marshall at one point seemed to believe it was. See *Gibbons v. Ogden* (1824). However, unlike the District Clause, which empowers Congress "To exercise exclusive Legislation," Art. I, §8, cl. 17, the language of the Commerce Clause gives no indication of exclusivity.

Nor can one assume generally that Congress' Article I powers are exclusive; many of them plainly coexist with concurrent authority in the States [citing cases referring to the patent power, copyright power, court-martial jurisdiction over the militia, and the bankruptcy power]. Furthermore, there is no correlative denial of power over commerce to the States in Art. I, §10, as there is, for example, with the power to coin money or make treaties. And both the States and Congress assumed from the date of ratification that at least some state laws regulating commerce were valid. The exclusivity rationale is infinitely less attractive today than it was in 1847. Now that we know interstate commerce embraces such activities as growing wheat for home consumption, *Wickard v. Filburn* (1942), and local loan sharking, *Perez v. United States* (1971), it is more difficult to imagine what state activity would survive an exclusive Commerce Clause than to imagine what would be precluded.

Another approach to theoretical justification for judicial enforcement of the Commerce Clause is to assert, as did Justice Curtis in dicta in *Cooley v. Board of Wardens* (1851) that "[w]hatever subjects of this power are in their nature national, or admit only of one uniform system, or plan of regulation, may justly be said to be of such a nature as to require exclusive legislation by Congress." That would perhaps be a wise rule to adopt (though it is hard to see why judges, rather than legislators, are fit to determine what areas of commerce "in their nature" require national regulation), but it has the misfortune of finding no conceivable basis in the text of the Commerce Clause, which treats "Commerce . . . among the several States" as a unitary subject. And attempting to limit the Clause's preemptive effect to state laws intended to regulate commerce (as opposed to those intended, for example, to promote health), see *Gibbons*, while perhaps a textually possible construction of the phrase "regulate Commerce," is a most unlikely one. Distinguishing between laws with the purpose of regulating commerce and "police power" statutes with that effect is, as Taney demonstrated in the *License Cases* (1847), more interesting as a metaphysical exercise than useful as a practical technique for marking out the powers of separate sovereigns.

The least plausible theoretical justification of all is the idea that, in enforcing the negative Commerce Clause, the Court is not applying a constitutional command at all, but is merely interpreting the will of Congress, whose silence in certain fields of interstate commerce (but not in others) is to be taken as a prohibition of regulation. There is no conceivable reason why congressional inaction under the Commerce Clause should be deemed to have the same preemptive effect elsewhere accorded only to congressional action. There, as elsewhere, "Congress' silence is just that — silence. . . ." *Alaska Airlines, Inc. v. Brock* (1987).

The historical record provides no grounds for reading the Commerce Clause to be other than what it says — an authorization for Congress to regulate commerce. The strongest evidence in favor of a negative Commerce Clause — that version of it which renders federal authority over interstate commerce exclusive — is Madison's comment during the Convention: "Whether the States are now restrained from laying tonnage duties depends on the extent of the power 'to regulate commerce.' These terms are vague, but seem to exclude this power of the States." 2 M. Farrand,

Records of the Federal Convention of 1787 (1937). This comment, however, came during discussion of what became Art. I, §10, cl. 3: "No State shall, without the Consent of Congress, lay any Duty of Tonnage. . . ." The fact that it is difficult to conceive how the power to regulate commerce would not include the power to impose duties; and the fact that, despite this apparent coverage, the Convention went on to adopt a provision prohibiting States from levying duties on tonnage without congressional approval; suggest that Madison's assumption of exclusivity of the federal commerce power was ill-considered, and not generally shared.

Against this mere shadow of historical support, there is the overwhelming reality that the Commerce Clause, in its broad outlines, was not a major subject of controversy, neither during the constitutional debates nor in the ratifying conventions. . . . Madison does not seem to have exaggerated when he described the Commerce Clause as an addition to the powers of the National Government "which few oppose and from which no apprehensions are entertained." The Federalist No. 45. I think it beyond question that many "apprehensions" would have been "entertained" if supporters of the Constitution had hinted that the Commerce Clause, despite its language, gave this Court the power it has since assumed. . . .

In sum, to the extent that we have gone beyond guarding against rank discrimination against citizens of other States — which is regulated not by the Commerce Clause but by the Privileges and Immunities Clause, U.S. Const., Art. IV, §2, cl. 1 ("The Citizens of each State shall be entitled to all Privileges and Immunities of Citizens in the several States") — the Court for over a century has engaged in an enterprise that it has been unable to justify by textual support or even coherent nontextual theory, that it was almost certainly not intended to undertake, and that it has not undertaken very well. It is astonishing that we should be expanding our beachhead in this impoverished territory, rather than being satisfied with what we have already acquired by a sort of intellectual adverse possession. . . .

United Haulers Association v. Oneida-Herkimer Solid Waste Management Authority

550 U.S. 330 (2007)

Justice Thomas, concurring in the judgment. . . .

[A]pplication of the negative Commerce Clause turns solely on policy considerations, not on the Constitution. Because this Court has no policy role in regulating interstate commerce, I would discard the Court's negative Commerce Clause jurisprudence.

I

Under the Commerce Clause, "Congress shall have Power . . . [t]o regulate Commerce with foreign Nations, and among the several States, and with the Indian Tribes." U.S. Const., Art. I, §8, cl. 3. The language of the Clause allows Congress not only to regulate interstate commerce but also to prevent state regulation of interstate commerce. *State Bd. of Ins. v. Todd Shipyards Corp.* (1962); *Gibbons v. Ogden*

(1824). Expanding on the interstate-commerce powers explicitly conferred on Congress, this Court has interpreted the Commerce Clause as a tool for courts to strike down state laws that it believes inhibit interstate commerce. But there is no basis in the Constitution for that interpretation. . . .

[T]he Court . . . analyze[s] whether the ordinances "discriminat[e] on [their] face against interstate commerce." Again, none of the cases the Court cites explains how the absence or presence of discrimination is relevant to deciding whether the ordinances are constitutionally permissible, and at least one case affirmatively admits that the nondiscrimination rule has no basis in the Constitution. *Philadelphia v. New Jersey* (1978) ("The bounds of these restraints appear nowhere in the words of the Commerce Clause, but have emerged gradually in the decisions of this Court giving effect to its basic purpose"). Thus cloaked in the "purpose" of the Commerce Clause, the rule against discrimination that the Court applies to decide this case exists untethered from the written Constitution. The rule instead depends upon the policy preferences of a majority of this Court.

The Court's policy preferences are an unsuitable basis for constitutional doctrine because they shift over time, as demonstrated by the different theories the Court has offered to support the nondiscrimination principle. In the early years of the nondiscrimination rule, the Court struck down a state health law because "the enactment of a similar statute by each one of the States composing the Union would result in the destruction of commerce among the several States." *Minnesota v. Barber* (1890). . . .

More recently, the Court has struck down state laws sometimes based on its preference for national unity, see, *e.g.*, *American Trucking Assns., Inc. v. Michigan Pub. Serv. Comm'n* (2005) (justifying the nondiscrimination rule by stating that "[o]ur Constitution was framed upon the theory that the peoples of the several states must sink or swim together"), and other times on the basis of antiprotectionist sentiment, see, *e.g.*, *Oregon Waste Systems, Inc. v. Department of Environmental Quality of Ore.* (1994) (noting the interest in "avoid[ing] the tendencies toward economic Balkanization"); *New Energy Co. of Ind. v. Limbach* (1988) (stating that the negative Commerce Clause "prohibits economic protectionism — that is, regulatory measures designed to benefit in-state economic interests by burdening out-of-state competitors"). . . .

Many of the above-cited cases . . . rest on the erroneous assumption that the Court must choose between economic protectionism and the free market. But the Constitution vests that fundamentally legislative choice in Congress. To the extent that Congress does not exercise its authority to make that choice, the Constitution does not limit the States' power to regulate commerce. In the face of congressional silence, the States are free to set the balance between protectionism and the free market. Instead of accepting this constitutional reality, the Court's negative Commerce Clause jurisprudence gives nine Justices of this Court the power to decide the appropriate balance.

II

As the foregoing demonstrates, despite more than 100 years of negative Commerce Clause doctrine, there is no principled way to decide this case under current law. Notably, the Court cannot and does not consider this case "[i]n light of the language of the Constitution and the historical context." *Alden v. Maine* (1999). Likewise, it cannot follow "the cardinal rule to construe provisions in context." And with no text to construe, the Court cannot take into account the Founders' "deliberate choice of words" or "their natural meaning." . . .

III

Despite its acceptance of negative Commerce Clause jurisprudence, the Court expresses concern about "unprecedented and unbounded interference by the courts with state and local government." It explains:

> The dormant Commerce Clause is not a roving license for federal courts to decide what activities are appropriate for state and local government to undertake, and what activities must be the province of private market competition. . . .
>
> There is no reason to step in and hand local businesses a victory they could not obtain through the political process.

I agree that the Commerce Clause is not a "roving license" and that the Court should not deliver to businesses victories that they failed to obtain through the political process. I differ with the Court because I believe its powerful rhetoric is completely undermined by the doctrine it applies.

In this regard, the Court's analogy to *Lochner v. New York* (1905), suggests that the Court should reject the negative Commerce Clause, rather than tweak it. In *Lochner* the Court located a "right of free contract" in a constitutional provision that says nothing of the sort. The Court's negative Commerce Clause jurisprudence, created from whole cloth, is just as illegitimate as the "right" it vindicated in *Lochner*. Yet today's decision does not repudiate that doctrinal error. Rather, it further propagates the error by narrowing the negative Commerce Clause for policy reasons — reasons that later majorities of this Court may find to be entirely illegitimate.

In so doing, the majority revisits familiar territory: Just three years after *Lochner*, the Court narrowed the right of contract for policy reasons but did not overrule *Lochner*. *Muller v. Oregon* (1908) (upholding a maximum-hours requirement for women because the difference between the "two sexes" "justifies a difference in legislation"). Like the *Muller* Court, today's majority trifles with an unsound and illegitimate jurisprudence yet fails to abandon it.

Because I believe that the power to regulate interstate commerce is a power given to Congress and not the Court, I concur in the judgment of the Court.

STUDY GUIDE

South-Central Timber Development, Inc. v. Wunnicke introduces two exceptions, where an otherwise discriminatory state law is permissible:

(1) If Congress has authorized the state regulation; or
(2) If the state is acting as a "market participant" rather than as a regulator.

South-Central Timber Development, Inc. v. Wunnicke

467 U.S. 82 (1984)

JUSTICE WHITE announced the judgment of the Court and delivered the opinion of the Court with respect to Parts I and II, and an opinion with respect to Parts III and IV, in which JUSTICE BRENNAN, JUSTICE BLACKMUN, and JUSTICE STEVENS joined.

I

In September 1980, the Alaska Department of Natural Resources published a notice that it would sell approximately 49 million board-feet of timber in the area of Icy Cape, Alaska, on October 23, 1980. The notice of sale, the prospectus, and the proposed contract for the sale all provided that "[p]rimary manufacture within the State of Alaska will be required as a special provision of the contract." Under the primary-manufacture requirement, the successful bidder must partially process the timber prior to shipping it outside of the State. The requirement is imposed by contract and does not limit the export of unprocessed timber not owned by the State. The stated purpose of the requirement is to "protect existing industries, provide for the establishment of new industries, derive revenue from all timber resources, and manage the State's forests on a sustained yield basis." When it imposes the requirement, the State charges a significantly lower price for the timber than it otherwise would.

The major method of complying with the primary-manufacture requirement is to convert the logs into cants, which are logs slabbed on at least one side. In order to satisfy the Alaska requirement, cants must be either sawed to a maximum thickness of 12 inches or squared on four sides along their entire length.

Petitioner, South-Central Timber Development, Inc., is an Alaska corporation engaged in the business of purchasing standing timber, logging the timber, and shipping the logs into foreign commerce, almost exclusively to Japan. It does not operate a mill in Alaska and customarily sells unprocessed logs. When it learned that the primary-manufacture requirement was to be imposed on the Icy Cape sale, it brought an action in Federal District Court seeking an injunction, arguing that the requirement violated the negative implications of the Commerce Clause. . . .

II

Although the Commerce Clause is by its text an affirmative grant of power to Congress to regulate interstate and foreign commerce, the Clause has long been recognized as a self-executing limitation on the power of the States to enact laws imposing substantial burdens on such commerce. It is equally clear that Congress may "redefine the distribution of power over interstate commerce" by "permit[ting] the states to regulate the commerce in a manner which would otherwise not be permissible." The Court of Appeals held that Congress had done just that by consistently endorsing primary-manufacture requirements on timber taken from federal land. Although the court recognized that cases of this Court have spoken in terms of express approval by Congress, it stated:

> But such express authorization is not always necessary. There will be instances, like the case before us, where federal policy is so clearly delineated that a state may enact a parallel policy without explicit congressional approval, even if the purpose and effect of the state law is to favor local interests.

We agree that federal policy with respect to federal land is "clearly delineated," but the Court of Appeals was incorrect in concluding either that there is a clearly delineated federal policy approving Alaska's local-processing requirement or that Alaska's policy with respect to its timber lands is authorized by the existence of a "parallel" federal policy with respect to federal lands. . . .

The requirement that Congress affirmatively contemplate otherwise invalid state legislation is mandated by the policies underlying dormant Commerce Clause doctrine. . . . The Commerce Clause was designed "to avoid the tendencies toward economic Balkanization that had plagued relations among the Colonies and later among the States under the Articles of Confederation." Unrepresented interests will often bear the brunt of regulations imposed by one State having a significant effect on persons or operations in other States. Thus, "when the regulation is of such a character that its burden falls principally upon those without the state, legislative action is not likely to be subjected to those political restraints which are normally exerted on legislation where it affects adversely some interests within the state." On the other hand, when Congress acts, all segments of the country are represented, and there is significantly less danger that one State will be in a position to exploit others. Furthermore, if a State is in such a position, the decision to allow it is a collective one. A rule requiring a clear expression of approval by Congress ensures that there is, in fact, such a collective decision and reduces significantly the risk that unrepresented interests will be adversely affected by restraints on commerce.

The fact that the state policy in this case appears to be consistent with federal policy — or even that state policy furthers the goals we might believe that Congress had in mind — is an insufficient indicium of congressional intent. Congress acted only with respect to federal lands; we cannot infer from that fact that it intended to authorize a similar policy with respect to state lands. Accordingly, we reverse the contrary judgment of the Court of Appeals.

III

We now turn to . . . whether Alaska's restrictions on export of unprocessed timber from state-owned lands are exempt from Commerce Clause scrutiny under the "market-participant doctrine."

Our cases make clear that if a State is acting as a market participant, rather than as a market regulator, the dormant Commerce Clause places no limitation on its activities. See *White v. Massachusetts Council of Construction Employers, Inc.* (1983); *Reeves, Inc. v. Stake* (1980); *Hughes v. Alexandria Scrap Corp.* (1976).

The precise contours of the market-participant doctrine have yet to be established, however, the doctrine having been applied in only three cases of this Court to date.

The first of the cases, *Hughes v. Alexandria Scrap Corp.* involved a Maryland program designed to reduce the number of junked automobiles in the State. A "bounty" was established on Maryland-licensed junk cars, and the State imposed more stringent documentation requirements on out-of-state scrap processors than on in-state ones. The Court rejected a Commerce Clause attack on the program, although it noted that under traditional Commerce Clause analysis the program might well be invalid because it had the effect of reducing the flow of goods in interstate commerce. The Court concluded that Maryland's action was not "the kind of action with which the Commerce Clause is concerned," because "[n]othing in the purposes animating the Commerce Clause prohibits a State, in the absence of congressional action, from participating in the market and exercising the right to favor its own citizens over others."

In *Reeves, Inc. v. Stake*, the Court upheld a South Dakota policy of restricting the sale of cement from a state-owned plant to state residents, declaring that "[t]he basic distinction drawn in *Alexandria Scrap* between States as market participants and States as market regulators makes good sense and sound law." The Court relied upon "the long recognized right of trader or manufacturer, engaged in an entirely private business, freely to exercise his own independent discretion as to parties with whom he will deal." In essence, the Court recognized the principle that the Commerce Clause places no limitations on a State's refusal to deal with particular parties when it is participating in the interstate market in goods.

The most recent of this Court's cases developing the market-participant doctrine is *White v. Massachusetts Council of Construction Employers, Inc.*, in which the Court sustained against a Commerce Clause challenge an executive order of the Mayor of Boston that required all construction projects funded in whole or in part by city funds or city-administered funds to be performed by a work force of at least 50% city residents. The Court rejected the argument that the city was not entitled to the protection of the doctrine because the order had the effect of regulating employment contracts between public contractors and their employees. Recognizing that "there are some limits on a state or local government's ability to impose restrictions that reach beyond the immediate parties with which the government transacts business," the Court found it unnecessary to define those limits because "[e]veryone affected by the order [was], in a substantial if informal sense, 'working for the city.'" The fact that the employees were "working for the city" was "crucial" to the market-participant analysis in *White*.

The State of Alaska contends that its primary-manufacture requirement fits squarely within the market-participant doctrine, arguing that "Alaska's entry into the market may be viewed as precisely the same type of subsidy to local interests that the Court found unobjectionable in *Alexandria Scrap*." However, when Maryland became involved in the scrap market it was as a purchaser of scrap; Alaska, on the other hand, participates in the timber market, but imposes conditions downstream in the timber-processing market. Alaska is not merely subsidizing local timber processing in an amount "roughly equal to the difference between the price the timber would fetch in the absence of such a requirement and the amount the state actually receives." If the State directly subsidized the timber-processing industry by such an amount, the purchaser would retain the option of taking advantage of the subsidy by processing timber in the State or forgoing the benefits of the subsidy and exporting unprocessed timber. Under the Alaska requirement, however, the choice is made for him: if he buys timber from the State he is not free to take the timber out of state prior to processing.

The State also would have us find *Reeves* controlling. It states that "*Reeves* made it clear that the Commerce Clause imposes no limitation on Alaska's power to choose the terms on which it will sell its timber." Such an unrestrained reading of *Reeves* is unwarranted. Although the Court in *Reeves* did strongly endorse the right of a State to deal with whomever it chooses when it participates in the market, it did not — and did not purport to — sanction the imposition of any terms that the State might desire. For example, the Court expressly noted in *Reeves* that "Commerce Clause scrutiny may well be more rigorous when a restraint on foreign commerce is alleged," that a natural resource "like coal, timber, wild game, or minerals," was not involved, but instead the cement was "the end product of a complex process whereby a costly physical plant and human labor act on raw materials," and that South Dakota did not bar resale of South Dakota cement to out-of-state purchasers. In this case, all three of the elements that were not present in *Reeves* — foreign commerce, a natural resource, and restrictions on resale — are present.

Finally, Alaska argues that since the Court in *White* upheld a requirement that reached beyond "the boundary of formal privity of contract," then, a fortiori, the primary-manufacture requirement is permissible, because the State is not regulating contracts for resale of timber or regulating the buying and selling of timber, but is instead "a seller of timber, pure and simple." Yet it is clear that the State is more than merely a seller of timber. In the commercial context, the seller usually has no say over, and no interest in, how the product is to be used after sale; in this case, however, payment for the timber does not end the obligations of the purchaser, for, despite the fact that the purchaser has taken delivery of the timber and has paid for it, he cannot do with it as he pleases. Instead, he is obligated to deal with a stranger to the contract after completion of the sale.

That privity of contract is not always the outer boundary of permissible state activity does not necessarily mean that the Commerce Clause has no application within the boundary of formal privity. The market-participant doctrine permits a State to influence "a discrete, identifiable class of economic activity in which [it] is a major participant." *White.* Contrary to the State's contention, the doctrine is not carte blanche to impose any conditions that the State has the economic power to dictate, and does not validate any requirement merely because the State imposes it upon someone with whom it is in contractual privity.

The limit of the market-participant doctrine must be that it allows a State to impose burdens on commerce within the market in which it is a participant, but allows it to go no further. The State may not impose conditions, whether by statute, regulation, or contract, that have a substantial regulatory effect outside of that particular market. Unless the "market" is relatively narrowly defined, the doctrine has the potential of swallowing up the rule that States may not impose substantial burdens on interstate commerce even if they act with the permissible state purpose of fostering local industry.

At the heart of the dispute in this case is disagreement over the definition of the market. Alaska contends that it is participating in the processed timber market, although it acknowledges that it participates in no way in the actual processing. South-Central argues, on the other hand, that although the State may be a participant in the timber market, it is using its leverage in that market to exert a regulatory effect in the processing market, in which it is not a participant. We agree with the latter position.

There are sound reasons for distinguishing between a State's preferring its own residents in the initial disposition of goods when it is a market participant and a State's attachment of restrictions on dispositions subsequent to the goods coming to rest in private hands. First, simply as a matter of intuition a state market participant has a greater interest as a "private trader" in the immediate transaction than it has in what its purchaser does with the goods after the State no longer has an interest in them. . . .

Second, downstream restrictions have a greater regulatory effect than do limitations on the immediate transaction. Instead of merely choosing its own trading partners, the State is attempting to govern the private, separate economic relationships of its trading partners; that is, it restricts the post-purchase activity of the purchaser, rather than merely the purchasing activity. In contrast to the situation in *White*, this restriction on private economic activity takes place after the completion of the parties' direct commercial obligations, rather than during the course of an ongoing commercial relationship in which the city retained a continuing proprietary interest in the subject of the contract. In sum, the State may not avail itself of the market-participant doctrine to immunize its downstream regulation of the timber-processing market in which it is not a participant. . . .

Viewed as a naked restraint on export of unprocessed logs, there is little question that the processing requirement cannot survive scrutiny under the precedents of the Court. . . .

ASSIGNMENT 3

B. THE PRIVILEGES AND IMMUNITIES CLAUSE OF ARTICLE IV

The Privileges and Immunities Clause of Article IV reads (emphasis added): "The citizens of each state shall be entitled to all privileges *and* immunities of citizens in the several states." (Don't confuse it with the Privileges *or* Immunities Clause of the Fourteenth Amendment.) The first noteworthy case on the Privileges and Immunities Clause of Article IV was *Corfield v.*

Justice Bushrod Washington was George Washington's nephew.

Coryell, decided by Justice Bushrod Washington while sitting on the Circuit Court for the District of Pennsylvania in 1823:

> The inquiry is, what are the privileges and immunities of citizens in the several states? We feel no hesitation in confining these expressions to those privileges and immunities which are, in their nature, fundamental; which belong, of right, to the citizens of all free governments; and which have, at all times, been enjoyed by the citizens of the several states which compose this Union, from the time of their becoming free, independent, and sovereign. What these fundamental principles are, it would perhaps be more tedious than difficult to enumerate. They may, however, be all comprehended under the following general heads: Protection by the government; the enjoyment of life and liberty, with the right to acquire and possess property of every kind, and to pursue and obtain happiness and safety; subject nevertheless to such restraints as the government may justly prescribe for the general good of the whole.
>
> The right of a citizen of one state to pass through, or to reside in any other state, for purposes of trade, agriculture, professional pursuits, or otherwise; to claim the benefit of the writ of habeas corpus; to institute and maintain actions of any kind in the courts of the state; to take, hold and dispose of property, either real or personal; and an exemption from higher taxes or impositions than are paid by the other citizens of the state; may be mentioned as some of the particular privileges and immunities of citizens, which are clearly embraced by the general description of privileges deemed to be fundamental: to which may be added, the elective franchise, as regulated and established by the laws or constitution of the state in which it is to be exercised. These, and many others which might be mentioned, are, strictly speaking, privileges and immunities, and the enjoyment of them by the citizens of each state, in every other state, was manifestly calculated (to use the expressions of the preamble of the corresponding provision in the old articles of confederation) "the better to secure and perpetuate mutual friendship and intercourse among the people of the different states of the Union."

Since the clause prohibits discrimination against citizens from out of state, it becomes necessary to determine whether discrimination has taken place. Given that "citizenship has its privileges," the mere existence of differential treatment between citizen and noncitizen is not sufficient to show a violation of the clause. *Hicklin v. Orbeck* examines what else needs to be demonstrated.

STUDY GUIDE

- The next case provides an overview of the case law that has developed around the Privileges and Immunities Clause of Article IV.
- How does the Court view the relationship between the Privileges and Immunities Clause and the Dormant Commerce Clause?

Hicklin v. Orbeck

437 U.S. 518 (1978)

MR. JUSTICE BRENNAN delivered the opinion of the Court.

In 1972, professedly for the purpose of reducing unemployment in the State, the Alaska Legislature passed an Act entitled "Local Hire Under State Leases." The key provision of "Alaska Hire," as the Act has come to be known, is the requirement that "all oil and gas leases, easements or right-of-way permits for oil or gas pipeline purposes, utilization agreements, or any renegotiation of any of the preceding to which the state is a party" contain a provision "requiring the employment of qualified Alaska residents" in preference to nonresidents.[12] This employment preference is administered by providing persons meeting the statutory requirements for Alaskan residency with certificates of residence — "resident cards" — that can be presented to an employer covered by the Act as proof of residency. Appellants [are] individuals desirous of securing jobs covered by the Act but unable to qualify for the necessary resident cards. . . .

Appellants' principal challenge to Alaska Hire is made under the Privileges and Immunities Clause of Art. IV, §2: "The Citizens of each State shall be entitled to all Privileges and Immunities of Citizens in the several States." That provision, which "appears in the so-called States' Relations Article, the same Article that embraces the Full Faith and Credit Clause, the Extradition Clause . . . , the provisions for the admission of new States, the Territory and Property Clause, and the Guarantee Clause," *Baldwin v. Montana Fish and Game Commn.* (1978), "establishes a norm of comity," *Austin v. New Hampshire* (1975), that is to prevail among the States with respect to their treatment of each other's residents.[13] The purpose of the Clause, as described in *Paul v. Virginia* (1869), is

> to place the citizens of each State upon the same footing with citizens of other States, so far as the advantages resulting from citizenship in those States are concerned. It relieves them from the disabilities of alienage in other States; it inhibits discriminating legislation against them by other States; it gives them the right of free ingress into other States, and egress from them; it insures to them in other States the same freedom possessed by the citizens of those States in the acquisition and enjoyment of property and in the pursuit of happiness; and it secures to them in other States the equal protection of their laws. It has been justly said that no provision in the Constitution has tended so strongly to constitute the citizens of the United States one people as this.

Appellants' appeal to the protection of the Clause is strongly supported by this Court's decisions holding violative of the Clause state discrimination against nonresidents seeking to ply their trade, practice their occupation, or pursue a common

---

[12] The regulations implementing the Act further require that all nonresidents be laid off before any resident "working in the same trade or craft" is terminated: "[T]he nonresident may be retained only if no resident employee is qualified to fill the position."

[13] Although this Court has not always equated state residency with state citizenship, it is now established that the terms "citizen" and "resident" are "essentially interchangeable," for purposes of analysis of most cases under the Privileges and Immunities Clause of Art. IV.

calling within the State. For example, in *Ward v. Maryland* (1871), a Maryland statute regulating the sale of most goods in the city of Baltimore fell to the privileges and immunities challenge of a New Jersey resident against whom the law discriminated. The statute discriminated against nonresidents of Maryland in several ways: It required nonresident merchants to obtain licenses in order to practice their trade without requiring the same of certain similarly situated Maryland merchants; it charged nonresidents a higher license fee than those Maryland residents who were required to secure licenses; and it prohibited both resident and nonresident merchants from using nonresident salesmen, other than their regular employees, to sell their goods in the city. In holding that the statute violated the Privileges and Immunities Clause, the Court observed that "the clause plainly and unmistakably secures and protects the right of a citizen of one State to pass into any other State of the Union for the purpose of engaging in lawful commerce, trade, or business without molestation." *Ward* thus recognized that a resident of one State is constitutionally entitled to travel to another State for purposes of employment free from discriminatory restrictions in favor of state residents imposed by the other State.

Again, *Toomer v. Witsell* (1948), the leading modern exposition of the limitations the Clause places on a State's power to bias employment opportunities in favor of its own residents, invalidated a South Carolina statute that required nonresidents to pay a fee 100 times greater than that paid by residents for a license to shrimp commercially in the three-mile maritime belt off the coast of that State. The Court reasoned that although the Privileges and Immunities Clause "does not preclude disparity of treatment in the many situations where there are perfectly valid independent reasons for it," "[i]t does bar discrimination against citizens of other States where there is no substantial reason for the discrimination beyond the mere fact that they are citizens of other States." A "substantial reason for the discrimination" would not exist, the Court explained, "unless there is something to indicate that noncitizens constitute a peculiar source of the evil at which the [discriminatory] statute is aimed." Moreover, even where the presence or activity of nonresidents causes or exacerbates the problem the State seeks to remedy, there must be a "reasonable relationship between the danger represented by non-citizens, as a class, and the . . . discrimination practiced upon them." *Toomer*'s analytical framework was confirmed in *Mullaney v. Anderson* (1952), where it was applied to invalidate a scheme used by the Territory of Alaska for the licensing of commercial fishermen in territorial waters; under that scheme residents paid a license fee of only $5 while nonresidents were charged $50.

Even assuming that a State may validly attempt to alleviate its unemployment problem by requiring private employers within the State to discriminate against nonresidents — an assumption made at least dubious by *Ward* — Alaska Hire's discrimination against nonresidents cannot withstand scrutiny under the Privileges and Immunities Clause. For although the statute may not violate the Clause if the State shows "something to indicate that noncitizens constitute a peculiar source of the evil at which the statute is aimed," *Toomer*, and, beyond this, the State "has no burden to prove that its laws are not violative of the . . . Clause," *Baldwin* (Brennan, J., dissenting), certainly no showing was made on this record that nonresidents were "a peculiar source of the evil" Alaska Hire was enacted to remedy, namely,

Alaska's "uniquely high unemployment." What evidence the record does contain indicates that the major cause of Alaska's high unemployment was not the influx of nonresidents seeking employment, but rather the fact that a substantial number of Alaska's jobless residents — especially the unemployed Eskimo and Indian residents — were unable to secure employment either because of their lack of education and job training or because of their geographical remoteness from job opportunities; and that the employment of nonresidents threatened to deny jobs to Alaska residents only to the extent that jobs for which untrained residents were being prepared might be filled by nonresidents before the residents' training was completed.

Moreover, even if the State's showing is accepted as sufficient to indicate that nonresidents were "a peculiar source of evil," *Toomer* and *Mullaney* compel the conclusion that Alaska Hire nevertheless fails to pass constitutional muster. For the discrimination the Act works against nonresidents does not bear a substantial relationship to the particular "evil" they are said to present. Alaska Hire simply grants all Alaskans, regardless of their employment status, education, or training, a flat employment preference for all jobs covered by the Act. A highly skilled and educated resident who has never been unemployed is entitled to precisely the same preferential treatment as the unskilled, habitually unemployed Arctic Eskimo enrolled in a job-training program. If Alaska is to attempt to ease its unemployment problem by forcing employers within the State to discriminate against nonresidents — again, a policy which may present serious constitutional questions — the means by which it does so must be more closely tailored to aid the unemployed the Act is intended to benefit. Even if a statute granting an employment preference to unemployed residents or to residents enrolled in job-training programs might be permissible, Alaska Hire's across-the-board grant of a job preference to all Alaskan residents clearly is not.

Relying on *McCready v. Virginia* (1877), however, Alaska contends that because the oil and gas that are the subject of Alaska Hire are owned by the State,[14] this ownership, of itself, is sufficient justification for the Act's discrimination against nonresidents, and takes the Act totally without the scope of the Privileges and Immunities Clause. As the State sees it "the privileges and immunities clause [does] not apply, and was never meant to apply, to decisions by the states as to how they would permit, if at all, the use and distribution of the natural resources which they own. . . ." We do not agree that the fact that a State owns a resource, of itself, completely removes a law concerning that resource from the prohibitions of the Clause. Although some courts, including the court below, have read *McCready* as creating an "exception" to the Privileges and Immunities Clause, we have just recently confirmed that "[i]n more recent years . . . the Court has recognized that the States' interest in regulating and controlling those things they claim to 'own' . . . is by no means absolute." *Baldwin*. Rather than placing a statute

[14] At the time Alaska was admitted into the Union on January 3, 1959, 99% of all land within Alaska's borders was owned by the Federal Government. In becoming a State, Alaska was granted and became entitled to select approximately 103 million acres of those federal lands. . . .

completely beyond the Clause, a State's ownership of the property with which the statute is concerned is a factor — although often the crucial factor — to be considered in evaluating whether the statute's discrimination against noncitizens violates the Clause. Dispositive though this factor may be in many cases in which a State discriminates against nonresidents, it is not dispositive here.

The reason is that Alaska has little or no proprietary interest in much of the activity swept within the ambit of Alaska Hire; and the connection of the State's oil and gas with much of the covered activity is sufficiently attenuated so that it cannot justifiably be the basis for requiring private employers to discriminate against nonresidents. . . .

Alaska Hire extends to employers who have no connection whatsoever with the State's oil and gas, perform no work on state land, have no contractual relationship with the State, and receive no payment from the State. The Act goes so far as to reach suppliers who provide goods or services to subcontractors who, in turn, perform work for contractors despite the fact that none of these employers may themselves have direct dealings with the State's oil and gas or ever set foot on state land. Moreover, the Act's coverage is not limited to activities connected with the extraction of Alaska's oil and gas. It encompasses, as emphasized by the dissent below, "employment opportunities at refineries and in distribution systems utilizing oil and gas obtained under Alaska leases." The only limit of any consequence on the Act's reach is the requirement that "the activity which generates the employment must take place inside the state." Although the absence of this limitation would be noteworthy, its presence hardly is; for it simply prevents Alaska Hire from having what would be the surprising effect of requiring potentially covered out-of-state employers to discriminate against residents of their own State in favor of nonresident Alaskans. In sum, the Act is an attempt to force virtually all businesses that benefit in some way from the economic ripple effect of Alaska's decision to develop its oil and gas resources to bias their employment practices in favor of the State's residents. We believe that Alaska's ownership of the oil and gas that is the subject matter of Alaska Hire simply constitutes insufficient justification for the pervasive discrimination against nonresidents that the Act mandates.

Although appellants raise no Commerce Clause challenge to the Act, the mutually reinforcing relationship between the Privileges and Immunities Clause of Art. IV, §2, and the Commerce Clause — a relationship that stems from their common origin in the Fourth Article of the Articles of Confederation[15] and

[15] That Article provided:

> The better to secure and perpetuate mutual friendship and intercourse among the people of the different states in this union, the free inhabitants of each of these states, paupers, vagabonds and fugitives from justice excepted, shall be entitled to all privileges and immunities of free citizens in the several states; and the people of each State shall have free ingress and regress to and from any other State, and shall enjoy therein all the privileges of trade and commerce, subject to the same duties, impositions, and restrictions, as the inhabitants thereof respectively; provided, that such restrictions shall not extend so far as to prevent the removal of property, imported into any State, to any other State of which the owner is an inhabitant; provided, also that no imposition, duties or restriction, shall be laid by any State on the property of the United States, or either of them.

their shared vision of federalism — renders several Commerce Clause decisions appropriate support for our conclusion. *West v. Kansas Natural Gas* (1911), struck down an Oklahoma statutory scheme that completely prohibited the out-of-state shipment of natural gas found within the State. The Court reasoned that if a State could so prefer its own economic well-being to that of the Nation as a whole, "Pennsylvania might keep its coal, the Northwest its timber, [and] the mining States their minerals," so that "embargo may be retaliated by embargo" with the result that "commerce [would] be halted at state lines." *West* was held to be controlling in *Pennsylvania v. West Virginia* (1923), where a West Virginia statute that effectively required natural gas companies within the State to satisfy all fuel needs of West Virginia residents before transporting any natural gas out of the State was held to violate the Commerce Clause. *West* and *Pennsylvania v. West Virginia* thus established that the location in a given State of a resource bound for interstate commerce is an insufficient basis for preserving the benefits of the resource exclusively or even principally for that State's residents. *Foster Packing Co. v. Haydel* (1928), went one step further; it limited the extent to which a State's purported ownership of certain resources could serve as a justification for the State's economic discrimination in favor of residents. There, in the face of Louisiana's claim that the State owned all shrimp within state waters, the Court invalidated a Louisiana law that required the local processing of shrimp taken from Louisiana marshes as a prerequisite to their out-of-state shipment. The Court observed that "by permitting its shrimp to be taken and all the products thereof to be shipped and sold in interstate commerce, the State necessarily releases its hold and, as to the shrimp so taken, definitely terminates its control."

West, Pennsylvania v. West Virginia, and *Foster Packing* thus establish that the Commerce Clause circumscribes a State's ability to prefer its own citizens in the utilization of natural resources found within its borders, but destined for interstate commerce. Like Louisiana's shrimp in *Foster Packing*, Alaska's oil and gas here are bound for out-of-state consumption. Indeed, the construction of the Trans-Alaska Pipeline, on which project appellants' nonresidency has prevented them from working, was undertaken expressly to accomplish this end. Although the fact that a state-owned resource is destined for interstate commerce does not, of itself, disable the State from preferring its own citizens in the utilization of that resource, it does inform analysis under the Privileges and Immunities Clause as to the permissibility of the discrimination the State visits upon nonresidents based on its ownership of the resource. Here, the oil and gas upon which Alaska hinges its discrimination against nonresidents are of profound national importance. On the other hand, the breadth of the discrimination mandated by Alaska Hire goes far beyond the degree of resident bias Alaska's ownership of the oil and gas can justifiably support. The confluence of these realities points to but one conclusion: Alaska Hire cannot withstand constitutional scrutiny. As Mr. Justice Cardozo observed in *Baldwin v. G. A. F. Seelig* (1935), the Constitution "was framed upon the theory that the peoples of the several states must sink or swim together, and that in the long run prosperity and salvation are in union and not division."

Reversed.

C. IMPLIED LIMITS ON STATE POWERS TO REGULATE ELECTIONS

ASSIGNMENT 4

We conclude our consideration of constraints imposed on state law by federalism with *U.S. Term Limits, Inc. v. Thornton*. This case returns us to the issue of sovereignty—first discussed in *Chisholm v. Georgia* (Chapter 1)—that runs throughout the materials in the first part of the casebook. *U.S. Term Limits* illustrates how disagreement about the nature of what the Court has described as a "fundamental principle of our representative democracy" can still lead to divergent results in important cases.

The term limits movement was a grassroots effort to achieve "rotation in office." Although some framers of the Constitution argued in favor of this position, it was not adopted in the original constitutional scheme. Notice that the principle of "rotation in office" now applies to the President according to the Twenty-Second Amendment, which says:

> No person shall be elected to the office of the President more than twice, and no person who has held the office of President, or acted as President, for more than two years of a term to which some other person was elected President shall be elected to the office of the President more than once. . . .

The "Contract with America," on which congressional Republicans ran for office in 1994, pledged the party to bring to a vote a constitutional amendment mandating term limits for members of Congress. While it received a majority of votes in the House,[16] it failed to muster the supermajority needed to submit the amendment to the states. While the attempt to achieve change at the federal level failed, the effort to achieve this result state by state continued.

STUDY GUIDE

- In the next case, do the majority opinion and the dissent disagree about who are "the People"? Or do they disagree about how "the People" are supposed to express their will?
- Does Justice Thomas adopt the "compact theory" of the national government? If so, wasn't this theory discredited by the Civil War? If not, what exactly is his theory?

[16] The Citizen Legislature Act failed by a vote of 227 in favor to 204 opposed along largely party lines: Republican (189-40); Democratic (38-163). That there were insufficient votes for passage was well known before the vote, so this count does not necessarily reflect how representatives would have voted if they had believed that passage was actually possible.

- Notice how this case raises the issue of how to construe the Constitution when the text and the historical record are largely silent about the particular issue at hand.
- Why is the majority so focused on the intentions of "the Framers"? Would a "living constitution" approach to constitutional interpretation justify the Court in upholding the Arkansas constitution? If not, why not?

U.S. Term Limits, Inc. v. Thornton

514 U.S. 779 (1995)

JUSTICE STEVENS delivered the opinion of the Court.

The Constitution sets forth qualifications for membership in the Congress of the United States. Article I, §2, cl. 2, which applies to the House of Representatives, provides:

> No Person shall be a Representative who shall not have attained to the Age of twenty five Years, and been seven Years a Citizen of the United States, and who shall not, when elected, be an Inhabitant of that State in which he shall be chosen.

Article I, §3, cl. 3, which applies to the Senate, similarly provides:

> No Person shall be a Senator who shall not have attained to the Age of thirty Years, and been nine Years a Citizen of the United States, and who shall not, when elected, be an Inhabitant of that State for which he shall be chosen.

Today's cases present a challenge to an amendment to the Arkansas State Constitution that prohibits the name of an otherwise eligible candidate for Congress from appearing on the general election ballot if that candidate has already served three terms in the House of Representatives or two terms in the Senate. The Arkansas Supreme Court held that the amendment violates the Federal Constitution. We agree with that holding. Such a state-imposed restriction is contrary to the "fundamental principle of our representative democracy," embodied in the Constitution, that "the people should choose whom they please to govern them." *Powell v. McCormack* (1969). Allowing individual States to adopt their own qualifications for congressional service would be inconsistent with the Framers' vision of a uniform National Legislature representing the people of the United States. If the qualifications set forth in the text of the Constitution are to be changed, that text must be amended.

At the general election on November 3, 1992, the voters of Arkansas adopted Amendment 73 to their State Constitution. Proposed as a "Term Limitation Amendment," its preamble stated:

> The people of Arkansas find and declare that elected officials who remain in office too long become preoccupied with reelection and ignore their duties as representatives of the people. Entrenched incumbency has reduced voter participation and has led to an

> electoral system that is less free, less competitive, and less representative than the system established by the Founding Fathers. Therefore, the people of Arkansas, exercising their reserved powers, herein limit the terms of the elected officials.
>
> . . .

Section 3, the provision at issue in these cases, applies to the Arkansas Congressional Delegation. It provides:

> (a) Any person having been elected to three or more terms as a member of the United States House of Representatives from Arkansas shall not be certified as a candidate and shall not be eligible to have his/her name placed on the ballot for election to the United States House of Representatives from Arkansas.
>
> (b) Any person having been elected to two or more terms as a member of the United States Senate from Arkansas shall not be certified as a candidate and shall not be eligible to have his/her name placed on the ballot for election to the United States Senate from Arkansas.

. . . First, we conclude that the power to add qualifications is not within the "original powers" of the States, and thus is not reserved to the States by the Tenth Amendment. Second, even if States possessed some original power in this area, we conclude that the Framers intended the Constitution to be the exclusive source of qualifications for members of Congress, and that the Framers thereby "divested" States of any power to add qualifications. . . .

Source of the Power

Contrary to petitioners' assertions, the power to add qualifications is not part of the original powers of sovereignty that the Tenth Amendment reserved to the States. Petitioners' Tenth Amendment argument misconceives the nature of the right at issue because that Amendment could only "reserve" that which existed before. As Justice Story recognized, "the states can exercise no powers whatsoever, which exclusively spring out of the existence of the national government, which the constitution does not delegate to them. . . . No state can say, that it has reserved, what it never possessed." 1 Story §627. . . .

With respect to setting qualifications for service in Congress, no such right existed before the Constitution was ratified. The contrary argument overlooks the revolutionary character of the government that the Framers conceived. Prior to the adoption of the Constitution, the States had joined together under the Articles of Confederation. . . . After the Constitutional Convention convened, the Framers were presented with, and eventually adopted a variation of, "a plan not merely to amend the Articles of Confederation but to create an entirely new National Government with a National Executive, National Judiciary, and a National Legislature." In adopting that plan, the Framers envisioned a uniform national system, rejecting the notion that the Nation was a collection of States, and instead creating a direct link between the National Government and the people of the United States. In that National Government, representatives owe primary allegiance not to the people of a State, but to the people of the Nation. As Justice Story observed, each Member of Congress is "an officer of the union, deriving his powers and qualifications from the constitution, and neither created by, dependent upon, nor controllable by, the states. . . . Those officers owe their existence and functions to the united voice of the whole, not of a portion, of the people." 1 Story §627. Representatives and Senators are as much officers of the entire union as is the President. States thus "have just as much right, and no more, to prescribe new qualifications for a representative, as they have for a president. . . . It is no original prerogative of state power to appoint a representative, a senator, or president for the union."

We believe that the Constitution reflects the Framers' general agreement with the approach later articulated by Justice Story. For example, Art. I, §5, cl. 1 provides: "Each House shall be the Judge of the Elections, Returns and Qualifications of its own Members." The text of the Constitution thus gives the representatives of all the people the final say in judging the qualifications of the representatives of any one State. For this reason, the dissent falters when it states that "the people of Georgia have no say over whom the people of Massachusetts select to represent them in Congress."

Two other sections of the Constitution further support our view of the Framers' vision. First, consistent with Story's view, the Constitution provides that the salaries of representatives should "be ascertained by Law, and paid out of the Treasury of the United States," Art. I, §6, rather than by individual States. The salary provisions reflect the view that representatives owe their allegiance to the people, and not to States. Second, the provisions governing elections reveal the Framers' understanding that powers over the election of federal officers had to be delegated to, rather than reserved by, the States. It is surely no coincidence that the context of federal elections provides one of the few areas in which the Constitution expressly requires action by the States, namely that "[t]he Times, Places and Manner of holding Elections for Senators and Representatives, shall be prescribed in each State by the legislature thereof." This duty parallels the duty under Article II that "each State shall appoint, in such Manner as the Legislature thereof may direct, a Number of Electors." Art II., §1, cl. 2. These Clauses are express delegations of power to the States to act with respect to federal elections. . . .

In short, as the Framers recognized, electing representatives to the National Legislature was a new right, arising from the Constitution itself. The Tenth Amendment thus provides no basis for concluding that the States possess reserved power to add qualifications to those that are fixed in the Constitution. Instead, any state power to set the qualifications for membership in Congress must derive not from the reserved powers of state sovereignty, but rather from the delegated powers of national sovereignty. In the absence of any constitutional delegation to the States of power to add qualifications to those enumerated in the Constitution, such a power does not exist.

The Preclusion of State Power

Even if we believed that States possessed as part of their original powers some control over congressional qualifications, the text and structure of the Constitution, the relevant historical materials, and, most importantly, the "basic principles of our democratic system" all demonstrate that the Qualifications Clauses were intended to preclude the States from exercising any such power and to fix as exclusive the qualifications in the Constitution. . . .

The Convention and Ratification Debates

The available affirmative evidence indicates the Framers' intent that States have no role in the setting of qualifications. In *Federalist Paper, No. 52,* dealing with the House of Representatives, Madison addressed the "qualifications of the electors and the elected." Madison first noted the difficulty in achieving uniformity in the qualifications for electors, which resulted in the Framers' decision to require only that the qualifications for federal electors be the same as those for state electors. Madison argued that such a decision "must be satisfactory to every State, because it is comfortable to the standard already established, or which may be established, by the State itself." Madison then explicitly contrasted the state control over the qualifications of electors with the lack of state control over the qualifications of the elected:

> The qualifications of the elected, being less carefully and properly defined by the State constitutions, and being at the same time more susceptible of uniformity, have been very properly considered and regulated by the convention. A representative of the United States must be of the age of twenty-five years; must have been seven years a citizen of the United States; must, at the time of his election be an inhabitant of the State he is to represent; and, during the time of his service must be in no office under the United States. Under these reasonable limitations, the door of this part of the federal government is open to merit of every description, whether native or adoptive, whether young or old, and without regard to poverty or wealth, or to any particular profession of religious faith.

Madison emphasized this same idea in *Federalist 57*:

> Who are to be the objects of popular choice? Every citizen whose merit may recommend him to the esteem and confidence of his country. *No qualification of wealth, of birth, of religious faith, or of civil profession is permitted to fetter the judgment or disappoint the inclination of the people.* (emphasis added).

The provisions in the Constitution governing federal elections confirm the Framers' intent that States lack power to add qualifications. The Framers feared that the diverse interests of the States would undermine the National Legislature, and thus they adopted provisions intended to minimize the possibility of state interference with federal elections. For example, to prevent discrimination against federal electors, the Framers required in Art. I, §2, cl. 1, that the qualifications for federal electors be the same as those for state electors. As Madison noted, allowing States to differentiate between the qualifications for state and federal electors "would have rendered too dependent on the State governments that branch of the federal government which ought to be dependent on the people alone." *The Federalist, No. 52.* Similarly, in Art. I, §4, cl. 1, though giving the States the freedom to regulate the "Times, Places and Manner of holding Elections," the Framers created a safeguard against state abuse by giving Congress the power to "by Law make or alter such Regulations." The Convention debates make clear that the Framers' overriding concern was the potential for States' abuse of the power to set the

"Times, Places and Manner" of elections. Madison noted that "[i]t was impossible to foresee all the abuses that might be made of the discretionary power." Gouverneur Morris feared "that the States might make false returns and then make no provisions for new elections." When Charles Pinckney and John Rutledge moved to strike the congressional safeguard, the motion was soundly defeated. As Hamilton later noted: "Nothing can be more evident than that an exclusive power of regulating elections for the national government, in the hands of the State legislatures, would leave the existence of the Union entirely at their mercy." *The Federalist, No. 59.*

The Framers' discussion of the salary of representatives reveals similar concerns. When the issue was first raised, Madison argued that congressional compensation should be fixed in the Constitution, rather than left to state legislatures, because otherwise "it would create an improper dependence." George Mason agreed, noting that "the parsimony of the States might reduce the provision so low that . . . the question would be not who were most fit to be chosen, but who were most willing to serve."

When the issue was later reopened, Nathaniel Gorham stated that he "wished not to refer the matter to the State Legislatures who were always paring down salaries in such a manner as to keep out of offices men most capable of executing the functions of them." Edmund Randolph agreed that "[i]f the States were to pay the members of the Nat[ional] Legislature, a dependence would be created that would vitiate the whole System." Rufus King "urged the danger of creating a dependence on the States," and Hamilton noted that "[t]hose who pay are the masters of those who are paid." The Convention ultimately agreed to vest in Congress the power to set its own compensation. See Art. I, §6.

In light of the Framers' evident concern that States would try to undermine the National Government, they could not have intended States to have the power to set qualifications. Indeed, one of the more anomalous consequences of petitioners' argument is that it accepts federal supremacy over the procedural aspects of determining the times, places, and manner of elections while allowing the states carte blanche with respect to the substantive qualifications for membership in Congress.

The dissent nevertheless contends that the Framers' distrust of the States with respect to elections does not preclude the people of the States from adopting eligibility requirements to help narrow their own choices. As the dissent concedes, however, the Framers were unquestionably concerned that the States would simply not hold elections for federal officers, and therefore the Framers gave Congress the power to "make or alter" state election regulations. Yet under the dissent's approach, the States could achieve exactly the same result by simply setting qualifications for federal office sufficiently high that no one could meet those qualifications. In our view, it is inconceivable that the Framers would provide a specific constitutional provision to ensure that federal elections would be held while at the same time allowing States to render those elections meaningless by simply ensuring that no candidate could be qualified for office. Given the Framers' wariness over the potential for state abuse, we must conclude that the specification of fixed qualifications in the constitutional text was intended to prescribe uniform rules that would preclude modification by either Congress or the States.

We find further evidence of the Framers' intent in Art. 1, §5, cl. 1, which provides: "Each House shall be the Judge of the Elections, Returns and Qualifications of its own Members." That Art. I, §5 vests a federal tribunal with ultimate authority to judge a Member's qualifications is fully consistent with the understanding that those qualifications are fixed in the Federal Constitution, but not with the understanding that they can be altered by the States. If the States had the right to prescribe additional qualifications — such as property, educational, or professional qualifications — for their own representatives, state law would provide the standard for judging a Member's eligibility. . . . The judging of questions concerning rights which depend on state law is not, however, normally assigned to federal tribunals. The Constitution's provision for each House to be the judge of its own qualifications thus provides further evidence that the Framers believed that the primary source of those qualifications would be federal law.

We also find compelling the complete absence in the ratification debates of any assertion that States had the power to add qualifications. In those debates, the question whether to require term limits, or "rotation," was a major source of controversy. The draft of the Constitution that was submitted for ratification contained no provision for rotation. In arguments that echo in the preamble to Arkansas' Amendment 73, opponents of ratification condemned the absence of a rotation requirement, noting that "there is no doubt that senators will hold their office perpetually; and in this situation, they must of necessity lose their dependence, and their attachments to the people." Even proponents of ratification expressed concern about the "abandonment in every instance of the necessity of rotation in office." At several ratification conventions, participants proposed amendments that would have required rotation. . . .

Regardless of which side has the better of the debate over rotation, it is most striking that nowhere in the extensive ratification debates have we found any statement by either a proponent or an opponent of rotation that the draft constitution would permit States to require rotation for the representatives of their own citizens. If the participants in the debate had believed that the States retained the authority to impose term limits, it is inconceivable that the Federalists would not have made this obvious response to the arguments of the pro-rotation forces. The absence in an otherwise freewheeling debate of any suggestion that States had the power to impose additional qualifications unquestionably reflects the Framers' common understanding that States lacked that power.

In short, if it had been assumed that States could add additional qualifications, that assumption would have provided the basis for a powerful rebuttal to the arguments being advanced. The failure of intelligent and experienced advocates to utilize this argument must reflect a general agreement that its premise was unsound, and that the power to add qualifications was one that the Constitution denied the States. . . .

Democratic Principles

Our conclusion that States lack the power to impose qualifications vindicates the same "fundamental principle of our representative democracy" . . . namely that "the people should choose whom they please to govern them." . . . This egalitarian theme echoes throughout the constitutional debates. In *The Federalist, No. 57*, for example, Madison wrote: "Who are to be the objects of popular choice? Every citizen whose merit may recommend him to the esteem and confidence of his country. No qualification of wealth, of birth, of religious faith, or of civil profession is permitted to fetter the judgment or disappoint the inclination of the people." *The Federalist, No. 57*. . . . State-imposed restrictions . . . violate a[n] . . . idea central to this basic principle: that the right to choose representatives belongs not to the States, but to the people. From the start, the Framers recognized that the "great and radical vice" of the Articles of Confederation was "the principle of LEGISLATION for STATES or GOVERNMENTS, in their CORPORATE or COLLECTIVE CAPACITIES, and as contradistinguished from the INDIVIDUALS of whom they consist." *The Federalist, No. 15* (Hamilton). Thus the Framers, in perhaps their most important contribution, conceived of a Federal Government directly responsible to the people, possessed of direct power over the people, and chosen directly, not by States, but by the people. . . . The Congress of the United States, therefore, is not a confederation of nations in which separate sovereigns are represented by appointed delegates, but is instead a body composed of representatives of the people. As Chief Justice John Marshall observed: "The government of the union, then, . . . is, emphatically, and truly, a government of the people. In form and in substance it emanates from them. Its powers are granted by them, and are to be exercised directly on them, and for their benefit." *McCulloch v. Maryland*. . . .

The Framers deemed this principle critical when they discussed qualifications. For example, during the debates on residency requirements, Morris noted that in the House, "*the people at large*, not the *States*, are represented." (emphasis in original). Similarly, George Read noted that the Framers "were forming a *Nati[ona]l* Gov[ernmen]t and such a regulation would correspond little with the idea that we were one people." (Emphasis in original.) . . . Consistent with these views, the constitutional structure provides for a uniform salary to be paid from the national treasury, allows the States but a limited role in federal elections, and maintains strict checks on state interference with the federal election process. The Constitution also provides that the qualifications of the representatives of each State will be judged by the representatives of the entire Nation. The Constitution thus creates a uniform national body representing the interests of a single people.

Permitting individual States to formulate diverse qualifications for their representatives would result in a patchwork of state qualifications, undermining the uniformity and the national character that the Framers envisioned and sought to ensure. Such a patchwork would also sever the direct link that the Framers found so critical between the National Government and the people of the United States. . . .

The merits of term limits, or "rotation," have been the subject of debate since the formation of our Constitution, when the Framers unanimously rejected a proposal to add such limits to the Constitution. The cogent arguments on both sides of the question that were articulated during the process of ratification largely retain their force today. . . . It is not our province to resolve this longstanding debate.

We are, however, firmly convinced that allowing the several States to adopt term limits for congressional service would effect a fundamental change in the constitutional framework. Any such change must come not by legislation adopted either by Congress or by an individual State, but rather — as have other important changes in the electoral process — through the Amendment procedures set forth in Article V. . . . In the absence of a properly passed constitutional amendment, allowing individual States to craft their own qualifications for Congress would thus erode the structure envisioned by the Framers, a structure that was designed, in the words of the Preamble to our Constitution, to form a "more perfect Union."

The judgment is affirmed.

Justice Kennedy, concurring.

. . . In my view, . . . it is well settled that the whole people of the United States asserted their political identity and unity of purpose when they created the federal system. . . .

Federalism was our Nation's own discovery. The Framers split the atom of sovereignty. It was the genius of their idea that our citizens would have two political capacities, one state and one federal, each protected from incursion by the other. The resulting Constitution created a legal system unprecedented in form and design, establishing two orders of government, each with its own direct relationship, its own privity, its own set of mutual rights and obligations to the people who sustain it and are governed by it. It is appropriate to recall these origins, which instruct us as to the nature of the two different governments created and confirmed by the Constitution.

A distinctive character of the National Government, the mark of its legitimacy, is that it owes its existence to the act of the whole people who created it. It must be remembered that the National Government too is republican in essence and in theory. . . . Once the National Government was formed under our Constitution, the same republican principles continued to guide its operation and practice. As James Madison explained, the House of Representatives "derive[s] its powers from the people of America," and "the operation of the government on the people in their individual capacities" makes it "a national government," not merely a federal one. *The Federalist, No. 39.* The Court confirmed this principle in *McCulloch v. Maryland* (1819), when it said, "The government of the Union, then . . . is, emphatically, and truly, a government of the people. In form and in substance it emanates from them. Its powers are granted by them, and are to be exercised directly on them, and for their benefit." . . .

In one sense it is true that "the people of each State retained their separate political identities," for the Constitution takes care both to preserve the States and to make use of their identities and structures at various points in organizing the federal union. It does not at all follow from this that the sole political identity of an American is with the State of his or her residence. It denies the dual character of the Federal Government which is its very foundation to assert that the people of the United States do not have a political identity as well, one independent of, though consistent with, their identity as citizens of the State of their residence. . . .

Of course, because the Framers recognized that state power and identity were essential parts of the federal balance, the Constitution is solicitous of the prerogatives of the States, even in an otherwise sovereign federal province. . . . Nothing in the Constitution or *The Federalist Papers*, however, supports the idea of state interference with the most basic relation between the National Government and its citizens, the selection of legislative representatives. . . .

The federal character of congressional elections flows from the political reality that our National Government is republican in form and that national citizenship has privileges and immunities protected from state abridgement by the force of the Constitution itself. . . . Federal privileges and immunities may seem limited in their formulation by comparison with the expansive definition given to the privileges and immunities attributed to state citizenship, see *Slaughter-House Cases*, but that federal rights flow to the people of the United States by virtue of national citizenship is beyond dispute. . . .

It is maintained by our dissenting colleagues that the State of Arkansas seeks nothing more than to grant its people surer control over the National Government, a control, it is said, that will be enhanced by the law at issue here. The arguments for term limitations (or ballot restrictions having the same effect) are not lacking in force; but the issue, as all of us must acknowledge, is not the efficacy of those measures but whether they have a legitimate source, given their origin in the enactments of a single State. There can be no doubt, if we are to respect the republican origins of the Nation and preserve its federal character, that there exists a federal right of citizenship, a relationship between the people of the Nation and their National Government, with which the States may not interfere. Because the Arkansas enactment intrudes upon this federal domain, it exceeds the boundaries of the Constitution.

JUSTICE THOMAS, with whom THE CHIEF JUSTICE, JUSTICE O'CONNOR, and JUSTICE SCALIA join, dissenting.

It is ironic that the Court bases today's decision on the right of the people to "choose whom they please to govern them." Under our Constitution, there is only one State whose people have the right to "choose whom they please" to represent Arkansas in Congress. The Court holds, however, that neither the elected legislature of that State nor the people themselves (acting by ballot initiative) may prescribe any qualifications for those representatives. The majority therefore defends the right of the people of Arkansas to "choose whom they please to govern them" by invalidating a provision that won nearly 60% of the votes cast in a direct election and that carried every congressional district in the State.

I dissent. Nothing in the Constitution deprives the people of each State of the power to prescribe eligibility requirements for the candidates who seek to represent them in Congress. The Constitution is simply silent on this question. And where the Constitution is silent, it raises no bar to action by the States or the people.

Because the majority fundamentally misunderstands the notion of "reserved" powers, I start with some first principles. Contrary to the majority's suggestion, the people of the States need not point to any affirmative grant of power in the Constitution in order to prescribe qualifications for their representatives in Congress, or to authorize their elected state legislators to do so.

Our system of government rests on one overriding principle: all power stems from the consent of the people. To phrase the principle in this way, however, is to be imprecise about something important to the notion of "reserved" powers. The ultimate source of the Constitution's authority is the consent of the people of each individual State, not the consent of the undifferentiated people of the Nation as a whole.

The ratification procedure erected by Article VII makes this point clear. The Constitution took effect once it had been ratified by the people gathered in convention in nine different States. But the Constitution went into effect only "between the States so ratifying the same," Art. VII; it did not bind the people of North Carolina until they had accepted it. In Madison's words, the popular consent upon which the Constitution's authority rests was "given by the people, not as individuals composing one entire nation, but as composing the distinct and independent States to which they respectively belong" *The Federalist, No. 39.*[17]

When they adopted the Federal Constitution, of course, the people of each State surrendered some of their authority to the United States (and hence to entities accountable to the people of other States as well as to themselves). They affirmatively deprived their States of certain powers, see, e.g., Art. I, §10, and they affirmatively conferred certain powers upon the Federal Government, see, e.g., Art. I, §8. Because the people of the several States are the only true source of power, however, the Federal Government enjoys no authority beyond what the Constitution confers: the Federal Government's powers are limited and enumerated. . . .

In each State, the remainder of the people's powers . . . are either delegated to the state government or retained by the people. The Federal Constitution does not specify which of these two possibilities obtains; it is up to the various state constitutions to declare which powers the people of each State have delegated to their state government. As far as the Federal Constitution is concerned, then, the States can exercise all powers that the Constitution does not withhold from them. The Federal Government and the States thus face different default rules: where the Constitution is silent about the exercise of a particular power — that is, where the Constitution does not speak either expressly or by necessary implication — the Federal Government lacks that power and the States enjoy it.

These basic principles are enshrined in the Tenth Amendment, which declares that all powers neither delegated to the Federal Government nor prohibited to the States "are reserved to the States respectively, or to the people." With this careful last phrase, the Amendment avoids taking any position on the division of power between the state governments and the people of the States: it is up to the people of each State to determine which "reserved" powers their state government may exercise. But the Amendment does make clear that powers reside at the state level except where the Constitution removes them from that level. All powers that the Constitution neither delegates to the Federal Government nor prohibits to the States are controlled by the people of each State.

---

[17] The ringing initial words of the Constitution — "We the People of the United States" — convey something of the same idea. (In the Constitution, after all, "the United States" is consistently a plural noun. See Art. I, §9, cl. 8; Art. II, §1, cl. 7; Art. III, §2, cl. 1; Art. III, §3, cl. 1.) . . .

To be sure, when the Tenth Amendment uses the phrase "the people," it does not specify whether it is referring to the people of each State or the people of the Nation as a whole. But the latter interpretation would make the Amendment pointless: there would have been no reason to provide that where the Constitution is silent about whether a particular power resides at the state level, it might or might not do so. In addition, it would make no sense to speak of powers as being reserved to the undifferentiated people of the Nation as a whole, because the Constitution does not contemplate that those people will either exercise power or delegate it. The Constitution simply does not recognize any mechanism for action by the undifferentiated people of the Nation. Thus, the amendment provision of Article V calls for amendments to be ratified not by a convention of the national people, but by conventions of the people in each State or by the state legislatures elected by those people. Likewise, the Constitution calls for Members of Congress to be chosen State by State, rather than in nationwide elections. Even the selection of the President — surely the most national of national figures — is accomplished by an electoral college made up of delegates chosen by the various States, and candidates can lose a Presidential election despite winning a majority of the votes cast in the Nation as a whole. See also Art. II, §1, cl. 3 (providing that when no candidate secures a majority of electoral votes, the election of the President is thrown into the House of Representatives, where "the Votes shall be taken by States, the Representatives from each State having one Vote"); Amdt. 12 (same).

In short, the notion of popular sovereignty that undergirds the Constitution does not erase state boundaries, but rather tracks them. The people of each State obviously did trust their fate to the people of the several States when they consented to the Constitution; not only did they empower the governmental institutions of the United States, but they also agreed to be bound by constitutional amendments that they themselves refused to ratify. See Art. V (providing that proposed amendments shall take effect upon ratification by three quarters of the States). At the same time, however, the people of each State retained their separate political identities. As Chief Justice Marshall put it, "[n]o political dreamer was ever wild enough to think of breaking down the lines which separate the States, and of compounding the American people into one common mass." *McCulloch v. Maryland* (1819).

Any ambiguity in the Tenth Amendment's use of the phrase "the people" is cleared up by the body of the Constitution itself. Article I begins by providing that the Congress of the United States enjoys "[a]ll legislative Powers herein granted," §1, and goes on to give a careful enumeration of Congress' powers, §8. It then concludes by enumerating certain powers that are *prohibited* to the States. The import of this structure is the same as the import of the Tenth Amendment: if we are to invalidate Arkansas' Amendment 73, we must point to something in the Federal Constitution that deprives the people of Arkansas of the power to enact such measures.

The majority disagrees that it bears this burden. But its arguments are unpersuasive.

The majority begins by announcing an enormous and untenable limitation on the principle expressed by the Tenth Amendment. According to the majority, the States possess only those powers that the Constitution affirmatively grants to them or that they enjoyed before the Constitution was adopted; the Tenth Amendment "could only 'reserve' that which existed before." From the fact that the States had not previously enjoyed any powers over the particular institutions of the Federal Government established by the Constitution,[18] the majority derives a rule precisely opposite to the one that the Amendment actually prescribes: "[T]he states can exercise no powers whatsoever, which exclusively spring out of the existence of the national government, which the constitution does not delegate to them."

The majority's essential logic is that the state governments could not "reserve" any powers that they did not control at the time the Constitution was drafted. But it was not the state governments that were doing the reserving. The Constitution derives its authority instead from the consent of the people of the States. Given the fundamental principle that all governmental powers stem from the people of the States, it would simply be incoherent to assert that the people of the States could not reserve any powers that they had not previously controlled.

The Tenth Amendment's use of the word "reserved" does not help the majority's position. If someone says that the power to use a particular facility is reserved to some group, he is not saying anything about whether that group has previously used the facility. He is merely saying that the people who control the facility have designated that group as the entity with authority to use it. The Tenth Amendment is similar: the people of the States, from whom all governmental powers stem, have specified that all powers not prohibited to the States by the Federal Constitution are reserved "to the States respectively, or to the people."

The majority is therefore quite wrong to conclude that the people of the States cannot authorize their state governments to exercise any powers that were unknown to the States when the Federal Constitution was drafted. Indeed, the majority's position frustrates the apparent purpose of the Amendment's final phrase. The Amendment does not pre-empt any limitations on state power found in the state constitutions, as it might have done if it simply had said that the powers not delegated to the Federal Government are reserved to the States. But the Amendment also does not prevent the people of the States from amending their state constitutions to remove limitations that were in effect when the Federal Constitution and the Bill of Rights were ratified. . . .

The majority also seeks support for its view of the Tenth Amendment in *McCulloch v. Maryland*. But this effort is misplaced. *McCulloch* did make clear that a power need not be "expressly" delegated to the United States or prohibited to the States in order to fall outside the Tenth Amendment's reservation; delegations and prohibitions can also arise by necessary implication. True to the text of the Tenth Amendment, however, *McCulloch* indicated that all powers as to which the Constitution does not speak (whether expressly or by necessary implication) are

---

[18] At the time of the Framing, of course, a Federal Congress had been operating under the Articles of Confederation for some 10 years. The States unquestionably had enjoyed the power to establish qualifications for their delegates to this body, above and beyond the qualifications created by the Articles themselves. It is surprising, then, that the concurring opinion seeks to buttress the majority's case by stressing the continuing applicability of "the same republican principles" that had prevailed under the Articles.

"reserved" to the state level. Thus, in its only discussion of the Tenth Amendment, *McCulloch* observed that the Amendment "leav[es] the question, whether the particular power which may become the subject of contest has been delegated to the one government, or prohibited to the other, to depend on a fair construction of the whole [Constitution]." *McCulloch* did not qualify this observation by indicating that the question also turned on whether the States had enjoyed the power before the framing. To the contrary, *McCulloch* seemed to assume that the people had "conferred on the general government the power contained in the constitution, and on the States the whole residuum of power."

The structure of *McCulloch*'s analysis also refutes the majority's position. The question before the Court was whether the State of Maryland could tax the Bank of the United States, which Congress had created in an effort to accomplish objects entrusted to it by the Constitution. Chief Justice Marshall's opinion began by upholding the federal statute incorporating the Bank. It then held that the Constitution affirmatively prohibited Maryland's tax on the Bank created by this statute. The Court relied principally on concepts that it deemed inherent in the Supremacy Clause. . . . In the Court's view, when a power has been "delegated to the United States by the Constitution," Amdt. 10, the Supremacy Clause forbids a State to "retard, impede, burden, or in any manner control, the operations of the constitutional laws enacted by Congress to carry [that power] into execution." *McCulloch*. Thus, the Court concluded that the very nature of state taxation on the Bank's operations was "incompatible with, and repugnant to," the federal statute creating the Bank.

For the past 175 years, *McCulloch* has been understood to rest on the proposition that the Constitution affirmatively barred Maryland from imposing its tax on the Bank's operations. For the majority, however, *McCulloch* apparently turned on the fact that before the Constitution was adopted, the States had possessed no power to tax the instrumentalities of the governmental institutions that the Constitution created. This understanding of *McCulloch* makes most of Chief Justice Marshall's opinion irrelevant; according to the majority, there was no need to inquire into whether federal law deprived Maryland of the power in question, because the power could not fall into the category of "reserved" powers anyway. . . .

[T]he only true support for [the majority's] view of the Tenth Amendment comes from Joseph Story's 1833 treatise on constitutional law. Justice Story was a brilliant and accomplished man, and one cannot casually dismiss his views. On the other hand, he was not a member of the Founding generation, and his Commentaries on the Constitution were written a half century after the framing. Rather than representing the original understanding of the Constitution, they represent only his own understanding. In a range of cases concerning the federal/state relation, moreover, this Court has deemed positions taken in Story's commentaries to be more nationalist than the Constitution warrants. . . . In this case too, Story's position that the only powers reserved to the States are those that the States enjoyed before the framing conflicts with both the plain language of the Tenth Amendment and the underlying theory of the Constitution.

The majority also sketches out what may be an alternative (and narrower) argument. Again citing Story, the majority suggests that it would be inconsistent with the notion of "national sovereignty" for the States or the people of the States to have any reserved powers over the selection of Members of Congress. The majority apparently reaches this conclusion in two steps. First, it asserts that because Congress as a whole is an institution of the National Government, the individual Members of Congress "owe primary allegiance not to the people of a State, but to the people of the Nation." Second, it concludes that because each Member of Congress has a nationwide constituency once he takes office, it would be inconsistent with the Framers' scheme to let a single State prescribe qualifications for him.

Political scientists can debate about who commands the "primary allegiance" of Members of Congress once they reach Washington. From the framing to the present, however, the selection of the Representatives and Senators from each State has been left entirely to the people of that State or to their state legislature. See Art. I, §2, cl. 1 (providing that members of the House of Representatives are chosen "by the People of the several States"); Art. I, §3, cl. 1 (originally providing that the Senators from each State are "chosen by the Legislature thereof"); Amdt. 17 (amending §3 to provide that the Senators from each State are "elected by the people thereof"). The very name "congress" suggests a coming together of representatives from distinct entities. In keeping with the complexity of our federal system, once the representatives chosen by the people of each State assemble in Congress, they form a national body and are beyond the control of the individual States until the next election. But the selection of representatives in Congress is indisputably an act of the people of each State, not some abstract people of the Nation as a whole.

The concurring opinion . . . protests that the exercise of "reserved" powers in the area of congressional elections would constitute "state interference with the most basic relation between the National Government and its citizens, the selection of legislative representatives." But when one strips away its abstractions, the concurring opinion is simply saying that the people of Arkansas cannot be permitted to inject themselves into the process by which they themselves select Arkansas' representatives in Congress.

The concurring opinion attempts to defend this surprising proposition by pointing out that Americans are "citizens of the United States" as well as "of the State wherein they reside," Amdt. XIV, §1, and that national citizenship (particularly after the ratification of the Fourteenth Amendment) "has privileges and immunities protected from state abridgement by the force of the Constitution itself." These facts are indeed "beyond dispute," but they do not contradict anything that I have said. Although the United States obviously is a Nation, and although it obviously has citizens, the Constitution does not call for Members of Congress to be elected by the undifferentiated national citizenry; indeed, it does not recognize any mechanism at all (such as a national referendum) for action by the undifferentiated people of the Nation as a whole. Even at the level of national politics, then, there always remains a meaningful distinction between someone who is a citizen of the United States and of Georgia and someone who is a citizen of the United States and of Massachusetts. The Georgia citizen who is unaware of this distinction will have it pointed out to him as soon as he tries to vote in a Massachusetts congressional election.

In short, while the majority is correct that the Framers expected the selection process to create a "direct link" between members of the House of Representatives and the people, the link was between the Representatives from each State and the people of that State; the people of Georgia have no say over whom the people of Massachusetts select to represent them in Congress. This arrangement must baffle the majority, whose understanding of Congress would surely fit more comfortably within a system of nationwide elections. But the fact remains that when it comes to the selection of Members of Congress, the people of each State have retained their independent political identity. As a result, there is absolutely nothing strange about the notion that the people of the States or their state legislatures possess "reserved" powers in this area.

The majority seeks support from the Constitution's specification that Members of Congress "shall receive a Compensation for their Services, to be ascertained by Law, and paid out of the Treasury of the United States." Art. I, §6, cl. 1. But the fact that Members of Congress draw a federal salary once they have assembled hardly means that the people of the States lack reserved powers over the selection of their representatives. Indeed, the historical evidence about the compensation provision suggests that the States' reserved powers may even extend beyond the selection stage. The majority itself indicates that if the Constitution had made no provision for congressional compensation, this topic would have been "left to state legislatures." Likewise, Madison specifically indicated that even with the compensation provision in place, the individual States still enjoyed the reserved power to supplement the federal salary. (Remarks at the Virginia ratifying convention.)

As for the fact that a State has no reserved power to establish qualifications for the office of President, it surely need not follow that a State has no reserved power to establish qualifications for the Members of Congress who represent the people of that State. Because powers are reserved to the States "respectively," it is clear that no State may legislate for another State: even though the Arkansas legislature enjoys the reserved power to pass a minimum wage law for Arkansas, it has no power to pass a minimum wage law for Vermont. For the same reason, Arkansas may not decree that only Arkansas citizens are eligible to be President of the United States; the selection of the President is not up to Arkansas alone, and Arkansas can no more prescribe the qualifications for that office than it can set the qualifications for Members of Congress from Florida. But none of this suggests that Arkansas cannot set qualifications for Members of Congress from Arkansas.

In fact, the Constitution's treatment of Presidential elections actively contradicts the majority's position. While the individual States have no "reserved" power to set qualifications for the office of President, we have long understood that they do have the power (as far as the Federal Constitution is concerned) to set qualifications for their Presidential electors — the delegates that each State selects to represent it in the electoral college that actually chooses the Nation's chief executive. Even respondents do not dispute that the States may establish qualifications for their delegates to the electoral college, as long as those qualifications pass muster under other constitutional provisions (primarily the First and Fourteenth

Amendments). As the majority cannot argue that the Constitution affirmatively grants this power, the power must be one that is "reserved" to the States. It necessarily follows that the majority's understanding of the Tenth Amendment is incorrect, for the position of Presidential elector surely "spring[s] out of the existence of the national government."

In a final effort to deny that the people of the States enjoy "reserved" powers over the selection of their representatives in Congress, the majority suggests that the Constitution expressly delegates to the States certain powers over congressional elections. Such delegations of power, the majority argues, would be superfluous if the people of the States enjoyed reserved powers in this area.

Only one constitutional provision — the Times, Places and Manner Clause of Article I, §4 — even arguably supports the majority's suggestion. ... Contrary to the majority's assumption, however, this Clause does not delegate any authority to the States. Instead, it simply imposes a duty upon them. The majority gets it exactly right: by specifying that the state legislatures "shall" prescribe the details necessary to hold congressional elections, the Clause "expressly requires action by the States." This command meshes with one of the principal purposes of Congress' "make or alter" power: to ensure that the States hold congressional elections in the first place, so that Congress continues to exist. ... Constitutional provisions that impose affirmative duties on the States are hardly inconsistent with the notion of reserved powers.

Of course, the second part of the Times, Places and Manner Clause does grant a power rather than impose a duty. As its contrasting uses of the words "shall" and "may" confirm, however, the Clause grants power exclusively to Congress, not to the States. If the Clause did not exist at all, the States would still be able to prescribe the times, places, and manner of holding congressional elections; the deletion of the provision would simply deprive Congress of the power to override these state regulations. ...

I take it to be established, then, that the people of Arkansas do enjoy "reserved" powers over the selection of their representatives in Congress. Purporting to exercise those reserved powers, they have agreed among themselves that the candidates covered by §3 of Amendment 73 — those whom they have already elected to three or more terms in the House of Representatives or to two or more terms in the Senate — should not be eligible to appear on the ballot for reelection, but should nonetheless be returned to Congress if enough voters are sufficiently enthusiastic about their candidacy to write in their names. Whatever one might think of the wisdom of this arrangement, we may not override the decision of the people of Arkansas unless something in the Federal Constitution deprives them of the power to enact such measures.

The majority settles on "the Qualifications Clauses" as the constitutional provisions that Amendment 73 violates. [B]ut the Qualifications Clauses are merely straightforward recitations of the minimum eligibility requirements that the Framers thought it essential for every Member of Congress to meet. They restrict state power only in that they prevent the States from abolishing all eligibility requirements for membership in Congress. ...

At least on their face, . . . the Qualifications Clauses do nothing to prohibit the people of a State from establishing additional eligibility requirements for their own representatives. Joseph Story thought that such a prohibition was nonetheless implicit in the constitutional list of qualifications, because "[f]rom the very nature of such a provision, the affirmation of these qualifications would seem to imply a negative of all others." This argument rests on the maxim *expressio unius est exclusio alterius*. When the Framers decided which qualifications to include in the Constitution, they also decided not to include any other qualifications in the Constitution. In Story's view, it would conflict with this latter decision for the people of the individual States to decide, as a matter of state law, that they would like their own representatives in Congress to meet additional eligibility requirements.

To spell out the logic underlying this argument is to expose its weakness. Even if one were willing to ignore the distinction between requirements enshrined in the Constitution and other requirements that the Framers were content to leave within the reach of ordinary law, Story's application of the *expressio unius* maxim takes no account of federalism. At most, the specification of certain nationwide disqualifications in the Constitution implies the negation of other *nationwide* disqualifications; it does not imply that individual States or their people are barred from adopting their own disqualifications on a state by state basis. Thus, the one delegate to the Philadelphia Convention who voiced anything approaching Story's argument said only that a recital of qualifications in the Constitution would imply that Congress lacked any qualification-setting power. . . .

The Qualifications Clauses do prevent the individual States from abolishing all eligibility requirements for Congress. This restriction on state power reflects the fact that when the people of one State send immature, disloyal, or unknowledgeable representatives to Congress, they jeopardize not only their own interests but also the interests of the people of other States. Because Congress wields power over all the States, the people of each State need some guarantee that the legislators elected by the people of other States will meet minimum standards of competence. The Qualifications Clauses provide that guarantee: they list the requirements that the Framers considered essential to protect the competence of the National Legislature.

If the people of a State decide that they would like their representatives to possess additional qualifications, however, they have done nothing to frustrate the policy behind the Qualifications Clauses. Anyone who possesses all of the constitutional qualifications, plus some qualifications required by state law, still has all of the federal qualifications. Accordingly, the fact that the Constitution specifies certain qualifications that the Framers deemed necessary to protect the competence of the National Legislature does not imply that it strips the people of the individual States of the power to protect their own interests by adding other requirements for their own representatives.

The people of other States could legitimately complain if the people of Arkansas decide, in a particular election, to send a 6 year old to Congress. But the Constitution gives the people of other States no basis to complain if the people of Arkansas elect a freshman representative in preference to a long-term incumbent. That being the case, it is hard to see why the rights of the people of other States have been violated when the people of Arkansas decide to enact a more general disqualification of long-term incumbents. Such a disqualification certainly is subject to scrutiny under other constitutional provisions, such as the First and Fourteenth Amendments. But as long as the candidate whom they send to Congress meets the constitutional age, citizenship, and inhabitancy requirements, the people of Arkansas have not violated the Qualifications Clauses. . . .

The majority responds that "a patchwork of state qualifications" would "undermin[e] the uniformity and the national character that the Framers envisioned and sought to ensure." Yet the Framers thought it perfectly consistent with the "national character" of Congress for the Senators and Representatives from each State to be chosen by the legislature or the people of that State. The majority never explains why Congress' fundamental character permits this state-centered system, but nonetheless prohibits the people of the States and their state legislatures from setting any eligibility requirements for the candidates who seek to represent them.

As for the majority's related assertion that the Framers intended qualification requirements to be uniform, this is a conclusion, not an argument. Indeed, it is a conclusion that the Qualifications Clauses themselves contradict. At the time of the framing, and for some years thereafter, the Clauses' citizenship requirements incorporated laws that varied from State to State. Thus, the Qualifications Clauses themselves made it possible that a person would be qualified to represent State A in Congress even though a similarly situated person would not be qualified to represent State B. . . .

Although the Qualifications Clauses neither state nor imply the prohibition that it finds in them, the majority infers from the Framers' "democratic principles" that the Clauses must have been generally understood to preclude the people of the States and their state legislatures from prescribing any additional qualifications for their representatives in Congress. But the majority's evidence on this point establishes only two more modest propositions: (1) the Framers did not want the Federal Constitution itself to impose a broad set of disqualifications for congressional office, and (2) the Framers did not want the Federal Congress to be able to supplement the few disqualifications that the Constitution does set forth. The logical conclusion is simply that the Framers did not want the people of the States and their state legislatures to be constrained by too many qualifications imposed at the national level. The evidence does not support the majority's more sweeping conclusion that the Framers intended to bar the people of the States and their state legislatures from adopting additional eligibility requirements to help narrow their own choices. . . .

The fact that the Framers did not grant a qualification-setting power to Congress does not imply that they wanted to bar its exercise at the state level. One reason why the Framers decided not to let Congress prescribe the qualifications of its own members was that incumbents could have used this power to perpetuate themselves or their ilk in office. . . . But neither the people of the States nor the state legislatures would labor under the same conflict of interest when prescribing qualifications for Members of Congress, and so the Framers would have had to use a different calculus in determining whether to deprive them of this power. . . .

In discussing the ratification period, the majority stresses two principal data. One of these pieces of evidence is no evidence at all — literally. The majority devotes considerable space to the fact that the recorded ratification debates do not contain any affirmative statement that the States can supplement the constitutional qualifications.[19] For the majority, this void is "compelling" evidence that "unquestionably reflects the Framers' common understanding that States lacked that power." The majority reasons that delegates at several of the ratifying conventions attacked the Constitution for failing to require Members of Congress to rotate out of office qualifications, the majority argues, they would have blunted these attacks by pointing out that rotation requirements could still be added State by State.

But the majority's argument cuts both ways. The recorded ratification debates also contain no affirmative statement that the States *cannot* supplement the constitutional qualifications. While ratification was being debated, the existing rule in America was that the States could prescribe eligibility requirements for their delegates to Congress, even though the Articles of Confederation gave Congress itself no power to impose such qualifications. If the Federal Constitution had been understood to deprive the States of this significant power, one might well have expected its opponents to seize on this point in arguing against ratification.

The fact is that arguments based on the absence of recorded debate at the ratification conventions are suspect, because the surviving records of those debates are fragmentary. We have no records at all of the debates in several of the conventions, and only spotty records from most of the others.

If one concedes that the absence of relevant records from the ratification debates is not strong evidence for either side, then the majority's only significant piece of evidence from the ratification period is *Federalist, No. 52*. Contrary to the majority's assertion, however, this essay simply does not talk about "the lack of state control over the qualifications of the elected," whether "explicitly" or otherwise.

It is true that *Federalist, No. 52* contrasts the Constitution's treatment of the qualifications of voters in elections for the House of Representatives with its treatment of the qualifications of the Representatives themselves. As Madison noted, the Framers did not specify any uniform qualifications for the franchise in the Constitution; instead, they simply incorporated each State's rules about eligibility to vote in elections for the most numerous branch of the state legislature. By contrast, Madison continued, the Framers chose to impose some particular qualifications that all members of the House had to satisfy. But while Madison did say that the qualifications of the elected were "more susceptible of uniformity" than the qualifications of electors, he did not say that the Constitution prescribes anything but uniform minimum qualifications for congressmen. That, after all, is more than it does for congressional electors. . . .

---

19 . . . Just as individual States could extend the vote to women before the adoption of the Nineteenth Amendment, could prohibit poll taxes before the adoption of the Twenty-fourth Amendment, and could lower the voting age before the adoption of the Twenty-sixth Amendment, so the Framers' decision not to impose a nationwide limit on congressional terms did not itself bar States from adopting limits of their own.

[W]hen Madison wrote that the state constitutions defined the qualifications of Members of Congress "less carefully and properly" than they defined the qualifications of voters, he could only have meant that the existing state qualifications did not do enough to safeguard Congress' competence: the state constitutions had not adopted the age, citizenship, and inhabitancy requirements that the Framers considered essential. Madison's comments readily explain why the Framers did not merely incorporate the state qualifications for Congress. But they do not imply that the Framers intended to withdraw from the States the power to supplement the list of qualifications contained in the Federal Constitution. . . .

It is radical enough for the majority to hold that the Constitution implicitly precludes the people of the States from prescribing any eligibility requirements for the congressional candidates who seek their votes. This holding, after all, does not stop with negating the term limits that many States have seen fit to impose on their Senators and Representatives. Today's decision also means that no State may disqualify congressional candidates whom a court has found to be mentally incompetent, who are currently in prison, or who have past vote fraud convictions. Likewise, after today's decision, the people of each State must leave open the possibility that they will trust someone with their vote in Congress even though they do not trust him with a vote in the election for Congress. . . .

[T]oday's decision reads the Qualifications Clauses to impose substantial implicit prohibitions on the States and the people of the States. I would not draw such an expansive negative inference from the fact that the Constitution requires Members of Congress to be a certain age, to be inhabitants of the States that they represent, and to have been United States citizens for a specified period. Rather, I would read the Qualifications Clauses to do no more than what they say. I respectfully dissent.

PART III

THE EXECUTIVE POWER

CHAPTER 6

The Executive Power

ASSIGNMENT 1

Congress's powers are limited by Article I, which imposes both external constraints like the Enumerated Powers doctrine (Chapter 3) and internal constraints like Federalism (Chapter 4). Likewise, Article I and the principles of federalism impose limitations on the powers of states (Chapter 5). We now turn our attention to doctrines that govern the "separation of powers." We begin by examining the scope of the executive power, particularly in the context of waging war and conducting foreign affairs. Article II, Section 1 begins: "The executive power shall be vested in a President of the United States of America." Article II, Section 2 further specifies the powers of the President as follows:

> Section 2. The President shall be commander in chief of the Army and Navy of the United States, and of the militia of the several states, when called into the actual service of the United States; he may require the opinion, in writing, of the principal officer in each of the executive departments, upon any subject relating to the duties of their respective offices, and he shall have power to grant reprieves and pardons for offenses against the United States, except in cases of impeachment.
>
> He shall have power, by and with the advice and consent of the Senate, to make treaties, provided two-thirds of the Senators present concur; and he shall nominate, and by and with the advice and consent of the Senate, shall appoint ambassadors, other public ministers and consuls, judges of the Supreme Court, and all other officers of the United States, whose appointments are not herein otherwise provided for, and which shall be established by law: but the Congress may by law vest the appointment of such inferior officers, as they think proper, in the President alone, in the courts of law, or in the heads of departments.

> The President shall have power to fill up all vacancies that may happen during the recess of the Senate, by granting commissions which shall expire at the end of their next session.

Article II, Section 3 adds:

> Section 3. He shall from time to time give to the Congress information of the state of the union, and recommend to their consideration such measures as he shall judge necessary and expedient; he may, on extraordinary occasions, convene both Houses, or either of them, and in case of disagreement between them, with respect to the time of adjournment, he may adjourn them to such time as he shall think proper; he shall receive ambassadors and other public ministers; he shall take care that the laws be faithfully executed, and shall commission all the officers of the United States.

Madison's notes on the Constitutional Convention indicate that the framers devoted far less time for debate about the powers of the President than about the powers of Congress. Many of the framers assumed that Congress would be the preeminent branch of the national government. Thus the definition of Congress's powers was central to establishing federalism, the vertical division of power between the national and state governments. The executive would only "execute" the laws that were within the limited enumerated powers of the national government. Further, it was commonly assumed that George Washington, whose sterling character was widely respected, would be the first President. By relinquishing his military command after the Revolutionary War, Washington had shown himself to be trustworthy in the exercise of power. Defining the specifics of Article II was not seen as a significant priority for the Framers. Though Washington set important precedents during his administration, other chief executives would not hold themselves to such lofty standards. In particular, tensions between the President and Congress have been particularly pronounced during times of war. Since the time of the framing, there has been endless debate over what role Congress has concerning foreign policy and war.

As you study the materials on the executive's war and foreign affairs powers and on the separation of powers, consider what the text of the Constitution does and does not tell us about these authorities. Article I, Section 1 provides "[a]ll legislative Powers *herein granted* shall be vested in a Congress of the United States." Note that Congress has only those powers that are "herein granted." In contrast, the President is not so limited. Article II, Section 1 states that "[t]he *executive power* shall be vested in a President of the United States of America." Does this provision merely name the office and specify that it would be held by one person? Or did it confer "the executive power" — a bundle of defined powers whose content at the time would have been understood — in a "unitary" (i.e., single) President? The remaining clauses in Article II vest the President with express grants of power to be sure, but in contrast with Article I, the framers did not specify a complete listing of the powers for the President. Could this mean that the President must logically have powers beyond those enumerated? What about areas where Congress has enumerated powers over foreign affairs, such as with respect to the ratification of treaties or the declaration of war?

Further, the meaning of the text of Article II may depend on the background assumption or "default rule" against which the drafters of the Constitution were writing.[1] Was it generally assumed that the President received all the "executive" or prerogative powers associated with the King of England *minus* those prerogative powers expressly delegated to Congress? Or was it generally assumed that the President, like Congress, only received the powers delegated to him by Article II, *plus* those powers authorized by Congress pursuant to its enumerated powers?

Finally, for a variety of reasons, the Supreme Court has said far less about the definition of executive power than it has said about the definition of legislative power. We will consider some of the reasons for this disparity in the chapters that discuss limits on the judicial power. There, we will study certain judicially defined limits on when courts will reach the merits of a case (for example, the "political questions" doctrine and the requirement of "standing"). Several of these justiciability limitations have been applied with particular force when challenges to executive power are raised — either because the Constitution requires it or because judges (in an exercise of prudence or self-restraint) have chosen to avoid involvement. We saw as early as *Marbury v. Madison* that the Court is willing, in the proper case, to review the actions of the executive branch. But often the Court has chosen to avoid deciding constitutional issues, particularly when the President's war and foreign affairs powers are implicated. And because Congress, as a coequal branch, has some ability to "fight its own battles," the Court has been more willing in this arena than others to defer to the political processes.

The scope of the Executive's power, much like the scope of Congress's powers, is subject to debates about the Constitution's text, intent, and structure, as well as whether changed conditions in the modern world should affect how those powers are construed. Where war and foreign affairs are implicated, these debates often take place only among scholars, politicians, and the public, as courts usually offer no clear resolution. But in certain contexts, the courts *have* addressed these, sometimes in great detail.

A. A SINGLE, VIGOROUS EXECUTIVE

In the following essay, Alexander Hamilton defends the framer's decision to create a single — as distinct from a divided — executive. His argument emphasizes two factors: energy and accountability. Some of this analysis will have further implications in the context of the separation of powers, which we will consider in Chapter 7. Hamilton's emphasis on a "vigorous" executive may surprise you. After all, the colonists had just fought a war against what they believed to be a tyrannical monarch. But keep in mind that at the time Hamilton wrote *Federalist No. 70*, the United States was a new and small country. It had no standing army. Spain, France, and Great Britain all had a continuing presence in North America. There was

[1] The role that such background assumptions should play in determining the original meaning of what the Constitution does say is a subject worthy of careful study. See Randy E. Barnett, The Misconceived Assumption About Constitutional Assumptions, 103 Nw. U. L. Rev. 615 (2009).

legitimate concern over the future safety and independence of the fledgling United States. Hamilton concluded that electing a strong executive was essential to preserving American interests at home, and abroad.

ALEXANDER HAMILTON, *FEDERALIST No. 70*, Saturday, March 15, 1788

To the People of the State of New York:

There is an idea, which is not without its advocates, that a vigorous Executive is inconsistent with the genius of republican government. The enlightened well-wishers to this species of government must at least hope that the supposition is destitute of foundation; since they can never admit its truth, without at the same time admitting the condemnation of their own principles. Energy in the Executive is a leading character in the definition of good government. It is essential to the protection of the community against foreign attacks; it is not less essential to the steady administration of the laws; to the protection of property against those irregular and high-handed combinations which sometimes interrupt the ordinary course of justice; to the security of liberty against the enterprises and assaults of ambition, of faction, and of anarchy. Every man the least conversant in Roman story, knows how often that republic was obliged to take refuge in the absolute power of a single man, under the formidable title of Dictator, as well against the intrigues of ambitious individuals who aspired to the tyranny, and the seditions of whole classes of the community whose conduct threatened the existence of all government, as against the invasions of external enemies who menaced the conquest and destruction of Rome.

There can be no need, however, to multiply arguments or examples on this head. A feeble Executive implies a feeble execution of the government. A feeble execution is but another phrase for a bad execution; and a government ill executed, whatever it may be in theory, must be, in practice, a bad government.

Taking it for granted, therefore, that all men of sense will agree in the necessity of an energetic Executive, it will only remain to inquire, what are the ingredients which constitute this energy? How far can they be combined with those other ingredients which constitute safety in the republican sense? And how far does this combination characterize the plan which has been reported by the convention?

The ingredients which constitute energy in the Executive are, first, unity; secondly, duration; thirdly, an adequate provision for its support; fourthly, competent powers.

The ingredients which constitute safety in the republican sense are, first, a due dependence on the people, secondly, a due responsibility.

Those politicians and statesmen who have been the most celebrated for the soundness of their principles and for the justice of their views, have declared in favor of a single Executive and a numerous legislature. They have with great propriety, considered energy as the most necessary qualification of the former, and have regarded this as most applicable to power in a single hand, while they have, with equal propriety, considered the latter as best adapted to deliberation and wisdom, and best calculated to conciliate the confidence of the people and to secure their privileges and interests.

That unity is conducive to energy will not be disputed. Decision, activity, secrecy, and despatch will generally characterize the proceedings of one man in a much more eminent degree than the proceedings of any greater number; and in proportion as the number is increased, these qualities will be diminished.

This unity may be destroyed in two ways: either by vesting the power in two or more magistrates of equal dignity and authority; or by vesting it ostensibly in one man, subject, in whole or in part, to the control and co-operation of others, in the capacity of counsellors to him. Of the first, the two Consuls of Rome may serve as an example; of the last, we shall find examples in the constitutions of several of the States. New York and New Jersey, if I recollect right, are the only States which have intrusted the executive authority wholly to single men. Both these methods of destroying the unity of the Executive have their partisans; but the votaries of an executive council are the most numerous. They are both liable, if not to equal, to similar objections, and may in most lights be examined in conjunction.

The experience of other nations will afford little instruction on this head. As far, however, as it teaches any thing, it teaches us not to be enamoured of plurality in the Executive. We have seen that the Achaeans, on an experiment of two Praetors, were induced to abolish one. The Roman history records many instances of mischiefs to the republic from the dissensions between the Consuls, and between the military Tribunes, who were at times substituted for the Consuls. But it gives us no specimens of any peculiar advantages derived to the state from the circumstance of the plurality of those magistrates. . . .

But quitting the dim light of historical research, attaching ourselves purely to the dictates of reason and good sense, we shall discover much greater cause to reject than to approve the idea of plurality in the Executive, under any modification whatever.

Wherever two or more persons are engaged in any common enterprise or pursuit, there is always danger of difference of opinion. If it be a public trust or office, in which they are clothed with equal dignity and authority, there is peculiar danger of personal emulation and even animosity. From either, and especially from all these causes, the most bitter dissensions are apt to spring. Whenever these happen, they lessen the respectability, weaken the authority, and distract the plans and operation of those whom they divide. If they should unfortunately assail the supreme executive magistracy of a country, consisting of a plurality of persons, they might impede or frustrate the most important measures of the government, in the most critical emergencies of the state. And what is still worse, they might split the community into the most violent and irreconcilable factions, adhering differently to the different individuals who composed the magistracy. . . .

In the legislature, promptitude of decision is oftener an evil than a benefit. The differences of opinion, and the jarrings of parties in that department of the government, though they may sometimes obstruct salutary plans, yet often promote deliberation and circumspection, and serve to check excesses in the majority. When a resolution too is once taken, the opposition must be at an end. That resolution is a law, and resistance to it punishable. But no favorable circumstances palliate or atone for the disadvantages of dissension in the executive department. Here, they are pure and unmixed. There is no point at which they cease to operate. They serve to embarrass and weaken the execution of the plan or measure to which they relate, from the first step to the final conclusion of it. They constantly counteract those qualities in the Executive which are the most necessary ingredients in its composition — vigor and expedition, and this without any counterbalancing good. In the conduct of war, in which the energy of the Executive is the bulwark of the national security, every thing would be to be apprehended from its plurality.

[T]hese observations apply . . . with considerable weight to the project of a council, whose concurrence is made constitutionally necessary to the operations of the ostensible Executive. An artful cabal in that council would be able to distract and to enervate the whole system of administration. If no such cabal should exist, the mere diversity of views and opinions would alone be sufficient to tincture the exercise of the executive authority with a spirit of habitual feebleness and dilatoriness.

But one of the weightiest objections to a plurality in the Executive, and which lies as much against the last as the first plan, is, that it tends to conceal faults and destroy responsibility. Responsibility is of two kinds — to censure and to punishment. The first is the more important of the two, especially in an elective office. Man, in public trust, will much oftener act in such a manner as to render him unworthy of being any longer trusted, than in such a manner as to make him obnoxious to legal punishment. But the multiplication of the Executive adds to the difficulty of detection in either case. It often becomes impossible, amidst mutual accusations, to determine on whom the blame or the punishment of a pernicious measure, or series of pernicious measures, ought really to fall. It is shifted from one to another with so much dexterity, and under such plausible appearances, that the public opinion is left in suspense about the real author. The circumstances which may have led to any national miscarriage or misfortune are sometimes so complicated that, where there are a number of actors who may have had different degrees and kinds of agency, though we may clearly see upon the whole that there has been mismanagement, yet it may be impracticable to pronounce to whose account the evil which may have been incurred is truly chargeable.

"I was overruled by my council. The council were so divided in their opinions that it was impossible to obtain any better resolution on the point." These and similar pretexts are constantly at hand, whether true or false. And who is there that will either take the trouble or incur the odium, of a strict scrutiny into the secret springs of the transaction? Should there be found a citizen zealous enough to undertake the unpromising task, if there happen to be collusion between the parties concerned, how easy it is to clothe the circumstances with so much ambiguity, as to render it uncertain what was the precise conduct of any of those parties? . . .

It is evident from these considerations, that the plurality of the Executive tends to deprive the people of the two greatest securities they can have for the faithful exercise of any delegated power, *first*, the restraints of public opinion, which lose their efficacy, as well on account of the division of the censure attendant on bad measures among a number, as on account of the uncertainty on whom it ought to fall; and, *second*, the opportunity of discovering with facility and clearness the misconduct of the persons they trust, in order either to their removal from office or to their actual punishment in cases which admit of it. . . . A council to a magistrate, who is himself responsible for what he does, are generally nothing better than a clog upon his good intentions, are often the instruments and accomplices of his bad and are almost always a cloak to his faults. . . .

I will only add that, prior to the appearance of the Constitution, I rarely met with an intelligent man from any of the States, who did not admit, as the result of experience, that the UNITY of the executive of this State was one of the best of the distinguishing features of our constitution.

B. THE POWER OF THE PRESIDENT TO SUSPEND THE WRIT OF HABEAS CORPUS

It is no exaggeration to say that the Civil War represented a sea change in the American constitutional order.[2] The founding generation feared national government; state governments were considered the guardians of liberty. The Civil War, which was waged over the issues of slavery and "states' rights," turned this founding era ideology upside down. Prosecuting the war required the creation of previously unimaginable federal agencies, the establishment of an enormous standing army, and the exercise of broad executive powers. As George Ticknor of Harvard observed at the time, "The civil war of '61 has made a great gulf between what happened before it in our century and what has happened since, or what is likely to happen hereafter. It does not seem to me as if I were living in the country in which I was born, or in which I received whatever I got of political education and principles."

The election of 1860 was a four-way race, with Southern and Northern Democrats backing two different candidates, plus an additional candidate of the Constitutional Unionist party running in the South. As a result of the fragmented ballot, Republican Abraham Lincoln was elected to the presidency without receiving a single electoral vote from a Southern state (and in fact was not even on the ballot in most of them). After his election, but before he took office, seven Southern states seceded from the Union: South Carolina was first, followed by Mississippi, Florida, Alabama, Georgia, Louisiana, and Texas. These states seized military and other federal facilities, including the New Orleans mint with its $500,000 in hard money. Only Fort Sumter in Charleston, South Carolina, and three other forts along the Florida coast remained in federal hands.

In February 1861, delegates from the states that had seceded drew up a constitution for a Confederate States of America. In his inaugural address on March 4, Lincoln attempted to alleviate the fears of the remaining slave states, which had not seceded, as to his intentions concerning slavery:

> Apprehension seems to exist among the people of the Southern States that by the accession of a Republican Administration their property and their peace and personal security are to be endangered. There has never been any reasonable cause for such apprehension. Indeed, the most ample evidence to the contrary has all the while existed and been open to their inspection. It is found in nearly all the published speeches of him who now addresses you. I do but quote from one of those speeches when I declare that —

[2] For an engaging and accessible account of the events surrounding the Civil War — including the Taney Court — and the effect of the war on the political system of the United States, see Jeffrey Rogers Hummel, Emancipating Slaves, Enslaving Free Men: A History of the American Civil War (1996). See also Daniel Farber, Lincoln's Constitution (2003), and Mark A. Graber, Dred Scott and the Problem of Constitutional Evil (2006).

I have no purpose, directly or indirectly, to interfere with the institution of slavery in the States where it exists. I believe I have no lawful right to do so, and I have no inclination to do so.

Those who nominated and elected me did so with full knowledge that I had made this and many similar declarations and had never recanted them; and more than this, they placed in the platform for my acceptance, and as a law to themselves and to me, the clear and emphatic resolution which I now read:

> Resolved, That the maintenance inviolate of the rights of the States, and especially the right of each State to order and control its own domestic institutions according to its own judgment exclusively, is essential to that balance of power on which the perfection and endurance of our political fabric depend; and we denounce the lawless invasion by armed force of the soil of any State or Territory, no matter what pretext, as among the gravest of crimes.

I now reiterate these sentiments, and in doing so I only press upon the public attention the most conclusive evidence of which the case is susceptible that the property, peace, and security of no section are to be in any wise endangered by the now incoming Administration. I add, too, that all the protection which, consistently with the Constitution and the laws, can be given will be cheerfully given to all the States when lawfully demanded, for whatever cause — as cheerfully to one section as to another. . . .

Despite Lincoln's assurances, on April 12, 1861, Fort Sumter was fired upon by Confederate forces. Unable to receive federal reinforcements, it was surrendered three days later. After the attack, President Lincoln called up the state militias. This decision would have pitted the militias of the remaining slave states, which had not yet seceded, against the armed forces of the Confederacy. In part because they were put to this choice, the slave states of Virginia, North Carolina, Tennessee, and Arkansas then joined the Confederacy.

Though it is called the Civil War, Congress never formally voted on a declaration of war. Rather, President Lincoln prosecuted the military campaign through broad and largely unprecedented executive powers. These exercises of power, and the judiciary's reaction to them, set the stage for modern treatments of the President and Congress's authority in times of war. In this section we consider two specific powers claimed by Lincoln — the power to suspend the writ of habeas corpus and the power to emancipate the slaves.

In the Anglo-American tradition, prisoners can ask a judge to determine the legality of their confinement by petitioning for a *writ of habeas corpus*. After hostilities began, President Lincoln suspended the writ of habeas corpus and imposed martial law within some areas that had not seceded from the Union. To appreciate why, one must consider timing and geography. When Lincoln acted, eleven states had already seceded from the United States. But four remaining slave states had yet to decide: Delaware, Kentucky, Missouri, and Maryland. Only Delaware was firmly loyal to the Union. The Lincoln administration considered retaining Maryland to be vital. Looking at a map it is easy to appreciate the strategic significance of Maryland, which was immediately adjacent to the nation's capital on three sides. Additionally, Virginia, which was located to the south of the District of Columbia, had already left the Union.

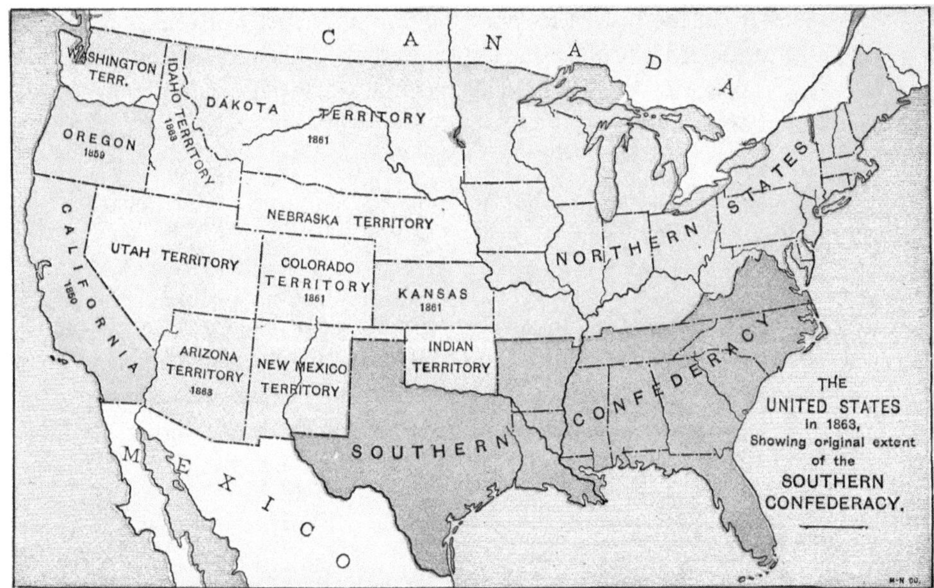

U.S. and Confederate states

Historian Jeffrey Rogers Hummel describes the situation:

> Maryland contained Baltimore, the country's third largest city; the state also isolated the nation's capital, itself a southern town, from the free states further north. No sizable regular army units were on hand for Washington's defense, and with Confederate flags already visible [in Virginia] across the Potomac River to the South, Lincoln feared he might have to flee.
>
> The arrival of the first regiment to answer Lincoln's call, the 6th Massachusetts, did nothing to dispel the panic. A mob had attacked the troops in Baltimore as they shuttled between train stations. In the ensuing melee shots were exchanged. Four soldiers and at least nine civilians died, with many more injured. While the 6th Massachusetts limped into Washington, Baltimore officials burned the railroad bridges and cut the telegraph wires.
>
> Not until more regiments began pouring into the beleaguered capital a week later was it truly secure. Lincoln then suspended the writ of *habeas corpus* along the "military line" between Philadelphia and the District of Columbia and clamped a military occupation down upon Maryland. The governor convened the legislature in the northwest part of the state, where unionism was strong. Although the legislature rejected secession, it came out for "the peaceful and immediate recognition of the independence of the Confederate States"; the state "hereby gives her cordial consent thereunto, as a member of the Union." The legislature also denounced "the present military occupation of Maryland" as a "flagrant violation of the Constitution." . . .

The text of the Constitution contains the following provision: "The privilege of the writ of habeas corpus shall not be suspended, unless when in cases of rebellion or invasion the public safety may require it." This clause does not specify whether the writ may be suspended by the President, by Congress, or by both acting in concert. However, it appears in Article I, which broadly concerns Congress's powers, and in Section 9 of that Article, which specifically limits the legislature's authority. Did President Lincoln have the unilateral power to suspend the writ?

In the case of *Ex parte Merryman*, Chief Justice Roger Brooke Taney sharply criticized Lincoln's suspension of the writ as unconstitutional. This case concerned a prisoner who was held by the Union Army at Fort McHenry in Maryland, Taney's home state.

STUDY GUIDE

- When Lincoln suspended the writ of habeas corpus, Congress was not in session and the nation confronted an obvious emergency. Are either of these facts relevant to the constitutionality of his actions?
- Notice that this opinion is rendered by Taney, who was serving at the Circuit Court, District of Maryland, and not the Supreme Court. In what capacity did Taney even render this decision?

Chief Justice Roger Taney

Ex parte Merryman

17 F. Cas. 144 (1861)

Circuit Court, District of Maryland

[On May 25, 1861, John Merryman, a citizen of Baltimore, was arrested by a military force, acting under orders of George Cadwalader, a major general of the United States Army detached to Fort McHenry in Maryland. On May 26, Chief Justice Taney issued a writ of habeas corpus directing the commandant of the fort to produce Merryman's body before him in Baltimore. General Cadwalader declined to produce the petitioner, instead sending the Chief Justice a letter explaining his reason for refusing. The letter read, in part:

> The prisoner was brought to this post on the 20th inst., by Adjutant James Wittimore and Lieut. Wm. H. Abel, by order of Col. Yohe, and is charged with various acts of treason, and with being publicly associated with and holding a commission as lieutenant in a company having in their possession arms belonging to the United States, and avowing his purpose of armed hostility against the government. He is also informed that it can be clearly established, that the prisoner has made often and unreserved declarations of his association with this organized force, as being in avowed hostility to the government, and in readiness to co-operate with those engaged in the present rebellion against the government of the United States. He has further to inform you, that he is duly authorized by the president of the United States, in such cases, to suspend the writ of habeas corpus, for the public safety. This is a high and delicate trust, and it has been enjoined upon him that it should be executed with judgment and discretion, but he is nevertheless also instructed that in times of civil strife, errors, if any, should be on the side of the safety of the country. He most respectfully submits for your consideration, that those who should co-operate in the present trying and painful position in which our country is placed, should not, by any unnecessary want of confidence in each other, increase our embarrassments. He, therefore, respectfully requests that you will postpone further action upon this case, until he can receive instructions from the president of the United States, when you shall hear further from him.

When informed that the general had not brought with him the body of John Merryman, the Chief Justice issued an order holding the general in contempt. When the marshal of the court was unable to secure entry into the fort to effectuate the general's arrest, Taney authorized him to summon the posse comitatus for assistance in seizing and bringing the general before the court where he would be liable to punishment by fine and imprisonment. Nevertheless, Taney excused the outmatched marshal from any further efforts because "the power refusing obedience was so notoriously superior to any the marshal could command." Afterwards, in an unusual move, Taney made arrangements for his written opinion "to be laid before the president, in order that he might perform his constitutional duty, to enforce the laws, by securing obedience to the process of the United States." — EDS.]

John Merryman later had a son and named him Roger Brooke Taney Merryman.

Taney, Circuit Justice.

The application in this case for a writ of habeas corpus is made to me under the 14th section of the judiciary act of 1789, which renders effectual for the citizen the constitutional privilege of the writ of habeas corpus. That act gives to the courts of the United States, as well as to each justice of the supreme court, and to every district judge, power to grant writs of habeas corpus for the purpose of an inquiry into the cause of commitment. . . .

The case, then, is simply this: a military officer, residing in Pennsylvania, issues an order to arrest a citizen of Maryland, upon vague and indefinite charges, without any proof, so far as appears; under this order, his house is entered in the night, he is seized as a prisoner, and conveyed to Fort McHenry, and there kept in close confinement; and when a habeas corpus is served on the commanding officer, requiring him to produce the prisoner before a justice of the supreme court, in order that he may examine into the legality of the imprisonment, the answer of the officer, is that he is authorized by the president to suspend the writ of habeas corpus at his discretion, and in the exercise of that discretion, suspends it in this case, and on that ground refuses obedience to the writ.

As the case comes before me, therefore, I understand that the president not only claims the right to suspend the writ of habeas corpus himself, at his discretion, but to delegate that discretionary power to a military officer, and to leave it to him to determine whether he will or will not obey judicial process that may be served upon him. No official notice has been given to the courts of justice, or to the public, by proclamation or otherwise, that the president claimed this power, and had exercised it in the manner stated in the return. And I certainly listened to it with some surprise, for I had supposed it to be one of those points of constitutional law upon which there was no difference of opinion, and that it was admitted on all hands, that the privilege of the writ could not be suspended, except by act of congress.

When the conspiracy of which Aaron Burr was the head, became so formidable, and was so extensively ramified, as to justify, in Mr. Jefferson's opinion, the suspension of the writ, he claimed, on his part, no power to suspend it, but communicated his opinion to congress, with all the proofs in his possession, in order that congress might exercise its discretion upon the subject, and determine whether the public safety required it. And in the debate which took place upon the subject, no one suggested that Mr. Jefferson might exercise the power himself, if, in his opinion, the public safety demanded it.

Having, therefore, regarded the question as too plain and too well settled to be open to dispute, if the commanding officer had stated that, upon his own responsibility, and in the exercise of his own discretion, he refused obedience to the writ, I should have contented myself with referring to the clause in the constitution, and to the construction it received from every jurist and statesman of that day, when the case of Burr was before them. But being thus officially notified that the privilege of the writ has been suspended, under the orders, and by the authority of the president, and believing, as I do, that the president has exercised a power which he does not possess under the constitution, a proper respect for the high office he fills, requires me to state plainly and fully the grounds of my opinion, in order to show that I have not ventured to question the legality of his act, without a careful and deliberate examination of the whole subject.

The clause of the constitution, which authorizes the suspension of the privilege of the writ of habeas corpus, is in the 9th section of the first article. This article is devoted to the legislative department of the United States, and has not the slightest reference to the executive department. It begins by providing "that all legislative powers therein granted, shall be vested in a congress of the United States, which shall consist of a senate and house of representatives." And after prescribing the manner in which these two branches of the legislative department shall be chosen, it proceeds to enumerate specifically the legislative powers which it thereby grants [and legislative powers which it expressly prohibits]; and at the conclusion of this specification, a clause is inserted giving congress "the power to make all laws which shall be necessary and proper for carrying into execution the foregoing powers, and all other powers vested by this constitution in the government of the United States, or in any department or officer thereof."

The power of legislation granted by this latter clause is, by its words, carefully confined to the specific objects before enumerated. But as this limitation was unavoidably somewhat indefinite, it was deemed necessary to guard more effectually certain great cardinal principles, essential to the liberty of the citizen, and to the rights and equality of the states, by denying to congress, in express terms, any power of legislation over them. It was apprehended, it seems, that such legislation might be attempted, under the pretext that it was necessary and proper to carry into execution the powers granted; and it was determined, that there should be no room to doubt, where rights of such vital importance were concerned; and accordingly, this clause is immediately followed by an enumeration of certain subjects, to which the powers of legislation shall not extend. The great importance which the framers of the constitution attached to the privilege of the writ of habeas corpus, to protect the liberty of the citizen, is proved by the fact, that its suspension, except in cases of invasion or rebellion, is first in the list of prohibited powers; and even in these cases the power is denied, and its exercise prohibited, unless the public safety shall require it.

It is true, that in the cases mentioned, congress is, of necessity, the judge of whether the public safety does or does not require it; and their judgment is conclusive. But the introduction of these words is a standing admonition to the legislative body of the danger of suspending it, and of the extreme caution they should exercise, before they give the government of the United States such power over the liberty of a citizen.

It is the second article of the constitution that provides for the organization of the executive department, enumerates the powers conferred on it, and prescribes its duties. And if the high power over the liberty of the citizen now claimed, was intended to be conferred on the president, it would undoubtedly be found in plain words in this article; but there is not a word in it that can furnish the slightest ground to justify the exercise of the power. . . .

[H]is powers in relation to the civil duties and authority necessarily conferred on him are carefully restricted, as well as those belonging to his military character. He cannot appoint the ordinary officers of government, nor make a treaty with a foreign nation or Indian tribe, without the advice and consent of the senate, and cannot appoint even inferior officers, unless he is authorized by an act of congress to do so. He is not empowered to arrest any one charged with an offence against the United States, and whom he may, from the evidence before him, believe to be guilty; nor can he authorize any officer, civil or military, to exercise this power, for the fifth article of the amendments to the constitution expressly provides that no person "shall be deprived of life, liberty or property, without due process of law" that is, judicial process. . . .

The only power, therefore, which the president possesses, where the "life, liberty or property" of a private citizen is concerned, is the power and duty prescribed in the third section of the second article, which requires "that he shall take care that the laws shall be faithfully executed." He is not authorized to execute them himself, or through agents or officers, civil or military, appointed by himself, but he is to take care that they be faithfully carried into execution, as they are expounded and adjudged by the coordinate branch of the government to which that duty is assigned by the constitution. It is thus made his duty to come in aid of the judicial authority, if it shall be resisted by a force too strong to be overcome without the assistance of the executive arm; but in exercising this power he acts in subordination to judicial authority, assisting it to execute its process and enforce its judgments.

With such provisions in the constitution, expressed in language too clear to be misunderstood by any one, I can see no ground whatever for supposing that the president, in any emergency, or in any state of things, can authorize the suspension of the privileges of the writ of habeas corpus, or the arrest of a citizen, except in aid of the judicial power. He certainly does not faithfully execute the laws, if he takes upon himself legislative power, by suspending the writ of habeas corpus, and the judicial power also, by arresting and imprisoning a person without due process of law.

Nor can any argument be drawn from the nature of sovereignty, or the necessity of government, for self-defence in times of tumult and danger. The government of the United States is one of delegated and limited powers; it derives its existence and authority altogether from the constitution, and neither of its branches, executive, legislative or judicial, can exercise any of the powers of government beyond those specified and granted; for the tenth article of the amendments to the constitution, in express terms, provides that "the powers not delegated to the United States by the constitution, nor prohibited by it to the states, are reserved to the states, respectively, or to the people."

Indeed, the security against imprisonment by executive authority, provided for in the fifth article of the amendments to the constitution, which I have before quoted, is nothing more than a copy of a like provision in the English constitution, which had been firmly established before the declaration of independence. Blackstone states it in the following words: "To make imprisonment lawful, it must be either by process of law from the courts of judicature, or by warrant from some legal officer having authority to commit to prison." 1 Bl. Comm. 137.

The people of the United Colonies, who had themselves lived under its protection, while they were British subjects, were well aware of the necessity of this safeguard for their personal liberty. And no one can believe that, in framing a government intended to guard still more efficiently the rights and liberties of the citizen, against executive encroachment and oppression, they would have conferred on the president a power which the history of England had proved to be dangerous and oppressive in the hands of the crown; and which the people of England had compelled it to surrender, after a long and obstinate struggle on the part of the English executive to usurp and retain it.

The right of the subject to the benefit of the writ of habeas corpus, it must be recollected, was one of the great points in controversy, during the long struggle in England between arbitrary government and free institutions, and must therefore have strongly attracted the attention of the statesmen engaged in framing a new and, as they supposed, a freer government than the one which they had thrown off by the revolution. From the earliest history of the common law, if a person were imprisoned, no matter by what authority, he had a right to the writ of habeas corpus, to bring his case before the king's bench; if no specific offence were charged against him in the warrant of commitment, he was entitled to be forthwith discharged; and if an offence were charged which was bailable in its character, the court was bound to set him at liberty on bail. The most exciting contests between the crown and the people of England, from the time of Magna Charta, were in relation to the privilege of this writ, and they continued until the passage of the statute of 31 Car. II., commonly known as the great habeas corpus act. . . .

If the president of the United States may suspend the writ, then the constitution of the United States has conferred upon him more regal and absolute power over the liberty of the citizen, than the people of England have thought it safe to entrust to the crown; a power which the queen of England cannot exercise at this day, and which could not have been lawfully exercised by the sovereign even in the reign of Charles the First. . . .

Such is the case now before me, and I can only say that if the authority which the constitution has confided to the judiciary department and judicial officers, may thus, upon any pretext or under any circumstances, be usurped by the military power, at its discretion, the people of the United States are no longer living under a government of laws, but every citizen holds life, liberty and property at the will and pleasure of the army officer in whose military district he may happen to be found.

In such a case, my duty was too plain to be mistaken. I have exercised all the power which the constitution and laws confer upon me, but that power has been resisted by a force too strong for me to overcome. It is possible that the officer who has incurred this grave responsibility may have misunderstood his instructions, and exceeded the authority intended to be given him; I shall, therefore, order all the proceedings in this case, with my opinion, to be filed and recorded in the circuit court of the United States for the district of Maryland, and direct the clerk to transmit a copy, under seal, to the president of the United States. It will then remain for that high officer, in fulfilment of his constitutional obligation to "take care that the laws be faithfully executed," to determine what measures he will take to cause the civil process of the United States to be respected and enforced.

Although it is commonly argued that President Lincoln invoked his executive power to defy Taney's order,[3] this claim has been challenged as among several myths surrounding the facts of *Merryman*. According to Seth Barrett Tillman, Chief Justice Taney never actually issued an *order* to the President, but only had his *opinion* sent to the President:

> The first and primary *Merryman* myth is that President Lincoln ignored or defied a judicial *order* from Chief Justice Taney to *release* John Merryman. However, Taney never ordered anyone to release Merryman. Taney's final order merely stated,
>
> > I shall, therefore, order all the proceedings in this case, with my opinion, to be filed and recorded in the [C]ircuit [C]ourt of the United States for the [D]istrict of Maryland, and direct the clerk to transmit a copy, under seal, to the [P]resident of the United States. It will then remain for that high officer, in fulfilment of his constitutional obligation to "take care that the laws be faithfully executed," *to determine what measures he will take* to cause the civil process of the United States to be respected and enforced.
>
> Again, Taney issued no order to release Merryman. It follows, therefore, that Lincoln could not have ignored or defied it, nor could anyone else for that matter. . . .
>
> [A]lthough Taney concluded that Merryman was entitled to be released, Taney did not order his release. Taney's opinion put forward only advice (or, perhaps, a legal position akin to an Office of Legal Counsel memorandum), not a traditional judicial order. In other words, *Merryman* was effectively an advisory opinion, and given the disparity between Taney's order (which left Merryman in jail) and his opinion (which asserted that Merryman was entitled to be freed), it was perhaps a good deal less. . . . In short, Lincoln had every reason to believe that there was no obligation to obey Taney's opinion.[4]

Though the President never formally acknowledged Taney's opinion, he would soon address Congress about his suspension of the writ of habeas corpus.

STUDY GUIDE

- President Lincoln defended his decision to suspend the writ of habeas corpus in his July 4 message to a special session of Congress.
- Subsequently, Congress formally enacted a statute "approving, legalizing, and making valid all the acts, proclamations, and orders of the President, &c., as if they had been issued and done under the previous express authority and direction of the Congress of the United States." Is this relevant to an assessment of Lincoln's previous actions?

---

[3] See, e.g., Michael Stokes Paulsen, The Merryman Power and the Dilemma of Autonomous Executive Branch Interpretation, 15 Cardozo L. Rev. 81, 83 (1993) (referring to "President Abraham Lincoln's refusal to honor judicial process, in the form of a writ of habeas corpus issued by Chief Justice Roger Taney in the case of *Ex parte Merryman*").

[4] Seth Barrett Tillman, Ex Parte Merryman: Myth, History, and Scholarship, 224 Mil. L. Rev. 481, 495-498, 505-506 (2016). For more background on the case, see Phillip W. Magness, Between Evidence, Rumor, and Perception: Marshal Lamon and the "Plot" to Arrest Chief Justice Taney, 42 J. Sup. Ct. Hist. 133 (2017).

- Was later congressional approval necessary? If so, what does this say about the propriety of Lincoln's earlier assertion of presidential power? Or is all's well that ends well?
- Consider what should be the effect, if any, of a state of emergency on interpreting the powers of the President or Congress.

ABRAHAM LINCOLN, MESSAGE TO CONGRESS IN SPECIAL SESSION, July 4, 1861. At the beginning of the present Presidential term, four months ago, the functions of the Federal Government were found to be generally suspended within the several States of South Carolina, Georgia, Alabama, Mississippi, Louisiana, and Florida, excepting only those of the Post Office Department.

Within these States, all the Forts, Arsenals, Dock-yards, Customhouses, and the like, including the movable and stationary property in, and about them, had been seized, and were held in open hostility to this Government, excepting only Forts Pickens, Taylor, and Jefferson, on, and near the Florida coast, and Fort Sumter, in Charleston harbor, South Carolina. The Forts thus seized had been put in improved condition; new ones had been built; and armed forces had been organized, and were organizing, all avowedly with the same hostile purpose. . . .

In the border States, so called — in fact, the middle states — there are those who favor a policy which they call "armed neutrality" — that is, an arming of those states to prevent the Union forces passing one way, or the disunion, the other, over their soil. This would be disunion completed. Figuratively speaking, it would be the building of an impassable wall along the line of separation. And yet, not quite an impassable one; for, under the guise of neutrality, it would tie the hands of the Union men, and freely pass supplies from among them, to the insurrectionists, which it could not do as an open enemy. At a stroke, it would take all the trouble off the hands of secession, except only what proceeds from the external blockade. It would do for the disunionists that which, of all things, they most desire — feed them well, and give them disunion without a struggle of their own. It recognizes no fidelity to the Constitution, no obligation to maintain the Union; and while very many who have favored it are, doubtless, loyal citizens, it is, nevertheless, treason in effect.

Recurring to the action of the government, it may be stated that, at first, a call was made for seventy-five thousand militia; and rapidly following this, a proclamation was issued for closing the ports of the insurrectionary districts by proceedings in the nature of Blockade. So far all was believed to be strictly legal. At this point the insurrectionists announced their purpose to enter upon the practice of privateering. Other calls were made for volunteers, to serve three years, unless sooner discharged; and also for large additions to the regular Army and Navy. These measures, whether strictly legal or not, were ventured upon, under what appeared to be a popular demand, and a public necessity; trusting, then as now, that Congress would readily ratify them. It is believed that nothing has been done beyond the constitutional competency of Congress.

Soon after the first call for militia, it was considered a duty to authorize the Commanding General, in proper cases, according to his discretion, to suspend the privilege of the writ of habeas corpus; or, in other words, to arrest, and detain, without resort to the ordinary processes and forms of law, such individuals as he might deem dangerous to the public safety. This authority has purposely been exercised but very sparingly. Nevertheless, the legality and propriety of what has been done under it, are questioned; and the attention of the country has been called to the proposition that one who is sworn to "take care that the laws be faithfully executed," should not himself violate them. Of course some consideration was given to the questions of power, and propriety, before this matter was acted upon. The whole of the laws which were required to be faithfully executed, were being resisted, and failing of execution, in nearly one-third of the States. Must they be allowed to finally fail of execution, even had it been perfectly clear, that by the use of the means necessary to their execution, some single law, made in such extreme tenderness of the citizen's liberty, that practically, it relieves more of the guilty, than of the innocent, should, to a very limited extent, be violated? To state the question more directly, are all the laws, but one, to go unexecuted, and the government itself go to pieces, lest that one be violated? Even in such a case, would not the official oath be broken, if the government should be overthrown, when it was believed that disregarding the single law, would tend to preserve it? But it was not believed that this question was presented. It was not believed that any law was violated. The provision of the Constitution that "The privilege of the writ of habeas corpus, shall not be suspended unless when, in cases of rebellion or invasion, the public safety may require it," is equivalent to a provision — is a provision — that such privilege may be suspended when, in cases of rebellion, or invasion, the public safety does require it. It was decided that we have a case of rebellion, and that the public safety does require the qualified suspension of the privilege of the writ which was authorized to be made. Now it is insisted that Congress, and not the Executive, is vested with this power. But the Constitution itself, is silent as to which, or who, is to exercise the power; and as the provision was plainly made for a dangerous emergency, it cannot be believed the framers of the instrument intended, that in every case, the danger should run its course, until Congress could be called together; the very assembling of which might be prevented, as was intended in this case, by the rebellion.

No more extended argument is now offered; as an opinion, at some length, will probably be presented by the Attorney General. Whether there shall be any legislation upon the subject, and if any, what, is submitted entirely to the better judgment of Congress. . . .

It was with the deepest regret that the Executive found the duty of employing the war-power, in defence of the government, forced upon him. He could but perform this duty, or surrender the existence of the government. No compromise, by public servants, could, in this case, be a cure; not that compromises are not often proper, but that no popular government can long survive a marked precedent, that those who carry an election, can only save the government from immediate destruction, by giving up the main point, upon which the people gave the election. The people themselves, and not their servants, can safely reverse their own deliberate decisions. As a private citizen, the Executive could not have consented that these institutions shall perish; much less could he, in betrayal of so vast, and so sacred a trust, as these free people had confided to him. He felt that he had no moral right to shrink; nor even to count the chances of his own life, in what might follow. In full view of his great responsibility, he has, so far, done what he has deemed his duty. You will now, according to your own judgment, perform yours. He sincerely hopes that your views, and your action, may so accord with his, as to assure all faithful citizens, who have been disturbed in their rights, of a certain, and speedy restoration to them, under the Constitution, and the laws. And having thus chosen our course, without guile, and with pure purpose, let us renew our trust in God, and go forward without fear, and with manly hearts.

C. THE POWER OF THE COMMANDER IN CHIEF TO USE MILITARY FORCE

We now look at a case that raises the question of whether the President can enter into, or respond to, hostilities without the advance consent of Congress. One of the few times the Court has specifically addressed the war-making power was in *The Prize Cases.*

Fort Sumter and a Civil War blockade warship

STUDY GUIDE

- What does the Court see as its role in adjudicating the legality of the blockade? What issue does it need to decide to determine the constitutionality of President Lincoln's actions? According to the Court, by what authority did the President act?
- To determine whether the blockade ordered by the President was constitutional, was it necessary for the Court to determine whether a state of war existed? If a state of war *did* exist, the President would be exercising his power as commander in chief. Yet the Court also takes the imposition of the blockade as evidence of the existence of a state of war. Is that circular reasoning?
- Is there a difference between a state of war and a declaration of war?
- If the President does have the power to repel invasion, does that necessarily mean that he had the authority to order the blockade?

The Prize Cases

67 U.S. (2 Black) 635 (1863)

[During the Civil War, President Lincoln ordered a naval blockade of Southern ports. American ships that were attempting to smuggle goods to the South were captured by Union ships. Under admiralty law, vessels seized during war can be kept as "prizes" (hence the name of the case). Though the case primarily dealt with the ownership of the seized ships, the Court had to reach the question of whether there was a state of war. If the Southern states were belligerents, then the seizures were valid. If there was not a state of war, however, then the seizures were acts of piracy, and were not valid. — EDS.]

MR. JUSTICE GRIER. . . .

The right of prize and capture has its origin in the "*jus belli*," and is governed and adjudged under the law of nations. To legitimate the capture of a neutral vessel or property on the high seas, a war must exist de facto, and the neutral must have knowledge or notice of the intention of one of the parties belligerent to use this mode of coercion against a port, city, or territory, in possession of the other.

Let us enquire whether, at the time this blockade was instituted, a state of war existed which would justify a resort to these means of subduing the hostile force. War has been well defined to be, "That state in which a nation prosecutes its right by force." The parties belligerent in a public war are independent nations. But it is not necessary to constitute war, that both parties should be acknowledged as

Notice that *The Prize Cases* were decided while the war was still being waged, by a 5-4 vote.

independent nations or sovereign States. A war may exist where one of the belligerents, claims sovereign rights as against the other.

Insurrection against a government may or may not culminate in an organized rebellion, but a civil war always begins by insurrection against the lawful authority of the Government. A civil war is never solemnly declared; it becomes such by its accidents — the number, power, and organization of the persons who originate and carry it on. When the party in rebellion occupy and hold in a hostile manner a certain portion of territory; have declared their independence; have cast off their allegiance; have organized armies; have commenced hostilities against their former sovereign, the world acknowledges them as belligerents, and the contest a *war. They* claim to be in arms to establish their liberty and independence, in order to become a sovereign State, while the sovereign party treats them as insurgents and rebels who owe allegiance, and who should be punished with death for their treason.

The laws of war, as established among nations, have their foundation in reason, and all tend to mitigate the cruelties and misery produced by the scourge of war. Hence the parties to a civil war usually concede to each other belligerent rights. They exchange prisoners, and adopt the other courtesies and rules common to public or national wars.

"A civil war," says Vattel,[5]

> breaks the bands of society and government, or at least suspends their force and effect; it produces in the nation two independent parties, who consider each other as enemies, and acknowledge no common judge. Those two parties, therefore, must necessarily be considered as constituting, at least for a time, two separate bodies, two distinct societies. Having no common superior to judge between them, they stand in precisely the same predicament as two nations who engage in a contest and have recourse to arms.
>
> This being the case, it is very evident that the common laws of war — those maxims of humanity, moderation, and honor — ought to be observed by both parties in every civil war. Should the sovereign conceive he has a right to hang up his prisoners as rebels, the opposite party will make reprisals, the war will become cruel, horrible, and every day more destructive to the nation.

As a civil war is never publicly proclaimed, *eo nomine*, against insurgents, its actual existence is a fact in our domestic history which the Court is bound to notice and to know.

The true test of its existence, as found in the writings of the sages of the common law, may be thus summarily stated: "When the regular course of justice is interrupted by revolt, rebellion, or insurrection, so that the Courts of Justice cannot be kept open, *civil war exists* and hostilities may be prosecuted on the same footing as if those opposing the Government were foreign enemies invading the land."

By the Constitution, Congress alone has the power to declare a national or foreign war. It cannot declare war against a State, or any number of States, by virtue of any clause in the Constitution. The Constitution confers on the President the

---

[5] [Vattel was an eighteenth-century Swiss philosopher who wrote about the law of nations, which is now referred to as international law. — EDS.]

whole Executive power. He is bound to take care that the laws be faithfully executed. He is Commander-in-chief of the Army and Navy of the United States, and of the militia of the several States when called into the actual service of the United States. He has no power to initiate or declare a war either against a foreign nation or a domestic State. But by the Acts of Congress of February 28th, 1795, and 3d of March, 1807, he is authorized to call out the militia and use the military and naval forces of the United States in case of invasion by foreign nations, and to suppress insurrection against the government of a State or of the United States.

If a war be made by invasion of a foreign nation, the President is not only authorized but bound to resist force by force. He does not initiate the war, but is bound to accept the challenge without waiting for any special legislative authority. And whether the hostile party be a foreign invader, or States organized in rebellion, it is none the less a war, although the declaration of it be "*unilateral*." . . .

The President was bound to meet [a civil war] in the shape it presented itself, without waiting for Congress to baptize it with a name; and no name given to it by him or them could change the fact. It is not the less a civil war, with belligerent parties in hostile array, because it may be called an "insurrection" by one side, and the insurgents be considered as rebels or traitors. It is not necessary that the independence of the revolted province or State be acknowledged in order to constitute it a party belligerent in a war according to the law of nations. . . .

The law of nations is also called the law of nature; it is founded on the common consent as well as the common sense of the world. It contains no such anomalous doctrine as that which this Court are now for the first time desired to pronounce, to wit: That insurgents who have risen in rebellion against their sovereign, expelled her Courts, established a revolutionary government, organized armies, and commenced hostilities, are not *enemies* because they are *traitors*; and a war levied on the Government by traitors, in order to dismember and destroy it, is not a *war* because it is an "insurrection."

Whether the President in fulfilling his duties, as Commander-in-chief, in suppressing an insurrection, has met with such armed hostile resistance, and a civil war of such alarming proportions as will compel him to accord to them the character of belligerents, is a question to be decided *by him*, and this Court must be governed by the decisions and acts of the political department of the Government to which this power was entrusted. "He must determine what degree of force the crisis demands." The proclamation of blockade is itself official and conclusive evidence to the Court that a state of war existed which demanded and authorized a recourse to such a measure, under the circumstances peculiar to the case. . . .

If it were necessary to the technical existence of a war, that it should have a legislative sanction, we find it in almost every act passed at the extraordinary session of the Legislature of 1861, which was wholly employed in enacting laws to enable the Government to prosecute the war with vigor and efficiency. And finally, in 1861, we find Congress . . . passing an act "approving, legalizing, and making valid all the acts, proclamations, and orders of the President, &c., as if they had been *issued and done under the previous express authority* and direction of the Congress of the United States." Without admitting that such an act was necessary under the circumstances, it is plain that if the President had in any manner assumed powers which it was necessary should have the authority or sanction of Congress, that ... this ratification has operated to perfectly cure the defect.... [W]e are of the opinion that the President had a right, *jure belli,* to institute a blockade of ports in possession of the States in rebellion, which neutrals are bound to regard....

MR. JUSTICE NELSON, dissenting.

In the case of a rebellion or resistance of a portion of the people of a country against the established government, there is no doubt, if in its progress and enlargement the government thus sought to be overthrown sees fit, it may by the competent power recognize or declare the existence of a state of civil war, which will draw after it all the consequences and rights of war between the contending parties as in the case of a public war.... But before this insurrection against the established Government can be dealt with on the footing of a civil war, within the meaning of the law of nations and the Constitution of the United States, and which will draw after it belligerent rights, it must be recognized or declared by the war-making power of the Government. No power short of this can change the legal status of the Government or the relations of its citizens from that of peace to a state of war, or bring into existence all those duties and obligations of neutral third parties growing out of a state of war. The war power of the Government must be exercised before this changed condition of the Government and people and of neutral third parties can be admitted. There is no difference in this respect between a civil or a public war....

Congress assembled on the call for an extra session the 4th of July, 1861, and among the first acts passed was one in which the President was authorized by proclamation to interdict all trade and intercourse between all the inhabitants of States in insurrection and the rest of the United States, subjecting vessel and cargo to capture and condemnation as prize, and also to direct the capture of any ship or vessel belonging in whole or in part to any inhabitant of a State whose inhabitants are declared by the proclamation to be in a state of insurrection, found at sea or in any part of the rest of the United States....

This Act of Congress, we think, recognized a state of civil war between the Government and the Confederate States, and made it territorial.... Congress on the 6th of August, 1862, passed an Act confirming all acts, proclamations, and orders of the President, after the 4th of March, 1861, respecting the army and navy, and legalizing them, so far as was competent for that body, and it has been suggested, but scarcely argued, that this legislation on the subject had the effect to bring into existence an *ex post facto* civil war with all the rights of capture and confiscation, *jure belli,* from the date referred to. An *ex post facto* law is defined, when, after an action, indifferent in itself, or lawful, is committed, the Legislature then, for the first time, declares it to have been a crime and inflicts punishment upon the person who committed it. The principle is sought to be applied in this case. Property of the citizen or foreign subject engaged in lawful trade at the time, and illegally captured, which must be taken as true if a confirmatory act be necessary, may be held and confiscated by subsequent legislation. In other words trade and commerce authorized at the time by acts of Congress and treaties, may, by *ex post facto* legislation, be changed into illicit trade and commerce with all its penalties and forfeitures annexed and enforced. . . .

Upon the whole, after the most careful consideration of this case which the pressure of other duties has admitted, I am compelled to the conclusion that no civil war existed between this Government and the States in insurrection till recognized by the Act of Congress 13th of July, 1861; that the President does not possess the power under the Constitution to declare war or recognize its existence within the meaning of the law of nations, which carries with it belligerent rights, and thus change the country and all its citizens from a state of peace to a state of war; that this power belongs exclusively to the Congress of the United States, and, consequently, that the President had no power to set on foot a blockade under the law of nations, and that the capture of the vessel and cargo in this case, and in all cases before us in which the capture occurred before the 13th of July, 1861, for breach of blockade, or as enemies' property, are illegal and void, and that the decrees of condemnation should be reversed and the vessel and cargo restored.

MR. CHIEF JUSTICE TANEY, MR. JUSTICE CATRON and MR. JUSTICE CLIFFORD, concurred in the dissenting opinion of MR. JUSTICE NELSON.

D. THE POWER OF THE PRESIDENT TO EXPROPRIATE PROPERTY IN TIME OF WAR

ASSIGNMENT 2

1. The Power to Emancipate Slaves

It has long been debated whether the Civil War was about saving the Union or about ending slavery. Perhaps the least controversial conclusion is that the motivations for the war differed between North and South, and evolved in the North over time. Despite Lincoln's assurances during his inaugural address, the Southern states feared that their slave system would be jeopardized. Under the Republican constitutional platform, which was devised by future Chief Justice Salmon P. Chase, the slave states would begin a process of political decline.

As for the North, while abolitionists urged Lincoln to make the war about slavery, he feared that doing so could push the border slave states that remained in the Union into the arms of the Confederacy. Lincoln also confronted a constitutional dilemma: neither he, nor Congress, had the authority to end slavery. Before the Civil War it was widely thought that only the states had the power to abolish slavery, as slaves were deemed to be a species of "property" to be defined by state law. In *Dred Scott v. Sandford*, decided in 1857 (just three years before the war began), the Supreme Court adopted this theory. Chief Justice Taney's majority opinion held that slavery could not be barred in the federal territories by Congress because doing so would amount to a deprivation of "property" without due process of law in violation of the Fifth Amendment.

For these reasons, Lincoln never claimed that the Civil War was justified by any cause except for the preservation of the Union. If Congress then lacked the power to abolish slavery, how could the President have the power to emancipate slaves? When he issued his Emancipation Proclamation, it was expressly done pursuant to his executive power as commander in chief; that is, as a war measure "warranted by the Constitution, upon military necessity."

The Emancipation Proclamation achieved several goals. First, it freed slaves in territory controlled by Confederate forces, though it did not emancipate slaves in territories controlled by Union forces. Why were slaves in the border states not freed? Because those states were not in rebellion, and thus Lincoln lacked the executive power to do so. Second, the Proclamation changed federal policy by expressly "enticing" slaves to flee to Union lines. Third, by ordering that "such persons of suitable condition, will be received into the armed service of the United States to garrison forts, positions, stations, and other places, and to man vessels of all sorts in said service," it allowed for slaves in border states to enter the U.S. Army. This decision had the legal effect of freeing them and their families. Attorney General Edward Bates, at the behest of Treasury Secretary Salmon Chase, issued an opinion explaining the constitutionality of this provision. By affirming that African Americans could be citizens of the United States, Bates was repudiating Chief Justice Taney's reasoning in *Dred Scott*.[6]

Still, the fact that the Emancipation Proclamation was issued as a war measure meant that it did not abolish the institution of slavery itself. To accomplish this, Republicans believed it was imperative to amend the written Constitution, which they did after the conclusion of the war with the Thirteenth Amendment. Such an amendment would also prevent courts from later ruling that, once the exigencies of war had passed, the slaveholders were entitled to the return of their emancipated "property."

Given the absence of such an amendment, Lincoln's Emancipation Proclamation raised serious constitutional questions about whether he was acting within the scope of the executive power of the President. It is to this controversy we now turn.

ABRAHAM LINCOLN, EMANCIPATION PROCLAMATION, WASHINGTON, D.C., January 1, 1863

By the President of the United States of America:

A Proclamation.

Whereas, on the twenty-second day of September, in the year of our Lord one thousand eight hundred and sixty two, a proclamation was issued by the President of the United States, containing, among other things, the following, to wit:

---

[6] For a detailed historical examination of the constitutional concerns of the Republicans; their sustained efforts to free slaves where they believed they had authority to do so, for example, in the District of Columbia; the opinion of Attorney General Bates that African Americans were citizens of the United States; and the consequential effects of the Emancipation Proclamation, see James Oakes, Freedom National: The Destruction of Slavery in the United States, 1861-1865 (2014).

That on the first day of January, in the year of our Lord one thousand eight hundred and sixty-three, all persons held as slaves within any State or designated part of a State, the people whereof shall then be in rebellion against the United States, shall be then, thenceforward, and forever free; and the Executive Government of the United States, including the military and naval authority thereof, will recognize and maintain the freedom of such persons, and will do no act or acts to repress such persons, or any of them, in any efforts they may make for their actual freedom.

That the Executive will, on the first day of January aforesaid, by proclamation, designate the States and parts of States, if any, in which the people thereof, respectively, shall then be in rebellion against the United States; and the fact that any State, or the people thereof, shall on that day be, in good faith, represented in the Congress of the United States by members chosen thereto at elections wherein a majority of the qualified voters of such State shall have participated, shall, in the absence of strong countervailing testimony, be deemed conclusive evidence that such State, and the people thereof, are not then in rebellion against the United States.

Now, therefore I, Abraham Lincoln, President of the United States, by virtue of the power in me vested as Commander-in-Chief, of the Army and Navy of the United States in time of actual armed rebellion against the authority and government of the United States, and as a fit and necessary war measure for suppressing said rebellion, do, on this first day of January, in the year of our Lord one thousand eight hundred and sixty three, and in accordance with my purpose so to do publicly proclaimed for the full period of one hundred days, from the day first above mentioned, order and designate as the States and parts of States wherein the people thereof respectively, are this day in rebellion against the United States, the following, to wit:

> Arkansas, Texas, Louisiana, (except the Parishes of St. Bernard, Plaquemines, Jefferson, St. Johns, St. Charles, St. James Ascension, Assumption, Terrebonne, Lafourche, St. Mary, St. Martin, and Orleans, including the City of New Orleans) Mississippi, Alabama, Florida, Georgia, South-Carolina, North-Carolina, and Virginia, (except the forty-eight counties designated as West Virginia, and also the counties of Berkley, Accomac, Northampton, Elizabeth-City, York, Princess Ann, and Norfolk, including the cities of Norfolk and Portsmouth[)], and which excepted parts, are for the present, left precisely as if this proclamation were not issued.

And by virtue of the power, and for the purpose aforesaid, I do order and declare that all persons held as slaves within said designated States, and parts of States, are, and henceforward shall be free; and that the Executive government of the United States, including the military and naval authorities thereof, will recognize and maintain the freedom of said persons.

And I hereby enjoin upon the people so declared to be free to abstain from all violence, unless in necessary self-defence; and I recommend to them that, in all cases when allowed, they labor faithfully for reasonable wages.

And I further declare and make known, that such persons of suitable condition, will be received into the armed service of the United States to garrison forts, positions, stations, and other places, and to man vessels of all sorts in said service.

And upon this act, sincerely believed to be an act of justice, warranted by the Constitution, upon military necessity, I invoke the considerate judgment of mankind, and the gracious favor of Almighty God.

The Emancipation Proclamation applied to 3.1 million slaves held in the Confederacy, and an estimated 20,000-50,000 slaves were freed in former rebel areas on the day it went into effect. Although it did not automatically free the approximately 900,000 slaves in the border states that had remained in the Union — Delaware, Maryland, Missouri, and Kentucky — it did provide for border state slaves to be enlisted in the Union Army, which had the effect of emancipating both them and their families.

In witness whereof, I have hereunto set my hand and caused the seal of the United States to be affixed.

Constitutional objections to the Emancipation Proclamation involving the proper extent of executive power were articulated forcefully by former-Justice Benjamin Curtis, who had been appointed to the Supreme Court by President Millard Fillmore. Born in 1809 in Watertown, Massachusetts, Curtis was educated at Harvard. As an Associate Justice of the Supreme Court, he had issued an impassioned dissent to the Court's decision in *Dred Scott*. He resigned from the Court that same year (1857) owing to his disagreement with Taney's opinion in that case.

STUDY GUIDE

- How does Curtis view the President's power during wartime? Can you see any difference between what he recognizes as the proper scope of that power and Lincoln's assertion of the power to suspend the writ of habeas corpus? If you object to one, must you also object to the other? Does it matter that these actions were taken as part of a "civil war" on American territory?
- Notice the seeming contradiction of claiming both that the South could not lawfully secede from the United States (and therefore never truly left) and the theory that the seceding states had forfeited all their rights. When thinking about this issue, consider the legal status of incarcerated criminals. They do not lose their citizenship, but they do forfeit many of their civil rights until those rights are later restored.
- This issue comes up again in the context of the readmission of Southern states to Congress, a legislative body from which (according to the North) they never legally departed. What is to be done in such circumstances? Does the Constitution tell us?

BENJAMIN CURTIS, OBJECTIONS TO EMANCIPATION PROCLAMATION, October, 1862. The war in which we are engaged is a just and necessary war. It must be prosecuted with the whole force of this government till the military power of the South is broken, and they submit themselves to their duty to obey, and our right to have obeyed, the Constitution of the United States as "the supreme law of the land." But with what sense of right can we subdue them by arms to obey the

Constitution as the supreme law of their part of the land, if we have ceased to obey it, or failed to preserve it, as the supreme law of our part of the land. . . .

Let us, then, analyze these proclamations and orders of the President; let us comprehend the nature and extent of the powers they assume. Above all, let us examine that portentous cloud of the military power of the President, which is supposed to have overcome us and the civil liberties of the country, pursuant to the will of the people, ordained in the Constitution *because we are in a state of war*. . . .

It must be obvious to the meanest capacity, that if the President of the United States has an *implied* constitutional right, as commander-in-chief of the army and navy in time of war, to disregard any one positive prohibition of the Constitution, or to exercise any one power not delegated to the United States by the Constitution, because, in his judgment, he may thereby "best subdue the enemy," he has the same right, for the same reason, to disregard each and every provision of the Constitution, and to exercise all power, *needful, in his opinion,* to enable him "best to subdue the enemy."

It has never been doubted that the power to abolish slavery within the States was not delegated to the United States by the Constitution, but was reserved to the States. If the President, as commander-in-chief of the army and navy in time of war, may, by an executive decree, exercise this power to abolish slavery in the States, because he is of opinion that he may thus "best subdue the enemy," what other power reserved to the States or to the people, may not be exercised by the President, for the same reason that he is of opinion he may thus best subdue the enemy? . . .

The President is the commander-in-chief of the army and navy, not only by force of the Constitution, but under and subject to the Constitution, and to every restriction therein contained, and to every law enacted by its authority, as completely and clearly as the private in his ranks.

He is general-in-chief; but can a general-in-chief *disobey any law of his own country*? When he can, he super-adds to his *rights* as commander the *powers* of a usurper; and that is military despotism. In the noise of arms have we become deaf to the warning voices of our fathers, to take care that the military shall always be subservient to the civil power? Instead of listening to these voices, some persons now seem to think that it is enough to silence objection, to say, true enough, there is no civil right to do this or that, but it is a military act. They seem to have forgotten that every military act is to be tested by the Constitution and laws of the country under whose authority it is done. And that under the Constitution and laws of the United States, no more than under the government of Great Britain, or under any free or any settled government, the mere authority to command an army, is not an authority to disobey the laws of the country. . . .

In time of war, a military commander, whether he be the commander-in-chief, or one of his subordinates, must possess and exercise powers both over the persons and the property of citizens which do not exist in time of peace. But he possesses and exercises such powers, *not in spite of the Constitution and laws of the United States, or in derogation from their authority, but in virtue thereof and in strict subordination thereto*. The general who moves his army over private property in the course of his operations in the field, or who impresses into the public service means of transportation, or subsistence, to enable him to act against the enemy, or who seizes persons within his lines as spies, or destroys supplies in immediate danger of falling into the hands of the enemy, uses authority unknown to the Constitution and laws of the United States in time of *peace*; but not unknown to that Constitution and those laws in time of *war*. The power to declare war, includes the power to use the customary and necessary means effectually to carry it on. As Congress may institute a state of war, it may legislate into existence and place under executive control the means for its prosecution. And, in time of war without any special legislation, not the commander-in-chief only, but every commander of an expedition, or of a military post, is lawfully empowered by the Constitution and laws of the United States to do whatever is necessary, and is sanctioned by the laws of war, to accomplish the lawful objects of his command. But it is obvious that this implied authority must find early limits somewhere. If it were admitted that a commanding general in the field might do whatever in his discretion might be necessary to subdue the enemy, he could levy contributions to pay his soldiers; he could force conscripts into his service; he could drive out of the entire country all persons not desirous to aid him; — in short, he would be the absolute master of the country for the time being.

No one has ever supposed — no one will now undertake to maintain — that the commander-in-chief, in time of war, has any such lawful authority as this.

What, then, is his authority over the persons and property of citizens? I answer, that, over all persons enlisted in his forces he has military power and command; that over all persons and property *within the sphere of his actual operations in the field*, he may lawfully exercise such restraint and control as the successful prosecution of his particular military enterprise may, in his honest judgment, absolutely require; and upon such persons as have committed offences against any article of war, he may, through appropriate military tribunals, inflict the punishment prescribed by law. *And there his lawful authority ends.*

The military power over citizens and their property is a power to act, not a power to prescribe rules for future action. It springs from present pressing emergencies, and is limited by them. . . . Apply these principles to the proclamations and orders of the President. They are not designed to meet an existing emergency in some particular military operation in the field; they prescribe future rules of action touching the persons and property of citizens. They are to take effect, not merely within the scope of military operations in the field, or in their neighborhood, but throughout the entire country, or great portions thereof. Their subject-matter is not military offences, or military relations, but civil offences, and domestic relations; the relation of master and servant; the offences of "disloyalty, or treasonable practices." Their purpose is not to meet some existing and instant military emergency, but to provide for distant events, which may or may not occur; and whose connections, if they should coincide with any particular military operations, are indirect, remote, casual, and possible merely. . . .

These conclusions concerning the powers of the President cannot be shaken by the assertion that "rebels have no rights." . . . The assertion itself is not true, in reference either to the seceding *States* or their *people*. . . . [T]he Government of the United States has never admitted, and cannot admit, that as States, they are in rebellion. . . . [T]he Constitution is as much the supreme law of the land in Tennessee to-day, as it was before the void act of secession was attempted by a part of its people. Else the act was effectual, and the State is independent of the Government of the United States, and the war is a war of conquest and subjugation. . . .

But, if it were conceded that "rebels have no rights," there would still be matter demanding the greatest consideration. For the inquiry which I have invited is not what are *their* rights, but what are *our* rights. . . . It is among the rights of all of us that the executive power should be kept within its prescribed constitutional limits, and should not *legislate*, by its decrees, upon subjects of transcendent importance to the whole people.

Whether such decrees are wise or unwise, whether their subjects are citizens or not, if they are usurpations of power, *our* rights are both infringed and endangered. They are infringed, because the power to decide and to act is taken from the people without their consent. They are endangered, because, in a constitutional government, every usurpation of power dangerously disorders the whole framework of the State. . . .

2. The Power to Seize Private Businesses

Youngstown Sheet & Tube Co. v. Sawyer is not technically a war powers case. However, it does raise the question of whether, during times of war, the President has the power to act independently of congressional authorizations. *Youngstown* is viewed as one of the Court's most important decisions affecting executive power, and the separation of powers more broadly. Indeed, far more than Justice Hugo Black's majority opinion, Justice Robert Jackson's concurrence has become the framework often used in subsequent judicial evaluations of executive power.

From 1950-1953, the United States was engaged in the Korean War, which is sometimes referred to as the "Korean Conflict." This was not a war declared by Congress, but instead was authorized by the United Nations Security Council. The United States joined the United Nations by virtue of a treaty approved by the Senate in 1945. Apart from the other issues in the case, the uncertain legal status of this "war" can be glimpsed at various points in these opinions. President Harry S. Truman ordered the seizure of American steel mills (the case is often referred to as *The Steel Seizure Case*). The President did so to prevent a labor strike that would have disrupted supply lines to the military.

> Future Chief Justice William Rehnquist was law clerk to Justice Robert Jackson when *Youngstown* was decided.

STUDY GUIDE

- Do your sympathies shift as we move from the emancipation of slave "property" to the seizure of the operations of a private company?
- The case features six different opinions by Justices in the majority plus a seventh opinion of the dissenters. How do the opinions by Justices in the majority differ from each other? (*Hint:* Do they disagree at all about the facts?)

- While constitutional interpretation can be difficult, one would think it would be easy enough to determine whether an act of the President has been authorized or prohibited by Congress, which it is necessary to do before concluding that the President has acted lawfully or unlawfully. Does the disagreement among the Justices, both in the majority and in dissent, tell us anything about the difficulty of discerning whether Congress has either authorized or forbidden the President to act?
- Can you discern the categories used by Justice Jackson in his opinion—an approach that future Justices have found so compelling?
- What did the dissenters say about congressional authorization? Does their argument cast any doubt on the practicality of Jackson's approach?

Youngstown Sheet & Tube Co. v. Sawyer

The Steel Seizure Case, 343 U.S. 579 (1952)

MR. JUSTICE BLACK delivered the opinion of the Court....

We are asked to decide whether the President was acting within his constitutional power when he issued an order directing the Secretary of Commerce to take possession of and operate most of the Nation's steel mills. The mill owners argue that the President's order amounts to lawmaking, a legislative function which the Constitution has expressly confided to the Congress and not to the President. The Government's position is that the order was made on findings of the President that his action was necessary to avert a national catastrophe which would inevitably result from a stoppage of steel production, and that in meeting this grave emergency the President was acting within the aggregate of his constitutional powers as the Nation's Chief Executive and the Commander in Chief of the Armed Forces of the United States. The issue emerges here from the following series of events:

In the latter part of 1951, a dispute arose between the steel companies and their employees over terms and conditions that should be included in new collective bargaining agreements. Long-continued conferences failed to resolve the dispute. On December 18, 1951, the employees' representative, United Steelworkers of America, C.I.O., gave notice of an intention to strike when the existing bargaining agreements expired on December 31. The Federal Mediation and Conciliation Service then intervened in an effort to get labor and management to agree. This failing, the President on December 22, 1951, referred the dispute to the Federal Wage Stabilization Board to investigate and make recommendations for fair and equitable terms of settlement. This Board's report resulted in no settlement. On April 4, 1952, the Union gave notice of a nation-wide strike called to begin at 12:01 A.M. April 9. The indispensability of steel as a component of substantially all weapons and other war materials led the President to believe that the proposed work stoppage would immediately jeopardize our national defense and that governmental seizure of the steel mills was necessary in order to assure the continued availability of steel.

Reciting these considerations for his action, the President, a few hours before the strike was to begin, issued Executive Order 10340. The order directed the Secretary of Commerce to take possession of most of the steel mills and keep them running. The Secretary immediately issued his own possessory orders, calling upon the presidents of the various seized companies to serve as operating managers for the United States. They were directed to carry on their activities in accordance with regulations and directions of the Secretary. The next morning the President sent a message to Congress reporting his action. Twelve days later he sent a second message. Congress has taken no action. . . .

II

The President's power, if any, to issue the order must stem either from an act of Congress or from the Constitution itself. There is no statute that expressly authorizes the President to take possession of property as he did here. Nor is there any act of Congress to which our attention has been directed from which such a power can fairly be implied. Indeed, we do not understand the Government to rely on statutory authorization for this seizure. There are two statutes which do authorize the President to take both personal and real property under certain conditions. However, the Government admits that these conditions were not met and that the President's order was not rooted in either of the statutes. . . .

Moreover, the use of the seizure technique to solve labor disputes in order to prevent work stoppages was not only unauthorized by any congressional enactment; prior to this controversy, Congress had refused to adopt that method of settling labor disputes. When the Taft-Hartley Act was under consideration in 1947, Congress rejected an amendment which would have authorized such governmental seizures in cases of emergency. . . .

It is clear that if the President had authority to issue the order he did, it must be found in some provision of the Constitution. And it is not claimed that express constitutional language grants this power to the President. The contention is that presidential power should be implied from the aggregate of his powers under the Constitution. Particular reliance is placed on provisions in Article II which say that "The executive Power shall be vested in a President . . ."; that "he shall take Care that the Laws be faithfully executed"; and that he "shall be Commander in Chief of the Army and Navy of the United States."

The order cannot properly be sustained as an exercise of the President's military power as Commander in Chief of the Armed Forces. The Government attempts to do so by citing a number of cases upholding broad powers in military commanders engaged in day-to-day fighting in a theater of war. Such cases need not concern us here. Even though "theater of war" be an expanding concept, we cannot with faithfulness to our constitutional system hold that the Commander in Chief of the Armed Forces has the ultimate power as such to take possession of private property in order to keep labor disputes from stopping production. This is a job for the Nation's lawmakers, not for its military authorities.

Nor can the seizure order be sustained because of the several constitutional provisions that grant executive power to the President. In the framework of our

Constitution, the President's power to see that the laws are faithfully executed refutes the idea that he is to be a lawmaker. The Constitution limits his functions in the lawmaking process to the recommending of laws he thinks wise and the vetoing of laws he thinks bad. And the Constitution is neither silent nor equivocal about who shall make laws which the President is to execute. The first section of the first article says that "All legislative Powers herein granted shall be vested in a Congress of the United States." . . .

The President's order does not direct that a congressional policy be executed in a manner prescribed by Congress — it directs that a presidential policy be executed in a manner prescribed by the President. The preamble of the order itself, like that of many statutes, sets out reasons why the President believes certain policies should be adopted, proclaims these policies as rules of conduct to be followed, and again, like a statute, authorizes a government official to promulgate additional rules and regulations consistent with the policy proclaimed and needed to carry that policy into execution.[7] The power of Congress to adopt such public policies as those proclaimed by the order is beyond question. It can authorize the taking of private property for public use. It can make laws regulating the relationships between employers and employees, prescribing rules designed to settle labor disputes, and fixing wages and working conditions in certain fields of our economy. The Constitution does not subject this lawmaking power of Congress to presidential or military supervision or control.

It is said that other Presidents without congressional authority have taken possession of private business enterprises in order to settle labor disputes. But even if

---

[7] [In an appendix to its opinion, the Court includes the wording of the executive order and the following preamble to it:

> WHEREAS American fighting men and fighting men of other nations of the United Nations are now engaged in deadly combat with the forces of aggression in Korea, and forces of the United States are stationed elsewhere overseas for the purpose of participating in the defense of the Atlantic Community against aggression; and
>
> WHEREAS the weapons and other materials needed by our armed forces and by those joined with us in the defense of the free world are produced to a great extent in this country, and steel is an indispensable component of substantially all of such weapons and materials; and
>
> WHEREAS steel is likewise indispensable to the carrying out of programs of the Atomic Energy Commission of vital importance to our defense efforts; and
>
> WHEREAS a continuing and uninterrupted supply of steel is also indispensable to the maintenance of the economy of the United States, upon which our military strength depends; and
>
> WHEREAS a controversy has arisen between certain companies in the United States producing and fabricating steel and the elements thereof and certain of their workers represented by the United Steel Workers of America, CIO, regarding terms and conditions of employment; and
>
> WHEREAS the controversy has not been settled through the processes of collective bargaining or through the efforts of the Government, including those of the Wage Stabilization Board, to which the controversy was referred on December 22, 1951, pursuant to Executive Order No. 10233, and a strike has been called for 12:01 A.M., April 9, 1952; and
>
> WHEREAS a work stoppage would immediately jeopardize and imperil our national defense and the defense of those joined with us in resisting aggression, and would add to the continuing danger of our soldiers, sailors, and airmen engaged in combat in the field; and
>
> WHEREAS in order to assure the continued availability of steel and steel products during the existing emergency, it is necessary that the United States take possession of and operate the plants, facilities, and other property of the said companies as hereinafter provided. . . . — EDS.]

this be true, Congress has not thereby lost its exclusive constitutional authority to make laws necessary and proper to carry out the powers vested by the Constitution "in the Government of the United States, or any Department or Officer thereof."

The Founders of this Nation entrusted the lawmaking power to the Congress alone in both good and bad times. It would do no good to recall the historical events, the fears of power and the hopes for freedom that lay behind their choice. Such a review would but confirm our holding that this seizure order cannot stand.

The judgment of the District Court is *Affirmed.*

Mr. Justice Frankfurter, concurring. . . .

A constitutional democracy like ours is perhaps the most difficult of man's social arrangements to manage successfully. Our scheme of society is more dependent than any other form of government on knowledge and wisdom and self-discipline for the achievement of its aims. For our democracy implies the reign of reason on the most extensive scale. The Founders of this Nation were not imbued with the modern cynicism that the only thing that history teaches is that it teaches nothing. They acted on the conviction that the experience of man sheds a good deal of light on his nature. It sheds a good deal of light not merely on the need for effective power if a society is to be at once cohesive and civilized, but also on the need for limitations on the power of governors over the governed.

To that end, they rested the structure of our central government on the system of checks and balances. For them, the doctrine of separation of powers was not mere theory; it was a felt necessity. Not so long ago, it was fashionable to find our system of checks and balances obstructive to effective government. It was easy to ridicule that system as outmoded — too easy. The experience through which the world has passed in our own day has made vivid the realization that the Framers of our Constitution were not inexperienced doctrinaires. These long-headed statesmen had no illusion that our people enjoyed biological or psychological or sociological immunities from the hazards of concentrated power. It is absurd to see a dictator in a representative product of the sturdy democratic traditions of the Mississippi Valley. The accretion of dangerous power does not come in a day. It does come, however slowly, from the generative force of unchecked disregard of the restrictions that fence in even the most disinterested assertion of authority. [The not-so-subtle reference is to President Harry Truman. The opinion is written in 1952, only a few short years after the war against dictators Adolf Hitler, Benito Mussolini, and Francisco Franco. — Eds.] . . .

The pole-star for constitutional adjudications is John Marshall's greatest judicial utterance that "it is *a constitution* we are expounding." *McCulloch v. Maryland* (1819). . . . Not the least characteristic of great statesmanship which the Framers manifested was the extent to which they did not attempt to bind the future. It is no less incumbent upon this Court to avoid putting fetters upon the future by needless pronouncements today. . . .

The Framers, however, did not make the judiciary the overseer of our government. They were familiar with the revisory functions entrusted to judges in a few of the States, and refused to lodge such powers in this Court. Judicial power can be exercised only as to matters that were the traditional concern of the courts at

Westminster, and only if they arise in ways that to the expert feel of lawyers constitute "Cases" or "Controversies." Even as to questions that were the staple of judicial business, it is not for the courts to pass upon them unless they are indispensably involved in a conventional litigation — and then only to the extent that they are so involved. Rigorous adherence to the narrow scope of the judicial function is especially demanded in controversies that arouse appeals to the Constitution. The attitude with which this Court must approach its duty when confronted with such issues is precisely the opposite of that normally manifested by the general public. So-called constitutional questions seem to exercise a mesmeric influence over the popular mind. This eagerness to settle — preferably forever — a specific problem on the basis of the broadest possible constitutional pronouncements may not unfairly be called one of our minor national traits. . . .

The path of duty for this Court, it bears repetition, lies in the opposite direction. Due regard for the implications of the distribution of powers in our Constitution and for the nature of the judicial process as the ultimate authority in interpreting the Constitution, has not only confined the Court within the narrow domain of appropriate adjudication. It has also led to "a series of rules under which it has avoided passing upon a large part of all the constitutional questions pressed upon it for decision." Brandeis, J., in *Ashwander v. Tennessee Valley Authority* (1936). A basic rule is the duty of the Court not to pass on a constitutional issue at all, however narrowly it may be confined, if the case may, as a matter of intellectual honesty, be decided without even considering delicate problems of power under the Constitution. It ought to be, but apparently is not, a matter of common understanding that clashes between different branches of the government should be avoided if a legal ground of less explosive potentialities is properly available. Constitutional adjudications are apt, by exposing differences, to exacerbate them. The issue before us can be met, and therefore should be, without attempting to define the President's powers comprehensively. . . .

We must therefore put to one side consideration of what powers the President would have had if there had been no legislation whatever bearing on the authority asserted by the seizure, or if the seizure had been only for a short, explicitly temporary period, to be terminated automatically unless Congressional approval were given. These and other questions, like or unlike, are not now here. I would exceed my authority were I to say anything about them. . . . In adopting the provisions which it did, by the Labor Management Relations Act of 1947, for dealing with a "national emergency" arising out of a breakdown in peaceful industrial relations, Congress was very familiar with Governmental seizure as a protective measure. On a balance of considerations, Congress chose not to lodge this power in the President. It chose not to make available in advance a remedy to which both industry and labor were fiercely hostile. . . .

In any event, nothing can be plainer than that Congress made a conscious choice of policy in a field full of perplexity and peculiarly within legislative responsibility for choice. In formulating legislation for dealing with industrial conflicts, Congress could not more clearly and emphatically have withheld authority than it did in 1947. . . . It cannot be contended that the President would have had power to issue this order had Congress explicitly negated such authority in formal legislation.

Congress has expressed its will to withhold this power from the President as though it had said so in so many words. . . . It would be not merely infelicitous draftsmanship but almost offensive gaucherie to write such a restriction upon the President's power in terms into a statute rather than to have it authoritatively expounded, as it was, by controlling legislative history. By the Labor Management Relations Act of 1947, Congress said to the President, "You may not seize. Please report to us and ask for seizure power if you think it is needed in a specific situation." . . .

Absence of authority in the President to deal with a crisis does not imply want of power in the Government. Conversely the fact that power exists in the Government does not vest it in the President. The need for new legislation does not enact it. Nor does it repeal or amend existing law. . . . To be sure, the content of the three authorities of government is not to be derived from an abstract analysis. The areas are partly interacting, not wholly disjointed. The Constitution is a framework for government. Therefore the way the framework has consistently operated fairly establishes that it has operated according to its true nature. Deeply embedded traditional ways of conducting government cannot supplant the Constitution or legislation, but they give meaning to the words of a text or supply them. It is an inadmissibly narrow conception of American constitutional law to confine it to the words of the Constitution and to disregard the gloss which life has written upon them. In short, a systematic, unbroken, executive practice, long pursued to the knowledge of the Congress and never before questioned, engaged in by Presidents who have also sworn to uphold the Constitution, making as it were such exercise of power part of the structure of our government, may be treated as a gloss on "executive Power" vested in the President by §1 of Art. II. . . .

No remotely comparable practice can be vouched for executive seizure of property at a time when this country was not at war, in the only constitutional way in which it can be at war. It would pursue the irrelevant to reopen the controversy over the constitutionality of some acts of Lincoln during the Civil War. Suffice it to say that he seized railroads in territory where armed hostilities had already interrupted the movement of troops to the beleaguered Capital, and his order was ratified by the Congress. The only other instances of seizures are those during the periods of the first and second World Wars. In his eleven seizures of industrial facilities, President Wilson acted, or at least purported to act, under authority granted by Congress. Thus his seizures cannot be adduced as interpretations by a President of his own powers in the absence of statute. Down to the World War II period, then, the record is barren of instances comparable to the one before us. Of twelve seizures by President Roosevelt prior to the enactment of the War Labor Disputes Act in June, 1943, three were sanctioned by existing law, and six others were effected after Congress, on December 8, 1941, had declared the existence of a state of war. In this case, reliance on the powers that flow from declared war has been commendably disclaimed by the Solicitor General. . . .

A scheme of government like ours no doubt at times feels the lack of power to act with complete, all-embracing, swiftly moving authority. No doubt a government with distributed authority, subject to be challenged in the courts of law, at least long enough to consider and adjudicate the challenge, labors under restrictions from which other governments are free. It has not been our tradition to envy such governments. In any event our government was designed to have such restrictions. The price was deemed not too high in view of the safeguards which these restrictions afford. I know no more impressive words on this subject than those of Mr. Justice Brandeis:

> "The doctrine of the separation of powers was adopted by the Convention of 1787, not to promote efficiency but to preclude the exercise of arbitrary power. The purpose was, not to avoid friction, but, by means of the inevitable friction incident to the distribution of the governmental powers among three departments, to save the people from autocracy." *Myers v. United States* (1924).

It is not a pleasant judicial duty to find that the President has exceeded his powers and still less so when his purposes were dictated by concern for the Nation's well-being, in the assured conviction that he acted to avert danger. But it would stultify one's faith in our people to entertain even a momentary fear that the patriotism and the wisdom of the President and the Congress, as well as the long view of the immediate parties in interest, will not find ready accommodation for differences on matters which, however close to their concern and however intrinsically important, are overshadowed by the awesome issues which confront the world. When at a moment of utmost anxiety President Washington turned to this Court for advice, and he had to be denied it as beyond the Court's competence to give, Chief Justice Jay, on behalf of the Court, wrote thus to the Father of his Country:

> "We exceedingly regret every event that may cause embarrassment to your administration, but we derive consolation from the reflection that your judgment will discern what is right, and that your usual prudence, decision, and firmness will surmount every obstacle to the preservation of the rights, peace, and dignity of the United States." Letter of August 8, 1793, 3 Johnston, Correspondence and Public Papers of John Jay (1891), 489.

In reaching the conclusion that conscience compels, I too derive consolation from the reflection that the President and the Congress between them will continue to safeguard the heritage which comes to them straight from George Washington.

Mr. Justice Douglas, concurring.

There can be no doubt that the emergency which caused the President to seize these steel plants was one that bore heavily on the country. But the emergency did not create power; it merely marked an occasion when power should be exercised. And the fact that it was necessary that measures be taken to keep steel in production does not mean that the President, rather than the Congress, had the constitutional authority to act. The Congress, as well as the President, is trustee of the national welfare. The President can act more quickly than the Congress. The President with the armed services at his disposal can move with force as well as with speed. All executive power — from the reign of ancient kings to the rule of modern dictators — has the outward appearance of efficiency.

Legislative power, by contrast, is slower to exercise. There must be delay while the ponderous machinery of committees, hearings, and debates is put into motion. That takes time; and while the Congress slowly moves into action, the emergency may take its toll in wages, consumer goods, war production, the standard of living of the people, and perhaps even lives. Legislative action may indeed often be cumbersome, time-consuming, and apparently inefficient. But as Mr. Justice Brandeis stated in his dissent in Myers v. United States (1926):

> The doctrine of the separation of powers was adopted by the Convention of 1787, not to promote efficiency but to preclude the exercise of arbitrary power. The purpose was not to avoid friction, but, by means of the inevitable friction incident to the distribution of the governmental powers among three departments, to save the people from autocracy.

We therefore cannot decide this case by determining which branch of government can deal most expeditiously with the present crisis. The answer must depend on the allocation of powers under the Constitution. . . .

A determination that sanctions should be applied, that the hand of the law should be placed upon the parties, and that the force of the courts should be directed against them, is an exercise of legislative power. In some nations that power is entrusted to the executive branch as a matter of course or in case of emergencies. We chose another course. We chose to place the legislative power of the Federal Government in the Congress. The language of the Constitution is not ambiguous or qualified. It places not *some* legislative power in the Congress; Article I, Section 1 says "All legislative Powers herein granted shall be vested in a Congress of the United States, which shall consist of a Senate and House of Representatives."

The legislative nature of the action taken by the President seems to me to be clear. When the United States takes over an industrial plant to settle a labor controversy, it is condemning property. The seizure of the plant is a taking in the constitutional sense. . . . The power of the Federal Government to condemn property is well established. . . . But there is a duty to pay for all property taken by the Government. The command of the Fifth Amendment is that no "private property be taken for public use, without just compensation." That constitutional requirement has an important bearing on the present case.

The President has no power to raise revenues. That power is in the Congress by Article I, Section 8 of the Constitution. The President might seize and the Congress by subsequent action might ratify the seizure. But until and unless Congress acted, no condemnation would be lawful. The branch of government that has the power to pay compensation for a seizure is the only one able to authorize a seizure or make lawful one that the President has effected. That seems to me to be the necessary result of the condemnation provision in the Fifth Amendment. . . .

If we sanctioned the present exercise of power by the President, we would be expanding Article II of the Constitution and rewriting it to suit the political conveniences of the present emergency. Article II which vests the "executive Power" in the President defines that power with particularity. . . . But . . . the power to execute the laws starts and ends with the laws Congress has enacted. . . .

We pay a price for our system of checks and balances, for the distribution of power among the three branches of government. It is a price that today may seem exorbitant to many. Today a kindly President uses the seizure power to effect a wage increase and to keep the steel furnaces in production. Yet tomorrow another President might use the same power to prevent a wage increase, to curb trade unionists, to regiment labor as oppressively as industry thinks it has been regimented by this seizure.

MR. JUSTICE JACKSON, concurring in the judgment and opinion of the Court.

That comprehensive and undefined presidential powers hold both practical advantages and grave dangers for the country will impress anyone who has served as legal adviser to a President in time of transition and public anxiety. While an interval of detached reflection may temper teachings of that experience, they probably are a more realistic influence on my views than the conventional materials of judicial decision which seem unduly to accentuate doctrine and legal fiction. . . .

A judge, like an executive adviser, may be surprised at the poverty of really useful and unambiguous authority applicable to concrete problems of executive power as they actually present themselves. Just what our forefathers did envision, or would have envisioned had they foreseen modern conditions, must be divined from materials almost as enigmatic as the dreams Joseph was called upon to interpret for Pharaoh. A century and a half of partisan debate and scholarly speculation yields no net result but only supplies more or less apt quotations from respected sources on each side of any question. They largely cancel each other.[8] And court decisions are indecisive because of the judicial practice of dealing with the largest questions in the most narrow way.

The actual art of governing under our Constitution does not and cannot conform to judicial definitions of the power of any of its branches based on isolated clauses or even single Articles torn from context. While the Constitution diffuses power the better to secure liberty, it also contemplates that practice will integrate the dispersed powers into a workable government. It enjoins upon its branches separateness but interdependence, autonomy but reciprocity. Presidential powers are not fixed but fluctuate, depending upon their disjunction or conjunction with those of Congress. We may well begin by a somewhat over-simplified grouping of practical situations in which a President may doubt, or others may challenge, his powers, and by distinguishing roughly the legal consequences of this factor of relativity.

1. When the President acts pursuant to an express or implied authorization of Congress, his authority is at its maximum, for it includes all that he possesses in his own right plus all that Congress can delegate. In these circumstances, and in these only, may he be said (for what it may be worth) to personify the federal sovereignty. If his act is held unconstitutional under these circumstances, it usually means that

---

[8] A Hamilton may be matched against a Madison. 7 The Works of Alexander Hamilton, 76-117; 1 Madison, Letters and Other Writings, 611-654. Professor Taft is counterbalanced by Theodore Roosevelt. Taft, Our Chief Magistrate and His Powers, 139-140; Theodore Roosevelt, Autobiography, 388-389. It even seems that President Taft cancels out Professor Taft. Compare his "Temporary Petroleum Withdrawal No. 5" of September 27, 1909, United States v. Midwest Oil Co., 236 U.S. 459, 467, 468, with his appraisal of executive power in "Our Chief Magistrate and His Powers" 139-140.

the Federal Government as an undivided whole lacks power. A seizure executed by the President pursuant to an Act of Congress would be supported by the strongest of presumptions and the widest latitude of judicial interpretation, and the burden of persuasion would rest heavily upon any who might attack it.

2. When the President acts in absence of either a congressional grant or denial of authority, he can only rely upon his own independent powers, but there is a zone of twilight in which he and Congress may have concurrent authority, or in which its distribution is uncertain. Therefore, congressional inertia, indifference or quiescence may sometimes, at least as a practical matter, enable, if not invite, measures on independent presidential responsibility. In this area, any actual test of power is likely to depend on the imperatives of events and contemporary imponderables rather than on abstract theories of law.

3. When the President takes measures incompatible with the expressed or implied will of Congress, his power is at its lowest ebb, for then he can rely only upon his own constitutional powers minus any constitutional powers of Congress over the matter. Courts can sustain exclusive presidential control in such a case only by disabling the Congress from acting upon the subject. Presidential claim to a power at once so conclusive and preclusive must be scrutinized with caution, for what is at stake is the equilibrium established by our constitutional system.

Into which of these classifications does this executive seizure of the steel industry fit? It is eliminated from the first by admission, for it is conceded that no congressional authorization exists for this seizure. That takes away also the support of the many precedents and declarations which were made in relation, and must be confined, to this category.

Can it then be defended under flexible tests available to the second category? It seems clearly eliminated from that class because Congress has not left seizure of private property an open field but has covered it by three statutory policies inconsistent with this seizure. . . .

This leaves the current seizure to be justified only by the severe tests under the third grouping, where it can be supported only by any remainder of executive power after subtraction of such powers as Congress may have over the subject. In short, we can sustain the President only by holding that seizure of such strike-bound industries is within his domain and beyond control by Congress. Thus, this Court's first review of such seizures occurs under circumstances which leave presidential power most vulnerable to attack and in the least favorable of possible constitutional postures.

I did not suppose, and I am not persuaded, that history leaves it open to question, at least in the courts, that the executive branch, like the Federal Government as a whole, possesses only delegated powers. The purpose of the Constitution was not only to grant power, but to keep it from getting out of hand. However, because the President does not enjoy unmentioned powers does not mean that the mentioned ones should be narrowed by a niggardly construction. Some clauses could be made almost unworkable, as well as immutable, by refusal to indulge some latitude of interpretation for changing times. I have heretofore, and do now, give to the enumerated powers the scope and elasticity afforded by what seem to be reasonable, practical implications instead of the rigidity dictated by a doctrinaire textualism.

The Solicitor General seeks the power of seizure in three clauses of the Executive Article, the first reading, "The executive Power shall be vested in a President of the United States of America." Lest I be thought to exaggerate, I quote the interpretation which his brief puts upon it: "In our view, this clause constitutes a grant of all the executive powers of which the Government is capable." If that be true, it is difficult to see why the forefathers bothered to add several specific items, including some trifling ones. The example of such unlimited executive power that must have most impressed the forefathers was the prerogative exercised by George III, and the description of its evils in the Declaration of Independence leads me to doubt that they were creating their new Executive in his image. Continental European examples were no more appealing. And if we seek instruction from our own times, we can match it only from the executive powers in those governments we disparagingly describe as totalitarian. I cannot accept the view that this clause is a grant in bulk of all conceivable executive power but regard it as an allocation to the presidential office of the generic powers thereafter stated.

The clause on which the Government next relies is that "The President shall be Commander in Chief of the Army and Navy of the United States. . . ." These cryptic words have given rise to some of the most persistent controversies in our constitutional history. Of course, they imply something more than an empty title. But just what authority goes with the name has plagued presidential advisers who would not waive or narrow it by nonassertion yet cannot say where it begins or ends. It undoubtedly puts the Nation's armed forces under presidential command. Hence, this loose appellation is sometimes advanced as support for any presidential action, internal or external, involving use of force, the idea being that it vests power to do anything, anywhere, that can be done with an army or navy.

That seems to be the logic of an argument tendered at our bar — that the President having, on his own responsibility, sent American troops abroad derives from that act "affirmative power" to seize the means of producing a supply of steel for them. To quote, "Perhaps the most forceful illustration of the scope of Presidential power in this connection is the fact that American troops in Korea, whose safety and effectiveness are so directly involved here, were sent to the field by an exercise of the President's constitutional powers." Thus, it is said, he has invested himself with "war powers."

I cannot foresee all that it might entail if the Court should indorse this argument. Nothing in our Constitution is plainer than that declaration of a war is entrusted only to Congress. Of course, a state of war may in fact exist without a formal declaration. But no doctrine that the Court could promulgate would seem to me more sinister and alarming than that a President whose conduct of foreign affairs is so largely uncontrolled, and often even is unknown, can vastly enlarge his mastery over the internal affairs of the country by his own commitment of the Nation's armed forces to some foreign venture. I do not, however, find it necessary or appropriate to consider the legal status of the Korean enterprise to discountenance argument based on it.

Assuming that we are in a war *de facto*, whether it is or is not a war *de jure*, does that empower the Commander in Chief to seize industries he thinks necessary to supply our army? The Constitution expressly places in Congress power "to raise and *support* Armies" and "to *provide* and *maintain* a Navy." (Emphasis supplied.) This certainly lays upon Congress primary responsibility for supplying the armed forces. Congress alone controls the raising of revenues and their appropriation and may determine in what manner and by what means they shall be spent for military and naval procurement. I suppose no one would doubt that Congress can take over war supply as a Government enterprise. On the other hand, if Congress sees fit to rely on free private enterprise collectively bargaining with free labor for support and maintenance of our armed forces, can the Executive, because of lawful disagreements incidental to that process, seize the facility for operation upon Government-imposed terms?

There are indications that the Constitution did not contemplate that the title Commander in Chief *of the Army and Navy* will constitute him also Commander in Chief of the country, its industries and its inhabitants. He has no monopoly of "war powers," whatever they are. While Congress cannot deprive the President of the command of the army and navy, only Congress can provide him an army or navy to command. It is also empowered to make rules for the "Government and Regulation of land and naval Forces," by which it may to some unknown extent impinge upon even command functions.

That military powers of the Commander in Chief were not to supersede representative government of internal affairs seems obvious from the Constitution and from elementary American history. Time out of mind, and even now in many parts of the world, a military commander can seize private housing to shelter his troops. Not so, however, in the United States, for the Third Amendment says, "No Soldier shall, in time of peace be quartered in any house, without the consent of the Owner, nor in time of war, but in a manner to be prescribed by law." Thus, even in war time, his seizure of needed military housing must be authorized by Congress. It also was expressly left to Congress to "provide for calling forth the Militia to execute the Laws of the Union, suppress Insurrections and repel Invasions. . . ." Such a limitation on the command power, written at a time when the militia rather than a standing army was contemplated as the military weapon of the Republic, underscores the Constitution's policy that Congress, not the Executive, should control utilization of the war power as an instrument of domestic policy. Congress, fulfilling that function, has authorized the President to use the army to enforce certain civil rights. On the other hand, Congress has forbidden him to use the army for the purpose of executing general laws except when expressly authorized by the Constitution or by Act of Congress. . . .

We should not use this occasion to circumscribe, much less to contract, the lawful role of the President as Commander in Chief. I should indulge the widest latitude of interpretation to sustain his exclusive function to command the instruments of national force, at least when turned against the outside world for the security of our society. But, when it is turned inward, not because of rebellion but because of a lawful economic struggle between industry and labor, it should have no such indulgence. His command power is not such an absolute as might be implied from that office in a militaristic system but is subject to limitations consistent with a constitutional Republic whose law and policy-making branch is a representative Congress. The purpose of lodging dual titles in one man was to insure that the civilian would control the military, not to enable the military to subordinate the presidential office. No penance would ever expiate the sin against free government of holding that a President can escape control of executive powers by law through assuming his military role. What the power of command may include I do not try to envision, but I think it is not a military prerogative, without support of law, to seize persons or property because they are important or even essential for the military and naval establishment.

The third clause in which the Solicitor General finds seizure powers is that "he shall take Care that the Laws be faithfully executed. . . ." That authority must be matched against words of the Fifth Amendment that "No person shall be . . . deprived of life, liberty or property, without due process of law. . . ." One gives a governmental authority that reaches so far as there is law, the other gives a private right that authority shall go no farther. These signify about all there is of the principle that ours is a government of laws, not of men, and that we submit ourselves to rulers only if under rules.

The Solicitor General lastly grounds support of the seizure upon nebulous, inherent powers never expressly granted but said to have accrued to the office from the customs and claims of preceding administrations. The plea is for a resulting power to deal with a crisis or an emergency according to the necessities of the case, the unarticulated assumption being that necessity knows no law.

Loose and irresponsible use of adjectives colors all nonlegal and much legal discussion of presidential powers. "Inherent" powers, "implied" powers, "incidental" powers, "plenary" powers, "war" powers and "emergency" powers are used, often interchangeably and without fixed or ascertainable meanings.

The vagueness and generality of the clauses that set forth presidential powers afford a plausible basis for pressures within and without an administration for presidential action beyond that supported by those whose responsibility it is to defend his actions in court. The claim of inherent and unrestricted presidential powers has long been a persuasive dialectical weapon in political controversy. While it is not surprising that counsel should grasp support from such unadjudicated claims of power, a judge cannot accept self-serving press statements of the attorney for one of the interested parties as authority in answering a constitutional question, even if the advocate was himself. But prudence has counseled that actual reliance on such nebulous claims stop short of provoking a judicial test. [Justice Jackson is referring to his own opinion, written while he was attorney general under President Roosevelt, which was cited in this case by the solicitor general. — Eds.] . . .

The appeal . . . that we declare the existence of inherent powers *ex necessitate* to meet an emergency asks us to do what many think would be wise, although it is something the forefathers omitted. They knew what emergencies were, knew the pressures they engender for authoritative action, knew, too, how they afford a ready pretext for usurpation. We may also suspect that they suspected that emergency powers would tend to kindle emergencies. Aside from suspension of the privilege of the writ of habeas corpus in time of rebellion or invasion, when the public safety may require it, they made no express provision for exercise of extraordinary authority because of a crisis. I do not think we rightfully may so amend their work, and, if we could, I am not convinced it would be wise to do so, although many modern nations have forthrightly recognized that war and economic crises may upset the normal balance between liberty and authority. Their experience with emergency powers may not be irrelevant to the argument here that we should say that the Executive, of his own volition, can invest himself with undefined emergency powers.

Germany, after the First World War, framed the Weimar Constitution, designed to secure her liberties in the Western tradition. However, the President of the Republic, without concurrence of the Reichstag, was empowered temporarily to suspend any or all individual rights if public safety and order were seriously disturbed or endangered. This proved a temptation to every government, whatever its shade of opinion, and in 13 years suspension of rights was invoked on more than 250 occasions. Finally, Hitler persuaded President Von Hindenberg to suspend all such rights, and they were never restored. . . .

In view of the ease, expedition and safety with which Congress can grant and has granted large emergency powers, certainly ample to embrace this crisis, I am quite unimpressed with the argument that we should affirm possession of them without statute. Such power either has no beginning or it has no end. If it exists, it need submit to no legal restraint. I am not alarmed that it would plunge us straightway into dictatorship, but it is at least a step in that wrong direction.

As to whether there is imperative necessity for such powers, it is relevant to note the gap that exists between the President's paper powers and his real powers. The Constitution does not disclose the measure of the actual controls wielded by the modern presidential office. That instrument must be understood as an Eighteenth-Century sketch of a government hoped for, not as a blueprint of the Government that is. Vast accretions of federal power, eroded from that reserved by the States, have magnified the scope of presidential activity. Subtle shifts take place in the centers of real power that do not show on the face of the Constitution.

Executive power has the advantage of concentration in a single head in whose choice the whole Nation has a part, making him the focus of public hopes and expectations. In drama, magnitude and finality his decisions so far overshadow any others that almost alone he fills the public eye and ear. No other personality in public life can begin to compete with him in access to the public mind through modern methods of communications. By his prestige as head of state and his influence upon public opinion he exerts a leverage upon those who are supposed to check and balance his power which often cancels their effectiveness.

Moreover, rise of the party system has made a significant extraconstitutional supplement to real executive power. No appraisal of his necessities is realistic which overlooks that he heads a political system as well as a legal system. Party loyalties and interests, sometimes more binding than law, extend his effective control into branches of government other than his own and he often may win, as a political leader, what he cannot command under the Constitution. . . . I cannot be brought to believe that this country will suffer if the Court refuses further to aggrandize the presidential office, already so potent and so relatively immune from judicial review, at the expense of Congress.

But I have no illusion that any decision by this Court can keep power in the hands of Congress if it is not wise and timely in meeting its problems. A crisis that challenges the President equally, or perhaps primarily, challenges Congress. If not good law, there was worldly wisdom in the maxim attributed to Napoleon that "The tools belong to the man who can use them." We may say that power to legislate for emergencies belongs in the hands of Congress, but only Congress itself can prevent power from slipping through its fingers.

The essence of our free Government is "leave to live by no man's leave, underneath the law" — to be governed by those impersonal forces which we call law. Our Government is fashioned to fulfill this concept so far as humanly possible. The Executive, except for recommendation and veto, has no legislative power. The executive action we have here originates in the individual will of the President and represents an exercise of authority without law. No one, perhaps not even the President, knows the limits of the power he may seek to exert in this instance and the parties affected cannot learn the limit of their rights. We do not know today what powers over labor or property would be claimed to flow from Government possession if we should legalize it, what rights to compensation would be claimed or recognized, or on what contingency it would end. With all its defects, delays and inconveniences, men have discovered no technique for long preserving free government except that the Executive be under the law, and that the law be made by parliamentary deliberations.

Such institutions may be destined to pass away. But it is the duty of the Court to be last, not first, to give them up.

MR. JUSTICE BURTON, concurring in both the opinion and judgment of the Court. . . .

In the case before us, Congress authorized a procedure which the President declined to follow. Instead, he followed another procedure which he hoped might eliminate the need for the first. Upon its failure, he issued an executive order to seize the steel properties in the face of the reserved right of Congress to adopt or reject that course as a matter of legislative policy. . . . Does the President, in such a situation, have inherent constitutional power to seize private property which makes congressional action in relation thereto unnecessary? We find no such power available to him under the present circumstances. The present situation is not comparable to that of an imminent invasion or threatened attack. We do not face the issue of what might be the President's constitutional power to meet such catastrophic situations. Nor is it claimed that the current seizure is in the nature of a military command addressed by the President, as Commander in Chief, to a mobilized nation waging, or imminently threatened with, total war.

The controlling fact here is that Congress, within its constitutionally delegated power, has prescribed for the President specific procedures, exclusive of seizure, for his use in meeting the present type of emergency. Congress has reserved to itself the right to determine where and when to authorize the seizure of property in meeting such an emergency. Under these circumstances, the President's order of April 8 invaded the jurisdiction of Congress. It violated the essence of the principle of the separation of governmental powers. Accordingly, the injunction against its effectiveness should be sustained.

MR. JUSTICE CLARK, concurring in the judgment of the Court. . . .

The limits of presidential power are obscure. However, Article II, no less than Article I, is part of "a constitution intended to endure for ages to come, and, consequently, to be adapted to the various *crises* of human affairs." . . . In my view . . . the Constitution does grant to the President extensive authority in times of grave and imperative national emergency. In fact, to my thinking, such a grant may well be necessary to the very existence of the Constitution itself. . . . As Lincoln aptly said, "[Is] it possible to lose the nation and yet preserve the Constitution?" In describing this authority I care not whether one calls it "residual," "inherent," "moral," "implied," "aggregate," "emergency," or otherwise. I am of the conviction that those who have had the gratifying experience of being the President's lawyer have used one or more of these adjectives only with the utmost of sincerity and the highest of purpose. [A defense of Jackson's opinion rendered while serving as attorney general to Franklin Roosevelt. — EDS.]

I conclude that where Congress has laid down specific procedures to deal with the type of crisis confronting the President, he must follow those procedures in meeting the crisis; but that in the absence of such action by Congress, the President's independent power to act depends upon the gravity of the situation confronting the nation. I cannot sustain the seizure in question because here . . . Congress had prescribed methods to be followed by the President in meeting the emergency at hand. . . . [T]he hard fact remains that neither the Defense Production Act nor Taft-Hartley authorized the seizure challenged here, and the Government made no effort to comply with the procedures established by the Selective Service Act of 1948, a statute which expressly authorizes seizures when producers fail to supply necessary defense materiel. . . .

MR. CHIEF JUSTICE VINSON, with whom MR. JUSTICE REED and MR. JUSTICE MINTON join, dissenting. . . .

This Court affirms. Some members of the Court are of the view that the President is without power to act in time of crisis in the absence of express statutory authorization. Other members of the Court affirm on the basis of their reading of certain statutes. Because we cannot agree that affirmance is proper on any ground, and because of the transcending importance of the questions presented not only in this critical litigation but also to the powers of the President and of future Presidents to act in time of crisis, we are compelled to register this dissent.

I

. . . Those who suggest that this is a case involving extraordinary powers should be mindful that these are extraordinary times. A world not yet recovered from the devastation of World War II has been forced to face the threat of another and more terrifying global conflict.

Accepting in full measure its responsibility in the world community, the United States was instrumental in securing adoption of the United Nations Charter, approved by the Senate by a vote of 89 to 2. The first purpose of the United Nations is to "maintain international peace and security, and to that end: to take effective collective measures for the prevention and removal of threats to the peace, and for the suppression of acts of aggression or other breaches of the peace. . . ." In 1950, when the United Nations called upon member nations "to render every assistance" to repel aggression in Korea, the United States furnished its vigorous support. For almost two full years, our armed forces have been fighting in Korea, suffering casualties of over 108,000 men. Hostilities have not abated. The "determination of the United Nations to continue its action in Korea to meet the aggression" has been reaffirmed. Congressional support of the action in Korea has been manifested by provisions for increased military manpower and equipment and for economic stabilization, as hereinafter described. . . .

Congress also directed the President to build up our own defenses. Congress, recognizing the "grim fact . . . that the United States is now engaged in a struggle for survival" and that "it is imperative that we now take those necessary steps to make our strength equal to the peril of the hour," granted authority to draft men into the armed forces. As a result, we now have over 3,500,000 men in our armed forces. . . .

Following the attack in Korea, the President asked for authority to requisition property and to allocate and fix priorities for scarce goods. In the Defense Production Act of 1950, Congress granted the powers requested and, *in addition*, granted power to stabilize prices and wages and to provide for settlement of labor disputes arising in the defense program. The Defense Production Act was extended in 1951, a Senate Committee noting that in the dislocation caused by the programs for purchase of military equipment "lies the seed of an economic disaster that might well destroy the military might we are straining to build." Significantly, the Committee examined the problem "in terms of just one commodity, steel," and found "a graphic picture of the over-all inflationary danger growing out of reduced civilian supplies and rising incomes." Even before Korea, steel production at levels above theoretical 100% capacity was not capable of supplying civilian needs alone. Since Korea, the tremendous military demand for steel has far exceeded the increases in productive capacity. This Committee emphasized that the shortage of steel, even with the mills operating at full capacity, coupled with increased civilian purchasing power, presented grave danger of disastrous inflation.

The President has the duty to execute the foregoing legislative programs. Their successful execution depends upon continued production of steel and stabilized prices for steel. . . . [T]he central fact of this case [is] that the Nation's entire basic steel production would have shut down completely if there had been no Government seizure. . . . [T]he uncontroverted affidavits in this record amply support the finding that "a work stoppage would immediately jeopardize and imperil our national defense."

Plaintiffs do not remotely suggest any basis for rejecting the President's finding that *any* stoppage of steel production would immediately place the Nation in peril. Moreover, even self-generated doubts that *any* stoppage of steel production constitutes an emergency are of little comfort here. The Union and the plaintiffs bargained for 6 months with over 100 issues in dispute — issues not limited to wage demands but including the union shop and other matters of principle between the parties. At the time of seizure there was not, and there is not now, the slightest evidence to justify the belief that any strike will be of short duration. The Union and the steel companies may well engage in a lengthy struggle. Plaintiffs' counsel tells us that "sooner or later" the mills will operate again. That may satisfy the steel companies and, perhaps, the Union. But our soldiers and our allies will hardly be cheered with the assurance that the ammunition upon which their lives depend will be forthcoming — "sooner or later," or, in other words, "too little and too late."

Accordingly, if the President has any power under the Constitution to meet a critical situation in the absence of express statutory authorization, there is no basis whatever for criticizing the exercise of such power in this case.

II

The steel mills were seized for a public use. The power of eminent domain, invoked in this case, is an essential attribute of sovereignty and has long been recognized as a power of the Federal Government. . . . Admitting that the Government could seize the mills, plaintiffs claim that the implied power of eminent domain can be exercised only under an Act of Congress; under no circumstances, they say, can that power be exercised by the President unless he can point to an express provision in enabling legislation. . . . [T]he President's only course in the face of an emergency is to present the matter to Congress and await the final passage of legislation which will enable the Government to cope with threatened disaster.

Under this view, the President is left powerless at the very moment when the need for action may be most pressing and when no one, other than he, is immediately capable of action. Under this view, he is left powerless because a power not expressly given to Congress is nevertheless found to rest exclusively with Congress. . . .

III

A review of executive action demonstrates that our Presidents have on many occasions exhibited the leadership contemplated by the Framers when they made the President Commander in Chief, and imposed upon him the trust to "take Care that the Laws be faithfully executed." With or without explicit statutory authorization, Presidents have at such times dealt with national emergencies by acting promptly and resolutely to enforce legislative programs, at least to save those programs until Congress could act. Congress and the courts have responded to such executive initiative with consistent approval.

Our first President displayed at once the leadership contemplated by the Framers. . . . When international disputes engendered by the French revolution threatened to involve this country in war, and while congressional policy remained uncertain, Washington issued his Proclamation of Neutrality. Hamilton, whose defense of the Proclamation has endured the test of time, invoked the argument that the Executive has the duty to do that which will preserve peace until Congress acts and, in addition, pointed to the need for keeping the Nation informed of the requirements of existing laws and treaties as part of the faithful execution of the laws. . . .

Jefferson's initiative in the Louisiana Purchase, the Monroe Doctrine, and Jackson's removal of Government deposits from the Bank of the United States further serve to demonstrate by deed what the Framers described by word when they vested the whole of the executive power in the President.

Without declaration of war, President Lincoln took energetic action with the outbreak of the War Between the States. He summoned troops and paid them out of the Treasury without appropriation therefor. He proclaimed a naval blockade of the Confederacy and seized ships violating that blockade. Congress, far from denying the validity of these acts, gave them express approval. The most striking action of President Lincoln was the Emancipation Proclamation, issued in aid of the successful prosecution of the War Between the States, but wholly without statutory authority.

In an action furnishing a most apt precedent for this case, President Lincoln without statutory authority directed the seizure of rail and telegraph lines leading to Washington. Many months later, Congress recognized and confirmed the power of the President to seize railroads and telegraph lines and provided criminal penalties for interference with Government operation. This Act did not confer on the President any additional powers of seizure. Congress plainly rejected the view that the President's acts had been without legal sanction until ratified by the legislature. Sponsors of the bill declared that its purpose was only to confirm the power which the President already possessed. Opponents insisted a statute authorizing seizure was unnecessary and might even be construed as limiting existing Presidential powers. . . .

This is but a cursory summary of executive leadership. But it amply demonstrates that Presidents have taken prompt action to enforce the laws and protect the country whether or not Congress happened to provide in advance for the particular method of execution. At the minimum, the executive actions reviewed herein sustain the action of the President in this case. . . . The fact that temporary executive seizures of industrial plants to meet an emergency have not been directly tested in this Court furnishes not the slightest suggestion that such actions have been illegal. Rather, the fact that Congress and the courts have consistently recognized and given their support to such executive action indicates that such a power of seizure has been accepted throughout our history.

History bears out the genius of the Founding Fathers, who created a Government subject to law but not left subject to inertia when vigor and initiative are required.

IV

Focusing now on the situation confronting the President on the night of April 8, 1952, we cannot but conclude that the President was performing his duty under the Constitution to "take Care that the Laws be faithfully executed." . . .

The President reported to Congress the morning after the seizure that he acted because a work stoppage in steel production would immediately imperil the safety of the Nation by preventing execution of the legislative programs for procurement of military equipment. And, while a shutdown could be averted by granting the price concessions requested by plaintiffs, granting such concessions would disrupt the price stabilization program also enacted by Congress. Rather than fail to execute either legislative program, the President acted to execute both.

Much of the argument in this case has been directed at straw men. We do not now have before us the case of a President acting solely on the basis of his own notions of the public welfare. Nor is there any question of unlimited executive power in this case. The President himself closed the door to any such claim when he sent his Message to Congress stating his purpose to abide by any action of Congress, whether approving or disapproving his seizure action. Here, the President immediately made sure that Congress was fully informed of the temporary action he had taken only to preserve the legislative programs from destruction until Congress could act.

The absence of a specific statute authorizing seizure of the steel mills as a mode of executing the laws — both the military procurement program and the anti-inflation program — has not until today been thought to prevent the President from executing the laws. Unlike an administrative commission confined to the enforcement of the statute under which it was created, or the head of a department when administering a particular statute, the President is a constitutional officer charged with taking care that a "mass of legislation" be executed. Flexibility as to mode of execution to meet critical situations is a matter of practical necessity. . . . Although more restrictive views of executive power, advocated in dissenting opinions of Justices Holmes, McReynolds and Brandeis, were emphatically rejected by this Court in *Myers v. United States* (1926), members of today's majority treat these dissenting views as authoritative.

There is no statute prohibiting seizure as a method of enforcing legislative programs. Congress has in no wise indicated that its legislation is not to be executed by the taking of private property (subject of course to the payment of just compensation) if its legislation cannot otherwise be executed. Indeed, the Universal Military Training and Service Act authorizes the seizure of any plant that fails to fill a Government contract or the properties of any steel producer that fails to allocate steel as directed for defense production. And the Defense Production Act authorizes the President to requisition equipment and condemn real property needed without delay in the defense effort. Where Congress authorizes seizure in instances not necessarily crucial to the defense program, it can hardly be said to have disclosed an intention to prohibit seizures where essential to the execution of that legislative program.

Whatever the extent of Presidential power on more tranquil occasions, and whatever the right of the President to execute legislative programs as he sees fit without reporting the mode of execution to Congress, the single Presidential purpose disclosed on this record is to faithfully execute the laws by acting in an emergency to maintain the status quo, thereby preventing collapse of the legislative programs until Congress could act. The President's action served the same purposes as a judicial stay entered to maintain the status quo in order to preserve the jurisdiction of a court. In his Message to Congress immediately following the seizure, the President explained the necessity of his action in executing the military procurement and anti-inflation legislative programs and expressed his desire to cooperate with any legislative proposals approving, regulating or rejecting the seizure of the steel mills. Consequently, there is no evidence whatever of any Presidential purpose to defy Congress or act in any way inconsistent with the legislative will.... There is no cause to fear Executive tyranny so long as the laws of Congress are being faithfully executed. Certainly there is no basis for fear of dictatorship when the Executive acts, as he did in this case, only to save the situation until Congress could act....

VI

The diversity of views expressed in the six opinions of the majority, the lack of reference to authoritative precedent, the repeated reliance upon prior dissenting opinions, the complete disregard of the uncontroverted facts showing the gravity of

When *Dames & Moore v. Regan* was decided in 1981, a young John G. Roberts, Jr. (far right), the future Chief Justice, clerked for Justice Rehnquist (second from the left). As noted earlier, Rehnquist had clerked for Justice Jackson when *Youngstown Sheet & Tube Co. v. Sawyer* was decided in 1952.

the emergency and the temporary nature of the taking all serve to demonstrate how far afield one must go to affirm the order of the District Court.

The broad executive power granted by Article II to an officer on duty 365 days a year cannot, it is said, be invoked to avert disaster. Instead, the President must confine himself to sending a message to Congress recommending action. Under this messenger-boy concept of the Office, the President cannot even act to preserve legislative programs from destruction so that Congress will have something left to act upon. There is no judicial finding that the executive action was unwarranted because there was in fact no basis for the President's finding of the existence of an emergency for, under this view, the gravity of the emergency and the immediacy of the threatened disaster are considered irrelevant as a matter of law. . . .

Faced with the duty of executing the defense programs which Congress had enacted and the disastrous effects that any stoppage in steel production would have on those programs, the President acted to preserve those programs by seizing the steel mills.

There is no question that the possession was other than temporary in character and subject to congressional direction — either approving, disapproving or regulating the manner in which the mills were to be administered and returned to the owners. The President immediately informed Congress of his action and clearly stated his intention to abide by the legislative will. No basis for claims of arbitrary action, unlimited powers or dictatorial usurpation of congressional power appears from the facts of this case. On the contrary, judicial, legislative and executive precedents throughout our history demonstrate that in this case the President acted in full conformity with his duties under the Constitution. Accordingly, we would reverse the order of the District Court.

ASSIGNMENT 3

E. THE DOMESTIC POWERS OF THE PRESIDENT WHEN HE ENTERS INTO AGREEMENTS WITH OTHER NATIONS

In *Dames & Moore v. Regan*, we shift our focus from the President's war power to his power to conduct foreign affairs. The Court revisits the doctrine adopted by the Court in *Youngstown Sheet & Tube Co. v. Sawyer*. Justice Rehnquist's majority opinion employs the framework presented in Justice Jackson's famous concurrence, though with a twist. As noted above, William Rehnquist clerked for Justice Jackson at the time that *Youngstown* was argued and decided. And in an even bigger coincidence, the current Chief Justice, John G. Roberts, served as a law clerk for Justice Rehnquist in 1981.

STUDY GUIDE

- Does Justice Rehnquist faithfully apply Justice Jackson's concurring opinion in *Youngstown*, or does he modify it?
- What constitutional power is the President exercising? Are executive agreements provided for in the text of the Constitution?
- How does Chief Justice Rehnquist address the problem of interpreting congressional silence?
- Does the Court's analysis suggest that, when Congress has not specifically addressed a particular circumstance it may not have anticipated, considerable caution must be taken before concluding that the President has acted "illegally"?

Dames & Moore v. Regan

453 U.S. 654 (1981)

Justice Rehnquist delivered the opinion of the Court.

The questions presented by this case touch fundamentally upon the manner in which our Republic is to be governed. Throughout the nearly two centuries of our Nation's existence under the Constitution, this subject has generated considerable debate. We have had the benefit of commentators such as John Jay, Alexander Hamilton, and James Madison writing in *The Federalist Papers* at the Nation's very inception, the benefit of astute foreign observers of our system such as Alexis de Tocqueville and James Bryce writing during the first century of the Nation's existence, and the benefit of many other treatises as well as more than 400 volumes of reports of decisions of this Court. As these writings reveal it is doubtless both futile and perhaps dangerous to find any epigrammatical explanation of how this country has been governed. Indeed, as Justice Jackson noted, "[a] judge . . . may be surprised at the poverty of really useful and unambiguous authority applicable to concrete problems of executive power as they actually present themselves." *Youngstown Sheet & Tube Co. v. Sawyer* (1952) (concurring opinion).

Our decision today will not dramatically alter this situation, for the Framers "did not make the judiciary the overseer of our government." *Id.* at 343 U.S. 594 (Frankfurter, J., concurring). We are confined to a resolution of the dispute presented to us. That dispute involves various Executive Orders and regulations by which the President nullified attachments and liens on Iranian assets in the United States, directed that these assets be transferred to Iran, and suspended claims against Iran that may be presented to an International Claims Tribunal. This action was taken in an effort to comply with an Executive Agreement between the United States and Iran. . . . As we now turn to the factual and legal issues in this case, we freely confess that we are obviously deciding only one more episode in the never-ending tension between the President exercising the executive authority in a world that presents each day some new challenge with which he must deal, and the Constitution under which we all live and which no one disputes embodies some sort of system of checks and balances.

I

On November 4, 1979, the American Embassy in Tehran was seized and our diplomatic personnel were captured and held hostage. In response to that crisis, President Carter, acting pursuant to the International Emergency Economic Powers Act (hereinafter IEEPA), declared a national emergency on November 14, 1979, and blocked the removal or transfer of "all property and interests in property of the Government of Iran, its instrumentalities and controlled entities and the Central Bank of Iran which are or become subject to the jurisdiction of the United States." . . . Exec. Order No. 12170.

On December 19, 1979, petitioner Dames & Moore filed suit in the United States District Court for the Central District of California against the Government of Iran, the Atomic Energy Organization of Iran, and a number of Iranian banks. In its complaint, petitioner alleged that its wholly owned subsidiary, Dames & Moore International, S. R. L., was a party to a written contract with the Atomic Energy Organization, and that the subsidiary's entire interest in the contract had been assigned to petitioner. Under the contract, the subsidiary was to conduct site studies for a proposed nuclear power plant in Iran. As provided in the terms of the contract, the Atomic Energy Organization terminated the agreement for its own convenience on June 30, 1979. Petitioner contended, however, that it was owed $3,436,694.30 plus interest for services performed under the contract prior to the date of termination. The District Court issued orders of attachment directed against property of the defendants, and the property of certain Iranian banks was then attached to secure any judgment that might be entered against them.

On January 20, 1981, the Americans held hostage were released by Iran pursuant to an Agreement entered into the day before and embodied in two Declarations of the Democratic and Popular Republic of Algeria. . . . The Agreement stated that "[i]t is the purpose of [the United States and Iran] . . . to terminate all litigation as between the Government of each party and the nationals of the other, and to bring about the settlement and termination of all such claims through binding arbitration." In furtherance of this goal, the Agreement called for the establishment of an Iran-United States Claims Tribunal which would arbitrate any claims not settled within six months. Awards of the Claims Tribunal are to be "final and binding" and "enforceable . . . in the courts of any nation in accordance with its laws." Under the Agreement, the United States is obligated "to terminate all legal proceedings in United States courts involving claims of United States persons and institutions against Iran and its state enterprises, to nullify all attachments and judgments obtained therein, to prohibit all further litigation based on such claims, and to bring about the termination of such claims through binding arbitration."

On April 28, 1981, petitioner filed this action in the District Court for declaratory and injunctive relief against the United States and the Secretary of the

Treasury, seeking to prevent enforcement of the Executive Orders and Treasury Department regulations implementing the Agreement with Iran. In its complaint, petitioner alleged that the actions of the President and the Secretary of the Treasury implementing the Agreement with Iran were beyond their statutory and constitutional powers and, in any event, were unconstitutional to the extent they adversely affect petitioner's final judgment against the Government of Iran and the Atomic Energy Organization, its execution of that judgment in the State of Washington, its prejudgment attachments, and its ability to continue to litigate against the Iranian banks. . . .

II

The parties and the lower courts, confronted with the instant questions, have all agreed that much relevant analysis is contained in *Youngstown*. Justice Black's opinion for the Court in that case, involving the validity of President Truman's effort to seize the country's steel mills in the wake of a nationwide strike, recognized that "[t]he President's power, if any, to issue the order must stem either from an act of Congress or from the Constitution itself." Justice Jackson's concurring opinion elaborated in a general way the consequences of different types of interaction between the two democratic branches in assessing Presidential authority to act in any given case. When the President acts pursuant to an express or implied authorization from Congress, he exercises not only his powers but also those delegated by Congress. In such a case the executive action "would be supported by the strongest of presumptions and the widest latitude of judicial interpretation, and the burden of persuasion would rest heavily upon any who might attack it." When the President acts in the absence of congressional authorization he may enter "a zone of twilight in which he and Congress may have concurrent authority, or in which its distribution is uncertain." In such a case the analysis becomes more complicated, and the validity of the President's action, at least so far as separation-of-powers principles are concerned, hinges on a consideration of all the circumstances which might shed light on the views of the Legislative Branch toward such action, including "congressional inertia, indifference or quiescence." Finally, when the President acts in contravention of the will of Congress, "his power is at its lowest ebb," and the Court can sustain his actions "only by disabling the Congress from acting upon the subject."

Although we have in the past found and do today find Justice Jackson's classification of executive actions into three general categories analytically useful, . . . Justice Jackson himself recognized that his three categories represented "a somewhat over-simplified grouping," and it is doubtless the case that executive action in any particular instance falls, not neatly in one of three pigeonholes, but rather at some point along a spectrum running from explicit congressional authorization to explicit congressional prohibition. This is particularly true as respects cases such as the one before us, involving responses to international crises the nature of which Congress can hardly have been expected to anticipate in any detail. . . .

III

[The government contended that the International Emergency Economic Powers Act of 1976 (IEEPA) gave the President the power to nullify the attachments and transfer the assets to the tribunal. The Court agreed, finding that IEEPA expressly gave the President the authority to "nullify" and "transfer" "transactions involving, any property in which any foreign country or a national thereof has any interest." — Eds.]

. . . Because the President's action in nullifying the attachments and ordering the transfer of the assets was taken pursuant to specific congressional authorization, it is "supported by the strongest of presumptions and the widest latitude of judicial interpretation, and the burden of persuasion would rest heavily upon any who might attack it." *Youngstown* (Jackson, J., concurring). Under the circumstances of this case, we cannot say that petitioner has sustained that heavy burden. A contrary ruling would mean that the Federal Government as a whole lacked the power exercised by the President, and that we are not prepared to say.

IV

Although we [decline] to conclude that the IEEPA or the Hostage Act directly authorizes the President's suspension of claims for the reasons noted, we cannot ignore the general tenor of Congress' legislation in this area in trying to determine whether the President is acting alone or at least with the acceptance of Congress. As we have noted, Congress cannot anticipate and legislate with regard to every possible action the President may find it necessary to take or every possible situation in which he might act. Such failure of Congress specifically to delegate authority does not, "especially . . . in the areas of foreign policy and national security," imply "congressional disapproval" of action taken by the Executive. *Haig v. Agee* (1981). On the contrary, the enactment of legislation closely related to the question of the President's authority in a particular case which evinces legislative intent to accord the President broad discretion may be considered to "invite" "measures on independent presidential responsibility," *Youngstown* (Jackson, J., concurring). At least this is so where there is no contrary indication of legislative intent and when, as here, there is a history of congressional acquiescence in conduct of the sort engaged in by the President. It is to that history which we now turn.

Not infrequently in affairs between nations, outstanding claims by nationals of one country against the government of another country are "sources of friction" between the two sovereigns. *United States v. Pink* (1942). To resolve these difficulties, nations have often entered into agreements settling the claims of their respective nationals. . . . Consistent with that principle, the United States has repeatedly exercised its sovereign authority to settle the claims of its nationals against foreign countries. Though those settlements have sometimes been made by treaty, there has also been a longstanding practice of settling such claims by executive agreement without the advice and consent of the Senate. Under such agreements, the President has agreed to renounce or extinguish claims of United States nationals against foreign governments in return for lump-sum payments or the establishment of arbitration procedures. . . . It is clear that the practice of settling claims continues today. Since 1952, the President has entered into at least 10 binding settlements with foreign nations, including an $80 million settlement with the People's Republic of China.

Crucial to our decision today is the conclusion that Congress has implicitly approved the practice of claim settlement by executive agreement. This is best demonstrated by Congress' enactment of the International Claims Settlement Act of 1949. The Act had two purposes: (1) to allocate to United States nationals funds received in the course of an executive claims settlement with Yugoslavia, and (2) to provide a procedure whereby funds resulting from future settlements could be distributed. To achieve these ends Congress created the International Claims Commission, now the Foreign Claims Settlement Commission, and gave it jurisdiction to make final and binding decisions with respect to claims by United States nationals against settlement funds. By creating a procedure to implement future settlement agreements, Congress placed its stamp of approval on such agreements. Indeed, the legislative history of the Act observed that the United States was seeking settlements with countries other than Yugoslavia and that the bill contemplated settlements of a similar nature in the future.

Over the years Congress has frequently amended the International Claims Settlement Act to provide for particular problems arising out of settlement agreements, thus demonstrating Congress' continuing acceptance of the President's claim settlement authority. . . . Finally, the legislative history of the IEEPA further reveals that Congress has accepted the authority of the Executive to enter into settlement agreements. . . . In addition to congressional acquiescence in the President's power to settle claims, prior cases of this Court have also recognized that the President does have some measure of power to enter into executive agreements without obtaining the advice and consent of the Senate. In *United States v. Pink*, for example, the Court upheld the validity of the Litvinov Assignment, which was part of an Executive Agreement whereby the Soviet Union assigned to the United States amounts owed to it by American nationals so that outstanding claims of other American nationals could be paid. . . .

In light of all of the foregoing — the inferences to be drawn from the character of the legislation Congress has enacted in the area, such as the IEEPA and the Hostage Act, and from the history of acquiescence in executive claims settlement — we conclude that the President was authorized to suspend pending claims pursuant to Executive Order No. 12294. As Justice Frankfurter pointed out in *Youngstown*, "a systematic, unbroken, executive practice, long pursued to the knowledge of the Congress and never before questioned . . . may be treated as a gloss on 'Executive Power' vested in the President by §1 of Art. II." Past practice does not, by itself, create power, but "long-continued practice, known to and acquiesced in by Congress, would raise a presumption that the [action] had been [taken] in pursuance of its consent." . . . *United States v. Midwest Oil Co.* (1915). Such practice is present here and such a presumption is also appropriate. In light of the fact that Congress may be considered to have consented to the President's action in suspending claims, we cannot say that action exceeded the President's powers. . . .

Just as importantly, Congress has not disapproved of the action taken here. Though Congress has held hearings on the Iranian Agreement itself, Congress has not enacted legislation, or even passed a resolution, indicating its displeasure with the Agreement. Quite the contrary, the relevant Senate Committee has stated that the establishment of the Tribunal is "of vital importance to the United States." We are thus clearly not confronted with a situation in which Congress has in some way resisted the exercise of Presidential authority.

Finally, we re-emphasize the narrowness of our decision. We do not decide that the President possesses plenary power to settle claims, even as against foreign governmental entities. . . . But where, as here, the settlement of claims has been determined to be a necessary incident to the resolution of a major foreign policy dispute between our country and another, and where, as here, we can conclude that Congress acquiesced in the President's action, we are not prepared to say that the President lacks the power to settle such claims. . . . The judgment of the District Court is accordingly affirmed, and the mandate shall issue forthwith.

F. THE POWER TO DETAIN AMERICAN CITIZENS WITHOUT TRIAL

ASSIGNMENT 4

President Roosevelt primarily selected his nominees to the Supreme Court based on their views of the constitutionality of his New Deal. With the outbreak of World War II, however, the "New Deal" Justices would soon have to pass upon the constitutionality of Roosevelt's war measures. *Hirabayashi v. United States* and *Korematsu v. United States* stand with *Dred Scott v. Sandford* and *Plessy v. Ferguson* as among the most reviled opinions issued by the Supreme Court. Yet, as with those cases, we must ask whether the fault lies with the Court, which always has limited knowledge about national security concerns, or with the Constitution itself, which vests ill-defined war powers with the President. Frank answers to these questions help to illuminate how the Constitution should be interpreted today.

STUDY GUIDE

- *Hirabayashi v. United States, Korematsu v. United States,* and *Ex parte Endo* involved the exclusion of American citizens of Japanese descent from large parts of the country declared to be military zones during a declared war. If you think these cases were wrongly decided at the time, on what basis should the Court have reached a different result?
- Note the Court's reliance on historic discrimination against Japanese-Americans as a basis for upholding the curfew.

- The Court observes that "[t]he Fifth Amendment contains no equal protection clause and it restrains only such discriminatory legislation by Congress as amounts to a denial of due process." Can the federal government, as opposed to the states, classify people based on race?
- To avoid confusion, you should note that the decision in this case concerns only the trial in civilian court of Hirabayashi for violating the curfew. The opinion does not involve his challenge to the exclusion zone scheme; the Court addressed this other component of the order fifteen months later in *Korematsu.*
- Finally, note that while there were three dissenting votes in *Korematsu*, the judgment in *Hirabayashi* was unanimous.

Hirabayashi v. United States

320 U.S. 81 (1943)

MR. CHIEF JUSTICE STONE delivered the opinion of the Court.

Appellant, an American citizen of Japanese ancestry, was convicted in the district court of violating the Act of Congress of March 21, which makes it a misdemeanor knowingly to disregard restrictions made applicable by a military commander to persons in a military area prescribed by him as such, all as authorized by an Executive Order of the President. The [question presented is] whether the restriction unconstitutionally discriminated between citizens of Japanese ancestry and those of other ancestries in violation of the Fifth Amendment.

The indictment is in two counts. The second charges that appellant, being a person of Japanese ancestry, had on a specified date, contrary to a restriction promulgated by the military commander of the Western Defense Command, Fourth Army, failed to remain in his place of residence in the designated military area between the hours of 8:00 P.M. and 6:00 A.M. The first count charges that appellant, on May 11 and 12, 1942, had, contrary to a Civilian Exclusion Order issued by the military commander, failed to report to the Civil Control Station within the designated area, it appearing that appellant's required presence there was a preliminary step to the exclusion from that area of persons of Japanese ancestry. . . .

[A]ppellant asserted that the indictment should be dismissed because he was an American citizen who had never been a subject of and had never borne allegiance to the Empire of Japan. . . . On the trial to a jury it appeared that appellant was born in Seattle in 1918, of Japanese parents who had come from Japan to the United States, and who had never afterward returned to Japan; that he was educated in the Washington public schools and at the time of his arrest was a senior in the University of Washington; that he had never been in Japan or had any association with Japanese residing there.

The evidence showed that appellant had failed to report to the Civil Control Station on May 11 or May 12, 1942, as directed, to register for evacuation from the military area. He admitted failure to do so, and stated it had at all times been his belief that he would be waiving his rights as an American citizen by so doing. The evidence also showed that for like reason he was away from his place of residence after 8:00 P.M. on May 9, 1942. The jury returned a verdict of guilty on both counts and appellant was sentenced to imprisonment for a term of three months on each, the sentences to run concurrently. . . .

The curfew order which appellant violated, and to which the sanction prescribed by the Act of Congress has been deemed to attach, purported to be issued pursuant to an Executive Order of the President. In passing upon the authority of the military commander to make and execute the order, it becomes necessary to consider in some detail the official action which preceded or accompanied the order and from which it derives its purported authority.

On December 8, 1941, one day after the bombing of Pearl Harbor by a Japanese air force, Congress declared war against Japan. On February 19, 1942, the President promulgated Executive Order No. 9066. The Order recited that "the successful prosecution of the war requires every possible protection against espionage and against sabotage to national-defense material, national-defense premises, and national-defense utilities. . . ." By virtue of the authority vested in him as President and as Commander in Chief of the Army and Navy, the President purported to "authorize and direct the Secretary of War, and the Military Commanders whom he may from time to time designate, whenever he or any designated Commander deems such action necessary or desirable, to prescribe military areas in such places and of such extent as he or the appropriate Military Commander may determine, from which any or all persons may be excluded, and with respect to which, the right of any person to enter, remain in, or leave shall be subject to whatever restrictions the Secretary of War or the appropriate Military Commander may impose in his discretion."

On February 20, 1942, the Secretary of War designated Lt. General J.L. DeWitt as Military Commander of the Western Defense Command, comprising the Pacific Coast states and some others, to carry out there the duties prescribed by Executive Order No. 9066. On March 2, 1942, General DeWitt promulgated Public Proclamation No. 1. The proclamation recited that the entire Pacific Coast "by its geographical location is particularly subject to attack, to attempted invasion by the armed forces of nations with which the United States is now at war, and, in connection therewith, is subject to espionage and acts of sabotage, thereby requiring the adoption of military measures necessary to establish safeguards against such enemy operations." It stated that "the present situation requires as matter of military necessity the establishment in the territory embraced by the Western Defense Command of Military Areas and Zones thereof"; it specified and designated as military areas certain areas within the Western Defense Command; and it declared that "such persons or classes of persons as the situation may require" would, by subsequent proclamation, be excluded from certain of these areas, but might be permitted to enter or remain in certain others, under regulations and restrictions to be later prescribed. Among the military areas so designated by Public Proclamation No. 1 was Military Area No. 1, which embraced, besides the southern part of Arizona, all the coastal region of the three Pacific Coast states, including the

City of Seattle, Washington, where appellant resided. Military Area No. 2, designated by the same proclamation, included those parts of the coastal states and of Arizona not placed within Military Area No. 1. . . .

An Executive Order of the President, No. 9102, of March 18, 1942, established the War Relocation Authority, in the Office for Emergency Management of the Executive Office of the President; it authorized the Director of War Relocation Authority to formulate and effectuate a program for the removal, relocation, maintenance and supervision of persons designated under Executive Order No. 9066, already referred to; and it conferred on the Director authority to prescribe regulations necessary or desirable to promote the effective execution of the program.

Congress, by the Act of March 21, 1942, provided: "That whoever shall enter, remain in, leave, or commit any act in any military area or military zone prescribed, under the authority of an Executive order of the President, by the Secretary of War, or by any military commander designated by the Secretary of War, contrary to the restrictions applicable to any such area or zone or contrary to the order of the Secretary of War or any such military commander, shall, if it appears that he knew or should have known of the existence and extent of the restrictions or order and that his act was in violation thereof, be guilty of a misdemeanor and upon conviction shall be liable" to fine or imprisonment, or both.

Three days later, on March 24, 1942, General DeWitt issued Public Proclamation No. 3. After referring to the previous designation of military areas by Public Proclamations No. 1 and 2, it recited that ". . . the present situation within these Military Areas and Zones requires as a matter of military necessity the establishment of certain regulations pertaining to all enemy aliens and all persons of Japanese ancestry within said Military Areas and Zones. . . ." It accordingly declared and established that from and after March 27, 1942, "all alien Japanese, all alien Germans, all alien Italians, and all persons of Japanese ancestry residing or being within the geographical limits of Military Area No. 1 . . . shall be within their place of residence between the hours of 8:00 P.M. and 6:00 A.M., which period is hereinafter referred to as the hours of curfew." It also imposed certain other restrictions on persons of Japanese ancestry, and provided that any person violating the regulations would be subject to the criminal penalties provided by the Act of Congress of March 21, 1942.

Beginning on March 24, 1942, the military commander issued a series of Civilian Exclusion Orders pursuant to the provisions of Public Proclamation No. 1. Each such order related to a specified area within the territory of his command. The order applicable to appellant was Civilian Exclusion Order No. 57 of May 10, 1942. It directed that from and after 12:00 noon, May 16, 1942, all persons of Japanese ancestry, both alien and non-alien, be excluded from a specified portion of Military Area No. 1 in Seattle, including appellant's place of residence, and it required a member of each family, and each individual living alone, affected by the order to report on May 11 or May 12 to a designated Civil Control Station in Seattle. Meanwhile the military commander had issued Public Proclamation No. 4 of March 27, 1942, which recited the necessity of providing for the orderly evacuation and resettlement of Japanese within the area, and prohibited all alien Japanese and all persons of Japanese ancestry from leaving the military area until future orders should permit.

Appellant does not deny that he knowingly failed to obey the curfew order as charged in the second count of the indictment, or that the order was authorized by the terms of Executive Order No. 9066, or that the challenged Act of Congress purports to punish with criminal penalties disobedience of such an order. His contentions are only that Congress unconstitutionally delegated its legislative power to the military commander by authorizing him to impose the challenged regulation, and that, even if the regulation were in other respects lawfully authorized, the Fifth Amendment prohibits the discrimination made between citizens of Japanese descent and those of other ancestry. . . .

The conclusion is inescapable that Congress, by the Act of March 21, 1942, ratified and confirmed Executive Order No. 9066. *Prize Cases* (1862). And so far as it lawfully could, Congress authorized and implemented such curfew orders as the commanding officer should promulgate pursuant to the Executive Order of the President. The question then is not one of Congressional power to delegate to the President the promulgation of the Executive Order, but whether, acting in cooperation, Congress and the Executive have constitutional authority to impose the curfew restriction here complained of. . . . For reasons presently to be stated, we conclude that it was within the constitutional power of Congress and the executive arm of the Government to prescribe this curfew order for the period under consideration. . . .

Executive Order No. 9066, promulgated in time of war for the declared purpose of prosecuting the war by protecting national defense resources from sabotage and espionage, and the Act of March 21, 1942, ratifying and confirming the Executive Order, were each an exercise of the power to wage war conferred on the Congress and on the President, as Commander in Chief of the armed forces, by Articles I and II of the Constitution. See *Ex parte Quirin* (1942). We have no occasion to consider whether the President, acting alone, could lawfully have made the curfew order in question, or have authorized others to make it. For the President's action has the support of the Act of Congress, and we are immediately concerned with the question whether it is within the constitutional power of the national government, through the joint action of Congress and the Executive, to impose this restriction as an emergency war measure. The exercise of that power here involves no question of martial law or trial by military tribunal. Cf. *Ex parte Milligan* (1866); *Ex parte Quirin*. Appellant has been tried and convicted in the civil courts and has been subjected to penalties prescribed by Congress for the acts committed.

The war power of the national government is "the power to wage war successfully." See Charles Evans Hughes, War Powers Under the Constitution. It extends to every matter and activity so related to war as substantially to affect its conduct and progress. The power is not restricted to the winning of victories in the field and the repulse of enemy forces. It embraces every phase of the national defense, including the protection of war materials and the members of the armed forces from injury and from the dangers which attend the rise, prosecution and progress of war. Since the Constitution commits to the Executive and to Congress the exercise of the war power in all the vicissitudes and conditions of warfare, it has necessarily given them wide scope for the exercise of judgment and discretion in determining the nature and extent of the threatened injury or danger and in the selection of the means for resisting it. Where, as they did here, the conditions call for the exercise of judgment and discretion and for the choice of means by those branches of the Government on which the Constitution has placed the responsibility of war making, it is not for any court to sit in review of the wisdom of their action or substitute its judgment for theirs.

The actions taken must be appraised in the light of the conditions with which the President and Congress were confronted in the early months of 1942, many of which, since disclosed, were then peculiarly within the knowledge of the military authorities. On December 7, 1941, the Japanese air forces had attacked the United States Naval Base at Pearl Harbor without warning, at the very hour when Japanese diplomatic representatives were conducting negotiations with our State Department ostensibly for the peaceful settlement of differences between the two countries. Simultaneously or nearly so, the Japanese attacked Malaysia, Hong Kong, the Philippines, and Wake and Midway Islands. On the following day their army invaded Thailand. Shortly afterwards they sank two British battleships. On December 13th, Guam was taken. On December 24th and 25th they captured Wake Island and occupied Hong Kong. On January 2, 1942, Manila fell, and on February 10th Singapore, Britain's great naval base in the East, was taken. On February 27th the battle for the Java Sea resulted in a disastrous naval defeat to the United Nations. By the 9th of March Japanese forces had established control over the Netherlands East Indies; Rangoon and Burma were occupied; Bataan and Corregidor were under attack.

Although the results of the attack on Pearl Harbor were not fully disclosed until much later, it was known that the damage was extensive, and that the Japanese by their successes had gained a naval superiority over our forces in the Pacific which might enable them to seize Pearl Harbor, our largest naval base and the last stronghold of defense lying between Japan and the west coast. That reasonably prudent men charged with the responsibility of our national defense had ample ground for concluding that they must face the danger of invasion, take measures against it, and in making the choice of measures consider our internal situation, cannot be doubted.

The challenged orders were defense measures for the avowed purpose of safeguarding the military area in question, at a time of threatened air raids and invasion by the Japanese forces, from the danger of sabotage and espionage. As the curfew was made applicable to citizens residing in the area only if they were of Japanese ancestry, our inquiry must be whether in the light of all the facts and circumstances there was any substantial basis for the conclusion, in which Congress and the military commander united, that the curfew as applied was a protective measure necessary to meet the threat of sabotage and espionage which would substantially affect the war effort and which might reasonably be expected to aid a threatened enemy invasion. The alternative which appellant insists must be accepted is for the military authorities to impose the curfew on all citizens within the military area, or on none. In a case of threatened danger requiring prompt action, it is a choice between inflicting obviously needless hardship on the many, or sitting passive and unresisting in the presence of the threat. We think that constitutional government, in time of war, is not so powerless and does not compel so hard a choice if those charged with the responsibility of our national defense have reasonable ground for believing that the threat is real.

When the orders were promulgated there was a vast concentration, within Military Areas Nos. 1 and 2, of installations and facilities for the production of military equipment, especially ships and airplanes. Important Army and Navy bases were located in California and Washington. Approximately one-fourth of the total value of the major aircraft contracts then let by Government procurement officers were to be performed in the State of California. California ranked second, and Washington fifth, of all the states of the Union with respect to the value of shipbuilding contracts to be performed.

In the critical days of March, 1942, the danger to our war production by sabotage and espionage in this area seems obvious. The German invasion of the Western European countries had given ample warning to the world of the menace of the "fifth column." Espionage by persons in sympathy with the Japanese Government had been found to have been particularly effective in the surprise attack on Pearl Harbor.[9] At a time of threatened Japanese attack upon this country, the nature of our inhabitants' attachments to the Japanese enemy was consequently a matter of grave concern. Of the 126,000 persons of Japanese descent in the United States, citizens and non-citizens, approximately 112,000 resided in California, Oregon and Washington at the time of the adoption of the military regulations. Of these approximately two-thirds are citizens because born in the United States. Not only did the great majority of such persons reside within the Pacific Coast states but they were concentrated in or near three of the large cities, Seattle, Portland and Los Angeles, all in Military Area No. 1.

There is support for the view that social, economic and political conditions which have prevailed since the close of the last century, when the Japanese began to come to this country in substantial numbers, have intensified their solidarity and have in large measure prevented their assimilation as an integral part of the white population.[10] In addition, large numbers of children of Japanese parentage are sent to Japanese language schools outside the regular hours of public schools in the locality. Some of these schools are generally believed to be sources of Japanese nationalistic propaganda, cultivating allegiance to Japan. Considerable numbers, estimated to be approximately 10,000, of American-born children of Japanese parentage have been sent to Japan for all or a part of their education.

---

[9] See "Attack upon Pearl Harbor by Japanese Armed Forces," Report of the Commission Appointed by the President, dated January 23, 1942.

[10] Federal legislation has denied to the Japanese citizenship by naturalization, and the Immigration Act of 1924 excluded them from admission into the United States. State legislation has denied to alien Japanese the privilege of owning land. It has also sought to prohibit intermarriage of persons of Japanese race with Caucasians. Persons of Japanese descent have often been unable to secure professional or skilled employment except in association with others of that descent, and sufficient employment opportunities of this character have not been available.

Congress and the Executive, including the military commander, could have attributed special significance, in its bearing on the loyalties of persons of Japanese descent, to the maintenance by Japan of its system of dual citizenship. Children born in the United States of Japanese alien parents, and especially those children born before December 1, 1924, are under many circumstances deemed, by Japanese law, to be citizens of Japan. No official census of those whom Japan regards as having thus retained Japanese citizenship is available, but there is ground for the belief that the number is large.[11]

The large number of resident alien Japanese, approximately one-third of all Japanese inhabitants of the country, are of mature years and occupy positions of influence in Japanese communities. The association of influential Japanese residents with Japanese Consulates has been deemed a ready means for the dissemination of propaganda and for the maintenance of the influence of the Japanese Government with the Japanese population in this country.

As a result of all these conditions affecting the life of the Japanese, both aliens and citizens, in the Pacific Coast area, there has been relatively little social intercourse between them and the white population. The restrictions, both practical and legal, affecting the privileges and opportunities afforded to persons of Japanese extraction residing in the United States, have been sources of irritation and may well have tended to increase their isolation, and in many instances their attachments to Japan and its institutions.

Viewing these data in all their aspects, Congress and the Executive could reasonably have concluded that these conditions have encouraged the continued attachment of members of this group to Japan and Japanese institutions. These are only some of the many considerations which those charged with the responsibility for the national defense could take into account in determining the nature and extent of the danger of espionage and sabotage, in the event of invasion or air raid attack. The extent of that danger could be definitely known only after the event and after it was too late to meet it. Whatever views we may entertain regarding the loyalty to this country of the citizens of Japanese ancestry, we cannot reject as unfounded the judgment of the military authorities and of Congress that there were disloyal members of that population, whose number and strength could not be precisely and quickly ascertained. We cannot say that the war-making branches of the Government did not have ground for believing that in a critical hour such persons could not readily be isolated and separately dealt with, and constituted a menace to the national defense and safety, which demanded that prompt and adequate measures be taken to guard against it. . . .

[A]ppellant insists that the exercise of the power is inappropriate and unconstitutional because it discriminates against citizens of Japanese ancestry, in violation of the Fifth Amendment. The Fifth Amendment contains no equal protection

---

[11] Statistics released in 1927 by the Consul General of Japan at San Francisco asserted that over 51,000 of the approximately 63,000 American-born persons of Japanese parentage then in the western part of the United States held Japanese citizenship. . . . A census conducted under the auspices of the Japanese government in 1930 asserted that approximately 47% of American-born persons of Japanese parentage in California held dual citizenship.

clause and it restrains only such discriminatory legislation by Congress as amounts to a denial of due process. Congress may hit at a particular danger where it is seen, without providing for others which are not so evident or so urgent.

Distinctions between citizens solely because of their ancestry are by their very nature odious to a free people whose institutions are founded upon the doctrine of equality. For that reason, legislative classification or discrimination based on race alone has often been held to be a denial of equal protection. *Yick Wo v. Hopkins* (1886). We may assume that these considerations would be controlling here were it not for the fact that the danger of espionage and sabotage, in time of war and of threatened invasion, calls upon the military authorities to scrutinize every relevant fact bearing on the loyalty of populations in the danger areas. Because racial discriminations are in most circumstances irrelevant and therefore prohibited, it by no means follows that, in dealing with the perils of war, Congress and the Executive are wholly precluded from taking into account those facts and circumstances which are relevant to measures for our national defense and for the successful prosecution of the war, and which may in fact place citizens of one ancestry in a different category from others. "We must never forget, that it is *a constitution* we are expounding," "a constitution intended to endure for ages to come, and, consequently, to be adapted to the various *crises* of human affairs." *McCulloch v. Maryland* (1819). The adoption by Government, in the crisis of war and of threatened invasion, of measures for the public safety, based upon the recognition of facts and circumstances which indicate that a group of one national extraction may menace that safety more than others, is not wholly beyond the limits of the Constitution and is not to be condemned merely because in other and in most circumstances racial distinctions are irrelevant.

Here the aim of Congress and the Executive was the protection against sabotage of war materials and utilities in areas thought to be in danger of Japanese invasion and air attack. We have stated in detail facts and circumstances with respect to the American citizens of Japanese ancestry residing on the Pacific Coast which support the judgment of the war-waging branches of the Government that some restrictive measure was urgent. We cannot say that these facts and circumstances, considered in the particular war setting, could afford no ground for differentiating citizens of Japanese ancestry from other groups in the United States. The fact alone that attack on our shores was threatened by Japan rather than another enemy power set these citizens apart from others who have no particular associations with Japan.

Our investigation here does not go beyond the inquiry whether, in the light of all the relevant circumstances preceding and attending their promulgation, the challenged orders and statute afforded a reasonable basis for the action taken in imposing the curfew. We cannot close our eyes to the fact, demonstrated by experience, that in time of war residents having ethnic affiliations with an invading enemy may be a greater source of danger than those of a different ancestry. Nor can we deny that Congress, and the military authorities acting with its authorization, have constitutional power to appraise the danger in the light of facts of public notoriety. We need not now attempt to define the ultimate boundaries of the war power. We decide only the issue as we have defined it — we decide only that the curfew order as applied, and at the time it was applied, was within the boundaries of the war power. In this case it is enough that circumstances within the knowledge of those charged with the responsibility for maintaining the national defense afforded a rational basis for the decision which they made. Whether we would have made it is irrelevant. . . .

Affirmed.

MR. JUSTICE DOUGLAS concurring:

While I concur in the result and agree substantially with the opinion of the Court, I wish to add a few words to indicate what for me is the narrow ground of decision. . . .

It is true that we might now say that there was ample time to handle the problem on the individual rather than the group basis. But military decisions must be made without the benefit of hindsight. The orders must be judged as of the date when the decision to issue them was made. To say that the military in such cases should take the time to weed out the loyal from the others would be to assume that the nation could afford to have them take the time to do it. But as the opinion of the Court makes clear, speed and dispatch may be of the essence. Certainly we cannot say that those charged with the defense of the nation should have procrastinated until investigations and hearings were completed. At that time further delay might indeed have seemed to be wholly incompatible with military responsibilities.

Since we cannot override the military judgment which lay behind these orders, it seems to me necessary to concede that the army had the power to deal temporarily with these people on a group basis. Petitioner therefore was not justified in disobeying the orders.

But I think it important to emphasize that we are dealing here with a problem of loyalty not assimilation. Loyalty is a matter of mind and of heart not of race. That indeed is the history of America. Moreover, guilt is personal under our constitutional system. Detention for reasonable cause is one thing. Detention on account of ancestry is another. . . . Obedience to the military orders is one thing. Whether an individual member of a group must be afforded at some stage an opportunity to show that, being loyal, he should be reclassified is a wholly different question. . . .

[I]f it were plain that no machinery was available whereby the individual could demonstrate his loyalty as a citizen in order to be reclassified, questions of a more serious character would be presented. The United States, however, takes no such position. We need go no further here than to deny the individual the right to defy the law. It is sufficient to say that he cannot test in that way the validity of the orders as applied to him.

MR. JUSTICE MURPHY, concurring:

In voting for affirmance of the judgment I do not wish to be understood as intimating that the military authorities in time of war are subject to no restraints whatsoever, or that they are free to impose any restrictions they may choose on the rights and liberties of individual citizens or groups of citizens in those places which may be designated as "military areas." While this Court sits, it has the inescapable duty of seeing that the mandates of the Constitution are obeyed. That duty exists in time of war as well as in time of peace, and in its performance we must not forget that few indeed have been the invasions upon essential liberties which have not been accompanied by pleas of urgent necessity advanced in good faith by responsible men.

Nor do I mean to intimate that citizens of a particular racial group whose freedom may be curtailed within an area threatened with attack should be generally prevented from leaving the area and going at large in other areas that are not in danger of attack and where special precautions are not needed. Their status as citizens, though subject to requirements of national security and military necessity, should at all times be accorded the fullest consideration and respect. When the danger is past, the restrictions imposed on them should be promptly removed and their freedom of action fully restored.

STUDY GUIDE

- *Korematsu* is far more famous than *Hirabayashi*. But the heart of the 1944 decision's legal analysis consists of reliance on the Court's earlier 1943 unanimous judgment.
- Would it surprise you to know that, however reviled, *Korematsu* is still regularly cited as precedent? See if you can identify the constitutional proposition for which it still stands as authority.
- Does Justice Murphy rely on hindsight in his dissent? What would his opinion be if matters were "as urgent as they have been represented to be"? Where does judicial deference fit into his approach? Had Justice Murphy's approach been adopted by the Court, would President Roosevelt have obeyed? What exactly is Justice Murphy proposing the Court do in such cases, and does his approach provide a way out of the morass? In light of the fact that the Fifth Amendment does not contain an equal protection clause, under what constitutional provision is the federal government barred from discriminating on the basis of race?
- What is Justice Jackson's response to the majority's reliance on *Hirabayashi*? Justice Jackson appears to be cognizant that making exceptions is dangerous in a legal system governed by precedent. Is his worry relevant to situations other than this one?
- Note that the decision in this case concerns only the exclusion zones, though Korematsu also tried to challenge his detention.
- *Korematsu* was decided on December 18, 1944. However, the day before, the Western Defense Command issued Public Proclamation No. 21, which lifted the exclusion order on the West Coast and allowed Japanese-Americans to return to their homes. Though the notice was not published in the Federal Register until January 2, 1945 (10 Fed. Reg. 53-01), there is some evidence that Chief Justice Stone, who was in touch with the executive branch, delayed the release of *Korematsu* and *Endo*.[12] How should this affect the way we read the majority opinion? Was the case moot before it was even decided?

---

[12] Patrick O. Gudridge, Remember *Endo*?, 116 Harv. L. Rev. 1933, 1935 n.11 (2003).

Manzanar Relocation Center in California, July 1, 1942

Eleanor Roosevelt visits the Gila River Internment Camp, April 23, 1943.

Gordon Hirabayashi

Fred Korematsu

Korematsu v. United States

323 U.S. 214 (1944)

Mr. Justice Black delivered the opinion of the Court.

The petitioner, an American citizen of Japanese descent, was convicted in a federal district court for remaining in San Leandro, California, a "Military Area," contrary to Civilian Exclusion Order No. 34 of the Commanding General of the Western Command, U.S. Army, which directed that after May 9, 1942, all persons of Japanese ancestry should be excluded from that area. No question was raised as to petitioner's loyalty to the United States. The Circuit Court of Appeals affirmed, and the importance of the constitutional question involved caused us to grant certiorari.

It should be noted, to begin with, that all legal restrictions which curtail the civil rights of a single racial group are immediately suspect. That is not to say that all such restrictions are unconstitutional. It is to say that courts must subject them to the most rigid scrutiny. Pressing public necessity may sometimes justify the existence of such restrictions; racial antagonism never can. . . .

In *Hirabayashi v. United States* (1943), we sustained a conviction obtained for violation of the curfew order. The *Hirabayashi* conviction and this one thus rest on the same 1942 Congressional Act and the same basic executive and military orders, all of which orders were aimed at the twin dangers of espionage and sabotage. . . .

In the light of the principles we announced in the *Hirabayashi* case, we are unable to conclude that it was beyond the war power of Congress and the Executive to exclude those of Japanese ancestry from the West Coast war area at the time they did. True, exclusion from the area in which one's home is located is a far greater deprivation than constant confinement to the home from 8 P.M. to 6 A.M. Nothing short of apprehension by the proper military authorities of the gravest imminent danger to the public safety can constitutionally justify either. But exclusion from a threatened area, no less than curfew, has a definite and close relationship to the prevention of espionage and sabotage. The military authorities, charged with the primary responsibility of defending our shores, concluded that curfew provided inadequate protection and ordered exclusion. They did so, as pointed out in our *Hirabayashi* opinion, in accordance with Congressional authority to the military to say who should, and who should not, remain in the threatened areas.

In this case the petitioner challenges the assumptions upon which we rested our conclusions in the *Hirabayashi* case. He also urges that by May 1942, when Order No. 34 was promulgated, all danger of Japanese invasion of the West Coast had disappeared. After careful consideration of these contentions we are compelled to reject them.

Here, as in the *Hirabayashi* case, ". . . we cannot reject as unfounded the judgment of the military authorities and of Congress that there were disloyal members of that population, whose number and strength could not be precisely and quickly ascertained. We cannot say that the war-making branches of the Government did not have ground for believing that in a critical hour such persons could not readily be isolated and separately dealt with, and constituted a menace to the national defense and safety, which demanded that prompt and adequate measures be taken to guard against it."

Like curfew, exclusion of those of Japanese origin was deemed necessary because of the presence of an unascertained number of disloyal members of the group, most of whom we have no doubt were loyal to this country. It was because we could not reject the finding of the military authorities that it was impossible to bring about an immediate segregation of the disloyal from the loyal that we sustained the validity of the curfew order as applying to the whole group. In the instant case, temporary exclusion of the entire group was rested by the military on the same ground. The judgment that exclusion of the whole group was for the same reason a military imperative answers the contention that the exclusion was in the nature of group punishment based on antagonism to those of Japanese origin. That there were members of the group who retained loyalties to Japan has been confirmed by investigations made subsequent to the exclusion. Approximately five thousand American citizens of Japanese ancestry refused to swear unqualified allegiance to the United States and to renounce allegiance to the Japanese Emperor, and several thousand evacuees requested repatriation to Japan.

We uphold the exclusion order as of the time it was made and when the petitioner violated it. . . . In doing so, we are not unmindful of the hardships imposed by it upon a large group of American citizens. But hardships are part of war, and war is an aggregation of hardships. All citizens alike, both in and out of uniform, feel the impact of war in greater or lesser measure. Citizenship has its responsibilities as well as its privileges, and in time of war the burden is always heavier. Compulsory exclusion of large groups of citizens from their homes, except under circumstances of direst emergency and peril, is inconsistent with our basic governmental institutions. But when under conditions of modern warfare our shores are threatened by hostile forces, the power to protect must be commensurate with the threatened danger. . . .

We are thus being asked to pass at this time upon the whole subsequent detention program in both assembly and relocation centers, although the only issues framed at the trial related to petitioner's remaining in the prohibited area in violation of the exclusion order. Had petitioner here left the prohibited area and gone to an assembly center we cannot say either as a matter of fact or law that his presence in that center would have resulted in his detention in a relocation center. Some who did report to the assembly center were not sent to relocation centers, but were released upon condition that they remain outside the prohibited zone until the military orders were modified or lifted. This illustrates that they pose different problems and may be governed by different principles. The lawfulness of one does not necessarily determine the lawfulness of the others. . . .

The Assembly Center was conceived as a part of the machinery for group evacuation. The power to exclude includes the power to do it by force if necessary. And any forcible measure must necessarily entail some degree of detention or restraint whatever method of removal is selected. But whichever view is taken, it results in holding that the order under which petitioner was convicted was valid.

It is said that we are dealing here with the case of imprisonment of a citizen in a concentration camp solely because of his ancestry, without evidence or inquiry concerning his loyalty and good disposition towards the United States. Our task would be simple, our duty clear, were this a case involving the imprisonment of a loyal citizen in a concentration camp because of racial prejudice. Regardless of the true nature of the assembly and relocation centers — and we deem it unjustifiable to call them concentration camps with all the ugly connotations that term implies — we are dealing specifically with nothing but an exclusion order. To cast this case into outlines of racial prejudice, without reference to the real military dangers which were presented, merely confuses the issue. Korematsu was not excluded from the Military Area because of hostility to him or his race. He *was* excluded because we are at war with the Japanese Empire, because the properly constituted military authorities feared an invasion of our West Coast and felt constrained to take proper security measures, because they decided that the military urgency of the situation demanded that all citizens of Japanese ancestry be segregated from the West Coast temporarily, and finally, because Congress, reposing its confidence in this time of war in our military leaders — as inevitably it must — determined that they should have the power to do just this. There was evidence of disloyalty on the part of some, the military authorities considered that the need for action was great, and time was short. We cannot — by availing ourselves of the calm perspective of hindsight — now say that at that time these actions were unjustified.

Affirmed.

MR. JUSTICE FRANKFURTER, concurring:

. . . I am unable to see how the legal considerations that led to the decision in *Hirabayashi v. United States* fail to sustain the military order which made the conduct now in controversy a crime. And so I join in the opinion of the Court, but should like to add a few words of my own.

The provisions of the Constitution which confer on the Congress and the President powers to enable this country to wage war are as much part of the Constitution as provisions looking to a nation at peace. . . . To recognize that military orders are "reasonably expedient military precautions" in time of war and yet to deny them constitutional legitimacy makes of the Constitution an instrument for dialectic subtleties not reasonably to be attributed to the hard-headed Framers, of whom a majority had had actual participation in war. If a military order such as that under review does not transcend the means appropriate for conducting war, such action by the military is as constitutional as would be any authorized action by the Interstate Commerce Commission within the limits of the constitutional power to regulate commerce. And being an exercise of the war power explicitly granted by the Constitution for safeguarding the national life by prosecuting war effectively, I find nothing in the Constitution which denies to Congress the power to enforce such a valid military order by making its violation an offense triable in the civil courts. To find that the Constitution does not forbid the military measures now complained of does not carry with it approval of that which Congress and the Executive did. That is their business, not ours.

Mr. Justice Roberts, dissenting:

I dissent, because I think the indisputable facts exhibit a clear violation of Constitutional rights. This is not a case of keeping people off the streets at night as was *Hirabayashi*, nor a case of temporary exclusion of a citizen from an area for his own safety or that of the community, nor a case of offering him an opportunity to go temporarily out of an area where his presence might cause danger to himself or to his fellows. On the contrary, it is the case of convicting a citizen as a punishment for not submitting to imprisonment in a concentration camp, based on his ancestry, and solely because of his ancestry, without evidence or inquiry concerning his loyalty and good disposition towards the United States. If this be a correct statement of the facts disclosed by this record, and facts of which we take judicial notice, I need hardly labor the conclusion that Constitutional rights have been violated. . . .

The predicament in which the petitioner thus found himself was this: He was forbidden, by Military Order, to leave the zone in which he lived; he was forbidden, by Military Order, after a date fixed, to be found within that zone unless he were in an Assembly Center located in that zone. General DeWitt's report to the Secretary of War concerning the programme of evacuation and relocation of Japanese makes it entirely clear, if it were necessary to refer to that document — and, in the light of the above recitation, I think it is not, — that an Assembly Center was a euphemism for a prison. No person within such a center was permitted to leave except by Military Order. In the dilemma that he dare not remain in his home, or voluntarily leave the area, without incurring criminal penalties, and that the only way he could avoid punishment was to go to an Assembly Center and submit himself to military imprisonment, the petitioner did nothing. . . .

We cannot shut our eyes to the fact that had the petitioner attempted to violate Proclamation No. 4 and leave the military area in which he lived he would have been arrested and tried and convicted for violation of Proclamation No. 4. The two conflicting orders, one which commanded him to stay and the other which commanded him to go, were nothing but a cleverly devised trap to accomplish the real purpose of the military authority, which was to lock him up in a concentration camp. The only course by which the petitioner could avoid arrest and prosecution was to go to that camp according to instructions to be given him when he reported at a Civil Control Center. We know that is the fact. Why should we set up a figmentary and artificial situation, instead of addressing ourselves to the actualities of the case? . . .

Mr. Justice Murphy, dissenting.

This exclusion of "all persons of Japanese ancestry, both alien and non-alien," from the Pacific Coast area on a plea of military necessity in the absence of martial law ought not to be approved. Such exclusion goes over "the very brink of constitutional power" and falls into the ugly abyss of racism. . . .

That this forced exclusion was the result in good measure of this erroneous assumption of racial guilt rather than bona fide military necessity is evidenced by the Commanding General's Final Report on the evacuation from the Pacific Coast area. In it he refers to all individuals of Japanese descent as "subversive," as belonging to "an enemy race" whose "racial strains are undiluted," and as constituting "over 112,000 potential enemies . . . at large today" along the Pacific Coast.[13]

In support of this blanket condemnation of all persons of Japanese descent, however, no reliable evidence is cited to show that such individuals were generally disloyal, or had generally so conducted themselves in this area as to constitute a special menace to defense installations or war industries, or had otherwise by their behavior furnished reasonable ground for their exclusion as a group.

Justification for the exclusion is sought, instead, mainly upon questionable racial and sociological grounds not ordinarily within the realm of expert military judgment, supplemented by certain semi-military conclusions drawn from an unwarranted use of circumstantial evidence. Individuals of Japanese ancestry are condemned because they are said to be "a large, unassimilated, tightly knit racial group, bound to an enemy nation by strong ties of race, culture, custom and religion." They are claimed to be given to "emperor worshipping ceremonies" and to "dual citizenship." . . .

The main reasons relied upon by those responsible for the forced evacuation, therefore, do not prove a reasonable relation between the group characteristics of Japanese Americans and the dangers of invasion, sabotage and espionage. The reasons appear, instead, to be largely an accumulation of much of the misinformation, half-truths and insinuations that for years have been directed against Japanese Americans by people with racial and economic prejudices — the same people who have been among the foremost advocates of the evacuation.[14] A military judgment based upon such racial and sociological considerations is not entitled to the great weight ordinarily given the judgments based upon strictly military considerations. Especially is this so when every charge relative to race, religion, culture,

---

[13] Further evidence of the Commanding General's attitude toward individuals of Japanese ancestry is revealed in his voluntary testimony on April 13, 1943, in San Francisco before the House Naval Affairs Subcommittee to Investigate Congested Areas:

> I don't want any of them [persons of Japanese ancestry] here. They are a dangerous element. There is no way to determine their loyalty. The west coast contains too many vital installations essential to the defense of the country to allow any Japanese on this coast. . . . The danger of the Japanese was, and is now — if they are permitted to come back — espionage and sabotage. It makes no difference whether he is an American citizen, he is still a Japanese. American citizenship does not necessarily determine loyalty. . . . But we must worry about the Japanese all the time until he is wiped off the map. Sabotage and espionage will make problems as long as he is allowed in this area. . . .

[14] Special interest groups were extremely active in applying pressure for mass evacuation. Mr. Austin E. Anson, managing secretary of the Salinas Vegetable Grower-Shipper Association, has frankly admitted that "we're charged with wanting to get rid of the Japs for selfish reasons. We do. It's a question of whether the white man lives on the Pacific Coast or the brown men. They came into this valley to work, and they stayed to take over. . . . They undersell the white man in the markets. . . . They work their women and children while the white farmer has to pay wages for his help. If all the Japs were removed tomorrow, we'd never miss them in two weeks, because the white farmers can take over and produce everything the Jap grows. And we don't want them back when the war ends, either." Quoted in "The People Nobody Wants," 214 Sat. Eve. Post 24, 66 (May 9, 1942).

geographical location, and legal and economic status has been substantially discredited by independent studies made by experts in these matters. . . .

No one denies, of course, that there were some disloyal persons of Japanese descent on the Pacific Coast who did all in their power to aid their ancestral land. Similar disloyal activities have been engaged in by many persons of German, Italian and even more pioneer stock in our country. But to infer that examples of individual disloyalty prove group disloyalty and justify discriminatory action against the entire group is to deny that under our system of law individual guilt is the sole basis for deprivation of rights.

Moreover, this inference, which is at the very heart of the evacuation orders, has been used in support of the abhorrent and despicable treatment of minority groups by the dictatorial tyrannies which this nation is now pledged to destroy. To give constitutional sanction to that inference in this case, however well-intentioned may have been the military command on the Pacific Coast, is to adopt one of the cruelest of the rationales used by our enemies to destroy the dignity of the individual and to encourage and open the door to discriminatory actions against other minority groups in the passions of tomorrow.

No adequate reason is given for the failure to treat these Japanese Americans on an individual basis by holding investigations and hearings to separate the loyal from the disloyal, as was done in the case of persons of German and Italian ancestry. It is asserted merely that the loyalties of this group "were unknown and time was of the essence." Yet nearly four months elapsed after Pearl Harbor before the first exclusion order was issued; nearly eight months went by until the last order was issued; and the last of these "subversive" persons was not actually removed until almost eleven months had elapsed. Leisure and deliberation seem to have been more of the essence than speed. And the fact that conditions were not such as to warrant a declaration of martial law adds strength to the belief that the factors of time and military necessity were not as urgent as they have been represented to be.

Moreover, there was no adequate proof that the Federal Bureau of Investigation and the military and naval intelligence services did not have the espionage and sabotage situation well in hand during this long period. Nor is there any denial of the fact that not one person of Japanese ancestry was accused or convicted of espionage or sabotage after Pearl Harbor while they were still free,[15] a fact which is some evidence of the loyalty of the vast majority of these individuals and of the effectiveness of the established methods of combatting these evils. It seems incredible that under these circumstances it would have been impossible to hold loyalty hearings for the mere 112,000 persons involved—or at least for the 70,000 American citizens—especially when a large part of this number represented children and elderly men and women.[16] Any inconvenience that may have

[15] The Final Report, makes the amazing statement that as of February 14, 1942, "The very fact that no sabotage has taken place to date is a disturbing and confirming indication that such action will be taken." Apparently, in the minds of the military leaders, there was no way that the Japanese Americans could escape the suspicion of sabotage.

[16] During a period of six months, the 112 alien tribunals or hearing boards set up by the British Government shortly after the outbreak of the present war summoned and examined approximately

accompanied an attempt to conform to procedural due process cannot be said to justify violations of constitutional rights of individuals.

I dissent, therefore, from this legalization of racism. Racial discrimination in any form and in any degree has no justifiable part whatever in our democratic way of life. It is unattractive in any setting but it is utterly revolting among a free people who have embraced the principles set forth in the Constitution of the United States. All residents of this nation are kin in some way by blood or culture to a foreign land. Yet they are primarily and necessarily a part of the new and distinct civilization of the United States. They must accordingly be treated at all times as the heirs of the American experiment and as entitled to all the rights and freedoms guaranteed by the Constitution.

MR. JUSTICE JACKSON, dissenting.

Korematsu was born on our soil, of parents born in Japan. The Constitution makes him a citizen of the United States by nativity and a citizen of California by residence. No claim is made that he is not loyal to this country. There is no suggestion that apart from the matter involved here he is not law-abiding and well disposed. Korematsu, however, has been convicted of an act not commonly a crime. It consists merely of being present in the state whereof he is a citizen, near the place where he was born, and where all his life he has lived. . . .

A citizen's presence in the locality, however, was made a crime only if his parents were of Japanese birth. Had Korematsu been one of four — the others being, say, a German alien enemy, an Italian alien enemy, and a citizen of American-born ancestors, convicted of treason but out on parole — only Korematsu's presence would have violated the order. The difference between their innocence and his crime would result, not from anything he did, said, or thought, different from they, but only in that he was born of different racial stock.

Now, if any fundamental assumption underlies our system, it is that guilt is personal and not inheritable. Even if all of one's antecedents had been convicted of treason, the Constitution forbids its penalties to be visited upon him, for it provides that "no attainder of treason shall work corruption of blood, or forfeiture except during the life of the person attained." Article III, §3, cl. 2. But here is an attempt to make an otherwise innocent act a crime merely because this prisoner is the son of parents as to whom he had no choice, and belongs to a race from which there is no way to resign. If Congress in peace-time legislation should enact such a criminal law, I should suppose this Court would refuse to enforce it.

But the "law" which this prisoner is convicted of disregarding is not found in an act of Congress, but in a military order. . . . It would be impracticable and dangerous idealism to expect or insist that each specific military command in an area of probable operations will conform to conventional tests of constitutionality. When an area is so beset that it must be put under military control at all, the paramount consideration is that its measures be successful, rather than legal. The armed services must protect a society, not merely its Constitution. . . . No court can

---

74,000 German and Austrian aliens. These tribunals determined whether each individual enemy alien was a real enemy of the Allies or only a "friendly enemy." About 64,000 were freed from internment and from any special restrictions, and only 2,000 were interned.

require . . . a commander in such circumstances to act as a reasonable man; he may be unreasonably cautious and exacting. . . .

But if we cannot confine military expedients by the Constitution, neither would I distort the Constitution to approve all that the military may deem expedient. This is what the Court appears to be doing, whether consciously or not. I cannot say, from any evidence before me, that the orders of General DeWitt were not reasonably expedient military precautions, nor could I say that they were. But even if they were permissible military procedures, I deny that it follows that they are constitutional. If, as the Court holds, it does follow, then we may as well say that any military order will be constitutional and have done with it.

The limitation under which courts always will labor in examining the necessity for a military order are illustrated by this case. How does the Court know that these orders have a reasonable basis in necessity? No evidence whatever on that subject has been taken by this or any other court. There is sharp controversy as to the credibility of the DeWitt report. So the Court, having no real evidence before it, has no choice but to accept General DeWitt's own unsworn, self-serving statement, untested by any cross-examination, that what he did was reasonable. And thus it will always be when courts try to look into the reasonableness of a military order.

In the very nature of things military decisions are not susceptible of intelligent judicial appraisal. They do not pretend to rest on evidence, but are made on information that often would not be admissible and on assumptions that could not be proved. Information in support of an order could not be disclosed to courts without danger that it would reach the enemy. Neither can courts act on communications made in confidence. Hence courts can never have any real alternative to accepting the mere declaration of the authority that issued the order that it was reasonably necessary from a military viewpoint.

Much is said of the danger to liberty from the Army program for deporting and detaining these citizens of Japanese extraction. But a judicial construction of the due process clause that will sustain this order is a far more subtle blow to liberty than the promulgation of the order itself. A military order, however unconstitutional, is not apt to last longer than the military emergency. . . . But once a judicial opinion rationalizes such an order to show that it conforms to the Constitution, or rather rationalizes the Constitution to show that the Constitution sanctions such an order, the Court for all time has validated the principle of racial discrimination in criminal procedure and of transplanting American citizens. The principle then lies about like a loaded weapon ready for the hand of any authority that can bring forward a plausible claim of an urgent need. Every repetition imbeds that principle more deeply in our law and thinking and expands it to new purposes. . . . A military commander may overstep the bounds of constitutionality, and it is an incident. But if we review and approve, that passing incident becomes the doctrine of the Constitution. There it has a generative power of its own, and all that it creates will be in its own image. Nothing better illustrates this danger than does the Court's opinion in this case.

It argues that we are bound to uphold the conviction of Korematsu because we upheld one in *Hirabayashi v. United States*, when we sustained these orders in so far as they applied a curfew requirement to a citizen of Japanese ancestry. I think we should learn something from that experience.

In that case we were urged to consider only that curfew feature, that being all that technically was involved, because it was the only count necessary to sustain Hirabayashi's conviction and sentence. We yielded, and the Chief Justice guarded the opinion as carefully as language will do. . . . However, in spite of our limiting words we did validate a discrimination on the basis of ancestry for mild and temporary deprivation of liberty. Now the principle of racial discrimination is pushed from support of mild measures to very harsh ones, and from temporary deprivations to indeterminate ones. And the precedent which it is said requires us to do so is *Hirabayashi*. The Court is now saying that in *Hirabayashi* we did decide the very things we there said we were not deciding. Because we said that these citizens could be made to stay in their homes during the hours of dark, it is said we must require them to leave home entirely; and if that, we are told they may also be taken into custody for deportation; and if that, it is argued they may also be held for some undetermined time in detention camps. How far the principle of this case would be extended before plausible reasons would play out, I do not know.

I should hold that a civil court cannot be made to enforce an order which violates constitutional limitations even if it is a reasonable exercise of military authority. The courts can exercise only the judicial power, can apply only law, and must abide by the Constitution, or they cease to be civil courts and become instruments of military policy.

Of course the existence of a military power resting on force, so vagrant, so centralized, so necessarily heedless of the individual, is an inherent threat to liberty. But I would not lead people to rely on this Court for a review that seems to me wholly delusive. . . . My duties as a justice as I see them do not require me to make a military judgment as to whether General DeWitt's evacuation and detention program was a reasonable military necessity. I do not suggest that the courts should have attempted to interfere with the Army in carrying out its task. But I do not think they may be asked to execute a military expedient that has no place in law under the Constitution. I would reverse the judgment and discharge the prisoner.

STUDY GUIDE

- Although *Korematsu* is sometimes said to have upheld detention of loyal American citizens in camps, we have seen that the case concerned only the constitutionality of the exclusion zones. In *Ex parte Endo*, decided the same day, the Court uses statutory construction to evaluate the detention policy.
- Why do you suppose the Court avoided the constitutional issues?
- As noted earlier, the Justices already knew that the Roosevelt administration would soon rescind the detention policies. What, then, is the significance of this unanimous judgment?

Mitsuye Endo

Ex parte Endo

323 U.S. 283 (1944)

MR. JUSTICE DOUGLAS delivered the opinion of the Court. . . .

Mitsuye Endo, hereinafter designated as the appellant, is an American citizen of Japanese ancestry. She was evacuated from Sacramento, California, in 1942, pursuant to certain military orders which we will presently discuss, and was removed to the Tule Lake War Relocation Center located at Newell, Modoc County, California. In July, 1942, she filed a petition for a writ of habeas corpus in the District Court of the United States for the Northern District of California, asking that she be discharged and restored to liberty. That petition was denied by the District Court in July, 1943. . . . Shortly thereafter appellant was transferred from the Tule Lake Relocation Center to the Central Utah Relocation Center located at Topaz, Utah, where she is presently detained. . . . Her petition for a writ of habeas corpus alleges that she is a loyal and law-abiding citizen of the United States, that no charge has been made against her, that she is being unlawfully detained, and that she is confined in the Relocation Center under armed guard and held there against her will. . . .

We are of the view that Mitsuye Endo should be given her liberty. In reaching that conclusion we do not come to the underlying constitutional issues which have been argued. For we conclude that, whatever power the War Relocation Authority may have to detain other classes of citizens, it has no authority to subject citizens who are concededly loyal to its leave procedure.

It should be noted at the outset that we do not have here a question such as was presented in *Ex parte Milligan* (1866), or in *Ex parte Quirin* (1942) where the jurisdiction of military tribunals to try persons according to the law of war was challenged in *habeas corpus* proceedings. Mitsuye Endo is detained by a civilian agency, the War Relocation Authority, not by the military. Moreover, the evacuation program was not left exclusively to the military; the Authority was given a large measure of responsibility for its execution and Congress made its enforcement subject to civil penalties by the Act of March 21, 1942. Accordingly, no questions of military law are involved.

Such power of detention as the Authority has stems from Executive Order No. 9066. That order is the source of the authority delegated by General DeWitt in his letter of August 11, 1942. And Executive Order No. 9102 which created the War Relocation Authority purported to do no more than to implement the program authorized by Executive Order No. 9066.

We approach the construction of Executive Order No. 9066 as we would approach the construction of legislation in this field. That Executive Order must indeed be considered along with the Act of March 21, 1942, which ratified and confirmed it as the Order and the statute together laid such basis as there is for participation by civil agencies of the federal government in the evacuation program. Broad powers frequently granted to the President or other executive officers by Congress so that they may deal with the exigencies of war time problems have been sustained. And the Constitution when it committed to the Executive and to Congress the exercise of the war power necessarily gave them wide scope for the exercise of judgment and discretion so that war might be waged effectively and successfully. *Hirabayashi v. United States.* At the same time, however, the Constitution is as specific in its enumeration of many of the civil rights of the individual as it is in its enumeration of the powers of his government. Thus it has prescribed procedural safeguards surrounding the arrest, detention and conviction of individuals. Some of these are contained in the Sixth Amendment, compliance with which is essential if convictions are to be sustained. And the Fifth Amendment provides that no person shall be deprived of liberty (as well as life or property) without due process of law. Moreover, as a further safeguard against invasion of the basic civil rights of the individual it is provided in Art. I, Sec. 9 of the Constitution that "The Privilege of the Writ of Habeas Corpus shall not be suspended, unless when in Cases of Rebellion or Invasion the public Safety may require it." See *Ex parte Milligan.*

We mention these constitutional provisions not to stir the constitutional issues which have been argued at the bar but to indicate the approach which we think should be made to an Act of Congress or an order of the Chief Executive that touches the sensitive area of rights specifically guaranteed by the Constitution. This Court has quite consistently given a narrower scope for the operation of the presumption of constitutionality when legislation appeared on its face to violate a specific prohibition of the Constitution. We have likewise favored that interpretation of legislation which gives it the greater chance of surviving the test of constitutionality. Those analogies are suggestive here. We must assume that the Chief Executive and members of Congress, as well as the courts, are sensitive to and respectful of the liberties of the citizen. In interpreting a war-time measure we must assume that their purpose was to allow for the greatest possible accommodation between those liberties and the exigencies of war. We must assume, when asked to find implied powers in a grant of legislative or executive authority, that the law makers intended to place no greater restraint on the citizen than was clearly and unmistakably indicated by the language they used.

The Act of March 21, 1942, was a war measure. The House Report stated, "The necessity for this legislation arose from the fact that the safe conduct of the war requires the fullest possible protection against either espionage or sabotage to national defense material, national defense premises, and national defense utilities." That was the precise purpose of Executive Order No. 9066, for, as we have seen, it gave as the reason for the exclusion of persons from prescribed military areas the protection of such property "against espionage and against sabotage." And Executive Order No. 9102 which established the War Relocation Authority did so, as we have noted, "in order to provide for the removal from designated areas of persons whose removal is necessary in the interests of national security." The purpose and objective of the Act and of these orders are plain. Their single aim was the protection of the war effort against espionage and sabotage. It is in light of that one objective that the powers conferred by the orders must be construed.

Neither the Act nor the orders use the language of detention. . . . And that silence may have special significance in view of the fact that detention in Relocation Centers was no part of the original program of evacuation but developed later to meet what seemed to the officials in charge to be mounting hostility to the evacuees on the part of the communities where they sought to go.

We do not mean to imply that detention in connection with no phase of the evacuation program would be lawful. The fact that the Act and the orders are silent on detention does not of course mean that any power to detain is lacking. Some such power might indeed be necessary to the successful operation of the evacuation program. At least we may so assume. Moreover, we may assume for the purposes of this case that initial detention in Relocation Centers was authorized. But we stress the silence of the legislative history and of the Act and the Executive Orders on the power to detain to emphasize that any such authority which exists must be implied. If there is to be the greatest possible accommodation of the liberties of the citizen with this war measure, any such implied power must be narrowly confined to the precise purpose of the evacuation program.

A citizen who is concededly loyal presents no problem of espionage or sabotage. Loyalty is a matter of the heart and mind not of race, creed, or color. He who is loyal is by definition not a spy or a saboteur. When the power to detain is derived from the power to protect the war effort against espionage and sabotage, detention which has no relationship to that objective is unauthorized. . . .

Detention which furthered the campaign against espionage and sabotage would be one thing. But detention which has no relationship to that campaign is of a distinct character. Community hostility even to loyal evacuees may have been (and perhaps still is) a serious problem. But if authority for their custody and supervision is to be sought on that ground, the Act of March 21, 1942, Executive Order No. 9066, and Executive Order No. 9102, offer no support. And none other is advanced. To read them that broadly would be to assume that the Congress and the President intended that this discriminatory action should be taken against these people wholly on account of their ancestry even though the government conceded their loyalty to this country. We cannot make such an assumption. As the President has said of these loyal citizens: "Americans of Japanese ancestry, like those of many other ancestries, have shown that they can, and want to, accept our institutions and work loyally with the rest of us, making their own valuable contribution to the national wealth and well-being. In vindication of the very ideals for which we are fighting this war it is important to us to maintain a high standard of fair, considerate, and equal treatment for the people of this minority as of all other minorities."

Mitsuye Endo is entitled to an unconditional release by the War Relocation Authority. . . .

The judgment is reversed and the cause is remanded to the District Court for proceedings in conformity with this opinion.

Mr. Justice Murphy, concurring.

I join in the opinion of the Court, but I am of the view that detention in Relocation Centers of persons of Japanese ancestry regardless of loyalty is not only unauthorized by Congress or the Executive but is another example of the unconstitutional resort to racism inherent in the entire evacuation program. . . . If, as I believe, the military orders excluding her from California were invalid at the time they were issued, they are increasingly objectionable at this late date, when the threat of invasion of the Pacific Coast and the fears of sabotage and espionage have greatly diminished. For the Government to suggest under these circumstances that the presence of Japanese blood in a loyal American citizen might be enough to warrant her exclusion from a place where she would otherwise have a right to go is a position I cannot sanction.

Mr. Justice Roberts.

I concur in the result but I cannot agree with the reasons stated in the opinion of the court for reaching that result.

As in *Fred Toyosaburo Korematsu v. United States*, the court endeavors to avoid constitutional issues which are necessarily involved. The opinion, at great length, attempts to show that neither the executive nor the legislative arm of the Government authorized the detention of the relator. . . . As the opinion discloses, the executive branch of the Government not only was aware of what was being done but in fact that which was done was formulated in regulations and in a so-called handbook open to the public. I had supposed that where thus overtly and avowedly a department of the Government adopts a course of action under a series of official regulations the presumption is that, in this way, the department asserts its belief in the legality and validity of what it is doing. I think it inadmissible to suggest that some inferior public servant exceeded the authority granted by executive order in this case. Such a basis of decision will render easy the evasion of law and the violation of constitutional rights, for when conduct is called in question the obvious response will be that, however much the superior executive officials knew, understood, and approved the conduct of their subordinates, those subordinates in fact lacked a definite mandate so to act. It is to hide one's head in the sand to assert that the detention of relator resulted from an excess of authority by subordinate officials. . . .

In the light of the knowledge Congress had as to the details of the programme, I think the court is unjustified in straining to conclude that Congress did not mean to ratify what was being done. . . . I conclude, therefore, that the court is squarely faced with a serious constitutional question, — whether the relator's detention violated the guarantees of the Bill of Rights of the federal Constitution and especially the guarantee of due process of law. There can be but one answer to that question. An admittedly loyal citizen has been deprived of her liberty for a period of years. Under the Constitution she should be free to come and go as she pleases. Instead, her liberty of motion and other innocent activities have been prohibited and conditioned. She should be discharged.

ASSIGNMENT 5

G. THE POWER TO TRY CITIZENS IN MILITARY TRIBUNALS

STUDY GUIDE

- Why exactly are the Nazi saboteurs in *Quirin* not entitled to invoke the Fifth and Sixth Amendments?
- What does the *Quirin* Court say about the commander-in-chief power of the President in the absence of congressional authorization? How does it distinguish *Ex parte Milligan*?
- How does the Court deal with the fact that one of the accused was a U.S. citizen?

Ex parte Quirin

317 U.S. 1 (1942)

[From July 8 to August 1, 1942, eight Nazi saboteurs were tried by a seven-member military commission in the Justice Department building in Washington, D.C. Two days after the trial ended, the commission found them guilty and issued death sentences. The Supreme Court, which heard oral arguments on July 29 and 30, issued an unsigned, two-page, per curiam opinion on July 31, finding that "the military commission was lawfully constituted." Chief Justice Stone's opinion, which appears below, was not published until October 29, 1942. At that time, however, six of the saboteurs had already been executed by the electric chair. — Eds.]

Mr. Chief Justice Stone delivered the opinion of the Court. . . .

The question for decision is whether the detention of petitioners by respondent for trial by Military Commission, appointed by Order of the President of July 2, 1942, on charges preferred against them purporting to set out their violations of the law of war and of the Articles of War, is in conformity to the laws and Constitution of the United States. . . .

The following facts appear from the petitions or are stipulated. Except as noted they are undisputed.

All the petitioners were born in Germany; all have lived in the United States. All returned to Germany between 1933 and 1941. All except petitioner Haupt are admittedly citizens of the German Reich, with which the United States is at war. Haupt came to this country with his parents when he was five years old; it is contended that he became a citizen of the United States by virtue of the naturalization of his parents during his minority and that he has not since lost his citizenship. The Government, however, takes the position that on attaining his majority he elected to maintain German allegiance and citizenship or in any case that he has by his conduct renounced or abandoned his United States citizenship. For reasons presently to be stated we do not find it necessary to resolve these contentions.

After the declaration of war between the United States and the German Reich, petitioners received training at a sabotage school near Berlin, Germany, where they were instructed in the use of explosives and in methods of secret writing. Thereafter petitioners, with a German citizen, Dasch, proceeded from Germany to a seaport in Occupied France, where petitioners Burger, Heinck and Quirin, together with Dasch, boarded a German submarine which proceeded across the Atlantic to Amagansett Beach on Long Island, New York. The four were there landed from the submarine in the hours of darkness, on or about June 13, 1942, carrying with them a supply of explosives, fuses and incendiary and timing devices. While landing they wore German Marine Infantry uniforms or parts of uniforms. Immediately after landing they buried their uniforms and the other articles mentioned and proceeded in civilian dress to New York City.

The remaining four petitioners at the same French port boarded another German submarine, which carried them across the Atlantic to Ponte Vedra Beach, Florida. On or about June 17, 1942, they came ashore during the hours of darkness wearing caps of the German Marine Infantry and carrying with them a supply of explosives, fuses, and incendiary and timing devices. They immediately buried their caps and the other articles mentioned and proceeded in civilian dress to Jacksonville, Florida, and thence to various points in the United States. All were taken into custody in New York or Chicago by agents of the Federal Bureau of Investigation. All had received instructions in Germany from an officer of the German High Command to destroy war industries and war facilities in the United States, for which they or their relatives in Germany were to receive salary payments from the German Government. They also had been paid by the German

Government during their course of training at the sabotage school and had received substantial sums in United States currency, which were in their possession when arrested. The currency had been handed to them by an officer of the German High Command, who had instructed them to wear their German uniforms while landing in the United States.[17]

The President, as President and Commander in Chief of the Army and Navy, by Order of July 2, 1942, appointed a Military Commission and directed it to try petitioners for offenses against the law of war and the Articles of War, and prescribed regulations for the procedure on the trial and for review of the record of the trial and of any judgment or sentence of the Commission. On the same day, by Proclamation, the President declared that "all persons who are subjects, citizens or residents of any nation at war with the United States or who give obedience to or act under the direction of any such nation, and who during time of war enter or attempt to enter the United States . . . through coastal or boundary defenses, and are charged with committing or attempting or preparing to commit sabotage, espionage, hostile or warlike acts, or violations of the law of war, shall be subject to the law of war and to the jurisdiction of military tribunals."

The Proclamation also stated in terms that all such persons were denied access to the courts.

Pursuant to direction of the Attorney General, the Federal Bureau of Investigation surrendered custody of petitioners to respondent, Provost Marshal of the Military District of Washington, who was directed by the Secretary of War to receive and keep them in custody, and who thereafter held petitioners for trial before the Commission.

On July 3, 1942, the Judge Advocate General's Department of the Army prepared and lodged with the Commission the following charges against petitioners, supported by specifications:

1. Violation of the law of war.
2. Violation of Article 81 of the Articles of War, defining the offense of relieving or attempting to relieve, or corresponding with or giving intelligence to, the enemy.
3. Violation of Article 82, defining the offense of spying.
4. Conspiracy to commit the offenses alleged in charges 1, 2 and 3. . . .

Petitioners' main contention is that the President is without any statutory or constitutional authority to order the petitioners to be tried by military tribunal for offenses with which they are charged; that in consequence they are entitled to be tried in the civil courts with the safeguards, including trial by jury, which the Fifth

---

[17] . . . On the night of June 12-13, 1942, members of the United States Coast Guard, unarmed, maintained a beach patrol along the beaches surrounding Amagansett, Long Island, under written orders mentioning the purpose of detecting landings. On the night of June 17-18, 1942, the United States Army maintained a patrol of the beaches surrounding and including Ponte Vedra Beach, Florida, under written orders mentioning the purpose of detecting the landing of enemy agents from submarines.

and Sixth Amendments guarantee to all persons charged in such courts with criminal offenses. . . .

The Government challenges each of these propositions. But regardless of their merits, it also insists that petitioners must be denied access to the courts, both because they are enemy aliens or have entered our territory as enemy belligerents, and because the President's Proclamation undertakes in terms to deny such access to the class of persons defined by the Proclamation, which aptly describes the character and conduct of petitioners. It is urged that if they are enemy aliens or if the Proclamation has force no court may afford the petitioners a hearing. But there is certainly nothing in the Proclamation to preclude access to the courts for determining its applicability to the particular case. And neither the Proclamation nor the fact that they are enemy aliens forecloses consideration by the courts of petitioners' contentions that the Constitution and laws of the United States constitutionally enacted forbid their trial by military commission. . . . [W]e have resolved those questions by our conclusion that the Commission has jurisdiction to try the charge preferred against petitioners. . . . We pass at once to the consideration of the basis of the Commission's authority. . . .

Congress and the President, like the courts, possess no power not derived from the Constitution. But one of the objects of the Constitution, as declared by its preamble, is to "provide for the common defence." As a means to that end the Constitution gives to Congress the power to "provide for the common Defence," "To raise and support Armies," "To provide and maintain a Navy," and "To make Rules for the Government and Regulation of the land and naval Forces." Congress is given authority "To declare War, grant Letters of Marque and Reprisal, and make Rules concerning Captures on Land and Water," and "To define and punish Piracies and Felonies committed on the high Seas, and Offenses against the Law of Nations." And finally the Constitution authorizes Congress "To make all Laws which shall be necessary and proper for carrying into Execution the foregoing Powers, and all other Powers vested by this Constitution in the Government of the United States, or in any Department or Officer thereof."

The Constitution confers on the President the "executive Power," and imposes on him the duty to "take Care that the Laws be faithfully executed." It makes him the Commander in Chief of the Army and Navy, and empowers him to appoint and commission officers of the United States.

The Constitution thus invests the President as Commander in Chief with the power to wage war which Congress has declared, and to carry into effect all laws passed by Congress for the conduct of war and for the government and regulation of the Armed Forces, and all laws defining and punishing offences against the law of nations, including those which pertain to the conduct of war. . . .

From the very beginning of its history this Court has recognized and applied the law of war as including that part of the law of nations which prescribes, for the conduct of war, the status, rights and duties of enemy nations as well as of enemy individuals. By the Articles of War, and especially Article 15, Congress has explicitly provided, so far as it may constitutionally do so, that military tribunals shall have jurisdiction to try offenders or offenses against the law of war in appropriate cases. Congress, in addition to making rules for the government of our Armed

Forces, has thus exercised its authority to define and punish offenses against the law of nations by sanctioning, within constitutional limitations, the jurisdiction of military commissions to try persons for offenses which, according to the rules and precepts of the law of nations, and more particularly the law of war, are cognizable by such tribunals. And the President, as Commander in Chief, by his Proclamation in time of war has invoked that law. By his Order creating the present Commission he has undertaken to exercise the authority conferred upon him by Congress, and also such authority as the Constitution itself gives the Commander in Chief, to direct the performance of those functions which may constitutionally be performed by the military arm of the nation in time of war.

An important incident to the conduct of war is the adoption of measures by the military command not only to repel and defeat the enemy, but to seize and subject to disciplinary measures those enemies who in their attempt to thwart or impede our military effort have violated the law of war. It is unnecessary for present purposes to determine to what extent the President as Commander in Chief has constitutional power to create military commissions without the support of Congressional legislation. For here Congress has authorized trial of offenses against the law of war before such commissions. We are concerned only with the question whether it is within the constitutional power of the national government to place petitioners upon trial before a military commission for the offenses with which they are charged. We must therefore first inquire whether any of the acts charged is an offense against the law of war cognizable before a military tribunal, and if so whether the Constitution prohibits the trial. We may assume that there are acts regarded in other countries, or by some writers on international law, as offenses against the law of war which would not be triable by military tribunal here, either because they are not recognized by our courts as violations of the law of war or because they are of that class of offenses constitutionally triable only by a jury. It was upon such grounds that the Court denied the right to proceed by military tribunal in *Ex parte Milligan* (1866). But as we shall show, these petitioners were charged with an offense against the law of war which the Constitution does not require to be tried by jury. . . .

By universal agreement and practice, the law of war draws a distinction between the armed forces and the peaceful populations of belligerent nations and also between those who are lawful and unlawful combatants. Lawful combatants are subject to capture and detention as prisoners of war by opposing military forces. Unlawful combatants are likewise subject to capture and detention, but in addition they are subject to trial and punishment by military tribunals for acts which render their belligerency unlawful. The spy who secretly and without uniform passes the military lines of a belligerent in time of war, seeking to gather military information and communicate it to the enemy, or an enemy combatant who without uniform comes secretly through the lines for the purpose of waging war by destruction of life or property, are familiar examples of belligerents who are generally deemed not to be entitled to the status of prisoners of war, but to be offenders against the law of war subject to trial and punishment by military tribunals.

Such was the practice of our own military authorities before the adoption of the Constitution,[18] and during the Mexican and Civil Wars.[19] Paragraph 83 of General Order No. 100 of April 24, 1863, directed that: "Scouts or single soldiers, if disguised in the dress of the country, or in the uniform of the army hostile to their own, employed in obtaining information, if found within or lurking about the lines of the captor, are treated as spies, and suffer death." And Paragraph 84, that "Armed Prowlers, by whatever names they may be called, or persons of the enemy's territory, who steal within the lines of the hostile army for the purpose of robbing, killing, or of destroying bridges, roads, or canals, or of robbing or destroying the mail, or of cutting the telegraph wires, are not entitled to the privileges of the prisoner of war." These and related provisions have been continued in substance by the Rules of Land Warfare promulgated by the War Department for the guidance of the Army. . . .

Our Government, by thus defining lawful belligerents entitled to be treated as prisoners of war, has recognized that there is a class of unlawful belligerents not entitled to that privilege, including those who though combatants do not wear "fixed and distinctive emblems." And by Article 15 of the Articles of War Congress has made provision for their trial and punishment by military commission, according to "the law of war."

By a long course of practical administrative construction by its military authorities, our Government has likewise recognized that those who during time of war pass surreptitiously from enemy territory into our own, discarding their uniforms upon entry, for the commission of hostile acts involving destruction of life or property, have the status of unlawful combatants punishable as such by military commission. This precept of the law of war has been so recognized in practice both here and abroad, and has so generally been accepted as valid by authorities on international law that we think it must be regarded as a rule or principle of the law of war recognized by this Government by its enactment of the Fifteenth Article of War. . . .

It is without significance that petitioners were not alleged to have borne conventional weapons or that their proposed hostile acts did not necessarily contemplate collision with the Armed Forces of the United States. . . . [T]he Rules of Land Warfare, already referred to, plainly contemplate that the hostile acts and purposes for which unlawful belligerents may be punished are not limited to assaults on the

[18] On September 29, 1780, Major John Andre, Adjutant-General to the British Army, was tried by a "Board of General Officers" appointed by General Washington, on a charge that he had come within the lines for an interview with General Benedict Arnold and had been captured while in disguise and traveling under an assumed name. The Board found that the facts charged were true, and that when captured Major Andre had in his possession papers containing intelligence, for the enemy, and reported their conclusion that "Major Andre . . . ought to be considered as a Spy from the enemy, and that agreeably to the law and usage of nations . . . he ought to suffer death." Major Andre was hanged on October 2, 1780.

[19] During the Mexican War military commissions were created in a large number of instances for the trial of various offenses. During the Civil War the military commission was extensively used for the trial of offenses against the law of war. . . . Soldiers and officers "now or late of the Confederate Army," were tried and convicted by military commission for "being secretly within the lines of the United States forces," and for "lurking about the posts, quarters, fortifications and encampments of the armies of the United States," although not "as a spy."

Armed Forces of the United States. Modern warfare is directed at the destruction of enemy war supplies and the implements of their production and transportation quite as much as at the armed forces. Every consideration which makes the unlawful belligerent punishable is equally applicable whether his objective is the one or the other. The law of war cannot rightly treat those agents of enemy armies who enter our territory, armed with explosives intended for the destruction of war industries and supplies, as any the less belligerent enemies than are agents similarly entering for the purpose of destroying fortified places or our Armed Forces. By passing our boundaries for such purposes without uniform or other emblem signifying their belligerent status, or by discarding that means of identification after entry, such enemies become unlawful belligerents subject to trial and punishment.

Citizenship in the United States of an enemy belligerent does not relieve him from the consequences of a belligerency which is unlawful because in violation of the law of war. Citizens who associate themselves with the military arm of the enemy government, and with its aid, guidance and direction enter this country bent on hostile acts are enemy belligerents within the meaning of the Hague Convention and the law of war. It is as an enemy belligerent that petitioner Haupt is charged with entering the United States, and unlawful belligerency is the gravamen of the offense of which he is accused.

Nor are petitioners any the less belligerents if, as they argue, they have not actually committed or attempted to commit any act of depredation or entered the theatre or zone of active military operations. The argument leaves out of account the nature of the offense which the Government charges and which the Act of Congress, by incorporating the law of war, punishes. It is that each petitioner, in circumstances which gave him the status of an enemy belligerent, passed our military and naval lines and defenses or went behind those lines, in civilian dress and with hostile purpose. The offense was complete when with that purpose they entered — or, having so entered, they remained upon — our territory in time of war without uniform or other appropriate means of identification. For that reason, even when committed by a citizen, the offense is distinct from the crime of treason defined in Article III, §3 of the Constitution, since the absence of uniform essential to one is irrelevant to the other.

But petitioners insist that, even if the offenses with which they are charged are offenses against the law of war, their trial is subject to the requirement of the Fifth Amendment that no person shall be held to answer for a capital or otherwise infamous crime unless on a presentment or indictment of a grand jury, and that such trials by Article III, §2, and the Sixth Amendment must be by jury in a civil court. Before the Amendments, §2 of Article III, the Judiciary Article, had provided: "The Trial of all Crimes, except in Cases of Impeachment, shall be by Jury," and had directed that "such Trial shall be held in the State where the said Crimes shall have been committed."

Presentment by a grand jury and trial by a jury of the vicinage where the crime was committed were at the time of the adoption of the Constitution familiar parts of the machinery for criminal trials in the civil courts. But they were procedures unknown to military tribunals, which are not courts in the sense of the Judiciary Article, and which in the natural course of events are usually called upon to function under conditions precluding resort to such procedures. ... [I]t was not the purpose or effect of §2 of Article III, read in the light of the common law, to enlarge the then existing right to a jury trial. The object was to preserve unimpaired trial by jury in all those cases in which it had been recognized by the common law and in all cases of a like nature as they might arise in the future, but not to bring within the sweep of the guaranty those cases in which it was then well understood that a jury trial could not be demanded as of right.

The Fifth and Sixth Amendments, while guaranteeing the continuance of certain incidents of trial by jury which Article III, §2 had left unmentioned, did not enlarge the right to jury trial as it had been established by that Article. . . .

We cannot say that Congress in preparing the Fifth and Sixth Amendments intended to extend trial by jury to the cases of alien or citizen offenders against the law of war otherwise triable by military commission, while withholding it from members of our own armed forces charged with infractions of the Articles of War punishable by death. It is equally inadmissible to construe the Amendments — whose primary purpose was to continue unimpaired presentment by grand jury and trial by petit jury in all those cases in which they had been customary — as either abolishing all trials by military tribunals, save those of the personnel of our own armed forces, or what in effect comes to the same thing, as imposing on all such tribunals the necessity of proceeding against unlawful enemy belligerents only on presentment and trial by jury. We conclude that the Fifth and Sixth Amendments did not restrict whatever authority was conferred by the Constitution to try offenses against the law of war by military commission, and that petitioners, charged with such an offense not required to be tried by jury at common law, were lawfully placed on trial by the Commission without a jury.

Petitioners, and especially petitioner Haupt, stress the pronouncement of this Court in the *Milligan* case, that the law of war "can never be applied to citizens in states which have upheld the authority of the government, and where the courts are open and their process unobstructed." Elsewhere in its opinion, the Court was at pains to point out that Milligan, a citizen twenty years resident in Indiana, who had never been a resident of any of the states in rebellion, was not an enemy belligerent either entitled to the status of a prisoner of war or subject to the penalties imposed upon unlawful belligerents. We construe the Court's statement as to the inapplicability of the law of war to Milligan's case as having particular reference to the facts before it. From them the Court concluded that Milligan, not being a part of or associated with the armed forces of the enemy, was a non-belligerent, not subject to the law of war save as — in circumstances found not there to be present and not involved here — martial law might be constitutionally established.

The Court's opinion is inapplicable to the case presented by the present record. We have no occasion now to define with meticulous care the ultimate boundaries of the jurisdiction of military tribunals to try persons according to the law of war. It is enough that petitioners here, upon the conceded facts, were plainly within those boundaries, and were held in good faith for trial by military commission, charged with being enemies who, with the purpose of destroying war materials and utilities, entered or after entry remained in our territory without uniform — an offense against the law of war. We hold only that those particular acts constitute an offense against the law of war which the Constitution authorizes to be tried by military commission. . . .

We need not inquire whether Congress may restrict the power of the Commander in Chief to deal with enemy belligerents. For the Court is unanimous in its conclusion that the Articles in question could not at any stage of the proceedings afford any basis for issuing the writ. . . .

[O]rders of the District Court should be affirmed, and that leave to file petitions for habeas corpus in this court should be denied.

On September 23, 2004, the United States Justice Department released Hamdi to Saudi Arabia on the condition that he give up his U.S. citizenship.

In the wake of the September 11, 2001 terrorist attacks, Congress enacted the Authorization for Use of Military Force (AUMF). This resolution gave the President the authority to "use all necessary and appropriate force against those nations, organizations, or persons he determines planned, authorized, committed, or aided the terrorist attacks that occurred on September 11, 2001." This resolution formally inaugurated the global war on terror, a conflict that has raised many questions about the scope of the national war power. The most vexatious issues arose because this did not seem to be the kind of "war" that could ever be won (and therefore can never be declared over). As a result, "extraordinary" wartime powers were at risk of becoming permanent fixtures of the American legal system. In *Hamdi v. Rumsfeld*, the Supreme Court wrestles with how to apply the doctrines developed in the previous cases in this arguably new context.

STUDY GUIDE

- As in *Youngstown*, in *Hamdi* there is some dispute about whether or not Congress has authorized the President's actions.
- On what basis does Justice Scalia conclude that the detention of an American citizen was not authorized by Congress's enactment of the Authorization for Use of Military Force? Notice the role that the writ of habeas corpus plays in his analysis.
- The vote breakdown in this case is very complex because there is no majority opinion that commands five votes. Justice O'Connor's *plurality* opinion—joined by the Chief Justice, Justice Kennedy, and Justice Breyer—concluded that Congress had authorized the detention of enemy combatants, but remanded the case to afford Hamdi the "opportunity to contest the factual basis for that detention before a neutral decisionmaker." Justice Scalia, joined by Justice Stevens, dissented, finding that Hamdi, a U.S. citizen, could not be detained. Justice Thomas, in dissent, would have upheld Hamdi's detention, and would not have remanded the case. Justice Souter, joined by Justice Ginsburg, disagreed with the plurality opinion's analysis, but to ensure that the judgment garnered five votes, joined the plurality's decision to remand the case. We told you it was complex.

Hamdi v. Rumsfeld

542 U.S. 507 (2004)

JUSTICE O'CONNOR announced the judgment of the Court and delivered an opinion, in which THE CHIEF JUSTICE, JUSTICE KENNEDY, and JUSTICE BREYER join.

At this difficult time in our Nation's history, we are called upon to consider the legality of the Government's detention of a United States citizen on United States soil as an "enemy combatant" and to address the process that is constitutionally owed to one who seeks to challenge his classification as such. The United States Court of Appeals for the Fourth Circuit held that petitioner's detention was legally authorized and that he was entitled to no further opportunity to challenge his enemy-combatant label. We now vacate and remand. We hold that although Congress authorized the detention of combatants in the narrow circumstances alleged here, due process demands that a citizen held in the United States as an enemy combatant be given a meaningful opportunity to contest the factual basis for that detention before a neutral decisionmaker. [The due process analysis is omitted. — EDS.]

On September 11, 2001, the al Qaeda terrorist network used hijacked commercial airliners to attack prominent targets in the United States. Approximately 3,000 people were killed in those attacks. One week later, in response to these "acts of treacherous violence," Congress passed a resolution authorizing the President to "use all necessary and appropriate force against those nations, organizations, or persons he determines planned, authorized, committed, or aided the terrorist attacks" or "harbored such organizations or persons, in order to prevent any future acts of international terrorism against the United States by such nations, organizations or persons." Authorization for Use of Military Force ("the AUMF"). Soon thereafter, the President ordered United States Armed Forces to Afghanistan, with a mission to subdue al Qaeda and quell the Taliban regime that was known to support it.

This case arises out of the detention of a man whom the Government alleges took up arms with the Taliban during this conflict. His name is Yaser Esam Hamdi. Born an American citizen in Louisiana in 1980, Hamdi moved with his family to Saudi Arabia as a child. By 2001, the parties agree, he resided in Afghanistan. At some point that year, he was seized by members of the Northern Alliance, a coalition of military groups opposed to the Taliban government, and eventually was turned over to the United States military. The Government asserts that it initially detained and interrogated Hamdi in Afghanistan before transferring him to the United States Naval Base in Guantanamo Bay in January 2002. In April 2002, upon learning that Hamdi is an American citizen, authorities transferred him to a naval brig in Norfolk, Virginia, where he remained until a recent transfer to a brig in Charleston, South Carolina. The Government contends that Hamdi is an "enemy combatant," and that this status justifies holding him in the United States indefinitely — without formal charges or proceedings — unless and until it makes the determination that access to counsel or further process is warranted. . . .

The threshold question before us is whether the Executive has the authority to detain citizens who qualify as "enemy combatants." There is some debate as to the proper scope of this term, and the Government has never provided any court with the full criteria that it uses in classifying individuals as such. It has made clear, however, that, for purposes of this case, the "enemy combatant" that it is seeking to detain is an individual who, it alleges, was "part of or supporting forces hostile to the United States or coalition partners" in Afghanistan and who "engaged in an armed conflict against the United States" there. We therefore answer only the narrow question before us: whether the detention of citizens falling within that definition is authorized.

The Government maintains that no explicit congressional authorization is required, because the Executive possesses plenary authority to detain pursuant to Article II of the Constitution. We do not reach the question whether Article II provides such authority, however, because we agree with the Government's alternative position, that Congress has in fact authorized Hamdi's detention, through the AUMF. . . .

The AUMF authorizes the President to use "all necessary and appropriate force" against "nations, organizations, or persons" associated with the September 11, 2001, terrorist attacks. There can be no doubt that individuals who fought against the United States in Afghanistan as part of the Taliban, an organization known to have supported the al Qaeda terrorist network responsible for those attacks, are individuals Congress sought to target in passing the AUMF. We conclude that detention of individuals falling into the limited category we are considering, for the duration of the particular conflict in which they were captured, is so fundamental and accepted an incident to war as to be an exercise of the "necessary and appropriate force" Congress has authorized the President to use.

The capture and detention of lawful combatants and the capture, detention, and trial of unlawful combatants, by "universal agreement and practice," are "important incident[s] of war." *Ex parte Quirin* (1942). The purpose of detention is to prevent captured individuals from returning to the field of battle and taking up arms once again.

There is no bar to this Nation's holding one of its own citizens as an enemy combatant. In *Quirin*, one of the detainees, Haupt, alleged that he was a naturalized United States citizen. We held that "[c]itizens who associate themselves with the military arm of the enemy government, and with its aid, guidance and direction enter this country bent on hostile acts, are enemy belligerents within the meaning of . . . the law of war." While Haupt was tried for violations of the law of war, nothing in *Quirin* suggests that his citizenship would have precluded his mere detention for the duration of the relevant hostilities. Nor can we see any reason for drawing such a line here. A citizen, no less than an alien, can be "part of or supporting forces hostile to the United States or coalition partners" and "engaged in an armed conflict against the United States"; such a citizen, if released, would pose the same threat of returning to the front during the ongoing conflict.

In light of these principles, it is of no moment that the AUMF does not use specific language of detention. Because detention to prevent a combatant's return to the battlefield is a fundamental incident of waging war, in permitting the use of "necessary and appropriate force," Congress has clearly and unmistakably authorized detention in the narrow circumstances considered here.

Hamdi objects, nevertheless, that Congress has not authorized the indefinite detention to which he is now subject. The Government responds that "the detention of enemy combatants during World War II was just as 'indefinite' while that war was being fought." We take Hamdi's objection to be not to the lack of certainty regarding the date on which the conflict will end, but to the substantial prospect of perpetual detention. We recognize that the national security underpinnings of the "war on terror," although crucially important, are broad and malleable. As the Government concedes, "given its unconventional nature, the current conflict is unlikely to end with a formal cease-fire agreement." The prospect Hamdi raises is therefore not far-fetched. If the Government does not consider this unconventional war won for two generations, and if it maintains during that time that Hamdi might, if released, rejoin forces fighting against the United States, then the position it has taken throughout the litigation of this case suggests that Hamdi's detention could last for the rest of his life.

It is a clearly established principle of the law of war that detention may last no longer than active hostilities. See Article 118 of the Geneva Convention (III) Relative to the Treatment of Prisoners of War, Aug. 12, 1949 ("Prisoners of war shall be released and repatriated without delay after the cessation of active hostilities").

Hamdi contends that the AUMF does not authorize indefinite or perpetual detention. Certainly, we agree that indefinite detention for the purpose of interrogation is not authorized. Further, we understand Congress' grant of authority for the use of "necessary and appropriate force" to include the authority to detain for the duration of the relevant conflict, and our understanding is based on longstanding law-of-war principles. If the practical circumstances of a given conflict are entirely unlike those of the conflicts that informed the development of the law of war, that understanding may unravel. But that is not the situation we face as of this date. Active combat operations against Taliban fighters apparently are ongoing in Afghanistan. The United States may detain, for the duration of these hostilities, individuals legitimately determined to be Taliban combatants who "engaged in an armed conflict against the United States." If the record establishes that United States troops are still involved in active combat in Afghanistan, those detentions are part of the exercise of "necessary and appropriate force," and therefore are authorized by the AUMF.

Ex parte Milligan (1866) does not undermine our holding about the Government's authority to seize enemy combatants, as we define that term today. In that case, the Court made repeated reference to the fact that its inquiry into whether the military tribunal had jurisdiction to try and punish Milligan turned in large part on the fact that Milligan was not a prisoner of war, but a resident of Indiana arrested while at home there. That fact was central to its conclusion. Had Milligan been captured while he was assisting Confederate soldiers by carrying a rifle against Union troops on a Confederate battlefield, the holding of the Court might well have been different. The Court's repeated explanations that Milligan was not a prisoner of war suggest that had these different circumstances been present he could have been detained under military authority for the duration of the conflict, whether or not he was a citizen.[20]

Moreover, as Justice Scalia acknowledges, the Court in *Ex parte Quirin* (1942) dismissed the language of *Milligan* that the petitioners had suggested prevented them from being subject to military process. . . . *Quirin* was a unanimous opinion. It both postdates and clarifies *Milligan*, providing us with the most apposite precedent that we have on the question of whether citizens may be detained in such circumstances. Brushing aside such precedent — particularly when doing so gives rise to a host of new questions never dealt with by this Court — is unjustified and unwise.

To the extent that Justice Scalia accepts the precedential value of *Quirin*, he argues that it cannot guide our inquiry here because "[i]n *Quirin* it was uncontested that the petitioners were members of enemy forces," while Hamdi challenges his classification as an enemy combatant. But it is unclear why, in the paradigm outlined by Justice Scalia, such a concession should have any relevance. Justice Scalia envisions a system in which the only options are congressional suspension of the writ of habeas corpus or prosecution for treason or some other crime. He does not explain how his historical analysis supports the addition of a third option — detention under some other process after concession of enemy-combatant status — or why a concession should carry any different effect than proof of enemy-combatant status in a proceeding that comports with due process. To be clear, our opinion only finds legislative authority to detain under the AUMF once it is sufficiently clear that the individual is, in fact, an enemy combatant; whether that is established by concession or by some other process that verifies this fact with sufficient certainty seems beside the point.

Further, Justice Scalia largely ignores the context of this case: a United States citizen captured in a foreign combat zone. Justice Scalia refers to only one case involving this factual scenario — a case in which a United States citizen-POW (a member of the Italian army) from World War II was seized on the battlefield in Sicily and then held in the United States. The court in that case held that the military detention of that United States citizen was lawful. See *In re Territo* (CA9 1946).

Justice Scalia's treatment of that case — in a footnote — suffers from the same defect as does his treatment of *Quirin*: Because Justice Scalia finds the fact of battlefield capture irrelevant, his distinction based on the fact that the petitioner "conceded" enemy combatant status is beside the point. Justice Scalia can point to no case or other authority for the proposition that those captured on a foreign battlefield (whether detained there or in U.S. territory) cannot be detained outside the criminal process.

[20] Here the basis asserted for detention by the military is that Hamdi was carrying a weapon against American troops on a foreign battlefield; that is, that he was an enemy combatant. The legal category of enemy combatant has not been elaborated upon in great detail. The permissible bounds of the category will be defined by the lower courts as subsequent cases are presented to them.

Moreover, Justice Scalia presumably would come to a different result if Hamdi had been kept in Afghanistan or even Guantanamo Bay. This creates a perverse incentive. Military authorities faced with the stark choice of submitting to the full-blown criminal process or releasing a suspected enemy combatant captured on the battlefield will simply keep citizen-detainees abroad. Indeed, the Government transferred Hamdi from Guantanamo Bay to the United States naval brig only after it learned that he might be an American citizen. It is not at all clear why that should make a determinative constitutional difference. . . .

JUSTICE SOUTER, with whom JUSTICE GINSBURG joins, concurring in part, dissenting in part, and concurring in the judgment.

[Justice Souter found Hamdi's "detention forbidden" by the Non-Detention Act, which "bars imprisonment or detention of a citizen 'except pursuant to an Act of Congress.'" But he did not agree with Justice O'Connor's plurality opinion. — EDS.]

. . . I would therefore vacate the judgment of the Court of Appeals and remand for proceedings consistent with this view. Since this disposition does not command a majority of the Court, however, the need to give practical effect to the conclusions of eight members of the Court rejecting the Government's position calls for me to join with the plurality in ordering remand on terms closest to those I would impose. See *Screws v. United States* (1945) (Rutledge, J., concurring in result). Although I think litigation of Hamdi's status as an enemy combatant is unnecessary, the terms of the plurality's remand will allow Hamdi to offer evidence that he is not an enemy combatant, and he should at the least have the benefit of that opportunity. It should go without saying that in joining with the plurality to produce a judgment, I do not adopt the plurality's resolution of constitutional issues that I would not reach. . . .

JUSTICE SCALIA, with whom JUSTICE STEVENS joins, dissenting.

Petitioner, a presumed American citizen, has been imprisoned without charge or hearing in the Norfolk and Charleston Naval Brigs for more than two years, on the allegation that he is an enemy combatant who bore arms against his country for the Taliban. His father claims to the contrary, that he is an inexperienced aid worker caught in the wrong place at the wrong time. This case brings into conflict the competing demands of national security and our citizens' constitutional right to personal liberty. Although I share the Court's evident unease as it seeks to reconcile the two, I do not agree with its resolution.

Where the Government accuses a citizen of waging war against it, our constitutional tradition has been to prosecute him in federal court for treason or some other crime. Where the exigencies of war prevent that, the Constitution's Suspension Clause, Art. I, §9, cl. 2, allows Congress to relax the usual protections temporarily. Absent suspension, however, the Executive's assertion of military exigency has not been thought sufficient to permit detention without charge. No one contends that the congressional Authorization for Use of Military Force, on which the Government relies to justify its actions here, is an implementation of the Suspension Clause. Accordingly, I would reverse the decision below.

I

The very core of liberty secured by our Anglo-Saxon system of separated powers has been freedom from indefinite imprisonment at the will of the Executive. . . . The gist of the Due Process Clause, as understood at the founding and since, was to force the Government to follow those common-law procedures traditionally deemed necessary before depriving a person of life, liberty, or property. When a citizen was deprived of liberty because of alleged criminal conduct, those procedures typically required committal by a magistrate followed by indictment and trial. . . .

These due process rights have historically been vindicated by the writ of habeas corpus. In England before the founding, the writ developed into a tool for challenging executive confinement. . . . The struggle between subject and Crown . . . culminated in the Habeas Corpus Act of 1679, described by Blackstone as a "second magna charta, and stable bulwark of our liberties." The Act governed all persons "committed or detained . . . for any crime." In cases other than felony or treason plainly expressed in the warrant of commitment, the Act required release upon appropriate sureties (unless the commitment was for a nonbailable offense). Where the commitment was for felony or high treason, the Act did not require immediate release, but instead required the Crown to commence criminal proceedings within a specified time. §7. If the prisoner was not "indicted some Time in the next Term," the judge was "required . . . to set at Liberty the Prisoner upon Bail" unless the King was unable to produce his witnesses. Able or no, if the prisoner was not brought to trial by the next succeeding term, the Act provided that "he shall be discharged from his Imprisonment." English courts sat four terms per year, so the practical effect of this provision was that imprisonment without indictment or trial for felony or high treason under §7 would not exceed approximately three to six months.

The writ of habeas corpus was preserved in the Constitution—the only common-law writ to be explicitly mentioned. See Art. I, §9, cl. 2. Hamilton lauded "the establishment of the writ of habeas corpus" in his *Federalist* defense as a means to protect against "the practice of arbitrary imprisonments . . . in all ages, [one of] the favourite and most formidable instruments of tyranny." *The Federalist, No. 84.* Indeed, availability of the writ under the new Constitution (along with the requirement of trial by jury in criminal cases, see Art. III, §2, cl. 3) was his basis for arguing that additional, explicit procedural protections were unnecessary. See *The Federalist, No. 83.*

II

The allegations here, of course, are no ordinary accusations of criminal activity. Yaser Esam Hamdi has been imprisoned because the Government believes he participated in the waging of war against the United States. The relevant question, then, is whether there is a different, special procedure for imprisonment of a citizen accused of wrongdoing by aiding the enemy in wartime.

Justice O'Connor, writing for a plurality of this Court, asserts that captured enemy combatants (other than those suspected of war crimes) have traditionally been detained until the cessation of hostilities and then released. That is probably an accurate description of wartime practice with respect to enemy aliens. The tradition with respect to American citizens, however, has been quite different. Citizens aiding the enemy have been treated as traitors subject to the criminal process.

As early as 1350, England's Statute of Treasons made it a crime to "levy War against our Lord the King in his Realm, or be adherent to the King's Enemies in his Realm, giving to them Aid and Comfort, in the Realm, or elsewhere." . . . The Founders inherited the understanding that a citizen's levying war against the Government was to be punished criminally. The Constitution provides: "Treason against the United States, shall consist only in levying War against them, or in adhering to their Enemies, giving them Aid and Comfort"; and establishes a heightened proof requirement (two witnesses) in order to "convic[t]" of that offense. Art. III, §3, cl. 1.

In more recent times, too, citizens have been charged and tried in Article III courts for acts of war against the United States, even when their noncitizen co-conspirators were not. For example, two American citizens alleged to have participated during World War I in a spying conspiracy on behalf of Germany were tried in federal court. A German member of the same conspiracy was subjected to military process. During World War II, the famous German saboteurs of *Ex parte Quirin*, received military process, but the citizens who associated with them (with the exception of one citizen-saboteur, discussed below) were punished under the criminal process. . . . The only citizen other than Hamdi known to be imprisoned in connection with military hostilities in Afghanistan against the United States was subjected to criminal process and convicted upon a guilty plea. See *United States v. Lindh* (E.D. Va. 2002).

There are times when military exigency renders resort to the traditional criminal process impracticable. . . . Where the Executive has not pursued the usual course of charge, committal, and conviction, it has historically secured the Legislature's explicit approval of a suspension. . . . Our Federal Constitution contains a provision explicitly permitting suspension, but limiting the situations in which it may be invoked: "The privilege of the Writ of Habeas Corpus shall not be suspended, unless when in Cases of Rebellion or Invasion the public Safety may require it." Art. I, §9, cl. 2. Although this provision does not state that suspension must be effected by, or authorized by, a legislative act, it has been so understood, consistent with English practice and the Clause's placement in Article I. See *Ex parte Merryman* (C.D. Md. 1861) (Taney, C.J., rejecting Lincoln's unauthorized suspension).

The Suspension Clause was by design a safety valve, the Constitution's only "express provision for exercise of extraordinary authority because of a crisis," *Youngstown* (Jackson, J., concurring). Very early in the Nation's history, President Jefferson unsuccessfully sought a suspension of habeas corpus to deal with Aaron Burr's conspiracy to overthrow the Government. During the Civil War, Congress passed its first Act authorizing Executive suspension of the writ of habeas corpus to the relief of those many who thought President Lincoln's unauthorized proclamations of suspension unconstitutional. Later Presidential proclamations of suspension relied upon the congressional authorization. During Reconstruction, Congress passed the Ku Klux Klan Act, which included a provision authorizing suspension of the writ, invoked by President Grant in quelling a rebellion in nine South Carolina counties. . . .

III

Of course the extensive historical evidence of criminal convictions and habeas suspensions does not necessarily refute the Government's position in this case. When the writ is suspended, the Government is entirely free from judicial oversight. It does not claim such total liberation here, but argues that it need only produce what it calls "some evidence" to satisfy a habeas court that a detained individual is an enemy combatant. Even if suspension of the writ on the one hand, and committal for criminal charges on the other hand, have been the only traditional means of dealing with citizens who levied war against their own country, it is theoretically possible that the Constitution does not require a choice between these alternatives.

I believe, however, that substantial evidence does refute that possibility. First, the text of the 1679 Habeas Corpus Act makes clear that indefinite imprisonment on reasonable suspicion is not an available option of treatment for those accused of aiding the enemy, absent a suspension of the writ. . . . §7 of the Act specifically addressed those committed for high treason, and provided a remedy if they were not indicted and tried by the second succeeding court term. That remedy was not a bobtailed judicial inquiry into whether there were reasonable grounds to believe the prisoner had taken up arms against the King. Rather, if the prisoner was not indicted and tried within the prescribed time, "he shall be discharged from his Imprisonment." The Act does not contain any exception for wartime. That omission is conspicuous, since §7 explicitly addresses the offense of "High Treason," which often involved offenses of a military nature.

Writings from the founding generation also suggest that, without exception, the only constitutional alternatives are to charge the crime or suspend the writ. In 1788, Thomas Jefferson wrote to James Madison questioning the need for a Suspension Clause in cases of rebellion in the proposed Constitution. His letter illustrates the constraints under which the Founders understood themselves to operate:

> Why suspend the Hab. corp. in insurrections and rebellions? The parties who may be arrested may be charged instantly with a well defined crime. Of course the judge will remand them. If the publick safety requires that the government should have a man imprisoned on less probable testimony in those than in other emergencies; let him be taken and tried, retaken and retried, while the necessity continues, only giving him redress against the government for damages.

A similar view was reflected in the 1807 House debates over suspension during the armed uprising that came to be known as Burr's conspiracy:

> With regard to those persons who may be implicated in the conspiracy, if the writ of habeas corpus be not suspended, what will be the consequence? When apprehended, they will be brought before a court of justice, who will decide whether there is any

> evidence that will justify their commitment for farther prosecution. From the communication of the Executive, it appeared there was sufficient evidence to authorize their commitment. Several months would elapse before their final trial, which would give time to collect evidence, and if this shall be sufficient, they will not fail to receive the punishment merited by their crimes, and inflicted by the laws of their country. (remarks of Rep. Burwell).

. . . President Lincoln, when he purported to suspend habeas corpus without congressional authorization during the Civil War, apparently did not doubt that suspension was required if the prisoner was to be held without criminal trial. In his famous message to Congress on July 4, 1861, he argued only that he could suspend the writ, not that even without suspension, his imprisonment of citizens without criminal trial was permitted.

Further evidence comes from this Court's decision in *Ex parte Milligan*. There, the Court issued the writ to an American citizen who had been tried by military commission for offenses that included conspiring to overthrow the Government, seize munitions, and liberate prisoners of war. The Court rejected in no uncertain terms the Government's assertion that military jurisdiction was proper "under the 'laws and usages of war'": "It can serve no useful purpose to inquire what those laws and usages are, whence they originated, where found, and on whom they operate; they can never be applied to citizens in states which have upheld the authority of the government, and where the courts are open and their process unobstructed."[21]

Milligan is not exactly this case, of course, since the petitioner was threatened with death, not merely imprisonment. But the reasoning and conclusion of *Milligan* logically cover the present case. The Government justifies imprisonment of Hamdi on principles of the law of war and admits that, absent the war, it would have no such authority. But if the law of war cannot be applied to citizens where courts are open, then Hamdi's imprisonment without criminal trial is no less unlawful than Milligan's trial by military tribunal. . . .

The proposition that the Executive lacks indefinite wartime detention authority over citizens is consistent with the Founders' general mistrust of military power permanently at the Executive's disposal. . . . A view of the Constitution that gives the Executive authority to use military force rather than the force of law against citizens on American soil flies in the face of the mistrust that engendered these provisions.

IV

The Government argues that our more recent jurisprudence ratifies its indefinite imprisonment of a citizen within the territorial jurisdiction of federal courts. It places primary reliance upon *Ex parte Quirin*, a World War II case

---

[21] As I shall discuss presently, the Court purported to limit this language in *Ex parte Quirin*. Whatever *Quirin*'s effect on *Milligan*'s precedential value, however, it cannot undermine its value as an indicator of original meaning.

upholding the trial by military commission of eight German saboteurs, one of whom, Hans Haupt, was a U.S. citizen. The case was not this Court's finest hour. The Court upheld the commission and denied relief in a brief per curiam issued the day after oral argument concluded; a week later the Government carried out the commission's death sentence upon six saboteurs, including Haupt. The Court eventually explained its reasoning in a written opinion issued several months later. . . .

In *Quirin* it was uncontested that the petitioners were members of enemy forces. They were "*admitted* enemy invaders" (emphasis added), and it was "undisputed" that they had landed in the United States in service of German forces. The specific holding of the Court was only that, "upon the *conceded* facts," the petitioners were "plainly within [the] boundaries" of military jurisdiction (emphasis added).[22] But where those jurisdictional facts are *not* conceded — where the petitioner insists that he is *not* a belligerent — *Quirin* left the pre-existing law [including *Milligan*] in place: Absent suspension of the writ, a citizen held where the courts are open is entitled either to criminal trial or to a judicial decree requiring his release.[23]

V

It follows from what I have said that Hamdi is entitled to a habeas decree requiring his release unless (1) criminal proceedings are promptly brought, or (2) Congress has suspended the writ of habeas corpus. A suspension of the writ could, of course, lay down conditions for continued detention, similar to those that today's opinion prescribes under the Due Process Clause. But there is a world of difference between the people's representatives' determining the need for that suspension (and prescribing the conditions for it), and this Court's doing so.

The plurality finds justification for Hamdi's imprisonment in the Authorization for Use of Military Force, which provides:

---

[22] The only two Court of Appeals cases from World War II cited by the Government in which citizens were detained without trial likewise involved petitioners who were conceded to have been members of enemy forces. The plurality complains that *Territo* is the only case I have identified in which "a United States citizen [was] captured in a foreign combat zone." Indeed it is; such cases must surely be rare. But given the constitutional tradition I have described, the burden is not upon me to find cases in which the writ was granted to citizens in this country who had been captured on foreign battlefields; it is upon those who would carve out an exception for such citizens (as the plurality's complaint suggests it would) to find a single case (other than one where enemy status was admitted) in which habeas was denied.

[23] The plurality's assertion that *Quirin* somehow "clarifies" *Milligan* is simply false. . . . [T]he *Quirin* Court propounded a mistaken understanding of *Milligan*; but nonetheless its holding was limited to "the case presented by the present record," and to "*the conceded facts*," and thus avoided conflict with the earlier case. (emphasis added). The plurality, ignoring this expressed limitation, thinks it "beside the point" whether belligerency is conceded or found "by some other process" (not necessarily a jury trial) "that verifies this fact with sufficient certainty." But the whole point of the procedural guarantees in the Bill of Rights is to limit the methods by which the Government can determine facts that the citizen disputes and on which the citizen's liberty depends. . . .

> That the President is authorized to use all necessary and appropriate force against those nations, organizations, or persons he determines planned, authorized, committed, or aided the terrorist attacks that occurred on September 11, 2001, or harbored such organizations or persons, in order to prevent any future acts of international terrorism against the United States by such nations, organizations or persons. §2(a).

This is not remotely a congressional suspension of the writ, and no one claims that it is. Contrary to the plurality's view, I do not think this statute even authorizes detention of a citizen with the clarity necessary to satisfy the interpretive canon that statutes should be construed so as to avoid grave constitutional concerns.[24] . . . But even if it did, I would not permit it to overcome Hamdi's entitlement to habeas corpus relief. . . . If the Suspension Clause does not guarantee the citizen that he will either be tried or released, unless the conditions for suspending the writ exist and the grave action of suspending the writ has been taken; if it merely guarantees the citizen that he will not be detained unless Congress by ordinary legislation says he can be detained; it guarantees him very little indeed. . . .

There is a certain harmony of approach in the plurality's making up for Congress' failure to invoke the Suspension Clause and its making up for the Executive's failure to apply what it says are needed procedures — an approach that reflects what might be called a Mr. Fix-it Mentality. The plurality seems to view it as its mission to Make Everything Come Out Right, rather than merely to decree the consequences, as far as individual rights are concerned, of the other two branches' actions and omissions. Has the Legislature failed to suspend the writ in the current dire emergency? Well, we will remedy that failure by prescribing the reasonable conditions that a suspension should have included. And has the Executive failed to live up to those reasonable conditions? Well, we will ourselves make that failure good, so that this dangerous fellow (if he is dangerous) need not be set free. The problem with this approach is not only that it steps out of the courts' modest and limited role in a democratic society; but that by repeatedly doing what it thinks the political branches ought to do it encourages their lassitude and saps the vitality of government by the people.

VI

. . . To be sure, suspension is limited by the Constitution to cases of rebellion or invasion. But whether the attacks of September 11, 2001, constitute an "invasion,"

---

[24] The plurality rejects any need for "specific language of detention" on the ground that detention of alleged combatants is a "fundamental incident of waging war." Its authorities do not support that holding in the context of the present case. Some are irrelevant because they do not address the detention of *American citizens.* The plurality's assertion that detentions of citizen and alien combatants are equally authorized has no basis in law or common sense. Citizens and noncitizens, even if equally dangerous, are not similarly situated. That captivity may be consistent with the principles of international law does not prove that it also complies with the restrictions that the Constitution places on the American Government's treatment of its own citizens. Of the authorities cited by the plurality that do deal with detention of citizens, *Quirin* and *Territo* have already been discussed and rejected. . . .

and whether those attacks still justify suspension several years later, are questions for Congress rather than this Court.[25] If civil rights are to be curtailed during wartime, it must be done openly and democratically, as the Constitution requires, rather than by silent erosion through an opinion of this Court. . . .

Many think it not only inevitable but entirely proper that liberty give way to security in times of national crisis — that, at the extremes of military exigency, *inter arma silent leges*. Whatever the general merits of the view that war silences law or modulates its voice, that view has no place in the interpretation and application of a Constitution designed precisely to confront war and, in a manner that accords with democratic principles, to accommodate it. Because the Court has proceeded to meet the current emergency in a manner the Constitution does not envision, I respectfully dissent.

Justice Thomas, dissenting.

The Executive Branch, acting pursuant to the powers vested in the President by the Constitution and with explicit congressional approval, has determined that Yaser Hamdi is an enemy combatant and should be detained. This detention falls squarely within the Federal Government's war powers, and we lack the expertise and capacity to second-guess that decision. As such, petitioners' habeas challenge should fail, and there is no reason to remand the case. . . .

I agree with the plurality that the Federal Government has power to detain those that the Executive Branch determines to be enemy combatants. But I do not think that the plurality has adequately explained the breadth of the President's authority to detain enemy combatants, an authority that includes making virtually conclusive factual findings. In my view, . . . we lack the capacity and responsibility to second-guess this determination. . . . [T]he Executive's decision that a detention is necessary to protect the public need not and should not be subjected to judicial second-guessing. Indeed, at least in the context of enemy-combatant determinations, this would defeat the unity, secrecy, and dispatch that the Founders believed to be so important to the war-making function.

I therefore cannot agree with Justice Scalia's conclusion that the Government must choose between using standard criminal processes and suspending the writ. Justice Scalia relies heavily upon *Ex parte Milligan*. . . . I admit that *Milligan* supports his position. But because the Executive Branch there, unlike here, did not follow a specific statutory mechanism provided by Congress, the Court did not need to reach the broader question of Congress' power, and its discussion on this point was arguably dicta, as four Justices believed (Chase, C.J., joined by Wayne, Swayne, and Miller, J.J., concurring in judgment).

More importantly, the Court referred frequently and pervasively to the criminal nature of the proceedings instituted against Milligan. . . . Because the

---

[25] Justice Thomas worries that the constitutional conditions for suspension of the writ will not exist "during many . . . emergencies during which . . . detention authority might be necessary." It is difficult to imagine situations in which security is so seriously threatened as to justify indefinite imprisonment without trial, and yet the constitutional conditions of rebellion or invasion are not met.

Government does not detain Hamdi in order to punish him, as the plurality acknowledges, *Milligan* . . . do[es] not control.

Justice Scalia also finds support in a letter Thomas Jefferson wrote to James Madison. I agree that this provides some evidence for his position. But I think this plainly insufficient to rebut the authorities upon which I have relied. In any event, I do not believe that Justice Scalia's evidence leads to the necessary "clear conviction that [the detention is] in conflict with the Constitution or laws of Congress constitutionally enacted," *Quirin*, to justify nullifying the President's wartime action.

Finally, Justice Scalia's position raises an additional concern. Justice Scalia apparently does not disagree that the Federal Government has all power necessary to protect the Nation. If criminal processes do not suffice, however, Justice Scalia would require Congress to suspend the writ. But the fact that the writ may not be suspended "unless when in Cases of Rebellion or Invasion the public Safety may require it," Art. I, §9, cl. 2, poses two related problems. First, this condition might not obtain here or during many other emergencies during which this detention authority might be necessary. Congress would then have to choose between acting unconstitutionally[26] and depriving the President of the tools he needs to protect the Nation. Second, I do not see how suspension would make constitutional otherwise unconstitutional detentions ordered by the President. It simply removes a remedy. Justice Scalia's position might therefore require one or both of the political branches to act unconstitutionally in order to protect the Nation. But the power to protect the Nation must be the power to do so lawfully.

Accordingly, I conclude that the Government's detention of Hamdi as an enemy combatant does not violate the Constitution. By detaining Hamdi, the President, in the prosecution of a war and authorized by Congress, has acted well within his authority. Hamdi thereby received all the process to which he was due under the circumstances. I therefore believe that this is no occasion to balance the competing interests, as the plurality unconvincingly attempts to do. . . . For these reasons, I would affirm the judgment of the Court of Appeals.

H. BALANCING NATIONAL SECURITY AND INDIVIDUAL LIBERTY

The Supreme Court's recent decision in *Ziglar v. Abbasi*, the facts of which began in the aftermath of September 11, 2001, presents two diametrically opposite perspectives on how judges should weigh the government's interest in promoting national security, and the potential risk to personal freedom. Compare Justice Kennedy's majority opinion with Justice Breyer's dissent.

---

[26] I agree with Justice Scalia that this Court could not review Congress' decision to suspend the writ.

STUDY GUIDE

- The Court's opinion in *Ziglar v. Abbasi* arose from the same facts as *Ashcroft v. Iqbal*, 556 U.S. 662 (2009), which you no doubt studied in Civil Procedure. Following the attacks of September 11, 2001, the federal government detained many Muslim-Americans without cause for days, weeks, and months on end. They were kept in deplorable conditions, and were physically abused. In *Iqbal*, the Supreme Court held that the detainees did not plead their case with "plausible" specificity. Following the remand, the plaintiffs pleaded their case again, and sought monetary damages against the federal officials, under the Court's precedent in *Bivens v. Six Unknown Agents of Federal Bureau of Narcotics*, 403 U.S. 388 (1971). Though the scope of the implied remedy for monetary damages is beyond your study in constitutional law, this case illustrates how the majority and dissent viewed national security considerations when reviewing executive branch actions.
- How does Justice Kennedy understand the impact of September 11 on the Court's review of the detention?
- Justice Breyer's dissent quotes a famous maxim that "amid the clash of arms, the laws are not silent. They may be changed, but they speak the same language in war as in peace." Two thousand years ago, Cicero in contrast observed, "In times of war, the laws fall silent." (Justice Scalia quoted this adage in *Hamdi*.) What does it mean?
- In 2015, Justice Breyer was asked if the Japanese internment at issue in *Korematsu* could happen again. He said, "I doubt it," citing the fact that "this country has developed a stronger tradition of civil liberties." One year earlier, Justice Scalia said, "[Y]ou are kidding yourself if you think [*Korematsu*] will not happen again." Who is right? Do the laws fall silent in times of war?
- The majority opinion was authored by Justice Kennedy. Chief Justice Roberts and Justice Alito joined the opinion its entirety. Justice Thomas concurred in the judgment, he noted, "in order for there to be a controlling judgment in this suit." (This decision was similar to Justice Souter's opinion in *Hamdi*.) Justice Breyer dissented, joined by Justice Ginsburg. This unique case yielded a 4-2 vote. Justice Sotomayor recused because she participated in this case during her tenure on the Second Circuit Court of Appeals. Justice Kagan recused because she participated in this case during her tenure as Solicitor General. Justice Gorsuch had not yet joined the Court when the case was argued.

Ziglar v. Abbasi

137 S. Ct. 1843 (2017)

JUSTICE KENNEDY delivered the opinion of the Court.

After the September 11 terrorist attacks in this country, and in response to the deaths, destruction, and dangers they caused, the United States Government ordered hundreds of illegal aliens to be taken into custody and held. Pending a determination whether a particular detainee had connections to terrorism, the custody, under harsh conditions to be described, continued. In many instances custody lasted for days and weeks, then stretching into months. Later, some of the aliens who had been detained filed suit, leading to the cases now before the Court.

The complaint named as defendants three high executive officers in the Department of Justice and two of the wardens at the facility where the detainees had been held. Most of the claims, alleging various constitutional violations, sought damages under the implied cause of action theory adopted by this Court in *Bivens v. Six Unknown Fed. Narcotics Agents* (1971). . . .

The suit was commenced in the United States District Court for the Eastern District of New York. After this Court's decision in *Ashcroft v. Iqbal* (2009), a fourth amended complaint was filed; and that is the complaint to be considered here. . . . The officials who must defend the suit on the merits, under the ruling of the Court of Appeals, are the petitioners here. The former detainees who seek relief under the fourth amended complaint are the respondents. The various claims and theories advanced for recovery, and the grounds asserted for their dismissal as insufficient as a matter of law, will be addressed in turn.

I

Given the present procedural posture of the suit, the Court accepts as true the facts alleged in the complaint. See *Iqbal*.

A

In the weeks following the September 11, 2001, terrorist attacks — the worst in American history — the Federal Bureau of Investigation (FBI) received more than 96,000 tips from members of the public. Some tips were based on well-grounded suspicion of terrorist activity, but many others may have been based on fear of Arabs and Muslims. FBI agents "questioned more than 1,000 people with suspected links to the [September 11] attacks in particular or to terrorism in general."

While investigating the tips — including the less substantiated ones — the FBI encountered many aliens who were present in this country without legal authorization. As a result, more than 700 individuals were arrested and detained on immigration charges. If the FBI designated an alien as not being "of interest" to the investigation, then he or she was processed according to normal procedures. In other words the alien was treated just as if, for example, he or she had been arrested at the border after an illegal entry. If, however, the FBI designated an alien as "of interest" to the investigation, or if it had doubts about the proper designation in a particular case, the alien was detained subject to a "hold-until-cleared policy." The aliens were held without bail.

Respondents were among some 84 aliens who were subject to the hold-until-cleared policy and detained at the Metropolitan Detention Center (MDC) in Brooklyn, New York. They were held in the Administrative Maximum Special Housing Unit (or Unit) of the MDC. The complaint includes these allegations:

Conditions in the Unit were harsh. Pursuant to official Bureau of Prisons policy, detainees were held in "tiny cells for over 23 hours a day." Lights in the cells were left on 24 hours. Detainees had little opportunity for exercise or recreation. They were forbidden to keep anything in their cells, even basic hygiene products such as soap or a toothbrush. When removed from the cells for any reason, they were shackled and escorted by four guards. They were denied access to most forms of communication with the outside world. And they were strip searched often — any time they were moved, as well as at random in their cells.

Some of the harsh conditions in the Unit were not imposed pursuant to official policy. According to the complaint, prison guards engaged in a pattern of "physical and verbal abuse." Guards allegedly slammed detainees into walls; twisted their arms, wrists, and fingers; broke their bones; referred to them as terrorists; threatened them with violence; subjected them to humiliating sexual comments; and insulted their religion.

Respondents are six men of Arab or South Asian descent. Five are Muslims. Each was illegally in this country, arrested during the course of the September 11 investigation, and detained in the Administrative Maximum Special Housing Unit for periods ranging from three to eight months. After being released respondents were removed from the United States. . . .

II

The first question to be discussed is whether petitioners can be sued for damages under *Bivens* and the ensuing cases in this Court defining the reach and the limits of that precedent.

A

In 1871, Congress passed a statute that was later codified at Rev. Stat. §1979, 42 U.S.C. §1983. It entitles an injured person to money damages if a state official violates his or her constitutional rights. Congress did not create an analogous statute for federal officials. Indeed, in the 100 years leading up to *Bivens,* Congress did not provide a specific damages remedy for plaintiffs whose constitutional rights were violated by agents of the Federal Government.

In 1971, and against this background, this Court decided *Bivens.* The Court held that, even absent statutory authorization, it would enforce a damages remedy to compensate persons injured by federal officers who violated the prohibition against unreasonable search and seizures. The Court acknowledged that the Fourth Amendment does not provide for money damages "in so many words." The Court noted, however, that Congress had not foreclosed a damages remedy in "explicit" terms and that no "special factors" suggested that the Judiciary should "hesitat[e]" in the face of congressional silence. The Court, accordingly, held that it could authorize a remedy under general principles of federal jurisdiction.

In the decade that followed, the Court recognized what has come to be called an implied cause of action in two cases involving other constitutional violations. In *Davis v. Passman* (1979), an administrative assistant sued a Congressman for firing her because she was a woman. The Court held that the Fifth Amendment Due Process Clause gave her a damages remedy for gender discrimination. And in *Carlson v. Green* (1980), a prisoner's estate sued federal jailers for failing to treat the prisoner's asthma. The Court held that the Eighth Amendment Cruel and Unusual Punishments Clause gave him a damages remedy for failure to provide adequate medical treatment. These three cases — *Bivens*, *Davis*, and *Carlson* — represent the only instances in which the Court has approved of an implied damages remedy under the Constitution itself.

[Justice Kennedy then concluded that the plaintiffs could not seek monetary damages for their detention following the attacks of September 11, 2011. — EDS.]

III

[Justice Kennedy discussed how national security interests affected his analysis. — EDS.]

In addition to this special factor, which applies to the claims against the Executive Officials, there are three other special factors that apply as well to the detention policy claims against all of the petitioners. First, respondents' detention policy claims challenge more than standard "law enforcement operations." *United States v. Verdugo-Urquidez* (1990). They challenge as well major elements of the Government's whole response to the September 11 attacks, thus of necessity requiring an inquiry into sensitive issues of national security. Were this inquiry to be allowed in a private suit for damages, the *Bivens* action would assume dimensions far greater than those present in *Bivens* itself, or in either of its two follow-on cases, or indeed in any putative *Bivens* case yet to come before the Court.

National-security policy is the prerogative of the Congress and President. See U.S. Const., Art. I, §8; Art. II, §1, §2. Judicial inquiry into the national-security realm raises "concerns for the separation of powers in trenching on matters committed to the other branches." *Christopher v. Harbury* (2002). These concerns are even more pronounced when the judicial inquiry comes in the context of a claim seeking money damages rather than a claim seeking injunctive or other equitable relief. The risk of personal damages liability is more likely to cause an official to second-guess difficult but necessary decisions concerning national-security policy.

For these and other reasons, courts have shown deference to what the Executive Branch "has determined . . . is 'essential to national security.'" *Winter v. Natural Resources Defense Council, Inc.* (2008). Indeed, "courts traditionally have been reluctant to intrude upon the authority of the Executive in military and national security affairs" unless "Congress specifically has provided otherwise." *Department of Navy v. Egan* (1988). Congress has not provided otherwise here.

There are limitations, of course, on the power of the Executive under Article II of the Constitution and in the powers authorized by congressional enactments, even with respect to matters of national security. See, *e.g.*, *Hamdi v. Rumsfeld* (2004) (plurality opinion) ("Whatever power the United States Constitution envisions for the Executive . . . in times of conflict, it most assuredly envisions a role for all three branches when individual liberties are at stake"); *Boumediene v. Bush* (2008) ("Liberty and security can be reconciled; and in our system they are reconciled within the framework of the law"). And national-security concerns must not become a talisman used to ward off inconvenient claims — a "label" used to "cover a multitude of sins." *Mitchell v. Forsyth* (1985). This "danger of abuse" is even more heightened given "the difficulty of defining" the "security interest" in domestic cases. . . .

* * *

If the facts alleged in the complaint are true, then what happened to respondents in the days following September 11 was tragic. Nothing in this opinion should be read to condone the treatment to which they contend they were subjected. The question before the Court, however, is not whether petitioners' alleged conduct was proper, nor whether it gave decent respect to respondents' dignity and well-being, nor whether it was in keeping with the idea of the rule of law that must inspire us even in times of crisis. Instead, the question with respect to the *Bivens* claims is whether to allow an action for money damages in the absence of congressional authorization. . . .

It is so ordered.

JUSTICE BREYER, with whom JUSTICE GINSBURG joins, dissenting.

[Justice Breyer would have found that the plaintiffs could seek monetary damages. — EDS.]

. . . I shall explain why I believe this suit falls well within the scope of traditional constitutional tort law and why I cannot agree with the Court's arguments to the contrary. I recognize, and write separately about, the strongest of the Court's arguments, namely, the fact that plaintiffs' claims concern detention that took place soon after a serious attack on the United States and some of them concern actions of high-level Government officials. While these facts may affect the substantive constitutional questions (*e.g.*, were any of the conditions "legitimate"?) or the scope of the qualified-immunity defense, they do not extinguish the *Bivens* action itself. If I may paraphrase Justice Harlan, concurring in *Bivens*: In wartime as well as in peacetime, "it is important, in a civilized society, that the judicial branch of the Nation's government stand ready to afford a remedy" "for the most flagrant and patently unjustified," unconstitutional "abuses of official power"; cf. *Boumediene v. Bush* (2008). . . . I would hold that the complaint properly alleges constitutional torts, *i.e.*, *Bivens* actions for damages. . . .

In my view, the Court's strongest argument is that *Bivens* should not apply to policy-related actions taken in times of national-security need, for example, during war or national-security emergency. As the Court correctly points out, the Constitution grants primary power to protect the Nation's security to the Executive and Legislative Branches, not to the Judiciary. But the Constitution also delegates to the Judiciary the duty to protect an individual's fundamental constitutional rights. Hence when protection of those rights and a determination of security needs conflict, the Court has a role to play. The Court most recently made this clear in cases arising out of the detention of enemy combatants at Guantanamo Bay. Justice O'Connor wrote that "a state of war is not a blank check." *Hamdi v. Rumsfeld* (2004) (plurality opinion). In *Boumediene*, the Court reinforced that point, holding that noncitizens detained as enemy combatants were entitled to challenge their detention through a writ of habeas corpus, notwithstanding the national-security concerns at stake.

We have not, however, answered the specific question the Court places at issue here: Should *Bivens* actions continue to exist in respect to policy-related actions taken in time of war or national emergency? In my view, they should.

For one thing, a *Bivens* action comes accompanied by many legal safeguards designed to prevent the courts from interfering with Executive and Legislative Branch activity reasonably believed to be necessary to protect national security. In Justice Jackson's well-known words, the Constitution is not "a suicide pact." *Terminiello v. Chicago* (1949) (dissenting opinion). The Constitution itself takes account of public necessity. Thus, for example, the Fourth Amendment does not forbid *all* Government searches and seizures; it forbids only those that are "unreasonable." Ordinarily, it requires that a police officer obtain a search warrant before entering an apartment, but should the officer observe a woman being dragged against her will into that apartment, he should, and will, act at once. The Fourth Amendment makes allowances for such "exigent circumstances." *Brigham City v. Stuart* (2006) (warrantless entry justified to forestall imminent injury). Similarly, the Fifth Amendment bars only conditions of confinement that are not "reasonably related to a legitimate governmental objective." *Bell v. Wolfish*. What is unreasonable and illegitimate in time of peace may be reasonable and legitimate in time of war. . . .

Given these safeguards against undue interference by the Judiciary in times of war or national-security emergency, the Court's abolition, or limitation of, *Bivens* actions goes too far. If you are cold, put on a sweater, perhaps an overcoat, perhaps also turn up the heat, but do not set fire to the house.

At the same time, there may well be a particular need for *Bivens* remedies when security-related Government actions are at issue. History tells us of far too many instances where the Executive or Legislative Branch took actions during time of war that, on later examination, turned out unnecessarily and unreasonably to have deprived American citizens of basic constitutional rights. We have read about the Alien and Sedition Acts, the thousands of civilians imprisoned during the Civil War, and the suppression of civil liberties during World War I. See W. Rehnquist, All the Laws but One: Civil Liberties in Wartime (1998); see also *Ex parte Milligan* (1866) (decided *after* the Civil War was over). The pages of the U.S. Reports themselves recite this Court's refusal to set aside the Government's World War II action removing more than 70,000 American citizens of Japanese origin from their west coast homes and interning them in camps, see *Korematsu v. United States* (1944) — an action that at least some officials knew at the time was unnecessary, see *id.* (Murphy, J., dissenting); P. Irons, Justice at War (1983). President Franklin Roosevelt's Attorney General, perhaps exaggerating, once said that "[t]he Constitution has not greatly bothered any wartime President."

Can we, in respect to actions taken during those periods, rely exclusively, as the Court seems to suggest, upon injunctive remedies or writs of habeas corpus, their retail equivalent? Complaints seeking that kind of relief typically come during the emergency itself, when emotions are strong, when courts may have too little or inaccurate information, and when courts may well prove particularly reluctant to interfere with even the least well-founded Executive Branch activity. That reluctance may itself set an unfortunate precedent, which, as Justice Jackson pointed out, can "li[e] about like a loaded weapon" awaiting discharge in another case. *Korematsu* (Jackson, J., dissenting).

A damages action, however, is typically brought after the emergency is over, after emotions have cooled, and at a time when more factual information is available. In such circumstances, courts have more time to exercise such judicial virtues as calm reflection and dispassionate application of the law to the facts. We have applied the Constitution to actions taken during periods of war and national-security emergency. See *Boumediene*; *Hamdi v. Rumsfeld*; cf. *Youngstown Sheet & Tube Co. v. Sawyer* (1952). I should think that the wisdom of permitting courts to consider *Bivens* actions, later granting monetary compensation to those wronged at the time, would follow *a fortiori*.

As is well known, Lord Atkins, a British judge, wrote in the midst of World War II that "amid the clash of arms, the laws are not silent. They may be changed, but they speak the same language in war as in peace." *Liversidge v. Anderson* (1942). The Court, in my view, should say the same of this *Bivens* action.

With respect, I dissent.

CHAPTER 7

The Separation of Powers

The previous chapter considered the balance between Congress and the President with respect to war-making and foreign affairs powers. In this chapter, we turn to the separation of the powers between the executive, legislative, and judicial branches in times of peace. We will examine a number of distinct issues that reveal a fundamental conflict in the way that the Justices support their conclusions. Keep in mind that the idea of "separation of powers" is itself not purely textual; those words do not appear in the Constitution. Some Justices offer a "functional" or practical analysis to evaluate the separation of powers. Others rely on a more "formal" analysis of the meaning and implications of various words in the text. The functional approach tends to support the branches *sharing* their powers. Doing so, according to functionalists, promotes an efficient and flexible system governance. The formal approach, in contrast, tends to emphasize that the powers must be kept separate, even if the legislature and executive agree to share them. In this chapter, consider how the Justices choose either, or both, of these approaches, and what effect that choice has on the administration of government.

ASSIGNMENT 1

A. THE APPOINTMENT POWER

The independent counsel law at issue in *Morrison v. Olson* was enacted by Congress in the wake of the Watergate scandal as part of the Ethics in Government Act of 1978. During the 1972 presidential campaign, the Committee for the Re-election of the

President (CRP, or what Nixon's critics dubbed *CREEP*) had enlisted several individuals to surreptitiously enter the Democratic National Headquarters located at the Watergate Hotel complex in Washington, D.C. What they were searching for remains a matter of controversy. Following the break-in, the men were arrested and charged with burglary. While they were in custody with their cases pending, arrangements were made to pay them to ensure their silence regarding their connection with the Nixon campaign. Although the burglary and investigation were reported before the election, President Nixon's involvement in the burglary was not disclosed until after he won re-election in a landslide victory. As evidence of Nixon's misbehavior mounted, impeachment proceedings were initiated in the House of Representatives on May 9, 1974.

Nixon's attorney general, Elliot Richardson, appointed Harvard law professor Archibald Cox as a special prosecutor. (Richardson had promised the Senate that he would do so during his confirmation hearing.) After a witness revealed during congressional hearings that there was a secret tape recording system in the Oval Office, Mr. Cox issued a subpoena to the White House for the recordings. The executive branch offered a compromise whereby the contents of the tapes would be summarized by a senior senator. Cox refused the deal.

Under the regulations in effect at the time, Nixon could not fire the special prosecutor himself; only the attorney general could. Nixon ordered Richardson to dismiss Cox. Richardson, citing the promise he had made to the Senate to support the independent investigation, refused to fire Cox, and resigned in protest. After Cox's resignation, the number two person at the Justice Department, Deputy Attorney General William Ruckelshaus, was elevated to the post of acting attorney general. Nixon then ordered Ruckelshaus to fire Cox. Ruckelshaus, who had also promised the Senate to support the independent special prosecutor, refused to fire Cox, and resigned. Neither Richardson nor Ruckelshaus thought that firing Cox would be illegal; rather, they refused to do the deed because of their commitments to the Senate.

Third in line at the Justice Department was Solicitor General Robert Bork. As acting head of the Justice Department, Bork agreed to fire Cox. Critically, Bork had made no similar pledge to the Senate. Bork later wrote that the President "had a clear legal authority to fire Cox and a good reason to do so," and testified before Congress that the regulations in effect were not "a bar to a presidential order." Indeed, Bork wrote in his autobiography that Richardson told the Solicitor General to fire Cox, because he could not.[1] Nevertheless, Bork too considered resigning to avoid being "perceived as a man who did the President's bidding to save my job." This rapid sequence of events, which all transpired on Saturday, October 20, 1973, came to be known as the "Saturday Night Massacre."

Democrats in Congress were infuriated. Nixon succumbed to the public outcry against his actions by allowing the appointment of a new special prosecutor. Leon Jaworski, who replaced Cox, continued to pursue the subpoenas for the tapes. The President objected to the request on the basis of "executive privilege" and the

[1] See Josh Blackman, Could Trump Remove Special Counsel Robert Mueller? Lessons from Watergate, Lawfare (May 23, 2017), https://www.lawfareblog.com/if-trump-fires-mueller-or-orders-his-firing.

separation of powers. On July 24, 1974, the Supreme Court ruled unanimously in *United States v. Nixon* that the President could not block the subpoena. As a result of what was disclosed on the tapes, President Nixon became the first President in American history to resign the office, stepping down less than three weeks later on August 9, 1974.

D.C. Circuit Court of Appeals Judge Lawrence Silberman, who authored the panel opinion invalidating the independent counsel law in *Morrison v. Olson* (over the dissent of then-appeals court judge Ruth Bader Ginsburg, who would have upheld the law), was later on the three-judge panel that appointed Kenneth Starr as independent counsel to investigate Bill and Hillary Clinton's involvement in the Whitewater land deal.

Four years later, Congress enacted the Ethics in Government Act of 1978 (EIGA), which provided a mechanism for judges, and not the executive branch, to appoint an "independent counsel." Note the change in terminology and structure; Cox and Jaworski were "special prosecutors" within the Justice Department. In 1986, Alexia Morrison was appointed as an "independent counsel" not by the attorney general, but by a panel of three federal judges, pursuant to the EIGA. *Morrison v. Olson* concerns the constitutionality of this arrangement (Morrison argued before the Supreme Court on her own behalf).

Postscript: The EIGA had a "sunset" provision requiring its periodic re-approval by Congress. In 1999, Congress allowed the law to lapse. Many attribute this decision to frustration over the prolonged and wide-ranging investigation by former-Judge Kenneth Starr, who served as independent counsel, into the alleged misconduct of President Bill Clinton. Many of the law's former supporters came to change their minds about its wisdom. Seventeen years later, after President Trump fired FBI Director James Comey, a "special counsel" was named by the deputy attorney general to investigate alleged collusion between the Trump presidential campaign and the Russian government. Soon enough, many changed their minds once again and supported the reintroduction of an independent counsel statute.

STUDY GUIDE

- The independent counsel law was upheld as constitutional by a 7-1 vote. (Justice Kennedy, who had been appointed recently to the bench, did not participate in the case.) If Justice Scalia's approach leads to what most consider to be the "correct" outcome (as demonstrated by later events), why does it garner only one vote — his?
- Do you agree with the outcome in *Morrison*? If so, is your agreement based on policy views on the merits of having such an office or on the Constitution (and what would be the difference between the two)? If not, can you account for how only Justice Scalia managed to reach what most now consider to be the "correct" outcome?
- The independent counsel law was in effect for over twenty years. If you think it was a constitutional or policy mistake, is there any way to resolve these situations without incurring the negative consequences that result from the "wrong" decision?

Morrison v. Olson

487 U.S. 654 (1988)

Chief Justice Rehnquist delivered the opinion of the Court, in which Justices Brennan, White, Marshall, Blackmun, Stevens, and O'Connor, joined.

This case presents us with a challenge to the independent counsel provisions of the Ethics in Government Act of 1978. We hold today that these provisions of the Act do not violate the Appointments Clause of the Constitution, Art. II, §2, cl. 2, or the limitations of Article III, nor do they impermissibly interfere with the President's authority under Article II in violation of the constitutional principle of separation of powers.

I

Briefly stated, Title VI of the Ethics in Government Act (Title VI or the Act), allows for the appointment of an "independent counsel" to investigate and, if appropriate, prosecute certain high-ranking Government officials for violations of federal criminal laws. The Act requires the Attorney General, upon receipt of information that he determines is "sufficient to constitute grounds to investigate whether any person [covered by the Act] may have violated any Federal criminal law," to conduct a preliminary investigation of the matter. When the Attorney General has completed this investigation, or 90 days has elapsed, he is required to report to a special court (the Special Division) created by the Act "for the purpose of appointing independent counsels." If the Attorney General determines that "there are no reasonable grounds to believe that further investigation is warranted," then he must notify the Special Division of this result. In such a case, "the division of the court shall have no power to appoint an independent counsel." If, however, the Attorney General has determined that there are "reasonable grounds to believe that further investigation or prosecution is warranted," then he "shall apply to the division of the court for the appointment of an independent counsel." The Attorney General's application to the court "shall contain sufficient information to assist the [court] in selecting an independent counsel and in defining that independent counsel's prosecutorial jurisdiction." Upon receiving this application, the Special Division "shall appoint an appropriate independent counsel and shall define that independent counsel's prosecutorial jurisdiction."

Theodore "Ted" Olson became the target of the investigation that gave rise to *Morrison v. Olson* due to his role in a scandal concerning the Environmental Protection Agency's Superfund program. The embattled Administrator of the EPA, who resigned from office amidst the controversy (though never charged with misconduct), was none other than Anne Gorsuch Burford — the mother of Justice Neil Gorsuch. A young Gorsuch told his mother in 1983, "You didn't do anything wrong. You only did what the president ordered. Why are you quitting? You raised me not to be a quitter."[2] Olson would go on to argue *Bush v. Gore* before the Supreme Court, and would serve as Solicitor General under President George W. Bush.

[2] Josh Blackman, The Connection Between Judge Gorsuch, Justice Scalia's Dissent in *Morrison v. Olson*, and *Chevron* Deference, Josh Blackman's Blog (Feb. 2, 2017), http://joshblackman.com/blog/2017/02/02/judge-gorsuch-and-justice-scalias-dissent-in-morrison-v-olson/.

With respect to all matters within the independent counsel's jurisdiction, the Act grants the counsel "full power and independent authority to exercise all investigative and prosecutorial functions and powers of the Department of Justice, the Attorney General, and any other officer or employee of the Department of Justice." The functions of the independent counsel include conducting grand jury proceedings and other investigations, participating in civil and criminal court proceedings and litigation, and appealing any decision in any case in which the counsel participates in an official capacity. The counsel's powers include "initiating and conducting prosecutions in any court of competent jurisdiction, framing and signing indictments, filing informations, and handling all aspects of any case, in the name of the United States." . . . The Act also states that an independent counsel "shall, except where not possible, comply with the written or other established policies of the Department of Justice respecting enforcement of the criminal laws." In addition, whenever a matter has been referred to an independent counsel under the Act, the Attorney General and the Justice Department are required to suspend all investigations and proceedings regarding the matter. An independent counsel has "full authority to dismiss matters within [his or her] prosecutorial jurisdiction without conducting an investigation or at any subsequent time before prosecution, if to do so would be consistent" with Department of Justice policy.

Two statutory provisions govern the length of an independent counsel's tenure in office. The first defines the procedure for removing an independent counsel[:]

> An independent counsel appointed under this chapter may be removed from office, other than by impeachment and conviction, only by the personal action of the Attorney General and only for good cause, physical disability, mental incapacity, or any other condition that substantially impairs the performance of such independent counsel's duties.

If an independent counsel is removed pursuant to this section, the Attorney General is required to submit a report to both the Special Division and the Judiciary Committees of the Senate and the House "specifying the facts found and the ultimate grounds for such removal." Under the current version of the Act, an independent counsel can obtain judicial review of the Attorney General's action by filing a civil action in the United States District Court for the District of Columbia. . . .

The other provision governing the tenure of the independent counsel defines the procedures for "terminating" the counsel's office. [T]he office of an independent counsel terminates when he or she notifies the Attorney General that he or she has completed or substantially completed any investigations or prosecutions undertaken pursuant to the Act. In addition, the Special Division, acting either on its own or on the suggestion of the Attorney General, may terminate the office of an independent counsel at any time if it finds that "the investigation of all matters within the prosecutorial jurisdiction of such independent counsel . . . have been completed or so substantially completed that it would be appropriate for the Department of Justice to complete such investigations and prosecutions."

Finally, the Act provides for congressional oversight of the activities of independent counsel. An independent counsel may from time to time send

Congress statements or reports on his or her activities. The "appropriate committees of the Congress" are given oversight jurisdiction in regard to the official conduct of an independent counsel, and the counsel is required by the Act to cooperate with Congress in the exercise of this jurisdiction. The counsel is required to inform the House of Representatives of "substantial and credible information which [the counsel] receives . . . that may constitute grounds for an impeachment." In addition, the Act gives certain congressional committee members the power to "request in writing that the Attorney General apply for the appointment of an independent counsel." The Attorney General is required to respond to this request within a specified time but is not required to accede to the request.

The proceedings in this case provide an example of how the Act works in practice. In 1982, two Subcommittees of the House of Representatives issued subpoenas directing the Environmental Protection Agency (EPA) to produce certain documents relating to the efforts of the EPA and the Land and Natural Resources Division of the Justice Department to enforce the "Superfund Law." At that time, appellee Olson was the Assistant Attorney General for the Office of Legal Counsel (OLC). . . . Acting on the advice of the Justice Department, the President ordered the Administrator of EPA to invoke executive privilege to withhold certain of the documents on the ground that they contained "enforcement sensitive information." [The Administrator of the EPA was Anne Gorsuch Burford — the mother of Justice Neil Gorsuch. — Eds.] The Administrator obeyed this order and withheld the documents. In response, the House voted to hold the Administrator in contempt, after which the Administrator and the United States together filed a lawsuit against the House. The conflict abated in March 1983, when the administration agreed to give the House Subcommittees limited access to the documents.

The following year, the House Judiciary Committee began an investigation into the Justice Department's role in the controversy over the EPA documents. During this investigation, appellee Olson testified before a House Subcommittee on March 10, 1983. Both before and after that testimony, the Department complied with several Committee requests to produce certain documents. Other documents were at first withheld, although these documents were eventually disclosed by the Department after the Committee learned of their existence. In 1985, the majority members of the Judiciary Committee published a lengthy report on the Committee's investigation. The report not only criticized various officials in the Department of Justice for their role in the EPA executive privilege dispute, but it also suggested that appellee Olson had given false and misleading testimony to the Subcommittee on March 10, 1983 . . . , thus obstructing the Committee's investigation. The Chairman of the Judiciary Committee forwarded a copy of the report to the Attorney General with a request . . . that he seek the appointment of an independent counsel to investigate the allegations against Olson. . . .

The Attorney General directed the Public Integrity Section of the Criminal Division to conduct a preliminary investigation. The Section's report concluded that the appointment of an independent counsel was warranted to investigate the Committee's allegations. . . . The Attorney General accordingly requested appointment of an independent counsel to investigate whether Olson's March 10, 1983, testimony "regarding the completeness of [OLC's] response to the

Judiciary Committee's request for OLC documents, and regarding his knowledge of EPA's willingness to turn over certain disputed documents to Congress, violated 18 U.S.C. 1505, 1001, or any other provision of federal criminal law." ...

[I]n May and June 1987, appellant caused a grand jury to issue and serve subpoenas *ad testificandum* and *duces tecum* on appellee[, who] moved to quash the subpoenas, claiming, among other things, that the independent counsel provisions of the Act were unconstitutional and that appellant accordingly had no authority to proceed. On July 20, 1987, the District Court upheld the constitutionality of the Act and denied the motions to quash. The court subsequently ordered that appellees be held in contempt ... for continuing to refuse to comply with the subpoenas. ... A divided Court of Appeals reversed. ... We now reverse. ...

III

The Appointments Clause of Article II reads as follows:

> [The President] shall nominate, and by and with the Advice and Consent of the Senate, shall appoint Ambassadors, other public Ministers and Consuls, Judges of the supreme Court, and all other Officers of the United States, whose Appointments are not herein otherwise provided for, and which shall be established by Law: but the Congress may by Law vest the Appointment of such inferior Officers, as they think proper, in the President alone, in the Courts of Law, or in the Heads of Departments.

... The initial question is, accordingly, whether appellant is an "inferior" or a "principal" officer. If she is the latter, as the Court of Appeals concluded, then the Act is in violation of the Appointments Clause.

The line between "inferior" and "principal" officers is one that is far from clear, and the Framers provided little guidance into where it should be drawn. We need not attempt here to decide exactly where the line falls between the two types of officers, because in our view appellant clearly falls on the "inferior officer" side of that line. Several factors lead to this conclusion.

First, appellant is subject to removal by a higher Executive Branch official. Although appellant may not be "subordinate" to the Attorney General (and the President) insofar as she possesses a degree of independent discretion to exercise the powers delegated to her under the Act, the fact that she can be removed by the Attorney General indicates that she is to some degree "inferior" in rank and authority.

Second, appellant is empowered by the Act to perform only certain, limited duties. An independent counsel's role is restricted primarily to investigation and, if appropriate, prosecution for certain federal crimes. Admittedly, the Act delegates to appellant "full power and independent authority to exercise all investigative and prosecutorial functions and powers of the Department of Justice," but this grant of authority does not include any authority to formulate policy for the Government or the Executive Branch, nor does it give appellant any administrative duties outside of those necessary to operate her office. The Act specifically provides that in policy matters appellant is to comply to the extent possible with the policies of the Department.

Third, appellant's office is limited in jurisdiction. Not only is the Act itself restricted in applicability to certain federal officials suspected of certain serious federal crimes, but an independent counsel can only act within the scope of the jurisdiction that has been granted by the Special Division pursuant to a request by the Attorney General. Finally, appellant's office is limited in tenure. There is concededly no time limit on the appointment of a particular counsel. Nonetheless, the office of independent counsel is "temporary" in the sense that an independent counsel is appointed essentially to accomplish a single task, and when that task is over the office is terminated, either by the counsel herself or by action of the Special Division. Unlike other prosecutors, appellant has no ongoing responsibilities that extend beyond the accomplishment of the mission that she was appointed for and authorized by the Special Division to undertake. In our view, these factors . . . are sufficient to establish that appellant is an "inferior" officer in the constitutional sense. . . .

This does not, however, end our inquiry under the Appointments Clause. Appellees argue that even if appellant is an "inferior" officer, the Clause does not empower Congress to place the power to appoint such an officer outside the Executive Branch. They contend that the Clause does not contemplate congressional authorization of "interbranch appointments," in which an officer of one branch is appointed by officers of another branch. The relevant language of the Appointments Clause is worth repeating. It reads: ". . . but the Congress may by Law vest the Appointment of such inferior Officers, as they think proper, in the President alone, in the courts of Law, or in the Heads of Departments." On its face, the language of this "excepting clause" admits of no limitation on interbranch appointments. Indeed, the inclusion of "as they think proper" seems clearly to give Congress significant discretion to determine whether it is "proper" to vest the appointment of, for example, executive officials in the "courts of Law." . . .

We also note that the history of the Clause provides no support for appellees' position. Throughout most of the process of drafting the Constitution, the Convention concentrated on the problem of who should have the authority to appoint judges. . . . [T]here was little or no debate on the question whether the Clause empowers Congress to provide for interbranch appointments, and there is nothing to suggest that the Framers intended to prevent Congress from having that power.

We do not mean to say that Congress' power to provide for interbranch appointments of "inferior officers" is unlimited. In addition to separation-of-powers concerns, which would arise if such provisions for appointment had the potential to impair the constitutional functions assigned to one of the branches, . . . Congress' decision to vest the appointment power in the courts would be improper if there was some "incongruity" between the functions normally performed by the courts and the performance of their duty to appoint. In this case, however, we do not think it impermissible for Congress to vest the power to appoint independent counsel in a specially created federal court. We thus disagree with the Court of Appeals' conclusion that there is an inherent incongruity about a court having the power to appoint prosecutorial officers.[3] We have recognized that courts may appoint private attorneys to act as prosecutor for judicial contempt

[3] Indeed, in light of judicial experience with prosecutors in criminal cases, it could be said that courts are especially well qualified to appoint prosecutors. This is not a case in which judges are given

judgments. . . . Lower courts have also upheld interim judicial appointments of United States Attorneys, and Congress itself has vested the power to make these interim appointments in the district courts.[4] Congress, of course, was concerned when it created the office of independent counsel with the conflicts of interest that could arise in situations when the Executive Branch is called upon to investigate its own high-ranking officers. If it were to remove the appointing authority from the Executive Branch, the most logical place to put it was in the Judicial Branch. In the light of the Act's provision making the judges of the Special Division ineligible to participate in any matters relating to an independent counsel they have appointed, we do not think that appointment of the independent counsel by the court runs afoul of the constitutional limitation on "incongruous" interbranch appointments.

IV

Appellees next contend that the powers vested in the Special Division by the Act conflict with Article III of the Constitution. We have long recognized that by the express provision of Article III, the judicial power of the United States is limited to "Cases" and "Controversies." As a general rule, we have broadly stated that "executive or administrative duties of a nonjudicial nature may not be imposed on judges holding office under Art. III of the Constitution." The purpose of this limitation is to help ensure the independence of the Judicial Branch and to prevent the Judiciary from encroaching into areas reserved for the other branches. . . .

In our view, Congress' power under the Clause to vest the "Appointment" of inferior officers in the courts may, in certain circumstances, allow Congress to give the courts some discretion in defining the nature and scope of the appointed official's authority. Particularly when, as here, Congress creates a temporary "office" the nature and duties of which will by necessity vary with the factual circumstances giving rise to the need for an appointment in the first place, it may vest the power to define the scope of the office in the court as an incident to the appointment of the officer pursuant to the Appointments Clause. This said, we do not think that Congress may give the Division unlimited discretion to determine the independent counsel's jurisdiction. In order for the Division's definition of the counsel's jurisdiction to be truly "incidental" to its power to appoint, the jurisdiction that the court decides upon must be demonstrably related to the factual circumstances that gave rise to the Attorney General's investigation and request for the appointment of the independent counsel in the particular case.

The Act also vests in the Special Division various powers and duties in relation to the independent counsel that, because they do not involve appointing the

---

power to appoint an officer in an area in which they have no special knowledge or expertise, as in, for example, a statute authorizing the courts to appoint officials in the Department of Agriculture or the Federal Energy Regulatory Commission.

[4] We note also the longstanding judicial practice of appointing defense attorneys for individuals who are unable to afford representation, notwithstanding the possibility that the appointed attorney may appear in court before the judge who appointed him.

counsel or defining his or her jurisdiction, cannot be said to derive from the Division's Appointments Clause authority. . . .

Some of these allegedly "supervisory" powers conferred on the court are passive: the Division merely "receives" reports from the counsel or the Attorney General, it is not entitled to act on them or to specifically approve or disapprove of their contents. Other provisions of the Act do require the court to exercise some judgment and discretion, but the powers granted by these provisions are themselves essentially ministerial. The Act simply does not give the Division the power to "supervise" the independent counsel in the exercise of his or her investigative or prosecutorial authority. And, the functions that the Special Division is empowered to perform are not inherently "Executive." . . .

V

We now turn to consider whether the Act is invalid under the constitutional principle of separation of powers. Two related issues must be addressed: The first is whether the provision of the Act restricting the Attorney General's power to remove the independent counsel to only those instances in which he can show "good cause," taken by itself, impermissibly interferes with the President's exercise of his constitutionally appointed functions. The second is whether, taken as a whole, the Act violates the separation of powers by reducing the President's ability to control the prosecutorial powers wielded by the independent counsel.

A

Two Terms ago we had occasion to consider whether it was consistent with the separation of powers for Congress to pass a statute that authorized a Government official who is removable only by Congress to participate in what we found to be "executive powers." *Bowsher v. Synar* (1986). We held in *Bowsher* that "Congress cannot reserve for itself the power of removal of an officer charged with the execution of the laws except by impeachment." A primary antecedent for this ruling was our 1926 decision in *Myers v. United States*. *Myers* had considered the propriety of a federal statute by which certain postmasters of the United States could be removed by the President only "by and with the advice and consent of the Senate." There too, Congress' attempt to involve itself in the removal of an executive official was found to be sufficient grounds to render the statute invalid. . . .

Unlike both *Bowsher* and *Myers*, this case does not involve an attempt by Congress itself to gain a role in the removal of executive officials other than its established powers of impeachment and conviction. The Act instead puts the removal power squarely in the hands of the Executive Branch; an independent counsel may be removed from office, "only by the personal action of the Attorney General, and only for good cause." There is no requirement of congressional approval of the Attorney General's removal decision, though the decision is subject to judicial review. In our view, the removal provisions of the Act make this case more analogous to *Humphrey's Executor v. United States* (1935), and *Wiener v. United States* (1958), than to *Myers* or *Bowsher*.

In *Humphrey's Executor*, the issue was whether a statute restricting the President's power to remove the Commissioners of the Federal Trade Commission (FTC) only for "inefficiency, neglect of duty, or malfeasance in office" was consistent with the Constitution. We stated that whether Congress can "condition the [President's power of removal] by fixing a definite term and precluding a removal except for cause, will depend upon the character of the office." . . . At least in regard to "quasi-legislative" and "quasi-judicial" agencies such as the FTC, "[t]he authority of Congress, in creating [such] agencies, to require them to act in discharge of their duties independently of executive control . . . includes, as an appropriate incident, power to fix the period during which they shall continue in office, and to forbid their removal except for cause in the meantime." In *Humphrey's Executor*, we found it "plain" that the Constitution did not give the President "illimitable power of removal" over the officers of independent agencies. Were the President to have the power to remove FTC Commissioners at will, the "coercive influence" of the removal power would "threate[n] the independence of [the] commission." . . . Similarly, in *Wiener* . . . we rejected the President's attempt to remove a Commissioner "merely because he wanted his own appointees on [the] Commission," stating that "no such power is given to the President directly by the Constitution, and none is impliedly conferred upon him by statute."

Appellees contend that *Humphrey's Executor* and *Wiener* are distinguishable from this case because they did not involve officials who performed a "core executive function." They argue that our decision in *Humphrey's Executor* rests on a distinction between "purely executive" officials and officials who exercise "quasi-legislative" and "quasi-judicial" powers. In their view, when a "purely executive" official is involved, the governing precedent is *Myers*, not *Humphrey's Executor*. And, under *Myers*, the President must have absolute discretion to discharge "purely" executive officials at will.

We undoubtedly did rely on the terms "quasi-legislative" and "quasi-judicial" to distinguish the officials involved in *Humphrey's Executor* and *Wiener* from those in *Myers*, but our present considered view is that the determination of whether the Constitution allows Congress to impose a "good cause"-type restriction on the President's power to remove an official cannot be made to turn on whether or not that official is classified as "purely executive." The analysis contained in our removal cases is designed not to define rigid categories of those officials who may or may not be removed at will by the President, but to ensure that Congress does not interfere with the President's exercise of the "executive power" and his constitutionally appointed duty to "take care that the laws be faithfully executed" under Article II. . . .

There is no real dispute that the functions performed by the independent counsel are "executive" in the sense that they are law enforcement functions that typically have been undertaken by officials within the Executive Branch. As we noted above, however, the independent counsel is an inferior officer under the Appointments Clause, with limited jurisdiction and tenure and lacking policymaking or significant administrative authority. Although the counsel exercises no small amount of discretion and judgment in deciding how to carry out his or her duties under the Act, we simply do not see how the President's need to control the exercise of that discretion is so central to the functioning of the Executive Branch as to require as a matter of constitutional law that the counsel be terminable at will by the President.

Nor do we think that the "good cause" removal provision at issue here impermissibly burdens the President's power to control or supervise the independent counsel, as an executive official, in the execution of his or her duties under the Act. This is not a case in which the power to remove an executive official has been completely stripped from the President, thus providing no means for the President to ensure the "faithful execution" of the laws. Rather, because the independent counsel may be terminated for "good cause," the Executive, through the Attorney General, retains ample authority to assure that the counsel is competently performing his or her statutory responsibilities in a manner that comports with the provisions of the Act. . . .

B

The final question to be addressed is whether the Act, taken as a whole, violates the principle of separation of powers by unduly interfering with the role of the Executive Branch. . . .

We observe first that this case does not involve an attempt by Congress to increase its own powers at the expense of the Executive Branch. . . . Unlike some of our previous cases, most recently *Bowsher v. Synar*, this case simply does not pose a "dange[r] of congressional usurpation of Executive Branch functions"; see also *INS v. Chadha* (1983). Indeed, with the exception of the power of impeachment — which applies to all officers of the United States — Congress retained for itself no powers of control or supervision over an independent counsel. The Act does empower certain Members of Congress to request the Attorney General to apply for the appointment of an independent counsel, but the Attorney General has no duty to comply with the request, although he must respond within a certain time limit. Other than that, Congress' role under the Act is limited to receiving reports or other information and oversight of the independent counsel's activities, functions that we have recognized generally as being incidental to the legislative function of Congress.

Similarly, we do not think that the Act works any judicial usurpation of properly executive functions. . . . [T]he Special Division has no power to appoint an independent counsel *sua sponte*; it may only do so upon the specific request of the Attorney General, and the courts are specifically prevented from reviewing the Attorney General's decision not to seek appointment. In addition, once the court has appointed a counsel and defined his or her jurisdiction, it has no power to supervise or control the activities of the counsel. As we pointed out in our discussion of the Special Division in relation to Article III, the various powers delegated by the statute to the Division are not supervisory or administrative, nor are they functions that the Constitution requires be performed by officials within the Executive Branch. The Act does give a federal court the power to review the Attorney General's decision to remove an independent counsel, but in our view this is a function that is well within the traditional power of the Judiciary. . . .

It is undeniable that the Act reduces the amount of control or supervision that the Attorney General and, through him, the President exercises over the investigation and prosecution of a certain class of alleged criminal activity. The Attorney General is not allowed to appoint the individual of his choice; he does not determine the counsel's jurisdiction; and his power to remove a counsel is limited. Nonetheless, the Act does give the Attorney General several means of supervising or controlling the prosecutorial powers that may be wielded by an independent counsel. Most importantly, the Attorney General retains the power to remove the counsel for "good cause," a power that we have already concluded provides the Executive with substantial ability to ensure that the laws are "faithfully executed" by an independent counsel. No independent counsel may be appointed without a specific request by the Attorney General, and the Attorney General's decision not to request appointment if he finds "no reasonable grounds to believe that further investigation is warranted" is committed to his unreviewable discretion. The Act thus gives the Executive a degree of control over the power to initiate an investigation by the independent counsel. In addition, the jurisdiction of the independent counsel is defined with reference to the facts submitted by the Attorney General, and once a counsel is appointed, the Act requires that the counsel abide by Justice Department policy unless it is not "possible" to do so. Notwithstanding the fact that the counsel is to some degree "independent" and free from executive supervision to a greater extent than other federal prosecutors, in our view these features of the Act give the Executive Branch sufficient control over the independent counsel to ensure that the President is able to perform his constitutionally assigned duties. . . .

Reversed.

Justice Kennedy took no part in the consideration or decision of the case.

Justice Scalia, dissenting.

It is the proud boast of our democracy that we have "a government of laws and not of men." Many Americans are familiar with that phrase; not many know its derivation. It comes from the First, Article XXX, of the Massachusetts Constitution of 1780, which reads in full as follows:

> In the government of this Commonwealth, the legislative department shall never exercise the executive and judicial powers, or either of them: The executive shall never exercise the legislative and judicial powers, or either of them: The judicial shall never exercise the legislative and executive powers, or either of them: to the end it may be a government of laws and not of men.

The Framers of the Federal Constitution similarly viewed the principle of separation of powers as the absolutely central guarantee of a just Government. In *No. 47* of *The Federalist*, Madison wrote that "[n]o political truth is certainly of greater intrinsic value, or is stamped with the authority of more enlightened patrons of liberty." *The Federalist, No. 47*. Without a secure structure of separated powers, our Bill of Rights would be worthless, as are the bills of rights of many nations of the world that have adopted, or even improved upon, the mere words of ours. . . .

[T]he Founders conspicuously and very consciously declined to sap the Executive's strength in the same way they had weakened the Legislature: by dividing the executive power. Proposals to have multiple executives, or a council of advisers with separate authority were rejected. Thus, while "[a]ll legislative Powers herein granted shall be vested in a Congress of the United States, which shall consist of a Senate *and* House of Representatives," U.S. Const., Art. I, §1 (emphasis added), "[t]he executive Power shall be vested in *a President of the United States*," Art. II, §1, cl. 1 (emphasis added).

That is what this suit is about. Power. The allocation of power among Congress, the President, and the courts in such fashion as to preserve the equilibrium the Constitution sought to establish — so that "a gradual concentration of the several powers in the same department," *Federalist, No. 51*, can effectively be resisted. Frequently an issue of this sort will come before the Court clad, so to speak, in sheep's clothing: the potential of the asserted principle to effect important change in the equilibrium of power is not immediately evident, and must be discerned by a careful and perceptive analysis. But this wolf comes as a wolf.

I

The present case began when the Legislative and Executive Branches became "embroiled in a dispute concerning the scope of the congressional investigatory power," which — as is often the case with such interbranch conflicts — became quite acrimonious. In the course of oversight hearings into the administration of the Superfund by the Environmental Protection Agency (EPA), two Subcommittees of the House of Representatives requested and then subpoenaed numerous internal EPA documents. The President responded by personally directing the EPA Administrator not to turn over certain of the documents, and by having the Attorney General notify the congressional Subcommittees of this assertion of executive privilege. In his decision to assert executive privilege, the President was counseled by appellee Olson, who was then Assistant Attorney General of the Department of Justice for the Office of Legal Counsel, a post that has traditionally had responsibility for providing legal advice to the President (subject to approval of the Attorney General). The House's response was to pass a resolution citing the EPA Administrator, who had possession of the documents, for contempt. Contempt of Congress is a criminal offense. The United States Attorney, however, a member of the Executive Branch, initially took no steps to prosecute the contempt citation. Instead, the Executive Branch sought the immediate assistance of the Third Branch by filing a civil action asking the District Court to declare that the EPA Administrator had acted lawfully in withholding the documents under a claim of executive privilege. The District Court declined (in my view correctly) to get involved in the controversy, and urged the other two branches to try "[c]ompromise and cooperation, rather than confrontation." After further haggling, the two branches eventually reached an agreement giving the House Subcommittees limited access to the contested documents.

Congress did not, however, leave things there. Certain Members of the House remained angered by the confrontation, particularly by the role played by the Department of Justice. . . . Accordingly, staff counsel of the House Judiciary Committee were commissioned (apparently without the knowledge of many of the Committee's members) to investigate the Justice Department's role in the controversy. That investigation lasted 2 1/2 years, and produced a 3,000-page report issued by the Committee over the vigorous dissent of all but one of its minority-party members. That report, which among other charges questioned the truthfulness of certain statements made by Assistant Attorney General Olson during testimony in front of the Committee during the early stages of its investigation, was sent to the Attorney General along with a formal request that he appoint an independent counsel to investigate Mr. Olson and others. . . .

Mr. Olson may or may not be guilty of a crime; we do not know. But we do know that the investigation of him has been commenced, not necessarily because the President or his authorized subordinates believe it is in the interest of the United States, in the sense that it warrants the diversion of resources from other efforts, and is worth the cost in money and in possible damage to other governmental interests; and not even, leaving aside those normally considered factors, because the President or his authorized subordinates necessarily believe that an investigation is likely to unearth a violation worth prosecuting; but only because the Attorney General cannot affirm, as Congress demands, that there are *no reasonable grounds to believe* that further investigation is warranted. The decisions regarding the scope of that further investigation, its duration, and, finally, whether or not prosecution should ensue, are likewise beyond the control of the President and his subordinates.

II

If to describe this case is not to decide it, the concept of a government of separate and coordinate powers no longer has meaning. The Court devotes most of its attention to such relatively technical details as the Appointments Clause and the removal power, addressing briefly and only at the end of its opinion the separation of powers. As my prologue suggests, I think that has it backwards. . . . Thus, while I will subsequently discuss why our appointments and removal jurisprudence does not support today's holding, I begin with a consideration of the fountainhead of that jurisprudence, the separation and equilibration of powers. . . .

To repeat, Article II, §1, cl. 1, of the Constitution provides: "The executive Power shall be vested in a President of the United States."

As I described at the outset of this opinion, this does not mean *some of* the executive power, but all of the executive power. It seems to me, therefore, that the decision of the Court of Appeals invalidating the present statute must be upheld on fundamental separation-of-powers principles if the following two questions are answered affirmatively: (1) Is the conduct of a criminal prosecution (and of an investigation to decide whether to prosecute) the exercise of purely executive power? (2) Does the statute deprive the President of the United States of exclusive control over the exercise of that power? Surprising to say, the Court appears to concede an affirmative answer to both questions, but seeks to avoid the inevitable conclusion that since the statute vests some purely executive power in a person who is not the President of the United States it is void.

The Court concedes that "[t]here is no real dispute that the functions performed by the independent counsel are 'executive,'" though it qualifies that concession by adding "in the sense that they are law enforcement functions that typically have been undertaken by officials within the Executive Branch." The qualifier adds nothing but atmosphere. In what *other* sense can one identify "the executive Power" that is supposed to be vested in the President (unless it includes everything the Executive Branch is given to do) *except* by reference to what has always and everywhere — if conducted by government at all — been conducted never by the legislature, never by the courts, and always by the executive. . . . Governmental investigation and prosecution of crimes is a quintessentially executive function.

As for the second question, whether the statute before us deprives the President of exclusive control over that quintessentially executive activity: The Court does not, and could not possibly, assert that it does not. That is indeed the whole object of the statute. Instead, the Court points out that the President, through his Attorney General, has at least some control. That concession is alone enough to invalidate the statute, but I cannot refrain from pointing out that the Court greatly exaggerates the extent of that "some" Presidential control. "Most importan[t]" among these controls, the Court asserts, is the Attorney General's "power to remove the counsel for 'good cause.'" This is somewhat like referring to shackles as an effective means of locomotion. As we recognized in *Humphrey's Executor v. United States* (1935) — indeed, what *Humphrey's Executor* was all about — limiting removal power to "good cause" is an impediment to, not an effective grant of, Presidential control. We said that limitation was necessary with respect to members of the Federal Trade Commission, which we found to be "an agency of the legislative and judicial departments," and "wholly disconnected from the executive department," because "it is quite evident that one who holds his office only during the pleasure of another, cannot be depended upon to maintain an attitude of independence against the latter's will." What we in *Humphrey's Executor* found to be a means of eliminating Presidential control, the Court today considers the "most importan[t]" means of assuring Presidential control. Congress, of course, operated under no such illusion when it enacted this statute, describing the "good cause" limitation as "protecting the independent counsel's ability to act independently of the President's direct control" since it permits removal only for "misconduct." H. R. Conf. Rep. (1987).

Moving on to the presumably "less important" controls that the President retains, . . . the Court points out that the Act directs the independent counsel to abide by general Justice Department policy, except when not "possible." The exception alone shows this to be an empty promise. Even without that, however, one would be hard put to come up with many investigative or prosecutorial "policies" (other than those imposed by the Constitution or by Congress through law) that are absolute. Almost all investigative and prosecutorial decisions — including the ultimate decision whether, after a technical violation of the law has been found, prosecution is warranted — involve the balancing of innumerable legal and practical considerations. Indeed, even political considerations (in the nonpartisan sense) must be considered, as exemplified by the recent decision of an independent counsel to subpoena the former Ambassador of Canada, producing considerable tension in our relations with that country. Another pre-eminently political decision is whether getting a conviction in a particular case is worth the disclosure of national security information that would be necessary. The Justice Department and our intelligence agencies are often in disagreement on this point, and the Justice Department does not always win. The present Act even goes so far as specifically to take the resolution of that dispute away from the President and give it to the independent counsel. . . .

As I have said, however, it is ultimately irrelevant *how much* the statute reduces Presidential control. . . . It is not for us to determine, and we have never presumed to determine, how much of the purely executive powers of government must be within the full control of the President. The Constitution prescribes that they *all* are.

The utter incompatibility of the Court's approach with our constitutional traditions can be made more clear, perhaps, by applying it to the powers of the other two branches. Is it conceivable that if Congress passed a statute depriving itself of less than full and entire control over some insignificant area of legislation, we would inquire whether the matter was "*so central* to the functioning of the Legislative Branch" as really to require complete control, or whether the statute gives Congress "sufficient control over the surrogate legislator to ensure that Congress is able to perform its constitutionally assigned duties"? . . . Or to bring the point closer to home, consider a statute giving to non-Article III judges just a tiny bit of purely judicial power in a relatively insignificant field, with substantial control, though not total control, in the courts. . . . Is there any doubt that we would not pause to inquire whether the matter was "*so central* to the functioning of the Judicial Branch" as really to require complete control, or whether we retained "sufficient control over the matters to be decided that we are able to perform our constitutionally assigned duties"? . . .

Is it unthinkable that the President should have such exclusive power, even when alleged crimes by him or his close associates are at issue? No more so than that Congress should have the exclusive power of legislation, even when what is at issue is its own exemption from the burdens of certain laws. No more so than that this Court should have the exclusive power to pronounce the final decision on justiciable cases and controversies, even those pertaining to the constitutionality of a statute reducing the salaries of the Justices. A system of separate and coordinate powers necessarily involves an acceptance of exclusive power that can theoretically be abused. . . . While the separation of powers may prevent us from righting every wrong, it does so in order to ensure that we do not lose liberty. The checks against any branch's abuse of its exclusive powers are twofold: First, retaliation by one of the other branch's use of its exclusive powers: Congress, for example, can impeach the executive who willfully fails to enforce the laws; the executive can decline to prosecute under unconstitutional statutes; and the courts can dismiss malicious prosecutions. Second, and ultimately, there is the political check that the people will replace those in the political branches. . . . Political pressures produced special prosecutors — for Teapot Dome and for Watergate, for example — long before this statute created the independent counsel.

The Court has, nonetheless, replaced the clear constitutional prescription that the executive power belongs to the President with a "balancing test." What are the standards to determine how the balance is to be struck, that is, how much removal of Presidential power is too much? . . . In my view, moreover, even as an ad hoc, standardless judgment the Court's conclusion must be wrong. . . .

Nothing is so politically effective as the ability to charge that one's opponent and his associates are not merely wrongheaded, naive, ineffective, but, in all probability, "crooks." And nothing so effectively gives an appearance of validity to such charges as a Justice Department investigation and, even better, prosecution. The present statute provides ample means for that sort of attack, assuring that massive and lengthy investigations will occur, not merely when the Justice Department in the application of its usual standards believes they are called for, but whenever it cannot be said that there are "no reasonable grounds to believe" they are called for. The statute's highly visible procedures assure, moreover, that unlike most investigations these will be widely known and prominently displayed. Thus, in the 10 years since the institution of the independent counsel was established by law, there have been nine highly publicized investigations, a source of constant political damage to two administrations. That they could not remotely be described as merely the application of "normal" investigatory and prosecutory standards is demonstrated by . . . the following facts: Congress appropriates approximately $50 million annually for general legal activities, salaries, and expenses of the Criminal Division of the Department of Justice. This money is used to support "[f]ederal appellate activity," "[o]rganized crime prosecution," "[p]ublic integrity" and "[f]raud" matters, "[n]arcotic & dangerous drug prosecution," "[i]nternal security," "[g]eneral litigation and legal advice," "special investigations," "[p]rosecution support," "[o]rganized crime drug enforcement," and "[m]anagement & administration." By comparison, between May 1986 and August 1987, four independent counsel (not all of whom were operating for that entire period of time) spent almost $5 million (one-tenth of the amount annually appropriated to the entire Criminal Division), spending almost $1 million in the month of August 1987 alone. . . .

In sum, this statute does deprive the President of substantial control over the prosecutory functions performed by the independent counsel, and it does substantially affect the balance of powers. That the Court could possibly conclude otherwise demonstrates both the wisdom of our former constitutional system, in which the degree of reduced control and political impairment were irrelevant, since all purely executive power had to be in the President; and the folly of the new system of standardless judicial allocation of powers we adopt today.

III

As I indicated earlier, the basic separation-of-powers principles I have discussed are what give life and content to our jurisprudence concerning the President's power to appoint and remove officers. . . .

[T]he Court does not attempt to "decide exactly" what establishes the line between principal and "inferior" officers, but is confident that, whatever the line may be, appellant "clearly falls on the 'inferior officer' side" of it. The Court gives three reasons: *First*, she "is subject to removal by a higher Executive Branch official," namely, the Attorney General. *Second*, she is "empowered by the Act to perform only certain, limited duties." *Third*, her office is "limited in jurisdiction" and "limited in tenure."

The first of these lends no support to the view that appellant is an inferior officer. Appellant is removable only for "good cause" or physical or mental incapacity. By contrast, most (if not all) *principal* officers in the Executive Branch may be removed by the President *at will*. I fail to see how the fact that appellant is more difficult to remove than most principal officers helps to establish that she is an inferior officer. And I do not see how it could possibly make any difference to her superior or inferior status that the President's limited power to remove her must be exercised through the Attorney General. If she were removable at will by the Attorney General, then she would be subordinate to him and thus properly designated as inferior; but the Court essentially admits that she is not subordinate. If it were common usage to refer to someone as "inferior" who is subject to removal for cause by another, then one would say that the President is "inferior" to Congress.

The second reason offered by the Court — that appellant performs only certain, limited duties — may be relevant to whether she is an inferior officer, but it mischaracterizes the extent of her powers. As the Court states: "Admittedly, the Act delegates to appellant [the] '*full power and independent authority to exercise all investigative and prosecutorial functions and powers of the Department of Justice*.'" Moreover, in addition to this general grant of power she is given a broad range of specifically enumerated powers, including a power not even the Attorney General possesses: to "contes[t] in court . . . any claim of privilege or attempt to withhold evidence on grounds of national security." Once all of this is "admitted," it seems to me impossible to maintain that appellant's authority is so "limited" as to render her an inferior officer. . . .

The final set of reasons given by the Court for why the independent counsel clearly is an inferior officer emphasizes the limited nature of her jurisdiction and tenure. Taking the latter first, I find nothing unusually limited about the independent counsel's tenure. To the contrary, unlike most high-ranking Executive Branch officials, she continues to serve until she (or the Special Division) decides that her work is substantially completed. This particular independent prosecutor has already served more than two years, which is at least as long as many Cabinet officials. As to the scope of her jurisdiction, there can be no doubt that is small (though far from unimportant). But within it she exercises more than the full power of the Attorney General. The Ambassador to Luxembourg is not anything less than a principal officer, simply because Luxembourg is small. And the federal judge who sits in a small district is not for that reason "inferior in rank and authority." . . .

More fundamentally, however, it is not clear from the Court's opinion why the factors it discusses — even if applied correctly to the facts of this case — are determinative of the question of inferior officer status. . . . I think it preferable to look to the text of the Constitution and the division of power that it establishes. These demonstrate, I think, that the independent counsel is not an inferior officer because she is not *subordinate* to any officer in the Executive Branch (indeed, not even to the President). Dictionaries in use at the time of the Constitutional Convention gave the word "inferiour" two meanings which it still bears today: (1) "[l]ower in place, . . . station, . . . rank of life, . . . value or excellency," and (2) "[s]ubordinate." S. Johnson, Dictionary of the English Language (6th ed. 1785). In a document dealing with the structure (the constitution) of a government, one would naturally expect the word to bear the latter meaning — indeed, in such a context it would be unpardonably careless to use the word unless a relationship of subordination was intended. If what was meant was merely "lower in station or rank," one would use instead a term such as "lesser officers." At the only other point in the Constitution at which the word "inferior" appears, it plainly connotes a relationship of subordination. Article III vests the judicial power of the United States in "one supreme Court, and in such *inferior* Courts as the Congress may from time to time ordain and establish." (emphasis added). In *Federalist, No. 81*, Hamilton pauses to describe the "inferior" courts authorized by Article III as inferior in the sense that they are "subordinate" to the Supreme Court.

That "inferior" means "subordinate" is also consistent with what little we know about the evolution of the Appointments Clause. As originally reported to the Committee on Style, the Appointments Clause provided no "exception" from the standard manner of appointment (President with the advice and consent of the Senate) for inferior officers. On September 15, 1787, the last day of the Convention before the proposed Constitution was signed, in the midst of a host of minor changes that were being considered, Gouverneur Morris moved to add the exceptions clause. No great debate ensued; the only disagreement was over whether it was necessary at all. Nobody thought that it was a fundamental change, excluding from the President's appointment power and the Senate's confirmation power a category of officers who might function on their own, outside the supervision of those appointed in the more cumbersome fashion. And it is significant that in the very brief discussion Madison mentions (as in apparent contrast to the "inferior officers" covered by the provision) "Superior Officers." Of course one is not a "superior officer" without some supervisory responsibility, just as, I suggest, one is not an "inferior officer" within the meaning of the provision under discussion unless one is subject to supervision by a "superior officer." It is perfectly obvious, therefore, both from the relative brevity of the discussion this addition received, and from the content of that discussion, that it was intended merely to make clear (what Madison thought already was clear) that those officers appointed by the President with Senate approval could on their own appoint their subordinates, who would, of course, by chain of command still be under the direct control of the President.

This interpretation is, moreover, consistent with our admittedly sketchy precedent in this area. For example, . . . in *United States v. Nixon* (1974), we noted that the Attorney General's appointment of the Watergate Special Prosecutor was made pursuant to the Attorney General's "power to appoint *subordinate officers* to assist him in the discharge of his duties." (emphasis added). . . . We explicitly stated that the Special Prosecutor was a "subordinate office[r]," because, in the end, the President or the Attorney General could have removed him at any time, if by no other means than amending or revoking the regulation defining his authority. . . .

To be sure, it is not a *sufficient* condition for "inferior" officer status that one be subordinate to a principal officer. Even an officer who is subordinate to a department head can be a principal officer. . . . But it is surely a *necessary* condition for inferior officer status that the officer be subordinate to another officer.

The independent counsel is not even subordinate to the President. The Court essentially admits as much. . . . Because appellant is not subordinate to another officer, she is not an "inferior" officer and her appointment other than by the President with the advice and consent of the Senate is unconstitutional.

IV

. . . Since our 1935 decision in *Humphrey's Executor v. United States* — which was considered by many at the time the product of an activist, anti-New Deal Court bent on reducing the power of President Franklin Roosevelt — it has been established that the line of permissible restriction upon removal of principal officers lies at the point at which the powers exercised by those officers are no longer purely executive. Thus, removal restrictions have been generally regarded as lawful for so-called "independent regulatory agencies," such as the Federal Trade Commission, the Interstate Commerce Commission, and the Consumer Product Safety Commission, which engage substantially in what has been called the "quasi-legislative activity" of rulemaking, and for members of Article I courts, such as the Court of Military Appeals, who engage in the "quasi-judicial" function of adjudication. It has often been observed, correctly in my view, that the line between "purely executive" functions and "quasi-legislative" or "quasi-judicial" functions is not a clear one or even a rational one. But at least it permitted the identification of certain officers, and certain agencies, whose functions were entirely within the control of the President. Congress had to be aware of that restriction in its legislation. Today, however, *Humphrey's Executor* is swept into the dustbin of repudiated constitutional principles. "[O]ur present considered view," the Court says, "is that the determination of whether the Constitution allows Congress to impose a 'good cause'-type restriction on the President's power to remove an official cannot be made to turn on whether or not that official is classified as 'purely executive.'" . . .

"[O]ur present considered view" is simply that any executive officer's removal can be restricted, so long as the President remains "able to accomplish his constitutional role." There are now no lines. If the removal of a prosecutor, the virtual embodiment of the power to "take care that the laws be faithfully executed," can be restricted, what officer's removal cannot? This is an open invitation for Congress to experiment. What about a special Assistant Secretary of State, with responsibility for one very narrow area of foreign policy, who would not only have to be confirmed by the Senate but could also be removed only pursuant to certain carefully designed restrictions? Could this possibly render the President "[un]able to accomplish his constitutional role"? Or a special Assistant Secretary of Defense for Procurement? The possibilities are endless. . . . The Court essentially says to the President: "Trust us. We will make sure that you are able to accomplish your constitutional role." I think the Constitution gives the President — and the people — more protection than that.

V

The purpose of the separation and equilibration of powers in general, and of the unitary Executive in particular, was not merely to assure effective government but to preserve individual freedom. Those who hold or have held offices covered by the Ethics in Government Act are entitled to that protection as much as the rest of us, and I conclude my discussion by considering the effect of the Act upon the fairness of the process they receive.

Only someone who has worked in the field of law enforcement can fully appreciate the vast power and the immense discretion that are placed in the hands of a prosecutor with respect to the objects of his investigation. Justice Robert Jackson, when he was Attorney General under President Franklin Roosevelt, described it in a memorable speech to United States Attorneys, as follows:

> [. . .] One of the greatest difficulties of the position of prosecutor is that he must pick his cases, because no prosecutor can even investigate all of the cases in which he receives complaints. If the Department of Justice were to make even a pretense of reaching every probable violation of federal law, ten times its present staff will be inadequate. We know that no local police force can strictly enforce the traffic laws, or it would arrest half the driving population on any given morning. What every prosecutor is practically required to do is to select the cases for prosecution and to select those in which the offense is the most flagrant, the public harm the greatest, and the proof the most certain.
>
> If the prosecutor is obliged to choose his case, it follows that he can choose his defendants. Therein is the most dangerous power of the prosecutor: that he will pick people that he thinks he should get, rather than cases that need to be prosecuted. With the law books filled with a great assortment of crimes, a prosecutor stands a fair chance of finding at least a technical violation of some act on the part of almost anyone. In such a case, it is not a question of discovering the commission of a crime and then looking for the man who has committed it, it is a question of picking the man and then searching the law books, or putting investigators to work, to pin some offense on him. It is in this realm — in which the prosecutor picks some person whom he dislikes or desires to embarrass, or selects some group of unpopular persons and then looks for an offense, that the greatest danger of abuse of prosecuting power lies. It is here that law enforcement becomes personal, and the real crime becomes that of being unpopular with the predominant or governing group, being attached to the wrong political views, or being personally obnoxious to or in the way of the prosecutor himself.

Under our system of government, the primary check against prosecutorial abuse is a political one. The prosecutors who exercise this awesome discretion are selected and can be removed by a President, whom the people have trusted enough to elect. Moreover, when crimes are not investigated and prosecuted fairly, nonselectively, with a reasonable sense of proportion, the President pays the cost in political damage to his administration. . . . That result, of course, was precisely what the Founders had in mind when they provided that all executive powers would be exercised by a single Chief Executive. As Hamilton put it, "[t]he ingredients which constitute safety in the republican sense are a due dependence on the people, and a due responsibility." *Federalist, No. 70.* The President is directly dependent on the people, and since there is only one President, he is responsible. The people know whom to blame, whereas "one of the weightiest objections to a plurality in the executive ... is that it tends to conceal faults and destroy responsibility."

That is the system of justice the rest of us are entitled to, but what of that select class consisting of present or former high-level Executive Branch officials? ... An independent counsel is selected, and the scope of his or her authority prescribed, by a panel of judges. What if they are politically partisan, as judges have been known to be, and select a prosecutor antagonistic to the administration, or even to the particular individual who has been selected for this special treatment? There is no remedy for that, not even a political one. Judges, after all, have life tenure, and appointing a surefire enthusiastic prosecutor could hardly be considered an impeachable offense. So if there is anything wrong with the selection, there is effectively no one to blame. The independent counsel thus selected proceeds to assemble a staff. ... [I]n the nature of things this has to be done by finding lawyers who are willing to lay aside their current careers for an indeterminate amount of time, to take on a job that has no prospect of permanence and little prospect for promotion. One thing is certain, however: it involves investigating and perhaps prosecuting a particular individual. Can one imagine a less equitable manner of fulfilling the executive responsibility to investigate and prosecute? What would be the reaction if, in an area not covered by this statute, the Justice Department posted a public notice inviting applicants to assist in an investigation and possible prosecution of a certain prominent person? Does this not invite what Justice Jackson described as "picking the man and then searching the law books, or putting investigators to work, to pin some offense on him"? To be sure, the investigation must relate to the area of criminal offense specified by the life-tenured judges. But that has often been (and nothing prevents it from being) very broad — and should the independent counsel or his or her staff come up with something beyond that scope, nothing prevents him or her from asking the judges to expand his or her authority or, if that does not work, referring it to the Attorney General, whereupon the whole process would recommence and, if there was "reasonable basis to believe" that further investigation was warranted, that new offense would be referred to the Special Division, which would in all likelihood assign it to the same independent counsel. It seems to me not conducive to fairness. But even if it were entirely evident that unfairness was in fact the result — the judges hostile to the administration, the independent counsel an old foe of the President, the staff refugees from the recently defeated administration — *there would be no one accountable to the public to whom the blame could be assigned*. ...

It is true, of course, that a similar list of horribles could be attributed to an ordinary Justice Department prosecution — a vindictive prosecutor, an antagonistic staff, etc. But the difference is the difference that the Founders envisioned when they established a single Chief Executive accountable to the people: the blame can be assigned to someone who can be punished.

It is ... an additional advantage of the unitary Executive that it can achieve a more uniform application of the law. Perhaps that is not always achieved, but the mechanism to achieve it is there. The mini-Executive that is the independent counsel, however, operating in an area where so little is law and so much is discretion, is intentionally cut off from the unifying influence of the Justice

Department, and from the perspective that multiple responsibilities provide. What would normally be regarded as a technical violation (there are no rules defining such things), may in his or her small world assume the proportions of an indictable offense. What would normally be regarded as an investigation that has reached the level of pursuing such picayune matters that it should be concluded, may to him or her be an investigation that ought to go on for another year. How frightening it must be to have your own independent counsel and staff appointed, with nothing else to do but to investigate you until investigation is no longer worthwhile — with whether it is worthwhile not depending upon what such judgments usually hinge on, competing responsibilities. And to have that counsel and staff decide, with no basis for comparison, whether what you have done is bad enough, willful enough, and provable enough, to warrant an indictment. How admirable the constitutional system that provides the means to avoid such a distortion. And how unfortunate the judicial decision that has permitted it. . . .

The ad hoc approach to constitutional adjudication has real attraction, even apart from its work-saving potential. It is guaranteed to produce a result, in every case, that will make a majority of the Court happy with the law. The law is, by definition, precisely what the majority thinks, taking all things into account, it ought to be. I prefer to rely upon the judgment of the wise men who constructed our system, and of the people who approved it, and of two centuries of history that have shown it to be sound. Like it or not, that judgment says, quite plainly, that "[t]he executive Power shall be vested in a President of the United States."

ASSIGNMENT 2

Senator Mark Warner (D-VA) presiding over an empty Senate during a pro-forma session on January 3, 2012. He would speak for roughly one minute before gaveling out the session until January 6. President Obama made the appointments on January 4.

STUDY GUIDE

- In January 2012, the House of Representatives was controlled by the Republicans, and the Senate was controlled by the Democrats. The Adjournment Clause, Art. I, §5, cl. 4, provides that "Neither House, during the Session of Congress, shall, without the Consent of the other, adjourn for more than three days." In order to block President Obama from making recess appointments to the National Labor Relations Board, and other positions, House Republicans relied on the Adjournment Clause to prevent the Senate from recessing for more than three days. As a result, during late December and early January, the Senate would break for three days, and return for a short, pro-forma session (that lasted less than a minute). President Obama's appointments were made between the January 3 and January 6 pro-forma sessions. Did it matter to the Court that no actual business was transacted during the brief, pro-forma session?
- Article II, Section 2, Clause 2 allows the President to fill all "vacancies that may happen during the Recess of the Senate." Is this clause limited to vacancies that arise "during" the recess, or does it also include vacancies that existed *before* the recess? What is the difference between "*the* Recess of the Senate" and "*a* Recess of the Senate"? Should it have made a difference? How many times does the Senate go into recess?
- Justice Breyer states that "[w]e therefore conclude, in light of historical practice, that a recess of more than 3 days but less than 10 days is presumptively too short to fall within the Clause." What does "presumptively" mean? When Justice Scalia died in February 2016, the Senate was on recess for roughly a week. Could President Obama have made a recess appointment to the Supreme Court?
- The judgment was unanimous, but Justice Scalia's concurring opinion reads more like a dissent. What is the biggest difference between Justice Breyer's majority opinion and Justice Scalia's concurring opinion?
- Justice Scalia refers to the gridlock in the Senate as "not a bug to be fixed by this Court, but a calculated feature of the constitutional framework"? Is he right? What is Justice Breyer's response?
- If the Senate acquiesces (that is, allows by inaction) to the President to make what are otherwise illegal recess appointments, should the Court give weight to that practice? (What could the Senate do to stop the practice?) Or should the Constitution be understood based on its original meaning? What if the two elements are in conflict?

National Labor Relations Board v. Noel Canning

134 S. Ct. 2550 (2014)

JUSTICE BREYER delivered the opinion of the Court.

Ordinarily the President must obtain "the Advice and Consent of the Senate" before appointing an "Office[r] of the United States." U.S. Const., Art. II, §2, cl. 2. But the Recess Appointments Clause creates an exception. It gives the President alone the power "to fill up all Vacancies that may happen during the Recess of the Senate, by granting Commissions which shall expire at the End of their next Session." Art. II, §2, cl. 3. We here consider three questions about the application of this Clause.

The first concerns the scope of the words "recess of the Senate." Does that phrase refer only to an inter-session recess (*i.e.*, a break between formal sessions of Congress), or does it also include an intra-session recess, such as a summer recess in the midst of a session? We conclude that the Clause applies to both kinds of recess.

The second question concerns the scope of the words "vacancies that may happen." Does that phrase refer only to vacancies that first come into existence during a recess, or does it also include vacancies that arise prior to a recess but continue to exist during the recess? We conclude that the Clause applies to both kinds of vacancy.

The third question concerns calculation of the length of a "recess." The President made the appointments here at issue on January 4, 2012. At that time the Senate was in recess pursuant to a December 17, 2011, resolution providing for a series of brief recesses punctuated by "*pro forma* session[s]," with "no business . . . transacted," every Tuesday and Friday through January 20, 2012. In calculating the length of a recess are we to ignore the *pro forma* sessions, thereby treating the series of brief recesses as a single, month-long recess? We conclude that we cannot ignore these *pro forma* sessions.

Our answer to the third question means that, when the appointments before us took place, the Senate was in the midst of a 3-day recess. Three days is too short a time to bring a recess within the scope of the Clause. Thus we conclude that the President lacked the power to make the recess appointments here at issue.

I

The case before us arises out of a labor dispute. The National Labor Relations Board (NLRB) found that a Pepsi-Cola distributor, Noel Canning, had unlawfully refused to reduce to writing and execute a collective-bargaining agreement with a labor union. The Board ordered the distributor to execute the agreement and to make employees whole for any losses.

The Pepsi-Cola distributor subsequently asked the Court of Appeals for the District of Columbia Circuit to set the Board's order aside. It claimed that three of the five Board members had been invalidly appointed, leaving the Board without the three lawfully appointed members necessary for it to act.

The three members in question were Sharon Block, Richard Griffin, and Terence Flynn. In 2011 the President had nominated each of them to the Board. As of January 2012, Flynn's nomination had been pending in the Senate awaiting confirmation for approximately a year. The nominations of each of the other two had been pending for a few weeks. On January 4, 2012, the President, invoking the Recess Appointments Clause, appointed all three to the Board.

The distributor argued that the Recess Appointments Clause did not authorize those appointments. It pointed out that on December 17, 2011, the Senate, by unanimous consent, had adopted a resolution providing that it would take a series of brief recesses beginning the following day. Pursuant to that resolution, the Senate held *pro forma* sessions every Tuesday and Friday until it returned for ordinary business on January 23, 2012. The President's January 4 appointments were made between the January 3 and January 6 *pro forma* sessions. In the distributor's view, each *pro forma* session terminated the immediately preceding recess. Accordingly, the appointments were made during a 3-day adjournment, which is not long enough to trigger the Recess Appointments Clause.

The Court of Appeals agreed that the appointments fell outside the scope of the Clause. But the court set forth different reasons. It held that the Clause's words "the recess of the Senate" do not include recesses that occur *within* a formal session of Congress, *i.e.*, intra-session recesses. Rather those words apply only to recesses *between* those formal sessions, *i.e.*, inter-session recesses. Since the second session of the 112th Congress began on January 3, 2012, the day before the President's appointments, those appointments occurred during an intra-session recess, and the appointments consequently fell outside the scope of the Clause.

The Court of Appeals added that, in any event, the phrase "vacancies that may happen during the recess" applies only to vacancies that come into existence during a recess. The vacancies that Members Block, Griffin, and Flynn were appointed to fill had arisen before the beginning of the recess during which they were appointed. For this reason too the President's appointments were invalid. And, because the Board lacked a quorum of validly appointed members when it issued its order, the order was invalid.

We granted the Solicitor General's petition for certiorari. We asked the parties to address not only the Court of Appeals' interpretation of the Clause but also the distributor's initial argument, namely, "[w]hether the President's recess-appointment power may be exercised when the Senate is convening every three days in *pro forma* sessions."

We shall answer all three questions presented.

II

Before turning to the specific questions presented, we shall mention two background considerations that we find relevant to all three. First, *the Recess Appointments Clause sets forth a subsidiary, not a primary, method for appointing officers of the United States.* The immediately preceding Clause — Article II, Section 2, Clause 2 — provides the primary method of appointment. It says that the President "shall nominate, *and by and with the Advice and Consent of the Senate*, shall appoint Ambassadors, other public Ministers and Consuls, Judges of the supreme Court, and all other Officers of the United States" (emphasis added).

The Federalist Papers make clear that the Founders intended this method of appointment, requiring Senate approval, to be the norm (at least for principal officers). Alexander Hamilton wrote that the Constitution vests the power of *nomination* in the President alone because "one man of discernment is better fitted to analise and estimate the peculiar qualities adapted to particular offices, than a body of men of equal, or perhaps even of superior discernment." The Federalist No. 76. At the same time, the need to secure Senate approval provides "an excellent check upon a spirit of favoritism in the President, and would tend greatly to preventing the appointment of unfit characters from State prejudice, from family connection, from personal attachment, or from a view to popularity." *Id.* Hamilton further explained that the

> ordinary power of appointment is confided to the President and Senate *jointly*, and can therefore only be exercised during the session of the Senate; but as it would have been improper to oblige this body to be continually in session for the appointment of officers; and as vacancies might happen *in their recess*, which it might be necessary for the public service to fill without delay, the succeeding clause is evidently intended to authorise the President *singly* to make temporary appointments. *Id.*, No. 67.

Thus the Recess Appointments Clause reflects the tension between, on the one hand, the President's continuous need for "the assistance of subordinates," *Myers v. United States* (1926), and, on the other, the Senate's practice, particularly during the Republic's early years, of meeting for a single brief session each year. We seek to interpret the Clause as granting the President the power to make appointments during a recess but not offering the President the authority routinely to avoid the need for Senate confirmation.

Second, *in interpreting the Clause, we put significant weight upon historical practice.* For one thing, the interpretive questions before us concern the allocation of power between two elected branches of Government. Long ago Chief Justice Marshall wrote that

> a doubtful question, one on which human reason may pause, and the human judgment be suspended, in the decision of which the great principles of liberty are not concerned, but the respective powers of those who are equally the representatives of the people, are to be adjusted; if not put at rest by the practice of the government, ought to receive a considerable impression from that practice. *McCulloch v. Maryland* (1819).

And we later confirmed that "[l]ong settled and established practice is a consideration of great weight in a proper interpretation of constitutional provisions" regulating the relationship between Congress and the President. *The Pocket Veto Case* (1929).

We recognize, of course, that the separation of powers can serve to safeguard individual liberty, and that it is the "duty of the judicial department" — in a separation-of-powers case as in any other — "to say what the law is," *Marbury v. Madison* (1803). But it is equally true that the longstanding "practice of the government," *McCulloch*, can inform our determination of "what the law is," *Marbury*.

That principle is neither new nor controversial. As James Madison wrote, it "was foreseen at the birth of the Constitution, that difficulties and differences of opinion might occasionally arise in expounding terms & phrases necessarily used in such a charter . . . and that it might require a regular course of practice to liquidate & settle the meaning of some of them." Letter to Spencer Roane (Sept. 2, 1819). And our cases have continually confirmed Madison's view.

These precedents show that this Court has treated practice as an important interpretive factor even when the nature or longevity of that practice is subject to dispute, and even when that practice began after the founding era.

There is a great deal of history to consider here. Presidents have made recess appointments since the beginning of the Republic. Their frequency suggests that the Senate and President have recognized that recess appointments can be both necessary and appropriate in certain circumstances. We have not previously interpreted the Clause, and, when doing so for the first time in more than 200 years, we must hesitate to upset the compromises and working arrangements that the elected branches of Government themselves have reached.

III

The first question concerns the scope of the phrase "*the recess* of the Senate." Art. II, §2, cl. 3 (emphasis added). The Constitution provides for congressional elections every two years. And the 2-year life of each elected Congress typically consists of two formal 1-year sessions, each separated from the next by an "inter-session recess." The Senate or the House of Representatives announces an inter-session recess by approving a resolution stating that it will "adjourn *sine die*," *i.e.*, without specifying a date to return (in which case Congress will reconvene when the next formal session is scheduled to begin).

The Senate and the House also take breaks in the midst of a session. The Senate or the House announces any such "intra-session recess" by adopting a resolution stating that it will "adjourn" to a fixed date, a few days or weeks or even months later. All agree that the phrase "the recess of the Senate" covers inter-session recesses. The question is whether it includes intra-session recesses as well.

In our view, the phrase "the recess" includes an intra-session recess of substantial length. Its words taken literally can refer to both types of recess. Founding-era dictionaries define the word "recess," much as we do today, simply as "a period of cessation from usual work." . . .

We recognize that the word "the" in "*the* recess" might suggest that the phrase refers to the single break separating formal sessions of Congress. That is because the word "the" frequently (but not always) indicates "a particular thing." But the word can also refer "to a term used generically or universally." The Constitution, for example, directs the Senate to choose a President *pro tempore* "in *the* Absence of the Vice-President." Art. I, §3, cl. 5 (emphasis added). And the Federalist Papers refer to the chief magistrate of an ancient Achaean league who "administered the government in *the* recess of the Senate." The Federalist No. 18 (J. Madison).

Reading "the" generically in this way, there is no linguistic problem applying the Clause's phrase to both kinds of recess. And, in fact, the phrase "the recess" was used to refer to intra-session recesses at the time of the founding.

The constitutional text is thus ambiguous. And we believe the Clause's purpose demands the broader interpretation. The Clause gives the President authority to make appointments during "the recess of the Senate" so that the President can ensure the continued functioning of the Federal Government when the Senate is away. The Senate is equally away during both an inter-session and an intra-session recess, and its capacity to participate in the appointments process has nothing to do with the words it uses to signal its departure.

History also offers strong support for the broad interpretation. We concede that pre-Civil War history is not helpful. But it shows only that Congress generally took long breaks between sessions, while taking no significant intra-session breaks at all (five times it took a break of a week or so at Christmas). Obviously, if there are no significant intra-session recesses, there will be no intra-session recess appointments. In 1867 and 1868, Congress for the first time took substantial, nonholiday intra-session breaks, and President Andrew Johnson made dozens of recess appointments. The Federal Court of Claims upheld one of those specific appointments, writing "[w]e have *no doubt* that a vacancy occurring while the Senate was thus temporarily adjourned" during the "first session of the Fortieth Congress" was "legally filled by appointment of the President alone." *Gould v. United States* (1884). Attorney General Evarts also issued three opinions concerning the constitutionality of President Johnson's appointments, and it apparently did not occur to him that the distinction between intra-session and inter-session recesses was significant. Similarly, though the 40th Congress impeached President Johnson on charges relating to his appointment power, he was not accused of violating the Constitution by making intra-session recess appointments.

In all, between the founding and the Great Depression, Congress took substantial intra-session breaks (other than holiday breaks) in four years: 1867, 1868, 1921, and 1929. And in each of those years the President made intra-session recess appointments.

Since 1929, and particularly since the end of World War II, Congress has shortened its inter-session breaks as it has taken longer and more frequent intra-session breaks; Presidents have correspondingly made more intra-session recess appointments. Indeed, if we include military appointments, Presidents have made thousands of intra-session recess appointments. . . . Not surprisingly, the publicly available opinions of Presidential legal advisers that we have found are nearly unanimous in determining that the Clause authorizes these appointments. . . .

What about the Senate? Since Presidents began making intra-session recess appointments, individual Senators have taken differing views about the proper definition of "the recess." But neither the Senate considered as a body nor its committees, despite opportunities to express opposition to the practice of intra-session recess appointments, has done so. Rather, to the extent that the Senate or a Senate committee has expressed a view, that view has favored a functional definition of "recess," and a functional definition encompasses intra-session recesses.

Most notably, in 1905 the Senate Committee on the Judiciary objected strongly to President Theodore Roosevelt's use of the Clause to make more than 160 recess appointments during a "fictitious" inter-session recess. At noon on December 7, 1903, the Senate President *pro tempore* had "declare[d]" a formal, "extraordinary session" of the Senate "adjourned without day," and the next formal Senate session began immediately afterwards. President Roosevelt made over 160 recess appointments during the instantaneous inter-session interval. The Judiciary Committee, when stating its strong objection, defined "recess" in functional terms as

> the period of time when the Senate is not sitting in regular or extraordinary session as a branch of the Congress . . . ; when its members owe no duty of attendance; when its Chamber is empty; when, because of its absence, it can not receive communications from the President or participate as a body in making appointments.

That functional definition encompasses intra-session, as well as inter-session, recesses. Justice Scalia is right that the 1905 Report did not specifically address the distinction between inter-session and intra-session recesses. But the animating principle of the Report — that "recess" should be practically construed to mean a time when the Senate is unavailable to participate in the appointments process — is inconsistent with the formalistic approach that Justice Scalia endorses.

Similarly, in 1940 the Senate helped to enact a law regulating the payment of recess appointees, and the Comptroller General of the United States has interpreted that law functionally. An earlier 1863 statute had denied pay to individuals appointed to fill up vacancies first arising prior to the beginning of a recess. The Senate Judiciary Committee then believed that those vacancies fell outside the scope of the Clause. In 1940, however, the Senate amended the law to permit many of those recess appointees to be paid. . . .

The upshot is that restricting the Clause to inter-session recesses would frustrate its purpose. It would make the President's recess-appointment power dependent on a formalistic distinction of Senate procedure. Moreover, the President has consistently and frequently interpreted the word "recess" to apply to intra-session recesses, and has acted on that interpretation. The Senate as a body has done nothing to deny the validity of this practice for at least three-quarters of a century. And three-quarters of a century of settled practice is long enough to entitle a practice to "great weight in a proper interpretation" of the constitutional provision. . . .

[S]ome argue that the Founders would likely have intended the Clause to apply only to inter-session recesses, for they hardly knew any other. See, *e.g.*, Brief for Originalist Scholars as *Amici Curiae*. Indeed, from the founding until the Civil War inter-session recesses were the only kind of significant recesses that Congress took. The problem with this argument, however, is that it does not fully describe the relevant founding intent. The question is not: Did the Founders at the time think about intra-session recesses? Perhaps they did not. The question is: Did the Founders intend to restrict the scope of the Clause to the form of congressional recess then prevalent, or did they intend a broader scope permitting the Clause to apply, where appropriate, to somewhat changed circumstances? The Founders knew they were writing a document designed to apply to ever-changing circumstances over centuries. After all, a Constitution is "intended to endure for ages to come," and must adapt itself to a future that can only be "seen dimly," if at all. *McCulloch*. We therefore think the Framers likely did intend the Clause to apply to a new circumstance that so clearly falls within its essential purposes, where doing so is consistent with the Clause's language. . . .

The greater interpretive problem is determining how long a recess must be in order to fall within the Clause. Is a break of a week, or a day, or an hour too short to count as a "recess"? The Clause itself does not say. And Justice Scalia claims that this silence itself shows that the Framers intended the Clause to apply only to an inter-session recess.

We disagree. For one thing, the most likely reason the Framers did not place a textual floor underneath the word "recess" is that they did not foresee the *need* for one. They might have expected that the Senate would meet for a single session lasting at most half a year. The Federalist No. 84 (A. Hamilton). And they might not have anticipated that intra-session recesses would become lengthier and more significant than inter-session ones. The Framers' lack of clairvoyance on that point is not dispositive. Unlike Justice Scalia, we think it most consistent with our constitutional structure to presume that the Framers would have allowed intra-session recess appointments where there was a long history of such practice . . . .

The Recess Appointments Clause seeks to permit the Executive Branch to function smoothly when Congress is unavailable. And though Congress has taken short breaks for almost 200 years, and there have been many thousands of recess appointments in that time, we have not found a single example of a recess appointment made during an intra-session recess that was shorter than 10 days. Nor has the Solicitor General. Indeed, the Office of Legal Counsel once informally advised against making a recess appointment during a 6-day intra-session recess. The lack of examples suggests that the recess-appointment power is not needed in that context.

There are a few historical examples of recess appointments made during inter-session recesses shorter than 10 days. . . . There may be others of which we are unaware. But when considered against 200 years of settled practice, we regard these few scattered examples as anomalies. We therefore conclude, in light of historical practice, that a recess of more than 3 days but less than 10 days is presumptively too short to fall within the Clause. We add the word "presumptively" to leave open the possibility that some very unusual circumstance — a national catastrophe, for instance, that renders the Senate unavailable but calls for an urgent response — could demand the exercise of the recess-appointment power during a shorter break. (It should go without saying — except that Justice Scalia compels us to say it — that political opposition in the Senate would not qualify as an unusual circumstance.)

In sum, we conclude that the phrase "the recess" applies to both intra-session and inter-session recesses. If a Senate recess is so short that it does not require the consent of the House, it is too short to trigger the Recess Appointments Clause. And a recess lasting less than 10 days is presumptively too short as well.

IV

The second question concerns the scope of the phrase "vacancies *that may happen* during the recess of the Senate." Art. II, §2, cl. 3 (emphasis added). All agree that the phrase applies to vacancies that initially occur during a recess. But does it also apply to vacancies that initially occur before a recess and continue to exist during the recess? In our view the phrase applies to both kinds of vacancy.

We believe that the Clause's language, read literally, permits, though it does not naturally favor, our broader interpretation. We concede that the most natural meaning of "happens" as applied to a "vacancy" (at least to a modern ear) is that the vacancy "happens" when it initially occurs. See 1 Johnson 913 (defining "happen" in relevant part as meaning "[t]o fall out; to chance; to come to pass"). But that is not the only possible way to use the word.

Thomas Jefferson wrote that the Clause is "certainly susceptible of [two] constructions." Letter to Wilson Cary Nicholas (Jan. 26, 1802). It "may mean 'vacancies that may happen to be' or 'may happen to fall'" during a recess. Jefferson used the phrase in the first sense when he wrote to a job seeker that a particular position was unavailable, but that he (Jefferson) was "happy that *another vacancy happens* wherein I can . . . avail the public of your integrity & talents," for "the office of Treasurer of the US. *is vacant* by the resignation of mr Meredith." Letter to Thomas Tudor Tucker (Oct. 31, 1801) (emphasis added). . . .

We can still understand this earlier use of "happen" if we think of it used together with another word that, like "vacancy," can refer to a continuing state, say, a financial crisis. A statute that gives the President authority to act in respect to "any financial crisis that may happen during his term" can easily be interpreted to include crises that arise before, and continue during, that term. Perhaps that is why the Oxford English Dictionary defines "happen" in part as "chance *to be*," rather than "chance to occur." OED (emphasis added); see also OED (defining "vacancy" as the "condition of an office or post being . . . vacant").

In any event, the linguistic question here is not whether the phrase can be, but whether it must be, read more narrowly. The question is whether the Clause is ambiguous. And the broader reading, we believe, is at least a permissible reading of a "'doubtful' phrase." We consequently go on to consider the Clause's purpose and historical practice.

The Clause's purpose strongly supports the broader interpretation. That purpose is to permit the President to obtain the assistance of subordinate officers when the Senate, due to its recess, cannot confirm them. . . . At the same time, we recognize one important purpose-related consideration that argues in the opposite direction. A broad interpretation might permit a President to avoid Senate confirmations as a matter of course. If the Clause gives the President the power to "fill up all vacancies" that occur before, and continue to exist during, the Senate's recess, a President might not submit any nominations to the Senate. He might simply wait for a recess and then provide all potential nominees with recess appointments. He might thereby routinely avoid the constitutional need to obtain the Senate's "advice and consent." . . .

While we concede that both interpretations carry with them some risk of undesirable consequences, we believe the narrower interpretation risks undermining constitutionally conferred powers more seriously and more often. It would prevent the President from making any recess appointment that arose before a recess, no matter who the official, no matter how dire the need, no matter how uncontroversial the appointment, and no matter how late in the session the office fell vacant. Overall, . . . we believe the broader interpretation more consistent with the Constitution's "reason and spirit."

Historical practice over the past 200 years strongly favors the broader interpretation. The tradition of applying the Clause to pre-recess vacancies dates at least to President James Madison. There is no undisputed record of Presidents George Washington, John Adams, or Thomas Jefferson making such an appointment, though the Solicitor General believes he has found records showing that Presidents Washington and Jefferson did so. We know that Edmund Randolph, Washington's Attorney General, favored a narrow reading of the Clause. Randolph believed that the "Spirit of the Constitution favors the participation of the Senate in all appointments," though he did not address — let alone answer — the powerful purposive and structural arguments subsequently made by Attorney General Wirt.

President Adams seemed to endorse the broader view of the Clause in writing, though we are not aware of any appointments he made in keeping with that view. See Letter to J. McHenry (Apr. 16, 1799). His Attorney General, Charles Lee, later informed Jefferson that, in the Adams administration, "whenever an office became vacant so short a time before Congress rose, as not to give an opportunity of enquiring for a proper character, they let it lie always till recess." We know that President Jefferson thought that the broad interpretation was linguistically supportable, though his actual practice is not clear. But the evidence suggests that James Madison — as familiar as anyone with the workings of the Constitutional Convention — appointed Theodore Gaillard to replace a district judge who had left office before a recess began. It also appears that in 1815 Madison signed a bill that created two new offices prior to a recess which he then filled later during the recess. He also made recess appointments to "territorial" United States attorney and marshal positions, both of which had been created when the Senate was in session more than two years before. Justice Scalia refers to "written evidence of Madison's own beliefs," but in fact we have no direct evidence of what President Madison believed. We only know that he declined to make one appointment to a pre-recess vacancy after his Secretary of War advised him that he lacked the power. On the other hand, he *did* apparently make at least five other appointments to pre-recess vacancies, as Justice Scalia does not dispute. . . .

Common sense also suggests that many recess appointees filled vacancies that arose before the recess began. We have compared the list of *intra*-session recess appointments in the Solicitor General's brief with the chart of congressional recesses. Where a specific date of appointment can be ascertained, more than half of those intra-session appointments were made within two weeks of the beginning of a recess. That short window strongly suggests that many of the vacancies initially arose prior to the recess. . . . Taken together, we think it is a fair inference that a large proportion of the recess appointments in the history of the Nation have filled pre-existing vacancies . . . .

The upshot is that the President has consistently and frequently interpreted the Recess Appointments Clause to apply to vacancies that initially occur before, but continue to exist during, a recess of the Senate. The Senate as a body has not countered this practice for nearly three-quarters of a century, perhaps longer. The tradition is long enough to entitle the practice "to great regard in determining the true construction" of the constitutional provision. *The Pocket Veto Case.* And we are reluctant to upset this traditional practice where doing so would seriously shrink the authority that Presidents have believed existed and have exercised for so long.

In light of some linguistic ambiguity, the basic purpose of the Clause, and the historical practice we have described, we conclude that the phrase "all vacancies" includes vacancies that come into existence while the Senate is in session.

V

The third question concerns the calculation of the length of the Senate's "recess." On December 17, 2011, the Senate by unanimous consent adopted a resolution to convene "*pro forma* session[s]" only, with "no business . . . transacted," on every Tuesday and Friday from December 20, 2011, through January 20, 2012. At the end of each *pro forma* session, the Senate would "adjourn until" the following *pro forma* session. During that period, the Senate convened and adjourned as agreed. It held *pro forma* sessions on December 20, 23, 27, and 30, and on January 3, 6, 10, 13, 17, and 20; and at the end of each *pro forma* session, it adjourned until the time and date of the next.

The President made the recess appointments before us on January 4, 2012, in between the January 3 and the January 6 *pro forma* sessions. We must determine the significance of these sessions — that is, whether, for purposes of the Clause, we should treat them as periods when the Senate was in session or as periods when it was in recess. If the former, the period between January 3 and January 6 was a 3-day recess, which is too short to trigger the President's recess-appointment power. If the latter, however, then the 3-day period was part of a much longer recess during which the President did have the power to make recess appointments.

The Solicitor General argues that we must treat the *pro forma* sessions as periods of recess. He says that these "sessions" were sessions in name only because the Senate was in recess as a *functional* matter. The Senate, he contends, remained in a single, unbroken recess from January 3, when the second session of the 112th Congress began by operation of the Twentieth Amendment, until January 23, when the Senate reconvened to do regular business.

In our view, however, the *pro forma* sessions count as sessions, not as periods of recess. We hold that, for purposes of the Recess Appointments Clause, the Senate is in session when it says it is, provided that, under its own rules, it retains the capacity to transact Senate business. The Senate met that standard here.

The standard we apply is consistent with the Constitution's broad delegation of authority to the Senate to determine how and when to conduct its business. The Constitution explicitly empowers the Senate to "determine the Rules of its Proceedings." Art. I, §5, cl. 2. And we have held that "all matters of method are open to the determination" of the Senate, as long as there is "a reasonable relation between the mode or method of proceeding established by the rule and the result which is sought to be attained" and the rule does not "ignore constitutional restraints or violate fundamental rights." *United States v. Ballin* (1892).

In addition, the Constitution provides the Senate with extensive control over its schedule. There are only limited exceptions. The Constitution thus gives the Senate wide latitude to determine whether and when to have a session, as well as how to conduct the session. This suggests that the Senate's determination about what constitutes a session should merit great respect . . . .

For these reasons, we conclude that we must give great weight to the Senate's own determination of when it is and when it is not in session. But our deference to the Senate cannot be absolute. When the Senate is without the *capacity* to act, under its own rules, it is not in session even if it so declares. In that circumstance, the Senate is not simply unlikely or unwilling to act upon nominations of the President. It is *unable* to do so. The purpose of the Clause is to ensure the continued functioning of the Federal Government while the Senate is unavailable. This purpose would count for little were we to treat the Senate as though it were in session even when it lacks the ability to provide its "advice and consent." Art. II, §2, cl. 2. Accordingly, we conclude that when the Senate declares that it is in session and possesses the capacity, under its own rules, to conduct business, it is in session for purposes of the Clause.

Applying this standard, we find that the *pro forma* sessions were sessions for purposes of the Clause. First, the Senate said it was in session. The Journal of the Senate and the Congressional Record indicate that the Senate convened for a series of twice-weekly "sessions" from December 20 through January 20. . . .

Second, the Senate's rules make clear that during its *pro forma* sessions, despite its resolution that it would conduct no business, the Senate retained the power to conduct business. During any *pro forma* session, the Senate could have conducted business simply by passing a unanimous consent agreement. The Senate in fact conducts much of its business through unanimous consent. Senate rules presume that a quorum is present unless a present Senator questions it. And when the Senate has a quorum, an agreement is unanimously passed if, upon its proposal, no present Senator objects. It is consequently unsurprising that the Senate *has* enacted legislation during *pro forma* sessions even when it has said that no business will be transacted. Indeed, the Senate passed a bill by unanimous consent during the second *pro forma* session after its December 17 adjournment. And that bill quickly became law.

By way of contrast, we do not see how the Senate could conduct business during a recess. It could terminate the recess and then, when in session, pass a bill. But in that case, of course, the Senate would no longer be in recess. It would be in session. And that is the crucial point. Senate rules make clear that, once in session, the Senate can act even if it has earlier said that it would not. . . .

The Recess Appointments Clause is not designed to overcome serious institutional friction. It simply provides a subsidiary method for appointing officials when the Senate is away during a recess. Here, as in other contexts, friction between the branches is an inevitable consequence of our constitutional structure. That structure foresees resolution not only through judicial interpretation and compromise among the branches but also by the ballot box.

VI

The Recess Appointments Clause responds to a structural difference between the Executive and Legislative Branches: The Executive Branch is perpetually in operation, while the Legislature only acts in intervals separated by recesses. The purpose of the Clause is to allow the Executive to continue operating while the Senate is unavailable. We believe that the Clause's text, standing alone, is ambiguous. It does not resolve whether the President may make appointments during intra-session recesses, or whether he may fill pre-recess vacancies. But the broader reading better serves the Clause's structural function. Moreover, that broader reading is reinforced by centuries of history, which we are hesitant to disturb. We thus hold that the Constitution empowers the President to fill any existing vacancy during any recess — intra-session or inter-session — of sufficient length.

Justice Scalia would render illegitimate thousands of recess appointments reaching all the way back to the founding era. More than that: Calling the Clause an "anachronism," he would basically read it out of the Constitution. He performs this act of judicial excision in the name of liberty. We fail to see how excising the Recess Appointments Clause preserves freedom. In fact, Alexander Hamilton observed in the very first Federalist Paper that "the vigour of government is essential to the security of liberty." The Federalist No. 1. And the Framers included the Recess Appointments Clause to preserve the "vigour of government" at times when an important organ of Government, the United States Senate, is in recess. Justice Scalia's interpretation of the Clause would defeat the power of the Clause to achieve that objective.

The foregoing discussion should refute Justice Scalia's claim that we have "embrace[d]" an "adverse-possession theory of executive power." Instead, as in all cases, we interpret the Constitution in light of its text, purposes, and "our whole experience" as a Nation. *Missouri v. Holland* (1920). And we look to the actual practice of Government to inform our interpretation.

Given our answer to the last question before us, we conclude that the Recess Appointments Clause does not give the President the constitutional authority to make the appointments here at issue. Because the Court of Appeals reached the same ultimate conclusion (though for reasons we reject), its judgment is affirmed.

It is so ordered.

Justice Scalia, with whom The Chief Justice, Justice Thomas, and Justice Alito join, concurring in the judgment. . . .

Today's Court agrees that the appointments were invalid, but for the far narrower reason that they were made during a 3-day break in the Senate's session. On its way to that result, the majority sweeps away the key textual limitations on the recess-appointment power. It holds, first, that the President can make appointments without the Senate's participation even during short breaks in the middle of the Senate's session, and second, that those appointments can fill offices that became vacant long before the break in which they were filled. The majority justifies those atextual results on an adverse-possession theory of executive authority: Presidents have long claimed the powers in question, and the Senate has not disputed those claims with sufficient vigor, so the Court should not "upset the compromises and working arrangements that the elected branches of Government themselves have reached."

The Court's decision transforms the recess-appointment power from a tool carefully designed to fill a narrow and specific need into a weapon to be wielded by future Presidents against future Senates. To reach that result, the majority casts aside the plain, original meaning of the constitutional text in deference to late-arising historical practices that are ambiguous at best. The majority's insistence on deferring to the Executive's untenably broad interpretation of the power is in clear conflict with our precedent and forebodes a diminution of this Court's role in controversies involving the separation of powers and the structure of government. I concur in the judgment only.

I. Our Responsibility

Today's majority disregards two overarching principles that ought to guide our consideration of the questions presented here.

First, the Constitution's core, government-structuring provisions are no less critical to preserving liberty than are the later adopted provisions of the Bill of Rights. Indeed, "[s]o convinced were the Framers that liberty of the person inheres in structure that at first they did not consider a Bill of Rights necessary." *Clinton v. City of New York* (1998) (KENNEDY, J., concurring). Those structural provisions reflect the founding generation's deep conviction that "checks and balances were the foundation of a structure of government that would protect liberty." *Bowsher v. Synar* (1986). It is for that reason that "the claims of individuals — not of Government departments — have been the principal source of judicial decisions concerning separation of powers and checks and balances." *Bond v. United States* (2011). Second and relatedly, when questions involving the Constitution's government-structuring provisions are presented in a justiciable case, it is the solemn responsibility of the Judicial Branch "'to say what the law is.'" *Zivotofsky v. Clinton* (2012) (quoting *Marbury v. Madison* (1803)). This Court does not defer to the other branches' resolution of such controversies; as Justice Kennedy has previously written, our role is in no way "lessened" because it might be said that "the two political branches are adjusting their own powers between themselves." *Clinton v. City of New York* (Kennedy, J., concurring). Since the separation of powers exists for the protection of individual liberty, its vitality "does not depend" on "whether 'the encroached-upon branch approves the encroachment.'" *Free Enterprise Fund v. Public Company Accounting Oversight Bd.* (2010). Rather, policing the "enduring structure" of constitutional government when the political branches fail to do so is "one of the most vital functions of this Court." *Public Citizen v. Department of Justice* (1989) (Kennedy, J., concurring). . . .

Likewise, when the charge is made that a practice "enhances the President's powers beyond" what the Constitution permits, "[i]t is no answer . . . to say that Congress surrendered its authority by its own hand." *Clinton* (Kennedy, J., concurring). "[O]ne Congress cannot yield up its own powers, much less those of other Congresses to follow. Abdication of responsibility is not part of the constitutional design." *Id.*

Of course, where a governmental practice has been open, widespread, and unchallenged since the early days of the Republic, the practice should guide our interpretation of an ambiguous constitutional provision. See, e.g., *Alden v. Maine* (1999); *Bowsher*; *Myers v. United States* (1926); *Youngstown Sheet & Tube Co. v.*

Sawyer (1952) (Frankfurter, J., concurring) (arguing that "a systematic, unbroken, executive practice, long pursued to the knowledge of the Congress and never before questioned" should inform interpretation of the "Executive Power" vested in the President) But "[p]ast practice does not, by itself, create power." *Medellín v. Texas* (2008) (quoting *Dames & Moore v. Regan* (1981)). That is a necessary corollary of the principle that the political branches cannot by agreement alter the constitutional structure. Plainly, then, a self-aggrandizing practice adopted by one branch well after the founding, often challenged, and never before blessed by this Court — in other words, the sort of practice on which the majority relies in this case — does not relieve us of our duty to interpret the Constitution in light of its text, structure, and original understanding.

Ignoring our more recent precedent in this area, which is extensive, the majority relies on *The Pocket Veto Case* (1929), for the proposition that when interpreting a constitutional provision "regulating the relationship between Congress and the President," we must defer to the settled practice of the political branches if the provision is "in any respect of doubtful meaning." The language the majority quotes from that case was pure dictum. The *Pocket Veto* Court had to decide whether a bill passed by the House and Senate and presented to the President less than 10 days before the adjournment of the first session of a particular Congress, but neither signed nor vetoed by the President, became a law. Most of the opinion analyzed that issue like any other legal question and concluded that treating the bill as a law would have been inconsistent with the text and structure of the Constitution. Only near the end of the opinion did the Court add that its conclusion was "confirmed" by longstanding Presidential practice in which Congress appeared to have acquiesced. We did not suggest that the case would have come out differently had the longstanding practice been otherwise.[5]

II. Intra-Session Breaks

The first question presented is whether "the Recess of the Senate," during which the President's recess-appointment power is active, is (a) the period between two of the Senate's formal sessions, or (b) any break in the Senate's proceedings. I would hold that "the Recess" is the gap between sessions and that the appointments at issue here are invalid because they undisputedly were made *during* the Senate's session. The Court's contrary conclusion — that "the Recess" includes "breaks in the midst of a session," — is inconsistent with the Constitution's text and structure, and it requires judicial fabrication of vague, unadministrable limits on the recess-appointment power (thus defined) that overstep the judicial role. And although the majority relies heavily on "historical practice," no practice worthy of our deference supports the majority's conclusion on this issue.

[5] The other cases cited by the majority in which we have afforded significant weight to historical practice, are consistent with the principles described above. Nearly all involved venerable and unchallenged practices, and constitutional provisions that were either deeply ambiguous or plainly supportive of the practice.

A. Plain Meaning

A sensible interpretation of the Recess Appointments Clause should start by recognizing that the Clause uses the term "Recess" in contradistinction to the term "Session." As Alexander Hamilton wrote: "The time within which the power is to operate 'during the recess of the Senate' and the duration of the appointments 'to the end of the next session' of that body, conspire to elucidate the sense of the provision." The Federalist No. 67.

In the founding era, the terms "recess" and "session" had well-understood meanings in the marking-out of legislative time. The life of each elected Congress typically consisted (as it still does) of two or more formal sessions separated by adjournments "*sine die*," that is, without a specified return date. The period *between* two sessions was known as "the recess." As one scholar has thoroughly demonstrated, "in government practice the phrase 'the Recess' *always* referred to the gap between sessions." Natelson, The Origins and Meaning of "Vacancies that May Happen During the Recess" in the Constitution's Recess Appointments Clause, 37 Harv. J.L. & Pub. Pol'y 199, 213 (2014) (hereinafter Natelson). By contrast, other provisions of the Constitution use the verb "adjourn" rather than "recess" to refer to the commencement of breaks *during* a formal legislative session. See, *e.g.*, Art. I, §5, cl. 1; *id.*, §5, cl. 4.

To be sure, in colloquial usage both words, "recess" and "session," could take on alternative, less precise meanings. A session could include any short period when a legislature's members were "assembled for business," and a recess could refer to any brief "suspension" of legislative "business." 2 N. Webster, American Dictionary of the English Language (1828). So the Continental Congress could complain of the noise from passing carriages disrupting its "daily Session," 29 Journals of the Continental Congress 1774-1789 (1785), and the House could "take a recess" from 4 o'clock to 6 o'clock, Journal of the House of Representatives, 17th Cong., 2d Sess. (1823). But as even the majority acknowledges, the Constitution's use of "the word 'the' in '*the* [R]ecess'" tends to suggest "that the phrase refers to the single break separating formal sessions."

More importantly, neither the Solicitor General nor the majority argues that the Clause uses "session" in its loose, colloquial sense. And if "the next Session" denotes a *formal* session, then "the Recess" must mean the break *between* formal sessions. As every commentator on the Clause until the 20th century seems to have understood, the "Recess" and the "Session" to which the Clause refers are mutually exclusive, alternating states.

Besides being linguistically unsound, the majority's reading yields the strange result that an appointment made during a short break near the beginning of one official session will not terminate until the end of the *following* official session, enabling the appointment to last for up to two years . . . .

One way to avoid the linguistic incongruity of the majority's reading would be to read both "the Recess" and "the next Session" colloquially, so that the recess-appointment power would be activated during any temporary suspension of Senate proceedings, but appointments made pursuant to that power would last only until the beginning of the next suspension (which would end the next colloquial session).

See, *e.g.*, Rappaport, The Original Meaning of the Recess Appointments Clause, 52 UCLA L. Rev. 1487, 1569 (2005) (hereinafter Rappaport, Original Meaning). That approach would be more linguistically defensible than the majority's. But it would not cure the most fundamental problem with giving "Recess" its colloquial, rather than its formal, meaning: Doing so leaves the recess-appointment power without a textually grounded principle limiting the time of its exercise.

The dictionary definitions of "recess" on which the majority relies provide no such principle. On the contrary, they make clear that in colloquial usage, a recess could include *any* suspension of legislative business, no matter how short. Webster even provides a stark illustration: "[T]he house of representatives had a *recess* of half an hour." The notion that the Constitution empowers the President to make unilateral appointments every time the Senate takes a half-hour lunch break is so absurd as to be self-refuting. But that, in the majority's view, is what the text authorizes.

The boundlessness of the colloquial reading of "the Recess" thus refutes the majority's assertion that the Clause's "purpose" of "ensur[ing] the continued functioning of the Federal Government" demands that it apply to intra-session breaks as well as inter-session recesses. The majority disregards another self-evident purpose of the Clause: to preserve the Senate's role in the appointment process — which the founding generation regarded as a critical protection against "despotism," *Freytag v. Commissioner* (1991) — by clearly delineating the times when the President can appoint officers without the Senate's consent. Today's decision seriously undercuts *that* purpose. In doing so, it demonstrates the folly of interpreting constitutional provisions designed to establish "a structure of government that would protect liberty," *Bowsher*, on the narrow-minded assumption that their only purpose is to make the government run as efficiently as possible. "Convenience and efficiency," we have repeatedly recognized, "are not the primary objectives" of our constitutional framework. *Free Enterprise Fund.*

Relatedly, the majority contends that the Clause's supposed purpose of keeping the wheels of government turning demands that we interpret the Clause to maintain its relevance in light of the "new circumstance" of the Senate's taking an increasing number of intra-session breaks that exceed three days. Even if I accepted the canard that courts can alter the Constitution's meaning to accommodate changed circumstances, I would be hard pressed to see the relevance of that notion here. The rise of intra-session adjournments has occurred in tandem with the development of modern forms of communication and transportation that mean the Senate "is always available" to consider nominations, even when its Members are temporarily dispersed for an intra-session break. Tr. of Oral Arg. (Ginsburg, J.). The Recess Appointments Clause therefore is, or rather, should be, an anachronism — "essentially an historic relic, something whose original purpose has disappeared." *Id.* (Kagan, J.). The need it was designed to fill no longer exists, and its only remaining use is the ignoble one of enabling the President to circumvent the Senate's role in the appointment process. That does not justify "read[ing] it out of the Constitution" and, contra the majority, I would not do so; but neither would I distort the Clause's original meaning, as the majority does, to ensure a prominent role for the recess-appointment power in an era when its influence is far more pernicious than beneficial.

To avoid the absurd results that follow from its colloquial reading of "the Recess," the majority is forced to declare that some intra-session breaks — though undisputedly within the phrase's colloquial meaning — are simply "too short to trigger the Recess Appointments Clause." But it identifies no textual basis whatsoever for limiting the length of "the Recess," nor does it point to any clear standard for determining how short is too short. It is inconceivable that the Framers would have left the circumstances in which the President could exercise such a significant and potentially dangerous power so utterly indeterminate. Other structural provisions of the Constitution that turn on duration are quite specific: Neither House can adjourn "for more than three days" without the other's consent. Art. I, §5, cl. 4. The President must return a passed bill to Congress "within ten Days (Sundays excepted)," lest it become a law. *Id.*, §7, cl. 2. Yet on the majority's view, when the first Senate considered taking a 1-month break, a 3-day weekend, or a half-hour siesta, it had no way of knowing whether the President would be constitutionally authorized to appoint officers in its absence. And any officers appointed in those circumstances would have served under a cloud, unable to determine with any degree of confidence whether their appointments were valid.[6]

Fumbling for some textually grounded standard, the majority seizes on the Adjournments Clause, which bars either House from adjourning for more than three days without the other's consent. *Id.*, §5, cl. 4. According to the majority, that clause establishes that a 3-day break is *always* "too short" to trigger the Recess Appointments Clause. It goes without saying that nothing in the constitutional text supports that disposition. If (as the majority concludes) "the Recess" means a recess in the colloquial sense, then it necessarily includes breaks shorter than three days. And the fact that the Constitution includes a 3-day limit in one clause but omits it from the other weighs strongly against finding such a limit to be implicit in the clause in which it does not appear. In all events, the dramatically different contexts in which the two clauses operate make importing the 3-day limit from the Adjournments Clause into the Recess Appointments Clause "both arbitrary and mistaken." Rappaport, Original Meaning.

And what about breaks longer than three days? The majority says that a break of four to nine days is "presumptively too short" but that the presumption may be rebutted in an "unusual circumstance," such as a "national catastrophe . . . that renders the Senate unavailable but calls for an urgent response." The majority

---

[6] The majority insists that "the most likely reason the Framers did not place a textual floor underneath the word 'recess' is that they did not foresee the *need* for one" because they did not anticipate that intra-session breaks "would become lengthier and more significant than inter-session ones." The majority's logic escapes me. The Framers' supposed failure to anticipate "length[y]" intra-session breaks might explain why (as I maintain) they did not bother to authorize recess appointments during intra-session breaks at all; but it cannot explain why (as the majority holds) they would have enacted a text that authorizes appointments during *all* intra-session breaks — even the short ones the majority says they *did* anticipate — without placing a temporal limitation on that power.

must hope that the *in terrorem* effect of its "presumptively too short" pronouncement will deter future Presidents from making any recess appointments during 4- to 9-day breaks and thus save us from the absurd spectacle of unelected judges evaluating (after an evidentiary hearing?) whether an alleged "catastrophe" was sufficiently "urgent" to trigger the recess-appointment power. The majority also says that "political opposition in the Senate would not qualify as an unusual circumstance." So if the Senate should refuse to confirm a nominee whom the President considers highly qualified; or even if it should refuse to confirm any nominee for an office, thinking the office better left vacant for the time being; the President's power would not be triggered during a 4- to 9-day break, no matter how "urgent" the President's perceived need for the officer's assistance. (The majority protests that this "should go without saying — except that Justice Scalia compels us to say it," seemingly forgetting that the appointments at issue in this very case were justified on those grounds and that the Solicitor General has asked us to view the recess-appointment power as a "safety valve" against Senatorial "intransigence." Tr. of Oral Arg.) . . .

If the Constitution's text empowers the President to make appointments during any break in the Senate's proceedings, by what right does the majority subject the President's exercise of that power to vague, court-crafted limitations with no textual basis? The majority claims its temporal guideposts are informed by executive practice, but a President's self-restraint cannot "bind his successors by diminishing their powers." *Free Enterprise Fund.*

An interpretation that calls for this kind of judicial adventurism cannot be correct. Indeed, if the Clause really did use "Recess" in its colloquial sense, then there would be no "judicially discoverable and manageable standard for resolving" whether a particular break was long enough to trigger the recess-appointment power, making that a nonjusticiable political question. *Zivotofsky.*

B. Historical Practice

For the foregoing reasons, the Constitution's text and structure unambiguously refute the majority's freewheeling interpretation of "the Recess." It is not plausible that the Constitution uses that term in a sense that authorizes the President to make unilateral appointments during *any* break in Senate proceedings, subject only to hazy, atextual limits crafted by this Court centuries after ratification. The majority, however, insists that history "offers strong support" for its interpretation. The historical practice of the political branches is, of course, irrelevant when the Constitution is clear. But even if the Constitution were thought ambiguous on this point, history does not support the majority's interpretation . . . .

Intra-session recess appointments were virtually unheard of for the first 130 years of the Republic, were deemed unconstitutional by the first Attorney General to address them, were not openly defended by the Executive until 1921, were not made in significant numbers until after World War II, and have been repeatedly criticized as unconstitutional by Senators of both parties. It is astonishing for the majority to assert that this history lends "strong support," to its interpretation of the Recess Appointments Clause. And the majority's contention that recent executive practice in this area merits deference because the Senate has not done more to oppose it is utterly divorced from our precedent. "The structural interests protected by the Appointments Clause are not those of any one branch of Government but of the entire Republic," *Freytag*, and the Senate could not give away those protections even if it wanted to.

Moreover, the majority's insistence that the Senate gainsay an executive practice "as a body" in order to prevent the Executive from acquiring power by adverse possession, will systematically favor the expansion of executive power at the expense of Congress. In any controversy between the political branches over a separation-of-powers question, staking out a position and defending it over time is far easier for the Executive Branch than for the Legislative Branch. All Presidents have a high interest in expanding the powers of their office, since the more power the President can wield, the more effectively he can implement his political agenda; whereas individual Senators may have little interest in opposing Presidential encroachment on legislative prerogatives, especially when the encroacher is a President who is the leader of their own party. And when the President wants to assert a power and establish a precedent, he faces neither the collective-action problems nor the procedural inertia inherent in the legislative process. The majority's methodology thus all but guarantees the continuing aggrandizement of the Executive Branch.

III. Pre-Recess Vacancies

The second question presented is whether vacancies that "happen during the Recess of the Senate," which the President is empowered to fill with recess appointments, are (a) vacancies that *arise* during the recess, or (b) all vacancies that *exist* during the recess, regardless of when they arose. I would hold that the recess-appointment power is limited to vacancies that arise during the recess in which they are filled, and I would hold that the appointments at issue here — which undisputedly filled pre-recess vacancies — are invalid for that reason as well as for the reason that they were made during the session. The Court's contrary conclusion is inconsistent with the Constitution's text and structure, and it further undermines the balance the Framers struck between Presidential and Senatorial power. Historical practice also fails to support the majority's conclusion on this issue.

A. Plain Meaning

As the majority concedes, "the most natural meaning of 'happens' as applied to a 'vacancy' . . . is that the vacancy 'happens' when it initially occurs." The majority adds that this meaning is most natural "to a modern ear," but it fails to show that founding-era ears heard it differently. "Happen" meant then, as it does now, "[t]o fall out; to chance; to come to pass." 1 Johnson, Dictionary of the English Language 913. Thus, a vacancy that *happened* during the Recess was most reasonably understood as one that *arose* during the recess. It was, of course, possible in certain contexts for the word "happen" to mean "happen to be" rather than "happen to occur," as in the idiom "it so happens." But that meaning is not at all natural when the subject is a vacancy, a state of affairs that comes into existence at a particular moment in time.[7]

In any event, no reasonable reader would have understood the Recess Appointments Clause to use the word "happen" in the majority's "happen to be" sense, and thus to empower the President to fill all vacancies that might *exist* during a recess, regardless of when they arose. For one thing, the Clause's language would have been a surpassingly odd way of giving the President that power. The Clause easily could have been written to convey that meaning clearly: It could have referred to "all Vacancies that may exist during the Recess," or it could have omitted the qualifying phrase entirely and simply authorized the President to "fill up all Vacancies during the Recess." Given those readily available alternative phrasings, the reasonable reader might have wondered, why would any intelligent drafter intending the majority's reading have inserted the words "that may happen" — words that, as the majority admits, make the majority's desired reading awkward and unnatural, and that must be effectively read out of the Clause to achieve that reading?

For another thing, the majority's reading not only strains the Clause's language but distorts its constitutional role, which was meant to be subordinate. As Hamilton explained, appointment with the advice and consent of the Senate was to be "the general mode of appointing officers of the United States." The Federalist No. 67. The Senate's check on the President's appointment power was seen as vital because "'manipulation of official appointments' had long been one of the American revolutionary generation's greatest grievances against executive power." *Freytag*. The unilateral power conferred on the President by the Recess Appointments Clause was therefore understood to be "nothing more than a supplement" to the "general method" of advice and consent. The Federalist No. 67.

If, however, the Clause had allowed the President to fill *all* pre-existing vacancies during the recess by granting commissions that would last throughout the following session, it would have been impossible to regard it — as the Framers plainly did — as a mere codicil to the Constitution's principal, power-sharing scheme for filling federal offices. On the majority's reading, the President would have had no need *ever* to seek the Senate's advice and consent for his appointments: Whenever there was a fair prospect of the Senate's rejecting his preferred nominee, the President could have appointed that individual unilaterally during the recess, allowed the appointment to expire at the end of the next session, renewed the appointment the following day, and so on *ad infinitum*. (Circumvention would have been especially easy if, as the majority also concludes, the President was authorized to make such appointments during any intra-session break of more than a few days.) It is unthinkable that such an obvious means for the Executive to expand its power would have been overlooked during the ratification debates. The original

[7] Despite initially admitting that the text "does not naturally favor" its interpretation, the majority halfheartedly suggests that the "happen to be" reading may be admissible when the subject, like "vacancy," denotes a "continuing state." That suggestion distorts ordinary English usage. It is indeed natural to say that an ongoing activity or event, like a war, a parade, or a financial crisis, is "happening" for as long as it continues. But the same is not true when the subject is a settled state of affairs, like death, marriage, or vacancy, all of which "happen" when they come into being.

understanding of the Clause was consistent with what the majority concedes is the text's "most natural meaning." . . .

More fundamentally . . . the majority [is] mistaken to say that the Constitution's "'substantial purpose'" is to "'keep . . . offices filled.'" The Constitution is not a road map for maximally efficient government, but a system of "carefully crafted restraints" designed to "protect the people from the improvident exercise of power." *INS v. Chadha* (1983). . . . [T]he majority's *argumentum ab inconvenienti* thus proves far too much. There are many circumstances other than a vacancy that can produce similar inconveniences if they arise late in the session: For example, a natural disaster might occur to which the Executive cannot respond effectively without a supplemental appropriation. But in those circumstances, the Constitution would not permit the President to appropriate funds himself. See Art. I, §9, cl. 7. Congress must either anticipate such eventualities or be prepared to be haled back into session. The troublesome need to do so is not a bug to be fixed by this Court, but a calculated feature of the constitutional framework. As we have recognized, while the Constitution's government-structuring provisions can seem "clumsy" and "inefficient," they reflect "hard choices . . . consciously made by men who had lived under a form of government that permitted arbitrary governmental acts to go unchecked." *Chadha.*

B. Historical Practice

For the reasons just given, it is clear that the Constitution authorizes the President to fill unilaterally only those vacancies that arise during a recess, not every vacancy that happens to exist during a recess. Again, however, the majority says "[h]istorical practice" requires the broader interpretation. And again the majority is mistaken. Even if the Constitution were wrongly thought to be ambiguous on this point, a fair recounting of the relevant history does not support the majority's interpretation. . . . In sum: Washington's and Adams' Attorneys General read the Constitution to restrict recess appointments to vacancies arising during the recess, and there is no evidence that any of the first four Presidents consciously departed from that reading. The contrary reading was first defended by an executive official in 1823, was vehemently rejected by the Senate in 1863, was vigorously resisted by legislation in place from 1863 until 1940, and is arguably inconsistent with legislation in place from 1940 to the present. The Solicitor General has identified only about 100 appointments that have ever been made under the broader reading, and while it seems likely that a good deal more have been made in the last few decades, there is good reason to doubt that many were made before 1940 (since the appointees could not have been compensated). I can conceive of no sane constitutional theory under which this evidence of "historical practice" — which is actually evidence of a long-simmering inter-branch conflict — would require us to defer to the views of the Executive Branch.

IV. Conclusion

What the majority needs to sustain its judgment is an ambiguous text and a clear historical practice. What it has is a clear text and an at-best-ambiguous historical practice. Even if the Executive could accumulate power through adverse possession by engaging in a *consistent* and *unchallenged* practice over a long period of time, the oft-disputed practices at issue here would not meet that standard. Nor have those practices created any justifiable expectations that could be disappointed by enforcing the Constitution's original meaning. There is thus no ground for the majority's deference to the unconstitutional recess-appointment practices of the Executive Branch.

The majority replaces the Constitution's text with a new set of judge-made rules to govern recess appointments. Henceforth, the Senate can avoid triggering the President's now-vast recess-appointment power by the odd contrivance of never adjourning for more than three days without holding a *pro forma* session at which it is understood that no business will be conducted. How this new regime will work in practice remains to be seen. Perhaps it will reduce the prevalence of recess appointments. But perhaps not: Members of the President's party in Congress may be able to prevent the Senate from holding *pro forma* sessions with the necessary frequency, and if the House and Senate disagree, the President may be able to adjourn both "to such Time as he shall think proper." U.S. Const., Art. II, §3. In any event, the limitation upon the President's appointment power is there not for the benefit of the Senate, but for the protection of the people; it should not be dependent on Senate action for its existence.

The real tragedy of today's decision is not simply the abolition of the Constitution's limits on the recess-appointment power and the substitution of a novel framework invented by this Court. It is the damage done to our separation-of-powers jurisprudence more generally. It is not every day that we encounter a proper case or controversy requiring interpretation of the Constitution's structural provisions. Most of the time, the interpretation of those provisions is left to the political branches — which, in deciding how much respect to afford the constitutional text, often take their cues from this Court. We should therefore take every opportunity to affirm the primacy of the Constitution's enduring principles over the politics of the moment. Our failure to do so today will resonate well beyond the particular dispute at hand. Sad, but true: The Court's embrace of the adverse-possession theory of executive power (a characterization the majority resists but does not refute) will be cited in diverse contexts, including those presently unimagined, and will have the effect of aggrandizing the Presidency beyond its constitutional bounds and undermining respect for the separation of powers.

I concur in the judgment only.

ASSIGNMENT 3

B. THE LEGISLATIVE VETO

Although the next case concerns the rather narrow issue of "one-house legislative vetoes" of presidential acts, it also provides another example of the disagreement about how such separation of powers issues are to be addressed. Justice White's opinion has become well known for its application of a "functional" approach, as compared with the more "formalist" analysis of Chief Justice Burger. The case also has broader implications since, as mentioned in the case itself, there are numerous laws that were enacted with some form of a "legislative veto."

STUDY GUIDE

- Can you identify what makes the "formalist" approach formalist, and the "functionalist" approach functionalist?
- Does the majority follow Justice Black's or Justice Jackson's framework from *The Steel Seizure Case*? Which approach does Justice White's dissent follow?
- Justice White's dissent suggests that the line-item veto is an appropriate response to the rise of the administrative state. What does his opinion suggest about the impact that executive branch agencies — "veritable fourth branch of the Government" — have had on the separation of powers?

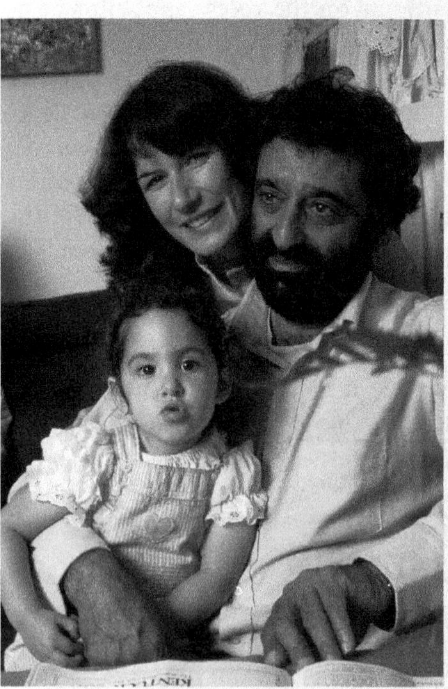

After the case, Jagdish Rai Chadha (above, with his wife and daughter) became a citizen of the United States and settled in a San Francisco suburb with his wife and two daughters.

INS v. Chadha

462 U.S. 919 (1983)

CHIEF JUSTICE BURGER delivered the opinion of the Court.

[This case] presents a challenge to the constitutionality of the provision in 244(c)(2) of the Immigration and Nationality Act, authorizing one House of Congress, by resolution, to invalidate the decision of the Executive Branch, pursuant to authority delegated by Congress to the Attorney General of the United States, to allow a particular deportable alien to remain in the United States. . . .

We turn now to the question whether action of one House of Congress under 244(c)(2) violates strictures of the Constitution. We begin, of course, with the presumption that the challenged statute is valid. Its wisdom is not the concern of the courts; if a challenged action does not violate the Constitution, it must be sustained. . . . By the same token, the fact that a given law or procedure is efficient, convenient, and useful in facilitating functions of government, standing alone, will not save it if it is contrary to the Constitution. Convenience and efficiency are not the primary objectives — or the hallmarks — of democratic government and our inquiry is sharpened rather than blunted by the fact that congressional veto provisions are appearing with increasing frequency in statutes which delegate authority to executive and independent agencies: "Since 1932, when the first veto provision was enacted into law, 295 congressional veto-type procedures have been inserted in 196 different statutes as follows: from 1932 to 1939, five statutes were affected; from 1940-49, nineteen statutes; between 1950-59, thirty-four statutes; and from 1960-69, forty-nine. From the year 1970 through 1975, at least one hundred sixty-three such provisions were included in eighty-nine laws." Abourezk, The Congressional Veto: A Contemporary Response to Executive Encroachment on Legislative Prerogatives, 52 Ind. L. Rev. 323, 324 (1977). . . .

The Constitution sought to divide the delegated powers of the new Federal Government into three defined categories, Legislative, Executive, and Judicial, to assure, as nearly as possible, that each branch of government would confine itself to its assigned responsibility. The hydraulic pressure inherent within each of the separate Branches to exceed the outer limits of its power, even to accomplish desirable objectives, must be resisted.

Although not "hermetically" sealed from one another, the powers delegated to the three Branches are functionally identifiable. When any Branch acts, it is presumptively exercising the power the Constitution has delegated to it. When the Executive acts, he presumptively acts in an executive or administrative capacity as defined in Art. II. And when, as here, one House of Congress purports to act, it is presumptively acting within its assigned sphere.

The legislative character of the one-House veto in these cases is confirmed by the character of the congressional action it supplants. Neither the House of Representatives nor the Senate contends that, absent the veto provision in 244(c)(2), either of them, or both of them acting together, could effectively require the Attorney General to deport an alien once the Attorney General, in the exercise of legislatively delegated authority,[8] had determined the alien should remain in the United States. Without the challenged provision in 244(c)(2), this could have been achieved, if at all, only by legislation requiring deportation. . . .

The nature of the decision implemented by the one-House veto in these cases further manifests its legislative character. After long experience with the clumsy, time-consuming private bill procedure, Congress made a deliberate choice to delegate to the Executive Branch, and specifically to the Attorney General, the authority to allow deportable aliens to remain in this country in certain specified circumstances. It is not disputed that this choice to delegate authority is precisely the kind of decision that can be implemented only in accordance with the procedures set out in Art. I. Disagreement with the Attorney General's decision on Chadha's deportation — that is, Congress' decision to deport Chadha — no less than Congress' original choice to delegate to the Attorney General the authority to make that decision, involves determinations of policy that Congress can implement in only one way; bicameral passage followed by presentment to the President. Congress must abide by its delegation of authority until that delegation is legislatively altered or revoked.

Finally, we see that when the Framers intended to authorize either House of Congress to act alone and outside of its prescribed bicameral legislative role, they narrowly and precisely defined the procedure for such action. There are four provisions in the Constitution, explicit and unambiguous, by which one House may act alone with the unreviewable force of law, not subject to the President's veto:

1. The House of Representatives alone was given the power to initiate impeachments. Art. I, §2, cl. 5;
2. The Senate alone was given the power to conduct trials following impeachment on charges initiated by the House and to convict following trial. Art. I, §3, cl. 6;
3. The Senate alone was given final unreviewable power to approve or to disapprove Presidential appointments. Art. II, §2, cl. 2;
4. The Senate alone was given unreviewable power to ratify treaties negotiated by the President. Art. II, §2, cl. 2.

---

[8] Congress protests that affirming the Court of Appeals in these cases will sanction "lawmaking by the Attorney General. . . . Why is the Attorney General exempt from submitting his proposed changes in the law to the full bicameral process?" . . . When the Attorney General performs his duties pursuant to §244, he does not exercise "legislative" power. . . . [T]he Attorney General acts in his presumptively Art. II capacity when he administers the Immigration and Nationality Act. Executive action under legislatively delegated authority that might resemble "legislative" action in some respects is not subject to the approval of both Houses of Congress and the President for the reason that the Constitution does not so require. That kind of Executive action is always subject to check by the terms of the legislation that authorized it; and if that authority is exceeded, it is open to judicial review, as well as the power of Congress to modify or revoke the authority entirely. A one-House veto is clearly legislative in both character and effect, and is not so checked; the need for the check provided by Art. I, §§1, 7, is therefore clear. Congress' authority to delegate portions of its power to administrative agencies provides no support for the argument that Congress can constitutionally control administration of the laws by way of a congressional veto.

Clearly, when the Draftsmen sought to confer special powers on one House, independent of the other House, or of the President, they did so in explicit, unambiguous terms. These carefully defined exceptions from presentment and bicameralism underscore the difference between the legislative functions of Congress and other unilateral but important and binding one-House acts provided for in the Constitution. These exceptions are narrow, explicit, and separately justified; none of them authorize the action challenged here. On the contrary, they provide further support for the conclusion that congressional authority is not to be implied and for the conclusion that the veto provided for in 244(c)(2) is not authorized by the constitutional design of the powers of the Legislative Branch.

Since it is clear that the action by the House under 244(c)(2) was not within any of the express constitutional exceptions authorizing one House to act alone, and equally clear that it was an exercise of legislative power, that action was subject to the standards prescribed in Art. I. The bicameral requirement, the Presentment Clauses, the President's veto, and Congress' power to override a veto were intended to erect enduring checks on each Branch and to protect the people from the improvident exercise of power by mandating certain prescribed steps. To preserve those checks, and maintain the separation of powers, the carefully defined limits on the power of each Branch must not be eroded. To accomplish what has been attempted by one House of Congress in this case requires action in conformity with the express procedures of the Constitution's prescription for legislative action: passage by a majority of both Houses and presentment to the President.

The veto authorized by 244(c)(2) doubtless has been in many respects a convenient shortcut; the "sharing" with the Executive by Congress of its authority over aliens in this manner is, on its face, an appealing compromise. In purely practical terms, it is obviously easier for action to be taken by one House without submission to the President; but it is crystal clear from the records of the Convention, contemporaneous writings and debates, that the Framers ranked other values higher than efficiency. The records of the Convention and debates in the states preceding ratification underscore the common desire to define and limit the exercise of the newly created federal powers affecting the states and the people. There is unmistakable expression of a determination that legislation by the national Congress be a step-by-step, deliberate and deliberative process.

The choices we discern as having been made in the Constitutional Convention impose burdens on governmental processes that often seem clumsy, inefficient, even unworkable, but those hard choices were consciously made by men who had lived under a form of government that permitted arbitrary governmental acts to go unchecked. There is no support in the Constitution or decisions of this Court for the proposition that the cumbersomeness and delays often encountered in complying with explicit constitutional standards may be avoided, either by the Congress or by the President. See Youngstown Sheet & Tube Co. v. Sawyer (1952). With all the obvious flaws of delay, untidiness, and potential for abuse, we have not yet found a better way to preserve freedom than by making the exercise of power subject to the carefully crafted restraints spelled out in the Constitution. . . .

Justice White, dissenting.

Today the Court not only invalidates 244(c)(2) of the Immigration and Nationality Act, but also sounds the death knell for nearly 200 other statutory provisions in which Congress has reserved a "legislative veto." For this reason, the Court's decision is of surpassing importance. And it is for this reason that the Court would have been well advised to decide the cases, if possible, on the narrower grounds of separation of powers, leaving for full consideration the constitutionality of other congressional review statutes operating on such varied matters as war powers and agency rulemaking, some of which concern the independent regulatory agencies.

The prominence of the legislative veto mechanism in our contemporary political system and its importance to Congress can hardly be overstated. It has become a central means by which Congress secures the accountability of executive and independent agencies. Without the legislative veto, Congress is faced with a Hobson's choice: either to refrain from delegating the necessary authority, leaving itself with a hopeless task of writing laws with the requisite specificity to cover endless special circumstances across the entire policy landscape, or in the alternative, to abdicate its law-making function to the Executive Branch and independent agencies. To choose the former leaves major national problems unresolved; to opt for the latter risks unaccountable policymaking by those not elected to fill that role. Accordingly, over the past five decades, the legislative veto has been placed in nearly 200 statutes. The device is known in every field of governmental concern: reorganization, budgets, foreign affairs, war powers, and regulation of trade, safety, energy, the environment, and the economy. . . .

The history of the legislative veto also makes clear that it has not been a sword with which Congress has struck out to aggrandize itself at the expense of the other branches — the concerns of Madison and Hamilton. Rather, the veto has been a means of defense, a reservation of ultimate authority necessary if Congress is to fulfill its designated role under Art. I as the Nation's lawmaker. While the President has often objected to particular legislative vetoes, generally those left in the hands of congressional Committees, the Executive has more often agreed to legislative review as the price for a broad delegation of authority. To be sure, the President may have preferred unrestricted power, but that could be precisely why Congress thought it essential to retain a check on the exercise of delegated authority.

For all these reasons, the apparent sweep of the Court's decision today is regretable. The Court's Art. I analysis appears to invalidate all legislative vetoes irrespective of form or subject. Because the legislative veto is commonly found as a check upon rulemaking by administrative agencies and upon broad-based policy decisions of the Executive Branch, it is particularly unfortunate that the Court reaches its decision in cases involving the exercise of a veto over deportation decisions regarding particular individuals. Courts should always be wary of striking statutes as unconstitutional; to strike an entire class of statutes based on consideration of a somewhat atypical and more readily indictable exemplar of the class is irresponsible.

If the legislative veto were as plainly unconstitutional as the Court strives to suggest, its broad ruling today would be more comprehensible. But, the constitutionality of the legislative veto is anything but clear-cut. The issue divides scholars, courts, Attorneys General, and the two other branches of the National Government. If the veto devices so flagrantly disregarded the requirements of Art. I as the Court today suggests, I find it incomprehensible that Congress, whose Members are bound by oath to uphold the Constitution, would have placed these mechanisms in nearly 200 separate laws over a period of 50 years.

The reality of the situation is that the constitutional question posed today is one of immense difficulty over which the Executive and Legislative Branches — as well as scholars and judges — have understandably disagreed. That disagreement stems from the silence of the Constitution on the precise question: The Constitution does not directly authorize or prohibit the legislative veto. Thus, our task should be to determine whether the legislative veto is consistent with the purposes of Art. I and the principles of separation of powers which are reflected in that Article and throughout the Constitution.

We should not find the lack of a specific constitutional authorization for the legislative veto surprising, and I would not infer disapproval of the mechanism from its absence. From the summer of 1787 to the present the Government of the United States has become an endeavor far beyond the contemplation of the Framers. Only within the last half century has the complexity and size of the Federal Government's responsibilities grown so greatly that the Congress must rely on the legislative veto as the most effective if not the only means to insure its role as the Nation's lawmaker. But the wisdom of the Framers was to anticipate that the Nation would grow and new problems of governance would require different solutions. Accordingly, our Federal Government was intentionally chartered with the flexibility to respond to contemporary needs without losing sight of fundamental democratic principles. This was the spirit in which Justice Jackson penned his influential concurrence in the *Steel Seizure Case*: "The actual art of governing under our Constitution does not and cannot conform to judicial definitions of the power of any of its branches based on isolated clauses or even single Articles torn from context. While the Constitution diffuses power the better to secure liberty, it also contemplates that practice will integrate the dispersed powers into a workable government." *Youngstown Sheet & Tube Co. v. Sawyer* (1952). This is the perspective from which we should approach the novel constitutional questions presented by the legislative veto.

In my view, neither Art. I of the Constitution nor the doctrine of separation of powers is violated by this mechanism by which our elected Representatives preserve their voice in the governance of the Nation.

The Court holds that the disapproval of a suspension of deportation by the resolution of one House of Congress is an exercise of legislative power without compliance with the prerequisites for lawmaking set forth in Art. I of the Constitution. Specifically, the Court maintains that the provisions of 244(c)(2) are inconsistent with the requirement of bicameral approval, implicit in Art. I, §1, and the requirement that all bills and resolutions that require the concurrence of both Houses be presented to the President. . . .

The power to exercise a legislative veto is not the power to write new law without bicameral approval or Presidential consideration. The veto must be authorized by statute and may only negative what an Executive department or independent agency has proposed. On its face, the legislative veto no more allows one House of Congress to make law than does the Presidential veto confer such power upon the President. . . .

The Court's holding today that all legislative-type action must be enacted through the lawmaking process ignores that legislative authority is routinely delegated to the Executive Branch, to the independent regulatory agencies, and to private individuals and groups. *FTC v. Ruberoid Co.* (1952) (Jackson, J. dissenting) ("The rise of administrative bodies probably has been the most significant legal trend of the last century. . . . They have become a veritable fourth branch of the Government, which has deranged our three-branch legal theories. . . ."). This Court's decisions sanctioning such delegations make clear that Art. I does not require all action with the effect of legislation to be passed as a law. Theoretically, agencies and officials were asked only to "fill up the details," and the rule was that "Congress cannot delegate any part of its legislative power except under the limitation of a prescribed standard." . . . In practice, however, restrictions on the scope of the power that could be delegated diminished and all but disappeared. In only two instances did the Court find an unconstitutional delegation. *Panama Refining Co. v. Ryan* (1935); *A. L. A. Schechter Poultry Corp. v. United States* (1935). . . .

The wisdom and the constitutionality of these broad delegations are matters that still have not been put to rest. But for present purposes, these cases establish that by virtue of congressional delegation, legislative power can be exercised by independent agencies and Executive departments without the passage of new legislation. For some time, the sheer amount of law — the substantive rules that regulate private conduct and direct the operation of government — made by the agencies has far outnumbered the lawmaking engaged in by Congress through the traditional process. There is no question but that agency rulemaking is lawmaking in any functional or realistic sense of the term. . . .

If Congress may delegate lawmaking power to independent and Executive agencies, it is most difficult to understand Art. I as prohibiting Congress from also reserving a check on legislative power for itself. Absent the veto, the agencies receiving delegations of legislative or quasi-legislative power may issue regulations having the force of law without bicameral approval and without the President's signature. It is thus not apparent why the reservation of a veto over the exercise of that legislative power must be subject to a more exacting test. In both cases, it is enough that the initial statutory authorizations comply with the Art. I requirements. . . .

The legislative veto provision does not "preven[t] the Executive Branch from accomplishing its constitutionally assigned functions." First, it is clear that the Executive Branch has no "constitutionally assigned" function of suspending the deportation of aliens. . . . Nor can it be said that the inherent function of the Executive Branch in executing the law is involved. The *Steel Seizure Case* resolved that the Art. II mandate for the President to execute the law is a directive to enforce the law which Congress has written. . . . Here, 244 grants the Executive only a qualified suspension authority, and it is only that authority which the President is constitutionally authorized to execute.

Moreover, the Court believes that the legislative veto we consider today is best characterized as an exercise of legislative or quasi-legislative authority. Under this characterization, the practice does not, even on the surface, constitute an infringement of executive or judicial prerogative. The Attorney General's suspension of deportation is equivalent to a proposal for legislation. The nature of the Attorney General's role as recommendatory is not altered because 244 provides for congressional action through disapproval rather than by ratification. In comparison to private bills, which must be initiated in the Congress and which allow a Presidential veto to be overriden by a two-thirds majority in both Houses of Congress, 244 augments rather than reduces the Executive Branch's authority. So understood, congressional review does not undermine, as the Court of Appeals thought, the "weight and dignity" that attends the decisions of the Executive Branch. . . .

I do not suggest that all legislative vetoes are necessarily consistent with separation-of-powers principles. A legislative check on an inherently executive function, for example, that of initiating prosecutions, poses an entirely different question. But the legislative veto device here — and in many other settings — is far from an instance of legislative tyranny over the Executive. It is a necessary check on the unavoidably expanding power of the agencies, both Executive and independent, as they engage in exercising authority delegated by Congress.

I regret that I am in disagreement with my colleagues on the fundamental questions that these cases present. But even more I regret the destructive scope of the Court's holding. It reflects a profoundly different conception of the Constitution than that held by the courts which sanctioned the modern administrative state. Today's decision strikes down in one fell swoop provisions in more laws enacted by Congress than the Court has cumulatively invalidated in its history. I fear it will now be more difficult to "insur[e] that the fundamental policy decisions in our society will be made not by an appointed official but by the body immediately responsible to the people," *Arizona v. California* (1963) (Harlan, J., dissenting in part). I must dissent.

Justice Rehnquist, with whom Justice White joins, dissenting.

A severability clause creates a presumption that Congress intended the valid portion of the statute to remain in force when one part is found to be invalid. *Carter v. Carter Coal Co.* (1936); *Champlin Refining Co. v. Corporation Comm'n of Oklahoma* (1932). A severability clause does not, however, conclusively resolve the issue. "[T]he determination, in the end, is reached by" asking "[w]hat was the intent of the lawmakers," *Carter*, and "will rarely turn on the presence or absence of such a clause." *United States v. Jackson* (1968). Because I believe that Congress did not intend the one-House veto provision of §244(c)(2) to be severable, I dissent. . . . By severing §244(c)(2), the Court permits suspension of deportation in a class of cases where Congress never stated that suspension was appropriate. I do not believe we should expand the statute in this way without some clear indication that Congress intended such an expansion. . . . Over the years, Congress consistently rejected requests from the Executive for complete discretion in this area. Congress always insisted on retaining ultimate control, whether by concurrent resolution, as in the 1948 Act, or by one-House veto, as in the present Act. Congress has never indicated that it would be willing to permit suspensions of deportation unless it could retain some sort of veto.

C. PRESIDENTIAL PRIVILEGES AND IMMUNITIES

ASSIGNMENT 4

Most of the doctrines discussed in this chapter concern the separation of powers between the legislative and executive branches. In this section we consider doctrines governing presidential immunity from lawsuits, which involves the executive's relationship to the judicial branch. In Chapters 8 and 9, we will consider some additional doctrines that involve the judiciary and its relationship to both the legislative and executive branches.

1. Executive Privilege

United States v. Nixon played an important role in the Watergate scandal involving President Richard Nixon, which was discussed earlier in this chapter, before *Morrison v. Olson*. There is no reason to believe that President Nixon had advance knowledge of the Watergate break-in. However, subsequent investigations by special prosecutors and by a committee of the House determined that Nixon had knowledge of and participated in the scheme to pay off the Watergate burglars. The most damning evidence consisted of conversations between the President and his subordinates in the Oval Office. They were recorded by a system that Nixon, like several previous Presidents, had secretly used to record conversations for historical purposes. The existence of these recordings was disclosed to the House investigation committee. Archibald Cox, who was appointed as special prosecutor by the attorney general, issued a subpoena to the President to produce them along with certain documents. The President resisted their production, asserting "executive privilege."

In the next case, the Supreme Court passed upon the constitutionality of subjecting the President to the judicial process by means of a subpoena. In compliance with the Court's ruling, the President turned over the tapes in late July 1974. One of the recordings, which became known as "the smoking gun" tape, confirmed the President's knowledge of the payments to the Watergate burglars. When the content of this tape was disclosed, several senior Republican congressmen privately urged the President to resign, which he did on August 9, 1974. Most observers believe that, without the evidence provided by the tapes, President Nixon might well have survived the controversy and served out his term.

STUDY GUIDE

- *United States v. Nixon* begins by considering the "justiciability" of this lawsuit, a topic we will return to in Chapter 8. If the special prosecutor was truly a subordinate of the President, was this issue justiciable?
- Why shouldn't the chief executive be able to overrule his subordinate without judicial interference? (Of course a congressional subpoena would raise different issues.)
- Did the Court override legitimate concerns about the role of the judiciary vis-à-vis the President to reach the "correct" result? How much of our assessment of this case comes from knowing what the subpoenaed tapes eventually revealed, or from dislike of Richard Nixon, or both?
- Presumably the President knew the information contained in the tapes, yet he turned them over anyway. Does this say anything about the *authority* of the Supreme Court as compared with the *power* of the executive branch?
- The case was obviously a "loss" for Richard Nixon himself. Was it also a "loss" for the presidency?

United States v. Nixon

418 U.S. 683 (1974)

MR. CHIEF JUSTICE BURGER delivered the opinion of the Court. . . .

On March 1, 1974, a grand jury of the United States District Court for the District of Columbia returned an indictment charging seven named individuals[9] with various offenses, including conspiracy to defraud the United States and to obstruct justice. Although he was not designated as such in the indictment, the grand jury named the President, among others, as an unindicted coconspirator. On April 18, 1974, upon motion of the Special Prosecutor, a subpoena *duces tecum* [a request to submit certain records — EDS.] was issued . . . to the President by the United States District Court and made returnable on May 2, 1974. This subpoena required the production, in advance of the September 9 trial date, of certain tapes, memoranda, papers, transcripts, or other writings relating to certain precisely identified meetings between the President and others. . . . On April 30, the President publicly released edited transcripts of 43 conversations; portions of 20 conversations subject to subpoena in the present case were included. On May 1,

[9] The seven defendants were John N. Mitchell [the attorney general], H.R. Haldeman, John D. Ehrlichman, Charles W. Colson, Robert C. Mardian, Kenneth W. Parkinson, and Gordon Strachan. Each had occupied either a position of responsibility on the White House staff or a position with the Committee for the Re-election of the President. Colson entered a guilty plea on another charge and is no longer a defendant.

1974, the President's counsel filed . . . a motion to quash the subpoena [on the grounds of executive privilege against disclosure of confidential communications.] . . .

II. Justiciability

In the District Court, the President's counsel argued that the court lacked jurisdiction to issue the subpoena because the matter was an intra-branch dispute between a subordinate and superior officer of the Executive Branch and hence not subject to judicial resolution. That argument has been renewed in this Court with emphasis on the contention that the dispute does not present a "case" or "controversy" which can be adjudicated in the federal courts. The President's counsel argues that the federal courts should not intrude into areas committed to the other branches of Government. He views the present dispute as essentially a "jurisdictional" dispute within the Executive Branch which he analogizes to a dispute between two congressional committees. Since the Executive Branch has exclusive authority and absolute discretion to decide whether to prosecute a case, it is contended that a President's decision is final in determining what evidence is to be used in a given criminal case. Although his counsel concedes that the President has delegated certain specific powers to the Special Prosecutor, he has not "waived nor delegated to the Special Prosecutor the President's duty to claim privilege as to all materials . . . which fall within the President's inherent authority to refuse to disclose to any executive officer." The Special Prosecutor's demand for the items therefore presents, in the view of the President's counsel, a political question . . . since it involves a "textually demonstrable" grant of power under Art. II. . . .

Our starting point is the nature of the proceeding for which the evidence is sought — here a pending criminal prosecution. It is a judicial proceeding in a federal court alleging violation of federal laws and is brought in the name of the United States as sovereign. Under the authority of Art. II, §2, Congress has vested in the Attorney General the power to conduct the criminal litigation of the United States Government. It has also vested in him the power to appoint subordinate officers to assist him in the discharge of his duties. Acting pursuant to those statutes, the Attorney General has delegated the authority to represent the United States in these particular matters to a Special Prosecutor with unique authority and tenure. The regulation gives the Special Prosecutor explicit power to contest the invocation of executive privilege in the process of seeking evidence deemed relevant to the performance of these specially delegated duties.

So long as this regulation is extant it has the force of law. . . . [I]t is theoretically possible for the Attorney General to amend or revoke the regulation defining the Special Prosecutor's authority. But he has not done so. So long as this regulation remains in force the Executive Branch is bound by it, and indeed the United States as the sovereign composed of the three branches is bound to respect and to enforce it. . . .

IV. The Claim of Privilege

A

[W]e turn to the claim that the subpoena should be quashed because it demands "confidential conversations between a President and his close advisors that it would be inconsistent with the public interest to produce." The first contention is a broad claim that the separation of powers doctrine precludes judicial review of a President's claim of privilege. The second contention is that if he does not prevail on the claim of absolute privilege, the court should hold as a matter of constitutional law that the privilege prevails over the subpoena *duces tecum*. . . .

B

In support of his claim of absolute privilege, the President's counsel urges two grounds, one of which is common to all governments and one of which is peculiar to our system of separation of powers. The first ground is the valid need for protection of communications between high Government officials and those who advise and assist them in the performance of their manifold duties; the importance of this confidentiality is too plain to require further discussion. Human experience teaches that those who expect public dissemination of their remarks may well temper candor with a concern for appearances and for their own interests to the detriment of the decisionmaking process.[10] Whatever the nature of the privilege of confidentiality of Presidential communications in the exercise of Art. II powers, the privilege can be said to derive from the supremacy of each branch within its own assigned area of constitutional duties. Certain powers and privileges flow from the nature of enumerated powers;[11] the protection of the confidentiality of Presidential communications has similar constitutional underpinnings.

The second ground asserted by the President's counsel in support of the claim of absolute privilege rests on the doctrine of separation of powers. Here it is argued that the independence of the Executive Branch within its own sphere, Humphrey's Executor v. United States (1935), insulates a President from a judicial subpoena in an ongoing criminal prosecution, and thereby protects confidential Presidential communications.

---

[10] There is nothing novel about governmental confidentiality. The meetings of the Constitutional Convention in 1787 were conducted in complete privacy. Moreover, all records of those meetings were sealed for more than 30 years after the Convention. Most of the Framers acknowledged that without secrecy no constitution of the kind that was developed could have been written.

[11] The Special Prosecutor argues that there is no provision in the Constitution for a Presidential privilege as to the President's communications corresponding to the privilege of Members of Congress under the Speech or Debate Clause. [Article I, Section 6, Clause 1, provides that Senators and Representatives shall "not be questioned in any other Place" for "any Speech or Debate in either House." — Eds.] But the silence of the Constitution on this score is not dispositive. "The rule of constitutional interpretation announced in *McCulloch v. Maryland*, that that which was reasonably appropriate and relevant to the exercise of a granted power was to be considered as accompanying the grant, has been so universally applied that it suffices merely to state it."

However, neither the doctrine of separation of powers, nor the need for confidentiality of high-level communications, without more, can sustain an absolute, unqualified Presidential privilege of immunity from judicial process under all circumstances. The President's need for complete candor and objectivity from advisers calls for great deference from the courts. However, when the privilege depends solely on the broad, undifferentiated claim of public interest in the confidentiality of such conversations, a confrontation with other values arises. Absent a claim of need to protect military, diplomatic, or sensitive national security secrets, we find it difficult to accept the argument that even the very important interest in confidentiality of Presidential communications is significantly diminished by production of such material for in camera inspection with all the protection that a district court will be obliged to provide.

The impediment that an absolute, unqualified privilege would place in the way of the primary constitutional duty of the Judicial Branch to do justice in criminal prosecutions would plainly conflict with the function of the courts under Art. III. In designing the structure of our Government and dividing and allocating the sovereign power among three co-equal branches, the Framers of the Constitution sought to provide a comprehensive system, but the separate powers were not intended to operate with absolute independence. . . .

C

Since we conclude that the legitimate needs of the judicial process may outweigh Presidential privilege, it is necessary to resolve those competing interests in a manner that preserves the essential functions of each branch. The right and indeed the duty to resolve that question does not free the Judiciary from according high respect to the representations made on behalf of the President.

The expectation of a President to the confidentiality of his conversations and correspondence, like the claim of confidentiality of judicial deliberations, for example, has all the values to which we accord deference for the privacy of all citizens and, added to those values, is the necessity for protection of the public interest in candid, objective, and even blunt or harsh opinions in Presidential decisionmaking. A President and those who assist him must be free to explore alternatives in the process of shaping policies and making decisions and to do so in a way many would be unwilling to express except privately. These are the considerations justifying a presumptive privilege for Presidential communications. The privilege is fundamental to the operation of Government and inextricably rooted in the separation of powers under the Constitution. . . .

But this presumptive privilege must be considered in light of our historic commitment to the rule of law. . . . We have elected to employ an adversary system of criminal justice in which the parties contest all issues before a court of law. The need to develop all relevant facts in the adversary system is both fundamental and comprehensive. The ends of criminal justice would be defeated if judgments were to be founded on a partial or speculative presentation of the facts. The very integrity of the judicial system and public confidence in the system depend on full disclosure of all the facts, within the framework of the rules of evidence. To ensure that justice is done, it is imperative to the function of courts that compulsory process be available for the production of evidence needed either by the prosecution or by the defense. . . .

In this case the President . . . does not place his claim of privilege on the ground they are military or diplomatic secrets. As to these areas of Art. II duties the courts have traditionally shown the utmost deference to Presidential responsibilities. In *C. & S. Air Lines v. Waterman S. S. Corp.* (1948), dealing with Presidential authority involving foreign policy considerations, the Court said:

> The President, both as Commander-in-Chief and as the Nation's organ for foreign affairs, has available intelligence services whose reports are not and ought not to be published to the world. It would be intolerable that courts, without the relevant information, should review and perhaps nullify actions of the Executive taken on information properly held secret.

. . .

No case of the Court, however, has extended this high degree of deference to a President's generalized interest in confidentiality. Nowhere in the Constitution, as we have noted earlier, is there any explicit reference to a privilege of confidentiality, yet to the extent this interest relates to the effective discharge of a President's powers, it is constitutionally based.

The right to the production of all evidence at a criminal trial similarly has constitutional dimensions. The Sixth Amendment explicitly confers upon every defendant in a criminal trial the right "to be confronted with the witnesses against him" and "to have compulsory process for obtaining witnesses in his favor." Moreover, the Fifth Amendment also guarantees that no person shall be deprived of liberty without due process of law. It is the manifest duty of the courts to vindicate those guarantees, and to accomplish that it is essential that all relevant and admissible evidence be produced.

In this case we must weigh the importance of the general privilege of confidentiality of Presidential communications in performance of the President's responsibilities against the inroads of such a privilege on the fair administration of criminal justice.[12] The interest in preserving confidentiality is weighty indeed and entitled to great respect. However, we cannot conclude that advisers will be moved to temper the candor of their remarks by the infrequent occasions of disclosure because of the possibility that such conversations will be called for in the context of a criminal prosecution.

---

[12] We are not here concerned with the balance between the President's generalized interest in confidentiality and the need for relevant evidence in civil litigation, nor with that between the confidentiality interest and congressional demands for information, nor with the President's interest in preserving state secrets. We address only the conflict between the President's assertion of a generalized privilege of confidentiality and the constitutional need for relevant evidence in criminal trials.

President Nixon (far right) in the Oval Office with aides (left to right) H.R. Haldeman, Dwight Chapin, and John D. Ehrlichman. Haldeman and Ehrlichman were among the seven defendants in United States v. Nixon.

On the other hand, the allowance of the privilege to withhold evidence that is demonstrably relevant in a criminal trial would cut deeply into the guarantee of due process of law and gravely impair the basic function of the courts. . . . Without access to specific facts a criminal prosecution may be totally frustrated. The President's broad interest in confidentiality of communications will not be vitiated by disclosure of a limited number of conversations preliminarily shown to have some bearing on the pending criminal cases.

We conclude that when the ground for asserting privilege as to subpoenaed materials sought for use in a criminal trial is based only on the generalized interest in confidentiality, it cannot prevail over the fundamental demands of due process of law in the fair administration of criminal justice. The generalized assertion of privilege must yield to the demonstrated, specific need for evidence in a pending criminal trial. . . .

MR. JUSTICE REHNQUIST took no part in the consideration or decision of these cases. [Rehnquist, the junior Justice at the time, had previously served in the Nixon administration. — EDS.]

2. Presidential Immunity from Civil Suits

United States v. Nixon raised the issue of whether presidential privilege could be used to quash a court's request for confidential information. *Nixon v. Fitzgerald* and *Clinton v. Jones* concern whether presidential immunity can be used to dismiss civil suits in the judicial branch. The former case concerns alleged acts that were committed within the official capacity of the office, while the latter case concerns the legality of alleged acts that were outside the President's official duties.

STUDY GUIDE

- Is there a compelling reason to distinguish between liability for acts committed within the President's official duties and acts committed outside those duties?
- Does immunity from civil liability literally place the President "above the law," as claimed by the dissent? Is there any other process to which the President is still subject?
- What is the difference between how Justice Powell's majority opinion and Chief Justice Burger's concurring opinion reach the same result? Can you see why one of those approaches might be considered "functional" (practical) and the other "formal" (more reliant on structure and the meaning of the text)?

Nixon v. Fitzgerald

457 U.S. 731 (1982)

JUSTICE POWELL delivered the opinion of the Court.

The plaintiff in this lawsuit seeks relief in civil damages from a former President of the United States. The claim rests on actions allegedly taken in the former President's official capacity during his tenure in office. The issue before us is the scope of the immunity possessed by the President of the United States.

In January 1970 the respondent A. Ernest Fitzgerald lost his job as a management analyst with the Department of the Air Force. Fitzgerald's dismissal occurred in the context of a departmental reorganization and reduction in force, in which his job was eliminated. In announcing the reorganization, the Air Force characterized the action as taken to promote economy and efficiency in the Armed Forces.

Respondent's discharge attracted unusual attention in Congress and in the press. Fitzgerald had attained national prominence approximately one year earlier, during the waning months of the Presidency of Lyndon B. Johnson. On November 13, 1968, Fitzgerald appeared before the Subcommittee on Economy in Government of the Joint Economic Committee of the United States Congress. To the evident embarrassment of his superiors in the Department of Defense, Fitzgerald testified that cost-overruns on the C-5A transport plane could approximate $2 billion. He also revealed that unexpected technical difficulties had arisen during the development of the aircraft. . . .

Fitzgerald's proposed reassignment encountered resistance within the administration. In an internal memorandum of January 20, 1970, White House aide Alexander Butterfield reported to Haldeman that "Fitzgerald is no doubt a top-notch cost expert, but he must be given very low marks in loyalty; and after all, loyalty is the name of the game." Butterfield therefore recommended that "[w]e should let him bleed, for a while at least." There is no evidence of White House efforts to reemploy Fitzgerald subsequent to the Butterfield memorandum. . . .

At a news conference on January 31, 1973, . . . President [Nixon] . . . took the opportunity to assume personal responsibility for Fitzgerald's dismissal:

> I was totally aware that Mr. Fitzgerald would be fired or discharged or asked to resign. I approved it and Mr. Seamans must have been talking to someone who had discussed the matter with me. No, this was not a case of some person down the line deciding he should go. It was a decision that was submitted to me. I made it and I stick by it.[13]

A day later, however, the White House press office issued a retraction of the President's statement. According to a press spokesman, the President had confused Fitzgerald with another former executive employee. . . . Fitzgerald filed a suit for damages in the United States District Court. . . .

This case now presents the claim that the President of the United States is shielded by absolute immunity from civil damages liability. In the case of the President the inquiries into history and policy, though mandated independently by our cases, tend to converge. Because the Presidency did not exist through most of the development of common law, any historical analysis must draw its evidence primarily from our constitutional heritage and structure. Historical inquiry thus merges almost at its inception with the kind of "public policy" analysis appropriately undertaken by a federal court. This inquiry involves policies and principles that may be considered implicit in the nature of the President's office in a system structured to achieve effective government under a constitutionally mandated separation of powers.

Here a former President asserts his immunity from civil damages claims of two kinds. He stands named as a defendant in a direct action under the Constitution and in two statutory actions under federal laws of general applicability. In neither case has Congress taken express legislative action to subject the President to civil liability for his official acts.

Applying the principles of our cases to claims of this kind, we hold that petitioner, as a former President of the United States, is entitled to absolute immunity from damages liability predicated on his official acts. We consider this immunity a functionally mandated incident of the President's unique office, rooted in the constitutional tradition of the separation of powers and supported by our history. Justice Story's analysis remains persuasive:

> There are . . . incidental powers, belonging to the executive department, which are necessarily implied from the nature of the functions, which are confided to it. Among these, must necessarily be included the power to perform them. . . . The president cannot, therefore, be liable to arrest, imprisonment, or detention, while he is in the discharge of the duties of his office; and for this purpose his person must be deemed, in civil cases at least, to possess an official inviolability.

J. Story, Commentaries on the Constitution of the United States (1833).

The President occupies a unique position in the constitutional scheme. Article II, §1, of the Constitution provides that "[t]he executive Power shall be vested in a President of the United States. . . ." This grant of authority

[13] A few hours after the press conference, Mr. Nixon repeated privately to Presidential aide Charles Colson that he had ordered Fitzgerald's firing. (recorded conversation of Jan. 31, 1973).

establishes the President as the chief constitutional officer of the Executive Branch, entrusted with supervisory and policy responsibilities of utmost discretion and sensitivity. These include the enforcement of federal law — it is the President who is charged constitutionally to "take Care that the Laws be faithfully executed"; the conduct of foreign affairs — a realm in which the Court has recognized that "[i]t would be intolerable that courts, without the relevant information, should review and perhaps nullify actions of the Executive taken on information properly held secret"; and management of the Executive Branch — a task for which "imperative reasons requir[e] an unrestricted power [in the President] to remove the most important of his subordinates in their most important duties."

In arguing that the President is entitled only to qualified immunity, the respondent relies on cases in which we have recognized immunity of this scope for governors and cabinet officers. We find these cases to be inapposite. The President's unique status under the Constitution distinguishes him from other executive officials.

Because of the singular importance of the President's duties, diversion of his energies by concern with private lawsuits would raise unique risks to the effective functioning of government. As is the case with prosecutors and judges — for whom absolute immunity now is established — a President must concern himself with matters likely to "arouse the most intense feelings." Yet, as our decisions have recognized, it is in precisely such cases that there exists the greatest public interest in providing an official "the maximum ability to deal fearlessly and impartially with" the duties of his office. This concern is compelling where the officeholder must make the most sensitive and far-reaching decisions entrusted to any official under our constitutional system. Nor can the sheer prominence of the President's office be ignored. In view of the visibility of his office and the effect of his actions on countless people, the President would be an easily identifiable target for suits for civil damages. Cognizance of this personal vulnerability frequently could distract a President from his public duties, to the detriment of not only the President and his office but also the Nation that the Presidency was designed to serve.

Courts traditionally have recognized the President's constitutional responsibilities and status as factors counseling judicial deference and restraint. For example, while courts generally have looked to the common law to determine the scope of an official's evidentiary privilege, we have recognized that the Presidential privilege is "rooted in the separation of powers under the Constitution." *United States v. Nixon* (1974). It is settled law that the separation-of-powers doctrine does not bar every exercise of jurisdiction over the President of the United States. *See, e.g., United States v. Nixon* . . . , *United States v. Burr* (Cir. Ct. Va. 1807); *cf. Youngstown Sheet & Tube Co. v. Sawyer* (1952). But our cases also have established that a court, before exercising jurisdiction, must balance the constitutional weight of the interest to be served against the dangers of intrusion on the authority and functions of the Executive Branch. When judicial action is needed to serve broad public interests — as when the Court acts, not in derogation of the separation of powers, but to maintain their proper balance, cf. *Youngstown*, or to vindicate the public interest in an ongoing criminal prosecution, *see United States v. Nixon* — the exercise of jurisdiction has been held warranted. In the case of this merely private suit for damages based on a President's official acts, we hold it is not.

A rule of absolute immunity for the President will not leave the Nation without sufficient protection against misconduct on the part of the Chief Executive. There remains the constitutional remedy of impeachment. In addition, there are formal and informal checks on Presidential action that do not apply with equal force to other executive officials. The President is subjected to constant scrutiny by the press. Vigilant oversight by Congress also may serve to deter Presidential abuses of office, as well as to make credible the threat of impeachment. Other incentives to avoid misconduct may include a desire to earn reelection, the need to maintain prestige as an element of Presidential influence, and a President's traditional concern for his historical stature.

The existence of alternative remedies and deterrents establishes that absolute immunity will not place the President "above the law."[14] For the President, as for judges and prosecutors, absolute immunity merely precludes a particular private remedy for alleged misconduct in order to advance compelling public ends. . . .

Chief Justice Burger, concurring. . . .

I join the Court's opinion, but I write separately to underscore that the Presidential immunity derives from and is mandated by the constitutional doctrine of separation of powers. Indeed, it has been taken for granted for nearly two centuries. In reaching this conclusion we do well to bear in mind that the focus must not be simply on the matter of judging individual conduct in a fact-bound setting; rather, in those familiar terms of John Marshall, it is a Constitution we are expounding. Constitutional adjudication often bears unpalatable fruit. But the needs of a system of government sometimes must outweigh the right of individuals to collect damages. . . .

It is one thing to say that a President must produce evidence relevant to a criminal case, as in *U.S. v. Burr*[15] and *United States v. Nixon*, and quite another

---

[14] [Footnote 41] The dissenting opinions argue that our decision places the President "above the law." This contention is rhetorically chilling but wholly unjustified. The remedy of impeachment demonstrates that the President remains accountable under law for his misdeeds in office. This case involves only a damages remedy. Although the President is not liable in civil damages for official misbehavior, that does not lift him "above" the law. The dissents do not suggest that a judge is "above" the law when he enters a judgment for which he cannot be held answerable in civil damages; or a prosecutor is above the law when he files an indictment; or a Congressman is above the law when he engages in legislative speech or debate. It is simply error to characterize an official as "above the law" because a particular remedy is not available against him.

[15] [Footnote 1. Aaron Burr, who was indicted for treason, asked President Jefferson to testify, and provide the courts with documents that could exonerate him. John Marshall, who presided over the trial as Circuit Justice, explained that "in no case of this kind would a court be required to proceed against the president as against an ordinary individual." Nonetheless, he ruled that Jefferson could be subpoenaed. The President provided some — but not all of the requested documents — citing his executive privilege. There is a lot of history between these three figures: in the presidential election of 1800, when Jefferson and Burr received the same number of electoral votes for President, Alexander Hamilton broke a logjam in the House, which needed to decide the matter, by throwing his support

to say a President can be held for civil damages for dismissing a federal employee. If the dismissal is wrongful the employee can be reinstated with backpay, as was done here.

The immunity of a President from civil suits is not simply a doctrine derived from this Court's interpretation of common law or public policy. Absolute immunity for a President for acts within the official duties of the Chief Executive is either to be found in the constitutional separation of powers or it does not exist. The Court today holds that the Constitution mandates such immunity and I agree.

The essential purpose of the separation of powers is to allow for independent functioning of each coequal branch of government within its assigned sphere of responsibility, free from risk of control, interference, or intimidation by other branches. Even prior to the adoption of our Constitution, as well as after, judicial review of legislative action was recognized in some instances as necessary to maintain the proper checks and balances. However, the Judiciary always must be hesitant to probe into the elements of Presidential decisionmaking, just as other branches should be hesitant to probe into judicial decisionmaking. Such judicial intervention is not to be tolerated absent imperative constitutional necessity. The Court's opinion correctly observes that judicial intrusion through private damages actions improperly impinges on and hence interferes with the independence that is imperative to the functioning of the office of a President.

Exposing a President to civil damages actions for official acts within the scope of the Executive authority would inevitably subject Presidential actions to undue judicial scrutiny as well as subject the President to harassment. The enormous range and impact of Presidential decisions — far beyond that of any one Member of Congress — inescapably means that many persons will consider themselves aggrieved by such acts. Absent absolute immunity, every person who feels aggrieved would be free to bring a suit for damages, and each suit — especially those that proceed on the merits — would involve some judicial questioning of Presidential acts, including the reasons for the decision, how it was arrived at, the information on which it was based, and who supplied the information. Such scrutiny of day-to-day decisions of the Executive Branch would be bound to occur if civil damages actions were made available to private individuals. Although the individual who claims wrongful conduct may indeed have sustained some injury, the need to prevent large-scale invasion of the Executive function by the Judiciary far outweighs the need to vindicate the private claims. . . .

Judicial intervention would also inevitably inhibit the processes of Executive Branch decisionmaking and impede the functioning of the Office of the President. The need to defend damages suits would have the serious effect of diverting the attention of a President from his executive duties since defending a lawsuit today — even a lawsuit ultimately found to be frivolous — often requires significant expenditures of time and money, as many former public officials have learned to their sorrow. This very case graphically illustrates the point. When litigation processes

---

to his nemesis Jefferson (believing Jefferson, for all his faults, was a patriot; Burr not so much); Burr later shot and killed Hamilton in a duel; Marshall, who was also Jefferson's nemesis — and a distant cousin — ultimately found Burr was not guilty of treason due to a lack of evidence. — EDS.]

are not tightly controlled — and often they are not — they can be and are used as mechanisms of extortion. Ultimate vindication on the merits does not repair the damage.

I fully agree that the constitutional concept of separation of independent coequal powers dictates that a President be immune from civil damages actions based on acts within the scope of Executive authority while in office. Far from placing a President above the law, the Court's holding places a President on essentially the same footing with judges and other officials whose absolute immunity we have recognized.

JUSTICE WHITE, with whom JUSTICE BRENNAN, JUSTICE MARSHALL, and JUSTICE BLACKMUN join, dissenting. . . .

Attaching absolute immunity to the Office of the President, rather than to particular activities that the President might perform, places the President above the law. It is a reversion to the old notion that the King can do no wrong. Until now, this concept had survived in this country only in the form of sovereign immunity. That doctrine forecloses suit against the Government itself and against Government officials, but only when the suit against the latter actually seeks relief against the sovereign. Suit against an officer, however, may be maintained where it seeks specific relief against him for conduct contrary to his statutory authority or to the Constitution. Now, however, the Court clothes the Office of the President with sovereign immunity, placing it beyond the law. . . . [T]he judgment in this case has few, if any, indicia of a judicial decision; it is almost wholly a policy choice, a choice that is without substantial support and that in all events is ambiguous in its reach and import. . . .

Taken at face value, the Court's position that as a matter of constitutional law the President is absolutely immune should mean that he is immune not only from damages actions but also from suits for injunctive relief, criminal prosecutions and, indeed, from any kind of judicial process. But there is no contention that the President is immune from criminal prosecution in the courts under the criminal laws enacted by Congress or by the States for that matter. Nor would such a claim be credible. The Constitution itself provides that impeachment shall not bar "Indictment, Trial, Judgment and Punishment, according to Law." Art. I, §3, cl. 7. Similarly, our cases indicate that immunity from damages actions carries no protection from criminal prosecution.

Neither can there be a serious claim that the separation-of-powers doctrine insulates Presidential action from judicial review or insulates the President from judicial process. No argument is made here that the President, whatever his liability for money damages, is not subject to the courts' injunctive powers. See, e.g., *Youngstown Sheet & Tube Co.* (1952); *Korematsu v. United States* (1944). . . . It is the rule, not the exception, that executive actions — including those taken at the immediate direction of the President — are subject to judicial review. Regardless of the possibility of money damages against the President, then, the constitutionality of the President's actions or their legality under the applicable statutes can and will be subject to review. . . .

Nor can private damages actions be distinguished on the ground that such claims would involve the President personally in the litigation in a way not necessitated by suits seeking declaratory or injunctive relief against certain Presidential actions. The President has been held to be subject to judicial process at least since 1807. [Justice White references Aaron Burr's subpoena of President Jefferson, addressed earlier in Chief Justice Burger's concurring opinion. — EDS.] . . . [N]either subjecting Presidential actions to a judicial determination of their constitutionality, nor subjecting the President to judicial process violates the separation-of-powers doctrine. Similarly, neither has been held to be sufficiently intrusive to justify a judicially declared rule of immunity. With respect to intrusion by the judicial process itself on executive functions, subjecting the President to private claims for money damages involves no more than this. If there is a separation-of-powers problem here, it must be found in the nature of the remedy and not in the process involved. . . .

The possibility of liability may, in some circumstances, distract officials from the performance of their duties and influence the performance of those duties in ways adverse to the public interest. But when this "public policy" argument in favor of absolute immunity is cast in these broad terms, it applies to all officers, both state and federal: All officers should perform their responsibilities without regard to those personal interests threatened by the possibility of a lawsuit. Inevitably, this reduces the public policy argument to nothing more than an expression of judicial inclination as to which officers should be encouraged to perform their functions with "vigor," although with less care.

The Court's response, until today, to this problem has been to apply the argument to individual functions, not offices, and to evaluate the effect of liability on governmental decisionmaking within that function, in light of the substantive ends that are to be encouraged or discouraged. In this case, therefore, the Court should examine the functions implicated by the causes of action at issue here and the effect of potential liability on the performance of those functions. . . .

Personnel decisions of the sort involved in this case are emphatically not a constitutionally assigned Presidential function that will tolerate no interference by either of the other two branches of Government. . . .

Absolute immunity is appropriate when the threat of liability may bias the decisionmaker in ways that are adverse to the public interest. But as the various regulations and statutes protecting civil servants from arbitrary executive action illustrate, this is an area in which the public interest is demonstrably on the side of encouraging less "vigor" and more "caution" on the part of decisionmakers. That is, the very steps that Congress has taken to assure that executive employees will be able freely to testify in Congress and to assure that they will not be subject to arbitrary adverse actions indicate that those policy arguments that have elsewhere justified absolute immunity are not applicable here. Absolute immunity would be nothing more than a judicial declaration of policy that directly contradicts the policy of protecting civil servants reflected in the statutes and regulations. . . .

The majority may be correct in its conclusion that "[a] rule of absolute immunity . . . will not leave the Nation without sufficient protection against misconduct on the part of the Chief Executive." Such a rule will, however, leave Mr. Fitzgerald without an adequate remedy for the harms that he may have suffered. More importantly, it will leave future plaintiffs without a remedy, regardless of the substantiality of their claims. The remedies in which the Court finds comfort were never designed to afford relief for individual harms. Rather, they were designed as political safety valves. Politics and history, however, are not the domain of the courts; the courts exist to assure each individual that he, as an individual, has enforceable rights that he may pursue to achieve a peaceful redress of his legitimate grievances.

I find it ironic, as well as tragic, that the Court would so casually discard its own role of assuring "the right of every individual to claim the protection of the laws," *Marbury v. Madison*, in the name of protecting the principle of separation of powers. Accordingly, I dissent.

JUSTICE BLACKMUN, with whom JUSTICE BRENNAN and JUSTICE MARSHALL join, dissenting.

I join JUSTICE WHITE's dissent. For me, the Court leaves unanswered his unanswerable argument that no man, not even the President of the United States, is absolutely and fully above the law. Until today, I had thought this principle was the foundation of our national jurisprudence. It now appears that it is not.

Nor can I understand the Court's holding that the absolute immunity of the President is compelled by separation-of-powers concerns, when the Court at the same time expressly leaves open, the possibility that the President nevertheless may be fully subject to congressionally created forms of liability. These two concepts, it seems to me, cannot coexist. . . .

STUDY GUIDE

- In *Clinton v. Jones* is President Clinton's claim of immunity weaker than that of President Nixon in *Nixon v. Fitzgerald*? In what respect is it stronger?
- On what basis does the *Jones* Court distinguish *Fitzgerald*?
- Is the Court's pragmatic or "functionalist" analysis of the impact of allowing civil suits while the President holds office confirmed or contradicted by subsequent events?
- Is there any alternative to the Court striking this sort of balance in a separation-of-powers case such as this?
- Justice Stevens found the "the risk that [his] decision will generate a large volume of politically motivated harassing and frivolous litigation" was not "serious." In light of the numerous lawsuits brought against President Trump, was this prediction well founded?
- *Clinton v. Jones* only concerned civil suits in federal court. Can the President be sued in state court during his term in office? Would such a suit be consistent with the Supremacy Clause?
- Can the President be indicted for a criminal offense while in office? Could the United States Attorney General hold the President for a criminal trial during his term? Consider whether a state attorney general could do so in state court.
- Could the President pardon himself for a criminal violation?

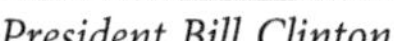

President Bill Clinton

Paula Jones

Clinton v. Jones

520 U.S. 681 (1997)

JUSTICE STEVENS delivered the opinion of the Court.

This case raises a constitutional and a prudential question concerning the Office of the President of the United States. Respondent, a private citizen, seeks to recover damages from the current occupant of that office based on actions allegedly taken before his term began. The President submits that in all but the most exceptional cases the Constitution requires federal courts to defer such litigation until his term ends and that, in any event, respect for the office warrants such a stay. Despite the force of the arguments supporting the President's submissions, we conclude that they must be rejected.

Petitioner, William Jefferson Clinton, was elected to the Presidency in 1992, and re-elected in 1996. His term of office expires on January 20, 2001. In 1991 he was the Governor of the State of Arkansas. Respondent, Paula Corbin Jones, is a resident of California. In 1991 she lived in Arkansas, and was an employee of the Arkansas Industrial Development Commission.

On May 6, 1994, she commenced this action in the United States District Court for the Eastern District of Arkansas by filing a complaint naming petitioner and Danny Ferguson, a former Arkansas State Police officer, as defendants. The complaint alleges two federal claims, and two state law claims over which the federal court has jurisdiction because of the diverse citizenship of the parties. As the case comes to us, we are required to assume the truth of the detailed — but as yet untested — factual allegations in the complaint.

Those allegations principally describe events that are said to have occurred on the afternoon of May 8, 1991, during an official conference held at the Excelsior Hotel in Little Rock, Arkansas. The Governor delivered a speech at the conference; respondent — working as a state employee — staffed the registration desk. She alleges that Ferguson persuaded her to leave her desk and to visit the Governor in a business suite at the hotel, where he made "abhorrent" sexual advances that she vehemently rejected. She further claims that her superiors at work subsequently dealt with her in a hostile and rude manner, and changed her duties to punish her for rejecting those advances. Finally, she alleges that after petitioner was elected President, Ferguson defamed her by making a statement to a reporter that implied she had accepted petitioner's alleged overtures, and that various persons authorized to speak for the President publicly branded her a liar by denying that the incident had occurred. Respondent seeks actual damages of $75,000, and punitive damages of $100,000. . . .

In response to the complaint, petitioner promptly advised the District Court that he intended to file a motion to dismiss on grounds of Presidential immunity, and requested the court to defer all other pleadings and motions until after the immunity issue was resolved. . . .

It is true that we have often stressed the importance of avoiding the premature adjudication of constitutional questions. That doctrine of avoidance, however, is applicable to the entire Federal Judiciary, not just to this Court, and comes into play after the court has acquired jurisdiction of a case. It does not dictate discretionary denial of every certiorari petition raising a novel constitutional question. It does, however, make it appropriate to identify two important constitutional issues not encompassed within the questions presented by the petition for certiorari that we need not address today.

First, because the claim of immunity is asserted in a federal court and relies heavily on the doctrine of separation of powers that restrains each of the three branches of the Federal Government from encroaching on the domain of the other two, it is not necessary to consider or decide whether a comparable claim might succeed in a state tribunal. If this case were being heard in a state forum, instead of advancing a separation of powers argument, petitioner would presumably rely on federalism and comity concerns,[16] as well as the interest in protecting federal officials from possible local prejudice that underlies the authority to remove certain cases brought against federal officers from a state to a federal court. Whether those concerns would present a more compelling case for immunity is a question that is not before us.

---

[16] [Footnote 13] Because the Supremacy Clause makes federal law "the supreme Law of the Land," Art. VI, cl. 2, any direct control by a state court over the President, who has principal responsibility to ensure that those laws are "faithfully executed," Art. II, §3, may implicate concerns that are quite different from the interbranch separation of powers questions addressed here.

Second, our decision rejecting the immunity claim and allowing the case to proceed does not require us to confront the question whether a court may compel the attendance of the President at any specific time or place. We assume that the testimony of the President, both for discovery and for use at trial, may be taken at the White House at a time that will accommodate his busy schedule, and that, if a trial is held, there would be no necessity for the President to attend in person, though he could elect to do so.[17]

Petitioner's principal submission — that "in all but the most exceptional cases," the Constitution affords the President temporary immunity from civil damages litigation arising out of events that occurred before he took office — cannot be sustained on the basis of precedent.

Only three sitting Presidents have been defendants in civil litigation involving their actions prior to taking office. Complaints against Theodore Roosevelt and Harry Truman had been dismissed before they took office; the dismissals were affirmed after their respective inaugurations. Two companion cases arising out of an automobile accident were filed against John F. Kennedy in 1960 during the Presidential campaign. After taking office, he unsuccessfully argued that his status as Commander in Chief gave him a right to a stay under the Soldiers' and Sailors' Civil Relief Act of 1940. The motion for a stay was denied by the District Court, and the matter was settled out of court. Thus, none of those cases sheds any light on the constitutional issue before us.

The principal rationale for affording certain public servants immunity from suits for money damages arising out of their official acts is inapplicable to unofficial conduct. In cases involving prosecutors, legislators, and judges we have repeatedly explained that the immunity serves the public interest in enabling such officials to perform their designated functions effectively without fear that a particular decision may give rise to personal liability. . . .

That rationale provided the principal basis for our holding that a former President of the United States was "entitled to absolute immunity from damages liability predicated on his official acts," *Nixon v. Fitzgerald* (1982). Our central concern was to avoid rendering the President "unduly cautious in the discharge of his official duties."

This reasoning provides no support for an immunity for unofficial conduct. As we explained in *Fitzgerald*, "the sphere of protected action must be related closely to the immunity's justifying purposes." Because of the President's broad responsibilities, we recognized in that case an immunity from damages claims arising out of official acts extending to the "outer perimeter of his authority." But we have never suggested that the President, or any other official, has an immunity that extends beyond the scope of any action taken in an official capacity.

Moreover, when defining the scope of an immunity for acts clearly taken within an official capacity, we have applied a functional approach. "Frequently our

[17] [Footnote 14] Although Presidents have responded to written interrogatories, given depositions, and provided videotaped trial testimony, no sitting President has ever testified, or been ordered to testify, in open court.

decisions have held that an official's absolute immunity should extend only to acts in performance of particular functions of his office." Hence, for example, a judge's absolute immunity does not extend to actions performed in a purely administrative capacity. As our opinions have made clear, immunities are grounded in "the nature of the function performed, not the identity of the actor who performed it." . . .

We are also unpersuaded by the evidence from the historical record to which petitioner has called our attention. He points to a comment by Thomas Jefferson protesting the subpoena duces tecum Chief Justice Marshall directed to him in the Burr trial,[18] a statement in the diaries kept by Senator William Maclay of the first Senate debates, in which then Vice President John Adams and Senator Oliver Ellsworth are recorded as having said that "the President personally [is] not . . . subject to any process whatever," lest it be "put . . . in the power of a common Justice to exercise any Authority over him and Stop the Whole Machine of Government," and to a quotation from Justice Story's Commentaries on the Constitution. None of these sources sheds much light on the question at hand.[19]

Respondent, in turn, has called our attention to conflicting historical evidence. Speaking in favor of the Constitution's adoption at the Pennsylvania Convention, James Wilson — who had participated in the Philadelphia Convention at which the document was drafted — explained that, although the President "is placed [on] high," "not a single privilege is annexed to his character; far from being above the laws, he is amenable to them in his private character as a citizen, and in his public character by impeachment." This description is consistent with both the doctrine of presidential immunity as set forth in *Fitzgerald*, and rejection of the immunity claim in this case. With respect to acts taken in his "public character" — that is official acts — the President may be disciplined principally by impeachment, not by private lawsuits for damages. But he is otherwise subject to the laws for his purely private acts.

In the end, as applied to the particular question before us, we reach the same conclusion about these historical materials that Justice Jackson described when confronted with an issue concerning the dimensions of the President's power.

---

[18] [Footnote 20] In Jefferson's view, the subpoena jeopardized the separation of powers by subjecting the Executive Branch to judicial command.

[19] [Footnote 23] . . . [T]his material is hardly proof of the unequivocal common understanding at the time of the founding. Immediately after mentioning the positions of Adams and Ellsworth, Maclay went on to point out in his diary that he virulently disagreed with them, concluding that his opponents' view "[s]hows clearly how amazingly fond of the old leven many People are." Finally, Justice Story's comments in his constitutional law treatise provide no substantial support for respondent's position. Story wrote that because the President's "incidental powers" must include "the power to perform [his duties], without any obstruction," he "cannot, therefore, be liable to arrest, imprisonment, or detention, while he is in the discharge of the duties of his office; and *for this purpose* his person must be deemed, in civil cases at least, to possess an official inviolability." (emphasis added). Story said only that "*an* official inviolability" (emphasis added) was necessary to preserve the President's ability to perform the functions of the office; he did not specify the dimensions of the necessary immunity. While we have held that an immunity from suits grounded on official acts is necessary to serve this purpose, see *Fitzgerald*, it does not follow that the broad immunity from all civil damages suits that petitioner seeks is also necessary.

"Just what our forefathers did envision, or would have envisioned had they foreseen modern conditions, must be divined from materials almost as enigmatic as the dreams Joseph was called upon to interpret for Pharoah. A century and a half of partisan debate and scholarly speculation yields no net result but only supplies more or less apt quotations from respected sources on each side. . . . They largely cancel each other." *Youngstown Sheet & Tube Co. v. Sawyer* (1952) (Jackson, J., concurring).

Petitioner's strongest argument supporting his immunity claim is based on the text and structure of the Constitution. He does not contend that the occupant of the Office of the President is "above the law," in the sense that his conduct is entirely immune from judicial scrutiny. The President argues merely for a postponement of the judicial proceedings that will determine whether he violated any law. His argument is grounded in the character of the office that was created by Article II of the Constitution, and relies on separation of powers principles that have structured our constitutional arrangement since the founding.

As a starting premise, petitioner contends that he occupies a unique office with powers and responsibilities so vast and important that the public interest demands that he devote his undivided time and attention to his public duties. He submits that — given the nature of the office — the doctrine of separation of powers places limits on the authority of the Federal Judiciary to interfere with the Executive Branch that would be transgressed by allowing this action to proceed.

We have no dispute with the initial premise of the argument. Former presidents, from George Washington to George Bush, have consistently endorsed petitioner's characterization of the office. . . . As Justice Jackson has pointed out, the Presidency concentrates executive authority "in a single head in whose choice the whole Nation has a part, making him the focus of public hopes and expectations. In drama, magnitude and finality his decisions so far overshadow any others that almost alone he fills the public eye and ear." *Youngstown Sheet & Tube Co. v. Sawyer* (1952) (Jackson, J., concurring). We have, in short, long recognized the "unique position in the constitutional scheme" that this office occupies. *Fitzgerald.* Thus, while we suspect that even in our modern era there remains some truth to Chief Justice Marshal's suggestion that the duties of the Presidency are not entirely "unremitting," *United States v. Burr* (Cir. Ct. Va. 1807), we accept the initial premise of the Executive's argument. . . .

It does not follow, however, that separation of powers principles would be violated by allowing this action to proceed. The doctrine of separation of powers is concerned with the allocation of official power among the three coequal branches of our Government. . . .

Of course the lines between the powers of the three branches are not always neatly defined. . . . *Morrison v. Olson* (1987); . . . *United States v. Nixon* (1974); *Youngstown.* But in this case there is no suggestion that the Federal Judiciary is being asked to perform any function that might in some way be described as "executive." Respondent is merely asking the courts to exercise their core Article III jurisdiction to decide cases and controversies. Whatever the outcome of this case, there is no possibility that the decision will curtail the scope of the official powers of the Executive Branch. The litigation of questions that relate entirely to the unofficial conduct of the individual who happens to be the President poses no perceptible risk of misallocation of either judicial power or executive power.

Rather than arguing that the decision of the case will produce either an aggrandizement of judicial power or a narrowing of executive power, petitioner contends that — as a by-product of an otherwise traditional exercise of judicial power — burdens will be placed on the President that will hamper the performance of his official duties. . . . As a factual matter, petitioner contends that this particular case — as well as the potential additional litigation that an affirmance of the Court of Appeals judgment might spawn — may impose an unacceptable burden on the President's time and energy, and thereby impair the effective performance of his office.

Petitioner's predictive judgment finds little support in either history or the relatively narrow compass of the issues raised in this particular case. As we have already noted, in the more than 200 year history of the Republic, only three sitting Presidents have been subjected to suits for their private actions. If the past is any indicator, it seems unlikely that a deluge of such litigation will ever engulf the Presidency. As for the case at hand, if properly managed by the District Court, it appears to us highly unlikely to occupy any substantial amount of petitioner's time.

Of greater significance, petitioner errs by presuming that interactions between the Judicial Branch and the Executive, even quite burdensome interactions, necessarily rise to the level of constitutionally forbidden impairment of the Executive's ability to perform its constitutionally mandated functions. . . .

The fact that a federal court's exercise of its traditional Article III jurisdiction may significantly burden the time and attention of the Chief Executive is not sufficient to establish a violation of the Constitution. Two long settled propositions, first announced by Chief Justice Marshall, support that conclusion. First, we have long held that when the President takes official action, the Court has the authority to determine whether he has acted within the law. Perhaps the most dramatic example of such a case is our holding that President Truman exceeded his constitutional authority when he issued an order directing the Secretary of Commerce to take possession of and operate most of the Nation's steel mills in order to avert a national catastrophe. *Youngstown*. Despite the serious impact of that decision on the ability of the Executive Branch to accomplish its assigned mission, and the substantial time that the President must necessarily have devoted to the matter as a result of judicial involvement, we exercised our Article III jurisdiction to decide whether his official conduct conformed to the law. Our holding was an application of the principle established in *Marbury v. Madison* (1803), that "[i]t is emphatically the province and duty of the judicial department to say what the law is."

Second, it is also settled that the President is subject to judicial process in appropriate circumstances. Although Thomas Jefferson apparently thought otherwise, Chief Justice Marshall, when presiding in the treason trial of Aaron Burr, ruled that a subpoena duces tecum could be directed to the President. *United*

States v. Burr.[20] We unequivocally and emphatically endorsed Marshall's position when we held that President Nixon was obligated to comply with a subpoena commanding him to produce certain tape recordings of his conversations with his aides. *United States v. Nixon*. As we explained, "neither the doctrine of separation of powers, nor the need for confidentiality of high level communications, without more, can sustain an absolute, unqualified Presidential privilege of immunity from judicial process under all circumstances."[21]

Sitting Presidents have responded to court orders to provide testimony and other information with sufficient frequency that such interactions between the Judicial and Executive Branches can scarcely be thought a novelty. . . . In sum, "[i]t is settled law that the separation of powers doctrine does not bar every exercise of jurisdiction over the President of the United States." *Fitzgerald*. If the Judiciary may severely burden the Executive Branch by reviewing the legality of the President's official conduct, and if it may direct appropriate process to the President himself, it must follow that the federal courts have power to determine the legality of his unofficial conduct. The burden on the President's time and energy that is a mere by-product of such review surely cannot be considered as onerous as the direct burden imposed by judicial review and the occasional invalidation of his official actions. We therefore hold that the doctrine of separation of powers does not require federal courts to stay all private actions against the President until he leaves office. . . .

We add a final comment on two matters that are discussed at length in the briefs: the risk that our decision will generate a large volume of politically motivated harassing and frivolous litigation, and the danger that national security concerns might prevent the President from explaining a legitimate need for a continuance.

We are not persuaded that either of these risks is serious. Most frivolous and vexatious litigation is terminated at the pleading stage or on summary judgment, with little if any personal involvement by the defendant. Moreover, the availability of sanctions provides a significant deterrent to litigation directed at the President in his unofficial capacity for purposes of political gain or harassment. History indicates that the likelihood that a significant number of such cases will be filed is remote. Although scheduling problems may arise, there is no reason to assume that the District Courts will be either unable to accommodate the President's needs or unfaithful to the tradition — especially in matters involving national security — of giving "the utmost deference to Presidential responsibilities." Several

---

[20] [Footnote 38] After the decision was rendered, Jefferson expressed his distress in a letter to a prosecutor at the trial, noting that "[t]he Constitution enjoins [the President's] constant agency in the concerns of 6. millions of people." He asked, "[i]s the law paramount to this, which calls on him on behalf of a single one?" For Chief Justice Marshall, the answer — quite plainly — was yes.

[21] [Footnote 39] Of course, it does not follow that a court may "proceed against the president as against an ordinary individual," *United States v. Nixon* (quoting *United States v. Burr*). Special caution is appropriate if the materials or testimony sought by the court relate to a President's official activities, with respect to which "[t]he interest in preserving confidentiality is weighty indeed and entitled to great respect." Id. We have made clear that in a criminal case the powerful interest in the "fair administration of criminal justice" requires that the evidence be given under appropriate circumstances lest the "very integrity of the judicial system" be eroded. Id.

Presidents, including petitioner, have given testimony without jeopardizing the Nation's security. In short, we have confidence in the ability of our federal judges to deal with both of these concerns.

If Congress deems it appropriate to afford the President stronger protection, it may respond with appropriate legislation. As petitioner notes in his brief, Congress has enacted more than one statute providing for the deferral of civil litigation to accommodate important public interests. If the Constitution embodied the rule that the President advocates, Congress, of course, could not repeal it. But our holding today raises no barrier to a statutory response to these concerns.

The Federal District Court has jurisdiction to decide this case. Like every other citizen who properly invokes that jurisdiction, respondent has a right to an orderly disposition of her claims. . . .

PART IV

THE JUDICIAL POWER

CHAPTER 8

The Political Question Doctrine

ASSIGNMENT 1

In Chapter 3, we studied the scope of the legislative power in Article I. In Chapters 4 and 5, we studied limitations that our system of federalism imposes on both federal and state power. In Chapters 6 and 7, we studied the scope of the executive power in Article II and how it is separated from the legislative and judicial branches. We now conclude the discussion of our constitutional structure by considering the judicial power in Article III.

Article III, Section 2 defines the scope of the jurisdiction of the federal courts as follows (note that the actual "judicial power" is never defined, rather, the Constitution only spells out where that power "extends"):

> Section 2. The judicial power shall extend to all cases, in law and equity, arising under this Constitution, the laws of the United States, and treaties made, or which shall be made, under their authority; — to all cases affecting ambassadors, other public ministers and consuls; — to all cases of admiralty and maritime jurisdiction; — to controversies to which the United States shall be a party; — to controversies between two or more states; — between a state and citizens of another state; — between citizens of different states; — between citizens of the same state claiming lands under grants of different states, and between a state, or the citizens thereof, and foreign states, citizens or subjects.
>
> In all cases affecting ambassadors, other public ministers and consuls, and those in which a state shall be party, the Supreme Court shall have original jurisdiction. In all

> the other cases before mentioned, the Supreme Court shall have appellate jurisdiction, both as to law and fact, with such exceptions, and under such regulations as the Congress shall make.

In Chapter 2, we read several key cases from the Marshall Court, including *Marbury v. Madison* and *McCulloch v. Maryland*, which interpreted this provision. These decisions affirmed a judicial power to invalidate unconstitutional laws enacted by Congress or the states, as well as to review the decisions of state courts. In Chapter 4, starting with *Hans v. Louisiana*, we saw how the Eleventh Amendment qualified the scope of the federal judiciary's power to adjudicate controversies between a state and citizens of another state. And in Chapter 7, we considered the extent to which the President might be immune from the judicial process when it is invoked to review his conduct. We now turn to some additional limitations on the power of federal courts that the Supreme Court itself has developed.

A. NO ADVISORY OPINIONS

Perhaps the earliest limitation that the Supreme Court imposed on its own jurisdiction was its refusal to issue "advisory opinions" to the other branches in advance of an actual case or controversy. In 1793, at the request of President Washington, Secretary of State Thomas Jefferson wrote to the Justices asking if the President could refer questions to them concerning the "construction of our treaties," "the laws of nature and nations," and "the laws of the land." In a letter to the President from Chief Justice John Jay, the Court declined Jefferson's request:

> Sir
>
> We have considered the previous Question stated in a Letter written to us by your Direction, by the Secretary of State, on the 18th of last month.
>
> The Lines of Separation drawn by the Constitution between the three Departments of Government — their being in certain Respects checks upon each other — and our being Judges of a court in the last Resort — are Considerations which afford strong arguments against the Propriety of our extrajudicially deciding the questions alluded to; especially as the Power given by the Constitution to the President of calling on the Heads of Departments for opinions, seems to have been purposely as well as expressly limited to the executive Departments.[1]

[1] Article II, Section 2 provides that the President "may require the Opinion, in writing, of the principal Officer in each of the executive Departments, upon any Subject relating to the duties of their respective Offices." Though Jay declined to provide the executive branch with advice in his capacity as Chief Justice, during his tenure on the Court, he negotiated the *Jay Treaty* between the United States and Great Britain. The Constitution's Incompatibility Clause in Article 1, Section 6, Clause 2, states that members of Congress are prohibited from serving in the executive branch, but that prohibition does not apply to the judiciary. As we discussed in Chapter 2, *Marbury v. Madison* arose when John Marshall simultaneously served as both Chief Justice and Secretary of State.

Artist's rendering of the first Supreme Court sitting in 1790 (from left, William Cushing, Chief Justice John Jay, John Blair, and James Wilson). Justices James Wilson and John Blair had been delegates to the Constitutional Convention in Philadelphia.

Old City Hall, Philadelphia, PA

The Supreme Court first assembled on February 1, 1790, in the Merchants Exchange Building (aka Royal Exchange Building) on the second floor. A brick arcade shaded the ground floor, an open-air market where Broad and Water Streets intersect today. Chief Justice John Jay was, however, forced to postpone the initial meeting of the Court until the next day since, due to transportation problems, some of the Justices were not able to reach New York until February 2. The earliest sessions of the Court were devoted to organizational proceedings — appointment of a court crier and a clerk, admission of lawyers to the bar, etc. By the time of the Correspondence of the Justices, it was sitting in the Old City Hall in Philadelphia, which you can visit today.

We exceedingly regret every Event that may cause Embarrassment to your administration; but we derive Consolation from the Reflection, that your Judgment will discern what is Right, and that your usual Prudence, Decision and Firmness will surmount every obstacle to the Preservation of the Rights, Peace, and Dignity of the United States.

John Jay
James Wilson
John Blair
Ja. Iredell
Wm Paterson

This important letter, which established the Court's practice of declining to issue advisory opinions, is referred to as the *Correspondence of the Justices.* To this day, federal courts will only consider issues that are raised in litigation. Many state courts, however, do provide advisory opinions.

In this chapter and the next we consider four additional limitations on the scope of the judiciary's power: (1) the political question doctrine, (2) standing, (3) ripeness, and (4) mootness. All four concepts are premised, at least in part, on the same considerations that led the first Justices to decline to provide advisory opinions: the federal courts have a specific, limited jurisdiction due to the separation of powers. This conclusion is bolstered by the fact that Article III, Section 2 expressly defines the judiciary's power in terms of "cases" and "controversies."

B. THE POLITICAL QUESTION DOCTRINE

Recall that in *Marbury v. Madison* (Chapter 2), Chief Justice Marshall articulated the following limitation on the judicial power:

> By the constitution of the United States, the President is invested with certain important political powers, in the exercise of which he is to use his own discretion, and is accountable only to his country in his political character, and to his own conscience. To aid him in the performance of these duties, he is authorized to appoint certain officers, who act by his authority and in conformity with his orders. In such cases, their acts are his acts; and *whatever opinion may be entertained of the manner in which executive discretion may be used, still there exists, and can exist, no power to control that discretion* [by the courts]. *The subjects are political.* They respect the nation, not individual rights, and being entrusted to the executive, the decision of the executive is conclusive. (emphasis added).

Although the cases in this section do not concern presidential power — which was touched upon in *United States v. Nixon* (Chapter 7) — they do concern the general reluctance of courts to decide "political" questions, and their occasional willingness to overcome that reluctance.

Baker v. Carr raised the question of whether the Guarantee Clause of Article IV, Section 4 can be applied to state governments by the judiciary of the United States.

The clause reads:

> The United States shall guarantee to every state in this union a republican form of government, and shall protect each of them against invasion; and on application of the legislature, or of the executive (when the legislature cannot be convened) against domestic violence.

Which branch of government, if any, is empowered to enforce the Guarantee Clause? Does "the United States" include the judiciary? In the 1849 case of *Luther v. Borden*, Chief Justice Taney seemed to say that the Guarantee Clause is not justiciable by the federal judiciary; at least that was how his decision was interpreted by some. In the next case, the Warren Court revisits this issue.

STUDY GUIDE

- Do you agree that the Guarantee Clause of Article IV should always be considered nonjusticiable?
- Why is Justice Frankfurter reluctant to have the judiciary involve itself in this kind of dispute?
- If the Court were to follow Justice Frankfurter's approach, would that limit the ability of the judiciary to fulfill its constitutional role in reviewing the constitutionality of governmental actions? Is that limitation a good or a bad thing?

Baker v. Carr

369 U.S. 186 (1962)

[The Tennessee state constitution required that legislative districts must be redrawn every ten years according to the federal census to provide for districts of substantially equal population. However, the state had not redistricted since the 1901 census. Plaintiff Charles Baker, a Republican who lived in Shelby County, Tennessee, filed suit in federal court, alleging that the state's refusal to redraw the electoral maps was unconstitutional. As tabulated by the 1960 census, the population had shifted such that Shelby County had about ten times as many residents as some of the rural districts — but its representation had not increased in six decades. Baker and the other plaintiffs contended there was no effective redress available in the Tennessee legislature because of the malapportionment. — EDS.]

MR. JUSTICE BRENNAN delivered the opinion of the Court. . . .

We hold that this challenge to an apportionment presents no nonjusticiable "political question." The . . . mere fact that the suit seeks protection of a political right does not mean it presents a political question. Such an objection "is little more than a play upon words." Rather, it is argued that apportionment cases, whatever the actual wording of the complaint, can involve no federal constitutional right except one resting on the guaranty [in Article IV, §4] of a republican form of government, and that complaints based on that clause have been held to present political questions which are nonjusticiable. . . .

Our discussion, . . . requires review of a number of political question cases, in order to expose the attributes of the doctrine — attributes which, in various settings, diverge, combine, appear, and disappear in seeming disorderliness. . . . That review reveals that . . . it is the relationship between the judiciary and the coordinate branches of the Federal Government, and not the federal judiciary's relationship to the States, which gives rise to the "political question." . . . The nonjusticiability of a political question is primarily a function of the separation of powers. Much confusion results from the capacity of the "political question" label to obscure the need for case-by-case inquiry. Deciding whether a matter has in any measure been committed by the Constitution to another branch of government, or whether the action of that branch exceeds whatever authority has been committed, is itself a delicate exercise in constitutional interpretation, and is a responsibility of this Court as ultimate interpreter of the Constitution. . . .

Foreign relations: There are sweeping statements to the effect that all questions touching foreign relations are political questions. Not only does resolution of such issues frequently turn on standards that defy judicial application, or involve the exercise of a discretion demonstrably committed to the executive or legislature, but many such questions uniquely demand single-voiced statement of the Government's views. Yet it is error to suppose that every case or controversy which touches foreign relations lies beyond judicial cognizance. Our cases in this field seem invariably to show a discriminating analysis of the particular question posed, in terms of the history of its management by the political branches, of its susceptibility to judicial handling in the light of its nature and posture in the specific case, and of the possible consequences of judicial action. . . .

Validity of enactments: In *Coleman v. Miller* (1939), this Court held that the questions of how long a proposed amendment to the Federal Constitution remained open to ratification, and what effect a prior rejection had on a subsequent ratification, were committed to congressional resolution and involved criteria of decision that necessarily escaped the judicial grasp.[2] Similar considerations apply to the enacting process: "[t]he respect due to coequal and independent departments,"

---

[2] [In a dissenting opinion in *Arizona State Legislature v. Arizona Indep. Redistricting Commn.* (2015), Justice Scalia characterized the Court's fragmented opinion in *Coleman v. Miller* (1939) in this fashion: "*Coleman* was a peculiar case that may well stand for nothing. The opinion discussing and finding standing, and going on to affirm the Kansas Supreme Court, was written by Chief Justice Hughes and announced by Justice Stone. Justice Frankfurter, joined by three other Justices, held there was no standing, and would have dismissed the petition (leaving the judgment of the Kansas Supreme Court in place). Justice Butler, joined by Justice McReynolds, dissented (neither joining Hughes's opinion nor separately discussing standing) and would have reversed the Kansas Supreme Court. That adds up to two votes to affirm on the merits, two to reverse on the merits (without discussing standing) and four to dismiss for lack of standing. . . . A pretty shaky foundation for a significant precedential ruling." — EDS.]

and the need for finality and certainty about the status of a statute contribute to judicial reluctance to inquire whether, as passed, it complied with all requisite formalities. . . .

It is apparent that several formulations which vary slightly according to the settings in which the questions arise may describe a political question, although each has one or more elements which identify it as essentially a function of the separation of powers. Prominent on the surface of any case held to involve a political question is found a textually demonstrable constitutional commitment of the issue to a coordinate political department; or a lack of judicially discoverable and manageable standards for resolving it; or the impossibility of deciding without an initial policy determination of a kind clearly for nonjudicial discretion; or the impossibility of a court's undertaking independent resolution without expressing lack of the respect due coordinate branches of government; or an unusual need for unquestioning adherence to a political decision already made; or the potentiality of embarrassment from multifarious pronouncements by various departments on one question.

Unless one of these formulations is inextricable from the case at bar, there should be no dismissal for nonjusticiability on the ground of a political question's presence. The doctrine of which we treat is one of "political questions," not one of "political cases." . . . [I]t is argued that this case shares the characteristics of decisions that constitute a category not yet considered, cases concerning the Constitution's guaranty, in Art. IV, §4, of a republican form of government. A conclusion as to whether the case at bar does present a political question cannot be confidently reached until we have considered those cases with special care. We shall discover that Guaranty Clause claims involve those elements which define a "political question," and, for that reason and no other, they are nonjusticiable. In particular, we shall discover that the nonjusticiability of such claims has nothing to do with their touching upon matters of state governmental organization.

Republican form of government: *Luther v. Borden* (1849), though in form simply an action for damages for trespass was, as Daniel Webster said in opening the argument for the defense, "an unusual case." The defendants, admitting an otherwise tortious breaking and entering, sought to justify their action on the ground that they were agents of the established lawful government of Rhode Island, which State was then under martial law to defend itself from active insurrection; that the plaintiff was engaged in that insurrection, and that they entered under orders to arrest the plaintiff. The case arose "out of the unfortunate political differences which agitated the people of Rhode Island in 1841 and 1842," and which had resulted in a situation wherein two groups laid competing claims to recognition as the lawful government. The plaintiff's right to recover depended upon which of the two groups was entitled to such recognition; but the lower court's refusal to receive evidence or hear argument on that issue, its charge to the jury that the earlier established or "charter" government was lawful, and the verdict for the defendants were affirmed upon appeal to this Court.

Chief Justice Taney's opinion for the Court reasoned as follows: (1) If a court were to hold the defendants' acts unjustified because the charter government had no legal existence during the period in question, it would follow that all of that government's actions — laws enacted, taxes collected, salaries paid, accounts settled, sentences passed — were of no effect, and that "the officers who carried their decisions into operation [were] answerable as trespassers, if not in some cases as criminals." . . . A decision for the plaintiff would inevitably have produced some significant measure of chaos, a consequence to be avoided if it could be done without abnegation of the judicial duty to uphold the Constitution.

(2) No state court had recognized as a judicial responsibility settlement of the issue of the locus of state governmental authority. Indeed, the courts of Rhode Island had in several cases held that "it rested with the political power to decide whether the charter government had been displaced or not," and that that department had acknowledged no change.

(3) Since "[t]he question relates, altogether, to the constitution and laws of [the] . . . State," the courts of the United States had to follow the state courts' decisions unless there was a federal constitutional ground for overturning them.

(4) No provision of the Constitution could be or had been invoked for this purpose except Art. IV, §4, the Guaranty Clause. Having already noted the absence of standards whereby the choice between governments could be made by a court acting independently, Chief Justice Taney now found further textual and practical reasons for concluding that, if any department of the United States was empowered by the Guaranty Clause to resolve the issue, it was not the judiciary:

> Under this article of the Constitution, it rests with Congress to decide what government is the established one in a State. For, as the United States guarantee to each State a republican government, Congress must necessarily decide what government is established in the State before it can determine whether it is republican or not. And when the senators and representatives of a State are admitted into the councils of the Union, the authority of the government under which they are appointed, as well as its republican character, is recognized by the proper constitutional authority. And its decision is binding on every other department of the government, and could not be questioned in a judicial tribunal. It is true that the contest in this case did not last long enough to bring the matter to this issue, and . . . Congress was not called upon to decide the controversy. Yet the right to decide is placed there, and not in the courts. . . .

Clearly, several factors were thought by the Court in *Luther* to make the question there "political": the commitment to the other branches of the decision as to which is the lawful state government; the unambiguous action by the President in recognizing the charter government as the lawful authority; the need for finality in the executive's decision, and the lack of criteria by which a court could determine which form of government was republican.

But the only significance that *Luther* could have for our immediate purposes is in its holding that the Guaranty Clause is not a repository of judicially manageable standards which a court could utilize independently in order to identify a State's lawful government. The Court has since refused to resort to the Guaranty Clause — which alone had been invoked for the purpose — as the source of a constitutional standard for invalidating state action.

We come, finally, to the ultimate inquiry whether our precedents as to what constitutes a nonjusticiable "political question" bring the case before us under the umbrella of that doctrine. A natural beginning is to note whether any of the common characteristics which we have been able to identify and label descriptively are present. We find none: the question here is the consistency of state action with the Federal Constitution. We have no question decided, or to be decided, by a political branch of government coequal with this Court. Nor do we risk embarrassment of our government abroad, or grave disturbance at home if we take issue with Tennessee as to the constitutionality of her action here challenged. Nor need the appellants, in order to succeed in this action, ask the Court to enter upon policy determinations for which judicially manageable standards are lacking. Judicial standards under the Equal Protection Clause are well developed and familiar, and it has been open to courts since the enactment of the Fourteenth Amendment to determine, if, on the particular facts, they must, that a discrimination reflects no policy, but simply arbitrary and capricious action.

This case does, in one sense, involve the allocation of political power within a State, and the appellants might conceivably have added a claim under the Guaranty Clause. Of course, as we have seen, any reliance on that clause would be futile. But because any reliance on the Guaranty Clause could not have succeeded, it does not follow that appellants may not be heard on the equal protection claim which, in fact, they tender. True, it must be clear that the Fourteenth Amendment claim is not so enmeshed with those political question elements which render Guaranty Clause claims nonjusticiable as actually to present a political question itself. But we have found that not to be the case here. . . .

We conclude, then, that the nonjusticiability of claims resting on the Guaranty Clause, which arises from their embodiment of questions that were thought "political," can have no bearing upon the justiciability of the equal protection claim presented in this case. Finally, we emphasize that it is the involvement in Guaranty Clause claims of the elements thought to define "political questions," and no other feature, which could render them nonjusticiable. Specifically, we have said that such claims are not held nonjusticiable because they touch matters of state governmental organization. . . . We conclude that the complaint's allegations of a denial of equal protection present a justiciable constitutional cause of action upon which appellants are entitled to a trial and a decision. The right asserted is within the reach of judicial protection under the Fourteenth Amendment.

The judgment of the District Court is reversed, and the cause is remanded for further proceedings consistent with this opinion.

Reversed and remanded.

MR. JUSTICE WHITAKER did not participate in the decision of this case.

MR. JUSTICE CLARK, concurring. . . .

I would not consider intervention by this Court into so delicate a field if there were any other relief available to the people of Tennessee. But the majority of the people of Tennessee have no "practical opportunities for exerting their political weight at the polls" to correct the existing "invidious discrimination." Tennessee has no initiative and referendum. I have searched diligently for other "practical opportunities" present under the law. I find none other than through the federal courts. The majority of the voters have been caught up in a legislative strait jacket. Tennessee has an "informed, civically militant electorate" and "an aroused popular conscience," but it does not sear "the conscience of the people's representatives." This is because the legislative policy has riveted the present seats in the Assembly to their respective constituencies, and by the votes of their incumbents a reapportionment of any kind is prevented. The people have been rebuffed at the hands of the Assembly; they have tried the constitutional convention route, but since the call must originate in the Assembly it, too, has been fruitless. They have tried Tennessee courts with the same result, and Governors have fought the tide only to flounder. It is said that there is recourse in Congress, and perhaps that may be, but, from a practical standpoint, this is without substance. To date, Congress has never undertaken such a task in any State. We therefore must conclude that the people of Tennessee are stymied, and, without judicial intervention, will be saddled with the present discrimination in the affairs of their state government.

MR. JUSTICE FRANKFURTER, whom MR. JUSTICE HARLAN joins, dissenting. . . .

From its earliest opinions, this Court has consistently recognized a class of controversies which do not lend themselves to judicial standards and judicial remedies. To classify the various instances as "political questions" is, rather, a form of stating this conclusion than revealing of analysis. Some of the cases so labelled have no relevance here. But from others emerge unifying considerations that are compelling.

1. The cases concerning war or foreign affairs, for example, are usually explained by the necessity of the country's speaking with one voice in such matters. While this concern alone undoubtedly accounts for many of the decisions, others do not fit the pattern. It would hardly embarrass the conduct of war were this Court to determine, in connection with private transactions between litigants, the date upon which war is to be deemed terminated. But the Court has refused to do so. . . . A controlling factor in such cases is that, decision respecting these kinds of complex matters of policy being traditionally committed not to courts but to the political agencies of government for determination by criteria of political expediency, there exists no standard ascertainable by settled judicial experience or process by reference to which a political decision affecting the question at issue between the parties can be judged. . . .

2. The Court has been particularly unwilling to intervene in matters concerning the structure and organization of the political institutions of the States. . . .

3. The cases involving Negro disfranchisement are no exception to the principle of avoiding federal judicial intervention into matters of state government in the absence of an explicit and clear constitutional imperative. For here the controlling command of Supreme Law is plain and unequivocal. An end of discrimination against the Negro was the compelling motive of the Civil War Amendments. . . . Thus, the Court, in cases involving discrimination against the Negro's right to vote, has recognized not only the action at law for damages, but, in appropriate circumstances, the extraordinary remedy of declaratory or injunctive relief.

4. The Court has refused to exercise its jurisdiction to pass on "abstract questions of political power, of sovereignty, of government." The "political question" doctrine, in this aspect, reflects the policies underlying the requirement of

"standing": that the litigant who would challenge official action must claim infringement of an interest particular and personal to himself, as distinguished from a cause of dissatisfaction with the general frame and functioning of government — a complaint that the political institutions are awry. What renders cases of this kind nonjusticiable is not necessarily the nature of the parties to them, for the Court has resolved other issues between similar parties; nor is it the nature of the legal question involved, for the same type of question has been adjudicated when presented in other forms of controversy. The crux of the matter is that courts are not fit instruments of decision where what is essentially at stake is the composition of those large contests of policy traditionally fought out in nonjudicial forums, by which governments and the actions of governments are made and unmade. . . .

5. The influence of these converging considerations — the caution not to undertake decision where standards meet for judicial judgment are lacking, the reluctance to interfere with matters of state government in the absence of an unquestionable and effectively enforceable mandate, the unwillingness to make courts arbiters of the broad issues of political organization historically committed to other institutions and for whose adjustment the judicial process is ill-adapted — has been decisive of the settled line of cases, reaching back more than a century, which holds that Art. IV, §4, of the Constitution, guaranteeing to the States "a Republican Form of Government," is not enforceable through the courts. . . .

The present case involves all of the elements that have made the Guarantee Clause cases nonjusticiable. It is, in effect, a Guarantee Clause claim masquerading under a different label. But it cannot make the case more fit for judicial action that appellants invoke the Fourteenth Amendment, rather than Art. IV, §4, where, in fact, the gist of their complaint is the same — unless it can be found that the Fourteenth Amendment speaks with greater particularity to their situation. We have been admonished to avoid "the tyranny of labels." Art. IV, §4, is not committed by express constitutional terms to Congress. It is the nature of the controversies arising under it, nothing else, which has made it judicially unenforceable. . . . [W]here judicial competence is wanting, it cannot be created by invoking one clause of the Constitution rather than another. . . .

Certainly "equal protection" is no more secure a foundation for judicial judgment of the permissibility of varying forms of representative government than is "Republican Form." Indeed, since "equal protection of the laws" can only mean an equality of persons standing in the same relation to whatever governmental action is challenged, the determination whether treatment is equal presupposes a determination concerning the nature of the relationship. This, with respect to apportionment, means an inquiry into the theoretic base of representation in an acceptably republican state. For a court could not determine the equal protection issue without, in fact, first determining the Republican Form issue, simply because what is reasonable for equal protection purposes will depend upon what frame of government, basically, is allowed. To divorce "equal protection" from "Republican Form" is to talk about half a question. . . .

Manifestly, the Equal Protection Clause supplies no clearer guide for judicial examination of apportionment methods than would the Guarantee Clause itself. Apportionment, by its character, is a subject of extraordinary complexity, involving — even after the fundamental theoretical issues concerning what is to be represented in a representative legislature have been fought out or compromised — considerations of geography, demography, electoral convenience, economic and social cohesions or divergencies among particular local groups, communications, the practical effects of political institutions like the lobby and the city machine, ancient traditions and ties of settled usage, respect for proven incumbents of long experience and senior status, mathematical mechanics, censuses compiling relevant data, and a host of others. . . . [T]hese are not factors that lend themselves to evaluations of a nature that are the staple of judicial determinations or for which judges are equipped to adjudicate by legal training or experience or native wit. Apportionment battles are overwhelmingly party or intra-party contests. It will add a virulent source of friction and tension in federal-state relations to embroil the federal judiciary in them.

STUDY GUIDE

- After *Baker v. Carr* and other Warren Court decisions, some observers came to doubt the continued vitality of the political question doctrine.
- In *Nixon v. United States* — which involved a former judge, not the former President — the Rehnquist Court reaffirmed the political question doctrine. How did it apply the factors identified in *Baker*?

Nixon v. United States

506 U.S. 224 (1993)

Chief Justice Rehnquist delivered the opinion of the Court.

Petitioner Walter L. Nixon, Jr., asks this court to decide whether Senate Rule XI, which allows a committee of Senators to hear evidence against an individual who has been impeached and to report that evidence to the full Senate, violates the Impeachment Trial Clause, Art. I, §3, cl. 6. That Clause provides that the "Senate shall have the sole Power to try all Impeachments." But before we reach the merits of such a claim, we must decide whether it is "justiciable," that is, whether it is a claim that may be resolved by the courts. We conclude that it is not.

Nixon, a former Chief Judge of the United States District Court for the Southern District of Mississippi, was convicted by a jury of two counts of making false statements before a federal grand jury and sentenced to prison. The grand jury investigation stemmed from reports that Nixon had accepted a gratuity from a Mississippi businessman in exchange for asking a local district attorney to halt the prosecution of the businessman's son. Because Nixon refused to resign from his office as a United States District Judge, he continued to collect his judicial salary while serving out his prison sentence.

On May 10, 1989, the House of Representatives adopted three articles of impeachment for high crimes and misdemeanors. The first two articles charged Nixon with giving false testimony before the grand jury and the third article charged him with bringing disrepute on the Federal Judiciary. After the House presented the articles to the Senate, the Senate voted to invoke its own Impeachment Rule XI, under which the presiding officer appoints a committee of Senators to "receive evidence and take testimony." The Senate committee held four days of hearings, during which 10 witnesses, including Nixon, testified. Pursuant to Rule XI, the committee presented the full Senate with a complete transcript of the proceeding and a report stating the uncontested facts and summarizing the evidence on the contested facts. Nixon and the House impeachment managers submitted extensive final briefs to the full Senate and delivered arguments from the Senate floor during the three hours set aside for oral argument in front of that body. Nixon himself gave a personal appeal, and several Senators posed questions directly to both parties. The Senate voted by more than the constitutionally required two-thirds majority to convict Nixon on the first two articles. The presiding officer then entered judgment removing Nixon from his office as United States District Judge.

Nixon thereafter commenced the present suit, arguing that Senate Rule XI violates the constitutional grant of authority to the Senate to "try" all impeachments because it prohibits the whole Senate from taking part in the evidentiary hearings. See Art. I, §3, cl. 6. Nixon sought a declaratory judgment that his impeachment conviction was void and that his judicial salary and privileges should be reinstated. . . .

A controversy is nonjusticiable — i.e., involves a political question — where there is "a textually demonstrable constitutional commitment of the issue to a coordinate political department; or a lack of judicially discoverable and manageable standards for resolving it. . . ." *Baker v. Carr* (1962). But the courts must, in the first instance, interpret the text in question and determine whether and to what extent the issue is textually committed. See *Powell v. McCormack* (1969). As the discussion that follows makes clear, the concept of a textual commitment to a coordinate political department is not completely separate from the concept of a lack of judicially discoverable and manageable standards for resolving it; the lack of judicially manageable standards may strengthen the conclusion that there is a textually demonstrable commitment to a coordinate branch.

In this case, we must examine Art. I, §3, cl. 6, to determine the scope of authority conferred upon the Senate by the Framers regarding impeachment. It provides:

> The Senate shall have the sole Power to try all Impeachments. When sitting for that Purpose, they shall be on Oath or Affirmation. When the President of the United States is tried, the Chief Justice shall preside: And no Person shall be convicted without the Concurrence of two-thirds of the Members present.

The language and structure of this Clause are revealing. The first sentence is a grant of authority to the Senate, and the word "sole" indicates that this authority is reposed in the Senate and nowhere else. The next two sentences specify requirements to which the Senate proceedings shall conform: the Senate shall be on oath or affirmation, a two-thirds vote is required to convict, and when the President is tried the Chief Justice shall preside. . . .

We think that the word "sole" is of considerable significance. Indeed, the word "sole" appears only one other time in the Constitution — with respect to the House of Representatives' "*sole* Power of Impeachment." Art. I, §2, cl. 5 (emphasis added). The common sense meaning of the word "sole" is that the Senate alone shall have authority to determine whether an individual should be acquitted or convicted. The dictionary definition bears this out. "Sole" is defined as "having no companion," "solitary," "being the only one," and "functioning . . . independently and without assistance or interference." Webster's Third New International Dictionary 2168 (1971). If the courts may review the actions of the Senate in order to determine whether that body "tried" an impeached official, it is difficult to see how the Senate would be "functioning . . . independently and without assistance or interference." . . .

The history and contemporary understanding of the impeachment provisions support our reading of the constitutional language. The parties do not offer evidence of a single word in the history of the Constitutional Convention or in contemporary commentary that even alludes to the possibility of judicial review in the context of the impeachment powers. This silence is quite meaningful in light of the several explicit references to the availability of judicial review as a check on the Legislature's power with respect to bills of attainder, *ex post-facto* laws, and statutes. See *The Federalist, No. 78* ("Limitations . . . can be preserved in practice no other way than through the medium of the courts of justice").

The Framers labored over the question of where the impeachment power should lie. Significantly, in at least two considered scenarios [the Virginia plan and the New Jersey plan] the power was placed with the Federal Judiciary. Indeed, Madison and the Committee of Detail proposed that the Supreme Court should have the power to determine impeachments. Despite these proposals, the Convention ultimately decided that the Senate would have "the sole Power to Try all Impeachments." Art. I, §3, cl. 6. According to Alexander Hamilton, the Senate was the "most fit depositary of this important trust" because its members are representatives of the people. See *The Federalist, No. 65.* The Supreme Court was not the proper body because the Framers "doubted whether the members of that tribunal would, at all times, be endowed with so eminent a portion of fortitude as would be called for in the execution of so difficult a task" or whether the Court "would possess the degree of credit and authority" to carry out its judgment if it conflicted with the accusation brought by the Legislature — the people's representative. In addition, the Framers believed the Court was too small in number: "The awful discretion, which a court of impeachments must necessarily have, to doom to honor or to infamy the most confidential and the most distinguished characters of the community, forbids the commitment of the trust to a small number of persons." *Id.*

There are two additional reasons why the Judiciary, and the Supreme Court in particular, were not chosen to have any role in impeachments. First, the Framers recognized that most likely there would be two sets of proceedings for individuals who commit impeachable offenses — the impeachment trial and a separate criminal trial. In fact, the Constitution explicitly provides for two separate proceedings. See Art. I, §3, cl. 7. The Framers deliberately separated the two forums to avoid raising the specter of bias and to ensure independent judgments:

> Would it be proper that the persons, who had disposed of his fame and his most valuable rights as a citizen in one trial, should in another trial, for the same offence, be also the disposers of his life and his fortune? Would there not be the greatest reason to apprehend, that error in the first sentence would be the parent of error in the second sentence? That the strong bias of one decision would be apt to overrule the influence of any new lights, which might be brought to vary the complexion of another decision?

The Federalist, No. 65.

Certainly judicial review of the Senate's "trial" would introduce the same risk of bias as would participation in the trial itself.

Second, judicial review would be inconsistent with the Framers' insistence that our system be one of checks and balances. In our constitutional system, impeachment was designed to be the only check on the Judicial Branch by the Legislature.... Judicial involvement in impeachment proceedings, even if only for purposes of judicial review, is counterintuitive because it would eviscerate the "important constitutional check" placed on the Judiciary by the Framers. See *id., No. 81.* Nixon's argument would place final reviewing authority with respect to impeachments in the hands of the same body that the impeachment process is meant to regulate.

Nevertheless, Nixon argues that judicial review is necessary in order to place a check on the Legislature. Nixon fears that if the Senate is given unreviewable authority to interpret the Impeachment Trial Clause, there is a grave risk that the Senate will usurp judicial power. The Framers anticipated this objection and created two constitutional safeguards to keep the Senate in check. The first safeguard is that the whole of the impeachment power is divided between the two legislative bodies, with the House given the right to accuse and the Senate given the right to judge.... The second safeguard is the two-thirds supermajority vote requirement....

In addition to the textual commitment argument, we are persuaded that the lack of finality and the difficulty of fashioning relief counsel against justiciability. We agree with the Court of Appeals that opening the door of judicial review to the procedures used by the Senate in trying impeachments would "expose the political life of the country to months, or perhaps years, of chaos." This lack of finality would manifest itself most dramatically if the President were impeached. The legitimacy of any successor, and hence his effectiveness, would be impaired severely, not merely while the judicial process was running its course, but during any retrial that a differently constituted Senate might conduct if its first judgment of conviction were invalidated. Equally uncertain is the question of what relief a court may give other than simply setting aside the judgment of conviction. Could it order the reinstatement of a convicted federal judge, or order Congress to create an additional judgeship if the seat had been filled in the interim? ...

For the foregoing reasons, the judgment of the Court of Appeals is

Affirmed.

Justice White, with whom Justice Blackmun joins, concurring in the judgment....

I concur in the judgment because the Senate fulfilled its constitutional obligation to "try" petitioner.... The majority states that the question raised in this case meets two of the criteria for political questions set out in *Baker v. Carr* (1962).... Of course the issue in the political question doctrine is not whether the Constitutional text commits exclusive responsibility for a particular governmental function to one of the political branches. There are numerous instances of this sort of textual commitment, e.g., Art. I, §8, and it is not thought that disputes implicating these provisions are nonjusticiable. Rather, the issue is whether the Constitution has given one of the political branches final responsibility for interpreting the scope and nature of such a power....

Even if the Impeachment Trial Clause is read without regard to its companion clause, the Court's willingness to abandon its obligation to review the constitutionality of legislative acts merely on the strength of the word "sole" is perplexing. Consider, by comparison, the treatment of Art. I, §1, which grants "All legislative powers" to the House and Senate. As used in that context "all" is nearly synonymous with "sole" — both connote entire and exclusive authority. Yet the Court has never thought it would unduly interfere with the operation of the Legislative Branch to entertain difficult and important questions as to the extent of the legislative power....

Justice Souter, concurring in the judgment.

I agree with the Court that this case presents a nonjusticiable political question. Because my analysis differs somewhat from the Court's, however, I concur in its judgment by this separate opinion.

As we cautioned in *Baker v. Carr*, "the 'political question' label" tends "to obscure the need for case-by-case inquiry." The need for such close examination is nevertheless clear from our precedents, which demonstrate that the functional nature of the political question doctrine requires analysis of "the precise facts and posture of the particular case," and precludes "resolution by any semantic cataloguing." ...

Whatever considerations feature most prominently in a particular case, the political question doctrine is "essentially a function of the separation of powers," existing to restrain courts "from inappropriate interference in the business of the other branches of Government," *United States v. Munoz Flores* (1990), and deriving in large part from prudential concerns about the respect we owe the political departments. Not all interference is inappropriate or disrespectful, however, and application of the doctrine ultimately turns, as Learned Hand put it, on "how importunately the occasion demands an answer." L. Hand, The Bill of Rights 15 (1958).

This occasion does not demand an answer. The Impeachment Trial Clause commits to the Senate "the sole Power to try all Impeachments," subject to three procedural requirements: the Senate shall be on oath or affirmation; the Chief Justice shall preside when the President is tried; and conviction shall be upon the concurrence of two-thirds of the Members present. U.S. Const., Art. I,

§3, cl. 6. It seems fair to conclude that the Clause contemplates that the Senate may determine, within broad boundaries, such subsidiary issues as the procedures for receipt and consideration of evidence necessary to satisfy its duty to "try" impeachments. Other significant considerations confirm a conclusion that this case presents a nonjusticiable political question: the "unusual need for unquestioning adherence to a political decision already made," as well as "the potentiality of embarrassment from multifarious pronouncements by various departments on one question." *Baker*. As the Court observes, judicial review of an impeachment trial would under the best of circumstances entail significant disruption of government.

Determining whether a ballot should be counted in Florida following the disputed 2000 presidential election

One can, nevertheless, envision different and unusual circumstances that might justify a more searching review of impeachment proceedings. If the Senate were to act in a manner seriously threatening the integrity of its results, convicting, say, upon a coin toss, or upon a summary determination that an officer of the United States was simply "a bad guy," judicial interference might well be appropriate. In such circumstances, the Senate's action might be so far beyond the scope of its constitutional authority, and the consequent impact on the Republic so great, as to merit a judicial response despite the prudential concerns that would ordinarily counsel silence. "The political question doctrine, a tool for maintenance of governmental order, will not be so applied as to promote only disorder." *Baker*.

STUDY GUIDE

- This excerpt from *Bush v. Gore* does not include the substance of the majority's reasoning in reversing the decision of the Florida Supreme Court. The excerpt is limited to the reasons why, despite the hotly contested political nature of the case, the majority thought it was appropriate for the Court to decide the matter, and why the dissenters disagreed.
- Does this case more closely resemble *Baker v. Carr* or *Nixon v. United States*? Do you need to know more about the substance of the constitutional issues to answer this question?
- Although Justice Breyer cites no political question doctrine cases, do you see how he might have used *Nixon v. United States* as authority for his objections?

Bush v. Gore

531 U.S. 98 (2000)

Per Curiam.

On December 8, 2000, the Supreme Court of Florida ordered that the Circuit Court of Leon County tabulate by hand 9,000 ballots in Miami-Dade County. It also ordered the inclusion in the certified vote totals of 215 votes identified in Palm Beach County and 168 votes identified in Miami-Dade County for Vice President Albert Gore, Jr., and Senator Joseph Lieberman, Democratic Candidates for President and Vice President. The Supreme Court noted that petitioner, Governor George W. Bush asserted that the net gain for Vice President Gore in Palm Beach County was 176 votes, and directed the Circuit Court to resolve that dispute on remand. The court further held that relief would require manual recounts in all Florida counties where so-called "undervotes" had not been subject to manual tabulation. The court ordered all manual recounts to begin at once. Governor Bush and Richard Cheney, Republican Candidates for the Presidency and Vice

Bush v. Gore was argued before the Supreme Court by Theodore "Ted" Olson (left) on behalf of George W. Bush and David Boies (right) on behalf of Al Gore. The two lawyers later joined forces to challenge the California law that limited marriage to opposite-sex couples. The Supreme Court ultimately dismissed the case, *Hollingsworth v. Perry*, finding that no parties had standing. Olson was also the subject of the independent counsel's investigation in *Morrison v. Olson*.

Presidency, filed an emergency application for a stay of this mandate. On December 9, we granted the application, treated the application as a petition for a writ of certiorari, and granted certiorari. . . .

Seven Justices of the Court agree that there are constitutional problems with the recount ordered by the Florida Supreme Court that demand a remedy. The only disagreement is as to the remedy. . . . None are more conscious of the vital limits on judicial authority than are the members of this Court, and none stand more in admiration of the Constitution's design to leave the selection of the President to the people, through their legislatures, and to the political sphere. When contending parties invoke the process of the courts, however, it becomes our unsought responsibility to resolve the federal and constitutional issues the judicial system has been forced to confront.

The judgment of the Supreme Court of Florida is reversed, and the case is remanded for further proceedings not inconsistent with this opinion.

Chief Justice Rehnquist, with whom Justice Scalia and Justice Thomas join, concurring. . . .

We deal here not with an ordinary election, but with an election for the President of the United States. . . . In most cases, comity and respect for federalism compel us to defer to the decisions of state courts on issues of state law. That practice reflects our understanding that the decisions of state courts are definitive pronouncements of the will of the States as sovereigns. Cf. *Erie R. Co. v. Tompkins* (1938). Of course, in ordinary cases, the distribution of powers among the branches of a State's government raises no questions of federal constitutional law, subject to the requirement that the government be republican in character. See U.S. Const., Art. IV, §4. But there are a few exceptional cases in which the Constitution imposes a duty or confers a power on a particular branch of a State's government. This is one of them. Article II, §1, cl. 2, provides that "[e]ach State shall appoint, in such Manner as the *Legislature* thereof may direct," electors for President and Vice President. (Emphasis added.) Thus, the text of the election law itself, and not just its interpretation by the courts of the States, takes on independent significance. . . . A significant departure from the legislative scheme for appointing Presidential electors presents a federal constitutional question. . . .

In Florida, the legislature has chosen to hold statewide elections to appoint the State's 25 electors. Importantly, the legislature has delegated the authority to run the elections and to oversee election disputes to the Secretary of State and to state circuit courts. Isolated sections of the code may well admit of more than one interpretation, but the general coherence of the legislative scheme may not be altered by judicial interpretation so as to wholly change the statutorily provided apportionment of responsibility among these various bodies. In any election but a Presidential election, the Florida Supreme Court can give as little or as much deference to Florida's executives as it chooses, so far as Article II is concerned, and this Court will have no cause to question the court's actions. But, with respect to a Presidential election, the court must be both mindful of the legislature's role under Article II in choosing the manner of appointing electors and deferential to those bodies expressly empowered by the legislature to carry out its constitutional mandate.

In order to determine whether a state court has infringed upon the legislature's authority, we necessarily must examine the law of the State as it existed prior to the action of the court. Though we generally defer to state courts on the interpretation of state law there are of course areas in which the Constitution requires this Court to undertake an independent, if still deferential, analysis of state law. . . .

This inquiry does not imply a disrespect for state courts but rather a respect for the constitutionally prescribed role of state legislatures. To attach definitive weight to the pronouncement of a state court, when the very question at issue is whether the court has actually departed from the statutory meaning, would be to abdicate our responsibility to enforce the explicit requirements of Article II.

JUSTICE BREYER, with whom JUSTICE STEVENS and JUSTICE GINSBURG join.

The Court was wrong to take this case. It was wrong to grant a stay. It should now vacate that stay and permit the Florida Supreme Court to decide whether the recount should resume. . . .

Despite the reminder that this case involves "an election for the President of the United States" (Rehnquist, C.J., concurring), no preeminent legal concern, or practical concern related to legal questions, required this Court to hear this case, let alone to issue a stay that stopped Florida's recount process in its tracks. . . . Of course, the selection of the President is of fundamental national importance. But that importance is political, not legal. And this Court should resist the temptation unnecessarily to resolve tangential legal disputes, where doing so threatens to determine the outcome of the election.

The Constitution and federal statutes themselves make clear that restraint is appropriate. They set forth a road map of how to resolve disputes about electors, even after an election as close as this one. That road map foresees resolution of electoral disputes by state courts. But it nowhere provides for involvement by the United States Supreme Court. To the contrary, the Twelfth Amendment commits to Congress the authority and responsibility to count electoral votes. A federal statute, the Electoral Count Act, enacted after the close 1876 Hayes-Tilden Presidential election, specifies that, after States have tried to resolve disputes (through "judicial" or other means), Congress is the body primarily authorized to resolve remaining disputes. See Electoral Count Act of 1887.

The legislative history of the Act makes clear its intent to commit the power to resolve such disputes to Congress, rather than the courts:

> The two Houses are, by the Constitution, authorized to make the count of electoral votes. They can only count legal votes, and in doing so must determine, from the best evidence to be had, what are legal votes. . . . The power to determine rests with the two Houses, and there is no other constitutional tribunal.

49th Cong., 1st Sess. (1886) (report submitted by Rep. Caldwell, Select Committee on the Election of President and Vice-President). . . .

The Act goes on to set out rules for the congressional determination of disputes about those votes. . . . Given this detailed, comprehensive scheme for counting electoral votes, there is no reason to believe that federal law either foresees or requires resolution of such a political issue by this Court. Nor, for that matter, is there any reason to think that the Constitution's Framers would have reached a different conclusion. Madison, at least, believed that allowing the judiciary to choose the presidential electors "was out of the question." Madison, July 25, 1787 (reprinted in 5 Elliot's *Debates on the Federal Constitution* 363 (2d ed. 1876)).

The decision by both the Constitution's Framers and the 1886 Congress to minimize this Court's role in resolving close federal presidential elections is as wise as it is clear. However awkward or difficult it may be for Congress to resolve difficult electoral disputes, Congress, being a political body, expresses the people's will far more accurately than does an unelected Court. And the people's will is what elections are about.

Moreover, Congress was fully aware of the danger that would arise should it ask judges, unarmed with appropriate legal standards, to resolve a hotly contested Presidential election contest. Just after the 1876 Presidential election, Florida, South Carolina, and Louisiana each sent two slates of electors to Washington. Without these States, Tilden, the Democrat, had 184 electoral votes, one short of the number required to win the Presidency. With those States, Hayes, his Republican opponent, would have had 185. In order to choose between the two slates of electors, Congress decided to appoint an electoral commission composed of five Senators, five Representatives, and five Supreme Court Justices. Initially the Commission was to be evenly divided between Republicans and Democrats, with Justice David Davis, an Independent, to possess the decisive vote. However, when at the last minute the Illinois Legislature elected Justice Davis to the United States Senate, the final position on the Commission was filled by Supreme Court Justice Joseph P. Bradley.

The Commission divided along partisan lines, and the responsibility to cast the deciding vote fell to Justice Bradley. He decided to accept the votes by the Republican electors, and thereby awarded the Presidency to Hayes.

Justice Bradley immediately became the subject of vociferous attacks. Bradley was accused of accepting bribes, of being captured by railroad interests, and of an eleventh-hour change in position after a night in which his house "was surrounded by the carriages" of Republican partisans and railroad officials. C. Woodward, *Reunion and Reaction* 159-160 (1966). . . . For present purposes, the relevance of this history lies in the fact that the participation in the work of the electoral commission by five Justices, including Justice Bradley, did not lend that process legitimacy. Nor did it assure the public that the process had worked fairly, guided by the law. Rather, it simply embroiled Members of the Court in partisan conflict, thereby undermining respect for the judicial process. And the Congress that later enacted the Electoral Count Act knew it.

This history may help to explain why I think it not only legally wrong, but also most unfortunate, for the Court simply to have terminated the Florida recount. Those who caution judicial restraint in resolving political disputes have described the quintessential case for that restraint as a case marked, among other things, by the "strangeness of the issue," its "intractability to principled resolution," its "sheer momentousness, . . . which tends to unbalance judicial judgment," and "the inner vulnerability, the self-doubt of an institution which is electorally irresponsible and has no earth to draw strength from." Bickel, [*The Least Dangerous Branch*, 184 (1962)]. Those characteristics mark this case.

I fear that in order to bring this agonizingly long election process to a definitive conclusion, we have not adequately attended to that necessary "check upon our own exercise of power," "our own sense of self-restraint." *United States v. Butler* (1936) (Stone, J., dissenting). Justice Brandeis once said of the Court, "The most important thing we do is not doing." Bickel, at 71. What it does today, the Court should have left undone. . . .

STUDY GUIDE

- Is the majority's opinion in *Zivotofsky v. Clinton* consistent with *Baker v. Carr*?
- What role does the fact that Congress created a statute play in the political question analysis?
- Quoting from *INS v. Chadha*, the Chief Justice writes, "No policy underlying the political question doctrine suggests that Congress or the Executive . . . can decide the constitutionality of a statute; that is a decision for the courts." Is this correct? Can an executive branch official decline to execute a statute he deems plainly unconstitutional, even if a court has not yet opined on it? Indeed, because the judiciary does not provide advisory opinions, what should the official do if the law is never challenged?
- Why would President Bush sign the Foreign Relations Authorization Act into law if he determined a provision was unconstitutional?
- In 2015, the Supreme Court heard this case a second time, and found that Congress could not require the executive branch to list Zivotofsky's place of birth as Israel, rather than as Jerusalem.

Zivotofsky ex rel. Zivotofsky v. Clinton

566 U.S. 189 (2012)

Chief Justice Roberts delivered the opinion of the Court.

Congress enacted a statute providing that Americans born in Jerusalem may elect to have "Israel" listed as the place of birth on their passports. The State Department declined to follow that law, citing its longstanding policy of not taking a position on the political status of Jerusalem. When sued by an American who invoked the statute, the Secretary of State argued that the courts lacked authority to decide the case because it presented a political question. The Court of Appeals so held.

We disagree. The courts are fully capable of determining whether this statute may be given effect, or instead must be struck down in light of authority conferred on the Executive by the Constitution.

I

A

In 2002, Congress enacted the Foreign Relations Authorization Act, Fiscal Year 2003. Section 214 of the Act is entitled "United States Policy with Respect to Jerusalem as the Capital of Israel." The first two subsections express Congress's "commitment" to relocating the United States Embassy in Israel to Jerusalem. The third bars funding for the publication of official Government documents that do not list Jerusalem as the capital of Israel. The fourth and final provision, §214(d), is the only one at stake in this case. Entitled "Record of Place of Birth as Israel for Passport Purposes," it provides that "[f]or purposes of the registration of birth, certification of nationality, or issuance of a passport of a United States citizen born in the city of Jerusalem, the Secretary shall, upon the request of the citizen or the citizen's legal guardian, record the place of birth as Israel."

The State Department's Foreign Affairs Manual states that "[w]here the birthplace of the applicant is located in territory disputed by another country, the city or area of birth may be written in the passport." The manual specifically directs that passport officials should enter "JERUSALEM" and should "not write Israel or Jordan" when recording the birthplace of a person born in Jerusalem on a passport.

Section 214(d) sought to override this instruction by allowing citizens born in Jerusalem to have "Israel" recorded on their passports if they wish. In signing the Foreign Relations Authorization Act into law, President George W. Bush stated his belief that §214 "impermissibly interferes with the President's constitutional authority to conduct the Nation's foreign affairs and to supervise the unitary executive branch." He added that if the section is "construed as mandatory," then it would "interfere with the President's constitutional authority to formulate the position of the United States, speak for the Nation in international affairs, and determine the terms on which recognition is given to foreign states." He concluded by emphasizing that "U.S. policy regarding Jerusalem has not changed." The President made no specific reference to the passport mandate in §214(d).

B

Petitioner Menachem Binyamin Zivotofsky was born in Jerusalem on October 17, 2002, shortly after §214(d) was enacted. Zivotofsky's parents were American citizens and he accordingly was as well, by virtue of congressional enactment. Zivotofsky's mother filed an application for a consular report of birth abroad and a United States passport. She requested that his place of birth be listed as "Jerusalem, Israel" on both documents. U.S. officials informed Zivotofsky's mother that State Department policy prohibits recording "Israel" as Zivotofsky's place of birth. Pursuant to that policy, Zivotofsky was issued a passport and consular report of birth abroad listing only "Jerusalem."

Zivotofsky's parents filed a complaint on his behalf against the Secretary of State. Zivotofsky sought a declaratory judgment and a permanent injunction ordering the Secretary to identify his place of birth as "Jerusalem, Israel" in the official documents. The District Court granted the Secretary's motion to dismiss the complaint on the grounds that Zivotofsky lacked standing and that his complaint presented a nonjusticiable political question. . . .

II

The lower courts concluded that Zivotofsky's claim presents a political question and therefore cannot be adjudicated. We disagree.

In general, the Judiciary has a responsibility to decide cases properly before it, even those it "would gladly avoid." *Cohens v. Virginia* (1821). Our precedents have identified a narrow exception to that rule, known as the "political question" doctrine. We have explained that a controversy "involves a political question . . . where there is 'a textually demonstrable constitutional commitment of the issue to a coordinate political department; or a lack of judicially discoverable and manageable standards for resolving it.'" *Nixon v. United States* (1993) (quoting *Baker v. Carr* (1962)). In such a case, we have held that a court lacks the authority to decide the dispute before it.

The lower courts ruled that this case involves a political question because deciding Zivotofsky's claim would force the Judicial Branch to interfere with the President's exercise of constitutional power committed to him alone. The District Court understood Zivotofsky to ask the courts to "decide the political status of Jerusalem." This misunderstands the issue presented. Zivotofsky does not ask the courts to determine whether Jerusalem is the capital of Israel. He instead seeks to determine whether he may vindicate his statutory right, under §214(d), to choose to have Israel recorded on his passport as his place of birth. . . .

The existence of a statutory right, however, is certainly relevant to the Judiciary's power to decide Zivotofsky's claim. The federal courts are not being asked to supplant a foreign policy decision of the political branches with the courts' own unmoored determination of what United States policy toward Jerusalem should be. Instead, Zivotofsky requests that the courts enforce a specific statutory right. To resolve his claim, the Judiciary must decide if Zivotofsky's interpretation of the statute is correct, and whether the statute is constitutional. This is a familiar judicial exercise.

Moreover, because the parties do not dispute the interpretation of §214(d), the only real question for the courts is whether the statute is constitutional. At least since *Marbury v. Madison* (1803), we have recognized that when an Act of Congress is alleged to conflict with the Constitution, "[i]t is emphatically the province and duty of the judicial department to say what the law is." That duty will sometimes involve the "[r]esolution of litigation challenging the constitutional authority of one of the three branches," but courts cannot avoid their responsibility merely "because the issues have political implications." *INS v. Chadha* (1983).

In this case, determining the constitutionality of §214(d) involves deciding whether the statute impermissibly intrudes upon Presidential powers under the Constitution. If so, the law must be invalidated and Zivotofsky's case should be dismissed for failure to state a claim. If, on the other hand, the statute does not trench on the President's powers, then the Secretary must be ordered to issue Zivotofsky a passport that complies with §214(d). Either way, the political question doctrine is not implicated. "No policy underlying the political question doctrine suggests that Congress or the Executive . . . can decide the constitutionality of a statute; that is a decision for the courts."

The Secretary contends that "there is 'a textually demonstrable constitutional commitment'" to the President of the sole power to recognize foreign sovereigns and, as a corollary, to determine whether an American born in Jerusalem may choose to have Israel listed as his place of birth on his passport. *Nixon* (quoting

Baker). Perhaps. But there is, of course, no exclusive commitment to the Executive of the power to determine the constitutionality of a statute. The Judicial Branch appropriately exercises that authority, including in a case such as this, where the question is whether Congress or the Executive is "aggrandizing its power at the expense of another branch." *Freytag v. Commissioner* (1991); see, *e.g.*, *Myers v. United States* (1926) (finding a statute unconstitutional because it encroached upon the President's removal power); *Bowsher v. Synar* (1986) (finding a statute unconstitutional because it "intruded into the executive function"); *Morrison v. Olson* (1988) (upholding a statute's constitutionality against a charge that it "impermissibly interfere[d] with the President's exercise of his constitutionally appointed functions").

Our precedents have also found the political question doctrine implicated when there is "'a lack of judicially discoverable and manageable standards for resolving'" the question before the court. *Nixon* (quoting *Baker*). Framing the issue as the lower courts did, in terms of whether the Judiciary may decide the political status of Jerusalem, certainly raises those concerns. They dissipate, however, when the issue is recognized to be the more focused one of the constitutionality of §214(d). Indeed, both sides offer detailed legal arguments regarding whether §214(d) is constitutional in light of powers committed to the Executive, and whether Congress's own powers with respect to passports must be weighed in analyzing this question.

For example, the Secretary reprises on the merits her argument on the political question issue, claiming that the Constitution gives the Executive the exclusive power to formulate recognition policy. She roots her claim in the Constitution's declaration that the President shall "receive Ambassadors and other public Ministers." U.S. Const., Art. II, §3. According to the Secretary, "[c]enturies-long Executive Branch practice, congressional acquiescence, and decisions by this Court" confirm that the "receive Ambassadors" clause confers upon the Executive the exclusive power of recognition.

The Secretary observes that "President Washington and his cabinet unanimously decided that the President could receive the ambassador from the new government of France without first consulting Congress." . . . The Secretary will not "list[] as a place of birth a country whose sovereignty over the relevant territory the United States does not recognize. Therefore, she claims, "listing 'Israel' as the place of birth would constitute an official decision by the United States to begin to treat Jerusalem as a city located within Israel."

For his part, Zivotofsky argues that, far from being an exercise of the recognition power, §214(d) is instead a "legitimate and permissible" exercise of Congress's "authority to legislate on the form and content of a passport." . . . Zivotofsky suggests that Congress's authority to enact §214(d) derives specifically from its powers over naturalization, U.S. Const., Art. I, §8, cl. 4, and foreign commerce, *id.*, §8, cl. 3. According to Zivotofsky, Congress has used these powers to pass laws regulating the content and issuance of passports since 1856. . . .

Further, Zivotofsky claims that even if §214(d) does implicate the recognition power, that is not a power the Constitution commits exclusively to the Executive.

Zivotofsky argues that the Secretary is overreading the authority granted to the President in the "receive Ambassadors" clause. He observes that in the Federalist Papers, Alexander Hamilton described the power conferred by this clause as "more a matter of dignity than of authority," and called it "a circumstance, which will be without consequence in the administration of the government." The Federalist No. 69. Zivotofsky also points to other clauses in the Constitution, such as Congress's power to declare war, that suggest some congressional role in recognition. . . .

Recitation of these arguments — which sound in familiar principles of constitutional interpretation — is enough to establish that this case does not "turn on standards that defy judicial application." Resolution of Zivotofsky's claim demands careful examination of the textual, structural, and historical evidence put forward by the parties regarding the nature of the statute and of the passport and recognition powers. This is what courts do. The political question doctrine poses no bar to judicial review of this case. . . .

Having determined that this case is justiciable, we leave it to the lower courts to consider the merits in the first instance. The judgment of the Court of Appeals for the D.C. Circuit is vacated, and the case is remanded for further proceedings consistent with this opinion.

JUSTICE SOTOMAYOR, with whom JUSTICE BREYER joins as to Part I, concurring in part and concurring in the judgment.

As this case illustrates, the proper application of *Baker*'s six factors has generated substantial confusion in the lower courts. I concur in the Court's conclusion that this case does not present a political question. I write separately, however, because I understand the inquiry required by the political question doctrine to be more demanding than that suggested by the Court. . . .

II

The court below held that this case presented a political question because it thought petitioner's suit asked the court to decide an issue "textually committed" to a coordinate branch — namely, "to review a policy of the State Department implementing the President's decision" to keep the United States out of the debate over the status of Jerusalem. Largely for the reasons set out by the Court, I agree that the Court of Appeals misapprehended the nature of its task. In two respects, however, my understanding of the political question doctrine might require a court to engage in further analysis beyond that relied upon by the Court.

First, the Court appropriately recognizes that petitioner's claim to a statutory right is "relevant" to the justiciability inquiry required in this case. In order to evaluate whether a case presents a political question, a court must first identify with precision the issue it is being asked to decide. Here, petitioner's suit claims that a federal statute provides him with a right to have "Israel" listed as his place of birth on his passport and other related documents. To decide that question, a court must determine whether the statute is constitutional, and therefore mandates the

Secretary of State to issue petitioner's desired passport, or unconstitutional, in which case his suit is at an end. Resolution of that issue is not one "textually committed" to another branch; to the contrary, it is committed to this one. In no fashion does the question require a court to review the wisdom of the President's policy toward Jerusalem or any other decision committed to the discretion of a coordinate department. For that reason, I agree that the decision below should be reversed.

That is not to say, however, that no statute could give rise to a political question. It is not impossible to imagine a case involving the application or even the constitutionality of an enactment that would present a nonjusticiable issue. Indeed, this Court refused to determine whether an Ohio state constitutional provision offended the Republican Guarantee Clause, Art. IV, §4, holding that "the question of whether that guarantee of the Constitution has been disregarded presents no justiciable controversy." *Ohio ex rel. Davis v. Hildebrant* (1916). A similar result would follow if Congress passed a statute, for instance, purporting to award financial relief to those improperly "tried" of impeachment offenses. To adjudicate claims under such a statute would require a court to resolve the very same issue we found nonjusticiable in *Nixon*. Such examples are atypical, but they suffice to show that the foreclosure altogether of political question analysis in statutory cases is unwarranted.

Second, the Court suggests that this case does not implicate the political question doctrine's concern with issues exhibiting "'a lack of judicially discoverable and manageable standards,'" because the parties' arguments rely on textual, structural, and historical evidence of the kind that courts routinely consider. But that was equally true in *Nixon*, a case in which we found that "the use of the word 'try' in the first sentence of the Impeachment Trial Clause lacks sufficient precision to afford any judicially manageable standard of review of the Senate's actions." We reached that conclusion even though the parties' briefs focused upon the text of the Impeachment Trial Clause, "the Constitution's drafting history," "contemporaneous commentary," "the unbroken practice of the Senate for 150 years," contemporary dictionary meanings, "Hamilton's Federalist essays," and the practice in the House of Lords prior to ratification. Such evidence was no more or less unfamiliar to courts than that on which the parties rely here.

In my view, it is not whether the evidence upon which litigants rely is common to judicial consideration that determines whether a case lacks judicially discoverable and manageable standards. Rather, it is whether that evidence in fact provides a court a basis to adjudicate meaningfully the issue with which it is presented. The answer will almost always be yes, but if the parties' textual, structural, and historical evidence is inapposite or wholly unilluminating, rendering judicial decision no more than guesswork, a case relying on the ordinary kinds of arguments offered to courts might well still present justiciability concerns.

In this case, however, the Court of Appeals majority found a political question solely on the basis that this case required resolution of an issue "textually committed" to the Executive Branch. Because there was no such textual commitment, I respectfully concur in the Court's decision to reverse the Court of Appeals.

JUSTICE ALITO, concurring in the judgment.

This case presents a narrow question, namely, whether the statutory provision at issue infringes the power of the President to regulate the contents of a passport. This case does not require the Judiciary to decide whether the power to recognize foreign governments and the extent of their territory is conferred exclusively on the President or is shared with Congress. Petitioner does not claim that the statutory provision in question represents an attempt by Congress to dictate United States policy regarding the status of Jerusalem. Instead, petitioner contends in effect that Congress has the power to mandate that an American citizen born abroad be given the option of including in his passport and Consular Report of Birth Abroad (CRBA) what amounts to a statement of personal belief on the status of Jerusalem. . . .

Under our case law, determining the constitutionality of an Act of Congress may present a political question, but I do not think that the narrow question presented here falls within that category. Delineating the precise dividing line between the powers of Congress and the President with respect to the contents of a passport is not an easy matter, but I agree with the Court that it does not constitute a political question that the Judiciary is unable to decide.

JUSTICE BREYER, dissenting.

. . . Justice Sotomayor [in her concurring opinion] adds that the circumstances in which these prudential considerations lead the Court not to decide a case otherwise properly before it are rare. I agree. But in my view we nonetheless have before us such a case. Four sets of prudential considerations, *taken together*, lead me to that conclusion.

First, the issue before us arises in the field of foreign affairs. . . . The Constitution primarily delegates the foreign affairs powers "to the political departments of the government, Executive and Legislative," not to the Judiciary. *Chicago & Southern Air Lines, Inc. v. Waterman S.S. Corp.* (1948); see also *Marbury v. Madison* (1803). And that fact is not surprising. Decisionmaking in this area typically is highly political. It is "delicate" and "complex." *Chicago & Southern Air Lines.* It often rests upon information readily available to the Executive Branch and to the intelligence committees of Congress, but not readily available to the courts. It frequently is highly dependent upon what Justice Jackson called "prophecy." And the creation of wise foreign policy typically lies well beyond the experience or professional capacity of a judge. *Ibid.* At the same time, where foreign affairs is at issue, the practical need for the United States to speak "with one voice and ac[t] as one," is particularly important. See *United States v. Pink* (1942) (Frankfurter, J., concurring). . . .

Second, if the courts must answer the constitutional question before us, they may well have to evaluate the foreign policy implications of foreign policy decisions. The constitutional question focuses upon a statutory provision, §214(d), that says: The Secretary of State, upon the request of a U.S. citizen born in Jerusalem (or upon the request of the citizen's legal guardian), shall "record" in the citizen's passport or consular birth report "the place of birth as Israel." And the question is whether this statute unconstitutionally seeks to limit the President's inherent constitutional authority to make certain kinds of foreign policy decisions. . . .

The Secretary of State argues that the President's constitutional authority to determine foreign policy includes the power to recognize foreign governments, that this Court has long recognized that the latter power belongs to the President exclusively, that the power includes the power to determine claims over disputed territory as well as the policy governing recognition decisions, and that the statute unconstitutionally limits the President's exclusive authority to exercise these powers. . . .

Zivotofsky, supported by several Members of Congress, points out that the Constitution also grants Congress powers related to foreign affairs, such as the powers to declare war, to regulate foreign commerce, and to regulate naturalization. See Art. I, §8, cls. 3, 4, 11. They add that Congress may share some of the recognition power and its attendant power of determining claims over disputed territory. And they add that Congress may enact laws concerning travel into this country and concerning the citizenship of children born abroad to U.S. citizens. They argue that these powers include the power to specify the content of a passport (or consular birth report). And when such a specification takes the form of statutory law, they say, the Constitution requires the President (through the Secretary of State) to execute that statute. See Art. II, §3.

Were the statutory provision undisputedly concerned only with purely administrative matters (or were its enforcement undisputedly to involve only major foreign policy matters), judicial efforts to answer the constitutional question might not involve judges in trying to answer questions of foreign policy. But in the Middle East, administrative matters can have implications that extend far beyond the purely administrative. Political reactions in that region can prove uncertain. And in that context it may well turn out that resolution of the constitutional argument will require a court to decide how far the statute, in practice, reaches beyond the purely administrative, determining not only whether but also the extent to which enforcement will interfere with the President's ability to make significant recognition-related foreign policy decisions. . . .

A judge's ability to evaluate opposing claims of this kind is minimal. At the same time, a judicial effort to do so risks inadvertently jeopardizing sound foreign policy decisionmaking by the other branches of Government. How, for example, is this Court to determine whether, or the extent to which, the continuation of the adjudication that it now orders will itself have a foreign policy effect?

Third, the countervailing interests in obtaining judicial resolution of the constitutional determination are not particularly strong ones. Zivotofsky does not assert the kind of interest, *e.g.*, an interest in property or bodily integrity, which courts have traditionally sought to protect. Nor, importantly, does he assert an interest in vindicating a basic right of the kind that the Constitution grants to individuals and that courts traditionally have protected from invasion by the other branches of Government. And I emphasize this fact because the need for judicial action in such cases can trump the foreign policy concerns that I have mentioned. . . .

The interest that Zivotofsky asserts, however, is akin to an ideological interest. . . . This is not to say that Zivotofsky's claim is unimportant or that the injury is not serious or even that it is purely ideological. It is to point out that those suffering somewhat similar harms have sometimes had to look to the political branches for resolution of relevant legal issues.

Fourth, insofar as the controversy reflects different foreign policy views among the political branches of Government, those branches have nonjudicial methods of working out their differences. The Executive and Legislative Branches frequently work out disagreements through ongoing contacts and relationships, involving, for example, budget authorizations, confirmation of personnel, committee hearings, and a host of more informal contacts, which, taken together, ensure that, in practice, Members of Congress as well as the President play an important role in the shaping of foreign policy. Indeed, both the Legislative Branch and the Executive Branch typically understand the need to work each with the other in order to create effective foreign policy. In that understanding, those related contacts, and the continuous foreign policy-related relationship lies the possibility of working out the kind of disagreement we see before us. Moreover, if application of the political-question "doctrine ultimately turns, as Learned Hand put it, on 'how importunately the occasion demands an answer,'" *Nixon* (Souter, J., concurring in judgment) (quoting L. Hand, The Bill of Rights 15 (1958)), the ability of the political branches to work out their differences minimizes the need for judicial intervention here.

The upshot is that this case is unusual both in its minimal need for judicial intervention and in its more serious risk that intervention will bring about "embarrassment," show lack of "respect" for the other branches, and potentially disrupt sound foreign policy decisionmaking. For these prudential reasons, I would hold that the political-question doctrine bars further judicial consideration of this case. And I would affirm the Court of Appeals' similar conclusion.

With respect, I dissent.

CHAPTER 9

Standing, Ripeness, and Mootness

The next three limitations on the judicial power we will consider — standing, ripeness, and mootness — grow out of the same concerns that led the first Supreme Court Justices to refuse to offer advisory opinions. Each doctrine ensures that there is a genuine "case or controversy" — an actual dispute — to be decided by a court and an actual injury that can be remedied by a judicial judgment.

ASSIGNMENT 1

A. STANDING

As we discussed in Chapter 8, federal judges can only decide issues that are brought to courts in adversarial proceedings; *advisory opinions* are prohibited. This practice is derived, in part, from Article III, Section 2, which provides that judicial power is limited to certain enumerated "cases" or "controversies":

> The judicial Power shall extend to all (1) *Cases*, in Law and Equity, arising under this Constitution, the Laws of the United States, and Treaties made, or which shall be made, under their Authority; — (2) to all *Cases* affecting Ambassadors, other public Ministers and Consuls; — (3) to all *Cases* of admiralty and maritime Jurisdiction; — (4) to *Controversies* to which the United States shall be a Party; — (5) to *Controversies* between two or more States; — (6) [to *controversies*] between a State and Citizens of another

> State; — (7) [to *controversies*] between Citizens of different States, — (8) [to *controversies*] between Citizens of the same State claiming Lands under Grants of different States, and (9) [to *controversies*] between a State, or the Citizens thereof, and foreign States, Citizens or Subjects. (emphasis added.)

Unless plaintiffs can show that their complaint is premised on one of these nine "heads," or areas of jurisdiction, the federal court cannot hear the case. From these requirements, the Supreme Court has developed the doctrine of *standing*; that is, plaintiffs can only bring suit in federal court if they have standing under Article III. This chapter offers a mere introduction to this fairly intricate doctrine. All students should consider taking a class in Federal Courts, even if they do not plan to practice in federal courts; all attorneys will need to know how to keep a case *in* state court, or remand a case *back* to state court.

The Supreme Court has explained that Article III imposes three requirements on plaintiffs in order to establish standing:

> Over the years, our cases have established that the irreducible constitutional minimum of standing contains three elements. First, the plaintiff must have suffered an "injury in fact" — an invasion of a legally protected interest which is (a) concrete and particularized; and (b) "actual or imminent, not 'conjectural' or 'hypothetical.'" Second, there must be a causal connection between the injury and the conduct complained of — the injury has to be "fairly . . . trace[able] to the challenged action of the defendant, and not . . . [the] result [of] the independent action of some third party not before the court. Third, it must be "likely," as opposed to merely "speculative," that the injury will be "redressed by a favorable decision." The party invoking federal jurisdiction bears the burden of establishing these elements. *Lujan v. Defenders of Wildlife* (1992) (citations omitted).

STUDY GUIDE

- When reading *Allen v. Wright*, consider whether the Court is properly limiting the jurisdiction of federal courts, or is, instead, preventing them from fulfilling their responsibility to protect constitutional rights and enforce limits on federal power.

Allen v. Wright

468 U.S. 737 (1984)

JUSTICE O'CONNOR delivered the opinion of the Court.

Parents of black public school children allege in this nationwide class action that the Internal Revenue Service (IRS) has not adopted sufficient standards and procedures to fulfill its obligation to deny tax-exempt status to racially discriminatory private schools. They assert that the IRS thereby harms them directly and interferes with the ability of their children to receive an education in desegregated public schools. The issue before us is whether plaintiffs have standing to bring this suit. We hold that they do not.

I

The IRS denies tax-exempt status under the Internal Revenue Code, and hence eligibility to receive charitable contributions deductible from income taxes to racially discriminatory private schools. The IRS policy requires that a school applying for tax-exempt status show that it

> admits the students of any race to all the rights, privileges, programs, and activities generally accorded or made available to students at that school and that the school does not discriminate on the basis of race in administration of its educational policies, admissions policies, scholarship and loan programs, and athletic and other school-administered programs.

To carry out this policy, the IRS has established guidelines and procedures for determining whether a particular school is in fact racially nondiscriminatory. Failure to comply with the guidelines "will ordinarily result in the proposed revocation of" tax-exempt status. . . .

In 1976, respondents challenged these guidelines and procedures in a suit filed in Federal District Court against the Secretary of the Treasury and the Commissioner of Internal Revenue. The plaintiffs named in the complaint are parents of black children who, at the time the complaint was filed, were attending public schools in seven States in school districts undergoing desegregation. They brought this nationwide class action

> on behalf of themselves and their children, and . . . on behalf of all other parents of black children attending public school systems undergoing, or which may in the future undergo, desegregation pursuant to court order [or] HEW regulations and guidelines, under state law, or voluntarily.

They estimated that the class they seek to represent includes several million persons.

Respondents allege in their complaint that many racially segregated private schools were created or expanded in their communities at the time the public schools were undergoing desegregation. According to the complaint, many such private schools, including 17 schools or school systems identified by name in the complaint (perhaps some 30 schools in all), receive tax exemptions either directly or through the tax-exempt status of "umbrella" organizations that operate or support the schools. . . . Respondents allege that the challenged Government conduct harms them in two ways. The challenged conduct

> (a) constitutes tangible federal financial aid and other support for racially segregated educational institutions, and
>
> (b) fosters and encourages the organization, operation and expansion of institutions providing racially segregated educational opportunities for white children avoiding attendance in desegregating public school districts, and thereby interferes with the

> efforts of federal courts, HEW and local school authorities to desegregate public school districts which have been operating racially dual school systems.

Thus, respondents do not allege that their children have been the victims of discriminatory exclusion from the schools whose tax exemptions they challenge as unlawful. Indeed, they have not alleged at any stage of this litigation that their children have ever applied or would ever apply to any private school. Rather, respondents claim a direct injury from the mere fact of the challenged Government conduct and, as indicated by the restriction of the plaintiff class to parents of children in desegregating school districts, injury to their children's opportunity to receive a desegregated education. The latter injury is traceable to the IRS grant of tax exemptions to racially discriminatory schools, respondents allege, chiefly because contributions to such schools are deductible from income taxes under §§170(a)(1) and (c)(2) of the Internal Revenue Code and the "deductions facilitate the raising of funds to organize new schools and expand existing schools in order to accommodate white students avoiding attendance in desegregating public school districts." . . .

II

A

Article III of the Constitution confines the federal courts to adjudicating actual "cases" and "controversies." As the Court explained in *Valley Forge Christian College v. Americans United for Separation of Church and State, Inc.* (1982), the "case or controversy" requirement defines with respect to the Judicial Branch the idea of separation of powers on which the Federal Government is founded. The several doctrines that have grown up to elaborate that requirement are "founded in concern about the proper — and properly limited — role of the courts in a democratic society." *Warth v. Seldin* (1975). . . . The case-or-controversy doctrines state fundamental limits on federal judicial power in our system of government.

The Art. III doctrine that requires a litigant to have "standing" to invoke the power of a federal court is perhaps the most important of these doctrines. "In essence, the question of standing is whether the litigant is entitled to have the court decide the merits of the dispute or of particular issues." *Warth v. Seldin.* Standing doctrine embraces several judicially self-imposed limits on the exercise of federal jurisdiction, such as the general prohibition on a litigant's raising another person's legal rights, the rule barring adjudication of generalized grievances more appropriately addressed in the representative branches, and the requirement that a plaintiff's complaint fall within the zone of interests protected by the law invoked. The requirement of standing, however, has a core component derived directly from the Constitution. A plaintiff must allege personal injury fairly traceable to the defendant's allegedly unlawful conduct and likely to be redressed by the requested relief.

Like the prudential component, the constitutional component of standing doctrine incorporates concepts concededly not susceptible of precise definition. The injury alleged must be, for example, "distinct and palpable," and not "abstract" or "conjectural" or "hypothetical." The injury must be "fairly" traceable to the challenged action, and relief from the injury must be "likely" to follow from a favorable decision. These terms cannot be defined so as to make application of the constitutional standing requirement a mechanical exercise. . . .

More important, the law of Art. III standing is built on a single basic idea — the idea of separation of powers. It is this fact which makes possible the gradual clarification of the law through judicial application. Of course, both federal and state courts have long experience in applying and elaborating in numerous contexts the pervasive and fundamental notion of separation of powers.

Determining standing in a particular case may be facilitated by clarifying principles or even clear rules developed in prior cases. Typically, however, the standing inquiry requires careful judicial examination of a complaint's allegations to ascertain whether the particular plaintiff is entitled to an adjudication of the particular claims asserted. Is the injury too abstract, or otherwise not appropriate, to be considered judicially cognizable? Is the line of causation between the illegal conduct and injury too attenuated? Is the prospect of obtaining relief from the injury as a result of a favorable ruling too speculative? These questions and any others relevant to the standing inquiry must be answered by reference to the Art. III notion that federal courts may exercise power only "in the last resort, and as a necessity," *Chicago & Grand Trunk R. Co. v. Wellman* (1892), and only when adjudication is "consistent with a system of separated powers and [the dispute is one] traditionally thought to be capable of resolution through the judicial process." *Flast v. Cohen* (1968).

B

Respondents allege two injuries in their complaint to support their standing to bring this lawsuit. First, they say that they are harmed directly by the mere fact of Government financial aid to discriminatory private schools. Second, they say that the federal tax exemptions to racially discriminatory private schools in their communities impair their ability to have their public schools desegregated. . . .

We conclude that neither suffices to support respondents' standing. The first fails under clear precedents of this Court because it does not constitute judicially cognizable injury. The second fails because the alleged injury is not fairly traceable to the assertedly unlawful conduct of the IRS.[1]

[1] The "fairly traceable" and "redressability" components of the constitutional standing inquiry were initially articulated by this Court as "two facets of a single causation requirement." To the extent there is a difference, it is that the former examines the causal connection between the assertedly unlawful conduct and the alleged injury, whereas the latter examines the causal connection between the alleged injury and the judicial relief requested. Cases such as this, in which the relief requested goes well beyond the violation of law alleged, illustrate why it is important to keep the inquiries separate if the "redressability" component is to focus on the requested relief. Even if the relief respondents request might have a substantial effect on the desegregation of public schools, whatever deficiencies exist in the opportunities for desegregated education for respondents' children might not be traceable to IRS violations of law — grants of tax exemptions to racially discriminatory schools in respondents' communities.

Respondents' first claim of injury can be interpreted in two ways. It might be a claim simply to have the Government avoid the violation of law alleged in respondents' complaint. Alternatively, it might be a claim of stigmatic injury, or denigration, suffered by all members of a racial group when the Government discriminates on the basis of race. Under neither interpretation is this claim of injury judicially cognizable.

This Court has repeatedly held that an asserted right to have the Government act in accordance with law is not sufficient, standing alone, to confer jurisdiction on a federal court. In *Schlesinger v. Reservists Committee to Stop the War* (1974), for example, the Court rejected a claim of citizen standing to challenge Armed Forces Reserve commissions held by Members of Congress as violating the Incompatibility Clause of Art. I, §6, of the Constitution. As citizens, the Court held, plaintiffs alleged nothing but "the abstract injury in nonobservance of the Constitution." . . . More recently, in *Valley Forge*, we rejected a claim of standing to challenge a Government conveyance of property to a religious institution. Insofar as the plaintiffs relied simply on "their shared individuated right" to a Government that made no law respecting an establishment of religion, we held that plaintiffs had not alleged a judicially cognizable injury. "[A]ssertion of a right to a particular kind of Government conduct, which the Government has violated by acting differently, cannot alone satisfy the requirements of Art. III without draining those requirements of meaning." Respondents here have no standing to complain simply that their Government is violating the law.

Neither do they have standing to litigate their claims based on the stigmatizing injury often caused by racial discrimination. There can be no doubt that this sort of noneconomic injury is one of the most serious consequences of discriminatory government action, and is sufficient in some circumstances to support standing. Our cases make clear, however, that such injury accords a basis for standing only to "those persons who are personally denied equal treatment" by the challenged discriminatory conduct. . . .

The consequences of recognizing respondents' standing on the basis of their first claim of injury illustrate why our cases plainly hold that such injury is not judicially cognizable. If the abstract stigmatic injury were cognizable, standing would extend nationwide to all members of the particular racial groups against which the Government was alleged to be discriminating by its grant of a tax exemption to a racially discriminatory school, regardless of the location of that school. All such persons could claim the same sort of abstract stigmatic injury respondents assert in their first claim of injury. A black person in Hawaii could challenge the grant of a tax exemption to a racially discriminatory school in Maine. Recognition of standing in such circumstances would transform the federal courts into "no more than a vehicle for the vindication of the value interests of concerned bystanders." *United States v. SCRAP* (1973). Constitutional limits on the role of the federal courts preclude such a transformation.

It is in their complaint's second claim of injury that respondents allege harm to a concrete, personal interest that can support standing in some circumstances. The injury they identify — their children's diminished ability to receive an education in a racially integrated school — is, beyond any doubt, not only judicially cognizable but, as shown by cases from *Brown v. Board of Education* (1954), to *Bob Jones University v. United States* (1983), one of the most serious injuries recognized in our legal system. Despite the constitutional importance of curing the injury alleged by respondents, however, the federal judiciary may not redress it unless standing requirements are met. In this case, respondents' second claim of injury cannot support standing, because the injury alleged is not fairly traceable to the Government conduct respondents challenge as unlawful.

The illegal conduct challenged by respondents is the IRS's grant of tax exemptions to some racially discriminatory schools. The line of causation between that conduct and desegregation of respondents' schools is attenuated, at best. From the perspective of the IRS, the injury to respondents is highly indirect, and "results from the independent action of some third party not before the court." *Simon v. Eastern Kentucky Welfare Rights Org.* (1974).

The diminished ability of respondents' children to receive a desegregated education would be fairly traceable to unlawful IRS grants of tax exemptions only if there were enough racially discriminatory private schools receiving tax exemptions in respondents' communities for withdrawal of those exemptions to make an appreciable difference in public school integration. Respondents have made no such allegation. It is, first, uncertain how many racially discriminatory private schools are in fact receiving tax exemptions. Moreover, it is entirely speculative, as respondents themselves conceded in the Court of Appeals, whether withdrawal of a tax exemption from any particular school would lead the school to change its policies. It is just as speculative whether any given parent of a child attending such a private school would decide to transfer the child to public school as a result of any changes in educational or financial policy made by the private school once it was threatened with loss of tax-exempt status. It is also pure speculation whether, in a particular community, a large enough number of the numerous relevant school officials and parents would reach decisions that collectively would have a significant impact on the racial composition of the public schools.

The links in the chain of causation between the challenged Government conduct and the asserted injury are far too weak for the chain as a whole to sustain respondents' standing. In *Simon v. Eastern Kentucky Welfare Rights Org.*, the Court held that standing to challenge a Government grant of a tax exemption to hospitals could not be founded on the asserted connection between the grant of tax-exempt status and the hospitals' policy concerning the provision of medical services to indigents. The causal connection depended on the decisions hospitals would make in response to withdrawal of tax-exempt status, and those decisions were sufficiently uncertain to break the chain of causation between the plaintiffs' injury and the challenged Government action. The chain of causation is even weaker in this case. It involves numerous third parties (officials of racially discriminatory schools receiving tax exemptions and the parents of children attending such schools) who may not even exist in respondents' communities and whose independent decisions may not collectively have a significant effect on the ability of public school students to receive a desegregated education.

The idea of separation of powers that underlies standing doctrine explains why our cases preclude the conclusion that respondents' alleged injury "fairly can be traced to the challenged action" of the IRS. That conclusion would pave the way generally for suits challenging, not specifically identifiable Government violations of law, but the particular programs agencies establish to carry out their legal obligations. Such suits, even when premised on allegations of several instances of violations of law, are rarely, if ever, appropriate for federal court adjudication. . . .

When transported into the Art. III context, that principle, grounded as it is in the idea of separation of powers, counsels against recognizing standing in a case brought, not to enforce specific legal obligations whose violation works a direct harm, but to seek a restructuring of the apparatus established by the Executive Branch to fulfill its legal duties. The Constitution, after all, assigns to the Executive Branch, and not to the Judicial Branch, the duty to "take Care that the Laws be faithfully executed." U.S. Const., Art. II, §3. We could not recognize respondents' standing in this case without running afoul of that structural principle. . . .

"The necessity that the plaintiff who seeks to invoke judicial power stand to profit in some personal interest remains an Art. III requirement." *Simon v. Eastern Kentucky Welfare Rights Org.* Respondents have not met this fundamental requirement. The judgment of the Court of Appeals is accordingly reversed, and the injunction issued by that court is vacated.

It is so ordered.

JUSTICE MARSHALL took no part in the decision of these cases.

JUSTICE STEVENS, with whom JUSTICE BLACKMUN joins, dissenting.

Three propositions are clear to me: (1) respondents have adequately alleged "injury in fact"; (2) their injury is fairly traceable to the conduct that they claim to be unlawful; and (3) the "separation of powers" principle does not create a jurisdictional obstacle to the consideration of the merits of their claim.

Respondents, the parents of black school children, have alleged that their children are unable to attend fully desegregated schools because large numbers of white children in the areas in which respondents reside attend private schools which do not admit minority children. . . . This kind of injury may be actionable whether it is caused by the exclusion of black children from public schools or by an official policy of encouraging white children to attend nonpublic schools. A subsidy for the withdrawal of a white child can have the same effect as a penalty for admitting a black child.

In final analysis, the wrong respondents allege that the Government has committed is to subsidize the exodus of white children from schools that would otherwise be racially integrated. The critical question in these cases, therefore, is whether respondents have alleged that the Government has created that kind of subsidy.

In answering that question, we must, of course, assume that respondents can prove what they have alleged. Furthermore, at this stage of the litigation, we must put to one side all questions about the appropriateness of a nationwide class action. The controlling issue is whether the causal connection between the injury and the wrong has been adequately alleged. . . .

We have held that, when a subsidy makes a given activity more or less expensive, injury can be fairly traced to the subsidy for purposes of standing analysis because of the resulting increase or decrease in the ability to engage in the activity. Indeed, we have employed exactly this causation analysis in the same context at issue here — subsidies given private schools that practice racial discrimination. . . .

This causation analysis is nothing more than a restatement of elementary economics: when something becomes more expensive, less of it will be purchased. Sections 170 and 501(c)(3) are premised on that recognition. If racially discriminatory private schools lose the "cash grants" that flow from the operation of the statutes, the education they provide will become more expensive, and hence less of their services will be purchased. Conversely, maintenance of these tax benefits makes an education in segregated private schools relatively more attractive by decreasing its cost. Accordingly, without tax-exempt status, private schools will either not be competitive in terms of cost or have to change their admissions policies, hence reducing their competitiveness for parents seeking "a racially segregated alternative" to public schools, which is what respondents have alleged many white parents in desegregating school districts seek. . . .

Considerations of tax policy, economics, and pure logic all confirm the conclusion that respondents' injury in fact is fairly traceable to the Government's allegedly wrongful conduct. The Court therefore is forced to introduce the concept of "separation of powers" into its analysis. The Court writes that the separation of powers "explains why our cases preclude the conclusion" that respondents' injury is fairly traceable to the conduct they challenge.

The Court could mean one of three things by its invocation of the separation of powers. First, it could simply be expressing the idea that, if the plaintiff lacks Art. III standing to bring a lawsuit, then there is no "case or controversy" within the meaning of Art. III, and hence the matter is not within the area of responsibility assigned to the Judiciary by the Constitution. . . . While there can be no quarrel with this proposition, in itself it provides no guidance for determining if the injury respondents have alleged is fairly traceable to the conduct they have challenged.

Second, the Court could be saying that it will require a more direct causal connection when it is troubled by the separation of powers implications of the case before it. That approach confuses the standing doctrine with the justiciability of the issues that respondents seek to raise. The purpose of the standing inquiry is to measure the plaintiff's stake in the outcome, not whether a court has the authority to provide it with the outcome it seeks. . . .

Third, the Court could be saying that it will not treat as legally cognizable injuries that stem from an administrative decision concerning how enforcement resources will be allocated. This surely is an important point. Respondents do seek to restructure the IRS's mechanisms for enforcing the legal requirement that discriminatory institutions not receive tax-exempt status. Such restructuring would dramatically affect the way in which the IRS exercises its prosecutorial discretion. The Executive requires latitude to decide how best to enforce the law, and in general the Court may well be correct that the exercise of that discretion, especially in the tax context, is unchallengeable.

However, as the Court also recognizes, this principle does not apply when suit is brought "to enforce specific legal obligations whose violation works a direct harm." For example, despite the fact that they were challenging the methods used by the Executive to enforce the law, citizens were accorded standing to challenge a pattern of police misconduct that violated the constitutional constraints on law enforcement activities in *Allee v. Medrano* (1974). Here, respondents contend that the IRS is violating a specific constitutional limitation on its enforcement discretion. There is a solid basis for that contention. . . .

In short, I would deal with the question of the legal limitations on the IRS's enforcement discretion on its merits, rather than by making the untenable assumption that the granting of preferential tax treatment to segregated schools does not make those schools more attractive to white students, and hence does not inhibit the process of desegregation. I respectfully dissent.

STUDY GUIDE

- The Supreme Court has held that Article III imposes three strict requirements for plaintiffs to establish standing: (1) injury in fact; (2) causal connection between the injury and the conduct complained of; and (3) the injury will likely be redressed by a favorable decision.
- Beyond these three requirements, the Court has further concluded that there are certain "prudential" considerations. Here, "prudential" means that courts have the option to hear the case, or not.
- *Federal Election Commission v. Akins* omits the Court's discussion of "prudential" considerations in granting standing (which are presumably applied at the discretion of the Court). It focuses on the treatment of "injury in fact," which the Court in *Allen v. Wright* said was a constitutionally required element of standing (which therefore presumably cannot be waived or ignored by the Court).
- On what basis did Justice Breyer conclude that such an injury existed? Why did Justice Scalia disagree?

Federal Election Commission v. Akins

524 U.S. 11 (1998)

JUSTICE BREYER delivered the opinion of the Court.

The Federal Election Commission (FEC) has determined that the American Israel Public Affairs Committee (AIPAC) is not a "political committee" as defined by the Federal Election Campaign Act of 1971 (FECA), and, for that reason, the Commission has refused to require AIPAC to make disclosures regarding its membership, contributions, and expenditures that FECA would otherwise require. We hold that respondents, a group of voters, have standing to challenge the Commission's determination in court, and we remand this case for further proceedings. . . .

This case arises out of an effort by respondents, a group of voters with views often opposed to those of AIPAC, to persuade the FEC to treat AIPAC as a "political committee." Respondents filed a complaint with the FEC, stating that AIPAC had made more than $1,000 in qualifying "expenditures" per year, and thereby became a "political committee." They added that AIPAC had violated the FEC provisions requiring "political committee[s]" to register and to make public the information about members, contributions, and expenditures to which we have just referred. Respondents also claimed that AIPAC had violated §441b of FECA, which prohibits corporate campaign "contribution[s]" and "expenditure[s]." They asked the FEC to find that AIPAC had violated the Act, and, among other things, to order AIPAC to make public the information that FECA demands of a "political committee."

AIPAC asked the FEC to dismiss the complaint. AIPAC described itself as an issue-oriented organization that seeks to maintain friendship and promote goodwill between the United States and Israel. AIPAC conceded that it lobbies elected officials and disseminates information about candidates for public office. But in responding to the §441b charge, AIPAC denied that it had made the kinds of "expenditures" that matter for FECA purposes (i.e., the kinds of election-related expenditures that corporations cannot make, and which count as the kind of expenditures that, when they exceed $1,000, qualify a group as a "political committee"). . . .

[We do not] agree with the FEC or the dissent that Congress lacks the constitutional power to authorize federal courts to adjudicate this lawsuit. Article III, of course, limits Congress' grant of judicial power to "cases" or "controversies." That limitation means that respondents must show, among other things, an "injury in fact" — a requirement that helps assure that courts will not "pass upon . . . abstract, intellectual problems," but adjudicate "concrete, living contest[s] between adversaries." *Coleman v. Miller* (1939) (Frankfurter, J., dissenting). In our view, respondents here have suffered a genuine "injury in fact."

The "injury in fact" that respondents have suffered consists of their inability to obtain information — lists of AIPAC donors (who are, according to AIPAC, its members), and campaign-related contributions and expenditures — that, on respondents' view of the law, the statute requires that AIPAC make public. There is no reason to doubt their claim that the information would help them (and others to whom they would communicate it) to evaluate candidates for public office, especially candidates who received assistance from AIPAC, and to evaluate the role that AIPAC's financial assistance might play in a specific election. Respondents' injury consequently seems concrete and particular. Indeed, this Court has previously held that a plaintiff suffers an "injury in fact" when the plaintiff fails to obtain information which must be publicly disclosed pursuant to a statute.

The FEC's strongest argument is its contention that this lawsuit involves only a "generalized grievance." The Solicitor General points out that respondents' asserted harm (their failure to obtain information) is one which is "shared in substantially equal measure by all or a large class of citizens." Brief for Petitioner. This Court, he adds, has often said that "generalized grievance[s]" are not the kinds of harms that confer standing. Brief for Petitioner 28; see also *Allen v. Wright* (1984). Whether styled as a constitutional or prudential limit on standing, the Court has sometimes determined that where large numbers of Americans suffer alike, the political process, rather than the judicial process, may provide the more appropriate remedy for a widely shared grievance.

The kind of judicial language to which the FEC points, however, invariably appears in cases where the harm at issue is not only widely shared, but is also of an abstract and indefinite nature — for example, harm to the "common concern for obedience to law." The abstract nature of the harm — for example, injury to the interest in seeing that the law is obeyed — deprives the case of the concrete specificity that characterized those controversies which were "the traditional concern of the courts at Westminster," *Coleman* (Frankfurter, J., dissenting); and which today prevents a plaintiff from obtaining what would, in effect, amount to an advisory opinion.

Often the fact that an interest is abstract and the fact that it is widely shared go hand in hand. But their association is not invariable, and where a harm is concrete, though widely shared, the Court has found "injury in fact." Thus the fact that a political forum may be more readily available where an injury is widely shared (while counseling against, say, interpreting a statute as conferring standing) does not, by itself, automatically disqualify an interest for Article III purposes. Such an interest, where sufficiently concrete, may count as an "injury in fact." This conclusion seems particularly obvious where (to use a hypothetical example) large numbers of individuals suffer the same common-law injury (say, a widespread mass tort), or where large numbers of voters suffer interference with voting rights conferred by law. We conclude that similarly, the informational injury at issue here, directly related to voting, the most basic of political rights, is sufficiently concrete and specific such that the fact that it is widely shared does not deprive Congress of constitutional power to authorize its vindication in the federal courts.

Respondents have also satisfied the remaining two constitutional standing requirements. The harm asserted is "fairly traceable" to the FEC's decision about which respondents complain. Of course, as the FEC points out, it is possible that even had the FEC agreed with respondents' view of the law, it would still have decided in the exercise of its discretion not to require AIPAC to produce the information. But that fact does not destroy Article III "causation," for we cannot know that the FEC would have exercised its prosecutorial discretion in this way. Agencies often have discretion about whether or not to take a particular action. Yet those adversely affected by a discretionary agency decision generally have standing to complain that the agency based its decision upon an improper legal ground. If a reviewing court agrees that the agency misinterpreted the law, it will set aside the agency's action and remand the case — even though the agency (like a new jury after a mistrial) might later, in the exercise of its lawful discretion, reach the same result for a different reason. Thus respondents' "injury in fact" is "fairly traceable" to the FEC's decision not to issue its complaint, even though the FEC might reach the same result exercising its discretionary powers lawfully. For similar reasons, the courts in this case can "redress" respondents' "injury in fact." . . .

In sum, respondents, as voters, have satisfied . . . constitutional standing requirements. They may bring this petition for a declaration that the FEC's dismissal of their complaint was unlawful. See 2 U.S.C. §437g(8)(A).

JUSTICE SCALIA, with whom JUSTICE O'CONNOR and JUSTICE THOMAS join, dissenting. . . .

The Constitution's line of demarcation between the Executive power and the judicial power presupposes a common understanding of the type of interest needed to sustain a "case or controversy" against the Executive in the courts. A system in which the citizenry at large could sue to compel Executive compliance with the law would be a system in which the courts, rather than of the President, are given the primary responsibility to "take Care that the Laws be faithfully executed," Art. II, §3. We do not have such a system because the common understanding of the interest necessary to sustain suit has included the requirement . . . that the complained-of injury be particularized and differentiated, rather than common to all the electorate. When the Executive can be directed by the courts, at the instance of any voter, to remedy a deprivation which affects the entire electorate in precisely the same way — and particularly when that deprivation (here, the unavailability of information) is one inseverable part of a larger enforcement scheme — there has occurred a shift of political responsibility to a branch designed not to protect the public at large but to protect individual rights. "To permit Congress to convert the undifferentiated public interest in executive officers' compliance with the law into an 'individual right' vindicable in the courts is to permit Congress to transfer from the President to the courts the Chief Executive's most important constitutional duty. . . ." *Lujan v. Defenders of Wildlife* (1992). If today's decision is correct, it is within the power of Congress to authorize any interested person to manage (through the courts) the Executive's enforcement of any law that includes a requirement for the filing and public availability of a piece of paper. This is not the system we have had, and is not the system we should desire. . . .

The next case, *Clapper v. Amnesty International USA* (2013), presents the Court's most recent discussion of whether a plaintiff suffered an "injury in fact," or whether the claimed injury was "hypothetical."

STUDY GUIDE

- Why should the Court hesitate before resolving the constitutionality of the warrantless surveillance program at issue in *Clapper*? What role does the standing doctrine play? Is this really a political question?
- Justice Breyer's dissent argues that the plaintiffs' injuries are not speculative but very likely to happen. Is he right? Does it matter that if standing is not found here, it may not be possible to challenge the surveillance program's constitutionality in other contexts?

Clapper v. Amnesty International USA

133 S. Ct. 1138 (2013)

Justice Alito delivered the opinion of the Court.

Section 702 of the Foreign Intelligence Surveillance Act of 1978, allows the Attorney General and the Director of National Intelligence to acquire foreign intelligence information by jointly authorizing the surveillance of individuals who are not "United States persons" and are reasonably believed to be located outside the United States. Before doing so, the Attorney General and the Director of National Intelligence normally must obtain the Foreign Intelligence Surveillance Court's approval. Respondents are United States persons whose work, they allege, requires them to engage in sensitive international communications with individuals who they believe are likely targets of surveillance under §1881a. Respondents seek a declaration that §1881a is unconstitutional, as well as an injunction against §1881a-authorized surveillance. The question before us is whether respondents have Article III standing to seek this prospective relief.

Respondents assert that they can establish injury in fact because there is an objectively reasonable likelihood that their communications will be acquired under §1881a at some point in the future. But respondents' theory of *future* injury is too speculative to satisfy the well-established requirement that threatened injury must be "certainly impending." E.g., *Whitmore v. Arkansas* (1990). And even if respondents could demonstrate that the threatened injury is certainly impending, they still would not be able to establish that this injury is fairly traceable to §1881a. As an alternative argument, respondents contend that they are suffering *present* injury because the risk of §1881a-authorized surveillance already has forced them to take costly and burdensome measures to protect the confidentiality of their international communications. But respondents cannot manufacture standing by choosing to make expenditures based on hypothetical future harm that is not certainly impending. We therefore hold that respondents lack Article III standing.

I

In 1978, after years of debate, Congress enacted the Foreign Intelligence Surveillance Act (FISA) to authorize and regulate certain governmental electronic surveillance of communications for foreign intelligence purposes. . . . In constructing such a framework for foreign intelligence surveillance, Congress created two specialized courts. In FISA, Congress authorized judges of the Foreign Intelligence Surveillance Court (FISC) to approve electronic surveillance for foreign intelligence purposes if there is probable cause to believe that "the target of the electronic surveillance is a foreign power or an agent of a foreign power," and that each of the specific "facilities or places at which the electronic surveillance is directed is being used, or is about to be used, by a foreign power or an agent of a foreign power." Additionally, Congress vested the Foreign Intelligence Surveillance Court of Review with jurisdiction to review any denials by the FISC of applications for electronic surveillance.

In the wake of the September 11th attacks, President George W. Bush authorized the National Security Agency (NSA) to conduct warrantless wiretapping of telephone and e-mail communications where one party to the communication was located outside the United States and a participant in "the call was reasonably believed to be a member or agent of al Qaeda or an affiliated terrorist organization." . . .

When Congress enacted the FISA Amendments Act of 2008, it left much of FISA intact, but it "established a new and independent source of intelligence collection authority, beyond that granted in traditional FISA." As relevant here, §702 of FISA, which was enacted as part of the FISA Amendments Act, supplements preexisting FISA authority by creating a new framework under which the Government may seek the FISC's authorization of certain foreign intelligence surveillance targeting the communications of non-U.S. persons located abroad. Unlike traditional FISA surveillance, §1881a does not require the Government to demonstrate probable cause that the target of the electronic surveillance is a foreign power or agent of a foreign power. And, unlike traditional FISA, §1881a does not require the Government to specify the nature and location of each of the particular facilities or places at which the electronic surveillance will occur. . . .

The present case involves a constitutional challenge to §1881a. Respondents are attorneys and human rights, labor, legal, and media organizations whose work allegedly requires them to engage in sensitive and sometimes privileged telephone and e-mail communications with colleagues, clients, sources, and other individuals located abroad. Respondents believe that some of the people with whom they exchange foreign intelligence information are likely targets of surveillance under §1881a. Specifically, respondents claim that they communicate by telephone and e-mail with people the Government "believes or believed to be associated with terrorist organizations," "people located in geographic areas that are a special focus" of the Government's counterterrorism or diplomatic efforts, and activists who oppose governments that are supported by the United States Government.

Respondents claim that §1881a compromises their ability to locate witnesses, cultivate sources, obtain information, and communicate confidential information to their clients. Respondents also assert that they "have ceased engaging" in certain telephone and e-mail conversations. According to respondents, the threat of surveillance will compel them to travel abroad in order to have in-person conversations. In addition, respondents declare that they have undertaken "costly and burdensome measures" to protect the confidentiality of sensitive communications.

On the day when the FISA Amendments Act was enacted, respondents filed this action seeking (1) a declaration that §1881a, on its face, violates the Fourth Amendment, the First Amendment, Article III, and separation-of-powers principles and (2) a permanent injunction against the use of §1881a. Respondents assert what they characterize as two separate theories of Article III standing. First, they claim that there is an objectively reasonable likelihood that their communications will be acquired under §1881a at some point in the future, thus causing them injury. Second, respondents maintain that the risk of surveillance under §1881a is so substantial that they have been forced to take costly and burdensome measures to protect the confidentiality of their international communications; in their view, the costs they have incurred constitute present injury that is fairly traceable to §1881a.

After both parties moved for summary judgment, the District Court held that respondents do not have standing. On appeal, however, a panel of the Second Circuit reversed. The panel agreed with respondents' argument that they have standing due to the objectively reasonable likelihood that their communications will be intercepted at some time in the future. In addition, the panel held that respondents have established that they are suffering "*present* injuries in fact — economic and professional harms — stemming from a reasonable fear of *future* harmful government conduct." The Second Circuit denied rehearing en banc by an equally divided vote.

Because of the importance of the issue and the novel view of standing adopted by the Court of Appeals, we granted certiorari, and we now reverse.

II

Article III of the Constitution limits federal courts' jurisdiction to certain "Cases" and "Controversies." As we have explained, "[n]o principle is more fundamental to the judiciary's proper role in our system of government than the constitutional limitation of federal-court jurisdiction to actual cases or controversies." *DaimlerChrysler Corp. v. Cuno* (2006); *Raines v. Byrd* (1997); see, e.g., *Summers v. Earth Island Institute* (2009). "One element of the case-or-controversy requirement" is that plaintiffs "must establish that they have standing to sue." *Raines*; see also *Summers*; *DaimlerChrysler Corp.*; *Lujan v. Defenders of Wildlife* (1992).

The law of Article III standing, which is built on separation-of-powers principles, serves to prevent the judicial process from being used to usurp the powers of the political branches. In keeping with the purpose of this doctrine, "[o]ur standing inquiry has been especially rigorous when reaching the merits of the dispute would force us to decide whether an action taken by one of the other two branches of the Federal Government was unconstitutional." "Relaxation of standing requirements is directly related to the expansion of judicial power," *United States v. Richardson* (1974) (Powell, J., concurring), and we have often found a lack of standing in cases in which the Judiciary has been requested to review actions of the political branches in the fields of intelligence gathering and foreign affairs, see, *e.g.*, *Richardson* (plaintiff lacked standing to challenge the constitutionality of a statute permitting the Central Intelligence Agency to account for its expenditures solely on the certificate of the CIA Director).

To establish Article III standing, an injury must be "concrete, particularized, and actual or imminent; fairly traceable to the challenged action; and redressable by a favorable ruling." *Monsanto Co. v. Geertson Seed Farms* (2010). "Although imminence is concededly a somewhat elastic concept, it cannot be stretched beyond its purpose, which is to ensure that the alleged injury is not too speculative for Article III purposes — that the injury is *certainly* impending." *Id.* Thus, we have repeatedly reiterated that "threatened injury must be *certainly impending* to constitute injury in fact," and that "[a]llegations of *possible* future injury" are not sufficient.

III

A

Respondents assert that they can establish injury in fact that is fairly traceable to §1881a because there is an objectively reasonable likelihood that their communications with their foreign contacts will be intercepted under §1881a at some point in the future. This argument fails. As an initial matter, the Second Circuit's "objectively reasonable likelihood" standard is inconsistent with our requirement that "threatened injury must be certainly impending to constitute injury in fact." *Whitmore*. Furthermore, respondents' argument rests on their highly speculative fear that: (1) the Government will decide to target the communications of non-U.S. persons with whom they communicate; (2) in doing so, the Government will choose to invoke its authority under §1881a rather than utilizing another method of surveillance; (3) the Article III judges who serve on the Foreign Intelligence Surveillance Court will conclude that the Government's proposed surveillance procedures satisfy §1881a's many safeguards and are consistent with the Fourth Amendment; (4) the Government will succeed in intercepting the communications of respondents' contacts; and (5) respondents will be parties to the particular communications that the Government intercepts. As discussed below, respondents' theory of standing, which relies on a highly attenuated chain of possibilities, does not satisfy the requirement that threatened injury must be certainly impending. See *Summers* (rejecting a standing theory premised on a speculative chain of possibilities). Moreover, even if respondents could demonstrate injury in fact, the second link in the above-described chain of contingencies — which amounts to mere speculation about whether surveillance would be under §1881a or some other authority — shows that respondents cannot satisfy the requirement that any injury in fact must be fairly traceable to §1881a.

First, it is speculative whether the Government will imminently target communications to which respondents are parties. Section 1881a expressly provides that respondents, who are U.S. persons, cannot be targeted for surveillance under §1881a. Accordingly, it is no surprise that respondents fail to offer any evidence that their communications have been monitored under §1881a, a failure that substantially undermines their standing theory. Indeed, respondents do not even allege that the Government has sought the FISC's approval for surveillance of their communications. Accordingly, respondents' theory necessarily rests on their assertion that the Government will target *other individuals* — namely, their foreign contacts.

Yet respondents have no actual knowledge of the Government's §1881a targeting practices. Instead, respondents merely speculate and make assumptions about whether their communications with their foreign contacts will be acquired under §1881a. . . . "The party invoking federal jurisdiction bears the burden of establishing" standing — and, at the summary judgment stage, such a party "can no longer rest on . . . 'mere allegations,' but must 'set forth' by affidavit or other evidence 'specific facts.'" *Defenders of Wildlife*. Respondents, however, have set forth no specific facts demonstrating that the communications of their foreign contacts will be targeted. Moreover, because §1881a at most *authorizes* — but does not *mandate* or *direct* — the surveillance that respondents fear, respondents' allegations are necessarily conjectural. Simply put, respondents can only speculate as to how the Attorney General and the Director of National Intelligence will exercise their discretion in determining which communications to target.

Second, even if respondents could demonstrate that the targeting of their foreign contacts is imminent, respondents can only speculate as to whether the Government will seek to use §1881a-authorized surveillance (rather than other methods) to do so. The Government has numerous other methods of conducting surveillance, none of which is challenged here. . . . Even if respondents could demonstrate that their foreign contacts will imminently be targeted — indeed, even if they could show that interception of their own communications will imminently occur — they would still need to show that their injury is fairly traceable to §1881a. But, because respondents can only speculate as to whether any (asserted) interception would be under §1881a or some other authority, they cannot satisfy the "fairly traceable" requirement.

Third, even if respondents could show that the Government will seek the Foreign Intelligence Surveillance Court's authorization to acquire the communications of respondents' foreign contacts under §1881a, respondents can only speculate as to whether that court will authorize such surveillance. In the past, we have been reluctant to endorse standing theories that require guesswork as to how independent decisionmakers will exercise their judgment. . . . We decline to abandon our usual reluctance to endorse standing theories that rest on speculation about the decisions of independent actors. . . .

Fourth, even if the Government were to obtain the Foreign Intelligence Surveillance Court's approval to target respondents' foreign contacts under §1881a, it is unclear whether the Government would succeed in acquiring the communications of respondents' foreign contacts. And fifth, even if the Government were to conduct surveillance of respondents' foreign contacts, respondents can only speculate as to whether *their own communications* with their foreign contacts would be incidentally acquired.

In sum, respondents' speculative chain of possibilities does not establish that injury based on potential future surveillance is certainly impending or is fairly traceable to §1881a.[2]

---

[2] Our cases do not uniformly require plaintiffs to demonstrate that it is literally certain that the harms they identify will come about. In some instances, we have found standing based on a "substantial risk" that the harm will occur, which may prompt plaintiffs to reasonably incur costs to mitigate or avoid that harm. *Monsanto Co. v. Geertson Seed Farms* (2010). But to the extent that the "substantial risk" standard is relevant and is distinct from the "clearly impending" requirement, respondents fall short of even that standard, in light of the attenuated chain of inferences necessary to find harm here. In addition, plaintiffs bear the burden of pleading and proving concrete facts showing that the defendant's actual action has caused the substantial risk of harm. Plaintiffs cannot rely on speculation about "'the unfettered choices made by independent actors not before the court.'" *Defenders of Wildlife*.

B

Respondents' alternative argument — namely, that they can establish standing based on the measures that they have undertaken to avoid §1881a-authorized surveillance — fares no better. Respondents assert that they are suffering ongoing injuries that are fairly traceable to §1881a because the risk of surveillance under §1881a requires them to take costly and burdensome measures to protect the confidentiality of their communications. The Second Circuit panel concluded that, because respondents are already suffering such ongoing injuries, the likelihood of interception under §1881a is relevant only to the question whether respondents' ongoing injuries are "fairly traceable" to §1881a. Analyzing the "fairly traceable" element of standing under a relaxed reasonableness standard, the Second Circuit then held that "plaintiffs have established that they suffered *present* injuries in fact — economic and professional harms — stemming from a reasonable fear of *future* harmful government conduct."

The Second Circuit's analysis improperly allowed respondents to establish standing by asserting that they suffer present costs and burdens that are based on a fear of surveillance, so long as that fear is not "fanciful, paranoid, or otherwise unreasonable." This improperly waters down the fundamental requirements of Article III. Respondents' contention that they have standing because they incurred certain costs as a reasonable reaction to a risk of harm is unavailing — because the harm respondents seek to avoid is not certainly impending. In other words, respondents cannot manufacture standing merely by inflicting harm on themselves based on their fears of hypothetical future harm that is not certainly impending. Any ongoing injuries that respondents are suffering are not fairly traceable to §1881a.

If the law were otherwise, an enterprising plaintiff would be able to secure a lower standard for Article III standing simply by making an expenditure based on a nonparanoid fear. . . . Thus, allowing respondents to bring this action based on costs they incurred in response to a speculative threat would be tantamount to accepting a repackaged version of respondents' first failed theory of standing. . . .

Because respondents do not face a threat of certainly impending interception under §1881a, the costs that they have incurred to avoid surveillance are simply the product of their fear of surveillance and our decision in *Laird* makes it clear that such a fear is insufficient to create standing. . . . For the reasons discussed above, respondents' self-inflicted injuries are not fairly traceable to the Government's purported activities under §1881a, and their subjective fear of surveillance does not give rise to standing.

IV

Respondents also suggest that they should be held to have standing because otherwise the constitutionality of §1881a could not be challenged. It would be wrong, they maintain, to "insulate the government's surveillance activities from meaningful judicial review." Respondents' suggestion is both legally and factually incorrect. First, "'[t]he assumption that if respondents have no standing to sue, no one would have standing, is not a reason to find standing.'" *Valley Forge Christian College*.

Second, our holding today by no means insulates §1881a from judicial review. As described above, Congress created a comprehensive scheme in which the Foreign Intelligence Surveillance Court evaluates the Government's certifications, targeting procedures, and minimization procedures — including assessing whether the targeting and minimization procedures comport with the Fourth Amendment. §1881a(a), (c)(1), (i)(2), (i)(3). Any dissatisfaction that respondents may have about the Foreign Intelligence Surveillance Court's rulings — or the congressional delineation of that court's role — is irrelevant to our standing analysis.

Additionally, if the Government intends to use or disclose information obtained or derived from a §1881a acquisition in judicial or administrative proceedings, it must provide advance notice of its intent, and the affected person may challenge the lawfulness of the acquisition. Thus, if the Government were to prosecute one of respondent-attorney's foreign clients using §1881a-authorized surveillance, the Government would be required to make a disclosure.[3] . . . In such a situation, unlike in the present case, it would at least be clear that the Government had acquired the foreign client's communications using §1881a-authorized surveillance. . . .

* * *

We hold that respondents lack Article III standing because they cannot demonstrate that the future injury they purportedly fear is certainly impending and because they cannot manufacture standing by incurring costs in anticipation of non-imminent harm. We therefore reverse the judgment of the Second Circuit and remand the case for further proceedings consistent with this opinion.

JUSTICE BREYER, with whom JUSTICE GINSBURG, JUSTICE SOTOMAYOR, and JUSTICE KAGAN join, dissenting.

The plaintiffs' standing depends upon the likelihood that the Government, acting under the authority of [the statute], will harm them by intercepting at least some of their private, foreign, telephone, or e-mail conversations. In my view, this harm is not "speculative." Indeed it is as likely to take place as are most future events that commonsense inference and ordinary knowledge of human nature tell us will happen. This Court has often found the occurrence of similar future events sufficiently certain to support standing. I dissent from the Court's contrary conclusion. . . .

---

[3] [When *Clapper* was argued, Solicitor General Donald B. Verrilli, Jr. represented to the Supreme Court that the government would notify defendants if it intended to use evidence obtained from warrantless wiretapping. However, after *Clapper* was decided, Verrilli learned that the executive branch would not disclose evidence that was "derived from" warrantless wiretapping. Charlie Savage, Federal Prosecutors, in a Policy Shift, Cite Warrantless Wiretaps as Evidence, N.Y. Times, Oct. 26, 2013. On the basis of his representation, Verrilli prevailed on the Obama administration to change this policy. Thereafter, the government would notify defendants if it relied on evidence "derived from" warrantless wiretapping; thus, the surveillance process could now in fact be challenged on a case-by-case basis, as Justice Alito concluded. — EDS.]

III

Several considerations, based upon the record along with commonsense inferences, convince me that there is a very high likelihood that Government, *acting under the authority of §1881a,* will intercept at least some of the communications just described. First, the plaintiffs have engaged, and continue to engage, in electronic communications of a kind that the 2008 amendment, but not the prior Act, authorizes the Government to intercept. These communications include discussions with family members of those detained at Guantanamo, friends and acquaintances of those persons, and investigators, experts and others with knowledge of circumstances related to terrorist activities. These persons are foreigners located outside the United States. They are not "foreign power[s]" or "agent[s] of . . . foreign power[s]." And the plaintiffs state that they exchange with these persons "foreign intelligence information," defined to include information that "relates to" "international terrorism" and "the national defense or the security of the United States."

Second, the plaintiffs have a strong *motive* to engage in, and the Government has a strong *motive* to listen to, conversations of the kind described. A lawyer representing a client normally seeks to learn the circumstances surrounding the crime (or the civil wrong) of which the client is accused. . . .

At the same time, the Government has a strong motive to conduct surveillance of conversations that contain material of this kind. The Government, after all, seeks to learn as much as it can reasonably learn about suspected terrorists (such as those detained at Guantanamo), as well as about their contacts and activities, along with those of friends and family members. And the Government is motivated to do so, not simply by the desire to help convict those whom the Government believes guilty, but also by the critical, overriding need to protect America from terrorism.

Third, the Government's *past behavior* shows that it has sought, and hence will in all likelihood continue to seek, information about alleged terrorists and detainees through means that include surveillance of electronic communications. As just pointed out, plaintiff Scott McKay states that the Government (under the authority of the pre-2008 law) "intercepted some 10,000 telephone calls and 20,000 email communications involving [his client] Mr. Al-Hussayen."

Fourth, the Government has the *capacity* to conduct electronic surveillance of the kind at issue. To some degree this capacity rests upon technology available to the Government. . . . This capacity also includes the Government's authority to obtain the kind of information here at issue from private carriers such as AT & T and Verizon. . . .

Of course, to exercise this capacity the Government must have intelligence court authorization. But the Government rarely files requests that fail to meet the statutory criteria. As the intelligence court itself has stated, its review under §1881a is "narrowly circumscribed." In re Proceedings Required by §702(i) of the FISA Amendments Act of 2008, No. Misc. 08-01 (Aug. 17, 2008), p. 3. There is no reason to believe that the communications described would all fail to meet the conditions necessary for approval. Moreover, compared with prior law, §1881a simplifies and thus expedites the approval process, making it more likely that the Government will use §1881a to obtain the necessary approval.

The upshot is that (1) similarity of content, (2) strong motives, (3) prior behavior, and (4) capacity all point to a very strong likelihood that the Government will intercept at least some of the plaintiffs' communications, including some that the 2008 amendment, §1881a, but not the pre-2008 Act, authorizes the Government to intercept.

At the same time, nothing suggests the presence of some special factor here that might support a contrary conclusion. The Government does not deny that it has both the motive and the capacity to listen to communications of the kind described by plaintiffs. Nor does it describe any system for avoiding the interception of an electronic communication that happens to include a party who is an American lawyer, journalist, or human rights worker. One can, of course, always imagine some special circumstance that negates a virtual likelihood, no matter how strong. But the same is true about most, if not all, ordinary inferences about future events. Perhaps, despite pouring rain, the streets will remain dry (due to the presence of a special chemical). But ordinarily a party that seeks to defeat a strong natural inference must bear the burden of showing that some such special circumstance exists. And no one has suggested any such special circumstance here.

Consequently, we need only assume that the Government is doing its job (to find out about, and combat, terrorism) in order to conclude that there is a high probability that the Government will intercept at least some electronic communication to which at least some of the plaintiffs are parties. The majority is wrong when it describes the harm threatened plaintiffs as "speculative."

IV

The majority more plausibly says that the plaintiffs have failed to show that the threatened harm is "*certainly impending*." But, as the majority appears to concede, *certainty* is not, and never has been, the touchstone of standing. The future is inherently uncertain. Yet federal courts frequently entertain actions for injunctions and for declaratory relief aimed at preventing future activities that are reasonably likely or highly likely, but not absolutely certain, to take place. And that degree of certainty is all that is needed to support standing here. . . .

More important, the Court's holdings in standing cases show that standing exists here. The Court has often *found* standing where the occurrence of the relevant injury was far *less* certain than here. . . .

In some standing cases, the Court has found that a reasonable probability of *future* injury comes accompanied with *present* injury that takes the form of reasonable efforts to mitigate the threatened effects of the future injury or to prevent it from occurring. Thus, in *Monsanto Co.*, plaintiffs, a group of conventional alfalfa growers, challenged an agency decision to deregulate genetically engineered alfalfa. They claimed that deregulation would harm them because their neighbors would plant the genetically engineered seed, bees would obtain pollen from the neighbors' plants, and the bees would then (harmfully) contaminate their own conventional alfalfa with the genetically modified gene. The lower courts had found a "reasonable probability" that this injury would occur.

Without expressing views about that probability, we found standing because the plaintiffs would suffer present harm by trying to combat the threat. *Ibid.* The plaintiffs, for example, "would have to conduct testing to find out whether and to what extent their crops have been contaminated." And they would have to take "measures to minimize the likelihood of potential contamination and to ensure an adequate supply of non-genetically-engineered alfalfa." We held that these "harms, which [the plaintiffs] will suffer even if their crops are not actually infected with" the genetically modified gene, "are sufficiently concrete to satisfy the injury-in-fact prong of the constitutional standing analysis."

Virtually identical circumstances are present here. Plaintiff McKay, for example, points out that, when he communicates abroad about, or in the interests of, a client (*e.g.*, a client accused of terrorism), he must "make an assessment" whether his "client's interests would be compromised" should the Government "acquire the communications." If so, he must either forgo the communication or travel abroad.

Since travel is expensive, since forgoing communication can compromise the client's interests, since McKay's assessment itself takes time and effort, this case does not differ significantly from *Monsanto.* And that is so whether we consider the plaintiffs' present necessary expenditure of time and effort as a separate concrete, particularized, imminent harm, or consider it as additional evidence that the future harm (an interception) is likely to occur. . . .

The Court has, of course, denied standing in other cases. But they involve injuries *less* likely, not more likely, to occur than here. In a recent case, *Summers v. Earth Island Institute* (2009), for example, the plaintiffs challenged a regulation exempting certain timber sales from public comment and administrative appeal. The plaintiffs claimed that the regulations injured them by interfering with their esthetic enjoyment and recreational use of the forests. The Court found this harm too unlikely to occur to support standing. The Court noted that one plaintiff had not pointed to a specific affected forest that he would visit. The Court concluded that "[t]here may be a chance, but . . . *hardly a likelihood*," that the plaintiff's "wanderings will bring him to a parcel about to be affected by a project unlawfully subject to the regulations."

In sum, as the Court concedes, the word "certainly" in the phrase "certainly impending" does not refer to absolute certainty. As our case law demonstrates, what the Constitution requires is something more akin to "reasonable probability" or "high probability." The use of some such standard is all that is necessary here to ensure the actual concrete injury that the Constitution demands. The considerations set forth in Parts II and III, *supra*, make clear that the standard is readily met in this case.

* * *

While I express no view on the merits of the plaintiffs' constitutional claims, I do believe that at least some of the plaintiffs have standing to make those claims. I dissent, with respect, from the majority's contrary conclusion.

ASSIGNMENT 2

B. RIPENESS

While the requirement of standing concerns the proper party to bring suit (the "who" question), the doctrine of ripeness concerns whether a lawsuit is premature because the injury is speculative and may never occur (the "when" question). Some of the most interesting constitutional cases are disposed of on ripeness grounds and never make it to the Supreme Court.

STUDY GUIDE

- Why did the court in the next case decline to apply the political question doctrine?
- What do you think the court would do if a similar case were brought after hostilities commenced?

Doe v. Bush

323 F.3d 133 (2003)

United States Court of Appeals for the First Circuit

LYNCH, CIRCUIT JUDGE.

Plaintiffs are active-duty members of the military, parents of military personnel, and members of the U.S. House of Representatives. (1) They filed a complaint in district court seeking a preliminary injunction to prevent the defendants, President George W. Bush and Secretary of Defense Donald Rumsfeld, from initiating a war against Iraq. They assert that such an action would violate the Constitution. The district court dismissed the suit, and plaintiffs appeal. We affirm the dismissal.

In October 2002, Congress passed the Authorization for Use of Military Force Against Iraq Resolution of 2002 (the "October Resolution"). Plaintiffs argue that the October Resolution is constitutionally inadequate to authorize the military offensive that defendants are now planning against Iraq. See U.S. Const. art. I, §8, cl. 11 (granting Congress the power "[t]o declare war"). They base this argument on two theories. They argue that Congress and the President are in collision — that the President is about to act in violation of the October Resolution. . . .

[P]laintiffs argue, judicial intervention is necessary to preserve the principle of separation of powers which undergirds our constitutional structure. Only the judiciary, they argue, has the constitutionally assigned role and the institutional competence to police the boundaries of the constitutional mandates given to the other branches: Congress alone has the authority to declare war and the President alone has the authority to make war.

The plaintiffs argue that important and increasingly vital interests are served by the requirement that it be Congress which decides whether to declare war. Quoting Thomas Jefferson, they argue that congressional involvement will slow the "dogs of war"; that Congress, the voice of the people, should make this momentous decision, one which will cost lives; and that congressional support is needed to ensure that the country is behind the war, a key element in any victory. They also argue that, absent an attack on this country or our allies, congressional involvement must come prior to war, because once war has started, Congress is in an uncomfortable default position where the use of its appropriations powers to cut short any war is an inadequate remedy.

The defendants are equally eloquent about the impropriety of judicial intrusion into the "extraordinarily delicate foreign affairs and military calculus, one that could be fatally upset by judicial interference." Such intervention would be all the worse here, defendants say, because Congress and the President are in accord as to the threat to the nation and the legitimacy of a military response to that threat.

The case before us is a somber and weighty one. We have considered these important concerns carefully, and we have concluded that the circumstances call for judicial restraint. The theory of collision between the legislative and executive branches is not suitable for judicial review, because there is not a ripe dispute concerning the President's acts and the requirements of the October Resolution passed by Congress. . . . [B]efore courts adjudicate a case involving the war powers allocated to the two political branches, they must be presented with a case or controversy that clearly raises the specter of undermining the constitutional structure. . . .

The Constitution reserves the war powers to the legislative and executive branches. This court has declined the invitation to become involved in such matters once before. Over thirty years ago, the First Circuit addressed a war powers case challenging the constitutionality of the Vietnam War on the basis that Congress had not declared war. *Massachusetts v. Laird* (1st Cir. 1971). The court found that other actions by Congress, such as continued appropriations to fund the war over the course of six years, provided enough indication of congressional approval to put the question beyond the reach of judicial review:

> The war in Vietnam is a product of the jointly supportive actions of the two branches to whom the congeries of the war powers have been committed. Because the branches are not in opposition, there is no necessity of determining boundaries. Should either branch be opposed to the continuance of hostilities, however, and present the issue in clear terms, a court might well take a different view. This question we do not face.

Applying this precedent to the case at hand today, the district court concluded, "[T]here is a day to day fluidity in the situation that does not amount to resolute conflict between the branches — but that does argue against an uninformed judicial intervention."

The lack of a fully developed dispute between the two elected branches, and the consequent lack of a clearly defined issue, is exactly the type of concern which causes courts to find a case unripe. In his concurring opinion in *Goldwater v. Carter* (1979), Justice Powell stated that courts should decline, on ripeness grounds, to decide "issues affecting the allocation of power between the President and Congress until the political branches reach a constitutional impasse." . . .

Ripeness doctrine involves more than simply the timing of the case. It mixes various mutually reinforcing constitutional and prudential considerations. One such consideration is the need "to prevent the courts, through avoidance of premature adjudication, from entangling themselves in abstract disagreements." *Abbott Labs. v. Gardner* (1967). Another is to avoid unnecessary constitutional decisions. A third is the recognition that, by waiting until a case is fully developed before deciding it, courts benefit from a focus sharpened by particular facts. The case before us raises all three of these concerns.

These rationales spring, in part, from the recognition that the scope of judicial power is bounded by the Constitution. . . . Article III of the Constitution limits jurisdiction to "cases" and "controversies," and prudential doctrines may counsel additional restraint.

The ripeness of a dispute is determined de novo. Ripeness is dependent on the circumstances of a particular case. Two factors are used to evaluate ripeness: "the fitness of the issues for judicial decision and the hardship to the parties of withholding court consideration." *Abbott Labs.* Ordinarily, both factors must be present.

The hardship prong of this test is most likely satisfied here; the current mobilization already imposes difficulties on the plaintiff soldiers and family members, so that they suffer "present injury from a future contemplated event." *McInnis-Misenor v. Me. Med. Ctr.* (1st Cir. 2003). Plaintiffs also lack a realistic opportunity to secure comparable relief by bringing the action at a later time.

The fitness inquiry here presents a greater obstacle. Fitness "typically involves subsidiary queries concerning finality, definiteness, and the extent to which resolution of the challenge depends upon facts that may not yet be sufficiently developed." *Ernst & Young* [*v. Depositors Econ. Prot. Corp.* (1st Cir. 1995)]. The baseline question is whether allowing more time for development of events would "significantly advance our ability to deal with the legal issues presented [or] aid us in their resolution." *Duke Power Co. v. Carolina Envtl. Study Group* (1978). "[T]he question of fitness does not pivot solely on whether a court is capable of resolving a claim intelligently, but also involves an assessment of whether it is appropriate for the court to undertake the task." *Ernst & Young.* These prudential considerations are particularly strong in this case, which presents a politically charged controversy involving momentous issues, both substantively (war and peace) and constitutionally (the powers of coequal branches).

One thrust of the plaintiffs' argument is that the October Resolution only permits actions sanctioned by the Security Council. In plaintiffs' view, the Resolution's authorization is so narrow that, even with Security Council approval of military force, Congress would need to pass a new resolution before United States participation in an attack on Iraq would be constitutional. At a minimum, according to plaintiffs, the October Resolution authorizes no military action "outside of a United Nations coalition."

For various reasons, this issue is not fit now for judicial review. For example, should there be an attack, Congress may take some action immediately. The purported conflict between the political branches may disappear. "[T]hat the future event may never come to pass augurs against a finding of fitness." *McInnis-Misenor.*

Many important questions remain unanswered about whether there will be a war, and, if so, under what conditions. Diplomatic negotiations, in particular, fluctuate daily. The President has emphasized repeatedly that hostilities still may be averted if Iraq takes certain actions. The Security Council is now debating the possibility of passing a new resolution that sets a final deadline for Iraqi compliance. United Nations weapons inspectors continue their investigations inside Iraq. Other countries ranging from Canada to Cameroon have reportedly pursued their own proposals to broker a compromise. As events unfold, it may become clear that diplomacy has either succeeded or failed decisively. The Security Council, now divided on the issue, may reach a consensus. To evaluate this claim now, the court would need to pile one hypothesis on top of another. We would need to assume that the Security Council will not authorize war, and that the President will proceed nonetheless.

Thus, even assuming that plaintiffs correctly interpret the commands of the legislative branch, it is impossible to say yet whether or not those commands will be obeyed. As was the situation in *Goldwater*, "[i]n the present posture of this case, we do not know whether there will ever be an actual confrontation between the Legislative and Executive Branches." (Powell, J., concurring).

Our analysis is based on ripeness rather than the political question doctrine. The political question doctrine — that courts should not intervene in questions that are the province of the legislative and executive branches — is a famously murky one. It has also been used fairly infrequently to block judicial review. The modern definition of the doctrine was established in the landmark case of *Baker v. Carr* (1962). In the forty years since that case, the Supreme Court has found a case nonjusticiable on the basis of the political question doctrine only twice. See *Nixon v. United States* (1993) (Senate procedures for impeachment of a federal judge); *Gilligan v. Morgan*, (1973) (training, weaponry, and orders of Ohio National Guard). Our court has been similarly sparing in its reliance on the political question doctrine.

Ultimately, however, the classification matters less than the principle. If courts may ever decide whether military action contravenes congressional authority, they surely cannot do so unless and until the available facts make it possible to define the issues with clarity.

C. MOOTNESS

We conclude this chapter by considering the requirement that a lawsuit present a live and continuing controversy. If a case is "moot," there is no longer any injury for a court to rectify (another "when" question). In a sense, the mootness doctrine is the mirror image of the ripeness doctrine; in the former, the case is brought too late, and in the latter, the case is brought too soon.

STUDY GUIDE

- Is there any compelling reason why the Court should not have reached the merits in *DeFunis v. Odegaard*, especially when both parties insisted that the case was not moot?
- Are you persuaded by the reasons the Court gives for refusing to apply the exception for injuries that are "capable of repetition, yet evading review"? (This doctrine is applied in cases involving abortion, which are seldom resolved during the nine months of pregnancy.)
- In 2016, the Supreme Court found that Abigail Fisher's challenge to the University of Texas's affirmative action policy was not moot, even though she had already graduated from college. Why? She sought a refund of her application fee, so there was (ostensibly) still a live controversy.
- Another exception to the mootness doctrine, not considered here, is for class-action lawsuits where the issues may have been rendered moot for the named plaintiffs, but where other members of the class continue to have a live controversy.

Marco DeFunis, Jr.

DeFunis v. Odegaard

416 U.S. 312 (1974)

Per Curiam . . .

In 1971 the petitioner Marco DeFunis, Jr., applied for admission as a first-year student at the University of Washington Law School, a state-operated institution. The size of the incoming first-year class was to be limited to 150 persons, and the Law School received some 1,600 applications for these 150 places. DeFunis was eventually notified that he had been denied admission. He thereupon commenced this suit in a Washington trial court, contending that the procedures and criteria employed by the Law School Admissions Committee invidiously discriminated against him on account of his race in violation of the Equal Protection Clause of the Fourteenth Amendment to the United States Constitution.

DeFunis brought the suit on behalf of himself alone, and not as the representative of any class, against the various respondents, who are officers, faculty members, and members of the Board of Regents of the University of Washington. He asked the trial court to issue a mandatory injunction commanding the respondents to admit him as a member of the first-year class entering in September 1971, on the ground that the Law School admissions policy had resulted in the unconstitutional denial of his application for admission. The trial court agreed with his claim and granted the requested relief.

DeFunis was, accordingly, admitted to the Law School and began his legal studies there in the fall of 1971. On appeal, the Washington Supreme Court reversed the judgment of the trial court and held that the Law School admissions policy did not violate the Constitution. By this time DeFunis was in his second year at the Law School.

He then petitioned this Court for a writ of certiorari, and Mr. Justice Douglas, as Circuit Justice, stayed the judgment of the Washington Supreme Court pending the "final disposition of the case by this Court." By virtue of this stay, DeFunis has remained in law school, and was in the first term of his third and final year when this Court first considered his certiorari petition in the fall of 1973. Because of our concern that DeFunis' third-year standing in the Law School might have rendered this case moot, we requested the parties to brief the question of mootness before we acted on the petition. In response, both sides contended that the case was not moot. The respondents indicated that, if the decision of the Washington Supreme Court were permitted to stand, the petitioner could complete the term for which he was then enrolled but would have to apply to the faculty for permission to continue in the school before he could register for another term.

We granted the petition for certiorari on November 19, 1973. The case was in due course orally argued on February 26, 1974. In response to questions raised from the bench during the oral argument, counsel for the petitioner has informed the Court that DeFunis has now registered "for his final quarter in law school." Counsel for the respondents have made clear that the Law School will not in any way seek to abrogate this registration. In light of DeFunis' recent registration for the last quarter of his final law school year, and the Law School's assurance that his registration is fully effective, the insistent question again arises whether this case is not moot, and to that question we now turn.

The starting point for analysis is the familiar proposition that "federal courts are without power to decide questions that cannot affect the rights of litigants in the case before them." . . . The inability of the federal judiciary "to review moot cases derives from the requirement of Art. III of the Constitution under which the exercise of judicial power depends upon the existence of a case or controversy." . . .

It might . . . be suggested that this case presents a question that is "capable of repetition, yet evading review," *Southern Pacific Terminal Co. v. ICC* (1911); *Roe v. Wade* (1973), and is thus amenable to federal adjudication even though it might otherwise be considered moot. But DeFunis will never again be required to run the gauntlet of the Law School's admission process, and so the question is certainly not "capable of repetition" so far as he is concerned. Moreover, just because this particular case did not reach the Court until the eve of the petitioner's graduation from law school, it hardly follows that the issue he raises will in the future evade review. If the admissions procedures of the Law School remain unchanged, there is no reason to suppose that a subsequent case attacking those procedures will not come with relative speed to this Court, now that the Supreme Court of Washington has spoken. This case, therefore, in no way presents the exceptional situation in which the Southern Pacific Terminal doctrine might permit a departure from "[t]he usual rule in federal cases . . . that an actual controversy must exist at stages of appellate or certiorari review, and not simply at the date the action is initiated." *Roe v. Wade.*

Because the petitioner will complete his law school studies at the end of the term for which he has now registered regardless of any decision this Court might reach on the merits of this litigation, we conclude that the Court cannot, consistently with the limitations of Art. III of the Constitution, consider the substantive constitutional issues tendered by the parties. Accordingly, the judgment of the Supreme Court of Washington is vacated, and the cause is remanded for such proceedings as by that court may be deemed appropriate.

STUDY GUIDE

- *Friends of the Earth v. Laidlaw Environmental Services* considers another exception to the mootness doctrine—voluntary cessation of the offending behavior, which could be resumed in the future.
- How does this exception square with the rationale for the mootness doctrine's requirement of a live controversy?

Friends of the Earth v. Laidlaw Environmental Services

528 U.S. 167 (2000)

[Friends of the Earth and other environmental groups brought suit to enforce the Clean Water Act (CWA) against Laidlaw Environmental Services, the holder of a National Pollution Discharge Elimination System (NPDES) permit, alleging that Laidlaw was violating mercury discharge limits. The plaintiffs used the citizen suit provision of the CWA to seek declaratory and injunctive relief, civil penalties, costs, and attorneys' fees. — EDS.]

JUSTICE GINSBURG delivered the opinion of the Court. . . .

The only conceivable basis for a finding of mootness in this case is Laidlaw's voluntary conduct — either its achievement by August 1992 of substantial compliance with its NPDES permit or its more recent shutdown of the Roebuck facility. It is well settled that "a defendant's voluntary cessation of a challenged practice does not deprive a federal court of its power to determine the legality of the practice." *City of Mesquite v. Aladdin's Castle, Inc.* (1982) "[I]f it did, the courts would be compelled to leave '[t]he defendant . . . free to return to his old ways.'" *Ibid.* In accordance with this principle, the standard we have announced for determining whether a case has been mooted by the defendant's voluntary conduct is stringent: "A case might become moot if subsequent events made it absolutely clear that the allegedly wrongful behavior could not reasonably be expected to recur." *United States v. Concentrated Phosphate Export Assn., Inc.* (1968). The "heavy burden of persua[ding]" the court that the challenged conduct cannot reasonably be expected to start up again lies with the party asserting mootness. *Ibid.* . . .

[A] defendant claiming that its voluntary compliance moots a case bears the formidable burden of showing that it is absolutely clear the allegedly wrongful behavior could not reasonably be expected to recur. By contrast, in a lawsuit brought to force compliance, it is the plaintiff's burden to establish standing by demonstrating that, if unchecked by the litigation, the defendant's allegedly wrongful behavior will likely occur or continue, and that the "threatened injury [is] certainly impending." *Whitmore v. Arkansas* (1990). . . .

Standing doctrine functions to ensure, among other things, that the scarce resources of the federal courts are devoted to those disputes in which the parties have a concrete stake. In contrast, by the time mootness is an issue, the case has been brought and litigated, often (as here) for years. To abandon the case at an advanced stage may prove more wasteful than frugal. This argument from sunk costs does not license courts to retain jurisdiction over cases in which one or both of the parties plainly lacks a continuing interest, as when the parties have settled or a plaintiff pursuing a nonsurviving claim has died. . . .

Laidlaw also asserts, in a supplemental suggestion of mootness, that the closure of its Roebuck facility, which took place after the Court of Appeals issued its decision, mooted the case. The facility closure, like Laidlaw's earlier achievement of substantial compliance with its permit requirements, might moot the case, but — we once more reiterate—only if one or the other of these events made it absolutely clear that Laidlaw's permit violations could not reasonably be expected to recur. The effect of both Laidlaw's compliance and the facility closure on the prospect of future violations is a disputed factual matter. FOE points out, for example—and Laidlaw does not appear to contest—that Laidlaw retains its NPDES permit. These issues have not been aired in the lower courts; they remain open for consideration on remand.

Table of Cases

Principal cases are italicized.

Index